Lecture Notes in Computer Science

Edited by G. Goos and J. Hartmanis
Series: GI, Gesellschaft für Informatik

26

GI - 4. Jahrestagung
Berlin, 9.–12. Oktober 1974

Herausgegeben im Auftrag der GI von D. Siefkes

Springer-Verlag
Berlin · Heidelberg · New York 1975

Editorial Board: D. Gries · P. Brinch Hansen
C. Moler · G. Seegmüller · N. Wirth

Prof. Dr. D. Siefkes
Technische Universität Berlin
Automatentheorie und Formale Sprachen
Fachbereich Kybernetik
1 Berlin 10
Otto-Suhr-Allee 18/20

AMS Subject Classifications (1970): 00A10, 68A05, 68A10, 68A20, 68A25, 68A30, 68A45, 68A50
CR Subject Classifications (1974): 1.50, 1.52, 3.63, 3.70, 3.73, 4.12, 4.22, 4.30, 4.32, 5.21, 5.23, 5.25, 6.20

ISBN 3-540-07141-5 Springer-Verlag Berlin · Heidelberg · New York
ISBN 0-387-07141-5 Springer-Verlag New York · Heidelberg · Berlin

This work is subject to copyright. All rights are reserved, whether the whole or part of the material is concerned, specifically those of translation, reprinting, re-use of illustrations, broadcasting, reproduction by photocopying machine or similar means, and storage in data banks.
Under § 54 of the German Copyright Law where copies are made for other than private use, a fee is payable to the publisher, the amount of the fee to be determined by agreement with the publisher.
© by Springer-Verlag Berlin · Heidelberg 1975. Library of Congress Catalog Card Number 73-13079. Printed in Germany.
Offsetdruck: Julius Beltz, Hemsbach/Bergstr.

VORWORT

Die 4. Jahrestagung der Gesellschaft für Informatik fand vom 9. bis 12. Oktober 1974 an der Technischen Universität Berlin statt. Auf dem Programm standen fünf Hauptvorträge und 65 Kurzreferate in ziemlich allen Gebieten der Informatik, eine Podiumsdiskussion über Informatik-Ausbildung und ein "Industrie-Programm".

Obwohl viele Fachausschüsse der GI inzwischen regelmäßig Spezial-Tagungen veranstalten, war die Beteiligung erfreulich (600 Teilnehmer). Die Zahl der Vortragsanmeldungen lag mit 170 sogar erheblich über der des Vorjahres. Man mag daraus schließen, daß die Jahrestagung nach wie vor eine wichtige Funktion hat.

Dem Programm-Ausschuß gehörten die Herren

R. Bayer, Technische Universität München

W. Brauer, Universität Hamburg

C.H.A. Koster, Technische Universität Berlin

A. Langseder, Landesamt für Datenverarbeitung München

C.L. Liu, University of Illinois

D.L. Parnas, TH Darmstadt

H. Rogge, Siemens A.G., München

H. Schappert, Bayer A.G., Leverkusen

D. Siefkes, Technische Universität Berlin (Vorsitzender)

an. Die Vortragsanmeldungen machten es nicht möglich, alle Gebiete der Informatik gleichmäßig durch Vorträge zu repräsentieren. Wir hoffen, daß die Tagung trotzdem diesen einen wichtigen Zweck erfüllt hat, die Kontakte zwischen den Spezialisten der verschiedenen Gebiete zu verbessern. Sehr erfreulich war dabei die hohe Beteiligung (etwa ein Drittel) der Vortragenden aus dem Ausland.

Leider reichten die Vortragsanmeldungen gerade im Bereich der Informatik-Anwendung nicht aus, um dieses Gebiet in dem ihm eigentlich zukommenden Umfang darzustellen. Einen gewissen Ausgleich lieferte nur das "Industrie-Programm", in dem Hersteller über neue Produkte und Techniken berichteten; diese Vorträge konnten im Tagungsband nicht abgedruckt werden. Auch die Podiumsdiskussion über Ausbildungsfragen zeigte, daß beiden Seiten, Forschern wie Anwendern, vielleicht nicht die Bereitschaft, aber noch (oder schon?) weitgehend die Fähigkeit fehlt, von einander zu lernen. Man kann es als symptomatisch ansehen, daß es keine Beziehungen gab zwischen der GI-Tagung und zwei Anwender-Tagungen, die kurz vorher bzw. gleichzeitig in West-Berlin stattfanden.

Mit zwei Hauptvorträgen, einer Vortragssitzung und einer Podiumsdiskussion war ein Tag fast ganz dem Thema "Informatik-Ausbildung" gewidmet. An der Podiumsdiskussion nahmen die Herren

C.H.A. Koster, Technische Universität Berlin (Diskussionsleitung)
K. Broadbent, ICL, Düsseldorf
V. Claus, Universität Dortmund
C. Hackl, IBM Deutschland, Sindelfingen
G. Lucas, TH Darmstadt, Student
S.G. van der Meulen, Rijksuniversiteit, Utrecht
P. Naur, Københavns Universitet
H. Oberquelle, Universität Hamburg, Student
M. Windfuhr, Hoesch Werke, Dortmund

teil. Diskutiert wurde vor allem das Problem einer mehr berufsbezogenen Informatik-Ausbildung.

Der vorliegende Band enthält nach den Hauptvorträgen die Kurzreferate, nach Sachgebieten geordnet. Die Untergliederung der Sachgebiete entspricht den einzelnen Sitzungen der Tagung.

An dieser Stelle sei noch einmal allen herzlich gedankt, die diese Tagung ermöglicht oder geholfen haben, sie vorzubereiten und durchzuführen, insbesondere
- dem Bundesminister für Forschung und Technologie
- der Technischen Universität Berlin
- den Firmen
   Computer Gesellschaft Konstanz
   IBM Deutschland GmbH
   Siemens A.G.
   Sperry Univac
- den Mitgliedern des Programm-Ausschusses
- vielen Angehörigen des Fachbereichs Kybernetik der Technischen Universität Berlin, vor allem dem Organisations-Komitee unter Leitung von Herrn E. Denert und dem lokalen Programm-Ausschuß
- den Sitzungsleitern
- und, last not least, allen Vortragenden und Diskussionsteilnehmern.

Dem Springer-Verlag einen herzlichen Dank, daß er diesen Tagungsband wieder in die "Lecture Notes in Computer Science" übernommen hat. Ganz besonders danke ich Herrn R. Hoffmann, Mitglied des lokalen Programm-Ausschusses, sowie unseren Sekretärinnen Frau M. Meier-Krege und Frau H. Barnewitz, die mir bei der Herausgabe dieses Bandes geholfen haben.

Berlin, Oktober 1974   Dirk Siefkes

INHALTSVERZEICHNIS SEITE

1. HAUPTVORTRÄGE:

J. HARTMANIS, J. SIMON 3
On the Structure of Feasible Computations

P. NEUMANN 52
Toward a Methodology for Designing Large Systems and
Verifying their Properties

H. FIEDLER 68
Datenschutz und Gesellschaft

P. NAUR 85
Trends in Computer Science Education

S.G. VAN DER MEULEN 94
How to Teach Computer Science to Students
Who don't Like Science

2. THEORETISCHE GRUNDLAGEN:

A. BERTONI 107
The Solution of Problems Relative to Probabilistic Automata
in the Frame of the Formal Languages Theory

M. HÖPNER 113
Eine Charakterisierung der Szilardsprachen und ihre Verwendung als Steuersprachen

M. KUDLEK 122
Comparing several ways of context-independent parallel
rewriting

S. HEILBRUNNER 131
Das Problem der 'unendlichen Modi' in ALGOL 68

P. RAULEFS 140
The D-Calculus: A System to Describe the Semantics of
Programs Involving Complex Data Types

W. BIBEL 153
Effizienzvergleiche von Beweisprozeduren

W. COY 161
Drei Komplexitätsmaße zweistufiger Normalformen
Boolescher Funktionen

3. PROGRAMMIERSPRACHEN UND COMPILER:

J. KLONK, H. A. SCHMID 173
Zwei BASIC-Systeme von unterschiedlicher Struktur -
Ein Vergleich ihrer Benutzerfreundlichkeit und Effizienz

F. KRÖGER 183
Speicherzuordnung an Datenstrukturen

	SEITE
H. J. SCHNEIDER Syntax-directed description of incremental compilers	192
E. DENERT, R. FRANCK, W. STRENG PLAN2D - Towards a Two-dimensional Programming Language	202
H.H. KRON, H.-J. HOFFMANN, G. WINKLER On a SLR(k)-Based Parser System which Accepts Non-LR(k)Grammars	214
H. FEUERHAHN A binary control structure and its relationship to grammars and side effects	224
C.H.A. KOSTER A technique for parsing ambiguous languages	233
D. NEEL, M. AMIRCHAHY, M. MAZAUD Optimization of Generated Code by Means of Attributes: Local Elimination of Common Redundant Sub-expressions.	247
R. WILHELM Code-Optimierung mittels attributierter Transformationsgrammatiken	257
J. MARTIN, Ch.FLOYD, R.NAGEL, P.SCHNUPP, O.WÖRZ, Die dynamische Datenbasis des HALORD Systems	267
H. ROTH Semantische Aspekte der Programmoptimierung	277

4. NICHTSEQUENTIELLE SYSTEME:

P. ANCILOTTI, M. FUSANI, N. LIJTMAER, C. THANOS Deadlock Conditions in Well Structured Modular Systems	289
K.-P. LÖHR Über die Lebensdauer von Prozessen in nichtsequentiellen Algorithmen	299
J. JÜRGENS Modularer Aufbau einer Familie von kooperierenden Prozessen	308
R. SCHROFF Vermeidung von Verklemmungen in bewerteten Petrinetzen	316
H. FUSS P-T-Netze zur numerischen Simulation von asynchronen Flüssen	326
H.-J. GOTTSCHALK Elementare Steuerknoten in Datenflußmodellen	336
H.J. BECKER, H. VOGEL E-V-Schemata Ein Ansatz zur formalen Behandlung paralleler Prozesse	345

		SEITE
	F. SCHWENKEL Zur Theorie unendlicher Parallelprozessoren	355

5. BETRIEBSSYSTEME:

J. HARMS 355
Fail-Softness Criteria in the Realization of a Minicomputer
Disk Operating System to be Used in an "Open-Shop" -
University Environment   367

R. ROSSI, M. SPADONI, P. TOTH   377
Operating Systems with Characteristics of Portability
for Minicomputers

S.W. SHERMAN, J.H. HOWARD Jr., J.C. BROWNE   386
Trace Driven Studies of Deadlock Control and Job Scheduling

S. HOENER   396
Zur Leistungsbewertung von Multiprozessor-Strukturen

S. SCHINDLER, S. BUDER   406
Memory and Processor Utilization in Safe States

M. HEINZ   416
Virtuelle Maschinen in einem allgemeinen Time-Sharing-
Betriebssystem

D. BAUM, H.-D. SCHRÖDTER   428
Ein Kommunikationsbetriebssystem für ein sternförmiges
Rechnernetz

6. RECHNERARCHITEKTUR UND BEWERTUNG:

W. HÄNDLER   439
On Classification Schemes for Computer Systems in the
Post-Von-Neumann-Era

W.M. DENNY   453
Micro-Programming Measurement Techniques for the
Burroughs B1700

P. KÜHN, M. LANGENBACH-BELZ   463
Über die Wirksamkeit zyklischer Abfertigungsstrategien
in Realzeitsystemen

7. INFORMATIONSSYSTEME:

J. CONRADI   475
Probleme der elektronischen Rechtsdokumentation - dargestellt
am Beispiel der Steuerrechtsdatenbank der DATEV e G

G. DATHE, K.-H. DRECKMANN   484
Entwurf eines Datenbanksystems für normierte Kennwerte
von Eisen- und Stahlwerkstoffen

	SEITE
J. J. MARTIN Aspects of Generality and Efficiency in Programming Language Implementation	494
J. SCHLÖRER Zum Problem der Anonymität der Befragten bei statistischen Datenbanken mit Dialogauswertung	502
P. HABERÄCKER, M. LEHNER Zugriffssicherung in Datenbanksystemen	512
A. PIROTTE, P. WODON A Query Language for a Relational Data Base	524
A. DÖRRSCHEIDT Konzept des Objektbeschreibungsbaums als Grundstruktur eines graphenorientierten Datenbankmodells	532
H. WEBER Beitrag zur Spezifikation der Funktion von generalisierten Datenbankmanagementsystemen	542
S.-A. TÄRNLUND A Structured Database	554
I.M. OSMAN The Partitioning of a Data Base into Subfiles Matching User's Queries	563

8. COMPUTER GRAPHICS:

H.U. LEMKE, A.P. ARMIT A Note on Advanced Software Techniques in Computer Graphics	579
U. TRAMBACZ Die Definition generalisierter, graphischer Eingabegeräte	589
H. M. AUS, V.ter MEULEN, M.KÄCKELL, W.SCHOLZ, K.KOSCHEL Pattern Recognition of Virus Induced Cell Changes	596
F. BRAKHAGEN Ein Programmsystem zur interaktiven Triangulierung zweidimensionaler Gebiete in der Methode der finiten Elemente	606
E. BECKER, F. REUTTER GIULIA-Ein System zum Verarbeiten analytisch gegebener Flächen	611
W. STRASSER Die Anwendung der B-Spline-Approximation in Computer Graphics	621

9. ANWENDUNG: GEOGRAPHIE, KONSTRUIEREN:

K. Ch. HASE Ein benutzerorientiertes Informationssystem für landesplanerische Applikationen	633

	SEITE

R. W. HESSDORFER 641
CAMS: Computer Augmented Mapping System

M.J.E. COOLEY 652
Computer Aided Design - Some Occupational and Social
Implications

H. FLESSNER, P. GORNY, H.-P. HAAKE, W. HANSMANN 659
Entwicklung und Einsatz eines interaktiven
Konstruktionsplatzes (IKP)

10. AUSBILDUNG:

W. COY 673
Bericht von einer dreisemestrigen Seminar-Reihe über ein
Thema aus dem Hardware-Bereich

S. E. BINNS, A.R. WEST 679
An Undergraduate Group Project in Software Engineering

R. LANGEBARTELS, O.HECKER, J.HINRICHS, S.MADALO, K.-H.RÖDIGER 686
Ein Dialogprogrammiersystem für den Unterricht in
Programmiersprachen

H.-Ch. ZEDLITZ 696
Berufsbild und Perspektiven des Informatikers

H. FRANCK, Th. SPITTA 703
Konzept und Studienplan für eine Fachrichtung "Wirtschaftsinformatik" im Studiengang "Informatik" der TU Berlin

Ch. FLOYD 713
Grundausbildung in Informatik

N. ORIS 716
Erfahrungen mit dem Versuch eines integrierten Informatik-
Grundstudiums

U. BOSLER, W.BOOKHAGEN, O.HECKER, W.KOCH, O.RABUS 730
Informatik an allgemeinbildenden Schulen
Überlegungen zur Gestaltung von Unterrichtsinhalten und
Erfahrungen bei der Organisation des Unterrichts

AUTORENVERZEICHNIS 741

1. HAUPTVORTRÄGE:

J. HARTMANIS AND J. SIMON
On the Structure of Feasible Computations

PETER G. NEUMANN
Toward a Methodology for Designing Large Systems and Verifying their Properties

H. FIEDLER
Datenschutz und Gesellschaft

PETER NAUR
Trends in Computer Science Education

S.G. VAN DER MEULEN
How to teach Computer Science to Students who don't like Science

ON THE STRUCTURE OF FEASIBLE COMPUTATIONS[†]

J. Hartmanis and J. Simon[††]

Department of Computer Science
Cornell University
Ithaca, New York 14853

Abstract:

During the last four years research on lower level computational complexity has yielded a rich set of interesting results which have revealed deep and unexpected connections between various problems and thus brought new unity to this area of computer science. This work has also yielded new techniques and insights which are likely to have further applications, and it has identified some very central problems in the quantitative theory of computing. The purpose of this paper is to give the reader an overview of these developments, an insight into some of these results and applications, as well as an appreciation of the unity and structure which has emerged in this area of research.

1. Introduction

In theoretical computer science we can identify several super problems whose solution is bound to contribute extensively to our understanding of the quantitative aspects of computations and could be of considerable practical value. Among these problems we certainly must include the problems dealing with :

1. The quantitative differences between deterministic and

[†] This research has been supported in part by the National Science Foundation Grant GJ-33171X and Grant 70/755 from Fundacao de Amparo a Pesquisa do Estado de Sao Paulo, and by Universidade Estadual de Campinas.
[††] On leave of absence from Universidade Estadual de Campinas, Campinas, S.P., Brazil.

nondeterministic computations.

    2. The time and memory trade-offs in computations.

    3. The computational speed gained by adding new operations to random access machines, such as multiplication.

    4. The change in descriptive power of formal languages as we add new features (operations).

The first problem area could also include the related problem of characterizing the quantitative differences between parallel and sequential computations as well as understanding the quantitative differences between "finding a proof" and "verifying that a given proof is correct" in a formal system.

    Considerable research effort has been dedicated to problems of this type during the last decade as part of a systematic development of the theory of computational complexity. The real progress, though, in this area of research has come since 1970. During the last four years research in this area has yielded a rich set of new results which have revealed unexpected and deep connections between different problems, including the four mentioned above. These results have brought new unity to the study of the computational complexity of feasible problems and have identified and isolated specific problems on whose solution many others depend. Furthermore, these results have yielded some powerful new techniques, interesting applications outside of computer science, and even insights about the nature of theoretical computer science.

    In this paper we will try to give the reader an overview of these developments, an insight into some of these results and their applications as well as an appreciation of the unity and structure which has emerged in this area of research.

2. Feasible computations and nondeterminism

From the early research on effective computability emerged in the first half of this century a consensus about the precise meaning of the concept "effectively computable". This consensus is expressed in Church's thesis which in essence asserts that: a function is _effectively computable_ (or simply _computable_) if and only if there exists a Turing machine which computes it.

Clearly, the class of effectively computable functions contains functions which are practically computable as well as functions which require arbitrarily large amounts of computing time (or any other resource by which we measure computational complexity) and thus these functions cannot be practically computed. So far there has not emerged any real consensus as to which functions are in principle practically computable. It is also not clear whether the concept of practically computable functions is in any sense fundamental and whether it has a mathematical invariance comparable to the class of effectively computable functions.

At the same time, there is already a general agreement that a process whose computation time (on a Turing machine) cannot be asymptotically bounded by a polynomial in the length of the input data is not a practical computation. For example, any function for which every Turing machine computing it requires at least a number of steps exponential in the length of the input is not practically computable. Thus we shall define below a computation to be _feasible_ iff it can be computed in polynomial time on a Turing machine. This definition of feasibility of computations, besides being intuitively acceptable, has some very nice mathematical properties and shows a very rugged invariance under changes of the underlying computing model. The last point will be particularly emphasized in Chapter 5 when we study random access machines with different sets of operations.

To make these concepts precise and to simplify our notation, we will consider all through this paper the computational problem of accepting languages or solving suitably encoded problems with "yes" and "no" answers, such as "Does the binary input string represent a prime number in binary notation?" or "Does the given regular expression designate the set of all finite binary sequences?" In all these problems the length of the input sequence is the number of symbols in the sequence and we express the amount of computing resource used in terms of the length of the input sequence.
Convention: A computation is _feasible_ iff it runs in polynomial time (in the length of the input) on a deterministic Turing machine.

To be able to talk about the class of all feasible computations we introduce
Definition: Let PTIME, or simply P, designate the family of languages accepted in polynomial time by deterministic Turing machines.

It is easily seen that the class of feasible computations, PTIME, includes a wide variety of languages and solutions of problems and that it is quite invariant under changes of computing models. We will return to the last point when we discuss random access machines in a later section and encounter the same polynomially bounded classes. On the other hand, there are very many other problems and languages about which we do not know whether they are feasible, that is, no polynomial time bounded algorithms have been discovered for them, nor has it been shown that such algorithms do not exist. Many of these problems are of considerable practical importance, and substantial effort has been expended to find deterministic polynomial time bounded algorithms for them.

A wide class of such important practical problems has the

property that they can be computed in polynomial time if the computations can be nondeterministic. Remember that a nondeterministic Tm may have several possible transitions from a given state, and it accepts a string w if there is a sequence of moves, starting with the initial configuration with input w and ending with a configuration in which the finite control is in a final state. The amount of resource used to accept w is the minimum over all such accepting sequences.

Thus a nondeterministic Turing machine can guess a solution and then verify whether it has guessed correctly. For example, consider the set

$$L = \{w | w \in 1(0 \cup 1)^* \text{ and } w \text{ does not denote a prime number}\}.$$

It is not known whether L is in PTIME but it is easily seen that L can be accepted in polynomial time by a nondeterministic Tm which guesses an integer (a binary sequence in $1(0 \cup 1)^*$ not longer than w) and then tests deterministically whether the integer divides w.

To give another, more theoretical computer science oriented example, let R_i and R_j be regular expressions over the alphabet consisting of $0, 1, \cdot, \cup$ and the delineators (,) and let $L(R_i)$ denote the set of sequences designated by R_i. Since we have not permitted the use of the Kleene star, *, in the regular expressions, we see that we can only describe finite sets and that the longest string in the set cannot exceed the length of the expression. Furthermore, the language

$$L_R = \{R_i, R_j) | L(R_i) \neq L(R_j)\}$$

can easily be recognized in polynomial time by a nondeterministic Tm which guesses a binary sequence w whose length does not exceed the length of the longest expression R_i or R_j, and then verifies that ∴ i L(R_i) or L(R_j) but not in both. So far no deterministic polynomial time algorithm has been discovered for this problem.

The multitude of problems and languages of this type has led to the definition of the corresponding nondeterministic class of languages.

Definition: Let NPTIME, or simply NP, denote the family of languages accepted in polynomial time by nondeterministic Turing machines.

To emphasize the importance of this class of problems or languages we list some such problems. In all these problems we assume that we have used a straightforward and simple encoding of the problem. For a detailed discussion of such problems see [6,16].

1. Given R_i,R_j regular expressions over $0,1,\cdot,\cup,(,)$. Determine if the sets of sequences denoted by R_i and R_j are different, i.e. if L(R_i) ≠ L(R_j).

2. Given a formula of the propositional calculus involving only variables plus connectives (or a Boolean expression in conjunctive normal form). Determine if it is 'true' for some assignment of the values 'false' and 'true' to its variables.

3. Given a (directed) graph G determine if the graph has a (directed) cycle which includes all nodes of G.

4. Given a graph G and integer k determine if G has k mutually adjacent nodes.

5. Given an integer matrix C and integer vector d determine if there exists a 0-1 vector x such that Cx = d.

6. Given a family of sets and a positive integer k. Determine if this family of sets contains k mutually disjoint sets.

7. Given a (n+1)tuple of integers $(a_1, a_2, \ldots, a_n, b)$. Does there exist a 0-1 vector x such that $\Sigma a_i x_i = b$?

It is easily seen that all of these problems are in NPTIME by a straightforward "guessing and verifying" method. On the other hand, no deterministic polynomial time algorithm is known for any of these problems. This list of problems can easily be extended and it is clear that it contains many practical problems for which we would very much like to have deterministic polynomial time algorithms [16, 1]. The question whether such algorithms exist is by now known as the
$$P = NP?$$
problem and it has to be considered as one of the central problems in computational complexity [6].

Intuitively, we feel that $P \neq NP$, though all attempts to prove it have failed. As we will show below, to prove that $P = NP$ we do not have to show that every problem in NP has an equivalent solution in P. All we have to show is that any one of the seven previously listed problems has a deterministic polynomially time bounded algorithm. This simplifies the $P = NP?$ problem considerably, but it still seems quite unlikely that such a deterministic polynomial time algorithm could exist. Of course, a proof that any one of these seven problems is not in P would prove that $P \neq NP$.

On the other hand, the exciting thing is that if $P = NP$ then its proof is very likely to reveal something fundamentally new about the nature of computing.

To emphasize this fact, recall that prime numbers have been studied for over two thousand years without discovering a fast (i.e. deterministic polynomial time) algorithm for their testing. Since the set of binary strings representing primes is in NP, this is just one more instance of the P = NP problem [26]. As an illustration we recall that in 1903 F. Cole showed that

$$2^{67} - 1 = 193707721 \times 76183825287$$

and claimed that it had taken him "three years of Sundays" to show that $2^{67} - 1$ was not a prime, as conjectured before. It is also striking how easily one can check whether the given factorization is correct, thus dramatically illustrating the difference between "finding a solution" and "verifying its correctness", which is the essence of the P = NP problem. For related problems see [10,11].

A very important property of the class NP was discovered by S.A. Cook [6] when he proved that there exists a language L in NP such that if there exists a deterministic polynomial time algorithm for the recognition of L, then P = NP and we can effectively find (from the deterministic polynomial time algorithm for L) deterministic polynomial time algorithms for every L' in NP.

To make these concepts precise we define complete languages in NP as those languages to which all other languages in NP can be "easily" reduced. Note that the concepts of complete languages and reducibility will be used repeatedly in this study and that they play important roles in recursive function theory and logic [30].

Definition: A language L is NP-complete (or complete in NP) iff L is in NP and for all L_i in NP there exists a function f_i, computable by a deterministic Tm in polynomial time, such that

$$w \text{ is in } L_i \text{ iff } f_i(w) \text{ is in } L.$$

Proposition 2.1: If L is a NP-complete language then L is in P iff P = NP.

Proof: To see this note that P = NP implies that L is in P. On the other hand, if L is in P then there exists a deterministic

Tm, M, which in polynomial time accepts L. For any other L_i in NP there exists, by definition of NP-completeness, a deterministic Tm M_i' which computes a function f_i such that

$$w \in L_i \text{ iff } f_i(w) \in L.$$

Let $M_{D(i)}$ be the deterministic Tm which on input w applies M_i' to compute $f_i(w)$ and then applies M on $f_i(w)$ to test whether $f_i(w)$ is in L. Clearly, the deterministic Tm $M_{D(i)}$ accepts L_i and operates in polynomial time since M_i' and M do. Thus L_i is in P, which completes the proof.

Next we prove that NP-complete languages actually exist by constructing a "universal NP" language L_U. This language is somewhat artificial but it reveals very clearly why NP-complete problems exist and demonstrates a technique which has many other applications. After this proof we show that there are also "natural" NP-complete languages. As a matter of fact, all the previously listed problems 1-7 are NP-complete.

<u>Theorem 2.2</u>: There exist NP-complete languages.

<u>Proof</u>: We will show that L_U defined below is NP-complete. Let

$$L_U = \{\#M_i \#\text{CODE}(x_1 x_2 \ldots x_n) \#^{3|M_i|t} \mid x_1 x_2 \ldots x_n \text{ is accepted by the one-tape, nondeterministic Tm } M_i \text{ in time } t\}$$

where M_i is given in some simple quintuple form, $|M_i|$ designates the length of the representation of M_i and $\text{CODE}(x_1 x_2 \ldots x_n)$ is a fixed, straightforward, symbol by symbol encoding of sequences over alphabets of arbitrary cardinality (the input and tape alphabet of M_i) into a fixed alphabet, say $\{0,1,\#\}$; with the provision that $|\text{CODE}(x_j)| \geq$ cardinality of the tape alphabet of M_i.

It is easily seen that a four-tape nondeterministic Tm M' can accept L_U in linear time. We indicate how M' uses its tapes: on the first sweep of the input M' checks the format of the input, copies M_i from the input on the first working tape and $\#^{3|M_i|}t$ on the second working tape. The third working tape is used to record the present state of M_i (in a tally notation) during the step-by-step simulation of M_i. It is seen that with the available information on its working tapes M' can simulate M_i on the input in time $2|M_i|t$ (for an appropriate, agreed upon representation of M_i). Thus M' operates in non-deterministic linear time and accepts L_U. Therefore, L_U is in NP and the assumption P = NP implies that L_U is accepted by a deterministic Tm M' operating in deterministic time n^p. Then for any nondeterministic Tm M_i working in time n^q we can recursively construct a Tm $M_{\sigma(i)}$ operating in polynomial time as follows:

1. for input $x_1 x_2 \ldots x_n$ $M_{\sigma(i)}$ writes down
   $\#M_i \#CODE(x_1 x_2 \ldots x_n) \#^{3|M_i|n^q}$
2. $M_{\sigma(i)}$ starts the deterministic machine M' on the sequence in (1) and accepts the input $x_1 x_2 \ldots x_n$ iff M' accepts its input.

Clearly, M_i and $M_{\sigma(i)}$ are equivalent, furthermore $M_{\sigma(i)}$ operates in time less than

$$2[3|M_i|n^q + |\#M_i \#CODE(x_1 x_2 \ldots x_n)|]^p \leq cn^{pq}.$$

Thus $M_{\sigma(i)}$ operates in deterministic polynomial time, as was to be shown.

The previous proof shows that if L_U is in P then we can recursively obtain for every M_i running in time n^q an equivalent deterministic Tm running in time $O[n^{pq}]$. Unfortunately, for a given Tm we cannot recursively determine the running time and thus we do not know whether M_i runs in polynomial time or not. Even if we know that M_i runs in polynomial time we still can not recursively determine the degree of the polynomial.

Our next result shows that, nevertheless, we can get a general translation result. For a related result see [9].

Theorem 2.3: P = NP iff there exists a recursive translation σ and a positive integer k, such that for every nondeterministic Tm M_i, which uses time $T_i(n) \geq n$, $M_{\sigma(i)}$ is an equivalent deterministic Tm working in time $O[T_i(n)^k]$.

Proof: The "if" part of the proof is obvious. To prove the "only if" part assume that P = NP. We will outline a proof that we can recursively construct for any M_i, running time $T_i(n) \geq n$, an equivalent deterministic Tm $M_{\sigma(i)}$ operating in time $O[T_i(n)^k]$ for a fixed k.

In our construction we use two auxiliary languages:

$B_i' = \{\#w\#^t |\ M_i$ accepts w in less than t time$\}$
$B_i'' = \{\#w\#^t |\ M_i$ on input w takes more than t time$\}$.

Clearly, the languages B_i' and $\Sigma^* - B_i''$ can be accepted in non-deterministic linear time. Therefore, by our previous result, we can recursively construct two deterministic machines M_i' and M_i''' which accept B_i' and $\Sigma^* - B_i''$ respectively, and operate in time $O[n^p]$. Now we obtain M_i'' from M_i''': M_i'' recognizes B_i''. M_i'' is a deterministic polynomial time bounded Tm since if $\Sigma^* - B_i''$ is in NP, it is in P (by hypothesis), and P is closed under complements.

From M_i' and M_i'' we can recursively construct the deterministic Tm $M_{\sigma(i)}$, which operates as follows:

1. For input w $M_{\sigma(i)}$ finds the smallest t_0 such that $\#w\#^{t_0}$ is not in B_i''. This is done by checking with M_i'' successively $\#w\#, \#w\#^2, \#w\#^3, \ldots$.

2. $M_{\sigma(i)}$ starts M_i' on input $\#w\#^{t_0}$ and accepts w iff M_i' accepts $\#w\#^{t_0}$.

Clearly, $M_{\sigma(i)}$ is equivalent to M_i and $M_{\sigma(i)}$ operates in time
$$O[\sum_{\ell=1}^{T_i(n)} \ell^p] = O[T_i(n)^{p+1}]$$

By setting $k = p+1$, we have completed the proof.

We conclude by observing that L_U is an NP-complete problem, as defined above.

Next we assert that there exist very many natural NP-complete problems and that finding fast algorithms for some of them is of considerable practical importance.

We will prove that

$$L_R = \{(R_i, R_j) \mid R_i, R_j \text{ are regular expressions over } 0, 1, \cdot, \cup, (\,,\,) \text{ and } L(R_i) \neq L(R_j)\}$$

is NP-complete. We have chosen to use this language since the proof utilizes a technique of describing Turing machine computations by means of regular expressions and this technique has interesting further applications.

<u>Theorem 2.4</u>: L_R is NP-complete and so are all the languages associated with the problems 1-7.

<u>Proof</u>: We prove only that the first problem on our list is NP-complete; for the other proofs see [16].

The proof that L_R is NP-complete relies heavily on the fact (proven below) that regular expressions can be used to describe the "invalid computations" of nondeterministic Tm's. More explicitly, for every nondeterministic Tm M_i operating in polynomial time there exists a deterministic Tm which for input $x_1 x_2 \ldots x_n$ in polynomial time writes out a regular expression describing the invalid computations of M_i on input $x_1 x_2 \ldots x_n$. Note that the input $x_1 x_2 \ldots x_n$ is accepted by M_i iff there exists a valid M_i computation on this input, which happens iff the set of invalid M_i computations on $x_1 x_2 \ldots x_n$ is not the set of all sequences (of a given length). Thus the test of whether $x_1 x_2 \ldots x_n$ is accepted by M_i can be reduced to a test of whether the regular expression, describing the invalid computations of M_i on $x_1 x_2 \ldots x_n$, does not describe all sequences (of a given length). This implies that if L_R is in P then P = NP and thus we see that L_R is NP-complete.

We now give the above outlined proof in more detail. Let M_i be a one-tape, nondeterministic Tm which operates in time n^k (we assume without loss of generality that M_i halts after exactly n^k steps). Let S be the set of states of M, q_0 the unique starting state, q_f the unique accepting final state, and let Σ be the tape alphabet of M_i. An <u>instantaneous description</u> of M_i is a sequence in $\Sigma^*(\Sigma \times S)\Sigma^*$ which indicates the tape content of M_i, the state M_i is in, and which symbol is being scanned. $\text{VCOMP}(x_1 x_2 \ldots x_n)$ denotes the set of <u>valid computations</u> of M_i on input $x_1 x_2 \ldots x_n$. A valid computation consists of a sequence of instantaneous descriptions

$$\# ID_1 \# ID_2 \# ID_3 \# \ldots \# ID_{n^k} \#$$

such that:

a) $ID_1 = (x_1, q_0) x_2 x_3 \ldots x_n b^{n^k - n}$

b) $ID_{n^k} \in \Sigma^t (\Sigma \times \{q_f\}) \Sigma^{n^k - t - 1}$

c) ID_{j+1} follows from ID_j, $1 \leq j \leq k-1$ by one move of M_i.

Note that for all i $|ID_i| = n^k$.

Define Γ as

$$\Gamma = \Sigma \cup \Sigma \times S \cup \{\#\}$$

and let the <u>invalid</u> set of computations be given by

$$\text{NVCOMP}(x_1 x_2 \ldots x_n) = \Gamma^{n^{2k}+n^k+1} - \text{VCOMP}(x_1 x_2 \ldots x_n).$$

We show next that there exists a deterministic Tm, M_D, which constructs for every input $x_1 x_2 \ldots x_n$ in polynomial time a regular ex-expression using only $\cdot, \cup$, denoting the set of sequences NVCOMP. To see this note that NVCOMP consists of:

R_1 = set of sequences which do not start correctly

R_2 = set of sequences which do not end correctly

R_3 = set of sequences which do not have a proper transition from ID_j to ID_{j+1}.

Thus

$$\text{NVCOMP}(x_1 x_2 \ldots x_n) = R_1 \cup R_2 \cup R_3.$$

Let $\bar{x}$ designate any y, $y \neq x$, $y \in \Gamma$. Note that the regular expression for $\bar{x}$ has length of the order of the size of Γ, i.e. a constant. Then

$$R_1 = \overline{\#}\Gamma^{n^{2k}+n^k} \cup \Gamma \overline{(x_1, q_0)} \Gamma^{n^{2k}+n^k-1} \cup \Gamma^2 \overline{x_2} \Gamma^{n^{2k}+n^k-2} + \ldots \cup \Gamma^{n^{2k}+n^k} \overline{\#}$$

$$R_2 = \{\Gamma - (S \times \{q_f\})\}^{n^{2k}+n^k+1}$$

$$R_3 = \bigcup_{p=0}^{n^{2k}-3} [\bigcup_{\sigma_1,\sigma_2,\sigma_3 \in \Gamma} \Gamma^p \sigma_1 \sigma_2 \sigma_3 \Gamma^{n^k-1} [\Gamma^3 - \text{CORRECT}(\sigma_1 \sigma_2 \sigma_3)]] \Gamma^{n^{2k}-p-4}]$$

where $\text{CORRECT}(\sigma_1 \sigma_2 \sigma_3)$ is the set of correct M_i transitions in one move from $\sigma_1 \sigma_2 \sigma_3$, in the following instantaneous description.

These triples are sufficient to specify the transitions, since in a single move only the square being scanned may be modified and the only other possible change in the ID is the position of the read/write head. Since the head moves at most one square, the set CORRECT suffices to charactrrize valid transitions. For example if the Tm in state q, upon reading a 0 may either print a 1 or a 0 and move right, then

$$\text{CORRECT}(\sigma_1(0,q)\sigma_3) = \{(\sigma_1 0(\sigma_3,q)),(\sigma_1 1(\sigma_3,q))\}$$
$$\text{CORRECT}((0,q)\sigma_2,\sigma_3) = \{(0(\sigma_2,q)\sigma_3),(1(\sigma_2,q)\sigma_3)\}$$
$$\text{CORRECT}(\sigma_1\sigma_2(0,q)) = \{(\sigma_1\sigma_2 0),(\sigma_1\sigma_2 1)\}.$$

It is easily seen that for any given Tm CORRECT is a finite set depending only on the alphabet and on the transition rules of the machine, but not on the input.

A straightforward computation shows that $R_1 \cup R_2 \cup R_3$ can be written out for input $x_1 x_2 \ldots x_n$ by a deterministic Tm in polynomial time in n. Thus the desired M_D exists.

If L_R is in P then we have a deterministic Tm M_C which in polynomial time accepts (R_i, R_j), provided $L(R_i) \neq L(R_j)$. But then combining M_D with this M_C we get a deterministic polynomial time Tm which for input $x_1 x_2 \ldots x_n$ writes out (using M_D)

$$\text{NVCOMP}(x_1 x_2 \ldots x_n)$$

and then checks (using M_C) whether the expressions are unequal. Clearly, the regular expressions are unequal iff there is a valid computation of M_i on $x_1 x_2 \ldots x_n$, but that happens iff M_i accepts this input. Since M_D and M_C operate in deterministic polynomial time, the combined machine accepting $L(M_i)$ also operates in deterministic polynomial time. Thus L_R in P implies P = NP. Clearly, P = NP implies that L_R is in P since it is easily seen that L_R is in NP. This completes the proof.

For the sake of completeness, we mention that it is not known whether the language

$$L_P = \{w \mid w \in 1(0 \cup 1)^* \text{ and } w \text{ designates a composite number}\}$$

is an NP-complete problem. It is easily seen that L_P is in NP, as stated before. A somewhat harder proof shows that, surprisingly,

$$\tilde{L}_p = \{w \mid w \in 1(0 \cup 1)^* \text{ and } w \text{ designates a prime}\}$$

is also in NP [26]. Thus the "guess and verify" method can be used to design (nondeterministic) polynomial time algorithms to test whether an integer is or is not a prime. Since L_p and $\tilde{L}_p$ (or $\bar{L}_p$ = $(0 \cup 1)^* - L_p$) are in NP, and for no NP-complete problem L is it known that $\bar{L}$ is in NP, it seems unlikely that either L_p or $\bar{L}_p$ could be NP-complete.

Note that, if we could show for an NP-complete problem L that $\bar{L}$ is not in NP, then we would have a proof that $P \neq NP$, since L' in P implies that $\overline{L'}$ is in P and thus in NP. A proof of this sort could possibly show that $P \neq NP$ without giving any insight into the actual deterministic time complexity of the class NP. Our current understanding of these problems is so limited that we cannot rule out either of the two extremes: a) that $P = NP$ and we need only polynomial time bounded deterministic algorithms, or (b) that there exist L in NP which require an exponential amount of time for their recognition.

As stated before, it appears that a proof that $P = NP$ will have to reveal something new about the nature of computation. Similarly, a proof that for all L in NP, $\bar{L}$ is in NP, which could happen even if $P \neq NP$, would have to reveal something unexpected about the process of computation. To emphasize this, consider again the set of unequal regular expressions over $0, 1, \cdot, \cup, (,)$:

$$L_R = \{(R_i, R_j) \mid L(R_i) \neq L(R_j)\} .$$

As observed before, L_R is easily seen to be in NP. On the other hand, it seems impossible (with our current state of knowledge about computing) that this computation could be carried out in deterministic polynomial time. Similarly, it seems impossible that the set of pairs of equal regular expressions,

$$L_{R\neg} = \{(R_i, R_j) \mid L(R_i) = L(R_j)\},$$

could be in NP, since in this case we would have to give a proof in nondeterministic polynomial time that there does not exist any sequence on which R_i and R_j differ. This appears to be a completely different situation than the proof that L_R is in NP and we do not know any methods which can exploit the power of nondeterminism to yield such a proof.

It may be shown that $L_{R\neg}$ has the same "completeness" property with respect to NP^c, i.e. the set of languages L such that $\Sigma^* - L$ is in NP, as L_R has with respect to NP; we will discuss such "complete" sets throughout the paper.

We conclude this section by observing that if $P \neq NP$ and NP is not closed under complementation, that then P and NP show a good low complexity level analogy to the recursive and recursively enumerable sets; P corresponding to the set of recursive sets and NP to the set of recursively enumerable sets.

3. Memory bounded computations

In the study of the complexity of computations there are two natural measures: the time or number operations and the tape or memory space used in the computation. It is strongly suspected that there exist interesting and important connections between these two complexity measures and that a central task of theoretical computer science is to understand the trade-offs between then [23].

In this section we discuss the problem of how much memory or tape is required for the recognition of the classes P and NP and some related problems. It will be seen that this study again leads us very quickly to some interesting open problems and reveals some interesting analogies with previous problems which will be further pursued in the chapter dealing with random access machines.

In analogy to the time bounded Tm computations we define memory bounded complexity classes.

<u>Definition</u>: Let PTAPE (NPTAPE) denote the family of languages accepted by deterministic (nondeterministic) Turing machines in polynomial tape.

Clearly, a Turing machine operating in polynomial time can visit only a polynomially bounded number of different tape squares and therefore we have

$$P \subseteq PTAPE \quad \text{and} \quad NP \subseteq NPTAPE.$$

Furthermore, any nondeterministic Tm M_i operating in time n^k can make no more than n^k different choices. On polynomial tape a deterministic Tm can successively enumerate all possible q^{n^k} sequences of choices M_i can make and for each sequence of choices simulate deterministically on polynomial tape the corresponding M_i computation. Therefore we obtain

<u>Proposition 3.1</u>: $NP \subseteq PTAPE$.

On the other hand, it is not known whether there exists an L in PTAPE which is not in NP. Intuitively, one feels that there must be such languages since in polynomial tape a Turing machine can perform an exponential number of operations before halting. At the same time, nobody has been able to prove that this exponential number of operations, restricted to polynomial tape, can be utilized effectively to accept something not in NP.

Thus we are led to another central problem in computational complexity: is NP = PTAPE or possibly P = PTAPE ?

At the present time we have to conjecture that NP $\neq$ PTAPE, since nothing in our knowledge of memory bounded computations suggests that PTAPE computations could be carried out in polynomial time. Furthermore, NP = PTAPE would have, as we will see later, some very strong and strange implications.

As stated in the previous chapter, it is not known whether P = NP, and this is a very important problem in complexity theory as well as for practical computing. The situation for tape bounded computations is different [31].

<u>Theorem 3.2</u>: Let $L(n) \geq \log n$ be the amount of tape used by a nondeterministic Tm M_i. Then we can effectively construct an equivalent deterministic Tm $M_{\sigma(i)}$ using no more than $[L(n)]^2$ tape.

From this result we get immediately

<u>Corollary 3.3</u>: PTAPE = NPTAPE.

In the last chapter we will give a new proof (without using Savitch's result) that PTAPE = NPTAPE, as part of our characterization of the computational power of multiplication in random access machines.

Next we will show that PTAPE has complete problems, just as NP did, and thus to show that NP = PTAPE we only have to show that one specific language in PTAPE is also in NP.

<u>Definition</u>: We say that a language L in PTAPE is <u>tape complete</u> iff for every L_i in PTAPE there exists a deterministic polynomial time computable function f_i such that

$w \in L_i$ iff $f_i(w) \in L$.

From this we immediately get

<u>Proposition 3.4</u>: NP = PTAPE (P = PTAPE) iff there exists a tape complete problem in NP (P).

We now show that tape complete problems exist. In order to emphasize the similarities with the NP case, we consider the following two languages:

$L_{UT} = \{\#M_i\#CODE(x_1x_2...x_n)\#^t | \ M_i$ accepts $x_1x_2...x_n$ using no more than $2+|M_i|+CODE(x_1x_2...x_n)+t$ tape squares$\}$

$L_R^* = \{R_i | \ R_i$ is a regular expression over $0,1,\cup,\cdot,*,(,)$ and $L(R_i) \neq (0 \cup 1)*\}$

Theorem 3.5: L_{UT} and L_R^* are tape complete languages. Thus

$$NP = PTAPE \ (P = PTAPE) \text{ iff } L_{UT} \in NP \ (P) \text{ iff } L_R^* \in NP \ (P).$$

Proof: It is easily seen that L_{UT} is accepted on the amount of tape needed to write down the input, if we permit nondeterministic operations. Thus L_{UT} is in PTAPE. Furthermore, if L_i is in PTAPE then there exists a deterministic Tm M_i which accepts L_i in n^k tape, for some k. But then there exists a Tm, $M_{\sigma(i)}$, which for input $x_1 x_2 \ldots x_n$ writes

$$\#M_i \#CODE(x_1 x_2 \ldots x_n) \#^{n^k - |CODE(x_1 x_2 \ldots x_n)| - 2 - |M_i|}$$

on its tape in deterministic polynomial time. Designate the function computed by $M_{\sigma(i)}$ by f_i. Then w is in L_i iff $f_i(w)$ is in L_{UT}, and we see that L_{UT} is tape complete.

To prove that L_R^* is tape complete observe that a nondeterministic Tm can guess a sequence and then on linear amount of tape (using standard techniques [19]) check that the sequence is not in R_i. Thus L_R^* is in PTAPE; as a matter of fact L_R^* is a context-sensitive language, as is L_{UT}. Now we again will exploit the power of regular expressions to describe invalid Tm computations efficiently.

For a Tm M_i which operates on n^k tape, we define

$$VCOMP(x_1 x_2 \ldots x_n) = \#ID_1 \#ID_2 \# \ldots \#ID_{HALT} \#$$

just as in Chapter 2, with $|ID_j| = n^k$. Since we now have the Kleene star available in our regular expressions, we define

$$NVCOMP = \Gamma^* - VCOMP.$$

Thus

$$NVCOMP(x_1 x_2 \ldots x_n) = R_1 \cup R_2 \cup R_3 \ ,$$

where R_1, R_2 and R_3 represent the sets of strings which do not start right, which do not end right, and where there is an incorrect transition from ID_i to ID_{i+1}, respectively. The details are quite similar to the proof in Chapter 2 and we write down the expressions for R_1, R_2 and R_3 to indicate the use of the $*$, which was not available in the other proof. It should be pointed out that M_i could perform an exponential number of steps before halting and therefore we cannot use the techniques of the previous proof. This proof makes an essential use of the Kleene star. Again $\bar{x}$ denotes any y, $y \neq x$ and y in $\Gamma = \Sigma \cup \{\#\} \cup \Sigma \times S$, q_0 the initial state and q_f the final state.

$$R_1 = \{\overline{\#} \cup \#[\overline{(x_1,q_0)} \cup (x_1,q_0)[\bar{x}_2 \cup x_2[\bar{x}_3 \cup x_3[\ldots \cup \overline{\#}]\ldots]\Gamma^*$$
$$R_2 = (\Gamma - \Sigma q_f)^*$$
$$R_3 = \Gamma^*\sigma_1\sigma_2\sigma_3\Gamma^{n^k-1}[\Gamma^3 - \text{CORRECT}(\sigma_1\sigma_2\sigma_3)]\Gamma^*$$

where $\text{CORRECT}(\sigma_1\sigma_2\sigma_3)$ is a correct sequence of the next ID if in the previous ID in the corresponding place appears $\sigma_1\sigma_2\sigma_3$.

It is easily seen that a deterministic Tm exists which for input $x_1x_2\ldots x_n$ writes out the regular expression $R_1 \cup R_2 \cup R_3$ on its tape in deterministic polynomial time. If we denote this function by f_i we see that

w is accepted by M_i iff $f_i(w) = R_1 \cup R_2 \cup R_3 \neq \Gamma^*$

since w is accepted by M_i iff there exists a valid computation of M_i on w, but this happens iff $\text{NVCOMP}(w) \neq \Gamma^*$. This concludes the proof that L_{UT} and L_R^* are tape complete languages and we see that NP = PTAPE (P = PTAPE) iff L_R^* or L_{UT} in in NP (P).

It should be pointed out that L_R^* is just one example of tape complete problems about regular expressions. We can actually state a very general theorem which characterizes a large class of such problems (or languages) [9], which shows that, for example,

$\{R|\ R$ regular expression and $L(R) \neq L(R^*)\}$

$\{R|\ R$ regular expression and $L(R)$ is cofinite$\}$

are two such tape complete languages; many others can be constructed using this result. It is interesting to note that

$$L_R = \{(R_i, R_j) \mid R_i, R_j \text{ regular expressions over } 0,1,\cup,\cdot,(\,,\,) \text{ and } L(R_i) \neq L(R_j)\}$$

is an NP-complete problem and if we added the expressive power of the Kleene star, *, the language

$$L_R^* = \{(R_i, R_j) \mid R_i, R_j \text{ regular expressions over } 0,1,\cup,\cdot,*,(\,,\,) \text{ and } L(R_i) \neq L(R_j)\}$$

became a tape complete language. Though we cannot prove that NP $\neq$ PTAPE, we conjecture that they are different, and therefore the Kleene star made the decision problem harder by the difference, if any, between NP and PTAPE.

It should be noted that without the Kleene star we cannot describe an infinite regular set and with $\cdot, \cup, *$ all regular sets can be described. From this alone we would suspect that the decision problem (recognition of) L_R^* should be harder than for L_R. Whether it really is harder, and by how much, remains a fascinating and annoying open problem.

To emphasize a further analogy between NP and PTAPE we take a quick look at logic. Recall that all the expressions in propositional calculus which for some assignment of variables become true form an NP-complete language. Thus we have

Theorem 3.6: The problem of recognizing the satisfiable formulas of the propositional calculus is an NP-complete problem [6]. Similarly, the set of true sentences (tautologies) of the propositional calculus is a complete language for $\overline{NP}$.

The next simplest theory, the first order propositional calculus with equality (1EQ) is a language that contains quantifiers but no function symbols or predicate symbols other than =. The following result characterizes the complexity of this decision problem.

Theorem 3.7: The problem of recognizing the set of true sentences for the first order predicate calculus (1EQ) is complete in PTAPE.

Proof: See [22].

Again we see that the difference in complexity between these two decision problems is directly related to the difference, if any, between NP and PTAPE.

Next we take a look at how the computational complexity of the decision problem for regular expressions changes as we permit further operations. We know that all regular sets can be described by regular expressions using the operators $\cup, \cdot, *$. At the same time, regular sets are closed under set intersection and set complementation. Therefore we can augment our set of operators used in regular expressions by $\cap$ and $\neg$ and we know from experience that these two operators can significantly simplify the writing of regular expressions. The surprising thing is that it is possible to prove that the addition of these operators makes the decision problems about regular expressions much harder [21]. In particular, as we will see the addition of the complementation operator makes the decision problem for equivalence of regular expressions practically unsolvable [34,14,22].

Theorem 3.8: The language

$$\tilde{L}_R = \{(R_i, R_j) \mid R_i, R_j \text{ regular expressions over } 0,1,\cdot,\cup,*,\neg,(,) \text{ and } L(R_i) \neq L(R_j)\}$$

cannot be recognized for any k in $2^{2^{\cdot^{\cdot^{\cdot^{2^n}}}}}/k$ tape. In other words, $\tilde{L}_R$ cannot be recognized on tape bounded by an elementary function.

The basic idea of the proof is very simple: if we can show that using extended regular expressions (i.e. with $\cdot,\cup,*,\neg$) we can describe the valid computations of Tm's using very large amounts of tape by very short regular expressions that are easily obtained from the Tm and its input, then the recognition of $\tilde{L}_R$ must require very large amounts of tape. To see this note that to test whether w is in $L(M_i)$ we can either run M_i on w, using whatever tape M_i requires, or else write down the regular expression, $R = \text{VCOMP}(w)$, describing the valid computations of M_i on w, and then test whether $L(R) = \emptyset$. Since w is accepted by M_i iff there exists a valid M_i computation in w, if the expression R is very short and the recognition of $\tilde{L}_R$ does not require much tape then this last procedure would save us a lot of tape. This is impossible, since there exist languages whose recognition requires arbitrarily large amounts of tape and these requirements cannot be (essentially) decreased [33,13]. Thus either method of testing whether w is in $L(M_i)$ must require a large amount of tape; which implies that the recognition of $\tilde{L}_R$ must require a large amount of tape.

The reason why the addition of complementation permits us to describe very long Turing machine computations economically is also easy to see, though the details of the proof are quite messy. The descriptive power is gained by using the complement to go from regular expressions describing invalid computations to regular expressions of (essentially) the same length describing valid computations. For example, consider a Tm M_i which, on any input of length n, counts up to 2^n and halts. Using the techniques from the proof of Theorem 3.5 we can write down

$$\text{NVCOMP}(x_1 x_2 \ldots x_n)$$

for this machine on cn tape squares, where c is fixed for M_i. But then

$$\neg \text{NVCOMP}(x_1 x_2 \ldots x_n) = \text{VCOMP}(x_1 x_2 \ldots x_n)$$

and we have a regular expression of length $\leq cn + 1 < Cn$, describing a computation which takes 2^n steps, and thus

VCOMP$(x_1 x_2 \ldots x_n)$ consists of a single string whose length is $\geq 2^{2n}$.

Next we indicate how the above regular expression is used to obtain a short regular expression for NVCOMP$(x_1 x_2 \ldots x_n)$ of Tm's using 2^n tape squares.

A close inspection of the proof of Theorem 3.5 shows that

$$\text{NVCOMP}(x_1 x_2 \ldots x_n) = R_1 \cup R_2 \cup R_3$$

and that the length of R_1 and R_2 grows linearly with n and does not depend on the amount of tape used by the Tm. Only R_3 has to take account of the amount of tape used in the computation since R_3 takes care of all the cases where an error occurs between successive instantaneous descriptions. In the proof of Theorem 3.5 we simply wrote out the right number of tape symbols between the corresponding places where the errors had to occur. Namely we used the regular expression

$$\Gamma^{n^k - 1}$$

as a "yardstick" to keep the errors properly spaced. The basic trick in this proof is to have short regular expressions for very long "yardsticks".

As indicated above, by means of complements we can write a regular expression for VCOMP$(x_1 x_2 \ldots x_n)$ of M_i which grows linearly in n and consists of a single sequence of length $\geq 2^n$. With a few ingenious tricks and the accompanying messy technical details we can use this regular expression as a yardstick to keep the errors properly spaced in a Tm computation using more than 2^n tape. Thus a regular expression which grows linearly in length can describe Tm computations using 2^n tape.

By iterating this process, we can construct for any k a regular expression whose length grows polynomially in n and which describes computations of Tm's using more than

$2^{2^{\cdot^{\cdot^{\cdot^{k}}}}2^n}$ tape squares for inputs of length n. From this we conclude by the previously outlined reasoning, that $\widetilde{L}_R$ cannot be recognized by any Tm using tape bounded by an elementary function.

For the sake of completeness we will mention a result [14] about regular expressions without ⌐, but with $\cup, \cdot, *$ and $\cap$.

Theorem 3.9: Let

$$L_R^{\hat{}} = \{(R_i, R_j) \mid R_i, R_j \text{ regular expressions over } 0, 1, \cup, \cdot, *, \cap, (,)$$
$$\text{and } L(R_i) \neq L(R_j)\}$$

Then the recognition of $L_R^{\hat{}}$ requires tape $L(n) \geq 2^{\sqrt{n}}$.

From the two previous results we see that the additional operator in regular expressions added considerably to the descriptive power of these expressions, in that the added operators permitted us to shorten regular expressions over $\cup, \cdot, *$ and that this shortening of the regular expressions is reflected in the resulting difficulty of recognizing $\widetilde{L}_R$ and $L_R^{\hat{}}$, respectively. Thus in a sense, these results can also be viewed as quantitative results about the descriptive powers of regular expressions with different operators.

Finally we note that the rather surprising result that for unrestricted regular expressions the equivalence is not decidable in elementary tape cannot be extended to single letter alphabets [29].

Theorem 3.10: The language

$$L_R^{SLA} = \{(R_i, R_j) \mid R_i, R_j \text{ regular expressions over } 1, \cup, \cdot, *, \neg, (,)$$
$$\text{and } L(R_i) = L(R_j)\}$$

can be recognized on

$$L(n) \leq 2^{2^{2^{2^{cn\log n}}}}$$

tape.

In the previous proofs we established the complexity of the recognition of unequal pairs of regular expressions by the following method: we described valid or invalid Tm computations by regular expressions and then related the efficiency of describing long Tm computations by short regular expressions to the complexity of the decision problem; the more powerful the descriptive power of our expressions (or languages) the harder the corresponding decision problem. We can actually state this somewhat more precisely as:

<u>Heuristic Principle</u>: If in some formalism one can describe with expressions of length n or less Tm computations using tape up to length $L(n)$, then the decision procedure for equality of these expressions must be of at least tape complexity $L(n)$.

For example, if a formalism enables us to state that a Tm accepts an input of length n using tape at most 2^n, and the length of such an expression is n^2, then any procedure that decides equality of two such expressions will have tape complexity at least $2^{\sqrt{n}}$. In [14] it is shown that regular expressions over $0,1,\cup,\cdot,\cap,*$ are such a formalism -- from which Theorem 3.9 follows.

Clearly, this principle also implies that if the formalism is so powerful that no computable function $L(n)$ can bound the length of tape used in Tm computations which can be described by expressions of length n, then the equivalence problem in this formalism is recursively undecidable. Thus this principle gives a nice view of how the expressive power of languages escalates the complexity of decision procedures until it becomes undecidable because the length of the Tm computations is no longer recursively bound to the length of the expressions describing them. Thus a formalism in which we can say "the i-th Tm halts", so that the length of this formula grows recursively in i, must have an undecidable decision problem. Very loosely speaking, as long as we can in our formalism make assertions about Tm computations, without describing the computations explicitly, we will have undecidable decision problems. As long as we must describe the Tm computations explicitly, the equivalence problem will be soluble and its computational difficulty depends on the descriptive power of the formalism.

Some of the most interesting applications of this principle have yielded the computational complexity of decision procedures for decidable logical theories. The results are rather depressing in that even for apparently simple theories the decision complexity makes them practically undecidable. We cite two such results.

We first consider the decision procedure for Pressburger arithmetic. We recall that Pressburger arithmetic consists of the true statements about integer arithmetic which can be expressed by using successor function S, addition, and equality. More formally, the theory is given by the axioms of first order predicate logic augmented by:

$(x = y) \rightarrow (\cdot(x) = S(y))$

$S(x) = S(y) \rightarrow (x = y)$

$S(x) \neq 0$

$x + 0 = x$

$x + S(y) = S(x + y)$

$A_{[x]}(0) \rightarrow [(\forall x) A \rightarrow A_{[x]}(S(x)) \rightarrow (\forall x)A]$ where x is not free in A and $A_{[x]}(y)$ means y substituted for every occurence of x in A (induction scheme)

The theory can express any fact about the integers that does not involve multiplication. For example, by writing

$(\underbrace{S...S(0)}_{i \text{ times}}...)$ we get a formula that denotes the integer i,

by writing $\underbrace{x + x + ... + x}_{n \text{ times}}$ where x is a formula, we may denote

nx (i.e. multiplication by a constant), by writing $(\exists x)[s + x = t]$ we express the fact that $s \leq t$, and by writing

$$(\exists x)[(r = s + \underbrace{x + x + \ldots + x}_{n \text{ times}}) \vee (s = r + \underbrace{x + x + \ldots + x}_{n \text{ times}})]$$

we are stating that $r \equiv s \pmod{n}$

It is a famous result of Pressburger's [28] that this theory is decidable: basically the reason is that all sentences of the theory can be effectively put into the form of a collection of different systems of linear diophantine equations, such that the original sentence is true iff one of the systems has a solution. Since linear diophantine equations are solvable, the theory is decidable. The transformation into and solution of the equations is costly in terms of space and time: the best known algorithm [25] has an upper bound of

$$2^{2^{2^{pn \log n}}}$$

on the deterministic time and storage required for a sentence of length n (p is a constant greater than 1).

Recently it has been shown [7] that any decision procedure will require at least a super exponential number of steps. More precisely

<u>Theorem 3.11</u>: There is a constant $c > 0$, such that for every (possibly nondeterministic) decision procedure A for Pressburger arithmetic, there is an integer n_0, such that for all $n > n_0$ there is a formula of length n which requires $2^{2^{cn}}$ steps of the procedure A to decide whether the formula is true.

The proof of this result is technically quite messy but again follows the principle of describing by short formulas in Pressburger arithmetic long Tm computations, thus forcing the decision procedure to be complex.

Next we look at a surprising result due to A. Meyer about the decision complexity of a decidable second order theory [20].

A logical theory is <u>second order</u> if we have quantifiers ranging over sets in the language. It is weak second order if set quantifiers range only over finite sets. All second order theories have, in addition to first order language symbols, a symbol, e.g. $\in$, to denote set membership. The weak monadic second order theory of one successor has the two predicates

$[x = S(y)]$ (or $x = y + 1$) and $[y \in X]$

with the usual interpretation. It was shown to be decidable by Buchi and Elgot [3],[4]. We shall abbreviate the theory by WS1S, and the set of sentences of its language by L_{S1S}.

Theorem 3.12: Let M be a Tm which, started with any sentence of L_{S1S} on its tape, eventually halts in a designated halting state iff the sentence is true. Then, for any $k \geq 0$, there are infinitely many n, for which M's computation requires more than

$$2^{2^{2^{\cdot^{\cdot^{\cdot^{2^n}}}}}} \Big\} k$$

steps and tape squares for some sentence of length n.

In other words, the decision procedure is not elementary recursive.

These asymptotic results actually hold for small n (of the order of the size of the Tm). Since they hold for the amount of tape used, the same bounds apply to lengths of proofs, in any reasonable formalism. Therefore, there are fairly short theorems in these theories (less than half a page long) that simply cannot be proven-- their shortest proofs are too long to write down.

The implications of these "practical undecidability" results are not yet well understood, but their philosophical impact on our ideas about formalized theories may turn out to be comparable to the impact of Goedel's undecidability result.

4. Nondeterministic tape computations and the lba problem

It is known, as pointed out before, that PTAPE = NPTAPE and that a nondeterministic $L(n)$-tape bounded computation ($L(n) \geq \log n$)

can be simulated deterministically on $L^2(n)$ tape [31]. On the other hand, it is not known whether we cannot do better than the square when we go from deterministic to nondeterministic tape bounded computations. As a matter of fact, we do not know whether we cannot eliminate nondeterminism in tape bounded computations by just enlarging the tape alphabet and not the amount of tape used.

This problem of how much memory we can save by using nondeterministic computations has been a recognized open problem since 1964 when it first appeared as a problem about context-sensitive languages or linearly bounded automata [24,18,17,9].

For the sake of completeness we recall that a <u>linearly bounded automaton</u> is a one-tape Turing machine whose input is placed between endmarkers and the Tm cannot go past these endmarkers. Thus all the computations of the lba are performed on as many tape squares as are needed to write down the input and since the lba can have arbitrarily large (but fixed) tape alphabet, we see that the amount of tape for any given lba (measured as length of equivalent binary tape) is linearly bounded by the length of the input word. If the Tm defining the lba operates deterministically we refer to the automaton as a <u>deterministic lba</u>, otherwise as a <u>nondeterministic lba</u> or simply an lba.

Since the connection between linearly bounded automata and context-sensitive languages is well-known [13], we will also refer to the languages accepted by nondeterministic and deterministic lba's as nondeterministic and deterministic context-sensitive languages, respectively. Let the corresponding families of languages be denoted by NDCSL and DCSL, respectively.

Then the lba <u>problem</u> is to decide whether NDCSL = DCSL. It is also an open problem to decide whether the nondeterministic context-sensitive languages are closed under complementation. Clearly if

NDCSL = DCSL then they are closed under complementation, but it still could happen that NDCSL $\neq$ DCSL and that the context-sensitive languages are closed under complementation.

We now show that there exist time and tape hardest recognizable context-sensitive languages. That is, the family NDCSL has complete languages and, as a matter of fact, we have already discussed such languages in this paper.

Recall that

$$L_R^* = \{R_i | R_i \text{ regular expression over } 0,1,\cup,*,(,) \text{ and } L(R) \neq (0 \cup 1)^*\}$$

and let

$$L_{LBA} = \{\#M_i\#CODE(x_1 x_2 \ldots x_n)\# | x_1 x_2 \ldots x_n \text{ is accepted by lba } M_i\}.$$

<u>Theorem 4.1</u>: 1. DCSL = NDCSL iff L_R^* is in DCSL iff L_{LBA} is in DCSL.

2. L in NDCSL implies $\bar{L}$ in NDCSL iff $\overline{L_{LBA}}$ is in NDCSL.

3. DCSL $\subseteq$ NP(P) iff L_{LBA} is in NP(P) iff L_R is in NP(P).

The proof is quite similar to the previous proofs that L_{UT} and L_R^* are complete in PTAPE.

It is interesting to note that if L_{LBA} of L_R^* can be recognized on a deterministic lba then all nondeterministic tape computations using $L_i(n) \geq n$ tape can be replaced by equivalent deterministic computations using no more tape. Furthermore, there is a recursive translation which maps the nondeterministic Turing machines onto the equivalent deterministic Turing machines.

<u>Corollary 4.2</u>: DCSL = NDCSL iff there exists a recursive translation σ such that for every nondeterministic Tm M_i which uses $L_i(n) \geq n$ tape, $M_{\sigma(i)}$ is an equivalent deterministic Tm using no more than $L_i(n)$ tape.

<u>Proof</u>: The proof is similar to the proof of Theorem 2.3. For details see [9].

From the above results we see that if DCSL = NDCSL then all

other deterministic and nondeterministic tape-bounded computations using more than a linear amount of tape are the same. On the other hand, we have not been able to force the equality downward. For example, we have not been able to show that if all deterministic and nondeterministic tape-bounded computations using $L_i(n) \geq 2^n$ tape are the same, that then DCSL = NDCSL.

Similarly, it could happen that DCSL = NDCSL but that the logn-bounded deterministic languages are properly contained in the non-deterministic logn-bounded computations.

It is worth mentioning that Greibach [8] has recently exhibited a context-free language which plays the same role among context-free languages as L_{LBA} does for context-sensitive languages. Namely, this context-free language is the hardest time and tape recognizable cfl and there also exist two recursive translations mapping context-free grammars into Turing machines recognizing the language generated by the grammar in the minimal time and on the minimal amount of tape, respectively, though at this time we do not know what is the minimal time or tape required for the recognition of context-free languages.

5. Random access machines

In this section we study random access machines which have been proposed as abstract models for digital computers and which reflect many aspects of real computing more directly than Turing machines do. On the other hand, as it will be seen from the results in this chapter, the study of the computational power of random access machines with different instruction sets leads us right back to the central problems which arose in the study of Tm computations. Thus, quite surprisingly, we will show that the difference in computing power of polynomially time bounded RAM's with and without multiplication is characterized by the difference between PTIME and PTAME for Tm's

More specifically, it is known that the computation time of random access machines without multiplication is polynomially related to the equivalent Tm computation time, and vice versa. Thus the question of whether the deterministic and nondeterministic polynomially time bounded random access machine computations are the same is equivalent to the question of whether P = NP for Tm computations, a problem we discussed before.

In contrast, when we consider random access machines with the power to multiply in unit time, the situation is completely different. We show that for these devices nondeterministic and deterministic computation time is polynomially related and therefore for random access machines with built-in multiplication, P = NP [32,12]. Furthermore, we give a complete characterization of the computational power of these devices: the family of languages accepted in polynomial time by random access machines with multiplication is exactly PTAPE, the family of languages accepted by Tm's in polynomial tape. Thus the additional computing power that a random access machine with multiplication has over such a machine without multiplication is characterized by the difference between PTIME and PTAPE for Tm computations. Recall that we do not know whether PTIME $\neq$ PTAPE and therefore, multiplication could be simulated in polynomial time by addition and boolean operations iff PTIME = PTAPE; again, an open problem which we have already discussed.

For related results about other random access machine models and for more detailed proofs than given in this paper see [12,32,27].

To make these concepts precise we now describe random access machines, RAM's, with different operation sets and step counting functions. Note that we again consider these devices as acceptors.

Definition: A RAM acceptor or RAM with instruction set O is a set of registers $R_0, R_1, \ldots$ each capable of storing a non-negative integer in binary representation, together with a finite <u>program</u> of (possibly labeled) <u>0-instructions</u>. If no two labels are the same, we say that the program is <u>deterministic</u>, otherwise it is <u>nondeterministic</u>. We call a RAM model deterministic if we consider only deterministic programs from the instruction set.

Our first instruction set consists of the following:

O_1

$R_i \leftarrow R_j$ (=k)	(assignment)
$R_i \leftarrow <R_j>$	(indirect addressing)
$R_i \leftarrow R_j + R_k$	(sum)
$R_i \leftarrow R_j \dot{-} R_k$	(proper subtraction)
$R_i \leftarrow R_j$ <u>bool</u> R_k	(boolean operations)
<u>if</u> R_i <u>comp</u> R_j label 1 <u>else</u> label 2	(conditional jump)
<u>accept</u>	
<u>reject</u>	

<u>comp</u> may be any of $<, \leq, =, \geq, >, \neq$. For boolean operations we consider the integers as bit strings and do the operations componentwise. Leading 0's are dropped at the end of operations: for example 11 <u>nand</u> 10 = 1. <u>bool</u> may be any binary boolean operation (e.g. $\wedge, \vee$, <u>eor</u>, <u>nand</u>, $\supset$, etc.). <u>accept</u> and <u>reject</u> have obvious meanings. An operand of =k is a literal and the constant k itself should be used.

The computation of a RAM starts by putting the input in register R_0, setting all registers to 0 and executing the first instruction of the RAM's program. Instructions are executed in sequence until a conditional jump is encountered, after which one of the instructions with label "label 1" is executed is the condition is satisfied and one of the instructions with label "label 2" is executed otherwise. Execution stops when an <u>accept</u> or <u>reject</u> instruction is met. A string $x \in \{0,1\}^*$ is accepted by the RAM if there is a finite computation ending with the execution of an <u>accept</u> instruction.

The complexity measures defined for RAM's are:

<u>(unit) time measure:</u> the complexity of an accepting computation is the number of instructions executed in the accepting sequence. The complexity of the RAM on input x is the minimal complexity of accepting computations.

<u>logarithmic, or length time measure</u>: the complexity of an accepting computation is the sum of the lengths of the operands of the instructions executed in the accepting sequence. When there are two operands, we take the length of the longer; when an operand has length 0 we use 1 in the sum. The complexity of the RAM on input x is the minimal complexity among accepting computations.

<u>memory measure</u>: the maximum number of bits used at any time in the computation. (The number of bits used at a given time is the sum of the number of significant bits of all registers in use at that time.)

Unless otherwise stated, time measure will mean unit time measure. We shall call RAM's with instruction set O_1 RAM_1's, or simply RAM's. For a discussion of RAM complexity measures, see [5] or [1].

We will consider another instruction set:

<u>O_2</u> is O_1 plus the instruction

$$R_i \leftarrow R_j \cdot R_k \qquad \text{(product)}$$

which computes the product of the two operands (which may be literals) and stores it in R_i. RAM's with instruction set O_2 will be called MRAM's (M for multiplication).

We denote by PTIME - MRAM and by NPTIME - MRAM, respectively, the families of languages accepted in polynomial time by deterministic and nondeterministic MRAM's.

We shall outline below the proof of the main results about MRAM's (for more detailed proofs and related results see [12,32,27])

Theorem 5.1: PTAPE $\supseteq$ NPTIME - MRAM

Theorem 5.2: PTIME - MRAM $\supseteq$ PTAPE.

Thus for MRAM's we have that deterministic and nondeterministic polynomial time computations are the same.

Corollary 5.3: PTAPE = NPTAPE.

This follows from the fact that the proofs of Theorems 5.1 and 5.2 actually imply that PTAPE $\supseteq$ NPTIME - MRAM and that PTIME - MRAM $\supseteq$ NPTAPE.

We now sketch a proof of Theorem 5.1.

Suppose the MRAM M operates in time n^k, where n is the length of the input. Our Tm simulator T will write out in one of its tapes a guess for the sequence of operations executed by M in its accepting computation and check that the sequence is correct. The sequence may be written down deterministically, by enumerating all such sequences of length n^k in alphabetical order. Since the number of instructions of M's program is a constant, the sequence will be of length cn^k for some constant c. To verify that such a sequence is indeed an accepting computation of M we need to check that one step follows from the previous one when M's program is executed -- which is only a problem in the case of conditional instructions, when we must find out the contents of a register. We shall define a function FIND(r,b,t) which will return the value of the b-th bit of register r at time t. Our theorem will be proved if this function is computable in polynomial tape -- the subject of the remainder of this part. Note that since we are testing for <u>an</u> accepting sequence, it does not matter whether we are simulating deterministic or nondeterministic machines.

First, let us prove that the arguments of FIND may be written down in polynomial tape. Note that in t operations the biggest possible number that may be generated is a^{2^t}, produced by successive multiplications: a, a^2, $a^2 \cdot a^2 = a^4$, $a^4 \cdot a^4 = a^8, \ldots, a^{2^t}$, where a is the maximum of x and the biggest literal in M's program. To address a bit of it, we need to count up to its length, that is, up to $\log_2(a^{2^t}) = 2^t \log_2 a$, which may be done in space $\log_2(2^t \log_2 a)$. In particular, for $t = n^k$, space n^{k+1} will suffice, so that b may be written down in polynomial tape. Clearly, t may also be written down in polynomial tape. There is a small difficulty with r: due to indirect addressing M might use high-numbered registers, even though it uses only a polynomial number of them. However, by using a symbol table, at a cost of a squaring of the running time, we may assume that a machine operating in time t uses only its t first registers. It is clear that in that case r may be written down in polynomial tape. Now let us describe FIND and prove that it operates in polynomial tape.

Informally, FIND works as follows: FIND(r,b,0) is easily computed given the input. We shall argue inductively. FIND(r,b,t) will be computed from previous values of FIND -- clearly the only interesting case is when r was altered in the previous move. For example, if the move at t-1 was $r \leftarrow pVs$, then FIND(r,b,t) = FIND(p,b,t-1) V FIND(s,b,t-1). This recursion in time does not cause any problems, because we may first compute FIND(p,b,t-1) and then reuse the tape for a call of FIND(s,b,t-1), so that if ℓ_{t-1} is the amount of tape needed to compute FIND's for time up to t-1, we have the recurrence $\ell_t = \ell_{t-1} + c$ ($\ell_0 = cn^{k+1}$) which has the solution $\ell_t = c'n^{k+1}$.

In the case of multiplication of two ℓ-digit numbers, we may have to compute up to ℓ factors and get the carry from the previous column in order to obtain the desired bit. Since ℓ may be 2^{n^k}, we must be able to take advantage of the regularity of operations in order to be able to compute within polynomial tape. Also, the carry from the previous column may be quite big: in the worst case, when we multiply $(1)^\ell$ by $(1)^\ell$ the carry may be ℓ. This is still manageable, since in time n^k, $\ell \leq 2^{n^k}$, an accumulator of length n^k will suffice. We also need to generate up to ℓ pairs of bits, multiply them in pairs, and add them up. This may be done as follows: we store the addresses of the two bits being computed, compute each of the two bits of the product separately, multiply the two results and update the addresses to get the addresses of the two bits of the next product. The product is added to an accumulator and the process is repeated until all product terms have been computed. Then we need the carry from the previous column.

We cannot compute this carry by a recursive call of FIND, because since the length of the register may be exponential, keeping track of the recursion would take exponential tape. Instead, we compute the carries explicitly from the bottom up --i.e., we first compute the carry at the rightmost column (finding the bits by recursive calls of FIND on pairs and multiplying them), and then, with that carry and FIND, we compute the carry from the second rightmost column, and so on. The space needed is only for keeping track of which column we are at, one recursive call of FIND, one accumulator and one previous carry holder. Each of these may be written down in space n^{k+1}, so that we have the recursion

$$\ell_t = \ell_{t-1} + cn^{k+1} \text{ with } \ell_0 = n$$

which implies $\ell_t \leq cn^{2k+1}$, and the simulation of multiplication may be carried out in polynomial space. The argument for + is similar but much easier, since only 2 bits and a carry of at most 1 are involved.

With the above comments in mind it is easy to write out a complete simulation program and see that it runs in polynomial time. This ends the proof of our theorem, i.e.

Theorem 5.1: Polynomial time bounded nondeterministic MRAM-recognizable languages are recognizable in polynomial tape by Turing machines.

Now we sketch the ideas behind the proof of Theorem 5.2. They are basically a set of programming tricks that enable us to do operations in parallel very efficiently.

To simplify our proof we will use a special RAM model referred to as CRAM (for concatenation). A CRAM is a RAM with the ability to concatenate the contents of two registers in one operation, and also has the operator SUBSTR(A,B) which replaces A by the string obtained from A by deleting the initial substring of the length ℓ, where ℓ is the length of B.

It can be seen that CRAM computations may be simulated easily by MRAM's, and that SUBSTR is not essential to the construction.

For any given Tm T operating in polynomial tape on input x, a CRAM can first generate all possible configurations of this Tm computation (a configuration of T on input x consists of the state of T, the contents of the work-tape and the positions of T's heads). From this set of all possible configurations, the CRAM can obtain the matrix of the relation "follow in one move" -- i.e. if A is the matrix of the relation, then $a_{ij} = 1$ iff T passes from the i-th to the j-th configuration in one move. Clearly, x is accepted by T iff $a^*_{be} = 1$ where A* is the transitive closure of A and b and e are initial and accepting final configurations respectively.

First we indicate how to compute efficiently the transitive closure of a matrix A. We suppose that initially the whole matrix is in a single register. Remember that $A^* = I \lor A \lor A^2 \lor A^3 \ldots \lor A^n \lor \ldots$, where A is n by n and A^i is the i-th power of A in the "and-or" multiplication (i.e. if $C = A \cdot B$, $c_{ij} = \bigvee_{k=1}^{n} a_{ik} \land b_{kj}$). Moreover, we may compute only the products

$(I \lor A), (I \lor A)^2, (I \lor A)^2 \cdot (I \lor A)^2 = (I \lor A)^4, \ldots$ where the exponent of $(I \lor A)$ is a power of 2. Since there are only $\log n$ of these $((I \lor A)^{n+1} = (I \lor A)^n)$, transitive closure of n by n matrices can be done in time $\log n$ times the time for multiplication. Throughout this proof, "multiplication" will mean "$\land$" and "multiplication of matrices", "and-or" multiplication. Also, for simplicity, we assume n to be a power of 2.

To multiply two matrices efficiently, we observe that if we have several copies of the matrix stored in the same register in a convenient way, we can obtain all products in a single "$\land$" operation: all we need is that for all i,j, and k, a_{ik} be in the same bit position as b_{kj}. For example, if we have

(row 0 of A)^n(row 1 of A)^n...(row n-1 of A)^n =

$(a_{0,0}a_{0,1}\cdots a_{0,n-1})^n (a_{1,0}a_{1,1}\cdots a_{1,n-1})^n \cdots (a_{n-1,0}a_{n-1,1}\cdots a_{n-1,n-1})^n$

in one register (where (row i)^n means n-fold concatenation) and

[(column 0 of b)(column 1 of B)...(column n-1 of B)]^n =

$[(b_{0,0}b_{1,0}\cdots b_{n-1,0})(b_{0,1}b_{1,1}\cdots b_{n-1,1})\cdots(b_{0,n-1}\cdots b_{n-1,n-1})]^n$

in the other, the "$\land$" of the two registers yields all terms $a_{ik} \land b_{kj}$. Supposing we are able to produce these forms of the matrices easily, all we have to do is collect terms and add ($\lor$) them up. To collect terms, if we are able to take advantage of the parallel operations at their fullest, we should not have to do more than $\log n$ operations, since each c_{ij} is the sum of n products. Note that in our case $c_{0,0}$ is the sum of the first n bits, $c_{0,1}$ of the next n, and in general c_{ij} is the sum of bits $i \cdot n + (j-1)n$ to $i \cdot n + jn - 1$.

We use the following idea: to add up a row vector of bits, take the second half of the row, add it in parallel to the first half and call the procedure recursively for the new first half. The reader is encouraged to write a routine, using the mask $M' = 0^{n/2}1^{n/2}$ to select the second half (n is the length of the vector) and prefixing strings of 0's to registers to get proper alignment. It is possible to design the algorithm in such a way that this procedure may be done in parallel for several vectors, stored concatenated to each other in a single register. In particular if one starts with n^2 copies of the mask M', then the following procedure obtains all terms of the matrix product C = A B from all the products $a_{ik} \wedge b_{kj}$:

ADDUP:PROC

$\qquad M = (0^{n/2} \cdot 1^{n/2})^{n^2}$

$\qquad K = n/2$

$\qquad \underline{\text{while}} \ K \geq 1 \ \underline{\text{do}}$

$\qquad\qquad B = A \wedge M$

$\qquad\qquad A = ((0^K \cdot A) \ V \ B) \wedge M$

$\qquad\qquad K = K/2$

$\qquad\qquad M = (0^K \cdot M) \wedge M$

$\qquad\qquad \underline{\text{end}}$

$\quad$ end:ADDUP

ADDUP uses 0^K and K/2 as primitive operations, but K/2 = SUBSTR(K,1) and 0^K may be obtained by successive concatenations of a string with itself: after p steps we get a string of 0's of length 2^p.

In order to perform matrix multiplication one must be able to expand matrices from some standard input form into the two forms we needed in forming the product. In addition, for transitive closure, we must "pack" the result back into standard form. We do not give the messy details: the sort of programming is illustrated by ADDUP. Basically one uses masks and logical operations to get the required bits from their original places, then using concatenations one "slides" a number of them simultaneously to where they belong. The masks and "sliding rules" are updated and the process repeated. It can be shown that all these operations require only time polynomial in the logarithm of the size of the matrix. In fact transitive closure of $n \times n$ boolean matrices may be found in $O(\log n^2)$ CRAM moves.

We still have to convince the reader that given a polynomial tape bounded Tm with input x, we can obtain the matrix of the "follow in one move" relation easily. We shall do this in an even sketchier way than our exposition of the method for computing transitive closures.

If a Tm operates on an input of length n in tape n^k, there are at most $O(2^{cn^k})$ different configurations. Let us take a convenient encoding of these in the alphabet $\{0,1\}$ and interpret the encodings as integers. By convenient encoding we mean one that is linear in the length of the tape used by the machine, where the positions of the heads and the state may be easily found, and which may be easily updated. Then, if we generate all the integers in the range $0 - (2^{cn^k}-1)$ (where c depends only on the encoding) we shall have produced encodings of all configurations, together with numbers that are not encodings of any configuration. The reader might amuse himself by writing a CRAM program that produces all integers between 0 and $m = 2^p-1$ in time p.

Now, in the operation of the Tm the character under the read-write head, the two symbols in the squares immediately to the right and left of it, the state of the finite control and the position of the input head uniquely determine the next configuration (i.e. $\text{CORRECT}(\sigma_1 \sigma_2 \sigma_3)$).

This is the sort of localized change that may be checked by boolean operations. More precisely, it is not hard to write a CRAM routine that checks that configuration c_i follows from configuration c_j in $O(\ell)$ moves, where ℓ is the length of the configurations. Moreover, the operations executed by the program do not depend on the contents of c_i or c_j -- in particular it may be adapted to check whether for vectors of configurations c_{it} $t = 0,1,\ldots,p$, c_{jk} $k = 0,1,\ldots p$ c_{jk} follows from c_{it} still using only $O(\ell)$ moves. Now the way to generate the transition matrix in time $O(n^{2k})$ where n is the length of the input is: first we generate all integers in the range $0 - (2^{n^k}-1)$, call these configurations c_i. Then, as in the matrix product routine, we form $(c_0)^m(c_1)^m\ldots(c_{m-1})^m$ where $m = 2^{n^k}$ and $(c_i)^m$ means m-fold concatenation, and $(c_0c_1\ldots c_{m-1})^m$ in $O(\log m) = O(n^k)$ operations, and in $O(n^k)$ operations determine simultaneously for all i and j whether c_j follows from c_i (i.e. obtain a vector of bits which is 1 iff c_j follows from c_i). This completes the description of our simulation algorithm: putting everything together we have a procedure which runs in polynomial time, since the matrix may be computed in $O((\log 2^{cn^k})^2)$ moves and its transitive closure in $O((\log 2^{cn^k})^2) = O(n^{2k})$ moves.

This completes the outline of the proof for the special CRAM used.

Let us restate the results of this chapter. We defined a reasonable RAM model -- the MRAM -- that has multiplication as a primitive operation, and proved two important facts about their power as recognizers:

1) deterministic and nondeterministic time complexity classes are polynomially related, i.e. PTIME - MRAM = NPTIME - MRAM .

2) time-bounded computations are polynomially related to Tm tape, i.e. PTIME - MRAM = PTAPE .

Since it can be proven that RAM time and Tm time are polynomially related, we also proved

3) RAM running times with and without multiplication are polynomially related if and only if Tm time and tape measures are polynomially related, i.e. PTIME = PTAPE iff PTIME - MRAM = PTIME - RAM_1.

This last observation is interesting, since it seems to imply that the elusive difference between time and memory measures for Tm's might perhaps be attacked by "algebraic" techniques developed in "low level" complexity theory.

We also note that RAM's may simulate MRAM's in polynomial time, as long as MRAM's operate in polynomial space and time. Therefore MRAM's are more powerful than RAM's if and only if the unit and logarithmic time measures are not polynomially related -- i.e. if (in our "polynomial smearing" language) the two are distinct measures.

Many "if and only if" type corollaries follow, in the same vein, from 1), 2) and 3). For example:

<u>Corollary 5.4</u>: The set of regular expressions whose complements are non-empty (i.e. L_R^* of section 3) is accepted in polynomial time by a deterministic Tm iff every language recognized by an MRAM in polynomial time is recognized by a deterministic RAM in polynomial time.

The reader may write down many of these: some of them sound quite surprising at first.

Minsky suggested [23] that one of the objectives of theoretical computer science should be the study of trade-offs (e.g. between memory and time, nondeterminism and time, etc.). Our constructions trade exponential storage for polynomial time (simulation of Tm's by MRAM's) and polynomial tape for exponential time in the other simulation. Whether this trade-off is real or the result of bad programming is not known, since P = PTAPE? is an open problem. If P $\neq$ PTAPE, then PTAPE would provide us with a class of languages which have a trade-off property: they may be recognized either in polynomial time or in polynomial storage, but not simultaneously.

<u>Corollary 5.5</u>: PTIME $\neq$ PTAPE iff there exists a language L which can be recognized by MRAM's in polynomial time and polynomial memory, but not simultaneously.

Note that if such an L exists, any tape complete problem may be chosen to be it, for example L_R^*.

As we saw, if MRAM's are different from RAM's, they must use more than a polynomial amount of storage (in our simulation it was an exponential amount). This suggests asking whether it is sufficient to have a RAM and exponential tape to get an MRAM's power, or, equivalently, to look at operations that make RAM - PTIME classes equivalent to PTAPE. The answer is that almost anything that expands the length of the registers fast enough will do, as long as we have parallel bit operations: multiplication, concatenation or shifting all have this property. In particular, concatenation, tests and parallel bit operations (no indirect addressing) will do. On the other hand, adding more and more powerful operations (indirect addressing, shifts by shift registers, division by 2, SUBSTR, multiplication, integer division) do not make the model more powerful, once we have a fast memory-augmenting device. The stability of this class of RAM's makes them a nice characterization of memory-bound complexity classes. We also think they might be useful for studying parallelism.

Since we believe that P $\neq$ NP (and therefore PTIME - RAM $\neq$ NPTIME - RAM) but PTIME - MRAM = NPTIME - MRAM it seems interesting to ask what happens to the P = NP? question in an abstract setting, when we allow a fixed but arbitrary set of recursive operations in a single step. The surprising result [2] is that there are instruction sets for which P = NP and instruction sets for which P $\neq$ NP -- in other words the problem becomes meaningless when asked in such a general setting. Since we have argued that P = NP? is a central problem of theoretical computer science, the result appears to us like a general warning that, by becoming too formal too soon, we can "generalize away" the problems of interest to computer science, and wind up with uninteresting abstractions.

In particular, a proof that P $\neq$ NP would have to deal somehow with the nitty-gritty combinatorics of the problem. We note that our technique for proving inclusion among sets -- diagonalization -- is usually insensitive to such details. The requirement that diagonal arguments be extremely efficient is peculiar to computer science, and the discovery of such a technique may be as big a breakthrough as the discovery of priority methods (nonrecursive but r.e. diagonal methods) was in recursion theory.

Bibliography

[1] Aho, A., J.E. Hopcroft and J.D. Ullman: The design and analysis of computer algorithms. Addison-Wesley, Reading, Mass. 1974

[2] Baker, T., J. Gill and R. Solovay: Relativization of the P =? NP question. To be published in SICOMP.

[3] Büchi, J.R.: Weak second order arithmetic and finite automata. Zeit. f. Math. Log. und Grund. der Math., 6(1960) 66-92.

[4] Büchi, J.R. and C.C. Elgot: Decision problems of weak second order arithmetics and finite automata, Part I. AMS Notices, 5(1959) Abstract 834.

[5] Cook, S.: Linear time simulation of deterministic two-way pushdown automata. Information Processing 71. North Holland, Amsterdam 1972. 75-80.

[6] Cook, S.: The complexity of theorem-proving procedures. Proc. 3rd Ann. ACM Symp. Th. Comp. 1971 151-158.

[7] Fisher, M.J. and M.O. Rabin: Super-exponential complexity of Pressburger arithmetic. Project MAC TM 43 (1974).

[8] Greibach, S.: The hardest context-free language. SIAM J. Comp. v.2, (1973) 304-310.

[9] Hartmanis, J. and H.B. Hunt III: The lba problem and its importance in the theory of computing. TR-171 Dept. Comp. Sci. Cornell University (1973). To be published by the AMS.

[10] Hartmanis, J. and H. Shank: Two memory bounds for the recognition of primes by automata. MST v.3 (1969) 125-129.

[11] Hartmanis, J. and H. Shank: On the recognition of primes by automata. JACM v.15(1968) 382-389.

[12] Hartmanis, J. and J. Simon: On the power of multiplication in random access machines. Conf. Rec. IEEE 15th SWAT (1974).

[13] Hopcroft, J.E. and J.D. Ullman: Formal languages and their relation to automata. Addison-Wesley, Reading, Mass. 1969.

[14] Hunt, H.B. III: On time and tape complexity of languages. Ph.D. Dissertation, 1973, Cornell University, Ithaca, N.Y.

[15] Hunt, H.B. III: On time and tape complexity of languages. 5th Ann. ACM Symp. Th. Comp. (1973)10-19.

[16] Karp, R.: Reducibilities among combinatorial problems. R. Miller and J. Thatcher (eds), Complexity of Computer Computations. Plenum Press (1972) 85-104.

[17] Kuroda, S.Y.: Classes of languages and linear bounded automata. Information and Control v.3 (1964) 207-223.

[18] Landweber, P.S.: Three theorems on phrase structure grammars of type 1. Information and Control v.2(1963) 131-136.

[19] McNaughton, R. and H. Yamada: Regular expressions and state graphs. E.F. Moore (ed) Sequential Machines: Selected Papers. Addison-Wesley, Reading, Mass. 1964.

[20] Meyer, A.: Weak monadic second order theory of successor is not elementary recursive. M.I.T. Project MAC TM 38(1973).

[21] Meyer, A. and L. Stockmeyer: The equivalence problem for regular expressions with squaring requires exponential space. Conf. Rec. IEEE 13th SWAT(1972) 125-129.

[22] Meyer, A. and L. Stockmeyer: Word problems requiring exponential tape. Proc. 5th Ann. ACM Symp. Th. Comp. (1973) 1-9.

[23] Minsky, M.: Form and content in computer science. JACM v.17 n.2 (1970) 197-215.

[24] Myhill, J.: Linearly bounded automata. WADD Technical Note 60-165 (June 1960).

[25] Oppen, D.C.: Elementary bounds for Pressburger arithmetic. Proc. 5th Ann. ACM Symp. Th. Comp.(1973) 34-37.

[26] Pratt, V.R.: Every prime has a succinct certification. Unpublished manuscript (January 1974).

[27] Pratt, V., L. Stockmeyer and M.O. Rabin: A characterization of the power of vector machines. Proc. 6th Ann. ACM Symp. Th. Comp. (1974) 122-134.

[28] Pressburger, M.: Über die Vollstandigkeit eines gewissen System der Arithmetik ganzen Zahlen, in welchen die Addition als einzige Operation hervortritt. Comptes-Rendus du I Congres des Mathematiciens des Pays Slavs. Warsaw, 1929.

[29] Rangel, J.L.: The equivalence problem for regular expressions over one letter alphabet is elementary. Conf. Rec. IEEE 15th SWAT (1974)

[30] Rogers, H. Jr.: Theory of recursive functions and effective computability. McGraw-Hill, New York. 1967.

[31] Savitch, W.J.: Relations between nondeterministic and deterministic tape complexities. JCSS v.4(1970) 177-192.

[32] Simon, J.: On the power of multiplication in random access machines. TR 74-205 Dept. of Comp. Sci. Cornell University (1974).

[33] Stearns, R.E., J. Hartmanis and P.M. Lewis: Hierarchies of memory limited computations. Conf. Rec. IEEE 6th SWAT (1965) 179-190.

[34] Stockmeyer, L.J.: The complexity of decision problems in automata theory and logic. Project MAC TR 133 (July 1974).

TOWARD A METHODOLOGY FOR DESIGNING LARGE SYSTEMS AND VERIFYING THEIR PROPERTIES

Peter G. Neumann
Computer Science Group
Stanford Research Institute
Menlo Park, California USA

Gesellschaft für Informatik
Berlin, West Germany
9-12 October 1974

ABSTRACT

This paper presents a rationale for a unified general approach to computer systems development, applicable to operating systems, applications subsystems, and hardware. A case is made for a formal methodology for design and implementation with which it is possible to verify system properties formally. Various goals for such a methodology are stated. Relevant existing work is cited. The potential effectiveness of this approach is discussed.

INTRODUCTION

This paper considers the task of designing, implementing, debugging, operating, modifying, and maintaining a large computer system (including its hardware and its operating system). It also considers the task of verifying that the system actually does what is expected of it--e.g., with respect to performance, security, and recovery from faults. It is the purpose of this paper to outline goals for, and steps toward, a methodology for this overall effort. The emphasis here is on a unified methodology to facilitate:

- Definition and design of a system or family of systems, represented as a structure of formally specified modules with formally specified interconnections.

- Implementation consistent with the design.

- Verification of asserted properties of the system design, implementation, and operation and other forms of validation.

- Graceful evolution, including facile handling of incremental changes.

This paper contains a discussion of the goals that such a methodology should attain. It briefly summarizes techniques, tools, and concepts that can contribute to the methodology. It also discusses a particular methodology. Such a methodology can be applicable not just to operating systems and hardware in large system developments, but also to smaller efforts such as special-purpose operating systems and their hardware, and to applications subsystems.

GOALS FOR THE METHODOLOGY

A general methodology for developing computer systems should be based on a clear statement of the desired goals for the methodology. The primary goals for such a methodology are that it should:

- Enhance the effectiveness of each resulting system, in terms of its cost-effectiveness and its correctness of operation (e.g., reliability, security, and recovery).

- Enhance the effectiveness of the development of each system or family of systems.

In order to achieve these primary goals, it is desirable that the methodology should:

- Enhance each phase of the overall effort, including design, implementation, debugging, testing, verification, operation, fault recovery, monitoring, tuning, maintenance, and evolution of the resulting system(s).

- Integrate these phases--e.g., using common languages and common formalizations.

- Provide successively increasing confidence throughout the development as to the goodness of the design and the implementation, and to the thoroughness of the verification.

- Inspire good management.

- Support relevant human needs (of users, system programmers, maintainers, managers, etc.).

Many contemporary system developments have suffered from the lack of such a methodology, or even from approaches for which some of these goals are in conflict. We thus next consider a collection of techniques that can be useful to attaining these goals.

APPROACHES USEFUL IN SUCH A METHODOLOGY

Various techniques and approaches have been emerging that are useful in developing such a methodology. Some are listed below, along with illustrative--but by no means comprehensive--references. Particularly relevant here is the use of:

- Structure in design and implementation. This includes notions of structured programming, top-down programming, levels of abstraction for data and procedures, such as hierarchical design and other functional decompositions of the system into abstract machines, formal mechanisms for handling abnormal conditions and error returns, and the systematic use of particular underlying concepts in hardware and software, such as a capability-addressing mechanism and a virtual machine approach. (Simon 62, Dijkstra 68a, 68b, 72a, 72b, Wirth 71b, Parnas 72b, 72c, 72d, 74, Parnas and Siewiorek 72, Horning and Randell 72, Hoare 72, Dahl 72, Dennis 73b, Goos 73a, 73b, Neumann 73, Neumann et al. 74, Bredt and Saxena 74, Brinch Hansen 74, Horning et al. 74, Linden 74)

- Formal specification languages and assertion languages for describing the desired behavior of each functional entity of the system, i.e., each abstract machine. Such languages are higher-level than programming languages and non-procedural, avoiding knowledge of implementation detail. They concern results, not how results are achieved. They include the ability to refer to data structures and operations of other abstract programs. (Parnas 72a, Glaser et al. 72, Giloi and Liebig 74, Robinson and Levitt 74) Formal descriptions of languages and language processors may also be useful. (Wegner 72, Hoare and Wirth 72)

- Suitable algorithmic programming languages for describing the implementations of abstract machines in terms of the operations and data structures of other (more primitive) abstract machines and corresponding language processors. Some of these languages may be highly constrained to avoid cumbersome constructs, or may have special constructs suitable for their applications. (Wegbreit 71, Wirth 71a, 74, Liskov and Zilles 73, Dennis 73a, Goos 73c, Wulf 74, Brinch Hansen 74, Clark and Horning 74, Dijkstra 74, Neumann et al. 74)

- Testing and debugging tools. (Rustin 71, Hetzel 73)

- Generation of assertions and verification conditions (i.e., theorems) to be verified. (Tlspas et al. 72b, Wegbreit, 73, Katz and Manna 73, Elspas 74, German and Wegbreit 74)

- Formal verification of theorems about the system and the language processors, and checking that proofs are correct (McCarthy 61, Floyd 67, Bledsoe and Gilbert 67, Good 70, Elspas et al. 72a, Waldinger and Levitt 73, Deutsch 73, Igarashi et al. 73, Milner 72, Weyhrauch 74, Boyer and Moore 75)

- Partial verification and simulation environments--e.g., with simulations for unimplemented portions. (Zurcher and Randell 68, Glaser et al. 72, Graham et al. 73, Snowdon 73, Henderson and Snowdon 74, Boehm 74)

- Hierarchical verification for large program complexes, reflecting the structure of the design and implementation. (Hoare 71, Spitzen 74, Robinson and Levitt 74)

- Other formal manipulations on programs--e.g., attaining efficient and correct programs by correctness-preserving transformations such as successive refinement and optimization (Knuth 74, Burstall and Darlington 74, Dikjstra 74, Neel and Amirchahy 74) and counterexample generators.

- Management techniques (including taking advantage of some of the above approaches); documentation aids; educational aids; and human-oriented development tools (graphic displays, editing environments, etc.). (Weinberg 71, Mills 71, 72, Baker 72a, 72b, Cammack and Rodgers 74)

Of somewhat less relevance here, but certainly of speculative interest for the future are:

- Other formal generative mechanisms such as automatic program synthesis. (Manna and Waldinger 71, Balzer 73, Spitzen 74)

For the interested reader, some of these papers cited have excellent bibliographies (e.g., Elspas et al. 72a, Gannon 73, Spitzen 74).

 These approaches are all of potential value to the desired methodology, although each by itself is deficient. For example, the development of an algorithmic language for designing (say) operating systems is inadequate unless it permits good design structure and also some form of verification. Thus, some combination (e.g., Floyd 71) of these and possibly other approaches is desired. Examples of combinations found in the literature include a collection of techniques used within IBM (Cammack and Rodgers, 73), the "TOPD" system for programming system development using partial verification and simulation of undeveloped portions (Henderson and Snowden 74); the design techniques of Parnas using formal specifications and an abstraction approach to design structure (e.g., Parnas 72a, 72b, 72c, 72d, 74, Parnas and Siewiorek 73); and the SRI methodology, providing a staged development process for hierarchical design and implementation with verification at each stage (Neumann et al. 74, Robinson and Levitt 74). These examples provide approaches toward the kind of methodology sought in this paper. Note that the goal of integrating the entire effort is very important here. For example, the design, implementation, and verification stages should all be compatible. The management function is greatly simplified by good design and implementation techniques, as is the verification effort.

A PROTOTYPE METHODOLOGY

The methodology currently being developed at SRI is being used in the development and verification of a secure system-operating system and hardware (see Neumann et al. 74). This methodology provides an approximation to the desired methodology outlined above. The methodology is divided into a design-and-implementation phase and a verification phase, with the two phases being overlapped. The design-and-implementation phase consists of five stages, as follows:

- S1 Structural decomposition of a system into abstract machines. Each abstract machine consists of an _internal state_ and a set of operations on that state.

- S2 Formal specification of each operation of each abstract machine in terms of _assertions_ about the state of the machine, before and after the operation takes place.

- S3 Formal correspondence between the state of each particular machine and the states of other machines whose (more primitive) operations will be used in the next stage (S4) to implement the operations of the particular machine. This correspondence is made for all but the most primitive operations.

- S4 Implementation of each operation of each abstract machine in terms of more primitive operations (_abstract implementation_), including (abstract) debugging.

- S5 If the most primitive operations already correspond to existing hardware instructions, the implementation is concluded. Otherwise, these operations must be programmed (or microprogrammed) and translated into executable code.

Note that the set of relations as to which operation is implemented out of which other operations induces an ordering on the abstract machines. This ordering need not be hierarchical. If we assume that there is no implementation loop--namely that no operation A can be implemented using an operation B which is implemented using operation A (directly or indirectly)--then this ordering is <u>hierarchical</u> (with respect to functional dependence). The use of a hierarchical ordering or of suborderings has great value in simplifying verification. It may in some cases have negative implications on efficiency in execution, but in most cases need not. Hierarchical design is strongly advocated here (see below).

The results of stage S3 provide a <u>complete design</u>, in that the structure of the system, the function of each abstract machine operation, and the interrelationships among the states of the abstract machines are specified but not implemented. The results of stage S4 provide an <u>abstract implementation</u>, since each operation is implemented out of lower-level operations not necessarily directly supported by any hardware. The results of stage S5 are called a <u>complete implementation</u>, for indeed the system is capable of execution. This staged design-and-implementation methodology is thus "software-first," in that many hardware considerations are basically deferred (although certainly not ignored) until the last stage (except possibly for the lowest level of the design). Note that in the absence of perfect wisdom, backtracking to earlier stages is not unusual.

The design phase by itself is essentially a two-dimensional formal generalization of "top-down programming." It has stages of increasing implementation specificity across multiple levels of operations. (Note that the design or implementation at any stage need not be top-down.) See Figure 1.

The verification phase of the methodology is closely integrated with the design-and-implementation methodology, and consists of four main stages, with a fifth stage available if desired:

- V1 Establishment of global assertions about the behavior of the abstract machines as specified in stages S2 and S3.

- V2 Verification that the assertions in V1 are satisfied by the complete design (S1, S2, S3).

- V3 Verification that the abstract programs in stage S4 are consistent with the complete design.

- V4 Verification that the abstract programs in stage S4 are correctly implemented in the hardware instructions (stage S5).

[• V5 Verification that the hardware instructions are correctly implemented.]

The SRI methodology thus outlined is addressed to the goals cited above. Although it is still too early to assess thesuccess of themethodology, several considerations deserve particular discussion here--namely, the importance of verification, the role of hierarchical design structure, the value of staged development, the attainment of graceful evolution, and support for developing a family of systems in software and hardware. Every one of the approaches outlined in the previous section is compatible with this methodology. Figure 1 provides a graphical summary of the methodology.

VERIFICATION

Although formal verification is at present extremely time-consuming and limited in scope, as well as unfavorably viewed by many, there is great need for it and good prospects for success as a practical technique. There is need because certain critical system functions cannot be adequately guaranteed by traditional testing means--e.g., the security of a system, or the ability to recover from hardware and software difficulties without crashing. There are good prospects because the combination of a highly structured design and a highly staged development make possible structured and staged verification techniques which vastly reduce the effort of verifying a system, compared with a nonstructured system with a nonstaged development. Recent results (Robinson and Levitt 74) show that with such an approach, complexity of verification need not grow exponentially with the complexity of the system. Thus, there is some hope for the verification of large systems.

In general, just as there is never 100 percent reliability or 100 percent security, there is never 100 percent verifiability. There are many potential reasons: assertions may be incomplete or incorrect; the conception itself may be faulty; there may be errors in the verification. Nevertheless, verification can greatly increase justifiable confidence in the system, most valuably, perhaps, for certain particularly critical applications. The methodology supports partial, or selective, verification and the isolation of less relevant operations, without their full involvement.

Recent results indicate that the potential for economical and useful formal testing may be somewhat limited. The notion of deriving sample test data so that each path in a program is traced at least once (path analysis) seems appealing in uncovering some program or design errors. However, Elspas et al. 74 show that:

- If data are generated automatically, then errors may remain undetected, even for the path in question.

- The effort involved in automatic generation of test cases can be equivalent in complexity to the effort required for formal verification.

These results thus strengthen the needs for effective verification.

There is no substitute for good design and good implementation, which can often simplify the verification effort still more noticeably than good verification techniques. Thus, again, there are great benefits to an integrated approach to design, implementation, and verification. The verification of poorly structured and badly implemented systems seems to be a futile exercise.

HIERARCHICALLY STRUCTURED DESIGN

As noted above, the design methodology can be constrained to result in a functionally hierarchical design, in which there is a partial ordering among the abstract machines as to which is implemented in terms of which others. (See, for example, Dijkstra 68a, Goos 73b, and Parnas 74.) The methodology need not be so constrained, but there are significant advantages. First, it appears feasible to achieve a hierarchical design in general, although in some cases an unnatural design can result if hardware is particularly inappropriate. In some cases, it may be desirable to distribute certain functions across several levels (possibly even redundantly), e.g. to avoid fixed-memory restrictions at high levels (e.g., Neumann et al. 74, Bredt and Saxena 74). Second, there are simplifications in the specification and implementation of the systems, and in understandability, monitorability, and maintainability. Third, great simplification arises in the verification, where a hierarchical design permits conceptually simple inductive and nonrecursive proofs of relatively small steps (e.g., see Robinson and Levitt 74). In particular, correctness of an abstract machine at one level depends on the correctness of only lower-level abstract machines, and is otherwise independent of the internal workings of the lower-level machines. Even if the design is not hierarchical throughout, hierarchical substructures can be of great value in simplifying verification. (The operating system described in Neumann et al. 74 is hierarchical throughout with respect to three relations, namely, functional dependence, protection, and correctness--cf. Parnas 74.)

STAGING OF THE DEVELOPMENT

The staged development is helpful in cleanly partitioning the overall effort, and provides many benefits for design, implementation, verification, and management. In particular, staging permits considerable overlapping of design and implementation on the one hand, and verification on the other. In particular, verification of the complete design (V2) relies on the completion of only S1, S2, S3, and V1, and provides verification that the design will work as asserted--assuming that it is then consistently implemented. Subsequently, verification of the abstract implementation (V3) relies on the completion of S4 but not of S5. (V3 also does not rely on the completion of V2, and could progress independently--although with some trepidation, in case V2 determines that any assertions are not satisfied.) Thus, the methodology provides what might be called <u>incremental</u> <u>confidence</u> in the design and in the implementation as the development progresses. Errors in design or in implementation can thus be caught soon after they are made, rather than persisting through latter phases of the development.

The staged development is also beneficial to system evolution subsequent to installation. For example, changes in hardware implementation that do not affect the instruction set are invisible to stages S1 to S5; changes in abstract programs that do not affect the design are invisible to stages S1 to S3. Note that the levels of functional abstraction provided by the hierarchy of abstract machines have a similar effect (cf. Dijkstra 68). Comparable effects are also noted with respect to verification. Potentially, any change in software and hardware may deleteriously affect the performance of the system. For example, such a change may incapacitate the system's ability to recover from an abnormal condition; may vitiate the security of the system; or may prevent a critical process from terminating at all. Thus, verification of the system is desirable following such changes. The staged development permits incremental verification of just those operations at just those stages where the effects of the changes may take place.

FAMILIES OF RELATED SYSTEMS

Enormously difficult problems arise in the development of not just a single system, but a set of related systems. A simple first approach suggests that hardware and software can be configured as needed from among a set of carefully designed modules ("building blocks"). However, widely varying requirements for processing, memory, and input-output can make the organization of such a "meta-design" extremely complicated.

A second approach is the "kernel" approach in which all systems have a suitably primitive common kernel (e.g., see Wulf et al. 74). A refinement of this approach recognizes multiple levels of the kernel, where different systems of the family share just those lowest levels (from the hardware instructions up, e.g., to the most primitive operating system functions) that are appropriate, but are independent above the shared levels. Note that the hardware-software boundaries may differ from one family member to another. These "kernel" approaches have numerous difficulties where the family is quite diverse.

A more general approach involves families of parameterized specifications for modules, rather than families of modules. This approach has been suggested by Parnas (Parnas 70), and appears to have great promise. The methodology discussed here supports such an approach, although it has not been so applied as yet. The above comments on the relatively small incremental effort required to carry out and verify small changes are also applicable to different members of a family of systems. In such a case, there are stages of verification that pertain to the family, and stages that are special to particular systems consistent with the family of specifications. Close relatives can share all of the former effort, and much of the latter.

CONCLUSIONS

This paper presents goals for and steps toward a methodology for the development and evolution of computer systems and families of systems. The following conclusions are offered, based on the author's experience.

- A formal unified approach should be used that integrates design, implementation and verification, as well as hardware and software.

- A staged development can provide continually increasing confidence in the expected product as it develops. It facilitates hardware-decoupled system design.

- Hierarchical levels of procedure abstraction and data abstraction are not only desirable, but generally feasible without loss of efficiency. Machine independence should be achieved wherever possible.

- Formal specification is advantageous, even in the absence of verification.

- Algorithmic language approaches are generally inadequate for large system developments unless techniques for globally structured design, data abstraction, and some form of verification are present. However, such a combination can be very powerful.

- Verification of properties of large systems is becoming feasible, especially with hierarchical structure.

- Good design, good implementation, wisdom, and common sense are invaluable. However, human frailties can be made less critical by the use of such a methodology.

There are, of course, significant problems that need to be solved by future research and development before the desired goals can be achieved. Particularly important is work on generating specifications and assertions and on new approaches to programming, e.g., on suitable languages facilitating structure, abstraction, successive transformations, and verification.

ACKNOWLEDGMENTS

This paper draws heavily on the experiences of various ongoing projects at SRI and on interactions with Lawrence Robinson, Robert S. Boyer, Karl N. Levitt, Theodore A. Linden, and John H. Wensley.

REFERENCES

Balzer 72 R. M. Balzer, "Automatic Programming," RR-73-1, USC/Information Sciences Institute, Marina del Rey, California (September 1972).

Baker 72a F. T. Baker, "Chief Programmer Teams," IBM Systems Journal, Vol. 11, No. 1 (1972).

Baker 72b F. T. Baker, "System Quality Through Structured Programming," AFIPS Proc. FJCC, pp. 339-343 (1972).

Bledsoe and Gilbert 67 W. W. Bledsoe and E. J. Gilbert, "Automatic Theorem Proof-Checking in Set Theory: a Preliminary Report," Sandia Corporation, Report SC-RR-67-525 (July 1967).

Boehm 74 B. W. Boehm," Some Steps toward Formal and Automated Aids to Software Requirements Analysis and Design," Information Processing 74 (IFIP), North-Holland Publishing, Vol. 2, pp. 192-197 (1974).

Boyer and Moore 75 R. S. Boyer and J. Moore, "Proving Theorems about LISP Functions," Journ. ACM, Vol. 22, No. 1 (1975).

Bredt and Saxena 74 T. H. Bredt and A. R. Saxena, "Heirarchical Design for Operating Systems," IEEE Computer Conference Fall (Fall COMPCON 74), Washington, D.C. (September 10-12, 1974).

Brinch Hansen 74 P. Brinch Hansen, "A Programming Methodology for Operating System Design," Information Processing 74 (IFIP), North-Holland Publishing, Vol. 2, pp. 394-397 (1974).

Clark and Horning 74 B. Clark and J. J. Horning, "Reflections on a Language for Operating System Design," Computer Science Research Group, University of Toronto Canada (1974).

Dahl 72 O. J. Dahl, in Structured Programming, C.A.R. Hoare Academic Press, New York, N.Y. (1972).

Dennis 73a	J. B. Dennis, The Design and Construction of Software Systems, <u>Advanced Course on Software Engineering</u>, <u>Lecture Notes in Economics and Mathematical Sciences</u> <u>81</u>, pp. 12-28, Springer-Verlag, Berlin [Heidelberg and New York] (1973).
Dennis 73b	J. B. Dennis, "Modularity," <u>loc. cit.</u> pp. 128-182 (1973).
Deutsch 73	L. P. Deutsch, "An Interactive Program Verifier," Ph.D. thesis, University of California, Berkeley, California (June 1973).
Dijkstra 68a	E. W. Dijkstra, "The Structure of the THE Multiprogramming System," <u>Comm. ACM</u>, Vol. 11, No. 5, pp. 341-346 (May 1968).
Dijkstra 68b	E. W. Dijkstra, "Co-operating Sequential Processes," in <u>Programming Languages</u>, F. Genuys, ed., pp. 43-112, Academic Press (1968).
Dijkstra 72a	E. W. Dijkstra, "Hierarchical Ordering of Sequential Process," in <u>Operating Systems Techniques</u>, pp. 72-93, Hoare and Perrott, eds., Academic Press, London (1972).
Dijkstra 72b	E. W. Dijkstra, "Notes on Structured Programming," in <u>Structured Programming</u>, C. A. Hoare, ed., Academic Press, New York, N.Y. (1972).
Dijkstra 74	E. W. Dijkstra, "Guarded Commands, Non-Determinacy and a Calculus for the Derivation of Programs," Nuenen, the Netherlands (June 26, 1974).
Elspas et al. 72a	B. Elspas, K. N. Levitt, R. J. Waldinger, and A. Waksman, "An Assessment of Techniques for Proving Program Correctness," <u>Computing Surveys</u>, Vol. 4, No. 2, pp. 97-147 (June 1972).
Elspas et al. 72b	B. Elspas, M. W. Green, K. N. Levitt, R. J. Waldinger, "Research in Interactive Program-Proving Techniques," Stanford Research Institute, Report-Phase II, Project 8398 (May 20, 1972).
Elspas 74	B. Elspas, "The Semiautomatic Generation of Inductive Assertions for Proving Program Correctness," Interim Report, Stanford Research Institute, Menlo Park, California (July 1974).
Elspas et al. 74	B. Elspas, R. S. Boyer, and K. N. Levitt, "SELECT--A System for Testing and Debugging Programs by Symbolic Execution," Stanford Research Institute, Menlo Park, California (September 1974).
Floyd 67	R. W. Floyd, "Assigning Meaning to Programs," <u>American Mathematical Society, Mathematical Aspects of Computer Science</u>, Vol. 19, pp. 19-32 (1967).
Floyd 71	R. W. Floyd, "Toward Interactive Design of Correct Programs," <u>Information Processing 71 (IFIP, Ljubliana)</u>, North-Holland Publishing (1971).
Gannon 73	J. D. Gannon, "An Annotated Bibliography on Computer Program Engineering," Technical Report 24, Computer Systems Research Group, University of Toronto (March 1973).
Giloi and Liebig 74	W. K. Giloi and H. Liebig, "A Formalism for the Description and Synthesis of Logical Algorithms and their Hardware Implementations," <u>IEEE Trans. Computer</u>, Vol. C-23, No. 9, pp. 897-906 (September 1974).
Glaser et al. 72	E. L. Glaser et al., "Papers in a Session Devoted to the LOGOS Project," <u>Digest of IEEE Conference (1972 COMPCON)</u>, pp. 175-192 (1972).

Good 70	P. I. Good, "Toward a Man-Machine System for Proving Program Correctness," Computation Center TSN-11, University of Texas, Austin (June 1970).
Goos 73a	G. Goos, "Some Basic Principles in Structuring Operating Systems," in *Operating Systems Techniques*, Hoare and Perrott (eds.), pp. 94-100, Academic Press, London (1973).
Goos 73b	G. Goos, "Hierarchies," *Advanced Course on Software Engineering, Lecture Notes in Economic and Mathematical Sciences* 81, pp. 29-46, Springer-Verlag, Berlin (1973).
Goos 73c	G. Goos, "Language Characteristics--Programming Languages as a Tool in Writing System Software," *loc. cit.*, pp. 47-69 (1973).
Graham et al. 73	R. M. Graham, G. L. Clancy, and D. B. DeVaney, "A Software Design and Evaluation System," *Comm. ACM*, Vol. 16, No. 2, pp. 110-116 (February 1973).
Henderson and Snowdon 74	P. Henderson and R. A. Snowdon, "A Tool for Structured Program Development," *Information Processing 74 (IFIP)*, North-Holland Publishing, Vol. 2, pp. 204-207 (1974).
Hetzel 73	W. C. Hetzel, ed., *Program Test Methods*, Prentice-Hall Inc. (1973).
Hoare 71	C.A.R. Hoare, "Procedures and Parameters: An Axiomatic Approach," *Symposium on Semantics of Algorithmic Languages, Lecture Notes in Mathematics* 188, E. Engeler (ed.), Springer-Verlag, Berlin (1971).
Hoare 72	C.A.R. Hoare, "Notes on Data Structuring," in *Structured Programming*, C.A.R. Hoare, ed., Academic Press, New York, N.Y. (1972).
Hoare and Wirth 72	C.A.R. Hoare and N. Wirth, "An Axiomatic Definition of the Programming Language PASCAL," Eidgenossiche Technische Hochshule, Report No. 6 (November 1972).
Horning and Randell 73	J. J. Horning and B. Randell, "Process Structuring," *Computing Surveys*, Vol. 5, No. 1, pp 5-30 (March 1973).
Horning et al. 73	J. J. Horning, H. C. Lauer, M. Meliar-Smith, and B. Randell, "Program Structure for Error Detection and Recovery," University of Newcastle, England (1973).
Igarashi et al. 73	S. Igarashi, R. London, and D. Luckham, "Automatic Verification of Programs I: A Logical Basis and Implementation," Memo AIM-200, Stanford Artificial Intelligence Lab., Stanford, California (May 1973).
Katz and Manna 73	S. M. Katz and Z. Manna, "A Heuristic Approach to Program Verification," Advance Papers of the Conference, Third International Joint Conference on Artificial Intelligence, Stanford University, Stanford, California, pp. 500-512 (August 1973).
Linden 74	T. A. Linden, "Capability-Based Addressing to Support Software Engineering and System Security," *Third Texas Conf. on Computing Systems*, Austin, Texas (November 7-8, 1974).
McCarthy 61	John McCarthy, "Computer Programs for Checking Mathematical Proofs," *Proc. AMS on Recursive Function Theory* (April 1961).
Manna and Waldinger 71	Z. Manna and R. J. Waldinger, "Towards Automatic Program Synthesis," *Comm. ACM*, Vol. 14, No. 3, pp. 151-165 (March 1971).

Mills 71	H. Mills, "Top Down Programming in Large Systems," in *Debugging Techniques in Large Systems* (R. Rustin (ed.), pp. 41-55, Prentice-Hall Inc. (1971).
Mills 72	H. D. Mills, "How to Write Correct Programs and Know It," IBM, Gaithersburg, Maryland (December 1972).
Milner 72	R. Milner, "Logic for Computable Functions; Description of a Machine Implementation," Artificial Intelligence Memo 169, Stanford University, Stanford, California (May 1972).
Neel and Armirchahy 74	M. Amirchahy and D. Neel, "Optimization of Generated Code by Means of Attributes," Proc. GI 74, Berlin, October 1974. Lecture Notes in Computer Science (Springer-Verlag, 1974).
Neumann 73	P. G. Neumann, "System Design for Computer Networks," Chapter 2 of *Computer-Communication Networks*, Abramson and Kuo, ed., pp. 29-81, Prentice-Hall, Inc. (1973).
Neumann et al. 74	P. G. Neumann, R. S. Fabry, K. N. Levitt, L. Robinson, and J. H. Wensley, "On the Design of a Provably Secure Operating System," IRIA, Rocquencourt, France, pp. 161-175 (August 13-14, 1974).
Parnas 71	D. L. Parnas (private communication).
Parnas 72a	D. L. Parnas, "A Technique for Software Module Specification With Examples," *CACM*, Vol. 15, No. 5, pp. 330-336 (May 1972).
Parnas 72b	D. L. Parnas, "On the Criteria to be Used in Decomposing Systems Into Modules," *Communications of the ACM*, Vol. 15, No. 12, pp. 1053-58 (December 1972).
Parnas 72c	D. L. Parnas, "Some Conclusions From an Experiment in Software Engineering Techniques," *Proc. FJCC*, pp. 325-329 (1972).
Parnas 72d	D. L. Parnas, "Response to Detected Errors in Well-Structured Programs," Technical Report, Department of Computer Science, Carnegie-Mellon University (July 1972).
Parnas and Siewiorek 72	D. L. Parnas and D. P. Siewiorek, "Use of the Concept of Transparency in the Design of Hierarchically Structured Systems," Technical Report, Department of Computer Science, Carnegie-Mellon University (July 1972).
Parnas 74	D. L. Parnas, "On a Buzzword: Hierarchical Structure," *Information Processing 74 (IFIP)*, Vol. 2, pp. 336-339, North-Holland Publishing (1974).
Robinson and Levitt 74	L. Robinson and K. N. Levitt, "Proof Techniques for Hierarchically Structured Programs," SRI working paper (July 1974).
Rustin 71	R. Rustin, ed., *Debugging Techniques in Large Systems*, Prentice-Hall, Inc. (1971).
Simon 62	H. A. Simon, "The Architecture of Complexity," *Proc. Am. Phil. Soc.*, Vol. 106, pp. 467-82 (December 1962).
Snowdon 73	R. A. Snowdon, "Pearl--A System for the Preparation and Validation of Structured Programs," in *Program Test Methods*, W. C. Hetzel, ed., Prentice-Hall, Inc., Englewood Cliffs, New Jersey (1973).
Spitzen 74	J. M. Spitzen, "Approaches to Automatic Programming," Harvard University Ph.D. Thesis, Center for Research in Computing Technology TR 17-74 (May 1974).

Waldinger and Levitt 73   R. J. Waldinger and K. N. Levitt, "Reasoning About Programs," *Proc. SIGACT/SIGPLAN Symposium on Principles of Programming Languages*, pp. 169-182, Boston, Massachusetts (October 1-3, 1973). Also to appear in *Artificial Intelligence*.

Wegbreit 71   B. Wegbreit, "The ECL Programming System," *Proc. AFIPS 1971 FJCC*, Vol. 39, pp. 253-262 (1971).

Wegbreit 73   B. Wegbreit, "Heuristic Methods for Mechanically Deriving Inductive Assertions," *Proceedings Third International Joint Conference on Artificial Intelligence*, Stanford University, pp. 524-536 (August 1973).

Wegner 72   P. Wegner, "The Vienna Definition Language," *ACM Computing Surveys*, Vol. 4, No. 1 (1972).

Weinberg 71   G. Weinberg, *The Psychology of Computer Programming*, Van Nostrand Reinhold Company, New York (1971).

Weyhrauch 74   R. Weyhrauch, "Manual for FOL (A Proof Checker for First Order Logic)," Stanford University, Artificial Intelligence Group, Stanford, California (January 1974).

Wirth 71a   N. Wirth, "The Programming Language Pascal," *Acta Information*, Vol. 1, No. 1, pp. 35-63 (1971).

Wirth 71b   N. Wirth, "Program Development by Stepwise Refinement," *Comm. ACM*, Vol. 14, No. 4, pp. 221-227 (April 1971).

Wirth 74   N. Wirth, "On the Design of Programming Languages," *Information Processing 74 (IFIP)*, Vol. 2, pp. 386-393, North-Holland Publishing (1974).

Wulf 74   W. A. Wulf, "ALPHARD, Toward a Language to Support Structured Programs," Carnegie-Mellon University, Pittsburgh, Pennsylvania (June 1974).

Wulf et al. 74   W. A. Wulf et al., "HYDRA: The Kernel of a Multiprocessor Operating System," *Comm. ACM*, Vol. 17, No. 6, pp. 337-345 (June 1974).

Zurcher and Randell 68   F. W. Zurcher and B. Randell, "Interactive Multilevel Modelling, A Methodology for Computer System Design," *Proceedings of IFIP* Congress 1968, North-Holland Publishing, pp. 138-142 (1968).

Burstall and Darlington 74   R.M. Burstall and J. Darlington, Systematic Development of Programs by Introducing Economies of Interaction, Department of Machine Intelligence, Univ. Edinburgh (1974).

Knuth 74   D. Knuth, Structured Programming with goto Statements, Computer Science Department, Stanford Univ., Palo Alto, California (May 1974).

FIGURE 1
SUMMARY OF THE SRI METHODOLOGY FOR COMPUTER SYSTEM DEVELOPMENT

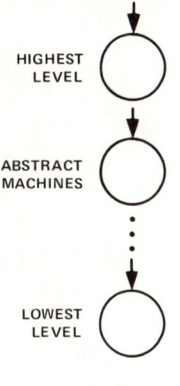

S1: DECOMPOSITION INTO OPERATIONS OF ABSTRACT MACHINES

HIGHEST LEVEL

ABSTRACT MACHINES

LOWEST LEVEL

(a)

S2: SPECIFICATION OF EACH OPERATION IN TERMS OF STATES OF ABSTRACT MACHINES

V1: ESTABLISHMENT OF GLOBAL ASSERTIONS
(b)

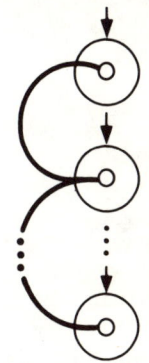

S3: MAPPINGS AMONG STATES OF ABSTRACT MACHINES (COMPLETE DESIGN)

V2: VERIFICATION OF COMPLETE DESIGN
(c)

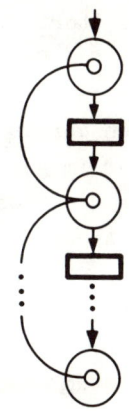

S4: ABSTRACT IMPLEMENTATION OF EACH OPERATION IN TERMS OF LOWER-LEVEL OPERATIONS

V3: VERIFICATION OF ABSTRACT IMPLEMENTATION
(d)

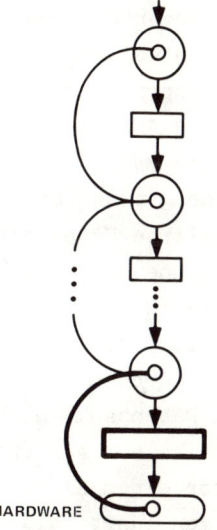

S5: ACTUAL IMPLEMENTATION

HARDWARE

V4: VERIFICATION OF ACTUAL IMPLEMENTATION
(e)

Datenschutz und Gesellschaft

H. FIEDLER

Zunächst einige Bemerkungen zur Motivierung der Fragestellung:

Die Datenschutzdiskussion betrifft heute die Gesamtheit der westlichen Industriestaaten[1]. Ursprünglich ist sie in USA entstanden, wo man etwa Mitte der sechziger Jahre auf skandalöse Mißstände im Kreditwesen hinwies. Dort existieren größenordnungsmäßig 100 Millionen Kreditdossiers, welche einen großen Teil aller Bürger betreffen. Diese enthalten auch etwa Merkmale wie "neurotisch" aufgrund von Auskünften durch Nachbarn. Man kann z.B. dadurch eine negative Bewertung bekommen, daß man wegen begründeter Reklamationen die Zahlung verweigert, und erhält dann keinen Kredit mehr[2]. In einer kreditorientierten Gesellschaft entspricht dies einer empfindlichen Strafe. Das ganze erschien als eine Art gesellschaftlichen Scherbengerichts - ohne alle Garantien eines fairen Verfahrens, auf die man doch gerade in USA ideologisch so großen Wert legt. Dabei ging es hier im Ansatz nicht um computerisierte Datenbestände; allerdings wurde die Problematik durch die beginnende Computerisierung verschärft. Andererseits gab es etwa zur gleichen Zeit eine ursprünglich durch eine DV-Planung veranlaßte Diskussion, nämlich diejenige um die "national data bank". Diese wurde um 1965 durch die US-Regierung ins Auge gefaßt - übrigens als statistische Datenbank, nicht als "intelligence system" über Personen. Nach einer Reihe von reports und hearings scheiterten diese Pläne an der Furcht vor einem allzu umfassend informierten DV-System der Regierung[3]. Dagegen führte die Kreditwesendiskussion schließlich zu einem auf dieses Spezialgebiet bezogenen Verbesserungsversuch durch eine gesetzliche Regelung, den "Fair Credit Reporting Act". Diese Regelung bezieht sich nicht speziell auf DV-Methoden; ob sie ausreichend und erfolgreich ist, bleibt noch zu klären[4].

Voraussetzung der Datenschutzdiskussion ist der Bestand der DV in ihrer heutigen Leistungsfähigkeit. Dabei haben natürlich große Datenverwaltungssysteme, Dstenfernverarbeitung und Realzeitbetrieb besondere Bedeutung. Gerade die durch die moderne DV gegebene Verknüpfungsmöglichkeit zwischen verschiedenen Benutzern und Systemen ist hier ein wesentlicher Punkt, nämlich die Leichtigkeit einer Weitergabe und Umfunktionierung personenbezogener Daten. Wie so oft in der DV scheint es allerdings auch hier, daß die Argumente großenteils mehr aus der Zukunft als aus der Erfahrung in Vergangenheit oder Gegenwart genommen sind.

Andererseits sind Wirkungen der Datenschutzdiskussion heute schon vielfach vorhanden. Dies gilt nicht nur von einer populären Bewußtseinsbildung in den Massenmedien. Neben einer unübersehbaren Literatur[5] gibt es international schon eine ganze Reihe großer projektartiger Studien, die z.T. analytisch und empirisch fundiert sind. In etwa einem Dutzend von Staaten und internationalen Organisationen haben derartige Vorarbeiten zu Vorschlägen normativer Regelungen oder zu diesen selbst geführt[6]. Von bereits vorhandenen gesetzlichen Regelungen möchte ich hier als Beispiele nennen:

- als erste Regelung das hessische Datenschutzgesetz von 1970
- als Spezialregelung den Fair Credit Reporting act der USA von 1970 (in Kraft 1971)
- als wohl weitestgehende Regelung das schwedische Datengesetz von 1973.

Heute kann danach die Datenschutzdiskussion als an sich bedeutsame Entwicklung bereits vorausgesetzt werden. Hier soll nicht nur ein Beitrag zu ihrer Weiterführung versucht, sondern z.T. gerade auf diese Diskussion selbst in ihrer gesellschaftlichen Bedeutung reflektiert werden - eine für den Informatiker sehr naheliegende Betrachtungsweise. In diesem Sinne werden i.folg. behandelt:

1. Datenschutz, Datensicherung und die zweifache Wurzel der Datenschutzdiskussion
2. Gesellschaftliche Tendenzen der Datenschutzdiskussion
3. Datenschutz im Konflikt gesellschaftlicher Ziele
4. Datenschutzrecht als Konfliktentscheidung und Operationalisierung
5. Datensicherung als gesellschaftliche Notwendigkeit und als Voraussetzung des Datenschutzes
6. Wege vom Datenschutz zu einem allgemeinen Recht der Information.

1. Datenschutz, Datensicherung und die zweifache Wurzel der Datenschutzdiskussion

1.1 Verschiedene Begriffe von Datenschutz und Datensicherung.

Während über die Abgrenzung der "Datensicherung" inzwischen doch weitgehend Einigkeit herrscht, ist die begriffliche Konzeption des "Datenschutzes" gerade in der Bundesrepublik noch recht kontrovers[7]. Einen sehr verbreiteten Ausgangspunkt der Differenzierung könnte man etwa folgendermaßen umschreiben: (vgl. hierzu Seidel a.a.O.)

- Datensicherung ist die Gesamtheit der Maßnahmen zur Sicherung von Daten gegen Zerstörung und unbefugten Gebrauch.
- Datenschutz ist die Gesamtheit der Maßnahmen zur Sicherung von datenbetroffenen Personen und Organisationen gegen Beeinträchtigung ihrer Interessen durch Datenverarbeitung (im weitesten Sinne).

Die Formulierungen zeigen schon, daß hier noch viele Unbestimmtheiten liegen. Besonders gilt dies für den "Datenschutz". Nach einer weitesten Auffassung[8] ist Datenschutz ganz umfassend "die Kehrseite der Datenverarbeitung", d.h. die Verhinderung ihrer gesellschaftlich unerwünschten Auswirkungen überhaupt. Etwas zugespitzt könnte man nach dieser weitesten Auffassung die Gegenüberstellung etwa so formulieren:

- Datensicherung ist die Sicherung der bestimmungsgemäßen Funktion von DV-Systemen im Sinne der Verfügungsbefugten (negativ: Sicherung gegen bestimmungswidrige Funktion)
- Datenschutz ist die Sicherung der wunschgemäßen Funktion von DV-Systemen im Sinne der Gesellschaft überhaupt (negativ: Sicherung gegen unerwünschte Funktion).

Während hier die Umschreibung der Datensicherung im wesentlichen mit der erstgenannten übereinstimmt und nur eine weitergehende Abstraktion bedeutet, zeigt die weite Konzeption des Datenschutzes gerade in dieser Gegenüberstellung ihre ganze Unbestimmtheit. Wie können solche Wünsche Außenstehender präzisiert werden, und wessen Wünsche sind es? Als solche außenstehende Interessenten kommen nicht nur die Datenbetroffenen infrage, sondern auch z.B. konkurrierende Personen und Institutionen oder partizipationswillige Bürger, usw..

1.2 Die zweifache Wurzel der Datenschutzdiskussion.

Historisch gesehen hat die Datenschutzdiskussion zwei verschiedene Wurzeln, insbesondere in ihrem amerikanischen Ursprungsland. Diese verschiedenen Wurzeln der Diskussion stehen auch in verschiedener Beziehung zum Begriffspaar Datenschutz-Datensicherung:

- Eine Wurzel liegt in der "privacy"-Problematik, wie sie auch ganz unabhängig von der automatisierten DV in der Diskussion um die "naked society"[9] zutage tritt. Hier geht es vor allem auch um Ermittlungs- und Abhörpraktiken wie z.B. im Kreditwesen, bei der Registrierung von Vietnamkriegsgegnern oder im Watergate-Fall, mit der dadurch bedingten Verletzung einer "Privatsphäre".

- Die zweite Wurzel liegt in der "Datenbank"-Problematik, wie sie anläßlich der Diskussion um ein national data center angesprochen wurde[10]. Hier geht es vor allem um die automatisierte Datenverwaltung als technologisches Mittel der Bürokratie in Staat und Wirtschaft.

Trotz ihrer gegenseitigen Abhängigkeit sind diese beiden Zusammenhänge recht verschieden. Der erste betrifft mehr die Stellung des Einzelnen in der Gesellschaft, der zweite mehr die Rolle einer bestimmten Technologie. Die Probleme der Privatsphäre einerseits, der DV-Technologie andererseits sind jedoch dann im Begriff der "computer-privacy" und in der Datenschutzdiskussion derart zusammengeflossen, daß hier eine Technologie als Antagonist eines Persönlichkeitswerts gesehen wird. Offensichtlich hat sich diese speziell gegen "den Computer" gerichtete Variante der Technologiekritik als sehr zugkräftig und publikumswirksam erwiesen. Es fragt sich aber gerade, ob hiermit nicht auch gewisse Gefahren verbunden sind. So etwa die irrige Hoffnung, durch bloße Technologiekritik soziale Konflikte lösen zu können. Vielleicht wird die weitere Arbeit zeigen, daß der stark "problemorientierte" Komplex des Datenschutzes doch wieder stärker in seine fachlichen Komponenten zurückverfolgt werden muß, nämlich einerseits den Schutz der Persönlichkeit im Bereich des Informationswesens (ob computerisiert oder nicht) und andererseits die Garantie der Transparenz und Beherrschbarkeit der DV-Technologie. Die letztere Komponente steht offensichtlich in enger Beziehung zur Forderung der "Datensicherheit".

Natürlich soll mit diesem Kritikansatz nicht geleugnet werden, daß eine bestimmte technologische Situation ohnehin vorhandene soziale Konflikte verschärfen kann - wie dies hier ganz offensichtlich der Fall ist.

2. Gesellschaftliche Tendenzen der Datenschutzdiskussion

Zur Betrachtung der Datenschutzdiskussion sollte man von der umfassendsten Konzeption ausgehen (nicht notwendig dabei stehenbleiben), um jedenfalls nichts außer acht zu lassen.

Danach ist Datenschutz die Gesamtheit der (artifiziellen, gewollten) Restriktionen und Verpflichtungen beim Umgang mit Daten zum Schutz gesellschaftlich anerkannter Zielsetzungen ("Interessen"). Was aber sind alles solche "gesellschaftlich anerkannte Interessen"? Insbesondere natürlich (bei uns) eine gewisse Autonomie der Einzelperson. Jedoch ist nicht einmal dies allgemein und selbstverständlich, auch in Bezug auf manche westliche Gesellschaften (Devise "Anpassung oder Vernichtung"). Eine der historischen Wurzeln der Datenschutzdiskussion war ja gerade die Verteidigung der als gefährdet oder verletzt gesehenen "privacy". Auch die Begründung zum gegenwärtigen Datenschutz-Gesetzentwurf der Bundesrepublik hat die "Privatsphäre" im Auge. Dazu kommen jedoch weitere Interessen. Der "Privatheit" entspricht z.B. antagonistisch die "Öffentlichkeit" mit ihren verschiedenen Ausprägungen, dem Geheimhaltungsinteresse das Interesse an Information und Transparenz. Aber auch auf dieses Gegensatzpaar läßt sich die Menge der gesellschaftlich relevanten Interessen am Status von Daten nicht beschränken. So spricht Steinmüller[11] von einem "magischen Dreieck widerstreitender Interessen" in der Datenschutzdiskussion, nämlich den Interessen an der Funktionsfähigkeit von Staat und Wirtschaft, der bestmöglichen Nutzung der DV und schließlich der Erhaltung gesellschaftlicher Freiräume. Steinmüller bemerkt gleich, daß auch damit die Problematik noch nicht erschöpft ist.

So macht allein schon die Aufzählung der beim Datenschutz (in dieser allgemeinsten Auffassung) involvierten Interessen Schwierigkeiten, erst recht natürlich dann ihre Bewertung und die Strukturierung der damit verbundenen Ziele. Dies alles hängt offensichtlich eng zusammen mit der jeweils betroffenen Gesellschaftsordnung. Schon die Artikulationsfähigkeit von Interessen ist je nach Gesellschaftsordnung verschieden. Auch die bei uns geführte Diskussion über den Wandel der Begriffe von "öffentlich" und "privat" ist dazu ein Beitrag[12]. Die Datenschutzproblematik und deren Lösung hängt ganz von der jeweiligen Gesellschaftsordnung und deren Typ ab, wäre z.B. für sozialistische Gesellschaften anders zu sehen als für die verschiedenen Ausprägungen der westlichen, usw.

Dies führt u.a. zu zwei möglichen Tendenzen:

- für eine mehr grundsätzliche Betrachtungsweise wird die Datenschutzdiskussion leicht zugleich zur Gesellschaftskritik, die Datenschutzregelung zum gesellschaftspolitischen Instrument. Als Zielsetzungen kommen hier sowohl eine Gesellschaftspolitik des Informationswesens infrage wie auch der Versuch einer direkten "Demokratisierung" der DV-Technologie.

- für eine mehr pragmatische Betrachtungsweise liegt es näher, sich auf die Randbedingungen der jeweils eigenen Gesellschaftsordnung zu konzentrieren. Dies gilt insbesondere für die übliche Strategie rechtlicher Regelung (Rechtspolitik). Aber selbst hierfür ist der Blick über die Grenzen des eigenen Gesellschaftssystems durchaus nützlich, wie ja die Tradition der "Rechtsvergleichung" zeigt. Heute könnte man auch von "vergleichender Systemanalyse" sprechen.

Ob man nun den Datenschutzbegriff etwas enger oder weiter ansetzt, den Kreis des Vergleichs größer oder kleiner zieht, jedenfalls sollte einer Datenschutzkonzeption die systematische Analyse der Zielstruktur im Rahmen der jeweiligen Gesellschaftsordnung vorangehen. Der Verweis auf den "Schutz der Privatsphäre" allein genügt hier nicht mehr. Man muß sich bewußt sein, daß es hier um die Entscheidung von Ziel- und Interessenkonflikten unter Berücksichtigung der Randbedingungen und Wertsysteme der jeweiligen Gesellschaftsordnung geht. Wesentlich ist dabei, daß diese Konflikte mehrere je für sich durchaus legitime Interessen betreffen. Es ist nicht einfach - wie so oft in der Datenschutzdiskussion geschehen - der "böse" Staat (oder die böse Technik) gegen den "guten" Bürger zu setzen.

3. Datenschutz im Konflikt gesellschaftlicher Zielsetzungen

3.1 Für den Datenschutz relevante Zielsetzungen.

Mag auch eine bestimmte Zielsetzung in den Vordergrund gestellt werden, so kann es doch beim Datenschutz nicht um eine einzige Zielsetzung alleine gehen. Betroffen sind vielmehr eine ganze Reihe gesellschaftlich legitimer Zielsetzungen, welche nichtsdestoweniger untereinander in Konflikt stehen können.

Hier seien einige solche Zielsetzungen aufgezählt, welche für den Datenschutz relevant sind oder in diesem Zusammenhang benannt wurden:

1. Erhaltung der "privacy" im weitesten Sinne, d.h. der "Privatsphäre" des Einzelnen, eventuell auch von Organisationen oder Gruppen. Dies ist der klassische, wenn auch inzwischen viel kritisierte Ausgangspunkt der Datenschutzdiskussion. Der Begriff der "Privatsphäre" ist relativ und wandelbar, liegt aber wohl zumindest für Einzelpersonen im Bereich des juristisch Definierbaren.

   Eine Variante hiervon ist darin zu sehen, daß man für den Umgang mit personenbezogenen Daten spezifizierte Beschränkungen postuliert (z.B. für die Ermittlung, Speicherung, Verarbeitung, Weitergabe). Hierin liegt eine auf die DV bezogene Spezialisierung und Präzisierung der "privacy".

2. Gewährleistung der Autonomie von Personen, Organisationen und Gruppen durch Einräumung gesellschaftlicher Freiräume. Diese Zielsetzung deckt sich nicht einfach mit der zu (1). Sie wird hier nicht als Ermöglichung des Rückzugs in die Privatsphäre gesehen, sondern als Hilfestellung für die aktive Teilnahme am gesellschaftlichen und insbesondere politischen Leben.

3. Erhaltung eines "Informationsgleichgewichts" zwischen verschiedenen Instanzen (insbesondere zwischen Exekutive und Legislative; man könnte aber ebenso etwa an das Verhältnis zwischen Bund und Ländern im föderalistischen System denken, oder an viele ähnliche Beziehungen).

   Hierbei ist nicht zu vergessen, daß in vielen gesellschaftlichen Beziehungen gerade ein systematisches Informationsgefälle besteht. Auch hat die Vorstellung des "Gleichgewichts" statischen Charakter und enthält deutliche Hinweise auf die Erhaltung des "status quo".

4. Gewährleistung der Funktionsfähigkeit und Konkurrenzfähigkeit der Wirtschaft, auch unter Ausnutzung der DV (u.a.: Kreditwesen, Zahlungsverkehr, Personalwirtschaft, Werbung).

5. Gewährleistung der Funktionsfähigkeit und Effizienz in Staat und öffentlicher Verwaltung, auch unter Ausnutzung der DV (u.a.: Meldewesen, Finanzwesen, Leistungswesen, Planung).

6. Gewährleistung gesellschaftlicher Transparenz und Kontrollfähigkeit. Dies versteht sich auch in einer "computerisierten" Gesellschaft keineswegs von selbst. Hierher gehört insbesondere die Kriminalitätsprophylaxe, z.B. der Wirtschaftskriminalität.

3.2 Notwendigkeit der methodischen Ordnung und Bewertung der Datenschutzziele.

Ein Blick auf die Auswahl der Ziele zeigt, daß diese auf recht verschiedenen Ebenen liegen und untereinander weitgehend antagonistisch wirken. Nach systemanalytischen Regeln müßte es um die genauere Analyse und Definition dieser Ziele, um ihre Bewertung und die Festlegung ihrer Relationen gehen. Dies alles wäre Voraussetzung für die Zuordnung geeigneter Maßnahmen etwa in einer Datenschutzregelung.

Leider ist es trotz des Umfangs der Datenschutzdiskussion mit diesen Vorarbeiten noch schlecht bestellt. Dies gilt sowohl für deren strukturelle wie empirische Komponente. Trotz mancher Ansätze zu einer methodischen Bearbeitung bleibt hier noch sehr viel zu tun.

4. Datenschutzrecht als Konfliktentscheidung und "Operationalisierung" des Datenschutzes

4.1 Erfordernisse rechtlicher Regelungen.

Eine rechtliche Regelung erfüllt ihren Zweck nur dann, wenn sie "operational" ist (oder "praktikabel"), d.h. praktisch anwendbar, entscheidbar, kontrollierbar. Das kann zu Beschränkungen oder zum Aufschub an sich erwünschter Regelungen führen, wenn sich Ziele oder Maßnahmen (noch) nicht klar genug definieren lassen, für die Lösung von Zielkonflikten noch keine überzeugende Konzeption gefunden ist. Innerhalb einer Rechtsordnung herrscht außerdem ein systematischer Zusammenhang, der für die Regelung einzelner Gegenstände Prinzipien aus höherrangigen Normen und Bewertungen vorgibt.

All dies ist insbesondere für eine Datenschutzregelung zu beachten. Natürlich sind hier nicht die jahrelangen Überlegungen z.B. zur Konstruktion des gegenwärtigen Entwurfs eines Datenschutzgesetzes der Bundesrepublik nachzuvollziehen[13]. Es soll aber anhand eines Schemas von Tiedemann und Sasse[14] versucht werden, wenigstens die Regelungsgegenstände zu bezeichnen. Hierbei zeigt sich schon, daß sich dieser Entwurf (BDSGE) - wie übrigens die meisten vorliegenden Regelungen oder Vorschläge - im Sinne der Zielauswahl oben zu (3) ganz auf das Gegensatzpaar privacy/ Effizienz konzentriert.

4.2 Regelungsgegenstände des Datenschutzes

Datenkategorien

A. Bereich geschützter Daten

    Nr. 1 Welche Art von Daten wird überhaupt gesetzlich geschützt? (z.B. persönliche, gewerbliche; evtl. nur elektronisch verarbeitete?)

Systeminterne DV

B. Sammlung und Speicherung von Daten

    Nr. 2 Welche Daten dürfen gesammelt und gespeichert werden?

    Nr. 3 Mit welchen Methoden dürfen Daten gesammelt werden?

    Nr. 4 Pflicht, die erste Erfassung von Daten dem Betroffenen mitzuteilen

    Nr. 5 Befugnis, Daten zu ändern

    Nr. 6 Befugnis, Daten zu löschen

C. Einsichts- und Auskunftsrecht hinsichtlich Speicherung

    Nr. 7 Einsichts- und Auskunftsrecht bezüglich gespeicherter Daten

    Nr. 8 Pflicht zur Offenlegung der Informationsquelle

Systemüberschreitende DV

D. Weitergabe von Daten

    Nr. 9   An wen und zu welchem Zweck dürfen Daten weitergegeben werden?

    Nr.10 Muß die Legitimation des Kunden überprüft werden?

    Nr.11 Auf welche Weise dürfen Daten weitergegeben werden?

    Nr.12 Welche Daten dürfen weitergegeben werden?

    Nr.13 Wie lange dürfen Daten weitergegeben werden?

    Nr.14 Pflicht zur Führung eines Protokolls

E. Informationspflichten bei der Weitergabe

    Nr.15 Mitteilungspflichten anläßlich der Weitergabe von Daten

    Nr.16 Anspruch auf Auskunft über die Weitergabe von Daten

Datenkorrektur

F. Ansprüche bei falschen, bestrittenen oder unzulässig gespeicherten Daten

    Nr.17 "Korrekturansprüche" (insbes. auf Löschung, Berichtigung, Gegendarstellung)

    Nr.18 Pflicht zur Mitteilung von Korrekturen an bisherige Datenempfänger

    Nr.19 Schadenersatzansprüche

Einzelne Schutzmaßnahmen

G. Organisatorischer Schutz gegen Mißbrauch

    Nr.2o Organisatorischer Schutz gegen Datenmißbrauch und Fremdzugriff

H. Anmeldung und Aufsicht
   Nr.21 Gewerbeanmeldung
   Nr.22 Aufsichtsinstanzen

I. Strafnormen
   Nr.23 Strafnormen

4.3 Einige Alternativen und strittige Punkte zum Entwurf eines Bundesdatenschutzgesetzes

Die hier angegebenen Regelungsgegenstände deuten zugleich einen Katalog von Maßnahmen an, die in einer Datenschutzregelung zu den schon genannten Zielen in Beziehung zu setzen sind. Hierbei ergeben sich in vielen Punkten Alternativen, so etwa:

- wird nur automatische oder auch konventionelle DV einbezogen?
- wird nur die DV öffentlicher Aufgabenträger oder auch die privater Firmen einbezogen?
- beschränkt man sich auf die Ziele des Privacy-Schutzes oder auch des "Informationsgleichgewichts" usw.?
- soll es einen allgemein zuständigen "Datenschutzbeauftragten" geben?

Im Entwurf eines Bundesdatenschutzgesetzes hat man sich zum Beispiel dafür entschieden, sich auf den Privacy-Schutz zu beschränken (personenbezogene Daten im Hinblick auf Einzelpersonen), dafür aber sowohl automatische wie konventionelle, öffentliche wie private DV einzubeziehen.

4.4 Kritik am BDSGE; Notwendigkeit weiterer Forschung

Den bisher genannten Entscheidungen des BDSGE wird man zustimmen können. Problematischer ist die Entscheidung, keinen Datenschutzbeauftragten als allgemein zuständige Instanz einzuführen. Bedenklich muß es schließlich scheinen, daß in vielen Punkten hier keine operationalisierte Lösung der zugrunde liegenden gesellschaftlichen Interessenkonflikte geboten wird.

So werden häufig Formeln wie "Erforderlichkeit", "überwiegendes Interesse", "schutzwürdige Belange" u.ä. gebraucht. Diese geben aber nicht selbst ein Lösungskonzept für Interessenkonflikte, sondern delegieren die Konfliktlösung an den Richter. Letztlich drückt sich darin eine Unsicherheit über die Bestimmung der Zielstruktur des Datenschutzes aus. Zugleich führt diese Unbestimmtheit und mangelnde Operationalisierung dazu, daß ein wichtiges Desiderat nicht erfüllt wird: Die Möglichkeit, Durchführung und Kontrolle von Datenschutzregelungen weitgehend durch DV zu unterstützen. Nach den Einsichten der Lehre von der "automationsgerechten Rechtssetzung" sind solche Klauseln der Automation nämlich nicht günstig.

Natürlich soll die Schwierigkeit der zu bewältigenden Aufgaben nicht unterschätzt werden. Allein der an Vorarbeiten zu investierende Aufwand ist außerordentlich groß (Strukturforschung, Datenschutz im Informationssystem; Rechtstatsachenforschung zur Klärung gesellschaftlicher Einstellungen und Interessen; usw.). Nichtsdestoweniger sollte dieser Aufwand im Interesse der Sache noch getrieben werden, vor oder neben einer rechtlichen Regelung (so z.B. für Ausführungsbestimmungen und spätere Novellierungen). In diesem Sinne der methodischen Vorarbeit für Datenschutzregelungen sind im internationalen Bereich wie in der Bundesrepublik bereits eine ganze Reihe von Untersuchungen zu nennen. Für die Bundesrepublik möchte ich aus neuester Zeit insbesondere eine Studie von Siemens und eine neu aufgenommene Untersuchung der GMD nennen[15].

5. Datensicherung als gesellschaftliche Notwendigkeit der DV und als Voraussetzung des Datenschutzes

Datensicherung ist vor allem in der Form der Sicherung gegen unbefugten Gebrauch (z.B. von Personaldaten) Voraussetzung für die Wirksamkeit des Datenschutzes nach jeder denkbaren Auffassung.

Andererseits dient Datensicherung natürlich auch weiteren Zielen als dem Datenschutz. Etwa nach ihrer verallgemeinerten Konzeption als Sicherung der bestimmungsgemäßen Funktion von DV-Systemen besitzt sie offensichtlich ganz grundlegende Bedeutung als Voraussetzung des gesellschaftlichen Vertrauens in die Datenverarbeitung. Hierbei geht es dann nicht nur um die Sicherheit von Daten in ihrem Bestand, sondern darüber hinaus um die Sicherheit von Funktionen.

Das Bedürfnis nach Datensicherung besteht sowohl für die über ein DV-System irgendwie Verfügungsbefugten (insbesondere die Halter eines DV-Systems, aber auch seine befugten Benutzer) wie auch für irgendwie betroffene Dritte (z.B. in einer Datenbank erfaßte Personen). Halter und Benutzer möchten sich auf die getroffenen Bestimmungen verlassen können. Betroffene Dritte sind darauf angewiesen, die Verfügungsbefugten eventuell zur Verantwortung ziehen zu können und dann nicht dem Einwand zu begegnen, die Systemfunktionen seien von diesen selbst nicht beherrschbar gewesen. Die Gesellschaft in ihrer Gesamtheit ist interessiert an der Verhütung "nicht verantwortbarer Systeme".

Zur Realisierung von Schutz- und Sicherheitspostulaten hat man teilweise die Entwicklung ethischer Regeln für das DV-Personal vorgeschlagen, also eine Art Standesethik wie z.B. auch für Ärzte.

Andererseits arbeitet man seit Jahren mit großem Aufwand an Sicherheitskonzepten für DV-Systeme auf einer kombinierten Basis von Maßnahmen der hardware, software und Organisation. Inzwischen hat sich eine ausgedehnte Sicherheitstechnik mit systemanalytischer Fundierung entwickelt, welche je nach den drohenden Risiken in ihrem Aufwand entsprechende Gegenmaßnahmen empfiehlt[16]. Die Sicherheitstechnik verspricht ein wichtiger Zweig der DV zu werden, der neben den Datenschutzerfordernissen u.a. noch die Drohung der "Computerkriminalität"[17] fördert.

Noch darüber hinaus dürfte sich aber die Frage stellen, ob man die "bestimmungsgemäße Funktion" von DV-Systemen in einer exakteren Weise definieren, garantieren und kontrollieren kann als durch die heute üblichen Methoden von Systementwicklung und Test. Hier könnte vielleicht gerade die theoretische Informatik einen wichtigen Beitrag zum gesellschaftlichen Vertrauen in die DV leisten, indem sie den Bereich "nicht verantwortbarer Systeme" begrenzt.

6. Wege vom Datenschutz zu einem allgemeinen Recht der Information

Die Probleme vorgeschlagener Datenschutzregelungen demonstrieren die Schwierigkeit, den Datenschutz im allgemeinen gegenwärtig zu operationalisieren. Tatsächlich ist man im Ausland z.T. schon den Weg einer spezialisierenden Beschränkung gegangen (z.B. in USA mit dem "fair credit reporting act). Im BDSGE zeigen sich die Schwierigkeiten der Operationalisierung selbst bei der Beschränkung auf die Zieldimension privacy-Effizienz. Es fragt sich, ob nicht als Alternative[18] zu einer allgemeinen Datenschutzregelung die folgende Aufteilung zu erwägen wäre:

- Einerseits ein <u>Datenverfahrensrecht</u> (Datensicherheits- und Ordnungsrecht), das insbesondere allgemein interessierende und konsensfähige Maßnahmen im Sinne der Transparenz, Effizienz und Kontrollierbarkeit einer gesellschaftlich grundlegend wichtigen Technologie regelt. Dies stände einer rechtlichen Regelung von Datensicherungsstandards nahe. Hier wären dann "technische" Überwachungsinstanzen zur Systemkontrolle zu installieren analog dem TÜV. Diese hätten für eine Art "Datenhygiene" zu sorgen.

- Andererseits ein <u>Informationsrecht</u> (im materiellen Sinne), das die inhaltlichen Zusammenhänge des Umgangs mit Daten in enger Abhängigkeit von den einzelnen Sachgebieten regelt. Dieses ist demgemäß nach einzelnen Gebieten zu spezialisieren und aufzuspalten: So z.B. nach Meldewesen, Personalwesen, Kreditwesen, Werbung.

Das letztere wäre in seinen zunächst allein greifbaren Spezialisierungen ein Schritt auf dem Weg zu einem allgemeinen Recht der Information, dessen Konturen sich erst nach und nach abzeichnen können. Zu diesem gehörte insbesondere auch das Recht der Informationsmedien (Presse, Rundfunk, Informationsvermittlungssysteme u.ä.).

Hiermit sind die Probleme der Informationstechnologie in der modernen Gesellschaft in ihrer ganzen Breite angesprochen. Mit vollem Recht hat man hierin Fragen von einer ganz grundsätzlichen Bedeutung gesehen[19]. Allerdings ist ihr volles Ausmaß und ihre Lösung heute noch kaum abzuschätzen.

Nach ihrem gesellschaftlichen Stellenwert bedeutet Datenverarbeitung nicht nur "Rationalisierung", sondern den Übergang zu einer neuen Stufe der Rationalität. Die DV tritt dem Menschen nicht nur als Werkzeug und spezieller Kommunikationspartner ("Roboter") gegenüber, sondern reguliert als Organisationsprinzip und Kommunikationsmedium wichtige Lebensvorgänge menschlicher Gemeinschaften. Sie mediatisiert Prozesse der zwischenmenschlichen Verständigung und kann dazu führen, daß die menschliche Lebenswelt nur noch in der Sichtweise einer bestimmten "Verdatung" aufgefaßt wird. Durch ihre allgemeine Verbreitung geht die Informationstechnologie weitgehend bereits in die Konstituierung gesellschaftlicher Verhältnisse ein und ermöglicht es, diese automatisch zu dokumentieren. Computer realisieren den "objektiven Geist" der Gesellschaft nicht nur als statische Struktur, sondern als Medium und als überindividuellen Prozeß[20].

Nichtsdestoweniger ist die Informationstechnologie nur eine Überlagerung alter gesellschaftlicher Probleme. Die notwendige Regelung informationeller Zusammenhänge kann von der Informatik nicht traditionslos neu konzipiert werden, sondern bedarf der konkreten Anknüpfung an die Ergebnisse überkommener Disziplinen (vor allem der Rechtswissenschaft, Soziologie, Politologie wie auch der Informationswissenschaft).

Insbesondere ins Juristische projiziert, ergibt sich so für eine Informationsregelung (Informationsrecht im objektiven Sinne) des DV-Bereichs die versuchsweise Systematik:

- DV-Organisationsrecht (z.B. die DV-Organisationsgesetze der deutschen Länder)
- DV-Verfahrensrecht (insbes. Recht der Datensicherheit und -kontrolle)
- Materielles Informationsrecht des DV-Bereichs (insbes. etwa ein Datenschutzrahmengesetz, speziellere Datenschutzregelungen einzelner Bereiche, aber auch Themen eines "Datenbereitstellungsrechts").

Alles hier geschilderte muß zugleich als Auftrag an die Informatik und die Informatiker verstanden werden. Die DV und die Informationssysteme der Zukunft werden wesentlich von den Forderungen nach Datensicherheit und Datenschutz sowie deren rechtlicher Ausgestaltung bestimmt und im Hinblick darauf konstruiert werden. Die Informatik wird so ein gesellschaftlich höchst wichtiges Betätigungsfeld hinzugewinnen, zugleich aber auch verstärkt mit den Gesellschaftswissenschaften kooperieren müssen.

7. Thesen

1. Die Datenschutzdiskussion ist sehr nötig und sollte sogar auf noch breiterer Basis geführt werden, enthält jedoch auch Gefahren:
   - Ablenkung von Problemen sozialer Konflikte durch Ernennung des Computers zum Sündenbock
   - Alibikonstruktion, indem man meint, durch Begrenzung der "Computermacht" genug für die Freiheit zu tun - während doch z.B. gerade die Tätigkeit der Geheimdienste aus Datenschutzregelungen ausgenommen wird
   - Unkalkulierte Wirkung, indem man etwa statt des politisch innovativen Bürgers im Effekt eher nur den "gewöhnlichen Verbrecher" (z.B. Wirtschaftskriminalität) schützt.

2. Es geht beim Datenschutz nicht um den Konflikt zwischen einem legitimen Interesse an persönlicher Freiheit und einem illegitimen Interesse an technologisch fundierter Herrschaft, sondern um den Konflikt mehrerer gesellschaftlich legitimer Interessen.

3. Terminologisch sollte Datenschutz auf die Problematik des Persönlichkeitsschutzes angesichts der Möglichkeiten der Informationstechnologie beschränkt werden. Fragen des "Informationsgleichgewichts" und des gesellschaftlich wunschgemäßen Funktionierens der Informationstechnologie überhaupt sollten aus Gründen der Klarheit nicht hier angehängt werden.

4. Datensicherung muß die Sicherung der bestimmungsgemäßen Funktion von DV-Systemen einschließen und ist in dieser Form Voraussetzung für

das gesellschaftliche Vertrauen in die DV. Die Entwicklung von Methoden zur Beschreibung, Garantie und Kontrolle dieser bestimmungsgemäßen Funktion ist eine Aufgabe von grundsätzlicher Bedeutung.

5. Die Datenschutzregelung des BDSGE enthält noch zu viele Unbestimmtheiten, welche auf ungelösten Konflikten wie auch auf immer noch unzureichender Vorarbeit durch die Forschung beruhen. Diese Regelung ist so nur als Rahmen aufzufassen, welcher alsbald durch weitere Regelungen ausgefüllt werden muß.

6. Die gesellschaftlichen Probleme der Informationstechnologie (und der hiervon unterstützten Methodik) drängen über den Datenschutz hinaus zu allgemeineren Überlegungen. Insbesondere geht es um Fragen einer Gesellschaft, die sich zum Teil bereits informationstechnologisch konstituiert und automatisch dokumentiert. Dies bedingt ganz neue Ansätze, deren Regelung auf den Komplex eines "Informationsrechts" hinweist. Die hier anstehenden Probleme sollten kooperativ in einer ganzen Reihe von Disziplinen aufgegriffen werden, wozu neben der Rechtswissenschaft und Informatik auch die Informationswissenschaften, die Politikwissenschaft und die Soziologie gehören.

7. Datenschutz und Datensicherheit müssen in der jeweils angemessenen Form für alle DV-betroffenen Disziplinen Ausbildungsinhalt werden, insbesondere also für Wirtschaftswissenschaftler, Juristen und Informatiker

----

Anmerkungen

1) Zum Umfang der Literatur vgl. neuestens die Bibliographie von Turn und Hunt (Privacy and Security in Databank Systems: An Annotated Bibliography 1970-1973. Rand, Santa Monica, 1974). Diese enthält, obwohl vorwiegend an der angelsächsischen Literatur orientiert, um 1000 Titel. Zum Hintergrund und zum Stand der Datenschutzbemühungen in den westlichen Industriestaaten vgl. neuestens den Bericht von Westin, Martin und Lufkin: The Impact of Computer Based Information Systems on Citizen Liberties in the Advanced Industrial Nations. A Report to the German Marshal Fund of the United States, New York 1973 (vorläufige Version). - Über die Datenschutzentwicklung im In- und Ausland berichtet regelmäßig der Hessische Datenschutzbeauftragte in seinen jährlichen Tätigkeitsberichten, die als Drucksachen des Hessischen Landtags veröffentlicht werden.

2) Seidel, Datenbanken und Persönlichkeitsrecht, Köln 1972, S.7 ff; Mallmann, Kreditauskunfteien und Datenschutz in den Vereinigten Staaten, in: Kilian-Lenk-Steinmüller, Datenschutz, Frankfurt 1973, S.311 ff.

3) Eine Dokumentation zu dieser Entwicklung findet sich bei Kamlah, Datenschutz im Spiegel der anglo-amerikanischen Literatur, Anlage 2 zur Bundestagsdrucksache VI/3826, Bonn 1972.

4) Vgl. z.B. Mallmann, a.a.O.

5) Vgl. z.B. Turn und Hunt, a.a.O., sowie Nagel, Bibliographie zum Fachgebiet Datensicherung-Datenschutz, Neuwied 1973 (über 7oo Titel).

6) Vgl. den Bericht von Westin, Martin und Lufkin, a.a.O.

7) Seidel, Das aktuelle Thema: Datenschutz, Teil II, in ONLINE (ZfD), 1973, S. 248 f. Vgl. schon Schneider, Datenschutz-Datensicherung, Siemens AG, 1971.

8) Steinmüller, u.a., Grundfragen des Datenschutzes (Gutachten im Auftrag des Bundesministeriums des Innern), Anlage 1 zur Bundestagsdrucksache VI/3826, Bonn 1972.

9) Packard, The Naked Society, New York 1964. Zum Zusammenhang mit der Datenschutzproblematik in der US-Literatur vor allem die bekannten Arbeiten von A.R. Miller und A.F. Westin, in der deutschen Literatur besonders Kamlah, Right of Privacy, Köln usw. 1969 sowie Seidel, Datenbanken und Persönlichkeitsrecht, a.a.O.

1o) Vgl. den Bericht bei Kamlah, Datenschutz im Spiegel der anglo-amerikanischen Literatur, a.a.O.

11) Schimmel-Steinmüller, Rechtspolitische Problemstellung des Datenschutzes, in: Dammann, Karhausen, Müller, Steinmüller, Datenbanken und Datenschutz, Frankfurt-New York 1974, S. 114.

12) Habermas, Strukturwandel der Öffentlichkeit, 5. Aufl. Neuwied 1971.

13) Entwurf eines Gesetzes zum Schutz vor Mißbrauch personenbezogener Daten bei der Datenverarbeitung (Bundes-Datenschutzgesetz-BDSG), von der Bundesregierung dem Bundestag vorgelegt am 2o.9.1973, Bundestagsdrucksache 7/1o27. Aus der neuesten Diskussion dazu seien hier genannt: Auernhammer, IBM-Nachr. Nr. 221, 1974, S. 167; Bühnemann, Beilage 1/1974 zu Heft 3/1974 des Betriebs-Beraters; Podlech, Beiheft 1 zu "Datenverarbeitung im Recht", Berlin 1973; Schimmel-Steinmüller, a.a.O., W. Schmidt, Juristenzeitung 1974, S. 241; Simitis, in: "Datenverarbeitung im Recht", Bd.2, 1973, S. 139; Tiedemann-Sasse (vgl. die folgende Anm.).

14) Tiedemann und Sasse: Delinquenzprophylaxe, Kreditsicherung und Datenschutz in der Wirtschaft, Köln usw. 1973, S. 75 f.

15) International bekannt geworden sind insbes. die folgenden Studien: Westin und Baker, Databanks in a Free Society, New York 1972; Younger, Report of the Committee on Privacy, London 1972; Privacy and Computers, A Report of a Task Force established jointly by Dept. of Communications/Dept. of Justice, Ottawa 1972; Niblett, Digital Information and the Privacy Problem, Informatics Studies, No. 2, Paris (OECD) 1971. In der Bundesrepublik handelt es sich um die noch unveröffentlichte Siemens-Studie "Datenschutz-Mittel und Maßnahmen für die Datenverarbeitung" sowie um eine von der Gesellschaft für Mathematik und Datenverarbeitung vor kurzem für das Bundesinnenministerium aufgenommenen Untersuchung über Auswirkungen geplanter Datenschutzregelungen.

16) Vgl. z.B. neuestens Turn, Privacy and Security in Personal Databank Systems, Rand, Santa Monica, 1974 (Bericht für die National Science Foundation).

17) Von zur Mühlen, Computerkriminalität, Neuwied 1973.

18) Eine potentielle Annäherung an diese Alternativkonzeption ist im BDSGE durch dessen "Subsidiaritätsklausel" (§ 37) angedeutet, wonach spezialgebietliche Datenschutzvorschriften des Bundes dem BDSG vorgehen. Man könnte hier an einen stärker differenzierenden Ausbau von Spezialgebieten des Datenschutzes denken.

19) Vgl. z.B. Westin (ed.): Information Technology in a Democracy, Cambridge (Mass.) 1971.

20) Fiedler, Rechtsinformatik und juristische Tradition, in: Festschrift für H.Welzel, Berlin 1974, S. 168 ff.

TRENDS IN COMPUTER SCIENCE EDUCATION

Peter Naur
Institute of Datalogy
Copenhagen University

Computer science and education

In these notes, what is meant by computer science is the discipline concerned with the hardware and software of computers, as well as with data, data representations, processes, algorithms, and programs, as directly inspired by the existence of computers. As education is regarded not merely such teaching and instruction that is given in the context of a curriculum called "computer science", "informatics", "datalogy", or a related name, but also more isolated activities of education as they take place both inside and outside the formal institutions of schooling and education.

The beginning around 1950

In the above sense computer science education dates back to the time when the first computers started running, about 1950. The earliest courses, given in Cambridge, England, by Maurice Wilkes and his collaborators, and in Philadelphia by people associated with the Moore School of Engineering, naturally had to be concerned chiefly with the computer at hand, with its structure, instructions, and programming in machine language. Two other topics were fairly prominent from the early beginning. One of them was numerical analysis. This is understandable when we remember that the early computers were chiefly thought of as tools for solving scientific problems. The early development in England was strongly influenced by Alan Turing, working at the National Physical Laboratory. Maurice Wilkes' earlier work was concerned with the physics of the atmosphere. The group at Cambridge also numbered D. R. Hartree, well known for his numerical methods for computing the structure of atoms and molecules. In the USA John Von Neumann was concerned with problems of mathematical physics, in addition to problems of pure mathematics.

Another topic of the early courses, prominent particularly in Cambridge, was methods for detecting programming errors. From the very start the group at Cambridge recognized the central importance of this aspect. They consequently set to work, and very successfully so, on establishing a library of well-tested subroutines. In this library they included a rich collection of programs for tracing the program execution and for obtaining "post mortem" print-outs.

Applications and higher-level languages

The stress on machine language and numerical analysis persisted during the mid 1950ies. During the late fifties the stress in computer science education was gradually changed and diversified in several directions. One new direction was a deliberate stress on the computer as a tool for a specialized application. A powerful contribution along this line was the project titled "The Use of Computers in Engineering Education" conducted by The College of Engineering, The University of Michigan, and running from 1960 to 1963. This project had two primary aims. First, the education of the engineering teaching staff in the use of the computer in each their particular special field, and second, the production of a rich collection of examples of the use of computers in the teaching of engineering.

A second new direction in computer science education from about 1958 was the replacement of machine language by higher-level languages. The Michigan project described above was based primarily on the language MAD, derived partly from the early version of Algol 60 (Algol 58). Fortran, introduced in 1957, also soon gained ground in education.

Automata and formal languages

Further diversification of the topics of education took place in the early 1960ies. In one direction, the formal and abstract aspects of the computer were the subject of increased attention. The roots of the computer in the theory of automata was stressed. This argument was founded solidly on Alan Turing's work on computable numbers from 1936. It found a new stimulus in the use of a formal notation for describing the syntax of Algol 60. It was further strongly supported by the rapidly growing interest in compilers for higher-level programming languages.

There was an upsurge of interest in the principles that would make it possible to write a program that would generate compilers of any one of a large class of languages. These principles were sought in the area of automata and formal languages.

Administrative data processing

While this drive in the direction of mathematical formalization was taking place, a rather different drive in the direction of the methods underlying administrative data processing was starting. In the early 1960ies it was still at its infancy. Cobol was still a novelty, and it was not at all certain what to put into an education that would support administrative data processing. Some of the issues discussed were "non-procedural languages" and the basic concepts of data processing (see, e.g. ref. 1).

ACM Curriculum 68

Much work done during the early 1960ies on computer science education at the university level was collected and organized in the ACM Curriculum Recommendation, appearing first in a preliminary form in 1965, and then in a definitive form in 1968 (ref. 2). This document does not describe the education as it is given in any one place, but is a proposal for a way to establish a system of courses. It is strongly tied in with the course structure of American universities. It may be considered uncertain whether this curriculum has been realized in detail anywhere. However, the report has had considerable influence on the thinking in many places inside and outside of the USA, and gives a picture of a number of important tendencies in computer science education in the late 1960ies. As a summary of the ACM Curriculum 68, these are the titles of the courses described in the curriculum:

Basic Computer Science Courses:
B1. Introduction to computing
B2. Computers and programming
B3. Introduction to discrete structures
B4. Numerical calculus

Intermediate Computer Science Courses:
I1. Data structures
I2. Programming languages
I3. Computer organization
I4. Systems programming
I5. Compiler construction
I6. Switching theory

I7. Sequential machines
I8. Numerical analysis I
I9. Numerical analysis II
   Advanced Computer Science Courses
A1. Formal languages and syntactic analysis
A2. Advanced computer organization
A3. Analog and hybrid computing
A4. System simulation
A5. Information organization and retrieval
A6. Computer graphics
A7. Theory of computability
A8. Large-scale information processing systems
A9. Artificial intelligence and heuristic programming

Generally speaking, the ACM Curriculum 68 tends to stressing those parts of the subject that lend themselves to formalization. It is weak in such aspects that are related to the experience and intuition of the practitioner, such as man/machine interface problems, the psychology of programming and of project work. Also, applications are practically absent from the curriculum.

Software engineering and programming methodology

Soon after its publication the attitude of the ACM Curriculum 68 met a strong, correcting view, in the growth of interest in what is called software engineering. This was initiated by a conference held in October 1968 (ref. 3). It was followed by other conferences, and soon the topics discussed at these conferences were included in courses in many places. The essence of software engineering is a stress on the problems of design and development of large software systems.

A related recent development of the university level teaching is the concern with programming methodology. This is conncected with software engineering, in that it starts from a concern with the quality, particularly the correctness, of computer programs. This aspect is pursued in several ways. In one direction, there is an interest in program proving, i.e. formal demonstrations that given programs yield results that have given properties. In another direction there is an interest in program style, in particular the use or avoidance of certain programming language features, such as go-to-statements and repetition clauses. This is further connected with a concern about the structure of programs and about ways of developing programs that will ensure that the results will be well structured, in some sense.

Specific algorithms

Yet another development of recent years is a deeper interest in specific algorithms. In university teaching this is strongly supported by the thorough treatments by D. E. Knuth of the algorithms of central importance in computer science (ref. 4). The most suitable way to introduce the basic, specific algorithms into a curriculum remains an open question, however. The point is that the treatment of a very basic method, such as an algorithm for sorting, as an isolated topic is unsound pedagogically, because the students lack motivation for grasping it. However, treating the same method in the context of a specific application also is unsatisfactory because it introduces a connection with that application that may prevent the students from realizing the general usefulness of the method.

This very common problem of education gets further complicated in computer science, where certain topics are at the same time a basic part of the discipline itself and examples of applications. Compiler design is perhaps the best example of this. Compilers are part of the basic tools of computer science and thus of great interest in computer science education. However, in many ways compilers raise problems that are found also in many applications. If compilers are stressed heavily in the curriculum there is a danger that the principles of general symbol manipulation that are employed in them become strongly tied to this particular context, instead of appearing to the students as methods of wide utility.

Computer architecture and operating systems

The treatment of the computer itself in recent education has changed in comparison with the practice of a few years back. On the one hand, the concentration on a single, or at most, a few computer designs has given place to broad, comparative views, covering all important ideas of computer design that have ever been realized. This development finds strong support in the appearance of the comprehensive handbook of computer architecture by Bell and Newell (ref. 5).

On the software side the idea of operating systems as indispensable parts of the tools has firmly established itself. In education this has created new requirements, not only for courses covering the complexities of present day operating systems, but for coverage of the underlying problems of organization and scheduling. This makes operations research a relevant topic for the computer scientist, not only as a fruitful field of application, but as a necessary tool in the development of computer systems.

Computers in application fields

As described above, computers were introduced into engineering education on a large scale about 1960. At about the same time, or even before, computers had found their way into natural science education. Since then, work on introducing computers has been continuing in many other fields, although at a slower pace. Among the next fields that have followed science and engineering in this development one may mention biological science, social science, and management. Management has been the subject of special attention from an ACM Curriculum Committee on Computer Education for Management, who have produced a curriculum proposal (ref. 6). As a summary of this proposal, these are the titles of the 13 courses comprising the curriculum:

Analysis of organizational systems:
A1. Introduction to systems concepts
A2. Organizational functions
A3. Information systems for operations and management
A4. Social implications of information systems

Background for systems development:
B1. Operations analysis and modeling
B2. Human and organizational behaviour

Computer and information technology:
C1. Information structures
C2. Computer systems
C3. File and communication systems
C4. Software design

Development of information systems:
D1. Information analysis
D2. System design
D3. System development projects

Education below university level

Besides the development of education at the university level in recent years there has been a steady movement of computer related topics into the education at less advanced levels. This has arisen first because it has been realized that the principles of algorithms, data processes, and programs, in themselves are of such interest, simplicity, and generality, that they find a natural place side by side with the concepts of elementary mathematics. Second, as computers have become widely available at ever lower costs, it has become natural to bring them in as tools for the work in secondary schools, in connection with the teaching of physics, biology, sociology, and other subjects that may profit from easy access to computation or data processing. Third, as computers have entered public and private enterprises on a large scale, the staff of these enterprises have a need for at least some knowledge of computers. For this reason computers and programming have been taken up as subjects in many schools of business and technology. Fourth, as the far reaching potentials of computers for society as a whole are increasingly becoming clear, it follows that a public that wants to decide on their own affairs in a well-informed manner must have some understanding of computers.

With a justification in one or several of these four considerations, computers and related topics have been taken up by numerous school systems at the vocational, secondary, and even primary level. The first experiments along these lines date back to before 1960, but the recent growth of activity did not get under way until after 1965. As of present, computers and programming form a regular part of the curriculum at many vocational schools. At the secondary and primary school levels the activity is still mostly experimental.

Trends and future prospects

The general trends of the activity in computer science education over the last quarter century may be summarized as follows. First, there has been a movement away from concern with special, ad hoc features of computers and their associated software, toward an interest in general principles. In the area of the computers themselves this is realized by stressing comparisons of many designs, rather than just a single one. In the field of programming the same trend manifests itself in an interest in the common concepts underlying the features of different programming languages, and similarly in a concern with programming methodology, underlying any programming activity, irrespective of the programming language that is used. In the field of specific algorithms, abstraction is achieved by concentrating on such problems that reccur in many application areas.

Second, while computer related topics are increasingly introduced into the curricula of many other fields, computer science education itself tends to concentrate more and more on problems of its own, such as data, data structures, programming languages, programming psychology, programming methodology, operating systems, and computer architecture. There is a decrease of stress on numerical analysis and on applications in natural science.

Third, computer related topics are rapidly being introduced at the more elementary levels of the education system, both as topics worthy of interest for their own sake and as a basis for applications in other fields.

As to the likely prospects it seems inevitable that these trends will continue into the nearer future. In the longer run it appears likely that the development in education will have to come to grips with the problems created by the vastly increasing complexities of present day computer systems. These complexities already today raise vexing problems in education. There is a widening contrast between the neatness and simplicity of the methods and principles that lend themselves well to the work in the class room and the facilities that are placed at the disposal of users of the huge black boxes of modern computer systems. For how long will it continue to make sense to teach the principles that underlie programming language translators of great elegance and reliability when the students have to do their practical work using systems that, by comparison, are crude and unreliable? Systems that, moreover, are practically inaccessible to detailed study and improvement because of their enormity.

In view of this contrast there is a very real danger that the strong tendency of present day education toward general principles will cause it to loose contact with the realities of the computer systems put on the market by the manufacturers. In other words, that the topics treated in education will become, in the worst sense, academic exercises. Similarly, there is a danger that the computer oriented topics that may find place in the more elementary education will be found to be increasingly out of touch with the way computers operate and are used in public and private institutions.

This problem cannot be solved by the educational institutions by themselves. In fact, it arises from the powerful forces of large manufacturing companies operating in a highly expansive and competitive market.

The way out of this problem can only be dimly perceived. As one possibility it may be found that the current dominance of computer systems of vast complexity and low reliability is temporary and that a new era, better in accordance with high academic and intellectual standards, will dawn. As another possibility, those responsible for the curricula may decide that the situation described above has to be accepted, and may conclude that the most reasonable topics of attention from the educational institutions in this context is the social implications of computers, rather than their technical aspects.

A final remark should be made. The education given at any educational institution depends deeply on the fundamental definitions of that institution, on its declared aims, on its system of control, rules of staff promotion, and decision procedure. Consequently, if you feel that the education offered at such an institution is in some way unsatisfactory, perhaps misguided or irrelevant, then it will not really help to put pressure on the staff of the institution. Instead you will have to address yourself to the basic law of that institution and have that altered. For example, if you want to weaken the stress on theory in universities, then you have to make sure that staff promotion does not depend on success in theoretical pursuits.

References
1. "An information algebra - Phase I report of the Language Structure Group of the CODASYL Development Committee." Comm.ACM 5,4 (Apr. 1962), 190-204.
2. "Curriculum 68 - Recommendations for academic programs in computer science. A report of the ACM Curriculum Committee on Computer Science." Comm.ACM 11, 3 (March 1968), 151-197.
3. Naur, P.; and Randell, B. (eds.) "Software Engineering." NATO Science Committee, Brussels, 1969.
4. Knuth, D.E. "The art of computer programming." Addison-Wesley, Reading Mass., vol. 1 1968, vol. 2 1969, vol. 3 1973.
5. Bell, C. G.; and Newell, A. "Computer structures: readings and examples." McGraw-Hill Book Co., New York, 1971.
6. "Curriculum recommendations for graduate professional programs in information systems - A report of the ACM Curriculum Committee on Computer Education for Management." Comm.ACM 15,5 (May 1972), 363-398.

HOW TO TEACH COMPUTER SCIENCE TO STUDENTS WHO DON'T LIKE SCIENCE

S.G. van der Meulen
Rijksuniversiteit Utrecht

The english word "Science" usually connotes the so-called "natural sciences", i.e. mathematics, astronomy, physics and perhaps also chemistry, but not, for instance, law, medicine, litterature. From this implied connotation of the word, it is clear where "computer science" fits in - precisely there where we always find it: in a department of "natural" sciences and (for historical reasons) even frequently in (or closely related to) the department of mathematics.

In the Netherlands we are used to a more detailed classification in "alpha"-, "bèta"- and "gamma"-sciences. The "bèta"-sciences are the "natural" sciences (including chemistry but not medicine), in the "alpha"-sciences we find theology, law, litterature, art etc. and in the "gamma"-sciences everything else (including medicine, pharmacy, biology, psychology and economy). A dutch "universiteit" embraces all the alpha-, bèta- and gamma-sciences; next to it we know the so called "technische hogeschool" (technical university) which is, essentially, a "bèta-engineering-academy". From the beginning on, computer science was assigned to these technical universities (Eindhoven, Delft, Twente) and not to the alpha-bèta-gamma-universities - an assignment which, though deplorabe in many respects, is justified by its historical logic which, of course, was hardware-logic (in the fifties), logically developing into firmware- and software-engineering.

And so computer science did not make its entry into the dutch university until the early seventies. Questions to answer were: is it a bèta-science? is the computer the subject of the science? and in particular: what shall we do for all the gamma- and alpha-students and staff members who already take courses in ALGOL and FORTRAN and use the tool for diverse and often very interesting purposes? A formal answer to these questions was given in the name: "informatica" rather than "computer science". In Utrecht (the largest university in the Netherlands) we also - though with some reluctance - adopted this name, with the understanding, however, that what is really meant is something like "algorithmic disciplines" supporting the whole university-gamma back to alpha. This was a decision in principle, nevertheless we can hardly take another standpoint due to the fact that many computer-using activities in gamma and alpha-departments have vested interests and the departments of mathematics and physics do not like to breed a cuckoo's egg.

So we are faced with the problem: "How to teach algorithmic disciplines to students who are not in science", which would have been a much better title of this lecture. The exordium "How to ----" suggests - in connection with many "How-to"-books - that, after hearing this lecture, you know how-to-do-it. I would really regret such an expectation. All I can - and want to - do is: give you an impression of how I try to teach "informatica" to students and staff members who are not necessary bèta's. You should know beforehand that it is my (present) educational faith that this may also be a (perhaps even very) good way to teach the fundamentals of computer science to Bèta's.

The environment of my ideal "informatica-instituut" is a university where nobody can do computer science as a major subject without having obtained at least a bachelor-degree in some discipline (alpha or bèta or gamma). Consequently, computer science should not take more than say 10% of the students time in his first two years. On the other hand, the university should be flexible enough to allow the student to take a not-more-than-10% course of algorithmic disciplines as a minor subject in exchange for another minor subject. To put it in another way: a modern university must recognize as a principle that algorithmic disciplines are of quite some (roughly: 10%) value for all studies and that (!) a computer is a tool to practise algorithmic disciplines. In order to make it a good deal, the lessequal 10% two-years course of computer science fundamentals must be 1°) substantial enough for bèta's, 2°) useful for gamma's and 3°) apprehensible (if not valuable) for alpha's.

This, of course, comes close to the quadrature of the circle. There is, however, one significant escape or - to give it more emphasis - this alpha-bèta-gamma-circle can be squared from the very nature of the algorithmic disciplines: in the choice of examples and programming excercises. On the ground of its purpose the two-years-course must consist of lectures constructing the circle and examples/excercises yielding the polygonal approximations. More concrete: sorting, searching and simulation is of importance for all, what to sort or search for or simulate may vary over many cases of greek letters. So we go to all the departments involved and ask them: what do you want your students to sort or search or simulate and what other wishes do you have? As far

as the little bit of experience goes until now, this might - on the
longer run - work out quite satisfactory (though you need diplomats
to ask the proper questions in well-shaped words and at the right moment). The central problem in the quadrature of this circle is, of
course, the proper choice of examples, exercises and problems for a
great variety of students.

We now come to the two-years program. Ten procent of a week is one
afternoon. We distinguish all-lecture afternoons (for all), all-practice
afternoons (division in several groups according to the provenance of
the student) and mixed afternoons. For the practice hours we need
assistance of the proper people from the students environment. In two
years we have four semesters and we call the courses A1 and A2 (first
year) and B1 and B2 (second year).

A1 replaces an introductory programming course, but it gives much
more (see below). A2 pursues the programming course, the major theme
is access algorithms (among which, of course, sorting and searching)
on fundamental data-structures (arrays, single- and double linked lists,
binary trees, queues and stacks) - examples, exercises and applications
as indicated above. The introduction of the stack (at the end of the
course) gives a good opportunity to survey the parsing of simple formulas (alpha-people are exited here) and to give a few examples of recursive problem-solving (e.g. towers of Hanoi). A1+A2 must form a more or
less complete whole for the benefit of those who want to quit here.
Therefore (and also to make a lock between A and B), A1+A2 is concluded
by a (multiple choice) test and/or a (not too difficult) programming
problem in the students field - teamwork is explicitly encouraged.

B1 is entirely devoted to "the course of a job through the computer
system". It is a broad - and sometimes more detailed - exposition of
what is the task of an operating system and how it works. Here we also
include a few fundamentals of parallel processing (interrupts and semaphores) and we give quite a bit of practical information about job-control language. We then describe the process of compilation and pay
some attention to error-detection and -recovery (and how, approximately, the compiler does it) and to code-optimization. The spirit of B1,
however, is that all this rather encyclopedic information (with a lot
of practical illustrations and small exercises) is not more nor less
than the background against which we deal with the major questions of
"how to divide your job" and "how to structure your program". The
major theme of B1 is "divide and rule". B2 is mainly devoted to practical work (division in diverse groups, of course), preparing the ground

for the final piece of work which is a more comprehensive programming
problem (to be authorized by a study-leader from the students environment). In B2 we give a small lecture-course (in principle for all) on
programming languages: a features-comparing orientation with a waft of
one- and two-level grammar.

The purpose of A+B is threefold:
1°) it is a complete whole, yielding a good insight in what are
   algorithmic disciplines (and activities) and also in what
   is going on in automatization, for those who do not want
   to come back to computer science in their further studies ,
2°) it gives a good foundation for those who want to take a
   minor "informatica"-subject in their field in the post-
   bachelor fase ,
3°) it is a sufficient minimum-basis for those who want to take
   computer science as a (perhaps even the) major subject .

For a good understanding of the general plan it may be important
to know that students in (numerical- and applied-) mathematics and in
physics have anyhow to do quite a bit of programming and computer-
oriented courses (mini-computers and real-time applications, for example,
in phyisics and chemistry) in their first years. A few synchronization-
problems between A+B and these more specific requirements have to be
solved; this can be done without difficulty (the practice-afternoons
have a broad margin).

Until here we discussed more the "What" than the "How". With regard
to the "What" it must be emphasized that the main theme of A+B is the
algorithmic processing of data (of all kinds) rather than the tool that
does it. My slogan is: "YOU do it, ----- with the aid of a tool -----
which, in most cases, is a computer". And here we arrive at the "How":
we teach algorithmic disciplines (plural, there are many). We consider
them as a valuable and - above all - practical approach to attack many
problems in all (alpha-bèta-gamma-)sciences. We conceive an automaton as
a technical device (the technology of which does not concern us) that
performs some "build-in" algorithm and we describe a computer-system
as a "commune of cooperating automata" (see below). The pivot on which
everything turns is that we explain the working of a computer in terms
of algorithms rather than the other way around. The computer is one -
though important - example of what can be done with algorithms.

This kind of lecturing on algorithmic disciplines requires a certain
breadth of cultivation and also a vivid imagination from the lecturer.
He must be able, for instance, to speak with some knowledge about a

musical score as a program: defining a number of parallel processes
(for ten fingers, or four voices, or a symphony-orchestra). He must
have enough insight in the material to defend the classical staff-
notation as a specimen of a programming language avant-la-lettre. Moreover, he must have enough imagination to realise the relevancy of such
a little elaboration (early in the A1-course), when a student in musicology comes to him with the intention to write a program which transcri-
bes an input musical score in some key to an output musical score in
another key: such a program has compiler-like features (there is quite
some syntax involved). It could be a very nice post-bachelor project,
provided it is given the proper general setting (for example transcribing also from say clavichord to grand-piano). But then this lecturer
must be able to convince a computer-hating professor in musicology, to
allow his student to take this project. The student, in his turn, must
first prove his ability and technical skill by solving a partial problem in this area, for example: the input- and internal coding of a
musical score. This could be a nice final test for A+B and this student
could happily work together with a plotter-devoted student. It will be
clear, that this is only one of many situations you will have to face
when you are going to teach computer science to students who --------
----- (well, who may become very enthusiastic).

More details on the "How" may be found in the following survey of
the A1-course. From an educational point of view, this was the most
difficult part of the program for me - I was faced with a yet completely
unknown population of students. It is, nowadays, very rare to find
alpha- and bêta- and gamma-students in one classroom.

The A1-course ranges over 15 afternoons (2 to 3 hours) and we fill
them as follows ("L"= Lecture, "P"= Practice)

1) L+L+L

Introduction to the concepts "information", "data", "information-
structure", "data-processing" (reading a book, subtracting numbers etc.),
"algorithm", "automaton" (as an algorithm-performing device), "computer"
(as an automaton with two inputs: an algorithm and data for that algorithm), "flowchart" (as a graph with command-nodes and branch-nodes).
A selection of daily-life algorithms (the protocol at the Royal Palace,
the conviction of road-offenders, a three-person game of heads or tails
and a few others). The Knuth-definition of "algorithm".

2) L+L+L

Further elaboration of the concept "automaton": the system-analysis

of the activities of a coffee- and cocoa- pouring buffet-lady, resulting in the algorithmic construction of a coffee- and cocoa- delivering
vending machine. The flowchart of this vending machine (an "automaton",
of course) is quite interesting. The possible choices are: coffee with
or without milk and/or sugar and cocoa with or without sugar. The
automaton always tries to serve you, provided that your coin is ok, and
gives your coin back if some supply is exhausted (nevertheless giving
you what is possible, in the worst case an empty cup). Moreover it checks
the presence of a new cup and the absence of the previous cup. Try to
design the minimal flowchart of this first non-capitalistic vending
machine. The flowchart contains three "waiting cycles". Here we find
a nice opportunity to introduce the concepts of "semaphore", "busy-"
and "not-busy-waiting" (i.e. "interrupt") and we say a few words about
traffic-regulation (cars are automata following their own algorithms
in their own timing, synchronized by traffic-lights and priority-rules).
Finally an encyclopedic introduction in what is automata-theory about
and a ten-minutes talk about Turings machine.

3) L+L+P

The introduction of a large computer-system (the CYBER 73/26) as
a "commune of synchronized cooperating automata": all input- and output-
devices are automata performing their build-in algorithms, and much the
same applies to magtape-units and discs. More detailed introduction of
a "processor" as "Siamese twins" composed of an "arithmetic unit" (an
automaton with build-in algorithms for arithmetic operations and many
more) and a "control unit" (playing the arithmetic unit like a pianist
playing the piano: the program is the score). The CYBER-machine has 10
peripheral processors and two CPU's (the Mao and the Brezjnev of the
world of automata).

The practice hour is devoted to the solution of problems given in
1 and 2: flowcharting of a few daily-life algorithms (some of them are
rather tricky).

1+2+3 is encyclopedic in its plan and prepares the ground for more
substantial work. Students must be able here to read (and design) simple
flowcharts and can be supposed to have some preliminary insight in what
is an automaton and also a vague idea of what is a processor and how
many automata can work together to yield a powerful tool for data-
processing.

4) L+L+P

A rather detailed treatment of a modern (Japanese) hand-calculator,
described with a detailed flowchart. The machine (FANCY-1 is its name)

has three registers: R (the goal-register of the build-in arithmetic operations), Q (an extra register to store results) and G (the memory-register). Input via digit-buttons. Operations via operation-buttons. Output via the windows R, Q and G. Arithmetic decimal, of course.

Here we are at a very important point. The operations of the machine (register-transports between R, Q and G, and the arithmetic operations) are described in a high-level language. This language will be used through the whole course A+B <u>as a reference-language</u> (only to <u>describe</u> algorithms). For this purpose we want to have as much comfort as possible, the use of the language is quite informal (I took ALGOL and use a few ALGOL68-features in A2 and B1). This reference language, however, does not force the students in any direction: depending on their taste and programming-needs, they will be as free as feasible to choose FORTRAN or even COMPASS if they want to.

In these two lectures we treat the concepts of "assignment" and "arithmetic operation" (R:=R'operator'G) and explain the working of FANCY-I in one detailed flowchart in which the machine-buttons are the branch-nodes. FANCY-I is a arithmetics-vending-machine.

The practice hour is devoted to a few algorithms with FANCY-I (mean and standard-deviation of a row of numbers), the algorithms to be defined by flowcharts, using the reference language.

5) L+L+P

FANCY-I gets a large memory (one million of number-cells) and becomes FANCY-II. We treat the concepts of "address" ("name") and "contents" ("value") and the concept of a "variable": a pair consisting of a name and a value it refers to. We give an example of an algorithm described with name-addressing. Then we introduce the address-register A and access the memory (still in reference-language notation) as G[A]. We introduce a very simple push-button language, which is the machine language of FANCY. We explain how, by a simple algorithm, you can transcribe a reference-language flowchart into this push-button language.

The practice hour is devoted to a few simple algorithms you can do with FANCY-II.

6) L+L+P

FANCY-II gets an input- and an output device (card-reader and line-printer) and becomes FANCY-III. We treat the coding of punch-cards and pay quite some attention to the two levels where the "data" are symbols and where the data are numbers. Introduction of two more buttons:

"SYMBIN":   G[A] := the next symbol of the card
"NUMBIN":   G[A] := the next number of the card
and, correspondingly, three buttons for output:
"SYMBEX":   print the symbol represented by G[A]
"NUMBEX":   print the number G[A]
"LINEX":   new line .

The important moment in these two lectures is the concept of symbols represented by numbers.

The practice hour is devoted two an algorithm with as input some text and as output the mean and standard-deviation of the word-length.

7) L+L+P

FANCY-III gets a control-unit, pushing its buttons and becomes FANCY. Once we know how texts can be represented in a memory, we can imagine an algorithm reading a "program" in the push-button language and then pushing the buttons. The input of the control-unit is a text in FANCY-code (read in the memory), its output is "pushing the buttons". FANCY is a "computer".

The important moment in these two lectures, of course, is the introduction of transfer- and branch-instructions for the control-unit and how to express them in FANCY-code (the machine-primitives) and in the reference-language (the concepts of "label", goto and if -- then --- else -- fi).

Practice hour devoted to "how to write a flowchart as a program".

8) L+L+L

The theme is the Von Neumann concept of a computer: the coding of machine-commands as "numbers" ("function" and "address") and the (very simple) algorithm of the control unit (the basic cycle). Nasty questions about the basic cycle: what is in the instruction counter before and after a jump and so on. The second and third lecture are about the very important consequences of the Von Neumann concept: the possibility of machinecode-generating programs (assemblers and compilers) and of program-manipulating programs (operating systems). Here we answer some of the many questions we left open in 3 .

One should notice at this point, that everything has been treated entirely in the framework of arithmetic discipline - even the working of a computer has been described in a machine-independent way! Moreover, the students have seen many little programs and even tried to write a few in the reference language. More than half of a programming course has been done — giving much more "inside-insight" as is the case in many traditional programming courses. Last, but not least, the student knows how texts can be manipulated and he even has some idea in why and how a compiler is possible.

9) L+P+P
10) L+P+P

A FORTRAN course. Surprise, surprise. But why not? We have seen a very primitive push button language and a high-level reference language (though only a little bit of both). We now introduce the worlds wildest used programming tool: a hammer, not a fencing-sword. Naturely, we also want to appease the physicists.

We make a lot of small programming excercises. The students can go to the machine, if they want to.

The afternoons 11 - 15 are (for P) devoted to many programming exercises (with a first branching-out for different applications) and (for L) to the theme "Mini-, Midi- and Maxi-Computers":

11) L+L+P

Binary coding of numbers and other data (radix-2, radix-8 and radix-16), the concepts of a "byte", the primitive types <u>bool</u>, <u>char</u>, <u>int</u> and <u>real</u> (and also <u>string</u>). Binary coding of machine-commands. A small, encyclopedic, talk on hardware (<u>and</u>- and <u>or</u>-gates).

12) L+L+P

The basic cycle revisited: the concepts of indirect addressing and, in relation to that, the subroutine-jump. The concepts of "open" and "closed" subroutine. The FORTRAN-subroutine (with the proper warnings).

12) L+P+P

Encyclopedic information about mini-computers (PDP8).

13) L+P+P

Encyclopedic information about midi-computers (PDP10).

14) L+L+P

Encyclopedic information about maxi-computers (IBM370/CYBER73).

15) L+L+L

Discussion and answer to yet unanswered questions. Many answers are very short: "wait and see ·in A , B1 and B2).

In the course A2 we begin with "structured programming": mainly banning the <u>goto</u> (and, consequently, warning for FORTRAN and other primitive programming systems). In particular, we pay attention to the concept of _procedure_ and the various ways to transfer a parameter.

Reference language features, treated in detail, are the conditional-, the case- and the loop-clauses. We also introduce the ALGOL68 mode-declaration - we need it for sufficient comfort in the lectures on data-structures like lists and binary trees. However, the didactic principle is always: never introduce a feature before you really need it to express an algorithm in a decent-structured way. The students are always free to choose their own language vehicle when they want to go to the machine (we try to treat them as grown up people with their own judgement). We enforce, however, more or less the use of the reference-language as the vehicle in which to think about the problem and in which to design the final program. Most students run away from FORTRAN and they know why!

Sofar the exposition of the "How" in A1 and A2. Hopefully you can figure out yourself the "How" of the B-course.

It is too early to report on results. With all proper reserve I could, however, express my personal faith that "computer science", conceived as a "practice of algorithmic disciplines", might on the long run appear to be a very valuable "inter-disciplinary" activity (if not ¬science). The only competor I can think of, is Philosophy - perhaps they have more in common than we can imagine nowadays.

Anyhow: teaching computer science to students who are assumed not to like science, is big fun.

2. THEORETISCHE GRUNDLAGEN

AUTOMATENTHEORIE UND FORMALE SPRACHEN
A. BERTONI

M. HÖPNER

M. KUDLEK

THEORIE DER PROGRAMMIERUNG
S. HEILBRUNNER

P. RAULEFS

KOMPLEXITÄTSTHEORIE
W. BIBEL

W. COY

THE SOLUTION OF PROBLEMS RELATIVE TO PROBABILISTIC AUTOMATA IN THE FRAME OF THE FORMAL LANGUAGES THEORY

A. Bertoni

Gruppo di Elettronica e Cibernetica - Facoltà di Scienze Fisiche - Università di Milano - Via Viotti, 5

INTRODUCTION

The concept of isolated cut-points [1], plays a fundamental role in the theory of probabilistic automata.
The following problem, suggested by [1] and by [2] is quite natural:
(1) "Can one device an algorithm to decide, for every given probabilistic automaton $\mathcal{A}$ (the automaton is given by matrices $A(\sigma)$, $\sigma \in \Sigma$, and we assume for semplicityn that these matrices have rational coordinates) and every (rational) λ, whether λ is an isolated cut-point of $\mathcal{A}$?"

In this paper we show that this problem is recursively unsolvable. In section 1 we introduce basic definitions, than (section 2) we proof the unsolvability of a problem on strings, which represents the foundamental lemma to show the unsolvability of (1). Finally (section 4) we suggest some problems, which remain open.

1. - BASIC DEFINITIONS

Let $\Sigma = \{\sigma_1, .., \sigma_n\}$ be a finite alphabet. $\langle \Sigma^+, \cdot \rangle$ and $\langle \Sigma^*, \cdot, \wedge \rangle$ are the free semi-group and the free monoid generated by Σ.
$\wedge$ is the empty string.

Given string x, the length $\ell(x)$ of x is the number of symbols in x. We assume $\ell(\wedge) = 0$. z is prefix of x, if there is an s such that zs = x.

Given two strings x and y, if z is the longest prefix common to x and y (i.e. $zs_1 = x$, $zs_2 = y$, $z's_1' = x$ and $z's_2' = y \implies \ell(z') \leq \ell(z)$), we write: $x \circ y = z$.

Let us give the set $\{0, 1, 2, ..., k-1, k\} \equiv K$. Each element $x \in K^+$ may be interpreted as "decimal in scale K+1" through the following rule: $k_{\partial_1} ... k_{\partial_s} = \sum_{\vartheta=1}^{s} k_{\partial_\vartheta}/(K+1)^\vartheta$
Ex.: In 2-scale (binary) 1/4 is represented by the string 01, while

in 10-scale (decimal) it is represented by the string 25.
Let $\mathcal{S}$ be a set, $|\mathcal{S}|$ is the cardinality of $\mathcal{S}$.

Def. 1. A probabilistic (stochastic) automaton A_p, is a set
$\langle \Pi, A(\sigma_j), \eta_T \rangle$, where

a) Π is a stochastic vector 1xn, i.e. $\Pi = (\Pi_1, \ldots, \Pi_n)$; $\sum_{k=1}^{n} \Pi_k = 1$; $\Pi_k \geq 0$

b) $A(\sigma_j)$ is, for all σ_j, a stochastic matrix, i.e.
$a_{ik}(\sigma_j) \geq 0$; $\sum_{k=1}^{n} a_{ik}(\sigma_j) = 1$ $(i = 1, 2, \ldots, n)$

c) η_T is a nx1 vector with 0 or 1 components.

From now on, we shall consider matrices and vectors, whose components are rational numbers.

Let A_p be a given stochastic automaton.

Def. 2. A stochastic matrix is specified to every $x \in \Sigma^*$:

a) $A(\Lambda) = I$; I is the identity matrix

b) $A(x\sigma_j) = A(x) A(\sigma_j)$

Def. 3. A stochastic event generated by the automaton A_p is the function p: $\Sigma^* \to [01]$, $p(x) = \Pi A(x) \eta_T$

We observe that the stochastic event is an application
p: $\Sigma^* \to [01]$

Def. 4. A rational number λ is said isolated for the event p if
$\exists \delta (\delta > 0; \forall x (|p(x) - \lambda| \geq \delta))$

2. UNSOLVABILITY OF A PROBLEM ON STRINGS

In this section we state the unsolvability of a problem on strings, similarly to the well-known Post Correspondence Problem.[5].
Let $\Sigma = \{\sigma_1, \ldots, \sigma_n\}$ and $K = \{0, 1, \ldots, k\}$ be two finite alphabets.
We consider the following two homomorphisms:

$\psi_1: \langle \Sigma^*, \cdot, \Lambda \rangle \to \langle K^*, \cdot, \Lambda \rangle$

$\psi_2: \langle \Sigma^*, \cdot, \Lambda \rangle \to \langle K^*, \cdot, \Lambda \rangle$

We set the following problems:

P_1: to decide whether $|\bigcup_{x \in \Sigma^*} \psi_1(x) \circ \psi_2(x)| = +\infty$

P_2: to decide whether $|\bigcup_{x \in \Sigma^*} \psi_1(\sigma_1 x) \circ \psi_2(\sigma_1 x)| = +\infty$

Th. 1. P_2 is recursively unsolvable $\Rightarrow P_1$ is recursively unsolvable.

Given an arbitrary configuration (ψ_1, ψ_2) of problem P_1, we associate in the same way as in [3], a configuration $(T\psi_1, T\psi_2)$ of problem P_2 such that $P_2(T\psi_1, T\psi_2)$ is solvable iff $P_1(\psi_1, \psi_2)$ is solvable. To show the unsolvability of P_1, it is enough to show the one of P_2, as stated in the following theorem.

Th. 2. P_2 is recursively unsolvable.

Proof: We assume reader's knowledge of Turing-machine concept and related problems. The proof goes on in the following way:

1) We join to each Turing machine MT a configuration (ψ_{1MT}, ψ_{2MT}) of problem P_2.
2) We show that $P_2(\psi_{1MT}, \psi_{2MT})$ has answer NO iff MT halts.

From the well-known results of unsolvability problems on Turing machines, the thesis follows.

A Turing Machine MT is a set $\langle Q, S \cup \{\#\}, \mathcal{P}, \#q_0 y \# \rangle$ where:

1) Q, S finite alphabet
2) $\#q_0 y \# \in \#q_0 S^+ \#$
3) $\mathcal{P}$ is a finite set of production rules of the type:
   a) $q_i S_j \to q_\ell S_k$
   b) $q_i S_j S_k \to S_d q_\ell S_k$
   c) $q_i S_j \# \to S_j q_\ell S_0 \#$
   d) $S_k q_i S_j \to q_\ell S_k S_d$
   e) $\# q_i S_j \to \# q_i S_0 S_d$
   f) $q_i S_j \to S_d$

together with a set of rules, which make the system deterministic [4].

Given the Turing machine MT, we construct the following configuration of problem P_2:

$\Sigma = \{\sigma_1; \ldots; \sigma_n\} \cup S \cup \{\#\}$
$K = S \cup Q \cup \{\#\} \cup \{*\}$

1) $\psi_1(\sigma_1) = *\#q_0 y \#$ $\psi_2(\sigma_1) = *$
2) $\psi_1(\sigma_\ell) = q_d S_k$ $\psi_2(\sigma_\ell) = q_i S_h$ iff $q_d S_k \to q_i S_h$ is a rule of type a), and likewise for all the rules of $\mathcal{P}$.
3) $\psi_1(S_m) = S_m$ $\psi_2(S_m) = S_m$

4) $\psi_1(\#) = \#$ $\psi_2(\#) = \#$

If $\psi_1(\sigma_1 x) \circ \psi_2(\sigma_1 x) = z$ then $z = *\#\omega_0\#\omega_1\#\omega_2\#\cdots\#\omega_m\#S$
where: $S \in \{S \cup Q\}^*$; $\ell(S) \leq \ell(\omega_m)+1$
$\omega_0 = q_0 y$; $\ell(\omega_i) \leq \ell(\omega_{i+1})-1$; $\forall i\ (\omega_i \xrightarrow{M.T.} \omega_{i+1})$

Observing that $m \leq \ell(z) \leq 3+4+\cdots+(m+1) = m\cdot(m+5)/2$ follows

$\left| \bigcup_{x \in \Sigma^*} \psi_1(\sigma_1 x) \circ \psi_2(\sigma_1 x) \right| < +\infty$ iff MT halts. Q.E.D.

3. UNSOLVABILITY OF A PROBLEM ON STOCHASTIC AUTOMATA

Let $\psi_1 : \langle \Sigma^*, \cdot, \Lambda \rangle \to \langle K^*, \cdot, \Lambda \rangle$ be a homomorphism of free monoids. If we interpret each string of K as a real number $\alpha \in [0\,1]$ described in a K+1 scale, ψ_1 is explainable as a function:

$$\psi_1 : \Sigma^* \to [0\,1]$$

Th. 1. Each homomorphism $\psi_1 : \langle \Sigma^*, \cdot, \Lambda \rangle \to \langle K^*, \cdot, \Lambda \rangle$ is explainable, in the above mentioned sense, as a stochastic event generated by a stochastic 2-states automaton.

Proof: it suffices observing that ψ_1 is the event generated by automaton:

$$A_p \equiv \left\langle \pi = (1,0);\ A(\sigma_j) = \begin{pmatrix} 0^{\ell(\psi_1(\sigma_j))} \cdot 1 & 1-0^{\ell(\psi_1(\sigma_j))} \cdot 1 \\ \psi(\sigma_j) & 1-\psi(\sigma_j) \end{pmatrix};\ \eta_T = \begin{pmatrix} 1 \\ 0 \end{pmatrix} \right\rangle$$

Now, let $x, y \in \{0;1;\ldots;K-1\}^*$ be interpreted as numbers in a K+1 basis. The following is a relation between numerical and on strings operations.

Th. 2. $|x-y| \leq 1/(K+1)^m \Rightarrow \ell(x \circ y) \geq m+1$

The proof follows immediately. We just observe that element K must **not** appear in the strings x and y, in order that the theorem continues holding.

Now let: $\psi_1 : \Sigma^* \to \{0,1,\ldots,K-1\}^*$
$\psi_2 : \Sigma^* \to \{0,1,\ldots,K-1\}^*$

be two given homomorphisms.

$\psi_1(x)$, interpreted in a K+1-scale, is a rational number. Similarly it holds for $\psi_2(x)$.
From Th. 2. follows immediately:

Th. 3. Number 0 is isolated as regards set $\bigcup_{x \in \Sigma^*} \{\psi_1(x) - \psi_2(x)\}$ iff
$|\bigcup_{x \in \Sigma^*} \psi_1(x) \circ \psi_2(x)| < +\infty$

Th. 4. It is recursively unsolvable if $\frac{1}{2}$ is an isolated cut-point for arbitrary 4-states stochastic automata.

Proof:

a) If ψ_1 and ψ_2 are the two above mentioned homomorphisms, then
$p = \frac{1}{2} + (\psi_1 - \psi_2)/2$ is a stochastic event defined by a 4-states automaton (it follows from Th. 1. and from the fact that, if ψ_1 and ψ_2 are stochastic events, also ψ_1 and $1-\psi_2$ have the same property, such as their convex linear combination $\frac{1}{2}\psi_1 + \frac{1}{2}(1-\psi_2)$

b) $\frac{1}{2}$ is isolated with respect to p, iff 0 does with respect to $\psi_1 - \psi_2$
Consequently from Th. 3.: $\frac{1}{2}$ isolated with respect to $p \Leftrightarrow$
$\Leftrightarrow |\bigcup_{x \in \Sigma^*} \psi_1(x) \circ \psi_2(x)| < +\infty$

c) If there is a procedure to decide whether $\frac{1}{2}$ is isolated as regards p, then there should be a procedure to decide whether
$|\bigcup_{x \in \Sigma^*} \psi_1(x) \circ \psi_2(x)| < +\infty$
differently from what stated in §2 -Th. 2

Th. 5. Let λ be a rational number, $0 < \lambda < 1$
It is recursively unsolvable if λ is isolated for a 4-states stochastic automaton.
Let $\lambda > \frac{1}{2}$. λ is isolated for p iff $\frac{1}{2}$ is isolated for $\lambda p/2$
Let $\lambda > \frac{1}{2}$. λ is isolated for p iff $1-\lambda$ is isolated for $1-p$, where $1-\lambda > \frac{1}{2}$.

CONCLUSION AND OPEN PROBLEMS

Substantially, the results of section 3 present the following lacks:

1. We do not consider the problem for $\lambda = 0$; $\lambda = 1$.
2. We proof the theorem (1) is recursively unsolvable, but we do not investigate the semi-decidability or the degrees of undecidability.
3. We limit the number of states (4 states), but we do not limit the cardinality of alphabet Σ.

Therefore we suggest:

1) Is the following problem solvable $\exists \delta (\delta > 0 ; \forall x (P(x) > \delta))$?
For automata with 1-symbol alphabet, there is a decision algorithm bound with the concept of transient state [2].
We believe it might be extended, but we have no proof for it.

2) Is there a procedure to generate recursively all the rational isolated cut-points for a given stochastic automaton?
This is surely true for stochastic quasi-defined automata [2] but it seems difficult to extend to arbitrary automata.

3) (1) is solvable for stochastic automata such that $|\Sigma| = 1$.
Is it solvable for stochastic automata such that $|\Sigma| = 2$?

BIBLIOGRAPHY

[1] RABIN Mathematical Theory of Automata. Proc. of Symb. in applied math. Ann. Math. Soc. Pg.166-168 (1967) 153-175

[2] PAZ Introduction to Probabilistic Automata. Academic Press, New York - London (1971)

[3] HOPCROFT, ULLMAN Formal Languages and their relation to Automata. Addison Wesley Publishing Co. (1969)

[4] NELSON Introduction to Automata. John Wiley - Sons, New.York - London - Sydney (1968)

[5] POST A variant of a recursively unsolvable problem. Bull. Am. Math. Soc. 52 (1946) 264-268

Eine Charakterisierung der Szilardsprachen

und ihre Verwendung als Steuersprachen

Matthias Höpner
Universität Hamburg
Institut für Informatik
Schlüterstraße 70

Viele Erweiterungen kontextfreier Grammatiken entstanden in letzter Zeit dadurch, daß man Kontrollmechanismen definierte, welche die Anwendung der Regeln steuern. Man versieht dabei jede Regel einer kontextfreien Grammatik (Abk.: cfG) mit Namen und ordnet dann jeder Ableitung ein "Kontrollwort" zu, indem man die Namen der verwendeten Regeln hintereinanderschreibt. Über der Namenmenge definiert man eine Steuersprache und läßt nur noch solche Ableitungen zu, deren Kontrollworte in der Steuersprache liegen.

Betrachtet man die Menge aller Kontrollworte, die eine cfG ohne jede Einschränkung hervorbringen kann, so erhält man die sogenannte "Szilardsprache" dieser Grammatik, deren Definition auf Stotzkij (1967) zurückgeht. Über die Familie der Szilardsprachen ist bisher nicht viel bekannt. Die Arbeiten von Fleck (1971) und Moriya (1973) liefern vollständige Charakterisierungen nur von den regulären bzw. kontextfreien Szilardsprachen.

In dieser Arbeit wird mit Hilfe der neuen Operationen "gesteuertes Mischen" und "Mischiteration" eine endliche Darstellung für alle Szilardsprachen und deren Bilder unter alphabetischen Homomorphismen abgeleitet, wie man sie ähnlich auch bei kontextfreien Sprachen kennt. Weiter wird eine enge Verbindung hergestellt zwischen den bekannten "regulären Baummengen" von Thatcher und Wright (1968) und den Szilardsprachen. Es wird gezeigt, wie sich jede Szilardsprache mit Hilfe einer regulären Baummenge und einer Abbildung "pick" darstellen läßt. Schließlich werden die Szilardsprachen selbst als Steuersprachen verwendet und gezeigt, daß man auf diese Weise die Familie der Matrixsprachen nicht verläßt.

Besonders dieser letzte Teil der vorliegenden Arbeit ging aus meiner, von Herrn Prof. Brauer betreuten Diplomarbeit hervor. Ihm und Herrn Dr. Monien möchte ich an dieser Stelle für ihre Hilfe danken, ohne die diese Arbeit nicht zustandegekommen wäre.

Definitionen und Vereinbarungen

Wir schreiben eine cfG als 4-Tupel in der Form $G = (N, T, R, S)$, wobei N die Menge der Nonterminals, T die Menge der Terminals, R die Regelmenge und S das Startsymbol ist. Es bezeichne ε das leere Wort, und es gelte $N \cap T = \emptyset$. Um den Regeln Namen geben zu können, definieren wir eine "Namenmenge" Lab und eine surjektive Abbildung $f : \text{Lab} \longrightarrow R$. Verschiedene Regeln erhalten auf diese Weise verschiedene Namen. Hat eine Regel $X \longrightarrow w \in R$ den Namen $r \in \text{Lab}$, so notieren wir kurz $X \xrightarrow{r} w \in R$. Die übliche Ableitungsrelation $\Longrightarrow^*$ wird durch die folgenden drei Vereinbarungen erweitert:

(1) $w_1 \underset{\varepsilon}{\Longrightarrow}^* w_2$, wenn $w_1 = w_2 \in (N \cup T)^*$.

(2) $w_1 \underset{r}{\Longrightarrow}^* w_2$ mit $r \in \text{Lab}$, wenn $w_1 = xXy$, $w_2 = xwy$ und $X \xrightarrow{r} w \in R$.

(3) $w_1 \underset{uv}{\Longrightarrow}^* w_3$ für $u, v \in \text{Lab}^*$, wenn $w_1 \underset{u}{\Longrightarrow}^* w_2$ und $w_2 \underset{v}{\Longrightarrow}^* w_3$.

Für eine Ableitung $w_1 \underset{u}{\Longrightarrow}^* w_2$ heißt u das "Kontrollwort" dieser Ableitung. Es gibt an, in welcher Reihenfolge die Regeln verwendet wurden, jedoch nicht, an welcher Stelle! Es können also zu einem Kontrollwort mehrere verschiedene Ableitungen gehören.

Als Szilardsprache $Sz(G)$ einer cfG G bezeichnet man die Menge aller Kontrollworte von terminalen Ableitungen. Also:

$$Sz(G) := \left\{ u \in \text{Lab}^* \mid S \underset{u}{\Longrightarrow}^* w, w \in L(G) \right\}.$$

Mit $\mathscr{S}_{\!\!\mathit{z}}$ werde die Familie aller Szilardsprachen von cfGs bezeichnet. Die Familie der kontextfreien Sprachen wird mit $\mathscr{C}_{\!\!f}$ und die Familie der regulären Mengen mit $\mathcal{R}$ abgekürzt. Für Sprachfamilien $\mathscr{L}_1$ und $\mathscr{L}_2$ über X^* sei:

$$\mathscr{L}_1 \wedge \mathscr{L}_2 := \left\{ L = L_1 \cap L_2 \mid L_1 \in \mathscr{L}_1, L_2 \in \mathscr{L}_2 \right\}.$$

Weiter sei:

$$\mathcal{H}^k(\mathscr{L}_1) := \left\{ L = h(L_1) \mid L_1 \in \mathscr{L}_1 \text{ und } \lg(h(a)) \leq k \in \mathbb{N} \text{ für alle } a \in X \right\}$$

und:

$$\mathcal{H}(\mathscr{L}_1) := \bigcup_{k=0}^{\infty} \mathcal{H}^k(\mathscr{L}_1).$$

Dabei bezeichnet $\lg(w)$ die Länge eines Wortes w. Die Potenzmenge von einer Menge X schreiben wir $\text{pot}(X)$.

Ausgehend von der Operation "Mischen", welche erstmals in anderem Zusammenhang von Ginsburg und Greibach (1970) erklärt wurde, definieren wir nun die neuen Operationen "gesteuertes Mischen" und "Mischiteration". Für die Operation Mischen benutzten Ginsburg und Greibach eine Präfixschreibweise mit dem Wortsymbol "shuff". Wir wollen hier die übersichtlichere Infixschreibweise mit dem Zeichen "⋙" benutzen.

Sei dazu X ein endliches Alphabet und M_1, $M_2 \subset X^*$ Wortmengen. Die Operation $⋊⋉$ wird wie folgt erklärt:

(1) $\quad M_1 ⋊⋉ M_2 := \left\{ w \in X^* \;\middle|\; \begin{array}{l} w = u_1 v_1 u_2 v_2 \ldots u_n v_n \\ \text{mit } u_i, v_i \in X^* \text{ so, daß} \\ u_1 u_2 \ldots u_n \in M_1 \text{ und} \\ v_1 v_2 \ldots v_n \in M_2 \text{ ist.} \end{array} \right\}$

Die Operation "$\overline{a}$" (gesteuertes Mischen) wird für jedes $a \in X$ wie folgt definiert:

(1) $\quad \{w\} \; \overline{a} \; M_2 := \{w\}$, wenn w kein a enthält.

(2) $\quad$ Wenn $w = xay$ mit $x, y \in X^*$ und x enthält kein a, so ist
$\{w\} \; \overline{a} \; M_2 := \{x\} \cdot (\, (\{y\} \; \overline{a} \; M_2) ⋊⋉ M_2 \,)$.

(3) $\quad M_1 \; \overline{a} \; M_2 := \bigcup_{w \in M_1} (\{w\} \; \overline{a} \; M_2)$.

Die rekursive Definition in (2) ist dabei zulässig, weil jedes Wort w ja immer nur endlich viele Zeichen a enthält. Die Mischiteration " $(\,)^{\overline{a}}$ " wird induktiv so definiert:

$(M_1)^{\overline{a}} := \bigcup_{n=0}^{\infty} Y_n$, wobei $Y_0 := \{a\}$ und $Y_{n+1} := Y_n \cup (M_1 \; \overline{a} \; Y_n)$.

Man beachte, daß die hier definierte Mischiteration eine andere ist, als die in Höpner (1974) verwendete. Hier gilt zum Beispiel: $\{ab\}^{\overline{a}} = \{b\}^* \{a\} \{b\}^*$ und $(\{0s1\}^{\overline{s}}) \; \overline{s} \; \{\varepsilon\} = D_1$, wobei D_1 die Dycksprache über dem Alphabet $\{0, 1\}$ ist.

Wie Penttonen (1974) bemerkt, haben die Terminals einer cfG keinerlei Einfluß auf die Szilardsprache dieser Grammatik. Wir wollen also hier nur cfGs betrachten, für die $T = \{\varepsilon\}$ gilt. Zur Formulierung des ersten Charakterisierungstheorems für Szilardsprachen wird noch der Begriff der "regulären Baumsprache" benötigt. Für Details siehe man Thatcher und Wright (1968) oder Brainerd (1969).

Eine "Operator-Menge" (ranked set) ist ein Paar (A, g), wobei A endliches Alphabet und $g : A \longrightarrow \mathbb{N}$ eine Abbildung in die natürlichen Zahlen ist. Mit $A_n := g^{-1}(n)$ werde die Menge aller "n-wertigen" Operatoren bezeichnet. In natürlicher Weise erklärt man nun Bäume über (A, g). Die Menge aller dieser Bäume werde mit $\mathcal{T}_A$ bezeichnet und wie folgt induktiv definiert:

(1) $\quad A_0 \subset \mathcal{T}_A$.

(2) $\quad$ wenn $t_1, \ldots, t_n \in \mathcal{T}_A$ sind und $x \in A_n$ ist, dann soll auch $xt_1 \ldots t_n \in \mathcal{T}_A$ sein.

Anstelle der hier verwendeten Präfixnotation wird für Bäume gerne eine graphische Darstellung verwendet.

Für Baumsprachen B_1, $B_2 \subset \mathcal{T}_A$ werden analog zum gewöhnlichen Komplexprodukt und der Kleenschen Hüllenbildung folgende Operationen definiert: (Thatcher und Wright (1968)) Wenn $a \in A_0$ ist, so ist das "a-Produkt" von B_1 und B_2, geschrieben als $B_1 \underset{a}{\circ} B_2$, die Menge aller Bäume, die man erhält, wenn man in den Bäumen aus B_1 für jedes a einen Baum aus B_2 einsetzt. Ebenfalls für $a \in A_0$ ist der "a-Abschluß" von B_1 die Menge $(B_1)^a := \bigcup_{i=0} Y_i$, wobei $Y_0 := \{a\}$ und $Y_{i+1} := Y_i \cup (B_1 \underset{a}{\circ} Y_i)$ ist. Eine Baumsprache heißt "regulär", wenn es ein Operator-Alphabet (A, g) gibt, derart, daß diese Baumsprache - ausgehend von endlichen Mengen von Bäumen aus $\mathcal{T}_A$ - mit Hilfe von Vereinigung, a-Produkt und a-Abschluß in endlich vielen Schritten gewonnen werden kann.

Reguläre Baummengen und Szilardsprachen

Mit Hilfe einer noch zu definierenden Abbildung "pick", die Bäume in Wortmengen abbildet, werden wir nun eine Verbindung zwischen den Szilardsprachen und den regulären Baummengen herstellen. Es gilt:

THEOREM 1

Ist B eine reguläre Baummenge, so ist pick(B) eine Szilardsprache. Umgekehrt gibt es zu jeder Szilardsprache $L \in \mathcal{L}_\mathcal{Z}$ eine reguläre Baumsprache B derart, daß $L = pick(B)$ ist.

Die Abbildung pick : $pot(\mathcal{T}_A) \longrightarrow pot(A^*)$ wird, ähnlich wie die bekannte Abbildung "yield", welche reguläre Baummengen in kontextfreie Sprachen abbildet, induktiv definiert:

(1) $pick(x) := \{x\}$ für jedes $x \in A_0$.

(2) $pick(xt_1t_2 \ldots t_n) := \{x\} \cdot (pick(t_1) \not\gtrless pick(t_2) \not\gtrless \ldots \not\gtrless pick(t_n))$
für $x \in A_n$; $t_1, t_2, \ldots, t_n \in \mathcal{T}_A$.

(3) $pick(B) := \bigcup_{t \in B} pick(t)$ für $B \subset \mathcal{T}_A$.

Als Beispiel sei t der folgende Baum: $t = aebdc$, wobei $A_0 := \{c, d, e\}$, $A_1 := \emptyset$ und $A_2 := \{a, b\}$ ist. Der Baum t hat die nebenstehende graphische Darstellung, und es gilt:

$pick(t) = \left\{ \begin{array}{l} aebdc, aebcd, abedc, abecd, \\ abdec, abced, abdce, abcde \end{array} \right\}$.

Die Abbildung pick liefert, auf einen Baum t angewendet, gerade die Menge aller linearen Aufschreibungen der Knoten, bei denen tieferliegende Knoten immer rechts von ihren oberen Nachbarn notiert werden. Die Operation Mischen tritt in (2) deshalb auf, weil bei Ableitungen in cfGs Regelumstellungen möglich sind. Im folgenden soll nun der Beweis von Theorem 1 skizziert werden.

Zu einer vorgegebenen cfG $G = (N, \{\varepsilon\}, R, S)$ mit der Namenmenge Lab konstruiert man ein sogenanntes "Tree generating regular System" (Brainerd (1969)) wie folgt. Man bildet das Operator-Alphabet $(A, g) := (N \cup Lab, g)$ indem man setzt:

(1) $g(X) := 0$ für alle $X \in N$.

(2) $g(r) := lg(w)$, wenn $X \xrightarrow{r} w$ eine Regel aus R ist.

Mit dieser Vereinbarung bestimmen folgende Regeln eindeutig ein Tree generating regular System (Abk.: T.g.r.S.) S′ im Sinne von Brainerd:

Für jede Regel $X \xrightarrow{r} w \in R$ sei $X \longrightarrow rw$ eine Regel des T.g.r.S. S′.

Man beachte, daß hier die Bäume in Präfixnotation geschrieben werden, und daß $w \in N^*$ ist, weil $T = \{\varepsilon\}$ ist.

Es ist nicht schwer zu sehen, daß die Abbildung pick aus den Bäumen, die das T.g.r.S. S′ erzeugt, Kontrollworte der cfG G macht, denn jede Ableitung in der cfG korrespondiert mit einer Ableitung im T.g.r.S.

Umgekehrt gibt es nach Brainerd (1969) zu jeder regulären Baumsprache B aus $\mathcal{T}_A$, wobei (A, g) ein Operator-Alphabet ist und $A′ \subset A$ eine Teilmenge von terminalen Operatoren, ein T.g.r.S. S′, dessen Regeln gerade die Form $X \longrightarrow x Y_1 Y_2 \ldots Y_n$ mit $x \in A'_n$ und $X, Y_1, \ldots, Y_n \in (A \smallsetminus A')_0$ haben. Dieses T.g.r.S. S′ kann sofort in eine kontextfreie Grammatik $G = (N, \{\varepsilon\}, R, S)$ umgeschrieben werden, indem man setzt:

$$N := (A \smallsetminus A')_0 \text{ , Lab} := A' \text{ sowie } R := \left\{ X \xrightarrow{r} w \,\middle|\, \begin{array}{l} X \longrightarrow rw \text{ ist Regel} \\ \text{des T.g.r.S. S′} \end{array} \right\}$$

pick(B) $\in \mathcal{L}$ ist dann wie eben zu zeigen, wobei B die Baummenge ist, die das T.g.r.S. S′ erzeugte. Als Korollare aus Theorem 1 erhält man:

<u>KOROLLAR 1</u> (Stotzkij (1967)) Für jede cfG G ist es entscheidbar, ob Sz(G) leer oder endlich ist.

Nach Theorem 1 gibt es eine reguläre Baummenge B derart, daß pick(B) = Sz(G) ist. Damit ist nun Sz(G) leer bzw. endlich genau dann, wenn B dies ist. Für reguläre Baummengen sind diese Fragen aber entscheidbar.

<u>KOROLLAR 2</u> (Höpner (1974)) Für jede Szilardsprache L ist $\psi(L)$ eine semilineare Menge. Dabei bezeichnet ψ die Parikh-Abbildung (siehe Salomaa (1973)).

Nach Brainerd (1969) liefern die Bäume einer regulären Baummenge in ihrer Präfixschreibweise eine kontextfreie Sprache. Ist nun B die reguläre Baummenge aus Theorem 1 mit pick(B) = Sz(G), dann gilt: $\psi(Sz(G)) = \psi(pick(B)) = \psi(B)$, wobei nun B als kontextfreie Sprache verstanden wird. Weil $\psi(B)$ nach dem Satz von Parikh eine semilineare Menge liefert, ist Korollar 2 bewiesen.

Penttonen (1974) zeigte, daß jede unendliche Szilardsprache einer cfG eine unendliche, reguläre Menge enthält. Wir erhalten:

KOROLLAR 3 Jede unendliche Szilardsprache $L \in \mathcal{S}z$ enthält eine unendliche, kontextfreie Sprache.

Es ist $B \subset \text{pick}(B)$ für jede Baummenge B. Für die reguläre Baummenge B aus Theorem 1 gilt zusätzlich $B \in \mathcal{R}\ell$.

Die endliche Darstellung der Sprachen aus $\mathcal{H}^1(\mathcal{S}z)$

Theorem 1 führt zu einer endlichen Darstellung der Szilardsprachen, wie man sie ähnlich bei den kontextfreien Sprachen kennt. Hier allerdings werden die Operationen gesteuertes Mischen und Mischiteration zugrundegelegt. Es gilt:

THEOREM 2

$\mathcal{H}^1(\mathcal{S}z)$ ist die kleinste Familie von Sprachen, die die endlichen Mengen enthält und abgeschlossen ist gegenüber den Operationen: Vereinigung, gesteuertes Mischen und Mischiteration.

Zum Beweis, daß sich jede Sprache aus $\mathcal{H}^1(\mathcal{S}z)$ mit den geforderten Operationen darstellen läßt, führen folgende Überlegungen: Sei G eine beliebige cfG und h ein alphabetischer Homomorphismus, dann gibt es nach Theorem 1 eine reguläre Baummenge B derart, daß $h(\text{pick}(B)) = h(\text{Sz}(G)) \in \mathcal{H}^1(\mathcal{S}z)$ ist. Für B kann man nun eine endliche Darstellung mit den Operationen a-Produkt, a-Abschluß und Vereinigung angeben (Thatcher und Wright (1968)). Dann zeigt man weiter, daß für Baummengen B_1 und B_2 folgendes zutrifft:

(1) $\text{pick}(B_1 \underset{a}{\circ} B_2) = \text{pick}(B_1) \overset{\frown}{a}\, \text{pick}(B_2)$.

(2) $\text{pick}(B_1{}^a) = (\text{pick}(B_1))^{\overset{\frown}{a}}$.

(3) $\text{pick}(B_1 \cup B_2) = \text{pick}(B_1) \cup \text{pick}(B_2)$.

Unter Berücksichtigung dieser Gleichungen kann man die endliche Darstellung für die reguläre Baummenge B in eine endliche Darstellung für die Szilardsprache Sz(G) umformen. In dieser endlichen Darstellung kommen die Zeichen, die für das gesteuerte Mischen und die Mischiteration verwendet werden, nur als Hilfszeichen vor und treten in der eigentlichen Szilardsprache nicht auf. Dies liegt an der Konstruktion der endlichen Darstellung für die reguläre Baumsprache, wie sie in Thatcher und Wright (1968) angegeben wird. Wegen dieses Sachverhalts kann nun auch noch der Homomorphismus h, der die Hilfszeichen ja nicht verändert, in die endliche Darstellung "hineingezogen" werden. Man erhält so die endliche Darstellung für die Sprache h(Sz(G)).

Umgekehrt zeigt man, daß die Familie $\mathcal{H}^1(\mathcal{S}z)$ alle endlichen (sogar alle regulären) Mengen enthält und gegenüber den Operationen Vereinigung, gesteuertes Mischen und Mischiteration abgeschlossen ist. Die Beweise findet man in Höpner

(1974). Da dort eine andere Form der Mischiteration verwendet wird, soll hier kurz gezeigt werden, daß mit der Sprache $L \in \mathcal{H}^1(\mathit{Sz})$ auch die Sprache $(L)^{\overline{a}}$ in $\mathcal{H}^1(\mathit{Sz})$ enthalten ist. Dazu sei $G = (N, \{\mathcal{E}\}, R, S)$ eine cfG mit Namenmenge Lab, für die $h(Sz(G)) \in \mathcal{H}^1(\mathit{Sz})$ gilt, und h sei ein alphabetischer Homomorphismus. Man bildet nun aus G eine neue Grammatik $G' = (N, \{\mathcal{E}\}, R', S)$, indem man für jede Regel $X \xrightarrow{r} w \in R$ mit $h(r) = a$ die Regel $X \xrightarrow{r} wS$ zu den Regeln von R hinzufügt. Es ist $(h(Sz(G)))^{\overline{a}} = h(Sz(G'))$.

Daß die Familie $\mathcal{H}^1(\mathit{Sz})$ echt kontextsensitive Sprachen enthält, sowie auch alle regulären Mengen, ist bekannt (Penttonen (1974), Stotzkij (1967)). Andererseits kann gezeigt werden, daß diese Familie gewisse kontextfreie Sprachen nicht enthält. Es gilt das

THEOREM 3

Jede Sprache L aus $\mathcal{H}(\mathit{Sz})$ mit der Eigenschaft $L \subset a_1^* \, a_2^* \, \ldots \, a_n^* \, a_{n+1}$ ist regulär.

Damit ist zum Beispiel die einfache, lineare Sprache $\{a^n b^n \mid n \geq 1\}$ nicht in $\mathcal{H}(\mathit{Sz})$ enthalten. Als Konsequenz dieses Theorems ergibt sich die Tatsache, daß die Familie $\mathcal{H}(\mathit{Sz})$ nicht gegenüber Durchschnittsbildung mit regulären Mengen und gsm-Abbildungen abgeschlossen ist. Die Dycksprache D_1 ist in $\mathcal{H}(\mathit{Sz})$ enthalten, und man gibt leicht eine reguläre Menge R an, so daß $D_1 \cap R = \{a^n b^n \mid n \geq 1\}$ ist. Eine gsm-Abbildung g kann gefunden werden, so daß $g(D_1) = \{a^n b^m \mid n \geq m \geq 1\}$ ist.

Szilardsprachen als Steuersprachen für cfGs

Betrachtet man kontextfreie Grammatiken mit Steuersprachen (Salomaa (1973)), so zeigt sich, daß man wesentlich kompliziertere Sprachen, als es die regulären Mengen sind, als Steuersprachen verwenden darf, ohne dadurch die Erzeugungskraft dieser Grammatiken zu erhöhen.

Es bezeichne $\mathcal{L}(2, \mathcal{K}, p)$ die Familie aller Sprachen, die von cfGs mit Steuersprachen aus der Familie $\mathcal{K}$ erzeugt werden können. Dabei steht die 2 für Typ-2-Sprache und $p \in \{0, 1\}$ gibt an, ob mit oder ohne sogenanntes "checking" abgeleitet werden soll. Detaillierte Definitionen entnimmt man Salomaa (1973). Die Familie $\mathcal{L}(2, \mathcal{R}, p)$ entspricht der Familie der Matrixsprachen und es ist $\mathcal{L}(2, \mathcal{R}, 1)$ genau die Familie der Phrasenstruktursprachen. Im Vergleich zu anderen Sprachklassen ist über die Familie $\mathcal{L}(2, \mathcal{R}, 0)$ noch nicht sehr viel bekannt. So weiß man z. B. nicht, ob $\mathcal{L}(2, \mathcal{R}, 0) = \mathcal{L}(2, \mathcal{C}f, 0)$ oder nicht. Durch Angabe einfacher Konstruktionen wurde in Höpner (1974) folgendes gezeigt:

THEOREM 4

$\mathcal{L}(2, \mathcal{R}, p) = \mathcal{L}(2, \mathit{Sz}, p) = \mathcal{L}(2, \mathcal{H}^k(\mathit{Sz}), p) = \mathcal{L}(2, \mathcal{H}^k(\mathit{Sz} \wedge \mathcal{R}), p)$
für alle $k \in \mathbb{N}$ und $p \in \{0, 1\}$.

Die Bedeutung dieses Theorems ergibt sich aus den folgenden gültigen Beziehungen:

$$\mathcal{R} \subsetneq \mathcal{H}^k(\mathcal{S}\!z) \quad \text{und} \quad \mathcal{H}^k(\mathcal{S}\!z) \subsetneq \mathcal{H}^k(\mathcal{S}\!z \wedge \mathcal{R}).$$

$\mathcal{S}\!z$ und $\mathcal{R}$ sind miteinander unvergleichbar, wie Penttonen (1974) gezeigt hat. Die Beweise für Theorem 4 benutzen Konstruktionen, die man nicht ohne weiteres auf den Fall ε-freier Regeln übertragen kann. Es ist also nicht gesagt, ob das Theorem 4 auch für jene gesteuerten cfGs gilt, die ausschließlich ε-freie Regeln enthalten.

Wir schreiben jetzt abkürzend $\mathcal{Z}^k$ für $\mathcal{H}^k(\mathcal{S}\!z \wedge \mathcal{R})$. Diese Abkürzung soll darauf hinweisen, daß man für diese Sprachfamilie Zählerautomaten angeben kann, die genau diese Sprachen akzeptieren. Diese Zählerautomaten sind in Höpner (1974) definiert, und man zeigt:

<u>THEOREM 5</u>

(1) $\mathcal{Z}^1 = \mathcal{Z}^k$ für alle $k \in \mathbb{N}$.

(2) $\mathcal{Z}^1 \subset \mathcal{L}(2, \mathcal{R}, 0)$.

(3) Zu jeder Sprache L aus $\mathcal{L}(2, \mathcal{R}, 0)$ gibt es eine Sprache Z aus $\mathcal{Z}^1$, so daß $\psi(L) = \psi(Z)$ ist.

Aus (3) von Theorem 5 folgt, daß in $\mathcal{Z}^1$ Sprachen enthalten sind, deren Parikh-Abbildung nicht mehr auf eine semilineare Menge führt. Die Familie $\mathcal{L}(2, \mathcal{R}, 0)$ enthält nämlich unter anderem die Sprache $Q := \{a^n b^m \mid n \geq 1, 1 \leq m \leq 2^n\}$. Daß auch $\mathcal{Z}^1$ diese Sprache Q enthält, zeigt das folgende Beispiel. Wir definieren eine Grammatik G, indem wir ihre Regeln angeben. Als Namenmenge fungiert die Menge Lab := $\{r_1, r_2, r_3, r_4, r_5, r_6, r_7, r_8, r_9, r_{10}, r_{11}, r_{12}, r_{13}\}$.

$r_1 := S \longrightarrow AE$ $\quad r_5 := A \longrightarrow A$ $\quad r_8 := A \longrightarrow CC$ $\quad r_{11} := E \longrightarrow \varepsilon$
$r_2 := A \longrightarrow B$ $\quad r_6 := D \longrightarrow EE$ $\quad r_9 := B \longrightarrow C$ $\quad r_{12} := C \longrightarrow C$
$r_3 := B \longrightarrow A$ $\quad r_7 := B \longrightarrow B$ $\quad r_{10} := C \longrightarrow \varepsilon$ $\quad r_{13} := D \longrightarrow \varepsilon$
$r_4 := E \longrightarrow DD$

Weiter wird ein Homomorphismus $h : \text{Lab} \longrightarrow \{a, b\}$ definiert:

$h(r_1) := h(r_2) := h(r_3) := a \,; \quad h(r_{11}) := h(r_{13}) := b \,;$

$h(r_i) := \varepsilon \quad$ für alle anderen $r_i \in \text{Lab}.$

Es ist nun:

$$Q = h(\ Sz(G) \cap \{r_1, r_2, r_3, r_4 r_5, r_6 r_7, r_8, r_9\}^* \cdot \{r_{11} r_{12}, r_{10}, r_{13} r_{14}\}^*)$$

Für die Familie $\mathcal{Z}^1$ lassen sich einige Abschlußeigenschaften zeigen. Es gilt:

<u>THEOREM 6</u>

Die Familie $\mathcal{Z}^1$ ist bezüglich der Operationen Vereinigung, Produkt, Durchschnitt, Substitution von regulären Mengen, inversen Homomorphismen, gsm-Abbildungen, gesteuertes Mischen und Mischiteration abgeschlossen.

Die Beweise hierzu werden besonders einfach, wenn man die Familie $\mathcal{Z}^1$ als die Menge der homomorphen Bilder der Szilardsprachen von Matrixgrammatiken charakterisiert. Dabei ist die Szilardsprache einer Matrixgrammatik analog zu der gewöhnlichen Szilardsprache definiert.

Der Beweis, daß mit $Z_1, Z_2 \in \mathcal{Z}^1$ auch $Z_1 \cdot Z_2 \in \mathcal{Z}^1$ ist, kann auch wie folgt geführt werden:

Es sei $Z_1 = h_1(L_1 \cap R_1)$, $Z_2 = h_2(L_2 \cap R_2)$ mit $L_1, L_2 \in \mathcal{L}$, $R_1, R_2 \in \mathcal{R}$ und $L_1 \subset Lab_1^*$, $L_2 \subset Lab_2^*$, wobei o.B.d.A. $Lab_1 \cap Lab_2 = \emptyset$ angenommen werden kann.

Nun ist $Z_1 \cdot Z_2 = (h_1(L_1 \cap R_1)) \cdot (h_2(L_2 \cap R_2)) = h((L_1 \cap R_1) \cdot (L_2 \cap R_2))$, wobei h eingeschränkt auf Lab_i wie h_i wirkt, $i \in \{1, 2\}$. Wegen $Lab_1 \cap Lab_2 = \emptyset$ gilt $(L_1 \cap R_1) \cdot (L_2 \cap R_2) = (L_1 \not\asymp L_2) \cap (R_1 \cdot R_2) = L \cap R$; denn es ist $\mathcal{L}$ gegenüber Mischen abgeschlossen, und $R = R_1 \cdot R_2$ ist eine reguläre Menge. Zusammenfassend gilt also $Z_1 \cdot Z_2 = h(L \cap R)$ wie verlangt.

Die Frage, ob $\mathcal{Z}^1$ auch gegenüber Kleenscher Hüllenbildung abgeschlossen ist, konnte bisher noch nicht beantwortet werden. Der obige Beweis läßt sich jedenfalls nicht einfach auf unendliche Produktbildung erweitern!

Ebenfalls unbewiesen ist für die Familie $\mathcal{H}(\mathcal{S}\mathcal{Z})$ die Vermutung, daß jede lineare Sprache, und in Verallgemeinerung von Theorem 3, jede überdeckbare Sprache in $\mathcal{H}(\mathcal{S}\mathcal{Z})$ schon regulär ist.

Literaturverzeichnis

W. Brainerd (1969), Tree generating regular Systems, Inf. & Control 14, 217-231.

A.C. Fleck (1971), On the combinatorial complexity of context-free grammars, Proceedings of IFIP Conference, Bocklet TA 2, 15-17.

S. Ginsburg und S.A. Greibach (1970), Principal AFL, J. Comput. System Sci. 4 308-338.

M. Höpner (1974), Über den Zusammenhang von Szilardsprachen und Matrixgrammatiken, Bericht Nr. 11, Institut für Informatik, Universität Hamburg.

E. Moriya (1973), Associate Languages and Derivational Complexity of Formal Grammars and Languages, Inf. & Control 22, 139-162.

M. Penttonen (1974), On derivation Languages corresponding to context-free Grammars, Acta Informatica 3, 285-293.

A. Salomaa (1973), Formal Languages, ACM Monograph Series, ACADEMIC PRESS New York and London.

E.D. Stotzkij (1967), On some restrictions on derivations in phrase-structure grammars, Akad. Nauk SSSR Nauchno-Tekhn. Inform. Ser 2, 35-38.

J.W. Thatcher und J.B. Wright (1968), Generalized finite automata theory with an application to a decision problem of second-order logic, Math. Systems Theory 2, 57-81.

COMPARING SEVERAL WAYS OF CONTEXT-INDEPENDENT PARALLEL REWRITING

Manfred Kudlek
Institut für Informatik
Universität Hamburg

1 Introduction, definitions, results.

Recently Lindenmayer systems have become a field of extensive study in theoretical informatics [1,2]. In such systems all symbols within a word have to be rewritten simultaneously. In this paper some special context-independent Lindenmayer systems (0L-systems) will be considered. They have to be placed between context-free Semi-Thue systems and 0L-systems. It is assumed that the basic terminology of L-systems is known [1,2,3].

As usual an alphabet V and a set R of context-free rules is given. The set of axioms may consist of more than one word, and in that case it will be denoted by the letter F, e.g. F0L. Without loss of generality it may be also assumed that for each symbol $x \in V$ there exists at least one rule $r \in R$ with x on its left-hand side. If this is not the case, the rule $x \to x$ may be added. The letters E, D, T will denote that there are non-terminals, that the system is deterministic, or that there are tables, respectively. If D and T are present this means that each table is deterministic, of course.

Now four ways of context-independent parallel rewriting may be introduced, namely :
  a) all symbols x within a word have to be rewritten simultaneously using one rule only for each symbol,
  b) one symbol has to be rewritten at every place of occurrence using one rule only,
  c) all symbols x within a word have to be rewritten using eventually several rules for one symbol,
  d) one symbol has to be rewritten at every place of occurrence using eventually several rules for that symbol.

To these the usual context-free rewriting may be added as e).

The language generated by these systems consists of all words derivable from the axioms including these (i.e. the sentential forms) if E is not present. If E is present this set has to be intersected with the free monoid over V_T, the set of terminal symbols, to get the generated language.

In the case of the usual context-free rewriting the generated languages will be denoted by sfFCF, sfCF, CF where sf means sentential forms. These abbreviations, as well as following ones, will also be used to denote families of languages.

The four ways of rewriting may be formulated in the OL-theory as follows [4] :
a) combinatorially complete DTFOL (ccDTFOL), i.e. all possible combinations of one rule for each symbol occur as a table (which is deterministic, of course),
b) symbol defined DTFOL (sdDTFOL), i.e. to each rule r∈R there is a table with that rule, but all other rules in that table being of the form x→x (for the other symbols), and there are no other tables except these,
c) FOL, or equivalently ccTFOL,
d) symbol defined unique TFOL (sduTFOL), i.e. to each symbol x there is a table only consisting of all rules r∈R with x on the left-hand side and y→y for the remaining symbols.

Besides these DTFOL, TFOL, and sdTFOL will be considered, as well as those systems without the letter F, and those with E.

In contrast to sduTFOL the system sdTFOL may contain more than one table of the kind defined in d) for a symbol x.

If $R = \{ x_i \to w_{ij} \mid j=1,\ldots,k(i); i=1,\ldots,n \}$ is a given set of context-independent rules, the tables of the systems defined above have the following forms :

ccDTFOL :

$x_1 \to w_{11}$	$x_1 \to w_{12}$		$x_1 \to w_{1k(1)}$
$x_2 \to w_{21}$	$x_2 \to w_{21}$	...	$x_2 \to w_{2k(2)}$
..	..		..
$x_n \to w_{n1}$	$x_n \to w_{n1}$		$x_n \to w_{nk(n)}$

sdDTFOL :

$x_1 \to w_{11}$	$x_1 \to w_{12}$		$x_1 \to x_1$		$x_1 \to x_1$
$x_2 \to x_2$	$x_2 \to x_2$	...	..	...	..
..	..		$x_{n-1} \to x_{n-1}$		$x_{n-1} \to x_{n-1}$
$x_n \to x_n$	$x_n \to x_n$		$x_n \to w_{n1}$		$x_n \to w_{nk(n)}$

FOL : One table consisting of all rules of R.

sduTFOL :

$x_1 \to w_{11}$		$x_1 \to x_1$
..		..
$x_1 \to w_{1k(1)}$	...	$x_{n-1} \to x_{n-1}$
$x_2 \to x_2$		$x_n \to w_{n1}$
..		..
$x_n \to x_n$		$x_n \to w_{nk(n)}$

sdTFOL :

$x_1 \to w_{111}$	$x_1 \to w_{121}$	
..	..	
$x_1 \to w_{11k(11)}$	$x_1 \to w_{12k(12)}$	...
$x_2 \to x_2$	$x_2 \to x_2$	
..	..	
$x_n \to x_n$	$x_n \to x_n$	

The following example shows the different ways of parallel rewriting giving the direct derivations from a single word ba^2b^2 :

$R = \{a \rightarrow a^2, a \rightarrow a^3, b \rightarrow b^2\}$

ccDTFOL : $b^2a^4b^4, b^2a^6b^4$

sdDTFOL : $ba^4b^2, ba^6b^2, b^2a^2b^4$

FOL : $b^2a^4b^4, b^2a^5b^4, b^2a^6b^4$

sduTFOL : $ba^4b^2, ba^5b^2, ba^6b^2, b^2a^2b^4$

CF : $ba^3b^2, ba^4b^2, b^2a^2b^2, ba^2b^3$

With the given definitions the following results hold, given as a diagram in which the abbreviations denote families of languages, and $\rightarrow$ proper inclusion, — inclusion, - - incomparability :

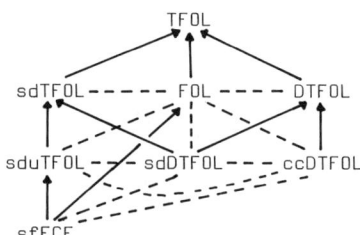

The same diagram holds for the families without F, and besides that CF is incomparable with all these families except sfFCF, sfCF which are properly included in CF. Furthermore all the families without F are proper inclusions of those with F. Adding E fewer results are known, and the following diagram may be given :

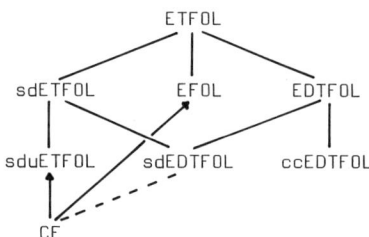

Of course, $Y \subset EY$ holds for each family Y.

2 Proofs.

1) DTFOL $⊊$ TFOL   (DTOL $⊊$ TOL)

   DTFOL⊂TFOL (DTOL⊂TOL) by definition.
   DTFOL≠TFOL (DTOL≠TOL). $L_1 = \{a^n | n \geq 1\}$ is a TFOL (TOL) by $A=\{a\}$, $R=\{\begin{array}{c} a \to a^2 \\ a \to a^3 \end{array}\}$
   but not a DTFOL (DTOL).

2) sdDTFOL $⊊$ DTFOL   (sdDTOL $⊊$ DTOL)

   sdDTFOL⊂DTFOL (sdDTOL⊂DTOL) by definition.
   sdDTFOL≠DTFOL (sdDTOL≠DTOL). $L_2 = \{a^{2^n} b^{2^n} | n \geq 0\}$ is a DTFOL (DTOL) by $A=\{ab\}$,
   $R=\{\begin{array}{c} a \to a^2 \\ b \to b^2 \end{array}\}$, but not a sdDTFOL (sdDTOL).

3) sduTFOL $⊊$ FOL   (sduTOL $⊊$ OL)

   a) sduTFOL≠FOL (sduTOL≠OL). L_2 is a FOL (OL) by $A=\{ab\}$, $R=\{a \to a^2, b \to b^2\}$,
      but not a sduTFOL (sduTOL).

   b) FOL≠sduTFOL (OL≠sduTOL). $L_3 = \{a^m b^{2^n} | m \geq 1, n \geq 0\}$ is a sduTFOL (sduTOL) by
      $A=\{ab\}$, $R=\{\begin{array}{c} a \to a \\ a \to a^2 \\ b \to b \end{array}, \begin{array}{c} a \to a \\ b \to b^2 \end{array}\}$, but not a FOL (OL).

      For $a \to \varepsilon$, $b \to \varepsilon$ cannot be rules of FOL (OL) ($\varepsilon, a, b \notin L_3$). Therefore the only
      possible rules are $a \to a^i$, $b \to b^j$ ($i, j \geq 1$). But there can exist only one rule
      $b \to b^j$, and $j = 2^k$ ($k \geq 1$), for if there would be more, there would be derivable
      $ab^{2^k + 2^l}$ from ab^2, and $2^k + 2^l \neq 2^m$ for $k \neq l$. How is derivable $a^m b$ ($m \geq 2$)?

4) sfFCF $⊊$ sduTFOL   (sfCF $⊊$ sduTOL)

   a) sfFCF⊂sduTFOL (sfCF⊂sduTOL). If R are the rules of sfFCF (sfCF) construct
      for sduTFOL (sduTOL) the following tables $\begin{array}{c} x \to w_i \\ x \to x \end{array}\}$ if $x \to w_i \in R$
      $y \to y$ for the other symbols

      Now, if $w \to w'$ in sfFCF (sfCF) then trivially $w \to w'$ in sduTFOL (sduTOL).
      If $w \to w'$ in sduTFOL (sduTOL) then by using successively $x \to w_i$ from R
      $w \overset{*}{\to} w'$ in sfFCF (sfCF).

   b) sfFCF≠sduTFOL (sfCF≠sduTOL). $L_4 = \{a^n bc^n a^n bc^n | n \geq 0\}$ is a sduTFOL (sduTOL) by
      $A=\{bb\}$, $R=\{\begin{array}{c} a \to a \\ b \to abc \\ c \to c \end{array}\}$, but not a sfFCF (sfCF).

5) FOL $⊊$ DTFOL   (OL $⊊$ DTOL)

   a) DTFOL≠FOL (DTOL≠OL). $L_5 = \{a^{2^m} b^{2^n} | m, n \geq 0\}$ is a DTFOL (DTOL) by $A=\{ab\}$,
      $R=\{\begin{array}{c} a \to a^2 \\ b \to b \end{array}, \begin{array}{c} a \to a \\ b \to b^2 \end{array}\}$. But L_5 is not a FOL (OL),
      for there can be only one rule $a \to a^i$ and only one rule $b \to b^j$ for FOL (OL).

b) FOL$\not\subset$DTFOL (OL$\not\subset$DTOL). $L_6=\{a^m b^{2^n}|m\geq n\geq 0\}$ is a FOL (OL) by A={ab}, R={a$\to$a, a$\to a^2$, b$\to b^2$}.

But L_6 is not a DTFOL (DTOL), for to get $a^m b$ (m$\geq$1) the tables to be used have to be of the form

a$\to a^i$
b$\to$b

But to get $a^p b$ (p prime) there either have to exist infinitely many axioms or infinitely many tables of the kind mentioned with i=p (prime).

6) OL $\subsetneq$ TOL

OL$\subset$TOL by definition.

OL$\neq$TOL. $L_7=\{a^{2^l 3^m}|l,m\geq 0\}$ is a TOL by A={a}, R={ a$\to a^2$, a$\to a^3$ }.

But L_7 is not an OL. For a$\to\epsilon$ cannot be a rule ($\epsilon\notin L_7$). Therefore the only possible rules are a$\to a^i$ (i$\geq$1), and the axiom has to be a. a$\to a^2$ has to be a rule ($a^2 \in L_7$), and a$\to$a cannot be a rule because $a^3 \in L_7$ would yield $a^5 \in L_7$. Therefore a$\to a^3$ has to be a rule. But now $a^2 \in L_7$ yields a^5 too.

7) FOL $\subsetneq$ TFOL

FOL$\subset$TFOL by definition.

FOL$\neq$TFOL. L_5 of 5a) is also a TFOL but not a FOL.

8) sfFCF $ \$ $ ccDTFOL   (sfCF $ \$ $ ccDTOL)

a) sfFCF$\not\subset$ccDTFOL (sfCF$\not\subset$ccDTOL). $L_8=\{a^m bc^m a^n bc^n|m,n\geq 0\}$ is a sfFCF (sfCF) by A={bb}, R={b$\to$abc}. But L_8 is not a ccDTFOL (ccDTOL).

b) ccDTFOL$\not\subset$sfFCF (ccDTOL$\not\subset$sfCF). L_4 of 4b) is a ccDTFOL (ccDTOL) by A={bb},

R={ | a$\to$a |
| --- |
| b$\to$abc |
| c$\to$c | }, but not a sfFCF (sfCF).

9) sfFCF $ \$ $ sdDTFOL   (sfCF $ \$ $ sdDTOL)

a) sfFCF$\not\subset$sdDTFOL (sfCF$\not\subset$sdDTOL). L_8 of 8a) is a sfFCF (sfCF) but not a sdDTFOL (sdDTOL).

b) sdDTFOL$\not\subset$sfFCF (sdDTOL$\not\subset$sfCF). L_4 of 4b) is a sdDTFOL (sdDTOL) by A={bb}, R the same as in 4b) or 8b), but not a sfFCF (sfCF).

10) sdDTFOL $ \$ $ ccDTFOL   (sdDTOL $ \$ $ ccDTOL)

a) sdDTFOL$\not\subset$ccDTFOL (sdDTOL$\not\subset$ccDTOL). $L_9=\{a\}\cup\{(a^m b)^n|m\geq 0, n\geq 1\}$ is a sdDTFOL (sdDTOL) by A={a}, R={ | a$\to$b |
| --- |
| b$\to$b | , | a$\to$a |
| --- |
| b$\to$ab | }

for a$\to$b$\to$ab$\to\ldots a^{n-1}b\to b^n \to (ab)^n \to \ldots (a^m b)^n \to \begin{array}{l} b^{n(m+1)} \\ (a^{m+1}b)^n \end{array}$

Suppose there exists a ccDTFOL (ccDTOL) generating L_9. As a,b$\in L_9$ all rules in a table have to be of the form a$\to(a^i b)^j$ (i$\geq$0, j$\geq$1)
b$\to(a^p b)^q$ (p$\geq$0, q$\geq$1).

Now ab$\in L_9$ gives $(a^i b)^j (a^p b)^q$, hence i=p. To get b^n there must be a rule a$\to b^r$ or b$\to b^s$. Now ab yields b^{r+s}. As the tables are combinatorially complete the only table is $\begin{bmatrix} a \to b^j \\ b \to b^k \end{bmatrix}$. But this doesn't generate any a.

11) sfFCF $\subsetneq$ FOL (sfCF $\subsetneq$ OL)

   a) sfFCF$\subset$FOL (sfCF$\subset$OL). If R are the rules of sfFCF (sfCF) take as the rules of FOL (OL) : $R' = R \cup \{x \to x | x \in V\}$.
   If $w \to w'$ in sfFCF (sfCF) then trivially $w \to w'$ in FOL (OL).
   If $w \to w'$ in FOL (OL) then $w \overset{*}{\to} w'$ in sfFCF (sfCF).

   b) sfFCF$\neq$FOL (sfCF$\neq$OL). L_2 of 2) is a FOL (OL) by A={ab}, $R = \{a \to a^2, b \to b^2\}$, but not a sfFCF (sfCF).

12) FOL $\not\subseteq$ ccDTFOL (OL $\not\subseteq$ ccDTOL)

   a) FOL$\not\subset$ccDTFOL (OL$\not\subset$ccDTOL). L_8 of 8a) is a FOL (OL) by A={bb}, $R = \{b \to abc, b \to b\}$.
   But L_8 is not a ccDTFOL (ccDTOL).

   b) ccDTFOL$\not\subset$FOL (ccDTOL$\not\subset$OL). $L_{10} = \{a^{2^m} b^{2^n} | 0 \leq m \leq n\}$ is a ccDTFOL (ccDTOL) by A={ab}, $R = \{\begin{bmatrix} a \to a \\ b \to b^2 \end{bmatrix}, \begin{bmatrix} a \to a^2 \\ b \to b^2 \end{bmatrix}\}$

   There can be only one rule $a \to a^{2^i}$ and only one rule $b \to b^{2^j}$ for FOL (OL).
   But how to generate ab^{2^n} (n≥0)? Therefore L_{10} is not a FOL (OL).

13) ccDTFOL $\subsetneq$ DTFOL (ccDTOL $\subsetneq$ DTOL)

   ccDTFOL$\subset$DTFOL (ccDTOL$\subset$DTOL) by definition.
   ccDTFOL$\neq$DTFOL (ccDTOL$\neq$DTOL). L_9 is a DTFOL (DTOL) by A={a}, $R = \{\begin{bmatrix} a \to b \\ b \to b \end{bmatrix}, \begin{bmatrix} a \to a \\ b \to ab \end{bmatrix}\}$.
   But L_9 is not a ccDTFOL (ccDTOL) by 10a).

14) ccDTFOL $\not\subseteq$ sduTFOL (ccDTOL $\not\subseteq$ sduTOL)

   a) ccDTFOL$\not\subset$sduTFOL (ccDTOL$\not\subset$sduTOL). L_2 of 2) is a ccDTFOL (ccDTOL) by A and R as in 2). But L_2 is not a sduTFOL (sduTOL).

   b) sduTFOL$\not\subset$ccDTFOL (sduTOL$\not\subset$ccDTOL). L_9 of 10a) or 13) is a sduTFOL (sduTOL) by A and R as in 10a) or 13).

15) sdDTFOL $\not\subseteq$ FOL (sdDTOL $\not\subseteq$ OL)

   a) sdDTFOL$\not\subset$FOL (sdDTOL$\not\subset$OL). L_5 of 5a) is a sdDTFOL (sdDTOL) by A and R as in 5a) but not a FOL (OL).

   b) FOL$\not\subset$sdDTFOL (OL$\not\subset$sdDTOL). L_2 of 2) is a FOL (OL) by A and R as in 3a) but not a sdDTFOL (sdDTOL).

16) sdDTFOL $\subsetneq$ sdTFOL (sdDTOL $\subsetneq$ sdTOL)

   sdDTFOL$\subset$sdTFOL (sdDTOL$\subset$sdTOL) by definition.
   sdDTFOL$\neq$sdTFOL (sdDTOL$\neq$sdTOL). L_1 of 1) is a sdTFOL (sdTOL) by A and R as in 1) but not a sdDTFOL (sdDTOL).

17) sdTFOL $\subsetneq$ TFOL (sdTOL $\subsetneq$ TOL)

   sdTFOL$\subset$TFOL (sdTOL$\subset$TOL) by definition.
   sdTFOL$\neq$TFOL (sdTOL$\neq$TOL). L_2 is a TFOL (TOL) by A and R as in 2) but not a sdTFOL (sdTOL).

18) sdTFOL $ FOL   (sdTOL $ OL)
   a) sdTFOL¢FOL (sdTOL¢OL). L_5 of 5a) is a sdTFOL (sdTOL) by A and R as in 5a) but not a FOL (OL).
   b) FOL¢sdTFOL (OL¢sdTOL). L_2 of 2) is a FOL (OL) by A and R as in 3a) but not a sdTFOL (sdTOL).
19) sduTFOL $ sdDTFOL   (sduTOL $ sdDTOL)
   a) sduTFOL¢sdDTFOL (sduTOL¢sdDTOL). If this would not be true, the following would hold : sfFCF⊂sdDTFOL (sfCF⊂sdDTOL) by 4). But that would contradict 9).
   b) sdDTFOL¢sduTFOL (sdDTOL¢sduTOL). L_7 of 6) is a sdDTFOL (sdDTOL) by A and R as in 6) but not a sduTFOL (sduTOL).
20) sduTFOL ⊊ sdTFOL   (sduTOL ⊊ sdTOL)
   sduTFOL⊂sdTFOL (sduTOL⊂sdTOL) by definition.
   sduTFOL≠sdTFOL (sduTOL≠sdTOL). This is an immediate consequence of 19) and 16).
21) sduTFOL $ DTFOL   (sduTOL $ DTOL)
   a) sduTFOL¢DTFOL (sduTOL¢DTOL). L_3 of 3b) is a sduTFOL (sduTOL) as in 3b) but not a DTFOL (DTOL) by the same arguments.
   b) DTFOL¢sduTFOL (DTOL¢sduTOL). L_2 of 2) is a DTFOL (DTOL) as in 2) but not a sduTFOL (sduTOL).

22) CF ¢ sfFCF   (CF ¢ sfCF)
   $L_{11} = \{a^n b^n | n \geq 1\}$ is a CF but not a sfFCF (sfCF).
23) CF ¢ TFOL   (CF ¢ TOL)
   L_{11} of 22) is a CF but not a TFOL (TOL). For suppose there exists a TFOL (TOL) generating L_{11}. Then in each table there can be only one rule for each a and b. But how to generate $a^p b^p$ for all primes p ?
24) CF ¢ sdDTFOL   (CF ¢ sdDTOL)
   CF ¢ sduTFOL   (CF ¢ sduTOL)
   CF ¢ ccDTFOL   (CF ¢ ccDTOL)
   CF ¢ DTFOL   (CF ¢ DTOL)
   CF ¢ FOL   (CF ¢ OL)
   CF ¢ sdTFOL   (CF ¢ sdTOL)
   This is a consequence of 1) to 21) and 23).
25) ccDTFOL ¢ CF   (ccDTOL ¢ CF)
   $L_{12} = \{a^{2^n} b^{2^n} c^{2^n} | n \geq 0\}$ is a ccDTFOL (ccDTOL) by $A = \{abc\}$, $R = \{\begin{array}{l} a \rightarrow a^2 \\ b \rightarrow b^2 \\ c \rightarrow c^2 \end{array}\}$
   but not a CF.
26) DTFOL ¢ CF   (DTOL ¢ CF)
   TFOL ¢ CF   (TOL ¢ CF)
   This is a consequence of 25) and 13), 1).

27) sduTFOL $\notsubseteq$ CF (sduTOL $\notsubseteq$ CF)
   L_4 of 4b) is a sduTFOL (sduTOL) but not a CF.
28) sdTFOL $\notsubseteq$ CF (sdTOL $\notsubseteq$ CF)
   This is a consequence of 27) and 20).
29) FOL $\notsubseteq$ CF (OL $\notsubseteq$ CF)
   L_{12} of 25) is a FOL (OL) by $A=\{abc\}$, $R=\{a \to a^2, b \to b^2, c \to c^2\}$.
   But L_{12} is not a CF.
30) sdDTFOL $\notsubseteq$ CF (sdDTOL $\notsubseteq$ CF)
   L_4 of 4b) is a sdDTFOL (sdDTOL) but not a CF.
31) sfFCF $ DTFOL (sfCF $ DTOL)
   a) sfFCF$\notsubseteq$DTFOL (sfCF$\notsubseteq$DTOL). L_8 of 8a) is a sfFCF (sfCF) but not a DTFOL (DTOL).
   b) DTFOL$\notsubseteq$sfFCF (DTOL$\notsubseteq$sfCF). This is a consequence of 26) and sfFCF CF (sfCF CF).
32) sdTFOL $ DTFOL (sdTOL $ DTOL)
   a) sdTFOL$\notsubseteq$DTFOL (sdTOL$\notsubseteq$DTOL). L_1 of 1) is a sdTFOL (sdTOL) by A and R as in 1), but not a DTFOL (DTOL).
   b) DTFOL$\notsubseteq$sdTFOL (DTOL$\notsubseteq$sdTOL). L_2 of 2) is a DTFOL (DTOL) but not a sdTFOL (sdTOL) as shown in 17).
33) sduTFOL $ DTFOL (sduTOL $ DTOL)
   a) sduTFOL$\notsubseteq$DTFOL (sduTOL$\notsubseteq$DTOL). L_1 of 1) is a sduTFOL (sduTOL) but not a DTFOL (DTOL).
   b) DTFOL$\notsubseteq$sduTFOL (DTOL$\notsubseteq$sduTOL). This is a consequence of 32b).
34) ccDTFOL $ sdTFOL (ccDTOL $ sdTOL)
   a) ccDTFOL$\notsubseteq$sdTFOL (ccDTOL$\notsubseteq$sdTOL). L_2 of 2) is a ccDTFOL (ccDTOL) but not a sdTFOL (sdTOL).
   b) sdTFOL$\notsubseteq$ccDTFOL (sdTOL$\notsubseteq$ccDTOL). L_9 of 10a) is a sdTFOL (sdTOL) but not a ccDTFOL (ccDTOL).
10)
   b) ccDTFOL$\notsubseteq$sdDTFOL (ccDTOL$\notsubseteq$sdDTOL). L_2 of 2) is a ccDTFOL (ccDTOL) by A and R as in 2) but not a sdDTFOL (sdDTOL).

35) sduETFOL $\subset$ sdETFOL $\subset$ ETFOL
   sdEDTFOL $\subset$ sdETFOL
   sdEDTFOL $\subset$ EDTFOL
   ccEDTFOL $\subset$ EDTFOL $\subset$ ETFOL
   By definition.
36) CF $ sduETFOL
   The proof is the same as in 4), for L_4 is not a CF.
37) CF $ EFOL $\subset$ ETFOL
   CF$\subset$EFOL$\subset$ETFOL. The proof of the first part is the same as in 11a), that of the second part by definition.
   CF$\neq$EFOL. L_{12} of 25) is also a EFOL as in 29), but not a CF.

38) $CF \$ sdEDTFOL$

This is proven in [5].

3 References

[1] L Systems. Edited by A. Salomaa, G. Rozenberg. Lecture Notes in Computer Science 15, Springer Berlin, Heidelberg, New York 1974
[2] M. Nielsen, G. Rozenberg, A. Salomaa, S. Skyum. Nonterminals, Homomorphisms and Codings in Different Variations of OL-systems. DAIMI PB-21, Aarhus 1974
[3] A. Salomaa. Formal Languages. Academic Press, New York, London 1973
[4] The names of the systems considered are due to a talk with G. Rozenberg
[5] S. Skyum. Parallel Context-free Languages. DAIMI PB-30, Aarhus 1974

Das Problem der 'unendlichen Modi' in ALGOL 68[§]

S. Heilbrunner
Hochschule der Bundeswehr München

1. EINLEITUNG

Nach der ursprünglichen Definition von ALGOL 68 ist die 'mode-declaration' **mode** $\underline{x}$ = **ref struct** ($\underline{x}$ p, **int** w, $\underline{x}$ q) nur dann erlaubt, wenn man eine terminale Produktion x_0 der Metavariablen MODE finden kann, die der Gleichung

$$x = \text{reference-to-structured-with-x-field-letter-p-and-integral-field-letter-w-and-x-field-letter-q}$$

oder kurz $x = rxpxq$ genügt (vgl. {1,2}). Es folgt, daß x_0 auch die Gleichungen

$$x = rrpxqprxpxqq$$
$$x = rrrxpxqprxpxqqprrxpxqprxpxqqq$$
$$\ldots$$
$$\ldots$$

erfüllen muß. Betrachtet man eine (kontextfreie) Grammatik mit der einzigen Regel $x ::= rxpxq$, der syntaktischen Variablen x und den terminalen Zeichen r,p und q, so folgt für jede aus x ableitbare Zeichenreihe z, daß x_0 die Gleichung $x = z$ erfüllen muß. Man schließt daraus, daß x_0 nicht von beschränkter Länge sein kann. Da ferner für beliebige Ordinalzahlen α gilt $1+\alpha+1+\alpha+1 > \alpha$ kann x_0 auch keine wohlgeordnete, transfinite Folge von Zeichen sein, sofern die Konkatenation solcher Folgen mit der Addition ihrer Ordnungstypen verträglich ist.

[§] Diese Arbeit ist teilweise im SFB49 -- Elektronische Rechenanlagen und Informationsverarbeitung -- der DFG in München entstanden.

5. ABLEITUNGSBÄUME

In diesem Abschnitt betrachten wir in informeller Weise die üblichen Strukturbäume für ableitbare Worte in kontextfreien Grammatiken. Wir bewerten die Knoten dieser Bäume mit rationalen Zahlen nach folgendem Schema:

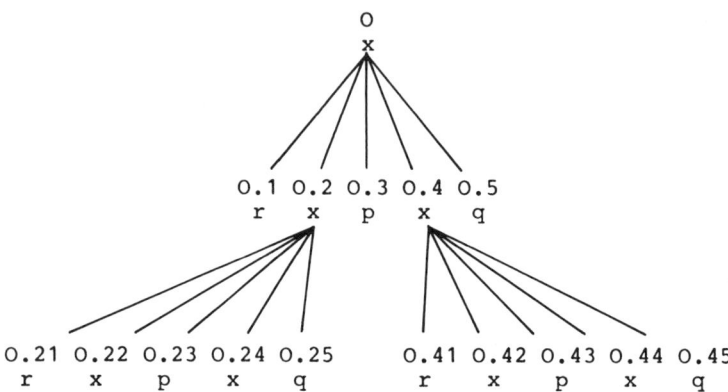

Für jeden Knoten K eines solchen Baumes B bilden wir das Paar (d_K, u_K), wobei d_K der zu dem Knoten K gehörige Dezimalbruch und u_K das zu dem Knoten K gehörige Zeichen ist. Die zu den Blättern (Endknoten) von B gehörigen Paare fassen wir zusammen:

$$X_B := \{(d_K, u_K) : K \text{ ist ein Blatt von } B\}$$

X_B ist eine Abbildung einer Teilmenge der rationalen Zahlen in die Menge der Zeichen. Wir fassen X_B als eine besondere Art der Darstellung derjenigen Produktion von x auf, die durch B definiert wird. So hat man bei dem oben gezeichneten Baum für X_B die folgende Tabelle:

d	0.1	0.21	0.22	0.23	0.24	0.25	0.3	0.41	0.42	0.43	0.44	0.45	0.5
$X_B(d)$	r	r	x	p	x	q	p	r	x	p	x	q	q

Wir stellen uns jetzt eine Folge $B_1, B_2, B_3, \ldots$ solcher Ableitungsbäume vor. Dabei soll jeweils B_{i+1} aus B_i durch Anwendung einer Produktionsregel entstehen. Definieren wir zu jedem dieser Bäume B_i die Menge

$$X_i := X_{B_i} := \{(d_K, u_K) : K \text{ ist ein Blatt von } B_i\}$$

wie oben, so ist die Frage nach dem Ergebnis des "unendlich" oftmaligen Anwendens von Produktionsregeln eine Frage nach dem Limes der Mengenfolge $X_1, X_2, X_3, \ldots$. Es erweist sich als zweckmäßig, als Grenzwert dieser Mengenfolge die Menge derjenigen Paare zu nehmen, die in fast jedem X_i enthalten sind, d.h.

$$X_o := X_\infty := \bigcup_{j=1}^{\infty} \bigcap_{i=j}^{\infty} X_i = \{(d,u) \mid \exists j \forall i > j : (d,u) \in X_i\} \, .$$

Es zeigt sich, daß X_o eine wohldefinierte Abbildung einer Teilmenge Def(X_o) der rationalen Zahlen in die Menge der Zeichen ist.

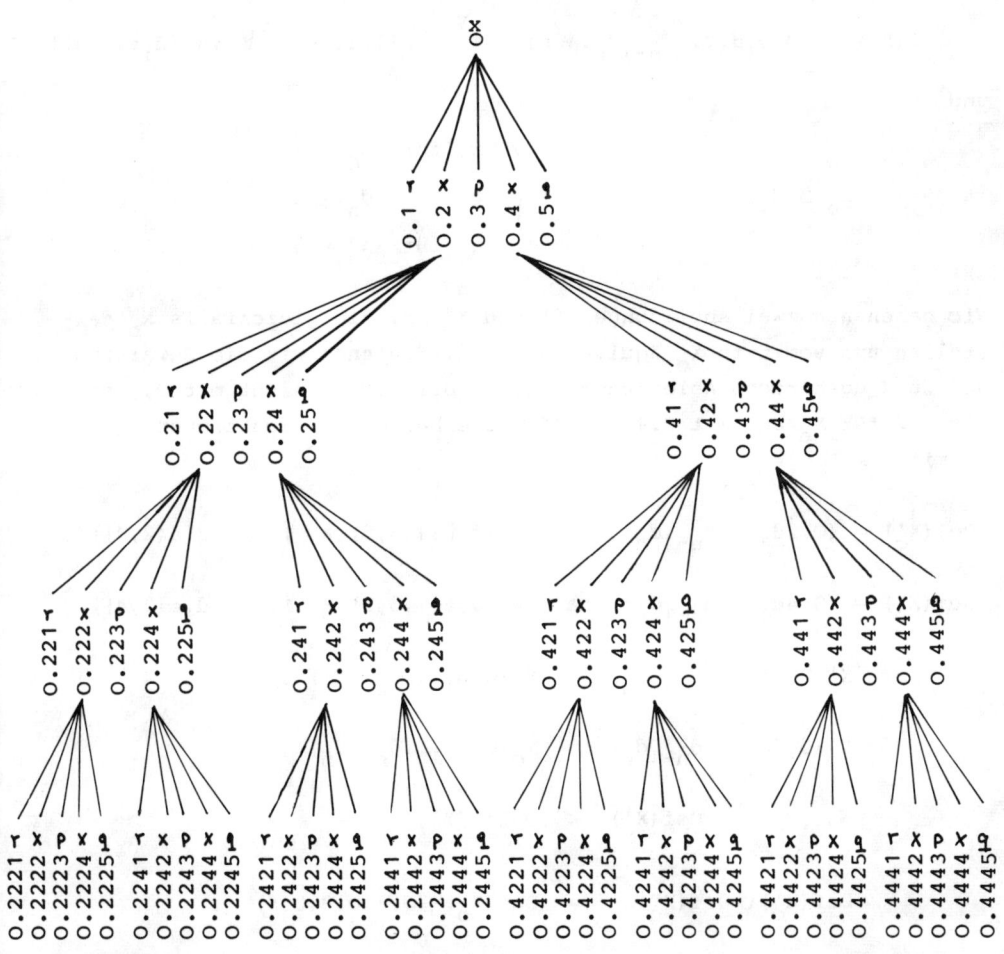

Wir wollen nun die Bäume der Folge einigermaßen gleichmäßig wachsen
lassen. Das soll heißen, daß die Folge der jeweils kürzesten Wege
zwischen der Wurzel des jeweiligen Baumes und seinen Blättern über
alle Grenzen wächst. Dann hat man:

$$\forall (d,x) \in X_i \; \exists \; j>i: \quad (d,x) \notin X_j \;\; .$$

Es folgt, daß x nicht mehr als Wert von X_o angenommen wird. Wir sagen,
X_o sei eine Darstellung einer terminalen Produktion x_o von x und zeigen, daß x_o die Gleichung $x = rxpxq$ in einem noch zu erklärenden
Sinne löst.

Untersucht man weitere Bäume (vgl. vorherige Seite) der Folge, so findet man für X_o im einzelnen:

$$\text{Def}(X_o) = \{0.d_1 d_2 \ldots d_{n-1} d_n : \; n \geq 1 \; \& \; d_n \in \{1,3,5\} \; \& \; \forall i \neq n: \; d_i \in \{2,4\}\}$$

und

$$X_o(0.d_1 d_2 \ldots d_{n-1} d_n) = \begin{cases} r & \text{für } d_n = 1 \\ p & \text{für } d_n = 3 \\ q & \text{für } d_n = 5 \end{cases}$$

Wir geben nun zwei Abbildungen X_o' und X_o'' an, die gleichfalls x_o darstellen und somit zu X_o äquivalent sind. Beginnen wir die Bewertung
der zu X_o gehörigen Ableitungsbäume an der Wurzel nicht mit 0, sondern
mit 0.2 für X_o' und mit 0.4 für X_o'', so erhalten wir Funktionen X_o' und
X_o'' mit

$$\text{Def}(X_o') = \{0.2d_1 \ldots d_{n-1} d_n : \; n \geq 1 \; \& \; d_n \in \{1,3,5\} \; \& \; \forall i \neq n: \; d_i \in \{2,4\}\} \;,$$

$$\text{Def}(X_o'') = \{0.4d_1 \ldots d_{n-1} d_n : \; n \geq 1 \; \& \; d_n \in \{1,3,5\} \; \& \; \forall i \neq n: \; d_i \in \{2,4\}\} \;,$$

$$X_o'(0.2d_1 \ldots d_{n-1} d_n) = X_o(0.d_1 \ldots d_{n-1} d_n) \;,$$

$$X_o''(0.4d_1 \ldots d_{n-1} d_n) = X_o(0.d_1 \ldots d_{n-1} d_n) \;,$$

$$\text{Def}(X_o') < \text{Def}(X_o'') \;,$$

$$\text{Def}(X_o') \cup \text{Def}(X_o'') = \text{Def}(X_o) \setminus \{0.1, 0.3, 0.5\} \;\; .$$

Wir definieren schließlich

$$R := \{(0.1, r)\} \;,\; P := \{(0.3, p)\} \;,\; Q := \{(0.5, q)\} \;.$$

und fassen R,P,Q als Darstellungen von r,p und q auf. Es gilt

$$\text{Def}(R) < \text{Def}(X_o') < \text{Def}(P) < \text{Def}(X_o'') < \text{Def}(Q) \;.$$

Wir wollen deshalb

$$R \cup X_o' \cup P \cup X_o'' \cup Q$$

als Darstellung von

$$r x_o p x_o q$$

auffassen. Aus den obigen Gleichungen folgt unmittelbar

$$X_o = R \cup X_o' \cup P \cup X_o'' \cup Q \;.$$

Da X_o ebenfalls eine Darstellung von x_o ist, schließen wir auf

$$x_o = r x_o p x_o q \;.$$

Zusammenfassend stellen wir fest: Es gibt eine terminale Produktion x_o von MODE, welche die Gleichung

$$x = \text{reference-to-structured-with-x-field-letter-p-and-}$$
$$\text{integral-field-letter-w-and-x-field-letter-q}$$

löst.

3. ZEICHENREIHEN

Es sei W eine nichtleere Menge. Zwei Funktionen

$$R: D \longrightarrow W \text{ und } S: E \longrightarrow W$$

auf (linear) geordneten Mengen D und E heißen __äquivalent,__ wenn es eine bijektive, isotone Abbildung H gibt mit $R = S \cdot H$. Der Betrachtung unterliegen nunmehr alle Funktionen, die irgendeine geordnete Menge nach W abbilden. Die zu verschiedenen Funktionen gehörigen geordneten Mengen können durchaus verschieden sein. Die Äquivalenzklassen dieser

Funktionen heißen <u>Zeichenreihen</u> bezüglich W. Zu jedem w∈W definieren wir eine <u>atomare Zeichenreihe</u> als Äquivalenzklasse der Funktion

$$R_w: \{1\} \longrightarrow W \quad \text{mit} \quad R_w(1) = w$$

und nennen die Menge der atomaren Zeichenreihen das <u>Vokabular</u>. Damit ist W entbehrlich, und wir sprechen von <u>Zeichenreihen über einem Vokabular</u>.[§]

Zur Definition der Konkatenation von Zeichenreihen erklären wir erst die Addition geordneter Mengen. Es sei $\{D_a : a \in A\}$ eine Menge disjunkter, geordneter Mengen. Außerdem sei A geordnet. Die Summe

$$\sum_{a \in A} D_a \quad \text{ist die Menge} \quad \bigcup_{a \in A} D_a \quad ,$$

wobei diese Vereinigung so angeordnet wird, daß die Ordnung in den einzelnen D_a erhalten bleibt und daß $a < ä$ stets $D_a < D_ä$ zur Folge hat. Ist jetzt zu jedem $a \in A$ eine Zeichenreihe r_a mit dem Repräsentanten

$$R_a: D_a \longrightarrow W$$

gegeben, so definieren wir

$$R: \sum_{a \in A} D_a \longrightarrow W \quad \text{durch} \quad R | D_a = R_a$$

für alle $a \in A$. Ist schließlich r die von R erzeugte Zeichenreihe, so wird Konkatenation definiert durch

$$r = \sum_{a \in A} r_a \quad .$$

Man zeigt, daß die Konkatenation für alle geordneten Mengen von Zeichenreihen wohldefiniert und assoziativ ist. Bei endlich vielen Summanden schreiben wir auch $r_1 + r_2 + \ldots + r_n$ etc.

Die Verwendung von Σ im Zusammenhang mit der Konkatenation hat einen historischen Grund. Enthält das Vokabular nämlich nur ein Zeichen, so reduziert sich die Theorie der Zeichenreihen über diesem Vokabular auf die Theorie der Ordnungstypen (vgl. {4}).

[§] Für Grundlagenprobleme im Zusammenhang mit dieser Definition verweisen wir auf {3}.

4. GRAMMATIKEN UND GLEICHUNGSSYSTEME

VS und VT seien zwei disjunkte Vokabulare. PR sei eine Menge von Paaren
(x,u), wobei x in VS liegt, und u eine Zeichenreihe über VS∪VT ist.
Diese Paare schreiben wir stets in der Form x ::= u. G = (VS, VT, PR)
heißt <u>Grammatik</u>. VS ist die Menge der <u>syntaktischen Variablen</u>,
VT die Menge der <u>terminalen</u> Zeichen und PR die Menge der <u>Produktions-
regeln</u>.

Eine Folge
$$\{ \sum_{a \varepsilon A_i} r_a \}_{i \leq \alpha} \ ,$$

wobei α eine beliebige Ordinalzahl ist, heißt <u>Ableitungsfolge</u> bezüglich G und $\{A_i\}$, wenn es Folgen $\{a_i\}$ und $\{D_i\}$ gibt, so daß gilt:

(i) $a_i \varepsilon A_i$ & $a_i \notin D_i$

(ii) $A_{i+1} = \{a \varepsilon A_i : a < a_i\} + D_i + \{a \varepsilon A_i : a > a_i\}$

(iii) $(r_{a_i} ::= \sum_{a \varepsilon D_i} r_a) \varepsilon \text{ PR}$

(iv) Für Limeszahlen β gilt:

$$A_\beta = \{a \varepsilon \bigcup_{i<\beta} A_i \mid \exists j \forall i: \ j<i<\beta \longrightarrow a \varepsilon A_i\}$$

Die ersten drei Bedingungen sind dem üblichen Ableitungsbegriff entnommen und entsprechen dem im zweiten Abschnitt betrachteten Auf-
stocken der Strukturbäume. Die letzte Gleichung wurde aus dem zweiten
Abschnitt übertragen und gestattet den Sprung auf die Limeszahlen. Es
ist anzumerken, daß die Bezugnahme auf $\{A_i\}$ wesentlich in die Definition mit eingeht. Andernfalls ist der Grenzwert nicht immer eindeutig
definiert. Wir sagen u sei aus t <u>ableitbar,</u> wenn es eine Ableitungs-
folge gibt, die mit t beginnt und mit u endet.

Wir betrachten nun Gleichungssysteme der Form

$$\{x_p = u_p : p \in P\}$$

in beliebig vielen Unbekannten x_p. Die rechten Seiten sollen durch Konkatenation von Konstanten und Unbekannten entstehen, wobei Konkatenation im eingeführten Sinne zu verstehen ist. Jedem Gleichungssystem ordnen wir eine Grammatik zu. Die Unbekannten gehen dabei in syntaktische Variable, die Konstanten in terminale Zeichen und die Gleichungen in Produktionsregeln über.

Es gilt folgender Satz:

> **Satz:** Gibt es eine konsistente Ersetzung der Unbekannten eines Gleichungssystems durch syntaktische Variable einer Grammatik, so daß nach der Ersetzung die rechten Seiten der Gleichungen aus den links stehenden syntaktischen Variablen ableitbar sind, so besitzt das Gleichungssystem im Sprachschatz der Grammatik eine Lösung.

Da die einem Gleichungssystem zugeordnete Grammatik immer eine Grammatik im Sinne dieses Satzes ist, folgt, daß alle Gleichungssysteme lösbar sind. Ein Beweis dieses Satzes findet sich in {5}. Wir wollen zum Schluß dieses Abschnittes erläutern, was unter der Lösung eines Gleichungssystemes zu verstehen ist.

Das Gleichungssystem $\{x_p = u_p : p \in P\}$ habe Unbekannte aus einem Vokabular VU und Konstante aus einem Vokabular VK. Die u_p seien in der Form

$$u_p = \sum_{q \in Q_p} u_{pq} \quad \text{mit} \quad u_{pq} \in \text{VU VK}$$

dargestellt. Man zeigt, daß eine solche Darstellung stets möglich ist. P sei wohlgeordnet. Eine Folge $\{t_p\}_{p \in P}$ heißt eine Lösung des Gleichungssystems, wenn alle t_p Zeichenreihen über VK sind und außerdem gilt:

$$t_p = \sum_{q \in Q_p} \ddot{u}_{pq} \quad \text{mit} \quad \ddot{u}_{pq} = \begin{cases} t_{\dot{p}} & \text{für } u_{pq} = x_{\dot{p}} \\ u_{pq} & \text{für } u_{pq} \in \text{VK} \end{cases}$$

5. ANWENDUNG AUF ALGOL 68

Für Algol 68 bedeutet der Satz des vorigen Abschnittes, daß alle 'mode-declarations' erlaubt sind, die man -- vermutlich -- hatte erlauben wollen. Die Syntax von Algol 68 hat nämlich die Eigenschaft, daß die rechten Seiten der zu lösenden Gleichungen aus der Meta-Variablen MODE abgeleitet werden können, sofern man alle Unbekannten durch MODE ersetzt.

Trotz dieser Tatsache ist die Anwendung der Theorie auf Algol 68 äußerst problematisch. Es zeigt sich nämlich, daß es Gleichungen mit sehr vielen verschiedenen Lösungen gibt, was für Algol 68 bedeuten würde, daß nicht jede 'mode-declaration' genau einen 'mode' definiert. Außerdem stellt sich heraus, daß die Lösungen sehr verschiedenartiger Gleichungen übereinstimmen. Für Algol 68 hätte das zur Folge, daß 'modes', die als verschieden beabsichtigt waren, gleich wären.

LITERATUR

{1} v. Wijngaarden, A. (ed.): Report on the Algorithmic Language Algol 68, Numerische Mathematik, vol.14, 1969, pp. 79-218.

{2} Baker, J.L.: An unintentional omission from Algol 68, Information Processing Letters, vol.1. 1972, pp. 229-232.

{3} Fraenkel; Bar-Hillel; Levy; v. Dalen: Foundations of Set Theory, 2nd ed., in Studies in Logic and the Foundations of Mathematics, vol.67, North-Holland, Amsterdam, 1973.

{4} Hausdorff, F.: Grundzüge der Mengenlehre, Leipzig, 1914.

{5} Heilbrunner, S.: Gleichungssysteme für Zeichenreihen, Bericht Nr. 7311, Abteilung Mathematik, TU München, 1973.

THE D-CALCULUS: A SYSTEM TO DESCRIBE THE SEMANTICS OF PROGRAMS INVOLVING COMPLEX DATA TYPES

- Summary -

Peter Raulefs

Institut für Informatik I, Universität Karlsruhe
D-7500 Karlsruhe 1, Postfach 6380, Fed. Rep. Germany

1. Introduction

Variants of the λ-calculus together with D. Scott's lattice-theoretic models have turned out to be a basic tool for describing the semantics of programming languages (e.g. [LANDIN 66], [REYNOLDS 72, 74], [SCOTT 74], [SCOTT-STRACHEY 71]). Based upon these approaches, in LCF [WEYHRAUCH-MILNER 72] a typed λ-calculus has been imbedded into a type theory providing a system in which properties about programs can be proven and programs can be constructed according to the properties being specified. The D-calculus presented in this paper contains essentially three new concepts that extend and refine the above systems:

(1) The D-calculus is an overtyped system combining the advantages of both typed and untyped systems without having the restrictions brought about by types. Hence, e.g. the semantics of programming language constructs having side effects and procedures taking arbitrary procedures as arguments as well as the intricacies of modes in ALGOL 68 can be adequately described in overtyped systems. A detailed account of overtyping the λ-calculus and such examples of applications is given in [RAULEFS 74].

(2) Abstract data types are introduced in terms of inverse systems of complete partially ordered sets (cpo-sets) that are refinements of the lattices developed by Scott and reflect the structure of data types more closely.

(3) The β-reduction mechanism of the λ-calculus is generalized to matching the binder to the argument - i.e. computing a substitution that makes the binder equal to the argument - and applying this substitution to the body of the λ-term. The control structure of "sugared" λ-calculi is generalized by using a pattern matching mechanism.

Section 2 contains an intuitive description of the computational model formalized by the D-calculus. Sections 3 and 4 give formal definitions of simple data types and the D-calculus. Preliminary studies indicate that the D-calculus can be successfully applied to investigate an astonishingly wide variety of phenomena e.g. in formal language theory, information structures, and semantics of programming languages. Some applications are indicated in Section 5.

All details as well as further applications can be found in [RAULEFS 75].

2. Intuitive Concept of Computation in the D-Calculus

(1) Each term t in the D-calculus starts processing information when receiving a package s of input information, where "t receives information s" is modelled by functional application of t to s, t:s, as usual.

(2) t changes (if necessary) so that its type fits the type of s for functional application. Transforming t into an object t' of suitable type is carried out by conversion rules taken from the overtyped λ-calculus. The transformation of t is done in such a way that t' still carries the meaning of t as far as it can be expressed by terms of the target type at all, and such that t can be retrieved from t' by transforming back.

Note that although each object of the D-calculus has a well-defined type, it adapts itself to almost anything changing contexts or environments require.

(3) A term in the D-calculus is a structured object that may contain components of "precise" as well as "vague" information, where "vague" information corresponds to typed variables. For terms s and t, a partial ordering is given by s $\sqsubseteq$ t iff s can be matched to t, i.e. there is a substitution type-consistently replacing variables in s by terms s.t. s and t become equal. Note that this partial ordering is defined on sets of terms of any type, including terms denoting functions, functionals, etc.

(4) A functional term consists of a binder, and triples being composed of a match term, an output term, and an output substitution. Upon receiving an incoming object, the functional term (1) matches the binder to the input object, (2) applies the matching substitution to the remaining triples, and (3) successively tries to match one match-term after another to the input object. After having obtained the first successful match, (4) the corresponding substitution is applied to the associated output term, and (5) the output substitution is applied to the term obtained after (4), yielding the resulting term.

In this way, control is administered by pattern matching and "computation" is done by substituting "more precise" for "vague" information.

3. **Simple Data Types**

A <u>simple data type</u> (SDT) (D,A) consists of

<u>1.</u> a 4-tuple $D = (A, V^o, C, M^o)$ where

   (1) A is a denumerable set ⎫ of <u>atomic constant symbols</u>
       V^o is an infinite, denumerable set ⎭   <u>(object) variable symbols</u>

    s.t. 1. $A \cap V = \emptyset$, and

         2. A contains a distinguished atomic constant symbol e called null object symbol;

   (2) $C = \{①, ②, \ldots, ⓚ\}$ ($K \in \mathbb{N}$) is a finite set of symbols called <u>constructor symbols</u>. Each $ⓚ \in C$ may or may not be assigned an arity $n_k \in \mathbb{N}_+$;

   (3) for any pair $\langle s,t \rangle$ of abstract data objects in $OB(D,A)$ as defined below, M^o determines a substitution $M^o\langle s,t \rangle$ matching s to t, where $M^o\langle s,t \rangle := \emptyset$ iff $s = t$ or s cannot be matched to t. M^o is called <u>matching function</u>.

   <u>Remark</u>: A set $\sigma = \{v_1 \leftarrow s_1, \ldots, v_K \leftarrow s_K\}$ with $v_k \in V^o, s_k \in OB(D,A)$ ($1 \leq k \leq K$) and $K \in \mathbb{N}$ is called a substitution. For any $t \in OB(D,A)$, σt denotes the object obtained by consistently replacing all occurrences of v_k by s_k ($1 \leq k \leq K$).

<u>2.</u> a set A of postulates about A, C, and $OB(D,A)$.

   <u>Remark</u>: A restricts the set of possible models of a SDT (D,A).

The set $OB(D)$ of <u>(abstract data) objects</u> belonging to a SDT (D,A) is inductively defined by:

   (1) $A, V^o \subset OB(D)$ (atomic objects)

   (2) $\forall ⓚ \in C: \{ⓚ[t_1, \ldots, t_N] \mid$ 1. $t_1, \ldots, t_N \in OB(D)$ and

          2. $N = n_k$ if specified and $N \in \mathbb{N}_+$ if not$\}$

          $\subset OB(D)$ (composite objects)

A partial ordering $\sqsubseteq_o$ among abstract data objects belonging to a SDT (D,A) is defined by:

$\forall t, t' \in OB(D): t \sqsubseteq_o t' :\Longleftrightarrow \exists$ substitution $\sigma: \sigma t = t'$

$\sqsubseteq_o$ is called <u>substitution order</u>

<u>Notation</u>: $t \equiv t' :\Longleftrightarrow t \sqsubseteq_o t' \wedge t' \sqsubseteq_o t$, i.e. $t \equiv t'$ iff t and t' are equal up to a renaming of variable symbols. We do not distinguish between objects $s, t \in OB(D)$ with $s \equiv t$.

$\forall X, Y \subseteq OB(D)$:

$S\{X \leftarrow Y\} := \{t \in OB(D) \mid \exists$ substitution $\sigma = \{v_1 \leftarrow y_1, \ldots, v_K \leftarrow y_K \mid y_1, \ldots, y_K \in Y\}$:

$\exists x \in X: \sigma x = t\}$

In particular, we consider

(1) $D_o^o := $

$$\begin{array}{c} A \\ \diagdown \\ v^o \end{array} \overline{\; \fbox{$①[v^o,\ldots,v^o] \cdot \quad \cdot \quad ⓚ[v^o,\ldots,v^o]$} \;}$$

where for each k, $1 \leq k \leq K$:

a. if n_k is specified: $ⓚ[v^o,\ldots,v^o]$ stands for $ⓚ[\underbrace{v^o,\ldots,v^o}_{n_k \text{ times}}]$

b. if n_k is unspecified: $ⓚ[v^o,\ldots,v^o]$ stands for $ⓚ[v^o], ⓚ[v^o,v^o], \ldots$

(2) $\forall m \in \mathbb{N}: D_{m+1}^o := S\{D_m^o \leftarrow D_o^o\}$

*3-1. $\forall m, n \in \mathbb{N}: m < n \Longrightarrow D_m^o \subsetneq D_n^o$.

*3-2. $\forall m \in \mathbb{N}: D_m^o$ is a complete partially ordered set (cpo-set).

*3-3. $\forall m \in \mathbb{N}: j_m^o: \begin{cases} D_{m+1}^o \to D_m^o \\ t \to j_m^o(t) := \max\{s \in D_m^o \mid s \sqsubseteq_o t\} \end{cases}$

is a well-defined continuous mapping.

*3-4. $\langle (D_m^o, j_m^o) \mid m \in \mathbb{N} \rangle$ is an inverse system.

Notation: The inverse system $\langle (D_m^o, j_m^o) \mid m \in \mathbb{N} \rangle$ associated with a SDT (D,A) is denoted by $I^o(D,A)$, and D_∞^o denotes its inverse limit.

Clearly, $OB(D,A) = D_\infty^o$.

A <u>model $M(D,A)$</u> of a SDT (D,A) is given by

$M(D,A) = (\langle (\underline{D}_m^o, \underline{j}_m^o) \mid m \in \mathbb{N} \rangle, \underline{M})$ where

$\langle (\underline{D}_m^o, \underline{j}_m^o) \mid m \in \mathbb{N} \rangle$ is an inverse system with

$$\underline{D}_o^o = \begin{array}{c} A \\ \diagdown \\ v^o \end{array} \overline{\; \fbox{$①[v^o,\ldots,v^o] \cdot \quad \cdot \quad ⓚ[v^o,\ldots,v^o]$} \;} \;,$$

$\forall m \in \mathbb{N}: \underline{D}_{m+1}^o := S\{\underline{D}_m^o \leftarrow \underline{D}_o^o\}$, and partial ordering given by the substitution ordering $\underline{\sqsubseteq}_o$. Here $\underline{A}$ is a set of atomic constants containing the null constant $\underline{e}$,

$\underline{C} = \{ \textcircled{1}, \ldots, \textcircled{K} \}$ is a set of constructors

s.t. $\forall \textcircled{k} \in \underline{C} : \textcircled{k} : \begin{cases} D_\infty^o \times \cdots \times D_\infty^o \to D_\infty^o \\ (t_1, \ldots, t_N) \to \textcircled{k}[t_1, \ldots, t_N] \end{cases}$, $(N = n_k$ resp. $N \in \mathbb{N}_t)$

and both $\underline{A}$ and $\underline{C}$ satisfy the postulates of A.

$\underline{M}$ is a mapping s.t.

(1) $\underline{M}: A \to \underline{A}$ where $\underline{M}[e] = \underline{e}$;

(2) $\underline{M}: V^o \to V^o$ is the identity map on V^o;

(3) $\underline{M}: C \to \underline{C}$ s.t. $\forall \textcircled{k} \in C: M[\textcircled{k}] = \underline{\textcircled{k}} \Rightarrow n_k = n_{\underline{k}}$ (if specified) and

$\forall t_1, \ldots, t_N \in D_\infty^o : \underline{M}[\textcircled{k}[t_1, \ldots, t_N]] = \underline{M}[\textcircled{k}][\underline{M}[t_1], \ldots, \underline{M}[t_N]]$

Clearly, $\forall t, t' \in D_\infty^o : t \sqsubseteq_o t' \iff \underline{M}[t] \underline{\sqsubseteq}_o \underline{M}[t']$.

4. The D-Calculus

We refer to a SDT (D,A) with associated inverse system

$I^o(D,A) = \langle (D_m, j_m) | m \in \mathbb{N} \rangle$.

4.1 Type System

The set T of types is inductively defined by

(1) $0, \infty \in T$;

(2) $\alpha, \beta \in T \wedge (\alpha, \beta) \neq (\infty, \infty) \Rightarrow (\alpha \to \beta) \in T$

Notation: 1. A type not containing any occurrence of ∞ is called a <u>finite type</u>.

Types containing at least one occurrence of ∞ are called <u>infinite types</u>. T_f and T_{inf} denote the sets of all finite resp. infinite types.

2. $\forall \alpha \in T_f : \alpha + 1 := (\alpha \to \alpha)$;

hence $T_f \iff \mathbb{N} \cup \{(n \to m) | n, m \in \mathbb{N} \wedge n \neq m\}$.

We define a partial ordering on T by

(1) $\forall \alpha \in T: 0 \leq \alpha, \alpha \leq \infty$;

(2) $\forall m, n \in T_f: m \leq n :\iff \bar{m} \, '\leq' \, \bar{n}$,

where $\bar{m}, \bar{n}$ are the integers that m, n denote and '$\leq$' is the usual less-or-equal relation on integers;

(3) $\forall (\alpha_1 \to \beta_1), (\alpha_2 \to \beta_2) \in T$:

$(\alpha_1 \to \beta_1) \leq (\alpha_2 \to \beta_2) : \iff \alpha_1 \leq \alpha_2 \wedge \beta_1 \leq \beta_2$

4.2 Terms

The terms of the D-calculus are constructed from objects in cpo-sets $OB^n(D,A)$ being defined next.

1. $\forall \alpha \in T : V^\alpha$ is an infinite and countable set of variable symbols of type α.

2.1 $E^1 := \{f | f = \lambda r. \langle (r_n, r'_n, \sigma_n) | 1 \leq n \leq N \rangle$ where

(1) $N \in \mathbb{N}$ and $\forall n. 1 \leq n \leq N: r, r_n, r'_n \in D_f^o \wedge \sigma_n \in SUB^o$;

(2) $\forall i,j . 1 \leq i,j \leq N:$ 1. $i \leq j \Rightarrow r_i \sqsubseteq_o r_j$

   2. $r_i \sqsubseteq_o r_j \Rightarrow \sigma_i r'_i \sqsubseteq_o \sigma_j r'_j \}$

where $D_f^o := \bigcup_{m \in \mathbb{N}} D_m^o$

and $SUB^o := \{\sigma | \sigma = \{v_k \leftarrow s_k | \forall k. 1 \leq k \leq K : v_k \in V^o, s_k \in D_f^o\}$ and $K \in \mathbb{N}\}$.

2.2 The set $OB^1(D,A)$ of first-order abstract data objects belonging to the SDT (D,A) is inductively defined by:

(1) $E^1, V^1 \subset OB^1(D,A)$;

(2) $\forall \circled{k} \in C: \{\circled{k}[t_1, \ldots, t_N] |$ 1. $t_1, \ldots, t_N \in OB(D)$ and

   2. $N = n_k$ if n_k specified and $N \in \mathbb{N}_+$ if not$\} \subset OB^1(D,A)$.

The substitution ordering $\sqsubseteq_1$ is defined in analogy to $\sqsubseteq_o$.

2.3. $D_o^1 :=$
$$
\begin{array}{c}
E^1 \\
\diagdown \\
V^1
\end{array}
\quad
\overline{\circled{1}[v^1, \ldots, v^1] \cdots \circled{K}[v^1, \ldots, v^1]}
$$

$\forall m \in \mathbb{N} : D_{m+1}^1 := S\{D_m^1 \leftarrow D_o^1\}$; $D_f^1 := \bigcup_{m \in \mathbb{N}} D_m^1$.

Similarly to *3-4, there are continuous mappings $j_m^1 : D_{m+1}^1 \to D_m^1$ s.t.

*4-1. $\langle (D_m^1, j_m^1) | m \in \mathbb{N} \rangle$ is an inverse system.

<u>Notation</u>: The inverse system of *4-1 is denoted by $I^1(D,A)$, its inverse limit by D_∞^1.

2.4. $SUB_V^1 := \{\sigma | \sigma = \{v_k \leftarrow f_k | \forall k. 1 \leq k \leq K : v_k \in V^1, f_k \in D_f^1\}, K \in \mathbb{N}\}$

$SUB_M^1 := \{\Sigma | \Sigma = (\theta, \{\langle 1, k_1, \eta_{1k_1} \rangle | l \in \underline{L}, k_1 \in \underline{K}_1, \eta_{1k_1} \in SUB^o\})$

where $\underline{L} \subset \mathbb{N}$ and $\forall l \in \underline{L} : \underline{K}_1 \subset \mathbb{N}$ are finite index sets$\}$

$SUB^1 := SUB_V^1 \cup SUB_M^1$

$\forall f \in E^1 . f = \lambda r. \langle (r_i, r'_i, \sigma_i) | 1 \leq i \leq I \rangle :$

$\forall \Sigma \in \text{SUB}_M^1 . \Sigma = (\theta, \{ \langle 1, k_1, \eta_{1k_1} \rangle \mid 1 \in \underline{L}, k_1 \in \underline{K}_1, \eta_{1k_1} \in \text{SUB}^o \})$:

$\Sigma f := \lambda \theta r. \langle (\eta_{nm_n} \circ \theta r_n, \eta_{nm_n} \circ \theta r'_n, \eta_{nm_n} \circ \theta [\sigma_n]), (r_i, r'_i, \sigma_i) \mid$

1. $n \in \underline{L} \cap \{1, \ldots, I\}$ and $\forall n \in \underline{L}: m_n \in \underline{K}_n$;
2. $i \in \{1, \ldots, I\} - \underline{N}$
3. all triples are ordered accdg. to cond. (2) of 2.1 $\rangle$

2.5. $\sqsubseteq_1$ extends to: $\forall t, t' \in D_\infty^1 : t \sqsubseteq_1 t' : \iff \exists \Sigma \in \text{SUB}^1 : \Sigma t = t'$.

2.6. M^o can be extended to the <u>first-order matching function</u>

$$M^1 : D_f^1 \times D_f^1 \longrightarrow \text{SUB}^1$$

3. Assume inductively that for some $n \in T$ the set $\text{OB}^n(D,A)$ of abstract n-th order objects, the partial ordering $\sqsubseteq_n$, the inverse system $I^n(D,A) = \langle (D_m^n, j_m^n) \mid m \in \mathbb{N} \rangle$ with inverse limit D_∞^n, the set SUB^n, and the n-th order matching function M^n have been defined.

3.1. $E^{n+1} := \{ f \mid f = \lambda r. \langle (r_n, r'_n, \Sigma_n) \mid 1 \leq n \leq N \rangle$ where

(1) $N \in \mathbb{N}$ and $\forall n. 1 \leq n \leq N : r, r_n, r'_n \in D_f^n \wedge \Sigma_n \in \text{SUB}^n$;

(2) $\forall i, j. 1 \leq j \leq N: 1. i \leq j \Rightarrow r_i \not\sqsubseteq_n r_j$

2. $r_i \sqsubseteq_n r_j \Rightarrow \Sigma_i r'_i \sqsubseteq_n \Sigma_j r'_j \}$

3.2. $\text{OB}^{n+1}(D,A)$, the inverse system $I^{n+1}(D,A)$ with inverse limit D_∞^{n+1}, the set SUB^{n+1}, $\sqsubseteq_{n+1}$, and M^{n+1} are defined similarly as in 2.1. - 2.6.

4. $\forall (k \to 1) \in T$:

$E^{kl} := \{ f \mid f = \lambda r. \langle (r_n, r'_n, \Sigma_n) \mid 1 \leq n \leq N \rangle$ where

(1) $N \in \mathbb{N}$ and $\forall n. 1 \leq n \leq N : r, r_n \in D_f^k \wedge r'_n \in D_f^l \wedge \Sigma_n \in \text{SUB}^1$;

(2) $\forall i, j. 1 \leq i, j \leq N: 1. i \leq j \Rightarrow r_i \not\sqsubseteq_k r_j$

2. $r_i \sqsubseteq_k r_j \Rightarrow \Sigma_i r'_i \sqsubseteq_l \Sigma_j r'_j \}$

4.1. Again $\text{OB}^{kl}(D,A), I^{kl}(D,A), D_\infty^{kl}, \text{SUB}^{kl}, \sqsubseteq_{kl}, M^{kl}$ are defined as above.

5. $\{ \theta_{\alpha\beta} \mid \alpha, \beta \in T \}$ is the set of transfer function symbols.

   τ maps each abstract data object to its type.

6. The <u>set $L(D,A)$ of all terms in the D-calculus</u> is inductively defined by:

(1) $\forall \alpha \in T: D_f^\alpha \subset L(D,A)$ is a set of terms of type α;

(2) $\forall \alpha, \beta, \gamma \in T: \lambda r_\alpha. \langle (s_{i_\beta}, t'_{i_\gamma}, \Sigma_{i_\gamma}) \mid 1 \leq i \leq I \rangle$ where

[1. $I \in \mathbb{N}; r_\alpha, s_{i_\beta}, t'_{i_\gamma}$ are terms of the subscripted types and

$\Sigma_{i_\gamma} \in SUB^\gamma$ $(1 \leq i \leq I)$;

2. $\forall k, 1.1 \leq k, 1 \leq I:$ 1. $k \leq 1 \Rightarrow s_{k\beta} \not\sqsubseteq_\beta s_{1\beta}$

2. $s_{k\beta} \sqsubseteq_\beta s_{1\beta} \Rightarrow \Sigma_{k\gamma} t'_{k\gamma} \sqsubseteq_\gamma \Sigma_{1\gamma} t'_{1\gamma}$]

is a term

(2.1) of type $(\alpha \rightarrow \gamma)$ if $(\alpha, \gamma) \neq (\infty, \infty)$;

(2.2) of type ∞ if $\alpha = \gamma = \infty$;

(3) $\forall \alpha, \beta \in T: \forall s_\alpha, t_\beta \in L(D,A):$

(3.1) $s_\alpha : t_\beta \in L(D,A)$ is a term of type γ if $\alpha = (\alpha_1 \rightarrow \gamma)$;

(3.2) $s_\alpha : t_\beta \in L(D,A)$ is a term of type α if $\alpha \in \{0, \infty\}$;

(4) $\forall \alpha, \beta \in T: \forall t_\alpha \in L(D,A): \Theta_{\alpha\beta}(t_\alpha) \in L(D,A)$ is a term of type β.

7. $\forall \alpha \in T: \forall v \in V^\alpha: \forall t \in L(D,A):$

An occurrence of v in t is <u>bound</u> iff this occurrence appears in a subterm $\lambda s. \langle (s_i, s'_i, \Sigma_i) | 1 \leq i \leq I \rangle$ of t and there is an occurrence of v in s that is not a bound occurrence of v in s.

An occurrence of v in t is <u>free</u> iff it is not a bound occurrence of v in t.

If $t = \lambda r. \langle (r_i, r'_i, \Sigma_i) | 1 \leq i \leq I \rangle$ and v has a free occurrence in r then any possible free occurrence of v in r_i, r'_i and (the rhs of) Σ_i $(1 \leq i \leq I)$ lies in the <u>scope</u> of the binder λr.

<u>Notation</u>: For any substitution Σ and any $t \in L(D,A):$

$\Sigma[t]_{free}$ denotes the term obtained by substituting accdg. to Σ only free occurrences of variables in v.

4.3 Conversion Rules

1. <u>α-conversion</u>: $\forall t \in L(D,A):$ if $f = \lambda r. \langle (r_i, r'_i, \Sigma_i) | 1 \leq i \leq I \rangle$ is a subterm of t then f may be replaced in t by

$\lambda \sigma[r]_{free} \cdot \langle (\sigma[r_i]_{free}, \sigma[r'_i]_{free}, \sigma[\Sigma_i]_{free}) | 1 \leq i \leq I \rangle$ where

$\sigma = \{v_1 \leftarrow v'_1, \ldots, v_K \leftarrow v'_K\}$ is a substitution s.t.

$\forall k. 1 \leq k \leq K:$ 1. $v_k, v'_k \in \bigcup_{\alpha \in T} V^\alpha_\lambda \quad \tau[v_k] = \tau[v'_k]$;

2. v_k has free occurrences in r;

3. v'_k does not have any free occurrence in f.

2. β-conversion:

2.1. Notation

$\forall \sigma, \tau \in SUB^0. \sigma = \{v_1 \leftarrow s_1, \ldots, v_K \leftarrow s_K\}, \tau = \{u_1 \leftarrow t_1, \ldots, u_L \leftarrow t_L\}$:

$\sigma \circ \tau := \{u_1 \leftarrow \sigma t_1 | 1 \leq l \leq L \wedge u_l \neq \sigma t_l\} \cup \{v_k \leftarrow s_k | 1 \leq k \leq K \wedge v_k \notin \{u_1, \ldots, u_L\}\}$

$\sigma[\tau] := \{\sigma u_l \leftarrow \sigma t_l | 1 \leq l \leq L \wedge \sigma u_l \in V^0\}$

$\forall \Sigma, T \in SUB^1. \Sigma = (\sigma, \{\langle i, j_i, \sigma_{ij_i}\rangle | i \in \underline{I}, j_i \in \underline{J}_i, \sigma_{ij_i} \in SUB^0\})$,

$T = (\tau, \{\langle k, l_k, \tau_{kl_k}\rangle | k \in \underline{K}, l_k \in \underline{L}_k, \tau_{kl_k} \in SUB^0\})$:

$\Sigma \circ T := (\sigma \circ \tau, \{\langle k, l_k, \sigma_{kl_k} \circ \tau_{kl_k}\rangle | k \in \underline{I} \wedge \underline{K} \& l_k \in \underline{I}_k \cap \underline{L}_k\}$

$\cup \{\langle i, j_i, \sigma_{ij_i}\rangle | i \in \underline{I}-\underline{K} \wedge j_i \in \underline{J}_i - \underline{L}_i\}$

$\cup \{\langle k, l_k, \tau_{kl_k}\rangle | k \in \underline{K}-\underline{I} \wedge l_k \in \underline{L}_k - \underline{J}_k\})$

$\Sigma[T] := (\sigma[\tau]$, (similarly as for $\Sigma \circ T$ with "$\sigma_{kl_k} \circ \tau_{kl_k}$" being replaced by

"$\sigma_{kl_k}[\tau_{kl_k}]$")

Composition ∘ and application [ ] of substitutions can be generalized straightforwardly to substitutions of arbitrary types.

2.2. $\forall t \in L(D,A)$: if $f_{(\alpha \to \beta)}: s_\alpha \in L(D,A)$ is a subterm of t and

$f = \lambda r_\alpha \cdot \langle (r_{i\alpha}, r'_{i\beta}, \Sigma_{i\beta}) | 1 \leq i \leq I\rangle$ then $f_{(\alpha \to \beta)}: s_\alpha$ may be replaced in t by $\bar{s}_\beta$,

where $\bar{s}_\beta$ is the object obtained by executing the following algorithm:

[1] *if* $r_\alpha \sqsubseteq_\alpha s_\alpha$ *then* $\Gamma_\alpha := M^\alpha \langle r_\alpha, s_\alpha\rangle$ *else goto* [2];

for $i = 1, \ldots, I$ *do* [*if* $\Gamma_\alpha r_{i\alpha} \sqsubseteq_\alpha s_\alpha$ *then goto* [3]];

[2] $\bar{s}_\beta := v_\beta$; *STOP*; (where $v_\beta \in V^\beta$ does not occur in t)

[3] $\Gamma_{i\alpha} := M^\alpha \langle r_{i\alpha}, s_\alpha\rangle \circ \Gamma_\alpha; \bar{s}_\beta := \Gamma_{i\alpha}[\Sigma_{i\beta}] \circ \Gamma_{i\alpha} r'_{i\beta}$; *STOP*;

2.3. ⓚ$[t_1, \ldots, t_N]: s \to$ ⓚ$[t_1:s, \ldots, t_N:s]$

3. θ-conversion: For any $\alpha, \beta, \gamma, \Gamma, \varepsilon \in T$ and terms with types subscripted:

3.1. $s_\alpha: t_\beta \to \Theta_{\alpha(\beta \to \alpha)}(s_\alpha): t_\beta$ if $\alpha \in \{0, \infty\}$

$s_\alpha: t_\beta \to \Theta_{(\alpha_1 \to \alpha_2)(\beta \to \alpha_2)}(s_\alpha): t_\beta$ if $\alpha = (\alpha_1 \to \alpha_2)$

3.2. $\Theta_{(\alpha \to \beta)(\gamma \to \delta)}(\lambda r_\alpha \cdot \langle (r_{i\varepsilon}, r'_{i\beta}, \Sigma_{i\beta}) | 1 \leq i \leq I\rangle)$

$\to TRANS_{(\alpha \to \beta)(\gamma \to \delta)}(\lambda r_\alpha \cdot \langle (r_{i\varepsilon}, r'_{i\beta}, \Sigma_{i\beta}) | 1 \leq i \leq I\rangle)$

(which is a term of the form $\lambda s_\gamma . \langle (s_{i\gamma}, s'_{i\delta}, \Sigma_{i\delta}) | 1 \leq i \leq I \rangle$)

Remark: $TRANS_{\alpha_1 \alpha_2}$ is an algorithm syntactically translating any term s_{α_1} into a term t_{α_2} s.t. the meaning of s_{α_1} is optimally preserved in t_{α_2} w.r.t. collective models and interpretations (see [RAULEFS 74]).

3.3. $\theta_{\alpha\beta}(\theta_{\beta\alpha}(t_\beta)) \to t_\beta$

4. η-conversion and other conversion rules of conventional λ-calculi can be straightforwardly carried over to a D-calculus-like system.

4.4. Models and Properties of D-calculi

1. Any model $M(D,A) = (\langle (\underline{D}^o_m, \underline{j}^o_m) | m \in \mathbb{N} \rangle, \underline{M})$ of an SDT (D,A) is extended to a model of a D-calculus on (D,A) as follows:

   (1) to the type 0 we assign the set $\underline{D}^o_\infty$;

   (2) $\forall \alpha, \beta \in T. \alpha, \beta \neq \infty$: to the type $(\alpha \to \beta)$ we assign the set $[\underline{D}^\alpha_\infty \to \underline{D}^\beta_\infty]$;

Following the usual construction given in e.g. [SCOTT 71] there are continuous functions $\psi_n \in [\underline{D}^{n+1}_\infty \to \underline{D}^n_\infty]$ ($n \in T$) s.t.

*4-2. $\langle (\underline{D}^n_\infty, \psi_n) | n \in T \rangle$ is an inverse system.

Notation: $\underline{D}^\infty_\infty$ denotes the inverse limit of $\langle (\underline{D}^n_\infty, \psi_n) | n \in T \rangle$.

   (3) to the type ∞ we assign the set $\underline{D}^\infty_\infty$;

   (4) $\forall \alpha, \beta \in T: \underline{M}(\theta_{\alpha\beta})$ is the usual transfer function (e.g. [REYNOLDS 72.1]) adapted to our system;

   (5) $\forall \alpha, \beta \in T: [\underline{M}(\theta_{\alpha\beta})|_{V^\alpha}]^{-1} = \underline{M}(\theta_{\beta\alpha})|_{V^\beta}$ holds;

Remark: The admissible models and interpretations of the D-calculus have to be slightly further restricted to <u>collective models and interpretations</u> as described in [RAULEFS 74].

2. The next theorems show that these models and their associated interpretations actually do the job:

*4-3. $\forall$ interpretations I : $\forall \alpha \in T : \forall t_\alpha \in L(D,A) : I[t_\alpha] \in \underline{D}^\alpha_\infty$.

*4-4. $\forall$ interpretations I: $\forall t, t' \in L(D,A)$:
   if t can be converted to t' then $I[t] = I[t']$.

3. $\forall \alpha, \beta \in T : \forall f_{(\alpha \to \beta)} \in L(D,A)$:

$D_{f(\alpha \to \beta)} := \{s \in L(D,A) \mid$ the β-conversion algorithm (4.3.2.2) applied to $f_{(\alpha \to \beta)}$:s does not terminate at step [2]$\}$

is called the <u>processing domain</u> of $f_{(\alpha \to \beta)}$.

*4-4. $\forall \alpha, \beta \in T : \forall f, g \in E^{\alpha\beta}$:

$$f \sqsubseteq_{(\alpha \to \beta)} g \Rightarrow (1) \; D_f \subseteq D_g, \quad \text{and}$$
$$(2) \; \forall s \in D_f : f:s \sqsubseteq_\beta g:s$$

I.e., a functional object f is less or equal than another functional object g in the usual sense if f can be matched to g.

5. Examples and Applications

(1) Examples of Simple Data Types

(1.1) <u>STRING</u> $:= (D, \{[\text{STRING } i] \mid 1 \leq i \leq 4\})$ s.t.

[STRING 1] $C = \{①\}$ and $n_1 = 2$;

[STRING 2] A is finite;

[STRING 3] $\forall s_1, s_2, s_3 \in D_f^o : ①[s_1, ①[s_2, s_3]] = ①[①[s_1, s_2], s_3]$

i.e. ① is an associative constructor symbol.

[STRING 4] $\forall s \in D_f^o : ① [s,e] = ① [e,s] = e$

For sets $X \subseteq D_f^o$ let $fr(X) := \{t \in X \mid$ no variable symbol occurs in t$\}$.

Then, $fr(D_f^o) = A^*$.

(1.2) <u>LIST</u> $:= (D, \{[\text{LIST } i] \mid 1 \leq i \leq 3\})$ s.t.

[LIST 1] $C = \{①, ②\}$, $n_1 = 2$, and n_2 unspecified;

[LIST 2] A is finite;

[LIST 3] ① is an associative constructor symbol, ② is not.

(1.3) <u>TREE</u> $:= (D, \{[\text{TREE } i] \mid 1 \leq i \leq 3\})$ s.t.

[TREE 1] $C = \{①\}$ and n_1 unspecified;

[TREE 2] A is finite;

[TREE 3] $D_f^o = $

$$\begin{array}{c} A \\ \diagdown \\ X \\ \diagdown \\ V^o \end{array} \quad ① [X, V, \ldots, V]$$

where X is an infinite, countable set of atomic variable symbols s.t. only symbols from $X \cup A$ may be substituted for atomic variable symbols from X.

Remark: For $n_1 = k(\geq 3)$, TREE describes the data type of k-ary trees.

(1.4) STACK $= (D,\{[STRING\ i],[STACK]\mid 1 \leq i \leq 4\})$ where

[STACK] $\quad D_o^o :=$
$$\begin{array}{c} A \\ \diagdown \\ \textcircled{1}\ [A,V^o] \\ \diagup \\ V^o \end{array}$$

(2) Formal Languages

Assuming the SDT STRING and an appropriate model, we obtain:

*5-1. For any recursively enumerable language L on the finite alphabet $\underline{A}$ there is an $f_L \in \underline{E}^1$ s.t.

$$L = \{\sigma_e(f_L^n:v) \mid n \in \mathbb{N}_+\}$$

(where σ_e denotes the substitution replacing any $v \in V^o$ by $\underline{e}$, and the β-reduction 4.3.2.2 is generalized to a nondeterministic control structure.)
I.e. <u>any r.e. language</u> is just the <u>set of all finite approximations to the least fixed-point of a functional term in $\underline{E}^1$</u>.

The Chomsky-hierarchy and similar families of formal languages can be easily described by sets of terms in $\underline{E}^1$.

(3) Semantics of Programming Languages

The D-calculus extends and refines the known concepts (e.g. [SCOTT-STRACHEY 71], [REYNOLDS 72,74], [TENNENT 73]) for describing the semantics of programming languages with definitional systems based on the λ-calculus. By founding a definitional interpreter on the D-calculus (instead of the λ-calculus),

(3.1) type conflicts arising when trying to describe things like side-effects and higher-order features in typed systems disappear while the advantages of having types remain.

(3.2) information structures employed in the defined programming language can be closely modelled. Composite objects in the defined language are represented by D-calculus terms containing corresponding constructors.

(3.3) the scope of environments in the defined language corresponds to the scope of binders of λ-terms in the D-calculus. The "structured" design of programs as well as the "structured" flow of control is almost trivially reflected in the corresponding D-calculus terms.

(3.4) the D-calculus can be straightforwardly imbedded into an "overtyped type theory" [RAULEFS 74] obtaining a mechanizeable system in which proofs about properties of programs can be carried out and mechanical program construction can be studied.

6. References

[LANDIN 66] Landin, P. A λ-calculus approach. In Advances in Programming and Non-Numerical Computation, L. Fox (ed.), Pergamon Press, 1966: 97-141.

[RAULEFS 74] Raulefs, P. The overtyped λ-calculus and its application for describing semantics of programming languages. Technical Report, Inst. f. Informatik I, Karlsruhe Univ., Nov. 1974.

[RAULEFS 75] Raulefs, P. Dissertation, 1975

[REYNOLDS 72] Reynolds, J.C. Definitional interpreters for higer-order programming languages. Proc. ACM 1972 Ann. Conf.:717-740

[REYNOLDS 72.1] Reynolds, J.C. Notes on a lattice-theoretic approach to the theory of computation. Tech. Rep., Systems and Information Science Dept., Syracuse University, 1972.

[REYNOLDS 74] Reynolds, J.C. On the relation between direct and continuation semantics. Proc. 2nd Coll. on Automata, Languages and Programming 1974 (ed. J. Loeckx), Springer Lecture Notes in Computer Science vol. 14 (1974): 141-156.

[SCOTT 74] Scott, D. Data types as lattices. Mimeographed notes, Kiel International Summer School and Logic Conference, 1974.

[SCOTT-STRACHEY 71] Scott, D. and C. Strachey. Towards a mathematical semantics for computer languages. Proc. Symp. Computer and Automata, Polytechnic Inst. of Brooklyn, 1971: 19-46.

[TENNENT 73] Tennent, R.D. Mathematical semantics of SNOBOL4. Proc. ACM Symp. Principles of Programming Languages, Boston, Oct. 1973:95-107.

[WEYHRAUCH-MILNER 72] Weyhrauch, R. and R. Milner. Program semantics and correctness in a mechanized logic. Proc. 1st USA-Japan Comp. Conf., 1972:384-392.

EFFIZIENZVERGLEICHE VON BEWEISPROZEDUREN

W. Bibel

Mathematisches Institut, Technische Universität München

0. Einleitung

Das Gebiet des automatischen Beweisens ist etwa seit 1965 zusehends unübersichtlicher geworden, da von Jahr zu Jahr neue Beweisprozeduren auftauchen, von denen die Autoren meistens behaupten, sie seien effizienter als die bis dahin bekannten Verfahren. Zur Begründung werden zwar nicht mehr die CPU-Zeiten von ein paar zufälligen Testbeispielen herangezogen, doch sehr viel überzeugender sind die Argumente oft auch heute noch nicht. Ausnahmen hiervon sind zum Beispiel die Arbeiten von KOWALSKI und KUEHNER [3] und LOVELAND [4], obwohl auch deren Vergleichsmethoden nicht allgemeiner Natur, sondern zugeschnitten sind auf die speziellen Verfahren, die dort verglichen werden.

Da der praktische Einsatz von Beweisverfahren noch immer nicht so recht in Gang gekommen ist, fehlt es überdies auch an einem durch viele Testbeispiele geprägten "Gefühl" für die Leistungsfähigkeit der verschiedenen Verfahren, wie es etwa bei gängigen Übersetzern vorhanden ist. Es ist daher verständlich, daß die Frage nach einem allgemeinen und praktikablen Maßstab für Effizienzvergleiche immer vordringlicher wird. Jedoch ist, wie auch LOVELAND in [4] feststellt, ein Ansatz in dieser Richtung bis heute nicht bekannt geworden.

Der Kern eines solchen Ansatzes besteht in der Präzisierung der Aussage "Verfahren X ist effizienter als Verfahren Y". Eine Präzisierung dieser und ähnlicher Aussagen wird in dieser Arbeit vorgeschlagen und motiviert (Abschnitt 1). Sie ist verfahrensunabhängig, also allgemein und dürfte den Sachverhalt genau treffen. Ob sie praktikabel ist, können naturgemäß erst eine Reihe von konkreten Anwendungen erweisen, was den Rahmen dieser Arbeit weit übersteigt. Jedoch werden mit ihr in Abschnitt 2 der Vergleich von 2 einfachen Prozeduren durchgeführt und in Abschnitt 3 weitere Anwendungen kurz skizziert, womit ein erster Schritt in dieser Richtung unternommen ist. Ein subtiler Vergleich zwischen hochgezüchteten Verfahren unterschiedlicher Herkunft dürfte allerdings äußerst mühsam sein, was jedoch kaum anders zu erwarten war.

1. Die Effizienzrelation

Die Schwierigkeiten, das Effizienzverhalten zweier vollständiger Verfahren quantitativ zu vergleichen, beruhen im wesentlichen auf dem folgenden Phänomen. Wird eine Prozedur P1 zu einer Prozedur P2 weiterentwickelt, so besteht die Verbesserung bezüglich Effizienz in aller Regel nicht in einer Senkung der Kosten an Speicherbedarf und/oder Zeitaufwand für *alle* Theoreme, vielmehr wirkt sich die Verbesserung nur auf eine Teilklasse T_1 von Theoremen positiv aus, während sie für eine andere Teilklasse T_2 im Gegenteil sogar eine Kostenerhöhung mit sich bringt. Trotzdem hat man oft das nicht unberechtigte Gefühl, daß der Gewinn den Verlust übertrifft.

Nun hat man es aber in der Praxis nie mit der Klasse T aller Theoreme zu tun, da den Kosten zum Beweis eines Theorems durch die gegebenen Möglichkeiten immer eine obere Grenze k gesetzt ist. Berücksichtigt man dies, dann wird man unter zwei gegebenen vollständigen Prozeduren P1 und P2 natürlicherweise P2 dann als *effizienter in Bezug auf* k als P1 (in Zeichen P1 $\triangleleft_k$ P2) bezeichnen, wenn die Wahrscheinlichkeit ein beliebig vorgegebenes und — zur Vermeidung von unendlichen Mengen — im Hinblick auf k realistisches Theorem T mit den durch k begrenzten Möglichkeiten zu beweisen, bei P2 größer ist als bei P1. Dies ist aber bei gleicher Gewichtung aller Theoreme genau dann der Fall, wenn die Gesamtzahl der durch P2 unterhalb k bewiesenen Theoreme diejenige von P1 echt übersteigt. Unter Verwendung der Funktion kst(P;T) für die Kosten zum Beweis von T mit P und der Theoremmenge $T(P;k) := \{T \in T : \text{kst}(P;T) \leq k\}$ ergibt sich also die folgende Definition:

Df1.   P1 $\triangleleft_k$ P2   gdw $|T(P1;k)| < |T(P2;k)|$

P1 $\bowtie_k$ P2   gdw $|T(P1;k)| = |T(P2;k)|$

Die Kosten $kst(P;T)$ setzen sich naturgemäß aus mehreren Komponenten zusammen, wobei insbesondere die Speicher- und Zeitkomponente interessiert; man wird annehmen, daß kst monoton wachsend in diesen Komponenten ist. Überdies kann man ohne Einschränkung annehmen, daß kst nur natürliche Zahlen als Werte annimmt.

Die durch k begrenzten Möglichkeiten in der Motivation zu Df1 kann man sich ganz anschaulich als eine genau bestimmte Situation an einer konkreten Rechenanlage vorstellen. Df1 ist also auf eine bestimmte Situation bezogen. Eine effizienzmäßig bessere Prozedur soll sich aber nicht nur in einer bestimmten Situation, sondern in allen denkbaren Situationen bewähren. Es ist also naheliegend sich nicht nur auf *eine* Kostenschranke k, sondern auf einen Bereich $\{k : k1 \leq k \leq k2\}$, kurz $k1 - k2$, denkbarer Kostenschranken zu beziehen, was die folgende Definition ergibt:

Df2. $\quad P1 \triangleleft_{k1-k2} P2 \quad gdw$
$\quad\quad \exists k(k1 \leq k \leq k2 \wedge P1 \triangleleft_k P2) \wedge \forall k(k1 \leq k \leq k2 \wedge \neg P1 \triangleleft_k P2 \rightarrow P1 \bowtie_k P2)$

$\quad\quad P1 \bowtie_{k1-k2} P2 \quad gdw \quad \forall k(k1 \leq k \leq k2 \rightarrow P1 \bowtie_k P2)$

Im Spezialfall $k1 = k2$ geht Df2 in Df1 über; außerdem gilt:

Th1. $\quad$ Die Relation $\triangleleft_{k1-k2}$ ist transitiv, antisymmetrisch und antireflexiv. Die Relation $\bowtie_{k1-k2}$ ist eine Äquivalenzrelation.

Nun bringt eine Verbesserung einer Prozedur meist eine gewisse Komplizierung des Verfahrens mit sich, so daß durch eine zu niedrig angesetzte untere Bereichsgrenze $k1$ folgende Situation entstehen könnte. Eine bei allen höheren k's im Vergleich zu P1 effizientere Prozedur P2 ist für $k = k1$ außerstande, überhaupt noch etwas zu beweisen, während P1 dort ein paar triviale Theoreme gerade noch durchbringt. Solche Grenzfälle sind natürlich völlig uninteressant und sollen im folgenden durch geeignete Wahl von $k1$ ausgeschlossen sein. Durch entsprechende Normierung kann überdies $k1$ immer als 1 angenommen werden. — Andererseits wird sich das Effizienzverhalten über einen großen Bereich $1 - k2$ auch über $k2$ hinaus fortsetzen, so daß die Obergrenze als unbeschränkt angenommen werden kann. Für diesen Fall sei die kürzere Notation $P1 \triangleleft P2$ vorbehalten.

Eine Reihe von Varianten dieser Definitionen bieten sich an, unter denen die folgenden erwähnt seien.

a) In wenigen Fällen ist es ja doch möglich, Verbesserungen *ohne* jede Kostenerhöhung durchzuführen, was als P1 ◁◁ P2 gekennzeichnet sei. Dies ist dann eine schärfere Aussage und impliziert natürlich auch P1 ◁ P2.

b) Anstatt sich auf die konkreten Speicher- und Zeitkosten zu beziehen, wird es in den meisten Fällen zur Durchführung von Beweisen nötig sein, modellartige Kosten anzugeben, wie es z.B. in [3] mit der rm-size oder in [1] mit dem Grad durchgeführt wurde. Solche Ansätze ordnen sich also zwanglos der gegebenen allgemeinen Definition unter.

c) Bisher wurde davon ausgegangen, daß die betrachteten Verfahren vollständig und alle Theoreme $T \in \mathcal{T}$ gleichwahrscheinlich sind. In der Praxis dürften sich künftig aber, wie auch RABIN in [7] mutmaßt, gerade solche Verfahren bewähren, die diese Eigenschaften nicht haben. Die gegebenen Definitionen können aber natürlich statt für ganz $\mathcal{T}$ auch auf Teilklassen $\mathcal{T}1$ eingeführt werden; ja, sie gestatten auch, Prozeduren, die sich auf verschiedene Teilklassen "spezialisieren", miteinander zu vergleichen (P1|$\mathcal{T}1$ ◁ P2|$\mathcal{T}2$). Bei einer Gewichtung der Theoreme mit unterschiedlichen Wahrscheinlichkeiten darf man zum Vergleich nicht die Anzahl, sondern die Summe der Wahrscheinlichkeiten der unterhalb von k bewiesenen Theoreme heranziehen. Df1 erscheint dann als Spezialfall, in dem alle Wahrscheinlichkeit gleich 1 sind.

2. Vergleich zweier einfacher Verfahren

Mag die im ersten Abschnitt eingeführte Vergleichsmethode noch so plausibel erscheinen, so wird sie nur dann zu einer Klärung unter der verwirrenden Fülle von Beweisverfahren wesentlich beitragen, wenn sie auch konkret anwendbar ist, d.h. wenn entsprechende Beweise nicht an unüberwindlichen Schwierigkeiten scheitern. Deshalb soll sie in diesem Abschnitt exemplarisch an zwei ganz einfachen Verfahren erprobt werden, von denen das eine dem anderen die Prawitzsche dummy-Idee [5] voraus hat, deren Vorteil allgemein anerkannt ist. Die in diesem Abschnitt bewiesene Aussage ist daher inhaltlich keineswegs originell oder von besonderem Interesse. Und doch kennzeichnet es die Situation, daß man auch für so einfache Fälle in der Literatur keine genaueren Begründungen findet.

Eine Beschreibung der beiden Verfahren findet sich in [2], Abschnitt 2; sie werden dort SSG (ein "Standard-" oder auch "British-museum-Verfahren") und DSG (im wesentlichen das in [5] beschriebene Verfahren) genannt und sollen hier nur anhand eines Beispiels T erläutert werden. T sei das Theorem $\forall x \neg px \land \forall y \neg qy \lor \exists z(pz \lor qz)$.

Dem ersten Verfahren liegt eine Standardaufzählung aller Terme zugrunde. Der Einfachheit halber nehmen wir ohne Einschränkung an, daß keine Funktionszeichen auftreten. SSG betrachtet das äußerste logische Zeichen im äußersten Minimalteil von T, der nicht Literal ist, also das $\land$ in $\forall x \neg px \land \forall y \neg qy$. Eine solche Konjunktion reduziert das Problem zu zwei Unterproblemen, nämlich den Beweis von $\forall x \neg px \lor \exists z(pz \lor qz)$ und von $\forall y \neg qy \lor \exists z(pz \lor qz)$. Hiervon wird zunächst das erstere untersucht und wieder das äußerste logische Zeichen im äußersten Minimalteil, der nicht Literal ist, betrachtet. Jetzt ist dies eine Allquantifizierung $\forall x$; dies ergibt die Reduzierung zu $\neg pa_1 \lor \exists z(pz \lor qz)$, wobei für x die Variable mit dem kleinsten Index in der Abzählung eingesetzt wird, die bisher nicht auftrat. Wie vorher kommt nun $\exists z$ an die Reihe und führt zu $\neg pa_1 \lor (pa_1 \lor qa_1) \lor \exists z(pz \lor qz)$; wobei a_1 als der Term mit dem kleinsten Index in der Abzählung gewählt wird, der für diesen Minimalteil bisher noch nicht verwendet wurde. Diese Formel ist tautologisch, also ein Axiom und das Verfahren nimmt nunmehr das obige 2.Unterproblem $\forall y \neg qy \lor \exists z(pz \lor qz)$ in Angriff und kommt analog zum Ziel.

DSG verfährt ganz analog, nur wird im Falle eines Existenzquantors nicht ein bestimmter Term, sondern eine Variable d_1 über alle Terme (ein "dummy") eingesetzt, also im Beispiel $\neg pa_1 \lor (pd_1 \lor pd_1) \lor \exists z(pz \lor qz)$ und es wird erst im nachhinein geprüft, ob d_1 so bestimmt werden kann, daß die Formel tautologisch wird, was hier mit $d_1 = a_1$ möglich ist. Ein solches dummy kann aber wegen der bekannten Variablenbedingung nicht mit jeder Variablen identifiziert werden, nämlich mit genau denjenigen nicht, die erst *nach* dessen Einführung durch Allquantoren eingeführt wurden. DSG ist also komplizierter als SSG, da es noch zusätzlich eine Reihenfolge unter den Variablen und dummies speichern muß und da die Axiombestimmung damit aufwendiger wird. Trotzdem bringt DSG gegenüber SSG eine erhebliche Verbesserung mit sich. Sei nämlich a_n die n-te Variable in der Aufzählung, dann benötigt SSG zum Beweis von $\neg pa_n \lor \exists z(pz \lor qz)$ genau n Reduktionen, bis eine tautologische Formel $\neg pa_n \lor (pa_1 \lor qa_1) \lor \ldots \lor (pa_n \lor qa_n) \lor \exists z(pz \lor qz)$ entsteht, während DSG durch die Identifizierung $d = a_n$ schon nach einer Reduktion wie oben fertig ist. Es muß also gezeigt werden, daß dieser Vorteil von DSG den oben erwähnten Nachteil überwiegt.

Th2. SSG ◁ DSG .

Beweis. Es ist klar, daß wir Formeln, die sich nur in der Bezeichnung von Prädikats- oder gebundenen Objektvariablen unterscheiden, identifizieren können. Wir wollen uns beim Beweis der Einfachheit halber auf echt prädikatenlogische Theoreme beschränken, d.h. aussagenlogische und quasiaussagenlogische Theoreme wie $\forall x \, (px \lor \neg px)$ — also Formeln, die nach Streichung aller Quantoren eine tautologische Form haben, wobei ohne Einschränkung angenommen ist, daß deren Allquantoren alle *verschiedene* Variable und Existenzquantoren immer *dieselbe* Variable binden und keine Negationszeichen vor Quantoren stehen — außer acht lassen.

Mit diesen Vereinbarungen zeigen wir nun, daß für alle k gilt SSG $\trianglelefteq_k$ DSG, also eine stärkere Aussage als Th2. Sei k beliebig gewählt und seien T1, ..., Tn, n ≥ 0, genau diejenigen Theoreme, die mit SSG, aber nicht mit DSG bewiesen werden können. Ti (ai1,...,aimi) entstehe aus Ti durch Streichen der mi Allquantoren in Ti und Ersetzung der von ihnen gebundenen durch die entsprechenden freien Variablen ai1, ..., wobei i = 1, ..., n. Die neuen Formeln sind als Spezialisierungen wieder Theoreme. Wählt man für ai1, ..., genau die freien Variablen, die auch P1 in einem Beweis von Ti einsetzt, dann verläuft ein Beweis der neuen Theoreme mit P1 wie für die ursprünglichen, nur entfallen alle Reduktionen, die vorher von Allquantoren verursacht waren. Diese neuen Theoreme sind also ebenfalls mit P1 unterhalb k beweisbar. Sie sind es aber auch mit P2, da die Komplizierung von P2 gegenüber P1 durch das Streichen aller Allquantoren verschwindet.

Wenn man nun statt dieser speziellen Variablen solche mit höherem Index in Ti(ai1, ..., aimi) verwendet und dabei von dem Einfluß von ihren Bezeichnungen auf den Beweisaufwand (durch ihre Codierung) absieht, da dieser für beide Verfahren in *gleicher* Weise eingeht, so erhöht sich der Aufwand von P1, während derjenige von P2 konstant bleibt, wie es am obigen Beispiel illustriert wurde. Dieser Mehraufwand kann beliebig gesteigert werden, so daß schließlich mehr als n Theoreme der Form Ti (ai1, ..., aimi) erreicht werden, die unterhalb k mit P1 nicht mehr, mit P2 jedoch bewiesen werden. Im Falle n = 0 argumentiert man analog mit dem Theorem $\neg paj \lor \exists x \, px$.

3. Ausblicke auf weitere Anwendungen

Nach der in Abschnitt 2 vorgeführten exemplarischen Anwendung der in dieser Arbeit vorgeschlagenen Vergleichsmethode, sollen schließlich

noch einige weitere Anwendungen in gebotener Kürze angedeutet werden.
Dabei ist klar, daß man nach Verlassen der Standardmethode alle Bezeichnungsvarianten von Theoremen miteinander identifiziert.

Die nach SSG ◁ DSG nächstliegende Frage ist die nach einem Vergleich von DSG mit der in [1] beschriebenen semi-systematischen Prozedur (hier kurz SSP genannt). Während DSG das gegebene Theorem stur von links nach rechts reduziert, erreicht SSP bei den All- und Existenzquantoren eine optimale Reihenfolge der zugehörigen Reduktionen, wodurch sich für SSP eine zusätzliche Komplizierung, insgesamt aber eine Verbesserung ergibt, die im Vergleich z.B. zu Resolution-Verfahren in etwa der Verwendung von Skolem-Funktionen entspricht.

Das Theorem $\exists x_1 \forall y_1\, px_1 y_1 \vee \forall y_2 \exists x_2 ((\neg py_2 x_2 \vee \exists x_3 \exists x_4 \neg px_3 x_4) \wedge \exists x_5 \neg px_2 x_5)$, kurz $A \vee B$, kann diese Situation illustrieren. Nach erstmaliger Reduktion der All- und Existenzquantoren und der Konjunktion, vergleicht DSG Literal L_1 (Zählung von links nach rechts in $A \vee B$) ohne Erfolg mit L_2, dann erfolgreich L_1 mit L_3 und L_1 mit L_4, insgesamt also 3 Vergleiche. SSP geht analog vor, ist nun aber beim Vergleich L_1 mit L_2 erfolgreich, scheitert damit jedoch bei L_1 und L_4, um schließlich ebenfalls mit L_1, L_3 und L_1, L_4 durchzukommen, mit insgesamt 4 Vergleichen.

Der Vorteil von SSP zeigt sich erst bei einer sogenannten Strukturvariante dieses Theorems, nämlich bei $B \vee A$. Hier ist DSG erst nach weiteren Reduktionen und insgesamt 22 Vergleichen erfolgreich, während SSP unverändert 4 Vergleiche durchzuführen hat. Dieses Beispiel deutet bereits die Grundidee an, die bei einem Beweis der folgenden Aussage Verwendung findet.

Th3.   DSG ◁ SSP

Und zwar geht man in analoger Weise wie beim Beweis von Th2 vor. Zu gegebenem k werden die Theoreme $T_1, \ldots, T_n$, die von DSG, nicht aber von SSP unterhalb k bewiesen werden, ohne Veränderung der Tautologiegraphen [7], die die zugrundeliegende tautologische Struktur widerspiegeln, so vereinfacht, daß die Komplizierung von SSP gegenüber DSG nicht mehr zum Tragen kommt (im obigen Beispiel würde dies eine Streichung von L_2 bedeuten). Ohne diese beiden Eigenschaften (gleiche Tautologiegraphen und Wegfall der Komplizierung) können diese Theoreme dann in trivialer Weise so zu $T_1, \ldots, T_n$ aufgebläht werden, daß sie für SSP unterhalb k gerade noch beweisbar sind. Für DSG gilt dann: Ti' oder eine Strukturvariante (vgl. obiges Beispiel) davon ist unterhalb k nicht mehr beweisbar, $i = 1, \ldots, n$.

In [2] ist eine weiter verbesserte Prozedur PRV beschrieben, für die SSP ◁ PRV vermutlich ähnlich zu beweisen ist. Allerdings dürften diese Beweise im Detail bereits erheblichen Umfang annehmen. Das Interesse konzentriert sich daher augenblicklich mehr auf die viel interessantere Frage, wie sich PRV in Bezug auf Effizienz im Vergleich zu den populären Resolution-Methoden verhält. Partielle Ergebnisse hierüber finden sich in [7] und [2]. Sie fügen sich ebenso zwanglos in den in dieser Arbeit gegebenen Rahmen wie die bereits im ersten Abschnitt erwähnten Ansätze anderer Autoren.

Es besteht daher Grund zur Hoffnung, daß die hier präsentierte Vergleichsmethode eine beschleunigende und vereinheitlichende Wirkung auf die Bemühungen ausübt, in die Fülle vorhandener Beweisverfahren eine gewisse Ordnung zu bringen, daß sie vielleicht sogar einen Ansatz zu einer "general theory of efficiency applicable to actual procedures" [4] darstellt. Ihre Anwendbarkeit wäre nicht auf Beweisverfahren beschränkt, sondern ließe sich offenbar auf andere Gebiete übertragen; das Gebiet der Formelmanipulation sei dafür als beliebig gewähltes Beispiel angeführt.

Literaturverzeichnis

[1] Bibel, W.: An approach to a systematic theorem proving procedure in first-order logic. Computing 12, 43-55 (1974).

[2] Bibel, W. und Schreiber J.: Proof search in a Gentzen-like system of first-order logic. Bericht Nr.7412, Abteilung Mathematik, TU München.

[3] Kowalski, R. und Kuehner, D.: Linear resolution with selection function. Artificial Intelligence 2, 227-260 (1971).

[4] Loveland, D.W.: A unifying view of some linear Herbrand procedures. JACM 19, 366-384 (1972).

[5] Prawitz, D.: An improved proof procedure. Theoria 26, 102-139 (1960).

[6] Rabin, M.O.: Theoretical impediments to artificial intelligence. Preprints IFIP Congress 74, 615-619.

[7] Schreiber, J.: Vergleichende qualitative und quantitative Untersuchungen von Beweisverfahren. Bericht Nr.7411, Abteilung Mathematik, TU München.

DREI KOMPLEXITÄTSMASSE ZWEISTUFIGER NORMALFORMEN BOOLESCHER FUNKTIONEN[†]

Wolfgang Coy, Technische Hochschule Darmstadt

1. GRUNDLEGENDE DEFINITIONEN

Ausgangspunkt der Untersuchung ist ein Satz von O.B.LUPANOW, der hier in abgeschwächter Form angegeben wird:

Satz 1
Zu jeder gegebenen, in allen 2^n Variablen wesentlichen Funktion $F:B^{2^n} \to B$ können 2^n (n+1)-stellige Funktionen $f_1,\ldots f_{2^n}$ konstruiert werden, so daß jede n-stellige Funktion $f(X)$ mit $X = <x_1,\ldots x_n>$ in der Form

$$f(X) = F(f_1(X,f(0,\ldots 0)), f_2(X,f(0,\ldots 0,1)),\ldots f_{2^n}(X,f(1,\ldots 1)))$$

darstellbar ist.

Einen Beweis des Satzes findet man in |4|.

Definition 1
Genügen die 2^n-stellige Funktion F und die 2^n (n+1)-stelligen Funktionen $f_1,\ldots f_{2^n}$ dem obigen Satz, so heißt $<F;f_1,\ldots f_{2^n}>$ eine zweistufige Normalform-Zerlegung.

Um zum Begriff der zweistufigen Normalform zu gelangen, werden zunächst die mehrstelligen Gatter definiert:

Definition 2
i) Eine Funktion $f:B^n \to B$ heißt Junktionsfunktion <u>gdw</u> γ und γ_i aus B existieren, so daß für alle Tupel $<\tau_1,\ldots \tau_{i-1},\tau_{i+1},\ldots \tau_n>$ und $<\sigma_1,\ldots \sigma_{i-1},\sigma_{i+1},\ldots \sigma_n>$ aus B^{n-1} mit $1 \leq i \leq n$ gilt:
$f(\tau_1,\ldots \tau_{i-1},\gamma_i,\tau_{i+1},\ldots \tau_n) = f(\sigma_1,\ldots \sigma_{i-1},\gamma_i,\sigma_{i+1},\ldots \sigma_n) = \gamma$.
Gilt für alle i die Beziehung $\gamma = \gamma_i$, dann heißt f reine Junktion.

ii) Eine Funktion $f:B^n \to B$ heißt Linearfunktion <u>gdw</u> für alle Tupel $<\tau_1,\ldots \tau_{i-1},\tau_{i+1},\ldots \tau_n>$ aus B^{n-1} mit $1 \leq i \leq n$ gilt:
$f(\tau_1,\ldots \tau_{i-1},0,\tau_{i+1},\ldots \tau_n) \neq f(\tau_1,\ldots \tau_{i-1},1,\tau_{i+1},\ldots \tau_n)$.

iii) Ein Schaltkreis S, der eine n-stellige Junktionsfunktion g realisiert, heißt n-stelliges Junktionsgatter (der Art g); ein Schalt- S, der eine n-stellige Linearfunktion h realisiert, heißt n-stelliges

---
[†] Bei der Untersuchung handelt es sich um einen Auszug einer Arbeit, die dem Fachbereich Informatik der Technischen Hochschule Darmstadt als Dissertation vorgelegt ist. Als Gutachter sind Prof.Dr.G.Hotz, Saarbrücken, Prof.Dr.-Ing. R.Piloty, Darmstadt und Prof.Dr. H.Walter, Darmstadt, bestellt worden.

Lineargatter (der Art h).

Offensichtlich gibt es für jedes n genau zwei n-stellige Linearfunktionen, nämlich $f_{L1}(x_1,\ldots x_n) = x_1 \oplus x_2 \oplus \ldots \oplus x_n$ und $f_{L2} = \overline{f_{L1}}$ und genau zwei reine Junktionsfunktionen, nämlich $f_{J1}(x_1,\ldots x_n) = x_1 \vee x_2 \vee \ldots \vee x_n$ für $\gamma=1$ und $f_{J2}(x_1,\ldots x_n) = x_1 \wedge x_2 \wedge \ldots \wedge x_n$ für $\gamma=0$. Weiterhin gibt es zwei Klassen von Junktionsfunktionen, nämlich: $f(x_1,\ldots x_n) = x_1^{\sigma_1} \vee \ldots \vee x_n^{\sigma_n}$ und $f(x_1,\ldots x_n) = x_1^{\sigma_1} \wedge \ldots \wedge x_n^{\sigma_n}$, die durch geeignete Komplementierung der Eingänge $x_1,\ldots x_n$ auf die reinen Junktionen zurückgeführt werden können.

Mit Hilfe der in Definition 2 beschriebenen mehrstelligen Gatter können nun die zweistufigen Normalformen definiert werden:

Definition 3
Eine zweistufige Normalform-Zerlegung $N = \langle F; f_1,\ldots f_{2^n} \rangle$ heißt zweistufige Normalform N gdw die Funktionen F und $f_1,\ldots f_{2^n}$ durch mehrstellige Junktions- oder Lineargatter realisierbar sind.

Zur Bestimmung zweistufiger Normalformen gilt der folgende Hilfssatz:

Hilfssatz 1
Sei $N = \langle F; f_1,\ldots f_{2^n} \rangle$ eine zweistufige Normalform; es gilt für $1 \leq i \leq n$:

i) Ist F eine Junktion, dann sind auch die f_i Junktionen.
ii) Ist F linear, dann sind die f_i Junktionen.

Der Beweis folgt im Fall i) aus der Notwendigkeit, mit einer durch γ charakterisierten Junktion F auch die durch $\bar{\gamma}$ charakterisierten Junktionen darstellen zu müssen. Im Fall ii) folgt der Beweis aus der Forderung, daß eine vollständige Basis logischer Funktionen mindestens eine nicht-lineare Funktion enthalten muß (vgl. |4|).

2. DREI KOMPLEXITÄTSMASSE

Es werden drei Maße der Komplexität zweistufiger Normalformen definiert und ihr Verhältnis zueinander untersucht.

Definition 4
Die Funktion $f: B^n \to B$ werde in der Normalform $N = \langle F; f_1,\ldots f_{2^n} \rangle$ durch den Schaltkreis $S_N(f)$ realisiert. Die Zahl der in $S_N(f)$ verwendeten mehrstelligen Gatter heißt Gatter-Komplexität $\Psi(S_N(f))$ des Schaltkreises

$S_N(f)$. Die Gatter-Komplexität $\Psi_N(f)$ der Funktion f in der Normalform N ist gleich dem Minimum der Gatter-Komplexitäten $\Psi(S_N^i(f))$ aller Schaltkreise $S_N^i(f)$, die die Funktion f in der Normalform N realisieren.

Dieses Komplexitätsmaß Ψ ist invariant gegen die Negation einzelner Leitungen (d.h. Negationsglieder verändern die Gatter-Komplexität nicht); es lassen sich drei Klassen gleich komplexer Normalformen (relativ zu Ψ) charakterisieren:

Definition 5
Eine Normalform $N_1 = \langle F; f_1, \ldots f_{2^n}\rangle$ heißt gleich komplex wie die Normalform $N_2 = \langle G; g_1, \ldots g_{2^n}\rangle$ <u>gdw</u> für alle $f: B^n \to B$ gilt: $\Psi_{N_1}(f) = \Psi_{N_2}(f)$.

Man sieht leicht, daß es genau drei Klassen gleich komplexer, zweistufiger Normalformen gibt:

Lemma 1
Es gibt genau drei Klassen gleich komplexer, zweistufiger Normalformen logischer Funktionen $f: B^n \to B$, die repräsentiert werden durch:

i) die kanonische disjunktive Normalform mit der Darstellung
$$f(x_1, \ldots x_n) = \bigvee_{i_1=0}^{1} \ldots \bigvee_{i_2=0}^{1} x_1^{i_1} \wedge \ldots \wedge x_n^{i_n} \wedge f(i_1, \ldots i_n);$$

ii) die kanonische konjunktive Normalform mit der Darstellung
$$f(x_1, \ldots x_n) = \bigwedge_{i_1=0}^{1} \bigwedge_{i_2=0}^{1} x^{i_1} \vee \ldots \vee x^{i_n} \vee f(i_1, \ldots i_n);$$

iii) die Polynomial-Normalform mit der Darstellung
$$f(x_1, \ldots x_n) = c_0 \oplus c_1 \wedge x_1 \oplus \ldots \oplus c_{n+1} \wedge x_1 \wedge x_2 \oplus \ldots c_{n(n+1)/2} \wedge x_{n-1} \wedge x_n \oplus$$
$$\oplus c_{n(n+1)/2+1} \wedge x_1 \wedge x_2 \wedge x_3 \oplus \ldots \oplus c_{2^n-1} \wedge x_1 \wedge \ldots \wedge x_n$$

Zum Beweis ist zu beachten, daß F stets als reine Junktion oder als Linearfunktion aufgefasst werden kann.

Über den Begriff des Schaltfehlers lassen sich zwei weitere Komplexitätsmaße definieren, die in der einschlägigen Literatur (vgl. |2|,|3|) geläufig sind. Es handelt sich um die Test-Komplexität der Einzelfehler (engl. *single faults*) und um die Test-Komplexität der Mehrfachfehler (engl. *multiple faults*).

Definition 6

i) Wird die Übertragungsfunktion $f:B^n \to B$ eines Schaltkreises $S_N(f)$ aus der zweistufigen Normalform N durch eine physikalisch-technische Störung H in die Funktion $f_H(x_1,\ldots x_n) \neq f(x_1,\ldots x_n)$ verwandelt, so heißt H logischer Fehler von $S_N(f)$;

ii) ist H dadurch erklärbar, daß genau eine Leitung in $S_N(f)$ den konstanten Wert k=0 oder k=1 annimmt, so heißt H Einzelfehler der Leitungen in $S_N(f)$ und zwar s-a-0-Fehler für k=0 und s-a-1-Fehler für k=1;

iii) ist H dadurch erklärbar, daß eine oder mehrere Leitungen in $S_N(f)$ einen (jeweils) konstanten Wert k=0 oder k=1 annehmen, so ist H ein Mehrfachfehler der Leitungen in $S_N(f)$;

iv) jedes n-Tupel $t = <\tau_1,\ldots\tau_n>$ mit $f_H(t) \neq f(t)$ heißt Test t von H in $S_N(f)$;

v) die minimale Anzahl von Tests zur Entdeckung aller Einzelfehler eines Schaltkreises $S_N(f)$ heißt Test-Komplexität $\phi_s(S_N(f))$ der Einzelfehler;

vi) die minimale Anzahl von Tests zur Entdeckung aller Mehrfachfehler eines Schaltkreises $S_N(f)$ heißt Test-Komplexität $\phi_m(S_N(f))$ der Mehrfachfehler.

3. EINIGE AUSSAGEN ZUR KOMPLEXITÄT ZWEISTUFIGER NORMALFORMEN

Zuerst wird der Begriff der Test-Komplexität für mehrstellige Gatter untersucht. Dann werden die Begriffe Gatter-Komplexität und Test-Komplexität für die zweistufigen Normalformen untersucht und zueinander in Beziehung gesetzt.

3.1 DIE TEST-KOMPLEXITÄT MEHRSTELLIGER GATTER

Für die Junktionsgatter gilt eine einfache Aussage:

Lemma 2
Für jedes n-stellige Junktionsgatter $G(f)$ gilt: $\phi_s(G(f)) = \phi_m(G(f)) = n+1$.
Beweis:
Man sieht leicht, daß die folgende Testmenge bezüglich der Entdeckung aller Einzelfehler der Eingangsleitungen und der Ausgangsleitung von $G(f)$ vollständig und minimal ist:

i) für $1 \leq j \leq n$: $t_j = \{<\tau_1,\ldots\tau_n>|\tau_j=\gamma_j$ und für alle $i \neq j$ mit $1 \leq i \leq n$: $\tau_i=\bar{\gamma}_i\}$
und

ii) $t_{n+1} = \{<\tau_1,\ldots\tau_n>|\tau_i=\bar{\gamma}_i$ für alle $1 \leq i \leq n\}$.

Die Testmenge $T = \{t_1, \ldots t_{n+1}\}$ entdeckt auch alle Mehrfachfehler. Enthält der Mehrfachfehler M einen Einzelfehler der Ausgangsleitung ist die Behauptung trivial. Enthält M einen s-a-γ_i-Fehler der Eingangsleitung x_i, dann entdeckt t_{n+1} diesen Fehler; enthält M keinen s-a-γ_i-Fehler, aber einen s-a-$\bar{\gamma}_i$-Fehler der Leitung x_i, dann entdeckt t_i den Mehrfachfehler M.

Lemma 3
Für alle n-stelligen EXOR-Gatter G gilt:
i) $\quad \Phi_s(G) = \begin{cases} 2 & \text{wenn n ungerade ist} \\ 3 & \text{sonst} \end{cases}$

ii) $\quad \Phi_m(G) = n+1$.

Beweis:
Offensichtlich genügen im Fall einer ungeraden Zahl von Eingängen die beiden Tests "alle Eingänge null" und "alle Eingänge eins", während im Fall einer geraden Zahl von Eingängen noch der Test "eine ungerade Zahl von Eingängen eins" zum Test des Gatterausgangs benötigt wird. Der Beweis von ii) kann |1| entnommen werden.

3.2 DIE GATTER-KOMPLEXITÄT ZWEISTUFIGER NORMALFORMEN

Lässt man Normalform-Darstellungen von Funktionen allein in der nach Definition 3 festgelegten Weise zu, so gibt es trivialerweise stets Funktionen mit exponentieller Gatter-Komplexität. In der Praxis werden natürlich möglichst viele Kürzungen der Gatter-Zahl vorgenommen, etwa durch Anwendung der Absorptionsregel (aVab) = a in der kanonischen, disjunktiven Normalform. Es sollen deshalb alle möglichen Kürzungen beim Schaltkreis-Entwurf mit zweistufigen Normalformen zulässig sein. Lässt eine Normalform $N = \langle F; f_1, \ldots f_{2^n} \rangle$ Kürzungen zu, so kann kein f_i-Gatter mehr als 2^n verschiedene Zustände seiner Eingangsleitungen $x_1, \ldots x_n$ annehmen, da jeder Eingang x_i entweder wesentlich oder nicht wesentlich für die realisierte Funktion f_i sein kann. Es ergeben sich also maximal $(2^n)^k$ verschiedene Schaltkreis-Darstellungen mit Hilfe der Gatter $S(F)$ und $S(f_1), \ldots S(f_k)$ (die die Funktionen $F, f_1, \ldots f_k$ realisieren) in N. Tatsächlich sind nicht alle diese Darstellungen verwendbar, da die Anwendung einer Kürzungsregel auf ein Gatter $S(f_i)$ im allgemeinen nicht unabhängig von den übrigen Gattern erfolgt; da aber im wesentlichen die Ordnung der Gatter-Komplexität untersucht werden soll, wird diese grobe Vereinfachung vorgenommen. Es folgt:

Lemma 4

Ist $N = \langle F; f_1, \ldots f_{2^n}\rangle$ eine zweistufige Normalform, dann gibt es für jedes rationale q mit $0 \leq q < 1$ von einem hinreichend großen n an mindestens $q \cdot 2^{2^n}$ n-stellige Funktionen mit $\Psi_N(f) > \frac{1}{n}(2^n + \text{ld}(1-q))$.

Beweis:
$(1-q) \cdot 2^{2^n}$ der 2^{2^n} darzustellenden n-stelligen Funktionen seien mit $\Psi_N(f) \leq x$ realisierbar. Ist x minimal, so stehen zur Realisierung der $(1-q) \cdot 2^{2^n}$ Funktionen nicht mehr als $(2^n)^x$ verschiedene Schaltkreise zur Verfügung. Aus $(2^n)^x \geq (1-q) \cdot 2^{2^n}$ folgt dann: $x \geq \frac{1}{n}(2^n + \text{ld}(1-q))$. Demnach müssen zumindest $q \cdot 2^{2^n}$ n-stellige Funktionen mit der Gatter-Komplexität $\Psi_N(f) > \frac{1}{n}(2^n + \text{ld}(1-q))$ realisiert werden. Dieser Ausdruck wird für ein hinreichend großes n bei festem q mit $0 \leq q < 1$ stets positiv.

Dieses Ergebnis lässt sich auf alle drei Klassen gleich komplexer Normalformen erweitern:

Satz 2

Es gibt für jedes rationale q mit $0 \leq q < 1$ von einem hinreichend großen n an mindestens $q \cdot 2^{2^n}$ n-stellige Funktionen, für die in allen zweistufigen Normalformen N_i gilt: $\Psi_{N_i}(f) > \frac{1}{n}(2^n + \text{ld}(1-q) - \text{ld}(3))$.

Beweis:
Der Beweis folgt direkt aus dem Beweis des vorhergehenden Lemmas und aus Lemma 1.

3.3 DIE TEST-KOMPLEXITÄT DER EINZELFEHLER IN ZWEISTUFIGEN NORMALFORMEN

Da die Gatter-Komplexität die Zahl der Eingänge des S(F)-Gatters in der Normalform $N = \langle F; f_1, \ldots f_{2^n}\rangle$ bestimmt, folgt direkt, daß Normalformen aus Junktionsgattern stets Funktionen mit exponentieller Test-Komplexität der Einzelfehler enthalten:

Lemma 5

Ist $N = \langle F; f_1, \ldots f_{2^n}\rangle$ eine zweistufige Normalform mit der Junktionsfunktion F, so gilt für alle Funktionen $f: B^n \to B$: $\Phi_S(S_N(f)) \geq \Psi_N(f)$.

Der Beweis folgt aus Lemma 2. Es gilt aber:

Satz 3

Es gibt für jede logische Funktion $f: B^n \to B$ eine Schaltkreis-Darstellung $S(f)$ in der Polynomial-Normalform mit $\Phi_S(S(f)) \leq 3n+2$.

Beweis:

Die Konstante c_0 der Polynomial-Normalform kann durch ein Negationsglied am Schaltkreis-Ausgang ersetzt werden. Der Beweis wird dann in drei Abschnitten geführt:

i) Es wird gezeigt, daß die 2^n-1 Konjunktionsgatter mit n+1 Tests vollständig testbar sind.

ii) Es wird gezeigt, daß für die n Eingangsleitungen eine vollständige Testmenge mit höchstens 2n Tests konstruierbar ist.

iii) Es wird gezeigt, daß für das Lineargatter eine vollständige Testmenge mit 3 Tests erzeugt werden kann.

zu i) Da alle Konjunktionsgatter nur nicht-negierte Leitungen besitzen, ist die im Beweis von Lemma 2 angegebene n+1-elementige Testmenge für das Gatter mit der vollen Konjunktion $x_1 \wedge ... \wedge x_n$ auch vollständige Testmenge aller Konjunktionsgatter des Schaltkreises S(f).

zu ii) Man betrachte die Leitung x_i ($1 \leq i \leq n$). Die Konjunktionsgatter K_j sollen den Index j tragen, der der Konstanten c_j der Konjunktion in der Polynomial-Normalform nach Lemma 1,iii entspricht. Sei K_m das Konjunktionsgatter mit dem niedrigsten Index m unter denjenigen Gattern, in die x_i mündet. Setzt man alle Eingänge von K_m (außer x_i) auf den Wert eins und alle anderen Eingangsleitungen auf den Wert null, so wird der Zustand von x_i, wie man leicht sieht, allein über das Gatter K_m zum Schaltkreisausgang übertragen. Mit $x_i=1$ und $x_i=0$ ergeben sich die gesuchten Tests. Für n Leitungen sind also 2n Tests konstruierbar.

zu iii) Nach Lemma 3 genügen maximal drei Tests zur vollständigen Einzelfehler-Erkennung bei Lineargattern. Die beiden Tests "alle Eingänge null" und "alle Eingänge eins" werden durch die Belegung "alle x_i null" bzw. "alle x_i eins" der Schaltkreis-Eingänge $x_1, ... x_n$ erreicht. Dabei ist der letzte Test schon unter i) durchgeführt worden. Schließlich wird noch das Konjunktionsgatter K_m mit dem niedrigsten Index m an allen Eingängen mit dem Wert eins belegt, während alle anderen Eingangsleitungen mit dem Wert null belegt werden; dies erzeugt den dritten Test "eine ungerade Anzahl von Eingängen eins". Dieser Test ist schon unter ii) durchgeführt worden. Man sieht, daß mit einem zusätzlichen Test das Lineargatter vollständig getestet wird.

Es folgt die Behauptung.

3.4 DIE MEHRFACHFEHLER-TESTKOMPLEXITÄT ZWEISTUFIGER NORMALFORMEN

Die Einzelfehler-Testkomplexität ließ sich im Fall der Polynomial-Normalform als im wesentlichen unabhängig von der Gatter-Komplexität zeigen. Im Fall der Mehrfachfehler-Testkomplexität gilt:

Lemma 6
Ist $N = \langle F; f_1, \ldots f_{2^n} \rangle$ eine (beliebige) zweistufige Normalform, dann gilt
für alle Funktionen f: $\Phi_m(S_N(f)) \geq \Psi_N(f)$, unabhängig von der speziellen
Wahl des Schaltkreises $S_N(f)$.

Der Beweis folgt aus Lemma 5 und Lemma 3, da zum vollständigen Test des
Gatters S(F) stets $\Phi_m(S(F)) \geq \Psi_N(f)$ Tests benötigt werden.

Es folgt:

Satz 4
Für jede rationale Zahl q mit $0 \leq q < 1$ gibt es von einem hinreichend großen
n an mindestens $q \cdot 2^{2^n}$ Funktionen $f: B^n \to B$, für die in allen Normalformen
N gilt: $\Phi_m(S_N(f)) \geq \frac{1}{n}(2^n + \text{ld}(1-q) - \text{ld}(3))$, unabhängig von der Wahl
des Schaltkreises $S_N(f)$.

Der Beweis folgt mit dem vorstehenden Lemma direkt aus Satz 2. Damit wurde gezeigt, daß die Gatter-Komplexität zweistufiger Normalformen eine untere Schranke der Mehrfachfehler-Komplexität bildet und daß somit bei wachsendem n ein immer grösserer Anteil der Funktionen $f: B^n \to B$ nur mit exponentieller Komplexität (bezüglich n) in irgendeiner zweistufigen Normalform realisierbar ist. Im Falle mehrstufiger Schaltkreise gilt dieses Ergebnis nicht (vgl. |1|).

4. ZUSAMMENFASSUNG UND AUSBLICK

Es wurden drei Komplexitätsmaße kombinatorischer Schaltkreise in zweistufiger Normalform-Darstellung untersucht. Dabei zeigte sich, daß die meisten Funktionen in dieser Darstellung sowohl exponentielle Gatter-Komplexität wie auch exponentielle Mehrfachfehler-Testkomplexität (relativ zur Zahl der Eingangsvariablen) besitzen. Dies ist auch nicht durch eine geschickte Wahl der jeweiligen Normalform zu verhindern. Bei der Einzelfehler-Testkomplexität ließ sich dagegen eine Normalform, nämlich die Polynomial-Normalform auszeichnen. In ihr lassen sich alle Funktionen mit linearer Test-Komplexität darstellen. Die Ergebnisse sind weitgehend auf zweistufige Normalform-Zerlegungen, wie sie durch den Satz von LUPANOW beschrieben werden, erweitern (vgl. |1|).

An dieser Stelle möchte ich H.Walter für seine Anregungen, sein Verständnis und seine Hilfe danken, die er mir während der Zeit der Ausarbeitung dieser Ideen zukommen ließ. Ebenso möchte ich meinen Kollegen und den

Studenten der Forschungsgruppe Automatentheorie und formale Sprachen an der TH Darmstadt danken.

LITERATUR

|1| Wolfgang Coy, Die Testkomplexität von Schaltkreisen, als Dissertation dem Fachbereich Informatik der Technischen Hochschule Darmstadt eingereicht, Juli 1974.

|2| A.D. Friedman / P.R. Menon, Fault Detection in Digital Circuits, Englewood Cliffs, 1971.

|3| J.P.Hayes, On realizations of boolean functions requiring a minimal or near-minimal number of tests, IEEE Trans. on Comp., Vol. C-20, No. 12, Dez. 1971, pp. 1506-1513.

|4| N.E.Kobrinski / B.A.Trachtenbrot, Einführung in die Theorie endlicher Automaten, Berlin(DDR), 1967.

3. PROGRAMMIERSPRACHEN UND COMPILER

IMPLEMENTIERUNG VON PROGRAMMIERSPRACHEN
J. KLONK und H.A. SCHMID

F. KRÖGER

ZWEIDIMENSIONALE SPRACHEN
H.J. SCHNEIDER

E. DENERT, R. FRANCK, W. STRENG

PARSER-ORIENTIERTE METHODEN
H.H. KRON, H.-J. HOFFMANN, G. WINKLER

H. FEUERHAHN

C.H.A. KOSTER

CODE-OPTIMIERUNG
D. NEEL, M. AMIRCHAHY, M. MAZAUD

R. WILHELM

IMPLEMENTIERUNGS- UND OPTIMIERUNGSTECHNIKEN
J. MARTIN, Ch. FLOYD, R. NAGEL, P. SCHNUPP, O. WÖRZ

H. ROTH

Zwei BASIC - Systeme von unterschiedlicher Struktur - Ein Vergleich
ihrer Benutzerfreundlichkeit und Effizienz

Jürgen Klonk und Hans Albrecht Schmid[*]
Fakultät für Informatik, Universität Karlsruhe

1. Einleitung

In dieser Arbeit werden zwei BASIC-Systeme von unterschiedlicher Struktur in Bezug auf ihre Benutzerfreundlichkeit und Effizienz verglichen. Beide Systeme sind auf der Burroughs B6700 der Fakultät für Informatik an der Universität Karlsruhe implementiert.

Das von Burroughs gelieferte System (im folgenden "BBASIC" genannt) besteht aus dem interaktiven Kommando und Text-Editing-System CANDE und einem BASIC-Compiler [1]. Mit Hilfe von CANDE wird eine Programm-(text-) Datei interaktiv erstellt und abgeändert. Dabei sammelt CANDE die einzelnen Eingaben eines Benutzers in eine für alle Benutzer gemeinsame Pufferzone; erst nach gewissen Kommandos (wie z.B. Übersetzen, oder auch umnumerieren des Programmes) werden diese Eingaben in die Programmdatei des Benutzers eingearbeitet. Vor einer Ausführung wird das auf der Programmdatei befindliche Programm vom BASIC-Compiler geschlossen übersetzt. Er erzeugt - ebenso wie im Stapelbetrieb verwendete Compiler - Maschinencode, bei dessen Ausführung keinerlei Benutzereingriffe möglich sind. Wie aus dieser kurzen Beschreibung hervorgeht, kann die Arbeitsweise dieses Systems als charakteristisch für den Großteil der heute verfügbaren Dialogsysteme betrachtet werden.

Das zweite BASIC-System (im folgenden "CBASIC" genannt) ist ein inkrementelles System und wurde von den Verfassern dieser Arbeit implementiert (siehe [7]). In diesem experimentellen System sind die Funktionen des Text-Editing, der Kompilierung, der Ausführung und des Debugging integriert. Seine Struktur ist speziell auf den Dialogbetrieb zugeschnitten und dessen Erfordernissen angepaßt. Die strukturellen Prinzipien, nach denen dieses System aufgebaut ist, sind erstmals in [9] beschrieben. In [10] wird theoretisch nachgewiesen, daß Systeme dieser Art die Vorteile kompilierender Systeme (Effizienz von Programmausführungen) und interpretierender Systeme (Benutzerfreundlichkeit und Effizienz bei Programmänderungen) verbinden. In dieser Arbeit soll nun untersucht werden, ob diese in der Theorie nachgewiesenen Vorteile auch in der Praxis vorhanden sind.

---

[*] jetzt: Department of Computer Science, University of Toronto, Toronto

2. Struktur des CBASIC-Systems

Das CBASIC-System hat eine einheitliche Dialogsprache, die sich aus den Anweisungen der Programmiersprache BASIC und aus Kommandos wie "Execute", "Resume", "List", "Save" usw. zusammensetzt. Die Sprache BASIC wurde in gewissen Punkten erweitert; so können z.B. Bezeichner beliebige Länge haben und als Marken gesetzt werden.

Zeilen können direkt oder indirekt eingegeben werden. Indirekt eingegebene Zeilen werden entsprechend ihrer Zeilennummer in das Programm eingefügt; direkt eingegebene Zeilen beginnen mit einem Fluchtsymbol und werden unmittelbar ausgeführt. Bei den meisten Zeilentypen ist entweder nur direkte oder indirekte Eingabe sinnvoll, bei einigen jedoch (wie z.B. "Let" oder "Print") sind beide Arten zulässig.

Wegen der inkrementellen Arbeitsweise des Systems wird zwischen der Korrektheit einer einzelnen Zeile ("lokale Syntax") und der des gesamten Programmes ("globale Korrektheit") unterschieden. Zur globalen Korrektheit gehören in BASIC die richtige Anordnung der FOR-NEXT-Zeilen und die konsistente Benutzung von Marken und Variablen.

Die lokale Syntax einer Zeile wird - auch bei indirekter Eingabe - unmittelbar nach der Eingabe überprüft. Inkorrekte Zeilen werden abgelehnt, und die Kontrolle wird an den Benutzer zurückgegeben. Korrekte Zeilen werden nicht in Textform gespeichert, sondern der Inhalt einer Zeile wird durch den Eingabeverarbeitungsmodul aufgespalten und in die Programmkontrolltafel ("PKT") und den Pseudocodebereich ("PC") eingetragen (vergleiche Abb. auf der folgenden Seite).

- Ein PKT-Eintrag enthält die Zeilennummer, den Zeilentyp, einen Zeiger auf den PKT-Eintrag mit der nächstgrößeren Zeilennummer und zwei Zeiger auf die zugehörigen Pseudocode- und Codestücke. Die Programmkontrolltafel enthält also die gesamte Information über die Struktur des erstellten Programmes.
- Der Pseudocode stellt eine verschlüsselte Form des Eingabetextes dar. Die Infixform ist beibehalten, aber alle Bezeichner sind durch Verweise auf die Variablentabelle ("VTAB") ersetzt. Dadurch ist der Quelltext leicht aus dem Pseudocode rekonstruierbar, und zu seiner Weiterverarbeitung ist keine lexikalische und Syntax-Analyse mehr erforderlich.

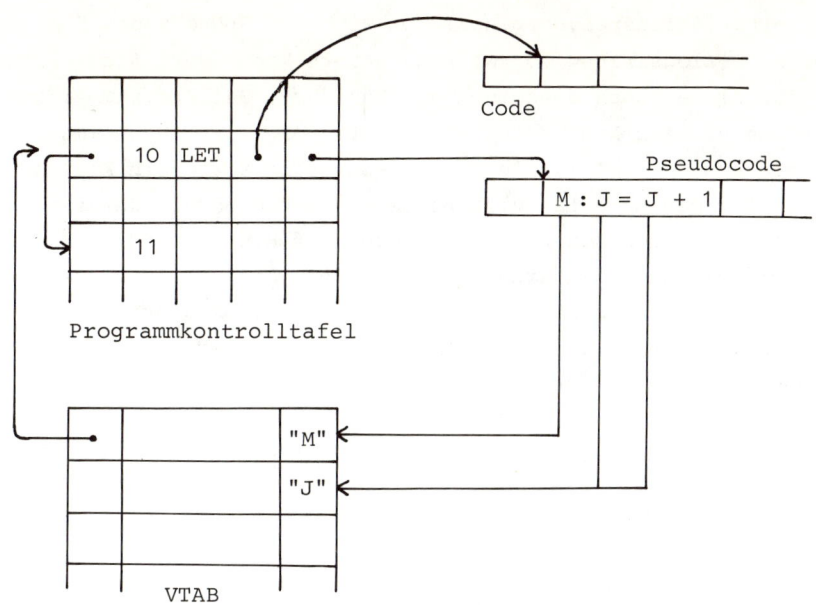

Bei der Eingabe eines "Execute"- oder "Resume"-Kommandos oder einer direkten BASIC-Zeile wird der Ausführungsmodul aufgerufen; erst jetzt wird die globale Korrektheit des Programmes überprüft. (Direkt eingegebene BASIC-Zeilen werden dabei als einzeilige Programme aufgefaßt.)

Bei der Ausführung wird der Übergang von einer Zeile zur nächsten interpretiert; die Codestücke, die den einzelnen Zeilen entsprechen, werden jedoch direkt ausgeführt. Jedes Codestück endet mit einem Sprung in einen - je nach Zeilentyp verschiedenen - Eingang des Kontrollinterpretierers. Der Index auf die laufende Zeile, den der Kontrollinterpretierer führt, wird entsprechend weitergeschaltet, und es wird mit Hilfe des Zeigers auf den Code im neuen laufenden PKT-Eintrag auf das nächste Codestück gesprungen.

In dem PKT-Eintrag für jede Zeile ist angezeigt, ob ein gültiges Codestück vorhanden ist. Dies wird bei der Kontrollfortschaltung überprüft; vor Ausführung von Zeilen, für die kein gültiger Code vorhanden ist, wird das Codeerzeugungsmodul aufgerufen, das die Zeile übersetzt und die Adresse des erzeugten Codestückes in die Kontrolltafel einträgt. Anschließend wird das neu erzeugte Codestück ausgeführt. Programmzeilen werden also erst unmittelbar vor ihrer Ausführung übersetzt, sofern es erforderlich ist.

Aus der obigen Beschreibung ergibt sich, daß ein Benutzerprogramm in fünf miteinander verkettete Datenzonen aufgespalten wird (PKT,VTAB,PC,

CODE, Benutzervariablenspeicherplatz). Da sich die Größe jeder Zone im Verlaufe einer Dialogsitzung fortwährend ändern kann, wird die Speicherverwaltung für diese Zonen dynamisch durchgeführt. Bei Programmeingabe und -abänderung und zur Ausführung der meisten Organisationskommandos werden nur die Kontrolltafel, die Variablentabelle sowie ein kleiner Pufferbereich für den momentan verarbeiteten Pseudocode im Kernspeicher benötigt. Die restlichen Zonen befinden sich auf Hintergrundspeicher und werden nur für Programmausführungen geladen. Das Ein- und Auslagern dieser Bereiche wird vom System selbst vorgenommen, um statistische Informationen über den Ablauf einer Dialogsitzung zum gezielten Ein- und Auslagern ausnützen zu können.

3. Spezifische Probleme bei der CBASIC-Implementierung

3.1 Verarbeitung von Deklarationen

Bei der Implementierung von BASIC treten bezüglich der Behandlung von Variablen Probleme auf, da Variable sowohl explizit als auch implizit deklariert werden können und sich explizite Deklarationen an beliebiger Stelle im Programm befinden können (also auch hinter dem ersten Auftreten einer Variablen).

Explizite Deklarationen (DIM- oder DEF-Zeilen oder Zeilen mit einer Bezeichnermarke) werden bei der Eingabe in die Variablentabelle eingetragen, und beim Entfernen der Zeile dort rückgängig gemacht. Implizite Deklarationen dagegen werden erst beim Übersetzen während der Ausführung realisiert. Wird beim Ändern einer Deklaration in der Variablentabelle festgestellt, daß bereits Code für diese Variable erzeugt worden ist, dann wird der gesamte Code ungültig gesetzt.

Das Rückgängigmachen einer impliziten Deklaration wird vom System nicht festgestellt, da beim Entfernen einer normalen Programmzeile der Pseudocode nicht untersucht wird. Daher ist beim Auftreten von impliziten Doppeldeklarationen (die sich bei einander widersprechenden Verwendungen desselben, nicht explizit deklarierten Bezeichners ergeben) eine völlige "Entdeklaration" der Variablen erforderlich, unter Verlust ihres Wertes und Ungültigsetzen des gesamten Codes.

3.2 Anpassung an das Burroughs B6700 System

Jedem Prozeß ist auf der Burroughs B6700 ein Keller zugeordnet, der im Wesentlichen die Variablen des Prozesses und die Deskriptoren der zugeordneten Segmente enthält. (Ein Segment wird aus der Spalte eines Arrays oder dem Code eines Blockes gebildet.) Codesegmente und Datensegmente

werden durch die Kennung ihrer Deskriptoren und zusätzlich durch die
Kennung jedes Wortes des Segments unterschieden. Das Betriebssystem betrachtet jedes Codesegment als unveränderlich und "reentrant".

Auf Hardwareebene gibt es bei der B6700 fast keinen Speicherschutz. Dieser wird dadurch gewährleistet, daß dem Benutzer nur Compiler für höhere Programmiersprachen, aber kein Assembler zur Verfügung stehen. Daher gibt es normalerweise keine Möglichkeit, daß Benutzerprogramme selbst erzeugten Code ausführen. Die privilegierte Systemprogrammiersprache ESPOL [3] ist normalen Benutzern nicht zugänglich.

Der größte Teil des CBASIC-Systems ist in Burroughs Extended ALGOL geschrieben und stellt für das Betriebssystem ein normales, eintrittsinvariantes Benutzerprogramm dar. Die Bedienung verschiedener Benutzer zur gleichen Zeit wird daher nicht vom CBASIC-System selbst, sondern vom Betriebssystem vorgenommen. Im Prozeßkeller jedes Benutzers befinden sich die Verwaltungsdaten des CBASIC-Systems, die Deskriptoren auf VTAB, PKT und CODE sowie die Variablen und Array-Deskriptoren der BASIC-Benutzerprogramme. Für die Datenbereiche VTAB, PKT und CODE ist jeweils ein eigenes Segment angelegt.

Die Codeerzeugung und -ausführung wird im CBASIC-System durch ein ESPOL-Intrinsic ermöglicht, das den Datendeskriptor des CODE-Segmentes und den Segmentdeskriptor einer Dummyprozedur vertauscht und die Kennungen der Speicherworte umsetzt. Ein anschließender Aufruf der Dummyprozedur führt dann zur Ausführung des erzeugten Codes.

Die Tatsache, daß das Code-Segment durch die Codeerzeugung abgeändert wird, im Burroughs-System Codesegmente jedoch als unveränderlich betrachtet werden, hat gewisse Schwierigkeiten zur Folge. Diese ließen sich lösen, wenn auch auf nicht ganz klare und saubere Art. Dies wird weniger durch die Rechnerarchitektur und die Struktur des Burroughs-System bedingt, sondern mehr dadurch, daß die Hardware-Operatoren allzu speziell auf den üblichen ALGOL-Gebrauch zugeschnitten sind, obwohl sie sich ohne Schwierigkeiten erweitern ließen.

Die Code-, Keller- und Segmentstruktur der B6700 erwies sich als recht aufwendig beim Zugriff auf einzelne, indizierte Worte eines Segmentes. Daher erfordert die Interpretation des Zeilenüberganges bei Ausführungen von BASIC-Programmen gegenüber konventionellen Maschinen mit Indexregistern relativ viel Aufwand.

4. Vergleich der Benutzerfreundlichkeit

Zur Programmerstellung und -abänderung sind beide Systeme gleich gut geeignet. Bei beiden ist die Eingabe von Programmzeilen jederzeit und in beliebiger Folge möglich. Im Gegensatz zu BBASIC wird jedoch bei CBASIC die Korrektheit einer Zeile sofort bei der Eingabe überprüft. Das ist vom benutzerpsychologischen Standpunkt aus günstig, da zwischen dem "Begehen" des Fehlers und seiner Korrektur keine anderen Aktivitäten liegen. Außerdem werden unnötige Kompilationen vermieden, die sonst zum Entdecken der Syntaxfehler erforderlich sind.

Die frühe Entdeckung von Syntaxfehlern ist jedoch wohl nicht der wichtigste Vorteil voll interaktiver Systeme, sondern eher die Eingriffsmöglichkeiten während der Ausführung. Untersuchungen dazu (siehe [5]) ergaben: "Syntactical errors do not represent a major source of delay in the development of programs. Our observations suggest that techniques that permit the user to make small changes to his program on the basis of information signaled during the program run might reduce the time required to program a given application". Diese Möglichkeiten sind jedoch in konventionellen, nicht interpretierenden Dialogsystemen nicht vorhanden. So wird im BBASIC-System ein Programm nach erfolgreicher Übersetzung wie im Stapelbetrieb geschlossen ausgeführt. Eingriffsmöglichkeiten in die Ausführung bestehen keine (abgesehen von der Ein- und Ausgabe von Daten während des Programmlaufes); ebenso ist die Programmumgebung nach Beendigung oder Abbruch einer Ausführung verloren.

Im CBASIC-System kann dagegen die Ausführung eines Programmes interaktiv kontrolliert werden. Programme können stückweise ausgeführt werden, oder es können Haltepunkte gesetzt werden, bei denen die Ausführung unterbrochen wird. Weitere Debugging-Hilfen wie z.B. Trace sind ebenfalls vorhanden. Die Programmumgebung bleibt nach Unterbrechung einer Ausführung stets erhalten, unabhängig davon, ob die Unterbrechung regulär erfolgt ist, durch einen asynchronen Interrupt oder durch einen von Hardware oder Ausführungsmodul festgestellten Fehler. Während der Unterbrechung kann der Benutzer durch direkte Eingabe von BASIC-Zeilen die Variablenwerte des unterbrochenen Programmes abfragen oder abändern; durch indirekte Eingabe von Zeilen kann er das Programm ändern und somit Fehler korrigieren. Die unterbrochene Ausführung kann - auch nach Änderungen am Programm - an der Unterbrechungsstelle wiederaufgenommen werden. Der folgende Ausschnitt aus einer Dialogsitzung soll diese Möglichkeiten illustrieren:

```
100 FOR I=1 TO 10
110 FOR J=0 TO 10
120 LET S=S+A(I,J)          Programmeingabe
130 NEXT J
140 NEXT I
@ EXEC                      Ausführungsbefehl
```

Fehler Zeile 120: Ungültiger Index	Laufzeit-Fehlermeldung vom CBASIC-System
@ PRINT I,J 1 0	Selektive Abfrage von Variablenwerten, um festzustellen, welcher Index falsch ist
@ LET J=1	Abänderung des falschen Indexwertes
110 FOR J=1 TO 10	Korrektur des Programmes
@ RESUME	Wiederaufnahme der Ausführung

5. Vergleich der Effizienz

Der Rechenzeitbedarf und Speicherbedarf beider Systeme bei Programmabänderungen und Ausführungen wird im folgenden an Hand von Messungen verglichen. Der Rechenzeitbedarf (CPU-Zeit) wird entweder direkt mit der eingebauten Uhr (Auflösung: $2,4*10^{-6}$ sek) gemessen oder den Accounting-Protokollen entnommen. Vom Burroughs-System wird zusätzlich zur CPU-Zeit die I/O-Zeit gemessen, die als Maß für die durch ein Programm verursachte Kanalbelastung dient.

Als Speicherbedarf wird das Integral der Kernspeicherbelegung über die Zeit betrachtet. Vom Betriebssystem wird der Speicherbedarf als Integral über CPU- und I/O-Zeit berechnet; diese Definition wurde von uns übernommen. Im folgenden soll in erster Linie der Speicherbedarf verglichen werden, der durch ein Benutzerprogramm (einschließlich Daten) verursacht wird. Der Systemspeicherbedarf hat demgegenüber eine geringere Bedeutung, da er sich wegen der eintrittsinvarianten Programmierung des Systems auf verschiedene Benutzer aufteilt. Das Betriebssystem mißt das Speicherintegral getrennt für Code- und Datenbereiche; daher sind genaue Werte für den Speicherbedarf des Dialog-Systems und des Benutzerprogramms verfügbar.

5.1 Ausführungs- und Abänderungseffizienz

Die Ausführungseffizienz von CBASIC-Programmen hängt stark von der jeweiligen Programmstruktur ab, da bei kurzen Zeilen die Interpretation der Zeilenübergänge stärker ins Gewicht fällt. Für die Ausführung des folgenden Programmstückes:

```
10 FOR I=1 TO 30000
20 LET C= (B+2*A)*(B+3*A)
30 LET C= (B+2*A)*(B+3*A)
40 LET C= (B+2*A)*(B+3*A)
50 LET C= (B+2*A)*(B+3*A)
60 LET C= (B+2*A)*(B+3*A)
70 NEXT I
```

benötigte das BBASIC-System 9.35 sek., das CBASIC-System 14.01 sek. Die Ausführung von CBASIC-Programmen ist also in diesem (günstigen) Fall um

den Faktor 1.5 langsamer. Im ungünstigsten Fall, etwa einer leeren FOR-
NEXT-Schleife, beträgt der Faktor 5.8. Bei realistischen Programmen
(die wir hier aus Platzgründen nicht wiedergeben können) ergeben sich
Faktoren etwa um 2. Da im BBASIC-System jedoch eine konstante Zeit von
etwa 0.05 bis 0.1 sek. zur Initialisierung einer Ausführung benötigt
wird, benötigt eine sehr kurze Ausführung in CBASIC sogar weniger Re-
chenzeit als in BBASIC.

Der Aufwand, der durch die Abänderung eines Programmes verursacht wird,
hängt von seiner Größe und (im CBASIC-System) davon ab, ob deklarative
oder andere BASIC-Zeilen abgeändert werden. Zur Übersetzung eines 80-
zeiligen Programmes (siehe [7]) benötigt der BASIC-Compiler 1.4 sek.
Der im CBASIC-System durch eine Abänderung verursachte Aufwand ist ver-
nachlässigbar gering, wenn keine Deklaration abgeändert wird. Bei der
Abänderung einer Deklaration werden zum Generieren des Codes für dasselbe Programm 0.28 sek. benötigt. Nimmt man an, daß etwa 10% aller Abänderungen Deklarationen betreffen, dann beträgt der Faktor, um den der
Änderungsaufwand beim CBASIC-System geringer ist, etwa 50.

Der Speicherbedarf bei Ausführungen und Abänderungen verhält sich ähnlich: Bei Programmausführungen ist der Speicherbedarf des CBASIC-Systems etwas größer, da zusätzlich zum Codebereich die Kontrolltafel und
Verwaltungsdaten im Kernspeicher benötigt werden. Bei Änderungen dagegen ist der Speicherbedarf im BBASIC-System um einen wesentlichen Faktor größer. Der genaue Wert dieses Faktors hängt allerdings stark von
der allgemeinen Struktur des Compilers ab, z.B. von seinen Tabellen-
mindestgrößen.

5.2 Beispieldialogsitzung

Mit den in der Literatur vorhandenen statistischen Daten über Rechnerbenutzung wurde versucht, eine Beispielsitzung zu konstruieren, die re-
präsentativ für einen großen Teil der Arbeiten an einem Universitäts-
rechenzentrum ist, und zwar für den Teil, für den der Dialogbetrieb besonders geeignet ist. ("Dialogsitzungen" zur Abwicklung langer "Produk-
tionsläufe" werden damit ausgeschlossen.)

An Universitätsrechenzentren sind wenig rechenintensive Arbeiten von
großer Bedeutung. Nach [6] benötigten 2/3 aller (im Stapelbetrieb) verarbeiteten Jobs weniger als 3,8 sek. Verarbeitungszeit; sie hatten eine
mittlere Programmgröße von 95 Karten. Nach [9] betrug (an einem Time-
Sharing-System) eine Interaktion im Durchschnitt 1 sek., einschließlich
der Ausführung rechenintensiver Jobs. Das Verhältnis von Kompilationszu Ausführungsgesamtzeiten, das für den Vergleich beider Systeme von

besonderer Bedeutung ist, betrug im Stapelbetrieb nach [11] für alle
Studentenarbeiten etwa 1:1, und für Programmierkurse 2,5:1 (bei erfolgreicher Programmausführung). Im Dialogbetrieb betrug es nach [8] etwa
1:1, einschließlich rechenintensiver Jobs. Da erfahrungsgemäß im Dialogbetrieb Kompilationen häufiger sind als im Stapelbetrieb, dürfte für
die uns interessierende Benutzerklasse ein Verhältnis von Kompilationszu Ausführungsaufwand von etwa 1,5 : 1 realistisch sein.

Weiterhin läßt sich der Literatur entnehmen, daß zwei Drittel bis drei
Viertel aller Kompilationen ohne Fehlermeldung ablaufen. (Siehe [5],[8])
Ein hoher Anteil von Editierkommandos (etwa 75%) wird allgemein bestätigt (Siehe [5],[8],[11]).

Die Beispieldialogsitzung entspricht bei Benutzung des BBASIC-Systems
den oben angegebenen Werten; sie wurde am CBASIC-System analog durchgeführt. In ihr wird ein 80 Zeilen langes Programm zur Berechnung von Π
erstellt. Die Dialogsitzung besteht aus 2 Sequenzen von Programmerstellung (oder -abänderung) und Übersetzen, aus 8 Sequenzen von Programmabänderung, -übersetzung und -ausführung, und 2 Ausführungen zu "Produktionszwecken". Insgesamt werden im Laufe der Sitzung 166 Zeilen eingegeben, davon 68 Editierkommandos und 98 BASIC-Zeilen. (Ein Protokoll
der Sitzung findet sich in [7].)

Die Meßergebnisse sind in der folgenden Tabelle zusammengefaßt:

	BBASIC	CBASIC
CPU-Zeit (sek.)	34,353	25,22
I/O-Zeit (sek.)	24,565	20,42
Speicherintegral für Benutzer (Worte sek.)	228342[1]	129580
CPU-Zeit Editieren (sek.)	10,057	7,17
CPU-Zeit Übersetzen (sek.)	14,396	0,81
CPU-Zeit Ausführen (sek.)	9,900	17,24[2]

(1) Summe der Integrale der BASIC-Compileraufrufe
(2) Enthält Zeiten für Aufrufe der ESPOL-Intrinsics

Wie erwartet verhält sich BBASIC nur bei der Ausführung, CBASIC jedoch
beim Editieren und Übersetzen von Programmen effizienter.

Der Rechenzeitbedarf ist in der obigen Tabelle getrennt aufgeschlüsselt.
Als BBASIC-Benutzerspeicherbedarf wird in der Tabelle nur das Integral
der Datenbereiche bei BBASIC-Compileraufrufen angegeben. Eigentlich
kommt noch der Speicherbedarf bei Ausführungen und der für die Benutzerdaten des CANDE-Systems hinzu, dessen Größe sich für einen einzelnen
Benutzer nicht genau ermitteln ließ.

Somit benötigt bei der Durchführung einer typischen Dialogsitzung das

BBASIC-System für jeden Benutzer 36% mehr CPU-Zeit, verursacht eine um 20% größere Kanalbelastung und hat einen um mehr als 70% größeren Speicherbedarf als das CBASIC-System. Dabei bietet das CBASIC-System - im Gegensatz zu BBASIC - denselben hohen Grad an Interaktivität wie ein Interpretierer. Der Vergleich der beiden unterschiedlich strukturierten Dialogsysteme ergibt also, daß Systeme, deren Struktur speziell den Erfordernissen des Dialogbetriebes angepaßt ist, eine größere Effizienz und gleichzeitig eine größere Benutzerfreundlichkeit als konventionell strukturierte Dialogsysteme besitzen.

Wir danken Herrn Bär, Herrn Schroth und Herrn Zorn vom Informatik-Rechenzentrum der Universität Karlsruhe für ihr freundliches Entgegenkommen und ihre Hilfe beim Umgang mit der Burroughs B6700.

Literatur

[1] Burroughs B6700, BASIC Information Manual, Form No.5000383

[2] Burroughs B6700, Reference Manual, Form No. 105 863

[3] Burroughs B6700, ESPOL Information Manual, Form No. 5000 094

[4] Burroughs B6700, Ext. ALGOL Information Manual, Form No.5000128

[5] Boies, S.J., User Behaviour on an Interactive Computer System
IBM Systems Journal, 1974, No. 1

[6] Hunt, B., Dichn, G., and Garnatz, D.: Who are the Users? An Analysis of Computer Use in an University Center, AFIPS, Vol.38,1971

[7] Klonk, J.: Implementierung eines Dialogsystems für BASIC
Diplomarbeit, Institut für Informatik II, Uni. Karlsruhe,Juni 1974

[8] Scherr, A.L.: An Analysis of Time Shared Computer Systems
Chapt. 2 + App. B, MIT-Press, Cambridge, Mass., 1967

[9] Schmid, H.A.: The Structure of a Flexible and Efficient Compiler for Algorithmic Conversational Languages
Springer Lecture Notes 75, Berlin 1972

[10] Schmid, H.A.: Zur Struktur von Dialogsystemen
Dissertation, Universität Karlsruhe, 1973

[11] Walter, E.S. and Wallace, V.L.: Further Analysis of a Computer Center Environment, Comm. ACM 10 (May 1967)

SPEICHERZUORDNUNG AN DATENSTRUKTUREN[*]

F. Kröger

Mathematisches Institut der Technischen Universität München

1. Einleitung

Die Deklaration einer Variablen in einem Programm bewirkt bei der Ausführung des Programms auf einer Maschine die Reservierung eines zugeordneten Speicherplatzes, der, ebenso wie die in der Deklaration definierte *Datenstruktur*, eine teils unmittelbar durch diese, teils durch Eigenschaften der vorliegenden Maschine oder implementierungstechnisch bedingte Struktur trägt. Trotz dieser verschiedenartigen Abhängigkeiten zeigt die Praxis, daß die Konstruktion der auftretenden *Speicherstrukturen* in einem gewissen Rahmen unabhängig von der Menge der in einer speziellen Quellsprache definierbaren Datenstrukturen und unabhängig von speziellen Maschineneigenschaften und Implementierungstechniken immer wiederkehrende Mechanismen benützt.

Um diese Tatsache nutzbar zu machen, wird derzeit in einer Arbeitsgruppe an der Konstruktion eines *Speicherzuordnungsmoduls* gearbeitet, der durch Kombination der grundlegenden Mechanismen eine Vielzahl von Speicherstrukturen erzeugen kann. Ein derartiger Modul könnte als Teil eines Übersetzers eingesetzt werden.

Wir wollen im folgenden in vereinfachter Weise die von uns verwendeten Grundbausteine zur Erzeugung von Speicherstrukturen anhand einer Sprache S skizzieren. Die Elemente dieser Sprache heißen *Normdeklaratoren*, haben ähnliche syntaktische Struktur wie die Deklaratoren in höhe-

---

[*] Diese Arbeit wurde teilweise durch den Sonderforschungsbereich 49 - Elektronische Rechenanlagen und Informationsverarbeitung - in München unterstützt.

ren Programmiersprachen wie etwa ALGOL und dienen zur Beschreibung der
Schnittstelle zwischen Benutzer und Modul.

2. Elementare Strukturen

Der Aufbau von Speicherstrukturen erfolgt induktiv, ausgehend von einem
Satz elementarer Strukturen. Als solche haben wir gewählt
— Bitreihen   und
— Wortreihen.
Sie werden beschrieben durch die *primitiven Normdeklaratoren*
      BIT[1], BIT[2], BIT[3], ...   bzw.
      WORD[1], WORD[2], WORD[3], ...
Die Zahlen geben die Länge der jeweiligen Reihe an, so daß also etwa
unter WORD[2] ein Doppelwort zu verstehen ist.

Wir setzen dabei den zugrundeliegenden Speicher als linear adressierbar
voraus. Ist er nicht bitadressierbar, so kann die Sprache entsprechend
eingeschränkt werden.

Zum größeren Komfort nehmen wir noch Normdeklaratoren
      BYTE[1], BYTE[2], BYTE[3], ...
und   HAWO[1], HAWO[2], HAWO[3], ...
hinzu, die die Reservierung von Bitreihen gewisser ausgezeichneter Längen, nämlich Reihen von Bytes bzw. Halbwörtern, bewirken sollen.

Zwischen diesen Normdeklaratoren gelten "metrische" Beziehungen (Anzahl
der Bits pro Byte, Halbwort, Wort), die maschinenabhängig sind und als
Parameter in die Beschreibung der Semantik der Normdeklaratoren eingehen (vgl. dazu das zweite Beispiel in Abschnitt 4).

Mögliche Quellsprachendeklaratoren, die auf die primitiven Normdeklaratoren abgebildet werden, sind z.B.:
      int, real, bool, char, ref real, ...
Mögliche Abbildungen sind etwa:

      int   ↦ WORD[1],
      real   ↦ WORD[2],
      bool   ↦ BIT[1]   oder   WORD[1],
      char   ↦ BYTE[1] oder   WORD[1],
   ref real ↦ WORD[1].

Kleinere Einheiten können innerhalb größerer adjustiert oder gepackt
auftreten (wir verwenden "adjustieren" für das englische "align"). So
bedeutet etwa der Normdeklarator

      AL(WORD[1]) - BIT[1]

die Reservierung eines Bits "linksbündig" in einem Wort. Allgemein lassen wir zu

      AL(μ[m]) - ν[n]

und   AR(μ[m]) - ν[n],

wobei (unter gewissen Einschränkungen) m und n für natürliche Zahlen stehen, und $\mu, \nu \in$ {BIT, BYTE, HAWO, WORD} gilt. AR bedeutet im Gegensatz zu AL "rechtsbündiges" Adjustieren.

In ähnlicher Weise gibt es in S Elemente der Form

      PA - ν[n],

wodurch Packungsvorschriften angesprochen werden, auf die wir hier nicht weiter eingehen wollen.

3. Zusammengesetzte Strukturen

Komplexere Speicherstrukturen können durch Zusammensetzen von einfacheren erzeugt werden. Hierfür gibt es im wesentlichen zwei Mechanismen:
- sequentielle Aneinanderfügung,
- Verknüpfung einer (genügend großen) elementaren Struktur mit einer anderen Struktur durch einen Verweis.

Wir wollen dies im weiteren anhand von graphischen Darstellungen von Speicherplätzen erläutern. Dazu beschränken wir uns der Einfachheit halber in der Menge der elementaren Strukturen auf Wortreihen und nehmen an, daß die Maschinenwörter mit natürlichen Zahlen adressiert sind, wobei zwei unmittelbar aufeinander folgende Wörter auch zwei aufeinander folgende Zahlen a, a+1 als Adressen haben. Ein Wort mit der Adresse a stellen wir dar durch

      a : ▭

und umfangreichere Strukturen (mit Anfangsadresse a) durch größere Rechtecke

      a : ☐
      b :

Die Angabe der Endadresse b lassen wir gegebenenfalls auch weg.

3.1. Sequentielle Zusammensetzung

Es seien z eine ("zur Übersetzungszeit" bekannte) natürliche Zahl und $\mu_1, \ldots, \mu_z$ Normdeklaratoren.

Die Speicherstruktur

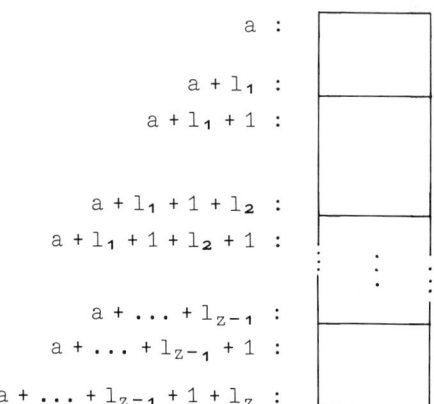

entsteht durch sequentielle Zusammensetzung der durch μ_i erzeugten Komponenten

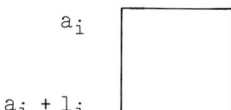

Ihre Erzeugung wird beschrieben durch den Normdeklarator
(1)   CART($\mu_1, \ldots, \mu_z$)
und im Spezialfall, daß alle μ_i gleich einem Normdeklarator μ sind, auch durch
(2)   MAT[z](μ).

Die typischen Datenstrukturen, die durch diese Elemente abgedeckt werden, sind Verbunde und (statische) Matrizen.

3.2. Verweise

Ist

eine durch den Normdeklarator μ beschriebene Speicherstruktur, so wird die Struktur

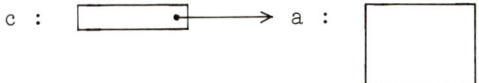

(Verweis "von c auf a")
repräsentiert durch den Normdeklarator
    LINK(WORD[1],μ).
Etwas allgemeiner lassen wir zu
(3)   LINK(ν,μ),
wo ν primitiver Normdeklarator von bestimmter Art sein kann.

Dieses Sprachelement dient nicht etwa zur Abarbeitung von Deklaratoren wie <u>ref</u> struct (...), sondern zur Erzeugung von *festen* Verweisen, wie sie beim Übersetzerbau immer wieder verwendet werden. Ein Beispiel ist der Verweis von einer Leitzelle auf eine dynamisch fixierte Matrix.

Um gerade dieses letzere Beispiel zu realisieren, ist es nötig, noch eine weitere Art von Elementen einzuführen, die zwar selbst keine Normdeklaratoren sind, aber als Komponente μ in (3) auftreten können:
(4)   DMAT[n](μ').
Dieses Element ist ein Analogon zu dem Normdeklarator
    MAT[z](μ),
mit dem Unterschied, daß n ein Identifikator (mit den natürlichen Zahlen als Wertebereich) ist. Das bewirkt einen semantischen Unterschied: Während die Bedeutung eines Normdeklarators (2) in der *Ausführung* eines bestimmten Algorithmus zur Erzeugung der zugehörigen Speicherstruktur besteht, bedeutet ein Element (4) (im wesentlichen) die *Codierung* des entsprechenden Algorithmus.

3.3. Der induktive Aufbau

Die beschriebenen Zusammensetz-Mechanismen kann man miteinander verzahnen und induktiv fortführen. So erhält man eine Vielfalt von Normdeklaratoren, deren entsprechende Speicherstrukturen eine große Zahl von gebräuchlichen Datenstrukturen abdecken.

Wir wollen den syntaktischen Aufbau andeuten, indem wir zu den Normdeklaratoren der Arten (1), (2), (3) angeben, von welcher Art jeweils die Komponenten sein können:

CART(μ_1, ..., μ_z) : μ_i primitiver Normdeklarator oder von der Art (1), (2) oder (3),

MAT[z](μ) : μ wie oben,

LINK(ν,μ) : ν = HAWO[1]   oder ν = WORD[z],
μ primitiver Normdeklarator oder von der Art (1), (2), (3) oder (4), wobei μ' in einer Komponente der Art (4) selbst wieder ein primitiver Normdeklarator oder von der Art (1), (2), (3) oder (4) sein kann.

3.4. Bildung von "Alternativen"

Im System S gibt es schließlich noch ein weiteres Konstruktionsprinzip, das sich nur in einem recht weiten Sinn unter die Überschrift "Zusammensetzung" eingliedern läßt. Sind μ_1, ..., μ_z Normdeklaratoren mit entsprechenden Speicherstrukturen, so soll es möglich sein, einen Speicherplatz von einem Umfang zu reservieren, der gleich dem Maximum über die einzelnen Speicherumfänge ist, und die einzelnen Strukturen, die diesem Platz vermöge μ_1, ..., μ_z aufgeprägt sein können, zu sammeln. Diese "Alternativensammlung" ermöglicht die Implementierung von Deklaratoren wie

        union(....)

und wird durch den Normdeklarator

(5)   ALT(μ_1, ..., μ_z)

beschrieben.
Wir erlauben allerdings nur eine recht restriktive Handhabung, indem wir die Syntax so einschränken, daß die μ_i selbst nicht von der Art (5) sein und auch keine Komponenten dieser Art enthalten dürfen, und daß (5) nicht als Komponente in einem Normdeklarator der Art (1) auftreten darf.

4. Zwei Beispiele

Es sei eine Datenstruktur gegeben durch
     struct([1:n,1:m]int u, struct(real x, int y) z).
Wir wollen der Einfachheit halber annehmen, daß die Matrix u mit Hilfe einer einzelnen Leitzelle (ohne weiteren Deskriptor) implementiert werden solle, also entsprechend folgendem Bild:

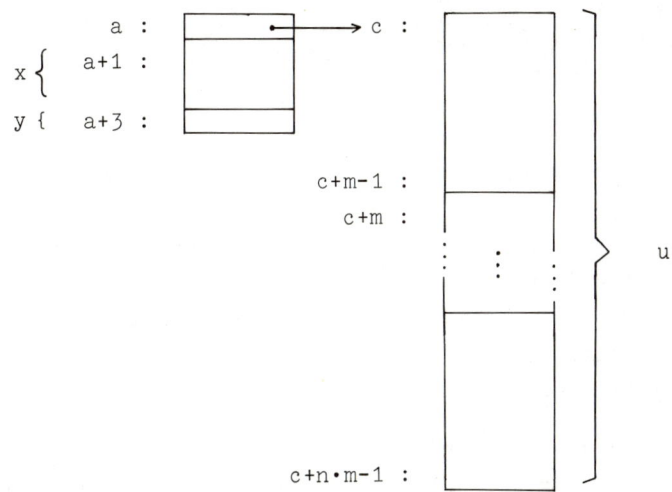

Diese Struktur wird erzeugt durch den Normdeklarator
     CART(LINK(WORD[1],DMAT[n](DMAT[m](WORD[1]))),CART(WORD[2],WORD[1])).

Als zweites Beispiel betrachten wir die PL/1-Struktur

     1 A,
       2 B bit(24),
       2 C char(2),
       2 D bit(6) aligned,
       2 E fixed.

Dies könnte übersetzt werden in den Normdeklarator
     CART(BIT[24],BYTE[2],AL(WORD[1])-BIT[6],WORD[1]).

Wie bereits erwähnt, gehen in die Abarbeitung dieses Ausdrucks gewisse Maschinenparameter ein. So ist die Semantik dieses Normdeklarators derart erklärt, daß sich etwa für eine Maschine mit 36 Bit pro Wort und 9 Bit pro Byte (in Erweiterung der obigen Vereinbarungen bezüglich graphischer Darstellung) das Bild

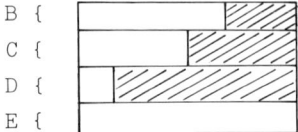

ergibt, dagegen für eine Maschine mit 48 Bit pro Wort und 8 Bit pro Byte:

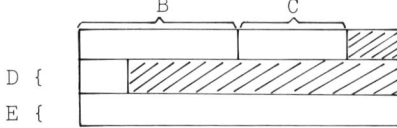

5. Zusammenfassung

Das System S der Normdeklaratoren bildet einen zentralen Teil der Eingabesprache eines geplanten Speicherzuordnungsmoduls. Dieser Modul ist — wie wir hoffen klar gemacht zu haben — fähig, eine große Klasse von Datenstrukturen, speziell aus ALGOL-ähnlichen Sprachen und z.B. PL/1, zu verarbeiten.

Die Entwicklung von S wurde an vielen Stellen besonders von der ALGOL 68 - Implementierung beeinflußt (vgl. BRANQUART/LEWI [1], HILL/SCHEIDIG/WÖSSNER [4]).

Wir haben die Normdeklaratoren in vereinfachter Weise dargestellt. Zwei besondere Mechanismen wollen wir an dieser Stelle noch erwähnen, zum einen die Möglichkeit der Speicherreservierung in verschiedenen *Speicherbereichen* (z.B. Keller und Halde), zum anderen die Möglichkeit, gewisse Reservierungen nicht vom Übersetzer, sondern vom Laufzeitsystem durchführen zu lassen. (Das ermöglicht etwa die Erfassung von Konstruktionen wie

$$xx := \underline{real} := 3.14$$

in ALGOL 68.)

Unterbleiben muß wegen des vorgegebenen Umfangs dieser Arbeit auch nur die Andeutung einer formalen Semantikzuordnung zu den Normdeklaratoren und erst recht ein Eingehen auf die sehr eng mit den Normdeklaratoren verknüpften Mechanismen zur *Selektion* von Komponenten aus Speicherstrukturen (zum letzteren vgl. WÖRLE [6]).

Die vorliegende Arbeit — als Teilprojekt einer Arbeitsgruppe — wäre nicht entstanden ohne die fortwährende Mithilfe kritischer Diskussionspartner. Ihnen, Fr.D.Maison, Frl.L.Wörle, sowie den Herren Prof.R.Bayer,

St.Heilbrunner, W.Niegel, Prof.M.Paul, Prof.K.Samelson, R.Schroff, sei an dieser Stelle gedankt.

Literatur

[1]　BRANQUART,P., LEWI,J.: A Scheme of Storage Allocation and Garbage Collection for ALGOL 68. In: PECK, J.E.L. (ed.): ALGOL 68 Implementation. Amsterdam: North-Holland 1971

[2]　GRAU,A.A., HILL,U., LANGMAACK,H.: Translation of ALGOL 60. Handbook for Automatic Computation, Vol.I, Part b. Berlin-Heidelberg-New York: Springer 1967

[3]　GRIES,D.: Compiler Construction for Digital Computers. New York: John Wiley & Sons 1971

[4]　HILL,U., SCHEIDIG,H., WÖSSNER,H.: An ALGOL 68 Compiler. Abteilung Mathematik der TU München, Interner Bericht, 1971

[5]　MILLER,P.: Automatic creation of a code generator from a machine description. MIT, Cambridge (Mass.), Project MAC TR-86, 1971

[6]　WÖRLE,L.: Selektion in Zugriffsgraphen. Abteilung Mathematik der TU München, Bericht Nr.7316, 1973

SYNTAX-DIRECTED DESCRIPTION OF INCREMENTAL COMPILERS

Hans Jürgen Schneider
University of Erlangen

o. Introduction

Program and data structures may be described formally by using graphs with labelled nodes and edges. The Vienna Definition Language [4] is a well-known example of such a system which uses a special type of graphs, namely trees. Implementing an incremental compiler, we must consider various lists and a lot of references between them in order to allow insertion, deletion, or substitution of increments (see e.g. [6]). (We consider increments to be some syntactical units still to be defined by the implementer.) Formally, these data constitute a graph with labelled nodes (increments and some special "nonterminal" symbols, e.g. pointers) and labelled edges (references of different types); however, the result is not always a tree. We may consider the following types of edges: surrounding block of an increment or block, applied occurrence of a declared entity, next increment, first increment of a block, etc. Establishing a syntax-directed concept for implementing incremental compilers, we need a formal system to describe the syntax of languages the words of which are labelled graphs.

1. Formal definitions

Generalizing the concept of Chomsky-grammars to graphs, the main problem is to specify the embedding and replacement of subgraphs in order to get direct derivation:

1.1 Definition: The graph H is called derivable from G iff we have the following pushout-construction

$$\begin{array}{ccccc} 'B & \xleftarrow{'p} & K & \xrightarrow{p'} & B' \\ {\scriptstyle 'd}\downarrow & \text{PO} & \downarrow d & \text{PO} & \downarrow{\scriptstyle \bar{d}'} \\ G & \xleftarrow{'\bar{p}} & D & \xrightarrow{\bar{p}'} & H \end{array}$$

where ('B,'p,K,p',B') is a production.

In addition to the left-hand and right-hand side ('B and B' resp.), we introduce a gluing-graph K, morphisms 'p and p', and an enlargement $(d:K\to D, m_D)$ to describe the embedding. In [2], this concept was introduced, using graphs 'B and B' in the usual sense. But we can give examples (even in the area of incremental compiling) which can be described better if the graphs 'B, K, and B' are allowed to be incomplete, i.e. there may be edges without a source or target node. Therefore, we must assume d, '$\tilde{d}$, and $\tilde{d}$' to be "weak" graph-morphisms preserving labels, but allowing an edge in G, D, or H resp. to have a source or target node although the pre-image does not.

1.2 Definition: A <u>graph</u> G = (E_G, V_G, q_G, z_G) consists of two finite sets E_G and V_G (edges and vertices) together with two partial mappings $q_G: E_G \to V_G$ and $z_G: E_G \to V_G$, determining the sources and targets of the edges. G is called <u>complete graph</u> iff $dom(q_G) = dom(z_G) = E_G$.

1.3 Definition: A <u>weak graph-morphism</u> (a <u>graph-morphism</u>) $f: G \to H$ is a pair $f = (f_E, f_V)$ of mappings $f_E: G_E \to H_E$, $f_V: G_V \to H_V$ where

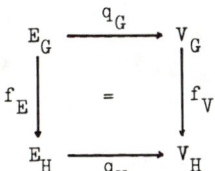
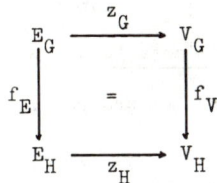

commute in the sense that $q_H(f_E(e))$ and/or $z_H(f_E(e))$ are defined if (if and only if) $q_G(e)$ and/or $z_G(e)$ resp. are defined.

Incomplete graphs together with weak graph-morphisms constitute a category GRAPH$^-$; composition of morphisms and identities are defined componentwise.

1.4 Definition: Let $\Omega := (\Omega_E, \Omega_V)$ be a pair of denumerable sets (<u>labelling alphabet</u>), G a graph, and $m_G := (m_E, m_V)$ a pair of partial mappings $m_E: E_G \to \Omega_E$, $m_V: V_G \to \Omega_V$ (<u>labelling mapping</u>). Then (G, m_G) is called <u>Ω^--graph</u>. Given Ω^--graphs (G, m_G) and (H, m_H), a graph-morphism $f: G \to H$ is called <u>Ω^--graph-morphism</u> iff $m_H \cdot f = m_G$ holds. G is called <u>Ω-graph</u> iff m_E and m_V are total.

In the category of sets a pushout-object may be constructed from the disjoint union $D \cup B$ using the equivalence relation R induced by $\{(d(k), p(k)): k \in K\}$:

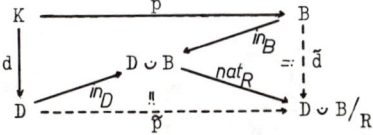

In the category of graphs the pushout-object (used in Def.1.1) may be constructed componentwise.

1.5 Theorem: Let be K an incomplete graph, (B, m_B) an incomplete Ω-graph, (D, m_D) a complete Ω^--graph, $d: K \to D$ an injective weak graph-morphism, $p: K \to B$ a graph-morphism where p and the domains of q_K, z_K, m_D satisfy some further properties. Then, there is a unique labelling m_H of the pushout-object H in

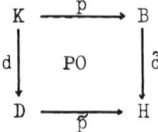

and H is a complete Ω-graph.

The proof is given in $[3]$. Thus, it is possible to construct G and H, if a production and an enlargement $(d:K \to D, m_D)$ are given (see Def.1.1). On the other hand, we have a necessary and sufficient condition for existence and explicit construction of an enlargement if $\tilde{d}$ is given and $\tilde{d}$, q_H, z_H satisfy some further properties. If p is injective, the enlargement is unique up to isomorphism. The proof is given in $[3]$, too.

2. Insertion and deletion of declarations

We consider an ALGOL-like programming language and the following part of a program:

```
begin dcl B;  dcl A; ...
      begin dcl C;  dcl B; ...
            ...A...B...C...
            begin dcl A;  dcl C; ...
                  ...B...C...
      end   end   end
```

In Fig.1, we describe some relations between the increments of this program by a labelled graph. Each node represents one increment; the edges show the relations:

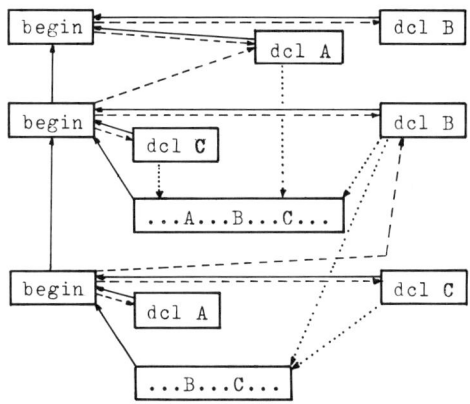

Fig.1

a ⟶ b: increment a is part of block b.
a --→ b: declaration b is valid in block a.
a ······→ b: increment b contains an applied occurrence of the identifier declared by increment a.

If we insert a new declaration for B in the third block, we obtain the graph of Fig.2:

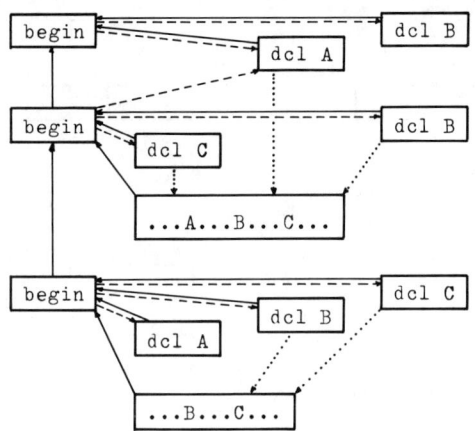

Fig.2

The subgraph 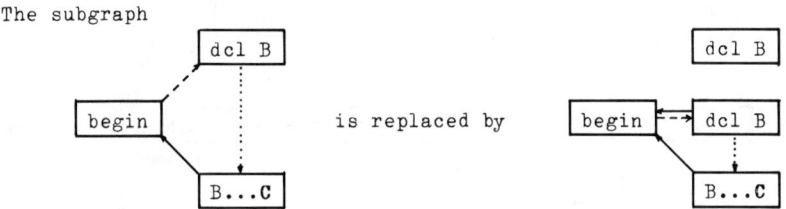 is replaced by

But these are not the left-hand and right-hand side of a suitable production realizing insertion of declarations because
- this "production" may be applied to blocks in which a declaration for B already exists,
- this "production" does not replace the references to applied occurrences which we find in blocks of a higher level.

It is not convenient to describe insertion of a new declaration by one production only, since the programmer may have an unrestricted number of possibly nested blocks. Therefore, we consider a programmed grammar: the command "INSERT DECLARATION" is described by a sequence of productions with success- and failure-fields:

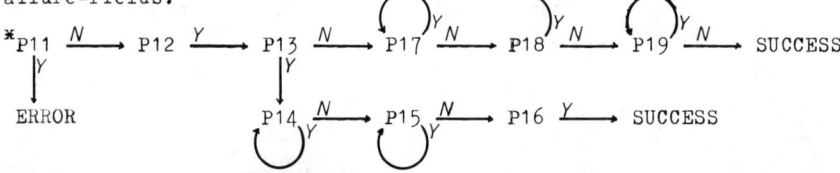

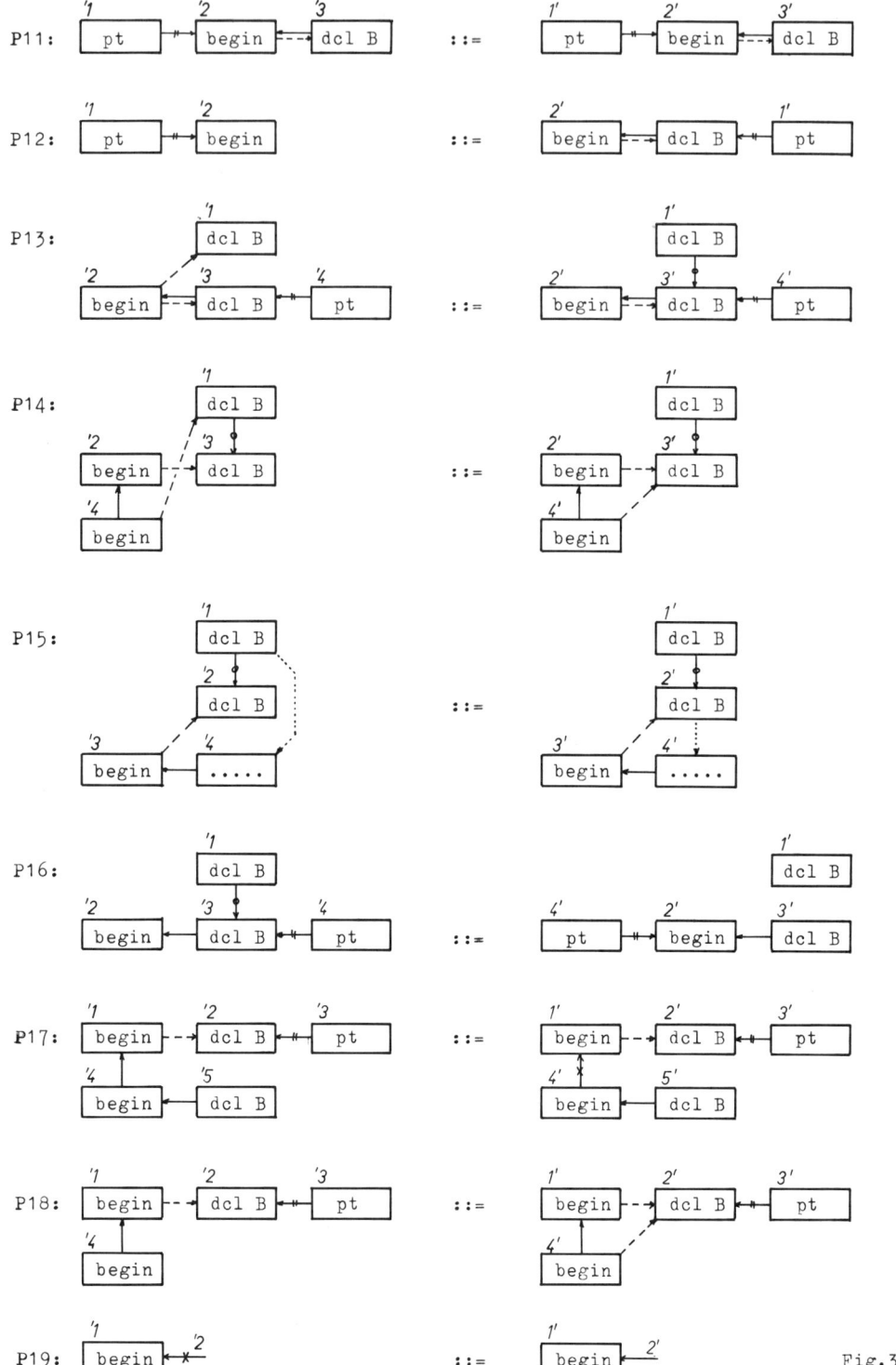

Fig.3

where Y denotes that the production was applied, and N that it was not applicable. The star marks the starting production. The productions P11-P19 are given in Fig.3. The gluing graph K and the <u>gluing conditions</u> 'p, p' are trivial and indicated by numbers: 'p(k) and p'(k) are identified by 'k and k' respectively. (Nodes and edges which are not numbered, do not possess a preimage in K.) <u>P11</u> tests whether a declaration for the same identifier (the letter B stands for an arbitrary identifier) exists already in the block selected. To identify the subgraph where a command must be applied, we assume existence of a <u>pointer</u> pt selecting by a ⟶-edge exactly one node. Production <u>P12</u> inserts the declaration; <u>P13</u> inserts an edge between the new declaration and the declaration which was valid in this block up till now, and deletes the edge which is now unvalid. The new edge is labelled by a nonterminal symbol and will be deleted by <u>P16</u>. (The idea of nonterminal edge-labels is due to Nagl [5].) <u>P14</u> selects a block which does not contain a declaration for the same identifier and is contained in a block already selected: now, the new declaration is valid in this block, too. <u>P15</u> transfers an applied-occurrence-edge to the new declaration. <u>P17</u> tests whether there is a suitable declaration in a block contained within the block considered. <u>P18</u> causes the new declaration to be valid in a block not selected by P17. Finally, <u>P19</u> deletes the nonterminal edges.

As an example of the application of such a production we consider P13. We get the derived graph in the following way: (a) Delete from the given graph all nodes and edges contained in the left-hand side of P13. (b) Add to the remaining the nodes and edges of the right-hand side of P13 connecting the new nodes and the new edges as in this right-hand side. (c) Edges previously connected with a 'k, are to be connected with the corresponding k'. Then, we may apply P14: step (a) yields an isolated edge (the ⟶-edge between '2 and '3); this edge is connected in step (c) with 2' and 3'. In general, the algorithm is more complicated, but in this paper we use very simple productions.

If we omit the ⟶-edges, we cannot use production P13. Then, we must search for the declaration valid in the selected block (see [1]).

In a similar way, we may describe the command "DELETE DECLARATION":

*P21 —N→ P23 —Y→ ERROR
│Y   ↘N
▼
P22 —Y→ SUCCESS   P24 —Y→ P25 ⟲Y N → SUCCESS

The productions are given in Fig.4. <u>P21</u> tests whether a declaration for the same identifier exists in a block containing the block with the selected declaration. If this is true, a nonterminal edge is inserted, and <u>P22</u> deletes the declaration. All edges previously connected with '1 or '2 are now connected with the same node. (Therefore, the ⟶-edge starting at the <u>dcl</u>-

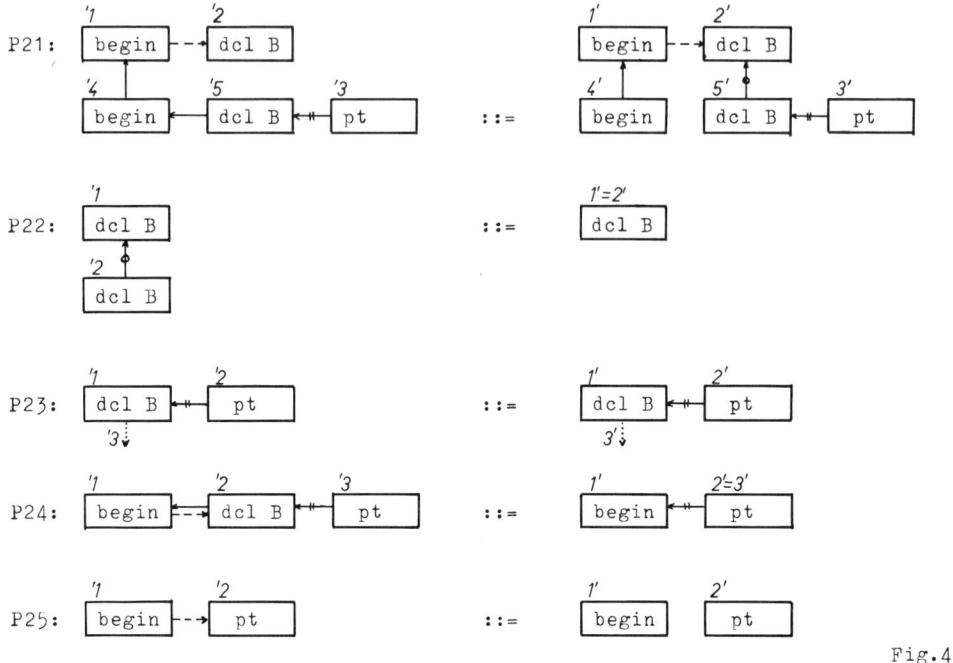

Fig.4

increment that is to be deleted, was already removed by P21.) Otherwise, P23 tests whether an applied occurrence of the declaration exists. If not, P24 deletes the declaration, and P25 deletes existing --→-edges from other blocks.

3. Modifying the block structure

First, we consider the insertion of a new block:

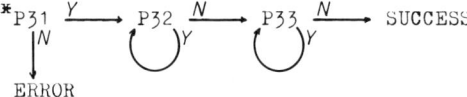

The productions are given in Fig.5. Productions P31 inserts the increments begin and end before the increment selected by the pointer. Now, we introduce the additional relation "next increment" (—→). Repeated application of P32 inserts the "valid"-edge from the new block to all declarations valid in the surrounding block. A nonterminal edge which will be replaced by P33, prevents multiple handling of a declaration. (This command may be formulated simpler using Nagl's system [5].)

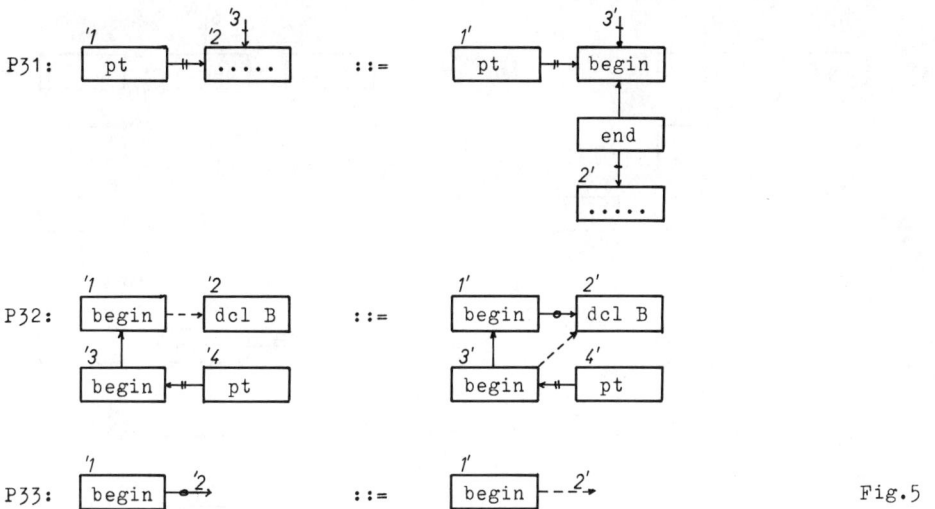

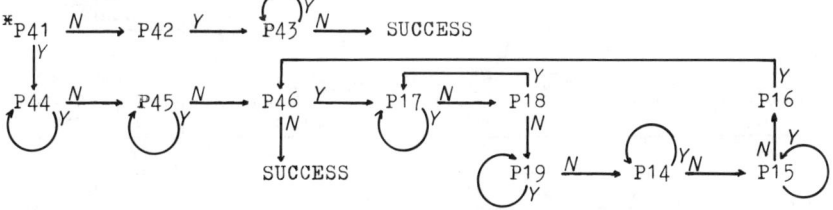

Fig.5

The increment <u>begin</u> may be shifted to another position (Fig.6) preserving the correctness of block structure:

*P41 $\xrightarrow{N}$ P42 $\xrightarrow{Y}$ P43 $\xrightarrow{N}$ SUCCESS
$\downarrow Y$
P44 $\xrightarrow{N}$ P45 $\xrightarrow{N}$ P46 $\xrightarrow{Y}$ P17 $\xrightarrow{N}$ P18 $\quad$ P16
$\qquad\qquad\qquad\qquad\downarrow N$
$\qquad\qquad\qquad$ SUCCESS $\qquad$ P19 $\xrightarrow{N}$ P14 $\xrightarrow{Y N}$ P15

<u>P41</u> tests whether the increment immediately preceding <u>begin</u> is the end of a block. If this is not true, this increment becomes part of the block (<u>P42</u>); <u>P43</u> transfers an applied occurrence. If there is a block preceding the <u>begin</u>, the whole block must be skipped and the scope of declarations must be updated: declarations contained in the block the begin of which was shifted, become valid in the block skipped and all blocks contained in it if there are no declarations for the same identifiers. <u>P44</u> selects declarations not to be transferred, <u>P45</u> transfers a "valid"-edge, and the application of <u>P46</u> allows us to use P14-P18.

4. Modifying a declaration

If we want to modify a declaration, we must take into account that possibly all increments with an applied occurrence of this declaration must be modified, too. We can distinguish three types of modifications:
a) There is no need to modify the applied occurrence, e.g. an array declaration where the storage class is altered (static, dynamic, controlled).
b) The applied occurrence must be modified, but this can be done immediately

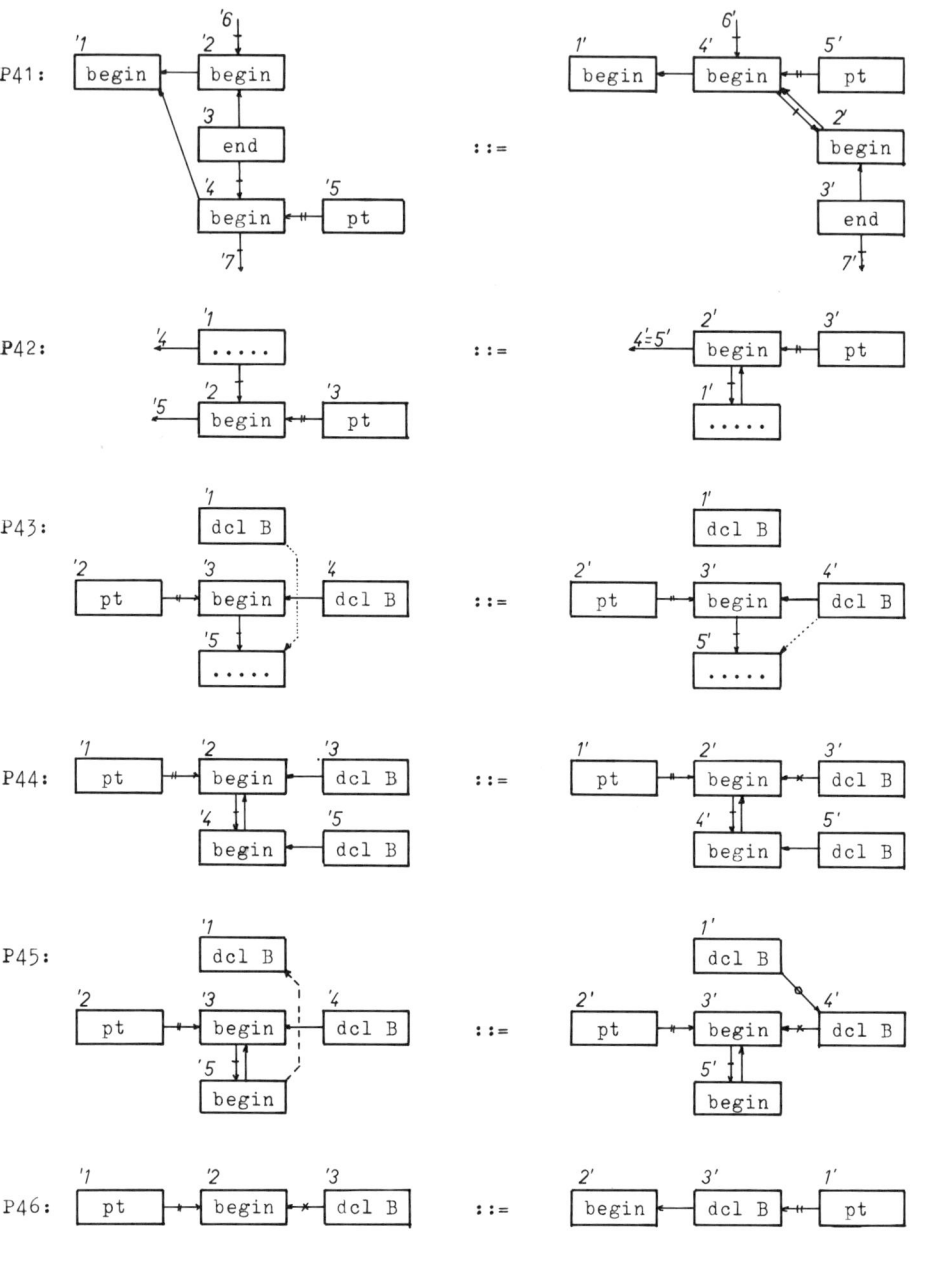

Fig.6

by the compiler, e.g. the change of precision. The applied occurrences must be recompiled since new coercions must be taken into account.

c) The applied occurrences must be modified, but this can be done only by the user himself, e.g. the replacement of a simple variable by a subscripted one. In such cases, we may insert nonterminal nodes which are not executable. On a display screen, there are different possibilities to call user's attention to these nonterminal increments (e.g. intensity of light).

These cases may be distinguished in a programmed grammar if we represent a declaration not by a single node, but by a tree, e.g.

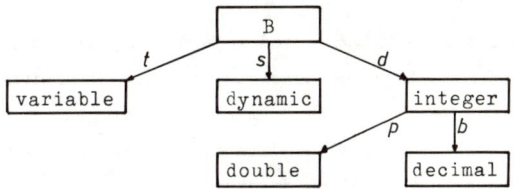

Then, we can test by productions which component (t, s, or d) is changed, and in each case a suitable sequence of productions follows.

5. Conclusion

Bunke has given in [1] a complete graph-grammar for an ALGOL-like language discussing many alternatives. Contrary to our paper, he uses the formalism introduced by Nagl [5].

References

[1] H. Bunke, Syntaxgesteuerte interaktive Programmierung
    Diplomarbeit, Univ. Erlangen, 1974

[2] H. Ehrig/M. Pfender/H.J. Schneider, Graph-grammars - an algebraic approach
    Proceed. Conf. Switch. Automat. Theory 1973, p.167-180

[3] H. Ehrig/M. Pfender/H.J. Schneider, Grammars on incomplete graphs
    To be published

[4] P. Lucas/K. Walk, On the formal description of PL/I
    Ann. Rev. Autom. Programming 6, 3 (1969)

[5] M. Nagl, Formale Sprachen von markierten Graphen
    Dissertation, Univ. Erlangen, 1974

[6] H.A. Schmid, A user oriented and efficient incremental compiler
    Int. Computing Symp. 1972, Venice, Preprints, p.259-269

PLAN2D - TOWARDS A TWO-DIMENSIONAL PROGRAMMING LANGUAGE

E. Denert, R. Franck, W. Streng
Technical University of Berlin
Department of Cybernetics

*One picture is worth more
than ten thousand words.*

1. INTRODUCTION

A program in a two-dimensional language is expressed in some diagrammatic, pictorial form, whereas a program in a "normal" language consists of a one-dimensional (linear) string of characters. To put it briefly, in the former case a program is "drawn", whilst in the latter case it is "written". A two-dimensional notation has been used or seems to be worthwhile at least in the following areas:

1. Mathematical expressions are much more readable, if their sub- and superscripts, fractional lines, summation and integration signs with lower and upper bounds, etc. can be written in their usual two-dimensional, not in a somehow linearized form. Due to its non-numeric nature PLAN2D does not deal with such features.

2. The most common use of a two-dimensional notation is the representation of control structures, especially with flow charts.[+] But there are still other possibilities for exploiting the two dimensions for describing the flow of control in algorithms. Besides the features used in PLAN2D, e.g. parallelism and synchronisation in non-sequential algorithms might be well expressed diagrammatically. No major effort in this direction is known to the authors.

3. Description and manipulation of linked data structures are the main concern of PLAN2D. There is a motivation for that, as simple as convincing: when dealing with linked data structures most programmers develop their algorithms with the aid of diagrams. In /Kn 68/, p. 256 Knuth recommends:"... it is helpful to draw "before and after" diagrams and to compare them to see which links need to be changed." But if these diagrams are so closely related to the problem, why translating them into the linear notation of some programming language instead of using them as programs directly understandable to the computer? So, the basic feature of PLAN2D consists of "before and after" diagrams which are merged into one diagram describing the desired manipulations of links and other entities. Matching the "before" diagram with the data structure is required, i.e. pattern matching is - besides the two-dimensional notation - the most important feature of PLAN2D.

[+] We should like to emphasize that PLAN2D has nothing to do with flow charts and to state our reluctance to them because they are one main source of "unstructured" programming.

These basic ideas used in PLAN2D are originally due to Carlos Christensen, who developed the AMBIT/G and AMBIT/L languages for list processing (see for example /Chr 68/, /Wo 72/). The main progress of PLAN2D in comparison to AMBIT is its formal definition of both syntax and semantics. An overview about the state of the art of two-dimensional programming languages is given in /We 72/.
Due to the fact that it heavily relies on pattern matching, PLAN2D gains some characteristics of a very high level language (see /LeSa 74/).

In order to preclude misunderstandings we should explicitly state that PLAN2D is not a graphical programming language, it does not deal with the manipulation of pictures. PLAN2D is related to Computer Graphics only in so far as it uses an interactive display system for input of programs.

Finally, we should emphasize that we do not consider PLAN2D to be the only two-dimensional programming language, but view it as a case study about how two dimensions could be exploited for programming.

2. Basic Features of PLAN2D

This paper does not provide an exhaustive description of PLAN2D, but only deals with its most important concepts, which are illustrated by an example in section 3. It might be hard to understand the concepts without knowing the example and vice versa. Therefore, the reader is recommended to read section 2 and 3 in parallel.

2.1 Graphical Representation of Data Structures

PLAN2D deals with structures, which are built up from elementary data types and pointers. Structures may themselves contain structures. A structure representing nodes of a binary tree would be defined e.g. in ALGOL 68 as

mode bintree = *struct* (*bool* mark, rightback, *ref bintree* llink, rlink)

The PLAN2D declaration of this structure is given in fig. 5. Such a declaration consists of a frame labeled with the name (type) of the structure (*bintree*). This frame contains an assembly of elements, which constitute the structure. Elementary data (*int, real, bool, string*) and structure components defined elsewhere are represented by rectangular boxes labeled with a field selector and containing the type description. Pointer components are depicted by hexagonal boxes with the type of the structure they are allowed to point to in it and also with a label as field selector.[+)]

Applied occurrences of the *bintree* structure declared in fig. 5 may be found in the PLAN2D program of fig. 6. The selector names need not to be used in applied occurrences of a structure if "selection by position" is unambiguously feasible.

[+)] We should like to acknowledge that parts of our two-dimensional notation are heavily influenced by the pictures S.G. van der Meulen introduced to the ALGOL 68 community.

Selection by position means that defining and applied occurrence of a structure are drawn with the same layout. Then e.g. the upper left boxes of the applied *bintree* structures always denote the *mark* component. Drawing always with the same layout may be well supported by an interactive graphics system which is used for editing PLAN2D programs. If for some reasons selection by position is ambiguous selector names have to be used.

If the content of a structure element is not important, i.e. if it is only used as a reference point for some pointers, it may be simply depicted by an empty rectangular box.

Not only structures, but also simple data elements are represented two-dimensionally.

2.2 Operating on the Data Structure by Means of Pattern Matching

Pattern matching means that a somehow defined data structure template is matched with (a part of) the data structure generated during execution of a program. If the pattern matches, some specific modifications are applied to the data structure, otherwise some other modifications take place. The pattern to be matched and the according modifications are drawn in one diagram, which is called a rule. More precisely, a rule semantically consists of five parts: the set of anchors, the if-part, the then-part, the else-part, the unconditional-part.

The first two parts must not be empty, whereas the last three parts may be.

1. The set of anchors in e.g. rule (R6) of fig. 6 consists of the pointers *prev* and *pres*. Generally, all variables in a rule are considered to be anchors. They are used for tying the rule at the appropriate part of the data structure.

2. Starting at the anchors a scan and comparison algorithm matches the if-part of the rule against the data structure. This matching is done according to the following two criteria, which constitute the if-part:
   - The structural criterion: The objects pointed to in the data structure are compared with those referenced by the fully drawn links in the rule. This criterion would not be met, e.g. if in rule (R6) *rlink (prev)* = *nil*, because *nil* is an object, which does not contain any components as *rlink (prev)* does. Another example is rule (R5), whose if-part matches successfully only if *pres* and *root* point to the same node.
   - The value criterion: Values of variables or components of structures can be compared with type conforming expressions. This can be done by inscribing the expression preceded by a relational operator in the variable or structure component to be compared. E.g. = *false* in the *mark* field of *rlink (prev)* is the (single) value criterion of rule (R6).

The if-part evaluates to true, if both, the structural and the value criterion evaluate to true. Then we say, the pattern (of the rule) matches, otherwise it does not match.

3. The <u>then-part</u> describes the modifications which have to take place in the data structure, if the if-part evaluates to true. Again, these modifications are concerned either with structure or with values:
   - <u>Structural modifications</u> means changing pointers according to dashed links.
   - <u>Value modifications</u> are assignments, which are denoted by single quoted expressions. E.g. the then-part of (R6) assigns the value $true$ to the $rightback$ field of $prev$.
4. The <u>else-part</u> is executed, if the pattern does not match. It is distinguished from the then-part by dashed-dotted links for structural and double quoted expressions for value modifications.
5. The <u>unconditional-part</u> describes modifications, which have to be executed regardless of the if-part. Pointer modifications are depicted by double dashed/dashed-dotted links, value modifications by unquoted expressions. E.g. rule (R2) unconditionally assigns $true$ to the $mark$ component of $llink(pres)$.

Table 1 summarizes the syntactic means for distinguishing the different parts of a rule.

	structure (links)	values (expressions)
if-part	⟶	expressions preceded by $=, \neq, <, \leq, >, \geq$
then-part	−−−⟶	single quoted expressions ('true')
else-part	−·−·−⟶	double quoted expressions ("true")
unconditional-part	=·=·=⟹	unquoted expressions (true)

<u>Table 1</u> Syntactic distinction of the parts of a rule

The introduction stated that PLAN2D is in some aspects a very high level language. This might be verified by noticing that
- no rule of the PLAN2D marking procedure (fig. 6) needs an auxiliary pointer as all one-dimensional versions use it for temporary referencing a node (e.g. $llink(pres)$ in (R2)) and that
- the PLAN2D programmer is not concerned with the order of the pointer modifications, which is of extreme importance in string language programs.

This meets the objective of very high level languages that the order of sequencing should not be specified by the programmer and, more generally, that he should state "what to do" not "how to do it" /LeSa 74/.

2.3 LANGUAGE AND CONTROL STRUCTURE

PLAN2D is a block oriented language, i.e. each block consists of a declarative and an operational part. The operational part which has to be drawn below the declarative part is a set of blocks and rules arbitrarily arranged in the two dimensions. The flow of control between these entities (blocks and rules) scattered within the frame of a block is governed by the following laws:

1. Unconnected entities one beneath the other are executed <u>sequentially</u>; the topmost first, the bottom most last.
2. The execution sequence of unconnected entities side by side is undefined, i.e. they may be executed <u>concurrently</u>.
3. A rule may select its <u>successor</u> entity according to the <u>pattern matching</u> (see fig. 1).

executed, if pattern matches — block or rule — executed, if pattern does not match

Fig. 1   Successor by condition rule

4. A rule may be executed as long as its pattern matches successfully, i.e. it may select itself as a successor. Such a rule is called a <u>repetitive rule</u> and is depicted by an arrow pointing to itself (rules (R2) and (R4)). If the pattern does no longer match, the successor entity is chosen according to one of the other laws.
5. PLAN2D has not goto, but instead provides the <u>leave rule</u> as an escape mechanism. See e.g. leave rules (R3) and (R5), which cause an escape from blocks (B3) and (B1), respectively. A leave may convey a value, which is then going to be the value of the block left (not present in fig. 6).
6. Similar to repetitive rules there exist <u>repetitive blocks</u>. There are blocks with unconditional repetition ((B2) and (B3)) and two cases of conditional repetition (fig. 2).

(a) WHILE cond DO....   (b) REPEAT .... UNTIL cond

Fig. 2 Conditional repetitive blocks

2.4 SOME OTHER FEATURES

Fig. 6 is an example of a <u>procedure</u> declaration in PLAN2D. A more general example can be found in fig. 3.

The orientation of the parameter flow links enables the specification of three kinds of parameters:
- input parameters ($i1$, $i2$, $root$), called by value,
- transient parameters ($flag$), called by value-result,
- output parameters ($node$, s), called by result.

If there are two or more paramters of one kind they have to be labeled by natural numbers in order to be able to appropriately match formal and actual parameters. Notice that in contrast to a linear procedure call the two-dimensional call explicitly bears information about the kind of parameter transmission (input, output, transient); a redundancy, which enhances program security.

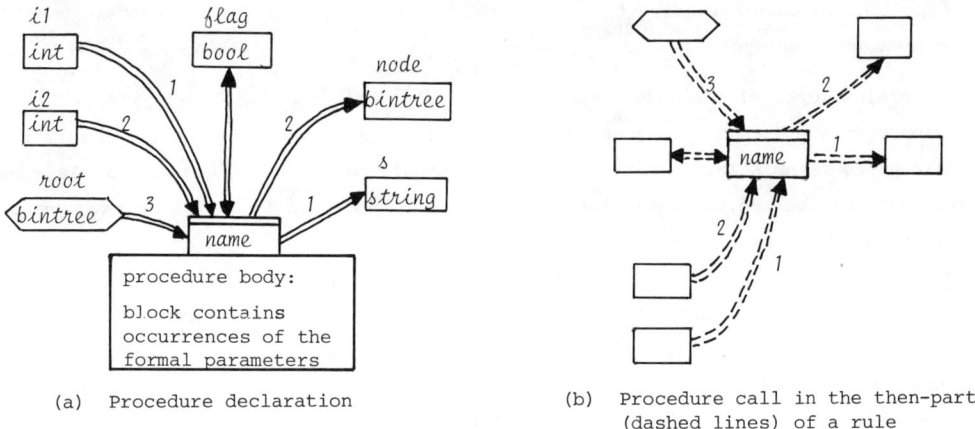

(a) Procedure declaration

(b) Procedure call in the then-part (dashed lines) of a rule

Fig. 3 Declaration and application of a procedure called *name*

Besides other features, e.g. the heap generator, also linear pieces of a guest language program are incorporated in PLAN2D.

3. An Example: Marking Algorithm without Auxiliary Stack

This section presents the PLAN2D version of a well known algorithm originally due to Schorr and Waite, who developed it for the purpose of garbage collection. A brief description may be found in /Kn 68/, p. 417.

The basic idea of that algorithm is to keep track of the way back through the data structure already traversed not by means of a stack, but by bending back one pointer of a node, to the predecessor (father) of that node. Taking a snapshot of a structure during traversal, it might look like fig. 4. The pointer couple *present* and *previous* is moved around so that *prev* always points to the node, where *pres* previously staid.

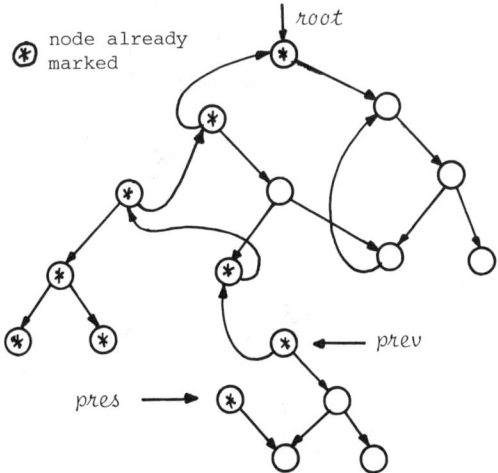

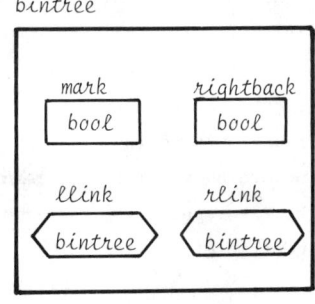

Fig. 4 Data structure during traversal

Fig. 5 Declaration of the node structure

Notice that we do not require the data structure to be a tree, it may contain shared subtrees and even cycles.

Our version works with a node structure as in fig. 5.
The *boolean* field *mark* is assumed to be *false* for all nodes in the memory before the *marking* algorithm starts. After its completion all nodes, which are accessible from the *root*, are marked, i.e. the *mark* field of these nodes is *true*. Of course, the link structure has to be the same as before.

The PLAN2D *marking* procedure is given in fig. 6.

After declaring the pointer couple (D1), *pres* and *prev* are initialized to point to the *root* (R1), which is also marked. The repetitive rule (R2) moves the pointer couple along the *llinks* until a node is encountered, which is either empty (*llink* (*pres*)=*nil*) or already marked (*mark* (*llink* (*pres*))= *true*). If one of these conditions occurs, the pattern of the rule does not match the data structure (else-part) whereby the repetition of (R2) is terminated. Otherwise (then-part), the *llink* is bent backward and accordingly the *rightback* field is set to *false*. *llink* (*pres*) is unconditionally marked.

In a similar manner rule (R3) causes one step to the right if possible, i.e. if *rlink* (*pres*) is not *nil* or marked. Then, due to the repetitive block (B3), rule (R2) is executed again. If it is impossible to move to the right, i.e. if pattern (R3) does not match, the repetition of block (B3) is terminated and control switches to rule (R4). Summarising, the effect of (B3) could be described by:

repeat: go left as far as possible (R2), then move one step to the right (R3)
until: no right son exists.

The repetitive rule (R4) causes an upward movement as long as *rlinks* are bent backward. This condition is checked by means of the truth value of the *rightback* field. This rule resets the bended pointers to its old position.

The leave rule (R5) terminates the program, if the *root* was encountered while climbing up its right subtree. Notice, that meeting the *root* from the left subtree must not stop the algorithm, because the right subtree has still to be visited.

Rule (R6) matches a situation where the *llink* is bent backward at any rate, because one is still climbing upward, but due to (R4) there is no more backward *rlink*. So (R6) resets the *llink* unconditionally. Whether one has to further climb up or to visit the right subtree depends on *rlink* (*prev*). If it is not *nil* and not marked (then-part), the right subtree is visited, the *rlink* is bent backward and the *rightback* field is set accordingly. The else-part causes a further upward movement.

Block (B2) repeats the alternating up and down moving until the whole structure, which is accessible from the *root*, is visited.

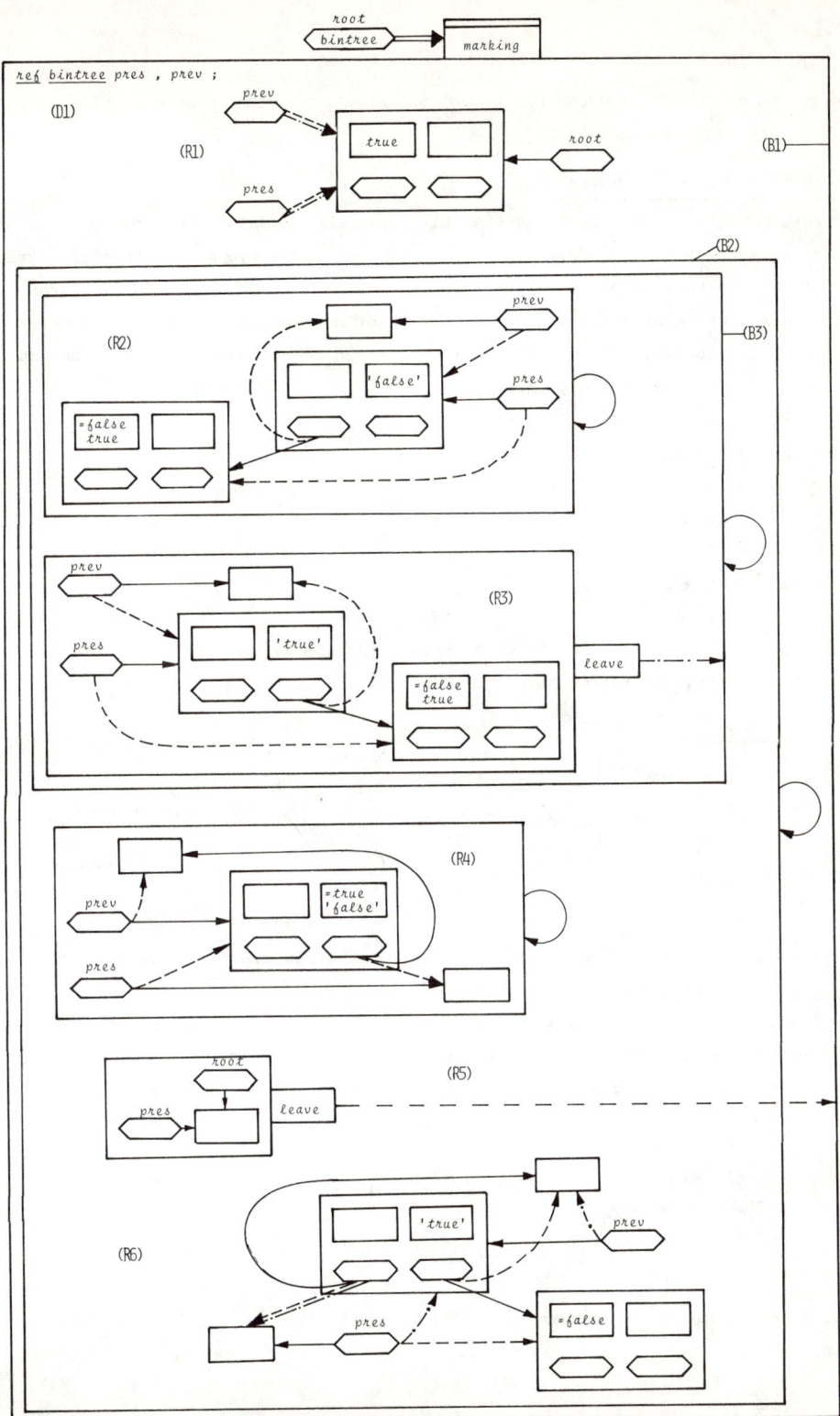

Fig.6 PLAN2D version of the marking algorithm
(symbols in paranthesis, like (B2), are references for the text, not part of the program)

4. Syntax of PLAN2D

The syntax of PLAN2D is described by use of Chomsky' systems over partially ordered symbol sets defined in /Sch 70/.

4.1 Description Method

For sake of brevity we cannot give in this paper the formal definitions of n-diagrams and n-grammars (see /Sch 70/). So we will give an intuitive description of n-grammars and how to use them to derive pictures. The most important idea with n-diagrams is to describe a picture by means of a fixed number of n relations between the single parts of the whole picture. We take the following seven relations to describe the important connections within a PLAN2D-program:

x	in	y	:⟺	x lies within y
x	hg	y	:⟺	x hangs on y
x	lf	y	:⟺	x lies left of, but neither over nor under y
x	ov	y	:⟺	x lies over y
x	fr	y	:⟺	x emanates from y
x	to	y	:⟺	x points to y
x	co	y	:⟺	x is concatenated with y

How to describe a PLAN2D-program with these relations we demonstrate in fig. 7 by showing the n-diagram representing rule (R5):

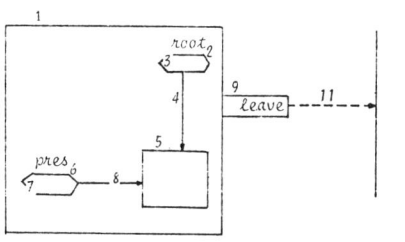
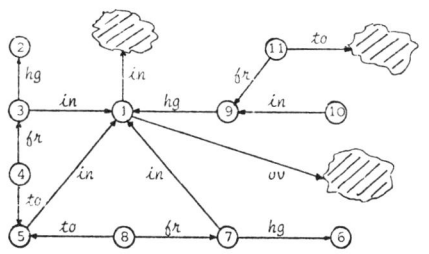

(a) Rule (R5) with labels   (b) n-diagram representing (R5)

Fig. 7 Formal description of rule (R5)

We give two examples to demonstrate how we describe grammar rules in the PLAN2D-syntax by using n-diagrams with these relations.

First fig. 8 shows the grammar rule from the application of which essentially the control structure feature described in section 2.3.3 and fig. 1 is derived.

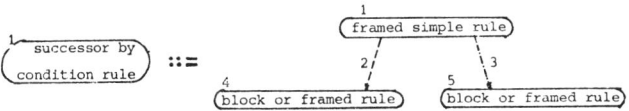

Fig. 8 An example of a grammar rule (The elements within a ⬭ frame are non-terminals.)

The relevant relations on the right side of this grammar rule are given by the graph of fig. 9a. The numbers of the nodes of this graph correspond to the numbering of the elements of the right side of the rule in fig. 8. So, e.g. the edge 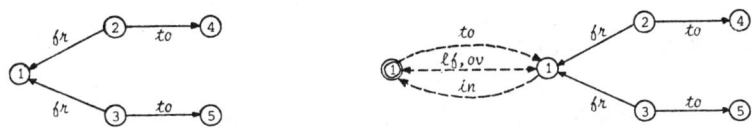 expresses that the element no. 2, the arrow -----▶, is related to the element no. 1 by the relation $from$. So far we got the description of the grammar rule itself. But if we want to apply this rule to an already derived node labeled (successor by condition rule) there might be some relations beginning or ending at this node. To complete the description of the rule we must prescribe which of these relations must be inherited to nodes of the right hand side of the rule after replacement. We give this supplementary description by the graph of fig. 9b. For the distinction between nodes representing parts of the left and the right hand side of the rule those for the left side will be

(a) Right hand side   (b) Complete rule

Fig. 9 Relational description of the grammar rule of fig. 8

encircled twice - in fig. 9b the single node ① .

The meaning of the three dashed edges is the following:
- if there is an edge pointing to the nonterminal (successor by condition rule) which is to be replaced then this edge has to point to node ① after replacement if the edge is labeled to, lf or ov.
- if there is an edge starting at (successor by condition rule) it has to start after replacement at node ① if this edge is labeled in, lf or ov.

Intuitively this means: If e.g. the nonterminal to be replaced lies within some element k i.e. there is an edge from (successor by condition rule) to k labeled in then after replacement the nonterminal (framed simple rule) lies within k, too, which is described by an edge from (framed simple rule) to k.

The second example shows a context-sensitive rule which ties together a data structure and a pointer to it derived independent of each other (fig. 10).

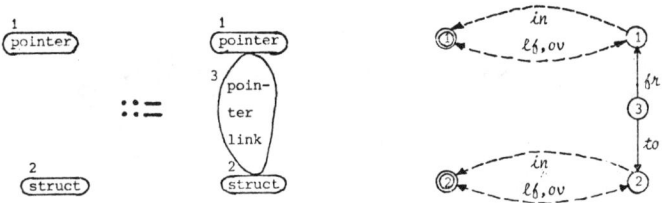

Fig. 10 A context-sensitive grammar rule of PLAN2D

These context-sensitivities are due to the two-dimensional notation of PLAN2D-programs.

4.2 Two-dimensional Precedence-Grammars and Syntax Analysis

We describe pictures by n-diagrams, i.e. by directed graphs with labeled nodes. So the syntax analysis in general and especially the search for a handle for reduction leads to the problem of searching sub-graphs in a given graph. It is well known that this problem is practically unsolvable in full generality for non trivial graphs. In analogy to the development of compiler construction for string-grammars about ten years ago we define precedence graph grammars in order to simplify the search for handles. We give the following intuitive description of our method.

The syntax analysis algorithm has as input data at any level a n-diagram, i.e. a rather unrestricted weighted directed graph. Traversing and modifying this graph we know at any node k

- the element of the symbol set belonging to k, e.g. ☐, ⌬, ---→, etc.
- the set of edges (relations) starting or ending at k.

We use these informations together with a precedence-cube to decide locally if k either belongs to a possible handle or in which direction to proceed to reach a handle in the following way:

For all edges starting at k, i.e. (k, l) ∈ rel where rel may be any of the n relations we know the symbols k' out of the symbol set belonging to k and l' belonging to l. Now we look up the precedence cube P at the entrance P (k', l', rel). If P (k',l',rel)=⋖ then k does not belong to a handle and we pass by to l. If P (k', l', rel) = ≐ then k belongs to a handle together with node l and possibly some other nodes which are found by looking at the rest of the edges by which k and l are connected to the n-diagram. If P(k', l', rel) = ⋗ we have to test the other edges. If for all connections the entry is also ⋗ then k alone is a handle; if not, see the other two possibilities above. For an edge ending at k we proceed analogously. For string grammars the precedence declaration leads to the enclosing of the handle in brackets like ⋖....⋗ . Consequently for our precedence n-grammars a handle is separated from the sets of the graph by brackets of the form ⋗ . In fig. 11 we show a n-diagram where the edges are labeled by symbols from the precedence cube and there we recognize four possible handles: node 5, node 8, nodes 10 and 11, nodes 1, 2 and 3.

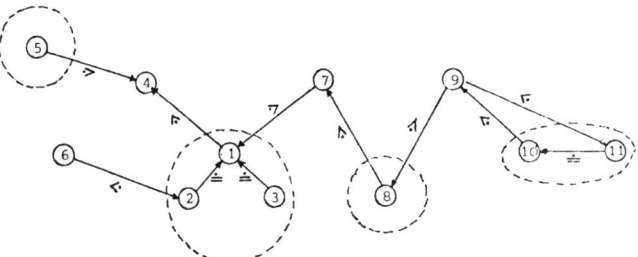

Fig. 11 A n-diagram with precedence relations

5. SEMANTICS OF PLAN2D

For the purpose of this paper it will suffice to sketch simply the basic framework of concepts currently under development and which will be reported in full elsewhere. The approach taken is the constructive one.

First a translator is defined which maps programs represented diagramatically by the PLAN2D-syntax into an abstract model. The translated program then becomes part of the initial state of an abstract machine. As far as we can see it seems to be possible to introduce the same basic definitional facility to model the abstract program and the states of the abstract machine as for the syntactic definitions (n-diagrams). This means that a general class of objects called semantic-n-diagram is defined in such a way that both the abstract program model and the states of a relevant class of abstract machines can be identified with subclasses of these objects.

Very informally a semantic-n-diagram can be viewed as an attributed n-diagram where some set of attributes defines the characteristics of the information contained in that n-diagram. A semantic-n-diagram in turn may consist of other semantic-n-diagrams where the dependencies between them are expressed by relations - this permits the structuring of the abstract program and data.

There is a diagramatic representation of semantic-n-diagrams and therefore we have a two-dimensional description method of the semantics of PLAN2D too.

6. REFERENCES

/TDMMC 72/   Proceedings of a Symposium on *Two-Dimensional Man-Machine Communication* (M.B.Wells, J.B.Morris, eds), Los Alamos, ACM SIGPLAN Notices, Vol.7, No.10, Oct.1972

/We 72/   Wells, M.B., *A Review of Two-Dimensional Programming Languages*, in: /TDMMC 72/, pp. 1-10

/Chr 68/   Christensen, C., *An Example of the Manipulation of Directed Graphs in the AMBIT/G Programming Language*, in: Klerer, M., Reinfelds, J.(eds), Interactive Systems for Experimental Applied Mathematics, Acad. Press, N.Y. 68

/Wo 72/   Wolfberg, M.S., *Fundamentals of the AMBIT/L List-Processing Language*, in: /TDMMC 72/, pp. 66-75

/LeSa 74/   Leavenworth, B.M., Sammet, J.E., *An Overview of Nonprocedural Languages*, Proceedings of a Symposium on Very High Level Languages, Santa Monica, Cal., ACM SIGPLAM Notices, Vol.9, No.4, April 74

/Sch 70/   Schneider, H.J., *Chomsky-Systeme für partielle Ordnungen*, Arbeitsberichte des Instituts für Math.Maschinen und Datenverarbeitung, Band 3, Nr.3, Erlangen, Aug. 1970

/Kn 68/   Knuth, D.E., *The Art of Computer Programming*, Vol.1, Addison-Wesley 1968

ON A SLR(k)-BASED PARSER SYSTEM WHICH ACCEPTS NON-LR(k)GRAMMARS

Hans H. Kron[+], Hans-Jürgen Hoffmann, Gerhard Winkler
Technische Hochschule Darmstadt, Fachbereich Informatik

Abstract

A context-free parser system based on DeRemer's SLR(k)-method is described. It consists of
(i) a *parser generator* constructing for any given context-free grammar SLR(k)-control tables as far as practicable and
(ii) a *parser* analysing sentences from left to right with occasional look-ahead. Emphasized is, by presenting some impressive examples, the treatment of non-LR(k) grammars in the system.

Introduction and relation to Knuth's and DeRemer's work; the LR-parser in our system

The fundamental concept of *LR(k)-grammars* as defined by Knuth[1] has proven ([2],[3]) to be a powerful tool for implementation of programming languages because the class of grammars successfully treatable is sufficiently large and still allows the use of efficient parser generating techniques. See [4] for a survey.

The parser in our system consists of two parts. One part is a traditional *LR-parser*. We discuss it in terms of DeRemer's paper[5] split into two machines, M_0 and M_1. We concentrate the discussion on parsing correct sentences as the behaviour of the machines with incorrect sentences is obvious.

The *LR(0) machine* M_0 consists of:
(i) A single cell for storing terminal or nonterminal symbols called *buffer*.
(ii) An *input tape* on which a sentence is written. The *input head* I_0 is able to *read* the contents of a cell into the buffer and to advance to the next cell.
(iii) A *finite control* C_0 in which the *"Characteristic finite-state machine"* (CFSM[5]) is embedded. C_0 is characterized by
  a) *states* $S_i \epsilon Z$, $i \geq 0$, Z finite, and
  b) *transitions* $t \epsilon T$, T finite, between states.
(iv) A stack for storing names of states, the *main stack*.

Whenever C_0 enters a state, the concatenated contents of main stack, buffer and unexamined portion of tape represents a sentential form (provided the sentence is correct). If the *current state* (i.e., the state whose name is on top of main stack) is a *read* or *reduce state* and determines together with the symbol in buffer a transition, M_0 performs that transition. If the current state is an *inadequate state*, M_0 must employ machine M_1 to determine a transition by look-ahead.

The *look-ahead machine* M_1 consists of:
(i) An *input head* I_1 which is able to *inspect* the contents of a cell of the input tape and to advance to the next cell atmost k times, $k \geq 1$, starting with the position of I_0.

[+] Present address: Dept. Information Sciences, University of California, Santa Cruz.

(ii) A *finite control* C_1 in which the *"look-ahead finite-state machine"* (LFSM) associated to the current, inadequate state, say S_i, of M_0 is embedded. C_1 associated to S_i is characterized by a *look-ahead tree* E_i with atmost k levels whose
   a) *edges* are labelled with symbols in V_T, V_T the terminal alphabet, and whose
   b) *leaves* bear a label identifying a transition from S_i.

When advancing I_1 through the tape, control C_1 of M_1 follows the sequence of edges in E_i which are labelled with the symbols read until a leaf is reached. Its label identifies the transition which M_0 has to perform.

We define the *k-look-ahead set* $K^k(t)$ of some transition t from an inadequate state S_i to be the set of strings achieved by concatenation of atmost k symbols along edges of E_i leading to any leaf labelled with t. The LR-parser formed by machines M_0 and M_1 will deterministically accept all sentences of a language if for all inadequate states the k-look-ahead sets for transitions in such a state are pairwise disjoint.

For a given grammar of a language there are different methods to construct (by the parser generator) the CFSM and LFSMs for its inadequate states. Each method defines a class of grammars for which the construction results in pairwise disjoint k-look-ahead sets in all inadequate states. One such grammar class is the class of SLR(k)-grammars as introduced by DeRemer[5]. The method which we use in our parser generator defines a class which we call FSLR(k); for details see [6]. We prove in [6] that
a) *FSLR(k) and SLR(k) are equivalent for k=0 and k=1*, and that
b) *FSLR(k) is a proper subclass of SLR(k) for k>1*.

We shall revert to the distinction between SLR(k) and FSLR(k) in the following section after presenting our construction method for LFSMs.

<u>Our method for construction of a CFSM and of LFSMs</u>

Prior to the discussion of the second part of our parser we briefly present our method for construction of a CFSM and of LFSMs associated to its inadequate states. The method yields for any grammar the same CFSM as DeRemer's method; it may yield different LFSMs. Therefore we concentrate on the LFSM construction.

Given the context-free *grammar* $G=(V_T,V_N,P,R)$ of a language L (without empty sentence λ in L); V_T the terminal and V_N the nonterminal alphabets, respectively, $V_T \cup V_N = V$; P the set of productions; and $R \in V_N$ the sentence symbol; $R \rightarrow \dashv R' \vdash$ the only production for R, $R' \in V_N$; "$\dashv$", "$\vdash$"$\in V_T$ unique terminator symbols. The parser generator defines a state $S_i \in Z$ of the LR(0) machine M_0 by an unique set of *configurations* $[p,m]$. Let S_1 be the initial and S_0 the final state of the CFSM. A configuration of S_i indicates that the first m symbols of the right-hand side of production $p(=A \rightarrow \omega) \in P$, $0 \leq m \leq |\omega|$, will match the portion of some valid sentence most recently read by M_0 when in state S_i.

A *read transition* from S_i is a triple $t=[S_i,v,S_j]$ where $S_i,S_j \in Z-\{S_0\}, v \in V$; we call S_j the *v-successor* of S_i.

A *reduce transition* from S_i is a triple $t=[S_i,p,S_0]$ where $S_i \in Z-\{S_0\}, p \in P$.

Our parser generator constructs the CFSM according to DeRemer's method (with some minor changes in the algorithm). Due to space limitations we refer to [6] for any details. States S_i are classified:

(i) S_i is a *read state* (R-state) if all transitions from S_i are read transitions.
(ii) S_i is a *reduce state* (P-state) if the only transition from S_i is a reduce transition.
(iii) Otherwise, S_i is an *inadequate state* (I-state).

If there are no I-states in Z, M_o with the CFSM constructed to be embedded in its control C_o is a parser for grammar G. G is FSLR(0) (and also SLR(0) and LR(0), respectively). Otherwise (and provided that the user of our parser system has set $k_{max}>0$, k_{max} a limit for look-ahead construction) the parser generator constructs for any I-state S_i a look-ahead tree E_i (with atmost k_{max} levels) which characterizes the LFSM associated to S_i. The leaves of E_i bear a label which either
a) identifies a transition from S_i or
b) is a special *indecision flag*, say "?".

An E_i with no "?" is called *final*, otherwise it is called *dropped* (if it has some leaf labelled with a transition) or it is called *undone* (if it has none). A grammar G is called FSLR(k), $k \leq k_{max}$, if the trees of all I-states of its CFSM are final and have atmost k levels; the first part of our parser, i.e., M_o and M_1 together, are a parser for G. If there is any E_i which is dropped or undone the first part of the parser is not sufficient (and the second part to be described in the next section is needed).

We need some auxiliary steps for the construction of LFSMs which we first define:

<u>procedure</u> set-Q'-*of-nonterminals-which-derive*-$(A \epsilon V_N)$-*in-a-rightmost-position*:
(i) Compute $Q(A)=\{B \epsilon V_N | B \to \alpha A \epsilon P$ for some $\alpha \epsilon V^*\}$ (by scanning productions in P).
(ii) Compute $Q'(A)=\{B \epsilon V_N | B \overset{*}{\Rightarrow} \alpha A$ for some $\alpha \epsilon V^*\}$ (by the recursive construction $Q'(A)=\{A\} \cup \{C \epsilon V_N | C \epsilon Q(B)$ for some $B \epsilon Q'(A)\})$.

<u>procedure</u> set-D-*of-terminal-transitions-achieved-by*-$(t \epsilon T)$:
(i) <u>case</u> t is
   (i.a) terminal transition <u>then</u> $D=\{t\}$.
   (i.b) nonterminal transition <u>then</u> $D=\emptyset$.
   (i.c) reduce transition, say $[S_i, A \to \omega, S_o]$ <u>then</u> $D=\{u \epsilon T | \exists B \epsilon Q'(A), \exists S_j \epsilon Z: S_j$ is a B-successor and u is a terminal transition from $S_j\}$
        (in other words: We collect terminal transitions u from each state $S_j \epsilon Z$ satisfying a) S_j not a P-state and b) S_j a B-successor for some $B \epsilon Q'(A)$).

<u>procedure</u> set-D_i-*of-terminal-transitions-achieved-in-state*-S_i:
(i) $D_i=\{u | u \epsilon D(t)$ for some transition t from $S_i\}$.

<u>procedure</u> leaf-W-*labelled-with*-$(t \epsilon T$ or $t=$"?")-*and-edge-from*-(N)-*under*$(v \epsilon V_T)$:
(i) Add to E_i a leaf, say M, labelled with t.
(ii) Add to E_i an edge from N under v to M.

Construct now <u>LFSM</u> for any I-state $S_i \epsilon Z$ as follows:
(i) Set k=1; establish (non-leaf) root N_o of E_i on level k.
(ii) <u>repeat</u> (ii.1) through (ii.2) <u>until</u> there are no non-leaves on level k:
    (ii.1) <u>for each</u> non-leaf N on level k <u>do</u>
        (ii.1.1) <u>if</u> k=1 <u>then</u> compute $H'=\{(u,t) | u \epsilon D(t)$ for some $t \epsilon T$ from $S_i\}$
             <u>else</u> compute $H'=\{(u,t) | \exists (S_j,t) \epsilon H_N : u \epsilon D_j\}$
             (In either case, a pair $(u,t) \epsilon H'$ means that transition u may be used to concatenate one terminal to the end of some look-ahead string belonging to t).

(ii.1.2) <u>for each</u> $b \epsilon V_T$ <u>do</u>
    (ii.1.2.1) Compute $H_N^{(b)} = \{(S_1,t) | \exists (u,t) \epsilon H', S_j \epsilon Z : u = [S_j,b,S_1]\}$
    (A pair $(S_1,t) \epsilon H_N^{(b)}$ means that S_1 will be entered after concatenating terminal b to the end of some look-ahead string belonging to t).
    (ii.1.2.2) <u>if</u> $\exists t_o \epsilon T : \forall (S_1,t) \epsilon H_N^{(b)} : t = t_o$ <u>then</u> $W(t_o,N,b)$.
    (ii.1.2.3) <u>if</u>($(\exists u,t\epsilon T, u \neq t; \exists S_1, S_m \epsilon Z, S_1 \neq S_m : (S_1,t),(S_m,u)\epsilon H_N^{(b)})$ <u>and</u> (b=⊢ <u>or</u> k=k_{max}) <u>or</u>
    $(\exists u,t\epsilon T, u \neq t; \exists S_1 \epsilon Z : (S_1,t),(S_1,u)\epsilon H_N^{(b)}))$ <u>then</u> $W("?",N,b)$(E_i is dropped!).
    (ii.1.2.4) <u>if</u>(<u>neither</u> condition in (ii.1.2.2) <u>nor</u> condition in (ii.1.2.3) holds) and $H_N^{(b)} \neq \emptyset$ <u>then do</u>
      (ii.1.2.4.1) Add to E_i a non-leaf, say M, on level k+1.
      (ii.1.2.4.2) Remember $H_M = H_N^{(b)}$.
      (ii.1.2.4.3) Add to E_i an edge from N under b to M.
(ii.2) Set k=k+1.
(iii) <u>while</u> $k \neq 1$ <u>do</u>
  (iii.1) Set k = k-1.
  (iii.2) <u>for each</u> non-leaf N on level k unless there is a path leading to some leaf labelled with $t \epsilon T$ <u>do</u>
    (iii.2.1) Remove all leaves with an edge <u>from</u> N.
    (iii.2.2) Remove all edges from N.
    (iii.2.3) Replace non-leaf N by a leaf N labelled with "?".
(iv) <u>if</u> N_o is a leaf labelled with "?", E_i is undone.

For a final E_i our construction leads to a k-look-ahead set $K^k(t)$ of a transition t from S_i which may be defined (by loss of some detail) recursively on the value of k to be:
(i) $K^k([S_i,v,S_j]) = \{v\eta | \exists \text{ transition t from } S_j : \eta \epsilon K^{k-1}(t)\}$,
(ii) $K^k([S_i,A\rightarrow\omega,S_o]) = \{v\eta | \exists S_j \epsilon Z \text{ which is B-successor from some state, } B \epsilon Q'(A):$
$\exists S_1 \epsilon Z : ([S_j,v,S_1]) \epsilon T \& (\exists \text{ transition t from } S_1 : \eta \epsilon K^{k-1}(t)))\}$
$(v \epsilon V_T, (A\rightarrow\omega) \epsilon P, K^o(t) = \{\lambda\}$ for all t).
The sets $K^k(t)$ (for distinction we use $K_{Kron}^k(t)$) are modifications of DeRemer's
simple-k-look-ahead sets associated to transitions t [5] ; remember his definition (rephrased in our terminology):
(i) $K_{DeRemer}^k([S_i,v,S_j]) = \{v\eta | \exists \text{ transition t from } S_j : \eta \epsilon K_{DeRemer}^{k-1}(t)\}$,
(ii) $K_{DeRemer}^k([S_i,A\rightarrow\omega,S_o]) = F_T^k(A) = \{\sigma \epsilon V_T^* | R \overset{*}{\Rightarrow} \alpha A \beta \& \sigma = k:\beta\}$.
From DeRemer's theorem ([5] , appendix) on $F_T^1(A)$ it follows that $K_{DeRemer}^1(t) = K_{Kron}^1(t)$; thus the class of FSLR(1)-grammars is equivalent to the class of SLR(1)-grammars. Note that the choice of k=1 in LR-parsers is common practice. However for k>1 relation $K_{DeRemer}^k(t) \subseteq K_{Kron}^k(t)$ holds as, in general, not all B-successor states of our construction play a role during construction of $F_T^k(A)$ in DeRemer's method (only those which are in a valid derivation sequence); $K_{DeRemer}^k(t_o)$ a smaller set than $K_{Kron}^k(t_o)$ for some transition t_o from any I-state S_i may cause the pairwise intersection of this set with all sets $K_{DeRemer}^k(t)$ of transition $t \neq t_o$ from S_i to yield $\emptyset$ in a case where the intersection of sets $K_{Kron}^k(t)$ does not yield $\emptyset$; thus the class of FSLR(k) grammars, k>1, is a subclass of the class of SLR(k)-grammars (Example 2 demonstrates that it is a proper subclass).

The multiple-stack machine in our parser

If the construction of CFSM and LFSMs for a given grammar G of a language L shows that G is not FSLR(k) for some $k \leq k_{max}$ the parser may still use the CFSM and LFSMs constructed in I-states with final look-ahead trees to control machines M_o and M_1 as long as no sentence $w \epsilon L$ is presented which requires M_o to enter an I-state with a dropped or undone tree. Moreover, if M_o enters a I-state, say S_i, with E_i dropped and if the inspection in w, done by M_1, leads to a leaf of E_i which is labelled by a transition t, M_o has to perform t. Otherwise M_1 reaches a leaf flagged with "?". M_o calls the second part of our parser, the *multiple-stack machine* M_2. M_2 uses stack contents during following-up all possible parser transitions. It constructs a look-ahead tree for w until the transition from S_i is uniquely identified[+]. M_2 has no limitation k_{max} for the number of levels in look-ahead tree construction. Netherthless M_2 always stops after a finite number of levels because w is of finite length. M_2 contains a finite, although potentially unlimited number of submachines (SMs) which we call *engaged*:

(i) A set $\{\nu_g\}$ of *submachine buffers* one buffer for each SM μ_g engaged.

(ii) An *input head* I_2 which is able to *inspect* the contents of a cell of the input tape, to copy the contents into any submachine buffer, and to advance to the next cell (although not across the right terminator symbol "⊢").

(iii) A *finite control* C_2 in which the CFSM is embedded.

(iv) A set $\{\bar{G}_g\}$ of *substacks* one substack for each SM μ_g engaged.

(v) A set $\{\kappa_g\}$ of *labels* one label for each SM μ_g engaged.

If M_o enters an I-state, say S_{i_o}, and M_1 is not able to identify a transition (rather delivers "?") M_2 is started by engaging a submachine, say μ_1. Engaging μ_1 means:

(i) put I_2 on the position occupied by I_o.

(ii) copy main stack of M_o into $\bar{G}_1$.

(iii) enter μ_1 into state S_{i_o} (which is on top of $\bar{G}_1$).

M_2 operates (roughly speaking) in R- and P-states and in I-states with a transition identified by M_1 for each engaged submachine as would M_o; we extract from [6], where the full algorithm is given, that part which treats an I-state with "?" delivered by the preceding call of M_1:

⋮
(iii.1) let $b \in V_T$ be the look-ahead symbol under I_2.
⋮
(iii.3) <u>while</u> there is at least one engaged SM μ_g with $\nu_g \neq b$ <u>do</u>
    (iii.3.1) let μ_{go} be such a SM with S_1 on top of $\bar{G}_{go}$.
    (iii.3.2) <u>case</u> S_1 is
⋮
        (iii.3.2c) I-state <u>then</u>
            (iii.3.2c.2)(M_1 has delivered "?")
                <u>for each</u> $u=[S_1, A\rightarrow\omega, S_o]$ <u>do</u> *create-new-SM-from-μ_{go}-for-reduce-transition-u*
                (i.e., engage another SM, say μ_h, for transition u and parallel follow-up.
                ... μ_h will continue in <u>while</u>-loop in some state).
            (iii.3.2c.3)μ_{go}-*performs-read-transition-from* S_1
              (which may remove μ_{go} from the <u>while</u>-loop or may disengage μ_{go} depending on a read transition under b possible or not).
⋮
(iii.5) <u>if</u> all engaged SM's have the same label, say t, <u>then</u> return to M_o with result "t".
⋮
(iii.7) advance I_2 one position.

The multiple-stack machine M_2 as implemented has two essential properties:

a) M_2 performs look-ahead as long as no unique identification of a transition is ob-

---
[+] The treatment of ambiguous grammars though implemented in our system is not discussed here further. See [6] for a detailed discussion.

tained by parallel follow-up of any possible derivation.

b) By stack control M_2 uses B-successor states for reductions $A \to \omega$, $B \in Q'(A)$ only if they could be involved in an actual LR-parse. The set of states entered by all engaged submachines in some position of I_2 may be understood to be the subset of states, "correct" for parsing w, on the corresponding level of the look-ahead tree in the I-state for which M_2 is called to identify a transition.

There are similarities of our parser (which consists of the LR-parser *and* the multiple-stack machine) with a parser as Earley described [7]. The essential difference is that we construct control tables for all parser states under those circumstances which lead to unique parsing decisions whereas Earley's algorithm maintains full configuration sets during the actual parse also under those circumstances. We reference a recent paper by Lang [8] with results suggesting an approach similar to our one.

Parser for language $L_1 = \{\dashv a^{2n+1} \vdash \mid n \geq 0\}$

We present CFSM and, as fas as required, LFSM's for three grammars G_1, G_1', G_1'' for L_1.

a) Left-recursive grammar G_1 which is FSLR(0) (and hence also SLR(0), LR(0)).

Productions in G_1:
$R \to \dashv S \vdash$
$S \to S\, a\, a$
$S \to a$

CFSM: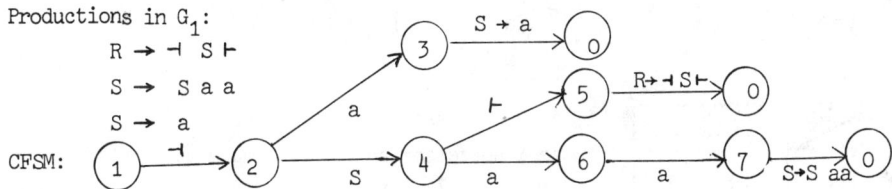

No inadequate state!

b) Right-recursive grammar G_1' which is FSLR(1) (and hence also SLR(1), LR(1)).

Productions in G_1':
$R \to \dashv S \vdash$
$S \to a\, a\, S$
$S \to a$

CFSM: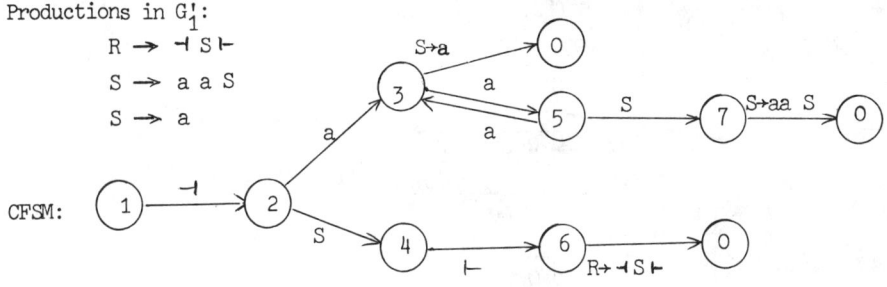

S_3 is an inadequate state!
To determine LFSM for state S_3 start with:

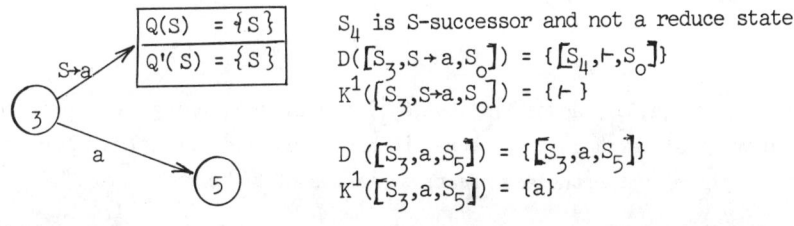

S_4 is S-successor and not a reduce state
$D([S_3, S \to a, S_0]) = \{[S_4, \vdash, S_0]\}$
$K^1([S_3, S \to a, S_0]) = \{\vdash\}$

$D([S_3, a, S_5]) = \{[S_3, a, S_5]\}$
$K^1([S_3, a, S_5]) = \{a\}$

LFSM for inadequate state S_3:

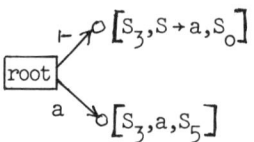

c) Self-embedding grammar G_1'' which is not FSLR(1) - it is not LR(k) for any finite k.
Productions in G_1'':

$R \rightarrow \dashv S \vdash$
$S \rightarrow aSa$
$S \rightarrow a$

CFSM:

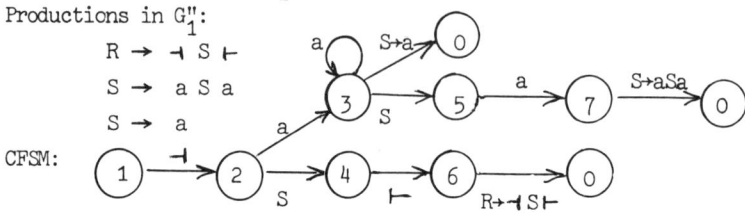

S_3 is an inadequate state!
Attempt to determine LFSM for state S_3 with $k_{max}=2$.
k=1:

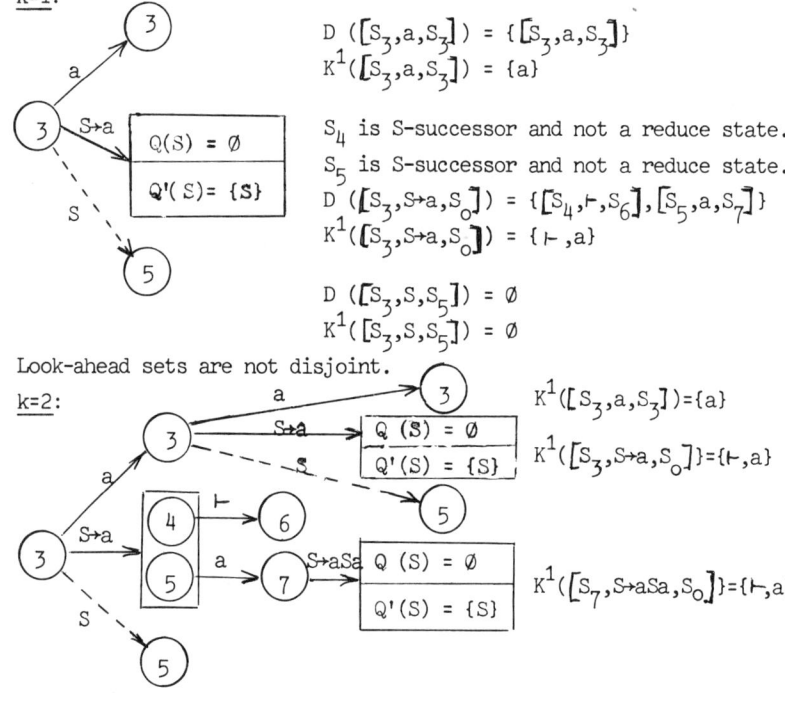

$D([S_3,a,S_3]) = \{[S_3,a,S_3]\}$
$K^1([S_3,a,S_3]) = \{a\}$

S_4 is S-successor and not a reduce state.
S_5 is S-successor and not a reduce state.
$D([S_3,S\rightarrow a,S_o]) = \{[S_4,\vdash,S_6],[S_5,a,S_7]\}$
$K^1([S_3,S\rightarrow a,S_o]) = \{\vdash,a\}$

$D([S_3,S,S_5]) = \emptyset$
$K^1([S_3,S,S_5]) = \emptyset$

Look-ahead sets are not disjoint.
k=2:

$K^1([S_3,a,S_3])=\{a\}$
$K^1([S_3,S\rightarrow a,S_o])=\{\vdash,a\}$
$K^1([S_7,S\rightarrow aSa,S_o])=\{\vdash,a\}$

Look-ahead sets $K^2([S_3,a,S_3])$ and $K^2([S_3,S\rightarrow a,S_o])$ remain overlapping as same states are again involved whatever k is chosen. See [6] for a parser protocol which demonstrates that the parser netherthless treats sentences of L_1 according to G_1''.

Parser for language $L_2 = \{\dashv abc\vdash, \dashv abd\vdash\}$

We present CFSM for a grammar G_2 for L_2 which is SLR(2) but not FSLR(k) for any finite k (Generalisation from k=2 to arbitrary k is obvious with $B \rightarrow b_1...b_{k-1}$). Thus in our system we have to utilize the capabilities of the second part of our parser in this example although a system with the first part only would also succeed if the parser generator would cover the full class of SLR(2)-grammars. We owe the example to a careful reader of a preliminary version of [6].

Productions in G_2:

$R \rightarrow \dashv S \vdash$
$S \rightarrow A B c$
$S \rightarrow A' B d$
$A \rightarrow a$
$A' \rightarrow a$
$B \rightarrow b$

CFSM:

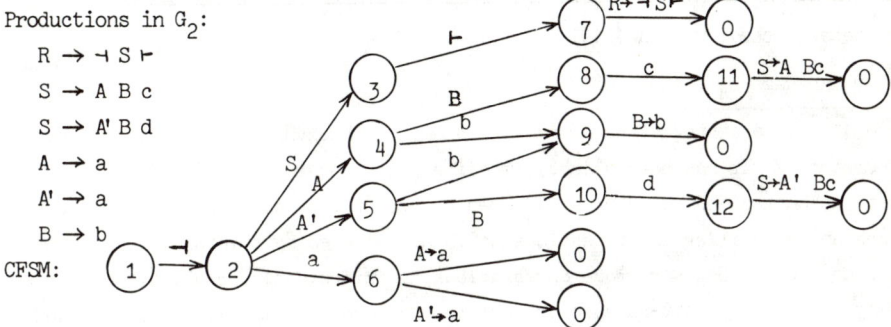

S_6 is an inadequate state!

Attempt to determine LFSM for state S_6.

k=1:

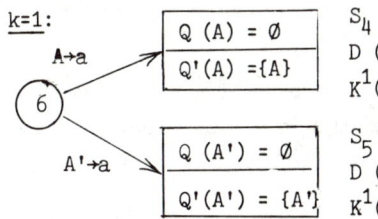

S_4 is A-successor and not a reduce state
$D([S_6, A \rightarrow a, S_o]) = \{[S_4, b, S_9]\}$
$K^1([S_6, A \rightarrow a, S_o]) = \{b\}$

S_5 is A'-successor and not a reduce state
$D([S_6, A' \rightarrow a, S_o]) = \{[S_5, b, S_9]\}$
$K^1([S_6, A' \rightarrow a, S_o]) = \{b\}$

Look-ahead sets are not disjoint.

k=2:

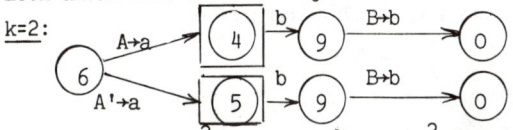

Look-ahead sets $K^2([S_6, A \rightarrow a, S_o])$ and $K^2([S_6, A' \rightarrow a, S_o])$ remain overlapping as both transitions lead to same state, S_9.

The parser, however, treats sentences of L_2 according to G_2 as is demonstrated by the parser protocol in [6].

Parser for language $L_3 \equiv$ ALGOL 60

We have run our parser generator with a grammar G_3 for ALGOL 60. G_3 has been prepared manually to achieve unambiguity for all programs. It assumes a lexical analysis and lexical substitution to be performed prior to the syntactical analysis of programs by our parser. Further we require arithmetic expressions which are conditioned to be parenthesised to the left or right of relational operators. G_3 was FSLR(1). We compared the result with some other parsers generated automatically. Furthermore we run the parser generator with an extension which performs some state minimisation [10].

figure of merit	LR(1) Korenjak [9]	LALR(1) Lalonde et.al.[2]	FSLR(1) 1st run	FSLR(1) 2nd run
number of terminal symbols	?	62	65	65
number of nonterminal symbols	?	82	62	62
number of productions	?	173	171	171
number of CFSM states	443	376	298	273

For more details see [10] and [11].

Parser for language $L_4 \equiv$ ALGOL 68

Grammar G_4 [12] is a context-free grammar of ALGOL 68 which has been developped by MBLE-Laboratories. It has been slightly modified with regard to the lexical analysis and substitution assumed. Of course, G_4 does not cover the semantics of *modes*, *context-conditions* and *priorities* in expressions which are covered by the two-level grammar in the defining report. However, *mode declarations*, *priority declarations* a.s.o. are syntactically included. <empty-rowed-coercend>, <empty-bound>, <empty-bound-pair>, and <empty-rowed-coercend-bound-pair> have to be identified in a program by terminal symbols introduced for that purpose prior to its submission to our parser (as to the MBLE-parser). There are some more modifications with regard to symbol representation; see [11] for details.

The final run of our parser generator with G_4 and $k_{max}=0$ (to avoid construction of look-ahead sets the documentation of which on about 2000 printer pages would have exceeded some spooling resources) on a SIEMENS 4004-46 was terminated normally with 3080 seconds CPU-time. We noticed:

75 terminal symbols,   170 nonterminal symbols,   170 productions.
754 CFSM-states including 118 inadequate states,   8767 transitions.
Tables constructed for the parser required 47 074 Bytes.

Some of the inadequate states have been investigated by hand. The grammar was found to be not FSLR(k) for any finite k (We did not expect to be!). We further noticed that the grammar was even not LR(k) for any finite k.

The parser was successfully used for parsing some programs. We give an example below with some interesting statistics:

```
begin
    proc innerproduct 1 = (int n, proc (int) real x,y) real:
    begin
        long real s:= long 0;
        for i to n do s plus leng x(i) * leng y (i);
        short s
    end;
innerproduct 1 (m,(int j) real: x1[j], y1)
end
```

222 reductions
74 look-aheads (by the parser) with k = 1
 5   "   ("   "   ") "   k = 2
 1 look-ahead   ("   "   ") "   k = 4 (in line 5 and 6)
 1   "   ("   "   ") "   k = 11 (in line 2, <formal parameter pack>).

The parser accepted the program after 55.8 seconds (time for producing documentation included).
We have run a similar experiment with a grammar G_5[13] of ALGOL 68 without essentially different results.

References

[1] D.E.Knuth: On the translation of languages from left to right; Inf.Control 8, 607-639 (1965).
[2] W.R.Lalonde, E.S.Lee, J.J.Horning: An LALR(k) parser generator; Proc.IFIP Congress 71, TA-3-183-187, North-Holland Publ. (1972).
[3] M.L.Joliat: Practical minimization of LR(k) parser tables; Proc.IFIP Congress 74, 376-380, North-Holland Publ. (1974).
[4] A.V.Aho, S.C.Johnson: LR parsing; ACM Comp.Surveys 6, 99-124 (1974).
[5] F.L.DeRemer: Simple LR(k) grammars; Comm.ACM 14, 453-460 (1971).
    ÷   : Practical translators for LR(k) languages; Project MAC, Oct.1969, MAC-TR-65, AD 699 501.
[6] H.H.Kron, H.-J.Hoffmann, G.Winkler: On an extension of SLR(k)-parsers to LR(k)-parsers with unbounded k; Research Report PU1R2/74, Comp.Science Dept., Techn. Univ. in Darmstadt, Sept. 1974.
[7] J.Earley: An efficient context-free parsing algorithm; Comm.ACM 13, 94-102 (1970).
[8] B.Lang: Deterministic techniques for efficient non-deterministic parsers; Lect. Notes in Comp.Sci.14, 255-269, Springer (1974).
[9] A.J.Korenjak: A practical method for constructing LR(k) parsers; Comm.ACM 12, 613-623 (1969).
[10] W.Mitteneder: Effizienter LR(1)-Parser; Diplomarbeit PÜ-S12, Comp.Science Dept., Techn. Univ. in Darmstadt, March 1974.
[11] H.H.Kron: Modifizierter LR(k)-Parser; Studienarbeit PÜ-S2, Comp.Science Dept., Techn. Univ. in Darmstadt, Dec. 1972.
[12] P.Branquart, et.al.: A context-free syntax of ALGOL 68; Inf.Proc.Letters 1, 141-148 (1972).
[13] M.Simonet: Une grammaire context-free d'ALGOL 68; Inst.Math.Appl. Grenoble (1970).

A Binary Control Structure and its Relationship to Grammars and Side Effects

H. Feuerhahn
Technische Universität Berlin

1. Introduction

In the theory of automatic parser generation for context free grammars, one parsing method has an outstanding position. Parsers based on this method, which has become known as no backup recursive descent parsing, may be generated from the grammar by a simple transcription process. This gives rise to the interpretation of grammars as programs with a simple binary control structure. If regular expressions as right sides are considered, this structure is powerful enough to express such structures as the _while_ ... _do_ structure or _do_ ... _until_ structure.

A graphic representation of grammar-based programs is introduced in an informal way. It gives rise to a "theory of side effects" and to the detection of structural errors. A formalization of similar systems can be found in [3].

An extension to affix grammars widens the idea of side effects and extends the control to parameters.

2. The interpretation of CF grammars as programs

2.1. Recursive descent parsing

The well-known parsing method of recursive descent is characterized by the fact that a parser can be obtained from a grammar by a simple transcription process, mapping each rule of the grammar into a parsing procedure for that rule [1, 2]. All those procedures simply consist of calls for other procedures in an order directly given by the structure of the corresponding CF rule. Such a procedure will be called a predicate.

More precisely:

By a predicate N we mean a Boolean procedure obtained by some transcription process from the (CF) rule, whose left hand side is a some nonterminal symbol n.

The transcription of a grammar is a parser, consisting of the predicates for all nonterminals embedded in an environment containing

a) A sequence of symbols and an input pointer ip pointing to some symbol in that sequence, the current symbol. Initially $ip = 1$, i.e. the first symbol in the input sequence is the current symbol.

b) One boolean procedure for each terminal symbol of the grammar, which tests whether the current symbol is equal to the demanded symbol and, if so, advances the input pointer. These procedures are called terminal predicates.

By the state of the parser we mean here the sequence of symbols in its environment together with the value of its input pointer. A state $\alpha_1 \alpha_2 \ldots \alpha_n, p$ will be pictorially represented as $\alpha_1 \alpha_2 \ldots \alpha_{p-1} \downarrow \alpha_p \ldots \alpha_n$.

A predicate, when called, in general has an effect (viz., a change in the state) and a value (viz., the boolean value delivered).

We say a predicate p recognizes a nonterminal n if, for any terminal production τ of n, a call of p in a state $\omega_1 \downarrow \tau \omega_2$, where ω_1 and ω_2 are (possibly empty) sequences of symbols, returns true with state $\omega_1 \tau \downarrow \omega_2$.

We say a predicate p strongly recognizes a nonterminal n if it recognizes n and, furthermore, returns *false* and a state $\omega_1 \nu \downarrow \omega_2$ when called in a state $\omega_1 \downarrow \nu \omega_2$, where ω_1, ν, and ω_2 are (possibly empty) sequences of symbols and $\nu\omega_2$ does not begin with a terminal production of n.

We say a predicate p exactly recognizes a nonterminal n if it strongly recognizes n, and does not change the state when returning *false* (i.e. ν is empty).

The difference between a strong recognizer and a recognizer lies purely in the reaction to incorrect input. Only a strong recognizer is guaranteed to reject all incorrect input. One may wonder, how many compilers are in existence that act as a recognizer instead of a strong recognizer.

2.2. A no backup parsing scheme

We will use the simplest transcription scheme, which leads to a parser that has become known as a no backup recursive descent parser. Taking a grammar in van Wijngaarden notation of BNF, the transcription of a rule

$$x: y_{11}, y_{12}, \ldots, y_{1n_1}; y_{21}, \ldots, y_{2n_2}; \ldots; y_{m1}, \ldots, y_{mn_m}.$$

is in an ALGOL 60 like language

$\underline{boolean}\ \underline{procedure}\ x;\ \underline{begin}$

$l_{11}:\ \underline{if}\ y_{11}\ \underline{then}\ \underline{goto}\ l_{12}\ \underline{else}\ \underline{goto}\ l_{21};$

$l_{12}:\ \underline{if}\ y_{12}\ \underline{then}\ \underline{goto}\ l_{13}\ \underline{else}\ \underline{goto}\ l_{21};$

.
.
.

$l_{1n_1}:\ \underline{if}\ y_{1n_1}\ \underline{then}\ \underline{goto}\ ltrue\ \underline{else}\ \underline{goto}\ l_{21};$

$l_{21}:\ \underline{if}\ y_{21}\ \underline{then}\ \underline{goto}\ l_{22}\ \underline{else}\ \underline{goto}\ l_{31};$

.
.
.

$l_{2n_2}:\ \underline{if}\ y_{2n_2}\ \underline{then}\ \underline{goto}\ ltrue\ \underline{else}\ \underline{goto}\ l_{31};$

.
.
.

$l_{m1}:\ \underline{if}\ y_{m1}\ \underline{then}\ \underline{goto}\ l_{m2}\ \underline{else}\ \underline{goto}\ lfalse;$

.
.
.

$l_{mn_m}:\ \underline{if}\ y_{mn_m}\ \underline{then}\ \underline{goto}\ ltrue\ \underline{else}\ \underline{goto}\ lfalse;$

$ltrue:\ x:=\ \underline{true};\ \underline{goto}\ lend;\ lfalse:\ x:=\ \underline{false};\ lend:\ \underline{end};$

This construction of a parser out of elements consisting of a call for a boolean procedure and two addresses has been described by Knuth [1]. Knuth showed that this parser is able to recognize the LL(1) languages, and, if slightly modified, even strongly recognizes the LL(1) languages.

Of course equivalent ALGOL 60 programs can be generated which avoid jumps and, hopefully, work more efficiently (see, e.g. [6]). This form has just been chosen for its perspicacity and simplicity.

The transcription may easily be extended to grammars with regular expressions as right sides. The resulting procedures will then obtain a more complicated structure involving loops. But they remain to be built up by the simple elements

$label1:\ \underline{if}\ p\ \underline{then}\ \underline{goto}\ label2\ \underline{else}\ \underline{goto}\ label3;$

and no further problems arise.

2.3. Recursive descent programs

The simple transcription process described above gives rise to the interpretation of CF-grammars as programs, using BNF as a programming language and interpreting BNF programs in the way described above. Of course the behaviour of such a program written in BNF is somewhat different from the behaviour of a CF grammar in formal language theory. The main points are, that the program proceeds deterministically and a program must terminate for any input. Ideally, the program should be able to recognize or even strongly recognize the language given by the grammar. This is of course not the fact for general CF grammars. A usual method is to investigate the grammar, whether it fulfills conditions essentially for the application of some parsing method (The LL(1) condition is for example such a condition).

We will go another way:
We interpret the grammar as a parsing program, which works in the given manner and then investigate whether that program contains any structural errors, such as endless loops, or branches, which will never be reached.

3. The binary control structure

The binary structure of CF rules, which is obtained by interpretation of the comma as the "Mc-Carthy" <u>and</u> and of the semicolon as the "Mc-Carthy" <u>or</u>, gives rise to a representation of a CF grammar as a hierarchy of binary graphs. The graphs are obtained from the rules of the grammar by a transcription process which is as simple as the one described above, and indeed the binary graphs can be seen as a graphic representation of the ALGOL 60 procedures yielded by the transcription above.

The nodes of the graphs are <u>members</u>, interpreted as calls for predicates. If the called predicate may succeed or fail (the normal case), two edges leave the member, one labelled t and one labelled f (the <u>true edge</u> and the <u>false edge</u>). All members of one alternative are interconnected sequentially by their true edges, while all false edges point to the first member of the next alternative. The true edge of the last member of each alternative points to the <u>*true exit*</u>, while the false edges of all members of the last alternative point to the <u>*false exit*</u>.

Thus, a rule
$$x: y_{11}, y_{12}, \ldots, y_{1n_1}; y_{21}, \ldots, y_{2n_2}; \ldots; y_{m1}, \ldots, y_{mn_m}.$$
yields the graph

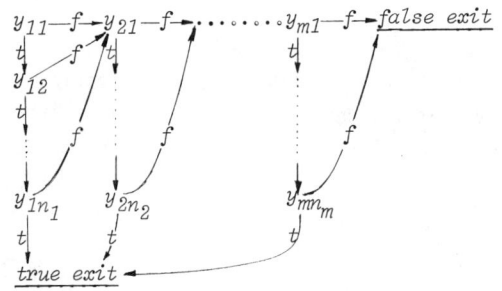

The terminal symbols correspond to predicates, which are not modelled further by graphs. They compare the current symbol of the input stream to the symbol wanted and have the effect of advancing the input pointer, if successful. The empty symbol ε corresponds to a predicate, which always succeeds (a so-called truth) and has no effect. Analogously a primitive falsehood is introduced, which always fails and has no effect. It may be said to correspond to a "forbidden symbol" ω. A predicate that has the ability to succeed or fail is called a test.

The graphs are then obtained by the combination of elements of the three types:

$$\text{test:} \quad a \; f \to \atop t \downarrow \qquad \text{truth:} \quad a \atop t \downarrow \qquad \text{falsehood:} \quad a \; f \to$$

This makes it obvious that the graphs may contain both exits, the true exit alone, or the false exit alone, and are then called tests, truths or falsehoods, respectively.

The direct correspondance between these graphs and the ALGOL 60 procedures given above is obvious. A description of the execution of the graphs is therefore omitted.

If we insert grouping and a repetition operator (*) into the grammar-like language, we obtain a more powerful control structure, that is still expressible by the binary graph system. It enables us to express not only various nested *if-then-else* constructions, but also *while-do* and *repeat-until* constructions, and is even more powerful. Let us demonstrate this by an example:

a) *act1: cond, stat, * ; .* $\qquad$ act1: cond—f →ε
$\qquad\qquad\qquad\qquad\qquad\qquad\qquad\qquad$ t↓ $\qquad$ t↓
$\qquad\qquad\qquad\qquad\qquad\qquad\qquad\qquad$ stat
$\qquad\qquad\qquad\qquad\qquad\qquad\qquad\qquad$ t↓ $\qquad$ true exit

$\qquad$ corresponds directly to *while* cond *do* stat;

b) *act2: cond; stat, * .* $\qquad$ act2: cond—f →stat
$\qquad\qquad\qquad\qquad\qquad\qquad\qquad\qquad$ t↓ $\qquad$ t↓
$\qquad\qquad\qquad\qquad\qquad\qquad\qquad\qquad$ true exit

$\qquad$ corresponds to $\qquad$ *repeat* stat *until* cond;

c) *act3: normal case, * ;* $\qquad$ act3: normal case—f →last case—f →report
$\qquad$ *last case ;* $\qquad\qquad\qquad\qquad\qquad\qquad$ t↓ $\qquad\qquad$ t↓ $\qquad\qquad$ t↓
$\qquad$ *report error, * .* $\qquad\qquad\qquad\qquad\qquad\qquad\qquad$ true exit

$\qquad$ is not expressible with the two constructions.

It may be remarked that the set of graphs constructible by transcription of CF-rules - even with regular expressions as right sides - is only a subset of all possible graphs.

4. Properties of the program

4.1. Effect and defect

One characteristic property of each predicate p is, whether it has an effect on the state if succeeding or failing. A change of state upon failing is directly related to the disability of the parser to recognize its language exactly. This makes such a <u>defect</u> normally unwanted. We may regard any change of the state upon failing as a bad <u>side effect</u> of the grammar based program. Clearly, an <u>effect</u> upon succeeding is a wanted behaviour of the program. We may model the effect and defect of each predicate in two sets $\textit{eff}_p$ and $\textit{def}_p$. The set $\textit{eff}_p$ ($\textit{def}_p$) is empty if the graph does not contain the *true exit (false exit)*. $\textit{eff}_p$ ($\textit{def}_p$) contains σ, (a "change of state symbol") if the *true exit (false exit)* can be reached after the state of the parser has been changed; it contains $\bar{\sigma}$ (a "no change symbol"), if the *true exit (false exit)* can be reached without affecting the state. This implies: if p is a terminal predicate, then

$$\textit{eff}_p = \{\sigma\}, \textit{def}_p = \{\bar{\sigma}\}.$$

For the predicate $p(\varepsilon)$ corresponding to the empty symbol ε, we get

$$\textit{eff}_{p(\varepsilon)} = \{\bar{\sigma}\}, \textit{def}_{p(\varepsilon)} = \emptyset$$

and analogously for the forbidden symbol

$$\textit{eff}_{p(\omega)} = \emptyset, \textit{def}_{p(\omega)} = \{\bar{\sigma}\}.$$

For the nonterminal predicates the sets $\textit{eff}_p$ and $\textit{def}_p$ can be computed recursively by first assuming the sets to be empty and updating them in several runs by only adding elements to them. The algorithm ends if in a run no set has been changed any more.

4.2. Classification of predicates:

By the sets $\textit{eff}_p$ and $\textit{def}_p$ we can classify the predicates into 8 types:

1) $\textit{def}_p = \emptyset$, $\textit{eff}_p \neq \emptyset$ truth
     a) $\sigma \notin \textit{eff}_p$ pure truth or <u>inert</u>
     b) $\sigma \in \textit{eff}_p$ active truth or <u>action</u>

2) $\textit{eff}_p = \emptyset$, $\textit{def}_p \neq \emptyset$ falsehood
     a) $\sigma \notin \textit{def}_p$ pure falsehood
     b) $\sigma \in \textit{def}_p$ reactive falsehood or <u>reaction</u>

3) $def_p \neq \emptyset$, $eff_p \neq \emptyset$ test
   a) $\sigma \notin def_p$, $\sigma \notin eff_p$ pure test
   b) $\sigma \notin def_p$, $\sigma \in eff_p$ active test
   c) $\sigma \in def_p$, $\sigma \notin eff_p$ reactive test
   d) $\sigma \in def_p$, $\sigma \in eff_p$ mixed test

4.3. Computation of properties of the program

Using the sets eff_p and def_p of the predicates, we are able to compute several properties of the program. One such property is the defect-freeness, already reflected above.

For every member m we are able to compute the set of all members which are accessible from m without changing the state. Let us call this set the set of effect-free accessible members $FAM(m)$. Clearly, if $m \in FAM(m)$, then the program contains an endless loop. Due to the irreversibility of the change of the state it is even necessary and sufficient for the Termination of a program that for every member m $m \notin FAM(m)$. If $m_2 \in FAM(m_1)$ for some m_1 and m_2, and m_1 and m_2 are calls for the same procedure, then the result of m_2 is known beforehand. A program with this property is called predictive. One simple property of a program is, whether all members are accessible from the first member of the starting predicate. A program, where this holds, is called reduced.

Returning to the theory of grammars, the reducedness implies that only the last alternative of each rule may produce the empty string. The termination forbids left recursion, while the unpredictiveness implies that the grammar must be left factored.

5. Extension to Affix Grammars

Affix Grammars [5] are an extension to CF grammars, designed to be parsable by (extended) parsing methods for CF grammars, but being much more powerful.

The parsing model for affix grammars used here is basically the same we used before for CF grammars.

Again each rule corresponds to a Boolean procedure designed to recognize the language of the nonterminal symbol on the left hand side. Those predicates are now equipped with parameters corresponding to the bound affixes connected with the symbols of the grammar, and local variables corresponding to the free affixes.

In the environment we have again a sequence of symbols and an input pointer with the same properties as before. But instead of the terminal predicates of the CF parser, we have primitive predicates which are equipped with (input and output) parameters and may be tests or actions.

As before the terminal predicates, the primitive predicates are not under control of the structure. They are regarded as defined outside the grammar and it lies in the responsibility of the programmer to formulate them correctly and to specify their type and their effect. In particular, they should have no defect.

The predicates are written in the usual grammar-like manner (again regular expressions are possible as right sides) and the corresponding binary control structure can be deduced from them in the same way as before.

The control over effects and defects is then extended to a control over the affixes. In this way, we are able to detect not only side effects but also such bad things as the use of an undefined value, two assignments to a variable in a row without intermediately using the value etc.

In the revised version of the programming language CDL [4], a language based on affix grammars, the structure described is used as an intermediate language, and a program is in preparation that checks CDL programs for structural errors and side effects.

References:

[1]   Knuth, D.E.: Top down syntax analysis
              Acta Informatica 1 (1971)

[2]   Foster, J.M.: A syntax improving program
              Computer Journal 11 (1968)

[3]   Lomet, D.B.: A formalization of transition diagram systems
              Journal ACM 20,2 (1973)

[4]   Koster, C.H.A.: A compiler Compiler
              Mathematisch Centrum Amsterdam MR 127 (1971)
          and CDL II - A revision of the Compiler Description Language (to appear)

[5]   Koster, C.H.A.: Affix Grammars, in Algol 68 Implementation
              North Holland Pub. Co., (1971)

[6] Koster, C.H.A.: A technique for parsing ambiguous language
        Proceedings of this conference

[7] Rosenkrantz, D.J., Stearns, R.E.: Properties of deterministic top down grammars
        Inf. & Control 17,3 ;1970)

[8] Feuerhahn, H.: Some reflections on structure and effects of CDL-rules.
        Paper presented at the CDL working conference, Berlin, March 1974.

A TECHNIQUE FOR PARSING AMBIGUOUS LANGUAGES

C.H.A. Koster
Technische Universität Berlin

Abstract

From a given context free grammar, it is possible in a variety of ways to generate automatically a program that acts as a recogniser for the language of that grammar. Under a number of conditions, depending on the particular technique used, this program is an "exact recogniser" of that language, accepting only sentences of the language and rejecting all other strings of symbols.

In the paper, a new technique for generating top-to-bottom parsers for context free grammars is proposed, the technique of recursive backup, which allows the automatic construction of parsers for any context free grammar which is free from left recursion. In particular it can cope with ambiguous grammars.

This technique is then extended to Affix Grammars, and its relationship to reversible programming exposed.

1. Recursive descent parsing of CF grammars

For parsing according to a Context-Free syntax, various algorithms are known, broadly divided into top-to-bottom and bottom-to-top methods [1]. Without going into relative merits and limitations of other methods, one specific top-to-bottom parsing method is of special interest here, because of its perspicacity and simplicity. This well-known parsing method, the method of "recursive descent", is characterized by the fact that a parser for a particular grammar is obtained from that grammar by a simple process of transcription, transcribing each rule of the grammar into a parsing procedure for that rule, recognizing terminal productions of that rule by (recursively) calling on parsing procedures.

Many such transcription methods are possible. Following the terminology in [8] we will call such a parsing procedure a predicate. Again following the terminology in [8], depending on the transcription method used and properties of the grammar, such a predicate may recognize or even exactly recognize the nonterminal symbol, of whose rule it is a transcription.

The aim in designing such a transcription is that the initial nonterminal symbol of the grammar should be exactly recognized.

1.1. No-backup scheme

The most straightforward scheme is the following (using as target language ALGOL 60; transcription to other languages can be made analoguously, in an obvious fashion).

We will describe the scheme by a 2-level transformational meta grammar:
On the left, we give a 2-level grammar [9,6] of CF grammars, on the right, for each alternative, we indicate the transcription, in a fashion which should be self-explanatory [10]. The function τ represents the transcription function.

A) TAG:: LETTER; TAG LETTER; TAG DIGIT.

B) LETTER:: letter ALPHA.

C) ALPHA:: a;b;c;d;e;f;g;h;i;j;k;l;m;n;o;p;q;r;s;t;u;v;w;x;y;z.

D) DIGIT:: digit CYPHER.

E) CYPHER:: 0;1;2;3;4;5;6;7;8;9.

F) EMPTY::.

G) SYMBOL:: letter s letter y letter m letter b letter o letter l.

a) rule: lhs, rhs, point symbol.	τ (lhs) τ (rhs) ;
b) lhs: nont, colon symbol.	*boolean procedure* τ (nont) ; τ (nont) :=
c) rhs: alt;	τ (alt)
alt, semicolon symbol, rhs.	*if* τ (alt) *then true else* τ (rhs)
d) alt: member;	τ (member)
member, comma symbol, alt;	*if* τ (member) *then* τ (alt) *else false*
EMPTY.	*true*
e) member: term;	τ (term)
nont.	τ (nont)
f) nont: TAG.	TAG
g) term: TAG SYMBOL.	*find symb* (TAG SYMBOL)

A suitable environment is assumed, which contains a *boolean procedure find symb (s);* which acts as an exact recognizer for the symbol it is called with, i.e.:

If the current input symbol is equal to its parameter s, then
the input is advanced by one symbol and the value *true* is returned;
otherwise, *false* is returned, without any effect on the input.

It is assumed that, through suitable renaming, there does not occur a nonterminal symbol find symb or a nonterminal symbol ending in symbol.

As an example, the rule

```
factor: identifier; number;
         open symbol, exp, close symbol.
```

has a transcription:

boolean procedure factor;

factor:= if identifier then true else
if number then true else
if find (open symbol) then
if exp then find (close symbol) else false else false;

Choosing as target language ALGOL 68, or any language including the "Mc-Carthy" *and* and *or*, allows a much simpler transcription, which is still essentially equivalent to the one given here (see the example P4 in [15]).

1.2. Shortcomings of the no-backup parsing method

The no-backup parsing method suffers from a number of shortcomings, which we will enumerate before trying to cure them.

1.2.1. Left-recursion

If the grammar has a nonterminal n which leftproduces into itself, i.e., there exists a string ω such that

$$n \rightarrow n \omega$$

then its transcription will execute in an endless loop.
As is well known, such left-recursion can always be removed by rewriting the grammar [3]. We will, therefore, consider only grammars which contain no left-recursive nonterminal.

1.2.2. Empty alternative

In a CF grammar, the order of alternatives is irrelevant, whereas its transcriptions will faithfully attempt to recognize in a canonical order implied by the ordering of alternatives. In particular, if in a rule some alternative produces empty, then it must come as the last alternative, because its transcription always yields <u>true</u>, so that any alternatives following it would never be considered. It is always possible to decide whether an alternative can produce empty, so that, without loss of generality, we can restrict ourselves to grammars in which only the last alternative in a rule may produce empty. (If more than one alternative in a rule can produce empty, then the grammar is ambiguous, see 1.2.5.).

1.2.3. Prefix-sharing

We say the terminal productions of two alternatives $a_{1_1}, \ldots, a_{1_n}$ and $a_{2_1}, \ldots, a_{2_m}$ for one same nonterminal n <u>share a prefix</u> if there are nonempty strings γ, ω_1 and ω_2 such that

$$n \rightarrow a_{1_1}, \ldots, a_{1_n} \overset{*}{\rightarrow} \gamma \omega_1$$
$$\text{and } n \rightarrow a_{2_1}, \ldots, a_{2_m} \overset{*}{\rightarrow} \gamma \omega_2$$
$$\text{where } \omega_1 \neq \omega_2$$

If two alternatives for one nonterminal symbol n share a prefix, then it is not possible to put those two alternatives into an order such that both are recognized. Sometimes, but not always, it can be eliminated by a suitable rewriting of the grammar [2]. In 1.3., we will demonstrate a way to solve the problem of prefix-sharing by introducing <u>back-up</u>.

1.2.4. Local ambiguity

A terminal production of one alternative $a_{1_1}, \ldots, a_{1_n}$ <u>is a prefix</u> of a terminal production of another alternative $a_{2_1}, \ldots, a_{2_m}$ for the same nonterminal n if there are nonempty strings γ and ω, such that

$$n \rightarrow a_{1_1}, \ldots, a_{1_n} \overset{*}{\rightarrow} \gamma$$
$$n \rightarrow a_{2_1}, \ldots, a_{2_m} \overset{*}{\rightarrow} \gamma \omega$$

If some rule in a grammar has this property, then we term that grammar <u>locally ambiguous</u>. Here again, there is an ordering problem but unlike with prefix sharing, we'll see in 1.3. it cannot always be solved by back-up.

It is not, in general, decideable whether a given CF grammar is not locally ambiguous.

1.2.5. Ambiguity

If two alternatives $a_{1_1}, \ldots, a_{1_n}$ and $a_{2_1}, \ldots, a_{2_m}$ have some terminal production in common, that is if there is a (possibly empty) string γ, such that

$$n \rightarrow a_{1_1}, \ldots, a_{1_n} \overset{*}{\rightarrow} \gamma$$
$$n \rightarrow a_{2_1}, \ldots, a_{2_m} \overset{*}{\rightarrow} \gamma$$

then we term the grammar <u>ambiguous</u>. In distinction to prefix-sharing and local ambiguity, ambiguity does not cause the parser to go astray, (whichever of the two alternatives appears first will shield off the other), but more than one parsing will never be found: the first one is always found according to some canonical order implied by the ordering of the alternatives.

We may, however, happen to be interested in another parsing, or even in all possible parsings, and then cannot use the simple scheme given.

It is not in general decideable whether a given CF grammar is ambiguous.

1.2.6. Conclusion

In order to overcome the shortcomings listed above, one can go a number of ways:

One can restrict the class of CF grammars to those, for which the scheme, or a scheme very near it [4], works. Or, alternatively, one can accept the scheme as gospel and interpret CF grammars as programs [8].

In this paper, we will investigate a different way, viz., to find more powerful schemes that do not suffer from the shortcomings mentioned, and which still lead to "reasonably" efficient parsers.

1.3. Partial-backup scheme

We will consider only those CF grammars, that are not left recursive, and of which only the last alternative in each rule may produce empty.

We recall that two alternatives $a_{1_1}, \ldots, a_{1_n}$ and $a_{2_1}, \ldots, a_{2_m}$ for one same nonterminal n share a prefix if there are nonempty strings γ, ω_1 and ω_2 ($\omega_1 \neq \omega_2$) that

$$n \rightarrow a_{1_1}, \ldots, a_{1_n} \overset{*}{\rightarrow} \gamma\omega_1$$
$$n \rightarrow a_{2_1}, \ldots, a_{2_m} \overset{*}{\rightarrow} \gamma\omega_2$$

If two consecutive alternatives in a rule share a prefix, then the wrong alternative might come first, accepting part of the input (γ) before discovering that it has no business doing so, and returning _false_.

In the partial-backup scheme, the value of the input pointer is noted at the beginning of the transcription of the rule, and restored upon unsuccessful exit from an alternative. Again, we give a two-level transformational metagrammar, using the same metanotions as in 1.1.

a) rule: TAG lhs, rhs, point symbol.
τ (lhs);
begin integer pold; _boolean_ b;
   pold:= pin; τ (rhs)
end: TAG:= b
end

b) TAG lhs: TAG nont, colon symbol.
boolean procedure TAG

c) rhs: alt;
    alt, semicolon symbol, rhs.
τ (alt)
τ (alt) τ (rhs)

d) alt: member;
    member, comma symbol, alt1;
    EMPTY.
b:= τ (member); _if_ b _then goto end_; pin:= pold;
b:= _if_ τ (member) _then_ τ (alt1) _else false_; _if_ b _then goto end_; pin:= pold;
b:= _true_; _goto_ end;

e) alt1: member;
    member, comma symbol, alt1.
τ (member)
_if_ τ (member) _then_ τ (alt1) _else false_

f) member: term;
    TAG nont.
τ (term)
τ (TAG nont)

g) TAG nont: TAG.
TAG

h) term: TAG SYMBOL.
find symb (TAG SYMBOL)

It is assumed that, through suitable renaming, no nonterminals b, pold, pin, etc., occur in the grammar. In the environment of the parser, _pin_ is assumed to be the input pointer. As an example, the rule

> program: begin symbol, block tail;
>   begin symbol, compound tail.

has as a transcription

> _boolean procedure_ program;
> _begin integer_ pold; _boolean_ b; pold:= pin;
>   b:= _if_ begin symbol _then_ block tail _else false_;
>   _if_ b _then goto_ end; pin:= pold;

```
            b:= if begin symbol then compound tail else false;
            if b then goto end; pin:= pold;
    end: program:= b
    end;
```

Of course, in this particular case it should have been simple to rewrite the rule in such a way that the no-backup scheme is applicable. Still, in this example the partial-backup method successfully copes with the shared prefix `begin symbol`.

1.3.1. Properties of partial backup parser

It can be shown that a partial-backup parser for a CF grammar G with starting symbol S recognizes S exactly if and only if G is not locally ambiguous. Trivially, it follows LL(1) languages are recognized exactly by a partial-backup parser.

The partial-backup method can cope only with those CF grammars that are not locally ambiguous, and cannot deliver more than one parsing for an ambiguous CF grammar.

The overhead involved in backup may be tremendous viz. if backup takes place over nonterminal symbols with productions of arbitrary length. (There are ways of reducing this overhead to practically zero viz. by left factoring or by making changes in the input string, which leads to a hybrid technique between top-down and bottom-up). Since it is undecideable whether a grammar is locally ambiguous, partial-backup parsers are not suitable for experimentation with grammars that are not definitely known to be free of local ambiguity. The only way we can establish a grammar to be free of local ambiguity, is to prove that it belongs to some further restricted class of CF grammars - but then much more efficient parsers are available.

Conclusion: there does not seem to be much point in using the partial-backup method: either a weaker or a more powerful parsing scheme must be used.

2. Recursive backup scheme

In a locally ambiguous rule, we don't know which one to choose out of several alternatives that are applicable. The only way to establish whether at some point a specific applicable alternative is the right one, is to choose that alternative, and then trying to perform the continuation of the parsing - if the rest of the parsing is successful, obviously the right alternative was taken, otherwise the parsing will have to be undone up to that same point so as to allow the choice of another alternative.

In other words, when parsing a rule

$$a: alt_1; alt_2; \ldots; alt_n.$$

at the end of each successful alternative we want to go off on a sideline, performing the continuation of the parsing to see whether the choice was right, but in such a fashion that, if that continuation is unsuccessful, we can continue with the next alternative of this rule as if nothing happened.

By a slight extension we can cope with ambiguity by <u>always</u> undoing each continuation completely, independent of whether it was successful or not.

2.1. <u>Recursive backup in ALGOL 60</u>

In order to accomplish this, we will equip each predicate with a by-name Boolean parameter q which is to hold at each point the continuation of the parsing.

We assume the environment to contain an array I holding the sequence of symbols to be parsed, the current symbol being indicated by the value of the input pointer pin, an integer variable. Futhermore it contains the following declaration in quasi-ALGOL:

<u>boolean procedure</u> req (symb, q);
      <u>symbol</u> symb; <u>boolean</u> q;
<u>if</u> I [pin]= symb <u>then</u>
<u>begin</u> pin:= pin + 1; req:= q; pin:= pin - 1 <u>end</u>
<u>else</u> req:= <u>false</u>;

A call $req\ (\alpha,\ q)$ in a state $\downarrow\alpha\omega$ results in a call of q in a state $\alpha\downarrow\omega$; after that call of q in a state $\alpha\downarrow\omega$, req returns in a state $\downarrow\alpha\omega$. The net effect on the input of req is nihil - provided the net effect of q is nihil.

The environment also contains

<u>boolean procedure</u> result;
<u>if</u> I [pin]= endmarker <u>then</u>
<u>begin</u> <report a successful parse>;
    result:= <u>true</u>
<u>end else</u> result:= <u>false</u>;

Note that this procedure also has no net effect on input. In this environment, the translated rules are embedded.

a) rule: lhs, rhs, point symbol.   τ (lhs) τ (rhs);

b) lhs: nont, colon symbol.   **boolean procedure** τ (nont)(q); **boolean** q;
                                                 τ (nont):=

c) rhs: alt;   τ (alt)
       alt, comma symbol, rhs.   τ (alt) ∨ τ (rhs)

d) alt: member;   τ (member) q)
       member, comma symbol, alt;   τ (member) τ (alt))
       EMPTY.   q

e) member: term;   τ (term)
       nont.   τ (nont)

f) term: TAG SYMBOL.   req (TAG SYMBOL,

g) nont: TAG.   TAG (

It is assumed that through suitable renaming no nonterminal q, pin, req, or ending on symbol occurs.

As an example, the highly ambiguous grammar:

         sent: <u>a</u>; <u>a</u>, <u>a</u>;
              <u>a</u>, sent;
              <u>a</u>, <u>a</u>, sent.

has a transcription

         boolean procedure sent (q); *boolean* q
         sent:= req (a, q) ∨ req (a, req (a, q)) ∨
                 req (a, sent (q)) ∨
                 req (a, req (a, sent (q)));

This procedure is invoked by *sent (result)*.

The parsing now proceeds through a rather sofisticated use of the call-by-name concept of ALGOL 60, which happens to allow the composition of procedures.

Assuming the input to consist of two a's followed by an endmarker, it is easy to verify the following equivalences:

         sent (result) in a state ↓aa↨
     ≡ *req (a, result) ∨ req (a, req (a, result)) ∨*
        req (a, sent (result)) ∨
        req (a, req (a, sent (result))) in a state ↓aa↨

$$\equiv result \text{ in state } a\downarrow a\ne \lor \quad \text{(a)}$$
$$result \text{ in state } aa\downarrow \ne \lor \quad \text{(b)}$$
$$sent\ (result) \text{ in state } a\downarrow a\ne \lor \text{(c)}$$
$$sent\ (result) \text{ in state } aa\downarrow \ne \quad \text{(d)}$$

Proceeding in this fashion, (a) and (d) deliver <u>false</u> and (b) and (c) deliver <u>true</u> once each. The number of successful parsings is the number of successful calls on *return*, in this case two.

In the same way, ↓aaaa≠ can be shown to lead to 5 successful parses. In general, in input string of n a's leads to Fn successfull calls on *result*, Fn being the n-th Fibonacci number

$$F_n = \begin{cases} n = 1 \to 1 \\ n = 2 \to 2 \\ n > 2 \to F_{n-1} + F_{n-2} \end{cases}$$

Note that the translation of each rule has the property that, for each successfully recognized alternative, an (implicit) boolean procedure is called. Provided this boolean procedure has no net effect, the translation of the alternative has no net effect. Since the actual parameter of the starting call has no net effect, and since in every further call the parameter is composed in such a way as to have no net effect, each procedure has no net effect.

2.2. Properties of recursive backup scheme

Any CF grammar which is not left-recursive can be recognized by means of the recursive backup scheme. In fact it can be seen as a compilative (instead of interpretive) realization of the most general top-down parsing algorithm [12].

The scheme allows the straight-forward realization of parsers for a very wide class of nondeterministic CF grammars, without rewriting of the grammar. It works efficiently for more restricted grammars (e.g., the parse is found in linear time for LL (1) grammars) but does not fail for less well-conditioned grammars. It is therefor a good vehicle for experimentation with grammars.

Even the restriction that the grammar must be free of left-recursion can be circummvented by a heuristic restriction on the recursion depth of the predicates.

Over the scheme of Earley as described in [13] it has the advantage of great simplicity, and of being compilative in nature.

If one is prepared to left-factorize the grammar, a great raise in efficiency can be obtained. As an example, the grammar from our previous example might be factorized as

> sent: a, (a, (sent;);
> sent;).

with a transcription

> *boolean procedure* sent (q); *boolean* q;
> sent:= req (a, req (a, sent (q) ∨ q) ∨
>   sent (q) ∨ q);

Further investigation of the efficiency of the recursive back-up scheme, and comparison to other schemes, is needed.

The drawback of the scheme is the large amount of memory space it may need. In a crude implementation of ALGOL 60, the stack may grow very fast, e.g. linearly with the length of the input string, and this may severely restrict the applicability of the algorithm.

A machine model for the algorithm can be given which is much more efficient.

3. Extension to Affix grammars

All three parsing schemes mentioned can easily be extended to affix grammars [14] - not surprising in view of the fact that affix grammars are intended as an extension of CF grammars to which parsing techniques applicable to CF grammars can be extended (see, e.g. [7] and [18]).

The extension of the no-backup scheme is the basis for the CDL Compiler Compiler [11]. We will briefly discuss here the extension of the recursive backup scheme to affix grammars.

The key step is to provide all predicates with parameters (input and output parameters, corresponding to the inherited and derived affixes). The primitive predicates and actions have to be predicates also, i.e., Boolean procedures with a continuation parameter q and no net effect upon return, e.g., for the primitive predicates equal and promitive action incr from [14].

> *boolean procedure* equal (a, b, q); *boolean* q;
> equal:= *if* a = b *then* q *else false*;

> *boolean procedure* incr (x, q); *boolean* q;
> *begin* x:= x + 1; incr:= q; x:= x - 1 *end*;

Notice in particular that any primitive must possess a unique inverse: it has to be undone after the elaboration of the continuation in order for the action to have no net effect.

As a further example, consider the assignation:

> *boolean procedure* ass (a, b, q); *boolean* q;
> *begin integer* local; local:= a; a:= b; ass:= q; a:= local *end*;

which is completely reversible (at the expense of local storage).

We will not here give the Metagrammar for the transcription (which is a straightforward extension of that in 2.1.) but will consider an example of a highly ambiguous affix grammar, viz. the grammar that walks mazes.

As primitives we have a predicate free + i + j which answers the question whether the position i, j of a checkerboard is free, as well as the action set + i + j for making the position i, j occupied and incr + x and decr + x for incrementing and decrementing x.

The following Affix grammar then gives an algorithm to parse a maze on the checkerboard, e.g. follow all paths starting at 1,1. We assume the affixes to range over the integers.

```
start: maze + 1 + 1.
maze + x + y: free + x + y, set + x + y, neighbours + x + y.
neighbours + x + y: incr + x, maze + x + y;
                    incr + y, maze + x + y;
                    decr + x, maze + x + y;
                    decr + y, maze + x + y.
```

With a transcription:

> *boolean procedure* start (q); *boolean* q;
>   start:= maze (1, 1, q);
> *boolean procedure* maze (x, y, q); *boolean* q;
>   maze:= free (x, y, set (x, y, neighbours (x, y, q)));
> *boolean procedure* neighbours (x, y, q); *boolean* q;
>   neighbours:= incr (x, maze (x, y, q)) ∨
>   incr (y, maze (x, y, q)) ∨
>   decr (x, maze (x, y, q)) ∨
>   decr (y, maze (x, y, q));

The primitives can be realized (presupposing a *boolean array* checkerboard $[1:n, 1:n]$ with suitable initialization) as

    boolean procedure free (i, j, q); *boolean* q;
        free:= *if* $i \geq 1 \wedge j \geq 1 \wedge i \leq n \wedge j \leq n$ *then*
            if checkerboard $[i, j]$ *then* q *else false*
        else false;

    boolean procedure set (i, j, q), *boolean* q;
      begin checkerboard $[i, j]:= $ *false*; set:= q; checkerboard $[i, j]:=$ *true end*;
    boolean procedure incr (x, q); *boolean* q;
      begin $x:= x + 1$; incr:= q; $x:= x - 1$ *end*;
    boolean procedure decr (x, q); *boolean* q;
      begin $x:= x - 1$; decr:= q; $x:= x + 1$ *end*;

This example should suffice to show that the recursive backup scheme can be extended straightforwardly to Affix grammars, allowing the construction of parsing automata for nondeterministic Affix grammars.

This opens a wide field of research:

1) The example shows that a nondeterministic interpretation of Affix grammars allows the writing of nondeterministic programs, without the bother of explicitly administering backup [16].

2) Observe that all predicates involved are fully reversible. Every Affix grammar can be realized on a fully reversible machine, at a much higher level than the reversible Turing machines investigated until now [17].

3) Affix grammars are powerful enough to serve as a formalization of semantics. Interpreting the Affix grammar nondeterministically allows the study of nondeterministic semantics.

References:

[1] J.M. Foster, Automatic Syntactic Analysis, Computer Monographs no. 7, Elsevier, 1970.

[2] J.M. Foster, A syntax improving program, Computer Journal, Vol. II, May 1968.

[3] R. Kurki-Suonio, On top-to-bottom recognition and left-recursion, CACM Vol. 9, July 1966

[4] D.E. Knuth, Top-Down Syntax Analysis, Acta Informatica 1, 1971.

[5] P. Naur (Ed.), Revised Report on the Algorithmic Language ALGOL 60, Num. Math. 4, 1963.

[6] A. van Wijngaarden(Ed.), Revised Report on the Algorithmic Language ALGOL 68, to appear 1974.

[7] D. Crowe, Generating Parsers for Affix Grammars, Comm. ACM 15, 8, August 1972.

[8] H. Feuerhahn, A binary control structure and its relationship to grammars and Side Effects, proceedings of this conference.

[9] C.H.A. Koster, Two-level grammars, Lecture Notes of an Advanced Course on Compiler Construction, Munich 1974, to appear as Springer Lecture Notes.

[10] F.L. De Remer, Transformational grammars, ibidem.

[11] C.H.A. Koster, Using the CDL Compiler Compiler, ibidem.

[12] T. Griffiths and S. Petrick, On the relative efficiencies of context-free grammar recognizers, Comm. ACM 8, 5, May 1965.

[13] J. Earley, An efficient context-free parsing Algorithm, Comm. ACM 13, 2, February 1970.

[14] C.H.A. Koster, Affix Grammars; in: Proceedings of the IFIP Working Conference on ALGOL 68 Implementation, Munich 1970, North Holland 1971.

[15] J.C. Boussard, J.J. Duby (Eds.), Rapport d'Evaluation à ALGOL 68, Revue Française d'Informatique et de Recherche opérationelle No. B-1, 1971.

[16] S.W. Golomb, L.D. Baumert, Backtrack programming, Journal of the ACM Vol.12 No.4, October 1965.

[17] C.H. Bennet, Logical Reversibility of Computation, IBM Journal Res. Develop., November 1973.

[18] D.A. Watt, LR Parsing of Affix Grammars, Report No. 7, Computing Department, University of Glasgow, August 1974.

OPTIMIZATION OF GENERATED CODE BY MEANS OF ATTRIBUTES :
Local elimination of common redundant sub-expressions.

D. Neel, M. Amirchahy and M. Mazaud
IRIA - BP.5, 78150 LE CHESNAY, France

ABSTRACT

This paper deals with the application of the notion of semantic attributes (as developped by D.E. KNUTH [1]) to generation of optimized code. Taking local elimination of common sub-expressions as a starting point, it is demonstrated by means of an example that meta-compilation by attributes allows semantic formalization of classical optimization algorithms. A redundancy attribute, $R\uparrow$, is defined to play an optimizing role in connection with redundant common sub-expressions during compilation without having to undergo a special treatment.

Extending these basic ideas the possibility of creating a set of attributes which define various desirable optimizations in algebraic languages is indicated. Thus a certain methodology, at the level of semantic description of a language, may be outlined. In addition such descriptions offer the advantage of being easy to write, clear and rigourous.

By code optimization we mean the treatment applied to a programme at compile time in order to generate the most efficient code possible for a given programme. Up to recent times most of the research works done in optimization field has been concerned with the writing of suitable algorithms. However, there are still not many optimizing compilers available (and none to our knowledge which uses the attributes method as we propose here). This is largely due to the fact that the application of most of the optimization algorithms involves the following risks :

1 - Programmers with a good understanding of the implementation of a language may allow themselves certain subtleties with potential side-effects in their programmes. Consequently some optimization processes may jeopardise this precarious equilibrium and lead to the generation of a semantically erroneous code with regards to the initial programme.

2 - Although the output programme on a macro-level ought not to be altered by the optimization processes, the statements' semantics are generally modified by the application of the optimization algorithms on a micro-level.

The risks mentioned above indicate that in order to set up a methodology of optimization, semantic aspects of programming languages have to be firmly tackled. For a long time now, syntactic rules (eg. BACKUS-NAUR Form) for the description of programming languages have been in use in compiler-writing systems while no such formalization has yet been achieved in the semantic field. Therefore it is difficult to mechanize the classical optimization methods as long as they are not included in the semantic description of a source language.

Now, D.E. KNUTH [1] has introduced the notion of semantic attributes as a vehicle for semantic description of each non-terminal in a grammar. We have tried in conjunction with a meta-compiler system research project (DELTA : DEscription de Langages et Traducteurs par Attributs) carried out at IRIA [2] to establish an optimization methodology by defining attributes capable of generation of optimized code. This research should help to eliminate the second risk mentioned earlier. As to the first one, it is automatically reduced since the application of algorithms is more closely controlled. Generaly, in order to produce optimized code several passes on the intermediate code (eg. triplets*) constituting the programme are required : in an initial stage the programme is divided up into basic blocks** on which the so called local optimizations may be applied. In a subsequent stage using these basic blocks, a unique set of disjoint intervals*** covering the overall programme graph can be determined. A more extended optimization may then be carried out on each of these intervals [3]. A major disadvantage of this classic method arises from the fact that the necessary readjustments and the handling of the intermediate code after each stage of optimization are quite cumbersome. According to different cases the following actions may be required :

- Propagation of constants and redundancy : triplet elimination.
- Invariant statements and expressions in loops : triplet displacement.
- Loop-dependant redundancies : triplet addition.

Later in this paper it will be shown how optimization by attributes reduces or eliminates this heavy but necessary triplet manipulations. We have voluntarily limited ourselves here to the presentation of a simple optimization case in order to allow the reader sufficient familiarization with the concepts introduced.

To begin with we shall give an example of local elimination of common sub--expressions by means of a classic optimization algorithm, then the same example is treated by the attributes method in order to set off a clear comparison between the two approches. Other publications [2] [4] present a set of major optimization described by attributes showing that such descriptions can lead to a methodology of optimization (Mrs D. NEEL's doctoral thesis (doctorat d'état) to be published : *Contribution à la formalisation de l'amélioration de code par attributs sémantiques*).

---

* The term triplet refers to a binary/unary operator and the two/one operand(s) which it controls immediately.

** Basic block is a linear sequence of programme instructions executed one after the other. It has unique entry and exit points (first and last statements respectively).

*** Interval refers to a maximal sub-graph with a single entry point through which all loops in the interval must necessarily pass.

I - CLASSICAL METHOD

The method chosen is that of *"dependencies number"* [5]. It enables local elimination of common redundant sub-expressions and is easily applicable to triplets.

Definition :

Let the dependencies number of each *variable* be initialized to zero. If triplet (t) assigns a value to the variable V (eg. (t) = V, 1) then by definition the dependencies number of V, dep(V), would take on the value t from triplet (t+1) on. The dependencies number of a *triplet* is : dep(t) = MAX(dep(operand1), dep(operand2)) + 1.

Theorem [5] :

Let triplets (i) and (j), with i < j, be identical (taking into account the commutativity of the operator) then (j) is redundant iff dep(i) = dep(j).

Method :

1 - Scan sequentially the triplets constituting the source text.
2 - If (j) is redundant with respect to (i) (cf. *theorem*) then replace triplet (j) by IDEM (i).
3 - If triplet (j) is of the type IDEM(i) then replace occurrences of operand (j) by (i).
4 - Compute the dependencies number of each triplet (cf. *definition*).
5 - No object code is produced in connection with IDEM-triplets.

Example :

DECLARE T(max1,max2) ;
....
T(I,J) = T(I,J+1) ;

Let ADR[T(1,1)] be the address of the first element of T. If we assume row-implementation of the table, then the address of an element designated by T(I,J) could be formulated as : ADR[T(I,J)] = ADR[T(1,1)] + (I-1) * max2 - 1 + J . The assignment statement T(I,J) = T(I,J+1) would give rise to the following triplets :

```
(1)    -    I           , 1
(2)    *    (1)         , max2
(3)    +    ADR[T(1,1)], (2)         evaluation of ADR[T(I,J)]
(4)    -    (3)         , 1
(5)    +    (4)         , J
(6)    -    I           , 1
(7)    *    (6)         , max2
```

```
          (8)   +    ADR[T(1,1)],  (7)
          (9)   -       (8)     ,   1
         (10)   +       (9)     ,   J
         (11)   +      (10)     ,   1           gives ADR[T(I,J+1)]
         (12)   =     T[(5)]    , T[(11)]       assignment
```

Applying the method :

Trip. n°	Triplets	dep(t)	redundancy detection	optimized triplets
(1)	- I , 1	1	- I , 1	- I , 1
(2)	* (1) , max2	2	* (1) , max2	* (1) , max2
(3)	+ ADR[T(1,1)], (2)	3	+ ADR[T(1,1)], (2)	+ ADR[T(1,1)], (2)
(4)	- (3) , 1	4	- (3) , 1	- (3) , 1
(5)	+ (4) , J	5	+ (4) , J	+ (4) , J
(6)	- I , 1	1	IDEM (1)	+ (5) , 1
(7)	* (6) , max2	2	IDEM (2)	= T[(5)], T[(6)]
(8)	+ ADR[T(1,1)], (7)	3	IDEM (3)	
(9)	- (8) , 1	4	IDEM (4)	
(10)	+ (9) , J	5	IDEM (5)	
(11)	+ (10) , 1	6	+ (5) , 1	
(12)	= T[(5)], T[(11)]	-	= T[(5)], T[(11)]	

The first redundant triplet found is (6) which is identical to (1), both having the same dependencies number. Consequently (6) is replaced by IDEM (1) and later all references to (6) will be replaced by those to (1). Thus triplets (7) and (2) can be detected to be identical with equal dependencies numbers making (7) redundant w.r.t. (2), etc... An additional scanning of the triplets is then required to eliminate those of IDEM-type.

II - *ATTRIBUTES METHOD*

Let us consider the production rules which define the syntax of the statement $T(I,J) = T(I, J+1)$:

```
      <P>  ::= <SL> ;        (P : Programme, SL : Statement List)
      <SL> ::= <SL'> ; <S>   (S : Statement)
      <SL> ::= <S>
      <S>  ::= <VV> = <E>    (VV : Vector Variable, E : Expression)
      <VV> ::= Name ( <E> , <E'> )
      <SV> ::= Name          (SV : Scalar Variable)
      <E>  ::= <E'> + <O>    (O : Operand)
```

```
<E>  ::= <O>
<O>  ::= <VV>
<O>  ::= <SV>
<O>  ::= Constant
```

On the corresponding tree representation (see page 6) the different occurrences of each non-terminal are numbered. Suppose FT (First Triplet) and LT (Last Triplet) to be the attribute-couple which carry the semantics of the source text into the intermediate **triplet** code. They serve to count the number of triplets produced for each non-terminal during the translation. As a general rule, if a non-terminal gives rise to n triplets, then LT = FT + n - 1.

Semantic description :

    `<P> ::= <SL> ;`

        FT(SL) = 1   (Let the first triplet produced from the programme be assigned the arbitrary value 1)

        LT(P) = LT(SL)   (The last triplet of the list SL is in fact the last programme triplet)*

    `<SL> ::= <S>`

        FT(S) = FT(SL)   (The first triplet of statement S constitutes the first SL list triplet)**

        LT(SL) = LT(S)

    `<SL> ::= <SL'> ; <S>`

        FT(SL') = FT(SL)

        FT(S) = LT(SL') + 1   (The first triplet of statement S follows syntactically the last triplet of the sub-list SL')

        LT(SL) = LT(S)

    `<VV> ::= Name ( <E> , <E'> )`

        FT(E) = FT(VV)

        FT(E') = LT(E) + 1

        LT(VV) = LT(E') + 5   (The evaluation of the address of VV requires 5 triplets corresponding to :
ADR(VV) + (LT(E) - 1) * max2 - 1 + LT(E') .
They are :

(LT(VV))	- LT(E)	, 1
(LT(VV)-1)	* LT(VV)	, max2
(LT(VV)-2)	+ ADR(VV)	, LT(VV)-1
(LT(VV)-3)	- LT(VV)-2	, 1
(LT(VV)-4)	+ LT(VV)-3	, LT(E'))

---

* Attribute LT is a synthesized attributes since its value depends on attributes from descending nodes of the syntactic tree. The notation LT↑ indicates that the attribute participates in synthesizing information from the leaves towards the tree-root.

** Attribute FT is an inherited attribute since its value depends on attributes from ascending nodes. The notation used in this case is FT↓.

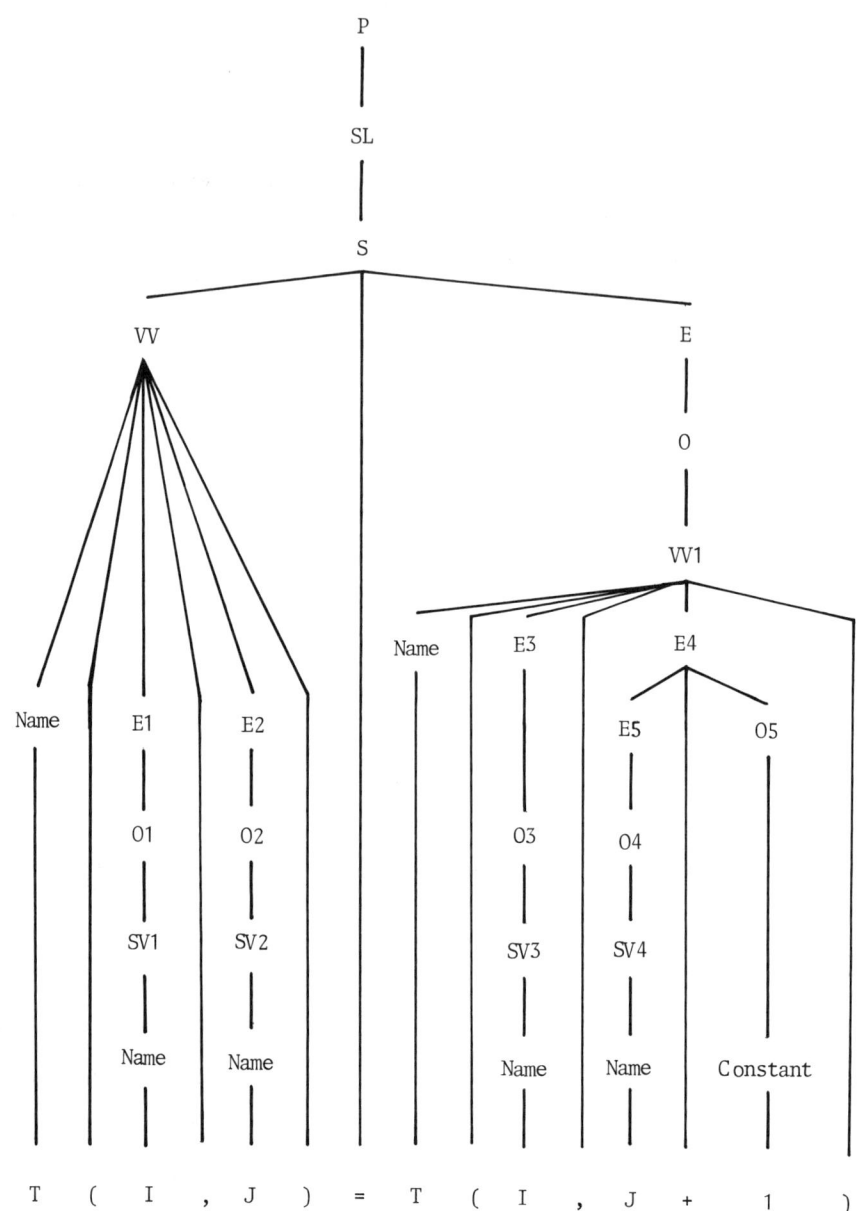

SYNTACTIC TREE

$\langle S \rangle ::= \langle W \rangle = \langle E \rangle$
   FT(W) = FT(S)
   FT(E) = LT(W) + 1   (Triplets in connection with E are produced after those of W)
   LT(S) = LT(E) + 1
   Produce triplet : (LT(S)) = LT(W) , LT(E)

$\langle E \rangle ::= \langle E' \rangle + \langle O \rangle$
   FT(E') = FT(E)
   FT(O) = LT(E') + 1
   LT(E) = LT(O) + 1
   Produce the triplet : (LT(E)) + LT(E') , LT(O)

$\langle E \rangle ::= \langle O \rangle$
   FT(O) = FT(E)
   LT(E) = LT(O)

$\langle O \rangle ::= \langle W \rangle$
   FT(W) = FT(O)
   LT(O) = LT(W)

$\langle O \rangle ::= \langle SV \rangle$
   LT(O) = FT(O) - 1   (No triplet is produced)

$\langle O \rangle ::= $ Constant
   LT(O) = FT(O) - 1

The semantics of each production rule is described by means of some of the attributes allotted to the various non-terminals involved. A sequence of statements in the semantic language establishes the relationships existing between these attributes in a production rule. Thus an implicit evaluation order for attributes is set up according to which the entire statement sequences may be rearranged in a coherent execution order. In a meta-compiler system the execution of this final semantic programme produces the object code corresponding to the source programme.

Optimizing attribute R↑ (Redundancy)

The function of this attribute consists of preventing the production of redundant triplets, so its definition should be inserted in the preceding semantic descriptions in such a way as to achieve this aim. The only candidates to redundancy would be expression-type non-terminals. In our example this would imply the following production rules :

$\langle E \rangle ::= \langle E' \rangle + \langle O \rangle$

$\langle W \rangle ::= $ Name ($\langle E \rangle$, $\langle E' \rangle$)

Method :

Let NT be a non-terminal generating a single triplet, then the triplet number would be given by LT(NT).

1 - If (LT(NT)) is redundant with respect to triplet (i) then R(NT) = i, else R(NT) = LT(NT).
2 - If R(NT) ≠ LT(NT) then no triplet is to be produced. This should be taken into account while evaluating LT(NT).
3 - If R(NT) = LT(NT) then produce the corresponding triplet, replacing all LT-type operands by their equivalent R-type.

Semantic description :

<E> ::= <E'> + <O>
FT(E') = FT(E)
FT(O) = LT(E') + 1
- If the triplet   +   R(E') , R(O)   is redundant w.r.t. triplet (i) then R(E) = i (no triplet is to be produced), else R(E) = LT(O) + 1 and produce the triplet   (R(E))   +   R(E') , R(O).
- If R(E) = LT(O) + 1 then LT(E) = LT(O) + 1, else LT(E) = LT(O).

Notice that triplet production now takes place in the semantic model describing R(E).

<VV> ::= Name (<E> , <E'>)
FT(E) = FT(VV)
FT(E') = LT(E)

Examine whether any of the triplets in connection with the address evaluation ADR(VV) + (R(E) - 1) * max2 - 1 + R(E') is redundant. Let nt be the number of triplets produced after optimization, initially nt = 0.

- If the triplet   -   R(E) , 1   is redundant with respect to triplet (i) then R(VV) = i (no triplet produced) , else nt = nt + 1   and R(VV) = LT(E') + nt and the relevent triplet is produced.
- If the triplet   *   R(VV) , max2   is redundant w.r.t. triplet (i) then R(VV) = i (no triplet produced) , else nt = nt + 1   and R(VV) = LT(E') + nt and the corresponding triplet is produced.
- The same procedure is repeated for the 3 remaining triplets :

   +   ADR(VV) , R(VV)
   -   R(VV)   , 1
   +   R(VV)   , R(E')   .

LT(VV) : R(VV)   (Evaluation of LT(VV) is postponed until nt becomes known, i.e. R(VV) has to be computed before)
LT(VV) = LT(E') + nt

III - A SURVEY OF THE TWO METHODS

In the classical method three distinct passes have to be effected : one on the source text and two others on the intermediate code. During the first pass non--optimized triplets are produced while the second pass consists of examining the triplets in a sequential order. However, before carrying out the redundancy test (cf. *theorem*), the operands which refer to triplets of the IDEM-type must be replaced which would mean an additional global reading of each triplet (*equivalent to still another pass*). Moreover the intermediate code would occupy a maximal storage space during this entire treatment : redundant triplets are not eliminated but simply marked as such. A third pass then permits the actual elimination of IDEM-triplets producing the optimized intermediate code.

The attribute method has the advantage of not requiring more than one effective pass on the source text to carry out the optimization. In fact the triplets produced are already optimized and hence the intermediate code occupies a minimum storage space. By its definition, the attribute R plays a similar role to IDEM-marking of the triplets : it replaces automatically each operand of triplet-type by its value, taking into account the optimizations already dealt with, and avoids the production of redundant triplets. This evidently reduces the number of triplets to consult during the redundancy test. The attribute R does not undergo any special treatment. It has been defined in such a way as to make the notion of redundancy a part of the semantics of the language : thus R acts as a natural optimizing agent during the compiling process.

Using the attributes method the programme topology is also re-established through attributes [4] and we can pass on information, relevent to the application of classical optimization algorithms, along the syntactic tree, thus alleviating the task of intermediate code handling. Indeed we offer compiler-writers a choice of attributes depending on nature of optimizations desired. The semantics of the optimizations being defined at the level of each syntactic rule benefit from the formalization of the latter. Consequently clarity and rigour are the two fundamental advantages of this method. The writing facility offered constitutes the third and not the most negligible advantage. Moreover, since the meta-compiler system DELTA is in charge of dealing with all attributes in the same way whether they serve to optimize code or not, optimization may be considered to be an integral part of language semantics. Finally, in providing users with a typical attribute-structure we set the foundation of a methodology which will allow them considerable disentanglement from implementation problems in order to concentrate their efforts more on optimization algorithms.

REFERENCES

[1] Mathematical Systems Theory, 2, *2*, 1968.
" Semantic of Context-free Languages ".
D.E. KNUTH

[2] Rapports de recherche LABORIA (IRIA) :
N° 20, juin 1973,
N° 35, octobre 1973,
N° 59, février 1974,
Séminaires Langages et Traducteurs, IRIA juin 1973.

[3] SIGPLAN Notices, July 1970.
" Control Flow Analysis ".
F.E. ALLEN

[4] ACM 74 Annual Meeting, November 11-13, 1974.
" Semantic Attributes and Improvement of Generated Code ".
D. NEEL and M. AMIRCHAHY

[5] John Wiley & Sons, Inc., New York, 1971.
" Compiler Construction for Digital Computers ".
G. GRIES

[6] Courant Institute of Mathematical Sciences, New York University, April 1970.
" Programming Languages and their Compilers ".
J. COCKE and J.T. SCHWARTZ

[7] Computer Science Group, Univ. of Washington, Seattle, Washington, Ph.D. 1972.
" Global Expression Optimization during Compilation ".
G.A. KILDALL

[8] The Computer Journal, *16*, 4, 1973.
" A FORTRAN to FORTRAN Optimizing Compiler ".
P.B. SCHNECK and E. ANGEL

[9] ACM Symposium, Boston, October 1973.
" Analysis of a Simple Algorithm for Global Flow Problems ".
M.S. HECHT and J.D. ULLMAN

CODE-OPTIMIERUNG MITTELS ATTRIBUTIERTER TRANSFORMATIONSGRAMMATIKEN

Reinhard Wilhelm
Technische Universität München
Abteilung Mathematik
8000 München 2
Arcisstraße 21

0. Einleitung

0.1. Motivation

Ein übersetzergenerierendes System sollte seinen Benutzern formale Modelle anbieten, mit denen die *Syntax und die Semantik von Programmiersprachen* beschrieben werden können. Zur Beschreibung der Syntax haben sich BNF und verwandte Beschreibungsverfahren schon seit vielen Jahren durchgesetzt. Der Fluß der semantischen Information läßt sich bequem durch *Knuth's Attribute* (Knuth 68) bzw. *Koster's Affixe* (Koster 71) darstellen. DeRemer (deRemer 73) schlägt vor, den Übersetzungsprozeß durch eine Menge von *Transformationsgrammatiken* zu beschreiben, wobei den Teilprozessen, wie Scanner, Parser usw., jeweils eine Transformationsgrammatik zugeordnet ist, welche den Prozeß beschreibt.

Ein solcher Teilprozeß ist auch die *sprachabhängige Code-Optimierung*. Der Benutzer des übersetzergenerierenden Systems sollte die Möglichkeit haben, die Optimierungsalgorithmen formal zu beschreiben, welche in den zu erzeugenden Übersetzer inkorporiert werden sollen.

Im hier gewählten Ansatz zur Lösung dieses Problems liege das zu optimierende Programm in Form eines Programmbaumes (computational tree) vor; die für die Optimierung notwendige Information sei in Form von Attributen mit den Knoten des Baumes assoziiert.

---

* Diese Arbeit ist im Sonderforschungsbereich 49 - Elektronische Rechenanlagen und Informationsverarbeitung - in München entstanden.

Die Optimierungsalgorithmen werden dargestellt durch Mengen von attributierten Transformationsregeln, das sind Regeln, deren Anwendbarkeit nicht nur vom Vorliegen eines bestimmten Musters im Programmbaum abhängt, sondern zusätzlich vom Erfülltsein von Prädikaten der Attribute im entsprechenden lokalen Bereich des Baumes.

In 0.2 werden attributierte Transformationsregeln (AT-Regeln), ihre Anwendbarkeit und ihre Anwendung definiert. Die Definitionen basieren teilweise auf (Rosen 73).

In 1 werden AT-Regeln angegeben für lokale Optimierungen. Am Beispiel der linearen Adreßfortschaltung in ALGOL60-for-Schleifen wird in 2 insbesondere das Sammeln der Optimierungsinformation in Attributen demonstriert. Für die Elimination redundanter Teilausdrücke in Basisblöcken werden in 3 dynamische, programmabhängige Mengen von AT-Regeln benutzt.

0.2. Definitionen

Sei $\underline{A}$ ein endlicher Symbolvorrat, $g : \underline{A} \to N$ eine Abbildung, die jedem Symbol aus $\underline{A}$ eine natürliche Zahl, genannt *Stelligkeit*, zuordnet.

Ein *Programmbaum* sei ein geordneter Baum, dessen Knoten mit Symbolen aus $\underline{A}$ markiert sind, so daß ein Knoten mit Markierung x genau $g(x)$ Söhne hat.

In einem *attributierten Programmbaum* sind mit den Knoten des Baumes semantische Attribute assoziiert (vgl. Knuth 68). Jedes Attribut A hat einen bestimmten Wertevorrat D_A.

Sei $\underline{V}$ eine endliche Menge von *Variablen* über der Menge der Programmbäume. Jede Variable hat eine i.a. nicht endliche Menge von Bäumen, deren Knoten mit Symbolen aus $\underline{A}$ markiert sind, als Wertevorrat.

Eine *Schablone* ist ein geordneter Baum, dessen Knoten markiert sind mit Elementen von $\underline{A} \cup \underline{V}$, wobei sich nur an Blättern des Baumes Variable aus $\underline{V}$ befinden.

Mit jedem Element aus $\underline{A}$ wird eine Menge von Attributen assoziiert, von denen einige <u>inherited</u> andere <u>derived</u> dort auftreten. (Koster 71).

Eine *attributierte Schablone* ist eine Schablone, in der mit Knoten, welche mit Symbolen aus $\underline{A}$ markiert sind, Attribute assoziiert sind. Die zu einer attributierten Schablone R gehörige attributfreie Schablone werde mit R_- bezeichnet.

Ist R eine attributierte Schablone mit Attributen $A_1, A_2, \ldots, A_n$, so sei

$$D_R =_{df} \underset{i}{\times} D_{A_i}$$

Eine *Transformationsregel* (T-Regel) ist ein Paar (R,S) von Schablonen, geschrieben $R \to S$ mit folgenden Eigenschaften:

- jedes $V \in \underline{V}$ tritt in R höchstens einmal auf,
- tritt ein $V \in \underline{V}$ in S auf, so muß es auch in R auftreten.

Eine *attributierte Transformationsregel* (AT-Regel) ist ein Quadrupel (R,S,P,F), geschrieben $R \overset{P}{\underset{F}{\Rightarrow}} S$, wobei $R_- \Rightarrow S_-$ eine T-Regel ist, R, S attributierte Schablonen sind,
P eine Menge von Prädikaten auf D_R ist,
F eine Menge von Funktionen von D_R in D_S ist.

Substituiert man in einer Schablone für alle Variable Bäume aus ihrem jeweiligen Wertebereich, so erhält man ein *Exemplar* der Schablone. Substituiert man in beiden Schablonen einer T-Regel $R \Rightarrow S$ konsistent für alle Variablen Bäume, so erhält man ein *Exemplar einer T-Regel*. Die dabei entstehenden Exemplare von R und S werden *korrespondierend* genannt.

Eine AT-Regel $R \overset{P}{\underset{F}{\Rightarrow}} S$ ist auf einen attributierten Programmbaum B *anwendbar*, wenn

- ein Exemplar von R_- in B auftritt,
- alle Prädikate von P, angewendet auf die aktuellen Attribute des Exemplars von R, den Wert <u>true</u> ergeben.

Eine *Anwendung* einer AT-Regel auf einen Baum B besteht in

- Ersetzung des Exemplars von R in B durch das korrespondierende Exemplar von S,
- Berechnen der Werte von Attributen von S mit Hilfe der Funktionen aus F.

Eine attributierte Transformationsgrammatik ist ein Paar $(\underline{B}, \underline{R})$, wobei
$\underline{B}$ eine i.a. nicht endliche Menge von attributierten Programmbäumen und
$\underline{R}$ eine Menge von AT-Regeln ist.

Zur Notation:

- In den folgenden Beispielen sind Symbole aus $\underline{A}$ durch Umrandung kenntlich gemacht.

— Es sind nicht alle Attribute aufgeführt, welche ein Knoten im Programmbaum hat, sondern nur jeweils die für die Anwendung einer AT-Regel relevanten.

1. Lokale Optimierung

Als solche werden Optimierungen bezeichnet, die unabhängig von der Umgebung vorgenommen werden können, z.B. Ausrechnen von Konstanten-Operationen zur Übersetzungszeit, Ersetzen von Divisionen und Multiplikationen mit Potenzen von 2 durch Shifts.

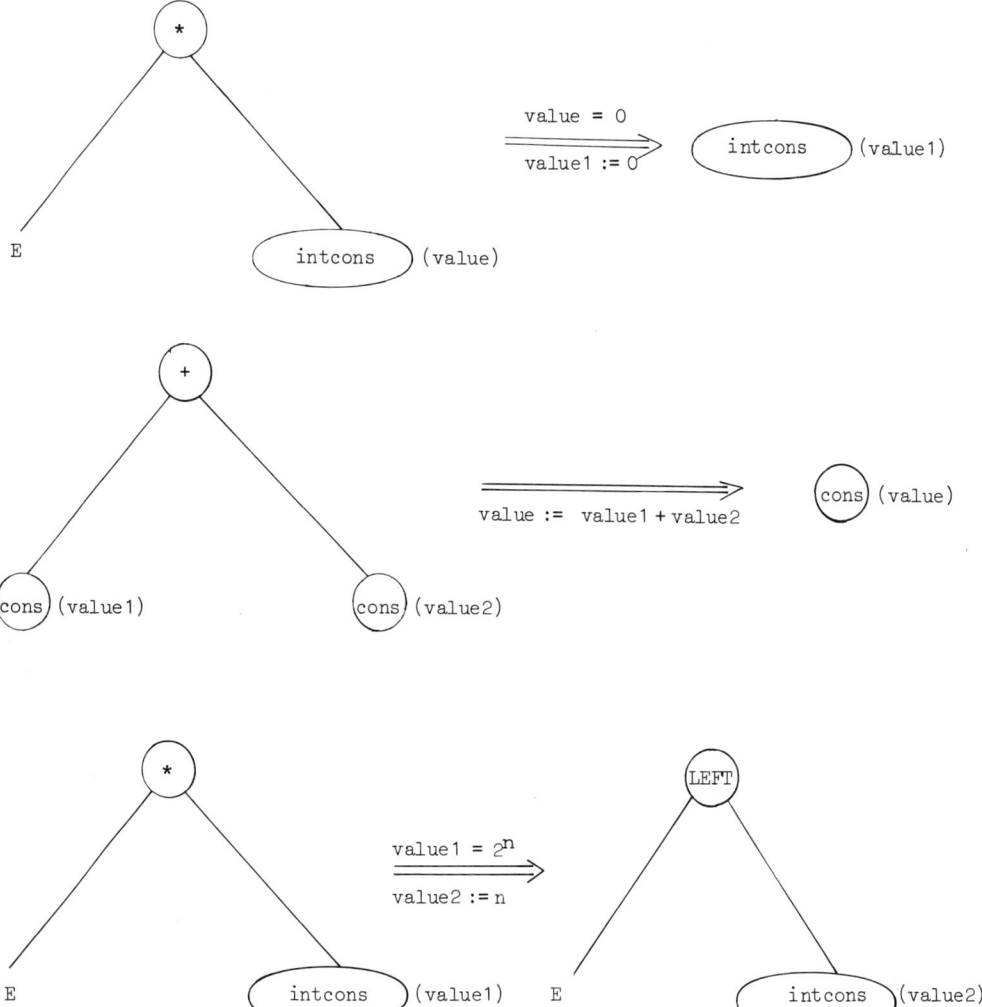

2. Lineare Adreßfortschaltung in ALGOL 60-for-Schleifen

Wir betrachten Schleifen der Form

      <u>for</u> lv := startexpr <u>step</u> stepexpr <u>until</u> endexpr <u>do</u> statement

Treten im Schleifenstatement S indizierte Variable auf, deren Indexausdrücke linear in der Schleifenvariablen lv sind, so kann unter gewissen Bedingungen die Neuberechnung der Adresse der indizierten Variablen bei jedem Schleifendurchlauf ersetzt werden durch die lineare Fortschaltung von Hilfsgrößen, die zusammen mit der Fortschaltung der Schleifenvariablen lv erfolgen (vgl.(Grau 67)).

Beispiel: Im Programm

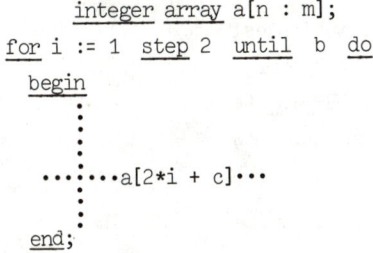

kann die Neuberechnung der Adresse von a[2*i + c] ersetzt werden durch die lineare Fortschaltung einer Hilfsgröße t um 4 , welche mit der Adresse von a[2+c] initialisiert wurde (Voraussetzung: c schleifenkonstant).

Wie im weiteren ersichtlich, hängt die Optimierbarkeit ab von

- den Attributen des <u>for</u>-Statements
- den Attributen der Indexausdrücke.

Das for-Statement sei im Programmbaum folgendermaßen dargestellt:

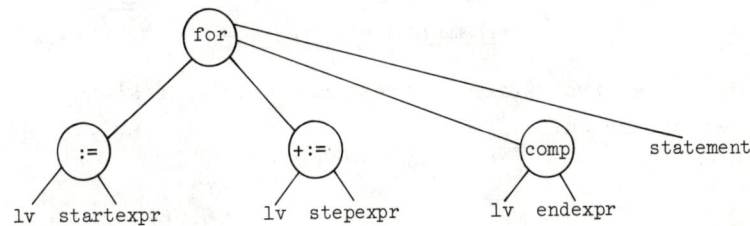

Zur Vereinfachung der Darstellung werden nur eindimensionale Felder betrachtet.

SFVI (Gries 71) sind: simple variable or simple formal parameter called by value with type integer.

Eine Produktion für das Nonterminal forstat, versehen mit Optimierungsattributen, ist:

```
forstat ("d" "int" loopvar, "bool" optimizable, no_proc_called,
               no_name_parameters, "set" assignedvariables):
    for,
    variable   ("d" "int" loopvar, loopvar_is_SFVI),
    :=,
    arithm_expr (...),
    step,
    arithm_expr ("d" "set" stepexprvariables,
                 "int" type_of_stepexpr,
                 "bool" only_SFVIs_in_stepexpr,
                        only-intconstants),
    until,
    arithm_expr (...),
    do,
    statement  ("i" "int" loopvar,
                "d" "set" assignedvariables,
                "bool" no_proc_called,
                       no_name_parameters),
    "op" assign (optimizable,
                 loopvar_is_SFVI                             and
                 type_of_stepexpr = integer                  and
                 stepexprvariables disjoint assignedvariables and
                 only_SFVIs_in_stepexpr                      and
                 only_intconstants                           and
                 not loopvar in assignedvariables            and
                 no_proc_called                              and
                 no_name_parameters).
```

Alle in dieser Produktion auftretenden Attribute können in einem Lauf ausgewertet werden.

Die Attributbesetzung des Nonterminals subscripted_variable ist:

>subscripted_variable ("i" "int" loopvar,
>   "bool" optimizable,
>   "set" assignedvariables,
>   "d" "set" indexpr_variables,
>   "bool" indexpr_lin_in_loopvar,
>   indexpr_with_loopvar,
>   only_SFVIs_in_indexpr)

Das inherited auftretende Attribut assignedvariables von subscripted_variable kann jedoch erst in einem <u>zweiten Lauf</u> durch das Schleifenstatement bis zu der subscripted variable gelangen.

In (Wilhelm 74) wird eine attributierte Grammatik für arithmetische Ausdrücke angegeben, welche die Besetzung der Attribute

>indexpr_lin_in_loopvar   und
>indexpr_with_loopvar   zeigt.

Für die folgenden Optimierungstransformationen werden optimierbare Indexausdrücke in folgender Form vorausgesetzt.

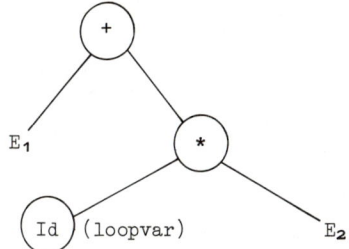

Diese Form läßt sich durch AT-Regeln herstellen.

Die nachfolgende Transformationsregel ersetzt im Baum die fortschaltbare indizierte Variable durch drei Teilbäume,
- einen, der eine neue Hilfszelle initialisiert (ivinit),
- einen, der die Hilfszelle linear fortschaltet (ivincr) und
- einen, der den Inhalt dieser Hilfsgröße, nämlich die Adresse der indizierten Variablen, holt.

Der letzte Teilbaum verbleibt im Baum an seiner Stelle, während die ersten beiden Teilbäume mit Hilfe zusätzlicher Regeln bis zum (for) - Knoten hinaufgeschoben werden.

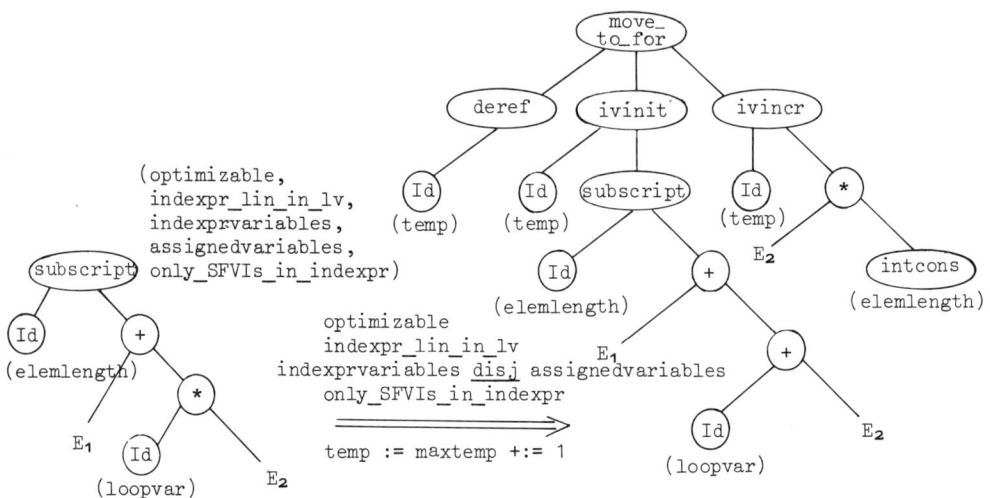

Mit Hilfe zwei weiterer AT-Regeln werden die Teilbäume mit den Wurzeln (ivinit) und (ivincr) an die Söhne des (for) – Knotens geschoben. Dort wird die Hilfszelle durch Substitution des Startexpression E_1 mit Hilfe der folgenden AT-Regel initialisiert.

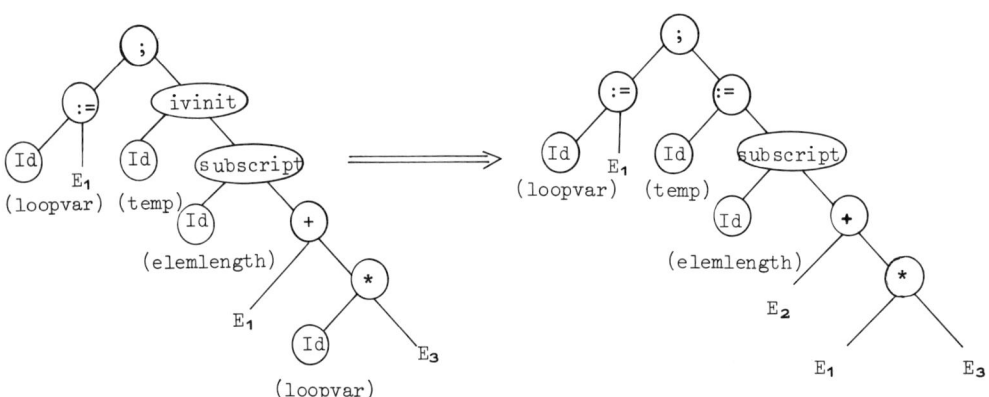

Um die Optimierung geschachtelter Schleifen zu ermöglichen, braucht man noch Regeln, welche indizierte Variable mit schleifenkonstanten Indexausdrücken in äußere Schleifen schieben. Die vollständige Regelmenge für die lineare Adreßfortschaltung findet sich in (Wilhelm 74).

3. Eliminierung gemeinsamer Teilausdrücke aus Basis-Blöcken

In den Kapiteln 1 und 2 wurden verschiedene Arten von Codeoptimierung durch Mengen von AT-Regeln beschrieben, welche abhängig von der Programmiersprache aber unabhängig vom jeweiligen Quellprogramm waren. Zur Eliminierung redundanter Teilausdrücke werden dynamische Mengen von AT-Regeln benutzt. Dabei entsprechen die in einem Basis-Block (basic block) zu einem bestimmten Zeitpunkt aktuellen AT-Regeln den zu diesem Zeitpunkt verfügbaren Teilausdrücken.

Mit jedem Identifier und jeder Zwischenspeicherzelle wird ein Attribut "value-number" (Cocke 70) assoziiert, welches die Zustände der jeweiligen Variablen identifiziert. Jede Variable, die in einem Basis-Block zum ersten Mal auftritt, bekommt eine bisher nicht benutzte value-number zugeordnet. Bei einer Wertzuweisung wird der Variablen auf der linken Seite die value-number der rechten Seite zugeordnet.
Wird ein noch nicht verfügbarer Ausdruck

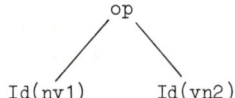

verarbeitet, so wird eine neue Zwischenspeicherzelle mit value-number vn:=vnmax+:=1 reserviert und eine Regel

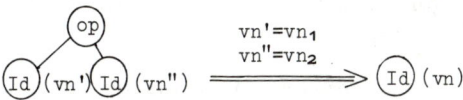

generiert.
Im Programmbaum wird ein Teilbaum

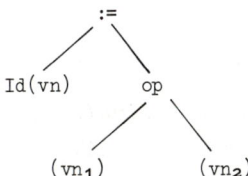

eingefügt.
Ist ein Ausdruck verfügbar, so gibt es eine anwendbare AT-Regel, welche ihn eliminiert.

4. Zusammenfassung und Ausblick

Attributierte Transformationsgrammatiken wurden vorgestellt, als ein Mittel zur formalen Beschreibung von Code-Optimierungsalgorithmen. Ein angestrebtes Ziel für weitere Arbeit ist der Beweis, daß gewisse durch AT-Regeln beschriebene Optimierungen Äquivalenztransformationen sind, d.h., daß optimierte Programme die gleichen Ergebnisse liefern wie die Ausgangsprogramme. Daß dieses bei existierenden optimierenden Compilern nicht immer der Fall ist, dürfte bekannt sein.

Ich möchte Frl.Dr.Hill, Herrn Dr.Schwald und Herrn Dieterich für wertvolle Diskussionen danken.

Bibliographie

(Cocke 70)   Cocke, J., Schwartz, J.T.: *Programming Languages and Their Compilers*. Prelim. Notes. Courant Institute of Mathematical Sciences 1970

(deRemer 73) deRemer, F.: *Transformational Grammars for Languages and Compilers*. Techn. Rep. No.50, Univ.of Newcastle upon Tyne 1973

(Grau 67)   Grau, A.A., Hill, U., Langmaack, H.: *Translation of ALGOL60*. Handbook for Automatic Computation Ib. Springer 1967

(Gries 71)   Gries, D.: *Compiler Construction for Digital Computers*. J. Wiley 1971

(Knuth 68)   Knuth, D.E.: *Semantics of Context-Free Languages*. Math. Systems Theory, 2, 1968

(Koster 71) Koster, C.H.A.: Affix-Grammars, in Peck (Ed.): *ALGOL68 Implementation*. North Holland 1971

(Rosen 73)   Rosen, B.K.: *Tree-Manipulating Systems and Church Rosser Theorems*. JACM Vol.20, No.1, 1973

(Wilhelm 74) Wilhelm, R.: *Codeoptimierung mit attributierten Transformationsgrammatiken*. Bericht Nr.7408, Abteilung Math. TU München

(Kron 74)   Kron, H.H.: *Partial Subtree Transformational Grammars*. Univ. of California, Santa Cruz 1974

Die dynamische Datenbasis des HALORD Systems

J. Martin   HALORG, Saarbrücken
Ch. Floyd, R. Nagel, P. Schnupp, O. Wörz   SOFTLAB, München

1. Einführung, Zielsetzung von HALORD

Das HALORD System bietet die Grundlage für ein integriertes Informationssystem zur Automatisierung der öffentlichen und betrieblichen Verwaltung.

Die dynamische Datenbasis (DDB) ist die zentrale Komponente des HALORD Systems. Sie verwaltet die Bewegungsdaten und gestattet gleichzeitig eine langfristige Auftragsplanung in Abhängigkeit von einer programmierten Organisationsbeschreibung einerseits und von eintreffenden Daten andererseits.

Die wesentliche Neuerung von HALORD besteht darin, daß nicht nur die Verwaltungsaufgaben von Programmen gelöst werden, sondern der organisatorische Ablauf selber automatisiert wird. Dabei ist ein neues Benutzerbild impliziert (Abb.1): Benutzer des HALORD Systems ist nicht in erster Linie der einzelne Programmierer (er "liefert" nur die verwendeten Algorithmen),

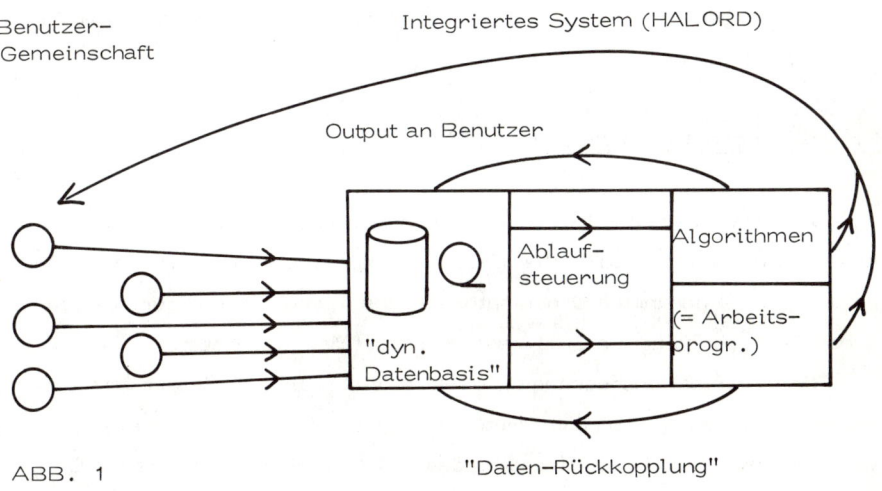

ABB. 1

der Benutzer ist vielmehr auf der einen Seite der Organisator des Betriebes, auf der anderen Seite der meist DV unerfahrene Sachbearbeiter. Der Sachbearbeiter liefert die Eingabedaten für das System. Ergebnisse von Programmläufen werden im Allgemeinen nicht an den Sachbearbeiter bzw. an den Programmierer zurückgeliefert, sondern nach Angaben des Organisators direkt an die zuständigen Dienststellen weitergeleitet oder zur weiteren Verarbeitung in der DDB behalten.

Die eigentlichen Verwaltungsaufgaben werden von Anwenderprogrammen, die unter HALORD laufen, durchgeführt. HALORD arbeitet im Stapelbetrieb und stellt eine Erweiterung des jeweiligen Herstellerbetriebssystems dar: HALORD Programme werden von der DDB aktiviert, sie können alle Möglichkeiten des ursprünglichen Systems ausnützen und darüber hinaus mit der DDB verkehren.

Bei der Planung von HALORD waren folgende Gesichtspunkte als Benutzeranforderungen maßgebend:

. Das System ist anwendungsneutral, nicht auf eine bestimmte Organisationsform zugeschnitten.
. Umstellung eines Betriebes auf HALORD kann schrittweise erfolgen.
. Die Bedienung für den EDV unerfahrenen Sachbearbeiter ist extrem einfach.
. Die dem Organisator gebotenen Möglichkeiten sind flexibel und differenziert genug, um nach und nach die Entwicklung einer optimalen Organisation zu ermöglichen.

2. Programmierte Organisation

Die Arbeit der DDB basiert auf einer Beschreibung des existierenden Datenflusses und der automatisierten Entscheidungsträger. Diese wird vom Organisator in der sogenannten Organisatorsprache formuliert und durch einen vorgeschalteten Übersetzer in DDB Beschreibungstafeln übersetzt.

Die Organisationsbeschreibung (Beispiel 1) kann bei Bedarf vom Organisator geändert werden. Änderungen treten einmal am Tag, zur Systemzeit, in Kraft, während des eigentlichen Einsatzes des HALORD Systems bleibt die Organisationsbeschreibung unverändert.

```
BEGIN
DATA     Rech      EFFECTIVE      74 - 1 - 11
DATA     Mahn      EFFECTIVE      74 - 1 - 11
DATA     Bezt      EFFECTIVE      74 - 1 - 11

PROGRAM  Billing   EFFECTIVE      74 - 1 - 11
PROGRAM  Remind    EFFECTIVE      74 - 1 - 11

JOB      Rechnung  EFFECTIVE      74 - 1 - 11
   EXEC     Billing    INPUT    Rech
   ACTIVATION TIME     RELATIVE TO   Rech      IMMEDIATE
   OUTPUT   Mahn       ON ABEND      RETRY

JOB      Mahnung   EFFECTIVE      74 - 1 - 11
   EXEC     Remind     INPUT    Bezt, Mahn
   ACTIVATION TIME     RELATIVE TO   Mahn      30 D
   OUTPUT   Bezt, Mahn ON ABEND      RETRY

END
```

Beispiel 1   Organisationsprogramm

Datenbeschreibung : Die von der DDB verwalteten Daten sind gekennzeichnet durch ihren Datentyp (Spalte 1-8 jedes Kartenbildes). Der Datentyp bildet das einzige Differenzierungsmerkmal, feinere Unterteilungen der Daten sind nicht vorgesehen. In der Organisatorsprache werden der Datentyp sowie eine eventuell geforderte Syntax für die Kartenbilder definiert. Paketbildung innerhalb eines Datentyps gestattet die Verwendung frei formatierter Records variabler Länge sowie erhebliche Steigerung der Effektivität bei der Verarbeitung.

Programmbeschreibung : Die unter HALORD laufenden Anwenderprogramme werden nicht von der DDB verwaltet, sondern stehen in einer Programmbibliothek zur Verfügung. In der Programmbeschreibung werden lediglich das Ein- Ausgabeverhalten der Anwenderprogramme sowie eventuelle Kriterien für eine erwünschte Vorsortierung der Eingabedaten beschrieben.

Auftragsbeschreibung : In einer Auftragsbeschreibung wird vom Organisator ein Auftragstyp definiert, aus dem die DDB eine Klasse von durchzuführenden Einzelaufträgen nach den Organisatorangaben generiert.

Ein Auftrag bildet die Verknüpfung zwischen dem zu aktivierenden Programm (Algorithmus), seinen Ein- und Ausgabedatentypen, seinem Aktivierungstermin, Voraussetzungen für die Aktivierung, sowie gewünschter Fehlerbehandlung.

Für den Aktivierungstermin gibt es drei Möglichkeiten :

Absolute Terminbeschreibung : Hier wird der Aktivierungstermin absolut, in Form von Kalenderdaten beschrieben. Dabei kann die Ausführung einmal oder periodisch (täglich, wöchentlich, monatlich usw.) verlangt werden.

Relative Terminbeschreibung: Ein relativer Termin bedeutet, daß der Auftrag eine bestimmte Zeit (Sonderfall : sofort) nach Eintreffen von Daten bzw. von Vollständigkeitsmeldungen für Daten ausgeführt werden soll. Terminbestimmende Daten heißen aktiv.

Anwendertermine : Ein Auftrag mit Anwendertermin kann zu einem beliebigen Zeitpunkt über die Steuersprachanweisung

... ACTIVATE

aktiviert werden (vgl. Abschnitt 3).

Die interne Termin-Behandlung für alle Aufträge ist einheitlich in dem Sinne, daß für jeden durchzuführenden Einzelauftrag der Termin entweder noch nicht festliegt oder in absoluter Form (Datum + Uhrzeit, bis auf Minute genau) gegeben ist. Dadurch wird erreicht, daß sowohl datengetriebene als auch terminbedingte Abläufe durch den gleichen Mechanismus verwaltet werden können.

Vollständigkeit von Daten : Im einfachsten Falle werden bei einer Auftragsaktivierung alle für diesen Auftrag eingetroffenen Daten verarbeitet. Die Gruppierung von Daten für einen Verarbeitungslauf entsteht also zufällig.

Wo eine solche willkürliche Gruppierung nicht sinnvoll erscheint, kann der Organisator Vollständigkeitskriterien für die einem Verarbeitungslauf zugeordneten Daten angeben. In einfachen Fällen (numerische Kriterien) kann die Vollständigkeit von Daten von der DDB automatisch geprüft werden, andernfalls ist eine Vollständigkeitsmeldung für Daten erforderlich. Die Vollständigkeit der Daten bildet dann eine zusätzliche Voraussetzung für die Aktivierung des Auftrags.

Zur Sicherung des Gesamtablaufs können Daten oder Vollständigkeitsmeldungen vorab angemahnt werden.

3. Steuer- und Änderungssprache

Wie schon erwähnt, bleibt die Organisationsbeschreibung während des Einsatzes von HALORD unverändert, die Organisatorsprache liefert also keine Möglichkeit, in den dynamischen Ablauf einzugreifen. Diesen Zweck erfüllt jedoch die Steuer- bezw. Änderungssprache.

Alle Anweisungen der Steuersprache haben die Form

... operation , parameter_liste

Über die Steuersprache werden Aufträge mit Anwenderterminen aktiviert:

... ACTIVATE , Auftragsname [, Termin]

oder die Vollständigkeit von Daten gemeldet:

... COMPLETE , Auftragsname [, Datentyp] .

Über die Steuersprache wird auch die Paketbildung von Daten erreicht (in der gegenwärtigen Version noch nicht implementiert).

Steuersprachanweisungen können (wie Daten) von außen oder von einem laufenden Programm eingegeben werden.

Anweisungen der Änderungssprache erlauben es, in die Daten- und Auftragswarteschlangen korrektiv einzugreifen.

4. Informationsfluß in der DDB

Abb. 2 zeigt den Informationsfluß der DDB.

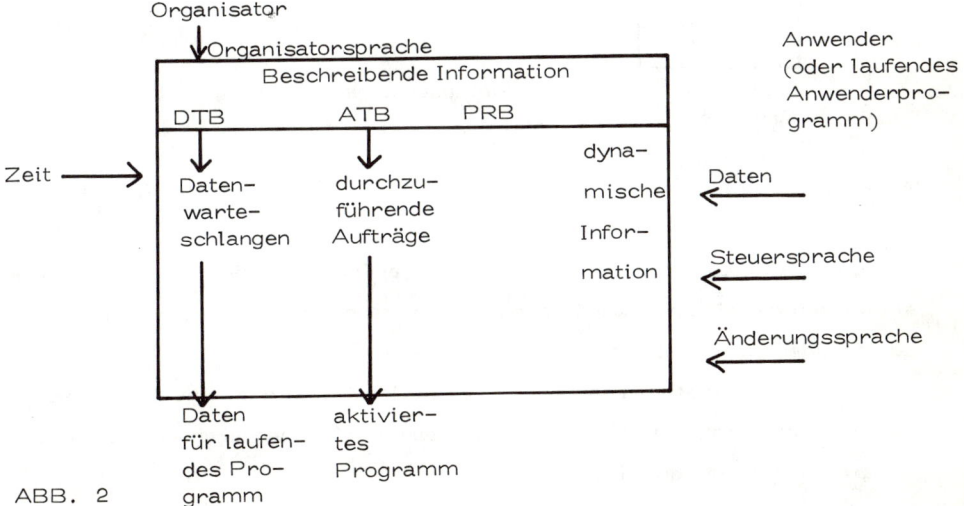

ABB. 2

Die Verwaltung der Daten und durchzuführenden Aufträge ist die eigentliche Funktion der DDB. Grundlage für die Verwaltung bildet die Organisationsbeschreibung. Zu jeder beschreibenden Struktur (Datentypbeschreibung, Auftragstypbeschreibung usw.) verwaltet die DDB eine Warteschlange.

Der interne dynamische Zustand der DDB wird durch Eintreffen von Daten und die externe Zeit bestimmt, und kann durch Anweisungen der Steuer- und Änderungssprache bei Bedarf modifiziert werden.

Die DDB liefert dem System sowohl zu aktivierende Programme als auch Daten für diese Programme.

5. Filekonzept

Für alle von der DDB verwalteten Objekte existiert ein einheitliches Filekonzept (Abb. 3). Für jedes Objekt gibt es eine beschreibende Struktur und eine von ihr verwaltete sequentielle Datei (Warteschlange).

In dieser Datei sind einzelne Records durch ihre laufende Nummer, ihren Eingangszeitpunkt und ihre Herkunft gekennzeichnet.

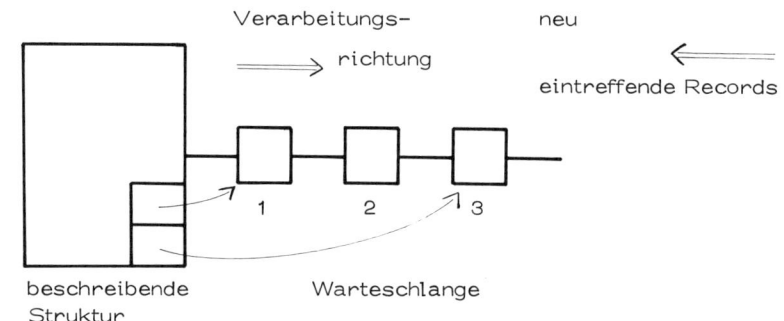

ABB. 3

6. Datenverwaltung

Daten erreichen die DDB entweder "von außen" über ein Eingabegerät oder sie werden von einem Anwenderprogramm erzeugt, die Behandlung der Daten ist in beiden Fällen identisch.

Daten (Einzelrecords bezw. Pakete) gehören jeweils zu einem Datentyp, der durch die Organisationsbeschreibung einem oder mehreren Aufträgen zur Verarbeitung zugeordnet ist.

Datenrecords werden in die Warteschlange ihres Typs eingeordnet. Aufträge greifen auf die Warteschlange sequentiell zu und verarbeiten jeden Datenrecord genau einmal.

Bei jedem Lauf eines Verarbeitungsauftrages wird daher ein Intervall aus der Datenwarteschlange verarbeitet. Ist ein Datentyp mehreren Aufträgen zugeordnet, so können sich die entsprechenden Intervallzerlegungen überschneiden (Abb. 4).

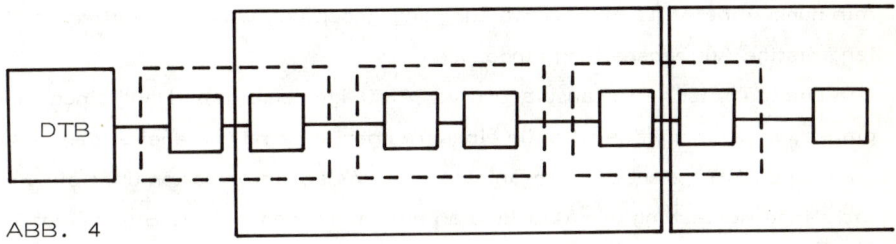

ABB. 4

Die Intervallzerlegung und damit die Zuordnung von Daten zu Verarbeitungsläufen wird von der DDB nach den Organisatorangaben (Termin, Vollständigkeitskriterien) automatisch durchgeführt.

7. Auftragsverwaltung

Durchzuführende Aufträge werden von der DDB generiert und durchlaufen eine Reihe von Zuständen, bevor sie ablauffähig sind. Die Reihenfolge, in der diese Zustände eintreten, hängt sowohl von den Angaben des Organisators als auch vom dynamischen Ablauf in der DDB ab. Auf alle Fälle müssen folgende Ereignisse eintreten, damit ein Auftrag ausgeführt werden kann:

- Der Auftrag wird geplant, d.h. sein Eintrag in der Auftragswarteschlange wird angelegt.
- Der Auftrag wird terminiert.
- Der Anfang des Datenintervalles wird festgelegt.
- Das Ende des Datenintervalles wird festgelegt.
- Der Termin wird erreicht.

Ein ablauffähiger Auftrag wird aktiviert, sobald die für den Auftrag notwendigen Betriebsmittel frei sind.

8. Terminierung

Bei Aufträgen mit absoluten und relativen Terminen liegt der Aktivierungstermin im Allgemeinen von vornherein fest, er wird unmittelbar nach Eintragen des Auftrages in die Warteschlange gesetzt.

Aufträge mit Anwenderterminen können längere Zeit ohne Termin im System existieren. Aufträge ohne Termin sind untereinander verkettet. Sobald der Termin durch eine ACTIVATE Anweisung angegeben ist, wird der Auftrag in die langfristige Auftragshaltung einbezogen.

Die langfristige Vorausplanung von Aufträgen erfolgt an Hand eines Jahresplanes, in den Aufträge, die für einen Tag geplant sind, untereinander verkettet sind. Die DDB liefert dem Organisator auf Wunsch Information über die voraussichtliche Auslastung der Maschine an einem gegebenen Tag. Sie verlegt Termine automatisch im Falle von Sonn- und Feiertagen und im Falle von Überlastung.

Täglich zur Systemzeit wird ein Tagesplan über alle an diesem Tag durchzuführenden Aufträge angelegt.

Dieser Tagesplan ist dynamisch veränderlich und dient der Ablaufsteuerung zur Auswahl des nächsten zu aktivierenden Auftrags.

9. Zuordnung von Daten zu Aufträgen

In der Auftragswarteschlange gibt es immer einen oder mehrere geplante Aufträge. Unter ihnen gibt es immer einen aktuellen Auftrag, dem neu eintreffende Daten zugespielt werden. Der aktuelle Auftrag ist normalerweise der mit dem spätesten Termin (oder noch nicht definiert). Die Datenintervalle für alle Aufträge des gleichen Termins mit früheren Aktivierungsterminen liegen schon fest.

Verarbeitet ein Auftrag mehr als einen Datentyp, dann ist der entsprechende aktuelle Auftrag nicht notwendig für alle Datentypen der selbe (Vollständigkeit von Daten kann selektiv definiert werden).

Passive Daten für einen Auftrag sind solche, die keinen Einfluß auf den Aktivierungstermin haben. Sie werden dem jeweils aktuellen Auftrag zugespielt. Der aktuelle Auftrag ändert sich durch Eintreffen von Terminen oder evtl. Vollständigkeitsmeldungen, nicht aber durch das Eintreffen neuer passiver Daten.

Aktive Daten werden dem jeweils aktuellen Auftrag solange zugeordnet, bis dessen Aktivierungstermin für sie nicht mehr richtig ist. Dann wird ein neuer aktueller Auftrag mit dem gewünschten Termin geplant. Abb. 5 liefert ein Beispiel eine dynamische Zuordnung von aktiven Daten zu einzelnen Verarbeitungsläufen.

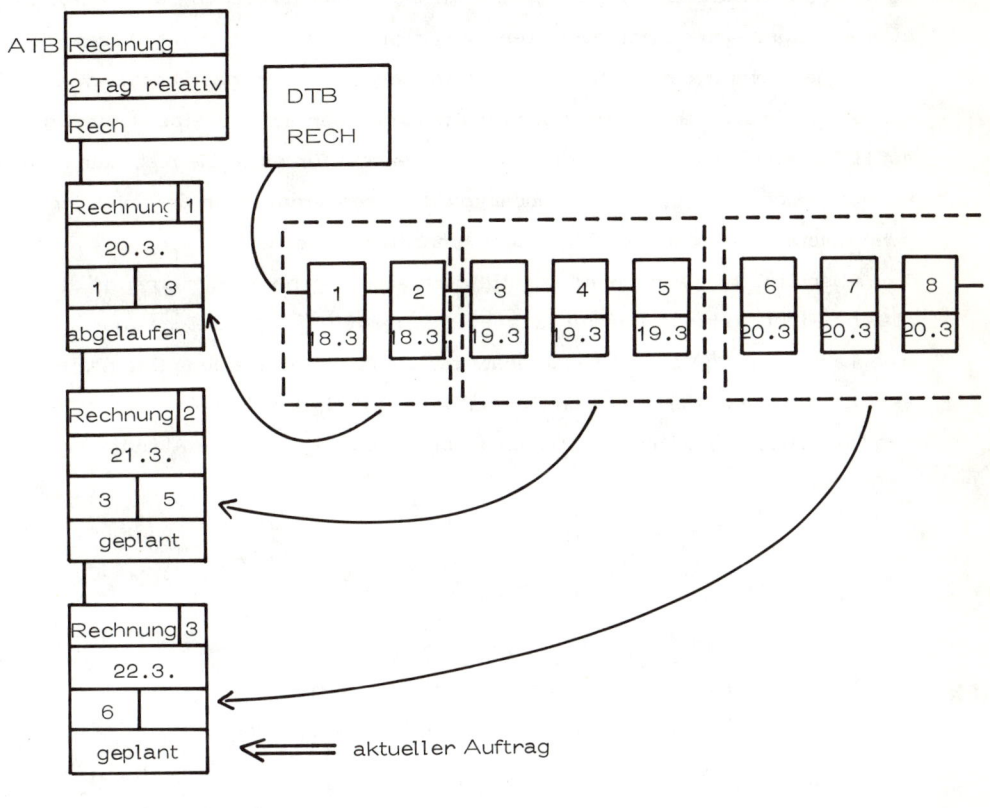

ABB. 5

10. Realisierungsstand

Eine Grundversion des HALORD Systems ist in PL/1 realisiert worden und läuft unter VS/1.

Das HALORD System wurde im Auftrag der HALBERGERHÜTTE AG entwickelt. Das Projekt wurde im Rahmen des 2. Bundesförderungsprogrammes für Datenverarbeitung unterstützt.

Der geplante weitere Ausbau des Systems wird vor allem Maßnahmen zur

Datensicherung und Effektivierung einschließen. Außerdem soll die Flexibilität der DDB als Organisationshilfe erhöht werden.

11. Schlußbetrachtungen

Mit dem HALORD System, insbesondere der dynamischen Datenbasis, ist ein neuartiges Automatisierungswerkzeug geschaffen worden, mit dessen Hilfe der immer komplexer werdende Ablauf in Rechenzentren gesichert und automatisiert werden kann. Wegen der Möglichkeit einer schrittweisen Umstellung auf HALORD bedeutet die Einführung des Systems für einen Betrieb kein großes Risiko. Wegen der leichten Änderbarkeit der programmierten Organisation kann schrittweise eine optimale Organisation entwickelt werden.

Abschließend sei noch auf parallele Entwicklungen von Systemen in die gleiche Richtung hingewiesen: das PASS System [1], welches nur absolute Terminierung von Aufträgen gestattet und über keine eigene Datenhaltung verfügt, und das Transaction Driven Operating System von CDC (Option des Betriebsystems Kronos), welches nur die datengetriebene Aktivierung von Aufträgen gestattet.

Literatur:

[1]: An automatic Scheduling System
W.C. Hoffer, Datamation 7/1974 pp. 75-83.

SEMANTISCHE ASPEKTE DER PROGRAMMOPTIMIERUNG
==

Helmut Roth
Lehrstuhl für mathematische Verfahrensforschung
und Datenverarbeitung der Universität Göttingen
D 34 Göttingen, Nikolausbergerweg 9b

0. Einführung und Motivation

Zur globalen maschinen- und sprachunabhängigen Programmoptimierung
werden bekanntlich im wesentlichen Algorithmen betrachtet, die ein
Programm von seinen syntaktischen Gegebenheiten her, wie etwa dem
(möglichen) Datenfluß und der Schleifenstruktur, bezüglich vorgegebener Kriterien verbessern. Es wird dabei versucht, für ein Programm
möglichst optimalen Objektkode zu erstellen, wie etwa in [1], [2],
[6] und [8], oder bereits das Quellenprogramm zu verbessern, wie
etwa in [4], [7] und zum Teil in [2]; die verwendeten Methoden sind
in beiden Fällen ähnlich.

Diesem Vorgehen sind bekanntlich durch Unentscheidbarkeitsresultate
Grenzen gesetzt; hinzu kommen aufwendigere Kompiler und längere
Kompilezeiten ([5]). Es liegt daher nahe, Programmoptimierung in
einem erweiterten Rahmen zu betrachten, in dem unter stärkerer Einbeziehung der Funktion eines Programmes vom Programmentwickler
(etwa in interaktiver Arbeitsweise) ein bezüglich vorgegebener Kriterien bereits möglichst optimales Quellenprogramm erstellt wird.
Das Ziel des Beitrags hier ist es nun, einige theoretische Aspekte
eines dafür geeigneten Optimierungsansatzes zu untersuchen.

1. Allgemeines zur Programmoptimierung

Es seien $u_1,\ldots,u_n$ Variable oder Konstante, denen Wortmengen $D(u_1)\ldots$
$\ldots,D(u_n)$, ihre Definitionsbereiche, im Falle einer Konstanten ein-
elementig, über endlichen Alphabeten zugeordnet seien; sei

$U := \{u_1,\ldots,u_n\}$. ω sei ein Symbol für "undefiniert", und erfülle
$\omega \notin D(u_i)$, $i = 1,\ldots,n$; für eine Variable u_i sei $\overline{D(u_i)} := D(u_i) \cup \{\omega\}$.
Eine <u>Zuordnungsanweisung</u> (abgekürzt: ZAW) sei eine Zeichenkette

$$u_i \longleftarrow f(u_{j_1},\ldots,u_{j_r}) \;,$$

wobei u_i eine Variable, $u_{j_1},\ldots,u_{j_r}$ Variable oder Konstante aus U und
f eine (partiell) berechenbare Abbildung

$$f : D(u_{j_1}) \times \ldots \times D(u_{j_r}) \longrightarrow \overline{D(u_i)}$$

bedeute. Weiterhin sei die Zeichenkette DUMMY eine ZAW.

Eine <u>bedingte Verzweigungsanweisung</u> (abgekürzt: BV) sei eine
Zeichenkette

$$\alpha(u_{j_1},\ldots,u_{j_s}) \;,$$

wobei $u_{j_1},\ldots,u_{j_s}$ Variable oder Konstante aus U und α eine entscheidbare binäre Relation sei.

Ist keine nähere Spezifikation erforderlich, werden Zuordnungs- und
bedingte Verzweigungsanweisungen, sowie zusätzlich die Zeichenketten
START und STOP als Anweisungen (abgekürzt: AW) bezeichnet.

Ein <u>Programm</u> $P = (P,x,z)$ mit den Programmvariablen $u_1,\ldots,u_n$ wird
gegeben durch:

a. einen endlichen gerichteten Graphen mit einer ausgezeichneten
   Anfangsecke mit Innengrad null und einer ausgezeichneten Endecke
   mit Außengrad null; jede Ecke außer der Endecke habe Außengrad
   eins oder zwei und liege auf einem Pfeilweg von der Anfangs- zur
   Endecke;

b. einer Bewertung der Anfangsecke mit START, der Endecke mit STOP,
   einer Ecke mit Außengrad eins mit einer ZAW und einer Ecke mit
   Außengrad zwei mit einer BV; in diesem Fall seien zusätzlich die
   beiden wegführenden Pfeile mit "+" bzw. "-" bewertet;

c. einem Tupel von Eingabevariablen $x = (x_1,\ldots,x_m), x_i \in U$, $i=1,\ldots,m$,
   und einem Tupel von Ausgabevariablen $z = (z_1,\ldots,z_l), z_i \in U$,
   $i =1,\ldots,l$.

Die Menge aller so definierten Programme sei mit P bezeichnet.

Für ein $P \in P$ läßt sich dann seine Funktion mit Hilfe der Funktionen
seiner Anweisungen definieren:
Die Funktion von START sei Zuordnen eines Wertetupels aus
$D(x):=D(x_1)\times\ldots\times D(x_m)$ an die Eingabevariablen x und Übergang zur

folgenden AW. Die Funktion einer ZAW $u_i \leftarrow f(u_{j1},\ldots,u_{jr})$ für ein Wertetupel $(u^o_{j1},\ldots,u^o_{jr})$ sei Ausführen der Berechnung, Zuordnung an u_i, falls das Resultat definiert und aus $D(u_i)$ ist, und Übergang zur folgenden AW; ist $f(u^o_{j1},\ldots,u^o_{jr}) \notin D(u_i)$, oder ist die Berechnung nicht definiert, so erfolge kein Übergang an die folgende AW, und u_i erhalte als Wert ω; ist die ZAW von der Gestalt DUMMY, so erfolge Übergang zur folgenden AW. Die Funktion einer BV $\alpha(u_{j1},\ldots,u_{js})$ für ein Wertetupel $(u^o_{j1},\ldots,u^o_{js})$ sei Übergang zu der auf den mit "+" bewerteten Pfeil folgenden AW, falls $\alpha(u^o_{j1},\ldots,u^o_{js})$ gilt und Übergang zu der auf den mit "-" bewerteten Pfeil folgenden AW, falls $\alpha(u^o_{j1},\ldots,u^o_{js})$ nicht gilt; ist die Berechnung der Relation nicht definiert, so erfolge kein Übergang. STOP bilde aus einem Wertetupel von Programmvariablen das Tupel der zu Ausgabevariablen gehörigen Werte.

Damit ist jedem $P = (P,x,z) \in \mathcal{P}$ eindeutig eine Abbildung F_P,

$$F_P : D(x) \longrightarrow \overline{D(z)} := \overline{D(z_1)} \times \cdots \times \overline{D(z_l)}$$

gegeben durch

$$F_P(x) := (z_1,\ldots,z_l) : \begin{cases} z_i \in D(z_i), \text{falls nach Initiierung von P bei START} \\ \text{mit x nach Berechnung endlich vieler AW STOP} \\ \text{mit dem Wert } z_i \in D(z_i) \text{ für die Ausgabevariable} \\ z_i \text{ erreicht wird,} \\ z_i = \omega \text{ sonst,} \end{cases}$$

die Funktion von P, zugeordnet.

Sei $P \in \mathcal{P}$; $P' \in \mathcal{P}$ stimme mit P funktionell überein - in Zeichen $P \vdash P'$ -, wenn P' die gleichen Eingabe- und Ausgabedefinitionsbereiche $D(x)$ und $D(z)$ wie P hat, und $F_{P'}(x) = F_P(x)$ für alle $x \in D(x)$ gilt, für die $F_P(x) \in D(z)$ ist. Die dadurch gegebene Relation auf $\mathcal{P}$ ist reflexiv und transitiv, aber nicht symmetrisch.

Eine Optimierung von Programmen aus $\mathcal{P}$ erfordert die Messung von Programmeigenschaften, wofür Programmkostenfunktionen (siehe auch [1]) geeignet sind.

<u>Definition 1</u>: Sei M eine mit der Relation $\geq_M$ teilweise geordnete

nichtleere Menge; eine Programmkostenfunktion (abgekürzt: PKF) ist
eine Abbildung

$$c : P \longrightarrow M$$

Für im folgenden vorkommende PKF sind die zugrundeliegende Menge M
und deren Ordnungsrelation jeweils aus dem Zusammenhang ersichtlich.

Definition 2:   Seien c eine PKF und P und P' Programme aus P.
P' heißt (echt) besser als P bzw. P heißt (echt) schlechter als P'
bezüglich c, wenn gilt:
 a. $c(P) \geq c(P')$, ($c(P) > c(P')$) ;
 b. $P \vdash P'$.
P' heißt c-optimal zu P, wenn P' besser als P ist und kein $P'' \in P$
existiert, so daß $c(P'') < c(P')$ und $P' \vdash P''$ gilt.
Sei nun c eine PKF; dann läßt sich c eine Menge $T(c)$ von Abbildungen

$$t : P \longrightarrow P$$

zuordnen, die die Eigenschaften
1. für alle $P \in P$ gilt $P \vdash t(P)$,
2. es existiert kein $P \in P$: $c(P) < c(t(P))$,
haben; offenbar ist $T(c) \neq \emptyset$ für alle PKF c.
Sei $\overset{\circ}{T}(c) := \{ t \in T(c) : \exists P \in P : c(P) > c(t(P)) \}$.

Für eine PKF c und ein $P_o \in P$ bedeutet dann Kenntnis von $T(c)$ die
Kenntnis aller Möglichkeiten, P_o bezüglich c zu verbessern. Im
Zusammenhang mit c-Optimalität gilt das folgende Lemma.

Lemma 1 : Seien c PKF und $P_o \in P$; ein c-optimales Programm zu P_o
existiert genau dann, wenn ein $t_o \in T(c)$ existiert, so daß P_o und
$t_o(P_o)$ vergleichbar sind und $c(t(P_o)) \geq c(t_o(P_o))$ für alle $t \in T(c)$
gilt, falls $t(P_o)$ und $t_o(P_o)$ bezüglich c vergleichbar sind.

Da eine Menge $T(c)$, c PKF, alle Verbesserungsmöglichkeiten bezüglich c
von Programmen aus P einschließt, ist es mit ihrer Hilfe leicht
möglich, gegenseitige Beeinflussung bei Optimierung bezüglich zweier
(und entsprechend auch mehrerer) PKF zu charakterisieren.

Lemma 2: Seien c und c' PKF;
 a. ist $T(c) \subset T(c')$, so ist für alle $P \in P$ mit $c(P) \geq_M c(t(P))$,
    $t \in T(c)$, nicht $c'(P) <_{M'} c'(t(P))$;

b. ist $\overset{o}{T}(c') \neq \emptyset$ und $T(c) \cap \overset{o}{T}(c') = \emptyset$, so ist für alle $P \in P$ mit $c'(P) >_{M'} c'(t(P))$, $t \in \overset{o}{T}(c')$, $c(P) <_M c(t(P))$, oder P und $t(P)$ sind bezüglich c nicht vergleichbar.

Für eine PKF c sind offenbar im allgemeinen die Mengen $T(c)$ und auch $\overset{o}{T}(c)$ beliebig "kompliziert", so daß keine sinnvolle Beschreibung, insbesondere im Hinblick auf Anwendungszwecke, möglich ist. Es ist daher für eine Anwendung von $T(c)$ und $\overset{o}{T}(c)$ zur Optimierung von Programmen aus P notwendig, zum einen nicht zu komplexe Programmkostenfunktionen zu betrachten, und zum anderen die Abbildungen, aus denen sich eine Menge $T(c)$ zusammensetzen kann, auf einzelne "Typen" einzuschränken, um Überschaubarkeit und einen gewissen Realitätsbezug zu erhalten.

2. Spezielle Programmtransformationen zur "schrittweisen" Optimierung.

Seien $P = (P,x,z) \in P$, f eine ZAW und g, h AW; dann bezeichne $\text{VER}_{f,(g,h)}(P)$ in P das Ersetzen von f durch die ZAW DUMMY, und Verschieben von f zwischen die Anweisungen g und h, falls f,g und h aus P sind und h direkt auf g in P folgt; $\text{LÖS}_f(P)$ in P das Ersetzen von f durch die ZAW DUMMY, falls f aus P ist; $\text{MOD}_{f,f'}(P)$ in P das Modifizieren einer ZAW der Form $i \leftarrow f(i)$ zu einer ZAW der Form $i \leftarrow f'(i)$, falls f in Programmteilen von P der Art

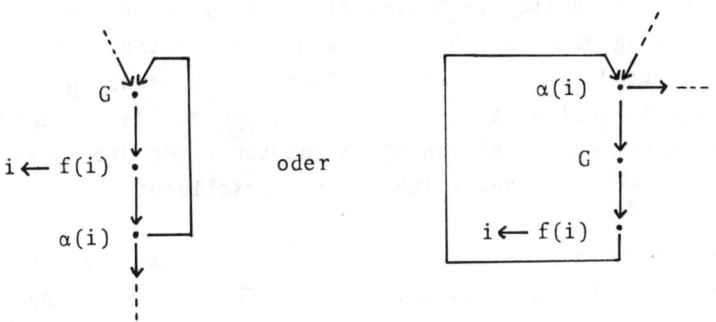

Figur 1

vorkommt, wobei G einen "Programmteil", i eine Programmvariable mit $D(i) = \mathbb{Z}$ und α eine BV von P bezeichnen. Die Ein- und Ausgabevariablen x und z von P bleiben bei allen drei Operationen fest.

Definition 3 : Eine Abbildung t : $P \to P$, die für (mindestens) ein
$P \in P$ die Gestalt $VER_{f,(g,h)}$ oder $LÖS_f$ oder $MOD_{f,f'}$ hat, alle weiteren
Programme aus P identisch abbildet und $P \vdash t(P)$ für alle $P \in P$ erfüllt,
heiße eine Programmtransformation.

Programmtransformationen aus Definition 3 werden entsprechend ihrer
Konstruktion mit $t_{f,(g,h)}$, t_f und $t_{f,f'}$ bezeichnet; die Menge aller so
gegebenen Programmtransformationen werde $A(P)$ genannt.

Für ein $P_o \in P$, eine ZAW f aus P_o und AW g und h aus P_o ist offenbar
im allgemeinen nicht entscheidbar, ob sie eine Abbildung $t_{f,(g,h)}$ oder
t_f oder $t_{f,f'}$, die alle weiteren Programme außer P_o identisch abbildet,
erzeugen. Die Betrachtung von Abbildungen aus $A(P)$ bedeutet jedoch
keine Einschränkung auf Abbildungen, die nur ein Programm nicht
identisch verändern, wie das folgende Lemma zeigt.

Lemma 3 : Seien f eine von DUMMY verschiedene ZAW und g und h AW;
dann existieren zu jedem $P \in P$ Programme P_1, P_2 und P_3 aus P, so daß
gilt:
a. $P \vdash P_i$, i=1,2,3;

b. $t_{f,(g,h)}(P_1) \neq P_1$, $t_f(P_2) \neq P_2$ und $t_{f,f'}(P_3) \neq P_3$.

Für eine PKF c seien $T(c) := T(c) \cap A(P)$ und $\overset{\circ}{T}(c) := \overset{\circ}{T}(c) \cap A(P)$.
Eine Beschreibung einer solchen Programmtransformationsmenge $T(c)$,
c PKF, erfordert damit offenbar eine Charakterisierung, unter welchen
Bedingungen eine Abbildung t aus $A(P)$ ist, und aus den so gefundenen
Abbildungen unter Benutzung von Eigenschaften von c die Auswahl derer,
die kein Programm aus P bezüglich c echt verschlechtern.

Für Anwendungszwecke sind vor allem auf ein Programm bezogene Transformationen aus $A(P)$ interessant. Für ihre Charakterisierung kann man
Methoden aus der Beschreibung der Semantik von Programmen heranziehen.

Sei $P = (P,x,z) \in P$; dann bestimmt jedes $x \in D(x)$ eindeutig einen Berechnungsweg $b(x)$, der, bei START anfangend, aus der Folge aller AW von P
besteht, die in P bei der Berechnung eines Resultates für den Eingabewert x durchlaufen werden. Für eine AW f von P sei
$B(f,P) := \{ b(x) : x \in D(x) \text{ und f ist AW aus } b(x) \}$.

Sei $P_o := (P_o, x, z) \in P$. Seien f eine ZAW und g,h AW von P_o; sei

$$\tilde{t}_{f,(g,h)}(P) := \begin{cases} VER_{f,(g,h)}(P), & \text{falls } P = P_o \\ P & \text{sonst.} \end{cases}$$

<u>Lemma 4</u> : $\tilde{t}_{f,(g,h)} \in A(P)$ gilt genau dann, wenn für alle $x \in D(x)$, für die $b(x) \in B(f, P_o) \cup B(g, P_o)$ und $F_{P_o}(x) \in D(z)$ ist, gilt:

$F_{P_o}(x) = F_{\tilde{t}_{f,(g,h)}(P_o)}(x)$.

Sei f wieder eine ZAW von P_o; sei

$$\tilde{t}_f(P) := \begin{cases} LÖS_f(P), & \text{falls } P = P_o \\ P & \text{sonst.} \end{cases}$$

<u>Lemma 5</u> : $\tilde{t}_f \in A(P)$ gilt genau dann, wenn für alle $x \in D(x)$, für die $b(x) \in B(f, P_o)$ und $F_{P_o}(x) \in D(z)$ ist, gilt: $F_{P_o}(x) = F_{\tilde{t}_f(P_o)}(x)$.

Sei nun s ein Programmteil gemäß Figur 1 aus P_o; sei

$$\tilde{t}_{f,f'}(P) := \begin{cases} MOD_{f,f'}(P), & \text{falls } P = P_o \\ P & \text{sonst} \end{cases}$$

<u>Lemma 6</u> : $\tilde{t}_{f,f'} \in A(P)$ gilt genau dann, wenn für alle $x \in D(x)$, für die $b(x)$ einen Teilweg aus s enthält und $F_{P_o}(x) \in D(z)$ ist, gilt:

$F_{P_o}(x) = F_{\tilde{t}_{f,f'}(P_o)}(x)$.

Die Lemmata 4 - 6 zeigen die Teile eines Programmes auf, die zu betrachten sind, wenn für auf ein Programm bezogene Programmtransformationen zur schrittweisen Optimierung nachgeprüft werden soll, ob ein abgebildetes Programm mit seinem Urbild funktionell übereinstimmt. Es ist klar, daß ihre Praktikabilität stark von der Gestalt eines Programmes abhängt und etwa für strukturierte Programme, wie sie in [8] betrachtet werden, größer ist, als für "unübersichtliche" Programme. Abschließend sollen nun anhand zweier Programmkostenfunktionen einige Überlegungen zur Schleifenoptimierung, insbesondere im Hinblick auf gegenseitige Beeinflussung, im Rahmen des hier dargestellten Optimierungsansatzes angestellt werden.

3. Schleifenoptimierung

Ein geschlossener Pfeilweg (im Flußdiagramm) eines $P \in \mathcal{P}$ heiße eine (Programm-) <u>Schleife</u>; weiter sei

$ES(P) := \{ s : s \text{ ist elementarer geschlossener Pfeilweg in } P \}$;

zur Definition der Begriffe siehe [6]; zur Bestimmung elementarer Schleifen siehe [3]. Es sei

$\mathcal{P}_n := \{ P \in \mathcal{P} : |ES(P)| = n \}$, $n = 0,1,2,..$

Dann ist offenbar $\mathcal{P} = \bigcup_{i=0}^{\infty} \mathcal{P}_i$.

Für $k = 1,2,..$ sei für $m^1, m^2 \in \mathbb{N}^k$ $m^1 \leq m^2$, wenn $m^1_j \leq m^2_j$ für alle Komponenten m^1_j, m^2_j von m^1 und m^2 gilt. Für $N := \bigcup_{i=1}^{\infty} \mathbb{N}^i$ und $m, m' \in N$ sei $m \leq m'$, wenn ein k existiert, so daß $m, m' \in \mathbb{N}^k$ und $m \leq m'$ in $\mathbb{N}^k$ gilt; damit ist N eine teilweise geordnete Menge.

Bezeichnen $z(s)$ bzw. $z(P)$ die Anzahl der von einem DUMMY verschiedenen ZAW in einer Schleife s bzw. in P, so wird durch

$$c_a(P) := \begin{cases} (z(s_1),...,z(s_n)), & \text{falls } ES(P) = \{s_1,...,s_n\}, n = 1,2,.. \\ z(P), & \text{falls } ES(P) = \emptyset, \end{cases}$$

eine PKF $c_a : \mathcal{P} \to N$ definiert. Da für alle $t \in A(P)$ $t(P) \in \mathcal{P}_n$ für alle $P \in \mathcal{P}_n$, $n = 0,1,...$, gilt, ist mit c_a eine sinnvolle Optimierungsmessung möglich, die insbesondere eine Verbesserung einer Schleife auf Kosten einer anderen ausschließt. Die bezüglich c_a erreichbaren Verbesserungen sind nicht nur Verbesserungen elementarer Schleifen:

<u>Lemma 7</u> : Seien $t \in T(c_a)$ und s eine Schleife eines $P \in \mathcal{P}$; dann ist $z(s) \geq z(s')$, wobei s' "das Bild von s in $t(P)$" sei.

Es ist dann
$\overset{o}{T}(c_a) = \{ t : \mathcal{P}_0 \to \mathcal{P}_0 : \exists P \in \mathcal{P}_0 \text{ und ZAW } f \text{ aus } P, \text{ so daß } t = t_f \}$
$\{ t : \mathcal{P}_n \to \mathcal{P}_n, n \geq 1 : \exists P \in \mathcal{P}_n \text{ und eine ZAW } f \text{ aus } s,$
$s \in ES(P), \text{ so daß } t = t_f \}$
$\{ t : \mathcal{P}_n \to \mathcal{P}_n, n \geq 1 : \exists P \in \mathcal{P}_n \text{ und eine ZAW } f \text{ aus } s, s \in ES(P)$
und AW g, h, nicht beide aus einem $s \in ES(P)$, so daß $t = t_{f,(g,h)} \}$.

Hinreichend zur Konstruktion einer auf ein Programm bezogenen Abbildung $t_f : P_n \to P_n$, $n \geq 0$, aus $\overset{\circ}{T}(c_a)$ entsprechend Lemma 5 sind etwa die "redundant instructions" aus [1]. Zur Konstruktion einer auf ein Programm bezogenen Abbildung $t_{f,(g,h)} : P_n \to P_n$, $n \geq 1$, aus $\overset{\circ}{T}(c_a)$ entsprechend Lemma 4 sind solche Anweisungen hinreichend, wie sie etwa in [1] u.a. zur "code motion" betrachtet werden; da c_a eine Abbildung in N ist, sind hier jedoch nur solche Verschiebungen zulässig, die Anweisungen aus einer Schleife nicht in eine andere bringen.

Für eine beliebige Schleife s eines Programmes $P = (P,x,z) \in P$ sei d'(s,x) die Anzahl, wieviel mal s Teilweg von b(x) ist; sei damit
$$d(s) := \max_{x \in D(x) \,:\, F_p(x) \in D(z)} d'(s,x) \quad ;$$
es ist $d(s) < \infty$ für jede Schleife s eines $P \in P$. Durch
$$c_d(P) := \begin{cases} (d(s_1),\ldots,d(s_n)), \text{ falls } ES(P) = \{s_1,\ldots,s_n\}, n = 1,2\ldots \\ 0 \text{ sonst,} \end{cases}$$
$P \in P$, wird eine PKF $c_d : P \to N$ definiert. Ebenso wie für c_a bringt eine Verbesserung bezüglich c_d nicht nur eine Verbesserung für elementare Schleifen:

<u>Lemma 8</u> : Seien $P = (P,x,z) \in P_n$ mit $ES(P) = \{s_1,\ldots,s_n\}$, $n \geq 1$ und s eine Schleife aus P; dann ist $d(s) \leq \sum d(s_i)$, wobei Summation über die s_i aus ES(P) erfolge, die Teilwege von s sind.

Die Möglichkeiten gegenseitiger Beeinflussung bei Optimierung bezüglich c_a und c_d beschreibt das folgende Lemma.

<u>Lemma 9</u> : Es gilt $\overset{\circ}{T}(c_d) \cap \overset{\circ}{T}(c_a) \neq \emptyset$, $\overset{\circ}{T}(c_a) \not\subset \overset{\circ}{T}(c_d)$ und $\overset{\circ}{T}(c_d) \not\subset \overset{\circ}{T}(c_a)$.

Für Anwendungszwecke bedeutet Lemma 9 zusammen mit Lemma 2, daß für eine Optimierung bezüglich c_a und c_d stets nachgeprüft werden muß, ob eine Programmtransformation aus $\overset{\circ}{T}(c_a)$ eine Verschlechterung bezüglich c_d ergibt, und ob eine Programmtransformation aus $\overset{\circ}{T}(c_d)$ eine Verschlechterung bezüglich c_a ergibt. Dies ist im zweiten Fall einfach, da offenbar für ein $t \in T(c_d)$ und ein $P \in P$ entscheidbar ist, ob $c_a(P) \geq c_a(t(P))$ ist; eine entsprechende Aussage für den ersten Fall gilt jedoch nicht.

Literatur

[1] Aho, A.V. und Ullman, D., The Theory of Parsing, Translation and Compiling, Part II : Compiling, Prentice Hall 1973;

[2] Allen, F.E., Program Optimization, Ann. Rev. Aut. Prog. $\underline{5}$ (1969), p. 239-279;

[3] Baer, J.-L., und Caughey, R., Segmentation and Optimization of Programs from Cyclic Structure Analysis, AFIPS Spring Joint Comput. Conference $\underline{40}$ (1972), p. 23-35;

[4] Clark, E.R., On the Automatic Simplification of Source-Language Programs, Proc. 21st ACM Nat. Conf. 1966, p. 313-319;

[5] Lowry, E.S. und Medlock, C.W., Object Code Optimization, CACM $\underline{12}$ (1969), p. 13-22;

[6] Schaefer, M., A Mathematical Theory of Global Program Optimization, Prentice Hall, Englewood Cliffs, 1973;

[7] Schneck, P.B. und Angel, E., A FORTRAN to FORTRAN Optimising Compiler, The Computer Journal $\underline{16}$ (1973), p. 322-330;

[8] Zellkowitz, M.V. und Bail, W.G., Optimization of Structured Programs, Software-Practice and Experience $\underline{4}$ (1974), p. 51-57.

4. NICHTSEQUENTIELLE SYSTEME

GEGENSEITIGE BEEINFLUSSUNG
P. ANCILOTTI, M. FUSANI, N. LIJTMAER, C. THANOS

K.-P. LÖHR

J. JÜRGENS

PETRI-NETZ-ÄHNLICHE MODELLE
R. SCHROFF

H. FUSS

H.-J. GOTTSCHALK

THEORIE
H.J. BECKER, H. VOGEL

F. SCHWENKEL

DEADLOCK CONDITIONS IN WELL STRUCTURED MODULAR SYSTEMS

P.Ancilotti, M.Fusani, N.Lijtmaer, C.Thanos
Istituto di Elaborazione dell'Informazione, C.N.R.
Pisa, ITALY

1. Introduction

Communication between program modules is a topic of great interest in the design and production of well structured modular systems. *Modules* may be thought of as logical components of the system, designed to carry out some tasks. To complete the description of a system we need to specify the *connections* between modules,"that are the assumptions which the modules make about each other" [1]. Systems in which the connections between modules contain little information are labeled *well structured* and in fact this property is essential to facilitate the changeability of the system and to prove system correctness [2].

This paper is concerned with some properties of well structured modular systems. In these systems each module is specified in terms of input/output behaviour and input/output interfaces are standardized. A single module becomes, during execution, a *sequential* process, while the whole system allows the *concurrent* execution of several processes which are themselves strictly sequential.

Following the input/output approach, synchronization is achieved by using the *message buffer mechanism* and the only communication primitives are *send* and *receive*. The main goal of this paper is to investigate the properties of such mechanism with respect to deadlock conditions.

Schemata are used as computation models: Cyclic sequential schemata are introduced to represent modules, while the model of the whole software system is obtained by a directed parallel composition of cyclic sequential schemata.

As far as deadlock is concerned, three different kinds of systems will be considered:

i) Data and time independent systems.

ii) Data dependent and time independent systems.

iii) Data and time dependent systems.

We shall show that in the first two types of systems reproducibility of deadlock conditions exists and is related to the connections between modules. Thus, any effort to provide an algorithm to avoid deadlock is a nonsense for systems having statically connected modules. On the basis of these results, an algorithm has been implemented as a procedure of the PSL dynamic nucleus (Pisa Software Laboratory). The PSL [3], is specially convenient to test the applicability of this algorithm since it generates an environment where a user may build and experiment well structured modular software systems.

2. Computation Schemata

" A *computation schema*, or *schema*, represents the manner in which functional elements and decision elements are interconnected, and their actions sequenced, to define an algorithm"[4].

More prcisely a schema is a triple $\Sigma = (A, V, C)$, where A is a set of *actors*, V is a set of *variables*, and C is a set of *control sequences* (*Control Set*[5]). The functional elements of a schema are called *operators* and the decision elements are called *deciders*. The set of operators and the set of deciders are denoted by O and D, respectively. These sets are disjoint ($D \cap O = \Phi$). Both, operators and deciders, are called *actors*. Then, actors are agents capable of transforming values and agents capable of testing values. To each actor a a *domain* X_a is associated, a finite subset of V. Similarly, to each operator o a *range* Y_o is associated, a finite subset of V.

A subset of variables ($I \subseteq V$) is called *schema input* if values are assigned to them before a computation begins.

Actors, operators and deciders, will be considered the units of computational activity, as characterized by their external behaviour. Associated with an operator o there are an *initiation event* $\bar{o}$ and a *termination event* $\underline{o}$. Associated with each decider d, there are an initiation event $\bar{d}$ and either the true or the false termination event, denoted by d_T and d_F respectively.

A *control sequence* of the schema is a string $\sigma = \alpha_1 \alpha_2 \ldots \alpha_n \ldots$
of actor initiation and termination events. The *control set* C represents
all the allowed sequences of events. The sequences in which operators
and deciders are permitted to act, may be specified by a precedence
graph [4].

Definition 2.1: Given a control sequence $\sigma = \alpha_1 \alpha_2 \ldots \alpha_{i-1} \alpha_i \ldots$, if
$\pi_{i-1} = \alpha_1 \ldots \alpha_{i-1}$ is a prefix of σ, after the occurrence of the
events in π_{i-1}, the only *feasible event* in σ is α_i, $i \geqslant 1$.

Note that if $\alpha_i = \underline{a}$ belongs to a control sequence, then $\underline{a}$ must be
present in the prefix π_{i-1}.

Definition 2.2: Given a control sequence σ of a schema Σ, a *chain of*
events in σ is a string γ of event occurrences in σ : $\gamma = \alpha_i \alpha_j \alpha_n \ldots$
such that $i < j < h < \ldots$.

We will refer to a schema Σ as a *data independent schema* if the
set of deciders is empty, otherwise Σ will be called a *data dependent*
schema.

A more detailed treatment about schemata is contained in [4,5].
In this paper we will be concerned with the control aspects of computation
schemata. In particular, we want to emphasize that our results are concerned with *control* and *sequencing* of a set of cooperating processes,
and not with their specific functions. For this purpose we refer to schemata as models of uninterpreted program modules. In this context any control sequence of a schema represents a particular process the program
module may give rise to, during execution.

To convert a schema into a specification of a particular program
module it is necessary to specify the value of the variables of the schema
and a function or predicate for each operator or decider.

Definition 2.4: An *interpretation* of a schema Σ is

i) for each variable $v \in V$, a value set $F(v)$;

ii) for each operator $o \in O$, a function $f_o: F(v_{x1}) \times F(v_{x2}) \times \ldots \times F(v_{xm})$
$\to F(v_{y1}) \times F(v_{y2}) \times \ldots \times F(v_{yn})$, where $X_o = \{v_{x1}, \ldots, v_{xm}\}$ and
$Y_o = \{v_{y1}, \ldots, v_{yn}\}$;

iii) for each decider $d \in D$ a predicate $P_d: F(v_{x1}) \times F(v_{x2}) \times \ldots \times F(v_{xm})$
$\to \{\text{true, false}\}$, where $X_d = \{v_{x1}, \ldots, v_{xm}\}$

Our attention will be focalized now on sequential processes. Parallel processes will be analized later as a combination of several processes which are themselves strictly sequential.

3. Sequential Schemata

<u>Definition 3.1</u>: A *sequential schema* is a schema $\Sigma=(A,V,C)$ where control sequences of C satisfy the following properties:
  i) For each $\sigma \in C$, after the ocurrence of $\bar{a}$, the feasible event is $\underline{a}$;
  ii) If an event $\underline{a}$ belongs to many control sequences of C, the feasible event after $\underline{a}$ is the same in all sequences;
  iii) If an event $\bar{a}$ belongs to many control sequences of C, the feasible event before $\bar{a}$ is the same in all sequences.

In the precedence graph of a sequential schema, each operator has at most one immediate successor and one immediate predecessor.

Note that if a sequential schema is data independent then there is only one possible control sequence σ in C.

<u>Definition 3.2</u>: A *finite sequential schema* is a sequential schema in which the set of actors is finite.

While the control sequences of this type of schemata allow to model the behaviour of sequential processes, a new type of schema must be introduced to handle cyclic sequential processes.

<u>Definition 3.3</u>: Given a finite sequential schema $\Sigma = (A,V,C)$, let us define a *cyclic sequential schema* $\Sigma^c = (A^c, V^c, C^c)$, where $A^c = A$, $V^c = V$ and $\sigma^c \in C^c$ iff $\sigma^c = \sigma_1 \sigma_2 \ldots \sigma_i \ldots$ with $\sigma_i \in C$ for any integer i. When a σ_i is composed by infinite events, then $\sigma^c = \sigma_1 \ldots \sigma_i$

If a cyclic sequential schema is data independent then there is only one possible control sequence σ^c in C^c: $\sigma^c = \sigma \sigma \ldots \sigma \ldots$ where σ is the unique control sequence of Σ. Note that while variables of schemata may be denoted, generally, by single memory cells, each input variable of a cyclic sequential schema is an array of infinite memory cells. Consecutive readings of an input variable involve consecutive array cells.

4. Parallel Composition of Cyclic Sequential Schemata

In a parallel schema a mechanism capable of describing concurrent, asynchronous activity is needed: This mechanism consists of allowing several initiations before a termination occurs, and of keeping track of such initiations.

Our attention will be focalized now on schemata whose control sequences model sets of concurrent processes. They can be conceived as a combination of several processes which are themselves strictly sequential.

In this section we introduce the *directed parallel composition of cyclic sequential schemata* to model the behaviour, and to point out special properties, of well structured software systems. In particular we will consider systems composed of several independent modules connected by a message buffer mechanism and where a single module becomes, during execution, a cyclic sequential process.

In order to point out some properties related to concurrency, let us introduce:

    i) A special type of variable, called *mailbox*;

    ii) Two new types of actors, *send* and *receive*.

Mailbox is a pair (c,N) where c is a memory cell that can assume only integer values between zero and n, and where N is an array of n memory cells. Note that n may be infinite. Here n represents the capacity of the mailbox. The pair of integers (w,n), where w is the actual value of c, is referred to as the *state* of the mailbox.

The actors *send* and *receive* may be defined as follows:

    i) The domain of any actor *send* (*receive*) is a set $X_s = \{x,m\}$ ($X_r = \{m\}$) where the variables x and m are a memory cell and a mailbox respectively. The range of any actor *send* (*receive*) is a set $Y_s = \{m\}$ ($Y_r = \{x,m\}$) where the mailbox m is the same in both the domain and the range.

    ii) Associated with each actor *send* (*receive*) there are an initiation event $\bar{s}$ ($\bar{r}$) and a termination event $\underline{s}$ ($\underline{r}$).

    iii) Given a control sequence $\sigma = \alpha_1 \ldots \alpha_i \ldots$ where $\alpha_i = \underline{s}$ ($\underline{r}$), α_i is *feasible* after the occurrence of all the events $\alpha_1, \ldots \alpha_{i-1}$ if the state of the mailbox m is such that w<n (w>0). When $\underline{s}$ ($\underline{r}$) occurs the state of m is modified as follows: w:=w+1 (w:=w-1).

Note that *send* and *receive* are the only actors that are allowed to modify the state of a mailbox.

The *state* of a schema is the set of states of all the mailboxes of the schema. Given an initial state and a control sequence we obtain a sequence of states of the schema. From now on the initial state is assumed to be such that for each mailbox w = 0.

<u>Definition 4.1</u>: A *Directed Parallel Composition* (DPC) of n cyclic sequential schemata $\Sigma_1,\ldots,\Sigma_n$ is a schema $\Sigma^P = (A^P, V^P, C^P)$ where:

   i) $A^P = \bigcup_{i=1}^{n} A_i$ and for any pair (Σ_i, Σ_j) of component schemata $A_i \cap A_j = \Phi$

   ii) $V^P = \bigcup_{i=1}^{n} V_i$ and for any *ordered* pair (Σ_i, Σ_j) of component schemata $V_i \cap V_j = M_{i,j}$

   iii) Any $\sigma^P \in C^P$ can be generated as follows: Given an n-tuple $\sigma_1, \ldots, \sigma_n$ where $\sigma_i \in C_i$ (i=1,...,n), for each integer $h \geq 0$ if $\tau_h = \alpha_1 \ldots \alpha_h$ is a prefix of σ^P, $\tau_{h+1} = \tau_h \alpha_{h+1}$ is a prefix of σ^P if α_{h+1} is the feasible event of a σ_i after the ocurrence of the events of σ_i in τ_h. Moreover, we assume that all the events that become feasible, must occur in σ^P at most after a finite number of event occurrences.

$M_{i,j}$ is a set, possibly empty, whose elements are mailboxes belonging to the range of actors *send* of the schema Σ_i and to the domain of actors *receive* of Σ_j. Mailbox $m_{i,j} \in M_{i,j}$ is said to *link* Σ_i with Σ_j. If $M_{i,j} = \Phi$ then Σ_i and Σ_j are not directly connected.

A DPC Σ^P can be represented by a *Connection Graph* G whose nodes are the component schemata and whose arcs are links among schemata, that is mailboxes.

We introduce now, some definitions on the connection graph and on deadlock.

<u>Definition 4.2</u>: A *terminal schema* of a DPC Σ^P is a schema Σ_i for which only one mailbox links Σ_i to some other schemata of Σ^P.

<u>Definition 4.3</u>: A *path* in the connection graph G of a DPC Σ^P is a collection of distinct schemata $\Sigma_1, \ldots, \Sigma_k$ linked through k-1 mailboxes: $m_{1,2}, m_{2,3}, \ldots, m_{k-1,k}$.

<u>Definition 4.4</u>: A *semipath* in G is a collection of distinct schemata $\Sigma_1, \ldots, \Sigma_n$ linked through k-1 mailboxes: $m_{1,2}$ or $m_{2,1}$, $m_{2,3}$ or $m_{3,2}, \ldots, m_{k-1,k}$ or $m_{k,k-1}$. If Σ_k coincides with Σ_1 the semipath is called a *semicycle*.

<u>Definition 4.5</u>: A mailbox is called *one-to-one* if it links only two

schemata.

Definition 4.6: Given a control sequence σ^p of a DPC Σ^p, a *deadlock* occurs in σ^p if at least one component schema Σ_k and an integer h exist such that for each integer t>h, $\alpha_t \notin \sigma_k$. Here σ_k is the control sequence of Σ_k in σ^p and σ_k is said a *deadlocked control sequence*. The first event of σ_k that follows the last event of σ_k in σ^p is called the *blocking event* of σ_k.

Note that the blocking events are unfeasible terminations of actors *send* or *receive* related to a mailbox whose state is (n,n) or (0,n) respectively.

Definition 4.7: For any blocking event e_i belonging to a deadlocked control sequence σ_i, if there is an event e_j belonging to a control sequence σ_j such that the occurrence of e_j in σ^p makes feasible e_i, then e_j is called an *awaking event* of e_i.

Obviously if σ_i is deadlocked in σ^p then also σ_j is deadlocked.

Definition 4.8: A deadlock in a control sequence σ^p of a DPC Σ^p is called a *partial deadlock* if σ^p is infinite. Otherwise it is called a *total deadlock*.

Definition 4.9: A DPC Σ^p is *well formed* if:

i) Any mailbox links at least two schemata.

ii) The connection graph G is connected.

From now on, any DPC will be tacitly considered well formed.

In the following sections distinctions among different kinds of DPC will be pointed out in order to find relevant properties of systems under deadlock conditions.

5. Data and Time Independent Systems

Definitions 5.1: A DPC Σ^p of n cyclic sequential schemata $\Sigma_1 \ldots \Sigma_n$ is of *type 1* if all the component schemata are *data independent* and all the mailboxes are one-to-one.

Any DPC Σ^p of type 1 is such that all its component schemata have only one control sequence. Furthermore, since Σ^p is well formed, it can be proved that if a deadlock occurs in some σ^p, for any blocking event e_i belonging to a deadlocked control sequence σ_i *there exists* one component schema Σ_j whose control sequence σ_j contains the awaking event of e_i. Thus, also σ_j is deadlocked in σ^P. In other words a *unique* deadlocked control sequence *can not exist* in σ^P.

More generally, the following lemma can be proved:

Lemma 5.1: Given a control sequence σ^P of a *DPC* Σ^P of type 1, if a deadlock occurs in σ^P, then for any Σ_i whose control sequence σ_i is deadlocked, every schema Σ_j such that a path exists in G from Σ_i to Σ_j, has the control sequence deadlocked.

In particular, if all the mailboxes of Σ^P have a finite capacity, then the following theorem can be proved:

Theorem 5.1: Given a control sequence σ^P of a *DPC* Σ^P of type 1, where all the mailboxes of Σ^P have a finite capacity, if a deadlock occurs in σ^P, then it is a total deadlock.

Now we give a necessary condition for the occurrence of a deadlock, both a partial and a total deadlock, in a control sequence σ^P of a *DPC* of type 1. This condition is related to the connection topology of the component schemata. For a proof of this and the following theorems, see [6].

Theorem 5.2: Given a control sequence σ^P of a *DPC* Σ^P of type 1, the existence of a semicycle in the connection graph G of Σ^P is a necessary condition for a deadlock in σ^P.

Let us state now, an important property of any *DPC* of type 1:

Theorem 5.3: Given a *DPC* of type 1, if a particular control sequence σ^P_* *is* finite and is composed of k events, then every control sequence σ^P is finite and is composed of the same number k of events.

The theorem 5.3 asserts that for a *DPC* of type 1, a total deadlock is independent of the particular control sequence. It only depends on both, the topology of the connections among component schemata and the structure of each component schema. Modular systems modelled by *DPC* of type 1 give rise, during execution, to a family of cooperating asynchronous processes. For these type of modular systems, a deadlock condition depends neither on the input data nor on the relative speeds of the component processes. For this reason we call this type of systems: *Data and time independent systems*.

6. Data Dependent and Time Independent Systems

Definition 6.1: A *DPC* Σ^P of n cyclic sequential schemata is of *type 2* if all the mailboxes in Σ^p are one-to-one.

Any DPC of type 1 is a particular case of DPCs of type 2, where all the component schemata are data independent. When deciders are present, it is no longer true that for any cyclic sequential schema there is only one possible control sequence. Therefore, for a DPC of type 2, if a deadlock occurs in some control sequence σ^p, it is not true that for a blocking event e_i of a deadlocked control sequence σ_i there exists a Σ_j whose control sequence σ_j contains the awaking event of e_i. In particular, a unique deadlocked σ_i can exist in σ^p. Thus, lemma 5.1 and theorem 5.1 are no longer true for a DPC of type 2. For the same reason also theorem 5.2 is false, in general. However we can prove that it is still true only for total deadlocks.

<u>Theorem 6.1</u>: Given a control sequence σ^p of a DPC Σ^p of type 2, a semicycle in the connection graph G of Σ^p is a necessary condition for a total deadlock in σ^p.

Theorem 5.3 is a consequence of the characteristics of a DPC of type 1, that is all the mailboxes are one-to-one and for each component schema there is only one control sequence. Here, theorem 5.3 is no longer true. However, an analogue theorem can be proved, if we choose a particular interpretation of actors *send* and *receive*, namely, values are written by *send* in the cells of the mailbox vector N, one at a time, and they are read by *receive* in exactly the same order. In other words the vector N is a FIFO queue. For any DPC of type 2, let us denote by Ω the set of interpretations for which, actors *send* and *receive* have the above specification.

We can prove that for any DPC of type 2, given an interpretation $\omega \in \Omega$ and an input assignment, there is only one possible control sequence for any component schema. Then, the following theorem can be proved

<u>Theorem 6.2</u>: Given a DPC of type 2 if, for some interpretation $\omega \in \Omega$ and for some input assignment, a particular control sequence σ^p_x is finite and composed by k events, then, for the same interpretation and for the same input assignement, every control sequence σ^p is finite and composed by the same number k of events.

This theorem enables us to say that in any modular system modelled by a DPC of type 2 a total deadlock is independent of the relative speeds of the component processes. However, a total deadlock depends on the input data. In other words if, for certain input data, a total deadlock occurs during a computation, then, for the same input data, the same deadlock condition occurs in any computation. For this reason we call this type of systems: *Data Dependent and Time Independent Systems*.

We want to emphasize that the above results hold only for an interpretation $\omega \in \Omega$. However, considering a mailbox as a FIFO queue is not a strong limitation.

A DPC of type 2 is a particular case of a DPC were all the mailboxes are one-to-one. If a DPC is not of type 2, theorem 6.2 is no longer true. In other words, for a modular system modelled by a general type of DPC a deadlock depends on the input data *and* on the relative speeds of the component processes. We call this type of systems *Data and Time dependent*.

7. Conclusions

This work arised from the design of the PSL [3], a software laboratory which aids an user to build well structured software systems. The above results can be tested on the PSL. In particular an algorithm for deadlock detection has been implemented [6].

Systems modelled by $DPCs$ of type 2 are particularly interesting. In fact, they are sufficiently general. Furthermore, for any interpretation $\omega \in \Omega$, they belong to the class of Patil's β systems [7]. That is, they are functinal systems.

8. References

[1] D.L.Parnas:" Information Distribution Aspects of Design Methodology" *IFIP, Proceedings - Ljubljana, Yugoslavia 1971*.
[2] D.L.Parnas:" On the problem of producing well structured programs". *Computer Science Research Review 1971-72. Carnegie Mellon University*.
[3] P.Ancilotti, R.Cavina, M.Fusani, F.Gramaglia, N.Lijtmaer, E.Martinelli C.Thanos: " Designing a Software Laboratory" *Proceedings 8th Yugoslav International Symposium on Information Processing, Bled, October 1973*.
[4] J.B.Dennis: *Course Notes "Computation Structures"* Department of Electrical Engineering, MIT 1967.
[5] J.P.Linderman:*"Productivity in Parallel Computation Schemata"*,MIT Project MAC - TR - 111, December 1973.
[6] P.Ancilotti, M.Fusani, N.Lijtmaer: *"Interprocess Communication: Deadlock Conditions"* IEI-CNR Internal Report (to be printed).
[7] S.S.Patil: "Closure properties of interconnections of determinate systems" *Record - Project MAC Conference on Concurrent Systems and Parallel Computation. ACM ,N.Y.1970*.

ÜBER DIE LEBENSDAUER VON PROZESSEN IN NICHTSEQUENTIELLEN ALGORITHMEN

Klaus-Peter Löhr

Technische Universität Berlin
Fachbereich Kybernetik

Abstract: *Semantics and implementation of* cobegin/coend-*constructs such as the "concurrent statement" (Dijkstra, Brinch Hansen) are investigated. It is shown that common interpretation of the concurrent statement confuses specification of concurrency and creation of processes. A language feature is proposed which allows for reducing the meaning of "concurrent blocks/compounds" to specification of concurrency while realizing implicit creation of processes in due time.*

1. Einleitung

Nur wenige Programmiersprachen gestatten die explizite Formulierung nebenläufiger ("paralleler") Prozesse, sei es für die Benutzung im Betriebssystem-Bereich, sei es für die Anwenderprogrammierung. Zur Darstellung von Nebenläufigkeit existieren verschiedene Varianten von im wesentlichen drei Sprachkonstruktionen:

fork/join [Conway 1963]: *sprachlich auf sehr elementarem Niveau, dem* goto *vergleichbar;*

create/wait [Dennis/van Horn 1966] [Burroughs 1968] [IBM 1966]: *realisiert im Burroughs Extended ALGOL und in PL/I;*

cobegin/coend [Dijkstra 1965] [van Wijngaarden 1968] [Brinch Hansen 1972]: *bei Brinch Hansen "concurrent statement", in ALGOL 68 "parallel clause".*

fork/join *wollen wir als für strukturierte Programmierung ungeeignet gleich wieder vergessen, die beiden anderen Konstruktionen werden wir im nächsten Abschnitt zur Lösung eines typischen Problems der nichtsequentiellen Programmierung heranziehen. Die dabei gewonnenen Kenntnisse über die Unzulänglichkeit von* create/wait *und über Implementierungsprobleme bei* cobegin/coend *zwingen zur begrifflichen Trennung zwischen Spezifi-*

kation von Nebenläufigkeit einerseits und Prozeßkreierung andererseits. Wenn ein Prozeß mit einer Warte-Operation beginnt, erweist sich bei der Implementierung eine verzögerte Kreierung als angebracht. Weiterhin ergeben sich Implikationen, die für eine Änderung der Semantik von cobegin/coend sprechen.

2. Ein elementares Pipelining-Problem

Wir betrachten eine Pipeline mit drei Stationen A,B,C, an denen Tätigkeiten a,b,c ausgeführt werden. Die Pipeline hat die folgende Struktur:

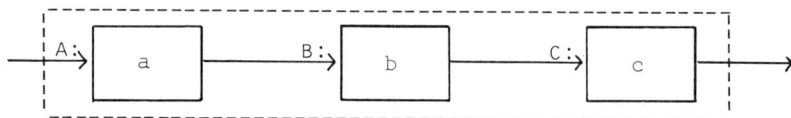

```
procedure a(p,q); mailbox p,q;
begin text x,y; comment possibly additional declarations;
      repeat receive (x,p);
             compute y using x;
             send (y,q)
      until x= notext
end of a
```

b und c haben eine analoge Struktur. send und receive dienen zur synchronisierten Kommunikation über Puffer[1], hier durch den Datentyp mailbox realisiert. - Mittels derartiger Prozeduren a,b,c und unter Verwendung von cobegin/coend kann die Pipeline wie folgt algorithmisch formuliert werden:

```
procedure pipeline (in,out); mailbox in,out;
cobegin procedure a(p,q);.........
        procedure b(p,q);.........
        procedure c(p,q);.........
        mailbox m1,m2;
        A: a(in,m1); B: b(m1,m2); C: c(m2,out)
coend of pipeline
```

Ein Objekt vom Typ mailbox werde hierbei als "leer" initialisiert. Für cobegin/coend wird folgende, gegenüber [Brinch Hansen 1972,1973] erweiterte Syntax und Semantik vorausgesetzt:

---

[1] vgl. [Brinch Hansen 1973]

Syntax *(hier als Erweiterung von ALGOL 60):*

    <concurrent compound>[1] ::= *cobegin* <concurrent tail>
    <concurrent tail>::= <process> *coend*|<process>;<concurrent tail>

    <concurrent block>::= <concurrent head>;<concurrent tail>
    <concurrent head> ::= *cobegin* <declaration>|<concurrent head>;<declaration>

    <process>::= <statement>
    <statement>::= <ALGOL statement>|<concurrent compound>|<concurrent block>

Semantik: Die konstituierenden Bestandteile "process" eines "concurrent compound/ block" werden nebenläufig ausgeführt; die Ausführung eines concurrent compound/block ist beendet, wenn die Ausführung aller seiner Bestandteile beendet ist. Im übrigen entspricht der concurrent block dem block (ALGOL 60 Revised Report 4.1.3). Sprünge über die Grenzen eines concurrent compound/block sind verboten (vgl. [Brinch Hansen 1973]); dies gilt auch für ein "restricted *goto*" in der Form eines *exit*, *leave* o.ä.

Terminologie: 1. Unter Prozeß wird im folgenden stets ein Abschnitt innerhalb eines Programms verstanden, der sich im Ableitungsbaum zu <process> reduzieren läßt.

    2. Analog zur Inkarnation eines Blocks (block instance) sprechen wir von der Inkarnation eines Prozesses[2]. Mittels Rekursion kann erreicht werden, daß mehrere Inkarnationen eines Prozesses koexistieren[3].

    3. Das Erzeugen einer Inkarnation eines Prozesses wird (sprachlich unpräzise) auch einfach Kreieren eines Prozesses genannt. Entsprechend ist mit Tod eines Prozesses stets die Beendigung der Ausführung einer Prozeß-Inkarnation gemeint. Der Zeitraum zwischen Kreieren und Tod heißt Lebensdauer des Prozesses. Beim Kreieren sind Betriebsmittel bereitzustellen (Speicher, Systemtabellen), beim Tod werden diese wieder freigegeben.

    4. Eine Anweisung (Prozeß, Prozedur) heißt sequentiell, wenn sie kein concurrent compound/block enthält, andernfalls nichtsequentiell. Eine Anweisung (Prozeß) heißt parallel, wenn sie ein concurrent compound/block ist; eine Prozedur

---

[1] bei [Brinch Hansen 1972,1973] "concurrent statement" genannt.

[2] Die vom Betriebssystem verwalteten "Prozesse" sind in diesem Sinne Inkarnationen von Prozessen.

[3] Bei Verwendung von *create* ist dies bereits mittels Iteration möglich.

heißt parallel, *wenn ihr Rumpf parallel ist. - Beachte, daß diese Begriffe sich auf den statischen Programmtext beziehen und somit beispielsweise ein sequentieller Prozeß durchaus die Kreierung weiterer Prozesse veranlassen kann (über Aufrufe nichtsequentieller Prozeduren).*

Die algorithmische Beschreibung der Pipeline mittels des concurrent block läßt nichts zu wünschen übrig: die Koexistenz der drei Stationen A,B,C und der lokale Charakter der Puffer m1,m2 werden adäquat wiedergegeben. Als keineswegs adäquat erweist sich jedoch die naheliegendste Implementierung: "Nach Aufruf der Prozedur pipeline *wird Speicherplatz für m1,m2 bereitgestellt und werden - mit Hilfe eines geeigneten Systemaufrufs - drei Prozesse kreiert, die wir der Einfachheit halber wieder mit A,B,C bezeichnen. Für B und C aber ist die Kreierung zu diesem Zeitpunkt sinnlos: nach den Prozeduraufrufen b(m1,m2) bzw. c(m2,out) blockieren die Prozesse sofort wieder (beim ersten* receive*). Die Kreierung ist offenbar erst dann sinnvoll, wenn Eingabedaten für B bzw. C bereitstehen.*

cobegin/coend *realisiert zwar in direktester Weise die Spezifikation nebenläufiger Prozesse, gibt dem Programmierer aber keine Möglichkeit zu zeitlich abgestufter Kreierung. Dies könnte die Befürworter des* create *auf den Plan rufen mit dem Vorschlag, statt des compound block an geeigneter Stelle Kreierungsanweisungen zu verwenden. Dies macht jedoch Eingriffe in die Prozeduren a und b erforderlich und hat insbesondere zur Folge, daß diese nicht mehr universell verwendbar sind. Ferner wird die Lesbarkeit des Algorithmus stark beeinträchtigt.*

Eine Lösung mittels create *hat somit gravierendere Nachteile als die mittels* cobegin/coend*, die lediglich eine Vergeudung von Betriebsmitteln zur Folge hat - jedenfalls bei der oben erwähnten Implementierung. Wir kehren daher zur Betrachtung des* cobegin/coend *zurück und versuchen alternative Implementierungen.*

Man beachte, daß eine Abkehr von der obigen Implementierung unumgänglich wird im Falle von rekursiven Prozeduren der folgenden Struktur:

  procedure recursive *(m);* mailbox *m;*
 cobegin mailbox *x;*
   A: begin text *t;* integer *i;*
     receive (t,m); i:= intval(t);
     if *i>0* then *send (textval(i-1),x)*
   end *of A;*
  B: *recursive (x)*
 coend *of recursive*

Allerdings ist derartiges auch nur sinnvoll bei einer Änderung der Semantik des concurrent block: seine Ausführung ist beendet, wenn jeder konstituierende Prozeß beendet o d e r noch nicht kreiert ist. Darauf wird unten näher eingegangen.

3. Verzögertes Kreieren von Prozessen

Um die Kreierung von Prozessen in concurrent blocks/compounds solange verzögern zu können, bis bestimmte Bedingungen erfüllt sind, führen wir die Konstruktion eines "delayed process" ein, der rein äußerlich der Hoare'schen conditional critical region [Hoare/Perrott 1973] und dem connection statement von SIMULA 67 [Dahl et al. 1970] ähnlich ist.

Syntax (hier als Erweiterung von 2. und SIMULA 67):

<process>::= <statement>|<delayed process>|<label>:<process>
<delayed process>::= *inspect* <object expression> *when* <boolean expression>
        do <statement>

Semantik: Die Funktion des delayed process

   inspect o *when* b *do* s

entspricht der von

   repeat with o *when* b *do*; *inspect* o *do* s *until false*

wobei die erste Anweisung in der Schleife eine conditional critical region, die zweite ein connection statement ist. Die Auswirkungen des Auftretens eines delayed process als Komponente eines concurrent block/compound werden im folgenden beschrieben.

Die Semantik eines concurrent block/compound, der als Komponente einen delayed process enthält, weicht von der in 2. beschriebenen Semantik ab: Ein delayed process *inspect* o *when* b *do* s wird erst dann kreiert, wenn b den Wert *true* hat. Die Ausführung eines concurrent block/compound ist als beendet zu betrachten, wenn alle seine Prozesse vom Typ "statement" beendet sind und alle seine Prozesse vom Typ "delayed process" sich im Ruhezustand befinden, d.h. auf ihr jeweiliges b warten. Das bedeutet, daß während des Ablaufs eines concurrent block/compound jedes "statement" genau einmal, jedes s eines delayed process hingegen unbestimmt oft (eventuell auch gar nicht) ausgeführt wird. Dies gilt unverändert, wenn s selbst ein concurrent block/compound ist.

Als Beispiel formulieren wir die Pipeline aus 2. unter Verwendung leicht veränderter Grundbausteine. Der Datentyp *mailbox* wird als Klasse im Sinne von SIMULA mit zugehörigen Prozedurattributen aufgefaßt. Jeder Zugriff auf ein Objekt vom Typ *mailbox* ist als (gegebenenfalls conditional) critical region bezüglich dieses Objektes realisiert (vergleiche [Brinch Hansen 1973]). Eine Operation m.send(x) kann daher einen mit *inspect* m *when not* empty *do* beginnenden delayed process kreieren.

    procedure a(p,q); *mailbox* p,q;
    begin text x,y;
        p.receive(x);
        compute y using x;
        q.send(y)
    end of a

    procedure pipeline (in,out); *mailbox* in,out;
    cobegin procedure a(p,q); ......
              procedure b(p,q); ......
              procedure c(p,q); ......
              mailbox m1,m2;
    A: *inspect* in *when not* empty *do* a(in,m1);
    B: *inspect* m1 *when not* empty *do* b(m1,m2);
    C: *inspect* m2 *when not* empty *do* c(m2,out)
    coend of pipeline

Diese Pipeline könnte in einem größeren System etwa wie folgt verwendet werden:

    cobegin
        ⋮
        inspect input *when not* empty *do* pipeline (input,output);
        ⋮
    coend

Beachte, daß die Pipeline in diesem Kontext nicht "voluntaristisch" aufgerufen oder kreiert wird, sondern "latent existiert" und genau dann aktiv wird, wenn Daten zu verarbeiten sind. Das gleiche gilt für die drei Bausteine der Pipeline. Da kein explizites Kreieren stattfindet, ist auch keine explizite Beendigung als Folge etwa eines eingelesenen *notext* nötig.

Auch eine einwandfreie Formulierung der Prozedur *recursive* aus 2. ist mit den hier bereitgestellten Mitteln möglich:

    procedure recursive (m); *mailbox* m;
    cobegin mailbox x;
      A: *begin* ....*end*;
      B: *inspect* x *when not* empty *do* recursive(x)
    coend of recursive

4. *Kreierung durch nebenläufige Operationen*

Eine Prozedur aus drei über Puffer kommunizierenden Prozessen mit der Struktur

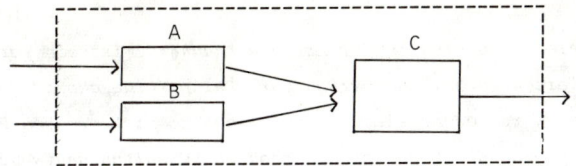

wäre wie folgt algorithmisch zu formulieren:

<u>procedure</u> combine (in1,in2,out); <u>mailbox</u> in1,in2,out;
<u>cobegin</u> <u>doublebox</u> d; <u>comment</u> object consisting of two mailboxes
                            first, second;
  A: <u>inspect</u> in1 <u>when</u> <u>not</u> empty <u>do</u>
          <u>begin</u> ..... receive(x); ..... d.first.send(y); ..... <u>end</u>;
  B: <u>inspect</u> in2 <u>when</u> <u>not</u> empty <u>do</u>
          <u>begin</u> ..... receive(x); ..... d.second.send(y); ..... <u>end</u>;
  C: <u>inspect</u> d <u>when</u> <u>not</u> (first.empty <u>or</u> second.empty) <u>do</u>
          <u>begin</u> ..... first.receive(x); second.receive(y); .....
              out.send(z)
          <u>end</u>
<u>coend</u> of combine

Beachte, daß für Anweisungen wie d.first.send(x) die semantische Äquivalenz mit <u>with</u> d <u>do</u> *first.send(x) (critical region bezüglich d) gefordert werden muß, wobei der Zugriff auf* first *keinen zusätzlichen kritischen Abschnitt benötigt.*

In einem größeren System werde combine *von zwei Prozessen gespeist, die etwa folgende Struktur haben:*

<u>procedure</u> a(out); <u>mailbox</u> out;
  <u>begin</u> <u>text</u> x; ...... out.send(x); ...... <u>end</u> of a

(und entsprechende Prozedur b). Die Kreierung einer Inkarnation von combine *erfolgt dann (nicht vorhersagbar) entweder durch eine send-Operation von* a *oder durch eine send-Operation von* b:

<u>cobegin</u> <u>doublebox</u> mm;
  X: a(mm.first);
  Y: b(mm.second);
  Z: <u>inspect</u> mm <u>when</u> <u>not</u> (first.empty <u>and</u> second.empty) <u>do</u>
              combine (first,second,output)
<u>coend</u>

Das einwandfreie Funktionieren dieser Konstruktion setzt voraus, daß die Parameterübergabe bei a,b und $combine$ durch call by name erfolgt!

5. *Bemerkungen*

a) *Für rekursive parallele Prozeduren in der Art von recursive ist ein Vorgehen gemäß der hier skizzierten Technik unverzichtbar. Falls keine derartige Rekursivität vorliegt, wird jedenfalls die Anzahl der koexistierenden Prozesse minimal gehalten - um den Preis eines erhöhten Verwaltungsaufwands.*

b) *Diese Technik kann somit als Analogon zur dynamischen Speicherverwaltung bei einem Programm ohne dynamische Feldvereinbarungen angesehen werden. Die strukturierte Parallelisierung durch geschaltete concurrent blocks/ compounds entspricht der strukturierten Speichervergabe durch die Blockschachtelung.*

c) *Die Verwandschaft der dargestellten Algorithmen zu Datenflußprogrammen ([Adams 1968], [Dennis/Fosseen 1973]) ist nicht zufällig. Die datenflußgesteuerte Koppelung nebenläufiger Prozesse ([Löhr 1973], [Ancilotti et al. 1974]) legt die Verwendung der hier entwickelten Prinzipien nahe. Diese sind im übrigen direkt auf Datenflußprogramme übertragbar.*

Literatur

[Adams 1968] D.A. Adams: A Computation Model with Data Flow Sequencing. Ph.D. thesis, Stanford Univ. 1968. Auszug in L.C. Hobbs et al.: Parallel Processor Systems, Technologies, and Applications. Spartan Books 1970.

[Ancilotti et al. 1974] P. Ancilotti/M. Fusani/N. Lijtmaer/C. Thanos: Deadlock Conditions in Well Structured Modular Systems. 4. GI-Jahrestagung Berlin 1974.

[Brinch Hansen 1972] P. Brinch Hansen: Structured Multiprogramming. CACM 15,7 (1972).

[Brinch Hansen 1973] P. Brinch Hansen: Operating System Principles. Prentice-Hall 1973.

[Burroughs 1968] Burroughs Corporation: Extended ALGOL Reference Manual. Detroit 1968.

[Conway 1963] M.E. Conway: A Multiprocessor System Design. Fall Joint Computer Conference 1963.

[Dahl et al. 1970] O.J. Dahl/B. Myhrhaug/K. Nygaard: SIMULA 67 Common Base Language. Norsk Regnesentral, Oslo 1970.

[Dennis/van Horn 1966] J.B. Dennis/E.C. van Horn: Programming Semantics for Multiprogrammed Computations. CACM 9,3 (1966).

[Dennis/Fosseen] J.B. Dennis/J.B. Fosseen: Introduction to Data Flow Schemas. Memo 81, Computation Structures Group, Project MAC, M.I.T. 1973.

[Dijkstra 1965] E.W. Dijkstra: Co-operating Sequential Processes. Report EWD 123, Dept. of Math., Techn. Univ. Eindhoven 1965. Abgedruckt im F. Genuys (ed.): Programming Languages. Academic Press 1968.

[Hoare/Perrott 1973] C.A.R. Hoare/R.H. Perrott: Operating Systems Techniques. Academic Press 1972.

[IBM 1966] IBM Corporation: PL/I Reference Manual, 1966.

[Löhr 1973] K.-P. Löhr: Datenflußgesteuerte Koppelung nichtsequentieller Systeme. Diss. Fachbereich Kybernetik, TU Berlin 1974.

[van Wijngaarden et al. 1968] A. van Wijngaarden/B.J. Mailloux/J.E.L. Peck/ C.H.A. Koster: Report on the Algorithmic Language ALGOL 68. Numerische Mathematik 14 (1969).

MODULARER AUFBAU EINER FAMILIE VON KOOPERIERENDEN PROZESSEN

(Bericht zum Projekt BSM[+])

Jürn Jürgens

Zusammenfassung

Das Konzept "Zustandssynchronisation" sowie das entsprechende Programmier-Hilfsmittel "Schleuse" werden eingeführt. Mittels Schleusen können die Synchronisationsbedürfnisse kooperierender Prozesse in natürlicher Weise formuliert werden, ohne daß dabei ein einzelner Prozeß auf andere Prozesse explizit Bezug zu nehmen braucht. Dies ermöglicht den modularen Aufbau von Prozeßfamilien. - Die Anwendung von Schleusen wird anhand von Beispielen demonstriert.

Die vorliegende Arbeit beruht auf Teilen der Dissertation des Autors [Jü 73], die in der Umgebung des Projekts BSM entstand und von Herrn Prof. Dr. G. Goos betreut wurde. Ihm sowie der Betriebssystemgruppe sei auch an dieser Stelle herzlich gedankt.

1. Modularität

Große Programmsysteme werden häufig strukturiert als Familien kooperierender sequentieller Prozesse (vgl.z.B. [Go 72]). Ziel einer solchen Strukturierung ist eine übersichtliche Zerlegung in eigenständige Bausteine mit klar definierten Schnittstellen.

Je einfacher dabei die Schnittstelle eines einzelnen Prozesses ist, desto leichter lassen sich solche Prozesse zu einem Gesamtsystem zusammensetzen. - Je enger und komplizierter andererseits die Verbindung eines Prozesses zu seiner Umgebung ist, desto schwieriger ist es, diesen Prozeß zu verstehen, zu programmieren, die Korrektheit des Programms zu prüfen, das Programm zu ändern. Je mehr Information über das Gesamtsystem in den Entwurf eines Prozesses eingeht, desto stärker wird dieser Prozeß mit seiner Umgebung verfilzt sein. Diese Verfilzung führt zu einem starren, fehleranfälligen und unhandlichen Aufbau des Gesamtsystems.

+) Die vorliegende Untersuchung wurde gefördert durch das Bundesministerium für Forschung und Technologie unter DV 2oo2

Aus diesen Gründen sollte ein Prozeß so wenig Information über das Gesamtsystem haben wie möglich, der Prozeß sollte zu einem abtrennbaren Modul [De 73] des Gesamtsystems gemacht werden. Parnas bezeichnet dieses Prinzip der Modularisierung als "information hiding" [Pa 72].

2. Zustandssynchronisation

Wenn Prozesse zusammenarbeiten, müssen sie einander synchronisieren, und damit müssen sie einander explitit oder implizit zur Kenntnis nehmen. In einer großen Zahl von Fällen läßt sich jedoch auf eine explizite Kenntnis anderer Prozesse verzichten, weil für die Synchronisation nicht eigentlich die Identität der beteiligten Prozesse wichtig ist, sondern weil es vielmehr auf bestimmte Zustände von Objekten (d.h. Variablen) ankommt, auf die die kooperierenden Prozesse gemeinsam zugreifen. Wir sprechen dann von Zustandssynchronisation. Die Problemstellung der Zustandssynchronisation lautet:

> Ein Prozeß kann einen bestimmten Teil seines Algorithmus erst durchlaufen, wenn ein bestimmtes Objekt aus seiner Umgebung in einen bestimmten Zustand versetzt wurde.

Ein Prozeß, der in dieser Weise sein Fortschreiten vom Zustand eines Objekts abhängig macht, wird als Interessent für dieses Objekt bezeichnet. Ein Interessent für ein Objekt kennt dieses Objekt, er kennt die Zustände des Objekts, die für ihn wichtig sind, und er weiß, in welchem Zusammenhang diese Zustände angenommen werden. - Welche Prozesse es allerdings sind, die diese Zustände herbeiführen, ist für den Prozeß irrelevant: Er braucht die Urheber dieser Zustände nicht zu kennen. Für den Interessenten ist allein wichtig zu wissen, daß es überhaupt Urheber gibt für die Zustände, die für ihn relevant sind.

Andererseits bedeutet Zustandssynchronisation auch, daß ein Urheber die Interessenten nicht zu kennen braucht. Der Urheber muß nur wissen, daß an einem Zustand grundsätzlich Interesse besteht, - wer die Interessenten sind, ja ob es in jedem Einzelfall überhaupt einen Interessenten gibt, ist unerheblich.

Die Verzögerung eines Prozesses bis zum Eintreten eines bestimmten Zustandes ist im allgemeinen nur sinnvoll, wenn der Prozeß die Möglichkeit erhält, Operationen an dem Objekt vorzunehmen, bevor der verlangte Zustand durch eine Operation eines anderen Prozesses wieder verlassen wird. Wo dies nicht bereits aus der Bedeutung des Zustandes folgt, muß es ausdrücklich verlangt werden. Die allgemeine Forderung der Zustandssynchronisation lautet daher:

> Ein Prozeß kann einen bestimmten Teil seines Algorithmus
> erst durchlaufen, wenn ein bestimmtes Objekt aus seiner
> Umgebung in einen bestimmten Zustand versetzt wurde. -
> Der Prozeß muß die Möglichkeit erhalten, Operationen an
> dem Objekt vorzunehmen, bevor der verlangte Zustand wieder
> verlassen wird.

3. Ein Beispiel: Erzeuger und Verbraucher

Folgende Variante des bekannten Erzeuger-Verbraucher-Problems [Di 68] kann als Beispiel für Zustandssynchronisation gedeutet werden: Ein Prozeß, der Erzeuger, schreibt Information in einen Puffer, damit diese später von einem anderen Prozeß, dem Verbraucher, aus dem Puffer gelesen werden kann. Das gemeinsame Objekt ist der Puffer; der Verbraucher muß sein Fortschreiten vom Zustand "Puffer gefüllt" abhängig machen; dieser Zustand wird vom Erzeuger hergestellt.

Wenn die Synchronisation in diesem Beispiel über den Zustand des Puffers hergestellt wird, brauchen Erzeuger und Verbraucher einander garnicht zu kennen: Der Verbraucher ist nicht betroffen, wenn sich die Identität des Erzeugers ändert; - sogar wenn der Erzeuger dynamisch bestimmt wird oder auch wenn der Puffer statt von einem Erzeuger von mehreren zusammenarbeitenden Prozessen gefüllt wird, hat dies keinen Einfluß auf den Verbraucher. Umgekehrt gehen Identität und Anzahl der Verbraucher nicht in den Algorithmus des Erzeugers ein.

Wenn mehrere Verbraucher um den Puffer konkurrieren in dem Sinne, daß nur einer den Pufferinhalt lesen darf, so wird neben dem Zustand "gefüllt" auch der Pufferzustand "belegt" relevant: Sobald ein Verbraucher (ggf. nach einer Verzögerung seines Fortschreitens) den Puffer als gefüllt vorgefunden hat, muß er ihn in den Zustand "belegt" überführen, noch bevor ein anderer Prozeß auf den Puffer zugreifen oder den Zustand des Puffers ändern kann.

4. Schleusen

Seinen $s_1,..,s_k$ Zustandsvariablen zur Beschreibung eines Objekts. Zu diesen Zustandsvariablen wird eine Schleuse γ implizit definiert durch Operationen der folgenden Art:

Sei B eine beliebige boolesche Funktion der Variablen $s_1,\ldots,s_k$, und sei S eine Anweisung, die ausschließlich auf die $s_1,\ldots,s_k$ zugreift. - Für jedes derartige Paar (B,S) ist eine Operation

$\quad\quad$ W(γ,B) <u>und</u> A(γ,S)

folgendermaßen definiert: Die Wirkung der Operation besteht in der Ausführung von S, jedoch wird S erst ausgeführt, wenn B = <u>true</u>. Das Feststellen von B = <u>true</u> und die Ausführung von S sind zusammen eine Elementaroperation, während derer kein anderer Prozeß auf γ zugreifen kann.

Eine Operation W(γ,B) <u>und</u> A(γ,S) wird eine <u>Durchfahrt</u> der Schleuse genannt.

Die Definition von γ ist nur sinnvoll, wenn auch das Auswerten einer Bedingung B mit dem Ergebnis <u>false</u> eine Elementaroperation ist und wenn auf die Variablen $s_1,\ldots,s_k$ ausschließlich durch Bedingungen B und Anweisungen S von Durchfahrten zugegriffen wird.

Wenn für die Bedingung B einer Durchfahrt zunächst B = <u>false</u> erkannt wird, so können danach andere Durchfahrten durch γ fortschreiten. Wenn dann später B = <u>true</u> erkannt wird, kann keine andere Durchfahrt fortschreiten, bis die Anweisung S dieser Durchfahrt ausgeführt ist.

Statt

$\quad\quad$ W(γ,<u>true</u>) <u>und</u> A(γ,S)

darf auch geschrieben werden

$\quad\quad$ A(γ,S).

Statt

$\quad\quad$ W(γ,B) <u>und</u> A(γ, <leere Anweisung>)

darf auch geschrieben werden

$\quad\quad$ W(γ,B).

5. Programme zum Erzeuger-Verbraucher-Problem

Sei ϒ die Schleuse, die durch die Variable

    Pufferzustand: (leer,voll)

gegeben ist. Dann lauten im Falle der o.a. einfachen Variante des Erzeuger-Verbraucher-Problems die Programme für Erzeuger und Verbraucher:

    Erzeuger: ...

                schreibe in Puffer;

                A(ϒ,Pufferzustand := voll);

                ...

    Verbraucher: ...

                W(ϒ, Pufferzustand = voll);

                lies aus Puffer;

                ...

    Initialisierung: Pufferzustand := leer;

Die Operation "W(ϒ,Pufferzustand = voll)" verzögert den Verbraucher so lange, bis die Bedingung "Pufferzustand = voll" erfüllt ist. Falls die Bedingung bereits bei ihrem Aufruf erfüllt ist, wird der aufrufende Prozeß unmittelbar fortgesetzt.

Die Operation "A(ϒ,Pufferzustand := voll)" weist der Variablen Pufferzustand den Wert voll zu und hebt ggf. die Verzögerung des Verbrauchers auf.

Eine allgemeinere Form des Erzeuger-Verbraucher-Problems ist folgende: Es gibt n Erzeuger E1,E2,..,En und m Verbraucher V1,V2,..,Vm, und die Erzeuger übergeben laufend Information an die Verbraucher. Es darf stets höchstens ein Erzeuger eine Informations-Portion in den Puffer schreiben; diese darf nur von einem Verbraucher gelesen werden; erst nachdem sie gelesen wurde, darf wieder ein Erzeuger eine Portion in den Puffer schreiben. Das Problem kann gelöst werden mittels der Schleuse ϒ, die zu der Variablen

    pufzust: (leer,wgef,voll,wgel)

gehört. Bei Benutzung dieser Schleuse lauten die Programme:

```
Ei: repeat begin
        ...
        W(ϒ,pufzust = leer) und A(ϒ,pufzust := wgef);
        schreibe in Puffer;
        A(ϒ,pufzust := voll);
    end;

Vj: repeat begin
        ...
        W(ϒ, pufzust = voll) und A(ϒ,pufzust := wgel);
        lies aus Puffer;
        A(ϒ,pufzust := leer);
    end;

Initialisierung:  pufzust := leer;
```

6. Das Handwerker-Problem

Eine Firma beschäftige einen Stab von Handwerkern, die verschiedenartige Aufträge ausführen. Ein Handwerker beginnt die Ausführung eines Auftrages damit, daß er sich im zentralen Werkzeuglager der Firma die nötigen Werkzeuge beschafft. Dann beginnt er zu arbeiten. Nach getaner Arbeit gibt er die entnommenen Werkzeuge wieder an das Lager zurück. Damit ist die Ausführung des Auftrages beendet, und der Handwerker kann den nächsten Auftrag ausführen.

Das zentrale Werkzeuglager besitzt Werkzeuge der Typen $W_1,...,W_n$. Für einen Handwerker, der einen Auftrag erhält, ist relevant, ob alle von ihm benötigten Werkzeuge im Lager vorhanden sind oder ob einige dieser Werkzeuge ausgeliehen sind. - Wenn ein Handwerker zu Beginn eines Auftrages im Lager nicht alle erforderlichen Werkzeuge vorfindet, so muß er warten, bis wieder genügend Werkzeuge der verlangten Typen im Lager sind. - Wir setzen voraus, daß ein Auftrag niemals mehr Werkzeuge erfordert als das Lager überhaupt besitzt und daß jeder Auftrag nach einer gewissen Zeit beendet wird.

Das Objekt, bezüglich dessen hier Sychronisation stattfinden soll, ist das Werkzeuglager. Die relevanten Zustände des Lagers lassen sich ausdrücken mittels einer Variablen

$$w \; : \; \underline{array} \, [1..n] \, \underline{of} \; \underline{integer},$$

wobei w[1] die Anzahl der Werkzeuge vom Typ W_i angibt, die im Lager verfügbar sind.

Der Werkzeugbedarf eines Auftrages A wird beschrieben durch die Konstante

$$a \; : \; \underline{array} \, [1..n] \, \underline{of} \; \underline{integer},$$

wenn für diesen Auftrag je a[i] Werkzeuge vom Typ W_i vonnöten sind.

Mit der Schreibweise w ⩾ a für
w[1] ⩾ a[1] $\underline{and}$ ... $\underline{and}$ w[n] ⩾ a[n] lautet dann das Programm für die Ausführung von Auftrag A:

$$\text{Auftrag A: } W(\Gamma, w \geqslant a) \; \underline{und} \; A(\Gamma, w := w-a);$$

$$\text{arbeiten;}$$

$$A(\Gamma, w := w+a);$$

Dies Programm für A ist unabhängig davon, welche weiteren Handwerker existieren und nach welchen Algorithmen diese arbeiten. Damit braucht A nicht geändert zu werden, wenn neue Handwerker in die Firma eintreten oder wenn andere die Firma verlassen. - Andererseits darf sich der innere Algorithmus von A ändern, ohne daß dies Rückwirkungen auf die Programme der anderen Handwerker oder auch nur auf die Schleuse Γ hätte.

Die Verwendung einer Schleuse hat zu einer natürlichen Modularisierung des gesamten Programms geführt, und diese Modularisierung bewirkt, daß das Programm leicht zu verstehen und leicht zu ändern ist.

Literatur

[De 73] Dennis, J.B.
Modularity
in: Advanced Course on Software Engineering
(Ed. F.L. Bauer)
Springer-Verlag, Berlin, Heidelberg, New York, 1973, 128-182

[Di 68] Dijkstra, E.W.
Cooperating Sequential Processes
in: Programming Languages
(Ed. F. Genuys)
Academic Press, London, 1968, 43-112

[Go 72] Goos,G., Jürgens,J. und Lagally,K.
The Operating System BSM, Viewed as a Community of Parallel Processes
Rechenzentrum der Technischen Universität München, Bericht 7208, 1972

[Jü 73] Jürgens, J.
Synchronisation paralleler Prozesse anhand von Zuständen
Dissertation Technische Universität München, 1973

[Pa 72] Parnas, D.L.
On the Criteria To Be Used in Decomposing Systems into Modules
CACM 15, 12 (December 1972), 1053-1058

VERMEIDUNG VON VERKLEMMUNGEN IN BEWERTETEN PETRINETZEN[1]

R. Schroff
Mathematisches Institut der Technischen Universität München

Einleitung

Unter den verschiedenen Hilfsmitteln zur Darstellung von kollateralen Vorgängen zeichnen sich Petrinetze in zweifacher Weise aus. Zum einen lassen sich mit ihnen häufig auftretende Situationen, wie der gegenseitige Ausschluß (engl.: mutual exclusion) oder das Erzeuger-Verbraucher-Problem, überzeugend einfach darstellen. Zum anderen eignen sie sich besonders für eine formale Behandlung von Fragestellungen aus dem Bereich der Koordination von kollateralen Prozessen.

In Systemen von kollateralen Prozessen kennt man das Problem der Verklemmung. Eine solche Situation liegt dann vor, wenn jeder aus einer betrachteten Menge von Prozessen auf das Fortschreiten (das Erzeugen eines Ereignisses) eines anderen wartet, d.h. sie warten unendlich lange. Sind alle Prozesse eines Systems an einer solchen Verklemmung beteiligt, dann handelt es sich um eine totale, ansonsten um eine partielle Verklemmung. Bei einer partiellen Verklemmung besteht grundsätzlich die Möglichkeit, daß sie durch einen nicht verklemmten Prozeß erkannt und aufgelöst werden kann. Gerät das System jedoch in eine totale Verklemmung, dann kann es sich selbst nicht mehr regenieren.

Wir werden an späterer Stelle den Begriff der Verklemmung auf Petrinetze übertragen und eine Regel zur Vermeidung von Verklemmungen angeben. Zunächst aber führen wir einige Definitionen ein.

Ein _bewertetes Petrinetz_ (im folgenden kurz Petrinetz genannt) ist ein Tupel $(S,T;Q,R,b)$. S und T sind endliche disjunkte Knotenmengen, die Knoten aus S heißen _Stellen_ und die aus T _Transitionen_

---
[1] Diese Arbeit ist im Sonderforschungsbereich 49 - Elektronische Rechenanlagen und Informationsverarbeitung - in München entstanden.

(in Abbildungen sind die Stellen durch Kreise, die Transitionen durch Rechtecke dargestellt). $Q \subset S \times T$ und $R \subset T \times S$ sind Mengen von gerichteten Bögen, sie verbinden Stellen mit Transitionen bzw. Transitionen mit Stellen. Die Abbildung $b : Q \cup R \to \mathbb{N}$ heißt <u>Bewertung</u> und ordnet jedem Bogen eine natürliche Zahl zu.

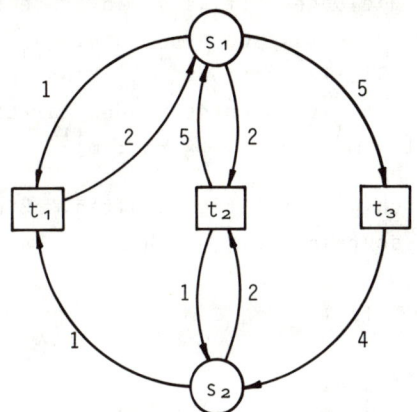

Abb.1 : Darstellung eines Petrinetzes

Die folgenden <u>Darstellungsmatrizen</u> $U = (u_{ij})$ und $V = (v_{ij})$ mit

$$u_{ij} = \begin{cases} b(s_i, t_j) & \text{falls} \quad (s_i, t_j) \in Q \\ 0 & \text{sonst} \end{cases}$$

$$v_{ij} = \begin{cases} b(t_j, s_i) & \text{falls} \quad (t_j, s_i) \in R \\ 0 & \text{sonst} \end{cases}$$

bilden eine äquivalente Beschreibungsform von Petrinetzen. Sie wird im weiteren verwendet, da man mit ihr direkten Zugang zur Linearen Algebra hat. Die Matrizen zu dem in Abb.1 dargestellten Petrinetz sind

$$U = \begin{vmatrix} 1 & 2 & 5 \\ 1 & 2 & 0 \end{vmatrix} \quad \text{und} \quad V = \begin{vmatrix} 2 & 5 & 0 \\ 0 & 1 & 4 \end{vmatrix} \; .$$

Eine <u>Markierung</u> m eines Petrinetzes ordnet jeder Stelle des Netzes Marken zu. Wir fassen m als Vektor mit nichtnegativen Komponenten

m_i auf : Auf der Stelle s_i befinden sich m_i Marken ($m \in N$, $N := \mathbb{N}_0 \times \mathbb{N}_0 \times \ldots \times \mathbb{N}_0$, $\mathbb{N}_0 := \mathbb{N} \cup \{0\}$). Durch das Schalten von Transitionen wird die Markierung verändert. Eine Transition t_j entnimmt beim Schalten den Stellen über die in sie hineinführenden Bögen (s_i, t_j) der Bewertung entsprechend je $b(s_i, t_j)$ Marken und gibt $b(t_j, s_i)$ Marken über die Bögen (t_j, s_i) ab. Die resultierende Markierung ist somit $m - u_j + v_j$, wenn u_j bzw. v_j die j-te Spalte von U bzw. V ist. Die Transition t_j kann jedoch nur dann schalten, wenn auf den Stellen die zu entnehmenden Marken vorhanden sind, d.h. wenn $m \geq u_j$ ist ($m^{(1)} \geq m^{(2)} \Leftrightarrow \forall i : m_i^{(1)} \geq m_i^{(2)}$).

Transitionen können auch gleichzeitig schalten. Eine nichtleere Menge M von Transitionen beschreiben wir durch einen Vektor d :

$$d_j := \begin{cases} 1 & \text{falls } t_j \in M \\ 0 & \text{sonst} \end{cases}$$

($d \neq 0$), und nennen ihn eine <u>Kombination</u> von Transitionen. Sie ist auf eine Markierung m <u>anwendbar</u>, wenn

$$m \geq Ud$$

ist. Alle durch d ausgewählten Transitionen sind dann <u>gleichzeitig schaltfähig</u>. Wenden wir d auf m an, dann erhalten wir

$$m' = m + (V - U)d$$

als Nachfolgemarkierung. Die Differenz $V - U$ bezeichnen wir mit W.

Sei das in Abb.1 dargestellte Petrinetz durch $m = (4,3)$ markiert, dann kann $d = (1,1,0)$ angewandt werden, d.h. t_1 und t_2 können gleichzeitig schalten. $m' = (8,1)$ ist die Nachfolgemarkierung. Auf die Markierung $m = (0,2)$ wäre dagegen keine Kombination anwendbar.

Wir verallgemeinern den Begriff der Anwendbarkeit auf Folgen von Kombinationen und nennen die Kombinationenfolge $\delta = \{d_i\}_{i \geq 0}$ auf eine Markierung $m(=m_0)$ <u>anwendbar</u>, wenn gilt:

$$\forall i \geq 0 : m_i \geq Ud_i \land m_{i+1} = m_i + Wd_i .$$

Die dadurch entstehende Markierungsfolge $\mu = \{m_i\}_{i \geq 0}$ nennen wir
<u>Fortsetzung</u> zu m.

In der Literatur werden vorwiegend Petrinetze mit der Bewertung $b \equiv 1$ diskutiert. Gelegentlich ist eine von 1 verschiedene Bewertung von Vorteil und gestattet die Darstellung von Problemen in direkter Weise. Möchte man zum Beispiel die Betriebsmittelvergabe behandeln und eine Betriebsmittelreservierung nur dann durchführen, wenn die Anforderungen eines Prozesses vollständig erfüllt werden können, dann läßt sich der Wunsch nach einer bestimmten Anzahl von Einheiten (wir interpretieren hier die Marken als Betriebsmitteleinheiten) durch die Bewertung ausdrücken.

Wir übertragen nun die oben eingeführten Begriffe für Verklemmungen auf Petrinetze. Hier verstehen wir unter einer Verklemmung eine Markierung, zu der es keine Fortsetzung gibt, die alle Transitionen immer wieder schaltet. Die Verklemmung ist total, wenn keine Fortsetzung exisistiert, die wenigstens eine Transition immer wieder schaltet. Alle Fortsetzungen einer totalen Verklemmung sind somit endlich. Jede ihrer Fortsetzungen führt zu einer Markierung, von der aus keine Transition mehr schalten kann. Wir definieren : m ist eine <u>partielle Verklemmung</u>, wenn m keine Fortsetzung besitzt, die alle Transitionen immer wieder schaltet; m ist eine <u>totale Verklemmung</u>, wenn alle Fortsetzungen zu m endlich sind. Eine totale Verklemmung ist auch eine partielle Verklemmung, aber nicht umgekehrt.

Entsprechend nennen wir m <u>verklemmungsfrei fortsetzbar</u> (vkf), wenn m keine Verklemmung ist, und verwenden die Indizes t und p, wenn wir zwischen der verklemmungsfreien Fortsetzbarkeit bezüglich totaler bzw. partieller Verklemmungen unterscheiden wollen. Die Menge aller vkf (vkf_t bzw. vkf_p) Markierungen bezeichnen wir mit VKF (VKF_t bzw. VKF_p). Unter dem <u>Verklemmungsproblem</u> verstehen wir die Frage nach einer verklemmungsfreien Fortsetzung.

<u>Vermeidung von Verklemmungen</u>

Wir untersuchen die Menge VKF und entwickeln eine Regel zur Vermeidung von Verklemmungen.

Zunächst stellen wir fest : Ist eine Folge δ auf eine Markierung m anwendbar, so kann sie auch auf jede größere Markierung m'(m' ≥ m) angewandt werden. Denn der Markierungsüberschuß m' - m bleibt bei der Anwendung von δ unberücksichtigt. Diese Feststellung trifft insbesondere auch für die Markierungen aus VKF zu, so daß jede um einen Vektor aus N vergrößerte Markierung m aus VKF ebenfalls zu VKF gehört :

(1)   VKF + N = VKF

($M_1 + M_2 := \{x_1 + x_2 : x_1 \in M_1, x_2 \in M_2\}$). Eine Markierung r ∈ VKF heißt <u>minimal</u>, wenn gilt :

$$\forall z \in N, z \neq 0 : r - z \notin VKF .$$

Die Menge aller minimalen Markierungen bezeichnen wir mit R. Aus (1) und der Definition für minimal folgt nun

(2)   VKF = R + N .

Mit dem <u>Hilfssatz</u> :

(3)   Sei $\{z_i\}_{i=0}^{\infty}$ eine unendliche Folge mit $z_i \in N$, dann gibt es Indizes i_1, i_2 mit $i_2 > i_1$, so daß gilt :

$$z_{i_1} \geq z_{i_2} .$$

(Beweis : vgl.[5]), zeigen wir, daß R endlich ist. Denn wäre R unendlich, dann würde eine Folge $r_0, r_1, \ldots$, gebildet aus verschiedenen Elementen aus R, besagen, daß $r_{i_2} \geq r_{i_1} \wedge r_{i_1} \neq r_{i_1}$ gilt, im Widerspruch zur Definition von minimal.

Die Mengen R und VKF des durch Abb.1 gegebenen Petrinetzes sind in Abb.2 dargestellt (in diesem Beispiel sind die partiellen Verklemmungen auch total, so daß VKF = VKF_p = VKF_t ist). Aus den Definitionen zum Verklemmungsbegriff folgt, daß es zu jeder vkf Markierung eine anwendbare Kombination gibt, so daß die entstehende Nachfolgemarkierung wieder vkf ist. Somit läßt sich die folgende

<u>Regel zur Vermeidung von Verklemmungen</u>

(4)
1) Wähle ein m_o aus VKF.
2) Wähle die Kombination d_i so, daß
   $m_i + Wd_i \geq r$ ist (r beliebig aus R).

angeben. Die dadurch erzeugte Fortsetzung zu $m(=m_o)$ ist verklemmungs-

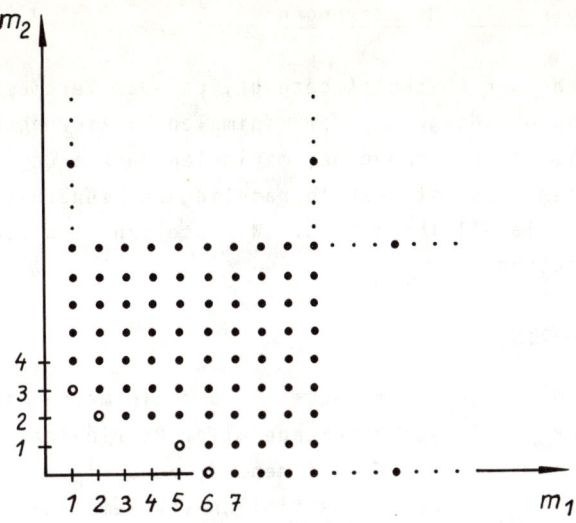

Abb.2 : minimale (o) und verklemmungsfrei fortsetzbare (•) Markierungen.

frei. Andererseits wird jede Folge, die gegen die Regel verstößt, in in eine Verklemmung geführt. Man beachte, daß im Schritt 2) der Regel im allgemeinen mehrere Kombinationen zur Auswahl anstehen. Es sind genau diese, die mit der Verklemmungsfreiheit verträglich sind. Wir folgern daraus : <u>Jede verklemmungsfreie Fortsetzung läßt sich mit der Regel erzeugen</u>.

Der hier beschrittene Weg zur Lösung des Verklemmungsproblems kann auf Systeme von Prozessen, die sich durch ein markiertes Petrinetz darstellen lassen, angewandt werden. Anhand der minimalen Markierungen kann dann sofort festgestellt werden, ob das Verklemmungsproblem lösbar ist, auch ist bekannt, wie im gegebenen Fall zu verfahren ist (vgl. Regel zur Vermeidung von Verklemmungen). In der Literatur wird das Problem vorwiegend durch die Untersuchung von lebendigen Markierungen (das sind vkf Markierungen, deren sämtliche Nachfolgemarkierungen wieder vkf sind - lebendig ist eine Verschärfung von vkf) behandelt. Dieser Weg führt nur dann zum Ziel, wenn die Markierung des Petrinetzes, das das gegebene Prozeßsystem darstellt, lebendig ist. Ist sie nicht lebendig, dann kann nicht gefolgert werden, daß das Verklemmungsproblem nicht lösbar ist, denn die Markierung könnte ja verklemmungsfrei fortsetzbar sein.

Zur Berechnung der minimalen Markierungen

Wir haben im vorangehenden Abschnitt gezeigt, daß das Verklemmungsproblem lösbar ist, wenn die Menge R der minimalen Markierungen bekannt ist. Die algorithmische Bestimmung der minimalen Markierungen ist ein nichttriviales Problem. Es ist deshalb naheliegend, zunächst einmal zu klären, ob es prinzipiell lösbar ist. Wir stellen also die Frage :
Ist die folgende Funktion

(5) $\quad f : P \rightarrow \mathcal{P}(N)$,

die jedem Petrinetz die zugehörige Menge R der minimalen Markierungen zuordnet, berechenbar ? (P sei die Menge aller Petrinetze). In Wirklichkeit handelt es sich um zwei Funktionen f_t und f_p, je nachdem, ob das Problem der totalen oder der partiellen Verklemmungen betrachtet wird. In [5] wurde ein Algorithmus zur Berechnung von R_t konstruiert und somit die Berechenbarkeit von f_t nachgewiesen (der Algorithmus dient dort nur zu Beweiszwecken und ist für eine praktische Anwendung nicht geeignet). Ob auch f_p berechenbar ist, konnte noch nicht beantwortet werden. Aus der Berechenbarkeit von f folgt die Entscheidbarkeit der Fragen :

> Ist eine Markierung m eines gegebenen Petrinetzes verklemmungsfrei fortsetzbar ? Gibt es zu einem gegebenen Petrinetz eine verklemmungsfrei fortsetzbare Markierung (diese Frage ist gleichbedeutend mit :
> Ist R nichtleer ?) ?

Die Behandlung des eben zitierten Algorithmus würde über den hier gegebenen Rahmen hinausführen. Wir wenden uns deshalb der einfacheren Frage :

(6) <u>Ist es entscheidbar, ob es zu einem Petrinetz eine vkf$_t$ Markierung gibt</u> ?

zu und beginnen mit der <u>Behauptung</u> :

(7) $\quad$ m ist genau dann vkf$_t$, wenn $m(=m_o)$ eine Fortsetzung $\{m_i\}_{i \geq 0}$ mit der Eigenschaft
$\exists i_1, i_2 \quad i_2 > i_1 : m_{i_2} \geq m_{i_1}$

besitzt.

Ist $m \in VKF_t$, dann gibt es zu m eine unendliche Fortsetzung $\{m_i\}_{i \geq 0}$. Nach Hilfssatz (2) gibt es dann Indizes i_1, i_2 mit $i_2 > i_1$, sodaß $m_{i_2} \geq m_{i_1}$ ist. - Sei umgekehrt $\delta = d_0, d_1, \ldots, d_n$ eine Kombinationenfolge, die angewandt auf m_{i_1} die Markierung m_{i_2} erzeugt, dann kann δ wegen $m_{i_2} \geq m_{i_1}$ auf m_{i_2} und danach immer wieder angewandt werden (der Markierungszuwachs $m_{i_2} - m_{i_1}$ wird dabei vervielfacht). Zu $m(=m_0)$ gibt es somit eine unendliche Fortsetzung, d.h. $m \in VKF_t$.

Wir fahren fort und zeigen:

R_t ist genau dann nichtleer, wenn das lineare Ungleichungssystem

(8) $\quad \begin{vmatrix} W \circ K \\ E \end{vmatrix} \cdot z \geq 0$

eine von Null verschiedene Lösung hat.

K ist eine Matrix, gebildet aus den $k = 2^n - 1$ möglichen Kombinationen, wenn n die Anzahl der Transitionen ist, E ist die Einheitsmatrix.

Sei R_t nichtleer und m aus VKF_t gewählt, dann gibt es nach (7) zu m eine Fortsetzung $\{m_i\}_{i \geq 0}$ und eine Folge $\delta = d_{i_1}, d_{i_2}, \ldots, d_{i_n}$ mit $n \geq 1$, die ein m_{i_1} überführt in $m_{i_2} = m_{i_1} + W \sum_{l=1}^{n} d_{i_l} (\geq m_{i_1})$. Sei z_j die Anzahl der in δ vorkommenden gleichen Schaltkombinationen d_j, dann ist

$$\sum_{l=1}^{n} d_{i_l} = \sum_{j=1}^{k} z_j d_j = K z$$

und wir erhalten $W K z \geq 0$. Da $z \neq 0$ ist (wegen $n \geq 1$) und alle z_j nichtnegativ sind, ist z eine von Null verschiedene Lösung des Ungleichungssystems (8).

Hat umgekehrt das Ungleichungssystem eine von Null verschiedene Lösung, dann hat es (wegen der ganzzahligen Matrix) auch eine ganzzahlige Lösung $z(\neq 0)$. Sei $\delta = d_1, \ldots, d_n$ eine Folge mit $\sum d_i = K z$, dann führt sie eine geeignete Markierung m über in $m + W K z (\geq m)$. Nach (7) ist somit m vkf_t und R_t nichtleer. Die Markierung m', deren Komponente m_i' gleich der Summe der Werte der i-ten Zeile von U ist, gestattet die Anwendung jeder Kombination (Spalte von K). Für alle größeren Markierungen gilt dasselbe. m ist demnach geeignet gewählt, wenn m und alle durch δ erzeugten Nachfolgemarkierungen größer als oder gleich m' sind, denn dann sind alle Kombinationen von δ anwendbar.

Da die Frage "Ist R_t nichtleer?" gleichbedeutend ist mit der Frage "Gibt es eine vkf_t Markierung ?", haben wir das oben gestellte Problem (6) auf die Lösbarkeit von linearen Ungleichungssystemen zurückgeführt. Für sie gibt es bekanntlich Lösungsverfahren (vgl.[3]), die Frage (6) kann somit bejaht werden.

Um festzustellen, ob R_t nichtleer ist, genügt es, statt dem Ungleichungssystem (8) folgendes einfachere

(9) $\qquad \left| \begin{matrix} W \\ E \end{matrix} \right| \cdot z \geq 0$

zu betrachten. Man überzeuge sich, daß wenn eine Kombinationenfolge δ auf eine Markierung m anwendbar ist, dann auch jede Sequentialisierung von δ auf m anwendbar ist. δ' heißt <u>Sequentialisierung</u> von δ, wenn jede Kombination d_i von δ durch eine Folge $d'_{i_1},\ldots,d'_{i_n}$ von Elementarkombinationen mit $d'_{i_1} + \ldots + d'_{i_n} = d_i$ ersetzt wird (Elementarkombinationen enthalten nur eine 1). Es ist also ausreichend, wenn wir nur Sequentialisierungen betrachten und in (8) W K durch W ersetzen.

Zusammenfassung

Das Verklemmungsproblem bei Petrinetzen wurde zurückgeführt auf die Bestimmung von minimalen verklemmungsfrei fortsetzbaren Markierungen. Eine Regel wurde angegeben mit der jede verklemmungsfreie Fortsetzung einer Markierung erzeugt werden kann. Die Funktion, die einem Petrinetz die Menge der minimalen Markierungen zuordnet, ist im Falle der totalen Veklemmungen berechenbar.

Eine naheliegende Fortführung dieser Arbeiten ist die Untersuchung der Berechenbarkeit im Falle der partiellen Verklemmungen und die Entwicklung von praktisch anwendbaren Algorithmen.

Literatur

[1] Computation Stuctures Group :
Progress Report 1969-70, Memo 53-1, MIT, 1972
Progress Report 1970-71, Memo 64, MIT, 1972
Progress Report, Memo 77, MIT, 1973

[2] Genrich, H.J.; Lautenbach, K.:
Synchronisationsgraphen.
Acta Informatica 2, 143-161, 1973

[3] Kuhn, H.W.; Tucker, A.W. (Eds.) :
Linear Inequalities and Related Systems.
Annals of Mathematics Studies, No. 38, 1956

[4] Lautenbach, K. :
Exakte Bedingungen der Lebendigkeit für eine Klasse
von Petri-Netzen.
Gesellschaft für Mathematik und Datenverarbeitung,
Bericht Nr. 82, Bonn, 1973

[5] Schroff, R. :
Vermeidung von totalen Verklemmungen in bewerteten
Petrinetzen.
Dissertation, Technische Universität München
Fakultät für Allgemeine Wissenschaften, 1974

P-T-NETZE
zur numerischen Simulation von asynchronen Fluessen

H. FUSS
Institut fuer Informationssystemforschung
in der
Gesellschaft fuer Mathematik und Datenverarbeitung (GMD), BONN

Modellbildung von nebeneinander ablaufenden Prozessen

Fuer das Verstaendnis dieser Ausfuehrungen ist eine gewisse Vertrautheit mit PETRI-Netzen nuetzlich. Die hier vorgestellten P-T-Netze (Puffer-Transaktions-Netze) leiten sich her aus den PETRIschen Stellen-Transitions-Netzen. Es wird hier auf den bekannten Definitionen aufgebaut, aber nicht alle Ergebnisse der Netztheorie sind uebertragbar, da die hier vorgelegte Betrachtung verschiedene Level der Theorie vereinigt durch die neu hinzukommende Veraenderlichkeit der Bewertung (durch eine Zusammenfassung von verschieden bewerteten, einander ausschliessenden Transitionen zu 'Transaktoren').
Dieser Standpunkt ergab sich durch Abwaegen der praktischen Belange (Simulationen mit variablen Stroemen) gegen die theoretischen Belange.

Es ergeben sich besondere Probleme, wenn man Modelle von nicht voll synchron nebeneinander ablaufenden Prozessen bilden will, denn die inneren Zusammenhaenge der Prozessteile sind dem Modellbildner haeufig nicht ausreichend bekannt. Dann behilft man sich damit, dass man statistische Zusammenhaenge abbildet statt kausale. Es ist offensichtlich, dass dadurch die Verhaltenstreue der Abbildung nur in beschraenktem Masse erhalten bleiben kann (Konfliktentscheidungen!). Eine weitere Schwierigkeit stellt sich oft ein, wenn man Modelle von nebeneinander ablaufenden Prozessen in Form eines mathematischen Systems vorliegen hat und sie durch ein Computerprogramm numerisch behandelt. Schon geringfuegige Aenderungen am mathematischen Modell ziehen u.U. langwierige Umprogrammierungen nach sich.
Bei Verwendung von Netzen treten viele dieser Schwierigkeiten nicht auf, Transparenz und Flexibilitaet der Abbildung werden erhoeht.

Markenfluss

Wenn in Netzen durch die Transitionen zwischen den Stellen Marken verschoben werden, so kann man, wie in PETRI-Netzen, sein Augenmerk mehr auf die markierten Stellen richten, die im einfachsten Fall als Vor- oder Nachbedingungen (etwas weiter gefasst als Voraussetzungen und Ergebnisse) von Ereignissen zu deuten sind.

Wir dagegen zielen hier auf eine spezielle Deutung der abstrakten Marken und erreichen das durch eine Spezialisierung der Transitionsregel, naemlich: zum Schalten gehoere auch, dass die Summe der Input-Marken gleich der Summe der Output-Marken ist (Markenzahl-Invarianz). Dann stehen die Marken fuer die Objekte, deren Fluss durch das System man verfolgt und simuliert.

Wir gehen aus von der Invarianz der Markenzahl gegenueber allem Geschehen im Netz, jedoch koennen die Marken an wohldefinierten Stellen (den Schnittstellen zwischen dem betrachteten System <Modell> und dessen Umwelt) aus dem betrachteten System heraustreten bzw. in dieses hineingeschleust werden.

P-T-Netze

Wir bilden durch Puffer-Transaktions-Netze, kurz: P-T-Netze, (Simulations-) Modelle der realen Welt nach folgenden Prinzipien:

Von gewissen Dingen (Systemteilen) der realen Welt ist fuer uns nur die Tatsache relevant, dass sie die Traeger von verschiedenen Zustaenden sein koennen, imdem sie eine veraenderliche Zahl (unbenannter) Objekte enthalten; die Bilder solcher Systemteile heissen Puffer.

Von gewissen anderen Teilen der realen Welt ist fuer uns nur die Tatsache relevant, dass sie Zustandsveraenderungen bewirken,
die Bilder der Traeger dieser Ereignisse heissen Transaktoren.

Bei "gleichzeitig" nebeneinander ablaufenden Vorgaengen wird unterschieden zwischen den schwach synchronisiert, concurrently nebeneinander ablaufenden Ereignissen und den streng synchronisierten, koinzidenten Ereignissen.

Prinzip der Vollstaendigkeit der Darstellung:
Alle relevanten Aspekte des Urbildes muessen in dem Modell dargestellt sein, und nur die Darstellung wird betrachtet.

Puffer

Ein Puffer entspricht einer PETRIschen Stelle, die mehr als eine Marke tragen kann. In einem Puffer koennen die Marken gezaehlt werden; ihre Anzahl kann seine Kapazitaet nicht ueberschreiten.

Def Bei der Modellbildung gehoert zu jedem <u>Puffer</u> P_n:
a) sein (individueller) Name,
b) sein Inhalt $i(P_n)$, mit $i(P_n) \in \{0,1,2,\ldots\}$
c) die Kapazitaet $c(P_n)$, mit $c(P_n) \in \{1,2,3,\ldots\}$
Es ist stets $i(P_n) \leq c(P_n)$.

Es werden $c(P_n)$ und ein Anfangs-Inhalt $i_0(P_n)$ bei der Modellbildung gesetzt. Die Kapazitaet eines Puffers im Modell ist unveraenderlich, dagegen koennen die Puffer zu verschiedenen "Zeiten" verschiedene Inhalte (=Zustaende) haben.
Welche Werte fuer $i(P_n)$ angenommen werden, ergibt sich (in Abhaengigkeit von dem Anfangswert) durch die Transaktions-Regel (s.dort).
Aus der Definition von $i(P_n)$ folgt: Pufferinhalte koennen nur um den Betrag natuerlicher Zahlen veraendert werden.

Ein Puffer wird durch einen <u>Kreis</u> dargestellt, der mit seinem Namen (Label) beschriftet und in den sein Inhalt eingetragen werden kann.

Beispiele: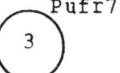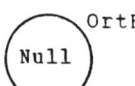

Die (unmittelbare) Umwelt eines Puffers, d.h. seine Nachbarn, sind die Transaktoren.

Transaktoren

Einer (PETRIschen) Transition entspricht hier ein <u>Transaktor</u>.

Das einmalige Wirken (das <u>Schalten</u>) eines Transaktors heisse eine <u>Transaktion</u> dieses Transaktors. Sie ist eine <u>elementare Veraenderung</u> in einem P-T-Netz und <u>veraendert koinzident</u> Pufferinhalte.

Die (unmittelbare) Umwelt eines Transaktors, d.h. seine Nachbarn, sind die Puffer. Die zwischen Puffern und Transaktoren herrschende Relation ist die Flussrelation. Sie wird als Pfeil zwischen ihnen dargestellt und ist gerichtet, die Pfeilspitze zeigt die Flussrichtung an.

<u>Def</u>   Bei der Modellbildung gehoert zu jedem <u>Transaktor</u> T_0:
  a) sein (individueller) Name,
  a) <u>(Input-) Puffer</u>, die zum Schalten Marken liefern,
  c) <u>(Output-) Puffer</u>, die die Marken aufnehmen, und
  d) <u>(Steuer oder K-) Puffer</u>, die bezueglich der Transaktion T_0 (in ihrem Inhalt) konstant sind; sie steuern die Inhalts-Veraenderungen in den unter b) und c) genannten Puffern gemaess der Transaktions-Regel.

Um die unter d) genannte Steuerung zu erzielen, wird jedem Puffer P_n, der mit einem Transaktor in Input- oder Output-Relation steht, ein Puffer K_n zugeordnet.
<u>Je ein P und ein K bilden ein fuer die Transaktion relevantes Paar.</u>
Die Inhalte der Puffer K_n koennen dann veraendert werden, wenn die Puffer statt in der K-Rolle (in einem anderen Level!) in der P-Rolle, d.h. als gewoehnliche Input- oder Output-Puffer P_n auftreten.
(K-Puffer sind verallgemeinerte Nebenbedingungen.)

Ein Transaktor T_n wird dargestellt durch ein <u>Rechteck</u>, das ggf. mit seinem Namen beschriftet werden kann; die dazugehoerigen Puffer werden wie bekannt durch Kreise dargestellt.

Ein Beispiel fuer die Darstellung eines Transaktors Tra_0 ist:

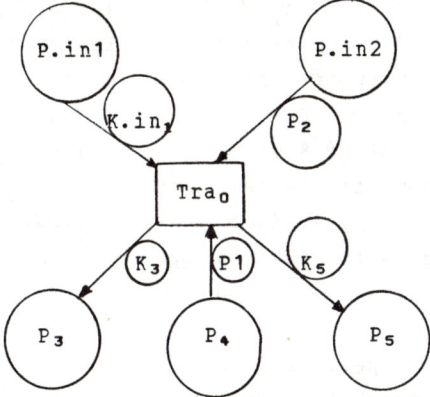

Da Marken Zustaende anzeigen, Ereignisse aber keinen Zustand haben koennen, sondern <u>stattfinden</u>, ist es sinnvoll festzulegen:

<u>Transaktoren koennen keine Marken speichern.</u>

Zur Erlaeuterung der <u>Transaktions-Regel</u> betrachten wir einen (festen) Transaktor T_0.

Die zu diesem Transaktor T_0 gehoerigen Input-Puffer seien mit P_{n_1}, $n_1=1,\ldots,N_1$, die zu ihm gehoerigen Output-Puffer mit P_{n_2}, $n_2=1,\ldots,N_2$ bezeichnet. (Dazu gehoeren jeweils die Steuerpuffer K_{n_1} bzw. K_{n_2}.)

Wir bezeichneten ja mit $i(P_n)$ die Inhalte der Puffer P_n. Wenn wir unterscheiden wollen zwischen dem Inhalt eines bestimmten Puffers P_n unmittelbar <u>vor</u> bzw. <u>nach</u> dem Stattfinden einer Transaktion T_0, so schreiben wir $i_1(P_n)$ bzw. $i_2(P_n)$.
(Die Unterscheidung zwischen $i_1(K_n)$ und $i_2(K_n)$ ist fuer die Puffer K_n unnoetig, da sich ihre Inhalte bei ihrer eigenen Transaktion, bei der sie in der K-Rolle auftreten, nach Def. nicht aendern.)

<u>Falls</u> eine Transaktion stattfindet, dann nach der folgenden Regel

<u>TR</u>: $i_1(P_{n_1}) - i(K_{n_1}) =: i_2(P_{n_1})$ fuer alle Input-Puffer P_{n_1} von T_0,
$i_1(P_{n_2}) + i(K_{n_2}) =: i_2(P_{n_2})$ fuer alle Output-Puffer P_{n_2} von T_0
<u>koinzident</u> fuer alle beteiligten Puffer P_{n_1} und P_{n_2}.

<u>Wann</u> eine Transaktion stattfinden kann, wird beschrieben durch die
<u>Transaktions-Regel</u>:

<u>Def</u> Ein <u>Transaktor T_0 kann gemaess der Regel TR genau dann schalten</u>, wenn folgende 3 Voraussetzungen erfuellt sind:
<u>a)</u> $i_1(P_{n_1}) - i(K_{n_1}) \geq 0$ fuer jedes $n_1=1,\ldots,N_1$;
d.h. der Inhalt der Input-Puffer P_{n_1} ist gross genug, um die erforderlichen Marken entnehmen zu koennen (T_0 aktiviert);
<u>b)</u> $\Sigma_{n_1} i(K_{n_1}) = \Sigma_{n_2} i(K_{n_2})$ fuer $n_1=1,\ldots,N_1$ und $n_2=1,\ldots,N_2$;
d.h. die Steuer-Puffer K der Input-Seite von T_0 muessen <u>gleich viel Marken</u> tragen wie die der Output-Seite (Invarianz);
<u>c)</u> $i_1(P_{n_2}) + i(K_{n_2}) \leq c(P_{n_2})$ fuer jedes $n_2=1,\ldots N_2$;
d.h. wenn in den Output-Puffern P_{n_2} genuegend Platz ist, um die ankommenden Marken aufnehmen zu koennen (T_0 sicher).

Man beachte die Korrespondenz zwischen a) und c), die fuer die Umkehrung der Flussrichtung (Rueckwaerts-Simulation) wichtig ist.

<u>Konflikte</u>

In engem Zusammenhang mit dem Begriff 'Transaktion' steht der Begriff "Konflikt". Er erscheint hier u.a. als ein "Streit" um die Marken eines Input-Puffers oder um die "Nicht-Marken", d.h. um den freien Inhaltsraum $c(P_n) - i(P_n)$ eines Output-Puffers.

Def Zwei Transaktoren T_1 und T_2, von denen jeder einzeln nach der Transaktions-Regel schalten koennte, stehen ueber einen Puffer P_0 in einem (Vorwaerts-) Konflikt, wenn
   a_1) sie P_0 als Input-Puffer gemeinsam haben und
   b_1) P_0 weniger Marken enthaelt, als sie zusammen fuer ihre Inputs brauchen.

Def Zwei Transaktoren T_1 und T_2, von denen jeder einzeln nach der Transaktions-Regel schalten koennte, stehen ueber einen Puffer P_0 in einem (Rueckwaerts-) Konflikt, wenn
   a_2) sie P_0 als Output-Puffer gemeinsam haben und
   b_2) P_0 weniger Marken aufnehmen kann, als diese Transaktoren zusammen mit ihren Outputs liefern.

Im nebenlaeufigen Zusammenwirken von Transaktoren (z.B. von T_0 und T_1) ist es ja moeglich, dass die Transaktion T_1 den Inhalt eines solchen ihrer (z.B. Output-) Puffer veraendert, der bei T_0 in der Funktion K wirkt. Dies ist ein Konflikt zwischen zwei verschiedenen Ebenen:

Def Zwei Transaktoren T_1 und T_2, von denen jeder einzeln nach der Transaktions-Regel schalten koennte, stehen ueber einen Puffer P_0 in einem (Level-) Konflikt, wenn P_0 bei T_1 in der Rolle P, bei T_2 in der Rolle K vorkommt.

Wir fordern axiomatisch:
   Konflikte muessen entschieden werden,
und zwar vom Modell-Bildner selbst waehrend der Simulation; oder er delegiert die Entscheidung (z.B. an einen Algorithmus), da sonst nicht die Invarianz des Simulations-Ergebnisses gewaehrleistet waere.

Das Entscheiden eines Konflikts (wozu Information gebraucht wird) bedeutet das Ermoeglichen einer Transaktion unter dadurch entstehender Unmoeglichkeit fuer andere Transaktionen, die mit der ausgewaehlten in Konflikt stehen.

Ob eine Transaktion stattfindet, haengt ausser von den in der Transaktions-Regel genannten Voraussetzungen davon ab, dass es keinen T_0 betreffenden Konflikt gibt oder alle ihn betreffenden Konflikte zu seinen Gunsten entschieden sind. Dann schaltet der Transaktor T_0 gemaess der Transaktions-Regel, solange nicht durch T_0 selbst oder nebenlaeufig durch andere Transaktionen die Voraussetzungen abgeaendert wurden.

Programmsystem

Zu dem vorgestellten Netztyp ist ein Programmsystem, bestehend aus einem Modell-Generator und einem Prozessor, entwickelt worden.
Es compiliert die Deklarationen (statements), die ein P bzw. T nebst seiner unmittelbaren Umgebung beschreiben, zu einem zusammenhaengenden Modell-Netz. In einer Deklaration ist genau das anzugeben, was bei den Definitionen fuer Puffer bzw. Transaktoren aufgefuehrt ist (s. dort).
Dabei werden eine Reihe von Vereinfachungen zur Bequemlichkeit des Benutzers zugelassen, z.B. die Verwendung von "Literals" (Konstanten-Puffern).
Das Programmsystem ist interaktiv angelegt, d.h. der Benutzer kann ueber einen Bildschirm und eine Schreibmaschine mit ihm in Kommunikation treten. Waehrend des Generierens des Netzes kann er schrittweise Veraenderungen vornehmen; das Ergebnis seiner Aenderungen wird ihm in einem speziellen Testprogramm angezeigt bzw. ausgedruckt.
Auch waehrend des Programmteils 'Processor' hat der Benutzer die Moeglichkeit, nun in eingeschraenkterem Masse, Variationen an seinem Modellnetz vorzunehmen. Insbesonders kann er waehrend der Simulation die Flussrichtung der Marken umkehren. Er muss dann eingreifen, wenn Konflikte zu entscheiden sind, die er keinem Algorithmus ueberlassen hat.
Das Programmsystem ist modular aufgebaut, in FORTRAN geschrieben und kann deshalb leicht nach den Wuenschen einer Benutzergruppe bzw. Installation abgeaendert werden.

Eine grosse Erleichterung, die aber nicht durch geschicktes Programmieren des Generators erreicht wird, sondern die durch die Struktur der Netze begruendet ist, ist die eingangs erwaehnte leichte Abaenderbarkeit der Modelle. Wenn man z.B. statt eines Puffers eine Verfeinerung anbringen moechte, z.B. ein puffer-berandetes Netz, so geht das ganz einfach, indem man die entsprechenden Verbindungen des Puffers zu seiner Umwelt loest, dafuer die Deklarationen des neuen Teilnetzes einfuegt und die neuen Verbindungen zwischen den beiden Teilen herstellt. Erfahrungsgemaess sind die Umprogrammierarbeiten (und damit Fehlerquellen) beim Abaendern von Aussagen in herkoemmlichen Programmiersprachen wesentlich groesser.

Ein Beispiel fuer ein solches Flussmodell, das ein oekonomisches Modell der BRD darstellt, ist das folgende:

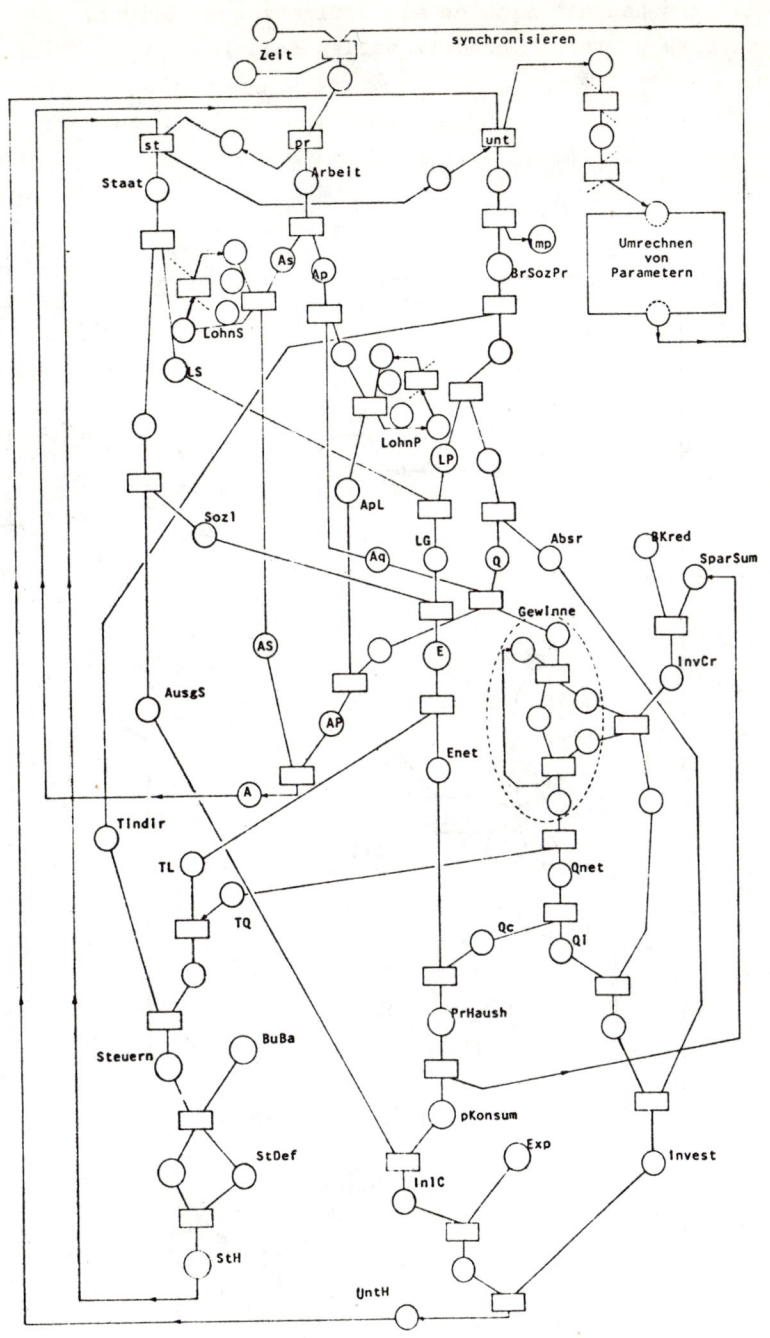

Wie man in P-T-Netzen rechnen kann, sieht man an dem folgenden Beispiel. (Es handelt sich um ein Teilnetz des obigen, in dem der Parameter L um p Prozent erhoeht werden soll.)

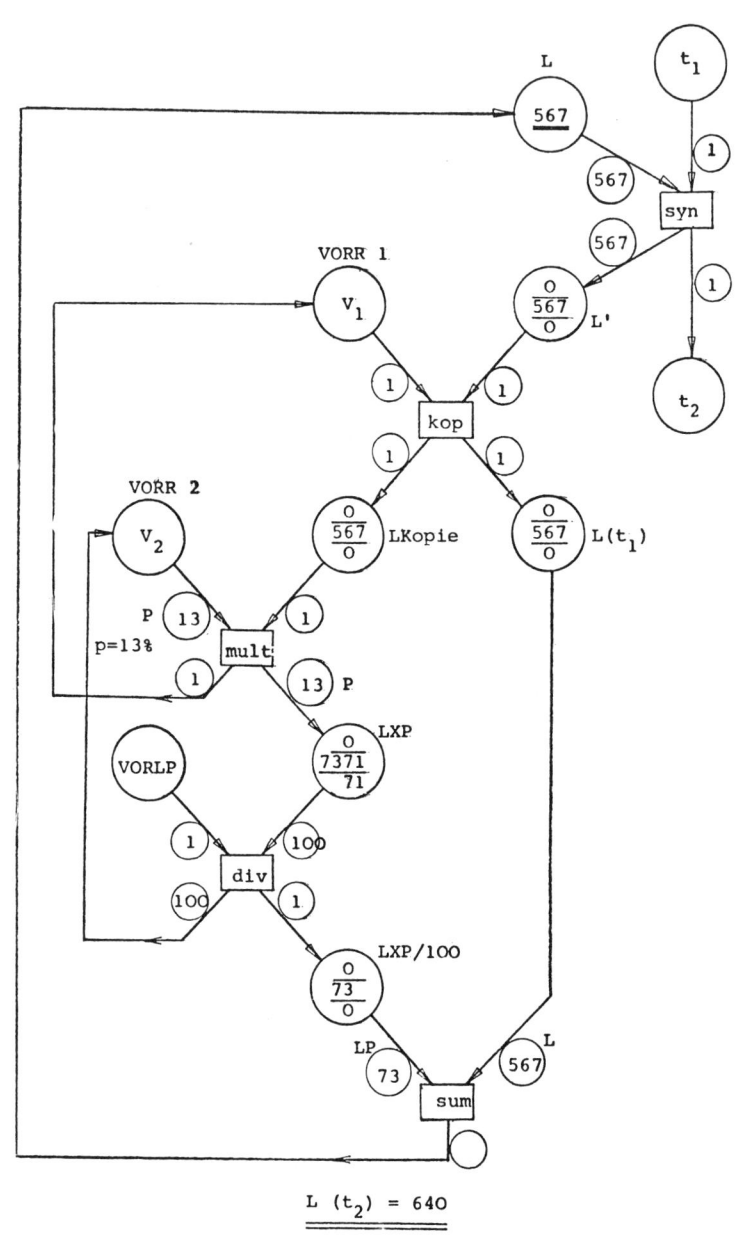

$\underline{\underline{L(t_2) = 640}}$

Literatur

Bernstein, P.A.:
Description Problems in the Modeling of Asynchronous Computer Systems
Technical Report No.48, Department of Computer Science, University of Toronto (1973)

Commoner, F.:
s. Holt, A.W. and Commoner, F.: Events and Conditions

Fuss, H.E.:
AFMG - Ein asynchroner Fluss-Modell-Generator
Berichte der GMD Nr... Bonn (1974) (in Druck)

Genrich, H.J.:
Ein Kalkuel des Planens und Handelns
Tagungsunterlage, GI/GMD-Fachtagung: Ansaetze zur Organisationstheorie rechnergestuetzter Informationssysteme (26.-28. 6. 1974)

Genrich, H.J,; Lautenbach, K.:
Synchronisationsgraphen
Acta Informatica 2, 143-161 (1973)

Hack, M.:
Analysis of Production Schemata by Petri Nets
MIT-Project MAC, TR-94 (1972)

Holt, A.W.; Commoner, F:
Events and Conditions
Information System Theory Project
Applied Data Research Inc., Princeton N.J. (1970)

Holt, A.W. et al.:
Final Report for the Project
'Development of Theoretical Foundations for Description and Analysis of Discrete Informationsystems', CADD-7405-2011
Volume I (Semantics) and Volume II (Mathematics)
Mass. Computer Ass., Inc., Wakefield, Mass. (1974)

Lautenbach, K.:
Exakte Bedingungen der Lebendigkeit fuer eine Klasse von Petri-Netzen
Berichte der GMD Nr.82, Bonn (1973)

Lautenbach, K.; Schmid, H.A.:
Use of Petri Nets for Proving Correctness of Concurrent Process Systems
Proceedings of IFIP Congress 74, pp. 187-191
North Holland Publ. Comp. (1974)

Petri, C.A.:
Concepts of Net Theory
Proc. Symp. on Math. Found. of Comp. Sc. (High Tatras), pp. 137-146 (1973)

Schroff, R.;
Vermeidung von totalen Verklemmungen in bewerteten Petrinetzen
Dissertation, Techn. Universitaet Muenchen (1974)

Shapiro, R.M.; Saint, H.:
A New Approach to Optimization of Sequencing Decisions
Ann. Rev. in Automatic Programming 6, Part 5 (1970)

Shapiro, R.M.; Saint, H.:
The Representation of Algorithms as Cyclic Partial Orderings
Final Report, Contract NASW-2097 (1971)

Yoeli, M.:
Petri Nets and Asynchronous Control Networks
Research Report CS-73-07,
Department of Applied Analysis and Computer Science
University of Waterloo (1973)

Elementare Steuerknoten in Datenflußmodellen

Hans-Jürgen Gottschalk

Informatik-FG. Programmiersprachen u. Compiler I
Technische Universität Berlin

1. Einleitung

Mit den in den letzten Jahren entwickelten und ständig weiter verbesserten integrierten Schaltkreisen können heute bereits komplette Zentraleinheiten für Minicomputer mit nur wenigen Chips aufgebaut werden. Es ist weiterhin abzusehen, daß in kurzer Zeit neben Prozessoren auch Halbleiter-Direktzugriffsspeicher ausreichender Kapazität zu einem Preis zur Verfügung stehen werden, der die Realisierung von Multiprozessorstrukturen mit einer sehr großen Anzahl solcher Komponenten erlaubt.

Demgegenüber sind bis heute Programmiersprachen, die eine problemorientierte Formulierung nichtsequentieller Algorithmen gestatten und bei geeigneter Implementierung die potentielle Leistungsfähigkeit solcher Systeme zu nutzen in der Lage sind, nur ansatzweise entwickelt worden. Die bisherigen Bemühungen um die theoretischen Grundlagen derartiger Programmiersysteme und einzelne Vorschläge zur praktischen Anwendung der Ergebnisse lassen sich hinsichtlich der Art und Weise, in der nebenläufige Aktivitäten repräsentiert bzw. erfaßt werden sollen, prinzipiell einem der drei Forschungsgebiete

    a) Automatische Programmanalyse
    b) Explizite Beschreibung kooperierender Prozesse
    c) Datenflußmodellierung

zuordnen. Während im Rahmen von a) Algorithmen zur automatischen Erfassung nebenläufiger Aktivitäten in "sequentiell" notierten Programmen angegeben werden, ist unter b) die Repräsentation nichtsequentieller Algorithmen mit Hilfe geeigneter Sprachelemente zu verstehen, die in eine ihrer sonstigen Struktur nach "sequentielle" Programmiersprache eingebettet werden.

2. Datenflußmodellierung

Eine grundsätzlich andere Vorstellung über das Wesen nichtsequentieller Rechenabläufe liegt den sogenannten Datenflußmodellen zugrunde, in denen man die Nebenläufigkeit von Aktionen nicht durch eine explizite Beschreibung des "control flow", d.h. der Ablaufsteuerung wie in 1.b) ausdrückt, sondern in natürlicher Weise vom Datenfluß abhängig macht. Die in diesem Zusammenhang entwickelten Modelle, von denen hier nur die "Program Graphs" von Rodriguez [1] die "Data Flow Schemas" von Dennis/Fosseen [2], die "Graph Programs" von Adams [3] sowie die asynchronen Netze von Luconi [4] und Bruno/Altman [5] erwähnt seien, haben eine zweifache Bedeutung: einerseits liefern sie die theoretischen Grundlagen für den Entwurf nichtsequentieller Rechnerstrukturen, andererseits geben sie den Anstoß zur Entwicklung neuartiger Programmiersprachen, die hier kurz als "Datenflußsprachen" bezeichnet werden sollen. Der letztgenannte Aspekt kommt bereits in den Arbeiten von Adams und Dennis/Fosseen zum Ausdruck; als weitere Vorschläge seien die Programmiersprachen DFPL von Kosinski [6] und COMPEL von Tesler/Enea [7] genannt.

Während die in 1.2 beschriebenen Sprachen in der vorliegenden Form bereits jetzt auf Mehrprozessoranlagen mit vergleichsweise konventioneller Architektur implementiert werden können, haben bisher weder die Entwicklung von Datenflußsprachen noch der Entwurf adäquater Rechnerstrukturen einen ähnlichen Stand erreicht.

Die weiteren Ausführungen beziehen sich auf die innere Struktur von Datenflußmodellen und sind als Versuch aufzufassen, die in ihrer äußeren Form sehr unterschiedlichen Modelle einer vergleichenden Betrachtungsweise zugänglich zu machen. Ein Grund, warum ein Vergleich der algorithmischen Eigenschaften oder die Beurteilung von Vor- und Nachteilen im Hinblick auf eine Implementierung nicht ohne weiteres möglich ist, ist offenbar darin zu sehen, daß die in den einzelnen Modellen vereinbarten Operatoren in Anzahl und Funktionsweise mehr oder weniger stark voneinander abweichen. Es liegt daher nahe, die Feinstruktur der verschiedenen Operatoren zu ergründen und daraus eine minimale Anzahl voneinander unabhängiger Operatorkonzepte abzuleiten. Als Ergebnis dieser Überlegung werden hier zwei elementare Operatoren eingeführt, mit denen Operatoren höherer Komplexität konstruiert werden können.

3. Aufbau von Datenflußgraphen

Der den verschiedenen Datenflußmodellen gemeinsame Kern besteht in der Darstellung von nichtsequentiellen Rechenabläufen durch gerichtete Graphen, in denen die Knoten Operatoren und die Kanten Datenkanäle repräsentieren.

Ein <u>Datenkanal</u> k transportiert in Kantenrichtung Daten aus der Menge V(k) der in k zulässigen Werte und ist zu jedem Zeitpunkt durch einen Belegungszustand gekennzeichnet. Die Menge B der möglichen Belegungszustände hat üblicherweise zwei Elemente, z.B. B={belegt, leer}, mit denen die An- bzw. Abwesenheit eines Datums im Kanal angezeigt wird (in [1] werden dagegen vier Zustände benötigt!)

Die interne Struktur eines <u>Operators</u> p aus der Menge der

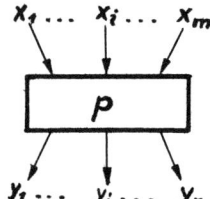

Abb. 1

im Modell vereinbarten Operatoren läßt sich wie folgt charakterisieren:

a) Jedem Operator p wird eine <u>Transitionsfunktion</u> T_p zugeordnet, die die Belegungszustände der Datenkanäle verändert. Diese Funktion wird z.B. in [2] und [6] graphisch durch "firing rules", in [1] und [3] in Form von Transitionstafeln angegeben.

b) Jeder Operator p erhält eine <u>Interpretation</u> durch Zuordnung einer totalen Funktion

$$F_p : \bigtimes_{i=1}^{m} V(x_i) \longrightarrow \bigtimes_{j=1}^{n} V(y_j) \; ,$$

die in endlicher Zeit berechenbar sein muß. Als Grenzfälle sind alternativ m=o oder n=o erlaubt, wodurch der Operator die Funktionseigenschaft verliert und in eine Daten-Quelle bzw. -Senke überführt wird. Quellen und Senken müssen ebenfalls in endlichen Zeitabständen Daten liefern bzw. aufnehmen können.

In Abhängigkeit von dem Effekt, der durch eine bestimmte Transitionsfunktion erzielt werden soll, teilt man die Operatoren zweckmäßigerweise in zwei Klassen ein, die im folgenden näher betrachtet werden.

3.1 Funktionsoperatoren

Ein Operator, für dessen Aktivierung alle Eingabekanäle den Zustand "belegt", alle Ausgabekanäle den Zustand "leer" aufweisen müssen, der jedem Eingabekanal ein Datum entnimmt und nach Berechnung von F_p in jeden Ausgabekanal ein Datum schreibt und schließlich die Belegungszustände aller mit ihm verbundenen Kanäle umkehrt, wird Funktionsoperator genannt. Bezüglich des Datenzugriffs liegen demnach eine UND-Eingangs- sowie eine UND-Ausgangslogik vor.

Die zugehörige Transitionsfunktion entspricht daher dem Schaltverhalten des folgenden Teilstücks eines Synchronisationsgraphen [8] (vergl. Abb. 1):

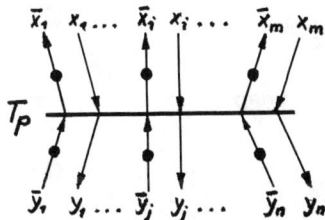

Abb. 2

Jeder Datenkanal k eines Operators wird hierin durch ein antiparalleles Kantenpaar $(\bar{k},k)$ dargestellt. Eine markierte $\bar{k}$-Kante bedeutet "Datenkanal k ist leer"; eine markierte k-Kante "Datenkanal k ist belegt". Mit dem wie in Abb.2 markierten Schaltelement läßt sich nun jedem azyklischen Datenflußgraph, dessen Knoten sämtlich Funktionsoperatoren sind, ein lebendiger und sicherer Synchronisationsgraph unterlegen. Da der im folgenden Beispiel angegebene Datenflußgraph Teilgraph einer größeren Struktur ist, gilt dies auch für den korrespondierenden Synchronisationsgraphen:

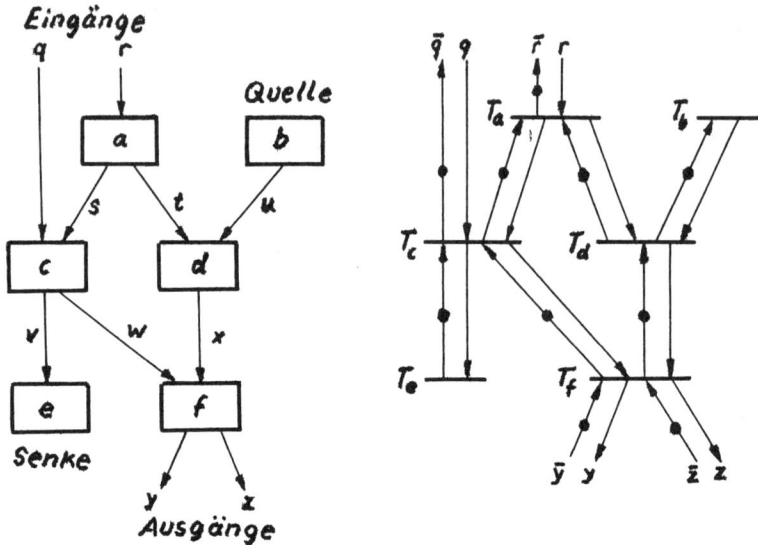

Abb. 3 Datenflußgraph und korrespondierender Synchronisationsgraph

Aus der Lebendigkeit und Sicherheit des unterliegenden Synchronisationsgraphen folgt unmittelbar, daß die möglichen Operationsfolgen des Datenflußgraphen verklemmungsfrei und die Wertefolgen in allen Datenkanälen deterministisch sind.

3.2 Steueroperatoren

Um Rechenabläufe mit datenabhängigen Verzweigungen und Wiederholungen - analog zu entsprechenden Anweisungen in "sequentiellen" Programmiersprachen - darstellen zu können, benötigt man Operatoren, die von dem für Funktionsoperatoren vereinbarten Verhalten abweichen. Während dort die Berechnung einer Funktion im Vordergrund steht und die Richtung des Datenflusses unveränderlich feststeht, ist hier der Funktionscharakter von untergeordneter Bedeutung, dagegen die Steuerung der Datenflußrichtung der entscheidende Aspekt. Operatoren mit diesen Eigenschaften werden als Steueroperatoren bezeichnet; ihre Eingangs- oder Ausgangslogik (oder beides) ist von UND verschieden. Mit anderen Worten: ein Steueroperator entnimmt während seiner Operation nicht allen Eingabekanälen Daten und/oder füllt nicht alle Ausgabekanäle mit Daten.

Dieser selektive Kanalzugriff hat mehrere Konsequenzen:

(1) Dem Steueroperator muß eine Information zugeführt werden, aufgrund der er die Kanalselektion vornimmt. Dies geschieht in fast allen

Fällen über einen zusätzlichen Eingabekanal, der hier <u>Steuerkanal</u> genannt werden soll. In einigen Datenflußmodellen haben Steuerkanäle andere Eigenschaften als Datenkanäle (in [1] und [2]), so daß zwei Kanaltypen betrachtet werden müssen, oder sie werden vom Modell nicht erfaßt (z.B. in [5]).

(2) Während die Determiniertheit der Wertefolgen in den Datenkanälen bei Beachtung der zulässigen Zustandsübergänge erhalten bleibt, kann schon für azyklische Datenflußgraphen, die Steueroperatoren enthalten, die Verklemmungsfreiheit der Operationsfolgen nicht mehr a priori garantiert werden. In [1] werden daher Prozeduren angegeben, die die Verklemmungsfreiheit für gewisse Strukturklassen entscheiden, in [2] und [5] wird das Problem mit Hilfe "wohlgeformter" Schemata konstruktiv gelöst, in [3] und [6] dagegen nicht behandelt.

Die Tabelle in Abb. 4 soll die hier informell und unter starken Vereinfachungen vorgenommene Modellcharakterisierung mit einer Gegenüberstellung abschließen. In der Spalte "Steueroperatoren" erscheinen nur Operatoren, die die hier erläuterten Eigenschaften aufweisen, und nicht immer die von den Urhebern als Steueroperatoren bezeichneten Elemente.

Modell nach	Steueroperatoren		Anzahl der Kanaltypen
	Bezeichnungen	Anzahl	
Rodriguez[1]	AND, OR, SELECTOR, JUNCTION, LOOPJUNCTION, LOOPOUTPUT	6	2
Dennis/ Fosseen[2]	AND, OR, T-GATE, F-GATE, MERGE	5	2
Adams[3]	COND ROUTE, BRANCH AND ROUTE, SELECT AND ROUTE, LOOP CONTROL	4	1
Bruno/ Altman[5]	SEQUENCE, ITERATION, SELECT	3	1
Kosinski[6]	OUTBOUND SWITCH, INBOUND SWITCH, LOOP, GATED PRESENCE	4	1

Abb. 4

4. Ein elementarer Steueroperator

Dem Entwurf des nachfolgend beschriebenen Steueroperators liegt die Überlegung zugrunde, daß man für die datenabhängige Kanalselektion zumindest zwei Operatoren benötigt, mit denen eine Ausgabe- und eine Eingabekanalselektion bezüglich zweier Kanäle dargestellt werden kann (Abb. 5 u. 6).

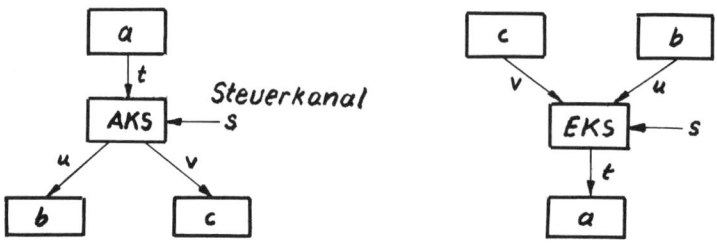

Abb. 5 Ausgabekanalselektion   Abb. 6 Eingabekanalselektion

Die Operatoren a, b und c repräsentieren drei paarweise disjunkte Datenflußgraphen, die in dieser Anordnung als Quellen bzw. Senken einzelner Kanaldaten fungieren. Die interne Struktur der Knoten AKS und EKS wird nun den Abbildungen 7 und 8

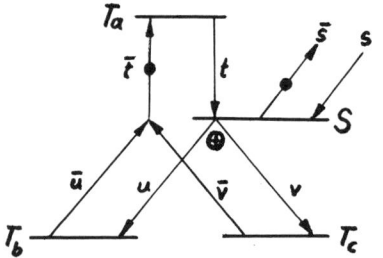 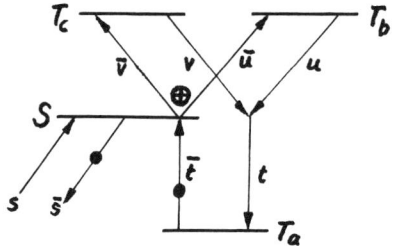

Abb. 7 Steueroperator AKS   Abb 8 Steueroperator EKS

entsprechend festgelegt. Sie unterscheidet sich von einem Petri-Netz nur durch die Verwendung einer Transition S mit <u>Exklusiv-Ausgangslogik</u> und hat die folgenden Eigenschaften:

1. Die Markierung im Innern von AKS(EKS) garantiert im Kontext der Abb.5 (Abb.**6**) Determiniertheit und Verklemmungsfreiheit.

2. Die beiden Steueroperatoren sind bezüglich ihrer Struktur identisch (180°-Drehung!). Sie unterscheiden sich nur durch die Anfangsmarkierung Es erscheint daher berechtigt, AKS und EKS nicht als zwei unterschiedliche Operatoren, sondern eher als zwei Verwendungsformen <u>eines</u> elementaren Steueroperators anzusehen.

3. Der Steuerkanal S arbeitet wie ein Datenkanal. Der über ihn einlaufende Datenwert wird als Entscheidungsinformation für S interpretiert.

4. Die Transition S beseitigt in AKS bei belegtem Kanal t (und in EKS bei leerem Kanal t) die Konfliktsituationen für T_b und T_c.

5. <u>Anwendungen</u>

Mit dem hier angegebenen elementaren Steueroperator lassen sich nun beliebige Operatoren definieren, deren Funktion eine Kanalselektion einschließt; insbesondere sind n-Kanalselektoren leicht realisierbar.

Die mit EKS- und AKS-Operatoren aufgebauten Verzweigungs- und Iterationsschemata enthalten gegenüber den in [2] angegebenen

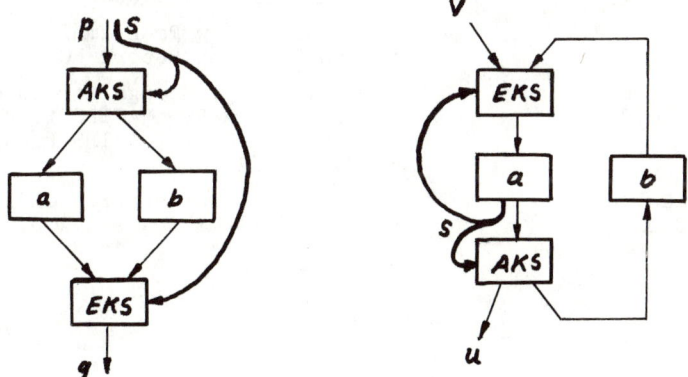

Abb. 9 Verzweigungsschema   Abb. 1o Iterationsschema
                              (in EKS ist $\bar{v}$ markiert!)

Schemata insgesamt eine geringere Anzahl operator-interner Transitionen und Kanäle. Darüberhinaus hat die Tatsache, daß anstelle der in der Tabelle für ein bestimmtes Modell angegebenen Anzahl von Steuerknoten und Kanaltypen - neben den gewöhnlichen Funktionsoperatoren - <u>ein</u> Steueroperatorentyp und <u>ein</u> Kanaltyp ausreichen, im Hinblick auf spätere Implementierungen auch eine praktische Bedeutung, weil für jeden Operator soft- oder hardwaremäßig die m+n Adressen seiner Vorgänger und Nachfolger sowie ein Ereigniszähler für die interne Transition realisiert werden müssen.

Literatur

[1] RODRIGUEZ, J.E. "A graph model for parallel computations". PhD Thesis, Massachusetts Institut of Technology, 1967

[2] DENNIS, J.B.; FOSSEEN, J.B. "Introduction to Data Flow Schemata". Project MAC, Computations Structures Group Memo 81, June 1973

[3] ADAMS, D.A. "A model for parallel computations". In Parallel processor systems, technologies and applications, L.C. Hobbs, et al. (Eds.), Spartan Books, New York, 1970. 311-334

[4] LUCONI, F.L. "Asynchronous computational structures". PhD Thesis, Massachusetts Institut of Technology, 1968

[5] BRUNO, J.; ALTMAN, M. "A theory of asynchronous control networks ". IEEE Trans. on Computers C-2o (June 1971) 629-638

[6] KOSINSKI, P.R. "A Data Flow Programming Language". IBM Research Report RC 4264, March 1973

[7] TESLER, L.G.; ENEA, H.G. "A language design for concurrent processes". In Proc AFIPS 1968 Spring Joint Computer Conf., AFIPS Press, Montvale, N.J., 4o2-4o8

[8] GENRICH, H.J.; LAUTENBACH, K. "Synchronisationsgraphen". Acta Informatica Vol.2, 143-161, Springer Verlag, 1973

E-V-Schemata

Ein Ansatz zur formalen Behandlung paralleler Prozesse

Hans J. Becker, Hagen Vogel
Oberregionales Forschungsprogramm Informatik
Universität Bonn

Abstract
Parallel program schemata in the sense of Keller are extended to E-V-schemata. Comparison of Petri-nets and E-V-schemata yields some interesting results.

0. Einleitung

Um Beschreibung und Konzipierung (Design) von parallelen Prozessen und Prozessoren effektiv zu gestalten, wurden in den letzten Jahren teilweise recht unterschiedliche formale Theorien paralleler Prozesse entwickelt. So gibt es einerseits Modelle, die den Prozessablauf mittels lokaler Kontrolle steuern, z.B. Petrinetze, andererseits Modelle, die dies durch globale Kontrolle bewirken, wie parallele Programmschemata nach R.M.Keller. Unser Ansatz verbindet diese beiden Konzepte, indem er, von Keller ausgehend, die globale Kontrolle beibehält und den wechselseitigen Übergang von Beschreibung mittels globaler Kontrolle zu lokaler Kontrolle ermöglicht, wodurch auch die jeweiligen Ergebnisse der einen Theorie für die andere nutzbar werden.

Unser Ansatz muß - mehr als bei R.M.Keller - so angelegt sein, daß, wie bei Petrinetzen, mehrere Operationen gleichzeitig beendet werden und daß aus der Gesamtmenge der als nächste ausführbaren Operationen bestimmte Teilmengen als gleichzeitig ausführbar ausgenommen werden können, was durch eine Verbotsstruktur V geschieht.

Um Petrinetze einbeziehen, insbesondere simulieren zu können, werden diese mit einer Speicherstruktur versehen. Die angenommene Speicherstruktur muß mit dem Petrinetz verträglich sein, d.h. sie darf keine neuen Konflikte, z.B. durch undefinierte Speicherzustände, hinzufügen. Umgekehrt sollten die im Petrinetz bestehenden Konflikte sich auch in der Speicherstruktur niederschlagen. Konfliktlösungsstrategien, zumindest wenn sie als Funktion formulierbar sind, können unmittelbar in einem entscheidungsbedingten E-V-Schema mitausgedrückt werden.

1. E-V-Schemata

Sei S eine abzählbare Menge. Eine endliche, nicht-leere Menge
Op = {a,b,...} heißt Operatorenmenge über dem Speicher S, falls gilt:

a) jedem a∈Op sind endliche Teilmengen D(a) und R(a) von S zugeordnet.
   D(a) ⊆ S heißt <u>Eingabe-</u> oder <u>Definitionsbereich</u> von a.
   R(a) ⊆ S heißt <u>Ausgabe-</u> oder <u>Bildbereich</u> von a.
   Sp = (D(a),R(a))$_{a∈Op}$ heißt <u>Speicherstruktur</u> der Operatorenmenge Op.
b) jedem a∈Op ist eine endliche, nicht-leere Menge
   $\Sigma(a) = \{a_1,...,a_{k(a)}\}$, $k(a) \in \mathbb{N}$ zugeordnet. $\Sigma(a)$ heißt Menge der
   <u>Terminierungen</u> von a.

Die Menge {Cond(C)|C ⊆ Op} heißt <u>Bedingungsraum</u> für Op, wobei Cond(C)
für die Bedingung steht, daß die Operatoren a∈C ausführbar sind.
Die Menge {Event(C_t)|$C_t \in \Gamma(C) \wedge C \subseteq Op$} heißt Ereignisraum für Op mit
$\Gamma(C) = \{C_t | C_t = \{a^1_{i_1},...,a^n_{i_n}\} \wedge 1 \leq i_j \leq k(a^j) \wedge 1 \leq j \leq n\}$ für $C = \{a^1,...,a^n\}$.
Event(C_t) steht für das <u>Ereignis</u>, daß die Operatoren $a^j \in C$ parallel aus-
geführt werden und die Terminierung $a^j_{i_j} \in \Sigma(a^j)$ liefern.

Ausgehend von der Vorstellung, daß Operationen, die gleichzeitig arbeiten und gemeinsame Speicherplätze - außer gemeinsamen Eingabespeicher-
plätzen - besitzen, im allgemeinen zu undefinierten Speicherzuständen
führen, werden die folgenden Einschränkungen von Ereignis- und Bedingungs-
raum definiert:
Sei $\Gamma(2^{Op}) = \bigcup \{\Gamma(C) | C \subseteq Op\}$.
Ein Ereignis Event(C_t), $C_t \in \Gamma(2^{Op})$ heißt <u>Speicherstruktur-verträglich</u>,
falls gilt:
$\bigwedge_{a_i,b_j} a_i,b_j \in C_t \Rightarrow R(a) \cap D(b) = R(b) \cap D(a) = R(a) \cap R(b) = \emptyset$.
Die Menge der Speicherstruktur-verträglichen Ereignisse wird mit $\mathcal{E}$
bezeichnet.
Die Bedingung Cond(C) mit C ⊆ Op heißt Speicherstruktur-verträglich,
falls Event(C_t) für ein $C_t \in \Gamma(C)$ Speicherstruktur-verträglich ist. (Es
gilt: Event(C_t) Sp.-verträglich => $\bigwedge_{C'_t \in \Gamma(C)}$ Event(C'_t) Sp.-verträglich.)
$\mathcal{L}$ bezeichnet die Menge der Sp.-verträglichen Bedingungen. Für Event(C_t)
können wir im folgenden kurz C_t setzen. Ebenso verwenden wir statt
Cond(C) im folgenden stets C, da eine Verwechselung der Bedingung Cond(C)
mit der Operatoren(teil-)menge C nicht zu befürchten ist.
Es gilt offensichtlich $\Gamma(\mathcal{L}) = \mathcal{E}$.

<u>Definition</u>: $\Phi_V = (\Phi,V)$ mit einer partiellen Funktion $\Phi : \mathcal{E}^* \longrightarrow 2^{Op}$
und einem zweistelligen Prädikat $V \equiv (V_1 \vee V_2)$ über $\Gamma(2^{Op})^* \times 2^{Op}$ mit
$\neg V(X,a)$ und $(V(X,C) \Rightarrow V(X,C \cup C'))$ für beliebige $a \in Op$, $C,C' \subseteq Op$,
$X \in \Gamma(2^{Op})^*$, heißt <u>Ereignisschema mit Verboten</u>, E-V-Schema, falls gilt:
1) $\bigwedge_{X \in \mathcal{E}^*} \bigwedge_{C \in \mathcal{L}} \bigwedge_{C_t \in \Gamma(C)} (<\Phi(X \cdot C_t)> <=> C \subseteq \Phi(X) \wedge \neg V(X,C))$

2) $\bigwedge_{X \in \mathcal{E}^*} \bigwedge_{C \in \mathcal{L}} \bigwedge_{C_t \in \Gamma(C)}$ $(<\Phi(X \cdot C_t)> \Rightarrow \Phi(X) - (C \cup K(X,C)) \subseteq \Phi(X \cdot C_t)$

mit $K(X,C) = \{a \mid a \in Op \wedge V_2(X, C \cup \{a\})\}$. Zur Notation: $<\Phi(X)> <=> X \in dom \, \Phi$.
Φ heißt <u>Funktion des E-V-Schemas</u> Φ_V. V heißt <u>Verbotsstruktur</u> von Φ_V.
Φ ordnet also einem (endlichen) Wort $X = X' \cdot C_t$ aus $\mathcal{E}^*$, d.h. einer Folge von zulässigen Ereignissen, eine Bedingung $\Phi(X) \subseteq Op$ zu, die dadurch gegeben wird, daß bei Bedingung $\Phi(X')$ das Ereignis C_t eingetreten ist.

Ist die Verbotsstruktur <u>V trivial</u>, d.h. gilt:
$(<\Phi(X)> \wedge C \subseteq \Phi(X)) \Rightarrow \neg V(X,C)$, dann heißt Φ_V <u>E-Schema</u>, d.h. Φ enthält schon die gesamte Information.

Sei $C \subseteq Op$; sei $X \in dom \, \Phi$, und gilt: $C \subseteq \Phi(X) \wedge (C \notin \mathcal{L} \vee V(X,C))$, so heißt (C,X) <u>Konflikt</u>. Gilt $(C \subseteq \Phi(X) \wedge C \notin \mathcal{L})$, so sprechen wir von einem <u>Speicher-(bedingten) Konflikt</u>.

Wir definieren noch folgenden Sonderfall:

<u>Definition</u>: Ein E-V-Schema Φ_V über Op heißt <u>entscheidungsfrei</u>, falls
gilt: $\bigwedge_{X \in \mathcal{E}^*} \bigwedge_{a_i \in \Gamma(Op)}$ $(X \cdot \{a_i\} \in dom \, \Phi \Rightarrow |k(a)| = 1)$.

Die Einschränkung von Φ auf Sp.-verträgliche Ereignisse scheint uns erforderlich zu sein, da das gleichzeitige Ausführen von in Speicherkonflikt stehenden Operationen notwendigerweise undefinierte Speicherzustände zur Folge haben muß. Darüber hinaus ist der Ausschluß von Ereignissen C_t mit $a,b \in C$ und $(R(a) \cap D(b)) \cup (D(a) \cap R(b)) = \emptyset$ insofern unwesentlich, als durch Einführen von neuen "Zwischen"-Speicherplätzen und zusätzlichen Operationen (mit reiner Transportfunktion) das alte Schema konfliktfrei bzgl. dieser Speicherkonflikte beschrieben werden kann.

<u>Definition</u>: $\Psi = (Q, q_0, f, g)$ heißt <u>Realisierung</u> des E-V-Schema Φ_V über Op, falls gilt:
1) Q abzählbare, nicht-leere Menge (<u>Kontrollzustände</u>),
2) $q_0 \in Q$ (<u>Anfangszustand</u>),
3) $f : Q \times \mathcal{E}^* \longrightarrow Q$, f partiell, wobei gilt:
   a) $f(q,e) = q$ (e leeres Wort über $\mathcal{E}^*$)
   ba) $<f(q, X \cdot C_t)> <=> \bigvee_{q' \in Q} f(q,X) = q' \wedge <f(q', C_t)>$
   bb) $<f(q, X \cdot C_t)> \Rightarrow f(q, X \cdot C_t) = f(f(q,X), C_t)$
   (f ist kanonische Erweiterung der auf $Q \times \mathcal{E}$ definierten Teilabbildung)
4) $g : Q \longrightarrow 2^{Op}$
5) $g(q_0) = \Phi(e)$
6) $\bigwedge_{X \in \mathcal{E}^*} \bigwedge_{C_t \in \mathcal{E}}$ $(<\Phi(X \cdot C_t)> <=> <f(q_0, X \, C_t)>$
7) $\bigwedge_{X \in \mathcal{E}^*} \bigwedge_{C_t \in \mathcal{E}}$ $(<f(q_0, X \cdot C_t)> \Rightarrow \Phi(X \cdot C_t) = g(f(q_0, X \cdot C_t)))$

Definition: Eine Struktur Ψ heißt E-V-Realisierung, falls es ein E-V-
Schema Φ_V gibt, so daß Ψ Realisierung von Φ_V ist.

Wie bei endlichen Automaten definiert man für die Realisierung einen
Realisierungsgraphen durch die Zuordnung : Knoten <-> Zustände, markierte Kanten <-> Ereignisse, Markierung von Knoten <-> Bedingungen g(q).
Keller schließt aus, daß mehrere Operationen echt gleichzeitig beendet
werden, da die Funktion Φ nur für Folgen von Terminierungen einzelner
Operationen definiert ist. Infolgedessen besitzen die Realisierungen
von Keller-Schemata Zustandsübergänge nur für einzelne Terminierungs-
symbole.
In unserem Modell ist die Funktion Φ für Folgen von Mengen von Terminie-
rungssymbolen definiert, d.h. wir lassen die gleichzeitige Beendigung
von mehreren Operationen zu, da auch bei Petri-Netzen Mutationen, die
eine Markierung in eine neue Markierung überführen, aus mehreren Transitionen bestehen können.
Die Darstellung von Konflikten ist bei Keller auf rein speicherbedingte
Konflikte beschränkt und mit einer nicht-deterministischen Sequentialisierung der im Konflikt befindlichen Operationen verbunden.
Die Hinzunahme der Verbotsstruktur in unserem Modell erlaubt auch solche
Konflikte darzustellen, in denen die im Konflikt befindlichen Ereignisse nur alternativ ausgeführt werden.

Korollar: Sei $\Phi_V = (\Phi,V)$ ein E-V-Schema, $V \equiv (V_1 \vee V_2)$. Sei V_2 trivial
und gelte für beliebige $X \varepsilon \mathcal{E}^*$ und $C \varepsilon \mathcal{L}$: $|C| \geq 2 <=> V_1(X,C)$, dann ist
Φ_V ein paralleles Programm-Schema nach Keller.

Für eine Struktur Ψ, die Punkt 1)-4) der vorigen Definition erfüllt, gilt:

Lemma: a) Φ ist E-V-Realisierung, falls gilt:

$\bigwedge_{X \varepsilon \mathcal{E}^*} \bigwedge_{C \varepsilon \mathcal{L}} \bigwedge_{C_t \varepsilon \Gamma(C)} \bigwedge_{q \varepsilon Q}$ $(f(q_0,X) = q \wedge <f(q,C_t)> =>$

(1) $(C \subseteq g(q) \wedge \bigwedge_{C' \subseteq C} \bigwedge_{C'_t \varepsilon \Gamma(C')} <f(q,C'_t)>) \wedge$

(2) $(g(q)-(C \cup K(q,C)) \subseteq g(f(q,C_t))))$ mit $K(q,C)=\{a_i | a \varepsilon g(q) \wedge \neg <f(q,C_t \cup \{a_i\})>\}$

Definition: Seien $\Phi_V = (\Phi,V)$ und $\Phi'_V = (\Phi',V')$ E-V-Schemata mit der Eigenschaft $\Phi = \Phi'$, dann heißen die Verbotsstrukturen V,V' R-äquivalent
($V \equiv_R V'$), falls gilt: $C \subseteq \Phi(X) \wedge C \varepsilon \mathcal{L} => (V(X,C) <=> V'(X,C))$.

Korollar: Jede E-V-Realisierung Ψ definiert ein bis auf R-Äquivalenz
eindeutiges E-V-Schema Φ_V.

Lemma: Seien Φ_V^1, Φ_V^2 E-V-Schemata. Dann gilt:

dom Φ^1 = dom Φ^2 => ($\Phi^1 = \Phi^2 \wedge V^1 \equiv_R V^2$).

<u>Korollar</u>: Sind Φ_V und Φ'_V E-V-Schemata mit gleicher Funktion Φ und R-äquivalenten Verbotsstrukturen, dann gilt für beliebige Ψ : Ψ ist Realisierung von Φ_V <=> Ψ ist Realisierung von Φ'_V.

Durch Zuordnung von konkreten Wertebereichen für die Speicherplätze und durch Interpretation der Operatoren durch konkrete Funktionen über diesen Wertebereichen wird aus einem E-V-Schema die formale Beschreibung eines konkreten parallelen Prozesses.

<u>Definition</u>: $I = (W, w_0, F, G)$ heißt <u>Interpretation</u> der Operatorenmenge Op, falls gilt:
1) $W = \underset{s \in S}{\times} W(s)$ mit Mengen $W(s)$. W heißt <u>Universum</u>, $W(s)$ heißt <u>Wertebereich</u> des Speicherplatzes s.
2) $w_0 \in W, w_0$ heißt <u>Anfangsspeicherbelegung</u>
3) $F = (F_a)_{a \in Op}$ mit Funktionen
   $$F_a : \underset{s \in D(a)}{\times} W(s) \longrightarrow \underset{s \in R(a)}{\times} W(s).$$
   F_a heißt <u>Datenfunktion</u> von a.
4) $G = (G_a)_{a \in Op}$ mit Funktionen
   $$G_a : \underset{s \in D(a)}{\times} W(s) \longrightarrow \Sigma(a) = \{a_1, \ldots, a_{k(a)}\}.$$
   G_a heißt <u>Entscheidungsfunktion</u> von a.

Int(Op) bezeichnet die Menge der Interpretationen über Op, $\Pi_A(W)$ die Projektion von W auf die Komponenten von $A \subseteq S$.

<u>Definition</u>: Sei $\Psi = (Q, q_0, f, g)$ eine E-V-Realisierung über einer Operatorenmenge Op und sei $I = (W, w_0, F, G)$ Interpretation dieser Operatorenmenge. Dann heißt:
1) (q_0, w_0) <u>Anfangskonfiguration</u>
2) $(q', w') = (q, w) \cdot C_t$ heißt <u>Folgekonfiguration</u> von (q, w), falls:
   1. $<f(q, C_t)> \wedge f(q, C_t) = q'$
   2. $\underset{a \in C}{\wedge} G_a(\Pi_{D(a)}(w)) = a_i \in C_t$
   3. $w'(s) = \begin{cases} w(s) & \text{falls } s \notin \bigcup \{R(a) | a \in C\} \\ \Pi_s(F_a(\Pi_{D(a)}(w))) & \text{falls } s \in R(a) \text{ für ein } a \in C \end{cases}$

(q, w) heißt <u>Konfiguration</u>, falls (q, w) entweder Anfangskonfiguration oder Folgekonfiguration einer Konfiguration ist.
Konf(Ψ, I) bezeichnet die Menge aller Konfigurationen der Realisierung Ψ bezüglich der Interpretation I.
Die Erweiterung der partiellen Abbildung $\cdot$: Konf$\times \mathcal{C} \longrightarrow$ Konf zu Konf$\times \mathcal{C}^* \longrightarrow$ Konf geschieht in kanonischer Weise.

Definition: Sei Ψ eine E-V-Realisierung über Op, I Interpretation von Op. Sei $\mathcal{L}^\omega$ die Menge der Wörter über $\mathcal{L}$ von unendlicher Länge und sei $\leq$ die Halbordnung über $\hat{\mathcal{L}} := \mathcal{L}^* \cup \mathcal{L}^\omega$ definiert durch:
$$Y \leq X \iff \bigvee_{Z \in \hat{\mathcal{L}}} Y \cdot Z \leq X \text{ für } Y \in \mathcal{L}^*, X \in \hat{\mathcal{L}}.$$
Dann heißt $X \in \hat{\mathcal{L}}$ I-Ausrechnung der Realisierung Ψ, falls gilt:
1) $\bigwedge_{Y \in \mathcal{L}^*} Y \leq X \Rightarrow <(q_0, w_0) \cdot Y>$
2) $X \in \mathcal{L}^* \Rightarrow g(f(q_0, X)) = \emptyset$
3) $X \in \mathcal{L}^\omega \Rightarrow \bigwedge_{a \in Op} \bigwedge_{Y \leq X} ((\bigwedge_{Z \in \mathcal{L}^*} Y \leq Z < X \Rightarrow a \varepsilon g(f(q_0, Z)))$
   $\Rightarrow \bigvee_{Z' \in \mathcal{L}^*} \bigvee_{C_t \in \mathcal{L}} (a \varepsilon C \wedge Y \leq Z' \cdot C_t < X))$

(3) heißt endliche Verzögerungseigenschaft.)

$P(\Psi, I) \subseteq \hat{\mathcal{L}}$ bezeichnet die Menge der I-Ausrechnungen der Realisierung Ψ.
Sei Pref $(\Psi, I) := \{X | <(q_0, w_0) \cdot X>, X \in \mathcal{L}^*\}$, dann gilt:

Korollar: Pref $(\Psi, I) = \{Y | \bigvee_{X \in \hat{\mathcal{L}}} X \in P(\Psi, I) \wedge Y \leq X\}$
d.h. Pref (Ψ, I) ist die Menge der Anfangsstücke der I-Ausrechnungen.

Lemma: Für Realisierungen Ψ_1, Ψ_2 eines E-V-Schema Φ_V gilt für beliebige Interpretationen $I \in Int(Op)$: $P(\Psi_1, I) = P(\Psi_2, I)$.
Damit auch: $Pref(\Psi_1, I) = Pref(\Psi_2, I)$.
Mit $P(\Psi) := \bigcup \{P(\Psi, I) | I \in Int(Op)\}$ und $Pref(\Psi)$ analog gilt weiter:
$P(\Psi_1) = P(\Psi_2)$ und $Pref(\Psi_1) = Pref(\Psi_2)$.

Deshalb kann man für E-V-Schemata Φ_V und eine beliebige Realisierung Ψ von Φ_V definieren:
Definition: $P(\Phi, I) := P(\Psi, I), Pref(\Phi, I) := Pref(\Psi, I)$, etc.

Satz: Für zwei E-V-Schemata Φ_V^1 und Φ_V^2 sind folgende Aussagen äquivalent:
 (a) $P(\Phi_V^1) = P(\Phi_V^2)$
 (b) $Pref(\Phi_V^1) = Pref(\Phi_V^2)$
 (c) $\bigwedge_{I \in Int(Op)} P(\Phi_V^1, I) = P(\Phi_V^2, I)$
 (d) $\bigwedge_{I \in Int(Op)} Pref(\Phi_V^1, I) = Pref(\Phi_V^2, I)$

Nach Definition von $Pref(\Phi_V)$ gilt: $Pref(\Phi_V, I) \subseteq dom \Phi_V$
Die Umkehrung gilt für entscheidungsfreie E-V-Schemata, nicht aber allgemein:

Lemma: Für ein entscheidungsfreies Schema Φ_V gilt bei beliebiger Interpretation $I \in Int(Op)$: $Pref(\Phi_V, I) = dom \Phi_V$.

Korollar: $Pref(\Phi_V, I_1) = Pref(\Phi_V, I_2) = Pref(\Phi_V)$.
$P(\Phi_V, I_1) = P(\Phi_V, I_2) = P(\Phi_V)$.

Korollar: Für zwei entscheidungsfreie E-V-Schemata Φ_V und Φ_V' gilt:
$P(\Phi_V) = P(\Phi_V') <=> (\Phi = \Phi' \wedge V \equiv_R V')$

2. Simulation

Sei $PN = ((S, T, \rho_1, \rho_2), m)$ ein __Petrinetz__.

Zu den Begriffen: Stellen (S), Transitionen (T), Eingangs-, Ausgangsstellen, Transitionen, schaltbereite Transition, schaltbare Transition, Markierung, Nachfolgemarkierung, tote Markierung, Markierungsklasse M, B-sicheres Petrinetz. etc., vgl. /G/ und /L/.

Definition: Sei PN Petrinetz mit der Markierung m. Eine Menge von Transitionen $T' \subseteq T$ heißt dann __m-schaltbar__, wenn es eine Markierung m' gibt, so daß gilt: (m,T',m') ist Mutationsregel (m[T'>m'), d.h. durch nebenläufiges Schalten der Transitionen $t \in T'$ geht die Markierung m in m' über (vgl. /G/, /L/).

Definition: $(m_i)_{i \in N'}$ (mit $m_i \in \mathbb{N}^P$ und N' nicht notwendig endliches Anfangsstück der natürlichen Zahlen $\mathbb{N}$) heißt __Markierungsfolge__ von PN, falls $m_0 = m$ ist und es eine Folge von Transitionenmengen $(T_{i+1})_{i \in N'}$ gibt, so daß gilt: $m_i[T_{i+1} > m_{i+1}$ für $i=0$, $i+1 \in N'$. Eine solche Folge $(T_{i+1})_{i \in N'}$ heißt (Anfangs-)__Schaltfolge__ des Petrinetzes.
$(T_{i+1})_{i \in N'}$ heißt __abgeschlossene Schaltfolge__,
a) für endliches N', falls $m_{N'}$ tot ist,
b) für unendliches N', falls jedes endliche Anfangsstück der Folge Anfangsschaltfolge ist und falls gilt:
$$\bigwedge_{t \in T} \bigwedge_{i \in N'} (\bigwedge_{j \in N'} (i \leq j => \{t\} \text{ ist } m_j\text{-schaltbar}) => \bigvee_{k \in N'} (i \leq k \wedge t \in T_k))$$

Im folgenden unterscheiden wir nicht zwischen der Schaltfolge $(T_{i+1})_{i \in N'}$ und dem Wort $x \in (2^T)^* \cup (2^T)^\omega$, dessen i-tes Zeichen T_i ist.
Bei unserem Vergleich von Petrinetzen und E-V-Schemata ordnen wir Transitionen und Operatoren einander zu. Wir definieren daher __Speicherstruktur__ Sp einer Transitionenmenge T eines Petrinetzes PN = $((S, T, \rho_1, \rho_2), m)$ wie oben für Op:
$Sp = (D(t), R(t))_{t \in T}$ mit $D(t) \subseteq M, R(t) \subseteq M$ für eine abzählbare Menge von Speicherplätzen M.

Definition: Sp heißt zulässig bezüglich PN, falls für $t,t' \in T$ gilt:
$$\bigwedge_{m \in M} \bigwedge_{T' \subseteq T} (t,t') \in T' \wedge T' \text{ ist m-schaltbar} \Rightarrow$$
$$D(t) \cap R(t') = R(t) \cap D(t') = R(t) \cap R(t') = \emptyset.$$

(PN,Sp) heißt <u>Petrinetz mit Speicherstruktur</u>, falls $Sp = (D(t),R(t))_{t \in T}$ zulässig bezüglich PN ist.

Definition: Sei $(PN,Sp) = (((S,T,\rho_1,\rho_2),m),(D(t),R(t))_{t \in T})$ Petrinetz mit Speicherstruktur, $\Phi_V = (\Phi,V)$ E-V-Schema über der Operatorenmenge Op. Φ_V <u>simuliert</u> (PN,Sp), falls gilt:
es gibt eine Abbildung $\lambda : Op \longrightarrow T$, die man kanonisch erweitert zu
$\lambda : \Gamma(2^{Op}) \longrightarrow 2^T$ durch $\lambda(C_t) = \bigcup\{\lambda(a) | a \in C\}$ und $\lambda : \widehat{\Gamma(2^{Op})} \longrightarrow \widehat{(2^T)}$
durch $\lambda((a_i)_{i \in N'}) = (\lambda(a_i))_{i \in N'}$, mit der Eigenschaft:
$\lambda(X)$ für $X \in \widehat{\Gamma(2^{Op})}$ ist abgeschlossene Schaltfolge von PN genau dann, wenn X Ausrechnung von Φ_V ist.

Satz: Jedes Petrinetz mit Speicherstruktur ist durch ein entscheidungs-freies E-V-Schema simulierbar.

$PN = ((S,T,\rho_1,\rho_2),m_0)$ induziert in folgender Weise eine Struktur:
$\Psi_{PN} = (M,m_0,f,g)$ mit:
M = Markierungsklasse von PN, m_0 (Anfangs-)Markierung von PN,
$f : M \times 2^T \longrightarrow M$, f partiell mit:
$<f(m,T')> \iff T'$ ist m-schaltbar,
$(<f(m,T')> \wedge m[T'>m') \Rightarrow f(m,T') = m'$;
$g : M \longrightarrow 2^T$, g total, wobei gilt: $g(m) = \{t | t \text{ ist m-schaltbar}\}$.

Satz: Für beliebiges Petrinetz mit Speicherstruktur (PN,Sp) ist Ψ_{PN} kommutative E-V-Realisierung.
Das eindeutig bestimmte E-V-Schema Φ_V ist entscheidungsfrei.
Dabei heißt Ψ <u>kommutativ</u>, falls gilt:
$$\bigwedge_{q \in Q} \bigwedge_{C_t,C_t' \in \mathfrak{C}} ((<f(q,C_t \cdot C_t')> \wedge <f(q,C_t' \cdot C_t)> \Rightarrow f(q,C_t \cdot C_t') = f(q,C_t' \cdot C_t))$$

Korollar: Für konfliktfreie Petrinetze mit Speicherstruktur ist Ψ_{PN} E-V-Realisierung mit trivialer Verbotsstruktur.

Lemma: Für beliebige Petrinetze mit Speicherstruktur ist die Verbotsstruktur von Ψ_{PN} nicht stets trivial.

Führt man für Petrinetze Interpretationen ein, analog zum Vorgehen bei E-V-Schemata, so zeigt sich, daß die Entscheidungsfunktionen $(G_t)_{t \in T}$ sinnvollerweise konstant anzunehmen sind, d.h. die den Ausrechnungen entsprechenden Schaltfolgen interpretationsunabhängig sind, was hier durch Simulierbarkeit mittels entscheidungsfreier Schemata zum Ausdruck kommt.

Definiert man analog zur Simulation von Petrinetzen durch E-V-Schemata die Simulation von E-V-Schemata durch Petrinetze und nennt man eine E-V-Realisierung bzw. ein E-V-Schema streng-kausal, falls die Operatoren nicht durch verschiedene minimale Ereignisse ausführbar werden, dann läßt sich der folgende Satz aussprechen:

<u>Satz</u>: Sei $\Psi = (Q, q_0, f, g)$ zustandsendliche, entscheidungsfreie, konfliktfreie, kommutative, streng-kausale Realisierung des E-V-Schema Φ_V. Dann gibt es ein Petrinetz, das Φ_V simuliert.

Die Kommutativität ist, anders als z.B. Konfliktfreiheit, eine notwendige Voraussetzung für die hier gewählte Form der Simulation von E-V-Schemata durch Petrinetze.

Sei $q_0, \ldots q_n$ der Weg im Realisierungsgraphen von Ψ, für den gilt: $q_{i+1} = f(q_i, g(q_i))$ für $i=o, \ldots n-1$ und $g(q_n) = \emptyset$. Dann definieren wir eine Folge von Petrinetzen $PN(-1), PN(0), PN(1), \ldots PN(n)$ wie folgt:

$PN(-1) := ((\{s^{-1}\}, \{t^{-1}\}, \rho_1^{-1}, \rho_2^{-1}), m^{-1})$ mit $\rho_1^{-1} = \{(s^{-1}, t^{-1})\}, \rho_2^{-1} = \emptyset$,

$\quad m^{-1} = \{(s^{-1}, 1)\}$

$PN(0) := ((S^0, T^0, \rho_1^0, \rho_2^0), m^0)$ mit:

$\quad S^0 = S^{-1} \cup \{s_a^0 \mid a \in g(q_0)\}$

$\quad T^0 = T^{-1} \cup \{t_a^0 \mid a \in g(q_0)\}$

$\quad \rho_1^0 = \rho_1^{-1} \cup \{(s_a^0, t_a^0) \mid a \in g(q_0)\}$

$\quad \rho_2^0 = \rho_2^{-1} \cup \{(s_a^0, t^{-1}) \mid a \in g(q_0)\}$

$\quad m^0 = m^{-1} \cup \{(s_a^0, 0) \mid a \in g(q_0)\}$

$PN(i+1) := ((S^{i+1}, T^{i+1}, \rho_1^{i+1}, \rho_2^{i+1}), m^{i+1})$ mit:

$\quad S^{i+1} = S^i \cup \bigcup \{S_a^{i+1} \mid a \in g(q_{i+1})\}$

$\quad T^{i+1} = T^i \cup \{t_a^{i+1} \mid a \in g(q_{i+1})\}$

$\quad \rho_1^{i+1} = \rho_1^i \cup \bigcup \{S_a^{i+1} \times \{t_a^{i+1}\} \mid a \in g(q_{i+1})\}$

$\quad \rho_2^{i+1} = \rho_2^i \cup \{(s_a^{t_b^i}, t_b^i) \mid b \in g(q_i) \wedge a \in g(q_{i+1})\}$

$\quad S_a^{i+1} = \{s_a^{t_b^i} \mid \bigvee_{C \subseteq Op} (a \in g(f(q_i, C)) \wedge \bigwedge_{c \in C} a \notin g(f(q_i, C-\{c\})) \wedge b \in C)\}$.

$\quad m^{i+1} = m^i \cup (S^{i+1} - S^i) \times \{0\}$

für $i=1, \ldots n-2$

$PN(n) := ((S^n, T^n, \rho_1^n, \rho_2^n), m^n)$ mit:

$S^n = S^{n-1} \cup \{s^n\}, T^n = T^{n-1}, \rho_1^n = \rho_1^{n-1}, m^n = m^{n-1} \cup \{(s^n, 0)\}$

$\rho_2^n = \rho_2^{n-1} \cup \{s^n\} \times (T^n - T^{n-2}).$

Satz: Das so konstruierte Petrinetz PN(n) simuliert Ψ.

3. Schlußbemerkung

Durch Fortführung obiger Untersuchungen, wie Charakterisierung der Klassen der E-V-simulierbaren Petrinetze und vor allem der PN-simulierbaren E-V-Schemata, sollen Zusammenhänge zwischen lokaler und globaler Kontrolle aufgezeigt werden.
Eine weitere durch Simulierbarkeit induzierte Klasseneinteilung liefert einen Äquivalenzbegriff für Schemata und Petrinetze, der wie andere wichtige Eigenschaften und Probleme, zum Beispiel Parallelitätsgrad von Schemata und Erhöhung von Parallelität (maximal parallelism) oder verschiedene Konfliktstrukturen und deren Auswirkungen, noch eingehender zu untersuchen bleibt.

Literatur:

/G/ H.J.Genrich: Einfache nicht-sequentielle Prozesse
Berichte der GMD Nr. 37, Bonn, 1971

/K/ R.M.Keller: Parallel Program Schemata and Maximal Parallelism
I.Fundamental Results
J.A.C.M., 20, July 73, pp. 514-537

/L/ K.Lautenbach: Exakte Bedingungen der Lebendigkeit für eine Klasse von Petri-Netzen
Berichte der GMD Nr. 82, Bonn, 1973

ZUR THEORIE UNENDLICHER PARALLELPROZESSOREN

F. Schwenkel

Institut für Informatik, Universität Hamburg

<u>Zusammenfassung</u>. Ein berechenbarkeitstheoretisches Modell paralleler Prozesse wird untersucht, bei dem die Koordination der laufenden Prozesse nur durch den lokalen Datenverkehr erfolgt. Dabei wird keinerlei Steuerinformation ausgetauscht, sondern nur die zu bearbeitenden Daten und daraus berechneten Resultate. Eine notwendige und hinreichende "Stabilitätsbedingung" (Einschränkung des Verhaltens der Einzelprozesse) wird abgeleitet, unter der das Koordinationsverfahren funktioniert. Das Koordinationsverfahren läßt sich mit jeder Strategie zur Zuteilung von Prozessoren kombinieren. Die zugrundegelegte Prozeßstruktur ist strikt hierarchisch; jeder Prozeß kommuniziert nur mit seinem unmittelbar übergeordneten Prozeß (von dem er gestartet wurde), sowie mit seinen unmittelbaren Unterprozessen (die von ihm gestartet wurden). Näher behandelt wird der Fall eines unendlichen Vorrats an Prozessoren, der es jedem laufenden Prozeß erlaubt, jederzeit beliebig viele Unterprozesse in Gang zu setzen. Dabei wurde ein Instruktionssatz und eine Programmierungsmethode zugrundegelegt, die es erlauben, LISP-artige Programmstrukturen zu realisieren, erweitert um globale Variable mit einmaliger Wertzuweisung.

1. <u>Einleitung</u>. Die Theorie und Praxis der Parallelprogrammierung hat sich auf dem komplexen Hintergrund der (Betriebs-)Systemprogrammierung entwickelt. Sie behandelt Probleme, die sich in der Systemprogrammierung - oder ganz allgemein in der höheren Programmierungstechnik - im Zusammenhang mit parallelen Prozessen ergeben. Die zugehörigen Ausdrucksmittel und Denkmodelle stammen einerseits aus dem Bereich der Programmsprachen (mit Sprachelementen zur Spezifikation und Kontrolle paralleler Prozesse), andererseits aus der Automaten- und Graphentheorie (zur abstrakten Modellierung und Verifikation von Systemen paralleler Prozesse). Demgegenüber ist uns kein Versuch bekannt, die Parallelprogrammierung aus einfachsten berechenbarkeitstheoretischen Grundlagen zu entwickeln, so wie wir die sequentielle Programmierung aus der Berechenbarkeitstheorie entwickeln können und wohl auch sollen. Der vorliegende Beitrag wird diesen Weg ein Stück weit verfolgen.

2. <u>Berechenbare Funktionen</u>. Unser Ausgangspunkt soll eine Systematik der berechenbaren Funktionen sein. Einfachheitshalber beschränken wir uns auf zahlentheoretische Funktionen; berechenbare Funktionen höherer Datentypen (Zeichenketten, Listen usf.) lassen sich darauf zurückführen oder analog dazu behandeln. Man erhält sämtliche berechenbaren (zahlentheoretischen) Funktionen aus einigen wenigen <u>Ausgangsfunktionen</u> mit Hilfe der Operatoren der <u>Substitution</u> und der <u>Rekursion</u> (s. Tabelle):[1]

---

[1] Mathematische Einzelheiten sind für die informale Behandlung in diesem Beitrag unwesentlich.

Elementarmanipulation	Zugehörige Ausgangsfunktion
Hinschreiben der Null	Konstante Funktion mit dem Wert 0
Kopieren eines Datums	Projektion $u_m^i(x_1,\ldots,x_m) = x_i$ $(1 \leq i \leq m)$
"Zusammensetzen" eines Datums	Nachfolgerfunktion $s(x) = x+1$
"Zerlegen" eines Datums	Vorgängerfunktion $v(x) = \max(0,x-1)$.

Aufbauprinzip für zusammengesetzte Datenmanipulationen	Zugeordnete Operation für Wortfunktionen
Hintereinanderausführung von Manipulationen G_i und H	Substitution von Funktionen $f(X) = h(g_1(X),\ldots,g_n(X))$, $X=(x_1,\ldots,x_m)$
Wiederholung der Manipulation H	Rekursion $f(X,y) = \begin{cases} g(X) & \text{falls } p(X,y)=0 \\ h(X,y,f(X,r(y))) & \text{sonst} \end{cases}$ Dabei sollen h, g_i, g, p und r Ausgangsfunktionen sein oder aus solchen durch Substitution und Rekursion abgeleitete Funktionen.

Die Ausgangsfunktionen beschreiben gewisse Elementarmanipulationen, die mit den Daten (hier: den natürlichen Zahlen) erlaubt sind. Substitution und Rekursion beschreiben Aufbauprinzipien, nach denen komplexe Datenmanipulationen aus elementaren zusammengesetzt werden können. Komplexe Abläufe von Datenmanipulationen werden so durch geschachtelte Funktionsdefinitionen beschrieben, genauer gesagt, durch endliche Folgen von Funktionsdefinitionen, die typischerweise mit einfachen Definitionen (in der Nähe der Ausgangsfunktionen) beginnen und zu höheren (indirekten, von den Ausgangsfunktionen um mehr Definitionsschritte entfernten, tiefer geschachtelten) Definitionen fortschreiten. Wir bezeichnen eine solche Definitionenfolge auch als ein __Programm__. Wir vereinbaren, daß eine __Ausführung__ eines Programms aus einer Serie von Datenmanipulationen besteht, die der einmaligen Auswertung der zuletzt definierten Funktion entspricht, angewandt auf einen gesondert anzugebenden Satz von __Eingabedaten__. Das sind im wesentlichen die Konventionen der Programmsprache LISP, genauer des Reinen LISP /1/.

Der Schachtelung der Funktionsdefinitionen entspricht eine zeitliche Staffelung der Manipulationen: die Ausgangsdaten sind zuerst den "inneren" Manipulationen zu unterziehen, dann (die Zwischenergebnisse) den "äußeren" Manipulationen. Im Fall von Substitutionen liegt dabei die Gesamtheit der auszuführenden Manipulationen ein für allemal fest. Im Fall von Rekursionen dagegen variiert sie in Abhängigkeit von den Daten (Abb. 1).

$$f(X,y) = \begin{cases} g(X) & \text{falls } p(X,y)=0 \qquad \text{Expliziter Fall} \\ h(X,y,f(X,r(y))) & \text{sonst} \qquad\qquad\quad \text{Reduktion} \end{cases}$$

$$\left. \begin{aligned} f(X,y) &= h(X,y,f(X,r(y))) \\ f(X,r(y)) &= h(X,r(y),f(X,r^2(y))) \\ &\vdots \end{aligned} \right\} \text{Reduktionsschritte}$$

$$f(X,r^n(y)) = g(X) \quad \left. \begin{aligned} &\text{falls } p(X,r^n(y))=0 \\ &\text{und } \quad p(X,r^i(y))\neq 0 \text{ für } 0 \leqq i < n \end{aligned} \right\} \text{Expliziter Fall}$$

$$\left. \begin{aligned} f(X,r^{n-1}(y)) &= h(X,r^{n-1}(y),g(X)) \\ &\vdots \end{aligned} \right\} \text{Rückwärtseinsetzungen}$$

$$f(X,y) = \underbrace{h(X,y, h(X,r(y), h(X,r^2(y),\ldots, h(X,r^{n-1}(y),g(X))\ldots)))}_{n \text{ mal } h \text{ angewandt}}$$

Sonderfall $X=x_1=x$, $h(x,y,z)$ unabh. v. x u. y , $g(x)=x$, $p(X,y)=y$, $r=v$:

$$f(x,y) = \begin{cases} x & \text{falls } y=0 \\ h(f(x,v(y))) & \text{sonst} \qquad \text{Reine Iteration} \end{cases}$$

$$= h^y(x)$$

<u>Abb. 1 Variable Wiederholung einer Datenmanipulation</u>

3. Sequentielle Ausführung von Programmen. Wegen der scheinbaren Priorität der "inneren" Manipulationen drängt sich das übliche Verfahren zur Auswertung von Funktionen auf, sequentiell von innen nach außen und von links nach rechts fortschreitend:

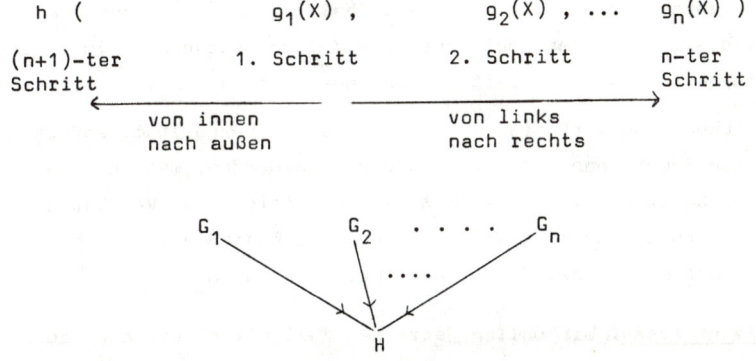

Bei Rekursionen muß man dabei allerdings i.a. zunächst durch eine variable Folge von Argument-Reduktionen zur "innersten" Manipulation vordringen (Abb.1). Als zugehöriges maschineninternes Implementationsverfahren bietet sich das Kellerverfahren an; der komplizierten Ineinanderschachtelung der Zwischenrechnungen entspricht dabei die übersichtliche Aufeinanderschichtung der Zwischenargumente und Zwischenresultate.

4. <u>Parallele Ausführung von Programmen</u>. Die prästabilierte Harmonie von Kellerverfahren und Funktionsauswertung von innen nach außen läßt die Täuschung entstehen, als ginge es gar nicht anders, als sei dies eine notwendige Folge der verlangten zeitlichen Staffelung der Teilmanipulationen. In Wirklichkeit bleibt diese auch bei ganz anderen Auswertungsverfahren erhalten, so z.B. bei der diametral entgegengesetzten Funktionsauswertung von "außen nach innen":

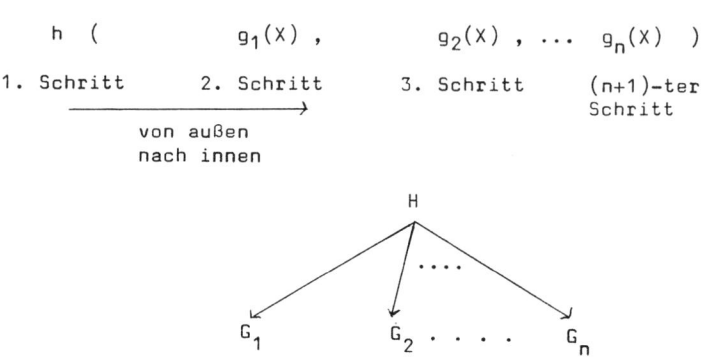

Abb. 2 <u>Funktionsauswertung von außen nach innen</u>

Dabei beginnt also die Auswertung der äußeren Teile einer Schachtelung v o r der Auswertung der inneren. Richtig ist, daß äußere Auswertungen nicht vor inneren abgeschlossen werden können, falls die inneren Zwischenresultate in den äußeren Rechnungen tatsächlich verwendet werden. Aber diese inneren Zwischenresultate mögen ja erst sehr spät oder überhaupt nicht benötigt werden. An dieser – a priori im allgemeinen unentscheidbaren – Eventualität hängt die Vernünftigkeit des Vorgehens von außen nach innen. Ähnlich kann man zugunsten von Verfahrensweisen argumentieren, bei denen die Zwischenrechnungen in irgendeiner anderen Abfolge – z.B. gleichzeitig – begonnen werden.

Alle diese Auswertungsverfahren liefern dasselbe Endresultat, sofern nur äußere Manipulationen immer dann vorläufig aufgehalten werden, wenn ein inneres Zwischenresultat benötigt wird, das im Moment noch nicht zur Verfügung steht. Genau dies ist der Kern der zeitlichen Staffelung der Manipulationen, die von der Schachtelung der Funktionsdefinitionen impliziert wird.

5. <u>Parallele Prozesse</u>. Wir wollen jetzt den Fall gleichzeitig ablaufender Zwischenrechnungen näher untersuchen. Da wir es in unserem Modell mit Funktionsschachtelungen zu tun haben, liegt es nahe, jede Funktionsauswertung als einen <u>Prozeß</u> – d.h. eine separate Zwischenrechnung – anzusehen, in programmierungstechnischen Termini zu definieren als eine Beschreibung der zu bearbeitenden Programme (Programmstücke) und Daten, sowie des augenblicklichen Bearbeitungszustands. Dabei können auch ohne weiteres mehrere separate Auswertungen ein und derselben Funktionsdefinition im Gange sein, die alle als getrennte Prozesse

zu betrachten sind. Offenbar läßt sich an jeder Substitutionsstelle und in jedem Rekursionsschritt ein separater Prozeß ansetzen. Eine feinere Struktur paralleler Prozesse läßt unser Modell nicht zu. Immerhin erfassen wir damit z.B. auch die parallele Ausführung arithmetischer Operationen in einem geschachtelten Ausdruck.

Ein Programm definiert eine natürliche baumstrukturierte Hierarchie von Prozessen, unabhängig von deren zeitlicher Staffelung oder Überlappung. Wir ordnen nämlich bei Substitutionen die inneren Zwischenrechnungen den äußeren unter (Abb.2). Bei Rekursionen ordnen wir jeden Rekursionsschritt seinem Vorgänger unter. Die Ausgangsdaten eines Prozesses in der Hierarchie bestehen erstens aus Argumenten, die vom unmittelbar übergeordneten Prozeß herabgereicht werden, zweitens aus den Zwischenresultaten der unmittelbar untergeordneten Prozesse. Die Argumente des obersten Prozesses sind die Eingabedaten.

6. **Datentransport und Prozeßkoordination**. Wir stellen jetzt Überlegungen zur maschinellen Ausführung paralleler Prozesse an. Wir setzen einen unbegrenzten Vorrat an **Prozessoren** voraus, autonomen Rechenautomaten, von denen jeder sämtliche Elementarmanipulationen ausführen kann, sowie eine Anzahl von Transport- und Kontrollfunktionen, die noch näher zu spezifizieren sind.[1] Wir denken uns (vorläufig) Prozesse und Prozessoren eineindeutig fest zugeordnet. Die Prozeßstruktur bildet sich damit isomorph in eine baumförmige Prozessorenhierarchie ab. Wir benutzen daher für Prozesse und Prozessoren dieselben Sprechweisen und Notationen.

Kümmern wir uns zunächst nicht darum, wann und wie die parallelen Prozesse gestartet werden und stellen uns vor, sie seien bereits in vollem Gang. Bleibt dafür zu sorgen, daß sie innerhalb des Spielraums der (von der Funktionsschachtelung) vorgeschriebenen zeitlichen Staffelung ablaufen. Zu diesem Zweck können die Daten – Argumente und Funktionswerte – herangezogen werden, die ohnehin zwischen den Prozessen ausgetauscht werden müssen. Wir reservieren dazu ein spezielles **uneigentliches Datum** Ω, das als Stellvertreter für noch nicht verfügbare Argumente und Resultate dient und von allen anderen **eigentlichen Daten** unterscheidbar sein muß. Die Prozessoren sollen vor jeder Manipulation, zu der eigentliche Daten erforderlich sind, in eine lokale Warteschleife gehen, falls sie auf uneigentliche Daten stoßen. Sobald das uneigentliche Datum in ein eigentliches **umschlägt**, soll die Rechnung weiterlaufen.

Damit ist die verlangte zeitliche Staffelung bereits gesichert. Wir müssen nur noch zusehen, daß eigentliche Daten von den Stellen, wo sie anfallen, auch stets dahin gelangen, wo sie zur weiteren Verarbeitung benötigt werden. Wir erreichen

---

[1] Ein möglicher Satz von Maschineninstruktionen für Prozessoren ist in /2/ näher untersucht.

dies durch einen ununterbrochenen Fluß von Argumentwerten (von oben nach unten in der Prozessorenhierarchie) und von Funktionswerten (von unten nach oben). Das Beispiel einer Substitution soll dies verdeutlichen:

$$f(X) = h(g_1(X),\ldots,g_n(X))$$

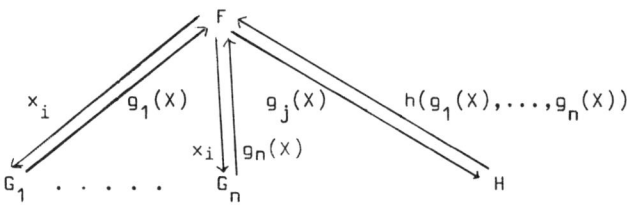

Abb. 3 Datenfluß bei einer Substitution

F sendet fortgesetzt seine eigenen Argumente zu den Prozessoren G_i hinab. Ferner holt F fortgesetzt die Resultate der G_i herauf und sendet sie wieder zum Prozessor H hinab. Schließlich holt F fortgesetzt das H-Resultat herauf und stellt es für den Weitertransport nach oben bereit. Der Prozessor F wird also fortgesetzt eine Programmschleife durchlaufen, die aus genau diesen Datentransporten (in irgendeiner Reihenfolge) besteht.

Zu Beginn der Rechnung sollen alle Daten uneigentlich sein. Nach und nach werden sie im Lauf einer erfolgreichen Rechnung durch eigentliche Daten ersetzt. Dabei kann es durchaus vorkommen, daß eigentliche Resultate aus der Prozeßhierarchie von unten angeliefert werden, bevor von oben eigentliche Argumentwerte zur Verfügung gestellt wurden.

Im Falle einer Rekursion lassen wir den Prozessor F nach dem folgenden Rechenplan verfahren (vgl. Abb. 4):

1. Transportiere X nach G, P, F' und H hinab.

2. Transportiere y nach R hinab.

3. Transportiere das Resultat von R nach F'.

4. Transportiere das Resultat von F' nach H.

5. Falls das Resultat von P gleich 0 ist: transportiere das Resultat von G herauf.

6. Falls das Resultat von P eigentlich und ungleich 0 ist: transportiere das Resultat von H herauf.

7. Fahre mit 1. fort.

$$f(X,y) = \begin{cases} g(X) & \text{falls} \quad p(X,y)=0 \\ h(X,y,f(X,r(y))) & \text{sonst} \end{cases}$$

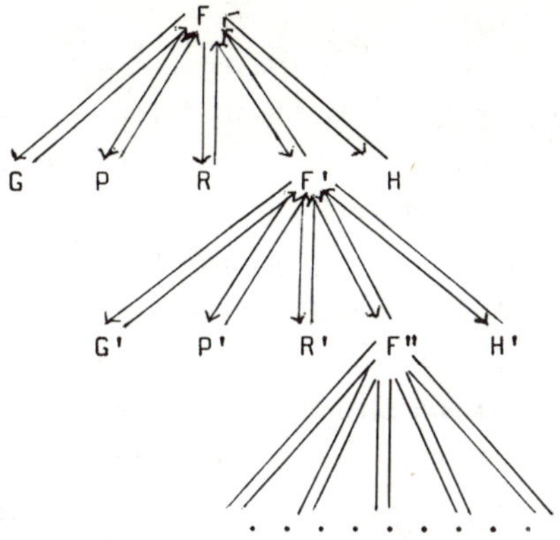

Abb. 4 Datenfluß im Falle einer Rekursion

Prozessoren, die zur Auswertung von Substitutionen und Rekursionen eingesetzt sind, halten also niemals an und geraten auch nicht in lokale Warteschleifen. Man braucht nun nur noch dafür zu sorgen, daß Prozessoren, die zur Ausführung einer Elementarmanipulation eingesetzt sind, diese stets ausführen (ihre lokale Warteschleife stets verlassen), sobald sie mit den zu manipulierenden eigentlichen Daten beliefert werden. Eine einfache Lösung besteht darin, auch diese Prozessoren endlose Programmschleifen durchlaufen zu lassen, in denen sie ständig versuchen, die aufgetragene Elementarmanipulation auszuführen, diese aber als Nulloperation behandeln, solange die vorliegenden Daten uneigentlich sind. Mehrere Prozessoren können dieselbe Programmschleife unabhängig voneinander durchlaufen (oder was dasselbe bedeutet, mehrere Prozesse können ein Programm gemeinsam haben). Das ist z.B. sinnvoll bei Rekursionen; alle Rekursionsschritte mit Ausnahme des letzten unterscheiden sich ja nur in den bearbeiteten Daten. Zu dem Zweck müssen Programme offenbar ablaufinvariant sein.

7. **Stabilität der Resultate.** Da dieselben Argumente und Resultate fortgesetzt auf- und abtransportiert werden, müssen wir verlangen, daß sie ihre Werte nicht verändern, sondern daß sie vielmehr <u>stabil</u> bleiben, d.h. im Lauf der Rechnung höchstens einmal von einem uneigentlichen Wert zu einem festen eigentlichen Wert <u>umschlagen</u>. Setzen wir aber die Argumente des obersten Prozessors (d.s. die Eingabedaten) als stabil voraus, so bleiben sie dies auch bei ihrem Abstieg durch die Prozessorenhierarchie. Falls die Elementarmanipulationen am unteren Ende der Hierarchie daraus stabile Zwischenresultate berechnen, so werden daraus beim Wiederaufstieg durch die Hierarchie weitere stabile Zwischenresultate

berechnet. So bleibt schließlich auch das Endresultat stabil.[1] Damit ist gezeigt, daß die Koordination einer bestehenden Hierarchie von Prozessen allein durch den natürlichen Fluß der Ausgangsdaten und Resultate mit erledigt werden kann.

8. **Anlagerung von Prozessoren.** Wir beschäftigen uns nun mit der Frage, wie neue Prozesse in Gang zu setzen sind, derart daß Prozeßhierarchien dynamisch von oben herab entfaltet werden können. Wir postulieren dazu einen in jedem Prozessor vorhandenen Mechanismus zur <u>Anlagerung</u> von Prozessoren. Wir stellen uns vor, daß Prozessoren reine Steuer- und Rechenwerke sind, die auf einem gemeinsamen Speicher für Programme und Daten operieren. Ein anzulagernder Prozessor ist dann lediglich auf die von ihm auszuführende Programmschleife anzusetzen, sowie auf den Speicherbereich, in dem der Datenaustausch mit dem unmittelbar übergeordneten Prozeß (d.i. der anlagernde Prozeß) erfolgen soll.

Eine Prozeßhierarchie läßt sich jetzt, wenn man will, aus einem einzigen Prozeß entfalten, indem

- jeder Substitutionsprozeß (Prozeß F in Abb. 3) sich zunächst Unterprozesse zur Berechnung der eingesetzten Funktionen anlagert,
- in jedem Reduktionsschritt einer Rekursion (Prozeß F^i in Abb. 4) zunächst Prozessoren (G^i, P^i, R^i, H^i in Abb. 4) zur Auswertung der Hilfsfunktionen angelagert werden, sowie ein Prozessor (F^{i+1}) zur Steuerung des nächsten Rekursionsschritts.

Die Speicherreservierung für den Datenaustausch und den sonstigen lokalen Bedarf des anzulagernden Prozessors soll der anlagernde Prozessor vornehmen. Setzen wir den Speicher sowie den Vorrat an Prozessoren als unendlich voraus, so ist die Anlagerungsoperation stets ausführbar. Da alle Prozessoren endlose Programmschleifen durchlaufen, Anlagerungen aber nur einmal stattfinden sollen, müssen Prozessoren die Fähigkeit zur Anlagerung nach dem ersten Schleifendurchgang verlieren. Die Alternative, Anlagerungsinstruktionen nach einmaliger Ausführung aus dem Programm zu löschen, verträgt sich nicht mit der Forderung der Ablaufinvarianz der Programme.

Die Unendlichkeitsvoraussetzung für Speicher und Prozessorenzahl garantiert, daß jede geschachtelte Funktionsdefinition für beliebige Ausgangsdaten ausgewertet werden kann. Will man umgekehrt diese Garantie geben, so ist die Unendlichkeitsforderung unvermeidlich, obwohl in jedem Einzelfall einer Funktionsauswertung nur ein endlicher Teil der Hilfsmittel benutzt wird. Wie groß dieser Teil sein wird, läßt sich im vorhinein i.a. nicht entscheiden.

---

[1] Genau nachweisen läßt sich dies nur nach Festlegung einer Maschinensprache und Angabe der Programmstücke für Elementarmanipulationen, Substitutionen und Rekursionen; s. dazu /2/.

9. <u>Endliche Multiprozessorsysteme</u>. Stehen nur endlich viele Prozessoren zur Verfügung, so führt unsere bisherige feste Zuordnung von Prozessen und Prozessoren i.a. zur Verklemmung (deadlock). Lösen wir dagegen die Prozesse von den Prozessoren los, so genügt im Prinzip ein einziger Prozessor, der nach irgendeinem Schema - z.B. reihum - von Prozeß zu Prozeß umgeschaltet wird. Damit sind wir beim konventionellen Betriebssystem, in dem Prozesse als selbständige Objekte manipuliert werden.[1] Es ist klar, daß diese Lösung für unser Ziel der engen Prozeßverzahnung nicht sonderlich attraktiv ist: die Prozessoranlagerung kann unter solchen Umständen schwerlich als eine sehr schnelle Operation realisiert werden. Es ist daher wichtig, an der Idee der permanenten Zuordnung von Prozessen und Prozessoren so weit als möglich festzuhalten. Dazu ist zweierlei zu bemerken.

Erstens haben wir bisher das natürliche Lebensende eines Prozesses nicht beachtet, nämlich den Augenblick, in dem er ein eigentliches Resultat produziert. Von da an kann der ganze untergeordnete Teilbaum der Prozeßhierarchie aufgelöst und die zugeordneten Prozessoren anderweitig eingesetzt werden. Wir halten damit immer noch an der permanenten Zuordnung von Prozessen und Prozessoren über die ganze Lebensdauer der Prozesse fest.

Zweitens kann man das Wachstum neuer Zweige der Prozeßhierarchie verzögern, bis bereits bestehende Zweige abgebaut sind. Im Prinzip können hier beliebig elaborate Zuweisungsverfahren angewandt werden, um die - i.a. prinzipiell unausweichliche - Verklemmung in günstig gelagerten Fällen zu vermeiden. Kostspielige Verfahren (wie der "Bankier-Algorithmus" /4/) verbieten sich aber, da ja die Prozessor-Anlagerung eine sehr schnelle Operation sein soll. Es könnte in der Praxis durchaus am besten sein, sich auf eine erfahrungsgemäß ausreichende (sehr große) Anzahl von Prozessoren zu verlassen und gelegentliche (hinreichend seltene) Verklemmungen in Kauf zu nehmen.

Immerhin kann nämlich bei eingetretener Verklemmung der Prozeßbaum beliebig amputiert werden. Die verbleibenden Prozesse laufen danach ungestört weiter. Die abgeschnittenen Teile wachsen wieder nach, sobald den Prozessoren an den Schnittstellen die Anlagerungsfähigkeit (für einen Schleifendurchlauf) zurückgegeben wird. Freilich kann auch diese Radikalkur i.a. keinen Erfolg garantieren. Die in amputierten Zweigen geleistete Arbeit geht überdies verloren; verfeinerte Verfahren zur geordneten Auslagerung und Wiederaufnahme temporär verdrängter Prozesse könnten daher doch vorzuziehen sein.

Der Vorschlag, Systemverklemmungen in der Praxis einfach abzuwarten, ist für kleine Prozessorenzahlen (bis zu einigen tausend) sicher absurd. Sollten sich aber die (vielleicht nicht ganz ernst gemeinten) Vorhersagen über das Dahin-

---
1) Eine Alternative ist in /3/ skizziert: Manipulation einzelner Maschineninstruktionen als selbständige Objekte, gesteuert durch das Vorliegen der zur zur Ausführung der Instruktionen erforderlichen (eigentlichen) Daten. Hier stellt sozusagen jede einzelne Instruktion einen separaten Prozeß dar.

schwinden der Hardwarekosten /5/ bewahrheiten, so werden wir gegen Ende der Dekade Systeme mit einigen 10^5 oder gar 10^6 Prozessoren sehen. Ein Prozessor hat dann nicht mehr die Bedeutung einer "Zentraleinheit", die in der Maschinenarchitektur durch andere "Einheiten", wie etwa einen ganzen Arbeitsspeicher aufzuwiegen ist. Vielmehr hat dann ein Prozessor nur noch das Gewicht einer einzelnen Speicher z e l l e . Bei Speichern sind wir aber durchaus gewohnt, es auf Verklemmung (Überlauf) ankommen zu lassen, gerade auch bei Prozessen mit unbegrenztem Speicherbedarf, wie Sprachübersetzern oder Beweisprogrammen. Realistische Abschätzungen darüber, bei was für Prozessorenanzahlen man möglichen Systemverklemmungen mit Gelassenheit entgegensehen kann, gibt es freilich noch nicht.

Ein ähnliches Argument ist vielleicht am Platz bezüglich des (mutmaßlich) verschwindend kleinen Ausnutzungsgrades eines einzelnen Prozessors in einem 10^6-fachen Multiprozessorsystem. Dieses Problem könnte durch bloße Änderung unserer Denkgewohnheiten verschwinden, sobald wir uns um die Ausnutzung eines wartenden Prozessors genau so wenig zu bekümmern brauchen wie um die Ausnutzung einer Speicherzelle, in der eine Konstante abgelegt ist. Mit anderen Worten, wir werden eines Tages völlig andere Definitionen von "Ausnutzung" anwenden, indem wir z.B. einen Prozessor als "ausgenutzt" ansehen, wenn er überhaupt irgendeinem Prozeß zugeordnet ist, auch wenn er mangels eigentlicher Daten auf der Stelle tritt.

10. **Weitere Entwicklungen.** Von unseren Überlegungen führt ein direkter Weg zu den Programmsprachen mit "einmaliger Wertzuweisung" ("single assignment" /6/, /3/), in denen während des Programmablaufs höchstens eine Wertzuweisung pro Variable erlaubt ist. In unserem Modell kann zwar eine Speicherzelle beliebig viele Wertzuweisungen erfahren, aber nur mit demselben stabilen Wert. Wir können daher unsere in Abschnitt 2 skizzierte Programmsprache ohne weiteres um globale Variable und einmalige Wertzuweisungen erweitern. Wenn man will, kann man unsere Entwicklungen als eine berechenbarkeitstheoretische Grundlegung des Verfahrens der einmaligen Wertzuweisung ansehen.

Wir vermuten, daß die (bisher nicht realisierten) Vorschläge zur Parallelprogrammierung mit einmaligen Wertzuweisungen - wenn überhaupt - am ehesten in der von uns vorgeschlagenen Form (feste Prozessorzuordnung, quasi-unendliches Multiprozessorsystem) zum Zuge kommen werden.

11. **Literatur.**

/1/ J. McCarthy. LISP 1.5 Programmer's Manual. MIT Press, Cambridge, 1965.

/2/ F. Schwenkel. Ein Modell zur Parallelprogrammierung. Technischer Bericht, Notre Dame Computer Science Department, Juni 1971.

/3/ D.D. Chamberlin. The "single-assignment" approach to parallel processing. AFIPS Conf. Proc. 39 (FJCC 1971), 263-269.

/4/ E.J. Dijkstra. Cooperating sequential processes. In: F. Genuys (Ed.). Programming Languages. Academic Press, London 1968.

/5/ C.C. Foster. A view of computer architecture. Comm.ACM 15 (1972), 557-565.

/6/ L.G. Tesler und H.J. Enea. A language for concurrent processes. AFIPS Conf. Proc. 32 (SJCC 1968), 403-408.

5. BETRIEBSSYSTEME

MINI-COMPUTERS
J. HARMS

R. ROSSI, M. SPADONI, P. TOTH

PERFORMANCE ANALYSIS
S.W. SHERMAN, J.H. HOWARD Jr., J.C. BROWNE

S. HOENER

S. SCHINDLER, S. BUDER

STRUKTUR
M. HEINZ

D. BAUM, H.-D. SCHRÖDTER

FAIL-SOFTNESS CRITERIA IN THE REALIZATION OF A MINICOMPUTER DISK OPERATING SYSTEM TO BE USED IN AN "OPEN-SHOP" UNIVERSITY ENVIRONMENT

J. Harms

CICE, Université de Genève

Abstract

In disk operating systems of computers without hardware protection, and when the system is used as an "open-shop" installation, the data on the disk must be protected entirely by software measures. Different types of incidents are analyzed which risk to destroy the data in such an environment. A combination of an automatic recovery procedure and of measures to be realized in the operating system is described. It guarantees the integrity of the operating system and of the structure of all files for the large majority of incidents. Any loss of data is limited to the file actually being modified while an incident occurs. If an automatic recovery is not possible, the system can be repaired with a disk scavenger whose main characteristics are outlined.

Introduction

A large amount of research has been done on the protection of data in a computer system shared by several users. Most protection schemes make two fundamental assumptions : (1) The hardware of the computer permits enforcing certain rules on user programs - they can only access memory within permitted "bounds", and they cannot execute "privileged instructions" relating to input/output or to the state of operation of the computer. (2) The computer is operated as a "closed-shop" installation - the users have no access to the computer site and cannot perform manual operations which might turn out to be harmful.

The basic models of many commonly used minicomputers provide neither memory protection nor privileged instructions. In minicomputer configurations including a disk and using a disk operating system, the disk is shared by the operating system and the individual user - even if the computer is monoprogrammed and used by one user at a time. Therefore, the data on the disk belonging to the operating system and to each user should be protected. Moreover, minicomputers are often used as "open-shop" installations : each user has physically control over the computer while he is running his programs (and he may be present and perform harmful operations while other users run their programs). In an open-shop installation, lacking memory protection and privileged instructions, full safety for the data on the disk cannot be obtained. This paper describes some considerations on how nevertheless a relatively fail-safe disk operating system can be realized. Data is very rarely lost and the losses, once they occur, can be confined within narrow limits and do not risk to damage the system as a whole.

Possible incidents

The above mentioned conditions can cause loss of data on the disk through several mechanisms.

Incidents due to the lack of memory protection :
1) The contents of a data buffer are destroyed while the data is still being transferred to the disk. For instance, a program re-uses a buffer before a transfer from this buffer to the disk is terminated, or the contents of the buffer are destroyed by clobbering.
2) The code of the supervisor is destroyed. The consequences are unpredictable, they may involve the loss of data on the disk through the mechanisms 1), 3) or 4). The reason for the destruction of the supervisor code is normally clobbering.

Incidents due to the execution of instructions that should be privileged :
3) An output operation to the disk is executed improperly. Subsequently, data on the disk can be lost either if another output operation already started but not finished is disturbed, or if the improper output operation itself writes data to the disk in an undesired fashion. The reason for the execution of such an instruction can be a user program trying to do its own input/output, or clobbering into executable code.
4) An instruction changing the state of the computer is accidentally executed. As a consequence, the supervisor may cease to function normally and needs to be restarted. For instance, if an instruction modifying the state of the interrupt system is accidentally executed, the supervisor will generally be unable to automatically correct the state of the interrupt system and will subsequently cease to operate normally.

Incidents due to improper manual interventions :

5) Due to an incorrect manipulation at the console of the computer, an executing output operation is not completed to its logical end. As a consequence, a disk sector may only be written partially, or the logical structure of the data on the disk may be wrong. Typically, a user manually stops the computer and re-bootstraps the system, possibly because his program hung up or because he wanted to stop the execution of his program.

Mechanisms 1) and 3) destroy the data stored on the disk. Recovery is not possible without introducing prohibitively complex redundancy. Moreover, these incidents normally cannot be detected automatically at the moment they occur. If the lost data belongs to the operating system, or if it relates to the structure of a user file, the whole system may become unusable. Some means of subsequent correction must be provided. For this subsequent correction we use a disk scavenger and a feature of the system generator which permits to regenerate single sectors with code of the operating system. Complete recovery of the data of damaged user files is not possible. Fortunately, errors due to the mechanism 3) occur extremely rarely : it is very improbable that clobbering will create output instructions for the disk, and so far, the few users capable of programming their own input/output could always be convinced to use the proper system requests. The most frequent incidents occur through the mechanism 1). They can only happen if user programs execute simultaneously with transfers to the disk. This parallelism does not occur often, never if user programs are written in FORTRAN or BASIC-like languages (the high-level languages generally available on minicomputers). In our system this kind of incident happens sufficiently seldom. We did not take the very restrictive measure of modifying the operating system, completely precluding the mentioned parallelism.

Mechanisms 2), 4) and 5) all have the same kind of interference : they cut off a sequence of operations modifying the contents of the disk before the logical termination. Mechanism 5) can produce partially written sectors (data channels of minicomputers normally access memory by "cycle stealing"; stopping the computer thus automatically halts data channel transfers). Partially written sectors can be avoided by means of a small hardware modification : the action of control panel keys stopping the computer is postponed until any current disk access has been terminated. For our NOVA computer this modification was very easy to realize.

If a logical sequence of transfers to the disk is cut off, two conditions can arrive. The structure (= sequence of sectors) of the file being modified did not change - for instance when a series of sectors is updated. Subsequently, the modification of the file may be incomplete, but the file can be reread or rewritten without any problem. Or the structure of the file did change (= sectors were reordered or reattributed). Generally, such a change takes at least two disk accesses. If they are interrupted, the structure of the file, and possibly of the free storage pool, will be incorrect. The file cannot be rewritten or reread beyond the point where the interruption occured. The consequence may be the truncation or loss of the data file, the reduction of the number of accessible sectors, or even the unability to use the system if system files are concerned. This type of event is the most frequent reason for the necessity to regenerate the disk, erasing all data already stored. Our main effort was spent on providing measures which automatically detect these conditions and recover the structure of the disk when the system is restarted.

Automatic recovery after the interruption of an output sequence

Generally, the operating system will be restarted after an incident interrupting a sequence of output operations to the disk. It may be necessary to reload the resident code of the operating system from the disk before the system can be restarted.

To initiate an automatic recovery when necessary, the restart procedure must have means to verify whether all output operations had been properly terminated before the system went down. Since information stored in the main memory may have been destroyed, the needed information must necessarily be stored on the disk. We use a permanent disk file consisting of a single sector : updating this file takes a single transfer to the disk and cannot be interrupted. The most evident procedure to provide and update the needed information is to log and unlog the beginning and the end of each transfer. This solution has been rejected because it triples the number of disk accesses for each output operation and prohibitively slows down the performance of the system.

A better way of providing the information for the detection of unterminated output operations is to use the "open" and "close" system requests, introducing a kind of "checkpoint-restart" procedure. These requests

exist in most operating systems. Their consequent use must be enforced
on user programs to permit reliably detecting any unfinished output operation. Each time a disk file is opened, a record is created in a one
sector file - the "Open-File-List". The record is erased when the file
is closed. The precedingly motivated restriction to one sector evidently
limits the number of disk files that can be simultaneaously open (in our
system this limit is 80). The mentioned record must contain the file
identifier of the opened file. The identifier enables the recovery procedure to find the corresponding entry in the file directory. If the record
concerns the free storage pool, some more information is needed, as will
be seen later. The "Open-File-List" is checked each time the operating
system is restarted; if it is found not to be empty, the recovery procedure is executed.

The implementation of the recovery procedure depends on the way the internal structure of the disk is implemented. It requires that sufficient
structure information is contained in each sector. Any error in the
structure of a file the can be detected by sequentially reading the
chain of sectors. In our system, each sector contains the physical address of the next sector and the unique identifier of the disk file (it
also contains the address of the preceding sector, but this information
is only used by the disk scavenger program when reconstructing a "lost"
data file from garbage sectors). The end of a file is indicated by a
special "next sector address". This kind of realization is used in several systems and permits the implementation of all necessary recovery
measures. The following discussion will assume this kind of structure.
A second requirement for our recovery procedure concerns the file directory : for each file it must also comprise the addresses of the first
and the last sector, and a file identifier, unique to the file, which
is repeated in each sector of the file.

The recovery procedure scans the "Open-File-List", for each record found,
checking the structure of the corresponding file. If the structure is
correct, the only action is the deletion of the record from the "Open-
File-List". If it is incorrect, a more complex correction is necessary.
The structure of a file can be verified by sequentially reading all
sectors of the file, checking the structure information of each sector,
and comparing it to the information in the file directory. In our system, the structure of files can only be modified by appending or deleting sectors at the end of a file : in this case the structure of the

file will be correct if the last sector, as determined by the directory, is an end-of-file sector with the correct identifier. The procedure adopted for the actual recovery of files with a bad structure makes two assumptions on the operating system : (1) The input/output routines only modify the structure of files at their end. (2) The system routines writing the end-of-file sector and updating the address of the last sector in the file directory observe the following sequence of actions : the end-of-file sector is written before updating the directory when a file is expanded, and after updating the directory when the length of a file is reduced. Under these conditions, the last sector as determined by the file directory will always be a sector inside the file if the structure of a file is incorrect. The next sectors will either be terminated by an end-of-file sector or will point into the free storage pool. The following sequence of actions then permits to recover the structure of files and of the free storage pool :
- open the free storage pool (see next chapter);
- convert into an end-of-file sector the sector determined by the file directory;
- delete in the "Open-List-File" the record concerning the recovered file;
- return all following sectors of the file to the free storage pool;
- close the free storage pool.

This recovery procedure also gives correct results if the recovery procedure itself is interrupted. Evidently, it cannot correct the contents of the corrected files. It therefore issues a message with the name of each recovered file, so that the user knows when a file should be rewritten.

Recovery procedure for the free storage pool

For data files, it is the user's responsibility to keep back-up data allowing to rewrite the file if necessary after an automatic recovery. The described procedure cannot recover an interrupted operation returning sectors to the free storage pool, because it does not know where the returning operation had been interrupted. Recording the address of each sector on the disk before it is returned to the pool solves the problem, but this is too slow. Therefore we had to provide a special recovery procedure for the free storage pool.

The basic principle of this procedure is to consider the free storage pool as a data file and to "open" it before sectors are returned, respectively to "close" it after the returning operation is finished. In order to resume the returning operation after the interruption, it must be possible to find the last sector actually returned before the interruption and the next sector that should have been returned. The necessary information is obtained by two operations : (1) The record in the "Open-File-List" created when opening the free storage pool also contains the address of the first sector to be returned. (2) While returning sectors to the free storage pool, some tracking data is generated; it can be stored in the sectors being returned since they do not contain any other significant data. The tracking data consists of the structure information of the chain of sectors before they were returned. The recovery procedure thus can follow the chain of sectors already returned to the free storage pool, starting at the sector indicated by the "Open-File-List". The last sector returned before the interruption will point to the first sector to be returned after the recovery. The two mentioned measures and the recovery procedure are easy to implement. The details depend on the form and structure of the free storage pool. We have made good experiences with a free storage pool in the form of a "free chain" with a structure identical to the data files.

Recovering the interruption of "Create" and "Delete"

With slight adaptations, the described procedures permit to recover the interruption of creation and deletion of files. This assumes that the operating system respects some rules, mainly concerning the sequence of actions during the creation and deletion of a file.

The actions during the creation of files and their sequence must be :
- determine an identifier for the new file;
- create a corresponding record in the "Open-File-List";
- create an entry in the file directory for a file with one sector (at this moment the sector still belongs to the free storage pool);
- update the structure of the free storage pool to remove the mentioned sector (this must be possible with a single disk access);
- convert the sector into an empty end-of-file sector;
- close the created file.

The recovery procedure must be adapted to tolerate the interruption of this sequence at any point. If no entry can be found in the file directory, the record must be cancelled right away. If the first (and only) sector indicated in the file directory belongs to the free storage pool, the creating sequence must be resumed at its fifth or fourth step, depending on whether the structure of the free storage pool is already modified or not.

The actions during the deletion of a file and their sequence must be :
- open the free storage pool;
- remove the entry concerning the file being deleted from the file directory;
- return all sectors of the file to the free storage pool;
- close the free storage pool.

The automatic recovery is already possible if this sequence is interrupted at any point, no adaptation of the recovery procedure is necessary.

Recovering the interruption of modifications of the file directory

Three types of operation modify the file directory : (1) An existing entry is updated. (2) A new entry is added. (3) An entry is deleted. It is very important that the interruption of any operation on the file directory will be automatically recovered - no operating system will function properly if its file directory is damaged. The modification of the file directory normally occurs as a part of a more complex operation; it should not be complicated by the preparation of data for an eventual recovery.

Our file directory has the form of a normal data file and contains a series of fixed length entries. The length of the file directory "file" is preset and does not change. Its last significant entry is followed by an end-of-information entry, distinguished by a file name whose first word is zero. All data between the end-of-information entry and the end-of-file is insignificant. This particular format of the file directory permits to achieve all modifications without the need for additional data for an eventual recovery. Unfinished modifications can be detected and corrected by adapting the recovery procedure. The recovery procedure must examine and repair the file directory before any other action. The preset length of the file directory "file" imposes a limit on the possible number of files.

An entry is deleted from the file directory by moving all following entries down, starting after the entry to be deleted and proceding entry by entry. During this process there will always be a duplicate entry.

The recovery procedure must find any duplicate entry and resume the process if necessary.

New entries are always added after the last significant entry. Due to the fixed length of the file directory no sectors need to be appended. The new entry is added by the following sequence of actions :
- add a second end-of-information entry;
- convert the original end-of-information entry into the desired entry, but leave a zero in the first word of the name field;
- correct the first word of the name field.

Thus, the new entry is logically introduced only after it is complete, even if two disk accesses are necessary to build an entry.

Updating an existing entry can take two disk accesses if the entry sits on the limit of two sectors. An automatic recovery of the interruption of these two accesses is only possible with additional recovery data. We therefore restrict the updating of the file directory to the updating of parts of an entry which never overlap sector limits. This restriction is not necessary if in a particular format of the file directory entries do not overlap sector limits.

The disk scavenger

The analysis of the possible incidents has shown that an automatic recovery is not always possible. Some other means of repairing the system must be provided which can be used if automatic recovery fails. A disk scavenger can serve this purpose. If needed, it will be loaded, using an "autoload" procedure. We developed such a program, its main features are shortly outlined.

During a first phase the disk scavenger reads all files indicated in the file directory and checks their structure. Any error is announced at the console and must be corrected by a systems programmer with an octal disk debugger. In the second phase the free storage pool is checked and a garbage collection is performed. All sectors are announced which neither belong to a known data file nor to the free storage pool; the systems programmer must decide what to do with each garbage sector.

The necessity for the intervention of a systems programmer is a critical aspect of this disk scavenger. During the first phase, automation is not possible. To aid the programmer, the scavenger displays all possible details on the file and on the error. Nevertheless, the most important fact for the correction is the systems programmer's knowledge of the way data is structured on the disk. During the second phase, the scavenger accomplishes the correction but leaves the decision to the programmer whether to ignore a garbage sector, to return it to the free storage pool, or to create an entry in the file directory for the found sector. This last option is only possible if the garbage sector (and any other garbage sectors linked to it) constitutes a complete file. If more than one garbage sector is concerned, the scavenger automatically assembles all sectors in the new file. This feature is very important, because it allows to save all data files even if the entire file directory had been lost.

Conclusion

The described measures present a good compromise between the safety of the data on the disk and the overhead necessary to obtain this safety. These measures are easy to implement in any system where the structure of the data on the disk is realized by chaining and where the individual sectors carry some information, characteristic and unique to their file. We have accordingly modified the disk operating system (Decision DDOS 1.5) of our Data General NOVA computers. We never had to rewrite a new system on our disks since the modifications have been introduced about two years ago. The disk scavenger is extremely rarely needed, in the average less than once every two months. This is particularly remarkable, since one NOVA is used as a self service system by research scientists and by students during practical courses on programming.

OPERATING SYSTEMS WITH CHARACTERISTICS OF PORTABILITY FOR MINICOMPUTERS

R. Rossi (·) - M. Spadoni (+) - P. Toth (·)

1 - INTRODUCTION

The purpose of this work is to delineate a technique of defining managing software, in the direction of multiprogrammed minicomputers, capable of distinguishing this software from the hardware on which it will operate and easily adaptable to various operative conditions.

2 - THE ARCHITECTURE OF THE SYSTEM

In the proposed system, the software in the direction of the computing system (O.S.) is articulated in two distinct sections: the first has the task of assuming all decisions for an optimum management of the system; the second, to make those decisions operating. The two complexes of programs responsible for developing these activities are here indicated respectively as "executive" and "monitor". The executive, which in the proposed architecture constitutes the portable part of O.S., operates basically by means of scheduling functions; these choices are made on the basis of algorithms which calculate the priority of the user requests of system resources. The scheduling functions are constructed using logical forms, called "basic activities"; the set of these activities, which will be presented below, is defined in a manner which consents an easy representation of an O.S. for multiprogrammed minicomputers /1/, /2/.

3 - THE MONITOR

The tasks assigned to the monitor are:
- to actuate the orders of the executive, furnishing procedures of transfer, of saving and restoring of the registers;
- to transform the hardware interrupts to software interrupts directed by the executive which organizes them in a structure on various levels.

The monitor procedures operate at inhibited hardware interrupts. The monitor does not possess the capacity of modifying autonomously the status of the processes present in the system. It is a structure determined by the hardware configuration of the computer.

(·) Istituto di Automatica - Università di Bologna
(+) Sogesta S.p.A. - Urbino

4 - THE EXECUTIVE

The executive operates by means of scheduling funcions for the management of the resources associated with the software levels/3/, and by means of a routine of examination of the levels, for their direction. From a logical point of view, each single scheduling function is composed of three distinct procedures: 1) the insertion in the queue by the user who formulated the request; 2) scheduling of the requested resources on the basis of an examination of the software levels; 3) removal from the queue of the satisfied request after having utilized the resource.

At the end of each of these phases, control is ceded to the routine of examination of the levels, which operates at non-inhibited interrupts. The choice of this operating technique was determined by the opportunity of operating at inhibited interrupts during each single procedure/4/, consenting at the same time the maximum interaction of the hardware with the monitor.

4.1) Software Levels

The degree of portability of the system is determined by the possibility of installing, with minimal modifications, the same executive in contact with various monitors and thus with various hardware configurations. It is evident that the lesser the flow of necessary information between executive and monitor, the easier it is to create conditions for the portability of the O.S. In particular, the monitor must be detached at the maximum from a knowledge of the structure of the executive in order to avoid the redefinition of the monitor itself at each modification of the managing techniques.

On the basis of such considerations, in the proposed system the flow of information between executive and monitor takes place solely by means of a set of software levels realized in analogy with the hardware circuits of responses to interrupt. The levels are organized in a hierarchic set; each of them is associated with a resource. A level is assigned to the user by means of an executive order transmitted by software interrupt to the monitor; consequently the level is defined active. The program of a user who takes advantage of a resource associated with one level can, with this organization, contemporaneously utilize resources associated with other levels. To avoid the occurrence of deadlock conditions /5/,/6/, algorithms of the "banker" type are used.

The single resource not associated with any level, and that thus can be shared contemporaneously by several users, is the work memory. The examination routine of the software levels, which operates on non-inhibited interrupts, declenches the execution of the procedure associated with the active level of highest priority. The levels are examined by this routine beginning from that with the highest priority and going to that with the lowest priority without skipping a level. On the other hand, it is possible to skip from one level to a higher level at the moment of organization of a hardware interrupt. A software level is deactivated when there are no longer requests for it or when the user who is utilizing it must await a particular event before being able to release the resource.

All the resources associated with software levels do not necessarily have to be hardware. The single difference in the management of software resources is that the software interrupt, which signals the executive an "end of use of resource" event, must be given by the user instead of by the monitor.

The executive is capable of changing the priority of the software levels.

The advantages one can obtain from such a structure are essentially of two sorts:
- uniformity in the treatment of resources, which permits structuring the executive by means of a single class of functions characterized by a single logical structure and operating with various procedures according to the resources;
- determination of a precise line beyond which the O.S. is determined by the hardware of the computer and is thus not portable.

One possible structure of software levels could be organized with a timer associated with those with highest priority, a disc with the next high, peripheral lens with lower levels, the CPU and an information set organized in files for the lowest levels. It is possible to take into consideration levels with which, as resources, are associated procedures which have the same structure as the programs of the user/2/; these are considered to be the exclusive propriety of the executive which may order their execution on the basis of internal evaluations or on request of authorized users. Such an operating technique was foreseen in order to permit, especially in systems of process control, the execution of high-priority alarm programs, bypassing the scheduling system of the CPU. If ever these programs request resources in common with other users who cannot be pre-empted, they are deferred to the decisions of the respective schedulers.

4.2) Basic activities

Having identified the basic elements of the structure af the "executive", we here propose their construction by means of a set of blocks that would permit a flexible organization of the system/3/. In such manner, in fact, one obtains an economy of memory, since the same model may be used with various modalities, permitting the realisation of different procedures.

This methodology lends itself to an easy realisation of new operative strategies not foreseen at the moment the system was defined /4/: in fact, insertions of new procedures or changes in the operating system reveal themselves easier in as much as the system subjected to the modifications was structured according to a modular type architecture.

We have so identified the set of "basic activities" that we believe necessary and sufficient to rappresent the functions of a minicomputer operating system. Each basic activity A_k consists of a logical structure defined by a procedure P_k, applicable to an information set D_k which has a non-empty intersection with the basic information set of the O.S.

By means of this method system function is univocally identified by the sequence of the basic activities which constitute it and by the related information sets.

The organization proposed for system functions allows easy realization of strategies connected with an evaluation of the system temporal bounds in their dynamic evolution.

For this purpose it is a good thing to synchronize the activities in such a way as to make a complete temporal independence possible in their execution, though respecting the logical bounds imposed by the function of the executive of which they are a part; the flow of informations between the activities A_j and A_k is therefore brought back to the variation of the parameters of the system which belong to the set $D_j \cap D_k = I_{jk}$. It follows that two activities interact within the common sub-set I_{jk}.

4.3) Definition of the basic activities

a) Executive - Monitor Interaction

Following the definition previously given of the executive/monitor relations, the basic activities realizing the interaction operations are here shown by | SL| (Set Level) and |RL| (Reset Level); |SS| (Set Scheduler) and | RS| (Reset Scheduler).

The first activates or deactivates a software level; the second requires or not the execution of the scheduler (scheduling procedure) of the resource for which the level was activated.

b) Access to the queues.

Resources are assigned to the processes according to a "priority" that may be established by the user or computed by means of suitable algorithms.

When the request priority is known, its insertion in the right queue takes place through an activity |AI| (Append Item), characterized by two basic operations: to put the necessary parameters in the appropriate memory locations where the "request forms" are placed and to provide for correct connection of the pointers among the forms themselves for good requests arrangement based on their priority.

The removal of the requests from the queues is accomplished by an activity |RI| (Remove Item), that provides for the descheduling through a modification of the pointers that link the request forms.

c) Queue management

The scheduling procedure that, in the projected model, has the task of the management of the requests and of the resources, can be realized with different modalities, but always by means of a defined set of basic activities.

Its tasks are of four types:
- individuation of the request with highest priority: the operation takes place by means of the basic activity |EQ| (Examine Queue);
- check of the real request execution possibility: basic activity |AC| (Availability Check);
- activation of other eventual scheduling procedures involved in the decisions of the executing one: basic activity |SI| (System Interaction analysis);
- formal assignment of the controlled resource: basic activity |RA| (Resource Assign).

The activity |EQ| consists in examining the elements of a queue ordered according to the priority.

The activity |AC| executes a test operation: it can be interpreted either as a check of the right of the user to operate (protection), or as an examination of a real change of situation of the user which invalidates his demand, or as a control of the situation of the semaphore which regulates the access to a critical region, or as a verification of the presence of requests in a queue.

The activity |SI| individuates, by means of a tabular research, the schedulers involved in thus becomes necessary.

The activity |RA| works on the resource descriptor to define its user. Between the basic activities there are four other activities which can concur in the definition of a scheduler: |AP|, |DP|, |AR|, |DR|, (Activate Process, Deactivate Process, Activate Resource, Deactivate Resource), which the system emploies respectively to activate and deactivate a process and to declare a semaphore free or blocked: they are mentioned here for greater formal clarity, even if, from a logical point of view, they can be considered analogous to |AI|, |AP|, and |DR|, and to |RI|, |DP|, and |AR|.

d) <u>Correlation functions between events and schedulers.</u>

The events that can lead to the execution of a generic scheduler are jointed to changes in the status of the resource or of the queue of the waiting processes.

The sets of activities to be executed in such cases are defined "correlation functions".

In Figure 1 are shown the correlation functions that take place in consequence of the events BI (Busy Idle) and QM (Queue Modify) in relation, respectively, to the release and to the presentation of a request for a common resource. The activities |RL| and |SL|, though not necessary, (the first for hardware resources, the second for software), are executed just the same because the execution of an activity |AC| for the individuation of the type resource requires a longer time for computation.

5 - SYSTEM REPRESENTATION

We have assumed following rules:
- with the symbols ⊏⊐ we mean "permanent conditions", which, once declared, are true if not implicitly or explicitly denied;
- with the symbols ⊂⊃ we mean "temporary conditions", which do not hold any more when the transition to which they refer takes place;
- vertical lines represent "events" (or transition times);
- the arrows represent logical connections between conditions and events;
- conditions and events must always alternate;
- when all conditions hold, that concur to an event, a transition takes place;
- conditions between the same events must be considered contemporary.

The symbol ⊕ represent an "exclusive OR" and must be applied to all arrows with the same symbol concurring to or coming from an event. We represent in Fig. 2 the life of an user job in the system.

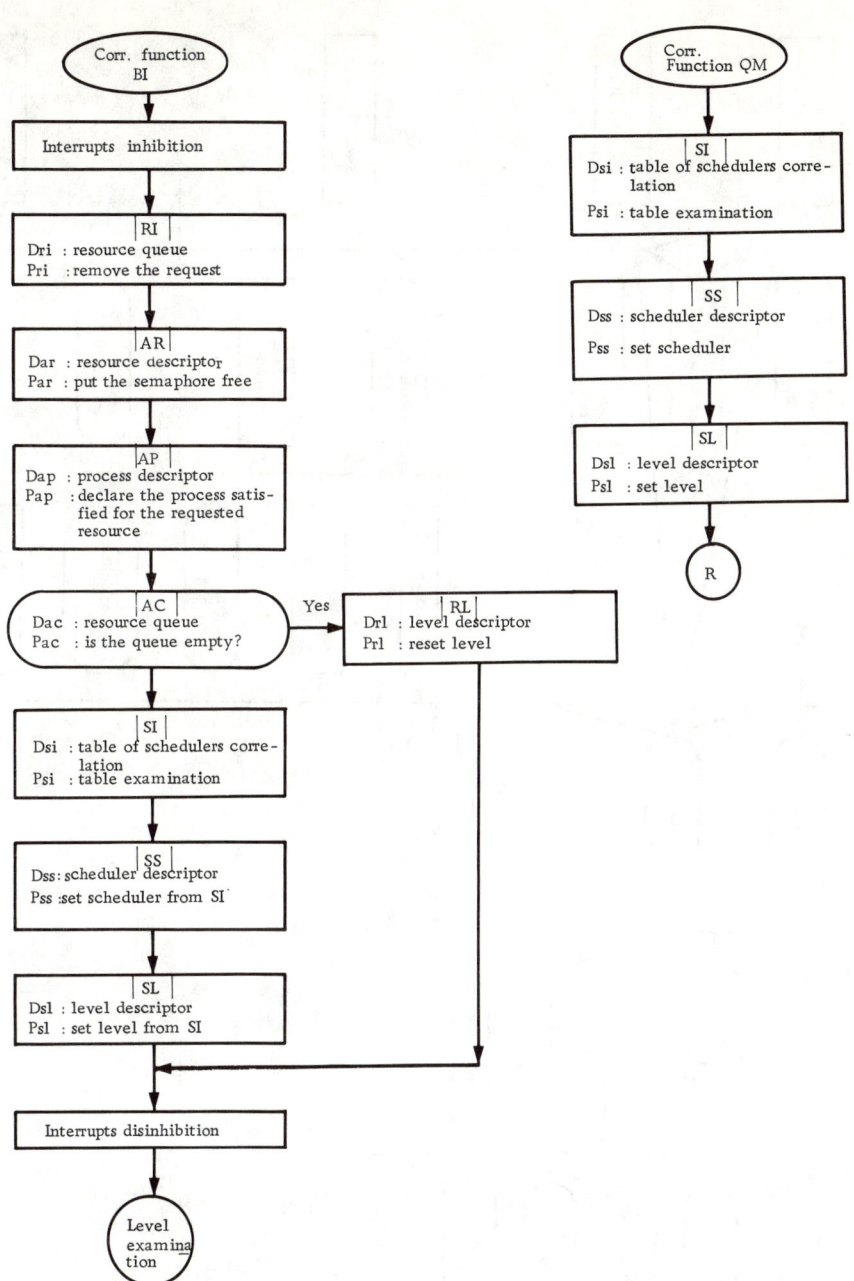

FIG. 1

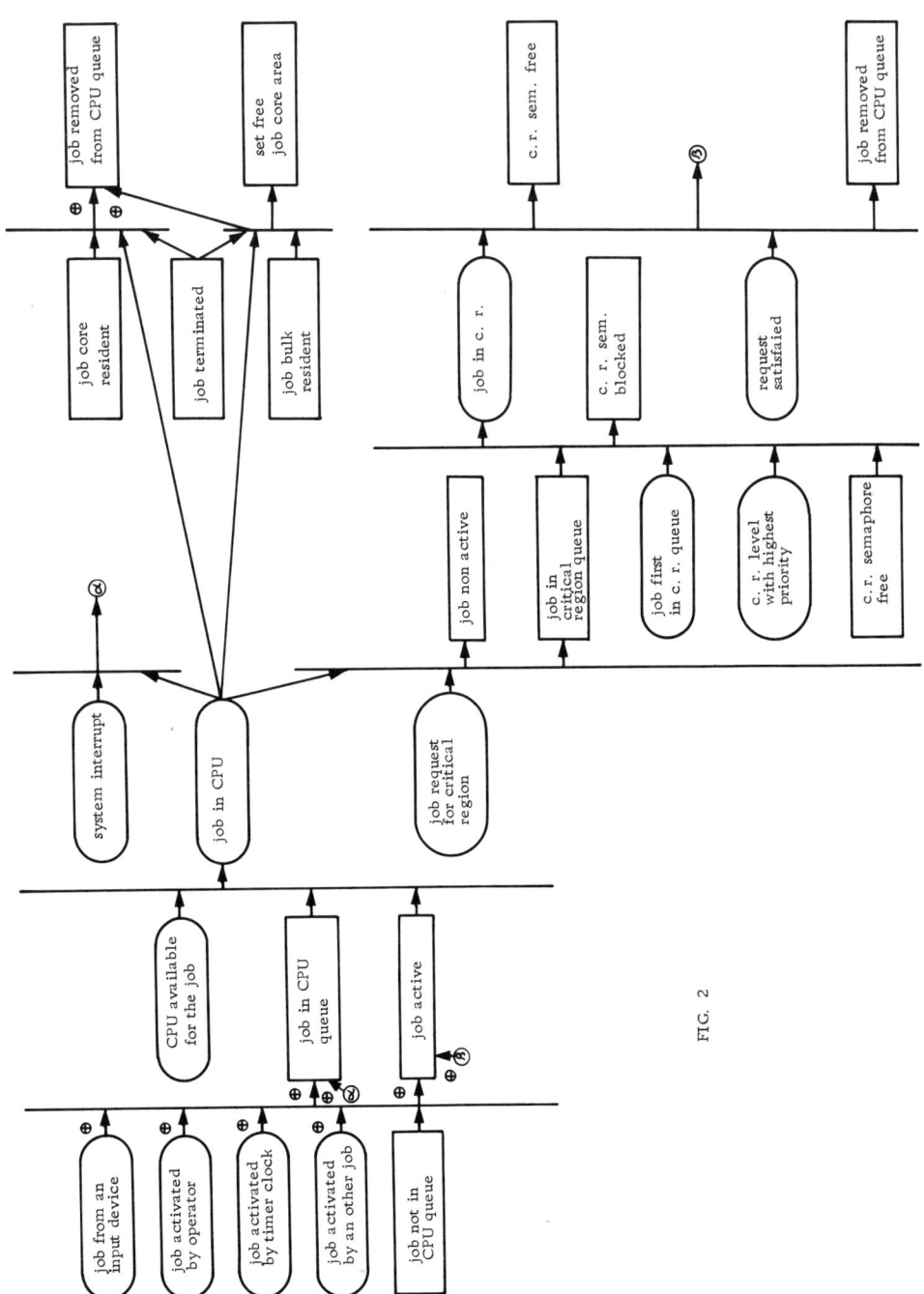

FIG. 2

LITERATURE

/1/ R.Rossi,M.Spadoni,P.Toth:"Sistemi operativi per minielaboratori" - Rapporto interno E7 - Istituto di Automatica - Università di Bologna (1973)

/2/ R.Rossi,M.Spadoni,P.Toth:"Criteri per la realizzazione di sistemi operativi con caratteristiche di portabilità per minielaboratori" - Rapporto interno E8 - Istituto di Automatica - Università di Bologna (1973)

/3/ L.Brizio,R.Rossi:"Generalizzazione dei sistemi operativi per minielaboratori" - Rapporto interno E5 - Istituto di Automatica - Università di Bologna (1972)

/4/ P.B.Hansen:"RC 4000 Software multiprogramming system" - RCSL No: 55-D140,Copenhagen,Regnecentralen (1971)

/5/ A.N.Habermann:"Prevention of system deadlocks" - Comm. ACM 13,7 (1969)

/6/ E.W.Dijkstra:"Cooperating sequential processes" - Programming Languages" - Ed. Genuys - Academic Press - pp. 43-112 - (1968)

TRACE DRIVEN STUDIES OF DEADLOCK CONTROL AND JOB SCHEDULING

Stephen W. Sherman*
Institute for Computer Applications in Science and Engineering
John H. Howard, Jr., and James C. Browne
The University of Texas at Austin

Abstract

A trace-driven model is used to study the effects of various schedulers and deadlock control algorithms in a general-purpose operating system. Jobs' requests for resources are extracted from a production load and used to drive a detailed simulation program. The simulation results show that the preemptive deadlock control algorithms give consistently good performance in terms of CPU utilization. The bankers algorithm and the detection and recovery deadlock control algorithms are susceptible to "knotting" (holding of resources by a blocked process) when there is no preemption, but their performance can be improved significantly by 1) allowing a moderate amount of preemption and 2) by forcing the job scheduler to limit the number of jobs competing for resources. When "knotting" is limited by either of the above methods, non-preemptive jobs scheduling improves CPU utilization. This paper extends and develops previous work and summarizes the interaction between some characteristics of job schedulers and deadlock control algorithms.

Acknowledgement

This research was supported by the National Science Foundation under grant GJ-1084, "Design and Analysis of Operating Systems" to the University of Texas at Austin and was made possible by the cooperation of the Computation Center of the University of Texas at Austin. The work was completed while the first author was in residence at ICASE, which is supported by NASA Grant NGR 47-102-001 at Langley Research Center.

I. Introduction

A variety of algorithms for dealing with the deadlock problem in operating systems have been proposed and compared qualitatively ([1][2][3][4]). This paper reports a quantitative study of the effects of deadlock control algorithms and job schedulers on CPU utilization.

CPU utilization is compared for two job loads of equal resource requirements. The actual job load had a number of interactive jobs which are reflected in an interactive model. Results from experiments with the interactive model are compared to results from a batch model which uses the same jobs as the interactive model but treats all jobs as if they were batch jobs.

Trace-driven modeling ([5][6][7]) is the vehicle used for this study. It is a simulation technique based on a detailed job load extracted from a production system, and is completely and historically described in [6]. It has also been used to study

---
*On leave from the University of Houston

other system algorithms such as CPU scheduling ([5][7]). A preliminary study of deadlock control algorithms in a batch environment, considering only the effect on CPU utilization, appears in [8]. The more sensitive measure of response time for interactive jobs was considered in [9].

This paper updates results from [8] and combines previous work ([5][9]) to develop new results on the positive effects of preemption on certain deadlock control algorithms. Further experiments are also presented which support conclusions in [9] concerning the need for an intelligent job scheduler preceding the deadlock control algorithm and the general good performance of preemptive deadlock control algorithms. The details of experimental precedures used to obtain the results reported in this paper have been previously reported in several papers ([5][6][7][8][9]) and are therefore only briefly sketched in this paper.

II. The Model and Environment

Trace-driven modeling is a technique whereby a recorded trace of system activities is directly used to define the environment and workload for a model of a computer system ([6]). Trace-driven modeling is a form of simulation which can be accurately validated. The model is validated by comparing its performance with the performance of the system whose data was recorded. Further information on trace-driven modeling in general can be found in [6] and very detailed information on this particular trace-driven modeling effort is in [5].

A CDC 6600 ([10]) was used to gather the trace data. The locally written operating system UT-2 ([5][11][12]) can support up to 13 user jobs and 3 system jobs concurrently. The user jobs have five peripheral processors for input/output, swapping, and system control functions.

The UT-2 system is a multiprogramming system that supports a mixed batch (5000 to 6000 jobs per day) and interactive (35 to 45 users simultaneously) load. Measurements used in the model were taken over a relatively long 30 minute period and a shorter 3 minute period with 1400 and 220 interactions respectively from the interactive users.

Two models are used to study the system. The first and earliest model ([5][8]) treats all jobs in the system as batch jobs. This model will be referred to as the batch model. The interactive jobs are included in this model in terms of their resource requirements, but they are not given any special priority and are not preempted for think time. That is, think time is assumed to be zero. The batch model was a reasonable model for the UT-2 system at the time the measurements were taken. Early versions of the system were completely batch oriented. A large majority of the users only used the batch system. The interactive system had only batch versions of language processors and utilities available to it. Figure 1 (without the interaction complete path) is an illustration of job processing in the batch model).

When the interaction complete path is included, Figure 1 shows a model of job processing in the interactive model. The interactive model is similar to the batch model in all respects except: 1) Interactive jobs are swapped out while waiting for input. 2) Think times are taken from the trace data and 3) The job scheduler treats interactive jobs in a slightly different way (explained below) than batch jobs. More detailed information on the interactive model may be found in [9].

The two job schedulers examined in the models are the preemptive scheduler (SP) that preempted jobs whenever less expensive jobs arrived in the job queue and a non-preemptive scheduler (SNP) which would not preempt at all in the batch model and limited preemption to interactive jobs in the interactive model. The actual scheduler used in the UT-2 system is very similar to the preemptive scheduler ([11]). Both the preemptive and non-preemptive schedulers had the following characteristics: 1) A cost was assigned to each job equal to the product of its current memory requirements and the amount of CPU time it needed before completing its current transaction. 2) The jobs were sorted in order of increasing cost. 3) The jobs were scanned least - cost first and any job that would fit into the available memory was selected. 4) At most 4 interactive jobs could be selected.

As in previous studies ([5][8][9]) four deadlock control algorithms are studied. The resources considered by the deadlock algorithms are central memory and peripheral processors. Immediate preemption, IP, is the technique used in the UT-2 system. If a job's request for memory cannot be satisfied immediately, the job is swapped out. Complete assignment, CA, prevents deadlocks by initially assigning to a job all of the resources it will ever need. Detection and recovery ([3]), DR, consists of running a deadlock detection algorithm whenever a job's request for additional resources cannot be satisfied and recovering if deadlock is detected. The "bankers algorithm" ([4]),BA, avoids deadlocks by assigning resources only when the system can find at least one safe sequence in which it can run all jobs.

III. Validation

In order not to distort the load presented to the simulated job scheduler ([6][9]), an initial queue of 55 jobs was selected from the pool of known jobs. The total amount of processing time used by the initial queue is stored as a threshold. Whenever the remaining processing in the simulated input queue drops below this threshold, new jobs are selected from the unused jobs.

Table 1 presents validation information for the relatively long measurement period. The first four columns represent data used in [9]. The actual and simulated interactive system performance measures (first two columns) agree to within 3.5%, with the measure most important here (CPU utilization) in agreement to within 1% relative error. The third column displays simulation results with the overhead associated with the software event recorder removed, showing that its effect was a degradation by approximately 2%. The fourth column gives results from a simulation with a different random ordering of the jobs, and again displays relative deviations of about 2%. The fifth column through the seventh column present the simulated batch system performance measures ([5]). Columns five and six correspond well to the simulated interactive system performance measures in columns two and three showing a slight improvement in performance due to fewer preemptions resulting in less overhead. The random ordering of the jobs in column seven was different from the ordering reflected in the results of the fourth column. The processing threshold for the initial set of jobs was about 11% of the threshold used in the initial ordering. This meant that the permuted batch model had a smaller number of jobs to consider throughout the run, and therefore the permuted batch model generated a lower degree of multiprogramming and utilized less memory. Even with this unfortunate random choice of the initial set of jobs, the model still agreed with the actual system in CPU utilization to within 2.5%. We conclude from this information that we have constructed a valid and stable simulation model of the actual system.

The short measurement period contains too few interactions and jobs to allow a convincing validation. Table 2 gives the comparison between actual and simulated system performance. The results based on the short period must be taken as showing trends only and as lending credence to the validated data from the longer measurement period.

IV. Results

Table 3 gives CPU utilizations for each combination of schedulers (SP and SNP), deadlock control algorithms (IP, CA, DR and BA) and models (interactive and batch) for the long measurement period. Table 4 gives the same set of CPU utilizations for the short measurement period.

In the interactive model in Table 3, the performance of each deadlock algorithm improved from 3.03% to 8.66% when the non-preemptive scheduler replaced the preemptive scheduler. The improvement in CPU utilization coincides with the decrease in overhead and delays caused by swapping. However, it is important to note that the non-preemptive scheduler, SNP, still swaps jobs in the interactive model due to the requirements for reasonable response time. (A parallel study ([9]) has shown that response times are worse using the SNP scheduler with the interactive model than with the SP scheduler). The batch model in Table 3 shows a performance improvement similar to the improvement in the interactive model using the IP and CA deadlock control algorithms with the SNP scheduler. However, the non-preemptive scheduler yields less CPU utilization than the preemptive scheduler using the DR and BA deadlock algorithms. This loss of CPU utilization for the detection and recovery algorithm (6.01%) and the bankers algorithm (18.40%) is not reflected in the batch model for the short measurement period in Table 4.

The significant characteristic which appeared in the DR and BA deadlock algorithms with the non-preemptive scheduler was the appearance of the "knotting" phenomenon. Knotting is the degradation of performance brought about by the tying up of resources by jobs which are not able to make effective progress ([8]). The deadlock algorithms DR and BA consider memory and peripheral processors as their non-preemptable resources and the number of peripheral processors being held by jobs requesting central memory is an indication of knotting. Table 5 shows that as the number of jobs holding peripheral processors and waiting for central memory increases, the CPU utilization decreases.

In the experiments in Table 3, the interactive model seems to have too much preemption activity using the preemptive scheduler. The performance was improved by using a non-preemptive scheduler and only preempting for a limited number (a maximum of 4 at one time) of interactive jobs. The decrease in preemption overhead overcame any tendency for the system to knot using the DR and BA algorithms. The performance of the batch model using the preemptive scheduler was almost equivalent to the interactive model. The non-preemptive scheduler was strictly non-preemptive in the batch environment and the lack of job preemption allowed knotting to dominate the resource environment for the DR and BA deadlock algorithms and more than compensate for any gains due to reduced overhead that were apparent in the IP and CA deadlock algorithms. Only a modest amount of preemption seemed to be needed to deter knotting since the interactive jobs averaged less than 1 interaction per second during the long measurement period. Statistical techniques ([5]) used to analyze the contributions of the deadlock control algorithms (IP, CA, DR, BA), job schedulers (SP, SNP), and models (batch, interactive) show that almost 60% of the observed variations in CPU utilization are accounted for by the interactions between variables. This large cross term indicates the significance of those interactions in designing an operating system. The need for preemption in the DR and BA algorithms is very unfortunate since these algorithms are usually used when preemption is difficult to achieve. The short measurement period in Table 4 was too short for knotting to develop. Jobs finished and resources were freed at a very rapid rate. Therefore, the non-preemptive scheduler always performed better than the preemptive scheduler.

In the batch model, some perturbations of the bankers algorithm and the detection and recovery algorithm were tried using the non-preemptive scheduler in an attempt to achieve better performance. Knotting had led to deadlocks in the detection and recovery algorithm. While only one deadlock was detected using the preemptive scheduler, 14 deadlocks occurred with the non-preemptive scheduler. The recovery procedure when a deadlock was detected was to preempt the resources currently held by the last job that caused the deadlock. When the recovery procedure was changed to preempt all of the jobs that held resources contributing to the deadlock, the CPU utilization increased from 61.40% to 67.45% using the non-preemptive scheduler.

An alternative technique for the bankers algorithm consisted of treating the peripheral processors requesting memory as preemptable resources. The batch model was changed to place the peripheral processor program that requested memory at the end of the queue of peripheral processor programs. The new technique returned an increase in CPU utilization of 9.02% over the CPU utilization of 48.15% presented in Table 3 for the non-preemptive scheduler.

In an attempt to reduce the contention for resources, the maximum number of user jobs is reduced in steps of 2 from 13 to 3 jobs. Three system jobs are always active. Table 6 shows the results of this experiment. The bankers algorithm steadily increased its performance under the non-preemptive scheduler until only a maximum of 3 user jobs were allowed. As a comparison, the same experiment was run using the preemptive scheduler with the immediate preemption deadlock control algorithm. The results of that experiment show little change in the CPU utilization with a barely perceptable downward trend when a maximum of 5 user jobs was allowed. Clearly, intelligent scheduling that removes congestion will aid the bankers algorithm. Similar results were found in [9].

The CPU utilizations of DR and BA reported here are markedly superior to those reported in the preliminary study ([8]). This is due both to the use of a model that is more comprehensive in its resolution of job characteristics and to the correction of an invalid implementation of DR and BA. Precise information on resource requirements, available and utilized in this trace-driven model, is highly favorable to the performance of CA and BA. Such precise information on resource requirements is not often available in normal production environments. The cost of preempting jobs on the system modeled in this study is very small since preempted jobs are swapped to extended core storage. The ease of preemption certainly helps the IP deadlock algorithm. The batch model was changed to assess the system a penalty in CPU time whenever a job was preempted in order to make preemption more expensive. Two experiments were conducted with system penalties of 100 milliseconds and 1 second using the SNP scheduler and the IP deadlock algorithm. CPU utilization dropped from 77.98% to 76.58% for the 100 millisecond penalty and to 60.29% for the 1 second penalty. One second of CPU time is a tremendous amount on a CDC 6600 and the performance of the IP deadlock mechanism under a penalty situation indicates that preemption should certainly be considered for deadlock control even if the cost is very high.

V. Conclusions

The simulation results presented here support the following conclusions. Non-preemptive job schedulers combined with the immediate preemption and complete assignment deadlock control algorithms yield better performance in terms of CPU utilization than preemptive job schedulers. The detection and recovery algorithm and the bankers algorithm are very susceptible to knotting when no preemption is allowed. A moderate amount of preemption can greatly improve the performance of both the detection and recovery algorithm and the bankers algorithm. The performance of deadlock control algorithms that are subject to knotting can also be improved by limiting the number of jobs competing for resources. CPU utilization can be improved in the detection and recovery algorithm by preempting all of the jobs that cause a deadlock rather than preempting the minimum number of jobs. The preemptive deadlock control algorithm gave consistently good performance even when a penalty for preemption was accessed.

References

1. Coffman, E. G., Elphick, M., and Shoshani, A., System deadlocks, Computing Surveys 3, 2 (June 1971), 67.

2. Holt, R. C., On deadlock in computer systems. Ph.D. dissertation, Department of Computer Science, Cornell University, Ithaca, N.Y., January 1971.

3. Shoshani, A., and Coffman, E. G. Detection and prevention of deadlocks. Fourth Annual Princeton Conf. on Information Sciences and Systems, Princeton, N. J., March 1970.

4. Habermann, A. N., Prevention of system deadlocks. Comm. ACM 12, 7 (July 1969), 373.

5. Sherman, S. W., Trace-driven modeling studies of the performance of computer systems. Ph. D. dissertation, Department of Computer Sciences, University of Texas, Austin, Texas, 1972.

6. Sherman, S. W. and Browne, J. C., Trace-driven modeling: Review and overview. Symposium on the Simulation of Computer Systems, Gaithersburg, Md., June 1973.

7. Sherman, S. W., Baskett, F., and Browne, J. C., Trace-driven modeling and analysis of CPU scheduling in a multi-programming system. Comm. ACM 15, 12 (Dec. 1972), 1063.

8. Sherman, S. W., Howard, J. H., and Browne, J. C., A comparison of deadlock prevention schemes using a trace-driven model. Sixth Princeton Conf. on Information Sciences and Systems, Princeton, N. J., March 1972, p. 604.

9. Sherman, S. W., Howard, J. H., and Browne, J. C., A study of response times under various deadlock algorithms and job schedulers. 1974 ACM National Conf., San Diego, Cal.

10. Thornton, J. E., Design of a Computer: The CDC 6600. Scott, Foresman and Co., Glenview, Ill., 1970.

11. Howard, J. H., A large-scale dual operating system. 1973 ACM National Conf., Atlanta, Ga., p. 242.

12. Johnson, D. S., A process-oriented model of resource demands in large multi-processing computer utilities. Ph.D. dissertation, Department of Computer Sciences, The University of Texas, Austin, Texas, 1972.

FIGURE 1 SYSTEM MODEL

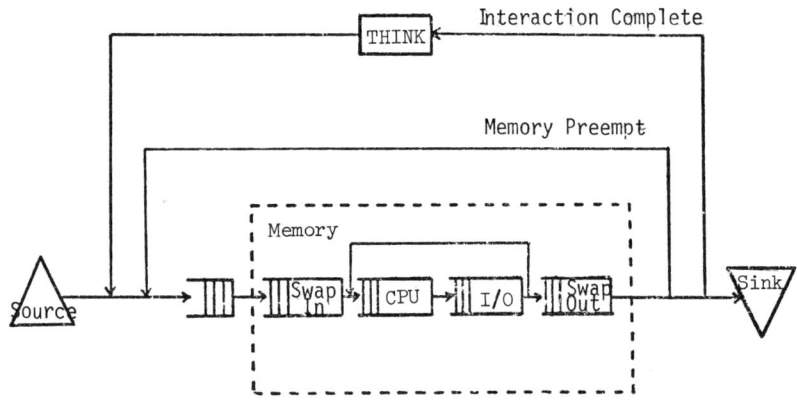

Table 1

VALIDATION OF LONG MEASUREMENT PERIOD

	Actual System	Interactive Model	Interactive Model Without Probe	Interactive Model Permuted	Batch Model	Batch Model Without Probe	Batch Model Permuted
ET^a	1637.719	1623.747	1578.504	1579.189	1589.34	1555.558	1697.027
CPU^b	69.73	70.32	72.34	73.30	71.84	73.40	67.28
PPU^c	82.6	85.5	81.5	83.3	85.9	84.4	79.9
DMP^d	8.38	8.28	8.33	8.43	8.72	8.76	7.06
Mem^e	121,880	120,027	115,443	115,346	116,510	116,457	95,617
RT^f	352	357	336	352			

a) running time in seconds
b) percentage of CPU utilized by user jobs
c) average percent of PPU resources utilized
d) degree of multiprogramming
e) average memory utilized (out of 131,072)
f) response time in milliseconds

Table 2

VALIDATION OF SHORT MEASUREMENT PERIOD

	Actual System	Interactive Model	Interactive Model Without Probe	Batch Model	Batch Model Without Probe
ET^a	199.172	207.518	202.402	193.353	189.530
CPU^b	47.16	45.26	46.40	48.58	49.56
PPU^c	96.7	97.0	94.0	97.8	98.1
DMP^d	10.17	10.48	10.23	10.79	9.74
Mem^e	116,930	114,291	109,791	113,194	105,801
RT^f	1373	1092	842		

Table 3

CPU UTILIZATION (PERCENT)
Long Measurement Period

	Interactive Model			
	IP	CA	DR	BA
SP	69.32	64.19	67.63	66.81
SNP	77.98	71.30	75.85	69.84

	Batch Model			
	IP	CA	DR	BA
SP	67.88	65.56	67.41	66.55
SNP	77.98	74.31	61.40	48.15

Table 4

CPU UTILIZATION (PERCENT)
Short Measurement Period

	Interactive Model			
	IP	CA	DR	BA
SP	42.31	40.83	40.14	38.83
SNP	48.13	45.66	47.03	45.12

	Batch Model			
	IP	CA	DR	BA
SP	44.57	42.62	43.67	42.80
SNP	50.73	49.33	47.71	45.62

Table 5

The effect of jobs holding peripheral processors and waiting for central memory using scheduler SNP and deadlock algorithms DR and BA. (Long Measurement Period)

Number of jobs holding and waiting	Percent of elapsed time using DR	Percent of time CPU was active using DR	Percent of elapsed time using BA	Percent of time CPU was active using BA
0	25.55	75.53	7.20	81.32
1	25.51	66.06	17.73	68.13
2	22.17	59.30	22.74	60.31
3	13.59	54.43	14.36	45.99
4	13.17	35.67	37.95	26.01

Table 6

Reduction of maximum number of user jobs from 13 to 3

Long Measurement Period

Maximum number of user jobs		13	11	9	7	5	3
CP scheduler and IP deadlock algorithm	Percent CPU utilization	67.88	67.88	67.88	67.91	67.81	
	DMP*	8.65	8.65	8.62	8.38	7.49	
SNP scheduler and BA deadlock algorithm	Percent CPU utilization	48.15	51.94	54.46	68.97	72.51	63.06
	DMP	10.91	10.67	10.30	9.32	7.86	5.96

*DMP - degree of multiprogramming includes the 3 system jobs

Zur Leistungsbewertung von Multiprozessor-Strukturen[*]

Siegfried Hoener
Informatik Forschungsgruppe 3
RWTH Aachen
Leiter: Prof. Dr. W. Ameling

1. Einleitung und Zusammenfassung

Zur Auswahl und Einsatzplanung von Datenverarbeitungsanlagen benötigt man Leistungs- oder Vergleichsmaßstäbe (vgl. z.B. BAUGUT [3], DWORATSCHEK und DONIKE [4], FLYNN [5]).
Die Ableitung geeigneter Bewertungsverfahren wird schwieriger mit zunehmender Komplexität der Rechnerstrukturen. Eine zweite Schwierigkeit besteht darin, für die große Streuung der möglichen Aufgaben allgemein gültige Aussagen zu treffen. Hier kann man zwei Fälle betrachten: Entweder eine Mittelwertuntersuchung für eine repräsentative Arbeitslast, oder eine Einzelproblemanalyse für wenige kritische Großprojekte.
In der vorliegenden Arbeit wird versucht, für den ersten Fall eine Systematik zu entwickeln, die bei Multiprozessorstrukturen eingesetzt werden kann. Dazu wird eine geeignete Erweiterung der Strukturbeschreibung von BELL und NEWELL [8] vorgenommen. Die Leistungsbewertung wird dann, nach Transformation des Strukturgraphen in einen Flußgraphen, zu einem Maximalflußproblem.
Neben der Leistungsbewertung kann ein Maß für die Ausfallempfindlichkeit angegeben werden.
Die Bewertung des Einzelproblemverhaltens kann im Rahmen dieser Arbeit nicht behandelt werden. Eine Veröffentlichung von dazu entwickelten Verfahren wird an anderer Stelle erfolgen.

2. Strukturdarstellung

Jede Datenverarbeitungsanlage setzt sich aus einer Reihe von Funktionseinheiten (Baugruppen) zusammen. Faßt man die Funktionseinheiten als abgeschlossene Gebilde auf, die durch ihre von außen erkennbaren Eigenschaften beschrieben werden können, dann wird die Struktur der DVA durch die Struktur der Verbindungen zwischen den einzelnen Funk-

---

[*] Die Arbeit wurde im Rahmen des Überregionalen Forschungsprogramms Informatik gefördert.

tionseinheiten beschrieben (z.B. PMS- (processor, memory, switch)-Darstellung von BELL und NEWELL [8]). Entsprechend dem jeweiligen Ziel der Untersuchungen können auch Betriebssystem-Module in die Menge der Funktionseinheiten einbezogen werden. Dieses ist eine wichtige Erweiterung, da z.B. in einer komplexen Struktur die gleichen Funktionen an der einen Stelle durch Software-Module ausgeführt werden können, während an einer anderen Stelle eine Hardwarebaugruppe dafür eingesetzt wird.

In der Struktur sind die Betriebssystem-Module entsprechend ihres Zusammenhangs miteinander und die Module der unteren Stufe mit den jeweiligen Prozessoren, durch die sie abgewickelt werden sollen, zu verbinden.
Etwas abstrakter ergibt sich damit die Strukturbeschreibung durch einen bewerteten Graphen.
Sei $\mathcal{F} = \{F_1, F_2, F_3, \ldots F_K\}$ die Menge der Funktionseinheiten, die an einem Datenverarbeitungssystem beteiligt sind, dann ist
$\mathcal{G}_S = (\mathcal{K}, \mathcal{Z}, BK)$ der <u>Strukturgraph</u> (Digraph [1]) mit:

$\mathcal{K} = \{K_1, \ldots, K_N\}$ Knotenmenge, nicht leer, endlich

$\mathcal{Z} = \{Z_1, \ldots, Z_M\}$ Zweigmenge endlich

$F : \mathcal{Z} \to \mathcal{K} \times \mathcal{K}$

$\phi_Z : \mathcal{Z} \to \mathcal{F} \times \mathcal{F}$

$\exists Z_m = (K_i, K_j)$ wenn zwischen den Urbildern von K_i und K_j eine von K_i nach K_j orientierte direkte Verbindung existiert.

BK = mehrwertige Knotenbewertungsfunktion (enthält die Eigenschaften der Funktionseinheiten),

F = (f_{im}) Inzidenzfunktion,

$f_{im} = \begin{cases} +1 & \text{für } \alpha Z_m = K_i \\ 0 & \alpha Z_m \neq K_i, \omega Z_m \neq K_i \\ -1 & \text{für } \omega Z_m = K_i \end{cases}$

αZ_m = Anfangsknoten von Z_m

ωZ_m = Endknoten von Z_m

$\mathcal{G}_S$ ist normalerweise zusammenhängend, wenn es sich um eine zusammenhängende Rechnerstruktur handelt.
Die Eigenschaften der Funktionseinheiten werden in der Knotenbewertungsfunktion festgehalten. Hier wird man in Abhängigkeit vom angestrebten Ziel eine mehr oder weniger detaillierte Darstellung wählen.

Die Strukturdarstellung erlaubt eine erste Bewertung verschiedener Systeme. So ist z.B. zu erkennen, welche Leistungen über welche Wege von welchen Knoten aus in Anspruch genommen werden können. Ein weiteres Kriterium ist der Grad des Zusammenhangs von $\mathcal{O\!f}_S$ für eine Abschätzung des Einflusses von Ausfällen einzelner Systemkomponenten (Funktionseinheiten) auf die Leistung der Struktur.

3. Leistungsbewertung

Häufig werden Großrechenanlagen in Rechenzentren für eine Vielzahl kleinerer oder mittlerer Aufgaben eingesetzt. Diese Betriebsart werde hier als Vielprogrammbetrieb bezeichnet. Kennzeichen dieser Betriebsart ist es, daß die Arbeitslast nur nach statistischen Gesichtspunkten gemessen werden kann. Entsprechendes gilt für die Leistungsbewertung.

3.1 Leistungsmaße, Ausfallempfindlichkeit

Zur Leistungsbewertung von Rechenanlagen bedient man sich häufig der sog. Mixkennzahlen ([3], GIBBSON Mix [5]), die ein Maß für die Verarbeitungsleistung bei Programmen mit einer entsprechenden Operationsverteilung darstellen.
Will man Aussagen für eine unterschiedlich strukturierte Arbeitslast ermitteln, zerlegt man zweckmäßig die Menge aller Programme
$\mathcal{R} = \{P_1 \ldots P_L\}$ in Klassen K_x $x = 1, \ldots X$ von Programmen mit näherungsweise gleichen Eigenschaften. Dann ermittelt man die mittleren Eigenschaften jeder Klasse und ordnet jeder Klasse einen Gewichtsfaktor g_x, $\sum_{x=1}^{X} g_x = 1$ entsprechend seiner Bedeutung oder Häufigkeit innerhalb der Arbeitslast zu. Gibt es ein Maß L_x für die Leistung einer Rechenanlage bei der Lösung von Aufgaben aus der Klasse K_x, dann kann man ein Leistungsmaß L für die gesamte Arbeitslast wie folgt ermitteln:

$$L = \sum_{x=1}^{X} g_x L_x$$

Statt eine Klassifizierung nach Programmen vorzunehmen, ist es oft besser, die Programme in Grundaufgaben (Tasks), wie z.B. Einlesen, Verarbeiten, Sortieren, Formatieren usw., zu zerlegen, die Tasks in Klassen einzuteilen und für jede Klasse die repräsentativen Merkmale zu bestimmen.
Ausgehend von einem eingeführten Leistungsmaß kann man die <u>Ausfallempfindlichkeit</u> einer Datenverarbeitungsanlage definieren:
Ist L die Leistung eines Systems im vollständig intakten Zustand und L_v die Leistungsfähigkeit nach Ausfall einer Komponente $K_v \in \mathcal{Q}$ (bzw. $Z_v \in \mathcal{Z}$) dann ist

$$E_v = \frac{L}{L_v} - 1$$

ein Maß für die Ausfallempfindlichkeit des Systems bei Ausfall der Komponente K_v (bzw. Z_v). E_v ist Null, wenn das System unempfindlich gegen Ausfall von K_v (bzw. Z_v) ist. E_v ist unendlich, wenn mit Ausfall einer Komponente das Gesamtsystem ausfällt.

3.2 Transformation auf ein Flußproblem

Multiprozessorsysteme sind i.a. sehr komplexe Anlagen, die häufig für Leistungsmessungen nicht zur Verfügung stehen. Es ergibt sich daher die Aufgabe, anhand der Leistungsangaben der einzelnen Komponenten, zu einer Leistungsbewertung zu kommen. Diese kann nur aus der Strukturbeschreibung gewonnen werden, da die Leistung des Systems nicht gleich der Summe der Komponentenleistungen gesetzt werden kann. Entscheidend ist vielmehr, wie gut die Kapazitäten der zusammenhängenden Funktionseinheiten bezüglich der Aufgabenstruktur aufeinander abgestimmt sind.

Aus diesen Gedanken ergibt sich der Ansatz, die Leistungsbewertung als ein Flußproblem anzusehen. Dazu ist der Strukturgraph in geeigneter Weise in einen Flußgraphen zu transformieren.
Die vorliegende Arbeit beschränkt sich auf die Betrachtung eines skalaren, homogenen Flußproblems. Für feinere Untersuchungen kann man zu inhomogenen vektorwertigen Flußgrößen übergehen. Die mathematische Behandlung wird dann erheblich schwieriger (vgl. z.B. HU [6]).

3.2.1 Bearbeitungsreihenfolge

Die Bearbeitung einer repräsentativen Aufgabe P_x aus einer Klasse K_x setzt sich aus einer Reihe von Teilschritten $(p_{x1}...p_{xn})$ zusammen, die jeweils Funktionseinheiten eines bestimmten Typs $f(F_k)$, $F_k \in \mathcal{F}$ erfordern (z.B. Arbeitsspeicher, E/A Verwaltung, Prozessor usw.). Zur Lösung muß daher die Aufgabe in einer bestimmten Reihenfolge die Funktionseinheiten der Rechenanlage durchlaufen, wobei i.a. nur die Reihenfolge der Funktionstypen von Bedeutung ist.
Unter <u>Bearbeitungsreihenfolge</u> T_x sei die den Aufgaben zuzuordnende Reihenfolge (t_i) der Funktionstypen $t_i = f(F_k)$ definiert : $T_x = (t_i)$, i=1,...,J. Die Bearbeitungsreihenfolge kann für verschiedene Klassen aus der Arbeitslast unterschiedlich sein.

3.2.2 Flußgraph

Ein Diagraph $\mathcal{G}_F = (\mathcal{K}_F, \mathcal{Z}_F, C)$ sei ein <u>Flußgraph</u> mit:
$\mathcal{K}_F$ = Knotenmenge, $|\mathcal{K}_F|$ endlich,
$\mathcal{Z}_F$ = Zweigmenge, $F_F : \mathcal{Z}_F \to \mathcal{K}_F \times \mathcal{K}_F$

C = Kapazitätsfunktion über $\mathcal{Z}_F$

$\exists\ K_q \in \mathcal{K}_F$: Quelle

$\exists\ K_s \in \mathcal{K}_F$: Senke

Die zu lösende Aufgabe besteht nun darin, den Strukturgraphen $\mathcal{G}_S$ in einen Flußgraphen $\mathcal{G}_F$ zu transformieren, und zwar unter Berücksichtigung der jeweiligen Bearbeitungsreihenfolge $T_x = (t_k)$, $k = 1,\ldots,J$. Dabei gelten folgende allgemeine Beziehungen:

a. $\{K_i\} \rightarrow \mathcal{Z}_j^* \subset \mathcal{Z}_F$, $K_i \in \mathcal{K}$

b. Die Eigenschaften von Teilmengen $\mathcal{Z}_j^*$ der Zweige in $\mathcal{G}_F$ gehen aus den Eigenschaften der Urbildknoten K_i durch Skalierung hervor (näheres s.u.).

Konstruktion:

1. Zerlegung von $\mathcal{K}$ in $\mathcal{K}_V$ und $\mathcal{K}_K$, $\mathcal{K} = \mathcal{K}_V \cup \mathcal{K}_K$, $\mathcal{K}_V \cap \mathcal{K}_K = \phi$
   $\mathcal{K}_V$ = Menge der Verarbeitungsknoten (Prozessor-, Speicher-, Ein-/ Ausgabeknoten usw.), $\mathcal{K}_K$ = Kanalknoten.

2. Konstruktion von Teilgraphen $\mathcal{T}_j$, $j=1\ldots J$.
   $\mathcal{T}_j$ disjunkt $\mathcal{T}_i$, $i\ \{1,\ldots J\}$, $j\ \{1,\ldots J\}$
   $\mathcal{T}_j = (\mathcal{K}_j^*, \mathcal{Z}_j^*, C_j^*)$, $\mathcal{Z}_j^* = \{Z_{ij}^*\}_{i=1,\ldots,dj}$
   $(\{\alpha Z_{ij}^*, \omega Z_{ij}^*\}, Z_{ij}^*, c_{ij}^*)$ disjunkt
   $(\{\alpha Z_{kj}^*, \omega Z_{kj}^*\}, Z_{kj}^*, c_{kj}^*)$,
   mit $Z_{ij}^* \in \mathcal{Z}_j^*$, $Z_{kj}^* \in \mathcal{Z}_j^*$
   und αZ = Anfangsknoten von Z,
   ωZ = Endknoten von Z.
   In den Teilgraphen $\mathcal{T}_j$ werden alle $K_n \in \mathcal{K}_V$ abgebildet, deren Typ t_j ist, d.h. die in der Stufe j der Bearbeitungsreihenfolge aktiv sein können.

3. Sind in $\mathcal{G}_S$ Prozessoren unterschiedlicher Leistung mit demselben Arbeitsspeicher S_i ohne Zwischenschaltung weitere Speicher verbunden, so ist in den entsprechenden Speicherteilgraphen für jeden Prozessortyp ein Bild von S_i einzutragen.

4. Abbildung $\mathcal{K}_K \rightarrow \mathcal{Z}_K$, derart, daß $Z_m \in \mathcal{Z}_K$, wenn $\alpha Z_m = \omega Z_{ij}^*$, $\omega Z_m = \alpha Z_{p,j+1}^*$ und $\exists K_n \in \mathcal{K}_K$, so daß K_n in $\mathcal{G}_S$ direkt, also über keine weiteren Knoten, mit den Urbildern von Z_{ij}^* und $Z_{p,j+1}^*$ verbunden ist.

5. Verbinden des Quellknotens K_q mit den Eingangszweigen Z^*_{i1} durch Zweige Z_{qi}, $\alpha Z_{qi} = K_q$, $\omega Z_{qi} = \alpha Z^*_{i1}$.

6. Verbinden der Z^*_{iJ} mit der Senke K_s durch Z_{is}, $\alpha Z_{is} = \omega Z^*_{iJ}$, $\omega Z_{is} = K_s$.

3.2.3 Skalierung

Da die Untersuchung der Leistung nur in Abhängigkeit von den Eigenschaften der einzelnen Aufgabenklassen erfolgen kann, ist es zweckmäßig, die Anforderungen $r^+_x(t_i)$ an die einzelnen Funktionseinheiten als Bezugsgrößen für deren Leistungsfähigkeit zu wählen.

Es sei $A_x = (r^+_x(t_i))$, $i=1,\ldots,I_x$, eine repräsentative Aufgabe für die Klasse K_x. Dann ergibt sich aus der angenommenen Kapazität $c^+(F_k)$ einer Funktionseinheit F_k die bezüglich K_x skalierte Kapazität:

$$c_x(F_k) = \frac{c^+(F_k)}{r^+_x(f(F_k))} \; .$$

Z.B. wird die skalierte Prozessorleistung in Tasks pro Zeiteinheit angegeben und kann damit als Kapazitätsgröße in das Flußnetz eingesetzt werden. Entsprechendes gilt für die anderen verarbeitenden oder übertragenden Funktionseinheiten, wie z.B. Ein- Ausgabe, Kanalwerk usw.

Eine Schwierigkeit ergibt sich bei der Betrachtung der Speicherkapazitäten, die man nicht ohne weiteres auf die Zeit beziehen kann. Bei den Massenspeichern kann man gegebenenfalls davon ausgehen, daß sie i.a. hinreichend groß ausgelegt werden, also von ihrer Kapazität keine Einschränkung der Leistung ausgeht.

Dieser Standpunkt ist bei den Arbeitsspeichern jedoch keinesfalls zulässig, da sie in sehr vielen Fällen knapp ausgelegt sind und damit die Leistung bestimmen.

Eine genaue Bestimmung des Durchsatzes an Tasks durch den Speicher ist schwierig und wird außer vom Speicher selbst, von der Kanalleistung, der Speicherstrategie und insbesondere von der Leistung der angeschlossenen Prozessoren bestimmt.

Kanaleinfluß und Speicherstrategie können durch einen Speicherladefaktor b erfaßt werden, der angibt, wieviel Speicherplatz über den Nettobedarf einer Tasks hinaus zur Verfügung gestellt werden muß, damit der Prozessor nach Beendigung einer Aufgabe sofort zur nächsten weitergehen kann. In erster Näherung sei hier b=2 gewählt (Wechselpufferbetrieb). Genauere Werte müssen durch Messung ermittelt werden.

Besteht eine direkte Verbindung zwischen einem Arbeitsspeicher S_i und einem Prozessor P_j, dann ergibt sich die transformierte Anforderung

$$r_x(f(F_k)) = \begin{cases} r_x^+(f(F_k)) & \text{bei } f(F_k) \neq \text{Speicher} \\ \dfrac{b \cdot r_x^+(f(F_k))}{c_x(P_j)} & \text{bei } f(F_k) = \text{Speicher} \end{cases}$$

Da eine Funktionseinheit verschiedene Schritte in der Bearbeitungsfolge ausführen kann (z.B. Kanalwerk), bzw. ein Speicher verschiedene Prozessoren bedienen kann, also das Bild eines Knotens $K_i \in \hat{\mathcal{R}}$ eine Zweigmenge $\mathcal{Z}_g = \{Z_{g1},\ldots,Z_{gMg}\}$, $\mathcal{Z}_g \subset \mathcal{Z}_F$ sein kann, ergibt sich aus den Eigenschaften von K_i eine <u>Gemeinschaftskapazität</u> (GK) c_g, $g \in \{1,\ldots,G\}$ (G = Anzahl der GK eines Flußgraphen), deren Aufteilung auf die einzelnen Z_{gm} nicht festliegt. Es muß gelten: $c_{gx}(K_i) \geq \sum_{m=1}^{M_g} a_{gm} \cdot w_{gm}$, wenn w_{gm} der Fluß im Zweig Z_{gm} und a_m der zugehörige Flußfaktor (s.u) ist.
Allgemein ergibt sich dann folgende Skalierungsformel für Gemeinschaftskapazitäten

$$c_{gx}(K_i) = \frac{c^+(K_i)}{\sum_{m=1}^{M_g} r_{xn}(f(K_i))}$$

mit den Anforderungen $r_{xm}(f(K_i))$ entsprechend der Stufe der Bearbeitungsreihenfolge, die durch den Zweig Z_{gm} repräsentiert wird.
Die Flußfaktoren a_m ergeben sich aus der Beziehung:

$$a_{gm} = \frac{r_{xm}(f(K_i))}{\sum_{n=1}^{M_g} r_{xn}(f(K_i))}$$

3.2.5 Reduktionen

Die Behandlung eines Flußgraphen wird durch geeignete Reduktionen erleichtert. Hier sollen einige Reduktionsregeln ohne Beweise vorgestellt werden:

a. Besitzt ein Flußgraph parallele Zweige, die keiner oder der gleichen GK angehören, dann lassen sich die Zweige mit der Summe der Einzelkapazitäten bzw. der Summe der Flußfaktoren zusammenfassen.
b. Zweiteilung von Zweigen lassen sich beseitigen, wenn:
    b1. keiner der Zweige einer GK angehört (der resultierende Zweig erhält das Minimum der beiden Einzelkapazitäten),
    b2. beide Zweige der gleichen GK angehören (der resultierende Zweig bleibt in der GK, die Flußfaktoren addieren sich).
c. Existiert eine fortlaufend orientierte Folge von Zweigen, deren gemeinsame Knoten vom Grade 2 sind (nur 2 inzidente Zweige), so können die Zweige gegeneinander vertauscht werden.
d. Gehen von einem Knoten zwei Zweige aus, so können die Endknoten der

beiden Zweige zusammengelegt werden, wenn die Endknoten keine weiteren zulaufenden Zweige besitzen und die beiden Zweige keiner oder der gleichen GK angehören. Die Kapazität des resultierenden Zweiges ergibt sich aus der Summe der Einzelkapazität bzw. aus einem Anteil an der GK.

e. Gehen von einem Knoten K_i zwei Zweige aus, die keiner oder der gleichen GK angehören, dann kann es zu Vereinfachungen führen, wenn man die Zweige durch Einführen von zusätzlichen Knoten zweiteilt und den mit K_i inzidenten Zweig die Kapazität beläßt, während die Hilfszweige unbegrenzte Kapazität erhalten.

f. In manchen Fällen kann eine Reduktion des Flußgraphen aufgrund von Symmetrieeigenschaften vorgenommen werden.

g. In Erweiterung der Regel d lassen sich auch Teilgraphen der folgenden Form vereinfachen, sofern die Zweige keiner oder der gleichen GK angehören.

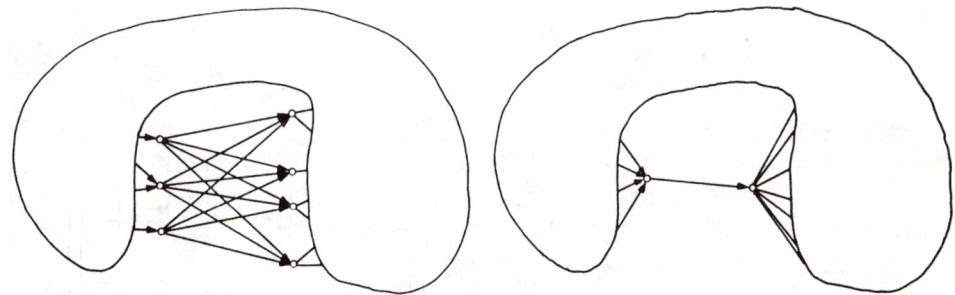

3.2.6 Ermittlung der Leistung

Nach der Transformation des Strukturgraphen in einen Flußgraphen ist die maximale Leistung der Multiprozessorstruktur durch die Bestimmung des maximalen Flusses (Durchsatzes) von der Quelle zur Senke zu ermitteln.

Gelingt es, durch Reduktion des Flußgraphen, alle Gemeinschaftskapazitäten zu beseitigen, dann liegt ein normales Maximalflußproblem vor, das mit dem Algorithmus von FORD und FULKERSON [6] gelöst werden kann.

Lassen sich die Gemeinschaftskapazitäten nicht beseitigen, dann kann versucht werden, mit dem "Out of Kilter"- Algorithmus [7] zur Lösung zu kommen, indem man die Gemeinschaftskapazitäten auf die beteiligten Zweige aufteilt und diesen Zweigen große Kostenfunktionen zuordnet. Findet man eine Aufteilung, bei der die Zweige mit Gemeinschaftskapazitäten an keiner Stelle den Fluß begrenzen (Engpaß bei nicht GK-Zweigen), dann ist der maximale Fluß gefunden.

Kann man diese Aufteilung nicht angeben, so kann mit einem heuristischen Verfahren versucht werden, eine Lösung zu finden. Darauf kann in diesem Zusammenhang nicht näher eingegangen werden. Bisher betrachtete Beispiele ließen sich mit einer mehrmaligen Anwendung des "Out of Kilter" Algorithmus lösen.
Entsprechend erfolgt die Ermittlung der Ausfallempfindlichkeiten, indem man, nach entfernen der Bildzweige der ausfallenden Funktionseinheit den reduzierenden Fluß bestimmt.

4. Beispiel

Die wesentlichen Schritte seien an einem einfachen Beispiel demonstriert. Gegeben sei eine Multiprozessorstruktur:
Der zugehörige Strukturgraph (ohne Berücksichtigung von Betriebssystemmodulen) ist in Bild 4.2 dargestellt (Paare antiparallel orientierter Zweige sind zur Vereinfachung der Darstellung durch Zweige ohne Orientierung ersetzt). Mit der stark vereinfachten Bearbeitungsreihenfolge (E, M, S, P, S, M, A) = (Einlesen, Massenspeicher, Arbeitsspeicher, Prozessor, Arbeitsspeicher, Massenspeicher, Ausgabe) kann folgender Flußgraph konstruiert werden: Bild 4.3 .
Durch mehrere Reduktionsschritte und durch Ausnutzung des sich bei einer Zusammenfassung der Ein- Ausgabe ergebenden Symmetrie kann man zu dem reduzierten Flußgraphen kommen. Die Kapazitätswerte ergeben sich aus einer ange-

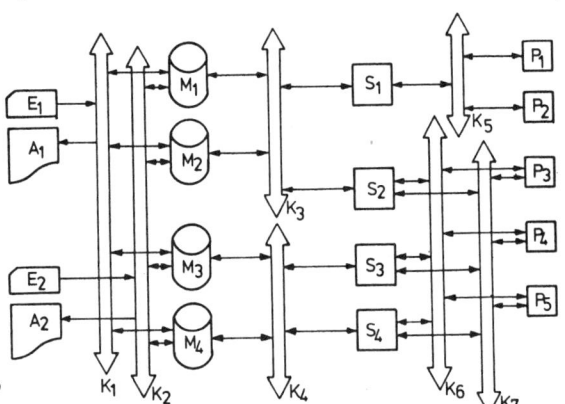

Bild 4.1 Multiprozessorstruktur

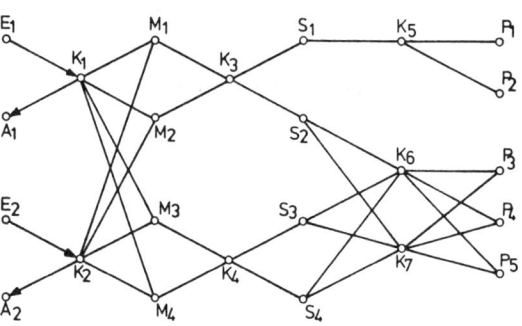

Bild 4.2 Strukturgraph

nommenen repräsentativen Aufgabe. Die einfache Darstellung bei den Arbeitsspeichern kommt aus der Annahme, daß alle 5 Prozessoren gleiche Leistung haben. Der Flußgraph läßt sich noch weiter reduzieren, wenn man Reduktionsregel f anwendet. Dabei lassen sich auch die beiden noch vorhandenen Gemeinschaftskapazitäten noch eliminieren. Die im Flußgraph

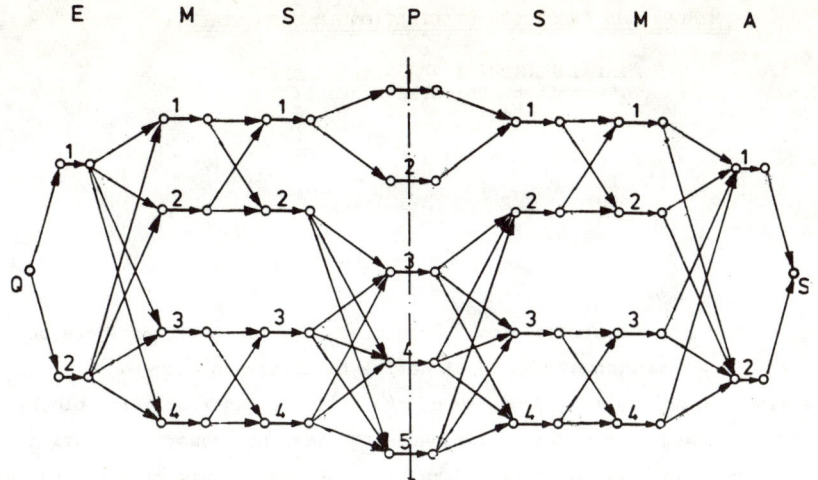

Bild 4.3   Flußgraph

nicht reduzierten Parallelzweige sind nur deshalb erhalten geblieben, weil zur Bestimmung der Ausfallempfindlichkeit einzelne Zweige entfernt werden müssen.

Es ergibt sich folgende Auswertung:

L = 780 Tasks / Zeiteinheit, Ausfallempfindlichkeit s. Tabelle.

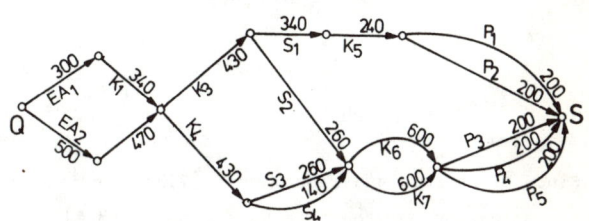

Bild 4.4   reduzierter Flußgraph

i	ausf. Funktionseinheit				
	EA_i	K_i	M_i	S_i	P_i
1	0.63	0.63	0	0.3	0
2	1.6	1.6	0	0.22	0
3	–	0.95	0	0.37	0.22
4	–	0.83	0	0.13	0.22
5	–	0.3	–	–	0.22
6	–	0	–	–	–
7	–	0	–	–	–

Tabelle Ausfallempfindlichkeit

5. Literaturverzeichnis

[1] HARARY,F.;NORMAN,R.,Z.;CARTWRIGHT,D.:Structural Models,Wiley&Sons, 1965
[2] SACHS,H.:Einf.in die Theorie der endl.Graphen,Hanser,München 1971
[3] BAUGUT,G.:Modelle zur Auswahl von DVA, Müller, Köln 1973
[4] DWORATSCHEK,S.;DONIKE,H.:Wirtschaftskeitsanalyse von Informationssystemen, de Gruyter, Berlin 1972
[5] FLYNN,M.J.:Trends and Problems in Computer Organization, IFIP 1974 North-Holland 1974, S.3-10
[6] HU,T.C.: Ganzzahlige Programmierung u.Netzwerkflüsse,Oldenburg, München 1972
[7] ELMAGHRABY,S.E.:Some Network Models in Management Science,Lecture Notes in Operations Research Nr.29, Springer 1970
[8] BELL,C.G.;NEWELL,A.: Computer Structures, McGraw-Hill, 1971

MEMORY AND PROCESSOR UTILIZATION IN SAFE STATES

Sigram Schindler and Steffen Buder
Technische Universität Berlin

Abstract: The paper describes tools developed in order to investigate the question whether - if preemption of memory of active tasks is not allowed - a restrictive task activation policy (avoiding any of the active tasks from being blocked for a while due to the memory constraints) reduces the mean processor utilization compared to a more liberal activation policy (implying the risk of blocking active tasks for a while due to memory constraints).

1. Introduction

Since Dijkstra's and Habermann's [1,2] work on deadlock prevention and Denning's investigations of the thrashing problem [3,4] a lot of knowledge concerning the multiprogramming problem has been accumulated [5]. Although the problems of deadlock prevention and thrashing prevention are of quite different nature it was shown in [6] that deadlock prevention algorithms can be used in paging algorithms in order to improve utilization of the central processor and memory (under certain circumstances).

In the next section - after introducing a very simple computer model - this dependency of the efficiency of nonpreemptive paging algorithms on the amount of information about program behaviour is discussed. At its end we explain briefly two alternatives for nonpreemptive paging algorithms based on such information, i.e. paging algorithms based on deadlock prevention.

The third section contains the detailed formulation of the problem investigated in this paper in terms of finite Markov chains. In order to obtain results with a reasonable amount of effort we focus our attention on the investigation of the average utilization of the processor by investigating the steady state only.

A very first quantitative result of this approach to the multiprogramming problem is explained in the fourth section. It is valid only under the assumptions formulated there and says that processor and memory utilization is not necessarily decreased as a consequence of applying a restrictive and very simple deadlock prevention algorithm (in the nonpreemptive paging algorithm), although the more liberal but more elaborate Banker's algorithm [1,2] could have been applied, too. In [10] the same result was obtained already previously by simulation (under quite realistic circumstances).

2. The Model and Definitions

The model of a computer used consists of working memory and a processor only. Let totmem denote its total number of identical memory units, i.e. page frames. The working load on this computer consists of a set of tasks independent of each other, denoted by $\underline{T}$, to be run on the computer. Obviously the notion of "task" has to be specified in more detail in order to allow the investigation of processor and memory utilization when executing $\underline{T}$, i.e. the efficiency of paging algorithms. A broad discussion of the notion of task used in this paper is given in [6]; therefore an informal introduction of tasks suffices here. For an extensive description of the relation between deadlock prevention algorithms and nonpreemptive paging algorithms see [6], too.

A task $T^{(j)}$ can be described by a set of random variables $X_t^{(j)}$, $t \in \underline{I}$, depending on a parameter t varying in a set of real numbers, denoted by $\underline{I}$. $X_t^{(j)}$ is the number of page frames needed by $T^{(j)}$ at time t. t here stands for real time or (virtual) $T^{(j)}$-time (see [4] or [6]); which one is relevant can always easily be seen from the context. The realization of task $T^{(j)}$ at time t is denoted by $x_t^{(j)}$. The tupel $(x_t^{(j)})_{t \in \underline{I}}$ represents the behaviour of the task $T^{(j)}$, i.e. we introduce

$$T^{(j)} := (x_t^{(j)})_{t \in \underline{I}} \ .$$

$x_t^{(j)}$ is the size of this tasks working set at time t. $T^{(j)}$'s maximal working set size is denoted by $mwss^{(j)}$, i.e. $mwss^{(j)} = \max_{t \in \underline{I}} \{x_t^{(j)}\}$. The set of "active" tasks, denoted by $\underline{T}_{a,t}$ is the subset of $\underline{T}$ consisting of all tasks holding page frames at time t. $\underline{T}_{a,t}$ is obtained by applying a memory allocation policy to $\underline{T}$. A task $T^{(j)}$ cannot be executed on the computer at time t unless it holds $x_t^{(j)}$ page frames at this time.

Throughout this paper we assume that all the tasks have the same mean processor utilization (see [6]), denoted by mpu, where $0 < mpu \leq 1$. This allows to define the mean utilization of the processor at time t, denoted by $MPU(m_t)$, where m_t denotes the number of active tasks holding all their x_t page frames at this time.
Then $MPU(1) = mpu$ and in general (see [9] for details)

$$MPU(m_t) = \frac{mpu}{mpu+(1-mpu)^{m_t}} \qquad (1)$$

Figure 1 shows the dependency of $MPU(m_t)$ on m_t for different values of mpu. Note that mpu can be increased by allowing larger x_t, whereas the reduction of a tasks working set sizes implies an increase in this tasks page traffic (see [4,6,11,12]) and therefore a reduction of its mpu.

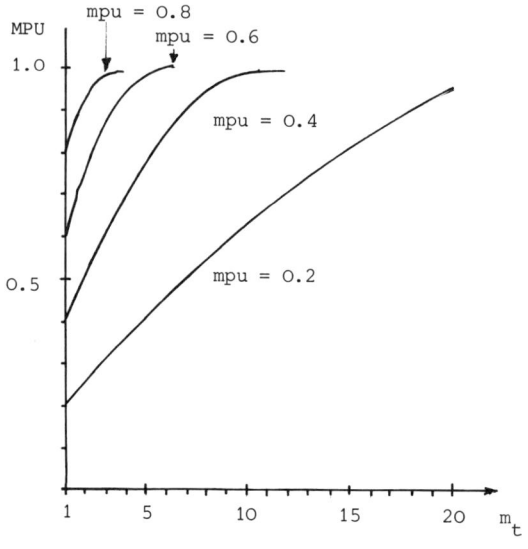

Figure 1

The utilization of memory at time t, denoted by $MU(m_t)$, then is

$$MU(m_t) = \frac{\sum_{j=1}^{m_t} x_t^{(j)}}{totmem}, \qquad (2)$$

where m_t is defined above.

a) <u>The Basic Nonpreemptive Task Activation Policy</u>

This task activation (and therefore: memory allocation) policy is characterized by the fact that a task $T^{(j)}$ - once activated - is guaranteed to get $x_t^{(j)}$ page frames at $T^{(j)}$-time t. Applying this policy restricts the number of tasks that can be active at any time t by implying $\sum_{T^{(j)} \in \underline{T}_{a,t}} mwss^{(j)} \leq totmem$. Let m_t' denote the maximal number of tasks for which this inequality holds, i.e.

$\sum_{j=1}^{m_t'} mwss^{(j)} \leq totmem \land \sum_{j=1}^{m_t'+1} mwss^{(j)} > totmem$, where the sequence, in which the tasks are to be executed is expressed by the indices 1,2,3,... . From (1) and (2) we obtain

$$MPU(m_t') = \frac{mpu}{mpu+(1-mpu)^{m_t'}} \quad , \quad MU(m_t') = \frac{\sum_{j=1}^{m_t'} x_t^{(j)}}{totmem} \quad (3)$$

b) The More Liberal Nonpreemptive Task Activation Policy

The only way to increase an unsatisfactorily small MPU is to increase m_t. For the case that in general $\sum_{j=1}^{m_t'} x_t^{(j)}$ is much less than $\sum_{j=1}^{m_t'} mwss^{(j)}$ we have a low memory utilization $MU(m_t')$ in general and one can hope to be able to activate more than m_t' tasks without running into a situation where one has to preempt memory occupied by the working set of an active task in order to become able to continue execution. The Banker's algorithm [1,2] allows to decide whether - for given $x_t^{(j)}$ and $mwss^{(j)}$ for $j=1,\ldots,m_t'$ - the task $T^{(m_t'+1)}$ can be activated, too, without running the risk of such preemptions although the $\sum_{j=1}^{m_t'+1} mwss^{(j)} > totmem$. Repeated application of the Banker's algorithm as an admission test eventually leads to a maximal $m_t'' := m_t' + i_t$, $i_t \geq 0$, such that at least one finishing sequence for the m_t'' activated tasks exists which does not involve any "unexpected" memory preemptions, [6].

Obviously it is no longer sure that all m_t'' active processes can get their x_t page frames at any time t; it is even no longer sure that m_t' active processes can get their x_t page frames - as was guaranteed by the basic task activation policy. The only guarantee we have now is that at any time t at least one task can get its x_t required page frames - the other $m_t''-1$ activated tasks being perhaps unable to continue execution thereby reducing the MPU and MU.

For ease of notation some abbreviations are introduced now. Let $\underline{T}_{b,t}$ denote the genuine subset of $\underline{T}_{a,t}$ consisting of all blocked tasks at time t, i.e. $T^{(j)} \in \underline{T}_{a,t}$ belongs to $\underline{T}_{b,t}$ iff the number of page frames held by $T^{(j)}$ at time t, $y_t^{(j)}$, is less than $x_t^{(j)}$. Let $m_t^b := |\underline{T}_{b,t}|$ and let $TNBPF_t$ be the total number of page frames held by blocked tasks at time t. Extending (1) and (2) to this case we obtain for $m_t'' > m_t'$

$$MPU(m_t'') = \frac{mpu}{mpu+(1-mpu)^{m_t'+i_t-m_t^b}} \quad (4)$$

$$MU(m_t'') = \frac{\sum_{j=1}^{m_t'} y_t^{(j)} + \sum_{j=m_t'+1}^{m_t''} y_t^{(j)} - TNBPF_t}{totmem} \quad (5)$$

Comparing (3) with (4) we see that an improvement of MPU is obtained iff

$$i_t > m_t^b \quad . \tag{6}$$

Comparing (3) with (5) we see that an improvement of MU is obtained iff

$$\sum_{j=1}^{m_t'} (x_t^{(j)} - y_t^{(j)}) + TNBPF_t < \sum_{j=m_{t+1}'}^{} y_t^{(j)} \quad ,$$

i.e.
$$\sum_{\substack{j=1 \\ T^{(j)} \in \underline{T}_{b,t}}}^{m_t'} x_t^{(j)} < \sum_{\substack{j=m_{t+1}' \\ T^{(j)} \notin \underline{T}_{b,t}}}^{m_t''} y_t^{(j)} \tag{7}$$

Therefore the more liberal nonpreemptive task activation policy improves mean processor utilization (respectively: mean memory utilization) - compared to the basic policy - only if it implies (6) (resp. (7)) to be true for a suffienctly large part of time while executing $\underline{T}$. Obviously this question can be investigated only if - in addition to the distribution, D, of the mwss$^{(j)}$ on $\{1,2,\ldots,\text{totmem}\}$, for $T^{(j)} \in \underline{T}$ - some information about the tasks' behaviours is known, too.

Talking about general purpose computers it seems to be unrealistic to assume the informations on D to be deterministic whereas by the scheduler certain probabilistic assumptions can be enforced to hold - especially in a large time sharing environment; these probabilistic assumptions will be explained in section 4 and are discussed in [6] and [9]. At the other hand it is quite realistic to assume deterministic informations on each task's individual behaviour (see [12]). This deterministic information can vary broadly from knowing - in addition to mwss$^{(j)}$ - for some or all tasks their minimal working sets sizes, their initial working sets, all their working sets, life times of working sets, etc. A discussion of the usefulness of such informations for designing nonpreemptive paging algorithms can be found in [6].

3. Steady State Probabilities

We first extend our notion of task slightly to include the information whether an active task is blocked or not. So let now $T^{(j)} := (y_t^{(j)}, b_t^{(j)})_{t \in \underline{I}}$, where

$$b_t^{(j)} := \begin{cases} + & \text{iff } T^{(j)} \text{ is blocked at time t} \\ - & \text{otherwise,} \end{cases}$$

and $\underline{I}$ is a subset of the integrals such that we look at the computer at equidistant points in time. This assumption on $\underline{I}$ is no restriction of generality if we consider mean utilization only (see [7]). Let for $t \in \underline{I}$ and for $T^{(j)} \in \underline{T}_{a,t}$ the $T^{(j)}$-time be

denoted by $t^{(j)}$. Then the "state $\underline{s}_t$ at time t" is defined to be
$\underline{s}_t := \{(y_{t^{(j)}}^{(j)}, b_{t^{(j)}}^{(j)}) | T^{(j)} \in \underline{T}_{a,t}\}$. As t is a discrete parameter and the total number
of states possible at all for this $\underline{T}_{a,t}$, S, is finite, we investigate mean processor and memory utilization for a fixed set of active tasks, $\underline{T}_a$, by finite Markov chains [8]. In [9] we discuss and justify the restrictions implied in this approach.

Let $p_{s,t}$ be the probability for state $\underline{s}$ at time t. Let the vector $\underline{p}_t$ denote the distribution of the state probabilities at time t, i.e.

$$\underline{p}_t := (p_{1,t}, p_{2,t}, \ldots, p_{S,t}).$$

Then $\sum_{s=1}^{S} p_{s,t} = 1$ for all t.

Let $\underline{M}$ denote the matrix of transition probabilities. Then $\underline{p}_{t+1} = \underline{p}_t \cdot \underline{M}$, where $m_{s,s'} = P(\underline{s}_{t+1} = \underline{s}' | \underline{s}_t = \underline{s})$ are the S^2 elements of $\underline{M}$. Under weak assumptions already after several transitions we approximate $\underline{p} = \underline{p} \cdot \underline{M}$ very good, (10)
where $\underline{p} := (p_1, p_2, \ldots, p_S)$ is the probability distribution for the steady state
(see [9] for details).

From (10) and from $\sum_{s=1}^{S} p_s = 1$ $\underline{p}$ can be computed, i.e.: in order to be able to compute the steady state probabilities for $\underline{T}_a$ we only need the transition matrix $\underline{M}$.

In the preceding section we computed MPU and MU for an arbitrary state $\underline{s}$ for an arbitrary $\underline{T}_a$. Observe now that the m_t required in (1) and (2) is given by the number of active tasks in state $\underline{s}$ which are not blocked, denoted by m_s. Moreover we are able at this point - as soon as we have the $\underline{M}$ for this $\underline{T}_a$ - to compute the probability p_s of the occurrance of $\underline{s}$ in the stationary case.

Therefore by

$$\text{MPU} = \sum_{s=1}^{S} \text{MPU}(m_s) \cdot p_s \quad \text{and} \quad (11)$$

$$\text{MMU} = \sum_{s=1}^{S} \text{MU}(m_s) \cdot p_s \quad (12)$$

the mean utilization of processor and memory are given, depending solely on $\underline{M}$ via the p_s, s=1,2,...,S.

But remember that $\underline{M}$ does depend on two parameters, namely

a) the memory allocation policy applied and

b) the maximal working set sizes of the tasks in $\underline{T}_a$,
$\underline{\text{MWSS}} := \{\text{mwss}^{(j)} | T^{(j)} \in \underline{T}_a\}$, if the Banker's algorithm is applied in a).

In order to see that $\underline{M}$ (and S and $p_1,..,p_S$) depends on b) we assume a fixed memory allocation policy, MAP. For different $\underline{MWSS}$ we obtain different states, different S and different $\underline{M}$ in general. I.e.: the above MPU and MMU in (11) and (12) are depending on $\underline{MWSS}$. In order to derive the mean utilization for this fixed memory allocation policy MAP we therefore have to compute

$$MPU(MAP) := \sum_{\forall \underline{MWSS}} MPU(\underline{MWSS}) \cdot p_{\underline{MWSS}} \tag{13}$$

and

$$MMU(MAP) := \sum_{\forall \underline{MWSS}} MMU(\underline{MWSS}) \cdot p_{\underline{MWSS}} \quad , \tag{14}$$

where $p_{\underline{MWSS}}$ is the probability for $\underline{MWSS}$ to occur during task execution on the computer (determined by the set of tasks $\underline{T}$ or the scheduler).

In order to see that $\underline{M}$ (and S and $p_1,...,p_S$) depends on a) assume an arbitrarily fixed $\underline{MWSS}$. It is seen from section 2 of this paper that there are several nonpreemptive task activation policies. Moreover there is the problem whether memory released by active tasks should be used for deblocking blocked tasks (and which of them) or whether it should be used for activating another task (which could be activated due to the nonpreemptive task activation policy in use) - requiring a "deblocking policy". Therefore MPU($\underline{MWSS}$) and MMU($\underline{MWSS}$) still depend on the task activation policy and on the deblocking policy.

Examples explaining the influence of both parameters a) and b) and a discussion of the feedbacks and other details omitted here are given in [9].

	$\underline{s}_t$ \ $\underline{s}_{t+1}$	1 1 1	1-1 1	1 1-1	0 2 1	1 2 0	1-1-1	0 1 2	1 0 2	0 2-1	0-1 2
	1 1 1	0.90	0.05	0.05	0.0	0.0	0.0	0.0	0.0	0.0	0.0
	1-1 1	0.0	0.94	0.0	0.00	0.00	0.05	0.0	0.0	0.0	0.0
	1 1-1	0.0	0.0	0.94	0.0	0.0	0.05	0.00	0.00	0.0	0.0
	0 2 1	0.05	0.0	0.0	0.90	0.00	0.0	0.0	0.0	0.05	0.0
$\underline{M}$ =	1 2 0	0.05	0.0	0.0	0.00	0.95	0.0	0.0	0.0	0.0	0.0
	1-1-1	0.0	0.0	0.0	0.0	0.0	1.00	0.0	0.0	0.00	0.0
	0 1 2	0.05	0.0	0.0	0.0	0.0	0.0	0.90	0.00	0.0	0.05
	1 0 2	0.05	0.0	0.0	0.0	0.0	0.0	0.00	0.95	0.0	0.0
	0 2-1	0.0	0.0	0.0	0.0	0.0	0.0	0.05	0.0	0.95	0.0
	0-1 2	0.0	0.0	0.0	0.05	0.0	0.0	0.0	0.0	0.0	0.95

$\underline{p}$ = (0.019, 0.017, 0.016, 0.011, 0.002, 0.841, 0.022, 0.003, 0.044, 0.022)

Figure 2: Steady state probability distribution, $\underline{p}$, for transition matrix, $\underline{M}$.

4. An Example

Under realistic restrictions concerning the allowed transitions (details see [9]) the number S of possible states increases very fast with totmem; therefore we were able only to investigate numerically the case totmem = 3. This allows 3^3 = 27 possible MWSS, ranging from $\{1,1,1\}$, ..., $\{3,3,3\}$, where we assume - again for simplicity - all p_{MWSS} to be the same, namely $\frac{1}{27}$. Moreover we had to impose the restrictions listed subsequently in order to obtain a manageable S and $\underline{M}$.

a)   At any point in time t either none of the active tasks' x_t is changed or the subsequent relation holds:

$$x_t^{(j)} = x_{t-1}^{(j)} - 1 \quad \text{or} \quad x_t^{(j)} = x_{t-1}^{(j)} + 1$$

can hold for at most one $T^{(j)} \in \underline{T}_{a,t}^{(j)}$ and then $x_t^{(k)} = x_{t-1}^{(k)}$ for all $k \neq j$. This implies especially that $x_t^{(j)} = 0$ is possible iff $x_{t-1}^{(j)} = 1$ was true and $T^{(j)}$ released one page frame. $T^{(j)}$ then is regarded to be completely executed and removed from $\underline{T}$. If $T^{(j)}$'s termination occurs then we assume that another task $T^{(k)}$ with mwss$^{(k)}$ = mwss$^{(j)}$ is activated immediately, unless an active task is blocked.

b)   If at time t $x_t^{(j)} = x_{t-1}^{(j)} - 1$ then by a cyclic scan the next blocked tasks is found and unblocked. If none of the active tasks is blocked the Banker's Algorithm from [1,2] is performed in order to determine, whether the next (based on a cyclic scan again) waiting task can be activated.

Note that these restrictions imply a deblocking policy and a task activation policy. We finally assumed in this case the probability for releases and requests (i.e. p_{rel} and p_{req}, resp.) to be equal to 0.05 each and that a task holding one page frame only terminates with a probability, p_{term}, such that the expectation value of the "running time" for all tasks is 500 transitions. In [9] it is shown how to construct automatically $\underline{M}$ under these assumptions for each of the 27 MWSS. Here we discuss $\underline{M}$ for the case MWSS := $\{1,2,2\}$, only.

In this case we obtain S = 10, namely (+1,+1,+1), (+1,-1,+1), (+1,+1,-1), (-0,+2,+1), (+1,+2,-0), (+1,-1,-1), (-0,+1,+2), (+1,-0,+2), (-0,+2,-1), (-0,-1,+2), where (±i,±j,±k) stands for the state $\{(i,\pm), (j,\pm), (k\pm)\}$. I.e.: For this MWSS for each t the state $\underline{s}_t$ is given by one of these 10 triples. The matrix of transition probabilities in this case, $\underline{M}$, then is given by Figure 2. Subsequently we explain the procedure applied for computing its elements.

Starting from $\underline{s}_t := (i,j,k)$ the $m_{\underline{s}_t, \underline{s}_{t+1}}$ is derived by means of the decision tree for this problem shown in Figure 3. In this tree $\underline{s}_t$ is the root, $\underline{s}_{t+1}$ is a leaf and the product of the probabilities on the path connecting them is $m_{\underline{s}_t, \underline{s}_{t+1}}$. Note that -

depending on $\underline{s}_t$, MWSS and the task activation policy in use - branches of this tree may be absent at each of its three levels. E.g.: the highest left branch does not exist iff i > 1; then the only remaining branch has probability 1. Note, moreover, that asymmetries are introduced by the cyclic left to right scan involved. Although for MWSS = $\{1,2,2\}$ the two states $(-0,+2,-1)$ and $(-0,-1,+2)$ are symmetric, the steady state probabilities for these two states have to be different because the first one can follow after the state $(+1,-1,-1)$, while the second one cannot. Indeed in the vector $\underline{p}$ describing the steady state probability distribution (printed below $\underline{M}$ in Figure 2) the last two components - describing the probabilities of the two above states - differ from each other. Computing MPU(m_s) for all 10 states by applying (1) and computing MPU($\{1,2,2\}$) by applying (11) and proceeding in the same way for other 26 MWSS we finally obtain from (13) for this example MPU(MAP) = 0.657 . Analoguous computations for decreased running times of the tasks show a slight increase in MPU(MAP), namely

running time	500	200	100	50
MPU(MAP)	0.657	0.666	0.676	0.687

In order to be able to compare these results to the mean processor utilization obtained by applying the basic nonpreemptive task activation policy we derive the MPU(MWSS) for this case directly by repeating the execution of the tasks involved in an MWSS periodically, e.g. for MWSS:= $\{1,2,2\}$ we execute tasks (according to the basic task activation policy) whose maximal working set sizes are $1,2,2,1,2,2,1,2,2,...$ in this sequence (see [9] for details). So now MPU($\{1,2,2\}$) = 0.69 . The result of this memory allocation policy, MAP', is MPU(MAP') = 0.67 and this MPU(MAP') is independent of p_{req}, p_{rel} and p_{term}. In [9] one finds a careful discussion of this method of comparing the efficiencies of memory allocation policies based on different task activation policies.

As a first result we see that there is no significant difference between the mean processor utilizations obtained from the two nonpreemptive task activation policies. Secondly we will see in [9] that the mean processor utilization can be improved considerably by allowing occasional preemptions for removing blocked tasks from memory, the probability of which to become unblocked within short time is very low, where the number of such preemptions required increases as $\sum_{T^{(j)} \in \underline{T}_{a,t}} mwss^{(j)}$ is increased (obviously it is zero for $\sum_{T^{(j)} \in \underline{T}_{a,t}} mwss^{(j)} \leq$ totmem). Both results were found empirically in [10] already.

References

[1] DIJKSTRA, E.W.: Cooperating Sequential Processes. In "Programming Languages", Academic Press, London 1968.
[2] HABERMANN, A.N.: Prevention of System Deadlocks, CACM, July 1969.

[3] DENNING, P.J.: Thrashing: Its Causes and Prevention. FJCC 1968.

[4] DENNING, P.J.: Virtual Memory. Computing Surveys 2,3, Sept. 1970.

[5] COFFMAN, DENNING: Operating Systems Theory. Prenctice-Hall 1973

[6] SCHINDLER, S.: Multiprogramming on M-Processor Systems, M ≥ 1. Basic Ideas. Sagamore Computer Conference on Parallel Processing, August 1974.

[7] KONDALL, D.G.: On the Use of the Characteristic Functional in the Analysis of Some Stochastic Processes Occuring in Physics and Biology. In: Proc. Comb. Phil. Soc., Vol. 47, 1951.

[8] KEMENY, SNELL: Finite Markov Chains, D. van Norstrand Publ., New Jersey 1960.

[9] BUDER, SCHINDLER: An Analysis of Memory Utilization by Finite Markov Chains. TR 74-28, FB 20, TU Berlin.

[10] SHERMAN, S.: Trace Driven Studies of Deadlock Control and Job Scheduling. 4. Jahrestagung der Gesellschaft für Informatik, Berlin 1974.

[11] LEW, A.: Optimal Resource Allocation and Scheduling Among Parallel Processes. Sagamore Computer Conference on Parallel Processing, August 1974.

[12] SCHINDLER, S.: Request Driven Versus Demand Driven Virtual Memory Organization. 8. Hawaii International Conference on System Sciences, January 1975.

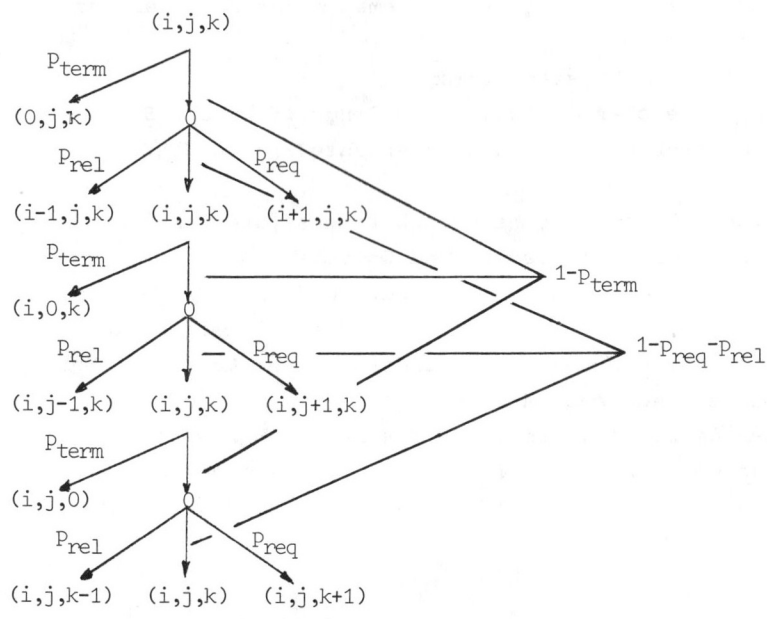

Figure 3: Decision Tree

VIRTUELLE MASCHINEN IN EINEM ALLGEMEINEN TIME-SHARING-BETRIEBSSYSTEM

Michael Heinz
Computer Gesellschaft Konstanz mbH

Einführung

Einige wichtige Anwendungen für Rechenanlagen werden von den heutigen Maschinen und konventionellen Betriebssystemen nicht oder nur unzureichend unterstützt:
- Entwicklung und Test von Systemsoftware
- Messungen an Hardware oder Software ohne Eingriff in die Systeme
- SW-Kompatibilitätsprobleme zwischen unterschiedlichen Betriebssystemen
- Übergang von einer alten auf eine neue Betriebssystemversion
- Ausbildung von Systemprogrammierern und Operateuren
- Erweiterung und Test von Systemen für neue HW-Konfigurationen etc.

Diese Anwendungen zeichnen sich dadurch aus, dass sie eigentlich den Einsatz jeweils eigener Rechner erfordern, deren Leistung aber nur zu einem Bruchteil ausgenützt würde.
Eine Lösung bieten Betriebssysteme, die die nackte Hardware-Schnittstelle mehrfach anzubieten in der Lage sind, Systeme, die mehrere "virtuelle Maschinen" (VM) zur Verfügung stellen /1/,/2/,/3/,/4/.

VM-Technik

Unter der Technik der virtuellen Maschinen versteht man das effiziente Zurverfügungstellen der Schnittstelle der nackten Hardware einer (Ziel)-Maschine auf einer Basismaschine /5/,/6/, insbesondere das gleichzeitige Zurverfügungstellen mehrerer solcher virtueller Maschinen. "Effizient" bedeutet, dass der überwiegende Teil der Befehle der "virtuellen" Hardware direkt auf der Basis-

Hardware abläuft und unterscheidet die VM-Technik von der Simulation durch Interpretation aller Befehle.

Dies erfordert eine gewisse Verwandtschaft der Hardware der gewünschten virtuellen Zielmaschine mit der Basismaschine und stellt weitere notwendige Bedingungen an die Hardware einer Maschine, die für die VM-Technik geeignet sein soll /7/,/8/.
Es gibt Ansätze für HW-Architekturen, die der VM-Technik besonders entgegenkommen /9/,/10/,/11/,/2/, doch soll im folgenden von einer normalen HW der "dritten Generation" mit zwei Privilegierungsmodi (Supervisor-/Problem-Status) und virtueller Adressierung (Paging) ausgegangen werden. Das bedeutet, dass alle "sensitiven" Operationen /7/ (z.B. privilegierte Befehle) der virtuellen Hardware simuliert werden müssen.

Schnittstellen

Ein konventionelles Betriebssystem (BS) legt über die - nur einmal vorhandene - Schnittstelle der nackten Hardware (HW-SS) mehrfach für seine Prozesse eine von ihm definierte Benutzer-Schnittstelle (SW-SS) (Fig 1: die Darstellungsweise ist von Goldberg /12/,/3/ übernommen).

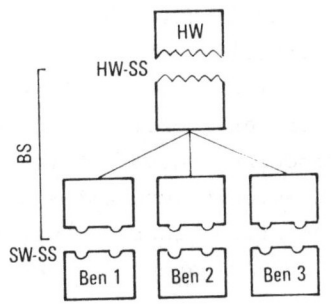

Fig. 1: Konventionelles BS

Ein Betriebssystem, das seinen Prozessen die gleiche Schnittstelle wie die nackte Hardware - virtuelle Maschinen - zur Verfügung stellt (Fig 2), nennt man einen VM-Monitor (VMM). Auf einer solchen virtuellen Hardware-Schnittstelle können jetzt wieder Betriebssysteme - z.B. auch ein VMM - aufsetzen.

VM-Monitor

Ein VMM hat die Aufgabe, die
einzelnen Komponenten für seine
virtuellen Maschinen zur Verfügung zu stellen:
- der Rechnerkern einer virtuellen Maschine entsteht durch
  Zuteilung des Rechnerkerns der
  Basismaschine zum direkten
  Ausführen von Befehlen bzw.
  zur Simulation von sensitiven
  Operationen der virtuellen
  Maschine durch den VMM.

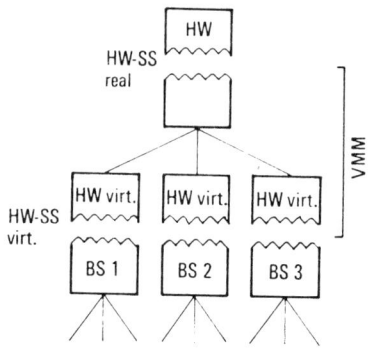

Fig. 2: VMM

- der Zentralspeicher einer
  virtuellen Maschine wird auf einen virtuellen Speicher des Basis-
  systems abgebildet.
- ein Peripheriegerät (bzw. dessen Datenträger) einer virtuellen
  Maschine wird entweder direkt auf ein funktionell ähnliches
  Gerät der Basiskonfiguration oder auf den Hintergrundspeicher der
  Basismaschine abgebildet (evtl. für eine zeitlich verschobene Abbildung auf ein verwandtes Gerät: Spooling).
- das Bedienfeld einer virtuellen Maschine wird über spezielle Kommandos und Ausgaben an einem Terminal der Basiskonfiguration simuliert.

Die aufgezählten Funktionen des VMM zur Realisierung von funktionellen
Abbildern der Komponenten seiner virtuellen Maschinen entsprechen den
normalen Aufgaben eines Betriebssystems, nämlich der Verteilung der
realen Betriebsmittel an seine Prozesse.
Bei genauer Betrachtung enthält ein VMM ein komfortables Time-Sharing-
Betriebssystem (TSBS), das über die gegebene Hardware-Schnittstelle
(Rechnerkern, Speicher, EA, Unterbrechungen) eine "höhere" Software-
Schnittstelle (Prozesse, virtuelle Speicher, Data Management, Warte-
zustände) legt, die aber nur intern, jedoch nicht an den externen
Schnittstellen des VMM erscheint; d.h. die virtuellen Maschinen sind
Prozesse, die die Dienstleistungen eines Time-Sharing-Systems über
das Format der Hardware-Schnittstelle ansprechen.

In der Vergangenheit wurde diese Eigenschaft - VMM als Time-Sharing-
Betriebssystem - ausgenutzt, indem für jeden Time-Sharing-Benutzer
des VMM eine virtuelle Maschine mit einem sehr einfachen Monopro-
gramming-Betriebssystem (MBS) /13/ vorgesehen wurde (Fig 3; die
Analogie zu Fig 1 ist evident).

VM-Monitor-Prozess

Nun ist es nicht einsichtig, warum ein normaler Terminalbenutzer eine

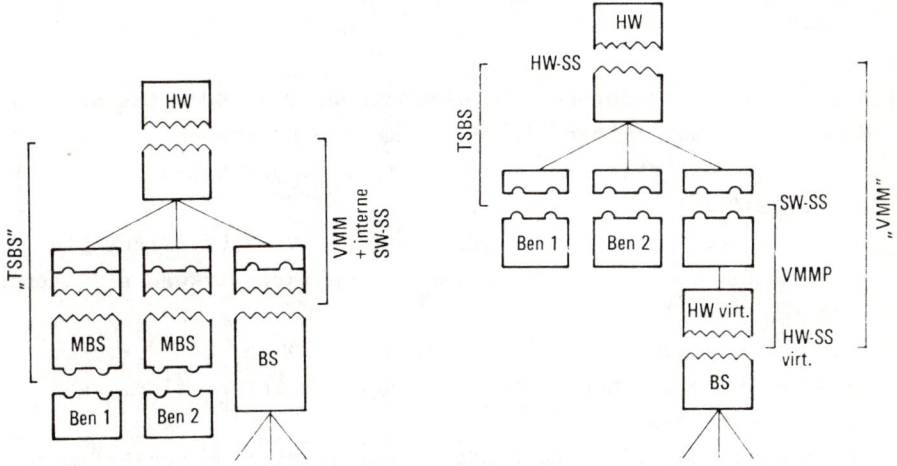

Fig. 3: VMM + MBS als TSBS   Fig. 4: VM im TSBS

Hardware-Schnittstelle zur Verfügung gestellt bekommen soll, die er
erst durch ein Betriebssystem (z.B. ein MBS) auf eine für ihn verwendbare Benutzer-Schnittstelle abbilden muss, insbesondere, wenn
bereits intern eine brauchbare Software-Schnittstelle vorliegt
(s. Fig 3).

Man kann anders vorgehen, von einem Time-Sharing-System ausgehen
und dieses so erweitern, dass für einen Prozess wahlweise anstelle
der normalen SW-Benutzer-Schnittstelle die Hardware-Schnittstelle
geboten werden kann: VM-Prozess (VMP). Die Abbildung der Hardware-
Schnittstelle - die der VM-Prozess sieht - auf die Software-Schnittstelle des Time-Sharing-Betriebssystems - die einzige Möglichkeit
innerhalb des TSBS an Betriebsmittel heranzukommen - wird durch
einen VM-Monitor-Prozess (VMMP) - einen normalen Prozess des TSBS -
vorgenommen (Fig 4; vgl. mit Fig 3).

Diese Abbildung der HW-Schnittstelle einer virtuellen Maschine auf eine explizite SW-Schnittstelle eines Betriebssystems entspricht einer Typ II-selbstvirtualisierenden virtuellen Maschine nach Goldberg /5/,/4/. Es sind einige virtuelle Maschinen vom Typ II bekannt /14/,/15/,/16/, die jedoch nicht selbstvirtualisierend sind.

SW-Anforderungen

Die Einbettung virtueller Maschinen durch VM-Prozesse (VMP) und VM-Monitor-Prozesse (VMMP) stellt zusätzliche Anforderungen an die Software-Schnittstelle des zugrundeliegenden Time-Sharing-Betriebssystems:

(1) Umleitung von synchronen Unterbrechungen des VMP - das sind die durch Befehlswirkungen direkt erzeugten Unterbrechungen wie z.B. SVC, privilegierter Befehl im nichtprivilegierten Zustand, Fehlseitenbedingung... - an den VMMP:
Diese Umleitung ist notwendig, damit der VMMP über sensitive Operationen des VMP informiert wird und ihre Wirkung simulieren kann.

(2) Lesender und schreibender Zugriff des VMMP auf den "Programmkontext" des VMP (Unterbrechungs- bzw. Fortsetzungsinformation, Register eines Prozesses):
Der Registerzugriff wird benötigt zur Simulation von Befehlswirkungen.

(3) Lesender und schreibender Zugriff des VMMP auf den (virtuellen realen und den virtuellen virtuellen) Adressenraum des VMP:
Dieser Speicherzugriff ist erforderlich zur Simulation von sensitiven Befehlen mit Speicherzugriff entsprechend dem jeweils eingestellten Adressierungsmodus.

(4) Mehrere virtuelle Adressenräume und insbesondere "leere" virtuelle Adressenräume:
einer virtuellen Maschine mit virtueller Adressierung oder mit einem Speichervollausbau entsprechend der Adressbreite können keinerlei Einschränkungen in der Belegung des Adressenraumes auferlegt werden, d.h. für einen VMP müssen Adressenräume ermöglicht werden, die "leer" - nicht von Objekten des Time-Sharing-Betriebssystems belegt - sind; hieraus folgt unmittelbar, dass eine Unterbrechungsroutine, die einen solchen VMP unterbricht, in einem anderen - weil die HW oft keine andere Wahl bietet: im realen - Adressenraum ablaufen muss.

(5) Manipulationen an den Adressraumbeschreibungen für den VMP durch
den VMMP (koordiniert mit dem Seiten-Supervisor des Time-Sharing-
Systems):
aus Effizienzgründen müssen möglichst viele Befehle der virtuellen HW auf der realen HW ablaufen es muss somit auch bei virtuellen Maschinen mit virtueller Adressierung die Adressumsetzung
von der HW der Basismaschine vorgenommen werden: das setzt voraus,
dass der VM-Monitor-Prozess für die HW die Doppelabbildung
"virtuelle virtuelle Adresse : reale Adresse" vorgibt. Diese
Doppelabbildung darf auch bei Manipulationen des Seiten-Super-
visors an dem virtuellen Adressenraum, der den Realspeicher der
virtuellen Maschine darstellt, nicht zu Fehlern führen.
(6) Parallele Aktivitäten innerhalb eines Benutzerauftrages:
es werden Dienste zur Unterstützung der Simulation von asynchronen
Vorgängen einer virtuellen Maschine (z.B. E/A) benötigt.
Entweder
- VMP und VMMP als eigenständige Prozesse des TSBS, da es sinnvoll ist, voneinander unabhängige Vorgänge als voneinander unabhängige Prozesse zu organisieren.
Zumindest aber
- VMP und VMMP innerhalb eines Prozesses des TSBS und Systemdienste
 (z.B. E/A, Weckdienste), die parallel zum auftraggebenden Prozess
 ablaufen und ihre Rückmeldungen dem Auftraggeber unterbrechungs-
 artig zustellen. Wird durch eine solche Rückmeldung der Prozess
 im "VMP-Zustand" unterbrochen, so muss - analog zu Forderung (1) -
 in den "VMMP-Zustand" umgeschaltet werden.

<u>Schluss</u>

Die beschriebenen System-Erweiterungen ermöglichen es
- falls das Betriebssystem in der genannten Art modifizierbar ist und
- falls die Hardware der zugrundeliegenden Maschine prinzipiell für
 die VM-Technik geeignet ist,
durch Hinzufügen von VM-Monitor-Prozessen die Technik der virtuellen
Maschinen in ein Time-Sharing-Betriebssystem einzubetten.

Literatur

/1/ Parmelee R.P., Peterson T.I., Tillman C.C., Hatfield D.J.
"Virtual Storage and Virtual Machine Concepts"
IBM Systems Journal, Vol 11, Nr 2, 1972, S.99-102

/2/ Goldberg R.P.
"Architecture of Virtual Machines"
AFIPS Conf. Proc., Vol 42, NCC 1973, S. 309-318

/3/ Goldberg R.P.
"Survey of Virtual Machine Research"
Computer, Vol 7, Nr 6, Juni 1974. S.34-45

/4/ Buzen J.P., Gagliardi U.O.
"The Evolution of Virtual Machine Architecture"
AFIPS Conf. Proc., Vol 42, NCC 1973, S. 291-299

/5/ Goldberg R.P.
"Virtual Machines: Semantics and Examples"
IEEE Computer Science Conference, Boston MA, 1971, S.141-142

/6/ Mallach E.G.
"On the Relationship between Virtual Machines and Emulators"
Proc. ACM SIGARCH-SIGOPS Workshop on Virtual Computer Systems,
Cambridge MA, 1973, S.117-126

/7/ Goldberg R.P.
"Hardware Requirements for Virtual Machine Systems"
Proc. 4th Hawaii International Conference on Systems Sciences,
Honululu, 1971, S.449-451

/8/ Popek G.J., Goldberg R.P.
"Formal Requirements for Virtualizable Third Generation
Architectures"
Comm. of the ACM, Vol 17, Nr 7, Juli 1974, S.412-421

/9/ Lauer H.C., Wyeth D.
"A Recursive Virtual Machine Architecture"
Proc. ACM SIGARCH-SIGOPS Workshop on Virtual Computer Systems,
Cambridge MA, 1973, S.113-116

/10/ Lauer H.C., Snow C.R.
"Is Supervisor-State Necessary?"
Proc. ACM AICA International Computing Symposium, Venedig, 1972,
S. 293-301

/11/ Gagliardi U.O., Goldberg R.P.
"Virtualizable Architectures"
Proc. ACM AICA International Computing Symposium, Venedig, 1972,
S. 527-538

/12/ Goldberg R.P. (Herausgeber)
Proc. ACM SIGARCH-SIGOPS Workshop on Virtual Computer Systems,
Cambridge MA, 1973

/13/ Klemenc H., Lochner H., Schönherr H-J.
"VM/370 = CP + CMS"
IBM Deutschland, 1972

/14/ Fuchi K., Hozuni T., Yuriko M., Toshitsugu Y.
"A Program Simulator by Partial Interpretation"
2nd ACM Symposium on Operating System Principles, Princeton
University, 1969, S.97-104

/15/ Srodawa R.J., Bates L.A.
"An Effizient Virtual Machine Implementation"
AFIPS Conf. Proc., Vol 42, NCC 1973, S.301-308

/16/ Galley S.W.
"PDP-10 Virtual Machines"
Proc. ACM SIGARCH-SIGOPS Workshop on Virtual Computer Systems,
Cambridge MA, 1973, S.30-34

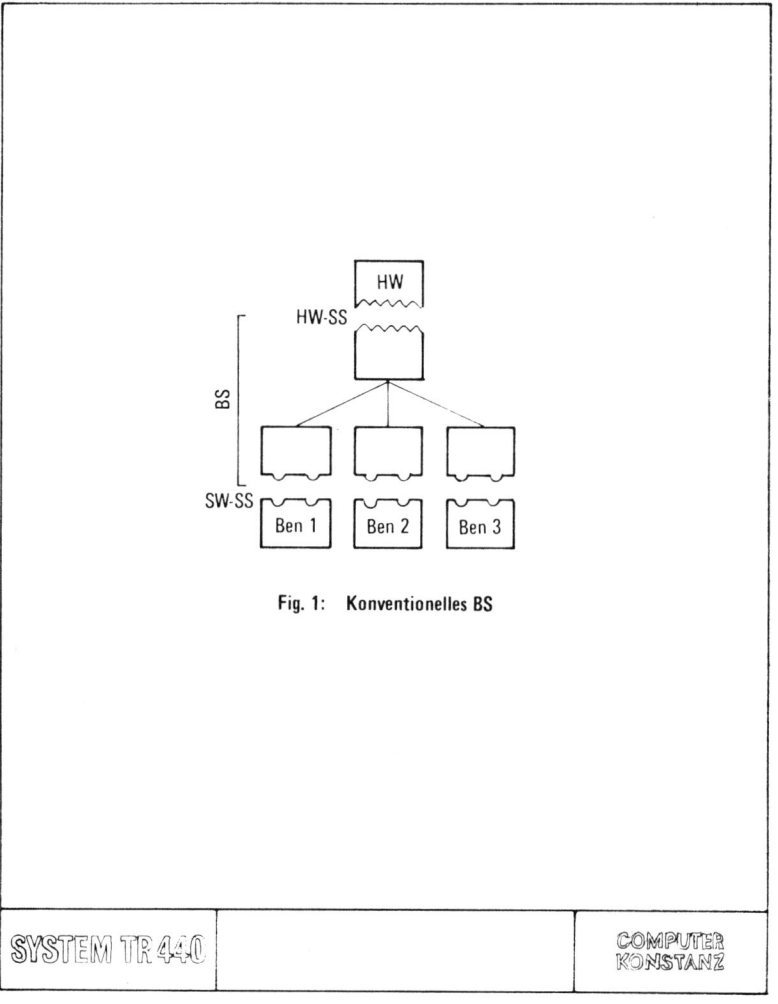

Fig. 1: Konventionelles BS

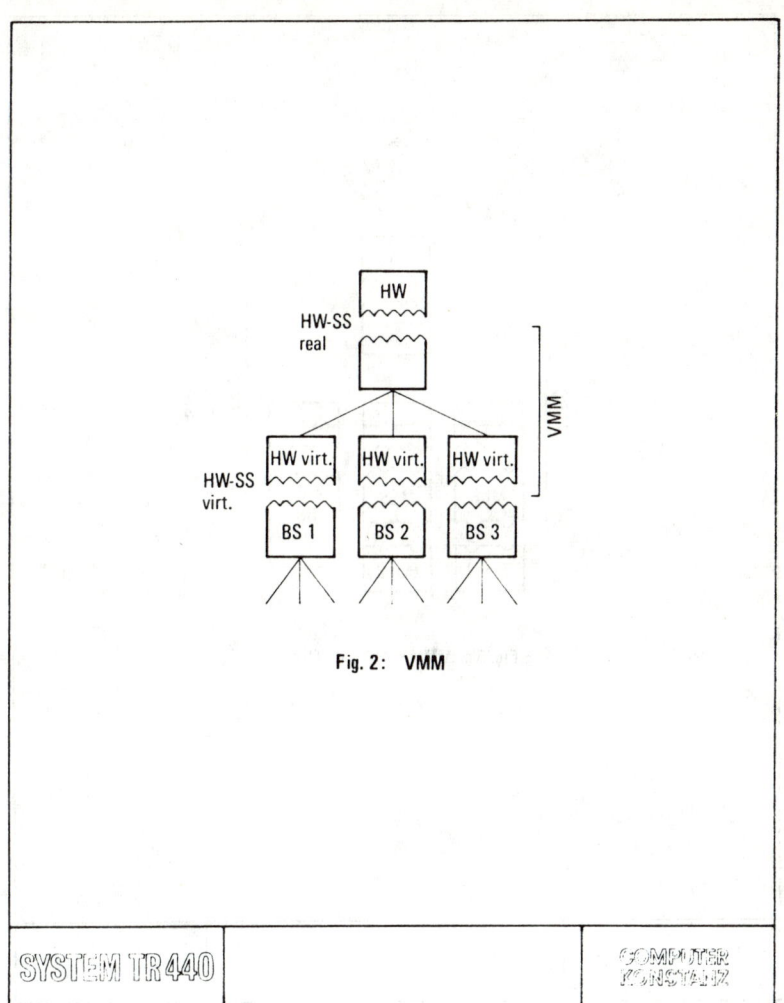

Fig. 2: VMM

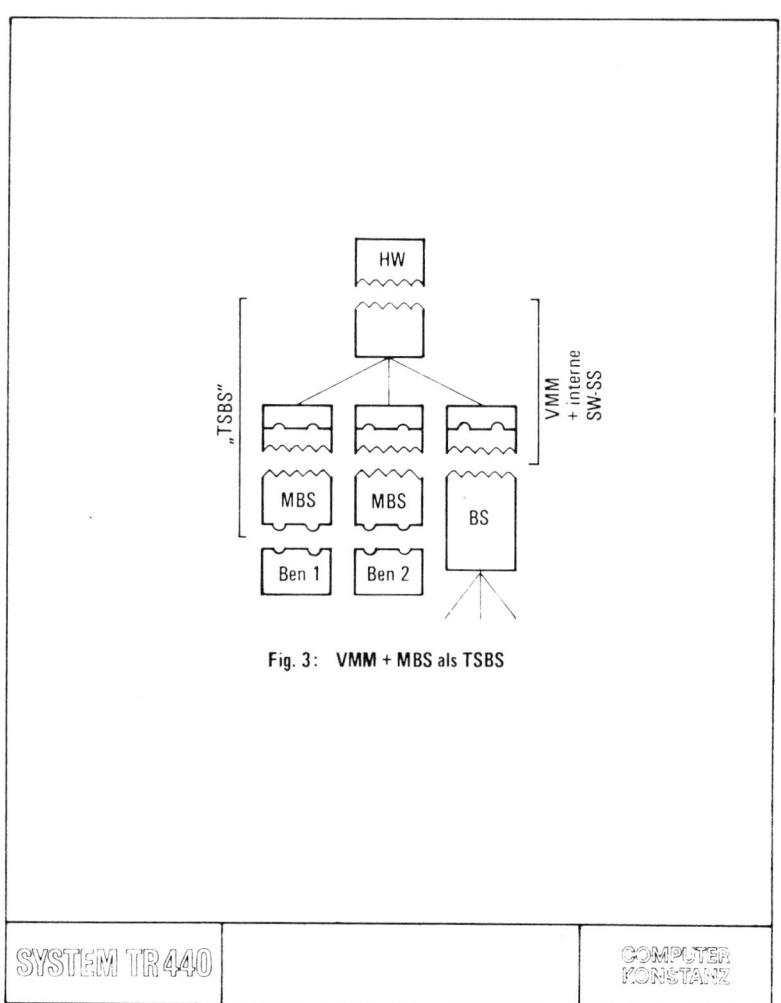

Fig. 3: VMM + MBS als TSBS

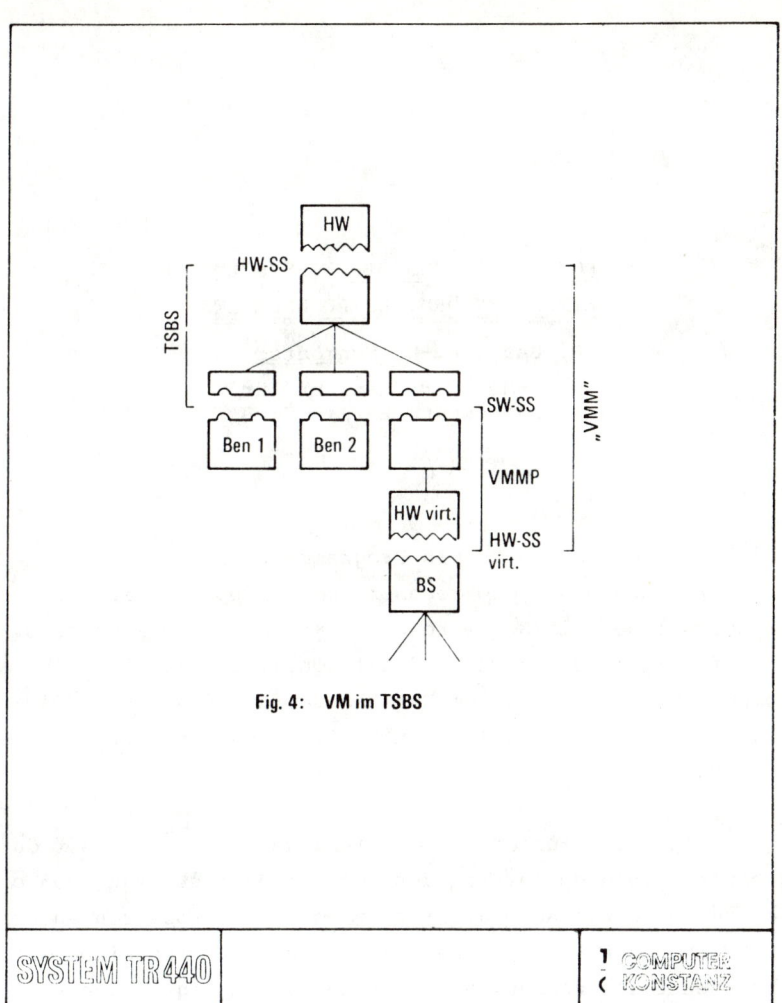

Fig. 4: VM im TSBS

EIN KOMMUNIKATIONSBETRIEBSSYSTEM FÜR
EIN STERNFÖRMIGES RECHNERNETZ

D. Baum, H.-D. Schrödter
Hahn-Meitner-Institut für
Kernforschung Berlin GmbH

Einleitung

In der vorliegenden Note wird ein Programmsystem zur Steuerung des Datenflusses zwischen einem Großrechner und gekoppelten Prozeßrechnern beschrieben, welches als Software eines Kommunikationsrechners (KR) in einem sternförmigen Rechnerverbundnetz konzipiert ist. Der Aufbau eines solchen Systems hängt vom Funktionsumfang des KR und damit im wesentlichen von der physikalischen Realisierung und der Zweckbestimmung des Verbundes ab.

Die Ausgangssituation für die Entwicklung war gekennzeichnet durch die Planung einer Rechnerspinne, in der für die Unterstützung von on-line-Experimenten sowie zur Automatisierung von Laborprozessen an experimentellen Schwerpunkten Prozeßrechner als Satelliten mit einem Großrechner über einen zentralen Kommunikationsknoten verbunden werden sollten [1], [7]. Die vollständige Einrichtung eines solchen Verbundsystems betrifft wesentlich mehr als das hier beschriebene Konzept; daher lag der Entwicklung auch hauptsächlich die Motivation zugrunde, Erfahrungen für den Entwurf entsprechender Bausteine zu sammeln und einen möglichen Lösungsweg vorzuschlagen. Zum angestrebten Leistungsumfang der Kommunikationssoftware gehört die Verwirklichung der gleichzeitigen Datenübertragung über k = 4 Leitungen mit mindestens 48 $\frac{KBit}{sec}$ Übertragungsgeschwindigkeit; dabei ist k Systemvariable. Ein denkbares Modell für die hardwaremäßige Realisierung der Kopplung bestand in folgender Vorstellung:

Ein Prozeßrechner des Typs PDP 11/45 stellt den zentralen Knoten des Netzes dar und ist über doppelt gepufferte DL11C-Interfaces der Fa. DEC (je Puffer 8 Bits = 1 Charakter) mit Prozeßrechnern sowie über ein DR11C-Interface (16 Bit Doppelpufferung) mit einem Siemens-Großrechner des Typs S 4004/151 verbunden. Dem DR11C-Interface (Übertragung 16 Bit parallel) ist ein zu entwickelnder Hardwarebaustein für die Verbindung zum Datenaustauschkanal DAK 1 (8 Bit Parallelübertragung) vorgeschaltet; der DAK1-Baustein hängt am Multiplex-Kanal der S 4004. Die Datenübertragung zu den Prozeßrechnern erfolgt über private Standleitungen ("twisted pairs") in Bit-seriellem Asynchronbetrieb (hardwaremäßige Vollduplex-Verbindung) mit einer Übertragungsgeschwindigkeit von 48 $\frac{KBit}{sec}$ pro Leitung. Die Verbindung Kommunikationsrechner - Großrechner erlaubt eine Übertragungsgeschwindigkeit von mehr als 100 $\frac{KByte}{sec}$.

Andere Hardware-Realisierungen - etwa bei Verwendung von DMA-Interfaces - können jedoch ebenso dem Konzept zugrunde gelegt werden. Der KR wird als "Packet-switching store and forward processor" angesehen. Die Gesamtheit der Kommunikationsfunktionen, d. h. das Komplement aller derjenigen Funktionen, die jeder der autonomen Rechner im Alleinbetrieb benötigen würde, ist einerseits durch die Netzkonfiguration, andererseits durch ihre Funktionsweise im Rahmen dieser Konfiguration bestimmt. Im Sinne von [2] werden diese Aufgaben wahrgenommen durch das "Verbundsteuersystem" und das "Datenübertragungssystem" der "Netzwerkmaschine" (in manchen Fällen wird vom "Kommunikations-Subsystem" [6], "Kommunikationsnetzwerk" [3] oder kurz "Netz" gesprochen). Sie lassen sich einteilen in Koordinationsaufgaben, Transformationsaufgaben und Transportaufgaben. Bis auf Code-Umwandlungen, die gemäß [2] ebenso wie Transportaufgaben vom Datenübertragungssystem durchgeführt werden, sind die Koordinations- und Transformationsaufgaben dem Verbundsteuersystem zuzurechnen. Dem Einsatz von kleinen bis mittleren Rechenanlagen als Kommunikationsrechner - und dabei in den verschiedenen Auslegungen, wie sie durch die Bezeichnungen "message-/packet-switching store and forward processor", "remote concentrator", "high-level front end processor" oder "ring interface" gekennzeichnet sind, liegt zweifellos der Gedanke zugrunde, möglichst viele der Funktionen der Netzwerkmaschine aus den einzelnen am Verbund teilhabenden Rechensystemen herauszuverlagern (vergl. auch [4], [5]). Diesem Anspruch wird das hier beschriebene System z. Z. nur in sehr geringem Umfang gerecht, und zwar nur insoweit, als es einen Vorschlag zur Realisierung eines sich selbst steuernden Systems von Kommunikationssoftware-Bausteinen repräsentiert, das bzgl.

Erweiterungen flexibel ist und die Möglichkeit dynamischer Prioritätsänderungen im Datenfluß per definitionem vorsieht.

1. Funktionsumfang und Systemstruktur

1.1 Abweichend von [2] werden die Funktionen einer KR-Software generell in zwei Hauptgruppen zusammengefaßt: Systemfunktionen und Kommunikationsfunktionen.

Die Systemfunktionen umfassen Systemeinleitungsaufgaben und Systemsteuerungsaufgaben. Die zweite Funktionsgruppe kann im Falle eines "store and forward node" am anschaulichsten durch die Stichworte "Datenempfang", "Datenbehandlung" und "Datenübertragung" gekennzeichnet werden. Datenempfangs- und Datenübertragungsfunktionen beinhalten die E/A-Steuerung ("flag detection", "handshaking", "time-out"-Behandlung), außerdem Übertragungsfehlererkennung, Mechanismen für physikalische Quittierungen bzw. Wiederholungsanforderungen sowie "header"- und Ende-Erkennungen. Teile solcher Funktionen können von Hardware-Bausteinen übernommen werden. Das "data handling" schließlich betrifft die Funktionen Interpretation, internes und externes "Routing", Packen und Entpacken, Transformation und Datenauslagerung. Im zur Diskussion stehenden System wurden nur einige der genannten Funktionen bisher implementiert. Abgesehen davon, daß in einem Sternnetz das Problem des "external routing" - sofern hierbei nur die Rechneradressierung, nicht die Task- oder Subsystemadressierung angesprochen wird - trivial ist, sind auch Statistikfragen, "network-control"-Funktionen, Transformationsfunktionen und Systemeinleitungsfunktionen zum Teil nicht berücksichtigt worden.

1.2 Die hierarchische Struktur des Systems ist dadurch gekennzeichnet, daß der die Modulsteuerung und Warteschlangenabarbeitung übernehmende Teil ("Scheduler") keinen Einfluß auf den "Ein-/Ausgabeteil" - bestehend jeweils aus "Interrupt-Service-Routinen" (ISR) und einem Eingabe-Initialisierungsmodul (E-INIT) bzw. Ausgabe-Initialisierungsmodul (S-INIT) - sowie den "Interpreter" nimmt.

Im Sinne des "data receiving - data handling - data transmitting"-
Ablaufes kann die Prioritätsstruktur wie folgt skizziert werden:

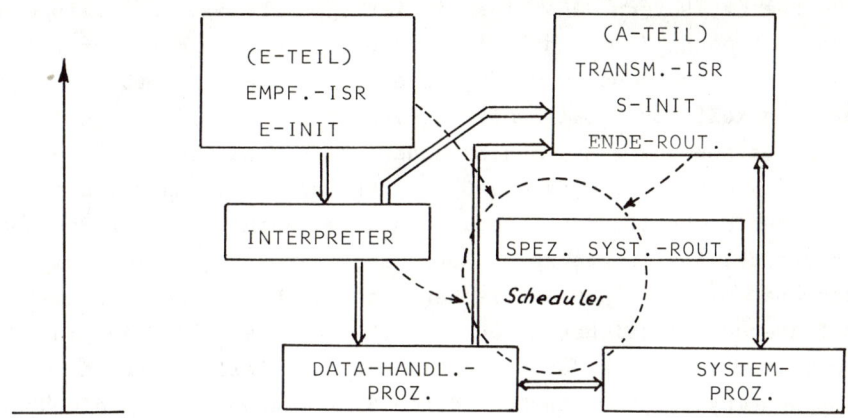

Syst.-Priorität

fig. 1

2. Systembeschreibung

2.1 Um den Systemaufbau leichter verdeutlichen zu können, sei auf die
Verfahrensweise bei Interfaces mit Charakter- oder Wortdoppelpufferung
hingewiesen (1 PDP11-Wort = 16 Bit). Im Gegensatz zum "Block-Interrupt-
Modell" (DMA-Interfaces oder E/A-Prozessoren) muß im genannten Fall die
"data-overrun"-Möglichkeit berücksichtigt werden, was insbesondere bei
softwaremäßiger Prozedurnachbildung zu erheblichen Zeitproblemen führt.

Bei Zugrundelegung der BSC-Prozedur wird der Eingabe-Teil im "Charak-
ter- bzw. Wort-Interrupt-Modell" durch folgenden Ablauf charakterisiert:
Die Anforderung zur Ermöglichung einer Datenübertragung (ENQ-Steuerzei-
chen) wird von einer speziellen ISR erkannt und nur bei freigegebener
Leitung durch ein "positives Acknowledgement" (ACK) angenommen. Ggf.
nach Austausch der ISR-Adresse im Interrupt-Vektor wird ein fest formatierter Nachrichtenkopf ("header" oder Etikett) über eine zweite ISR
empfangen. Der "header" wird byteweise (bzw. wortweise beim DR11C-

Interface) quittiert, um "data overrun" auszuschließen. Auf diese Weise ist es der KR-Software möglich, zu beliebiger Zeit und unabhängig von der Belastung durch k aktive Leitungen Kopfinformationen entgegenzunehmen. Nach Empfang des Kopfes wird in die Eingabe-Initialisierungsroutine E-INIT verzweigt (sofern diese inaktiv ist), welche die Initialisierung der Datenübertragung "versucht", d. h. die Zahl der bereits aktiven Leitungen, das Vorhandensein von Speicherplatz u. ä. überprüft und je nach Verfügbarkeit der Betriebsmittel durch Einsetzen der neuen ISR-Adresse für Datenempfang und Abgabe einer Positiv-Quittung bzw. durch Abgabe einer Negativ-Quittung die DÜ anstößt bzw. verhindert. Das Verfahren hat den Nachteil, daß sich aufgrund der zusätzlichen Bedeutung der Quittung für das letzte Byte (Wort) des Etiketts die "logische Prozedurebene" mit der "physikalischen Prozedurebene" überschneidet. Die das Textende-Kennzeichen erkennende ISR veranlaßt den Einsprung in den Interpreter. Im Falle des "Block-Interrupt-Modells" erfolgt der Einsprung in den Interpreter, nachdem durch Systemunterbrechung die Übernahme eines Paketes gemeldet wurde. Von dieser Schnittstelle an gehen beide Modelle ineinander über.

E-INIT und Interpreter werden somit von Interrupt-Service-Routinen direkt angesprungen, sofern sie nicht schon aktiv sind; im letzteren Fall erfolgt jeweils ein WS-Eintrag. Beide Moduln - wie auch S-INIT - sind so lange aktiv, bis die Maximalzahl k aktiver Übertragungsleitungen erreicht oder aber die jeweilige WS leer ist. Der Interpreter veranlaßt WS-Einträge für "data-handling"-Prozesse und prüft anschließend, ob die eben empfangene Nachricht vorrangig vor anderen Daten zu behandeln ist.

2.2 Der Grundgedanke des Systemkonzepts besteht darin, daß jedem Prozeß des Systems eine Dringlichkeitsstufe oder Priorität p <u>dynamisch</u> zugeordnet wird. Zu jedem p gibt es eine Reihe von Prozessen, die zyklisch durchlaufen wird, sofern eine Anforderung für mindestens einen dieser Prozesse vorliegt und die Priorität p die z. Z. höchste Priorität ist, unter der Prozesse des Systems auf die "run"-Möglichkeit warten. Die zyklisch zu durchlaufende Reihe von Prozessen der Priorität p wird als p-Schleife bezeichnet; ihr zugeordnet ist eine Schleifen-Warteschlange (WS). Jeder Prozeß besitzt zusätzlich einen Ereigniszähler und/oder eine Eingangs-WS. Wird die p-Schleife aktiviert, so bedeutet dies die Aktivierung des ersten Prozesses mit nicht-leerer WS, und zwar stets gerechnet von einem als "ersten" in der Schleife ausgezeichneten Prozeß. Die WS der Prozesse sind jedoch aufgrund der Schleifenzugehörigkeit insofern zusätzlich "strukturiert", als auch "Nulleinträge" zugelassen sind und die Abarbeitung eines WS-Eintrages durch einen Prozeß A weder die Abarbeitung des nächsten wesentlichen WS-Eintrages (nicht-Nulleintrages) von A noch die Abarbeitung eines wesentlichen WS-Eintrages des nächstfolgenden Prozesses in der p-Schleife zur Folge haben muß. Dies sei an einem Beispiel erläutert: Eine Nachricht von einem Prozeßrechner wird aufgrund einer Kopf-Interpretation der Dringlichkeitsstufe (Priorität) p zugerechnet. Der Empfang der vollständigen Nachricht bzw. des letzten (Steuer-)Zeichens der Übertragung ist durch Unterbrechung des Ablaufes irgendeines Prozesses möglich geworden. Lief dieser unterbrochene Prozeß unter einer Priorität q < p ab, so erfolgt nach Vollzug von WS-Eintragungen (i. a. aufgrund der Kopfauswertung) kein Rücksprung zum unterbrochenen Programm, sondern - auf dem Umweg über den Scheduler - die Aktivierung der p-Schleife. Im Falle q ≥ p können andere Nachrichten der gleichen Dringlichkeitsstufe, die wegen der Aktivität "dringlicherer" oder "gleich dringlicher" Prozesse bisher nicht bearbeitet werden konnten, vorher bereits WS-Einträge für die Prozesse der p-Schleife verursacht haben. Um zu garantieren, daß etwa alle "handling"-Prozesse für eine Nachricht während der Aktivität der p-Schleife hintereinander durchlaufen werden, werden durch jede solche Nachricht WS-Einträge für <u>jeden</u> Prozeß der p-Schleife veranlaßt, auch wenn einige der Prozesse gar nicht beansprucht werden sollten; das bedeutet, daß Nulleinträge gegeben werden. Berücksichtigt man die Nulleinträge mit, so wird nach Abarbeitung eines WS-Eintrages der nächste WS-Eintrag (der gleichen Nachricht) des nächsten Prozesses der p-Schleife abgearbeitet. Die Realisierung dieser Konzeption sieht allerdings vor, daß die WS der Prozesse - soweit es sich um Datenbehandlungs-Prozesse handelt - in die nachrichtenspezifischen Tabellen (vergl. u. "BSL") eingeordnet sind; die Einträge bedeuten die Durchführung des "internal routing".

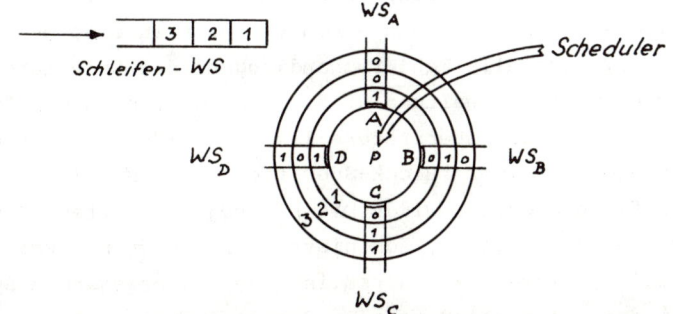

In Figur 2 ist eine p-Schleife mit den 4 Prozessen A, B, C, D und den
zugehörigen WS skizziert. Drei Nachrichten-Eingaben in der Reihenfolge
1 (innerer Ring), 2 und 3 (mittlerer bzw. äußerer Ring) haben WS-Einträge bewirkt. Die Abarbeitung beginnt mit Prozeß A, WS-Eintrag der Nachricht 1; dann folgt Prozeß D, WS-Eintrag der gleichen Nachricht 1, darauf Prozeß B, WS-Eintrag der Nachricht 2 usw.. Das Setzen von "event flags" für Prozesse durch andere Prozesse ist mit diesem Verfahren ebenfalls möglich.

Einige Bemerkungen: 1. Die hier eingeführten Prioritäten oder Dringlichkeitsstufen bestehen neben den möglichen HW- und SW-Prioritäten,
die dem Programmierer der PDP 11/45 zur Verfügung stehen. Dadurch erst
wird die dynamische Prioritätenvergabe bei der Nachrichtenbehandlung
und -übertragung in dieser Form möglich. 2. "Data-handling"-Prozesse
und andere mit variabler Dringlichkeit zu durchlaufende Prozesse sind
physikalisch nur einmal realisiert; die verschiedenen p-Schleifen
($p \in \mathbb{N}_o \subset \mathbb{N}$) werden durch verschiedene WS-Ebenen und die Einsprung-Priorität des Schedulers gebildet. Schleifen-Prozesse müssen stets reentrant
programmiert sein. 3. Das System steuert sich selbst: Im Anfangszustand
wird eine Warteschleife unterster Priorität p_o durchlaufen. Eine Unterbrechung kann in eine p_1-Schleife mit $p_1 > p_o$ verzweigen, eine nächste
Unterbrechung führt ggf. zur Aktivität einer p_2-Schleife mit $p_2 > p_1$
usw.. Ist eine p_n-Schleife abgearbeitet, so wird in die nächstniedrige
Schleife mit nicht-leerer Schleifen-WS verzweigt.

2.3 Die Hauptbausteine sind Eingabe-Teil (E-Teil) und Ausgabe-Teil
(A-Teil), Systemprozesse, Datenbehandlungsprozesse, Interpreter und
Scheduler.

Dem A-Teil zuzurechnen ist eine ENDE-Routine, zu deren Aufgaben Speicher-Freigabe, "table-updating" und Löschen spezifischer Einträge bzw.
- bei Nichtfreigabe - das Eintragen eines Vermerks in eine Quittungswarteliste gehören. Spezielle Fehlerbehandlungen, das Generieren von
Meldungen, Betriebsmittelverwaltung u. ä. sind Funktionen der Systemprozesse. Die Aufgaben des Interpreters lauten: Etikett-Auswertung,
Setzen von Einträgen in einer "Block-Specification-List" (BSL), die
nachrichtenspezifisch angelegt wird. Die Einträge betreffen: "internal routing", Nachrichtenart (Daten, Administration, Quittung) Priorität,
Blockidentifikation, Hinweis auf Adreßliste des zu belegenden Speicherrasters. Stellt der Interpreter fest, daß ein Datenblock keiner Bearbeitung bedarf, so wird sofort der A-Teil angesprungen. Der Interpreter un-

tersucht, ob die zuletzt "unterbrochene Priorität" größer oder gleich der Priorität des jetzt vorliegenden Blockes ist. Wenn ja, erfolgt der Rücksprung, anderenfalls wird der Scheduler mit der gefundenen "Block-Priorität" angesprungen.

Aufgaben des Schedulers: Abarbeitung der p-Schleifen, d. h. Schleifen-WS-Behandlung, Abarbeitung der Einträge der BSL, die die WS der Schleifenprozesse für "data-handling" repräsentieren. Ermittlung der prioritätsmäßig nächstniedrigen nicht-leeren Schleifen-WS, Vergleich der "unterbrochenen Priorität" q mit der Priorität p dieser Schleife, Aktivierung der Schleifenprozesse im Falle p > q. Die vom Scheduler aufgerufenen Moduln können u. U. Betriebsmittel anfordern (z. B. Speicherplatz, wenn eine Meldung zu generieren ist) oder freigeben (z. B. wenn eine logische Quittung bearbeitet wurde). In diesen Fällen werden WS-Einträge für System-Prozesse bzw. für die ENDE-Routine vorgenommen. Der Scheduler hat Aktivierungsaufgaben wahrzunehmen, ein CPU-Scheduling kann unabhängig davon durchgeführt werden.

3. Schlußbemerkung

Nur Teile des Systems sind realisiert. Testergebnisse können daher nicht angegeben werden. Die Interrupt-Service-Routinen sind so konzipiert, daß die kritischen Zeiten (Nichtunterbrechbarkeit) in der Größenordnung zwischen 19,08 µsec und 23,04 µsec liegen. Jeder aktiven Leitung ist eine Gruppe von Eingabe-ISR und eine Gruppe von Ausgabe-ISR zugeordnet. Die Pufferverwaltung wird dynamisch über eine effektiv einsetzbare Verfügbarkeitsliste gesteuert.

Literatur

[1] Busse, W. und Klessmann, H.: Überlegungen zu den Leistungsmerkmalen der Datenübertragungsperipherie beim Projekt "Zentrale Datenverarbeitung im HMI Berlin"
HMI-Bericht Nr. HMI-B 106, 3.71.

[2] Jotzoff, R., Langer, W., Müller, B. und Winkler, H.:
Über Theorie und Technik von Rechnerverbundsystemen
Angewandte Informatik 9/1973.

[3] Pouzin, L.: CIGALE, the Packet Switching Machine of the CYCLADES Computer Network
Proc. IFIP Congr. Stockholm (1974), 155 - 159.

[4] Pyke, T. N. und Blanc, R. P.: Computer Networking Technology - a State of the Art Review
COMPUTER Vol. 6, No. 8 (1973), 12 - 19.

[5] Roberts, L. G. und Wessler, B. D.: Computer Network Development to Achieve Resource Sharing
AFIPS Conf. Proc. Vol. 36/SJCC (1970).

[6] Scantlebury, R. A. und Wilkinson, P. T.: The National Physical Laboratory Data Communication Network
Proc. 2. Int. Conf. Comp. Com., Stockholm (1974), 223 - 228.

[7] Töpfer, H.-J.: Anforderungen an eine "Zentrale Datenverarbeitung"
HMI-Intern 6.72.

Nachtrag:

[8] Conrads, D., Moritz, H. E. und Mühlstroh, R.: JOKER - Ein System zur Kopplung von Experimentrechnern verschiedener Fabrikate mit einem zentralen Timesharingrechner
Kernforschungsanlage Jülich, Zentralinstitut für Angewandte Mathematik, Jül-1004-MA, Oktober 1973.

6. RECHNERARCHITEKTUR UND BEWERTUNG

W. HÄNDLER

W. M. DENNY

P. KÜHN, M. LANGENBACH-BELZ

ON CLASSIFICATION SCHEMES FOR COMPUTER SYSTEMS IN THE POST-VON-NEUMANN-Era[x]

Wolfgang Händler
Institut für Mathematische Maschinen
und Datenverarbeitung
der Universität Erlangen-Nürnberg

Michael Flynn [1] proposed a classification scheme consisting of the following components:

    SI   Single instruction stream
    MI   Multi instruction stream
    SD   Single data stream
    MD   Multi data stream

In this nomenclature one can classify some known examples of unconventional computers [xx] as follows:

SOLOMON	SIMD	[2]
ILLIAC IV	SIMD	[3]
PRIME	MIMD	[4]
DARE	MISD	[5]
MAPI	MISD	[6]
C.mmp	MIMD, SIMD and MISD	[7]
STARAN	SIMD	[8]
CD STAR 1oo	MISD	[9]
TIASC	MISD	[10]

---

[x] This work was partially supported by the Fraunhofer Gesellschaft zur Förderung der angewandten Forschung e.V., under contract No. T 0230/12340/11061

[xx] We have to assume for this short paper that the reader is familiar with some of the following structures.

The well known PRINCETON-Type Computer [11] falls into the class SISD. The classification scheme nevertheless is not entirely satisfactory for the needs of computer specialists. For instance such structurally different computer systems as SOLOMON, ILLIAC IV, and STARAN fall into only one class (SIMD). The classification scheme does not distinguish between the three types of pipelines: macropipeling, instruction-pipelining and arithmetic-pipelining. More than one of these three types of pipelining can be implemented in one computer system. As it offers only four classes the Flynn-Classification scheme cannot reflect the variety of all possible structures. Also the special position of the C.mmp-project which covers three of the possible four points in the diagramm (Fig. 1) is anomalous. In order to overcome this shortcoming we suggest below a new classification scheme.

While the Flynn-Scheme can be represented as a square (Fig. 1), a modification could provide a differentiation between bitwise processing (B) and wordwise processing (W) (Fig. 2), now spanning a cube. This makes the classification more distinctive. For instance ILLIAC IV is separated from STARAN. C.mmp covers now three of the possible eight points, SIMW, MIMW and MISW, where the latter characterizes the macro-pipelining-mode of operation. Thus the C.mmp-system can operate in three different modes depending on the application. At any time the C.mmp occupies only that state or mode of operation which is best suited to the application.

Nevertheless this slight modification of M. Flynn's classification scheme cannot be regarded as satisfactory. A more basic consideration shows that unconventional systems are characterized in the first place by

- k   the number of independently working programs directed by control units K   in accordance with the PMS/ISP-Notation [12].
- d   the number of arithmetic and logic units (data manipulators) D related to one control unit K, and
- w   the number of bit positions, which are processed in parallel (or simultaneously) by a unit D.

w is simply the wordlength of a parallel processor, which in most cases reflects the hardware structure of the appropriate primary memory.

With these 3 letters, which take integer values, one can form a triple (k, d, w), which now represents the mode of operation of a system. In this triple-notation the systems considered above become e.g.

```
          SOLOMON        (1, 1024, 1)
          ILLIAC IV      (1, 64, 64)
          PRIME          (5, 1, 16)
          DARE           (n, 1, 16) ⎫ n is the number of connected
          MAPI           (n, 1, w)  ⎭ processors
          C.mmp          (16, 1, 16)
                 and     (1, 16, 16)
          STARAN         (1, 8192, 1)
```

In this classification scheme the C.mmp-project covers more than one point. Unfortunately the notation does not, as yet reflect pipelining properties.

Including pipelining cannot result in a choice between parallism and pipelining. Rather we have to add classification elements to the above scheme, because obviously both features can be present in one structure. Corresponding to the three types of pipelining, i.e.

```
          macropipelining              (k')
          instruction pipelining       (d')
          and arithmetic pipelining    (w')
```

we supplement the triple given above by adding 3 factors in the following way:

$$(k \times k', d \times d', w \times w')$$

- k' is the number of programm-controlled units working separately on different tasks of one problem (this is the definition of macropipelining)

- d' is the number of function-units, which can work simultanously (adding units, logical units, indexing units etc.)[x]

- w' is the number of steps which the arithmetic pipelining unit contains.

---

[x] This is normally associated with a unit called scoreboard which imposes sequenciality to prevent conflicts.

In this notation the known pure pipelining computer-systems CD STAR 1oo and TIASC bear the following characteristics:

>CD STAR 1oo :   (1 x 1, 2 x 1, 64 x 4)
>TI ASC   (1 x 1, 4 x 1, 64 x 8)

By this classification the early approaches to an instruction pipelining occupy a significant place:

>CD 6600   (1 x 1, 1 x 1o, 6o x 1)
>(central part without PP's)

or:

>CD 7600   (1 x 1, 1 x 9, 6o x 1)
>(central part without PP's)

It is clear we can omit all the 1's. For instance the four examples mentioned above can be written:

>CD STAR 1oo   (1, 2, 64 x 4)
>TI ASC   (1, 4, 64 x 8)

or:

>CD 6600   (1, x 1o, 6o)
>(central part without PP's)
>CD 7600   (1, x 9, 6o)
>(central part without PP's)

The multiplication cross remains in order to signify the second position for pipelining for each of the three elements. For instance we have replaced 1 x 9 by x 9 etc. A further advantage of this convention is that pipelining features are shown only if present, in the second position of each element, so that the representation of the other examples which we have developed earlier (SOLOMON etc.) do not require alteration. All these examples have their essential properties or capabilities in the area of parallelism, in spite of the fact that, for instance, ILLIAC IV has a lookahead feature in connection with an instruction pipeline. In connection with Flynn's classification (Fig.1) and with the slightly modified Flynn classification (Fig. 2), we have already indicated that the C.mmp-structure can be used also for macro-pipelining-applications (MISD resp. MISW).

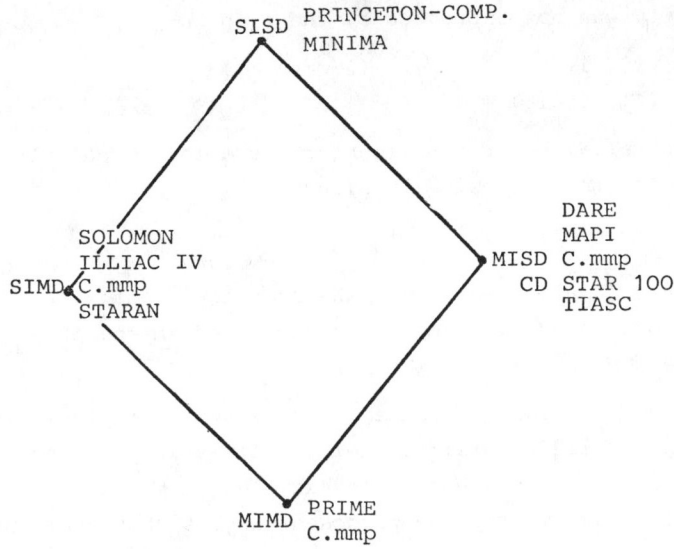

Fig.1: Classification Scheme as presented by M. Flynn.

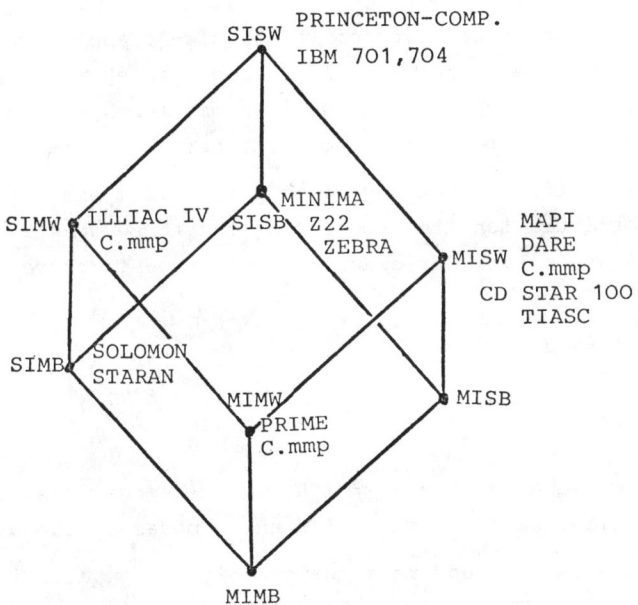

Fig.2: Modified Classification Scheme.

This property was not expressed by the triples

   (16, 1, 16)   (C.mmp)
 and (1, 16, 16)

as given above. With our supplementary notation for pipelining we now can write also the following triple

   (x 16, 1, 16)

The fact that in all these cases the same equipment, i.e. the same configuration, is used, seems to be expressed in the three triples above. We shall return to this point below.

For the present we forego further consideration of pipelining in order to focus on parallelism (simultaneity). It is left to the reader to try out the classification scheme with examples of his choice. As any classification scheme the one proposed has its shortcomings. For instance the triple does not contain any information about the interconnection of the elements, the memory structure, or the I/O-capability. We must assume that in such cases there is a reasonable balance between the system as characterized by the classification triple and the residue of the system.

We discuss below some properties of the triple-nomenclature. Finally we discuss in more detail an example in order to show the advantages of the notation. In both cases we derive some further conclusions as to the information content of the classification scheme.

As a rough estimation of the degree of parallelism exhibited by a particular configuration, the product of the three to six factors in the triple can be taken. For example, the C.mmp-structure is characterized by the three triples:

   (16, 1, 16),
   (1, 16, 16),
 and (x 16, 1, 16).

For all 3 cases we have 16 x 16 = 256, which demonstrates that the degree of parallelism is constant for the 3 modes of operation.

Of course there may be good reasons to modify the evaluation of the triple in practice. This point will not be investigated in this paper. Other aspects of the use of the classification scheme are discussed below in connection with a concept which is alled E̲rlangen Version of a G̲eneral P̲urpose P̲rocessor (EGPP).

There are several possible interpretations of the triples. Because there are in fact always 6 entities in the triple, i.e. k,k',d,d',w,w', (combined to (kxk', dxd', wxw')) we could interpret the classification scheme as being a set of points in $\mathbb{N}^6$ (points in a 6-dimensional space of natural numbers). Then most of the computer systems we have discussed so far occupy a certain point in $\mathbb{N}^6$. The appropriateness of a system for a certain application depends on this. If, for instance, some application, i.e. some algorithm developed for a certain application, requires the parallel execution of, say, n=66 operations the systems of the following characteristics are not best suited to this algorithms:

    (1, 1o24, 1)   (SOLOMON)
    (1, 8192, 1)   (STARAN)   or possibly even
    (1, 16, 16)   (C.mmp, one of the modes)

(where other systems are even less suited). In other words: As a <u>computer-system</u> is represented by one or more than one point in the classification scheme, so each phase of an <u>algorithm</u>^{x)} can be represented by a certain point in a corresponding scheme.

Without going into too much detail, it must be stated that the classification scheme is also applicable to an algorithm which defines an application program and that in general we have to investigate the relationship between a given algorithm (defining a problem) on the one hand and a possible available computer system on the other hand.

How does a certain computer system cover the application space? That seems to be an important question for evaluating computer systems.

We were very conscious of this question when developing the EGPP-concept [13,14,15] (Erlangen General Purpose Processor). In order to cover a broad variety of applications we have designed a computer system whose standard processor offers two modes of operations, namely to function as a conventional processor with N bits in parallel or to function as N processors which operate on only one bit at a time. Connecting many such processors as an array of, say, M processors, finally makes it possible to run MxN processor elements simultaneously, where each operates on only one bit. With this design, which is achieved by modifying the set of microprograms, the system can work as an ILLIAC IV, PRIME, STARAN, or a C.mmp configuration.

---

x) The algorithm must, of course, reflect entirely the intrinsic paralellism of the application.

This particular property is a considerable extension of contemporary (parallel) general purpose processors because it achieves a significant gain in flexibility, which is seen in its position in the classification scheme which we have described above. As a start we can think of an EGPP-Array [14] as a C.mmp configuration with the additional feature that it can operate in a 'vertical mode'. This means that each bit position in all the (parallel) processors is processing separately but simultaneously vertical data. These data are stored vertically in machine-words of the conventional primary memory, as it is shown in Fig. 3 for one of the processors. An essential aspect of this arrangement is that programming methods, operating systems and other features similar to those of conventional computers, are used in order to achieve efficient associative processing (in the sense of STARAN) as well as conventional (parallel) processing (in the sense of ILLIAC IV). There is also no need for many different dedicated memories [13,14,15] .

The nature of the connections between the elements of an E.G.P.P.-Array is quite different from that used in the C.mmp-project. While the latter uses crossbar switching to connect each processor with each memory block, the EGPP-Array provides only connections in a very close neighbourhood, mainly N,S,E,W, as shown in Fig. 4.

Let us assume as a simple example that 16 EGPP's, each one containing 64 bit positions, or, in the sense of this paper 64 processing elements, configure the array. Some additional EGPP's act as separate I/O and operating system processors, to schedule the array and ensure some synchronism. Then we can think of this arrangement (the EGPP-Array) as representing, at any time, one of

- a) 16 computers, 64 bit wordlength and parallel operation with an appropriate amount of (neighboured) memory allocated to each processor, working separately (PRIME-mode)
- b) 1 computer, processing in parallel 16 x 64 = 1o24 bits, performing associative functions (STARAN-mode).
- c) 1 computer, containing 16 arithmetic units with 64 bit positions each, working in parallel on one programm (ILLIAC IV-mode).
- d) a chain of 16 processors, each one processing in parallel 64 bits, forming a macropipelining system, operating on different tasks of one problem at the same time (macropipeling mode of C.mmp).

It is also possible to partition the array into several elements, each one working separately in one of the modes a) to d).

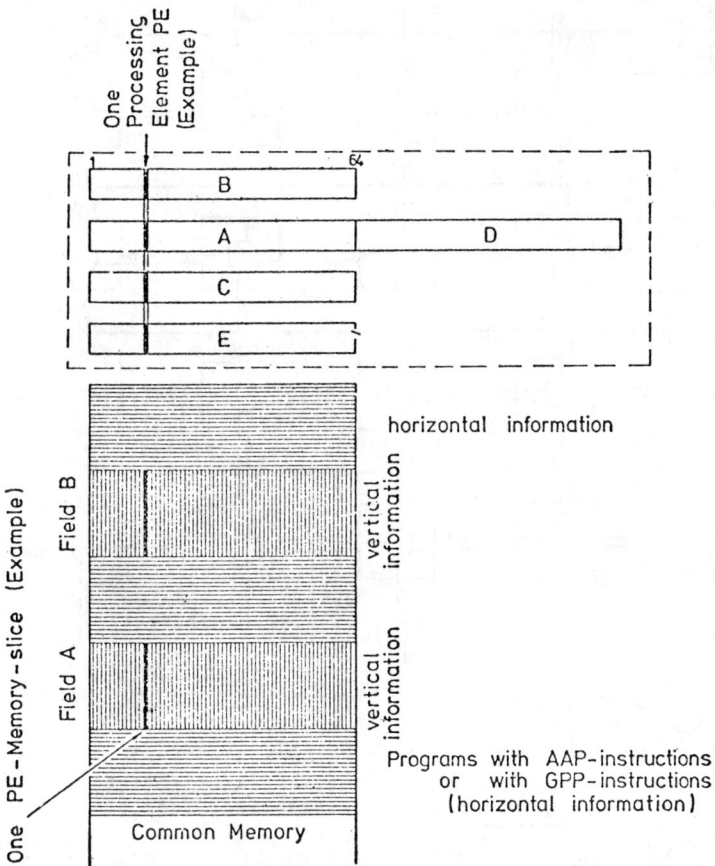

Fig.3: Erlangian General Purpose Processor (EGPP).

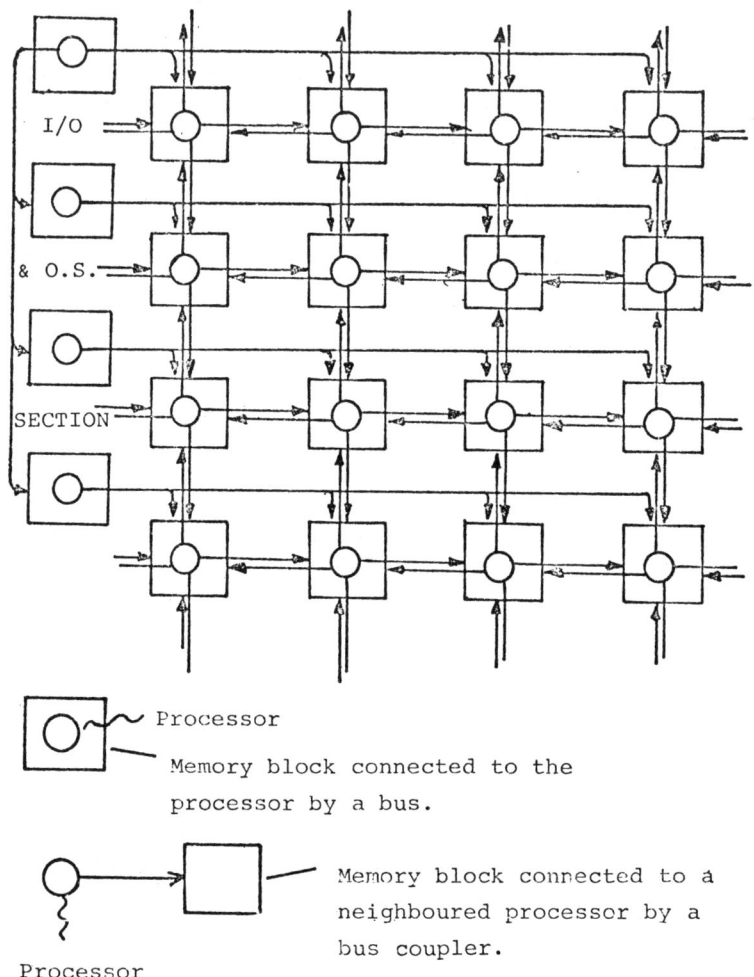

Fig.4: E.G.P.P.-Array. Interconnections are provided to directly neighboured elements and to the I/O - OS - Section.

Regarding the EGPP-Array as an object of the proposed classification scheme, we can state: The EGPP-Array can be at one time in one of the following states z:

z_1 = (16, 1, 64) = 16 (1, 1, 64)   compare a) above

z_2 = (1, 1o24, 1)   compare b)

z_3 = (1, 16, 64)   compare c)

z_4 = (x 16, 1, 64)   compare d)

or if we include partitions, then we have, for instance,

z' = (1, 1, 64) + (4, 1, 64) + (1, 512, 1)   or

z'' = 6 (1, 1, 64) + (1, 64, 1) + (x 3, 1, 64) + (x 2, 1, 64).

Since we call such expressions the states z of a computer system, the multiplication and addition rules are apparently defined as follows:

    1. (k x k', d x d', w x w') = k (x k', d x d', w x w') (multiplication)
    2. (k_1 x k', d x d', w x w') + (k_2 x k', d x d', w x w') =
                  ((k_1 + k_2) x k', d x d', w x w').   (addition)

So far we have assumed that d x d', w x w', are constant. This applies if we consider a structure like C.mmp. But if we consider the EGPP-structure [x)] we also have:

    3. (k x k', d_1 x d', w_1 x w') = (k x k', d_1.c x d', w_1/c x w').

For the actual EGPP-structure, we have in detail:

    z = (k, d_1, w_1) = (k, d_1·c, w_1/c).

c must be a divisor of w_1. Further the resulting d = d_1 · c and w = w_1/c have to be permitted integer values. For instance we can provide for the EGPP-structure the values   w = 1,
                                  w = 8,
                        or   w = 64.

This gives a broad variety of operation modes, which enable us to process data bitwise, byte-wise, or wordwise.

[x)]   disregarding in this paper the fact that we have not so far assumed pipelining for the EGPP-Structure.

This parallelism is of greatest value if data is processed bitwise (e.g. 1o24 bits), and of least value if we process the data wordwise.

For the classification triple we can write:

$$z = (16, 1, 64) =$$
$$z = (1, 1o24, 1) = (1, 128, 8) = (1, 16, 64).$$

By extending the concept of multiprogramming to the EGPP-Array we can change the state (or operation mode) at intervals of several milliseconds, and this can guarentee a tolerable utilization of the EGPP-Array for a broad variety of problems, demanding highly different degrees of parallelism.

The EGPP-Array-Project has been partially simulated using an Interdata 7o which is about to be replaced by an Interdata 85. Moreover we are investigating how the EGPP-Array can be best designed by using only elements, e.g. processors, and multiport-memories, which are currently available.

This seems to us to be a very promising endeavour. We draw the attention of the reader to related work in this field, described in detail in [16], and, with special reference to some problems of synchronism in the array to [17].

I wish to acknowledge the assistance of Robert Bell, both with the contents and with the final English version of this paper.

References

[1] FLYNN, M.J.: Some Computer Organisations and their Effectiveness, IEEE Trans. on Comp., C-21, Nr. 9, Sept. 1972 (compare also: Hobbs et al.: Parallel Processor Systems Technologies and Applications, New. York, Washington 1970)

[2] MURTHA, J.C.: Highly Parallel Information Processing Systems, in Advances in Computers, Vol. 7, 1966, pp. 11-20

[3] SLOTNICK, D.L. et al.: The ILLIAC IV computer, IEEE Trans. on Comp., C-17, Vol. 8, August 1968, pp. 746 - 757

[4] BASKIN, H.B. et al.: PRIME- A modular architecture for terminal-oriented systems. Proceedings S.J.C.C. 1972, pp. 431 - 437

[5] KORN, G.: Back to parallel computations:proposal for a completely new on-line simulation system using standard minicomputers for low-cost multiprocessing, Simulation, August 1972, pp. 37 - 45

[6] HÄNDLER, W.: The concept of Macro-Pipelining with high availability, Elektronische Rechenanlagen 15, 1973, pp. 269 - 274

[7] WULF, W.A. and BELL, C.G.: C.mmp - A multi-mini-processor, Proceedings F.J.C.C. 1972, pp. 765 - 777

[8] RUDOLPH, J.A.: A Production Implementation of an Associative Array Processor-STARAN, Proceedings F.J.C.C., 1972, pp. 229 - 241

[9] HINTZ, R.G., and TATE, D.P.: CONTROL DATA STAR-100 Processor Design. in IEEE, Compcon 72, Digest of papers, Innovative Architecture

[10] WATSON, W.J.: The TIASC- A highly modular and flexible super computer architecture, Proceedings F.J.C.C. 1972, pp. 221 - 228

[11] BURKS, A.W., GOLDSTINE, H.H. and von NEUMANN, J.: Preliminary Discussions of an Electronic Instrument Institute for Advanced Studies. Princeton, 1947.

[12] BELL, C.G. and NEWELL, A.: Computer Structures: Readings and Examples, New York 1971, pp. 15 - 36

[13] HÄNDLER, W.: Unconventional Computation by Conventional Equipment, NATO-Defence Research Group Seminar, Design and Evaluation of Information Systems, Athen 1974

[14] HÄNDLER, W.: A unified associative and von-Neumann processor EGPP and the EGPP-array, to appear in Proceedings of 1974 Sagamore Computer Conference

[15] HÄNDLER, W.: A conventional Processor Appearing as Associative
By Microprogramming,
Micro 7, The Seventh Annual Microprogramming
workshop, ACM
to appear in
Micro- News letters

[16] HEART, F.E. et al.: A New Minicomputer / Multiprocessor for the
ARPA-Network,
Proceedings AFIPS 1973 NCC

[17] SCHECHER, H.: Vorschläge für die Organisation einer flexiblen
Multiprocessoranlage.
GI-NTG Fachtagung Struktur und Betrieb von Rechner-
systemen, Braunschweig 1974,
Lecture Notes in Computer Science, 8,
Springer-Verlag, Berlin, pp. 64 - 78

MICRO-PROGRAMMING MEASUREMENT TECHNIQUES
FOR THE BURROUGHS B1700

W. Michael Denny
Burroughs Corporation
Goleta, CA 93017/USA

INTRODUCTION

Without adequate theoretical concepts, performance measurement is a sorcerer's art. Until information energy can be measured, we can never compare the effectiveness with which different computer architectures or programs process information.[3] Indeed, for all but the simplest information processing tasks, neither internal speeds, nor simulation, nor benchmarks reliably indicate the performance of the widely varying architectures currently marketed. Comparison of different software faces a similar impasse. Competing programs are, therefore, often judged on bases other than how effectively they process information; reliability and ease of use are common criteria.

The most a user can expect from performance measurement is some indication of relative performance of _his_ programs running on _his_ system. Then he can incrementally add hardware or modify software to improve relative performance. If the measurer is a computer manufacturer, he can modify the hardware and software or evaluate the relative impact of state of the art advances on relative performance.

Traditionally, there have been two different approaches to computer performance evaluation: hardware monitoring and software measurement.

I. HARDWARE MONITORING

These techniques are distinguished by the fact that instrumentation is connected directly to the hardware being measured. Such measurements normally do not interfere at all with the system being measured, nor do special programs need to be created for the purpose of measurement. This allows complex collections of programs (e.g., telecommunication systems) to be run exactly as written while the measurement proceeds in real time. Advocates of these hardware techniques point to their non-interfering qualities as well as the fact that little, if any, modification of existing software is necessary. The recent appearance of instrumentation selling for $5K to $20K has made such hardware measurements very popular; however, measurements made with such systems tend to be very hardware-oriented: one can measure things as channel utilization, processor load, some simple aspects of memory utilization, etc. Furthermore, each new measurement requires a thorough examination of the logic flows of the machine and usually a chancy re-connection of the monitoring hardware to the computer in question. Moreover, it is generally difficult to measure variables which are the result of complex system interrelationships with hardware measurement techniques.

This problem is aggravated by the progress of modern computer architecture, where more and more "hard" system resources remain bound to a particular piece of software for shorter and shorter periods of time and will be traded among competing pieces of software many times during the life of a job. Usually, this means that purely hardware measurements are increasingly irrelevant-- we require more correlation with the software being run.

This brings us to the second approach to performance measurement:

II. SOFTWARE MEASUREMENT

These techniques are usually characterized by the insertion (automatic or otherwise) of extra code into existing programs. This code then keeps track of run-time histories and makes them available to the user. Such soft measurement systems are often very useful to programmers in that they can often re-structure their code based on the histories obtained. Soft measurement techniques can often reveal complex system relationships (e.g., paging size and rates), but suffer from two disadvantages:

First, code must be modified to be measured. Usually, the modifications result in negligible additional overhead, but just as usually, the modifications are not trivial and should, therefore, be automatically inserted. The automatic insertion mechanism is rarely available in all the languages to which the user has access. Thus, soft measurement techniques become the province of a few specialized languages - usually the languages used by the elite rather than by the common user. How many commercial data processing systems have software monitoring facilities? Yet, RPG and COBOL account for about 65% of all programs written in the U.S.A.[4]

A second fault of purely soft measurement techniques is similar to that suffered by the purely hardware techniques: as hardware and software become more integrated, "pure" measurements of either kind become less relevant. This is especially true for modern micro-programmed systems where the architectures of the computer can be varied to suit the programs being run. We no longer are just interested in where we spend the most time. We now need to know how we got there and where we usually go once we are there, and how often and by whom we are interrupted, once we are there. These are all questions which require that the measurer examine the intimate processor and I/O hardware registers - but only at the appropriate time, that is, only when he is executing one interesting piece of code out of a much larger

system. Such a modern measurement system must combine the intimate touch
with the hardware with the ability to synthesize general system software
relationships.

III. MICRO-PROGRAMMED MEASUREMENT TOOLS

Micro-programmable computers offer great benefits to much of data processing.
Whereas traditional computers were designed to solve one or two classes of
information processing problems well, micro-programmable machines are adaptable
to a wide range of information processing tasks, exhibiting a specific bias
towards none.[6]

It is easier to write software for a micro-programmed system since, from the
viewpoint of the software, the "hard" system underlying it can be made and
re-made to more closely resemble the programmer's notion of the ideal machine
for his data processing problem.[3]

Furthermore, once written, the software in general runs better on a micro-
programmed system because fewer of the systems resources are wasted solving
classes of problems which do not resemble the problem at hand.[7]

Seen in this light, performance evaluation has perhaps more to gain from micro-
programming than the more usual areas of information processing. At least,
users of traditional machines found an occasional machine dedicated to their
region of interest. FORTRAN users had the 7090, ALGOL devotees had the B5500,
and COBOL programmers the B3500. But performance measurement has never seemed
quite sure enough of what is wanted to demand hard-wiring many measurement
features into a machine. Any one hard-wired feature usually lacked either the
generality which allowed it to be applied over several regions of interest or
the specific properties which allowed one region to be explored in great detail.
Furthermore, no manufacturer wanted to devote a great deal of hardware to
measurement; not all users wanted to measure their machines and certainly not
all of the time. Once the measurement was made, measurement hardware was the
most unused part of the computer.

In a micro-programmed computer, measurement tools may be designed into the
micro-program structure to carry the data processing advantages of micro-
programming over into the area of measurement. The firmware can be tailored to
yield a machine whose general systemic relationships can be explored. Then as
the investigation becomes more refined, the micro-program can be revised to
reveal the details.

In general, the measurements are easier to make when the computer's architecture can be varied to suit the measurements and the measurements are more relevant because hardware and software characteristics can be more easily combined.[5] Furthermore, once the measurement is completed, the measurement micro-program can be replaced with the standard firmware. In fact in some cases the measurement features of the firmware occupy so little space and time that they can be permanently imbedded in the system.

IV. THE B1700 MICRO-PROGRAM MEASUREMENT SYSTEM

In the B1700, programs reside in 666 ns S-memory along with an operating system which supports a virtual memory, variable page size, multi-programming environment. User programs and the operating system residing in S-memory are said to be comprised of S-code-- a code which is interpreted by the firmware. M-memory (a 167 ns writable control store) contains a micro-program interpreter for each different language residing in S-memory plus routines to do elementary handling of interrupt, I/O processing, etc.

Figure 1 illustrates the basic B1700 architecture which allows this. The advantage of making measurements in micro-code on the B1700 is that the micro-code underlies all the S-code via the interpreters and all the I/O activity via a micro-programmed interrupt handler. Since all programs and I/O activity are completely interpreted by the micro-code, all measurements of the details of S-code and I/O can be imbedded in the firmware.

A special hardware monitro micro op-code developed for internal Burroughs software development use lies at the heart of performance measurement on the B1700. Micro operations on the B1700 are all 16 bits long. In half of the micro instructions the first eight bits represent an operation code and the next eight bits contain the address of the operand. The hardware monitor micro operation makes use of the fact that when a micro no-op is encountered, the machine has no use for the eight bits of operand field, even though it has fetched them and loaded them into the operand register. The hardware monitor micro op is a variation on the micro no-op in which the contents of the operand field have been chosen (dynamically) by the programmer to represent whatever he wants. Then the contents of the operand register appear on the backplane of the B1700, where they can be decoded by instrumentation traditionally used for hardware measurements.

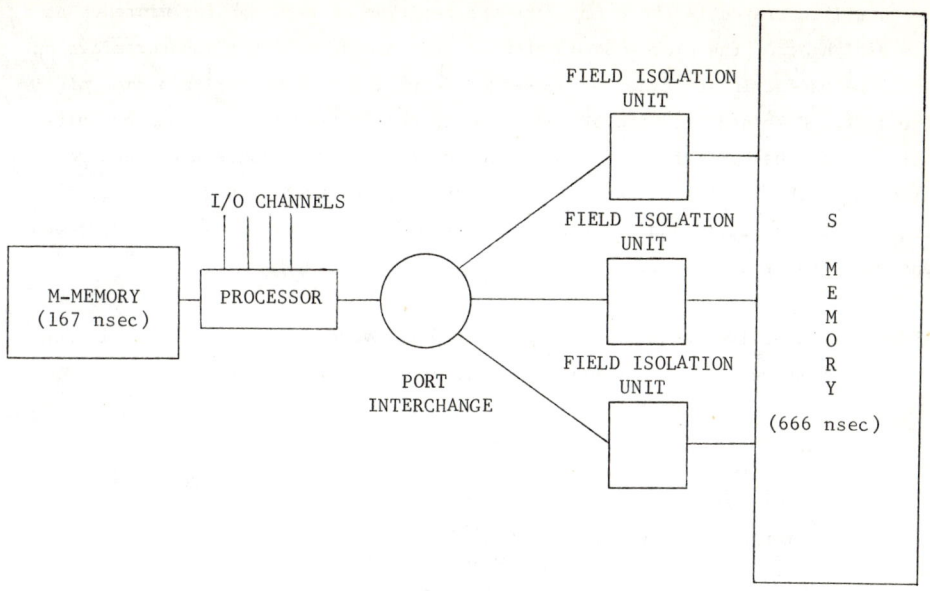

Figure 1

B1700 Organization
The Field Isolation Units Allow
Defined Field[6] Memory Requests

The hardware monitor op has been made available as an internal software development capability in the B1700 within SDL and MIL, the software development languages used internally by Burroughs Corporation. This feature has also been included by special implementation in the commonly used high-level languages (COBOL, RPG, FORTRAN IV, BASIC, UPL) for Burroughs' own measurement use.

Figure 2 illustrates the progress of a monitor micro-op from its insertion in either a high-level language program or a language interpreter micro-program to its use by the hardware performance monitor. In the example illustrated, monitor ops whose operand values are $5E_{16}$ and $5F_{16}$ have been inserted at the beginning and end of a piece of interesting code. These monitor statements reside in S-memory and are interpreted at run time by one of the several language interpreters residing in M-memory. Each time the firmware encounters such a monitor statement in the S-code, a hardware monitor op with the appropriate operand is executed.

Further illustrated in the example is the addition of a 3C monitor micro op at the beginning of the micro-coded fetch of each S-code. Such a monitor micro op would be useful in counting the number of S-ops interpreted during a time of interest. Combined with the 5E and 5F micro ops in Figure 2, we can, by suitably wiring the hardware performance monitor plugboard, measure the frequency with which the high-level S-code is executed, the distribution of the time required to interpret and execute this code and the number of S-ops interpreted and executed at run time.

There are several advantages to using such a hardware monitor operation in conjunction with an inexpensive hardware performance monitor.

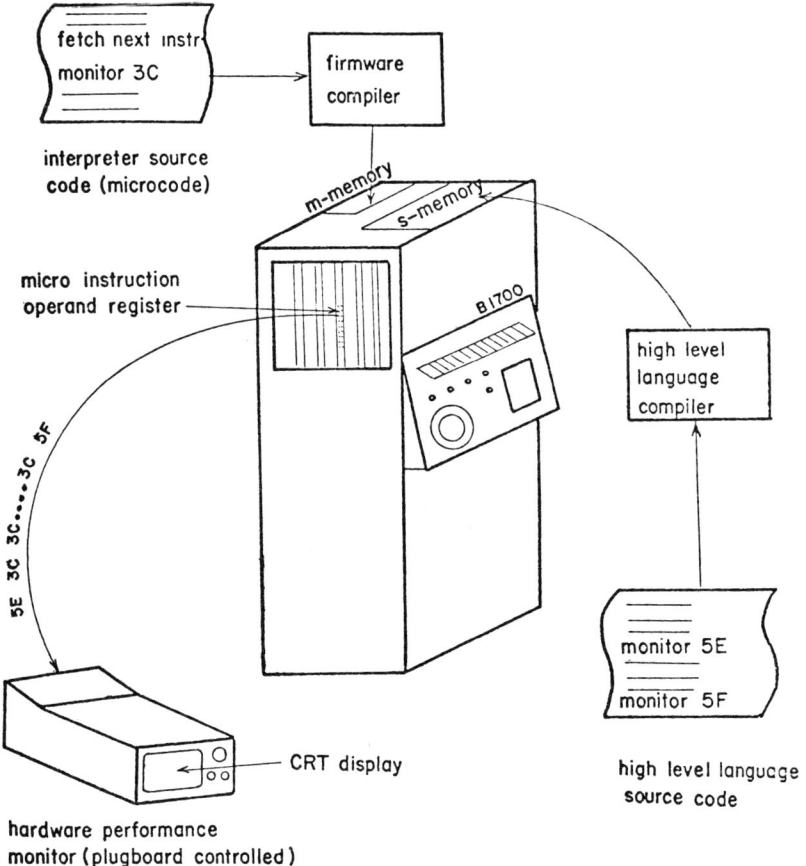

Figure 2

(1) Software measurement is possible in all software development languages. The programmer brackets interesting pieces of code with hardware monitor statements, wires his hardware performance monitor to measure the time between the appropriate monitor ops or the frequency of their occurrence, and runs his program. If he wants, he can almost always leave these monitor statements in the final version of his program for future performance evaluations. Monitor ops represent only about .001% of the executed code of the operating system and micro-programmed interrupt handler. Each monitor op takes only one processor clock to execute, making its addition negligible.

(2) For most performance questions, even those of a traditionally hardware nature, the hardware monitor uses the same connections to the backplane of the B1700. Thus, the measurer is spared the onerous task of tracking down special backplane connections for special problems and following the hardware logic flows of the computer. Usually the only connections to the B1700 are the eight pins corresponding to the eight bits of the operand register and a ninth pin which is true when the register contains the operand of a hardware monitor op.

(3) Measurements which traditionally fell within the realm of strictly hardware can now be combined with the appropriate software measurements making the results more meaningful. An example of this kind of measurement is given on the following page.

V. COMBINED HARDWARE - SOFTWARE MEASUREMENT ON THE B1700

The memory structure of the B1700 allows the processor to execute micro code from either (fast) M-memory or (relatively slow) S-memory through mechanisms which once set up are transparent to the micro code. To take advantage of this flexibility, therefore, the various language interpreters are divided into parts and the most often executed part kept in M-memory. The least often used parts reside in and are executed out of S-memory.

To see whether the division of the FORTRAN and COBOL language interpreters was a good one, it was necessary to measure the percent of fetches of its micro code from the S-memory. But since several language interpreters are normally present, it is important to measure these fetches only when the FORTRAN interpreter was active.

To accomplish this, hardware monitor ops were inserted in the operating system at those points when (1) the operating system reinstated a job, (2) interrupts of programs are recognized, (3) jobs communicate service requests to the operating system. Then using a hardware performance monitor, we were able to decode these hardware monitor ops and tell when the FORTRAN jobs of interest were executing. We then ANDed this condition with the hardware indication that a micro op was being fetched from memory. The results are shown below:

We measured the amount of time spent executing micro ops from S-memory using the original FORTRAN interpreter and varied the available M-memory from 1KB to 8KB. The results are shown by the solid line in Figure 3.

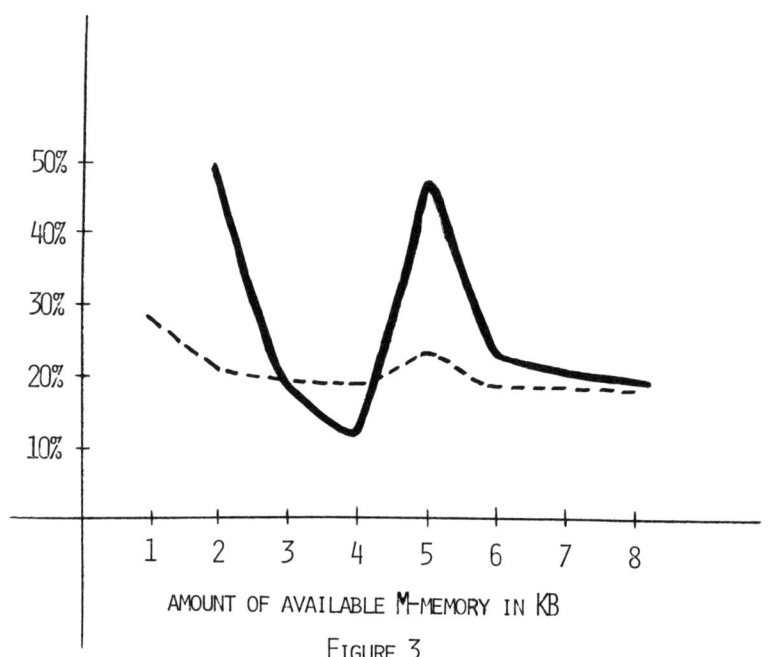

FIGURE 3

PERCENTAGE OF TIME SPENT EXECUTING MICRO CODE FROM S-MEMORY AS A FUNCTION OF AVAILABLE M-MEMORY

The figure shows that an increase in the amount of M-memory from 4KB to 5KB causes an unwanted increase in the amount of time spent executing micro code from S-memory. This indicated that in the 5KB region, the M-memory allocation algorithm still left some often-executed micro code in S-memory.

The FORTRAN group then re-studied the FORTRAN interpreter and re-organized it hoping to put the most often executed code in M-memory. After their re-organization, the measurements were repeated yielding the dotted line in

Figure 3. The re-organized FORTRAN interpreter provides greatly improved performance for small values of M-memory and eliminates the strong oscillation around 5KB. In general, FORTRAN users would see an increase in performance when the newly re-organized FORTRAN interpreter was released.

VI. MONITORED SOFTWARE REMAINS UNCHANGED

It is significant that in this case it was not necessary to modify existing software to set up the appropriate hardware monitor ops. Since we have found the communicate, interrupt and reinstate points so generally useful for measurement, and since hardware monitor ops consume so little time, it has been the customary practice of our software development group to always run with an operating system which also has these measurement ops inserted. So to make the above measurement, it was only necessary to properly wire the hardware performance monitor and make the connections which indicated a micro fetch from S-memory. Contrast this with the onerous software modifications and wiring efforts usually required for measurements of this sort.

VII. CONCLUSION

The addition of a special hardware monitor micro op to a micro-programming computer solves several problems traditionally associated with both hardware and software measurement. Since such micro ops consume so little time, they can often be placed where measurements are anticipated in running software. Such properly placed op-codes make it possible to measure many system functions without the burden of specially compiled or modified measurement programs. Such monitor operations also make it possible to collect data which is both hardware and software oriented and is, thus, more relevant to modern computers. Finally, by implementing such monitor op-codes in high level languages, the developer can with very minor additions to existing programs determine which pieces of code contribute most to the program's running time. The monitor functions consume so little time and space that he can leave them in the finished product so that he can readily investigate performance problems under real-data conditions.

BIBLIOGRAPHY

1. Belgard, R. "An Implementation of BLAISE on the Burroughs 1726". Master project at S.U.N.Y.-Buffalo, New York, June 1974.

2. Bell, T. E. "Computer Performance Analysis Measurement Objectives and Tools". Rand Corporation, Santa Monica, California, February 1971 (R-584 NASA/PR).

3. Johnson, R. R. "Measure and Evaluation". Grenoble University, France, August 1969, Lecture notes for three lectures.

4. Phillippakis, A. "Programming Language Usage". Datamation - October 1973, p. 109.

5. Saal, H. J. and Shustek, L. J. "Microprogrammed Implementation of Computer Measurement Techniques". Stanford University, SLAC Publication 1972 CS 294 (misc.), July 1972.

6. Wilner, W. T. "Design of the Burroughs B1700". FJCC 1973, pp. 489-498.

7. Wilner, W. T. "Burroughs B1700 Memory Utilization". FJCC 1973, pp. 579-586.

ÜBER DIE WIRKSAMKEIT ZYKLISCHER ABFERTIGUNGSSTRATEGIEN
IN REALZEITSYSTEMEN

Paul Kühn und Manfred Langenbach-Belz
Institut für Nachrichtenvermittlung und Datenverarbeitung
Universität Stuttgart

1. EINLEITUNG

In Realzeitsystemen tritt sowohl in der Peripherie als auch in der Zentraleinheit häufig das Problem auf, daß mehrere Anforderungen aus verschiedenen Geräten bzw. Warteschlangen gleichzeitig dasselbe Betriebsmittel in Anspruch nehmen wollen. Als Beispiele seien genannt: a) der von Teilnehmerstationen erzeugte Verkehr in Teilnehmerrechensystemen, b) die aus der Peripherie kommenden Meldungen bei der Prozeßdatenverarbeitung in Realzeitrechnern, c) der Zugriff von Vorverarbeitungseinheiten auf zentrale Verarbeitungs- oder Speichereinheiten in Nachrichtenvermittlungssystemen. Zur Organisation des Verkehrs ist deshalb eine Strategie anzugeben, nach der die einzelnen wartenden Anforderungen nacheinander bedient werden. Außer den bekannten Strategien wie FIFO (first in, first out) oder auch unterbrechenden bzw. nichtunterbrechenden Prioritäten werden in der Praxis aus Gründen der einfachen hardwaremäßigen Realisierbarkeit häufig auch zyklische Abfertigungsstrategien angewendet [1]. Hierbei werden aus verschiedenen Warteschlangen in zyklisch wiederkehrender Reihenfolge wartende Anforderungen zur Bedienung abgeholt.

In diesem Beitrag wird anhand von Warteschlangenmodellen die Wirksamkeit verschiedener zyklischer Abfertigungsstrategien untersucht und der Wirksamkeit anderer Strategien vergleichend gegenübergestellt. Zu diesem Zweck werden numerische Ergebnisse für mittlere Wartezeiten, Wartezeitverteilungsfunktionen und Verlustwahrscheinlichkeiten angegeben, welche z.T. mit Hilfe der Simulation und z.T. aus der Warteschlangentheorie gewonnen wurden. Die erzielten Ergebnisse und Erkenntnisse sollen dazu beitragen, die Auswahl einer zu implementierenden Abfertigungsstrategie bei der Entwicklung eines Systems zu erleichtern.

2. UNTERSUCHTE WARTESCHLANGENMODELLE

2.1 Modellstruktur

In Bild 1 ist die grundsätzliche Struktur des Warteschlangenmodells dargestellt. Die durch g verschiedene Ankunftsprozesse erzeugten Anforderungen werden in dafür zugeordneten Warteschlangen zwischengespeichert. Die einzelnen Warteschlangen werden jeweils bei Freiwerden der Bedienungseinheit nach einer bestimmten Abfertigungsstrategie (z.B. zyklisch oder nach Prioritäten) nach wartenden Anforderungen abgefragt, welche dann die Bedienungseinheit wieder belegen können.

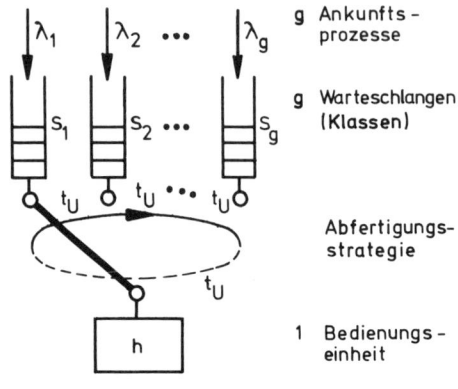

Bild 1. Struktur des Warteschlangenmodells

Die Auswahl einer der wartenden Anforderungen innerhalb einer Warteschlange zur Bedienung erfolge entweder nach den Warteschlangendisziplinen FIFO (first in, first out) oder RANDOM (zufällig).

Für das Umschalten der Bedienungseinheit von einer zur nächsten Warteschlange wird eine konstante Umschaltzeit $t_U \geq 0$ berücksichtigt, welche z.B. der vom Betriebssystem benötigten Verwaltungszeit (overhead) entspricht.

2.2 Abfertigungsstrategien

2.2.1 Zyklische Abfertigungsstrategien ohne Prioritäten

Unter "Abfertigungsstrategie ohne Prioritäten" sei hier verstanden, daß jede der Warteschlangen gleichartig behandelt wird. Dies ist bei folgenden zyklischen Abfertigungsstrategien der Fall:

CYCLIC ORDINARY: Die Bedienungseinheit bearbeitet aus den einzelnen Warteschlangen jeweils nur <u>eine</u> Anforderung (falls vorhanden) und geht dann nach Bedienungsende mit der Umschaltzeit t_U zur nächsten Warteschlange über.

CYCLIC EXHAUSTIVE: Die Bedienungseinheit fertigt <u>alle</u> wartenden Anforderungen einer Warteschlange nacheinander ab und geht erst dann mit der Umschaltzeit t_U zur nächsten Warteschlange über. Diese Abfertigungsstrategie ist in der Literatur auch als alternierende oder relative Priorität bekannt [2].

CYCLIC CLOCKED: Die Bedienungseinheit wird in festen Taktzeitpunkten mit konstantem Abstand an die einzelnen Warteschlangen in zyklischer Reihenfolge angeschaltet und übernimmt eine Gruppe von wartenden Anforderungen zur Bedienung.

Die Abfertigungsstrategie CYCLIC CLOCKED wurde in [9] behandelt.

2.2.2 Zyklische Abfertigungsstrategien mit Prioritäten

In einem Modell nach Bild 1 sollen nun bestimmte Warteschlangen bevorzugt abgefertigt werden, wodurch sie Priorität gegenüber anderen Warteschlangen erhalten:

CYCLIC PRIORITY: Die Bedienungseinheit frägt während eines Zyklus bestimmte Warteschlangen mehrmals ab, wobei die Häufigkeit der "Besuche" einer Warteschlange innerhalb eines Zyklus deren Priorität bestimmt.

Dabei werde noch zwischen folgenden zwei Fällen unterschieden:

a) Geordneter Prioritätszyklus:

Die Gesamtzahl der Besuche einer Warteschlange pro Zyklus wird von der Bedienungseinheit unmittelbar nacheinander durchgeführt. Bei 3 Warteschlangen und einer Zykluslänge 6 könnte z.B. die Reihenfolge der besuchten Warteschlangen innerhalb des Zyklus lauten: (1,1,1,2,2,3).

b) Gemischter Prioritätszyklus:

Die Bedienungseinheit verteilt die Gesamtzahl ihrer Besuche bei einer bestimmten Warteschlange über den gesamten Zyklus nach einem vorgeschriebenen Gesetz (z.B. gleichmäßig verteilt). Die Reihenfolge der besuchten Warteschlangen eines zu a) entspr. Beispiels könnte daher lauten: (1,2,1,3,1,2).

Die Gesamtzahl der Besuche der einzelnen Warteschlangen innerhalb eines Zyklus werde durch geschweifte Klammern gekennzeichnet; für obiges Beispiel also $\{3,2,1\}$.

2.2.3 Nichtzyklische Abfertigungsstrategien für Vergleichszwecke

Zum Vergleich mit den zyklischen Abfertigungsstrategien werden folgende nichtzyklischen Prioritätsstrategien herangezogen:

PREEMPTIVE PRIORITY: Abfertigung der Warteschlangen (Klassen) mit unterbrechenden Prioritäten [2].

NONPREEMPTIVE PRIORITY: Abfertigung der Warteschlangen mit nichtunterbrechenden Prioritäten [3].

PREEMPTION-DISTANCE (PD)-PRIORITY: Kombination aus unterbrechenden und nichtunterbrechenden Prioritäten; Anforderungen einer betrachteten Klasse j unterbrechen Anforderungen der Klassen $\geq j+\xi$, haben aber gegenüber Anforderungen der Klassen $j+1,\ldots,j+\xi-1$ nur nichtunterbrechende Priorität [4] (ξ = Unterbrechungs-Distanz).

PROBABILISTIC PRIORITY: Abfertigung der einzelnen Warteschlangen nach beliebig vorschreibbaren Wahrscheinlichkeiten [10].

2.3 Bezeichnungen und charakteristische Größen

Zur übersichtlicheren und kurzen Kennzeichnung des Warteschlangenmodells werde eine erweiterte KENDALL'sche Notation verwendet. Es bedeute z.B.

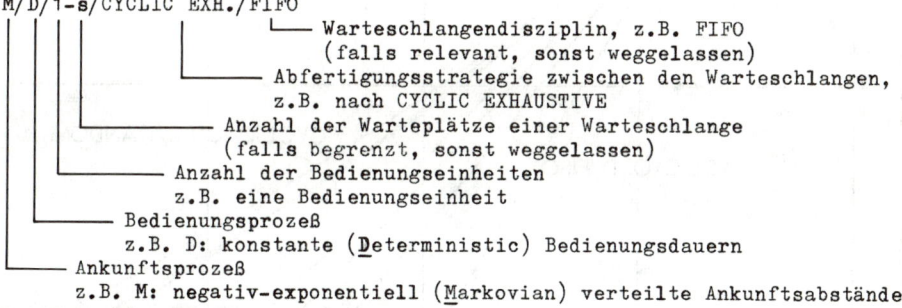

M/D/1-s/CYCLIC EXH./FIFO
- Warteschlangendisziplin, z.B. FIFO (falls relevant, sonst weggelassen)
- Abfertigungsstrategie zwischen den Warteschlangen, z.B. nach CYCLIC EXHAUSTIVE
- Anzahl der Warteplätze einer Warteschlange (falls begrenzt, sonst weggelassen)
- Anzahl der Bedienungseinheiten z.B. eine Bedienungseinheit
- Bedienungsprozeß z.B. D: konstante (**D**eterministic) Bedienungsdauern
- Ankunftsprozeß z.B. M: negativ-exponentiell (**M**arkovian) verteilte Ankunftsabstände.

Ferner bedeuten:

λ_j Ankunftsrate des Ankunftsprozesses für Anforderungen der Klasse j

h   Mittlere Bedienungsdauer

$A_j = \lambda_j h$ Angebot der Klasse j

A   Gesamtangebot, $A = A_1 + A_2 + \ldots + A_g$

w_j Mittlere Wartezeit aller Anforderungen der Klasse j

t_{w_j} Mittlere Wartezeit der wartenden Anforderungen der Klasse j

B_j Verlustwahrscheinlichkeit für Anforderungen der Klasse j

$W_j(>t)$ Verteilungsfunktion (VF) der Wartezeiten aller Anforderungen der Klasse j, $j = 1,2,\ldots,g$.

3. WIRKSAMKEIT ZYKLISCHER ABFERTIGUNGSSTRATEGIEN

In diesem Kapitel werden anhand einer Reihe von Beispielen die Eigenschaften der zyklischen Abfertigungsstrategien nach Abschn. 2.2 aufgezeigt und Eigenschaften anderer Strategien vergleichend gegenübergestellt. Ferner wird kurz auf die Anwendungsbezüge hingewiesen.

3.1 Einfluß der Anzahl von Warteschlangen und der Warteschlangendisziplin bei zyklischer Abfertigung ohne Prioritäten

Als Beispiel werde das Wartesystem M/D/1/CYCLIC ORD./FIFO bzw. RANDOM zugrundegelegt. Bild 2 zeigt den Einfluß der Anzahl g von Warteschlangen sowie der Warteschlangendisziplinen FIFO bzw. RANDOM auf die VF der Wartezeiten der Wartenden $W_j(>t)/W_j(>0)$. Hierzu sei vorausgeschickt, daß die Warteschlangendisziplin und die Abfertigungsstrategie (letztere wegen der hier gleichen Angebotswerte

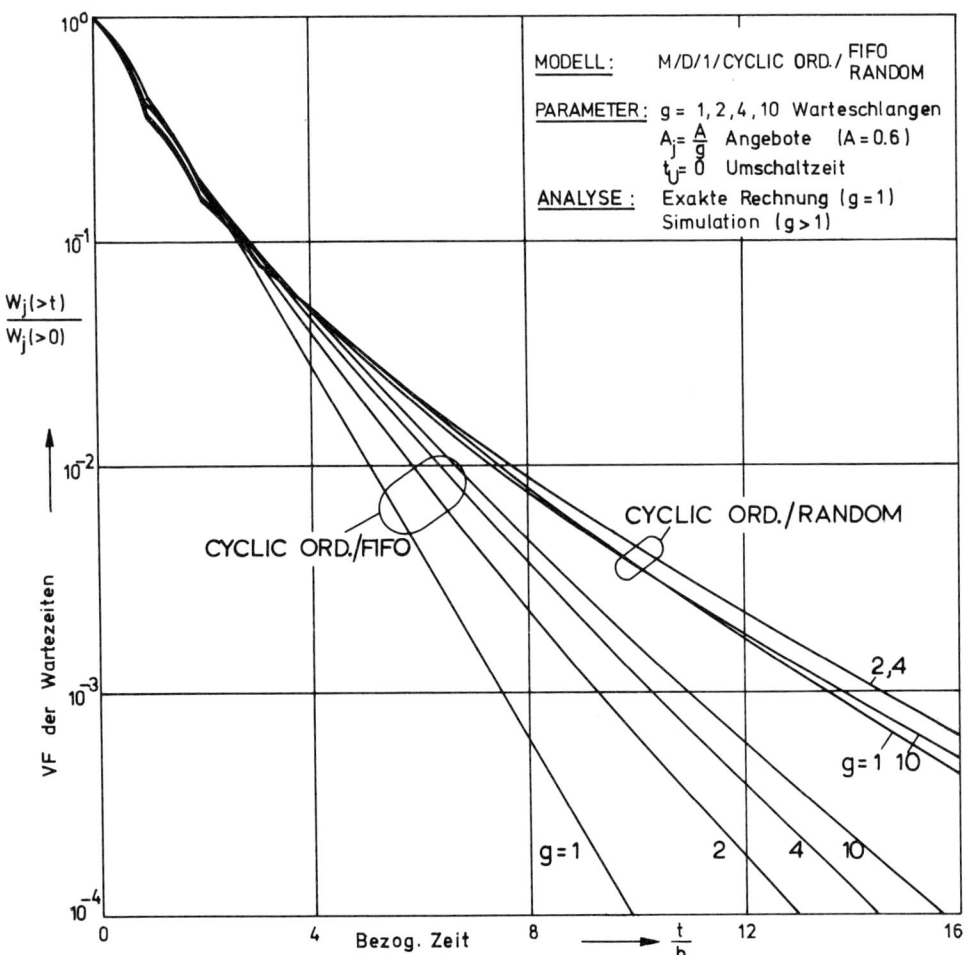

Bild 2. Einfluß der Anzahl von Warteschlangen und der Warteschlangendisziplin auf die VF der Wartezeiten

je Gruppe) keinen Einfluß auf die mittleren Wartezeiten haben, d.h. die mittlere Wartezeit der Wartenden ist einheitlich t_{Wj} = h/2(1-A), j=1,2,...,g, wie bei g = 1. Der Einfluß drückt sich vielmehr in den höheren Momenten der VF der Wartezeiten wie folgt aus:
- CYCLIC ORD./FIFO erzeugt eine mit g zunehmende Streuung der Wartezeiten
- CYCLIC ORD./RANDOM hat generell größere Streuungen als CYCLIC ORD./FIFO, der Einfluß von g ist jedoch offenbar begrenzt (für g→∞ gehen beide Strategien aus theoretischen Überlegungen heraus gegen dieselbe Grenzkurve).

In bestimmten Anwendungsfällen der Realzeit-Datenverarbeitung (z.B. Datenvermittlungen nach dem asynchronen Zeitmultiplex-Verfahren) ist es von großer Wichtigkeit, die Streuung von Wartezeiten in bestimmten Grenzen zu halten, um Zeichenverzerrungen oder -verluste zu vermeiden. Man kann mit Hilfe dieser Untersuchungen den Einfluß praktisch realisierter Strategien bestimmen und den Verbesserungsspielraum gegenüber der günstigen Strategie FIFO (g=1) abschätzen.

3.2 Vergleich zyklischer Abfertigungsstrategien ohne Prioritäten

Betrachtet werde das Wartesystem M/D/1 mit den Abfertigungsstrategien CYCLIC ORD./FIFO bzw. CYCLIC EXH./FIFO. Bei gleichen Angebotswerten je Warteschlange werden die mittleren Wartezeiten von diesen Strategien nicht beeinflußt, d.h. t_{Wj} = h/2(1-A), j = 1,2,...,g. Vielmehr war zu erwarten, daß sich

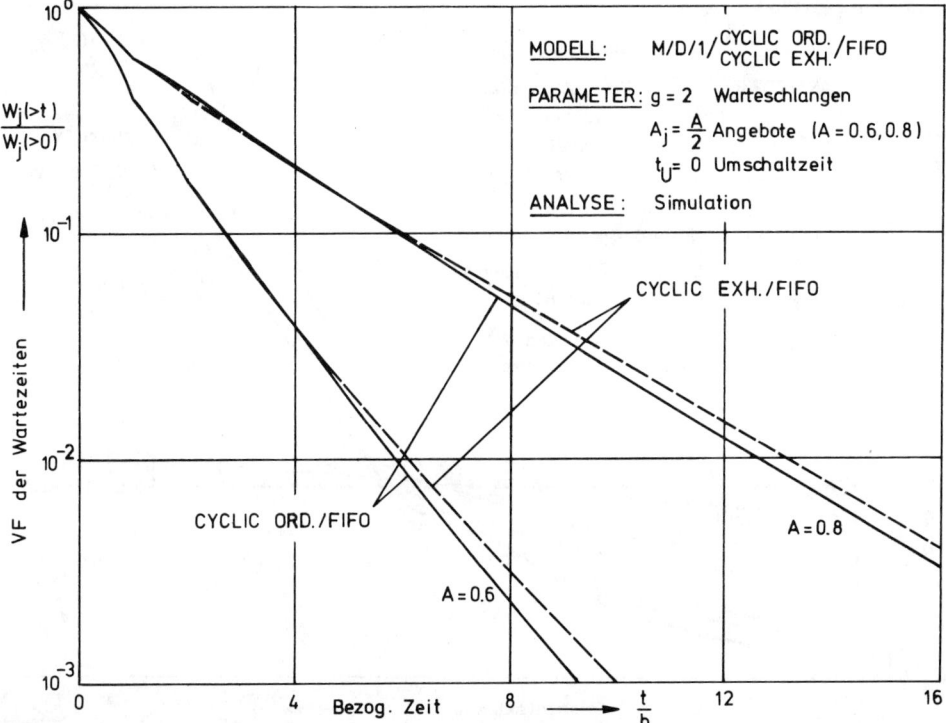

Bild 3. Einfluß zyklischer Abfertigungsstrategien ohne Prioritäten auf die VF der Wartezeiten

die Streuung der Wartezeiten bei diesen extremen Strategien deutlich unterscheidet. Bild 3 zeigt den Einfluß der beiden Abfertigungsstrategien auf die VF der Wartezeiten für den Fall g = 2 Gruppen. Entgegen der Erwartung führt CYCLIC EXH./FIFO nur auf eine wenig höhere Streuung der Wartezeiten verglichen mit CYCLIC ORD./FIFO. Für g > 2 waren die Unterschiede sogar noch geringer.

Für die praktische Anwendung bedeutet dies, daß die Strategie CYCLIC EXH. bevorzugt werden kann, da diese Strategie weniger Umschaltungen zwischen den Warteschlangen benötigt und bei endlich großer Umschaltzeit t_U somit leistungsfähiger ist (siehe auch Abschn. 3.4).

3.3 Vergleich der zyklischen Abfertigungsstrategie mit Prioritäten mit anderen Prioritätsstrategien

Die Einhaltung vorgeschriebener Bedingungen bezüglich der Antwortzeit verschiedener Klassen von Anforderungen wird i.a. durch Einführung von Prioritäten gewährleistet. Die zwei bekanntesten Fälle sind unterbrechende (PREEMPTIVE) bzw. nichtunterbrechende (NONPREEMPTIVE) Prioritäten. Bild 4 zeigt am Beispiel eines Wartesystems M/D/1 die mittleren Wartezeiten für unterbrechende und nichtunterbrechende Prioritäten, Unterbrechungs-Distanz (PD)-Prioritäten, zyklische Prioritäten sowie für den Grenzfall ohne Prioritäten.

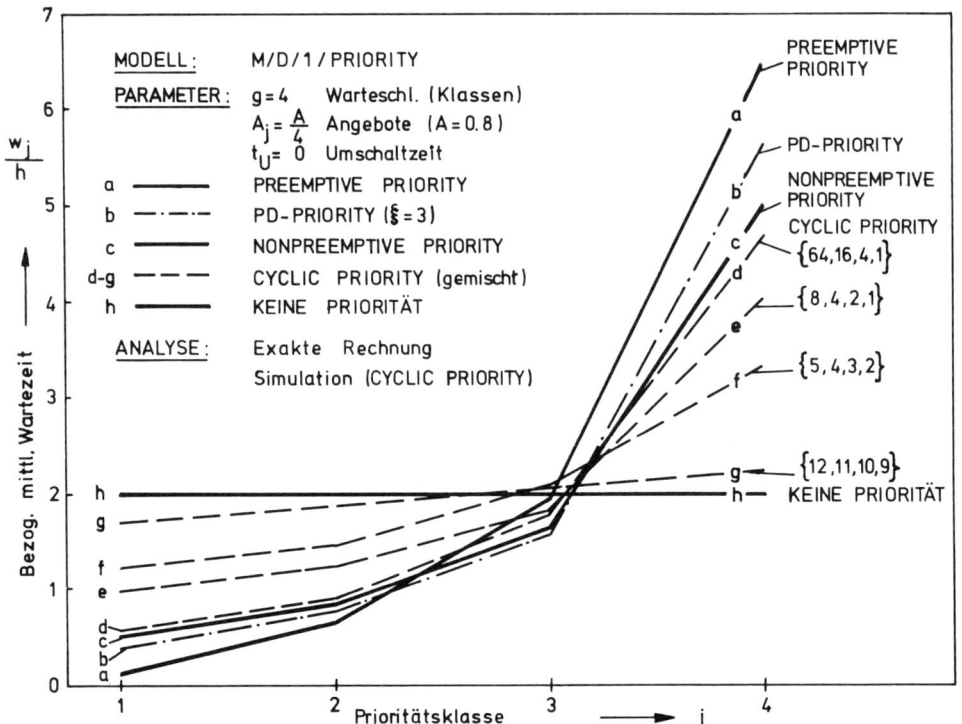

Bild 4. Vergleich verschiedener Prioritätsstrategien

Sind die Bedingungen für die hochprioritären Klassen nicht so streng wie etwa
bei NONPREEMPTIVE PRIORITY, so kann mit CYCLIC PRIORITY praktisch jedes beliebige Gewicht zwischen NONPREEMPTIVE PRIORITY und der Gleichbehandlung aller
Klassen (keine Prioritäten) eingestellt werden, vergl. Bild 4. Somit wird durch
PD-Prioritäten einerseits und zyklische Abfertigung mit Prioritäten andererseits das gesamte Spektrum zwischen den beiden Extremfällen unterbrechender bzw.
gar keiner Priorität ausgefüllt. Weitere Prioritätsstrategien, welche ebenfalls
dieses Spektrum ausfüllen, sind einerseits Unterbrechungs-Verzögerungs-Priori-
täten [11], andererseits wahrscheinlichkeitsmäßige Prioritätsstrategien [10],
vergl. auch Abschn. 4.3.

3.4 Einfluß von Zyklusfolge und Umschaltzeit bei zyklischen Abfertigungsstrategien mit Prioritäten

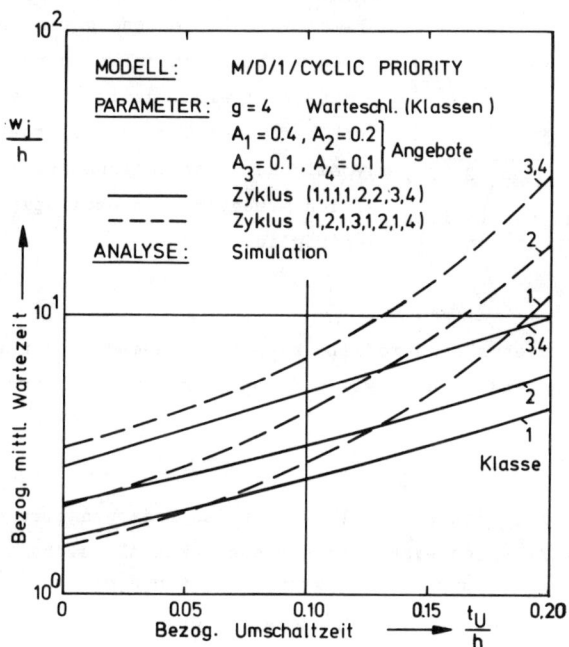

Bild 5. Einfluß von Zyklusfolge und Umschaltzeit auf die mittleren Wartezeiten

Der Einfluß von geordneter
bzw. gemischter Zyklusfolge
sowie der (konstanten) Umschaltzeit t_U werde am Beispiel des Wartesystems
M/D/1/CYCLIC PRIORITY gezeigt
(Parameter vergl. Bild 5).
Für $t_U = 0$ wird die hochprio-
ritäre Klasse 1 durch den ge-
mischten Prioritätszyklus zu
Lasten der Klassen niedrigster
Priorität leicht bevorzugt.
Mit zunehmender Umschaltzeit
t_U jedoch zeigt sich der geordnete Prioritätszyklus infolge seiner geringeren Anzahl
von Umschaltungen überlegen,
vergl. Bild 5. Aus dem gleichen Grund ermöglicht der geordnete Prioritätszyklus einen
höheren Maximaldurchsatz als
der gemischte.

3.5 Einsatz zyklischer Abfertigungsstrategien mit Prioritäten zum Ausgleich
der Auswirkungen ungleicher Angebotswerte

Abschließend soll anhand eines Warteverlustsystems M/D/1-s mit ungleichen Angeboten (Parameter vergl. Bild 6) gezeigt werden, wie mit Hilfe zyklischer Abfertigungsstrategien mit Prioritäten die Auswirkungen ungleicher Angebotswerte
je Klasse ausgeglichen werden können. In Bild 6 sind hierzu die Verlustwahrscheinlichkeiten B_j der einzelnen Klassen für CYCLIC ORD. und CYCLIC PRIORITY
angegeben (Verlustwahrscheinlichkeit = Wahrscheinlichkeit für Abweisen einer

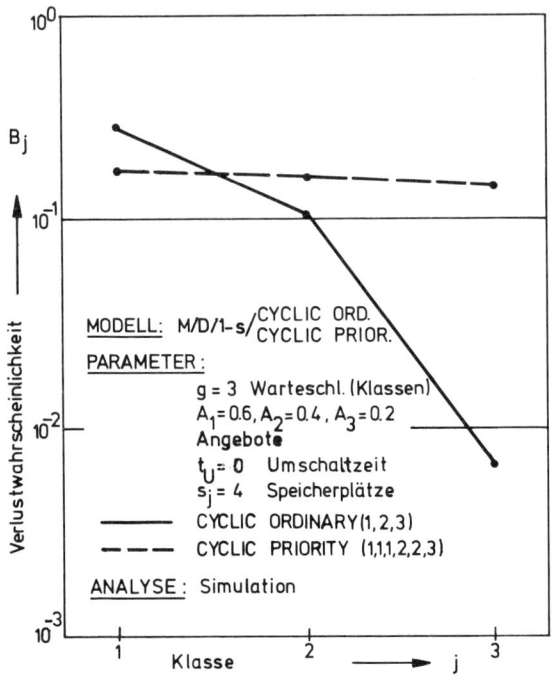

Bild 6. Ausgleich der Verlustwahrscheinlichkeiten bei ungleichen Angeboten

eintreffenden Anforderung infolge Speicherknappheit). Während CYCLIC ORD. zu sehr unsymmetrischen Verlusten führt, gleicht CYCLIC PRIORITY (mit Besuchs-Häufigkeiten entsprechend den Angeboten) sehr gut aus. Entsprechend könnte der Ausgleich z.B. auch bezüglich der mittleren Wartezeiten erfolgen.

In der Praxis könnte dieser Effekt z.B. so angewendet werden, daß der Zyklus in gewissen Zeitabständen entsprechend der momentanen Warteschlangenlängen neu eingestellt wird; damit wäre eine auch hardwaremäßig realisierbare dynamische Priorität zum Ausgleich momentaner Angebotsspitzen möglich.

4. ANALYSEVERFAHREN

Über die Analyseverfahren der Warteschlangenmodelle kann in diesem Rahmen nur ein Überblick gegeben werden. Es sind dies exakte und approximative Rechenverfahren sowie die Simulation.

4.1 Exakte Rechenverfahren

Für das Wartesystem M/G/1 (G: allgemeine (General) VF für den Bedienungsprozeß) sind für folgende Abfertigungsstrategien exakte Ergebnisse bekannt, welche in dieser Arbeit verwendet wurden: M/G/1/PREEMPTIVE PRIORITY nach R.G.MILLER [2], M/G/1/NONPREEMPTIVE PRIORITY nach A.COBHAM [3], M/G/1/PD-PRIORITY nach U.HERZOG [4] sowie M/G/1/CYCLIC EXHAUSTIVE nach B.AVI-ITZHAK, W.L.MAXWELL und L.W.MILLER [5], L.TAKÁCS [6], R.B.COOPER [7] und M.EISENBERG [8]. Die Lösungen für CYCLIC EXHAUSTIVE sind zwar prinzipiell bekannt, aber sehr schwierig auswertbar. Die Lösungen für CYCLIC ORDINARY und CYCLIC PRIORITY stehen für den allgemeinen Fall M/G/1 noch ganz aus.

Für den Sonderfall M/M/1-s können jedoch exakte Lösungsverfahren angegeben werden, welche in allen Fällen zyklischer Abfertigungsstrategien ohne Takt anwendbar sind. Sie bauen auf der Lösungsmethodik auf, welche zur exakten Behandlung von Mehrschlangen-Modellen des Typs M/M/n-s/PROBABILISTIC PRIORITY angewendet wurde [10]. Hierzu werden mehrdimensionale Zustände definiert, welche die Belegungszustände der Bedienungseinheit (d.h. deren momentane Stellung im Zyklus) sowie die einzelnen Warteschlangenlängen charakterisieren. Für die stationären Zustandswahrscheinlichkeiten ist ein lineares Zustandsgleichungssystem und zur Bestimmung der VF der Wartezeiten ein lineares Differentialgleichungssystem aufzulösen, welche bei der Betrachtung der zugrundeliegenden Markoff-Prozesse für die Systemzustände bzw. Wartezeiten gewonnen werden.

4.2 Approximative Rechenverfahren

Grundlage der Approximation ist die Ersetzung der zyklischen Abfertigungsstrategien durch wahrscheinlichkeitsmäßige Abfertigungsstrategien, wobei die Abfertigungswahrscheinlichkeiten für einzelne Warteschlangen entsprechend deren Prioritätshäufigkeiten im Zyklus gewählt werden. Bild 7 vergleicht für den Fall des Modells M/M/1-s die exakten Rechenergebnisse für PROBABILISTIC PRIORITY nach [10] mit Simulationsergebnissen für CYCLIC PRIORITY, woraus eine akzeptable Übereinstimmung abzulesen ist.

4.3 Simulation

Für die zyklischen Abfertigungsstrategien wurden die Ergebnisse mit Hilfe eines Simulationsprogrammes [12,13] gewonnen, wobei je Parameterkombination zwischen 100 000 und 400 000 "Rufe" erzeugt wurden. Die statistischen Vertrauensintervalle wurden aus Übersichtlichkeitsgründen (mit Ausnahme von Bild 7) weggelassen.

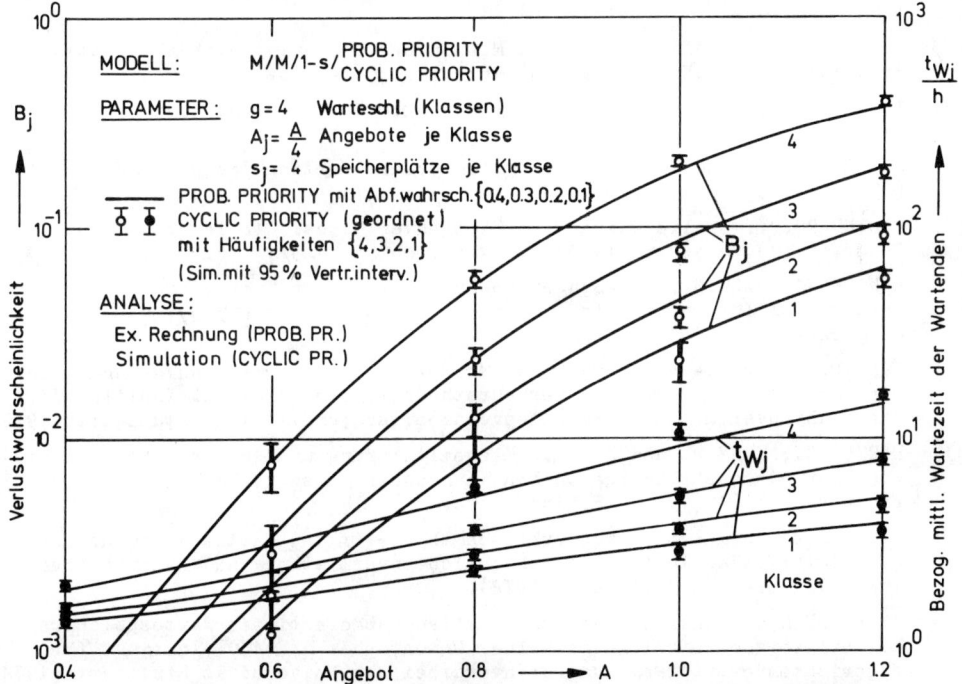

Bild 7. Vergleich von approximativer Rechnung mit Simulationsergebnissen

ZUSAMMENFASSUNG

In dem vorliegenden Beitrag wurden drei verschiedene zyklische Abfertigungsstrategien bezüglich ihrer Wirksamkeit untersucht und anderen bekannten Strategien vergleichend gegenübergestellt. Ferner wurde auf praktische Anwendungsmöglichkeiten sowie auf exakte und approximative Lösungsverfahren hingewiesen. Die erzielten Ergebnisse und Erkenntnisse sollen dazu beitragen, die Auswahl einer zu implementierenden Abfertigungsstrategie durch qualitative als auch quantitative Argumente zu unterstützen.

Die Autoren möchten an dieser Stelle Herrn Dipl.-Ing. Helmut Weisschuh für die Anregung zur Behandlung der zyklischen Prioritätsstrategie danken.

SCHRIFTTUM

[1] KRUSKAL,J.B.: Work-Scheduling Algorithms: A Nonprobabilistic Queuing Study (with possible Application to No.1 ESS). BSTJ, Vol.48(1969), S. 2963 - 2974.

[2] MILLER,R.G.Jr.: Priority Queues. The Annals of Math. Stat., Vol.31(1960), S. 86 - 103.

[3] COBHAM,A.: Priority Assignment in Waiting Line Problems. Opns.Res., Vol.2(1954), S. 70 - 76.

[4] HERZOG,U.: Verkehrsfluß in Datennetzen. 21.Bericht über verkehrstheoretische Arbeiten. Institut für Nachrichtenvermittlung und Datenverarbeitung , Universität Stuttgart (1973).

[5] AVI-ITZHAK,B., MAXWELL,W.L. und MILLER,L.W.: Queuing with Alternating Priorities. Opns.Res., Vol. 13(1965), S. 306 - 318.

[6] TAKÁCS,L.: Two Queues Attended by a Single Server. Opns.Res., Vol.16 (1968), S. 639 - 650.

[7] COOPER,R.B.: Queues Served in Cyclic Order: Waiting Times. BSTJ, Vol.49 (1970), S. 399 - 413.

[8] EISENBERG,M.: Cyclic Queue with Changeover Times. 6th Intern. Teletr. Congr. (ITC), München (1970), Congressbook S. 423/1 - 6.

[9] LANGENBACH-BELZ,M.: Two-Stage Queuing System with Sampled Parallel Input Queues. 7th Intern. Teletr. Congr. (ITC), Stockholm (1973), Congressbook S. 434/1 - 8.

[10] KÜHN,P.: Über die Berechnung der Wartezeiten in Vermittlungs- und Rechnersystemen. 15. Bericht über verkehrstheoretische Arbeiten. Institut für Nachrichtenvermittlung und Datenverarbeitung,Universität Stuttgart (1972).

[11] HERZOG,U., KÜHN,P. und ZEH,A.: Klassifizierung und Analyse von Verkehrsmodellen für das Ablaufgeschehen in Rechnersystemen. Nachrichtentechn. Fachber., Vol.44(1972), S. 181 - 198.

[12] BASTIAN,D.: Simulation von zyklisch abgefertigten Wartespeichern. Monographie Nr. 374. Institut für Nachrichtenvermittlung und Datenverarbeitung, Universität Stuttgart (1972).

[13] ARMBRUSTER,K.: Untersuchung von zyklisch abgefertigten Wartespeichern mit beliebigem Abfertigungszyklus. Monographie Nr. 430. Institut für Nachrichtenvermittlung und Datenverarbeitung,Universität Stuttgart (1974).

7. INFORMATIONSSYSTEME

ANWENDUNGEN
J. CONRADI

G. DATHE, K.-H. DRECKMANN

J.J. MARTIN

SICHERHEIT
J. SCHLÖRER

P. HABERÄCKER, M. LEHNER

THEORY
A. PIROTTE, P. WODON

A. DÖRRSCHEIDT

H. WEBER

UNTERTEILUNG VON DATENBANKEN
S.-Å. TÄRNLUND

I.M. OSMAN

Probleme der elektronischen Rechtsdokumentation - dargestellt am Beispiel der Steuerrechtsdatenbank der DATEV e G
Dr. J. Conradi
DATEV eG, 85 Nürnberg

1. Einführung

Die Probleme elektronischer Dokumentationssysteme sind heutzutage kaum noch datenverarbeitungsspezifisch. Die Anforderungen an inhaltserschliessende Dokumentationssysteme sind weitgehend bekannt; sie lassen sich etwa folgendermaßen skizzieren:

a) Formatierte und unformatierte Daten.

Die Verarbeitung nicht formatierter Daten ist ein Hauptkennzeichen von Dokumentationssystemen (im Unterschied zu sonstigen Datenbanksystemen). Formatierte Daten sind daneben von geringerer Bedeutung, aber in gewissem Umfange unerläßlich. Der Schwerpunkt liegt jedoch auf nicht formatisierbaren fortlaufenden Texten, deren Formatisierung schon aus dokumentarischer Sicht gar nicht angängig erscheint. Dies gilt auch für Systeme, die sich weitgehend auf die Verarbeitung konventioneller bibliographischer Daten beschränken. (Titeldokumentation).

b) Flexible Datenbankverwaltung

Der Inhalt einer Dokumentation ist kein statischer, sondern ein dynamischer Bestand, nicht nur im Hinblick auf die Vorwärtsdokumentation, sondern auch zur Pflege des gespeicherten Bestandes. Das Updating-Problem ist heutzutage wohl allgemein erkannt, wenn auch bei den bestehenden Systemen nicht hinreichend berücksichtigt. Das Erfordernis größerer Flexibilität erstreckt sich auch auf die Hilfsdateien und invertierten Bestände (Wörterbücher, Thesaurus): Hier bedarf es zumindest unterschiedlicher Optionsmöglichkeiten für den einzelnen Anwender, die durch Parameter- und Tebellentechniken eröffnet werden können.

c) Teilnehmer-Konzept

Der Benutzer greift auf Bestände zu, die von einer Dokumentationszentrale gespeichert worden sind und nur dort verwaltet werden. Das Bedürfnis zum Aufbau und zum parallelen Betrieb benutzereigener Datenbanken - Teilhaber-Konzept - ist bisher nicht artikuliert, aber im Bereich der Rechtsanwendung wohl zu erwarten (behördeninterne Vorgänge, Prozeßakten eines Rechtsanwaltes etc.).

d) Dialogsystem

Der Online-Dialog-Betrieb bei der Nutzung der Datenbank ist fester Bestandteil aller neueren Dokumentationssysteme. Die ergänzende Möglichkeit der Stapelverarbeitung ist in der Regel vorhanden oder leicht zu realisieren.

e) Einfache und universelle Abfragelogik

Formatierte und nicht formatierte Bestände werden mit Boole'schen Operatoren, angereichert um die sogn. Positionslogik und Wortfragmentmethoden abgefragt. Möglichkeiten und Grenzen dieser Abfragelogik sind gut erkennbar. Sie erscheint dem gegenwärtigen Stand der Erkenntnisse über die Effizienz unterschiedlicher Auffindungsstrategien angemessen.

f) Arithmetische Funktionen

Arithmetische Funktionen spielen derzeit bei den internen Retrieval-Funktionen eine größere Rolle als beim unmittelbar durch den Benutzer gesteuerten Einsatz. Sie sind als Bestandteil eines Dokumentationssystems unerläßlich, ihre Bedeutung wird im Hinblick auf absehbare Datenmanagement-Funktionen künftig wohl noch zunehmen.

g) Hoher Ausgabekomfort

Die Anzeige oder Ausgabe von Zielinformationen (gefundenen Dokumenten) ist eine wichtige Funktion neben der eigentlichen Retrieval-Funktion. Im Hinblick auf die für die Rechtsanwendung oft unerläßliche iterative Ermittlungsmethodik erscheint die hierdurch ermöglichte Überwindung der organisatorischen Trennung von Suche und Relevanzprüfung geradezu als Tauglichkeitskriterium für den Einsatz automatisierter Systeme.

h) Dienstleistungsfunktionen

Die derzeit im Vordergrund stehenden Nutzungstechniken lassen sich in vielfacher Hinsicht ergänzen und erweitern. (z.B. automatischer Ablauf von Fragen, die erfahrungsgemäß häufig gestellt werden; programmierte Unterweisung in der Benutzung des Dokumentationssystems). Solche Dienstleistungsfunktionen sind in Ansätzen bereits vorhanden; ihre Fortentwicklung ist eine der wichtigsten aus der jeweils dokumentierten Fachdisziplin heraus anzugehenden künftigen Forschungsaufgaben.

2. Aufgabe und Zielsetzung elektronischer Rechtsdokumentationen

Elektronische Dokumentationen im juristischen Bereich sind aus dem Bedürfnis heraus entstanden, dem Praktiker in der Rechtsanwendung ein wirksames Mittel zur raschen und zuverlässigen Lösung konkreter Einzelprobleme an die Hand zu geben. Infolge ihrer Praxisbezogenheit rückt die juristische Dokumentation in den Bereich des öffentlichen Interesses: Die Gleichheit aller vor dem Gesetz kann gefährdet erscheinen, wenn ein leistungsfähiges Dokumentationssystem monopolistisch gehandhabt wird. Die bestehenden Dokumentationen im In- und Ausland werden deshalb entweder von öffentlichen Institutionen oder von Einrichtungen der anwaltlichen oder steuerberatenden Berufe oder in enger Zusammenarbeit mit solchen betrieben.

Das Erfordernis der sehr aufwendigen Aufbereitung und Erfassung des Dokumentationsmaterials bedingt andererseits eine starke Objektbezogenheit jeglicher auf Verwirklichung abzielender Projektierung. Die Probleme sind sowohl quantitativer als qualitativer Natur. Dem Mengenproblem läßt sich durch Beschränkung auf einzelne Rechtsgebiete begegnen; inwieweit und unter welchen Bedingungen das gesamte wissenschaftliche Material mit seinen unterschiedlichen Dokumenttypen (z.B. Gesetze, Gerichtsurteile, Monographien) der für den Datenbankbetrieb erforderlichen Homogenisierung zugänglich ist, ist aber noch weitgehend ungeklärt. Die gegenwärtige Entwicklung in Deutschland tendiert deshalb zu institutionsgebundenen Einzelprojekten mit jeweils fachlicher (Steuerrechtsdatenbank, Sozialrechtsdatenbank) oder funktioneller (Urteilsdokumentation, Parlamentsdokumentation) Beschränkung. An übergreifenden Forschungs- und Entwicklungsarbeiten fehlt es weitgehend.

3. Die Steuerrechtsdatenbank der DATEV e G

a) Entwicklung

Die Steuerrechtsdatenbank der DATEV geht zurück auf Entwicklungsarbeiten der Forschungsgesellschaft DOCUMENTA Steuer und Recht, die zwischen 1968 und 1971 gemeinsam mit drei bedeutenden steuerrechtlichen Verlagen und den Finanzverwaltungen des Bundes und einiger Bundesländer durchgeführt worden waren. Ein hierbei durchgeführter

Test ergab im wesentlichen folgende Resultate, die sich als richtungsweisend auch für andere Dokumentationsprojekte erwiesen haben:

aa) Bei der Verarbeitung juristischer Dokumente ist in weiten Bereichen die sogn. Volltextspeicherung den herkömmlichen Indizierungsmethoden vorzuziehen.

bb) Die bibliothekarische und fachliche Erschließung muß über das bisher übliche Maß hinaus erweitert und verfeinert werden.

cc) Die Informationswiedergewinnung muß durch den Suchenden unmittelbar im Dialogbetrieb möglich sein.

dd) Die vorhandenen universellen Programmsysteme verschiedener Hersteller erscheinen geeignet, die juristische Dokumentation über das Experimentierstadium hinaus zur praktischen Anwendung zu bringen.

1971 übernahm die DATEV von der Forschungsgesellschaft die Ergebnisse der DOCUMENTA-Arbeit und hat die Einspeicherung steuerrechtlicher Materialien mit Unterstützung der Bay. Finanzverwaltung fortgesetzt. Ab 1975 soll die Dokumentation auf kommerzieller Grundlage zum Einsatz gelangen.

b) Der Inhalt der Datenbank

In ihrer gegenwärtigen Konzeption erstreckt sich die Datenbank auf Dokumente, die für den Praktiker von besonderer Bedeutung sind, sich in ihrem inhaltlichen Aufbau und ihrer Länge ähneln und deren bisherige bibliographische Erschließung besonders unbefriedigend erscheint. Es handelt sich um

aa) Gerichtsurteile zum Steuerrecht, und zwar sowohl der Bundesgerichte (Bundesfinanzhof, Bundesverfassungsgericht) als auch der erstinstanzlichen Finanzgerichte.

bb) Verfügungen und Erlasse der Finanzverwaltungen

cc) Aufsätze und Kurzbeiträge aus der Zeitschriftenliteratur zum Steuerrecht.

Die Materialien zu aa) und bb) werden - mit Ausnahme der erstinstanzlichen Gerichtsentscheidungen - zeitunabhängig gespeichert, d.h. seit dem Bestehen der Bundesrepublik. Material, das infolge von Gesetzesänderungen für die heutige und künftige Rechtsanwendung vollkommen ohne Bedeutung erscheint, wird hierbei ausgeschieden. Erstinstanzliche Entscheidungen und Literaturbeiträge werden von einem Stichtag an (1.1.1974) eingespeichert; Teilbestände, die zu Testzwecken aufgebaut wurden, datieren auch aus der Zeit vor diesem Stichtag.

Die höchstrichterlichen Steuerentscheidungen sind bereits nahezu vollständig auch nach rückwärts dokumentiert. Es handelt sich um rd. 9.000 Dokumente. Der jährliche Neuanfall an veröffentlichten Gerichtsentscheidungen erster und zweiter Instanz ist auf rd. 1.300 zu veranschlagen. Bei der Zeitschriftenliteratur ist mit mindestens 2.500 zu dokumentierenden Einzelbeiträgen jährlich zu rechnen. Die Zahl der vorliegenden und der laufend neu anfallenden Verwaltungserlasse ist noch nicht bekannt. In ihrem gegenwärtigen Ausbaustand umfaßt die Datenbank rd. 14.000 Dokumente. Diese sind weitüberwiegend im Volltext eingespeichert; lediglich bei der Zeitschriftenliteratur wird auf die Volltexterfassung verzichtet und stattdessen eine Zusammenfassung (Kurzfassung, Annotation) erstellt und gespeichert.

c) Dokumentationsschema

Die Dokumente werden nach einem Schema aufbereitet, das für alle Dokumenttypen im wesentlichen gleich ist:

1. Autor
2. Dokumenttyp
3. Titel / Geschäftszeichen
4. Datum
5. Fundstelle(n)
6. Zitate
7. Redaktionelle Anmerkungen
8. Streitjahr (bei Gerichtsentscheidungen)
9. Schlüsselwörter
10. Betroffene Vorschriften
11. - 13. Textteile

Die Elemente 1 bis 5 bilden die Bibliographie jedes Dokumentes; die Elemente 8 bis 10 - und in vielen Fällen auch der erste Textteil (Leitsatz, Zusammenfassung) enthalten inhaltsbezogene klassifikatorische Angaben. Die Elemente 6 und 7 lassen sich je nach Inhalt und Betrachtungsweise der Bibliographie oder Klassifikation zurechnen. Der Quellentext - soweit eingespeichert - ist immer in den letzten Elementen der Dokumentationseinheit enthalten.

Die meisten Elemente sind sowohl für die Wiederauffindung als auch für die unmittelbare Information im Zusammenhang mit der Dokumentenanzeige von Bedeutung; bei einigen Elementen beschränkt sich die Bedeutung jedoch auf die eine oder andere Funktion. Entsprechende Determinierungen sind im Zuge des Aufbaus der Datenbank möglich (sogn. Datenbankdesign). Der Inhalt des Feldes 10 (Schlüsselwörter) wird beispielsweise beim Suchvorgang mit ausgewertet, erscheint aber in der Regel bei der Anzeige des Dokumentes nicht.

Ebenfalls frei determinierbar ist die Formatierung einzelner Elemente oder Teile von Elementen. Die Formatierung mit der Folge arithmetischer Vergleichsoperationen ist nur für das Datum von wesentlicher Bedeutung. Wichtiger als die Formatisierung ist die Normierung einzelner Feldinhalte im Hinblick auf terminologische Klarheit und leichte Handhabung bei der Wiederauffindung. So sind z.B. die betroffenen gesetzlichen Vorschriften in dem entsprechenden Feld in einer von der herkömmlichen Form abweichenden zusammenfassenden Schreibweise aufgeführt (für 4 Abs. 1 Satz 3 des Einkommensteuergesetzes beispielsweise steht EStG:4/1/3), da bei der herkömmlichen Ausdrucksform die exakte Ansprechbarkeit der Vorschrift nicht gewährleistet bzw. außerordentlich erschwert ist. Es wird jedoch Wert darauf gelegt, daß solche Normierungen dem Benutzer keine wesentlichen zusätzlichen Chiffrierungsfähigkeiten abverlangen.

Auf interne Ordnungsmerkmale der Dokumentation wird bewußt verzichtet, da die Möglichkeit des direkten Zugriffs aufgrund beliebiger anderer Merkmale sie als überflüssigen Ballast erscheinen läßt. Eine interne Dokumentnummer ist zwar vorhanden und wird stets mit angezeigt, sie enthält jedoch keinerlei Strukturmerkmale.

d) Aufbau der Dateien (Grundlinien)

Für den Aufbau des Dokumentationssystems und das Retrieval wird weitestgehend das Programmsystem STAIRS der IBM eingesetzt. Nachstehend sind die wichtigsten Aspekte dieser Anwendung zusammengefaßt.

aa) Die inhaltliche Erschließung erfordert keine Strukturierung oder Formatierung innerhalb der Dokumentationseinheit. Das vorstehend dargestellte Dokumentationsschema hat für die Erschließung eine nur untergeordnete Bedeutung. Erschließungskriterien sind lediglich die Leerstelle als Worttrennungszeichen sowie die Satz- und Absatzkennzeichnung (im grammatikalischen Sinne).

bb) Volltexterschließung bedeutet weitgehenden Verzicht auf aktive

Selektion der Wiederauffindungsmerkmale. Die Maschine definiert automatisch jedes in dem Text vorkommende Wort als Suchwort und ordnet es dem betreffenden Dokument - ggf. auch mehrfach - zu. Der Anwender hat lediglich die Möglichkeit, eine in ihrem Umfang beschränkte Liste von Worten aufzustellen, die von der Indizierung ausgenommen sein sollen (sogn. Stopwortliste).

cc) Eine Strukturierung des Wortbestandes (Thesaurusarbeit) ist derzeit in nur geringem Umfange möglich (Bildung sogn. Synonymringe).

e) Nutzung der Datenbank
Die Datenbank soll von Anfang an über eine größere Anzahl dezentral aufgestellter Datenstationen direkt abgefragt werden. Die Datenstationen sollen von den Steuerberatern bzw. sonstigen Steuerfachleuten ohne Einschaltung eines Dokumentars direkt bedient werden. Bei den Datenstationen handelt es sich um Geräte der mittleren Datentechnik mit Schreib- und Rechenwerk, Tastatur, Druckwerk und -wahlweise- Bildschirm. Diese Datenstationen werden in den Steuerkanzleien primär für andere Zwecke (insbesondere Datenerfassung zur Finanzbuchhaltung) eingesetzt, so daß die Wirtschaftlichkeit der Datenbankabfragen in der Regel nicht durch den Investitionsaufwand für diese technische Ausrüstung belastet ist. Die Verbindung zur zentral gespeicherten Dokumentation wird im jeweiligen Bedarfsfalle über das öffentliche Telefonnetz im Wählleitungsverkehr hergestellt. Die Verbindungswege sind derzeit als Sternnetz mit dem Zentrum Nürnberg konzipiert.

Das Beispiel einer Abfrage ist in der folgenden Abb. dargestellt.

4. Zusammenfassung der wichtigsten Erkenntnisse aus den bisherigen Arbeiten

a) Elektronische Dokumentationssysteme erscheinen heute hinreichend ausgereift, um zum praktischen Einsatz zu gelangen. Ihre Vorteile liegen auf dem Gebiet der Rechtsanwendung insbesondere in der Schnelligkeit der Informationsvermittlung (einschließlich Aktualität des Bestandes), der Zugriffsbreite (Redundanz) infolge intensiver Erschließung und der Ausrichtung auf die für Juristen besonders wichtige iterative Suchmethodik.

b) Der nicht mediatisierte unmittelbare Zugang des Einzelnen zu der Dokumentation setzt eine Lösung von den im Bibliothekswesen dominierenden institutionellen Organisationsprinzipien insbesondere bei

DOCUMENTA - Abfrage

```
ççç    Bitte Eingabe DFV-Kennwort/Programm-ID und Anwählen
▷  AQUA DAGL DEMO
   SIGN ON IS COMPLETE
   R0102 ENTER DATA BASE NAME
▷  STR1 SESAM
   R0201 ENTER ONE OF THE FOLLOWING COMMANDS:
   ..BROWSE   ..SEARCH   ..SELECT   ..EXEC   ..RANK   ..HELP   ..CHANGE
▷  ..search
   AQUARIUS - SEARCH MODE - BEGIN YOUR QUERY AFTER THE STATEMENT NUMBER
   00001
▷  studienreise
   RESULT                               70 OCCURRENCES       24 DOCUMENTS
   00002

▷  1 and betrieblich$2 with veranlass$3
   RESULT                                7 OCCURRENCES        7 DOCUMENTS
   00003

▷  ..select
   AQUARIUS - SELECT MODE - ENTER EXTENT AND CRITERIA AFTER THE STATEMENT
      NUMBER OR ENTER EXPLAIN
   00003

▷  2 datum nl 72
   12516  NUMBER OF SELECTED DOCUMENTS = 000002
   00004

▷  ..browse 3 1,2,3,4,5,13
GERICHT    Bundesfinanzhof
DOKART     Urteil
AKTENZ     VI-R-274/70
DATUM      72.08.11
FUNDST1    BStBl-1972-11-0917
LEITSATZ        Die Reise eines Arbeitnehmers, die auf Weisung des Arbeitgebers
           und auf dessen Kosten ausgefuehrt wird, ist fuer die Besteuerung
           nicht ohne weiteres als Dienstreise anzusehen, wenn besondere
           Umstaende, wie z. B. die Art der Reise oder nahe verwandtschaftliche
           Beziehungen zwischen dem Arbeitgeber und dem Arbeitnehmer die
           dienstliche Veranlassung der Reise zweifelhaft erscheinen lassen.
           Weist die Reise wesentliche Merkmale einer Studienreise auf, so ist
           die dienstliche Veranlassung in Anlehnung an die Grundsaetze, die die
           Rechtsprechung zur Anerkennung von Studienreisen aufgestellt hat, zu
           ueberpruefen.
                EStG § 3 Nr. 16; LStDV § 4 Nr. 3; LStR Abschn. 21 Abs. 2
GERICHT    Bundesfinanzhof
DOKART     Urteil
AKTENZ     VIII-R-63/71
DATUM      73.10.11
FUNDST1    BStBl-1974-11-0198
LEITSATZ        Ueberwiegt nach dem Programm und dem aeusseren Erscheinungsbild
           der private Charakter einer Studienreise in die USA, so spricht schon
           die allgemeine Lebenserfahrung gegen die Annahme einer betrieblichen
           Veranlassung.
                EStG §§ 4 Abs. 4, 12 Nr. 1.

R0601 * END OF DOCUMENTS IN LIST - ENTER RETURN OR ANOTHER COMMAND.

▷  ENDE
   SIGN OFF IS COMPLETE
```

der Informationserschließung voraus. Die Dokumentation muß von synthetischen Klassifikationen und Codierungsformen, die aus der Sicht der Dokumentationsstelle zweckmäßig erscheinen, dem Benutzer aber aus seiner täglichen Arbeit nicht von vornherein geläufig sind, weitgehend freigehalten werden.

c) Die dokumentarische Forschungs- und Entwicklungsarbeit wird durch die Erkenntnis zu b) nicht überflüssig; sie wird sich voraussichtlich in den Bereich fachspezifischer Begriffs- und Terminologieprobleme hinein verlagern. Zweifellos bedarf die automatisierte Dokumentation neuer Dienstleistungsformen, deren Grundlagen noch weitgehend unerforscht sind.

Literaturhinweise:

Bundesjustizministerium (Hrsg.):	Das juristische Informationssystem, Analyse Planung Vorschläge, Karlsruhe 1972
ders.:	Informationsverhalten und Informationsbedarf von Juristen, Berlin 1973
Conradi:	DOCUMENTA - Konzept einer elektronischen Steuerrechtsdatenbank, Datenverarbeitung in Steuer, Wirtschaft und Recht (DSWR) 1972, S.85
ders.:	Zur Praxis der Informationswiedergewinnung, DSWR 1972, S. 451
Eckert/ Kreppel,	Plan, Aufbau und Funktion einer Steuerrechtsdatenbank, DSWR 1972, S. 373, 381, 427, 457

Entwurf eines Datenbanksystems für normierte Kennwerte von Eisen- und Stahlwerkstoffen

G.Dathe, K.-H.Dreckmann

Zusammenfassung

Es werden die wesentlichen Aufgaben des datenbankgestützten Informationssystems für Eisen- und Stahlwerkstoffe beschrieben und das Datenmaterial, auf dem das System arbeiten muß. Die Stellung des Datenbanksystems im Informationssystem wird abgegrenzt. Es werden die Überlegungen geschildert, die zur Konzeption wichtiger Teile der Datenbank und des Datenbankverwaltungssystems führten. Alternativen werden aufgezeigt und im Rahmen der Aufgabenstellung und des Datenmaterials bewertet.

1. Einleitung

Seit 1969 baut das Betriebsforschungsinstitut (BFI) des Vereins Deutscher Eisenhüttenleute (VDEh) ein Werkstoff-Informationssystem für Eisen- und Stahlwerkstoffe (WIS) auf. Ein erstes Teilsystem basiert auf Eigenschaftswerten von Stählen, so wie sie bei den einzelnen Versuchsanstalten und Qualitätsprüfstellen gemessen werden. Die Möglichkeiten dieses Teilsystems umfassen auch statistische Auswertungen wie Häufigkeitsverteilungen und Regressionsanalysen mit Vertrauens- und Prognosebereich. Damit können z.B. bei der Normungsarbeit Gewährleistungswerte festgelegt werden. Eine komfortable grafische Ausgabe erleichtert die Arbeit mit dem System, das seit 1972 in Betrieb ist und ständig weiterentwickelt wird. Einige Einsatzmöglichkeiten des Systems zeigt /1/. Der Aufbau des zugrunde liegenden Datenbanksystems wird in /2/ erläutert.

Ein zweites Teilsystem basiert auf genormten Eigenschaften von Eisen- und Stahlwerkstoffen. Dieses Teilsystem ist in der Entwurfsphase und wird im folgenden vorgestellt.

2. Aufgabenstellung

Das Teil-Informationssystem für genormte Kennwerte von Eisen- und Stahlwerkstoffen soll die Benutzung von Normenwerken bei zwei Aufgaben erleichtern:
- Ermittlung von Werkstoffen, die bestimmten Vorgaben genügen,
- Darstellung von Eigenschaften, die für einen bestimmten Werkstoff genormt sind.

Bei den Benutzern des Systems sollen nur minimale Kenntnisse über den Aufbau der Normenwerke erforderlich sein. Es soll z.B. kein Wissen darüber vorausgesetzt werden, welche Eigenschaften von bestimmten Werkstoffgruppen überhaupt genormt sind. Andererseits wird vorausgesetzt, daß eine Ergänzung der Ergebnisse i.a. anhand der Originaldokumente - z.B. DIN-Blätter - erfolgt, da es zumindest nicht ökonomisch ist, den gesamten Informationsgehalt der Normenwerke in Daten zu repräsentieren.

Die genannten Aufgaben treten auf
- bei der Auswahl eines Werkstoffes für ein Produkt, wobei die Gebrauchseigenschaften des Produktes und sein Fertigungsverfahren ein bestimmtes Eigenschaftprofil (Zugfestigkeit, Analysenwerte usw.) erfordern,
- bei der Umsetzung von Normen, wenn z.B. in einem Auftrag für ein Hüttenwerk eine ausländische Norm spezifiziert ist und nach DIN gefertigt werden soll,
- bei der Normungsarbeit, wenn z.B. mehrere nationale Normen durch eine internationale Norm ersetzt werden sollen.

Ein anderer Zugang zu den Normenwerken ist mit Dokumentationsmethoden möglich. Diesen Weg hat der Deutsche Normenausschuß (DNA) mit seinem System DINST (DIN Informationssystem Technik) beschritten /3/. Beide Systeme ergänzen sich: DINST ermöglicht den Zugang über bibliographische Angaben und Schlagwörter, das hier dargestellte System über Eigenschaftsprofile.

Einige weitere Forderungen ergeben sich aus dem Wunsch nach möglichst breiter Einsetzbarkeit des Systems:
- nicht-prozedurale Handhabung durch den Endbenutzer (Werkstoff-Fachmann), d.h. Steuerung des Zugriffsweges durch das System;
- Dialogverkehr, z.B. zur Ausgabe von Zwischenergebnissen an den Benutzer und Eingabe modifizierter Anweisungen, etwa eines geänderten Eigenschaftsprofiles;

- Mehrfachbenutzbarkeit;
- einfache Erweiterbarkeit des Datenbestandes, z.B. um weitere ausländische Normenwerke;
- Übertragbarkeit der Benutzer-Schnittstelle und möglichst vieler Systemteile.

3. Das Datenmaterial

Die im Sinne der Aufgabenstellung relevanten Eigenschaften der Eisen- und Stahlwerkstoffe sind in den Normenwerken i.a. tabellarisch dargestellt. In den Tabellen sind die - nicht notwendig numerischen - Werte einer Eigenschaft von der Spezifikation der Eigenschaft getrennt. Die Spezifikation einer Eigenschaft geschieht durch einen selbstdefinierenden Namen (z.B."Werkstoff-Nr.", "Streckgrenze in N/mm^2"), der als Name einer Variablen aufgefaßt wird, und durch Nebenbedingungen (z.B. bei "T = 20°C", "im Behandlungszustand G"), die Parameter heißen sollen. Die Spezifikation kann beliebig viele Parameter enthalten; bis zu fünf Parameter wurden festgestellt.

Ein hinreichend allgemeines Tabellenformat zeigt Bild 1:
- Der Kopf identifiziert die Tabelle und spezifiziert je Spalte eine Eigenschaft. Spalten können zu Gruppen zusammengefaßt sein, z.B. "mechanische Eigenschaften".
- Im Rumpf stehen die Eigenschaftswerte. Die Werte einer Zeile gehören zu einem bestimmten Werkstoff, ausnahmsweise auch zu mehreren Werkstoffen. In jeder Zeile ist angegeben, zu welchem Werkstoff sie gehört, was auch als Eigenschaft aufgefaßt wird. Ein Tabellen- (Matrix-) element kann enthalten:
  - genau einen Wert,
  - mehrere Werte,
  - eine Schranke (<Wert, >Wert),
  - einen Bereich (Wert - Wert),
  - einen Wert mit Verweis auf Fußnote,
  - Irrelevanzanzeiger (-, leer, usw.)

Im Fuß stehen Fußnoten, die sich auf Kopf oder Rumpf beziehen können.

Die Tabellen sind für eine unmittelbare Benutzung durch den Menschen konzipiert. Es bestand daher keine Notwendigkeit für ein einheitliches Format, selbst wenn in mehreren Tabellen gleiche Eigenschaften, z.B. Zugfestigkeiten, dargestellt werden.

Der Umfang der deutschen Normen für Eisen- und Stahlwerkstoffe läßt sich abschätzen mit ca. 500 Tabellen für 2000 Werkstoffe. Insgesamt existieren ca. 50 Variablen. Die Angaben zu einem Werkstoff sind über durchschnittlich 5 Tabellen verstreut. Etwa 1.000.000 Zeichen sind in den genannten Normen enthalten.

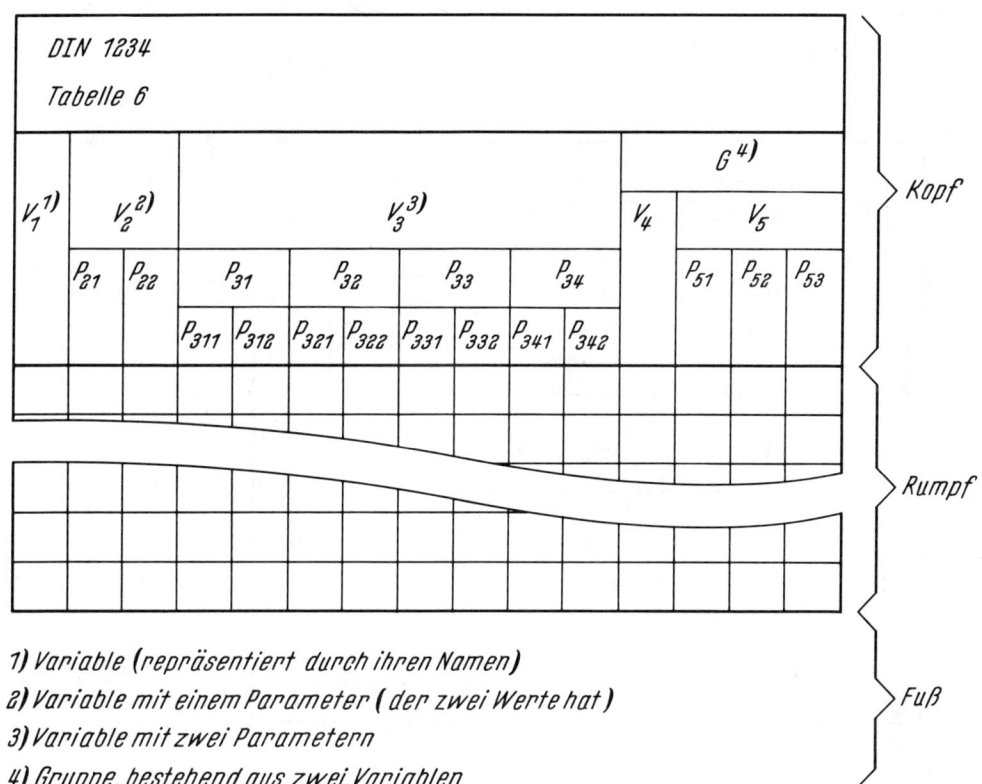

Bild 1 Allgemeines Tabellenformat.

4. Gesamtkonzept

Das Datenbanksystem wird nach Bild 2 als Teil eines datenbankgestützten Informationssystems betrachtet. Die einzelnen Bausteine sind wie folgt gegeneinander abgegrenzt:
- Das Datenbankverwaltungssystem (DBVS) ist ein Standard-Softwaresystem, das Daten zentral und nach einheitlichen Regeln verwaltet.
- Die Datenbank umfaßt die Daten, die durch das DBVS verwaltet werden.

- Die Standard-Anwendungsprogramme benutzen eine Schnittstelle zum DBVS, die von der allgemein zugänglichen Schnittstelle abweichen kann, um wichtige Aufgaben besonders effizient zu lösen. Hierzu gehören z.B. Programme, die den Dialog mit den Endbenutzern ermöglichen und damit das Datenbanksystem aus der Sicht des Endbenutzers zu einem geschlossenen System machen.
- Die Anwendungsprogramme benutzen eine allgemein zugängliche Schnittstelle zum DBVS. Aus ihrer Sicht ist das Datenbanksystem ein Wirtssprachensystem.

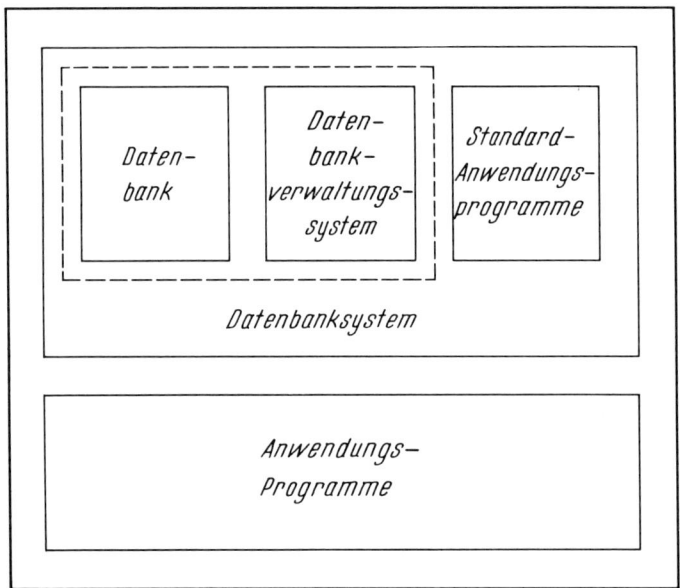

Bild 2 Bausteine eines datenbankgestützten Informationssystems

5. Die Datenbank

Ein grundlegender Schritt beim Entwurf einer Datenbank ist die Festlegung der Struktur von Daten. Dabei sind zu berücksichtigen:
- Struktur, Menge und Verarbeitung des ursprünglichen Datenmaterials;
- Möglichkeiten zur Strukturierung der Datenbank, die ein DBVS zuläßt;
- Aufwand für Speicherung und Verarbeitung unterschiedlich strukturierter Daten durch das DBVS.

In einer Datenbank kann man gewöhnlich unterscheiden zwischen:
- Primärdaten. Sie repräsentieren das ursprüngliche Datenmaterial.

- Sekundärdaten. Sie sind aus den Primärdaten abgeleitet, um die Funktionen des DBVS zu unterstützen (z.B. Zeiger, Adreßlisten).
- Strukturdaten. Sie beschreiben die Struktur der Daten in der Datenbank, soweit sie nicht durch das DBVS der Datenbank fest aufgeprägt wird.

Für die Gliederung des ursprünglichen Datenmaterials in Sätze bieten sich zwei Möglichkeiten an:
- genau ein Satz je Werkstoff,
- genau ein Satz je Tabellenzeile.

Vorteile der ersten Möglichkeit sind: Eine Recherche bezieht sich auf einen einzigen bekannten Satztyp; alle gespeicherten Eigenschaften eines bestimmten Werkstoffes sind mit einem einzigen Aufruf der Lesefunktion verfügbar. Der Satzaufbau wird jedoch kompliziert, weil er so viele Felder vorsehen muß, wie es den auftretenden Kombinationen von 50 Variablen mit unterschiedlichen und unterschiedlich vielen Parametern entspricht. Daraus folgen einige Nachteile: Die Aufbereitung der erfaßten Daten wird aufwendig; die Aufnahme weiterer Normen führt in aller Regel zur Änderung des Satztypes; die Daten lassen sich nur aufwendig in ihrem ursprünglichen Tabellenzusammenhang darstellen; die Aufbereitung des Satzes durch das DBVS wird aufwendiger.

Vorteile der zweiten Möglichkeit sind: Relativ einfache Aufbereitung der erfaßten Daten; einfache Darstellung der Daten im Tabellenzusammenhang wegen der weitgehenden Korrespondenz zwischen Zeilen- und Satzaufbau; bei Aufnahme weiterer Normen werden in den Strukturdaten weitere Satztypen definiert, während existierende Satztypen unverändert bleiben. Durch die Vielzahl von Satztypen ergeben sich folgende Nachteile: Bei einer Recherche ist nicht bekannt, welche Satztypen davon betroffen sind; gespeicherte Eigenschaften zu einem bestimmten Werkstoff stehen in einer nicht bekannten Anzahl von Sätzen unterschiedlichen Typs; die Strukturdaten werden relativ umfangreich.

Mit existierenden DBVS ist keine der beiden Möglichkeiten realisierbar. Es ist auch nicht möglich, die Aufgabenstellung ohne große Abstriche an existierende Systeme anzupassen. Daher wurde die Eigenentwicklung eines DBVS begonnen. Für die Darstellung des Datenmaterials erscheint die zweite Möglichkeit - 1 Satz je Tabellenzeile - bei der vorliegenden Aufgabenstellung günstiger. Daraus ergeben sich folgende Punkte, die den weiteren Entwurf der Datenbank beeinflussen:
- hohe Zahl von Satztypen,

- wenige Satzexemplare eines bestimmten Typs,
- häufiger Zugang von Satztypen,
- assoziative Zugriffsmöglichkeit auf Sätze unbekannten Typs.

Je Satztyp - das bedeutet auch je Tabelle des Datenmaterials - wird eine Satzbeschreibung in den Strukturdaten angelegt. Diese enthält alle Daten des Tabellenkopfes, insbesondere darüber, für welche Variable und welchen Parametersatz jeder Wert in den Primärdaten gilt. Die Struktur der Satzbeschreibung ist der Datenbank durch das DBVS aufgeprägt.

Die Sätze erhalten vom DBVS eine Satznummer als symbolische Adresse. Ihre Speicherung erfolgt in Blöcken fester Länge, die ebenfalls vom DBVS durchnummeriert werden und Objekt der Ein- und Ausgabefunktionen des Betriebssystems sind. Die Transformation von Satz- in Blocknummern erfolgt durch das DBVS. Damit wird die Speicherorganisation unabhängig von Satzschlüsseln des Benutzers; der eigentliche Zugriff auf die peripheren Speicher wird so einfach, daß er in jedem Betriebssystem realisierbar ist.

Ziel einer Recherche ist primär ein Werkstoff, nicht etwa ein Satz. Alle Sätze, die zu demselben Werkstoff gehören, müssen daher vom DBVS als eine Einheit erkannt werden können. Allgemeiner soll eine Datengesamtheit, die durch Verkopplung von Sätzen nach einem systembekannten Kriterium entsteht,
- Verband

heißen. Das Koppelkriterium für den Werkstoffverband besteht in der Übereinstimmung von Werkstoffnummern. Die Realisierung dieses Verbandes erfolgt durch Teilinversion der Sätze nach dem Koppelkriterium; bei Verkettung wären besondere Überlegungen für diejenigen Sätze erforderlich, die zu mehreren Verbänden gehören.

Eine (Teil-) Inversion der Primärdaten nach Eigenschaften als geeignete Technik zur Unterstützung des assoziativen Zugriffs ist nur für Eigenschaften sinnvoll, die keine Parameter enthalten. Das Ergebnis der Inversion sind Adreßlisten in der Form
    Variablenname, Eigenschaftswert, Adresse, Adresse,...
Der Variablenname wird selbstverständlich nicht redundant gespeichert. Bei Eigenschaften mit Parametern könnte man zunächst daran denken, die Parameter zwischen Variablenname und Eigenschaftswert einzuschieben. Dann ergeben sich Schwierigkeiten bei der Definition eines Ord-

nungskriteriums für die Adreßlisten und beim Zugriff auf die Adreßlisten, wenn für die Recherche z.B. der erste Parameter irrelevant ist. Der Ausweg, die Parameter zu permutieren, erscheint zu aufwendig, weil die Anzahl der Adressen in der einzelnen Adreßliste durchschnittlich gering ist. Eine Inversion ohne Berücksichtigung der Parameter als weitere Alternative ergibt eine zu große Unschärfe, weil die Eigenschaftswerte i.a. stark mit den Parametern variieren. Die Lösung besteht darin, daß die Satzbeschreibungen in den Strukturdaten nach Variablennamen invertiert werden. Die zugehörigen Adreßlisten haben die Form
    Variablenname, Adresse, Adresse, ...,
wobei Adresse auf eine Satzbeschreibung führt.

Die Fußnoten sind ein Teil der Primärdaten. Für die Recherche wird ihr Inhalt nicht berücksichtigt, obwohl er oft parameterähnliche Information darstellt. Bei der Datenerfassung wird entschieden, ob eine Fußnote, die sich auf den Tabellenkopf bezieht, so wichtig ist, daß sie explizit als Parameter aufgenommen werden muß. Das gilt im übrigen auch für den freien Text der Norm, soweit er sich auf Tabellen bezieht. Die Fußnoten bilden einen Verband mit den Sätzen, in denen sie zitiert werden.

6. Das Datenbankverwaltungssystem

Von den Funktionen des DBVS (Suchen, Lesen, Neuzugang, Ändern, Löschen, Datensicherheit, Datenschutz) werden nur die Funktionen Suchen und Lesen genauer betrachtet, die aus der Sicht des Endbenutzers am interessantesten sind.

Die Suchfunktion liefert als Ergebnis Nummern von Sätzen, die in ihrer Gesamtheit das Suchkriterium (vorgegebenes Eigenschaftsprofil) befriedigen und i.a. zu mehreren Werkstoffen gehören. Für die Interpretation eines Suchkriteriums durch das DBVS werden bestimmte Vereinbarungen getroffen, um möglichst alle Werkstoffe zu finden, die der Anforderung genügen:
- Diskrete numerische Werte im Suchkriterium werden für bestimmte Variable in einen Wertebereich transformiert, dessen Ausdehnung von der Variablen abhängt.
- Ein Wertebereich im Suchkriterium deckt sich bereits mit einem Wertebereich der genormten Eigenschaft, wenn sich beide Bereiche teilweise

überlappen.
- Analog wird mit Parameterwerten verfahren.
- Parameter, die im Suchkriterium angegeben sind, die aber in einer genormten Eigenschaft nicht vorkommen, gelten als irrelevant.
- Parameter, die in einer genormten Eigenschaft vorkommen, im Suchkriterium aber nicht angegeben sind, gelten als irrelevant.

Das Suchkriterium wird also weit ausgelegt und eine eventuell erforderliche weitere Einschränkung dem Endbenutzer überlassen, der sich jederzeit die genormten Eigenschaften ausgeben lassen kann.

An Stellen, wo die Interpretation des Suchkriteriums durch das System kritisch wird, sind Systemmeldungen und Eingriffsmöglichkeiten durch den Benutzer vorgesehen.

Ein Suchkriterium insgesamt stellt einen booleschen Ausdruck dar, in dem eine einzelne Solleigenschaft ein elementarer Bestandteil ist. Das Suchkriterium enthält keine prozeduralen Bestandteile: Es zielt auf Werkstoffe, enthält aber keine Angaben über den Ablauf des Suchvorgangs, z.B. keinen Hinweis auf bestimmte Satztypen.

Die systeminterne Umsetzung in eine Prozedur erfolgt derart, daß für jede einzelne Solleigenschaft die Menge der zutreffenden Sätze ermittelt wird. Die Satznummern werden in Werkstoffnummern transformiert. Auf die Mengen der Werkstoffnummern werden Mengenoperationen entsprechend den Operatoren im Suchkriterium angewendet. Zur Optimierung wird die Reihenfolge der Mengenoperationen so gewählt, daß als Zwischenergebnisse Mengen mit möglichst wenigen Elementen entstehen.

Zur Ermittlung der Menge zutreffender Satznummern für eine einzelne Solleigenschaft sind zwei unterschiedliche Vorgehensweisen erforderlich: Für eine Eigenschaft, nach der die Primärdaten invertiert wurden, kann die Menge der zutreffenden Satznummern ohne Rückgriff auf die Primärdaten über die Adreßlisten ermittelt werden. Bei allen anderen Eigenschaften erfolgt über den Variablennamen der Zugriff auf eine Adreßliste aus der Inversion der Satzbeschreibungen. Jede Adresse dieser Adreßliste führt zu einer Satzbeschreibung, in der geprüft werden kann, ob die relevanten Parameter in der gespeicherten Eigenschaft die Vorgabe in der jeweiligen Solleigenschaft erfüllen. Nur wenn das der Fall ist, werden die Eigenschaftswerte in den Primärdaten selbst überprüft. Das wird dadurch ermöglicht, daß die Satzbeschreibung mit den Tabellenzeilen einen weiteren Verband bildet. Die Satznummern derjenigen Tabellenzeilen, die Eigenschaftswerte entsprechend der Vorgabe enthalten, sind Elemente der gesuchten Menge.

Die Lesefunktion ist von der Suchfunktion strikt getrennt und bildet eine selbständige Funktion. Der Wunsch nach vielfältigen Darstellungsformaten rechtfertigt das. Der Endbenutzer kann z.B. verlangen:
- alle gespeicherten Daten zu einem Werkstoff,
- die gesamte Tabelle, in der ein Werkstoff vorkommt,
- einzelne spezifizierte Eigenschaften eines Werkstoffes.

Das letzte Format ist insofern interessant, als die Menge der für die Lesefunktion spezifizierten Eigenschaften keine Untermenge der Eigenschaften sein muß, die im Suchkriterium einer vorausgegangenen Suchfunktion spezifiziert werden. Es ist also nicht sicher, daß für den bestimmten Werkstoff die Eigenschaft überhaupt genormt ist. Die Datendarstellung im Dialog ist wünschenswert, damit der Endbenutzer die Daten möglichst freizügig durchkämmen und dann gegebenenfalls ein Druckformat festlegen kann.

Alle Ausgabeformate für den Endbenutzer können durch ein Standard-Anwendungsprogramm aus Sätzen aufgebaut werden, die das eigentliche Objekt der Lesefunktion sind. Vom Satz aus sind durch den Verbandszusammenhang die Satzbeschreibung mit allen Daten für den Tabellenkopf und die zugehörigen Fußnoten erreichbar.

Dank

Die Entwicklung des Informationssystems für Eisen- und Stahlwerkstoffe wird seit 1971 durch das Institut für Dokumentationswesen mit Mitteln des Bundesministeriums für Forschung und Technologie gefördert.

Schrifttum

/1/ NN: Aus der Arbeit mit der Werkstoffdatenbank.
    Stahl und Eisen 92 (1972) S. 211-214

/2/ Mommertz, K. H.; Radestock, J.; Kremer, K.-J.: Entwicklung einer Datenbank als Informationssystem über die Eigenschaften von Stählen.
    Stahl und Eisen 90 (1970) S. 1339-1346

/3/ Grothstück, W.; Hoffmann, W.; Nerlich, T.; Urbach, B.: Der kurze Weg zur Datenbank. Schrift des Deutschen Normenausschusses (DNA)

ASPECTS OF GENERALITY AND EFFICIENCY IN

PROGRAMMING LANGUAGE IMPLEMENTATION

Johannes J. Martin

Department of Computer Science
Virginia Polytechnic Institute and State University
Blacksburg, Va. 24061

1. Introduction

Composing and documenting voluminous programs is a difficult and time consuming task despite the multitude of existing programming languages. It is still the exception that a programmer finds a language that has all the properties he likes to have to his disposal for a given project. Further, many programmers show a very understandable reluctance toward learning a new notation since mastering all its inevitable pitfalls and idiosyncrasies frequently takes more time than programmers deem justifiable.

In this context, extensible languages are a promising branch on the tree of programming systems. These languages are supposed to permit the user to define his own notation and, hence, to create a language, custom tailored to his problem. The many advantages of such a system have been extensively discussed and praised by others [N71, W71, I70, S67, L66]. Only two points shall be added:

1) With the propagation of extensible systems, language design can be expected to become a new style of programming that will decisively improve the reliability and transparency of large programs.

2) For the academic world, extensible languages will make language design a better discipline to teach and especially to practice.

However, the extraordinary flexibility offered by the concept of extensible languages causes its own special problems. Used unwisely, it leads to slow compilations and inefficient code. These problems have been considered by some workers who offer the following measures as solutions:

1) restricting extension mechanisms to the very competent programmer by e.g. only providing a changeable (extensible) compiler rather than linguistic extension features [S71],

2) complementing the extension mechanisms by restriction mechanisms that permit the user to disable existing features and, hence, to freeze a language at some state of extension [W71, S70].

A different method, discussed by van Gils [G71], is derived from design principles of ALGOL 68. Although not specifically introduced for the sake of efficiency, this method seems to be most attractive for the purpose. By restricting extensions to certain non-insidious types, it not only helps efficiency but also promotes simplicity of rules and rather systematic error handling.

The generality/efficiency trade-off is the underlying theme for the following discussion of some design aspects of the programming system EPOS (Eine Programmiersprache Ohne Semantik), currently under development in the Computer Science Department of VPI&SU. This project has been greatly influenced by the works of van Gils [G71], Jorrand [J71], and by ALGOL 68 [L71, W69]. It is assumed that the reader is familiar with these publications as well as with the basic problems of compiler design.

2. On Defining Programming Languages

2.1 Conventional languages

The designer of a conventional programming language usually defines

1) a set of data objects, operations for these objects and control constructs, and

2) a suitable notation for the above components and rules for their assembly.

The notation rules form the grammar of the language; the data objects, operations and control constructs form the semantics.

To the author's knowledge, the grammars of programming languages ever formalized are context-free and, thus, definable by the Backus-Naur-Formalism (BNF). The precise description of the semantics can be accomplished by means of some hypothetical computer. The connection between the grammar and the hypothetical computer may then be established by a translation schema that maps syntactic elements of the grammar into sequences of instructions of the hypothetical computer (There are a number of translation schemata described in the literature, a good summary is found in Aho and Ullman [A73] who also furnish a comprehensive listing of the primary literature.).

Thus, we can define a conventional programming language as a triple

(1) $L_c = (G, C, T)$

where

G is a (context-free) grammar,

C a computer and

T a translation schema.

Being well known, methods for formalizing G, C and T will not be further discussed here.

2.2 Extensible languages

Extensible languages have been looked on as relatively small conventional base languages with additional mechanisms for specifying extensions. It seems, therefore, that the method of language definition for conventional languages, outlined above, should easily be applicable to extensible systems. A closer analysis reveals, however, that this is not true.

From the three components of the above definition only the hypothetical computer is equally useful for both, conventional and extensible languages as the basis for the description of the semantics whereas (i) the grammar and (ii) the translation schema cannot simply be transferred.

(i) For conventional languages, it is a priori possible to define a complete context-free grammar that permits the linear structure of the input text to be transformed into the hierarchical structure of the derivation tree. This transformation prepares the final translation into object code by isolating and ordering the translatable phrases.

For extensible languages, only the grammar of the base language can be completely described whereas, for possible extensions, only the class of permissible grammars can a priori be determined.

(ii) A quite analogous argument holds for the translation schema.

Therefore, extensible languages founded on higher level base languages are 5-tuples

(2) $\qquad L_{eb} = (G_b, H, C, T_b, U)$

where

$\quad G_b \quad$ is the grammar of the base language,

$\quad H \quad$ the class of grammars that may be used for extensions,

$\quad C \quad$ a hypothetical computer,

$\quad T_b \quad$ the translation schema of the base language,

$\quad U \quad$ the class of translation schemata that may be used for extensions.

The class H of permissible grammars decisively influences the complexity of the compiler. It is well known that parsers for arbitrary context-free grammars are much more complex and take more time and space than a parser for, say, operator precedence grammars. In section 3, we will discuss criteria for selecting a grammar class in more detail.

> Note: One might suspect that the classes H and U should not be mentioned in the definition because both seem to be implicitly defined by the extension mechanisms contained in the base language. However, there are two different classes of grammars as well as of translations:
> 1) the class of grammars (translations) that can be specified,
> 2) the class of grammars (translations) that can be handled by the parser (code generator)
> H and U represent the classes that can be handled.

2.3 Significance of the base language

We will now consider a simplification of the definition schema for extensible languages. The very nature of extensible languages makes it possible to use the extension mechanism not only for adding new features to the language but also for introducing new notations for existing (base language) features. Thus, if a user does not like the way declarations, operations or control structures are denoted in the base language he may tie some or all of these features to his own notations (i.e. redefine the features by means of the extension mechanisms).

Because of this flexibility, the usual criteria for sound language design like conciseness and natural or traditional denotation are of very little importance for base language design. Thus, pursuing other qualities like simplicity, transparency, generality and adaptability, we may simplify and generalize extensible systems by uniting the definition of the base language with the definition of the hypothetical computer i.e. by declaring the instruction set of the hypothetical computer to be the base language of the extensible system.

> Note: In order to make the definition of declaration statements possible, the instruction set of the hypothetical computer must, of course, contain instructions for storage allocation and rather sophisticated bookkeeping.

Because of the unification of the base language and the hypothetical computer the definition schema again becomes a triple:

(3) $L_e = (H, C, U)$

where

    H   is a class of grammars,

    C   a hypothetical computer and

    U   a class of translation schemata.

The general structure of the system is depicted in fig. 1. The general compiling algorithms update and interrogate a data base that contains the specific information about the language used and the program processed.

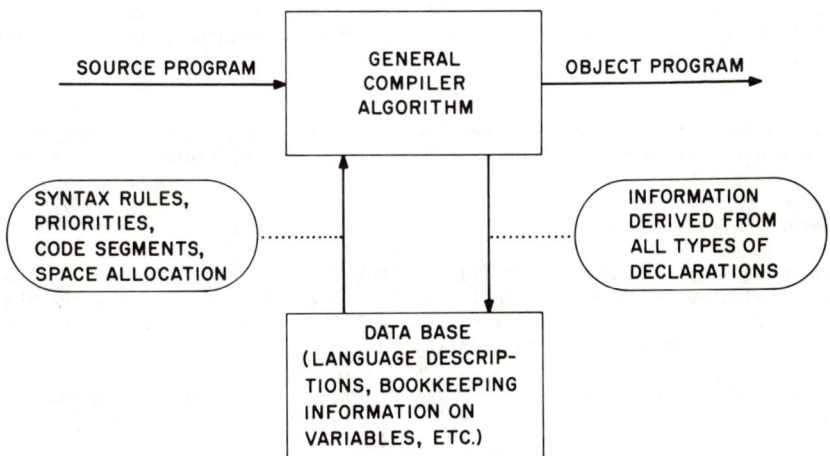

FIGURE 1   Overall structure of the compiler

Besides simplicity and transparency, the concept offers the programmer the opportunity to resort at any time to the low level base of the system and, hence, insure that critical code is implemented in the most efficient manner. Further, new operating system functions can be made available by adding the necessary instructions to the instruction set of the hypothetical computer.

3. The Choice of the Grammatical Class

We should now discuss the criteria for choosing the classes for the grammar and the translation schema and describe the hypothetical computer and the data base. Because of the limited space we shall, however, be content with an analysis of the first problem, i.e. choosing the grammar class. An in depth discussion of the other design criteria, developed in the context of the EPOS system, will be the subject of a report available in the near future.

The grammatical class chosen determines the simplicity of the parsing algorithm needed as well as the notational flexibility of the system. Since flexibility and simplicity are both desirable but, unfortunately, conflicting goals a compromise must be found.

Of the two extreme classes of grammars, (i) the regular grammars and (ii) all context-free grammars, neither is acceptable.

(i) Regular grammars do not permit nesting to be denoted and, therefore, are totally insufficient.

(ii) The class of all context-free grammars is not recommended for theoretical and practical reasons.

The theoretical problem is in ambiguity. It is not always possible to detect potential ambiguities by analysing the grammar rules added. Hence, we can possibly never tell whether a grammar is free of ambiguities. Perhaps, this problem is not too severe as there are rather simple responses to ambiguities later detected. For instance, one of the parses could be taken at random and a message issued. Nevertheless the problem should be avoided if it can be done without sacrificing essential advantages.

More serious is the fact that even the best general parsing algorithms (e.g. Earley's [E70]) are rather slow because of their high overhead, also for grammars that can be parsed in a time proportional to n. Moreover, some unambiguous grammars require proportional to n^2 parsing steps which is intolerable if long input sentences are considered.

Finally, the fact that parsing overhead increases with the size of the grammar makes general context-free grammars an undesirable class: actual grammars of extensible languages may grow unpredictably.

3.1 Operator precedence grammars

Van Gils [G71] suggested the use of (i) operator precedence grammars as a class whose precedence relation is defined by left and right priorities for finding the skeletal parse (i.e. the structure of the parse tree) and (ii) mode resolution with coercion for modifying and labelling the parse tree.

Since we feel that the simplicity of operator precedence parsing is very attractive but that its limitations are too severe, we will suggest two additions (target modes and environment parameters) that do not complicate the parser noticeably but enhance the flexibility considerably.

3.2 Target modes

Consider the grammar G_a

$V_T = (a|b|v|,|;)$ $V_N = (S'|S|D|E)$

S' → S;

S → D|S,D   D → a E|b E   E → v|E,v

and the sentence

a v,v,v,b v,v;

This resembles the problem which occurs with the extended form of the collateral identity declaration in ALGOL 68:

(4)   <u>int</u> i, j, k, <u>real</u> x, y;

G_a--or the grammar that describes (4)--is not an operator precedence grammar since the relation between <u>a</u> and <u>b</u> on the one hand and , on the other is not unique. As a consequence operator precedence parsing cannot detect the right hand side of the handle that starts with <u>a</u>--or <u>int</u> in (4) respectively.

It is therefore suggested to add the following parsing rule:

For finding the end of its handle, a prefix-like symbol (i.e. a symbol with maximal left priority) may specify the mode (target mode) of the first symbol outside of the handle. If the symbol with the specified mode is preceded by an infix operator (e.g. a comma) the handle ends before the infix symbol. If a target mode is specified, the end of a handle is found if a symbol with a sufficiently low left priority or with the specified (target) mode is encountered. As an example consider the identity declaration above assuming that <u>int</u> and <u>real</u> have the mode <u>mode</u> and also specify <u>mode</u> as a target mode.

Note: In order to properly handle symbols that are not yet declared we assume that they have, by default, maximal left and right priorities and the mode <u>undefined</u>.

Another problem occurs in statements that declare properties of symbols to which priorities have already been assigned like operators in operation declarations of ALGOL 68. Here priority oriented precedence parsing must fail. This problem, too, can be solved by target modes. However, in this case we want the symbol with the specified target mode to be the <u>last</u> element of the current handle rather than the first of the next handle.

In both cases, finding the right end of a handle requires that the mode of a symbol be considered <u>before</u> its priorities.

3.3 Environment parameters

We will use the following simple grammar in order to illustrate the motiviation of the second proposed addition to precedence parsing rules:

V_T = (a|b|v|.) V_N = (S|A|B)

S → a A|b B   A → v|A . v   B → v|v . B

This grammar is unambiguous and parseable in linear time. It is not an operator precedence grammar, though, because the relations between <u>v</u> and <u>.</u> as well as <u>.</u> and <u>v</u> are not unique. The problem, however, can easily be resolved if the parser is made to remember whether it has previously encountered an <u>a</u> or <u>b</u>. This is accomplished by environment parameters subject to the following rules:

1) A prefix-like symbol P may specify an environment parameter. This parameter is applicable to all elements of the handle that has P as its first constituent.

2) If a symbol P defines a new parameter it automatically disables temporarily (for the remainder of the handle) the parameter that is defined for an outer handle. At the right of the end of the handle the outer parameter is restored.

3) All attributes of a symbol can be made dependent on the current environment parameter (i.e. mode, priorities, target mode, the new environment parameter, the syntactic pattern of the handle governed by the symbol and the code to be generated for the handle). Thus, the same symbol can mean quite different things under the influence of different parameters.

4) The outer most parameter (i.e. the parameter of the whole program) has some predetermined value e.g. zero.

Environment parameters enhance the flexibility without complicating the parsing problem. Moreover, they can be used to improve parsing efficiency and program clarity by giving 'hints' to the compiler and the human reader.

Further, environment parameters permit different sublanguages to be envoked and dismissed within the same program. This feature will be used to distinguish between programs for the hypothetical computer and programs of the extended system. It is considered for incorporating assembly and microprogramming into the system.

Finally, it is contemplated to direct the lexical scanner (i.e. the rules that govern the forming and separating of symbols) by environment parameters.

3.4 Multiple use of symbols

The problem that some operators are used as both infix and prefix operators can be solved either in the manner suggested by van Gils i.e. by considering the modes of neighboring symbols or by using the following fact:

The right priority of a symbol immediately preceding an infix (a prefix) operator is always (never) maximal. Thus, if a symbol may be both, an infix and a prefix operator, the right priority of the preceding symbol resolves the question.

3.5 Error recovery

One of the compiler problems without a good solution is error handling in general and the continuation of parsing after an error has been detected in particular. The latter problem has a rather systematic solution if operator precedence grammars—pure or with the additions suggested—are used. If all precedence decisions are based on priorities and/or target modes, a unique parse tree is found for every possible string of symbols. Thus, the part of the parser that identifies the structure of the input program never detects errors. All error handling must therefore be done by the following, mode resolving, step. Since the structure of the input is already determined before any error is found the question of parse continuation after error detection never occurs.

3.6 Mode resolution and coercion

The purpose of mode resolution is labeling the parse tree uniquely with addresses to code segments. Mode resolution is a simple bottom-up procedure as long as the modes required at the nodes of the tree match those that are delivered by the roots of their respective subtrees. If the modes do not match, an error has been found or a conversion should be performed (i.e. inserted) by the compiler. The complexity and generality of the procedures that select these conversions is determined (i) by the amount of context that may be considered for making the selection and (ii) by the relation that holds among the modes and indicates whether a conversion exists. In ALGOL 68 the context that may be considered is practically unlimited; the mode structure is hierarchical.

(i) From the standpoint of efficiency it would be very desirable to limit the context sensitivity to the handle processed such that the code for a handle can be generated as soon as the end of that handle is found. Limiting the context considered to just one handle is justified particularly because it does not seem to cost us any essential flexibility.

(ii) Limitations of the hierarchical mode structure have been discussed by Jorrand [J71]. He suggests a scheme that permits an arbitrary graph structure to be used for defining the conversion rules among nodes (classes, as he terms them). His scheme requires that the base language be type-less, a demand which can be met in a very natural way if the base language is represented by the hypothetical computer. It is being investigated if the price that must be paid for the flexibility gained is not too high. In order to determine whether some given mode can be converted into some required mode, a path must be found in the graph that describes the conversion rules. Since the time complexity of path finding algorithms that work on arbitrary graphs can reach k^n (n being the length of the path) the problem of efficiency is very real.

4. Conclusion

Built on a clean definition scheme, the system sketched combines flexibility and efficiency in a balanced manner. It should be pointed out that no time consuming macro facilities but a homogeneous compile algorithm accomodates the extension facilities.

One of the purposes of this paper is to stimulate a discussion on combining considerations of generality and efficiency in a meaningful way, and we shall be grateful for any suggestions or criticism offered.

It is recognized that this paper is too short to do justice to the subject matter. As mentioned before, an in depth discussion on (i) the selection of classes of translations, (ii) the primitives furnished by the hypothetical computer, and (iii) the structure of the data base will be found in a report on the EPOS system.

References

A73   Aho, A. V. and Ullman, J. D., "The theory of parsing, translation, and compiling", Vol. II, Prentice-Hall, Englewood Cliffs, N.J. 1973.
E70   Earley, J., "An efficient context-free parsing algorithm", CACM 13, 2, Feb. 1970, pp. 94-102.
G71   van Gils, T., "Syntactic definition mechanisms,", SIGPLAN Notices, Vol. 6, Number 12, Dec. 1971, pp. 67-74.
I70   Irons, E. T., "Experience with an extensible language", CACM 13, 1, Jan. 1970, pp. 31-40.
J71   Jorrand, P., "Data types and extensible languages", SIGPLAN Notices, Vol. 6, Number 12, Dec. 1971, pp. 75-83.
L66   Leavenworth, B. M., "Syntax macros and extended translation", CACM 9, 11, Nov. 1966, pp. 790-793.
L71   Lindsey, C. H. and van der Meulen, S. G., "Informal introduction to ALGOL 68", North-Holland Publishing Co., Amsterdam, London, 1971.
N71   Notley, M. G., "A model of extensible language systems", SIGPLAN Notices, Vol. 6, Number 12, Dec. 1971, pp. 29-38.
S67   Standish, T. A., "A data definition facility for programming languages", Ph.D. Thesis, Carnegie Institute of Technology, May 1967.
S70   Schuman, S. A., and Jorrand, P., "Definition mechanisms in extensible programming languages", AFIPS Conference Proceedings, Vol. 37, AFIPS Press 1970, pp. 9-20.
S71   Scowen, R. S., "Babel, an application of extensible compilers", SIGPLAN Notices, Vol. 6, Number 12, Dec. 1971, pp. 1-7.
W69   van Wijngaarden, A. (Ed.) et al., "Report on the algorithmic language ALGOL 68, MR.101, Mathematisch Centrum, Amsterdam, Oct. 1969.
W71   Wegbreit, B., "An overview of the ECL programming system", SIGPLAN Notices, Vol. 6, Number 12, Dec. 1971, pp. 26-28.

ZUM PROBLEM DER ANONYMITÄT DER BEFRAGTEN
BEI STATISTISCHEN DATENBANKEN MIT DIALOGAUSWERTUNG

J. Schlörer
Abteilung für Med. Statistik, Dokumentation
und Datenverarbeitung der Universität
79 Ulm-Wiblingen, Schloßbau 38

Seit einigen Jahren weiß man, daß die Möglichkeit, einen statistischen Individualdatenbestand per Dialog auszuwerten, Wege eröffnet, um Informationen über Einzelpersonen aus einer statistischen Datenbank herauszuholen (6). Die Grenze zwischen im engeren Sinn personenbezogenen Daten und statistischen Individualdaten - also anonym, aber nach Einzelpersonen gespeicherten Daten - ist verschwommen geworden.

Das auf der PDP 15 unserer Abteilung implementierte Datenbanksystem (11,12), das zur Dialogauswertung statistischer Individualdatenbestände aus dem medizinischen Bereich dient, bot eine gute Gelegenheit, die mit solchen Systemen verbundenen Risiken näher zu untersuchen. Die hier mitgeteilten Ergebnisse werden an anderer Stelle detaillierter dargestellt (9,10). Für das Identifikationsexperiment wurde ein Bestand von 31 465 anonymen Datensätzen verwendet, der aus einer Vorsorgeuntersuchung stammt (3). Es sei vorweg betont, daß bei diesem Versuch niemandes Anonymität tatsächlich durchbrochen wurde, denn das zu jeder Identifikation nötige Vorwissen (siehe unten) war simuliert und stammte aus dem Datenbestand selbst. Überdies repräsentierte der Datenbestand nur eine Stichprobe mir unbekannter Zusammensetzung.

Damit ein Benutzer per Auswertungsdialog Information über Herrn oder Frau X aus einem statistischen Individualdatenbestand herausholen kann, müssen folgende Voraussetzungen erfüllt sein:

1. Der Eindringling bringt genug Vorwissen über Herrn X mit, um ihn eindeutig, mindestens aber annähernd zu identifizieren; die als Vorwissen dienende Information muß auch im Datensatz von Herrn X enthalten sein. Wenn das Vorwissen Herrn X nur annähernd identifiziert, lassen sich nur solche Eigenschaften in Erfahrung bringen, die Herr X mit allen

im Datenbestand vertretenen Doppelgängern - auf die auch das ganze verfügbare Vorwissen zutrifft - teilt (9). Wir gehen hier davon aus, daß das Vorwissen zur Identifikation ausreicht, d.h., nur auf einen Datensatz im Datenbestand treffen alle als Vorwissen bekannten Eigenschaften zu.

2. Der Benutzer kann mit Hilfe logischer Operatoren - logisch UND, NICHT, ODER - Bedingungen bzw. Anfragen formulieren.

3. Das System antwortet dem Benutzer mit der Zahl der Personen, die die eingegebene Bedingung erfüllen, also mit absoluten Häufigkeiten. Es sind auch "Schnüffeltechniken" bekannt, die zusätzliche Fähigkeiten des Systems (etwa die Berechnung von Mittelwerten) voraussetzen (8); es genügt aber schon, wenn nur absolute Häufigkeiten ausgegeben werden.

Angenehm für einen Eindringling, aber nicht zwingend nötig ist:

4. Der Eindringling weiß von vornherein, daß ein Datensatz über Herrn X im Datenbestand vorhanden ist.

5. Der Datenbestand ist fehlerfrei.

6. Das System erlaubt die Generierung neuer Variabler, d.h., der Benutzer kann zum Beispiel eine Bedingung $A \land B \land C$ eingeben, das Ergebnis unter dem Namen D zwischenspeichern und D bei späteren Anfragen wieder als Operanden verwenden.

Wir nehmen hier an, daß auch die Voraussetzungen 4 - 6 erfüllt sind; der Platz erlaubt nicht, darauf einzugehen, was ein Eindringling unternehmen kann, wenn sie fehlen (9, 10). Der Eindringling steht nun vor zwei Teilproblemen. Er muß

a) Herrn X - besser: den Datensatz von Herrn X - identifizieren und

b) bisher unbekannte Information aus diesem Datensatz herausholen, also das bisher bekannte Dossier ergänzen.

Am Teilproblem "Identifikation" interessiert vor allem, wieviel Vorwissen ein Eindringling denn nun mitbringen muß, um einen gesuchten Datensatz zu identifizieren. Um darüber eine Vorstellung zu gewinnen, wurden per Zufall 100 Datensätze aus dem schon erwähnten Datenbestand ausgewählt; jedem Datensatz wurden die Ausprägungen der 10 in Tabelle 1 aufgelisteten Merkmale entnommen. Gerade diese Variablen wurden verwendet, weil sie sich relativ leicht aus diversen Quellen besorgen lassen, also auch praktisch als Vorwissen für einen echten Eindringling geeignet wären. Mit Hilfe von Zufallszahlen wurde für jeden Datensatz eine andere Numerierung $a_1, a_2 \ldots a_{10}$ der zehn entnommenen Eigenschaften festgelegt. Für jeden Datensatz wurde dann die Anfragenserie

Merkmal	Zahl der Klassen	Relative Häufigkeit p_i der einzelnen Merkmalsausprägungen
1 Sitz (Ort) der Krankenkasse	6	0.0195 - 0.3724
2 Geschlecht	2	0.4943 - 0.5057
3 Alter (5J.-Klassen; nur Pat. von 15 - 59 Jahren)	9	0.0736 - 0.1352
4 Familienstand	5	0.0406 - 0.6944
5 Kinder im eigenen Haushalt	4	0.0884 - 0.5185
6 Einwohnerzahl d. Wohnsitzes	4	0.1829 - 0.3731
7 Berufliche Qualifikation	3	0.0481 - 0.4843
8 Art des Beschäft.-Betriebes	9	0.0002 - 0.5234
9 Geburtsdatum (Tag)	31	0.0192 - 0.0350
10 Geburtsdatum (Monat)	12	0.0760 - 0.0930

Tabelle 1. Die als simuliertes Vorwissen dienenden Merkmale

$$A_i = a_1 \wedge a_2 \wedge \ldots \wedge a_i \quad (i = 1, 2 \ldots k; k \leq 10)$$

durchgeführt. Bezeichnet man die Zahl der Personen, die eine eingegebene Bedingung A_i erfüllen, mit $f(A_i)$, dann galt $f(A_k) = 1$ und $f(A_{k-1}) > 1$. Mit anderen Worten: A_k ist jeweils die erste Anfrage einer Serie, die den fraglichen Datensatz identifiziert. k, also die Zahl der zur Identifizierung nötigen Eigenschaften, lag zwischen 4 und 10, in 65 der 100 Fälle zwischen 6 und 8 (einschließlich). In 2 Fällen reichten die 10 Eigenschaften nicht zur Identifikation aus. Als nächstes wurde für alle idenfizierenden Anfragen A_k der Wert

$$D = n \cdot \prod p_i \quad (i = 1, 2 \ldots k; n = 31\ 465)$$

berechnet. Es ergaben sich folgende Zahlen:

$D = n \cdot \prod_{i=1}^{k} p_i$	Zahl der identifizierten Datensätze	
	f	cum f
1.0 - < 10.0	13	13
0.1 - < 1.0	40	53
0.01 - < 0.1	33	86
0.001 - < 0.01	10	96
< 0.001	2	98
Keine Identifikation	2	100

Je niedriger D, desto größer der Umfang des zur Identifikation nötigen Vorwissens. Ein $D \geq 1.0$ reichte in 13 %, ein $D \geq 0.01$ in 86 % der Fälle zur Identifikation aus. Natürlich werden die Abhängigkeiten zwischen den als Vorwissen verwendbaren Eigenschaften in so gut wie jedem Datenbestand etwas anders aussehen; die hier gefundenen Werte kann man nicht ohne weiteres verallgemeinern. Akzeptiert man sie aber mit aller Vorsicht als ungefähre Richtwerte, dann scheint es interessant zu überlegen, wie viele und wie häufige oder seltene Eigenschaften von Herrn oder Frau X ein Eindringling kennen muß, damit bei Datenbeständen mit verschiedenem Umfang n D einen bestimmten Wert erreicht. Zur Vereinfachung sei dabei angenommen, daß jeweils alle als Vorwissen bekannten Eigenschaften die gleiche relative Häufigkeit p_x aufweisen; k läßt sich dann sehr einfach über die Gleichung

$$D = n \cdot p_x^k$$

errechnen. Tabelle 2 enthält k für verschiedenes p_x und n, und zwar in der linken Hälfte für D = 0,01 und in der rechten Hälfte für D = 1,8. Im gerade beschriebenen Experiment reichte der erste Wert in 86 %, der zweite Wert in 5 % der Fälle zur Identifikation des gesuchten Datensatzes. Alle Werte in Tabelle 2 sind zur nächsten ganzen Zahl aufgerundet.

D \ n	0,01				1,8			
p_x	0,5	0,3	0,2	0,1	0,5	0,3	0,2	0,1
31 465	22	13	10	7	15	9	7	5
1 000 000	27	16	12	8	20	11	9	6
60 000 000	33	19	14	10	25	15	11	8

Tabelle 2: Zahl der Eigenschaften (k), die bei verschiedenem Umfang n des Datenbestandes und bei verschiedenen relativen Häufigkeiten p_x nötig sind, um einen bestimmten Wert für D zu erreichen.

Natürlich steigt k mit steigendem n, steigendem p_x und fallendem D. Wenig erfreulich an diesen Zahlen scheint mir zweierlei: Einmal steigt k nur mit dem Logarithmus von n; um also Herrn X unter 60 Millionen Personen zu identifizieren, ist gar nicht so sehr viel mehr Vorwissen erforderlich, als wenn man ihn unter nur etwa 30 000 Personen herausfinden möchte. Zweitens sind die absoluten Werte für k nicht eben hoch; das wird noch deutlicher, wenn man daran denkt, daß alle drei Bestandteile eines Geburtsdatums (Tag, Monat, Jahr) - die alle auch Bestandteil des geplanten Personenkennzeichens sind - eine relative Häufigkeit p_x von unter 0,1, zum Teil sogar erheblich unter 0,1 haben.

Wie gesagt ist nicht bewiesen, daß etwa ein D von 0,01 bei jedem Datenbestand zur Identifikation von 80 - 90 % der Datensätze genügt. Aber auch wenn dafür ein D von 0,0001 nötig wäre, stiege die Zahl der erforderlichen Eigenschaften nicht allzu stark an: bei einem p_x von 0,1 und einem

n von 1 000 000 zum Beispiel betrüge k dann 10 anstatt 8 bei D = 0,01.
Wer einen statistischen Individualdatenbestand in der Hand hat und in jeder gewünschten Weise auswerten kann, ist natürlich bereits am Ziel, sobald er eine identifizierende Anfrage des oben beschriebenen Typs A_k formulieren kann. Er kann sich dann den betreffenden Datensatz sofort als Ganzes ansehen. Ein Normalbenutzer einer statistischen Datenbank, der auf einen Auswertungsdialog angewiesen ist und keine kompletten Datensätze geliefert bekommt, hat etwas mehr Arbeit vor sich.

Zuerst muß ich die von HOFFMAN und MILLER (6) beschriebene Technik erläutern, die ausschließlich logisches UND verwendet. Angenommen, der Eindringling kenne k Eigenschaften von Herrn X, die zu dessen Identifikation ausreichen; die Bedingung $A = a_1 \wedge a_2 \wedge \ldots \wedge a_k$ trifft nur auf einen Datensatz zu, eben auf den von Herrn X; $f(A) = 1$. Angenommen, jeder Datensatz enthalte eine Angabe darüber, ob die betreffende Person die Eigenschaft x besitzt. Der Eindringling will herausfinden, ob Herr X diese Eigenschaft besitzt. Er braucht nur die Anfrage $B = A \wedge x$ einzugeben; es kann nur zwei Antworten geben:

(1) $f(B) = 1 \longleftrightarrow$ Herr X hat x

(2) $f(B) = 0 \longleftrightarrow$ Herr X hat x nicht

Diese Technik ist allerdings leicht zu unterbinden. Das Programm braucht bloß auf jede Anfrage B die Antwort zu verweigern, bei der f(B) ein bestimmtes Minimum - in der Folge als Z_{min} bezeichnet - unterschreitet. Ein Z_{min} von 2 genügt schon. Es gibt eine - ebenfalls nur mit logischem UND arbeitende - Variante der HOFFMAN-MILLERschen Technik, mit der man Z_{min} partiell unterlaufen kann (6). Ich kann sie hier nicht im Detail darlegen, aber auch diese Variante läßt sich unterbinden, wenn man den Wert für Z_{min} entsprechend höher ansetzt. Von wenigen, sehr speziellen Situationen abgesehen, dürfte ein Z_{min} in der Größenordnung von 100 dafür ausreichen (9,10).

Wenn der Benutzer neben logischem UND noch andere logische Operationen in seine Bedingungen einbauen kann, wird der Schutz vor Eindringlingen schwieriger, und mit einer Einrichtung wie Z_{min} ist nichts mehr zu erreichen. Zunächst ist Folgendes leicht einzusehen: Sobald logisches NICHT greifbar ist, muß Z_{min} mit einem $Z_{max} = n - Z_{min}$ gekoppelt werden, wobei n den Umfang des Datenbestandes bedeutet, also die Zahl der enthaltenen Datensätze. Der Benutzer kann sonst jede Anfrage A mit $f(A) < Z_{min}$ durch $\neg A$ ersetzen und erhält dann $f(\neg A) = n - f(A)$ zur Antwort.

Ab sofort gehen wir also von einem System aus, das die Ausgabe jeder absoluten Häufigkeit $f(V) < Z_{min}$ und $f(V) > Z_{max} = n - Z_{min}$ verweigert.

Ein zusätzliches Hindernis für unseren Eindringling bestehe darin, daß auch die Generierung neuer Variabler V, deren f(V) im gesperrten Bereich liegt, unterbunden wird. Wenn also f(V) für die Ausgabe gesperrt bleibt, kann der Eindringling V auch nicht zwischenspeichern und in einer späteren Anfrage als logischen Operanden verwenden.

Wenn dem Eindringling UND, NICHT und ODER zur Verfügung stehen, und wenn sein Vorwissen zur Identifikation von Herrn X genügt, behindern in diese Schutzmaßnahmen nicht. Es genügen übrigens auch die Kombinationen UND/ODER, UND/NICHT, in manchen Fällen sogar NICHT/ODER; der Aufwand des Eindringlings wird allerdings bei den letzten beiden Kombinationen höher (Näheres siehe 9, 10). Der Eindringling wird sich - auf das Wie kommen wir noch zu sprechen - zwei Bedingungen A_1 und T mit folgenden Eigenschaften aufbauen:

1. A_1 trifft auf den Datensatz von Herrn X zu.
2. $Z_{min} < f(A_1) \leq Z_{max}$.
3. T trifft auf alle Datensätze zu, auf die auch A_1 zutrifft, nur nicht auf den Datensatz von Herrn X. Also $f(T) \geq Z_{min}$.
4. $f(T) \leq Z_{max}$.

Bezeichnet man die Mengen der Datensätze, die die Bedingungen A_1 und T erfüllen, als $S(A_1)$ und $S(T)$, ferner die Menge, die nur den Datensatz von Herrn X enthält, als $S(X)$, dann sieht das als VENN-Diagramm folgendermaßen aus:

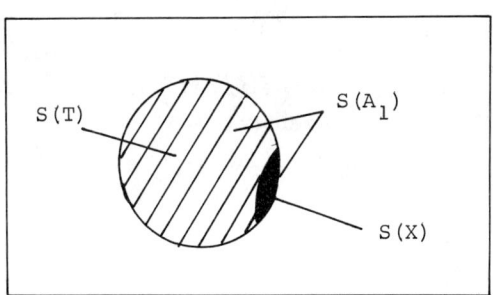

Abgesehen von den erwähnten, durch Z_{min} und Z_{max} bedingten Beschränkungen ist das Entscheidende, in Mengenbegriffen ausgedrückt, daß

$S(T \wedge A_1) = S(A_1) \setminus S(X)$

In obigem Diagramm ist sogar, der Einfachheit halber

$S(T) = S(A_1) \setminus S(X)$

Das ist jedoch nicht zwingend nötig. S(T) könnte also in dem Diagramm über $S(A_1)$ hinausgreifen, nur S(X) darf nicht darin enthalten sein.

Die Bedingung T wird im Folgenden als Trecker bezeichnet, weil sie tatsächlich eine Art Zugmaschine darstellt, mit deren Hilfe der Eindringling peu à peu den kompletten Datensatz von Herrn X herausziehen kann, ohne daß ihn die Sicherungen, die wir gerade in unser System eingebaut haben, im geringsten dabei stören. Um herauszufinden, ob Herr X die Eigenschaft x besitzt, stellt der Eindringling die Anfrage

$$B = (T \lor x) \land A_1$$

Darauf können wieder nur zwei Antworten kommen:

(1) $f(B) = f(A_1)$ $\longleftrightarrow$ Herr X hat x

(2) $f(B) = f(A_1) - 1$ $\longleftrightarrow$ Herr X hat x nicht

Dieses Spiel kann man natürlich mit jeder im Datenbestand vorkommenden Eigenschaft wiederholen. Es wird nur bei nichtgruppierten quantitativen Variablen etwas langwierig, falls der Benutzer sie nicht ad hoc klassifizieren oder aber auf eine weitere, von PALME beschriebene Technik ausweichen kann, die allerdings zusätzliche Fähigkeiten des Systems voraussetzt, etwa die Berechnung von Mittelwerten für vom Benutzer definierte Gruppen von Datensätzen (8).

In Abbildung 1 sind einige Verfahren des Treckeraufbaus skizziert. Sie sind funktionell gleichwertig, können aber beim Umgehen eines Kontrollalgorithmus oder von Beschränkungen der Abfragesyntax eine Rolle spielen (9, 10). In der Abbildung ist angenommen, daß $f(A_1 \land A_2) = 1$, genauer: $S(A_1 \land A_2) = S(X)$. Die Maske M darf bei der Variante 3 (siehe Abb. 1) nicht auf Herrn X zutreffen; wenn also Herr X beispielsweise geschieden ist, läßt sich die Eigenschaft "verheiratet" als Maske verwenden. Bei der Variante 2 (Abb.1) muß M dagegen der Bedingung

$$[S(A_1) \setminus S(X)] \cap S(M) = \emptyset$$

beziehungsweise

$$f(M \land (\neg A_2) \land A_1) = 0$$

genügen. Im übrigen müssen die Bedingungen natürlich wieder so konstruiert werden, daß kein auszugebendes Ergebnis und keine neu zu generierende Variable Z_{min} unter- oder Z_{max} überschreitet; das macht aber weiter keine Schwierigkeiten.

Es wird übrigens so gut wie immer möglich sein, $f(T)$, $f(A_1)$ und $f(M)$ in der Nähe von n/2 anzusiedeln (n = Zahl der Datensätze im Datenbestand). Bei annähernder Gleichverteilung der Geschlechter im Datenbestand genügt dafür schon, daß man als Bedingung A_1 ausschließlich das Geschlecht der

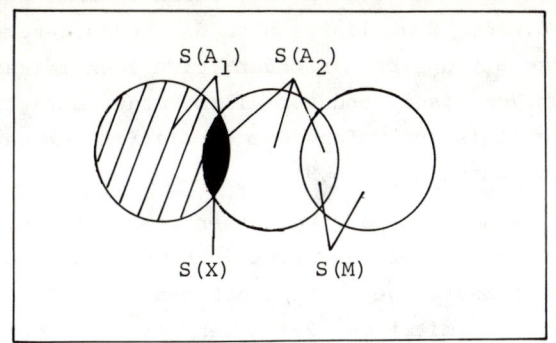

	Treckeraufbau:	Treckeranwendung:
(1)	$T = (\neg A_2) \wedge A_1$	$B = (T \vee x) \wedge A_1$
(2)	$T = (\neg (A_2 \vee M)) \wedge A_1$	$B = (T \vee x) \wedge A_1$
(3)	$T = M$	$B = (T \vee x) \wedge C$
	$C = (A_1 \wedge A_2) \vee M$	

Abbildung 1: Einige Varianten des Treckeraufbaus. Bei den Varianten (1) und (2) kann beim Treckeraufbau der Term $\wedge A_1$ weggelassen werden, falls Z_{min} und Z_{max} das zulassen.

fraglichen Person und als Maske das entgegengesetzte Geschlecht verwendet. Es gibt auch andere Möglichkeiten (10). Praktisch spielt das keine besondere Rolle, weil Werte für Z_{min} und Z_{max} in der Nähe von n/2 völlig unpraktikabel sind - jegliche statistische Auswertung wird damit lahmgelegt. Immerhin ist dies etwas beunruhigend: Man kann Ausgabesperren so wählen, daß keine statistische Auswertung des Datenbestandes mehr möglich ist - Dossiers kann man trotzdem noch herausziehen.

Es werden jetzt noch einige mögliche Schutzmaßnahmen gestreift; der knappe Raum läßt allerdings keine Details zu (Literaturhinweise bei 1,2, 7,9,10). Vorweg sei gesagt, daß - vom Standpunkt des Normalbenutzers aus tragbare - Beschränkungen der Abfragesyntax, aber auch Kontrollalgorithmen, soweit ich im Augenblick sehen kann, keine Aussicht auf Erfolg versprechen (10). Als Schutzmaßnahmen kommen unter anderen in Frage:

1. Beschränkung des Zugangs zur statistischen Datenbank. Dieser Weg scheint mir mindestens in manchen Fällen - zum Beispiel bei Planungsinformationssystemen - nicht völlig unbedenklich.

2. Der gespeicherte statistische Individualdatenbestand repräsentiert keine Population, sondern nur eine Stichprobe, deren Zusammensetzung dem Benutzer verborgen bleibt. Zwar lassen sich die beschriebenen Techniken auch auf solche Stichproben anwenden; eine Identifikation erfordert dann aber mehr Vorwissen, und vor allem werden derartige Attacken bei - im Verhältnis zum Umfang der Population - genügend kleinen Stichproben recht unrentabel (5,9).

3. Man kürzt den Datensatz um so viele als Vorwissen geeignete Merkmale, daß Identifikationen kaum noch oder gar nicht mehr möglich sind. Das ist übrigens eine der Voraussetzungen dafür, daß einige raffinierte Techniken zum Schutz der Anonymität der Befragten bei Longitudinalstudien (2,7) auch wirklich sicher funktionieren.

4. Einbringen von Zufallsfehlern in den Datenbestand, entweder nach einem von WARNER (13) vorgeschlagenen und inzwischen weiterentwickelten Prinzip schon bei der Datenerhebung oder erst in den fertigen Datenbestand (Übersicht bei 1).

5. Einbringen von Fehlern nicht in die Daten, sondern in den Output der Datenbank; es werden also keine echten absoluten Häufigkeiten mehr ausgegeben. Auch das ist nicht völlig narrensicher, außer es gelingt, wie von PALME (8) vorgeschlagen, eine Hashfunktion einzubauen, die bewirkt, daß jede Anfrage A, sooft sie wiederholt wird und wie immer sie der Benutzer durch Umstellen der Operanden umformt, stets den gleichen Fehler im Ergebnis nach sich zieht.

6. Mikroaggregation der Daten (4). Anschließend hat man freilich keine statistischen Individualdaten mehr vor sich.

Jede dieser Maßnahmen hat ihren Preis. Sie kostet in irgendeiner Form ein Stück Information, ein Stück Informationsfreiheit. Eine offene Gesellschaft braucht aber beides: Informationsfreiheit und "privacy".

Literatur:

(1) BORUCH, R.F.: Relations among statistical methods for assuring confidentiality of social research data. Social Sci. Res. 1 (1972), 403-414.
(2) BORUCH, R.F.: Strategies for eliciting and merging confidential research data. Policy Sci. 3 (1972), 275-297.
(3) EIMEREN, W.VAN, SELBMANN, H.K., ÜBERLA, K.: Modell einer allgemeinen Vorsorgeuntersuchung im Jahre 1969/70 - Schlußbericht. W.E.Weinmann Druckerei GmbH, Bonlanden bei Stuttgart 1972.

(4) FEIGE, E.L. and WATTS, H.W.: An investigation of the consequences of partial aggregation of micro-economic data. Econometrica $\underline{2}$ (1972), 343-360.

(5) FELLEGI, I.P.: On the question of statistical confidentiality. J.Amer.Statist.Ass. $\underline{67}$ (1972), 7-18.

(6) HOFFMAN, L. and MILLER, W.F.: Getting a personal dossier from a statistical data bank. Datamation $\underline{16}$, 5 (May 1970), 74-75.

(7) MÜLLER, P.J.: Datenschutz und Sicherung der Individualdaten der empirischen Sozialforschung. Datenverarbeitung in Steuer, Wirtschaft und Recht $\underline{3}$, 1 (Jan.1974), 2-11.

(8) PALME, J.: Software security. Datamation $\underline{20}$, 1 (Jan.1974), 51-55.

(9) SCHLÖRER, J.: Schnüffeltechniken und Schutzmaßnahmen bei statistischen Datenbank-Informationssystemen mit Dialogauswertung. Materialien Nr.29 der Abt.f.Med. Statistik, Dokumentation und Datenverarbeitung, Ulm März 1974.

(10) SCHLÖRER, J.: Identification and retrieval of personal records from a statistical data bank. In preparation.

(11) SELBMANN, H.K.: Ein Datenbanksystem zur Auswertung statistischer Datenbestände. Materialien Nr. 15 der Abteilung für Med. Statistik, Dokumentation und Datenverarbeitung, Ulm August 1972.

(12) SELBMANN, H.K.: Bitstring processing for statistical evaluation of large volumes of medical data. Meth. Inform. Med. $\underline{13}$ (1974), 61-64.

(13) WARNER, S.L.: Randomized response: a survey technique for eliminating evasive answer bias. J.Amer.Statist.Ass. $\underline{60}$ (1965), 63-69.

ZUGRIFFSSICHERUNG IN DATENBANKSYSTEMEN
P. Haberäcker, M. Lehner
Rechenzentrum Oberpfaffenhofen der Deutschen Forschungs-
und Versuchsanstalt für Luft- und Raumfahrt e.V.
8031 Oberpfaffenhofen Post Weßling

1. Einleitung

Mit dem Einsatz von DV-Anlagen in öffentlichen und privaten Verwaltungen treten verstärkt Forderungen nach Datenschutz auf. Dieser bedarf zu seiner Verwirklichung der Entwicklung vielfältiger technischer Hilfsmittel zur Zugriffssicherung. Das Gesamtspektrum der notwendigen Maßnahmen zur Zugriffssicherung umfaßt

- organisatorische Maßnahmen
- Hardware-Einrichtungen und
- Software.

Im Rechenzentrum Oberpfaffenhofen (RZO) wurden hauptsächlich die softwareseitigen Möglichkeiten der Zugriffssicherung untersucht. Derartige Mechanismen können in Betriebssysteme und in Anwendersysteme eingebaut werden. Zur Zugriffskontrolle in Betriebssystemen, die auch die Grundlage für alle Kontrollmechanismen auf der Ebene der Anwendersysteme bildet, liegen schon eine Reihe von Untersuchungen vor (z.B. [1], [2], [3], [4]). Eine wichtige Klasse von Anwendersystemen sind die Datenbanksysteme. Da sie in wachsendem Maße für die Verwaltung großer Datenmengen eingesetzt werden, ist die Entwicklung von Zugriffssicherungsmechanismen für Datenbanksysteme sehr wichtig. Darauf lag der Schwerpunkt der im RZO zur Zugriffssicherung durchgeführten Arbeiten. Das Ziel war die Entwicklung eines möglichst flexiblen und doch praktikablen Systems der Zugriffssicherung bei Datenbanksystemen, das auch in bestehende Datenbanksysteme eingegliedert werden kann.

2. Prinzipielle Erwägungen

Ein Datenbanksystem im hier verwendeten Sinn des Wortes (vgl. [8]) erlaubt es, mit Hilfe einer Datenbeschreibungssprache (DDL: data description language) das Strukturschema einer Anwender-Datenbank festzulegen und über die Anweisungen der Datenmanipulationssprache (DMS: data

---

Die Untersuchungen zu diesem Thema wurden vom Bundesministerium für Forschung und Technologie als Forschungsvorhaben DV 5.003 gefördert.

manipulation language), die meist in eine Gastsprache eingebettet sind, das <u>Datenbank-Management-System</u> zu den gewünschten Datentransporten zwischen dem Arbeitsspeicher des Benutzerprogramms und dem Hintergrundspeicher, auf dem sich die Datenbank befindet, zu veranlassen.

Datenbanksysteme sind Hilfsmittel allgemeiner Natur, die vielfältig verwendbare Software für die Verwaltung und Nutzung großer Datenbestände bereitstellen. Will man daher zu einem gegebenen Datenbanksystem ein Zugriffssicherungssystem hinzufügen - oder besser bei der Entwicklung eines Datenbanksystems ein Zugriffssicherungssystem integrieren, so muß auch letzteres den Charakter des universellen Hilfsmittels besitzen, somit vielfältige Möglichkeiten zur Realisierung individueller Anforderungen an eine Zugriffssicherung anbieten. Sonst besteht die Gefahr, daß Forderungen an die Zugriffssicherung entweder überhaupt nicht oder nur dadurch befriedigt werden können, daß man Abstriche an der freien Kombinierbarkeit der vom Datenbanksystem zur Strukturierung der Datenbank zur Verfügung gestellten Möglichkeiten macht. Die Struktur einer Datenbank sollte jedoch vom Anwenderproblem her bestimmt werden. Wir stellen daher folgendes Prinzip auf:

(P1)   Das Zugriffssicherungssystem darf von seiner Konstruktion her keine Auswirkungen auf die Struktur einer Anwender-Datenbank haben.

Durch das sich mehrende Verständnis für die Datenschutz-Problematik und durch die von Seiten der Gesetzgeber auf die Anwender zukommenden Datenschutzverpflichtungen werden die Anforderungen an die Zugriffssicherung laufend erhöht. Daher muß ein Zugriffssicherungssystem auch komplexere Methoden der Zugriffssicherung bieten, um mit den wachsenden Anforderungen Schritt halten zu können. Andernfalls beschränkt das Zugriffssicherungssystem die Anwendbarkeit des zugrundeliegenden Datenbanksystems. Wir gewinnen folgendes Prinzip:

(P2)   Ein allgemein verwendbares Zugriffssicherungssystem muß auch großen Anforderungen genügen können; dazu müssen komplexe Mechanismen der Zugriffssicherung angeboten werden.

Jeder Anwender wird bestrebt sein, die Kosten für den Unterhalt seiner Datenbanken und deren Benutzung zu minimieren. Dies gilt natürlich insbesondere für den Zugriffsschutz. Geringe Anforderungen an die Zugriffssicherung müssen sich mit entsprechend geringem Aufwand realisieren lassen. Es ergibt sich folgendes Prinzip:

(P3)   Die nach (P2) geforderten komplexeren Mechanismen der Zugriffssicherung sollten für ein Anwendersystem nur dann belastend wirken, wenn sie wirklich verwendet werden.

Bei Entscheidungen über die Gestaltung des Zugriffssicherungssystems werden die vorstehenden Prinzipien herangezogen.

3. Konstruktionsentscheidungen für ein allgemeines Zugriffssicherungssystem

3.1 Dynamische Zugriffskontrolle bis hinab zur Feldebene

Ausgehend von der Datenhierarchie einer Datenbank:

Datenbank
Teile der Datenbank, die einem Subschema entsprechen (vgl. [8])
Bereiche
Sätze (als Repräsentanten von Satztypen)
Felder (als Repräsentanten von Feldtypen)

stellt sich uns die Frage, welche dieser Stufen in Entscheidungen der Zugriffskontrolle einbezogen werden müssen. Wir werden zeigen, daß Zugriffsspezifikationen bis hinunter zur Feldebene angeboten werden müssen. Nehmen wir dazu im Beispiel einer Personaldatenbank an, daß das Zugriffssicherungssystem Zugriffsentscheidungen nur bis zur Satzebene zuläßt und wir in der Datenbank einen Satztyp der folgenden Gestalt haben:

PERSONENSATZ = (NAME, VORNAME, GEBURTSTAG,...,FUNKTION, GEHALT,...,
VORSTRAFEN, MEDIZINISCHE DATEN,...)

Ein Sachbearbeiter, der bei der Gehaltsabrechnung mitwirken soll, muß den PERSONENSATZ bearbeiten können, da er daraus die für seine Aufgaben wichtigen Daten bezieht. Man will aber verhindern, daß er auch die Felder VORSTRAFEN oder MEDIZINISCHE DATEN ausliest. Im Falle des angenommenen beschränkten Zugriffssicherungssystems müßte man dazu den Satztyp PERSONENSATZ in mindestens zwei verschiedene Satztypen aufteilen. Die Zugriffssicherung hätte also Auswirkungen auf die Struktur der Datenbank, was Prinzip (P1) widerspricht. Ein genügend allgemeines System der Zugriffssicherung muß daher Zugriffsentscheidungen bis auf Feldebene zulassen.

Dabei muß die Zugriffskontrolle <u>dynamisch</u> erfolgen, d.h. bei jedem Zugriff eines Benutzers auf die Datenbank muß die Berechtigung geprüft werden. Im zuletzt betrachteten Beispiel ließe sich nämlich das Zugriffssicherungsproblem auch dadurch lösen, daß man für die Lohnabrechnung ein geeignetes Subschema nach den in [8] gemachten Vorschlägen definiert. Dann müßte nur einmal zu Beginn einer in sich abgeschlossenen Arbeits-

phase des Sachbearbeiters abgeprüft werden, ob er das für ihn definierte
Subschema verwendet. Man könnte von einer statischen Zugriffssicherung
sprechen. Ein allgemeines Zugriffssicherungssystem läßt sich aber nicht
nur durch geeignete Definition solcher Subschemata aufbauen. Hat man
nämlich eine Feldtyp X der Datenbankbeschreibung nicht in das Subschema
eines Benutzerkreises einbezogen, so hat man den betreffenden Benutzern
jegliche Zugriffsmöglichkeit auf X genommen. Man möchte ihnen aber vielleicht nur den verändernden Zugriff auf X verbieten. Diese Kontrolle
der Zugriffsart, die nach Prinzip (P2) unbedingt gefordert werden muß,
läßt sich durch Subschemata nicht mehr lösen.

Ein allgemein verwendbares Zugriffssicherungssystem muß es also ermöglichen, Zugriffsspezifikationen bis auf Feldebene (<u>lokale Zugriffs-
kontrolle</u>) zu geben, wobei die Zugriffe selbst <u>dynamisch</u> abgeprüft werden, da sonst die Zugriffsart nicht ausreichend in die Vergabe von Zugriffsrechten einbezogen werden kann.

Es gibt aber durchaus Anwendungen, bei denen zumindest teilweise
keine feine Abstufung der Zugriffsberechtigungen bis zur Feldebene nötig
ist. Für diese Fälle muß nach Prinzip (P3) eine Möglichkeit vorhanden
sein, die Zugriffskontrolle durch eine Beschränkung auf die Ebene der
Sätze, Bereiche und Subschemata zu vergröbern (<u>globale Zugriffskontrolle</u>).

3.2 Zugriffsarten

Für Entscheidungen der Zugriffskontrolle ist das Wissen um die
Art des Zugriffs genauso wesentlich wie die Kenntnis des Objekts, auf
das zugegriffen wird. Daher müssen als Elemente der Zugriffssicherung
immer Paare betrachtet werden, die aus einem Objekt (bei Datenbanken:
Teil der Datenbank, auf den zugegriffen wird) und einer Zugriffsart
(Aktion) bestehen. Die gewöhnlich getroffene Unterscheidung in

        lesende und
        verändernde Zugriffe

genügt bei Datenbanken nicht. So ist das Verändern des Inhalts einer
Datenbank auf grundsätzlich verschiedene Weise möglich: Einspeichern
eines Repräsentanten eines Satztyps - Verändern bereits vorhandener
Repräsentanten - Löschen von Repräsentanten eines Satztyps. Da alle
diese Aktionen durch den Aufruf eines Befehls der Datenmanipulationssprache ausgeübt werden, wählen wir als Zugang zur Zugriffsart den Aufruf eines DMS-Befehls. Es bedeutet dann auch keine Schwierigkeit mehr,
über den Befehlsvorrat der DMS hinauszugehen und den Begriff Aktion auf
Programme auszudehnen, die mit Hilfe der DMS und eventuell einer Gast-

sprache erstellt worden sind.

Betrachten wir dazu die oben genannten, durch Befehle der DMS verwirklichten Veränderungsmöglichkeiten einer Datenbank. Wegen der inhaltlichen und strukturellen Verknüpfungen zwischen den Bereichen, Sätzen und Feldern einer Datenbank können solche Änderungen zahlreiche Auswirkungen auf den Rest des Datenmaterials haben. So wirkt sich bei einer Personaldatenbank das Ausscheiden eines Angestellten aus der betreffenden Firma sicher nicht nur im Löschen des zugehörigen Personalsatzes aus. Zum Beispiel müssen auch Daten über die Eingliederung des Angestellten in Abteilungen des Betriebes und Angaben für die betroffenen Abteilungen mitgeändert werden. Für einen so komplexen Vorgang wird man ein Programm erstellen, das alle Änderungen berücksichtigt und damit die Konsistenz des Datenmaterials der Datenbank aufrecht erhält. Einer Datenbank wird daher im allgemeinen eine sogenannte Methodenbank angegliedert sein, in der Programme für komplexe Auswertungs- und Veränderungsvorgänge bereitliegen. Diese Programme müssen nun genauso der Zugriffssicherung unterworfen werden können wie die Befehle der DMS. Zunächst scheint es für die Zugriffssicherung zu genügen, die Kontrolle bei der untersten Stufe der Aktionen, also bei den DMS-Befehlen, vorzunehmen. Dagegen sprechen aber mehrere Gründe. Zunächst umfaßt eine der genannten komplexen Aktionen oft sehr viele DMS-Befehle. Hat ein Benutzer das Recht, eine ganze Reihe der ersten DMS-Befehle auszuführen, aber nicht einen der nachfolgenden, so würde bei reiner Kontrolle der Einzelbefehle die Zeit für die Ausführung der ersten DMS-Befehle vergeudet. Handelt es sich darüber hinaus bei unserer komplexen Aktion um einen Vorgang, der Veränderungen in der Datenbank hinterläßt, so stellen sich beim erwähnten Fall der nur teilweisen Berechtigung auf DMS-Ebene schwierige Konsistenzprobleme ein. Es müßten in solchen Fällen alle schon erlaubten Veränderungen rückgängig gemacht werden, wenn eine damit zusammenhängende Datenkorrektur nicht mehr gestattet werden kann. Dies ist in der Praxis wohl unmöglich.

Effektivität des gesamten Anwendersystems und die Konsistenz der Datenbank fordern damit die Einbeziehung der Methodenbank in das Zugriffssicherungssystem. Es gibt aber von Seiten des Zugriffsschutzes noch einen tieferliegenden Grund. Man kommt damit zu einer Kontrolle ganzer Auswertungsvorgänge. Darf ein Benutzer nämlich die DMS-Befehle mit lesendem Zugriff verwenden, so kann er mit Hilfe darauf aufbauender Programme die vielfältigsten Auswertungen des Datenbestandes vornehmen. Werden jedoch nur gezielt erstellte Auswertungsprogramme aus einer Methodenbank zur Verfügung gestellt, so können darüber hinausgehende unerwünschte

Auswertungen sehr erschwert oder gar verhindert werden.

Unsere oben entwickelte Forderung, die Methodenbank in den Verfügungsbereich der Zugriffskontrollmechanismen zu bringen, hat Auswirkungen auf die Konstruktion von Datenbanksystemen. Diese müssen nämlich dann in der Lage sein, neben der Datenbank auch eine Methodenbank zu verwalten.

3.3 Zugriffsbedingungen

Eine weitere im Sinne von Prinzip (P2) wichtige Möglichkeit zur verfeinerten Abstufung von Zugriffsrechten ist die Einführung von Zugriffsbedingungen. Man kann zwei verschiedene Arten von Bedingungen unterscheiden:

- Bedingungen, bei deren Abprüfung das aktuell angesprochene Datenmaterial mit einbezogen werden muß: inhaltsabhängige Bedingungen
- Bedingungen anderer Art: kontextabhängige Bedingungen

Um die Nützlichkeit der ersten Bedingungsart einzusehen, können wir uns wieder des Beispiels der Personalverwaltung bedienen. Man will hier im allgemeinen nicht, daß jeder Angestellte der Personalabteilung die Personalsätze aller Betriebsangehörigen, insbesondere die der leitenden Angestellten, bearbeitet. Man muß also die Möglichkeit vorsehen, den Zugriff auf Repräsentanten des Satztyps PERSONALSATZ vom Inhalt des Feldes FUNKTION oder GEHALT abhängen zu lassen, was durch die Formulierung einer inhaltsabhängigen Bedingung möglich ist.

Bei den kontextabhängigen Bedingungen können wir eine weitere Unterscheidung vornehmen:

- Bedingungen, die zwar nicht das direkt angesprochene Datenmaterial einbeziehen, aber vom übrigen Inhalt der Datenbank abhängen: kontextabhängige Bedingungen im engeren Sinn
- Bedingungen, in deren Formulierung der Inhalt der Datenbank nicht eingeht: kontextabhängige Bedingungen im weiteren Sinn.

Ein Beispiel für die erste Art ergibt sich, wenn man die Bearbeitung eines Personalsatzes durch einen Angestellten nur dann gestatten will, wenn dessen eigener Personalsatz im Feld FUNKTION eine genügend hohe Stufe in der Hierarchie des Betriebes anzeigt. Kontextabhängige Bedingungen im weiteren Sinn sind alle Beschränkungen des Zugriffs auf gewisse Zeiträume innerhalb von Wochentagen oder auf Datumsintervalle.

4. Zugriffsmatrizen

4.1 Die primäre Zugriffsmatrix

Für die Zugriffssicherung muß zu jeder Datenbank mit geschützten Daten eine Zugriffssicherungsdatei aufgebaut werden. In dieser sind für jeden zugelassenen Benutzer der Datenbank die Zugriffsrechte eingetragen. Man kann sich die Zuordnung von Zugriffsrechten zu Benutzern am besten in Form einer Matrix veranschaulichen:

	Datenbank		Bereich 1		...	Satz 1		...	Feld 1	
	ZA1	...	ZA1	...		ZA1	...		ZA1	...
Benutzer 1										
.	Die Elemente der Zugriffsmatrix zeigen an, ob der Benutzer das angegebene Objekt mit der jeweiligen Zugriffsart ansprechen darf oder nicht, wobei eventuell auf Zugriffsbedingungen verwiesen wird.									
.										
.										
Benutzer m										

ZA: Zugriffsart (Aktion)

Diese Matrix besitzt für die Implementierung zwei große Nachteile:

(1) sie ist im allgemeinen äußerst umfangreich
(2) ihre Größe und ihr Inhalt sind wegen der Abhängigkeit vom aktuellen Inhalt der Datenbank einem raschen Wechsel unterworfen, so daß die Verwaltung dieser Zugriffsmatrix ein extrem schwieriges Problem darstellt.

Für eine Implementierung müssen wir diese Probleme verringern, ohne wichtige Möglichkeiten der Zugriffssicherung einzubüßen.

4.2 Reduktion der Zugriffsmatrix

Die Reduktion kann in Zeilen- und Spaltenrichtung erfolgen. Gleiche Zeilen in der Zugriffsmatrix gehören zu Benutzern mit identischen Zugriffsrechten. Diese werden zu Benutzerkategorien zusammengefaßt.

In Spaltenrichtung wird ein Übergang von Feldern und Sätzen zu Feldtypen und Satztypen vollzogen. Durch diesen Schritt wird die systembelastende Dynamik der Zugriffsmatrix weitgehend vermieden, da nun die Spaltenzahl nur mehr von der Struktur der Datenbank und nicht mehr von derem aktuellen Inhalt abhängt. Vom Feld- und Satztyp aus kann eine Verfeinerung der Zugriffsrechte mit Hilfe der Zugriffsbedingungen erfolgen, mit denen dann auch einzelne Felder erfaßt werden können.

5. Benutzeridentifizierung

In der Zugriffsmatrix sind die Zugriffsrechte der Benutzerkategorien festgelegt. Neben der Zugriffsmatrix muß die Zugriffssicherungsdatei auch eine Liste der zulässigen Benutzer enthalten, in der für jeden dieser Benutzer angegeben ist, unter welcher Kategorie (bzw. unter welchen Kategorien) er auf die Datenbank zugreifen darf. Bei der Aufnahme der Arbeit mit der Datenbank muß nun sichergestellt werden, daß der aktuelle Benutzer wirklich - wie er vorgibt! - mit dem registrierten Benutzer identisch ist. Dies ist das große Problem der Benutzeridentifizierung. Eine sichere Lösung kann hier nur durch das Zusammenwirken von organisatorischen Maßnahmen, Hardware-Einrichtungen und Software erreicht werden. Das Prinzip der Benutzeridentifizierung mit Hilfe von Software ist der Vergleich gespeicherter "Benutzermerkmale" mit aktuell eingegebenen, wobei die verschiedensten Verfahren denkbar sind. Hier sollen die implementierten Verfahren kurz dargestellt werden:

- einfaches Paßwort
- Paßwortauswahl: Für den Benutzer ist ein Paßwortsatz (Liste von Paßwörtern) und eine Zahl r gespeichert. Bei der Identifizierung muß der Benutzer Paßwörter eingeben, die er durch Anwendung bestimmter Algorithmen auf die Zahl r aus dem Paßwortsatz auswählt. Sind die eingegebenen mit den vom Zugriffssicherungssystem errechneten Paßwörtern identisch, so wird die Identifizierung als gelungen angesehen und ein neuer Wert für r zwischen Rechner und Benutzer vereinbart.
- Buchstabenauswahl: Es liegt der gleiche Paßwortsatz wie oben zu Grunde. Ausgehend von einer Zahl r und unter Kenntnis bestimmter Algorithmen müssen aus Einzelbuchstaben des Paßwortsatzes neue Paßwörter gebildet werden. Auch hier wird nach gelungener Identifizierung der Wert von r geändert.
- Frage-Antwort-Verfahren (speziell für den Dialogbetrieb): Für den Benutzer sind Fragen und zugehörige Antworten (n Paßwortpaare) gespeichert. Bei der Identifizierung werden dem Benutzer Fragen gestellt, die nach einem Zufallsverfahren aus den gespeicherten Fragen ausgewählt werden. Nach erfolgreicher Identifizierung wird vom Benutzer ein neues Frage-Antwort-Paar eingegeben.

Die Auswahl des jeweiligen Verfahrens ist dabei kategoriespezifisch, kann also dem Berechtigungsumfang angepaßt werden.

6. Erfahrungen aus der Implementierung

6.1 Problematik des nachträglichen Einbaus eines Zugriffssicherungssystem in ein bestehendes Datenbanksystem

Zur Gewinnung praktischer Erfahrungen wurde im RZO für das Datenbanksystem DBS 440 (vgl.[7]) ein Kontrollmechanismus implementiert, wobei jedoch weitgehende Unabhängigkeit vom verwendeten Rechner- und Datenbanksystem angestrebt wurde. Es zeigte sich, daß beim nachträglichen Einbau eines Zugriffssicherungssystems in ein Datenbanksystem folgende Probleme auftreten:

- Unterbringung der Zugriffssicherungsdatei
- Ansprung der Prozedur zur Benutzeridentifizierung und Berücksichtigung des Ergebnisses durch das Datenbank-Management-System
- Ansprung und richtige Versorgung der Zugriffskontroll-Prozedur zur dynamischen Überprüfung der Zugriffe (z.B. Zugang zu Datenpuffern für die Abprüfung inhaltsabhängiger Bedingungen)
- Ersatz der bei DBS 440 fehlenden Befehle für den lesenden Zugriff auf einzelne Felder durch das Löschen solcher Felder, auf die der anfragende Benutzer keine Zugriffsberechtigung hat
- Schutz des Programmkomplexes gegenüber den Benutzerprogrammen
- Übernahme der von der Zugriffssicherungsprozedur aufgezeichneten Journalinformation

6.2 Der entwickelte Programmkomplex

Die erstellten Programme können in drei Klassen eingeteilt werden:
- Programme für die Verwaltung der Zugriffssicherungsdatei
- Programme für die aktuelle Überprüfung der Zugriffsberechtigungen
- Programme zur Auswertung der Journaldaten

Im einzelnen ergaben sich folgende Programme:

Verwaltungsprogramme (FORTRAN): Aufbau und Verwaltung der Information für die Benutzeridentifizierung - Aufbau und Verwaltung der Zugriffsmatrix

Kontrollprogramme (FORTRAN, BCPL): Programm für die Benutzeridentifizierung - Prozedur für die dynamische Abprüfung der Zugriffe (bisheriger Ausbaustand: Zugriffssicherung auf Satztypebene unter Einbeziehung kontextabhängiger Bedingungen im weiteren Sinn)

<u>Journalprogramme (FORTRAN)</u>: Programme für die Auswertung der bei der Benutzeridentifizierung anfallenden Journaldaten

Den Einsatz der Kontrollprogramme bei der Benutzung einer Datenbank zeigt Bild 1.

6.3 Zeitmessungen

An den implementierten Kontrollprogrammen und am DBS-Prozessor wurden umfangreiche Zeitmessungen angestellt. Da die Messungen von sehr vielen Parametern abhängen (insbesondere natürlich vom verwendeten Rechner, dem Datenbanksystem, von den benutzten Programmiersprachen, von der ersten und zweiten Strukturebene der verwendeten konkreten Datenbanken, u.a.), können die hier angegebenen Werte nur als Richtwerte angesehen werden. Da nur höhere Programmiersprachen verwendet wurden, dürften die bei den Kontrollprogrammen erzielten Meßwerte relativ grobe obere Schranken des Erreichbaren sein.

<u>Zeiten für die Benutzeridentifizierung:</u>

    Rechnerkernzeit: 1 sec
    Verweilzeit im Dialog: 1.5 min

<u>Zeiten für die Überprüfung eines Zugriffs auf die Datenbank:</u>

    ohne Bedingungen: 1 msec
    mit Bedingungen: 1 - 3 msec

<u>Vergleichszeiten für die Erledigung eines Auftrags an den DBS-Prozessor:</u>

    lesende Zugriffe: Mittelwerte der einzelnen Befehle zwischen 1 und 1.5 msec;

    schreibende Zugriffe: Mittelwerte zwischen 0.5 und 74 msec (beim Befehl SPEICH (Einspeichern neuer Repräsentanten von Satztypen) beträgt die gemessene Spanne 0.5 bis 400 msec mit Mittelwert bei 74 msec).

Literatur:

1. Saltzer, J.H.; Schroeder, M.D.: "A Hardware Architecture for Implementing Protection Rings" CACM Vol. 15, Nr. 3 1972

2. Bransted, D.K.: "Privacy and Protection in Operating Systems" National Security Agency, 1972

3. Weissman, C.: "System Security Analysis / Certification Methodology and Results" System Development Corporation, Santa Monica, Cal., Report SP-3728, 8. Oktober 1973

4. Weissman, C.: "Security Controls in the ADEPT-50 time-sharing system" FJCC 1969

5. Hoffman, L.J.: "The formulary model for flexible privacy and access controls" FJCC 1971

6. Conway, R.W., Maxwell, W.L., Morgan, H.L.: "On the Implementation of Security Measures in Information Systems" CACM April 1972

7. DBS 440 - Benutzerbeschreibung, Telefunken Computer GmbH

8. CODASYL, Data Base Task Group, April 71 Report

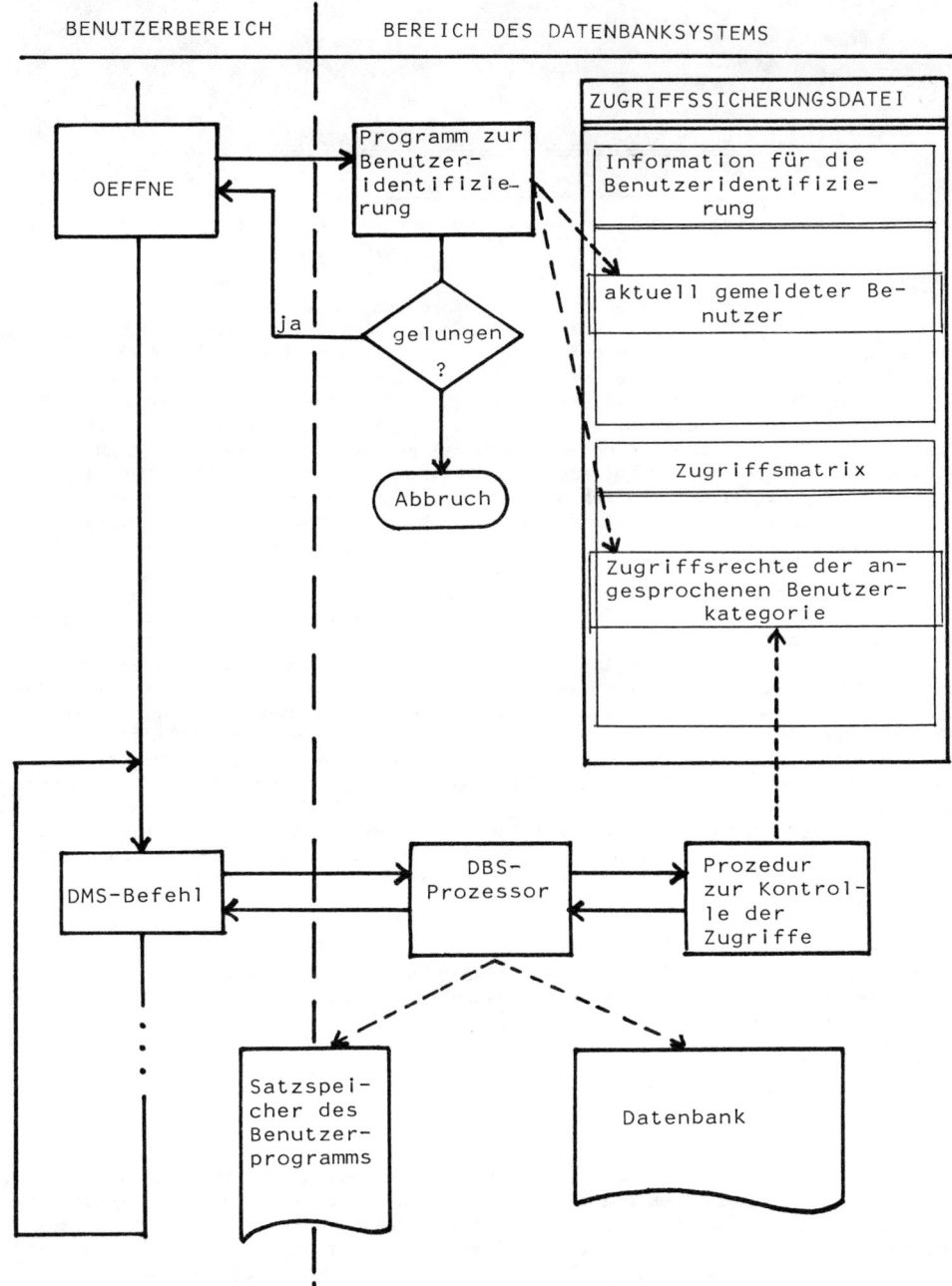

Bild 1: Einsatz der Kontrollprogramme bei der Benutzung einer Datenbank (mit dem DMS-Befehl OEFFNE wird bei DBS 440 die Arbeit mit einer bestimmten Datenbank eröffnet)

A QUERY LANGUAGE FOR A RELATIONAL DATA BASE

A. PIROTTE and P. WODON

MBLE Research Laboratory, 2 av. Van Becelaere, 1170 Brussels, Belgium.

0. Introduction

This paper is short description of two components of a question-answering system: a logical data structure for a data base and a formal query language. Both components must be understood by a user before he can request information from the system. Together, they define a formal model of an existing or supposed part of the world.

Any formal model has a structure for which many choices are to be made. All of them share the impossibility of capturing all the shades of reality. What can be done, however, is to try to make the model as natural as possible. Although a vague concept, "naturalness" is the first requirement for the model. It certainly implies simplicity (and, of course, independence from any detail of implementation).

Another requirement is independence from subject matter : the same logical structure for the data and semantic structures for the language should be usable whatever the subject matter.

For the logical data structures, a version of relational model[2] was chosen. It is indeed simple and subject independent. A careful choice of the relation forms makes it rather natural as well.

The semantics of the query language is designed to match as closely as possible what is known of the semantics of sensible questions expressed in natural languages. This leads to a non procedural language which shields its users from any consideration below the relational data structure. The various choices were made with two, in the long run possibly conflicting, aims : make the language easy to use by non-programmers, and make it a good target for ultimately translating questions expressed in "natural" language.

As it is now, the query language is not yet addressed to "casual users", i.e. users who are both non-programmers and infrequent. Too many details, mainly syntactic, are still to be remembered. The language presented here is only a step towards casual users.

1. Data base logical structure

Information to be entered into a data base is made of descriptions of events, situations, facts, properties, etc. For example, "company XYZ bought a MIX3 computer in 1973" , or "MIX3 computers have 5-bytes words".

Such pieces of information concern distinguishable entities which are in some relationship with one another. The information model formalizes just that : it is made of items representing distinct entities and of relations between sets of items, representing situations, facts, events, properties, etc. involving entities.

1.1. Items and classes.

In the model, "items" represent the entities (objects, concepts, etc ...) which must be distinguishable from one another. This should be understood in the context of a particular application. A data base is an arbitrary sketch of a part of real life designed for a specific purpose, and deciding which entities are distinct is a design decision. For example, if the subject matter is computing machinery, one may want to distinguish each physical computer installation and each cpu model, but not each installed cpu.

Not all the real world entities which are to be modelled have the same set of properties. For this reason, items are grouped into "classes" and each item belongs to exactly one class. Nested classes might be useful but they are not considered in this paper. Entities modelled by items of a given class share similar properties. For example, cpu models would belong to one class and configurations to another.

Throught this paper, a simple information system will be used in the examples.

Classes for this system are listed in Table 1.

Class identifier	Entities represented.
cpu	catalogued cpu models
conf	physical computer configurations
lgge	programming languages
opsys	operating systems
propcat	property categories (owns,rents,etc.)
date	dates
comp	companies
country	countries

Table 1.

1.2. Relations

Entities of the real world have properties and are related to other entities, by situations, facts, events, properties etc. This is modelled by "relations".

For example, companies may use computer installations. This can be modelled by a relation "use (x,y)" where x and y represent items of classes "comp" (companies) and "conf" (configurations), respectively. If company A uses configuration B, then the pair (A,B) belongs to relation "use". Thus a relation is a set of n-tuples, or tuples.

A relation is not a function : a company may use several computers and a computer may be shared by several companies.

Precisely, a relation is a subset of an indexed Cartesian product of classes:
use $\subset i_1$: comp $\times i_2$: conf
or, in general,
$R \subset i_1 : C_1 \times i_2 : C_2 \times ... \times i_n : C_n$
The pairs $i_j : C_j$ are the "domains" of the relation R. They are constituted of an index i_j and a class C_j. The same class may appear in several domains which are then distinguished by the index. Very often, such an index is called an attribute.

Such relations are in first normal form [4].

The user of a question answering system, however, should not look at relations in that mathematical fashion. He should know, for example, that "some companies make cpu's", not necessarily that "makecpu $\subset$ comp X cpu".

Relation name	Attributes of domains	Intended meaning
cpuconf	(cpu, conf)	cpu model of configuration
implunder	(lgge, conf, opsys)	language implemented on configuration under operating system
usedunder	(conf, comp, propcat)	configuration used by company under property category
installed	(conf, date)	configuration installed on date
makecpu	(comp, cpu)	company makes cpu model
address	(comp, country)	company located in country

Table 2

Table 2 shows the relations in the example system. Domain attributes are represented here by the associated class identifiers.

Before writing down Tables 1 and 2, one has to decide which information the system will contain. This being done, it remains to distribute this information between classes and relations in a "natural" way, and more or less arbitrary decisions have to be made in that process. For example, the information contained in class "propcat" and relation "usedunder" could have been distributed otherwise, introducing as many binary relations like "company owns configuration", "company rents configuration", etc ..., as there are elements in class "propcat". This would be natural, since "propcat" presumably has very few elements and, more importantly, since the number of these elements is not likely to vary during the lifetime of the data base. It is conceivable but completely unnatural to apply the same treatment to e.g. class "conf" in the same relation.

In Table 2, most relations are binary. This is due, on the one hand, to the simplicity of the example and, on the other hand, to the decision that relations should model as closely as possible the simplest ways in which users relate entities in the universe. This leads to relations with the smallest number of domains compatible with the information to be described. For example, which cpu model a configuration has is independent of its date of installation. Hence, these pieces of information are represented by two binary relations, "cpuconf" and "installed" instead of a ternary relation with domains : "cpu", "conf", "date" which might represent the same information.

It is not possible in general, however, to use only unary and binary relations without introducing unnatural classes.

Relations are used to represent any kind of relationship between entities. Whether these relationships are facts, events, hierarchies, etc. is not relevant within the formal model. In other words, it is left to the user to interpret a given relation as modelling a situation, or a hierarchy, or any other kind of actual relationship.

1.3 Basic operations on relations.

A few more notations will now be convenient. Letters, with subscripts when needed, will be used as follows : R for a relation ; C for a class ; x for an attribute ; a for a constant, i.e. a given item belonging to a particular class ; Γ for a compound class, i.e. a Cartesian product of classes ; X for a compound attribute, i.e. a tuple of attributes ; A for a compound constant.

A relation R will be denoted equivalently as e.g. R, R(X), $R(X_1, X_2)$, $R(x_1,...,x_n)$ with the automatic conventions that the compound class of X is $\Gamma(\Gamma_1$ and Γ_2 for X_1 and X_2) and the class of x_i is C_i.

In [5], several operations on relations are defined. They constitute an algebra which is itself a suitable collection of primitives for searching a relational data base. Of these operations only projection and natural join will be used here.

Projection.

Given a relation $R(X_1, X_2)$, the X_1-projection of R is a relation whose value is : $\{A_1 \mid A_1 \in \Gamma_1$ and $(\exists A_2) \in \Gamma_2$ such that $(A_1, A_2) \in R\}$

Natural join.

Given two relations $R_1(X_1, X_2)$ and $R_2(X_1, X_3)$ with a common (compound) domain X_1, the natural join of R_1 and R_2 is a relation $R_3(X_1, X_2, X_3)$ whose value is : $\{(A_1, A_2, A_3) \mid (A_1, A_2, A_3) \in \Gamma_1 \times \Gamma_2 \times \Gamma_3$ and $(A_1, A_2) \in R_1$ and $(A_1, A_3) \in R_2\}$

If the X_1-projections of R_1 and R_2 are equal, then R_1 and R_2 are joinable without loss of information, in the sense that R_1 and R_2 are projections of R_3.

If X_1 is empty, then the join $R_3(X_2, X_3)$ is the Cartesian product of the X_2-projection of R_1 and the X_3-projection of R_2.

The natural join is associative and commutative.

1.4. Minimal normal form.

We have insisted on having the simplest and most natural relations. Thus, the following two properties will be required:
(1) no relation can be decomposed into relations containing the same information as the parent relation ;
(2) the data base must be non-redundant : it may not contain a relation which can be obtained from other relations as a value for a query addressed to the data base.

Condition (2) is clear enough, although it can be described precisely only after a query language like that of section 2 has been defined.

Condition (1) requires further explanation. A relation $R(X_1, X_2, X_3)$ can be replaced without loss of information by its (X_1, X_2) and (X_1, X_3)-projections if the natural join of the projections is the relation R itself. Condition (1) demands that such a replacement be performed whenever possible. An example was given in section 1.2 : the cpu model of a configuration is independent of its date of installation. A user should not be forced to deal with both informations when he needs only one.
A single relation is said to be in minimal form if it verifies condition (1) above. Relations in minimal form enjoy interesting properties, two of which are given here

without proof.

Property 1: in most cases, a relation in minimal form has only one candidate key [4].
Property 2: a relation in minimal form is in third normal form [4].
    The converse of both properties is not true in general.

2. Query language.

   This section presents a formal query language (FQL for short) for requesting information from a data base structured as described in Section 1.
   Criteria for the design of FQL are :
(a) <u>completeness</u> : the language is complete if it can express any query whose answer can be "semantically deduced" from information contained in a data base. Proving anything about completeness requires a formal model of the information contents of a data base to be built on top of the logical data structure definition. In [5] a relational algebra is proposed for measuring the information contents of a relational data base : a query facility is complete if every operation of the relational algebra can be defined in it. It can be easily shown that FQL fulfils this condition;
(b) <u>naturalness</u> : this is a subjective criterion meaning that the semantics of the language constructs should be close to that of queries expressed in natural language. At this stage, little attention was paid to obtain a natural syntax ;
(c) <u>subject independence</u> : the language should fit the model of Section 1 but not a particular data base ;
(d) <u>nonsense filtering</u> : nonsense queries and queries which do not make much sense should not be expressible in the language.

2.1 <u>Closed questions, predicates, and relations</u>.

   Questions can be classified into open and closed ones [7]. Open questions, for example "What do you know about computers?", have no clear-cut answer. With respect to a data base, the only complete answer is a dump of all data. Open questions are therefore excluded from the language.
   On the contrary, closed questions have clear and, given a data base, unique answers. For example, "Does XYZ make computers?", "Are all the computers used by ABC made in the USA?", "What are the cpu models made by XYZ?", are closed questions. The first two are "yes-no" questions, the third one a "list" question : its answer is a list of appropriate cpu models.
   A yes-no question can be seen as a predicate with a truth value [7] : "does a value A satisfy a predicate P?" or "do all values A that satisfy P also satisfy Q?". In terms of relations, this becomes : "does a tuple A belong to relation R?" or "do all tuples A that belong to R_1 also belong to R_2?".
   A list question can be seen as a predicate with free variables : "What are the values X that satisfy P(X)?". In terms of relations, it becomes : "What are the tuples that belong to R?".
   These observations link this language outlined in Section 2 with the data structure presented in Section 1. The predicates to be verified, i.e. the questions, will be FQL expressions constructed according to certain rules. Associated to these rules are operations on relations which will construct, from the relations in the data base, a new relation answering the question.

2.2 <u>Basic notions</u>.

   FQL expressions are built from predicate names, functions, constants, variables, quantifiers, and operators. For example, the question
(Q1) Which languages are implemented on the computers used by Aro?
becomes, in FQL,
   <u>take all</u> (x) <u>st</u> *implunder* (x, conf,*) <u>and</u> *used under* (conf,"Aro",*) <u>end</u>
In that, *makecpu* is a predicate name, "Aro" a constant, x and *conf* variables, *all* a quantifier, *take* ... *st* and *and* operators, and * an "irrelevant variable".

<u>Types</u> To each class in the data base, there corresponds a type for constants and variables. Types are used to control well-formedness.

<u>Constants</u> A constant is the name of an item. It has a unique value, the named item, and a unique type, that of the class of the item. In this paper, constants appear between quotation marks: *"Aro"*.

Variables Variables, written as Algol identifiers, have a unique type and represent
sets of possible values of the corresponding class. They are used to indicate how
expressions must be evaluated and to control their well-formedness. When a variable is only used for well-formedness, it is called "irrelevant", and represented
by a star.

Model predicates Model predicates are the simplest expressions of the language.
They consist of a predicate name and a list of arguments. For example, *make cpu*
("Philips",x) is a model predicate.

The predicate name names a data base relation (In what follows, the relation
names in Table 2 are used as predicate names). The arguments are variables, constants, or irrelevant variables. For well-formedness, there must be as many arguments as there are domains in the relation, and the type of each argument must be
the type of the corresponding domain. (In this paper, the correspondence is indicated by the order of the arguments, although this is undesirable in practice).
Thus *make cpu ("Philips",x)* is well formed if *"Philips"* is a constant of type *comp*
and x a variable of type *cpu*. (Since a variable like x is not declared, it is the
context which gives it a type, and it must have the same type in all its occurrences).

The value of a model predicate is either a truth-value, when no argument is
a variable, or a relation when there are variables. The values of *make cpu ("Philips",*
"P1000") is 'true' if the relation *make cpu* contains the pair *("Philips", P1000")*
'false' otherwise. The value of *make cpu (Philips",x)* is the set of all constants
"A" such that *("Philips","A")* belongs to the relation *make cpu*.

In short, let *predname(X_1,A_2, -)* be a model predicate, where X_1 represents
the string of variables, A_2 the string of constants, - the string of irrelevant
variables. Let $R(X_1,X_2,X_3)$ be the named relation.
The value of *predname* X_1 instead of A_1 ,A_2, -) is
$\{A_1 \mid \exists A_3 : (A_1,A_2,A_3) \in R\}$
This is a set of tuples, i.e. a relation. If X_1 is empty (no variables), this becomes
$\exists A_3 : (A_2,A_3) \in R$.
Examples :
   implunder ("ALGOL", conf, opsys), produces a set of pairs *(conf,opsys)*, representing the configurations and operating systems on which ALGOL is implemented,
   implunder ("ALGOL",$*$,opsys)
produces only the operating systems.

2.3 FQL expressions.

A complete descriptions of FQL cannot be given here. This section illustrates,
mainly with examples, important constructs.

2.3.1. Predicates.

Several FQL expressions are "predicates". They have a relational value, where
domains are specified by variables, the variable types corresponding to the domain
classes. Model predicates are the simplest form of predicates. A conjunction is
another form.

2.3.2 Conjunctions.

Example Q1 contains an example of conjunction :
   implunder (x,conf,$*$) and usedunder (conf, "Aro", $*$)
The condition for well-formedness is that the conjunction be "connected". In this
simple example, this reduces to the condition that at least one variable be common
to both conjuncts. In general, when there are several conjuncts, the condition means
that it must be possible starting from any conjunct to reach all the others, a transition from one conjunct to another being possible if both contain a common variable.

This well-formedness rule is a "nonsense filter" : predicates connected by *and*
should be about a common subject.
The value of the above example is
   $\{(a_1,a_2) \mid (a_1,a_2) \in R_1 \text{ and } a_2 \in R_2\}$
where R_1 is the value of *implunder (x,conf,$*$)* and R_2 the value of *usedunder (conf,*
"Aro", $*$).

This value is the natural join of the relational values of the conjuncts, where variables play the role of domain attributes. When conjuncts are more complex and when conjunctions have more than two conjuncts, the value remains a natural join of the relational values of all conjuncts.

Disjunction is defined in a similar fashion.

Other forms of predicates are presented after the discussion of "queries".

2.3.3 Queries.

A query is the FQL form of a closed question. Roughly a query is a predicate plus, in the case of a list question, a specification of the variables of interest.

List queries, an example of which is Q1, have the form

<list> : <u>take all</u> (X_1) <u>st</u> <predicate (X_1, X_2)> <u>end</u>

If $R(X_1, X_2)$ is the value of the predicate, the value of the list query is given by
$\{A_1 \mid \exists A_2 : (A_1, A_2) \in R\}$

This is the X_1-projection of R. In Q1, only the languages are requested : the configurations have to be projected out.

The well-formedness rule for the list query is that the variables following <u>take all</u> occur in the predicate. Again, this acts as a nonsense filter.

More generally, <u>all</u> can be replaced by a positive integer, which requests only the corresponding number of elements from the X_1-projection of R.

Yes-no queries have two forms. The simplest one is

<yes-no> : <model predicate $(A, -)$>

i.e. a model predicate without variables. Its value is that of the model predicate, as defined in 2.2.

The other form of yes-no question is illustrated by
Q2 : "Are all the cpu models made by XYZ used in the USA?"
In FQL :
  <u>for</u> all(c) <u>st</u> make cpu ("XYZ", c)
      <u>holds</u> usedunder (conf,comp,*) <u>and</u> address (comp, "USA")
          <u>and</u> cpuconf(c,conf) <u>end</u>

The general form is
  <u>for</u> all (X_1) <u>st</u> <predicate$_1 (X_1, X_2)$> <u>holds</u> <predicate$_2 (X_1, X_3)$> <u>end</u>

Its value is 'true' if the X_1-projection of the value of predicate$_1$ is included in the X_1-projection of the value of predicate$_2$. In the case, however, where the first projection is empty (no X_1 verifies predicate$_1$), it is meaningless to give a 'true' (yes) answer. (In Q2, XYZ does not make computers'). In that case, the answer "abolishes the presupposition" [7] : "XYZ is not a maker of cpu's!"

2.3.4 Verification predicates.

Question Q2 can be generalized into Q3 : "What are the companies for which all the cpu models they make are used in the USA?"
In FQL, this becomes
  <u>take</u> all (comp) <u>st</u>
      <u>for</u> all(c) <u>st</u> make cpu (comp,c)
          <u>holds</u> usedunder (conf,firm,*) <u>and</u> address(firm,"USA")
              <u>and</u> cpuconf(c,conf)<u>end end</u>

The difference is that, within the <u>for</u> expression, the constant "XYZ" has been replaced by the variable comp , specified in <u>take all</u>(comp).

The <u>for</u> expression, in that case, is a "verification predicate" whose value is the set of tuples that verify it.

It can be shown that the operation of division introduced in [5] and the extensional quantifiers of [8] are particular forms of verification predicates.

A general definition and the properties of the verification cannot be given here. A few examples will illustrated its use.

Q4 : "List the companies which make all the cpu models they use".

  <u>take</u> all (comp)<u>st</u>
      <u>for</u> all (cpu) <u>st</u> usedunder(conf,comp,*) <u>and</u> cpuconf(cpu,conf)
          <u>holds</u> make cpu(comp,cpu) <u>end end</u>

Q5 : "Give the configurations which have one language common to all their systems."

<u>take</u> all(conf) <u>st</u>
  implunder(lang,conf,*) <u>and</u>
  <u>for</u> all(s) <u>st</u> implunder (*,conf,s)
    <u>holds</u> implunder(lang,conf,s) <u>end</u> <u>end</u>

2.3.5 Negation

Negation applied to a predicate produces the complement of a relation. The value of <u>not</u> predicate (X) is $\{A \mid A \in \Gamma \text{ and } A \notin R\}$, where R is the value of predicate (X) and Γ its compound domain.

Q7 : "List cpu manufacturers all of whose cpu models are used outside of the USA".

<u>take</u> <u>all</u> (comp) <u>st</u>
  make cpu(comp,*)
  <u>and</u> <u>for</u> <u>all</u> (cpu) <u>st</u> makecpu(comp,cpu)
    <u>holds</u> usedunder(conf, acomp,*) <u>and</u> cpuconf (cpu,conf)
    <u>and</u> <u>not</u> address (acomp, "<u>USA</u>") <u>end</u> <u>end</u>

The negated predicate <u>not</u> address(acomp, "USA") produces a set of companies A such that ("A", "USA") does not belong to address. These companies either have an address which is not "USA" or are not reported to have an address. Let us suppose that the latter possibility does not occur for relation address, but, in general, this behaviour of negation entails interesting properties of negated predicates and the action of negation on every kind of predicate has to be investigated. Results are not reported here.

2.3.6 Functions.

Functions include sums, counts, averages, etc. They fit rather well in the FQL predicate mechanism.

Q8. "Give, for each cpu model, the manufacturer of the model and the number of configurations having that cpu model".

<u>take</u> all (manuf,cpu,nb)<u>st</u>
  make cpu(manuf,cpu)
  <u>and</u> <u>let</u> nb = <u>count</u> (conf)<u>in</u>
    usedunder (conf,*,*)
    <u>and</u> cpuconf(cpu,conf) <u>end</u> <u>end</u>

In this example, variable nb gets typed and is made available by the <u>count</u> predicate, and, for other FQL constructs, it behaves like other variables.

3. Overview.
3.1 Data structure.

The two major characteristics of the data structure outlined in this paper are its simplicity and its naturalness. Simplicity is aimed at by the minimal form : associating items in a relation always models a genuine elementary association of entities in the universe. Naturalness is approached by defining classes as representations of sets of meaningful "observable" entities. Elements of relations are not representations of entities : they only describe links between entities.

This distinction between entity and links between entities is not always very clear in data base systems. Traditionally, records are used to describe relations but also to describe complex entities in terms of elementary items, themselves defined as strings or integers. The latter usage of records often entails the definition of artificial keys (such as for example the code number of a configuration) whose purpose is to ensure uniqueness of the complex entity but which are meaningless for a casual user. These extra items really belong to implementation considerations, and a user need only know for example that configurations have a cpu, that they have a date of installation, etc... without bothering about how each configuration will practically be represented and differentiated from other configurations.

Thus, the present model frees the users from interfering with characteristics of entities which are not explicitly needed in a partial reference to the data base. This has not always been the case in other formulations of the relational model.

Finally, it should be obvious, although the matter is not dealt with in this paper, that minimal form entails a minimum interaction of insertion and deletion of tuples, creation and deletion of relations with the current set of relations and with a set of currently existing queries.

On the other hand, it can be argued that minimal form forces users to refer to many small relations when formulating queries of some complexity. A classical solution consists here in defining a library of derived, redundant relations which take care of frequent cross-referencing between basic relations.

3.2. Query language.

FQL requires relations to be only in first normal form, and not necessarily in minimal form, and it can thus be effectively compared with other query languages for relations in first normal form.

In [6], several types of query languages are compared, which are called element-by-element, mapping oriented, relational calculus, algebraic and natural language.

FQL definitely has a flavor of predicate calculus with predicates, functions, variables, quantifiers and usual connectives. But the similarity is often superficial. FQL also has a flavor of relational algebra : predicates produce relation values, and the various constructs combine predicates in ways that strongly suggest operations of a relational algebra. Primitives in FQL were also chosen to match the semantics of important constructs in natural languages.

The number of primitive concepts and operations in FQL was kept to a strict minimum, and a complete syntactic and semantic definition is very short. Central to FQL design is the concept of predicate, which can take several different forms, and is used to define most FQL constructs in a recursive manner. Simple queries in natural language remain simple in FQL, but the set of primitives is the same for all queries regardless of their complexity. For example, variables are always present, unlike, for example, in SQUARE [1] where they can be dispensed with in the simplest queries. Completely absent from FQL are the undesirable "linking terms" of the ALPHA language [3]. Linking in FQL is implicit trough two or more occurrences of the same variable.

As it is, FQL requires a (reasonable) amount of training, but our contention is that some training effort will always be required of the users of a data base system, whatever the query language. In particular, a successful natural language capability will require from the users at least a deep knowledge of the universe of discourse and maybe familiarity with an interactive facility.

References

[1] Boyce R. F., Chamberlin D. D., King W. F., Hammer M. M., Specifying queries as relational expressions : SQUARE, IBM San Jose Report RJ 1291, October 1973.

[2] Codd E. F., A relational model of data for large shared data banks, Comm. ACM June 1970.

[3] Codd E. F., A data base sublanguage founded on the relationalcalculus, 1971 ACM-SIGFIDET workshop on data description, access and control, November 1971.

[4] Codd E. F., Further normalization of the data base relational model, in : Data Base Systems, Rustin Editor, Prentice-Hall 1972.

[5] Codd E. F., Relational completeness of data base sublanguages, in : Data Base Systems, Rustin Editor, Prentice-Hall 1972.

[6] Codd E. F., Recent investigations in relational data base systems, IFIP congress 1974, Stockholm.

[7] Janta-Polczynski M., Dialectics of questions and answers, MBLE Report R265, September 1974.

[8] Kuhns J. L., Quantification in query systems, Proc. ACM Symposium on information storage and retrieval, April 1971.

Konzept des Objektbeschreibungsbaums als Grundstruktur eines graphenorientierten Datenbankmodells

Arno Dörrscheidt
Technische Universität Berlin

1. Problemstellung

Datenbanksysteme sollen einer Mehrzahl von Benutzern Operationen auf einer Beschreibung eines Teilbereichs der realen Welt erlauben.

Die wichtigsten heute diskutierten Datenbankmodelle von CODD (Relationenmodell, /2/), CODASYL/DBTG (Record-Schema-Konzept, /1/) und FELDMAN/ROVNER (LEAP: ALGOL-Erweiterung für assoziative Speicherverwaltung, /5/) unterscheiden sich wesentlich durch die Datenstrukturen, die sie zur Beschreibung von Ausschnitten der realen Welt zulassen.

Wir wollen zunächst diese Unterschiede herausarbeiten und dann als Alternative zu den drei Modellen ein "graphenorientiertes Datenbankmodell" /4/ vorschlagen, dessen Grunddatenstruktur wir als Objektbeschreibungsbaum bezeichnen.

2. Datenstrukturen zur Beschreibung von Ausschnitten der realen Welt

Wir betrachten die reale Welt als eine Menge von Objekten zwischen denen Relationen bestehen. Als Objekte fassen wir alle Dinge auf, über die wir reden wollen. Objekte können konkret oder abstrakt sein. Beispiele für konkrete Objekte sind: ein Mensch, ein Haus, eine Maschine etc., Beispiele für abstrakte Objekte sind: ein Begriff, eine Zahl, eine Rechtsnorm, ein Algorithmus etc.

Wir unterscheiden außerdem atomare Objekte, - d.h. solche, die wir in einem bestimmten Zusammenhang als Ganzheiten auffassen wollen - und komplexe Objekte, die aus atomaren Objekten nach bestimmten Konstruktionsprinzipien zusammengesetzt sind. Beispiele für atomare Objekte: ein Mensch, ein Haus, ein Begriff, Beispiele für komplexe Objekte: eine Menge von Menschen, eine Häuserzeile, eine Begriffshierarchie, eine Warteschlange von Schiffen.

Ehe wir über atomare Objekte reden können, müssen wir sie mit eindeutigen Namen kennzeichnen. Beispiele: M100, 25, EHRE, §218StGB, SINUS. Haben wir das getan, können wir die Namen der atomaren Objekte zu Symbolisierungen komplexer Objekte zusammensetzen.

Beispiele:

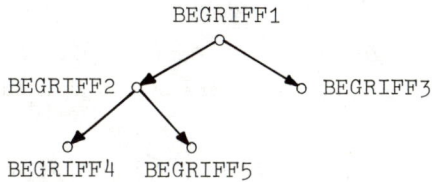

Relationen zwischen Objekten unterscheidet man üblicherweise

(1) nach der Stellenzahl in einstellige, zweistellige und n-stellige (n ⩾ 1) Relationen.

(2) danach, ob die Objekte atomar oder komplex sind in Relationen mit atomarem bzw. komplexen Definitionsbereichen.

In unserem Denken spielen offensichtlich zweistellige Relationen zwischen atomaren Objekten eine besondere Rolle, da wir über elementare Sachverhalte in der Form

"Subjekt" "Prädikat" "Objekt"

reden, wobei im einfachsten Fall sowohl das "Subjekt" als auch das "Objekt" atomare Objektsymbole sind.

Eine Datenstruktur, die auf zweistellige Relationen zwischen atomaren Objekten beschränkt ist, können wir definieren als ein Tripel

$$D = (O, R, \delta)$$

worin O eine Menge von atomaren Objektsymbolen, R eine Menge von Relationsnamen und δ eine dreistellige Relation

$$\delta \subset O \times R \times O$$

ist. (Vgl. hierzu MEALY /8/ und EHRICH /6/.)

D definiert einen gerichteten Graphen mit benannten Kanten. Die Tripel $(o_i, r_j, o_k) \in \delta$ sind die Kanten. Die Objektsymbole $o_i \in O$ sind die Anfangsknoten, die $o_k \in O$ die Endknoten und die $r_j \in R$ die Benennungen der Kanten.

Es gibt grundsätzlich drei Möglichkeiten zur Darstellung von δ:

(1) Man stellt δ als eine Menge von Tripeln (o_i, r_j, o_k) dar:

$$\delta_1 = \{(o_i, r_j, o_k) \mid (o_i, r_j, o_k) \in \delta\}$$

LEAP von FELDMAN/ROVNER benutzt solche Tripel als Grunddatenstruktur ("assoziative Tripel")

(2) Man faßt alle Tripel $(o_i, r_j, o_k) \in \delta$, die denselben Relationsnamen r_j enthalten, zusammen und stellt dann mit jedem Relationsnamen die Paarmenge

$$P_1(r_j) = \{(o_i, o_k) \mid (o_i, r_j, o_k) \in \delta\}$$

dar. Eine zweistellige Relation $\text{Rel}(r_j)$ wird dann angegeben als die Konkatenation des Relationsnamens mit der zugehörigen Menge $P_1(r_j)$:

$$\text{Rel}(r_j) = r_j \{(o_i, o_k) \mid (o_i, r_j, o_k) \in \delta\}$$

Die zweite Darstellungsart von δ ist dann die Menge aller $\text{Rel}(r_j)$

$$\delta_2 = \{\text{Rel}(r_j) \mid r_j \in R\}$$

Das ist - zunächst für zweistellige Relationen - die Grundstruktur des Relationenmodells von CODD.

(3) Wir stellen mit jedem Objektsymbol o_i die Paarmenge

$$P_2(o_i) = \{(r_j, o_k) \mid (o_i, r_j, o_k) \in \delta\}$$

dar. Die Konkatenation des Objektsymbols o_i mit $P_2(o_i)$ bezeichnen wir als Objektbeschreibung $B(o_i)$:

$$B(o_i) = o_i \{(r_j, o_k) \mid (o_i, r_j, o_k) \in \delta\}$$

δ_3 ist dann die Menge aller Objektbeschreibungen:

$$\delta_3 = \{B(o_i) \mid o_i \in O\}.$$

Diese Art der Darstellung entspricht einer Zerlegung des Graphen D in eine Menge von Bäumen, deren Wurzeln die Objektknoten o_i und deren Zweige die aus einem Objektknoten o_i herausweisenden Kanten sind. Wir sprechen deshalb auch von Objektbeschreibungsbäumen.

Das Record-Schema-Konzept der CODASYL/DBTG kann aus δ_3 entwickelt werden, indem man alle Objektbeschreibungen, die dieselben Relationsnamen r_j enthalten, als Sätze (records) eines bestimmten Typs auffaßt, die Relationsnamen zusammenfaßt als das "Schema" dieses Satztyps und dann mit jedem o_i nicht mehr die Paare (r_j, o_k), sondern nur noch die o_k in der durch das Schema vorgegebenen Reihenfolge als "record occurrence" darstellt.

Alle vier hier betrachteten Datenbankmodelle lassen die Darstellung von Elementarsachverhalten zu. Sie unterscheiden sich stark darin, wie sie komplexe Sachverhalte - d.h. Sachverhalte, die durch n-stellige Relationen zwischen komplexen Objekten gekennzeichnet sind - behandeln:

(1) In LEAP sind als komplexe Objekte lediglich "assoziative Tripel" zugelassen, n-stellige Relationen sind nicht darstellbar.

(2) CODD's Relationenmodell benutzt als Grundstruktur n-stellige Relationen, deren Definitionsbereiche aber nur atomare Objekte enthalten dürfen (simple domains). Relationen mit "non-simple Domains" werden durch "Normalisierung" in Relationen mit ausschließlich "simple domains" überführt. (vgl. /2/, /3/).

(3) Der CODASYL/DBTG-Vorschlag läßt als Elemente von Records neben atomaren Objekten (items) Vektoren und "Wiederholungsgruppen" (repeating groups) zu. Wiederholungsgruppen könnten aufgefaßt werden als n-stellige Relationen, die auch komplexe Definitionsbereiche - nämlich wieder Vektoren und Wiederholungsgruppen - enthalten dürfen.

(4) Wir benutzen als Grundstruktur Objektbeschreibungsbäume, d.h. atomare Objektsymbole o_i gefolgt von einer Menge von Paaren (r_j, o_k). Die Paare (r_j, o_k) bezeichnen wir als Merkmal-Ausprägungspaare und schreiben sie als (m,a).

Im Gegensatz zu CODD sind wir der Meinung, daß komplexe Objekte auch als solche dargestellt werden müssen. Wir lassen deshalb als Merkmalsausprägungen alle strukturierten Zusammenfassungen von Objektsymbolen zu, für die

(1) eine Syntax angebbar ist und
(2) "sinnvolle" Operationen definiert sind.

Als Konstruktionsprinzipien für komplexe Objekte kommen in erster Linie die bekannten Strukturkonzepte der Mathematik, der Logik und der Informatik in Frage. Wir betrachten also insbesondere Mengen, n-Tupel, n-stellige Relationen, Vektoren, Matrizen, Listen, Bäume, Netzwerke, Graphen, prädikatenlogische Ausdrücke und auch Programme als Merkmalsausprägungen. Außerdem lassen wir zu, daß Merkmalsausprägungen wieder (m,a)-Paare sind. Jeder Benutzer kann darüber hinaus eigene Datenstrukturen verwenden, sofern sie die Bedingungen (1) und (2) erfüllen.

3. Syntax des Objektbeschreibungsbaums

Wir beschreiben die möglichen Strukturen von Objektbeschreibungsbäumen durch eine etwas erweiterte BNF-Syntax.

Der auf das Wesentliche reduzierte Kern dieser Syntax ist in Abb.1 dargestellt. Darin sollen die Symbole ... und *** bedeuten, daß Null oder

(S1) ⟨objektbeschreibungsbaum⟩::=⟨grundobjekt⟩{⟨mapaar⟩...⟨mapaar⟩}
(S2) ⟨grundobjekt⟩ ::=⟨atomares symbol⟩|⟨ganze zahl⟩
(S3) ⟨mapaar⟩ ::=⟨m-name⟩ ⟨m-ausprägung⟩
(S4) ⟨m-name⟩ ::= ref⟨grundobjekt⟩
(S5) ⟨m-ausprägung⟩ ::= ref⟨ausprägung⟩
(S6) ⟨ausprägung⟩ ::=⟨atomare ausprägung⟩|⟨komplexe ausprägung⟩
(S7) ⟨atomare ausprägung⟩ ::=⟨grundobjekt⟩|⟨reelle zahl⟩
(S8) ⟨komplexe ausprägung⟩ ::=⟨menge⟩|
$\qquad\qquad\qquad$ ⟨ntupel⟩|
$\qquad\qquad\qquad$ ⟨relation⟩|
$\qquad\qquad\qquad$ ⟨mapaare⟩|
$\qquad\qquad\qquad$ ⟨vektor⟩|
$\qquad\qquad\qquad$ ⟨matrix⟩|
$\qquad\qquad\qquad$ ⟨liste⟩|
$\qquad\qquad\qquad$ ⟨binärbaum⟩|
$\qquad\qquad\qquad$ ⟨baum⟩
(S9) ⟨menge⟩ ::={⟨m-ausprägung⟩...⟨m-ausprägung⟩}
$\quad\subseteq A_i \qquad\qquad \in A_i \qquad\qquad \in A_i$
(S10) ⟨ntupel⟩ ::=(⟨m-ausprägung⟩$_1$***⟨m-ausprägung⟩$_n$)
$\quad \in A_1 \times A_2 \times ... \times A_n \qquad \in A_1 \qquad\qquad \in A_n$
(S11) ⟨relation⟩ ::={⟨ntupel⟩ ... ⟨ntupel⟩}
$\quad \subset A_1 \times A_2 \times ... \times A_n \quad \in A_1 \times A_2 \times ... \times A_n \quad \in A_1 \times A_2 \times ... \times A_n$
(S12) ⟨mapaare⟩ ::={⟨mapaar⟩...⟨mapaar⟩}
$\quad \subset M \times A \qquad\qquad \in M \times A \qquad \in M \times A$
(S13) ⟨vektor⟩ ::=(⟨m-ausprägung⟩$_1$***⟨m-ausprägung⟩$_n$)
$\quad \in A_i^n \qquad\qquad \in A_i \qquad\qquad \in A_i$
(S14) ⟨matrix⟩ ::=(⟨vektor⟩$_1$***⟨vektor⟩$_m$|
$\quad \in A_i^{n \cdot m} \qquad\qquad \in A_i^n \qquad \in A_i^n$
$\qquad\qquad$ (⟨matrix⟩$_1$***⟨matrix⟩$_m$)
$\qquad\qquad\quad \in A_i^n \qquad \in A_i^n$
(S15) ⟨liste⟩ ::=(⟨m-ausprägung⟩...⟨m-ausprägung⟩)
(S16) ⟨binärbaum⟩ ::=() | (⟨wurzel⟩ ⟨binärbaum⟩ ⟨binärbaum⟩)
(S17) ⟨baum⟩::=⟨wurzel⟩{⟨baum⟩...⟨baum⟩}
$\qquad$ ⟨wurzel⟩::=⟨m-ausprägung⟩
$\qquad\qquad\qquad \in A_i$

Abb. 1 : Syntax des Objektbeschreibungsbaums

mehr Elemente (...) bzw. genau n Elemente (***) des angegebenen syntaktischen Typs auftreten dürfen. Bei der Definition von komplexen Ausprägungstypen ist jeweils angegeben, aus welcher/welchen Menge(n) die Komponenten sein dürfen. Die A_i bezeichnen Teilmengen der Menge aller Ausprägungen, M ist die Menge der Merkmalsnamen.

Danach ist ein <objektbeschreibungsbaum> ein <grundobjekt> gefolgt von einer Menge von Null oder mehr <mapaar>en (S1).

Als <grundobjekt> lassen wir ein <atomares symbol> oder eine <ganze Zahl> zu (S2).

Von Grundobjekten verlangen wir
- daß sie nur einmal in der Datenbank definiert sind;
- daß sie einfach referenziert werden können;
- daß sie mit einer Menge von Merkmal-Ausprägungspaaren verknüpft werden können.

Ein <mapaar> besteht aus einem <m-name>n und einer <m-ausprägung> (S3).

Sowohl Merkmalsnamen als auch Merkmalsausprägungen stellen wir nicht als Zeichenketten, sondern als Verweise auf Grundobjekte (<u>ref</u> <grundobjekt>) bzw. auf Ausprägungen (<u>ref</u> <ausprägung>) dar (S4),(S5). <ausprägung>en sind entweder <atomare ausprägung> oder <komplexe ausprägung> (S6). Atomare Ausprägungen sind die Endknoten (Blätter) der Objektbeschreibungsbäume.

Dadurch, daß als Endknoten neben reellen Zahlen auch Grundobjekte zugelassen sind (S7), die wieder Wurzelknoten von Objektbeschreibungsbäumen sind, werden die Objektbeschreibungsbäume zum Datenbankgraphen verknüpft.

Als komplexe Ausprägungen lassen wir strukturierte Zusammenfassungen von <m-ausprägung>en, d.h. von Zeigern auf <ausprägung>en, zu. (S8)-(S17).

Die wichtigsten Typen von komplexen Ausprägungen sind:

(S9) : <menge>, d.h. eine endliche Aufzählung von wohlunterschiedenen <m-ausprägung>en.
Auf Mengen sind alle Operationen der Mengenalgebra definiert.

(S10) : <ntupel>, d.h. eine geordnete Folge von genau n <m-ausprägung>en, wobei die erste Komponente des n-Tupels aus einer Menge A_1, die zweite aus einer Menge A_2 usf. sein muß. Das n-Tupel ist dann ein Element aus $A_1 \times A_2 \times ... \times A_n$. Auf n-Tupeln sind als wesentliche Operationen definiert: Test auf Gleichheit, Selektieren einer vorgegebenen Komponente.

(S11) : <relation>, d.h. eine Teilmenge aus $A_1 \times A_2 \times ... \times A_n$. Die Elemente einer <relation> sind <ntupel> $\in A_1 \times A_2 \times ... \times A_n$.

Auf Relationen sind neben allen Mengenoperationen alle Operationen der Relationenalgebra (vgl. hierzu insb. CODD /2/.) definiert.

(S12) : ⟨mapaare⟩ sind eine endliche Menge von Null oder mehr ⟨mapaar⟩en. Wesentliche Operationen auf ⟨mapaare⟩n sind: Selektieren eines ⟨mapaar⟩es, das einen bestimmten ⟨m-name⟩n und/oder eine bestimmte ⟨m-ausprägung⟩ enthält; Hinzufügen, Löschen, Verändern eines bestimmten ⟨mapaar⟩es.

Durch Zulassen von ⟨mapaare⟩ als ⟨m-ausprägung⟩ erhalten wir die Möglichkeit, Merkmale mit schlecht definierten Wertebereichen zu beschreiben.

(S13) : ⟨vektor⟩en sind Zusammenfassungen von genau n ⟨m-ausprägung⟩en. Im Gegensatz zu ⟨ntupel⟩n sind alle Ausprägungen aus derselben Menge A_i. Ein Vektor ist ein Element aus A_i^n. Auf Vektoren sind alle Operationen der Vektoralgebra definiert.

(S14) : Eine ⟨matrix⟩ ist entweder ein Vektor von Vektoren oder ein Vektor von Matrizen. Durch diese Definition sind Matrizen beliebiger Dimension zugelassen.

Auf Matrizen sind alle Operationen der Matrizenalgebra erlaubt.

(S15) : Eine ⟨liste⟩ ist eine endliche Folge von Null oder mehr ⟨m-ausprägung⟩en. Im Gegensatz zu Mengen brauchen die Elemente einer Liste nicht "wohlunterschieden" zu sein.

Auf Listen sind die bekannten Operationen auf linearen Listen einschließlich speziellen linearen Listen wie Kellern, Warteschlangen, Deques definiert.

Außerdem können Listen zur Darstellung beliebiger Strukturen benutzt werden. (Alle hier definierten Strukturen können als spezielle Listen dargestellt werden).

(S16) : Ein ⟨binärbaum⟩ ist definiert als eine endliche Menge von Knoten, die entweder leer ist, oder eine Wurzel und einen linken und einen rechten Binärbaum enthält. Eine ⟨wurzel⟩ kann eine beliebige ⟨m-ausprägung⟩ sein.

(S17) : Ein ⟨baum⟩ ist eine ⟨wurzel⟩ zusammen mit einer endlichen Menge von Null oder mehr Bäumen (Unterbäumen.)

Auf Bäumen und Binärbäumen sind im wesentlichen Operationen zum Traversieren definiert.

4. Datenbeschreibung

Damit wir Objektbeschreibungsbäume richtig interpretieren können müssen wir außer den Objektbeschreibungsbäumen selbst noch Informationen über die Objektbeschreibungsbäume bereithalten und zwar

(1) zu jedem Merkmalsnamen eine Angabe über die Vorbereichsmenge und die Nachbereichsmenge, für die das Merkmal definiert ist;

(2) zu jeder als Vorbereich bzw. als Nachbereich angegebenen Menge:
   - den Typ der Elemente der Menge (z.B. GANZEZAHL, MENGE, NTUPEL)
   - bei atomarem Typ eine Angabe darüber, welche Elemente zu der Menge gehören, entweder

     (1) als Aufzählung der Elemente oder
     (2) als Teilabschnitt aus einer bekannten geordneten Menge oder
     (3) durch ein die Menge definierendes Prädikat.

   - bei komplexem Typ eine Angabe darüber, aus welcher/welchen Grundmenge(n) die Menge aufgebaut ist.

5. Ein Beispiel zur Darstellung eines Datenbankgraphen durch Objektbeschreibungsbäume

(1) Datenbankgraph, der einen Ausschnitt der für ein Luftverkehrsunternehmen relevanten Realität widerspiegelt.

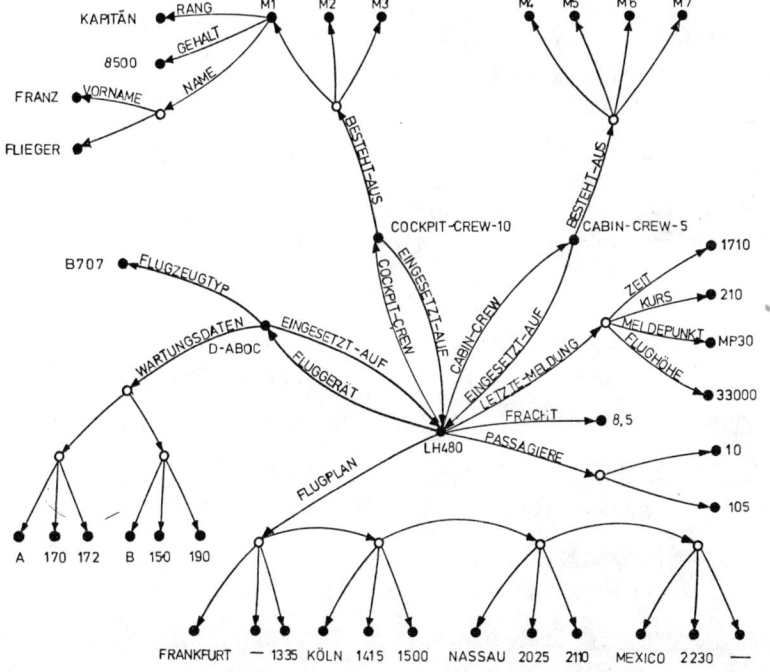

(2) Objektbeschreibungsbäume zu Flug-Nr LH480, Flugzeug D-ABOC,
Besatzungen COCKPIT-CREW-10 und CABIN-CREW-5, Mitarbeiter M1 :

LH480 (flugplan ((FRANKFURT - 1335)
               (KÖLN   1415 1500)
               (NASSAU 2025 2110)
               (MEXICO 2230 -))
       fluggerät D-ABOC
       cockpit-crew COCKPIT-CREW-10
       cabin-crew CABIN-CREW-5
       letzte-meldung (zeit 1710 meldepunkt MP30
           kurs 210 flughöhe 33000 besondere-ereignisse "1640 BRAND
           IN TRIEBWERK 1 GELÖSCHT UND STILLGELEGT UM 1641")
       fracht 8,5
       passagiere (10 105))

D-ABOC (flugzeugtyp B-707
        wartungsdaten ((A 170 172) (B 150 190))

COCKPIT-CREW-10 (besteht-aus (M1 M2 M3) eingesetzt-auf LH480))

CABIN-CREW-5 (besteht-aus (M4 M5 M6 M7) eingesetzt-auf LH480))

M1 (rang KAPITÄN gehalt 8500 name (FRANZ FLIEGER))

(3) Auszug aus der Datenbeschreibung:

1. Merkmale und dazugehörige Definitionsbereiche (Vorbereich, Nachbereich):
   FLUGGERÄT (ist-m-name (FLUG-NRN FLUGGERÄT-NRN))
   FLUGPLAN (ist-m-name (FLUG-NRN FLUGPLANDATEN))
   LETZTE-MELDUNG (ist-m-name (FLUG-NRN MAPAARE))

2. Definition der Definitionsbereiche
   FLUG-NRN (ist-menge (typ ATOMSYMBOL
              elemente (LH002...LH480...LH902)))

   FLUGGERÄT-NRN (ist-menge (typ ATOMSYMBOL
              elemente (D-ABED ...D-ABOC ...D-ABYZ))

   FLUGPLANDATEN (ist-menge (typ LISTE von FLUGPLANZEILEN))

   FLUGPLANZEILEN (ist-menge (typ NTUPEL
              struktur (ORTE ANKUNFTSZEITEN ABFLUGZEITEN)))

   ORTE (ist-menge (typ ATOMSYMBOL
              elemente (ABU-DHABI ...FRANKFURT ...ZÜRICH)))

   ANKUNFTSZEITEN (ist-menge (typ GANZEZAHL teilabschnitt (0 - 2400))

6. Schlußbemerkung

Das Konzept des Objektbeschreibungsbaums ist nicht eigentlich neu: Es entspricht in seiner Grundidee dem LISP-Konzept der "property list" /7/. Die wesentliche Erweiterung gegenüber dem LISP-Konzept liegt in der Einführung einer Anzahl für die Beschreibung realer Systeme "nützlicher" Datenstrukturen für "property values" (Merkmalsausprägungen).

In /4/ werden außer dem hier umrissenen Datenmodell noch wichtige Operationen auf Objektbeschreibungsbäumen und eine ansatzweise Implementierung in LISP beschrieben.

7. Literatur

/1/ CODASYL Data Base Task Group Report to the CODASYL Programming Language Committee, April 1971.

/2/ CODD, E.F. : A Relational Model of Data for Large Shared Data Banks; CACM 6(1970), S. 377 - 387.

/3/ CODD, E.F. : Further Normalization of the Data Base Relational Model; in "Data Base Systems" Prentice Hall, 1971.

/4/ DÖRRSCHEIDT, A. : Konzept eines graphenorientierten Datenbanksystems und ein Implementierungsansatz in LISP, Diss. TU Berlin; gepl. 1974.

/5/ FELDMAN, J.A., ROVNER, P.D. : An ALGOL-Based Associative Language; CACM 12 (1969), S. 439 - 499.

/6/ EHRICH, H.-D. : Datenstrukturen und Q-Systeme - Eine mathematische Studie; Vortrag GI-Jahrestagung 1973, Hamburg.

/7/ MCCARTHY et al. : LISP 1.5 programmer's manual, MIT Press, 1965.

/8/ MEALY, G.H. : Another Look at Data, Proc. AFIPS 1967, FJCC, Vol. 31.

BEITRAG ZUR SPEZIFIKATION DER FUNKTION
VON GENERALISIERTEN DATENBANKMANAGEMENTSYSTEMEN

Herbert Weber
Technische Universität Berlin

1. Einleitung

Unter "Generalisierten Datenbankmanagementsystemen (GDBMS)" werden Programmsysteme zum Aufbau und zur Manipulation von "generalisierten Datenbanken (DB)" verstanden. Generalisierte Datenbanken enthalten die Datenbestände mehrerer voneinander unabhängiger Benutzer in integrierter Form. Jeder Benutzer darf seinen Datenbestand definieren, ihn in die Datenbank einfügen und verändern oder auf eine beliebige Untermenge der in der Datenbank existierenden Datenbestände zugreifen.* Der Benutzer soll entsprechend seiner Interpretation der gespeicherten Daten eine von der Struktur der "Gesamtdatenbank" abweichend strukturierte "Teildatenbank" definieren dürfen. Mit einem solchen Konzept soll die Doppelspeicherung identischer Datenbestände vermieden werden und die nur _einmalige_ und _gleichzeitige_ Manipulation zur Aktualisierung der Datenbank ermöglicht werden.

Ein Programmsystem zur Verwaltung einer solchen Datenbank muß interfaces für jeden der möglichen Benutzertypen zur Verfügung stellen. Neben der Möglichkeit zur Definition einer Teildatenbank sollen die interfaces so definiert sein, daß Benutzerprogramme in verschiedenen - dem Benutzer vertrauten - Programmiersprachen (COBOL oder PL/1, aber auch nicht-prozedurale QUERY-Languages) geschrieben sein dürfen. In der Literatur sind - in Anlehnung an den CODASYL/DBTG-Report [CODA 71] - für dieses interface die Termini DDL/DML (Data-Definition-language/Data-manipulation-language) weit verbreitet. Die Interaktion eines Benutzers mit der Datenbank läßt sich nach diesem Konzept durch die folgende Prinzipskizze grob beschreiben.

---

* Auf beabsichtigte Einschränkungen dieser allgemeinen Forderung aufgrund von Datensicherungsmaßnahmen soll hier nicht eingegangen werden.

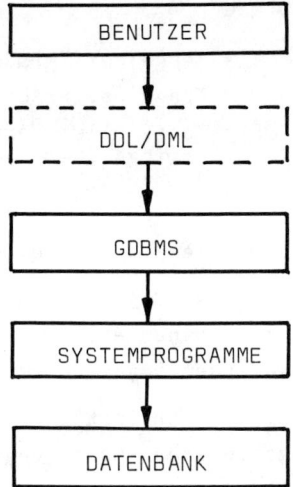

(Die durch die Systemprogramme definierte Sprache ist hier nicht eingezeichnet.)

In diesem Beitrag wird zunächst untersucht, wie in verschiedenen Datenbankkonzepten [CODA 71, CODD 70, DATE 72] die Interaktion zwischen Benutzer und GDBMS präzisiert wird. Daraus werden Spezifikationen der Funktionen des GDBMS abgeleitet, so daß eine korrekte Implementierung ermöglicht wird. Die hier verwendete Spezifikationsmethode ist von Parnas [PARN 72] vorgeschlagen worden und wird - soweit nötig - kurz dargestellt.

2. Terminologie

Die nicht einheitliche Nomenklatur in der Literatur macht die Definition einiger weiterer Begriffe notwendig:

(I) Ein strukturiertes Datenobjekt besteht aus atomaren Datenobjekten, die nach festgelegten Strukturierungsvorschriften zusammengefügt sind. Strukturierte Datenobjekte repräsentieren reale Objekte des Datenbankbenutzers.

(II) Als atomare Datenobjekte werden solche Datenobjekte bezeichnet, deren Struktur für die Lösung der relevanten Probleme des Datenbankbenutzers unerheblich ist. Als Menge der zulässigen atomaren Datenobjekte AD bezeichnen wir deshalb

$$AD = I \cup R \cup C$$

mit I = Menge der INTEGER
R = Menge der REAL
C = Menge aller Worte (character strings über einem beliebigen Alphabet)

(III) Die Beschreibung von strukturierten Datenobjekten erfolgt durch:

- die Menge von Namen der atomaren Objekte und eine Menge von Kompositionsvorschriften, nach denen atomare Objekte zu einem strukturierten Datenobjekt zusammengefaßt werden

- den aktuellen "Inhalt" der strukturierten Datenobjekte, das sind die der Struktur zugeordneten Ausprägungen (instances) der atomaren Datenobjekte.

(IV) Eine Menge von Vorschriften, die den Aufbau einer bestimmten Klasse von strukturierten Datenobjekten beschreiben (unabhängig vom Namen und dem zugeordneten Wert der atomaren Datenobjekte, nennen wir Schema-Typ oder Datenstrukturtyp.

(V) Die Menge der Vorschriften, die den Aufbau der Datenbank beschreiben (aus einer Menge von Schematypen), nennen wir Schema.

(VI) Die Menge der Vorschriften, die den Aufbau einer Teildatenbank eines oder mehrerer Benutzer beschreiben, nennen wir Subschema.

3. Spezifikation der Funktionen eines GDBMS

Auch wenn bei der Spezifikation der Funktionen eines Programmsystems feste Vorstellungen von der Implementierungssprache vorliegen, ist es weder sinnvoll noch hilfreich, die Spezifikation der Datenstrukturen und der Algorithmen unabhängig voneinander vorzunehmen.

In dieser Arbeit wird deshalb die These vertreten, daß Datenstrukturen und die Operationen auf diesen Strukturen in engem Zusammenhang gesehen werden müssen. Die Bedeutung eines Elementes in einem strukturierten Datenobjekt ist keineswegs allein durch den ihm zugeordneten Wert und die zwischen ihm und anderen Elementen existierenden Relationen definiert. Vielmehr ist seine Bedeutung auch durch die Menge der auf diesem Element zugelassenen Operationen bestimmt.

Im Gegensatz zu anderen Ansätzen [CODA 71] wird hier ein GDBMS deshalb

nicht so konzipiert, daß erst eine Sprache zur Beschreibung von "Inhalten"
der Datenbank und daran anschließend eine Sprache zur Manipulation der
Inhalte entwickelt wird. Dem hier vorgeschlagenen Vorgehen liegt dagegen
die Vorstellung zugrunde, daß der "Inhalt" der Datenbank durch die Menge
aller Funktionen des GDBMS bestimmt wird. Die genaue Beschreibung des
Inhaltes erfolgt durch die Spezifikation der Funktionen des GDBMS und
ein Benutzer arbeitet mit der Datenbank, indem er in seinem Anwenderprogramm eine Menge solcher Funktionen aufruft.

Die hier gewählte Methode zur Beschreibung von strukturierten Datenbeständen durch eine Menge von Funktionen eines Software-Systems, daß auf
diesen strukturierten Datenbeständen operiert, soll deutlich machen, daß
die verschiedenen Funktionen eines solchen Systems nicht voneinander unabhängig sind und daß damit hinsichtlich der Operationen auf strukturierten Datenbeständen Restriktionen existieren, die in der Funktionsspezifikation präzisiert werden können.

Diese Methode läßt sich durch das folgende Schema grob charakterisieren.

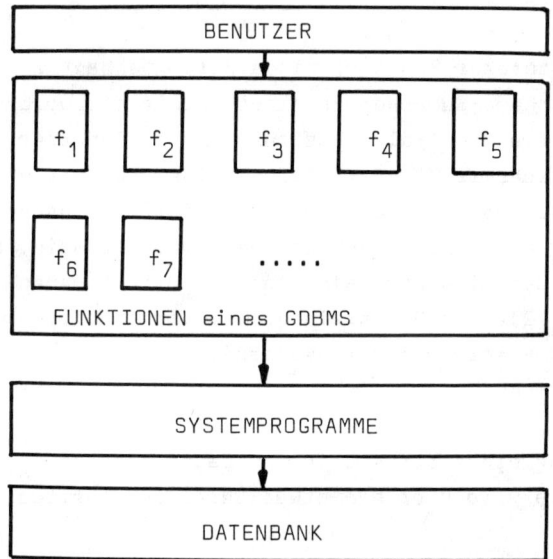

Parnas [PARN 72] hat ein solches Konzept zur Beschreibung der Funktionen
angegeben und an einigen Beispielen demonstriert. Die Beschreibung von
strukturierten Datenobjekten erfolgt in diesem Konzept dadurch, daß
eine Menge von Funktionen zu ihrer Charakterisierung spezifiziert wird.

Die Spezifikation der Funktion erfolgt durch

- die Menge der möglichen Werte, die diese Funktion zu vorgegebenen Argumentwerten annehmen kann (z. B. real, integer etc.)
- die Initialwerte, die diese Funktion annimmt (diese müssen nicht spezifiziert sein)
- die Menge der zulässigen Parameter (Argumente) für die die möglichen Funktionswerte angegeben werden
- die Beschreibung des "Verhaltens" dieser Funktion, d. h. die Beschreibung des Effektes, den der Aufruf dieser Funktion auf andere Funktionen oder auf Fehler-Routinen hat.

Dieses Verfahren wurde für die hier gestellte Aufgabe übernommen und wurde im wesentlichen im Hinblick auf eine korrekte Implementierung eines GDBMS ausgewählt.

4. Charakterisierung strukturierter Datenobjekte in einer generalisierten Datenbank

Um die Interaktion mehrerer Benutzer mit einer Datenbank zu ermöglichen, ist das sogenannte Schema-Subschema-Konzept entwickelt worden [CODA 71]. Mit diesem Konzept wird das Ziel angestrebt, jedem Benutzer mit der Definition eines Subschemas die Definition seiner Teildatenbank zu ermöglichen. Darüber hinaus soll jedes der definierten Subschemata gegenüber bestimmten Änderungen des Schemas invariant sein, eine Eigenschaft, die in der Literatur als "logical-data-independence" bezeichnet wird [DATE 72]. Die Beschreibung der Struktur einer Teildatenbank im Subschema soll von der Beschreibung dieser Struktur im Schema abweichen dürfen.

Zur Charakterisierung eines strukturierten Datenobjektes in einem Schema bzw. Subschema wird hier ein etwas verallgemeinertes Konzept vorgeschlagen:

1. Jedes Datenobjekt ist dadurch gekennzeichnet, daß es von einem bestimmten Schematyp (ST) ist. Ein Schematyp beschreibt all jene strukturierten Objekte, die nach den gleichen Kompositionsregeln aufgebaut worden sind.

2. Jedes Datenobjekt aus der Menge derer, die durch einen Schematyp beschrieben wird, ist eine spezielle Ausprägung des Schematyps -

ein Schematyp-instance (STI).

3. Ist einer Schematyp-instance von einem Benutzer eine bestimmte Bedeutung zugeordnet worden, so sprechen wir von einem Objekttyp (OT).

4. Und schließlich kann dem strukturierten Objekt vom Objekttyp OT ein Wert zugeordnet sein und man erhält so eine Objekttyp-instance (OTI).

ST und STI können wir, da ihnen keine durch einen Benutzer definierte Bedeutung zugeordnet ist, als abstrakte Datenobjekte und OT und OTI als konkrete Datenobjekte bezeichnen.

In den hier zur Diskussion stehenden Konzeptvorschlägen [CODA 71, CODD 70] erfolgt die Charakterisierung der strukturierten Datenobjekte in einer davon abweichenden Form.

In den in Abs. 5 beschriebenen Kompositionsfunktionen wird aber deutlich, wie die hier eingeführten Termini ST, STI, OT, OTI mit den dort verwendeten Charakterisierungen korrespondieren.

Beispiel:

G-ST : group mit 5 Elementen
G-STI : group mit 5 Elementen des Formates $F_1 - F_5$
G-OT : NAME, VORNAME, GEBTAG, GEBORT, FAMSTAND
G-OTI : XMANN, Y, 10/10/10, ZSTADT, VERH

5. Funktionen zur Komposition strukturierter Datenobjekte

Die erste und wichtigste Kategorie von Operationen, durch die strukturierte Datenobjekte definiert werden, sind solche zur Komposition komplexerer aus einfacheren Strukturtypen. Mit der Spezifikation der Funktionen zur Komposition strukturierter Datenobjekte spezifizieren wir - wie in Abs. 3 dargestellt - als das "Verhalten" dieser Operationen, nicht jedoch einen Algorithmus, der die Operationen repräsentiert.

Die bisher undefinierten Begriffe "Operation", "Funktion" und "Verhalten" werden durch den folgenden einfachen Formalismus präzisiert. Unter einer Operation verstehen wir den folgenden Ausdruck:

$$n :: func (P)$$

Bedeutung:

n   Name eines ST, STI, OT, OTI

:: kann zugeordnet werden das Ergebnis von

<u>func</u> (P) Funktionsaufruf mit der Parametermenge P

P   Menge von Parametern

oder den Ausdruck

$$n < x\ y\ z >$$

Bedeutung:

n   = Name einer OTI

xyz = Wert, der dieser OTI zugeordnet wird

Wir können hier von einer speziellen Operation, nämlich der assignment-operation sprechen.

Unter der Funktion verstehen wir das durch die Funktionsspezifikation beschriebene Ergebnis eines Funktionsaufrufes.

Innerhalb einer Funktionsspezifikation wird beschrieben, welche Effekte der Aufruf dieser Funktion auf andere definierte Funktionen hat. Die Menge der Effekte eines Funktionsaufrufes wird das Verhalten einer Operation genannt.

Eine vollständige Beschreibung der Operationen zur Komposition eines strukturierten Datenobjektes enthält dann die folgenden Komponenten:

<u>Schema-Typ (ST)-Komposition</u>

$$n\ (ST)\ ::\ \underline{func_1}\ (P_1)$$

<u>Schema-Typ-instance (STI)-Komposition</u>

$$n\ (STI)\ ::\ \underline{func_2}\ (P_2)$$

<u>Objekt-Typ (OT)-Komposition</u>

$$n\ (OT)\ ::\ \underline{func_3}\ (P_3)$$

<u>Objekt-Typ-instance (OTI)-Komposition</u>

$$n\ (OT) < value >$$

Mit den folgenden Kompositionsfunktionen lassen sich alle im DBTG- und Relationenkonzept definierten strukturierten Datenobjekte aufbauen.

Schematyp: Element

en:: $\underline{el_1}$(ADO, P_{11})

$\underline{el_1}$

poss.val.: $\{z|z \in ADO \land P_{11}(z)\}$

$P_{11}(z)$: z ist von bestimmter Charakteristik

parameter: ADO, P_{11}

effect: $\underline{el_2} = \{u|u \in \{z\}\}$

$\left.\begin{array}{c}\underline{tup_1}\\ \underline{seq_1}\end{array}\right\}$ unspezifiziert

Schematyp-instance: Elementinstance

ein:: $\underline{el_2}$(A, P_{12})

$\underline{el_2}$

poss.val.: $\{y|y \in A \land P_{12}(y)\}$

$P_{12}(y)$: y hat bestimmtes Format

parameter: A, P_{12}

effect: $\underline{el_3} = \{v\} = \{y\}$

$\left.\begin{array}{c}\underline{tup_2}\\ \underline{seq_2}\end{array}\right\}$ unspezifiziert

Objekttyp: Elementtyp

etn:: $\underline{el_3}$(B, P_{13})

$\underline{el_3}$

poss.val.: $\{x|x \in B \land P_{13}(x)\}$

$P_{13}(x)$: x ist ein bestimmter Wertebereich W zugeordnet

parameter: B, P_{13}

effect: $<\,> = \{(w \rightarrow x)|w \in W, x \in \{x\}\}$

$\left.\begin{array}{c}\underline{tup_3}\\ \underline{seq_3}\end{array}\right\}$ unspezifiziert

Objekttyp-instance: Element-Typ-instance

etin:: <val>

poss.val.: $\{(val \rightarrow pl)|val \in VAL, pl \in PL\}$

parameter: VAL, PL

effect: $\left.\begin{array}{c}\underline{tup_4}\\ \underline{seq_4}\end{array}\right\}$ unspezifiziert

Erläuterungen:

$\underline{el_1}$ Aus der Menge aller atomarer Datenobjekte (ADO) wird eine Untermenge so gebildet, daß alle ADO der Untermenge Z die gleichen charakteristischen Merkmale haben.

effect: Jede zu diesem Schematyp zu bildende Schema-typ-instance muß die durch el_1 festgelegten Charakteristika haben.

$\underline{el_2}$ Aus der Untermenge Z von ADO mit einer bestimmten Charakteristik wird eine Untermenge Y gebildet. Die ADO dieser Untermenge Y sind von einer bestimmten Dimension.

effect: Jede zu dieser Schematyp-instance zuordenbare Objekttyp muß die durch $\underline{el_2}$ festgelegten Dimensionen haben.

el_3 Jedem ADO aus der Untermenge Y wird ein Wertebereich zugeordnet.

effect: Einem Element mit einem festgelegten Schematyp, einer festgelegten Schematyp-instance und von einem bestimmten Objekttyp werden nur solche Werte zugeordnet, die zulässige Werte aus dem Wertebereich jedes ADO, der durch el_3 festgelegt wurde, sind.

el_4 Jedem durch Schematyp, Schematyp-instance und Objekttyp gekennzeichneten Element wird ein Wert aus dem vorgegebenen Wertebereich zugeordnet.

Schematyp: Tupel

tu:: $tup_1(Z, i, P_{21})$

tup_1

poss.val.: $\{Z_n | Z_n \subseteq Z \wedge P_{21}(z) \wedge z \in Z_n \wedge 1 \leq n \leq i\}$

$P_{21}(z)$: jedes z aus Z_n hat eine durch el_1 definierte Charakteristik

parameter: Z, i, P_{21}

effect: $tup_2 = \{U_n | U_n \subseteq Z \wedge 1 \leq n \leq i\}$

set_1 unspezifiziert

Sequenz-Schematyp

sn:: $seq_1(Z, i, P_{31})$

seq_1

poss.val.: $\{Z_n | Z_n \subseteq Z \wedge P_{31}(z) \wedge z \in Z_n \wedge 1 \leq n \leq i\}$

$P_{31}(z)$: jedes z aus Z_n hat die gleiche durch el_1 definierte Charakteristik und auf Z_n existiert eine Ordnung

parameter: Z, v, P_{31}

effect: $\left.\begin{array}{c}seq_2 \\ \overline{tup_1}\end{array}\right\}$ unspezifiziert

Relationen-Schematyp

rn: $rel_1(Z, i, P_{41})$

rel_1

poss.val.: $\{(z_1 \rightarrow z_2 \rightarrow \ldots \rightarrow z_n) | z_1, z_2 \ldots z_n \in Z \wedge P_{41}(z_i), 1 \leq i \leq n\}$

$P_{41}(z_i)$: die z_i haben eine durch el_1 definierte Charakteristik

parameter: Z, P_{41}

effect: rel_2 unspezifiziert

Set-Schematyp

setn:: $set_1(R, i, j, k, P_{51})$

set_1

poss.val.: $\{r_i \rightarrow \{r_j\},$
$r_i \rightarrow \{r_j\} \wedge r_j \rightarrow \{r_k\},$
$r_i \rightarrow (\{r_j\} \wedge r_k,$
$r_i, r_j \rightarrow \{r_k\} |$
$\{r_i\}, \{r_j\}, \{r_k\} \subseteq R,$
$r_i, r_j, r_k \in R \wedge P_{51}(r)\}$

$P_{51}(r)$: jedes r aus $\{r_i\}$, $\{r_j\}, \{r_k\}$ hat eine durch tup_1 definierte Charak-

teristik
parameter: R, i, j, k, P_{51}
effect: unspezifiziert

Die durch die Funktionsspezifikationen definierten Abhängigkeiten zwischen den Kompositionsfunktionen lassen sich durch das folgende Schema beschreiben. (Im Schema sollen die in den beiden diskutierten Konzepten zugelassenen Strukturkompositionen markiert werden.)

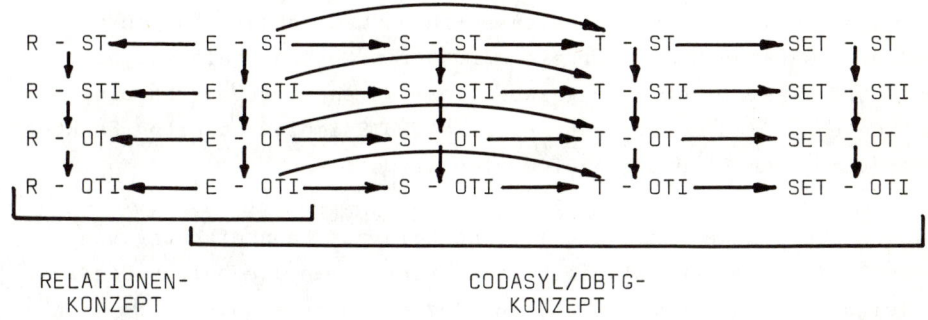

Beispiele:

```
      Element-Spezifikation      Tupel-Spezifikation

           CH-STRING              (CH-STRING, INT)
              ↓                          ↓
          [CH-STRING]            ([CH-STRING], [INT])
              ↓                          ↓
            NAME                    (NAME, ALTER)
              ↓                          ↓
           MUELLER                   (MUELLER, 27)
```

6. Funktionen zur Manipulation strukturierter Datenobjekte

Die vollständige Charakterisierung strukturierter Datenobjekte in einer Datenbank erfordert neben der Spezifikation von Kompositionsfunktionen die Spezifikation von Manipulationsfunktionen (Veränderung und Wiederauffindung).

Beispiel:

Ein sequentieller Schematyp wird weiter spezifiziert dadurch
- ob Manipulationen nur am ersten Element vorgenommen werden dürfen oder
- ob Manipulationen am ersten und am letzten Element vorgenommen werden dürfen etc.

Die Spezifikation solcher Manipulationsfunktionen ist nicht mehr Gegenstand dieser Arbeit.

7. Schlußfolgerungen

In den Konzeptvorschlägen von CODASYL/DBTG bzw. Codd/DATE erfolgt die Beschreibung von strukturierten Datentypen durch ein Schema (für den sog. data-base-administrator) und durch Subschemata (für die Benutzer).

Das Schema bzw. die Subschemata enthalten eine Aufzählung aller strukturierten Datenobjekte und die Darstellung von Relationen zwischen diesen Objekten. Im Gegensatz dazu werden in dieser Arbeit alle Datenobjekte als Ergebnis von Funktionsaufrufen betrachtet. Zu jedem vom Benutzer gewählten Namen für ein strukturiertes Datenelement wird eine Zuordnungsvorschrift angegeben, dem Namen wird dadurch eine Funktion des GDBMS zugeordnet. Alle im GDBMS implementierten Funktionen dürfen von jedem Benutzer aufgerufen werden.

Will man die Schema/Subschema-Terminologie zur Kennzeichnung von Flexibilität eines GDBMS beibehalten, könnte man die beiden Begriffe wie folgt auf das hier entwickelte Konzept übertragen:

Das Datenbank-Schema ist die Menge aller deklarierten Zuordnungen von Namen (Identifizierern) zu GDBMS-Funktionen. (Das Schema enthält also auch Vorschriften für die Manipulation von Datensätzen.)

Das Datenbank-Subschema ist eine näher zu spezifizierende Untermenge aller im Schema deklarierten Zuordnungen.

Im folgenden soll aufgezählt werden, inwieweit die im Subschema deklarierten Zuordnungen von denen im Schema abweichen dürfen:

(I) Namen im Subschema dürfen von den Namen im Schema verschieden sein, wenn eine Zuordnungsvorschrift für Namen existiert.

(II) Eine in einem Schema deklarierte Zuordnung legt den Bereich von possible values der zugeordneten Funktion fest und abweichend davon darf im Subschema eine Zuordnung deklariert werden, die eine Untermenge der possible values für die zugeordnete Funktion festlegt.

(III) Aus den im Schema deklarierten Elementen lassen sich im Schema und im Subschema unterschiedlich aufgebaute komplexere Strukturen deklarieren. (Eine Ausnahme stellen die im DBTG definierten owner-cupled-sets dar, für die besondere Restriktionen beachtet werden müssen.)

Die im Subschema deklarierten Zuordnungen sind deshalb invariant
gegenüber

- Änderungen von Namen im Schema
- Vergrößerungen des Bereiches der possible values der zugeordneten
  Funktion in der Zuordnung des Schemas und
- (mit Einschränkungen für owner-cupled-sets)
  veränderten Zusammenfassungen von Elementen zu komplexeren
  Strukturen im Schema.

Mit der hier gewählten Beschreibung der Implementierungsaufgabe wird
eine Darstellung, die die Korrektheitsprüfung der erstellten Programme erlauben soll, angestrebt. Ihre Anwendbarkeit wird in einem
Projekt überprüft werden.

Literatur

CODA 71	CODASYL/DBTG April 71-Report, verfügbar ACM New York
CODD 70	E. F. CODD, A Relational Model of Data for Large Shared Data Banks, CACM, Vol. 13 No. 6, Juni 1970
DATE 72	DATE, HEATH, HOPEWELL, A Collection of Papers on Data Independence, Techn. Rep. TR.12.094 IBM United Kingdom März 1972
PARN 72	D. L. PARNAS, A Technique for Software Module Specification with Examples, CACM, Vol. 15 No. 5, Mai 1972

A STRUCTURED DATABASE

Sten-Åke Tärnlund

University of Stockholm, Sweden

Abstract

A general outline of a structured data base contains a meta data base and its underlying structures. The meta data base should hold interesting facts leading to discoveries of regularities related to other facts that don't occur isolated but closed connected to each other. This idea is presented in two sections of which the second gives an illustration by an example.

1.1 A meta data base

The meta data base constitutes the top level of the data base and is generally supported by underlying structures ultimately defined by built-in primitives.

The meta data base should contain a representation of knowledge about the world (a micro-theory). It holds both general and pragmatic knowledge necessary for effective problem-solving.

Surprisingly often it is not only necessary but even sufficient for successful problem-solving to make use of only a few simple core descriptions. Some good examples are found in Minsky and Papert [1]. This phenomenon has important consequences on a creation of a meta data base.

Procedures operating on key descriptions embed general and pragmatic knowledge of a problem into a meta data base.

The presented idea with a meta data base is illustrated in section two by a simple procedure operating on three core descriptions called line, Y-line and triangle for playing the Piet Hein game CON-TAC-TIX.

1.2 Underlying structures

A meta data base typically has several underlying structures that ultimately connect the meta data base with primitives and built-in functions. We want all these connections not only to be correct but also to be able to be proved correct. In this way it is an equivalent problem to structure a data base and a program. It is generally known that the verification process is highly dependent on different structures. It makes sense to say that a data base (program) is more well structured than any others if it is easier to prove its correctness. An example of how good descriptions (data types) facilitate the verification process is found in Janning et al., [2].

1.3 Data base correctness

Having the meta data base it remains to show that the procedure invocations are correct i.e., to prove the correctness of the programs using the data base. To pursue this endevour we want a data base language that gives heavy support i.e., it should contain both well developed data structures for defining meta data base descriptions and sound formal language semantics. Moreover during creation of the meta data base we want to be able to implement it as fast as possible to test its problem-solving capabilities.

1.4 Data base languages

Some languages with powerful data structures for descriptions are LISP and SIMULA. They have also sound formal semantics.

Our program playing the CON-TAC-TIX is written in LISP.

Meta data bases for complex problem-solving need also capabilities for deductive reasoning. A subset of PLANNER [3] has been used for natural language communications [4]. An interesting proposal is to use predicate calculus as a programming language [5].

Data base languages with limited description power and confusing semantics apparently are blind-alleys towards sound data bases.

2 An example of a structured data base

We have written a program that plays the game CON-TAC-TIX. The play-board consists of 12x12 points that could be free or occupied by a black or white piece. A black (white) player wins when he connects two opposite black (white) edges in the playboard. Only one player can win and there is no draw.

Here follows a picture of the play-board with a black winning line (which is the case if every black piece with exception of the edge points has two black neighbours:

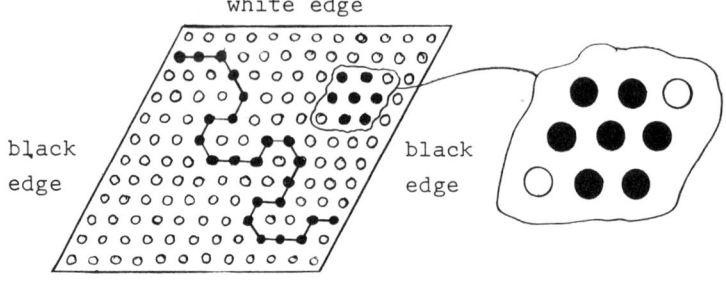

Fig 1 Showing the play-board. The local picture shows neighbour holes to a center hole

2.1 Meta data base

The meta data base consists of knowledge of the game embedded in procedures operating on descriptions.

2.1.1 Descriptions

These are called <u>line</u>, <u>Y-line</u> and <u>triangle</u>.
(i) <u>line</u>: a sequence of one-colour neighbour pieces (points).

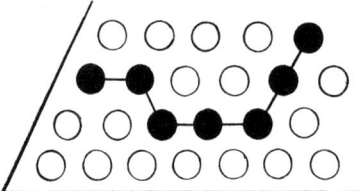

Fig 2 A part of the play-board with a line (the connected black dots).

The simpliest line contains only one point.
(ii) <u>Y-line</u>: A sequence of one or more one-colour Y-steps. Two pieces make one Y-step, if there are two possibilities to form a line between these pieces with another piece.

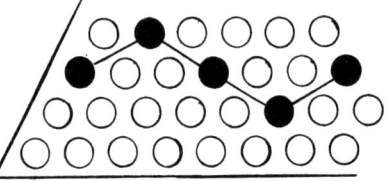

Fig 3 Part of the play-board with a Y-line (the connected black dots)

To reach a winning state of the game it is not necessary to have a complete winning line, it is sufficient with a Y-line.

(iii) <u>triangle</u>: three pieces that give three possibilities to form a
line between two of them with another piece.

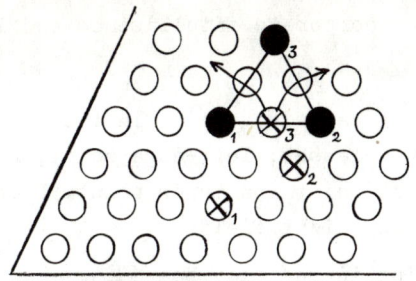

Fig 4   A part of the play-board showing a triangle (the connected black dots)

<u>Line</u>, <u>Y-line</u> and <u>triangle</u> are the only data types in the meta data base
so they should contain the core descriptions of the problem. At this
point two questions arise: is the meta data base a relevant theory of
the problem, and could the descriptions in the meta data base be defined correctly by the data base primitives?

2.1.2   Procedures

There are two different strategies to win the game. One is to look for
combinations that lead to a win; the other is to prevent the opponent
from winning.

A locally very efficient tactic for the latter strategy is to use the
description triangle. Figure 4 illustrates three consecutive moves from
white (crossed mark) and black (dots). First white makes his first move
(cross one) trying to form a Y-line. Black tries to stop that plan with
dot one. White revises his plan a little and moves cross two. Black stops
that Y-line with dot two. In his third move white tries to pass blacks
defence by cross three. By his third move black locally stops white's
attack. Now white can only continue in the directions shown by the arrows
in figure 4 and these are typically of local favour to black.

Every second time the program makes a move (i.e., puts a piece in a node)
which is found by reasoning in the meta data base. An illustrative procedure runs:

p1. If possible in three moves (a small look-ahead is assumed) create
a winning chain. (The game is terminating in a few moves.)

p2. Try to stop the most powerful chain in the most favourable end by
a <u>triangle</u> or <u>Y-line</u> or <u>line</u> respectively.

p3. Expand the most powerful chain of your own.

A winning chain is defined as a combination of a line or a Y-line. Open phrases as "most powerful chain" and "the most favourable end" give this procedure a chance to incorporate intelligence and learning.

2.3 Underlying structures

The most basic element in the data base is a point in the play-board. All the 144 points fall into five classes; left-edge point, right-edge point, upper-edge point, down-edge point and inner point. Each point is represented by a node containing eight fields:

PIECE
NO
α
β
γ
δ
ε
λ

Fig 5 A point in the play-board is represented in the data base by a node containing eight information fields: PIECE, NO, $\alpha,\beta,\gamma,\delta,\varepsilon$ and λ.

The PIECE-field represents the status of a point i.e., whether it is free or occupied by a black or white piece. The NO-field contains the unique number ($1 \leq NO \leq 144$) of a point in the play-board. The fields $\alpha,\beta,\ldots$ and λ are pointers that hold addresses to neighbour holes according to the following figure:

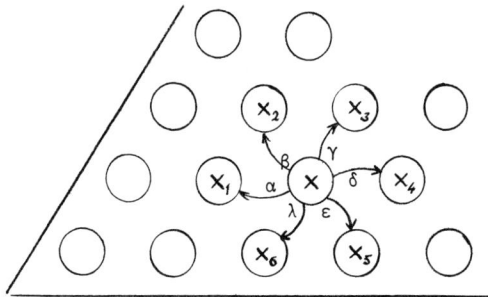

Fig 6 Shows the pointers $\alpha,\beta,\ldots$ and λ of a node x

There are six pointers of each node (point) in the play-board with the exception of the edge nodes. With these pointers we can define six primitive functions $\alpha-\lambda$, e.g.,

$$\beta[x] = \begin{cases} x_2 & \text{iff } x \text{ is not a left or an upper edge point} \\ \text{NIL} & \text{otherwise} \end{cases}$$

and with these primitives it is possible to reach any of the immediate neighbours of a node x.

After creating these relations between the points in the play-board we have a low level structure of the points in the data base.

Functions for play-board travelling

However, we are interested in any travel from a node x, but of course some of the nodes that can be reached from a node x are of special interest.

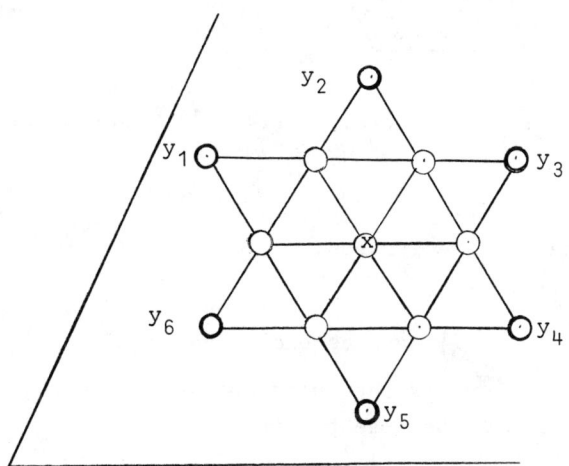

Fig 7 Shows the y nodes of a node x and their pointers.
Travels from a x point to a y_i-point ($1 \leq i \leq 6$)

The primitive functions $\alpha-\lambda$ are commutative in the following way e.g.,

$\beta[\alpha[x]] = \alpha[\beta[x]] = y_1$; $\gamma[\beta[x]] = \beta[\gamma[x]] = y_2$;

$\delta[\gamma[x]] = \gamma[\delta[x]] = y_3$; $\epsilon[\delta[x]] = \delta[\epsilon[x]] = y_4$;

$\lambda[\epsilon[x]] = \epsilon[\lambda[x]] = y_5$; $\alpha[\lambda[x]] = \lambda[\alpha[x]] = y_6$

It is useful to define some new but equivalent functions e.g., $\alpha[\beta[x]] = \alpha\beta[x]$ and so on.

2.2.1 Bottom-up definition of the meta data base

By the basic concept we can now express the top level descriptions: <u>line</u>, <u>Y-line</u> and <u>triangle</u>.

Line

A line[x] is defined as a set of points:

$\quad$ line[x] = $\{x, f_1[x], f_2[f_1[x]], \ldots, f_n[\ldots f_1[x]]\}$ $\qquad$ where

$\quad f_i = \alpha|\beta|\gamma|\delta|\epsilon|\lambda \qquad$ (| denotes exclusive or)

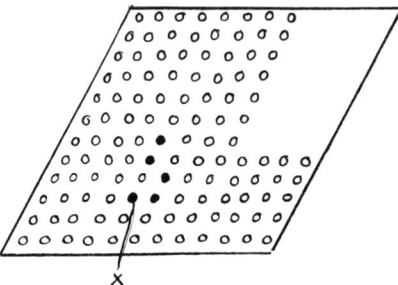

Fig 8 Shows the line[x] = {x,δ[x] γ[δ[x]] β[γ[δ[x]]] γ[β[γ[x]]]}

Y-line

A Y-line is defined as one or more Y-steps.

A Y-step of x is Y-step[x] = g[x]

where g = αβ|βγ|δε|ελ|λα   (| denotes exclusive or)

and whenever g is equal to one of the functions αβ - λα e.g., γδ then the points γ[x] and δ[x] must be free points.

A Y-line of x is then defined as

Y-line[x] = {x,g_1[x],...,g_n[...[g_1[x]]...]}

where each g_i ($1 \leq i \leq n$) are defined as g above.

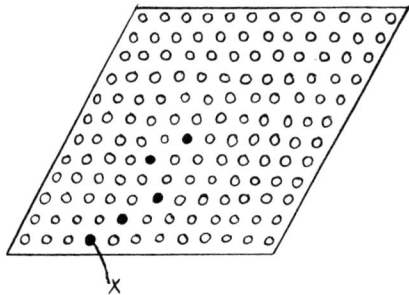

Fig 9 A Y-line containing the following points
{x, γδ[x], γδ[γδ[x]], γβ[γδ[γδ[x]]], δγ[γβ[γδ[γδ[x]]]]}

Triangle

For each suitable chosen point x there are six triangles.

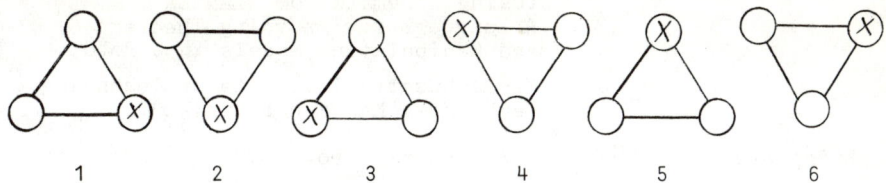

Fig 10 Showing the six triangles of a point x.

These six triangles of a point x are defined as follows:

triangle$_1$[x] = {x, α[α[x]] β[β[x]]},   triangle$_2$[x] = { x, β[β[x]] γ[γ[x]] }

triangle$_3$[x] = {x, γ[γ[x]] δ[δ[x]]},   triangle$_4$[x] = { x, δ[δ[x]] ε[ε[x]] }

triangle$_5$[x] = {x, ε[ε[x]] λ[λ[x]]},   triangle$_6$[x] = { x, λ[λ[x]] α[α[x]] }

These six triangles fall into two equivalence classes. One has the triangle members 2, 4 and 6. The other has 1, 3 and 5. Making use of these two classes the choice of triangle reduces to only two possibilities.

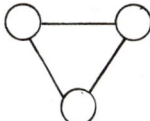 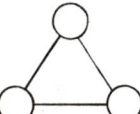

Fig 11 Shows the two equivalence classes of triangles {2,4,6} and {1,3,5}.

A program making use of these descriptions plays the game fairly well.

2.2 Data base correctness

The correctness of the data base remains still to be proved. The few and clean data types (descriptions) make us hopeful in front of that problem.

2.3 Data base language

The data base is written in LISP.[6]

Acknowledgment

To Å. Hansson for many good suggestions and corrections.

REFERENCES:

3. Hewitt C., Description and Theoretical Analysis (Using Schemata) of PLANNER: A Language for Provning Theorems and Manipulating Models in a Robot,

   Massachusetts Institute of Technology, Cambridge, Massachusetts, 1972.

2. Janning et. al., A Structured Program,

   University of Stockholm, 1974.

5. Kowalski R., Predicate logic as programming language,

   IFIP Proc. 1974.

6. Lynn and Whitfield, Stanford LISP 1.6 Manual,

   Stanford Artificial Intelligence Lab.

1. Minsky and Papert, Artificial Intelligence, Progress Report, 1972,

   Massachussets Institute of Technology Cambridge, Massachusetts, 1972.

4. Winograd, T., Understanding Natural Language,

   Academic Press, 1972.

THE PARTITIONING OF A DATA BASE INTO SUBFILES MATCHING USER'S QUERIES.

I.M. OSMAN

Computing Department, Durham University, Durham DH1 3LE, U.K.

(On a study leave from the Computer Centre, University of Khartoum, Sudan)

ABSTRACT: This paper discusses the splitting of files into smaller portions as dictated by the usage pattern in order to improve the data base performance. The feasibility of the splitting is shown. The treatment is within the context of the relational model of data [1].

INTRODUCTION.

In a data base whose files (relations) have a large number of fields (domains) or a large number of records (tuples), queries may only require a subset of the whole relation. The distribution pattern of references to the domains is usually nonuniform and therefore it is more efficient to separate the parts which are frequently referenced from those which are only occasionally referenced. This is conceptually similar to a well-known method in data processing where records are kept in two separate files: one for the moving hit group (e.g. moving customer's file) and the other for the records which are not referenced during a certain period of time (e.g. dead customer's file). Here, the case is more complex because we consider varying frequencies of reference for different groups of fields or records and the grouping is automatic and is not 'seen' by the user.

The possible ways and levels in which a relation may be split are as follows:

A. DOMAINWISE SPLIT

This method is suitable for relations having a large number of domains (e.g. relation Property in Fig. 1 whose degree is 42). The domains that are frequently requested together are kept in one portion. This may lead to saving in access time. The splitting can take place at one of the following levels:

I. Physical Storage Level (the splitting of files):
Traditionally data base files are stored record by record. In this type of splitting the file is partitioned when the data base is reorganised. Each partition holds the fields which are requested by the same query. The records are linked by pointers or by position. In the extreme case of partitioning single fields are stored separately, in

A data base relation   PROPERTY

(Street#, Propp, Olduse, ..., etc.)

degree   = 42

cardinality = 27323

tuple size = 124 bytes

The relation is sorted on the primary key (St#).
The following portions were formed:

A = projection of PROPERTY on domains 1 and 2

B = projection of PROPERTY on domains 1 and 3

Query	Response time (sec) IBM370/145	Relation used in answering the query
1 i) select(Street#=53&Prop=99X)	168	PROPERTY
	49	A
ii) select(Olduse=8)	181	PROPERTY
		B The resulting relation D=select from B(Olduse=8)
2 i) select(St#=53)	46 (av.)	PROPERTY
	1.2	A The resulting relation C=select from A(St#=53)
3 i) select(St#=53&Olduse=8)	124	PROPERTY
ii) join relation C & D on the equality of St#	5	C cardinality=125 D cardinality= 5
4 i) select(St#=53 Olduse=8)	128 (av.)	PROPERTY
ii) join A and B on equality of St#	88	A and B The resulting relation E=equijoin of A & B on St#
iii) select(St#=53 Olduse=8)	48	E

Results

Queries requiring more than one portion:

(a) Conjunctive queries:

   Time to answer query 3(i) from PROPERTY = 124 sec.

   Time to answer query 3(i) from portions
   by means of selections from A and B
   and then joining the results   = 41 sec.

                       ∴ clearcut gain

(b) Disjunctive queries:

   Time to answer query 4(i) from PROPERTY = 128 sec.

   Time to answer query 4(i) from portions
   A and B by means of equijoining on
   the sorted primary key domain and then
   answering the query from the result   = 136 sec.

                       ∴ a relatively small loss

FIGURE 1

which case the file is stored field by field, i.e. the records are completely transposed. An example of this extreme case is the ROBOT system (Record Organisation Based on Transposition)[2] This type of splitting is not discussed in this paper.[3]

II. Logical Level (the splitting of relations):

In this type of partitioning the relation is broken into a smaller number of relations (obtained by projections including the key domain) in such a way that the initial relation can be regenerated by logical operations, e.g. join, union, etc.

B. TUPLEWISE SPLIT

Here the partitioning is effected on the basis of the object value of a particular domain. By selections on the object value of a domain the relation is resolved into smaller relations such that it is possible to recover the first relation by forming the union of the constituent relations.

A. DOMAINWISE SPLIT:
LOGICAL LEVEL (The splitting of relations):

This will be discussed in the context of the relational model of data. Some concepts of relational data bases will be explained first.

1. The theoretical analysis:-

The theoretical analysis, justification and proofs for the domain-wise decomposition of relations at a logical level has been thoroughly worked out [4][5]. However, here we aim at improving the data base performance by splitting the relations in accordance with the way in which the user's queries reference the domains of relations. Thus the recommendations arrived at will be applicable to realistic situations.

2. Defined relations:-

Some data base madels patterned after relational concepts, for example, the IS/1 system [6] and SEQUEL [7] allow the user or the system to create relations as subsets of the main data. The definition of these relations is expressed in terms of existing data base relations using relational operators (e.g. the relation PEOPLE might be defined as the UNION of relation MALES and relation FEMALES). The system stores the definition and the defined relation is available to the user at the same logical level as the other data base relations. The defined relation remains a stored definition (i.e. implicit) until it is requested by a query. The implicit form takes negligible disk space. When the defined relation in its implicit form is referenced by a query it is then created, i.e. made <u>explicit</u>, by carrying out the indicated operations on stored data. The processing cost to create the relation varies with the complexity of the definition and the size of the relations involved in the definition. The explicit form may take a substantial amount of disk space. However, if the defined relation is available in its explicit form when requested by a query no additional cost is incurred.

The facility of defined relations allows the sharing of disk space among a number of relations at a processing cost incurred whenever a change is made from implicit to explicit representation. At some stage in the process of creating and querying relations one or more explicit relations will have to be deleted in order to free space for other requested relations. A replacement algorithm deletes the relation which has the least expected cost per unit size, i.e. that relation for which

$$G = \frac{\text{(the frequency of reference x cost of creating the relation)}}{\text{size of the relation}}$$

is minimum. [8] It is possible to estimate the probability of a defined relation remaining explicit if G for that relation is known. [3]

3. The splitting:-

The relation is partitioned by projections, e.g. consider relation S whose first domain is its original primary key or a system generated primary key such as the tuple number. Relation S has domains $(\underline{d_1}, d_2 .. d_n)$. To split S as follows:

$$S_1 = \text{projection } (\underline{d_1}, d_2 ... d_m) \text{ of S}$$
$$S_2 = \text{projection } (\underline{d_1}, d_{m+1} ... d_r) \text{ of S}$$
$$S_3 = \text{projection } (\underline{d_1}, d_{r+1} ... d_n) \text{ of S}$$

S_1, S_2 and S_3 are set up and stored as base relations.
Relation S is now defined in terms of its projections.
S = equijoin on d_1 of S_1, S_2 and S_3.

Generally, if a query requires domains in portions (relations) S_1 and S_2 simulatneously, a new relation S_{12} will be defined as:
S_{12} = equijoin on d_1 of S_1 and S_2.

The defined relation (S_{12}) will be explicit in the first place and the query will be answered. The defined relation (S_{12}) may then be maintained explicit and can answer similar queries. For how long S_{12} will remain explicit depends on its G value and the availability of space.

The partitioning will be beneficial if the major overhead (the equijoin time) can somehow be minimised. If the relations are stored with tuples sorted on some key the join time will be reduced significantly. In the discussion that follows we are concerned with relations which are sorted on their primary key domains.

4. Boolean Filters

Consider a relation S having k subsets $(S_1, S_2 \ldots S_k)$ where $S, S_1, \ldots S_k$ are defined as above.
Consider the queries involving i subsets taken, for convenience as $(S_1, S_2, \ldots S_i)$.

(a) For a boolean filter with conjunctions (AND)

Let $R = S_1$ join* S_2 join* S_3 ... join* S_i (i)

select $(R:B_1 \& B_2 \& B_3 \ldots B_i)$ = select $(S_1:B_1)$ join* select $(S_2:B_1)$ .... join* select $(S_i:B_i)$ (ii)

Where: join* is an equijoin on the primary key

B_i is a boolean term involving one domain or more of S_i.

If any select $(S_j:B_j)$ = NULL then the whole expression (ii) will be equal to NULL. In other words, the selections are performed on the individual portions and the result of the selections are joined on the primary key if no result is a NULL. The maximum number of equijoins = i-1.

Each relation resulting from a selection has a reduced cardinality (number of tuples). This reduction in the cardinality is designated r. The portions are joined in the ascending order of their sizes i.e. the smaller ones are joined first. (This reduces the size of data traded off between the disk and the work space during the joins.)

(b)   For a boolean filter with disjunctions (OR)

Similarly, select $(R:B_1 V B_2 V B_3 \ldots B_i)$ = select $(S_1:B_1)$ join* S_2 join* $S_3 \ldots$

join* S_i....U select $(S_2:B_2)$ join* S_1...............

join* S_i....U select $(S_i:B_i)$ join* $S_1 \ldots$ join* S_{i-1} (iii)

In this case the number of equijoins = i (i-1).

Also a large number data movements will be required. It is therefore sensible to define a relation on the subsets required by the query (by means of an equijoin) and then perform the selection on the explicit form of the defined relation.

i.e. select $(R:B_1 V B_2 V B_3 \ldots B_i)$ without splitting
= select $(Q:B_1 V B_2 V B_3 \ldots B_i)$
where $Q = S_1$ join* S_2 join* $S_3 \ldots$ join* S_i

5. An algorithm:-

The flow diagram in Figure 2 describes an algorithm for the management of queries requiring a partitioned relation. There is a definite

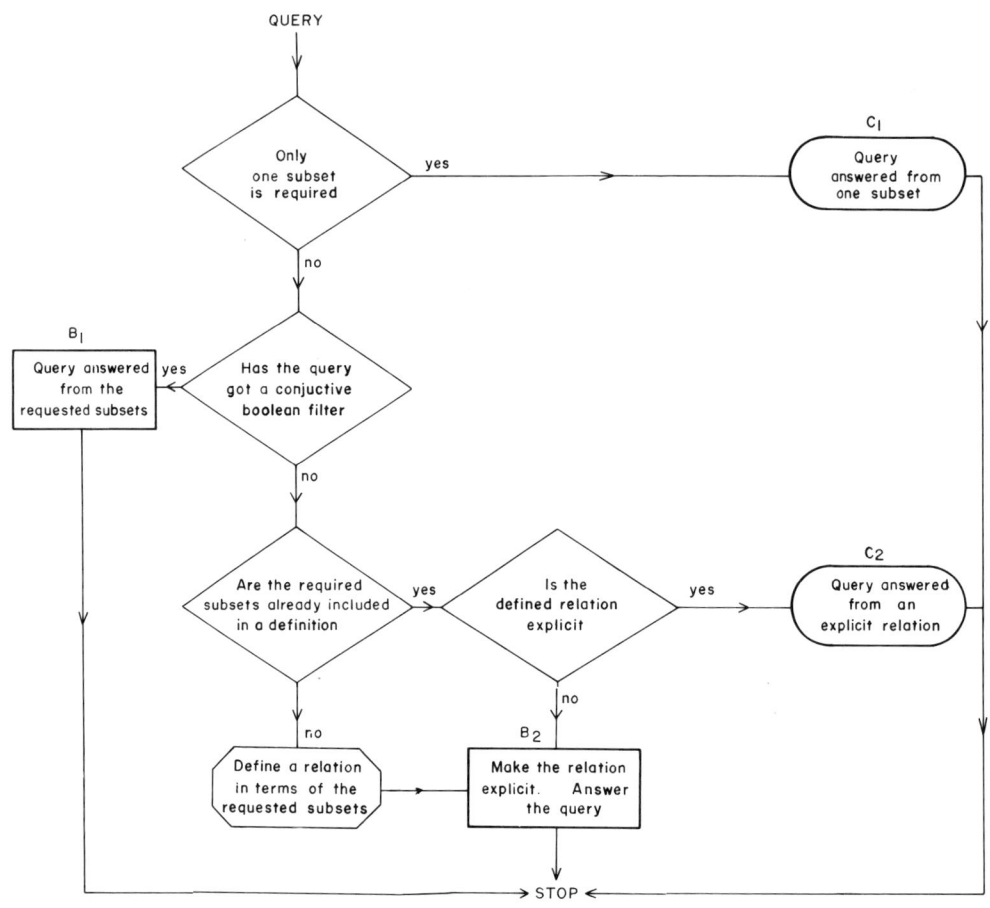

Figure 2

performance improvement due to splitting in the following cases:
  (i) When the query is answered from only one subset
      (C1 in the diagram).
  (ii) When the query is answered from an _explicit_ relation defined
       as the equijoin of the requested subsets (C2 in the diagram).
However, when the query requires more than one subset and the selection
boolean filter is conjunctive (Box B1 in the diagram), cpu time
due to comparisons is traded off for gain in access time. This
case does not always improve the performance. The gain in performance depends on: (a) the size of the whole relation, (b) the
number and sizes of the portion requested in the query, (c) the
value of the parameter r, (d) the charging algorithm of the installation (i.e. how cpu time is weighted against the access time)
and (e) the judicious choice of the portions and their constituent domains.

When the subsets have to be equijoined to answer a query (box B2
in the diagram), the loss or gain in performance depends on (a),
(b), (d) and (e) above.

The frequency of each of the above mentioned four types of queries is needed in order to estimate the gain in access time due to such splitting. (This is explained in [3]).

6. An experiment

The example shown in Figure 1 gives the response time of queries on a relation with and without splitting. This gives a feel of the magnitude of the potential gain which can be achieved by judicious splitting.

7. The Formation of Subsets for Domainwise splitting

When relation R is a candidate for splitting, some information describing the reference pattern of the domains has to be recorded. This information includes the frequency of usage and the concurrency of reference to the domains. When the data base is reorganised this information is used to evaluate a splitting criterion. Accordingly, if the splitting is viable, the optimum configuration of subsets will be determined.

We need to store the number of times (i) each domain was referenced as a single domain, (ii) each particular combination of domains was requested by a query.

For a relation of n domains (i) will only require n locations while (ii) will require $2^n - 1$ locations, the latter is too storage consuming. The access of such a huge number of locations whenever the relation is referenced is a serious overhead.

However, the following method is recommended. A bit vector of length n is stored for every type of query. The vector has 1's in the positions corresponding to the domains involved in the query. In Figure 3 the first query type requires domain seven and eight. This bit table method works as follows:

(i) When a query requiring relation R is decoded the positions of the referenced domains of R are marked by 1's in a bit vector X.
i.e. $X_i = \text{'1'}$; for all $i \in I$ where I is the set of the domains of R involved in the query, and
$X_j = \text{'0'}$; $j \notin I$.

(ii) The bit table is searched for a match between vector X and the vectors of the queries so far recorded. If no match is found vector X is added to the table to increase the number of types of query by 1.

The storage overhead of the bit table method is relatively small. It is only n bits times the number of the types of query.
The queries requiring single domains are stored separately.

From observations the type of queries rarely exceeds 2n. This gives a storage overhead of $\frac{n^2}{4}$ bytes which can be accommodated in core for processing. Another overhead is the cpu time of matching a new query as in (ii) above. The condition for a match is the equality of vector X to a query type vector (a table column). The number of comparisons depends on the type of search used,[9] for this standard table problem.

At time=t when Vector X equals column c of the table, the following is updated: (1) the number of references to column c, (2) the last reference ($L_c = t$), (3) the recency weighted frequency ($w_c = w_c + t$).

At time=T when all the table columns have been used up, the new vector X should replace column p which has the least w_p of all the columns that have not been referenced during the last 2n-1 references (i.e. $L_p < T - (2n-1)$.

In this way the old reference pattern is discarded to make way for the more recent pattern.

The choice of the optimum set of partitions:-

A clustering technique [10] is used to give n possible choices of portions. Using the bit table of fig. 3 the cost of answering the queries is evaluated for each solution set. The set having the minimum cost is chosen.

Figure 4 shows the cpu time taken to cluster and choose the optimum splitting set for relations of different degrees. It should be noted that this will be the actual overhead incurred by a data base system at the time of reorganisation because exactly the same process

Example:

Relation name : USE

degree = 13

cardinality = 64501

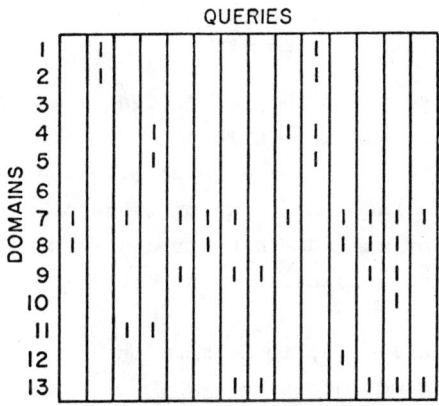

Select from Use (domain (7) = α & domain (8) = β); is a Query of type 1 for any value of α and β and whether the logical operator is AND or OR.

Number of queries examined = 136

Number of multi-domain queries = 82

Number of single-domain queries = 54

Figure 3

No. of Domains	No. of Query Types	Fortran Program cpu time (sec) IBM 360/67	Virtual Memory Kb
13	14	$\simeq 1$	less than 142
42	84	12	142
100	200	167	180

The overhead of choosing the subsets of a relation

Figure 4

will be followed. A better mathematical optimisation model may give a better choice at a similar overhead.

It is therefore appropriate to conclude that the overhead cost of splitting is small compared with the costs related to processing relations of large degrees, and that the splitting can be performed automatically at a tolerable overhead.

B. TUPLEWISE SPLITTING

A relation R is split according to the value of a given domain. The resulting subsets are themselves relations. These portions are formed by selections specifying a certain value or a range of values of the splitting domain. Relation R is seen as the union of these portions and the relation, R_{rem}, formed by the remaining tuples which do not satisfy the selections. i.e. for a relation of n portions $R = T_1 \cup T_2 \cup \ldots \cup R_{rem}$; where T_i is subset i of R.
The splitting is on one domain only i.e. it forms a one level hierarchy. This splitting has the following advantages:-
  (i)   It reduces the cpu and the access times for queries requiring the splitting domain or selections with conjunctive boolean filters containing the splitting domain,
  (ii) It is possible to save storage space by removing the objects of the splitting domain in the subsets. This can be achieved if the relation is split on specific values of the splitting domain rather than a range of values.
The disadvantages of tuplewise splitting are the following:-
  (i)   Each update requires some comparisons (of the order $n\log_2 n$ or $n/2$ comparisons depending on the organisation of the index of the subsets). Updates may also need to access more than one portion depending on the values of the splitting domain and of the updating tuples.
  (ii) Queries requiring the other domains or selections having disjunctive boolean filters containing the splitting domain will need to access more than one portion. This increases the access time.

The choice of the splitting domain.

The splitting domain is chosen automatically when the data base is reorganised. The frequencies of reference to the domain alone and in conjunctive boolean filters are kept for each domain. The splitting is performed on the domain with the highest frequency count.

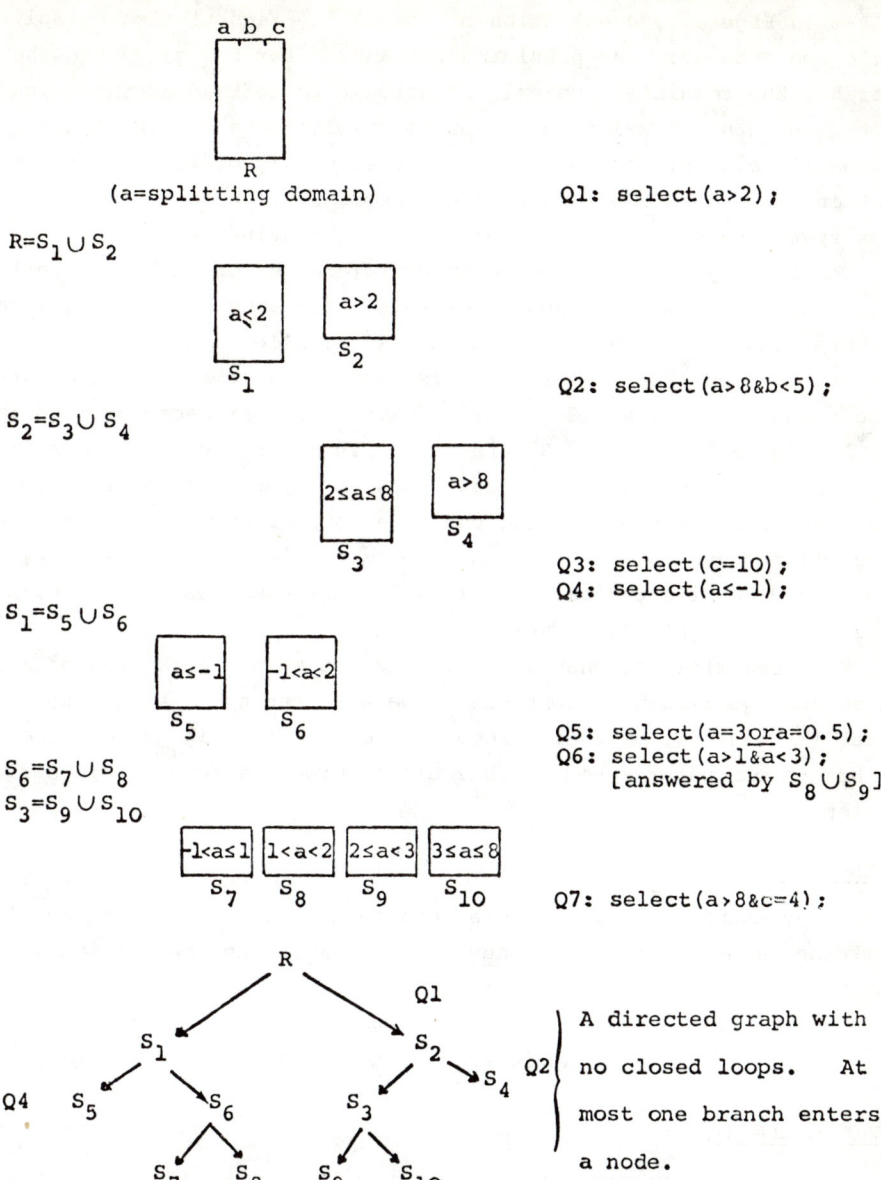

Figure 5

The formation of portions.

As in Figure 5, a selection on domain 'a' is satisfied by splitting R into two subsets; one providing the answer for the query and the other has the remaining tuples. Relation R is defined as the union of the two subsets. A selection leads to a split of a subset if its boolean filter contains the splitting domain only or if it contains the splitting domain in a conjunctive expression. In both cases the value range specified for the selection should be continuous.

The recency weighted frequency of reference for each portion is kept. When the number of subset exceeds a predetermined value, some of the subsets are pruned and the others are allowed to grow (split) further. The pair of leaves (subsets) having the smallest frequency of reference is united and the definition of its predecessor is deleted. e.g. In Figure 5 if S_7 and S_8 are to be pruned, S_6 is made a base relation and its definition is deleted. No major overhead is incurred when subsets are set up because one of each pair answers a query. Also, since all the generated definitions contain union operations only, complicated queries can be dealt with no further complications. E.g. A join R will give: A join $S_1 \cup$ A join S_2...etc.

The tree will permanently be influenced by the first few splits and so some queries will continue to be answered by more than one subset irrespective of their frequency, e.g. Q7 in Fig. 5, because only one branch can enter a node. This disadvantage is removed by reorganisation.

CONCLUSION

(i) By using the defined relations capability the advantages of splitting relations can be gained without impairing the utilization of disk space.

(ii) The process of monitoring the usage pattern and the choice of optimum splitting may be achieved at a tolerable overhead.

ACKNOWLEDGEMENT

I gratefully acknowledge encouragement and valuable guidance of: Dr. T.W. Rogers of IBM UK Scientific Centre, Peterlee, Co. Durham, Mr. J.S. Roper of the Department of Computing, Durham University and Dr. P. Hall of London University.

REFERENCES

[1] Codd, E.F. "A relational model of data for large shared data banks", Communication of ACM, Vol 13, No.6, June 1970.

[2]   Burns, D.   "ROBOT - A new approach to database management", Fourth European Conference on EDP Developments in Department Stores, London, November 1972.

[3]   Osman, I.M.   "Matching the storage to usage pattern in relational data bases" Ph.D. thesis, Durham University, October 1974.

[4]   Delobel, C
      Casey, R.G.   "Decomposition of a data base and the theory of boolean switching functions", IBM Journal of Research and Development, Vol. 17, No. 5, September 1973, pp 374-386.

[5]   Rissanen, J.
      Delobel, C.   "Decomposition of files, a basis for data storage and retrieval", IBM Research Report, RJ-1220, May 1973.

[6]   Notley, M.G.   "The Peterlee IS/1 System" IBM (UK) Scientific Centre Report, March 1972, UKSC 0018.

[7]   Boyce, Raymond F.
      Chaimberlin,
      Donald D.   "Using a STRUCTURED English query language as a data definition facility", IBM San Jose (California), December 10, 1973, RJ-1318.

[8]   Casey, R.G.
      Osman, I.M.   "Generalised page replacement algorithms in a relational data base", Proceedings 1974 ACM-SIGFIDET Workshop on Data Description, Access and Control, to be available from ACM HQ, 1974.

[9]   Knuth, D.E.   "The art of computer programming", Vol. 3, "Sorting and searching", Addison-Wesley, 1973, pp. 506-542.

[10] Wishart, David "CLUSTAN USER", Computing Laboratory, University of St. Andrews, St. Andrews, Fife, Scotland, 1969 (obtainable from the author.)

8. COMPUTER GRAPHICS

SOFTWARE
H.U. LEMKE, A.P. ARMIT

U. TRAMBACZ

ANWENDUNGEN
H.M. AUS, V. ter MEULEN, M. KÄCKELL, W. SCHOLZ, K. KOSCHEL

F. BRAKHAGEN

APPROXIMATIONS-TECHNIKEN
E. BECKER, F. REUTTER

W. STRAßER

A NOTE ON ADVANCED SOFTWARE TECHNIQUES IN COMPUTER GRAPHICS

H.U.Lemke and A.P.Armit
Graphical Software Ltd., London

1. Introduction

When designing an interactive computer graphics (IG) system as part of a research project, the development of new hardware or software techniques is often required. If, however, the IG system is designed as part of a commercial development, emphasis is on the evaluation and selection of existing and tested software techniques and hardware. The problem then is one of software engineering and the techniques selected for such a project may be determined by the following criteria:

a) The specification of the user facilities of the system.
b) A statement on the design objectives for the system, for example, its flexibility, maintainability and performance.
c) Available resources, e.g. manpower, design and implementation time and computer hardware, i.e. costs of all kinds.

If the system under development is fairly complex it will be difficult, if not impossible, to take account of these criteria in all design decisions. After completion of the project, however, and with the advantage of hindsight, it is possible to examine the consequences of the design decisions and to observe any shortcomings easily.

The system discussed in this paper is one of the very few complex IG systems developed in a commercial environment and therefore appears to be worthy of examination. Of particular interest are the effects on the design objectives of software techniques such as paged programs and data structures (1), pseudo machines and their structures (2) and the use of BCPL as a high level implementation language (3,4).

Before discussing these, a general description of the system is given.

2. Systems description

Worldwide developments in the field of computerised structural analysis have produced a number of program packages for finite element analysis. One of the larger programs is NASTRAN which is used or operated by many organisations in the US and Europe.

NASTRAN was originally developed for the NASA organisation in the US at the Goddard Space Flight Centre in Maryland for the analysis of space vehicles. Its development started in 1965 and took about five years to complete while occupying the time of some 26 programmers.

Functionally, NASTRAN is organised into an executive system and 14 modules each of which can be used in any order for a particular type of problem solution. For some finite element structures (FES) solution times can exceed many hours even on large computer systems. Data preparation for FES is conventionally on punched cards or card images on magnetic tape. Generally, these are many thousands of cards and it is easily appreciated how costly non-automatic card preparation or errors in cards can become.

To speed up and reduce the cost of data preparation and checking of FES for analysis with NASTRAN an interactive computer graphic system has been produced by Graphical Software Ltd. for Lloyd's Register of Shipping, London. With some 300 distinct and (according to the user) necessary commands, space limitation in this paper precludes full description. Therefore, only a statement on the overall objectives of the system is offered.

User specification

The basic task of the IG system is to allow a user to interactively modify and/or generate a representation of a ship's structure suitable for input to NASTRAN. In achieving this, IG is able both to accept and produce information in the NASTRAN input format. From the user point of view the IG system was designed to satisfy the following objectives:

    a) To provide means of altering or correcting a NASTRAN data deck for a ship's structural idealisation prepared elsewhere.
    b) To enable a NASTRAN data deck to be built up either by use of light-pen and keyboard or by a combination of light-pen, keyboard and card or tape input.
    c) To provide storage for structural idealisations so that they can be recalled and modified as necessary.

    d)   To be sufficiently flexible (in so far as it is practicable) to accept new techniques for idealising ship's structures.
    e)   To enable NASTRAN plotter data to be displayed.

Systems chart

A brief systems chart of the IG system is given in Fig.1. Central to the system is the data structure. It is generated by the input module (IG1) from a NASTRAN Bulk Data Deck or by the interactive module (IG2) from user input on the display. NASTRAN Bulk Data Decks are produced by the output module (IG3) from the data structure and are appended to the Executive and Case Control cards which may have been set up by IG1.

In addition to the data editing and generation facilities of IG2 further modification may be carried out using the scope text editor (EDITOR) which is a slightly modified version of the RAINBOW editor (5). This allows editing of Executive and Case Control cards.

Deformed finite element structures, etc. can be displayed on the screen with IGP after the NASTRAN plot tape has been converted from IBM 370 to PDP11 format by FRMNSP. Other conversion programs are FRMNSB and TONSB which convert from IBM to PDP11 and from PDP11 to IBM format respectively. Special structure filing facilities are provided by IGF.

BCPL is used as implementation language of IG1, IG3, EDITOR, IGP IGF and part of IG2.

NASTRAN analysis is carried out on an IBM 370/155.

Hardware

The computer hardware selected for implementing the IG system is a DEC PDP11/45 with memory segmentation, a floating point processor, 32K of core memory and a number of peripherals including discs, magnetic tape drive, card reader, paper tape reader and punch and a teletypewriter.

The display equipment consists of a 3D3 Vector General display with a three-dimensional rotation and transformation generator, phosphor protection, 10 mil spot, intensity modulation, character generator and an interface to the PDP11/45. An alphanumeric keyboard, 3-D joystick and light-pen are also attached to the display.

3. Design objectives

Although the user facilities to be provided by the IG system have been specified in some detail, no explicit specification of design objectives had to be met. Nevertheless, in the design and implementation of the system special effort was made to optimise towards the following design objectives:

    a) Modularity
    b) Flexibility
    c) User convenience
    d) Machine independance and mobility.

Modularity

This is concerned with breaking the system down into program modules such that each may be written, compiled and tested as an independent activity. Modularity was considered important mainly because of the systems expected high complexity and the relatively short time (18 months) available for its design and implementation.

Modularity is achieved by partitioning the system into functionally independent units which themselves may be further partitioned into units of different linguistic levels. A very idealised example for the modules IG1, IG2 and IG3 is given in Fig.2. Here the functional modules IG1 and IG2 are built from submodules of various linguistic levels.

Unfortunately, the boxes do not show the sizes of the program modules, otherwise the disproportionately large size of the assembler part of IG2 could be observed. Some of the facilities provided by this submodule could be grouped into:

    a) Initialisation routines (for the system and devices)
    b) Picture generation routines (points, lines, texts, tables etc.)
    c) Picture grouping routines (substructures, 3D elements etc.)
    d) Picture transformation routines (scaling, translation, rotation, dither, Z-slide etc.)
    e) Picture editing routines (move, delete, copy, update of points etc.)

f) Interrupt handling routines (light-pen, keyboard, joystick etc.)
g) Language processor facilities.

A modular structure which would reflect all such groupings would require a fairly general interface between these routines and the rest of the system. For highly interactive and real-time sensitive systems such as IG2 very general interfaces have to be avoided to preserve efficiency. Different hardware, particularly a faster subroutine calling mechanism and argument transfer could, however, improve this situation.

Flexibility

Flexibility of a system may be assessed by the ease of adaption to satisfy different user requirements, e.g. a change in the user facility specification. Frequently this requires modification to the flow of control, algorithms or graphic and applications data structures of the system.

Ideally, few program modules should be affected by any particular change.

A powerful technique to increase flexibility of an IG system is structure directed program control and data access. In the IG system, structures are available for the syntax description of NASTRAN Bulk Data Deck cards, control of user interaction on the display and for running display files while controlling display devices. These structures are processed by programs termed pseudo machines. For example, the interaction machine runs on a structure determining the flow of control in the system.

The structures have been generated "by hand" from the user specification and therefore may not necessarily represent the users real wishes. A more formal user specification and possibly a higher level of pseudo machine structure could improve the possibility of automatic translation.

Changes to algorithms are simplified if implementation is in an algorithmic language which supports some kind of hierarchical ordering.

BCPL is considered to be such a language and this is one of the reasons why it has been used extensively in the implementation of the system.

This, however, does not imply that BCPL is a suitable programming language for interactive graphic systems generally. Some features which are not available but could improve its graphics programming capability are:

- a) Graphic data types for points, lines etc.
- b) Graphic operators for general 2D and 3D transformations.
- c) A mechanism for interrupt handling of graphic and other devices.
- d) An easy to use and efficient interface to machine oriented code.
- e) A general facility for segmentation, protection and information sharing of program code and data.

User facility changes which affect the syntax or semantics of the application data structures, i.e. the representation of finite element structures, are far more difficult to contain within one program module and typically require considerable effort in reprogramming. It is mainly here that the limitations in flexibility can be found.

User convenience

User convenience in a graphics system is concerned principally with aspects of man-machine communication such as the selection of communication language, visual aids and real-time response.

As might be expected, real-time response has become the most critical aspect of user convenience in the system, particularly in the processing of very large finite element structures. The information contained in such structures can exceed 200K,16 bit words.

For the benefit of real-time response, finite element structures are represented by two interrelated application data structures. A block type structure has been selected to represent the NASTRAN Bulk Data Deck (Card structure). Each card is represented in a block of appropriate length.

Finite element geometry is held in a different structure (Line-Point structure). Typically, the length of this structure is only a fraction, say one tenth, of the size of the Card structure. It is just this reduced size (max 20K, 16 bit words) which allows the Line-Point structure to contain internal pointers. References are allowed only from the Card structure to the Line-Point structure.

Access to elements in the Line-Point structure is by generating a virtual address which is then "realised" by a demand paging mechanism. This is one of the facilities provided by a special purpose co-ordinator program of the IG system. Graphic programs are also paged into core. Display files, however, are locked into core and therefore can produce, together with other core resident parts of the system, a shortage of space for the execution of certain user requests. Although no thrashing is produced the response time can be unsatisfactory.

Suitable facilities for segmenting programs and data structures would probably provide a more satisfactory long term solution to reducing swapping time than, for example, simply enlarging core or experimenting with page sizes.

Machine independence and mobility

Machine independence and mobility is influenced by the degree to which special purpose hardware and special purpose features of the operating system are used in the implementation of the system.

Whenever possible, programming has been carried put in BCPL not only to secure machine independence and mobility but also to take advantage of its self documenting feature. The structures of pseudo machines can also be considered to provide machine independence.

For efficiency reasons, however, large parts of the IG system had to be written in assembler and have reduced machine independence and restricted mobility. Also, the decision to design the system around virtual memory increases the dependence upon hardware which provides paging.

4. Conclusion

It is clearly unsatisfactory to simply optimise the selection of software techniques towards a number of design objectives without some statement on the relative importance of these objectives. This is even more important when one considers in addition to modularity, flexibility, user convenience and machine independence design objectives such as generality, maintainability, reliability, security and performance.

Some type of numeric relationship should be established between the design objectives and the different software techniques which may be selected.

References

1. Grant, J.S.   A system for the PDP11/45. RAINBOW Memo No.62, 1972. University of Cambridge, Computer Laboratory.

2. Armit, A.P.   Organisation and Control of Interactive Systems. IRIA Conference. December, 1973. Rocquencourt, France.

3. Richards M.   BCPL: A tool for compiler writing and systems programming. Proc.S.J.C.C., 1969.

4. Richards M.   BCPL reference manual, Technical Memorandum 69/1, 1969. University of Cambridge, Computer Laboratory.

5. Wiseman N.E. RAINBOW Editor, RAINBOW Memo No.101, 1974 University of Cambridge, Computer Laboratory.

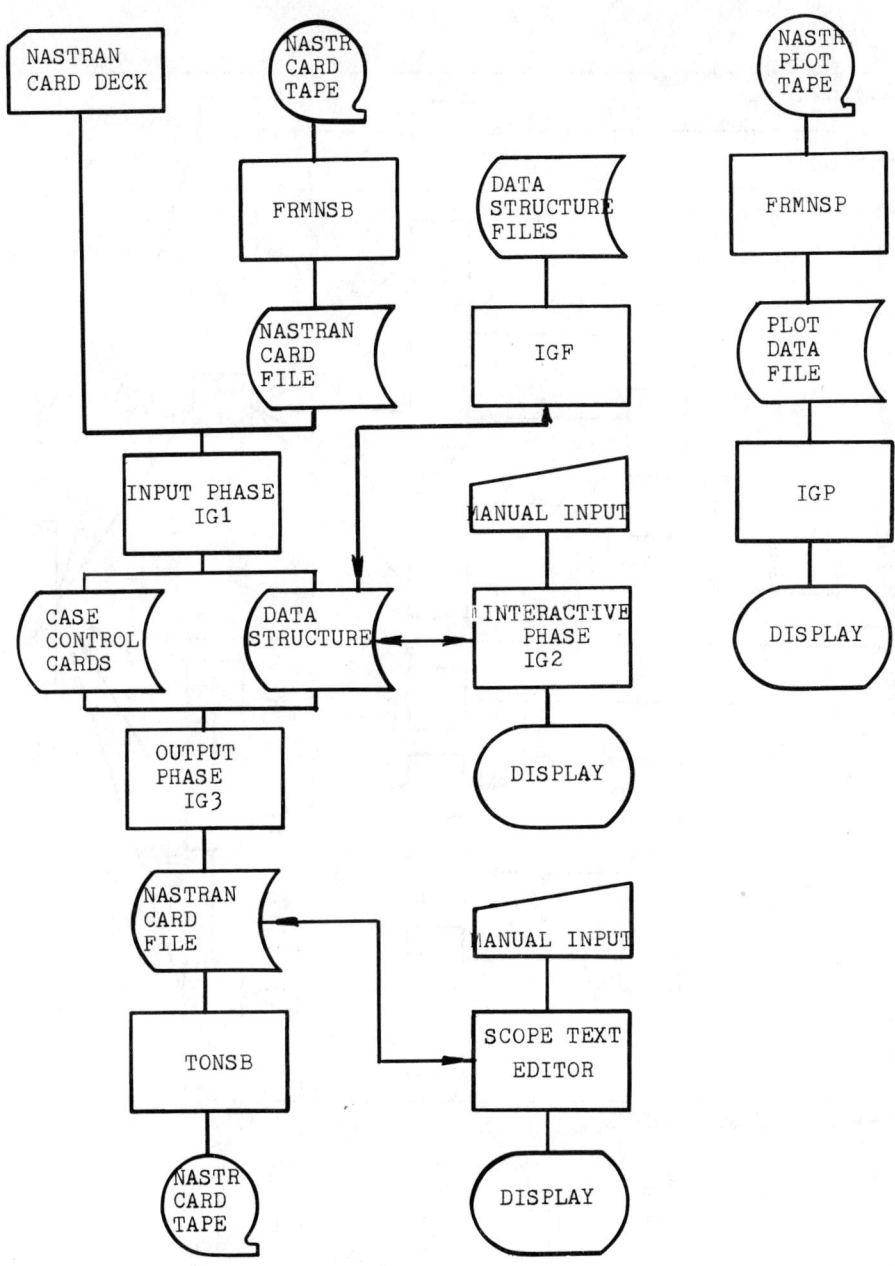

Fig. 1 SYSTEMS CHART OF IG SYSTEM

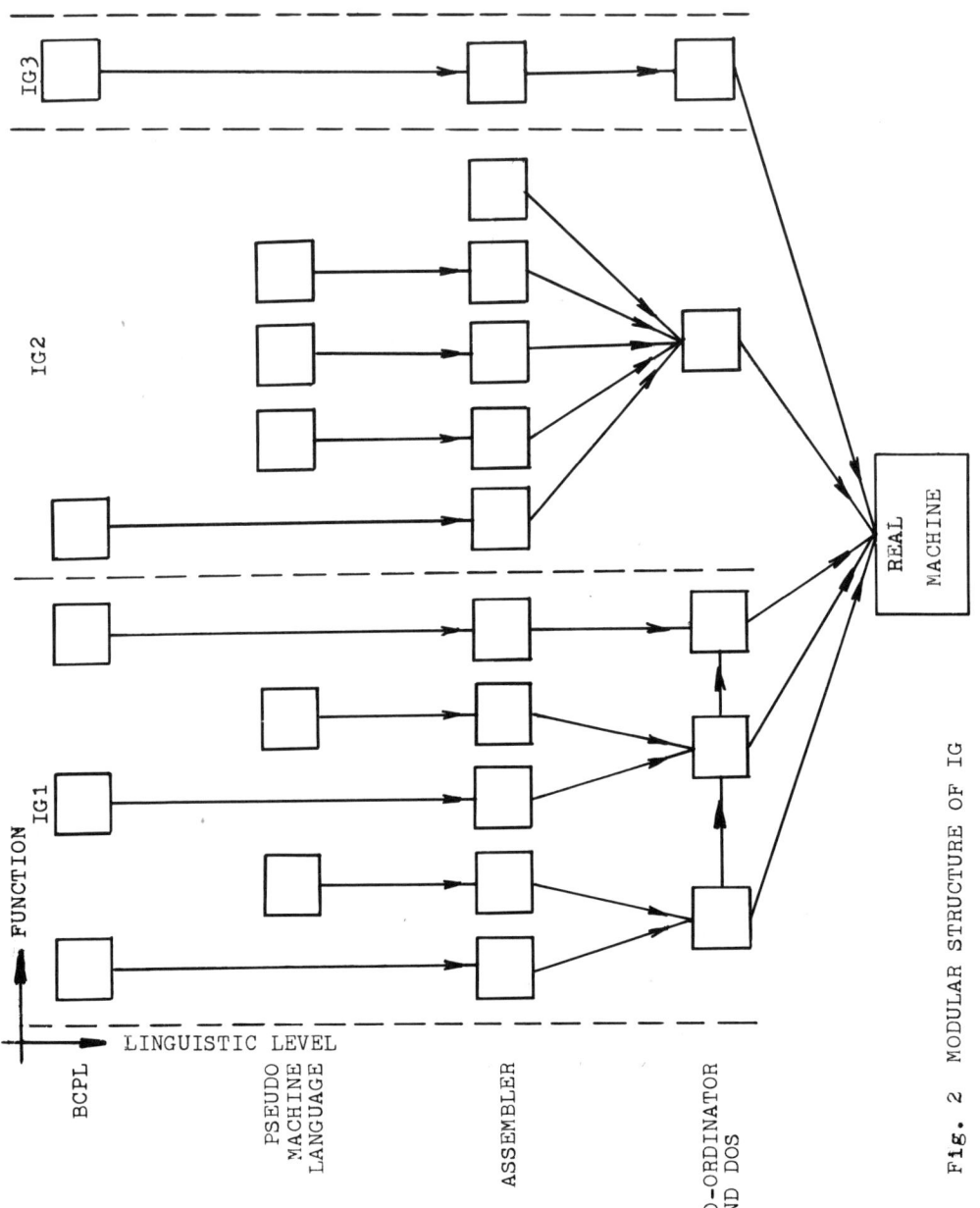

Fig. 2 MODULAR STRUCTURE OF IG

DIE DEFINITION GENERALISIERTER, GRAPHISCHER EINGABEGERÄTE

Ulrich Trambacz
Technische Universität Berlin
Fachbereich Kybernetik
D-1 Berlin 10, Einstein-Ufer 35-37

EINLEITUNG

"Warum konnte Computer Graphics den in dieses Fach gesetzten Erwartungen immer noch nicht entsprechen, deren Erfüllung seit langem für das nächste Jahr angekündigt wird ?" Zumindest zwei Antworten gibt es auf dieses Leit- (oder: Leid-)thema einer mehrtägigen Tagung im Sommer 1973.

Erstens: Es gibt eine Vielfalt graphischer Terminals kombiniert mit verschiedenen graphischen Eingabegeräten. Bei dem Entwurf der Software für diese Systeme waren die Hersteller bestrebt, die Vorteile der jeweiligen Hardware-Eigenschaften auszunutzen und deren Nachteile zu umgehen. Deshalb sind Anwendungsprogramme für diese Systeme in einem hohen Grad geräteabhängig und lassen sich kaum auf andere Maschinen übertragen. Geräteunabhängigkeit ist daher die erste Voraussetzung für höhere und universelle graphische Systeme /1/.

Und die zweite Antwort: Die Kenntnisse über Arbeitsabfolgen und die Arbeitsweise des Benutzers sowie über die Anpassung der Maschine an den Menschen sind immer noch sehr dürftig. WALLACE /2/ fordert als Voraussetzung für interaktive Eingabefolgen an graphischen Systemen, daß mit der Kommandosprache "kontinuierliche Bewegungs- und Blickrichtungsabfolgen" in "strukturierten Sätzen" beschreibbar sein müssen. Um diese Forderung zu erfüllen, müssen die anthropotechnischen Unterschiede der verschiedenen Eingabegeräte erforscht und diejenigen bekannten oder zukünftigen Geräte gefunden werden, die sich für eine bestimmte Anwendung am besten eignen. Eine geeignete Klassifizierung der Eingabegeräte kann auch unter diesem Gesichtspunkt zur Geräteunabhängigkeit von Eingabegeräten führen.

LOGISCHE EINGABEGERÄTE

1968 definierte NEWMAN /3/ erstmals sieben Kategorien von Benutzereingaben:
>   Textketten mit und ohne eingebetteten Wagenrücklauf,
>   dezimale und octale Werteeingabe,
>   das Zeigen auf dargestellte Objekte,
>   Positionseingabe und
>   Drucktastenfeld.

1972 reduzierte COTTON /4/ die Zahl der graphischen Eingabegeräte auf vier physikalische Geräte:
>   Drucktaste,
>   Analogeingabegerät,
>   Tablett und
>   Lichtstift.

1973 schlug wiederum NEWMAN /5/ vor, fünf höhere Grundfunktionen vorzusehen, die jeweils für eine bestimmte Interaktionsform verwendet werden:
>   Positionieren,
>   das Auswählen dargestellter Objekte,
>   Freihandzeichnen (inking),
>   Zeichenerkennung und
>   Verschieben von dargestellten Objekten.

Auf derselben Tagung wurde eine Klassifizierung der graphischen Eingabegeräte nach Benutzeraktionen vorgeschlagen /6/:
>   Objektidentifikation,
>   Positionsangabe,
>   Eingabe von Bedingungen und
>   dynamische Parametereingabe.

Kürzlich haben FOLEY und WALLACE /2/ ein sehr hübsches und vielversprechendes Konzept vorgelegt. Sie definieren vier virtuelle Eingabegeräte:
>   Zeigestift (= pick),
>   Wahltaste (= button),
>   Positionierer (= locator) und
>   Wertegeber (= valuator),

denen bestimmte physikalische Eingabegeräte als Prototypen entsprechen.

Bereits COTTON /4/ hat festgestellt, daß die physikalischen Eingabegeräte gegeneinander austauschbar sind und oft ausgetauscht werden müssen, da sie nicht immer mit jedem Ausgabegerät kombinierbar sind. Aber dieses oft notwendige Austauschen zeigt sich, von einem anderen Gesichtspunkt aus betrachtet, als sehr nützlich. Die physikalischen Eingabegeräte eignen sich aus anthropotechnischen Gründen unterschiedlich gut für die einzelnen interaktiven Benutzeraktionen an einem graphischen Terminal, so daß jeweils das Gerät ausgewählt werden kann, das dem Benutzer am ehesten kontinuierliche Bewegungs- und Blickrichtungsabfolgen erlaubt. Zur Untersuchung solcher Aktionsfolgen unter der Voraussetzung, daß Programmsysteme übertragbar bleiben, eignet sich ein Ansatz mit logischen Eingabegeräten.

Aufbauend auf die Terminologie von FOLEY und WALLACE, jedoch mit einigen Definitionsänderungen und etwas anderer Zuordnung der physikalischen Eingabegeräte zu den logischen Eingabegeräten, wird die folgende Formalisierung vorgeschlagen:

<Eingabegerät> ::= <Anzeiger eines Objektes, das während der Benutzung des Anwendungssystems definiert wurde> |
    <Anzeiger einer Position> |
    <Anzeiger eines Objektes, das im Anwendungssystem definiert wurde> |
    <Anzeiger eines Wertes>

<Anzeiger eines Objektes, das während der Benutzung des Anwendungssystems definiert wurde> ::= <Zeigestift>
<Anzeiger einer Position> ::= <Positionierer>
<Anzeiger eines Objektes, das im Anwendungssystem definiert wurde>
    ::= <Wahltaste>
<Anzeiger eines Wertes> ::= <Wertegeber>

Geräteunabhängigkeit bezüglich der Eingabegeräte wird dadurch erreicht, daß das System nur die logischen Eingabegeräte sieht. Auf der Benutzerseite werden die logischen Eingabegeräte von einer größeren Anzahl physikalischer Realisierungen oder deren logische Äquivalente vertreten, die mit den logischen Geräten entweder über Makros /7/ oder über einen Eingabemikroprozessor /6/ verknüpft sind.

Die logischen Äquivalente und die physikalischen Realisierungen der logischen Eingabegeräte sind in Tabelle 1 aufgeführt:

Tabelle 1: Die Definition logischer Eingabegeräte

<Eingabegerät> ::= <Anzeiger eines Objektes, das während der Benutzung des Anwendungssystems definiert wurde>|<Anzeiger einer Position>|<Anzeiger eines Objektes, das im Anwendungssystem definiert wurde>|<Anzeiger eines Wertes>

<Anzeiger eines Objektes, das während der Benutzung des Anwendungssystems definiert wurde>::= <Zeigestift>

<Anzeiger einer Position> ::= <Positionierer>

<Anzeiger eines Objektes, das im Anwendungssystem definiert wurde> ::= <Wahltaste>

<Anzeiger eines Wertes> ::= <Wertegeber>

<Zeigestift> ::= <physikalischer Zeigestift>|<logisches Äquivalent zum physikalischen Zeigestift>

<physikalischer Zeigestift> ::= Lichtstift

<logisches Äquivalent zum physikalischen Zeigestift> ::= Ausblenden überwacht von <Positionierer>| Ausblenden überwacht von <Wahltaste>| Eingabe des Namens mit <Wahltaste>| durchlaufende Helligkeitserhöhung gesteuert von <Wahltaste>| Ausblenden überwacht von <Wertegeber>

Tabelle 1 (Fortsetzung)

<Positionierer> ::= <physikalischer Positionierer>|<logisches Äquivalent zum physikalischen Positionierer>

<physikalischer Positionierer> ::= Tablettstift

<logisches Äquivalent zum physikalischen Positionierer> ::= Ziehkreuz gesteuert von <Zeigestift>| Laufmarke gesteuert von <Wahltaste>| Laufmarke gesteuert von <Wertegeber>

<Wahltaste> ::= <physikalische Wahltaste>|<logisches Äquivalent zur physikalischen Wahltaste>

<physikalische Wahltaste> ::= Tastatur|Lichtstiftschalter|Tablettstiftschalter|programmierte Knöpfe|Pedal|Spracheingabeanalysator

<logisches Äquivalent zur physikalischen Wahltaste> ::= Menuauswahl mit <Zeigestift>|vorformulierter Bewegungsablauf von <Zeigestift>|vorformulierter Bewegungsablauf von <Positionierer>|Drehwahl mit <Wertegeber>

<Wertegeber> ::= <physikalischer Wertegeber>|<logisches Äquivalent zum physikalischen Wertegeber>

<physikalischer Wertegeber> ::= Potentiometer|Steuerknüppel|Rollkugel

<logisches Äquivalent zum physikalischen Wertegeber> ::= Werteauswahl aus dargestellter Skala mit <Zeigestift>|numerische Eingabe mit <Wahltaste>

Folgende Überlegungen haben zu Modifikationen der in /2/ gegebenen Definitionen geführt: FOLEY und WALLACE definieren den Zeigestift als ein Gerät, das "vom Benutzer definierte Objekte" auswählt, und die Wahltaste als ein Gerät, das "vom System definierte Objekte" auswählt. Es könnten aber Systeme existieren, die es z.B. nicht nur dem Anwendungsprogrammierer sondern auch dem Benutzer erlauben, die Kommandos in einem Menu oder vorformulierte Bewegungsabläufe des Zeigestifts oder des Positionierers selbst festzulegen. Obwohl diese Objekte vom Benutzer definiert sind, besitzen sie die Eigenschaften von systemdefinierten Objekten. Um diesen Gegensatz aufzulösen, wurde die Wahltaste definiert als "Anzeiger eines Objektes, das im Anwendungssystem definiert wurde" und der Zeigestift als "Anzeiger eines Objektes, das während der Benutzung des Anwendungssystems definiert wurde".

Wie bereits festgestellt wurde, kann mit dem vorgelegten Formalismus einerseits Geräteunabhängigkeit auf der Eingabeseite erzielt und andererseits die Austauschbarkeit der physikalischen Eingabegeräte unter psychologischen und physiologischen Gesichtspunkten untersucht werden. Beim Austauschen eines Gerätes gegen ein anderes lassen sich einige interessante Methoden entdecken. Aber man findet natürlich auch weniger sinnvolle Ersetzungen, z.B. den Austausch des Zeigestiftes durch die Wahltaste und deren Austausch wieder gegen den Zeigestift. Und es treten Pleonasmen auf:

<Zeigestift> ::= ....
.... |Ausblenden überwacht von <Positionierer>| Ausblenden überwacht
                                                von <Wahltaste>|....
.... ::= .... |Laufmarke gesteuert von <Wahltaste>| ....

Hier ist das "Ausblenden (= boxing) überwacht von einer Laufmarke (= cursor), die gesteuert wird von <Wahltaste>", ein Umweg und Pleonasmus zum "Ausblenden überwacht von <Wahltaste>".

Ein besonderes Eingabegerät, das "Light Handle", wurde von NEWMAN /8/ beschrieben. Auch dies kann mit dem vorgelegten Formalismus nach einer mehrstufigen Ersetzung gefunden werden:

<Wertegeber> ::= ....
.... |numerische Eingabe mit <Wahltaste>
.... ::= .... |vorformulierter Bewegungsablauf von <Positionierer>|....
.... ::= .... Ziehkreuz gesteuert von <Zeigestift>|....

ZUSAMMENFASSUNG

Die vorgelegte Definition logischer Eingabegeräte ermöglicht es, auf der Eingabeseite geräteunabhängige und sehr flexible graphische Systeme zu entwerfen. An ihnen können die psychologischen und physiologischen Unterschiede logisch äquivalenter Eingabegeräte studiert und verwertet werden, so daß "in einem Jahr" ein Benutzer an Systemen arbeiten kann, die ihn weniger als bisher bei der Entfaltung seiner Fähigkeiten behindern.

LITERATUR

/1/ W.M. Newman: Where Are We ? SIGGRAPH-ACM Computer Graphics, Vol.8, No.1, Spring 1974, pp.12-29
/2/ J.D.Foley and V.L.Wallace: The Art of Natural Man-Machine Conversation, Proc. IEEE, April 1974
/3/ W.M. Newman: A system for interactive graphical programming, Proc. AFIPS 1968 SJCC, Vol. 32, pp. 47-54
/4/ I.W.Cotton: Network graphic attention handling, ONLINE 72 Conf. Proc., pp. 465-49o
/5/ W.M.Newman: An Approach to Graphics System Design, Proc. of AFCET-IRIA journées graphiques 1973, pp. 23-26
/6/ J.Encarnacao and U.Trambacz: The Design and Organization of a General-Purpose Display Processor, Proc. of AFCET-IRIA journées graphiques 1973, pp. 37-5o
/7/ C.H.A. Koster: Portable compilers and the UNCOL problem, Proc.IFIP Working Conf. on Machine Oriented High Level Languages, Trondheim, Aug. 1973
/8/ W.M.Newman: A graphical technique for numerical input, Computer Journal, Vol.11, May 1968, pp. 63-64

PATTERN RECOGNITION OF VIRUS INDUCED CELL CHANGES

Hans M. Aus, Volker ter Meulen, Mathilda Käckell, Wolfgang Scholz and
Klaus Koschel

Institute of Virology, University of Würzburg, Würzburg;
Max-Planck-Institute of Biophysical Chemistry, Göttingen;
Department of Pediatrics and Department of Neuro-Pathology,
University of Göttingen, Medical Center, Göttingen, Germany

ABSTRACT

Pattern recognition techniques have been applied in virology to extract virus dependent information from digitized images of cells and cell cultures. The successful application of these methods has been possible because viruses can induce marked biochemical and morphological changes in the cells. These changes can be measured and quantitatively analyzed. Preliminary investigations indicate that a considerable improvement in significant data extraction is possible if the extracted data and biological cells can be viewed simultaneously. Interactive image enhancement using TV scanning or mirror scanning methods and stored black/white differential maps of the target area and/or differential maps of the cells obtained by prescanning at other wavelengths greatly improves the subsequent feature extraction.

INTRODUCTION

Sophisticated programs and complete image analysis system have been developed and successfully applied to quantitatively analyze digitized, optical density images of chromosomes, cervix smears, and blood cells (1,2). Our own work, using a universal microspectrophotometer with a scanning stage and off-line analysis, has shown that the visible morphological alterations of the cells resulting from virus infection can be measured, analyzed and correlated to the known biological changes occurring in the cells (refs. 3-7). The texture of the biologically important, highly complex, sub-cellular, virus induced structural changes could not, however, be separated from the relatively unimportant cell structures by off-line, automatic feature extraction programs.

Recent hardware developments and cost reductions have made possible television image analysis systems complete with TV camera, computer, and video display monitors. Such systems offer the advantage of displaying both the specimen and computer output superimposed on the same monitor. The user can interact with the system using a joystick or lightpen. These systems enable the investigator to visually inspect and control what is being measured and analyzed. It has been of interest to us to apply such systems in our work in order to improve our measurement and analysis techniques. Unfortunately, the variation from point to point in the photo sensitive target area of the TV camera is too large relative to the biological variations and contrasts found in cell populations. Briefly stated, a cell measured in 15 different areas of the camera's field of view can produce up to 15 different, uncorrelated readings. To help eliminate the problem with the manufacturing variations in the camera's target area Bausch and Lomb has recently introduced a differential shading corrector in their Omnicon Image Analysis System. Black and white paper, respectively, are placed in front of the TV camera and the corresponding signals as recorded from the photosensitive target area are stored in fast memory as black and white calibration maps of the camera. The subsequent images are then measured as gray values (optical densities) relative to these absolute calibration maps.

An additional, challenging complexity for the image analysis systems occurs in cell-biology; since cells are very inhomogeneous, virus induced changes might have the same absolute optical gray values as the regular cell structures. Separation of the biologically interesting and important areas of the cell with respect to virus infection is, therefore, not possible using decision criteria based on absolute gray values. Preliminary work shows that it is possible to locate organelles and virus induced changes within a cell and to improve the subsequent image analysis by storing a map of the inhomogeneous cell structure as-well-as TV target area corrections in the black calibration map.

Two specific examples from Virology are included here to demonstrate the complexity of the problem, and the feasibility and usefulness of employing interactive techniques to provide specific information about biological entities, events and relationships. The interested reader is referred to the references for details concerning the biochemical, histochemical and cytophotometric material and methods (4-6).

IMAGE ENHANCEMENT AND FEATURE EXTRACTION

One area of interest in Virology is the measurement of the affect of polio virus infection on the various organelles found in the host cell. Lysosomes are one class of such intra cellular organelles which, in certain virus-host cell systems, are affected by the polio virus. During the cycle of polio infection the permeability of the thin lysosomal membranes surrounding the lysosomal enzymes is increased. Increased amounts of the digestive enzymes are, therefore, released into the cell cytoplasm and, eventually, destroy the cell by digesting the outer membrane of the cell. It is of interest, therefore, to isolate, measure, count, determine the distribution of, and otherwise analyze the lysosomes in the cells during the cycle of polio infection. Fig. 1a is a photograph of a Hela cell stained for the lysosomal enzyme acid phosphotase which appears as red granules in the visible light microscope. The image of this cell in the Omnicon monitor is shown in Fig. 1b. The white areas have been selected by the computer as having optical densities greater than a value set by the investigator. The granularity, or texture, due to the stained lysosomes is intermixed with the cell structure. In order to localize the lysosomes the gray values due to the granules must be separated from the gray values due to the cell structure. Fig. 1c is a map of the structure of the cell obtained by refreshing the black calibration memory with the cell (instead of the black paper) in the camera's field of view. The averaged structure of the cell is stored because the calibration map set-up routine averages over a neighborhood of approximately 200 picture points. The computed difference between Fig. 1a and 1c is shown in Fig. 1d and indicates a significant improvement in separating the texture of the cell due to the lysosomes from the structural background using differential mapping techniques.

A quantitative measure and analysis of the effect of Polio infection of the cell nucleic acid distribution in the cytoplasm is also of interest in virology. Computer analysis of the pronounced disintegration of the cell morphology (cytopathic effect) which occurs in Hela cells 7 to 8 hours after polio infection is relatively easy (ref. 5).

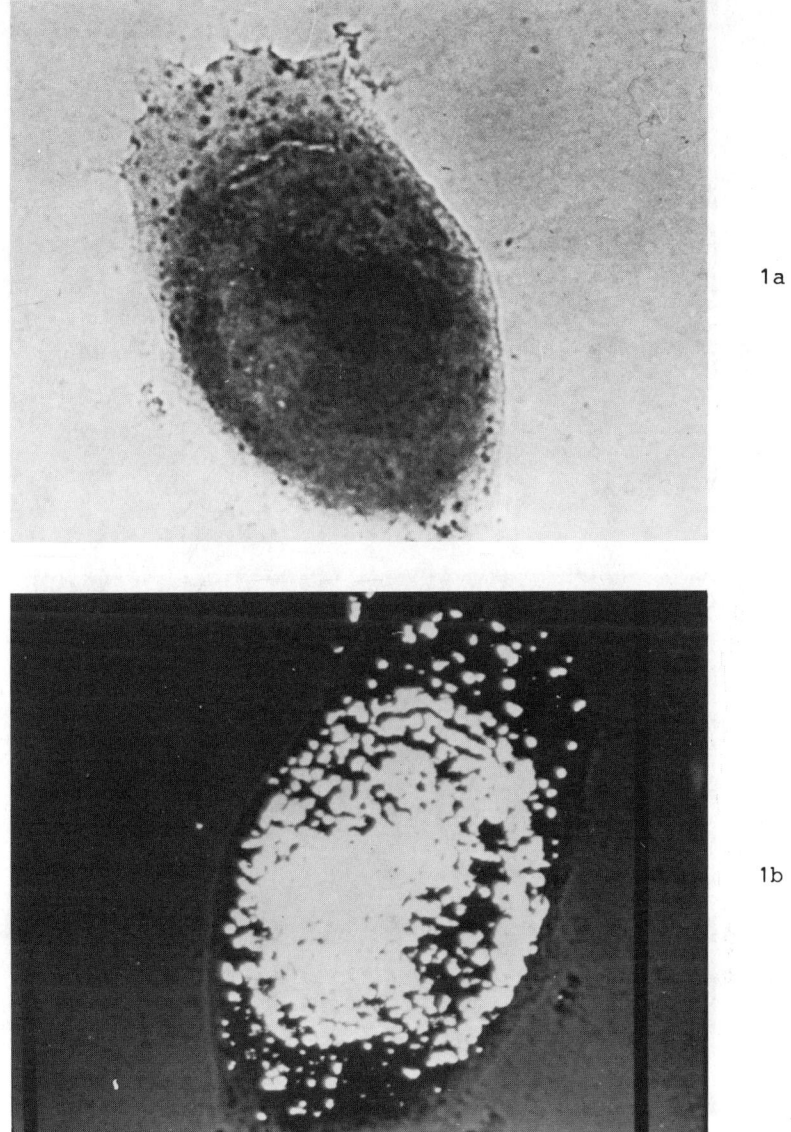

Fig. 1: Photograph of a Hela cell stoichiometrically stained to show the lysosomal enzyme acid phosphatase as viewed at 510 nm in the light microscope (a) and in the Omnicon monitor without differential mapping (b). The white spots (b,d) represent all picture points with an optical density greater than a selected density.

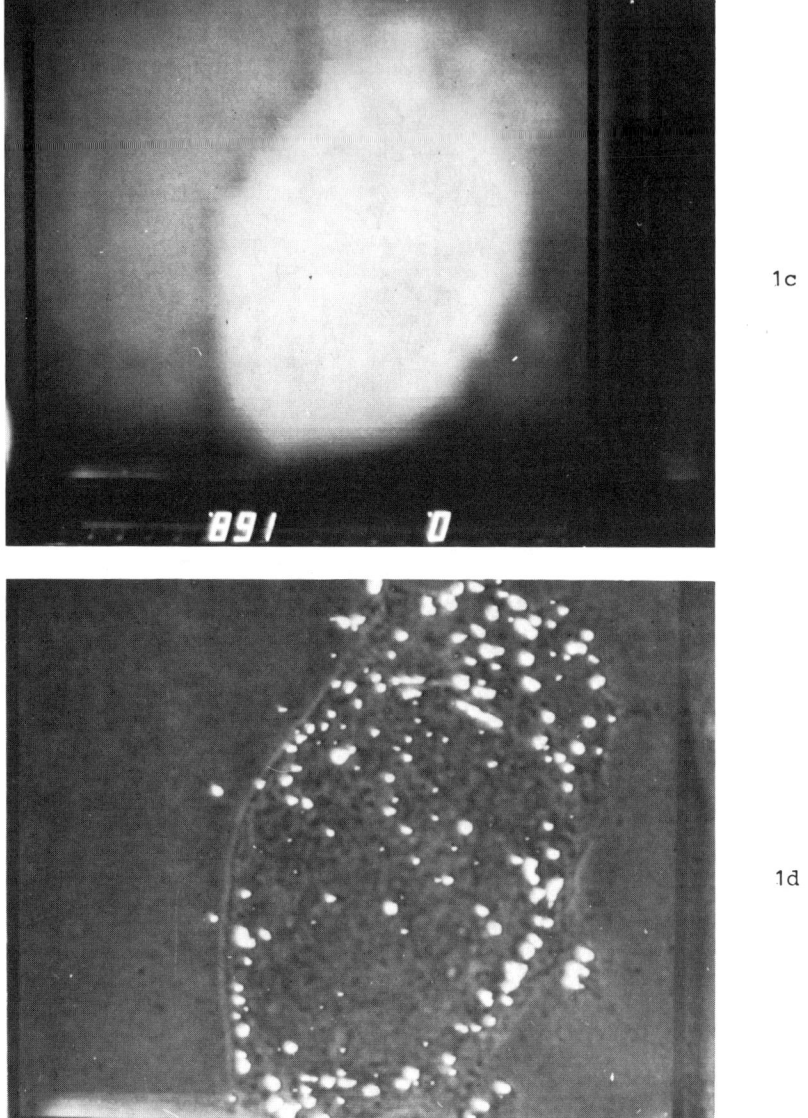

Fig. 1 continued: The inhomogeneous structure of the cell (c) stored in the calibration map. The difference (d) of (b) and (c) showing improved extraction of the lysosomes in the cell.

A more difficult problem, however, is to analyze the morphological and structural changes occurring in the host cell before such pronounced cytopathic effect occurs.

Typcial uninfected Hela cells as visualized in the ultraviolet microscope at 260 nanometers are shown in Fig. 2a. The darkest spots are nucleoli located within the nuclei. Note the relatively smooth appearance of the nuclei and cytoplasm. A Hela cell population four hours after polio virus infection is shown in Fig. 2b (also viewed at 260 nm). The image of this cell population as viewed in the Omnicon monitor without shading correction is shown in Fig. 2c. The visible, light gray, small granules appearing in most of the cells in 2b and 2c, but not in 2a, are polio virus induced changes in the cell nucleic acid distribution.

Note that the different areas of the cells are lighter than, as equally dark as, and darker than the virus induced granules (i.e. texture); that is, the cytoplasm, the nuclei and the nucleoli have absolute gray values that are smaller, equal, and greater than the virus induced changes.

The texture of the cells cannot be separated from the cell structure by the use of histograms and linear decision surfaces based on absolute gray value criteria. Fig. 2d shows the result of refreshing the black calibration storage with Fig. 2b in the camera's field of view. The tiny, almost invisible granules in Fig. 2c are now quite pronounced and the larger, unimportant cell structures have become background. The investigator can now set a critical gray value to separate the granules from the background, Fig. 2e. The larger dark spots due to the nucleoli can be eliminated from the subsequent computer analysis by selecting the appropriate particle size limits.

COMMENTS

Interactive image enhancement using differential mapping techniques can be employed to substantially improve the feature extraction of complex, virus induced, visual changes in a cell population. This type of pre-processing image enhancement shows that individual, intracellular granules can be localized and therefore counted, sized and otherwise quantitatively analyzed. It is worth noting that no special scene analysis programs were used to obtain these improvements. The investigator must, however, determine where the biologically interesting information is located.

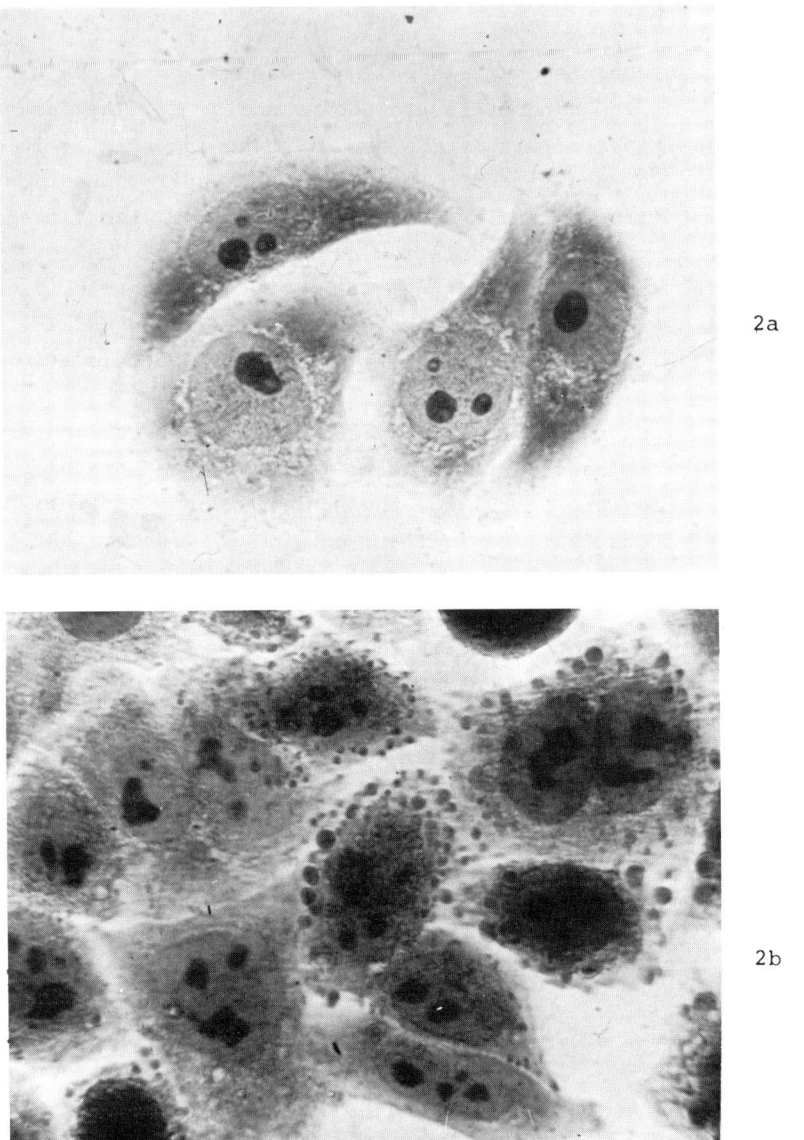

Fig. 2: Ultraviolet microscope view (260 nm) of control Hela cells (a) and Hela cells 4 hours post polio virus infection (b).

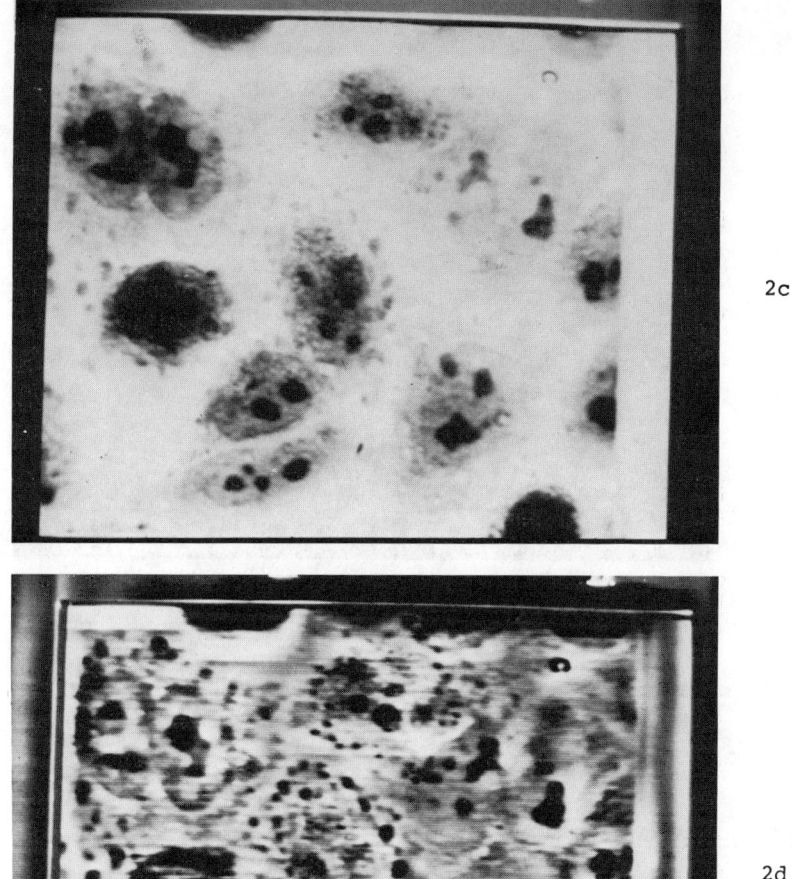

Fig. 2 continued: Hela cells in (b) as seen in Omnicon monitor (c). Enhanced image of polio induced granular activity (d) and subsequent extraction (e).

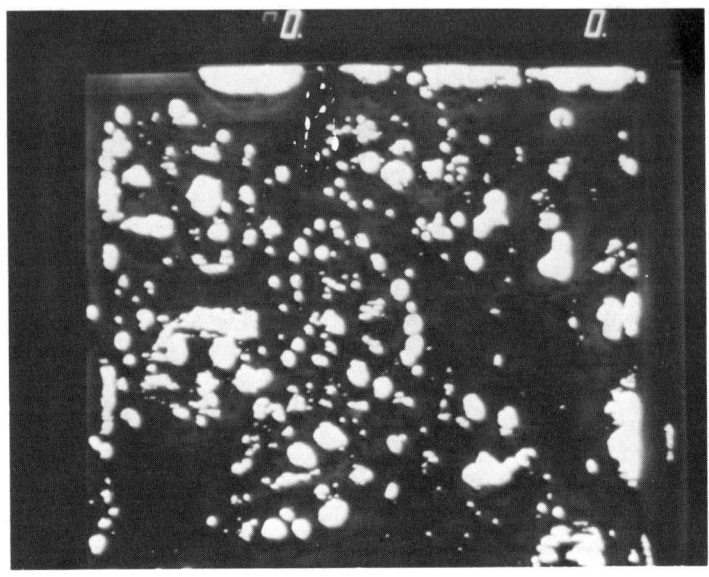

2e

Fig. 2 continued.

ACKNOWLEDGEMENTS

We wish to thank Bausch and Lomb Analytical System Division for granting us permission to use the Omnicon equipment at their plant in Rochester, N.Y., to obtain Figures 1b - d and 2c - e.

Supported in part by the Deutsche Forschungsgemeinschaft, Sonderforschungsbereich 33, Göttingen, Sonderforschungsbereich 105, Würzburg, and by Stiftung Volkswagenwerk.

REFERENCES

General Reviews of Automatic Image Analysis:
1. The Microscope, Vol. 22, No. 1, 1974, Microscope Publication Ltd., London and Chicago
2. Journal Histochemistry and Cytochemistry, Vol. 22, No. 7, 1974, Williams & Wilkins Co., Baltimore

Our work:

3. Aus, H.M.; ter Meulen, V.; Käckell, M.; Scholz, W.; and Koschel, K.: "Techniques Applicable to Computer-Aided Cytophotometry in Virology". J. Histochemistry and Cytochemistry, July 1974.

4. Aus, H.M.; Koschel, K.; ter Meulen, V.; Bartels, P.H.: "Approaches to computer analysis of polio infection in Hela cells". Proceedings of the International Computer Symposium, Davos, Switzerland, Vol. 1, North-Holland/American Elsevier Amsterdam, 1973, p. 407.

5. Aus, H.M.; ter Meulen, V.; Bartels, P.H.; Wied, G.L.: "Problems and approaches in computer aided analysis of virus infected cells". Chapter 14 in New Approaches to the Identification of Microorganisms. Proceedings Symposium on Rapid Methods and Automation in Microbiology, Stockholm, 1973, John Wiley, New York, 1974.

6. Koschel, K.; Aus, H.M.; ter Meulen, V.: "Lysosomal activity in polio infected Hela cells and VSV infected L-cells: a biochemical and histochemical analysis with computer-aided cytophotometric techniques". General Virology, in press.

7. ter Meulen, V.; Bartels, P.H.; Bahr, G.F.; Bibbo, M.; Cremer, N.; Lennette, E.H.; Wied, G.L.: "Computer assisted analysis of a carrier culture infected with Moloney leukemia virus". Acta Cytol (Baltimore) 16:5, 1972.

Ein Programmsystem zur interaktiven Triangulierung zweidimensionaler Gebiete in der Methode der finiten Elemente

F. Brakhagen
Institut für Grafische Datenverarbeitung und
Strukturerkennung der Gesellschaft für Mathematik
und Datenverarbeitung m.b.H. Bonn, 5205 St. Augustin

Die Methode der finiten Elemente ist eine häufig angewendete und sehr effektive Methode zur numerischen Lösung von Randwertproblemen bei partiellen Differentialgleichungen. Die Anwendung dieser Methode erfordert als Vorarbeit die Zerlegung des Gebiets, für das die Randwertaufgabe gestellt ist, in ein System von Dreiecken.

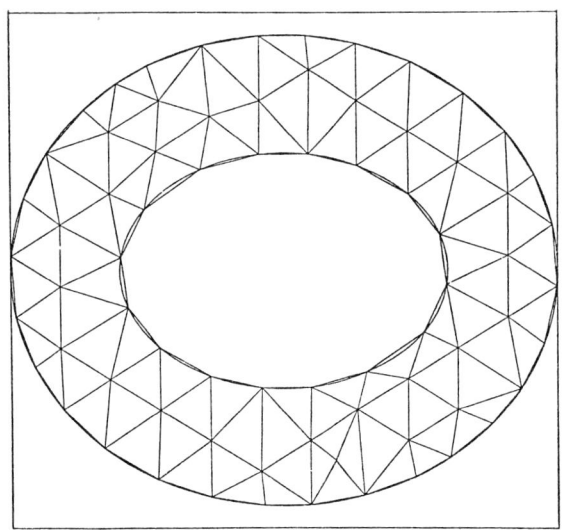

Beispiel eines triangulierten Gebiets

Um eine gute Approximation der exakten Lösung durch die numerische Lösung zu gewährleisten, sollte die Triangulierung vor allem die folgenden beiden Voraussetzungen erfüllen:

1. Jede geschlossene Randkurve ist möglichst gut durch einen Polygonzug von Dreiecksseiten zu approximieren.

2. Extrem kleine Winkel sind zu vermeiden.

Eine Ausführung der Triangulierung von Hand ist im allgemeinen mit einem sehr großen Arbeitsaufwand verbunden, insbesondere bei unregelmäßigen Gebieten und bei Verwendung feinmaschiger Dreiecksnetze. Vorhandene Programme zur vollautomatischen Triangulierung führen bei unregelmäßigen Gebieten zu unbefriedigenden Ergebnissen. Bei dieser Arbeit ist eine Reihe von logischen Entscheidungen zu fällen, die geometrischer Natur sind. Diese Entscheidungen können in einem beschränkten Umfang einprogrammiert werden. Man erhält dabei sehr unübersichtliche und sehr rechenaufwendige Programme, die nur dann zufriedenstellende Ergebnisse liefern, wenn die Gebiete bestimmte einschränkende Voraussetzungen erfüllen. Es ist wohl schwerlich möglich, in einem Programm alle denkbaren Unregelmäßigkeiten von Gebieten zu berücksichtigen. Das menschliche Auge ist hier offenbar dem Computer überlegen. Deshalb haben wir ein Programmsystem erstellt, das es erlaubt, die Triangulierung interaktiv am Bildschirm durchzuführen.

Dieses Programmsystem benutzt die IBM 2250 (ein grafisches Datensichtgerät) in Verbindung mit der IBM 360-50. Als Eingabevorrichtungen benutzt das System ein alphanumerisches Keyboard zur Eingabe bestimmter Kommandos und ein Grafacon zum Fixieren von Punkten. Als Programmiersprache wurde FORTRAN IV gewählt. Der Benutzer des Systems hat lediglich zur Gebietsdefinition ein FORTRAN-Unterprogramm zu erstellen und dem Programmpaket beizufügen.

Der Dialog dieses Programmsystems ist folgendermaßen aufgebaut. Es ist ein Grundzustand gegeben. In diesem Grundzustand wird ein Menue vorgelegt. Durch Eingabe bestimmter Kommandos können verschiedene Aktionen aufgerufen werden. Die diesen Eingabekommandos entsprechenden Programmteile können in folgende Klassen eingeteilt werden:

1. Gebietsdefinition
2. Netzerzeugung
   (i)   Einfügen einzelner Punkte
   (ii) Einfügen einzelner Linien
   (iii) Erzeugung eines regelmäßigen Dreiecksnetzes

3. Auslöschen von Netzteilen
   (i)   Auslöschen einzelner Punkte
   (ii) Auslöschen einzelner Linien
   (iii) Auslöschen größerer Netzteile und ganzer Netze

4. Bewegung von Netzteilen
   (i) Bewegung einzelner Punkte
   (ii) Bewegung ganzer Netze

5. Automatische Randanpassung

6. Datenorganisation
   (i) Reorganisation der Netzdaten zur Speicherplatzeinsparung
   (ii) Abspeichern der Netzdaten auf einem externen Speicher

7. Vergrößern und Verkleinern des Bildes

8. Programmsteuerung
   (i) Neuer Start
   (ii) Beendigung eines Laufs des Programmsystems

Nach Aufruf einer bestimmten Aktion werden alle weiteren Angaben durch das System vom Benutzer erfragt. Die einzelnen Programmteile bieten einen Kommandovorrat, mit dem die gewünschte Aktivität gesteuert werden kann. Die Steuerung kann bestehen in

1. Wahl aus einer vorgelegten Menuekarte,

2. Ja-Nein-Entscheidungen,

3. Fixieren von Punkten.

Nach Ausführung einer bestimmten Aktivität kehrt das System in den Grundzustand zurück.

Bei der Wahl einer passenden Datenstruktur für die Gebietsränder war in erster Linie zu berücksichtigen, daß die Gebietsdefinition vom Benutzer durch ein FORTRAN-Unterprogramm durchgeführt werden muß. Es war daher eine Darstellungsform zu wählen, mit der jedes beliebige Gebiet leicht darstellbar ist. Deshalb wurde folgendes Verfahren angewendet. Der Rand wird durch eine endliche Menge von Punkten dargestellt. Zwei benachbarte Randpunkte werden durch eine Strecke miteinander verbunden. Der Gebietsrand ist also als eine Menge von geschlossenen Polygonzügen gegeben.

Für die Wahl einer geeigneten Datenstruktur für die Dreiecksnetze
waren folgende Überlegungen maßgebend. Es ist auf jeden Fall sinnvoll,
die Netzknotenpunkte durchzunumerieren und ihre Koordinaten in Listen
abzuspeichern. Darüber hinaus benötigt das System eine Information
darüber, welche Knotenpunkte durch eine Dreiecksseite miteinander
verbunden sind. Wegen der grafischen Interaktion ist es notwendig,
daß die Datenstruktur für die grafische Ausgabe geeignet ist. Man
kann das Netz als Vereinigung von Dreiecken oder als Menge von sich
schneidenden Streckenzügen auffassen. Hier wurde die letzte Darstellungsform gewählt: Die Indexfolgen der Knotenpunkte auf den
einzelnen Streckenzügen werden in einer Liste abgespeichert, wobei
Indizes von Anfangspunkten der Polygonzüge besonders gekennzeichnet
werden. Diese Darstellungsform hat den Vorteil, daß jede Dreiecksseite nur einmal aufgelistet wird. Ferner kann dadurch das Dreiecksnetz in wenigen zusammenhängenden Streckenzügen gezeichnet werden,
d.h. es muß beim Zeichnen relativ selten neu aufgesetzt werden. Dadurch wird die Menge der Zeichenbefehle klein gehalten.

Die Triangulierung vollzieht sich im allgemeinen in folgenden drei
Schritten.

1. Das gegebene Gebiet wird von einem geeigneten Dreiecksnetz über-
   deckt.
   Zur Netzerzeugung bestehen verschiedene Möglichkeiten. Es kann
   ein Netz aus gleichseitigen Dreiecken, ein Netz aus rechtwinkli-
   gen Dreiecken oder ein Netz nach der speziellen Wahl des Benutzers
   erzeugt werden. Welches Netz die besten Ergebnisse liefert, hängt
   natürlich von den geometrischen Eigenschaften des Gebiets ab.
   Häufig ist es sinnvoll, das Dreiecksnetz in bestimmten Teilgebieten
   zu verfeinern. Dazu besteht die Möglichkeit, verschiedene Teilgebiete mit verschiedenen Dreiecksnetzen zu überdecken, deren
   Maschenweite diesen Teilgebieten angepaßt ist. Ferner können
   einzelne Knotenpunkte und Linien eingefügt werden.

2. Das Dreiecksnetz wird dem Verlauf des Gebietsrandes
   angepaßt.
   Ziel der Randanpassung ist es, jede geschlossene Randkurve möglichst gut durch einen Polygonzug von Dreiecksseiten zu approximieren. Dabei sind extrem kleine Winkel zu vermeiden. Bei regelmäßigen Gebieten mit glatten Rändern kann die Randanpassung
   automatisch durchgeführt werden. Bei der automatischen Randan-

passung werden die Knotenpunkte eines geeigneten Streckenzuges
des ursprünglichen Dreiecksnetzes auf den Rand verschoben. Um
bei diesem Prozeß das ursprüngliche Dreiecksnetz, das im allgemeinen eine mathematisch günstige Gestalt hat, möglichst wenig zu
verändern, wird folgendes Prinzip angewendet: Es werden Gitterpunkte, die möglichst nahe am Rand liegen, auf den ihnen am nächsten
gelegenen Randpunkt verschoben. Zur Behandlung unregelmäßiger
Gebietsteile bestehen folgende Möglichkeiten:
(i)   Verschiebungen einzelner Knotenpunkte,
(ii) Bewegungen ganzer Netze,
(iii) Einfügen einzelner Punkte und Linien,
(iv) Auslöschen einzelner Punkte und Linien.

3. Die Netzknotenpunkte, die nach Abschluß der Randanpassung außerhalb des Gebiets liegen, werden ausgelöscht.
Der Benutzer bezeichnet die auszulöschenden Netzteile, indem er
einen geschlossenen Polygonzug auf den Bildschirm zeichnet. Alle
Netzknotenpunkte innerhalb dieses Polygonzuges werden gelöscht.

Nach Abschluß der Triangulierung können die Netzdaten zur Weiterverarbeitung auf einem externen Speicher abgelagert werden.

Eine Beschreibung der Arbeitsweise des Programmsystems mit Hilfe von
Bildern ist unter [2] zu finden.

Literatur

[1] F. Brakhagen, G. Schmitgen: FEIA. Ein Programmsystem zur interaktiven Triangulierung zweidimensionaler Gebiete im Rahmen der Methode der finiten Elemente. Interner Bericht I3, Nr. 7/73, Gesellschaft für Mathematik und Datenverarbeitung m.b.H. Bonn.

[2] F. Brakhagen: Interaktive Triangulierung zweidimensionaler Gebiete in der Methode der finiten Elemente.
Erscheint in den Bonner Mathematischen Schriften in einem Tagungsband der Arbeitstagung "Numerische Behandlung von Variations- und Steuerungsproblemen" vom 18.-20.2.1974 an der Universität Bonn.

GIULIA - EIN SYSTEM ZUM VERARBEITEN ANALYTISCH GEGEBENER FLÄCHEN

ERHARD BECKER

FORSCHUNGSGRUPPE 15 (SPEZIELLE ANWENDUNGEN)
des überregionalen Forschungsprogramms Informatik an der RWTH Aachen

Prof. Dr. F. REUTTER

D-5100 Aachen, Seffenter Weg 23 (Rechenzentrum)

Graphische Interaktive Verarbeitung für LIniendarstellung Analytisch gegebener gekrümmter Flächen

Ziel von GIULIA ist es, eine möglichst große Anzahl häufig verwendeter analytisch gegebener gekrümmter Flächen besser verarbeitbar zu machen für den entwerfenden Ingenieur, als es mit den bisherigen Rasterdarstellungen möglich ist. Diejenigen Aufgabenstellungen sollen vereinfacht werden, in denen die geometrischen Eigenschaften primär die Funktion eines Objektes bestimmen. Zu diesem Zweck wurde GIULIA als Konstruktionsmittel für:

- Entwurf von gekrümmten Flächen
- Bestimmung von Verschneidungen beim Zusammensetzen von komplexen Flächen

sowie als Darstellungsmittel für:

- Darstellung der erzeugten Flächen

entworfen.

Unter einer "gekrümmten Fläche" soll im folgenden, in Anlehnung an die Bezeichnungen in /7/, aber in Ausweitung der dort gegebenen Definition, eine Fläche verstanden werden, deren Krümmung in mindestens einer Richtung variiert (oder in mathematisch einwandfreier Formulierung: Eine Fläche, deren Normalkrümmung in jedem Flächenpunkt, mit Ausnahme endlich vieler Richtungen, von Null verschieden ist). Durch diese Definition, die implizit in Übereinstimmung mit /15/ steht, sind alle Flächen zweiter Ordnung sowie auch Regel-, Röhren-, verallgemeinerte Röhrenflächen (einschließlich der allgemeinen Rotationsflächen) höherer als zweiter Ordnung einbezogen. Die Ausweitung der Definition gegenüber /7/ war durch die Zielsetzung, häufig verwendete Flächen zu verarbeiten, notwendig. Dem Autor sind außer den Häufigkeitsuntersuchungen /16/, die durch ihre spezielle Zielsetzung hier nur eingeschränkte Aussagekraft besitzen, weitere Häufigkeitsuntersuchungen nicht bekannt.

Analyse bisheriger Systeme und ihre Abgrenzung gegenüber GIULIA

Bisherige Systeme zum Verarbeiten gekrümmter Flächen lassen sich einteilen in:
A.1 Sichtbarkeitsklärende Systeme mit darstellungsbezogener Objektbeschreibung,
A.2 statisches und dynamisches Verhalten ermittelnde Systeme mit entsprechender eigenschaftsbezogener Objektbeschreibung,
A.3 werkstückbeschreibende Systeme mit fertigungsorientierter Objektbeschreibung.

Eine vergleichende Analyse bisheriger Systeme, in der nach Tabelle A. vorgegangen wird, findet sich in /3/. Eine ausführliche Aufzeichnung findet sich auch in /12/, ein Vergleich von 10 Algorithmen zur Sichtbarkeitsklärung in /17/. Auf die Flächenbeschreibung /2/, /4/, /5/, Sichtbarkeitsklärung und Datenhaltung /6/ allgemein bekannter Veröffentlichungen soll in diesem Rahmen nicht näher eingegangen werden.

Eine Verbindung zweier Systeme nach Tabelle A. wurde selten vorgenommen. Erst in letzter Zeit wird auch die Darstellung bei einigen Systemen nach A.3 /7/, /10/, /11/ sowie auch bei einigen nach A.2 stärker betrieben /1/, /18/.

Teilt man entsprechend Tabelle A. nach den Gesichtspunkten
- Darstellung eines Objektes
- Funktion eines Objektes
- Fertigung eines Objektes

ein, so erkennt man, daß bei der Funktion eines Objektes bisher statische und dynamische Eigenschaften - sekundär aus geometrischen Eigenschaften resultierend - im Vordergrund standen. Es war meist mit stark erhöhtem oder auch nicht realisierbarem Rechenaufwand verbunden, die primäre Abhängigkeit der Funktion von den geometrischen Eigenschaften eines Objektes zu ermitteln, wie z.B. die Frage, ob sich zwei gekrümmte Flächen im Raum schneiden, wenn die Flächen in einer stark unterteilten Rasterdarstellung - der gebräuchlichsten Flächeneingabe für diese Aufgaben - gegeben waren.

Im Falle der Rasterung wird die Fläche mit einem Netz überzogen und in kleine Flächenelemente aufgeteilt. Diese Aufteilung ist der erste Schritt der Flächenverarbeitung, in den folgenden Rechengängen wird also meist nur noch mit der Näherungsdarstellung der Flächenelementekombination gearbeitet. Eine n-fache Genauigkeitserhöhung bedeutet eine n^2-fache Erhöhung der Anzahl der Punkte auf der Fläche. Kennzeichen dieser Flächendarstellung sind:
- Große Anzahl von Punkten schon bei mittlerer Genauigkeit,
- einfache Darstellung jeden beliebigen Flächentyps nach der gleichen Art. Dementsprechend sind auch zur Weiterverarbeitung für die verschiedenen Flächentypen keine unterschiedlichen Algorithmen notwendig.

Dagegen arbeitet die in GIULIA verwendete *Liniendarstellung* nur mit den geometrisch aussagefähigen Linien einer Fläche:

B.1 Umriß
B.2 Endbegrenzung
B.3 ggf. erzeugende Kurven auf der Fläche
B.4 bei Flächenkombination die Durchdringungskurve(n) beider Flächen

Die Kurven auf der Fläche werden im Bild auch durch die Näherungsdarstellung eines Polygonzuges dargestellt; das Abspeichern des geometrischen Erzeugungsprinzips einschließlich seiner charakteristischen Daten ermöglicht aber eine Linienberechnung, z.B. des Umrisses und der Durchdringungskurve, aus dem geometrischen Erzeugungsprinzip und nicht aus der Näherungsdarstellung der gerasterten Fläche. Eine n-fache Genauigkeitserhöhung bewirkt einen n-fachen Anstieg der Punktzahl.

Der höhere Aufwand der Rasterdarstellung ist begründet in der

- Datenhaltung, weil alle erzeugten Punkte auf der Fläche einschließlich ihrer Beziehungen zueinander (zum Zeichnen der Linien) abgespeichert werden müssen,
- Darstellung, weil alle Linienstücke dargestellt werden, die das Netz auf dieser Fläche bilden,
- Weiterverarbeitung, weil bei einer Operation auf dieser Fläche jedes Rasterelement verarbeitet werden muß.

Ein Zahlenbeispiel soll dies erläutern: Zur Darstellung eines geraden Kreiszylinderstückes genügen beide Umrißmantellinien und beide endbegrenzenden Kreise. Vergleicht man diese Liniendarstellung mit einer Rasterdarstellung, die 20 achsennormale Kreisschnitte mit je 40 Punkten verwendet, so ergibt sich für die Rasterdarstellung ein Bedarf an 800 Punkten, 760 Flächenelementen, 1560 Linienstücken. Dem steht folgender Speicherbedarf für die Liniendarstellung gegenüber:

Zum Abspeichern der Flächendaten des Zylinders eine 4 x 4 Matrix, für die endbegrenzenden Ebenen 2 x 4 Werte; d.h. für die Flächendaten 24 Zahlenwerte. Dazu kommen 40 + 40 + 20 + 20 = 120 Punkte und 40 + 40 + 19 + 19 = 118 Linienstücke. Trotz dieser Vorteile wird die Liniendarstellung bisher nur wenig angewandt /9/, /14/.

Als spezifisches Einsatzgebiet von Rasterdarstellungen können alle nicht analytisch beschreibbaren Flächen angesehen werden (Karosserieflächen, Geländeflächen). Bei Darstellung von analytisch beschreibbaren Einzelflächen sollte geprüft werden, ob der Aufwand der Rasterdarstellung lohnt. Bei Verarbeitung von Zusammensetzungen von mehreren analytisch gegebenen Flächen empfiehlt sich meist eine Liniendarstellung, zumal ihre Anschaulichkeit, wenn nötig, durch zusätzliche erzeugende Kurven auf der Fläche noch erhöht werden kann (vgl. D.3).

Möglichkeiten von GIULIA und daraus resultierender Lösungsansatz

Die Erzeugung (im geometrischen Sinn) einer Fläche kann als Bewegung einer erzeugenden Kurve auf einer Leitkurve definiert werden. Um der Anforderung, häufig verwendete Flächen zu verarbeiten, gerecht zu werden, wurden für GIULIA als erzeugende Kurven Kegelschnitte und als Leitkurven beliebige (analytisch) beschreibbare Raumkurven vorgesehen. Daraus ergeben sich die in C. folgenden zulässigen algebraischen und transzendenten Flächen, wobei die Ebene nur wegen der Operationen D.1 und D.2 eingeführt wird. Der Benutzer kann beliebige Flächen aus der genannten Gruppe erzeugen, kombinieren oder auch löschen. Vom Algorithmus her ist die Anzahl der gleichzeitig darzustellenden Flächen nicht begrenzt; nur aus Speicherplatzgründen ist ihre Anzahl auf maximal fünf festgelegt.

C.1 Ebenen
C.2 Flächen zweiter Ordnung, z.B. Zylinder, Kegel, Kugel, Hyperboloide
C.3 Regelflächen: Erzeugende ist eine Gerade. Beispiel: Wendelfläche, einschaliges Rotationshyperboloid
C.4 Kugelhüllflächen: Erzeugende ist der Berührkreis einer Kugel. Beispiel: Torus
C.5 Verallgemeinerte Röhrenflächen: Erzeugende ist ein beliebiger Kegelschnitt. Auf diese Weise sind auch allgemeine Rotationsflächen erfaßt, d.h. als Meridiankurve ist jede beliebige (analytisch) beschreibbare ebene Kurve zulässig; Erzeugende ist in diesem Fall ein Kreis.

Die Flächen nach C.4 sind zwar eine Untermenge der Flächen nach C.5; sie werden nur wegen einfacherer weiterverarbeitender Algorithmen als getrennte Gruppe geführt.

Über diesen Flächen wurden Operationen vorgesehen, die Raumkurven auf den Flächen oder deren Bildkurven erzeugen und den Linien B.1 bis B.4 entsprechen; die Operationen seien hier in Beziehung gesetzt zu den eben genannten Flächen:

D.1 *Umrißkurvenbestimmung* über den Flächen zu C.2 bis C.5

D.2 Bestimmung ebener und räumlich gekrümmter *Endbegrenzungen* an Flächen zu C.1 bis C.5. Diese Operation kann für die ebene Endbegrenzung entweder durch Zeichnen des erzeugenden Kegelschnittes am Anfangs- und Endwert des Laufparameters der Leitkurve oder durch Abfragen eines linearen Ungleichungssystems erfolgen. Dieses lineare Ungleichungssystem wird bestimmt durch ein beliebiges konvexes Polyeder, das um die darzustellenden Flächen gelegt wird (Abb. 5). Für die räumlich gekrümmte Endbegrenzung, erzeugt durch eine Quadrik, wird eine quadratische Ungleichungsabfrage durchgeführt (Abb. 3).

D.3 Bestimmung erzeugender Kurven auf den Flächen zu C.1 bis C.5
Primär ist an Erzeugende im geometrischen Sinne gedacht, also hier an Kegelschnitte. Durch die Sichtbarmachung des speziellen erzeugenden Kegelschnittes

kann die Struktur der Fläche deutlich gemacht werden. Es besteht aber auch die Möglichkeit, die Fläche durch erzeugende ebene Schnitte (Höhen-, Quer- oder Diagonalschnitte) zu verdeutlichen (Abb. 6).

D.4 *Durchdringungskurvenermittlung* bei einer Flächenkombination von einer Fläche nach C.2 bis C.5 mit einer Fläche nach C.1 oder C.2.
Um in dieser Operation immer den günstigsten Algorithmus ausnutzen zu können, wird den Flächen nach C.1, C.2, C.3, C.4, C.5 nach Möglichkeit eine Zweitdarstellung zugeordnet. So kann z.B. ein schiefer Kreiszylinder als Quadrik, als Regelfläche oder als verallgemeinerte Röhrenfläche aufgefaßt werden. Für die weiterverarbeitenden Algorithmen ist die Darstellung als Quadrik und als Regelfläche günstig. Konstruiert der Benutzer also interaktiv diesen Zylinder, so werden ohne weiteres Zutun des Benutzers beide Darstellungsweisen in den Flächendaten des Zylinders abgespeichert. Beispiele zur Durchdringungskurvenermittlung finden sich in Abb. 2 und Abb. 5.

Es ist eine *Sichtbarkeitsklärung* über den Operationen D.1 bis D.4 zugelassen. Diese Sichtbarkeitsklärung über Einzelflächen und Flächenkombinationen ist z.Zt. noch in der Erprobungsphase.

Zulässige Projektionsarten sind:
E.1 Parallelprojektion für Zweitafelprojektion und axonometrische (anschauliche) Darstellung.
E.2 Zentralprojektion für perspektivische Darstellung.

Ein Lösungsansatz muß befriedigende Lösungen für folgende Aufgaben enthalten: Umsetzen der Operationen nach D., also der Kurvenerzeugungsbefehle, in einen gesteuerten Arbeitsablauf, der den günstigsten Algorithmus (in Abhängigkeit der beteiligten Flächen) für die Kurvenerzeugung auswählt und seine Durchführung überwacht. Die dabei anfallenden Probleme der Datenhaltung sind zu lösen.

Ein Satz von geometrischen Grundprogrammen (einschließlich der notwendigen numerischen Hilfsprogramme) zum Verarbeiten der folgenden Elemente (Kurven und Flächen) ist notwendig:
F.1 Kegelschnitt (mit dem vereinfachenden Sonderfall des Geradenpaares bzw. der Geraden), gegeben in Bezug auf seine Basis im Raum
F.2 Ebene
F.3 Quadrik

In Bezug auf die geometrischen Grundprogramme konnte auf der Forschungsarbeit /14/ aufgebaut werden.

Im folgenden Kapitel soll, ausgehend von der Datenhaltung, auf die Frage einer befriedigenden Steuerung, insbesondere für die Durchführung des einzelnen Kurvenerzeugungsbefehls, neben anderen Fragen der Implementation stärker eingegangen werden.

Implementation und bisherige Erfahrungen

GIULIA ist z.Zt. auf zwei Großrechnern implementiert. In beiden Fällen wird eine fast gleiche Fortran-Version verwendet.

Um eine möglichst hohe Flexibilität des Systems zu gewährleisten, werden die drei Datengruppen:
- *Ausgangsdaten*; sie bewirken den Start des Systems mit vom Benutzer vorgegebenen Daten,
- *Rechnungsdaten*; sie werden während der Rechnung gewonnen und auch wiederverwendet,
- *Ergebnisdaten*; sie stehen dem Benutzer zur Auswertung zur Verfügung und sind bei GIULIA eine Untermenge der Rechnungsdaten,

in getrennten Bereichen gespeichert.

Da alle drei Datengruppen den rechnungsdurchführenden Rechner durchlaufen, kann hier jede Art von Archivierung, d.h. Erzeugung von Reproduzierbarkeit eines Zustandes oder Ausgabe von Rechnungs- oder Ergebnisdaten durchgeführt werden. Die Benutzerdaten (Ausgangs- und Ergebnisdaten) können auch an der Benutzerseite archiviert oder ausgegeben werden. Somit kann entweder eine Stand-alone-Version oder verschiedene Arten von Rechnerkopplung verwendet werden.

Gestartet wird das System durch Einlesen der Ausgangsdaten, die in folgenden drei Datenblöcken abgespeichert sind:
- Daten der darzustellenden Flächen,
- Abbildungsdaten,
- Liniendaten, d.h. Angaben, welche Typen von Kurven berechnet werden sollen.

Die Einteilung der Ausgangsdaten ergibt sich aus den Tabellen C., D. und E.

Der Benutzer braucht nur die gewünschte Operation und die notwendigen Daten einzugeben. Das Einlesen der Ausgangsdaten bewirkt ein Abarbeiten der Kurvenerzeugungsbefehle, entsprechend Tabelle D., wobei das System das jeweils günstigste Verfahren, z.B. für Durchdringungs- oder Umrißkurvenermittlung, aufgrund einer verfeinerten internen Flächentypunterscheidung auswählt.

Ergebnisdatei ist je nach Benutzerwunsch eine Folge von Raum- oder Bildkurven, die zur weiteren Verarbeitung auf einen beliebigen Datenträger aufgezeichnet werden kann. Auf dieser Basis sind noch folgende Abbildungsvarianten möglich:
- Zeichenrahmengebung und -verschiebung,
- Maßstabsveränderung,
- bei Raumdaten: Veränderung der Abbildungsdaten.

Durch diese Schnittstellen kann GIULIA zu einem späteren Zeitpunkt in ein in Arbeit befindliches allgemeines interaktives System "PRIAMOS" /13/, das auf gekoppelten Rechnern arbeitet, eingebracht werden.

Zwei Programmteile bestimmen also innerhalb des Systems den Arbeitsablauf:
Der erste, bereits oben erwähnt, setzt die Benutzerwünsche in Kurvenerzeugungsbefehle
unter Verwendung des optimalen Verfahrens um und bildet somit eine äußere Steuerung.
Der andere, die innere Steuerung pro Kurvenerzeugungsbefehl, ist gekoppelt mit einer
Steuerung des Laufparameters; denn beide in GIULIA angewandten Möglichkeiten zur Erzeugung von Punkten einer Raumkurve:

- Die Raumkurve liegt als geschlossene Gleichung vor. Zu der Erzeugung der Punkte
  wird ein Laufparameter verwendet.
- Die Punkte der Raumkurve sind durch Schnitte zweier geometrischer Elemente nach
  F. festgelegt. Art und Maße der Elemente sind in Abhängigkeit des Laufparameters
  der Leitkurve gegeben.

basieren auf einer Parameterdarstellung. Somit durchläuft für jeden einzelnen Kurvenerzeugungsbefehl ein Parameter ein vorgegebenes Intervall. Dabei entstehen folgende
Aufgaben:

G.1 Abspeichern der maximal 4 Raumpunkte pro Parameterwert (maximal 4 Punkte können
bei dem Schnitt zweier Kegelschnitte entstehen, vgl. Tabelle F.).

G.2 Fortgesetzte Intervallteilung bei einem Wechsel in der Anzahl der erzeugten
Raumpunkte zwischen zwei aufeinanderfolgenden Parametern.

G.3 Durchführen der Ungleichungsabfragen nach Operation D.1

G.4 Ebenfalls fortgesetzte Intervallteilung bei einem Wechsel in der Anzahl der
verbleibenden Raumpunkte zwischen zwei aufeinanderfolgenden Parameterwerten.

G.5 Zuordnung der zum aktuellen Parameterwert ermittelten Raumpunkte zu den bisherigen Raumkurven.

G.6 Überbrücken von Fehlstellen oder Unstetigkeiten, die durch numerische Ungenauigkeiten entstehen.

G.7 Einhaltung der zulässigen Krümmung der Bild- oder Raumkurve überwachen.

G.8 Abspeichern der fertigen Kurven in einer Datenhaltung für anschließende Sichtbarkeitsklärung der gesamten Bildkurven, sowie zur Ausgabe der Ergebnisdaten.

Bei Tests zeigten zwei realisierte Steuerungen mit direkt einsetzenden Intervallteilungsprozessen bei Vorgängen nach G.2, G.4, G.6, G.7 im Fall von Überschneidungen
solcher Vorgänge nicht die notwendige Sicherheit.

Aus diesem Grund wurden die Intervallteilungsabläufe für die inzwischen implementierte
Steuerung in einen nachgeschalteten Algorithmus verlagert. Eine Ringstruktur ermöglicht ein beliebiges Einfügen der durch Intervallteilung ermittelten Punkte. Neben
diesen Längsverbindungen zwischen den Punkten zweier verschiedener Parameterwerte
sind auch Querverbindungen zwischen den (maximal 4) Punkten des gleichen Parameterwertes zugelassen. Der Ring wird durch Zeiger von den letzten zu den ersten Kurvenpunkten geschlossen; dieses ist für Kurven wichtig, die ihrem Erzeugungsprinzip
nach geschlossen sind.

Eine Kleinrechnerversion mit starker Segmentierung (1 Segment pro Flächentyp und Operation), keiner nachzuschaltenden Sichtbarkeitsklärung, Verfahrensangabe von Seiten des Benutzers, aber sonst nur kleineren Einschränkungen war ca. 1 Jahr im Test auf einer Kleinrechenanlage (32 K, 16bit). Hier wurde neben überhöhtem Rechenzeitbedarf fehlende Genauigkeit bei Durchdringungskurvenermittlung an Flächenkombinationen, bei denen Flächen nach C.4 oder C.5 verwendet wurden, als wesentlicher Hinderungsgrund für weiteren Einsatz erkannt. Eine zweite Kleinrechnerversion, die nur Ebenen und Flächen zweiter Ordnung verarbeitet, allerdings ohne Endbegrenzungen im Durchdringungsbereich, läuft bisher zufriedenstellend.

Unter Berücksichtigung dieser Ergebnisse wird z.Zt. an einer Kleinrechnerversion mit den Operationen D.1 bis D.4, Flächen zu 1.1, 1.2, 1.3 und beiden Projektionsarten gearbeitet. Ihr wesentliches Einsatzgebiet wird die Vermeidung von Überschneidungen von Bohrungen in einem Werkstück sein. Geplant ist eine Zahl von max. 100 Bohrungen, die miteinander auf Durchdringungen untersucht werden sollen. Ein Reduzieren der Flächendaten auf ca. 80 bit (5 Wörter) pro Fläche erscheint nach weiterer Flächentypunterteilung für diesen Fall möglich.

Die Weiterverarbeitung im Sinne der Systeme nach A.2 und A.3 wird durch die zulässigen Operationen vereinfacht. Durch Zeichnen der Erzeugenden und der Leitkurven kann die Struktur der Fläche sichtbar gemacht werden. Außerdem können ebene Schnitte als Höhen- oder Querschnitte eingeführt werden. Die Flächen nach C.1, C.2, C.3 (mit Einschränkungen) sind APT-verträglich.

Auch eine gemischte Verarbeitung von graphischen und analytisch gegebenen Flächen ist dem Prinzip nach durchführbar, da entstehende Durchdringungen unter Verwendung paralleler ebener Schnitte durch beide beteiligten Flächen konstruierbar sind.

Zusammenfassung

Ausgehend von einem Vergleich bestehender Systeme zum Verarbeiten gekrümmter Flächen, wird den bisherigen Rasterdarstellungen eine Lineardarstellung mit Linientypunterscheidung für algebraische und transzendente Flächen gegenübergestellt. Verarbeitbare Flächen sind Ebenen, Quadriken, Regel-, Kugelhüll- und verallgemeinerte Röhrenflächen. Die Flächen können durch Umrisse, Endbegrenzungen und Erzeugende, bei Flächenkombinationen auch Durchdringungskurven, dargestellt werden. Fragen der Datenhaltung und Programmsteuerung eines solchen Systems werden erläutert.

Danksagung

Herrn Professor Dr. F. Reutter, dem Leiter der Forschungsgruppe, sei an dieser Stelle für die Anregung zu dem vorliegenden System sowie für seine wohlwollende Unterstützung gedankt.

Herrn Professor Dr. R. Koller, dem Leiter des Instituts für Allgemeine Konstruktionslehre des Maschinenbaus, dankt der Verfasser für seine wertvollen Hinweise, die zur Erstellung einer speziellen Version zur Verarbeitung von Regelflächen, Quadriken und Ebenen führten.

Herrn Dipl.-Math. E. Heyne gebührt der Dank des Verfassers für das Überlassen der geometrischen Grundprogramme sowie für seine kollegiale Zusammenarbeit.

Innerhalb der Forschungsgruppe möchte der Verfasser Herrn Dr. H. Petersen und Herrn Dipl.-Ing. W. Moze für ihre stete Diskussionsbereitschaft danken.

Literaturangaben:

/ 1/ ARGYRIS, J.H., I. GRIEGER, E. SCHREM: Structural Analysis by Problemoriented Languages, ISD-Report No. 95, Stuttgart 1971

/ 2/ BEZIER, P.: Numerical Control - Mathematics and Applications, New York 1972

/ 3/ BECKER, E.: Interaktive graphische Verarbeitung analytisch gegebener gekrümmter Flächen, Arbeitsbericht der Informatikforschungsgruppe 15, RWTH Aachen, erscheint 1975

/ 4/ BÖHM, W.: Zur Darstellung von Flächen in der Datenverarbeitung, Angewandte Informatik 8/71

/ 5/ COONS, S.A., B. HERZOG: Surfaces for Computer-Aided Aircraft Design AIAA-Paper No. 67-895, New York, Oktober 1967

/ 6/ ENCARNACAO, J.: Datenstrukturen für Graphische Informationsverarbeitung, Symposium über Computer-Graphics, Berlin 1971

/ 7/ ENGELI, M.: Eine Methode zur Beschreibung gekrümmter Flächen, Technische Rundschau - Fertigungstechnik, Juni 1973, Bern

/ 8/ FORREST, A.R.: Curves and Surfaces for Computer-Aided design, Cambridge CAD-Group, Ph. D. Thesis, July 1968

/ 9/ GRIMM, W.: Darstellende Geometrie, Teil 1, Mathematisches Institut I, Universität Karlsruhe, 1974

/10/ KURTH, J.: Rechnerorientierte Werkstückbeschreibung, Diss. Berlin 1971

/11/ LACOSTE, J.P.: Rechnerangepaßte Werkstückdarstellung für den automatisierten Produktionsprozeß, Diss. Aachen 1971

/12/ NEWMAN, W., R.F. SPROULL: Principles of Interactive Computer Graphics, New York 1973

/13/ PETERSEN, H., W. MOZE: PRIAMOS - Programmsystem zum interaktiven Arbeiten mit Hilfe von Sichtgeräten, Arbeitsunterlagen, Aachen 1974

/14/ REUTTER, F., E. HEYNE: Untersuchungen über die automatische Lösung von Aufgaben der konstruktiven Geometrie, Forschungsbericht des Landes NRW No. 2300, 1973

/15/ SCHWEGLER, H.: NC - Fräsen gekrümmter Flächen, Berlin - Heidelberg - New York 1972

/16/ SIMON, R.: Rechnerunterstütztes Konstruieren, Diss. Aachen 1968

/17/ SUTHERLAND, I.E., R.F. SPROULL, R.A. SCHUMACKER: A Characterization of Ten Hidden-Surface Algorithms, ACM Comp. Surveys, Vol.6, No.1, March 1974

/18/ WALTHER, H.: Numerische Darstellung von Oberflächen unter Verwendung eines Optimalprinzips, Diss. München 1971

Abbildungen:

Folgende Bilder wurden mit GIULIA auf der Rechenanlage CD 6400 des Rechenzentrums der RWTH Aachen erzeugt und am Display der RA CD 1700 fotografiert.

Abb. 1 Umriß und ebene Endbegrenzung einer halben Kreisringfläche (Torus)

Abb. 2 Durchdringungskurve des Torus mit einem schiefen Kreiszylinder

Abb. 3 räumlich gekrümmte Endbegrenzung des Torus entlang der Schnittkurve mit dem Zylinder

Abb. 4 Durchdringung Torus/Zylinder unter Weglassen aller Punkte des Torus innerhalb des Zylinders

Abb. 5 ebene Endbegrenzung mehrerer gerader Kreiszylinder sowie die gegenseitigen Durchdringungen

Abb. 6 Rotationsfläche mit Darstellung der erzeugenden Kreise und paralleler ebener Schnitte

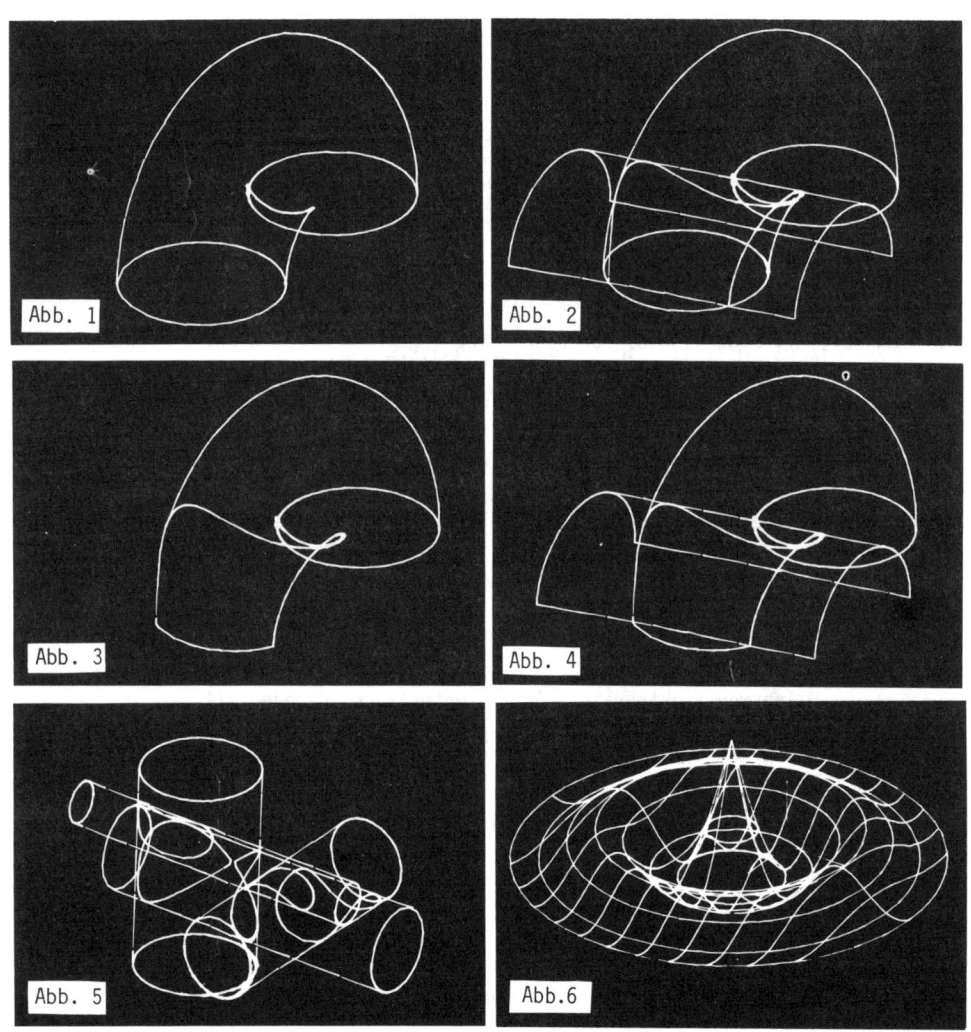

DIE ANWENDUNG DER B-SPLINE-APPROXIMATION
IN COMPUTER GRAPHICS

W. Straßer

Heinrich-Hertz-Institut Berlin

1. Einleitung

Seit den ersten Anfängen auf dem Gebiet Computer Graphics in den sechziger Jahren bemüht man sich, grafische Sichtgeräte (graphic displays) im computergestützten Entwurf (CAD) einzusetzen. Besondere Anstrengungen wurden unternommen um dreidimensionale Gebilde darstellen, interaktiv entwerfen und verändern zu können. Die Grundlage für die notwendigen mathematischen Verfahren wurde von Coons 1964 mit der Veröffentlichung seiner Arbeit "Surfaces for computer-aided design of space figures" /1/ geliefert. Flächen werden danach in Parameterform definiert. Durch Zusammensetzen von Teilflächen - auch patches oder Pflaster genannt - erhält man grössere Flächen. Die Darstellung der Flächen erfolgt durch Projektion einiger ihrer Parameterlinien auf den Bildschirm.

Die Coons'sche Flächendefinition erfordert vom Anwender erhebliche mathematische Kenntnisse. Zum Beispiel müssen, um ein kontinuierliches Aneinanderfügen von Teilflächen zu ermöglichen, Tangentenvektoren angegeben werden. Normalerweise wird der Anwender aber nur Tangenten, also Steigungen angeben können. Der Einfluss der Länge des Tangentenvektors lässt sich sehr schwer abschätzen. Eine wesentliche Verbesserung der interaktiven Entwurfsmöglichkeiten wurde mit der von Bézier angegebenen Approximation /2/ erreicht. Hierbei definiert der Benutzer die von ihm gewünschte Form in einem ersten Schritt grob durch ein Polygon (Bild 1). Die das Polygon approximierende Bézierkurve wird dann interaktiv durch Verschieben der Polygonstützstellen in die gewünschte Form gebracht.

Die Vorteile der Bézierapproximation sind:

1) Einfache Definition durch Polygone.
2) Pflaster können ohne die Angabe von Tangentenvektoren kantenfrei zusammengefügt werden.
3) Glättende Wirkung.

Als Nachteile sind zu nennen:

1) Der Grad der Kurve oder Fläche und somit auch der Rechenaufwand ist abhängig von der Anzahl der vorgegebenen Stützstellen.
2) Bei Veränderung einer Stützstelle ändert sich die gesamte Form. Lokale Änderungen sind nicht möglich.

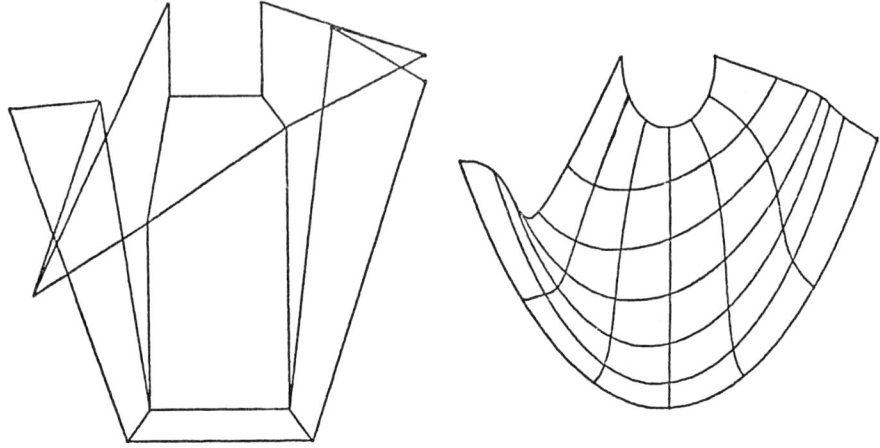

Bild 1: Bézierfläche und definierendes Polygonnetz

Die Suche nach einem Verfahren zum interaktiven Gestalten von Formen, das die o.g. Vorteile der Bézierapproximation und die der kubischen Splines

- Segmentweise definiertes Polynom

- Erhöhung des Freiheitsgrades ohne Erhöhung des Polynomgrades

in sich vereint, führte auf die B-Spline-Approximation /3/, /4/.

2. Eigenschaften der B-Splines

Eine B-Spline-Funktion (kurz: B-Spline) der Ordnung k ist ein stückweise (segmentweise) definiertes Polynom vom Grad (k-1), das an den Knoten (Segmentübergängen) (k-2)-mal stetig differenzierbar ist. k zusammenhängende Segmente sind von Null verschieden (Bild 2). Die Werte p_i der unabhängigen Variablen an den Knoten der Spline seien im Intervall (p_o, p_e) wie folgt gegeben:

$$p_o \leq p_1 \leq \ldots p_i \leq p_{i+1} \ldots \leq p_e \qquad (1)$$

$\mathcal{P} = (p_o, p_1, \ldots, p_i, \ldots, p_e)$ heisst Knotenvektor.

Der normierte B-Spline $N_{i,k}(p)$ mit der Eigenschaft

$$\sum_i N_{i,k}(p) \equiv 1 \qquad (2)$$

wird nach der Rekursionsformel /5/

$$N_{i,k}(p) = \frac{p-p_i}{p_{i+k-1}-p_i} \cdot N_{i,k-1}(p) + \frac{p_{i+k}-p}{p_{i+k}-p_{i+1}} \cdot N_{i+1,k-1}(p) \qquad (3)$$

berechnet. Der Index i gibt den Knoten an, bis zu welchem der Spline noch den Wert Null besitzt. Für den Spline erster Ordnung gilt:

$$N_{i,1}(p) = \begin{cases} 1 & p_i \leq p < p_{i+1} \\ 0 & \text{sonst} \end{cases} \qquad (4)$$

Dies impliziert, dass für zusammenfallende Knoten $p_i = p_{i+1}$ der Spline $N_{i,1}(p) \equiv 0$ ist. Bild 3 zeigt für k = 3 alle Möglichkeiten für das Zusammenfallen von Knoten.

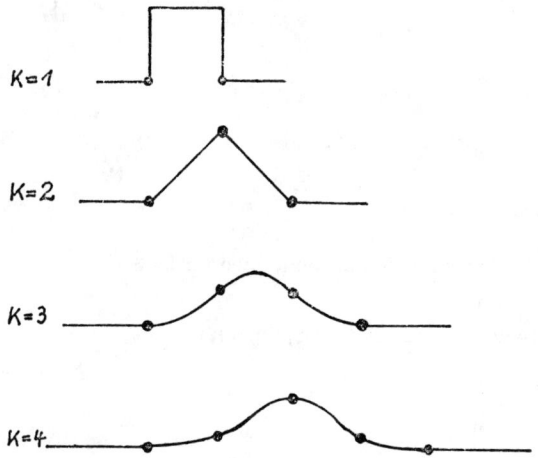

Bild 2: B-Splines für k = 1 bis k = 4

Das Arbeiten mit B-Splines wird wesentlich vereinfacht, wenn die Knoten p_i nach Gl. (1) positive ganze Zahlen sind. Zu diesem Zweck werden neue Koordinaten eingeführt:

$$p'_i = j \quad , \quad j \in 0, 1, 2, \ldots, e \qquad (5)$$

Zwischen den Knoten soll gelten

$$0 \leq p \leq 1$$

also $\quad p \equiv p' \pmod{1}$

B-Splines mit einfachen Knoten sind periodische Funktionen mit der Periode k:

$$N_{i,k}(p') = N_{i+k}(p') = N_{(i+k)\bmod e, k}(p') \qquad (6)$$

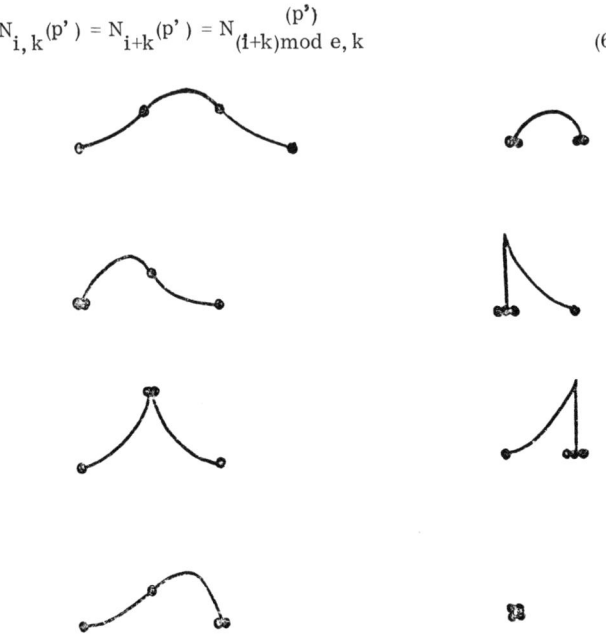

Bild 3: Zusammenfallen von Knoten für k= 3

Bild 4 zeigt die Familie der periodischen B-Splines für

$e = 4$ und $k = 3$: $N_{i,3} \Big|_{i=0}^{3}$

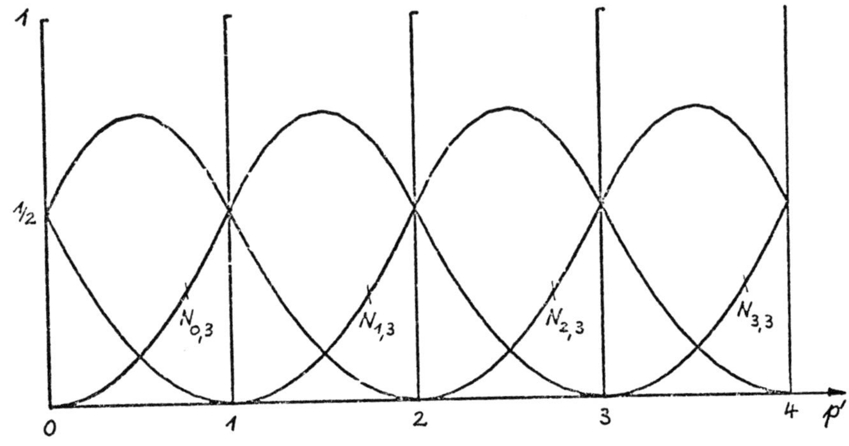

Bild 4: Periodische B-Splines $N_{i,3} \Big|_{i=0}^{3}$ mit $p = (p'_i \bmod 4)$

B-Splines mit mehrfachen Knoten sind dagegen keine periodischen Funktionen. Dies erkennt man aus Bild 5, das die Familie der nichtperiodischen B-Splines mit e = 8, k = 3 und k-fachem Knoten am Anfang und Ende des Intervalls (0, e) zeigt.

N' bedeutet 2-fach Knoten

N'' bedeutet 3-fach Knoten etc.

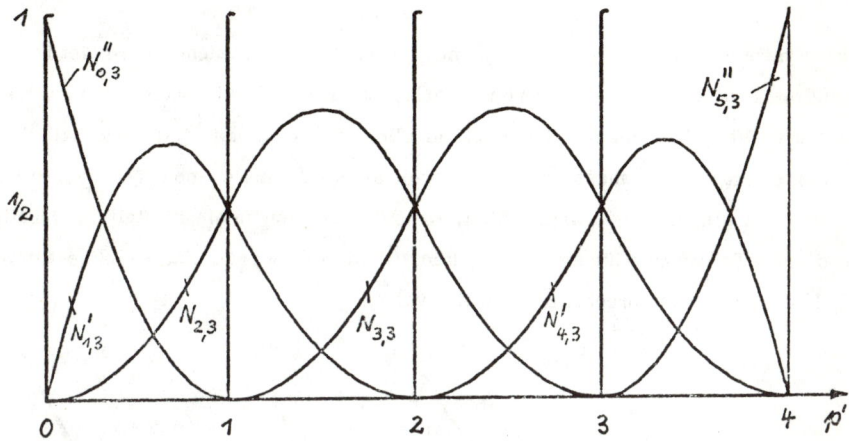

Bild 5: Nichtperiodische B-Splines $N''_{i,3} \big|_{i=0}^{5}$

mit $\mathcal{P} = (p'_0 = p'_1 = p'_2, p'_3, p'_4, p'_5, p'_6 = p'_7 = p'_8)$

3. B-Spline-Kurven und -Flächen /6/

Analog zur Bézierapproximation werden Kurven und Flächen durch Polygone definiert. Der Benutzer kann zwischen periodischen und nichtperiodischen B-Splines wählen und deren Ordnung vorschreiben. Im folgenden werden mit S(u', v') die Polygonstützstellen und mit Q(u', v') die Punkte des berechneten Pflasters bezeichnet.

3.1 Approximation mit nichtperiodischen B-Splines

Soll ein Polygon aus (m+1) Stützstellen S_i mit B-Splines k-ter Ordnung $N_{i,k}(u') \in C^{k-2}$ so approximiert werden, dass Anfangs- und Endpunkt von Polygon und Kurve zusammenfallen, so muss der Knotenvektor folgende Form besitzen:

$$\mathcal{U} = (\underbrace{u'_0 = u'_1 = \ldots u'_{k-1}}_{\text{k-fach}}, u'_k, u'_{k+1} \ldots u'_m, \underbrace{u'_{m+1} = u'_{m+2} = u'_{m+k}}_{\text{k-fach}}) \qquad (7)$$

Die Kurve wird nach

$$Q(u') = \sum_{i=0}^{m} N_{i,k}(u') \cdot S_i = \left[N_{i,k}(u') \right]^T \cdot \bar{S} \qquad (8)$$

berechnet und ist überall (k-2)-mal stetig differenzierbar. Sie besteht aus

$$B = m - k + 2 \qquad (9)$$

Kurvensegmenten. Da jede Stützstelle nur mit einem B-Spline gewichtet wird, ist ihr Einfluss auf maximal k Kurvensegmente beschränkt. Damit sind lokale Änderungen am Kurvenverlauf durch Verschieben einer Stützstelle möglich. Soll eine Stützstelle innerhalb des Polygons interpoliert werden, muss der Knotenvektor an dieser Stelle einen (k-1)-fachen Knoten aufweisen. Der gleiche Effekt wird erzielt, wenn das Polygon an dieser Stelle in 2 Teile zerlegt und jedes Teilpolygon für sich approximiert wird. Bild 6 zeigt eine B-Spline-Kurve mit m = 5, k = 3 und die entsprechende Bézierkurve.

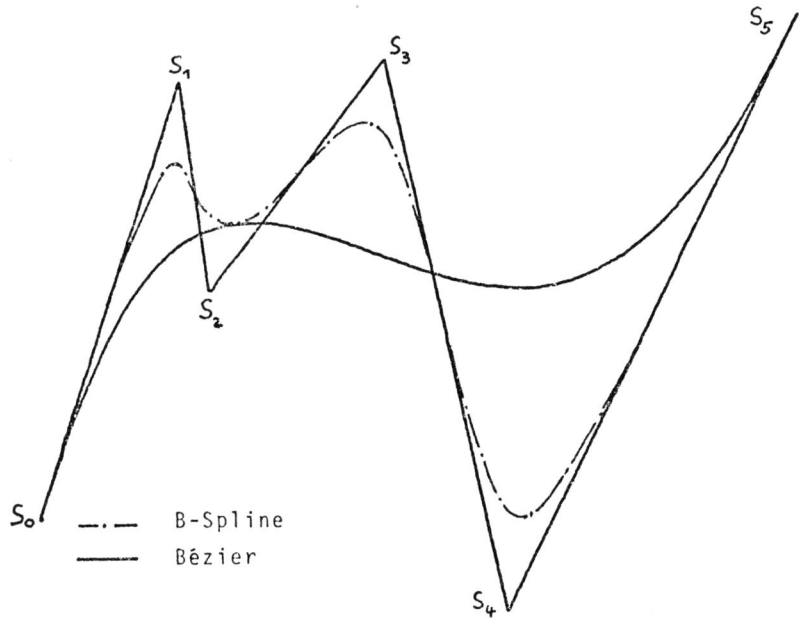

Bild 6: Bézier- und B-Spline-Kurve für m = 5, k = 3

Die für Kurven gemachten Aussagen lassen sich unmittelbar auf Flächen übertragen. Die Fläche

$$Q(u', v') = \sum_{i=0}^{m} \sum_{j=0}^{n} N_{i,k}(u') \cdot S_{ij} \cdot N_{j,l}(v') \qquad (10)$$

$$= U^T \cdot \bar{\bar{S}} \cdot V$$

besteht aus B · C = (m − k + 2) · (n − l + 2)   (11)

Pflastern. Wird eine Stützstelle $S_{i,j}$ verändert, ändert sich im Gegensatz zur Bézierapproximation nicht die gesamte Fläche, sondern höchstens k · l Pflaster.

Die Approximation mit nichtperiodischen B-Splines hat den Nachteil, dass die Kurven bzw. Flächen am Rand mit anderen Polynomen approximiert werden als in der Mitte und deshalb eine einheitliche Darstellung nicht möglich ist. Dieser Mangel tritt bei den periodischen B-Splines nicht auf.

3.2 Approximation mit periodischen B-Splines

Der periodische B-Spline $N_{i,k}(u')$ hat sein Maximum beim Parameterwert $u' = u'_i + \frac{k}{2}$ (Bild 4). Für die Kurvenapproximation wird Gl. (10) so modifiziert, dass für geradzahliges k der mit S_i korrespondierende Kurvenpunkt $P_i = Q(u'_i)$ ist.

$$Q(u') = \left[N_{(i-\frac{k}{2}) \bmod (m+1), k}(u') \right]^T \cdot \bar{S} \qquad (12)$$

mit $\frac{k}{2} = \begin{cases} \frac{k}{2} & \text{k gerade} \\ \text{entier}(\frac{k}{2}) & \text{k ungerade} \end{cases}$ für

Approximiert man ein Polygon aus (m+1) Stützstellen nach Gl. (12), so erhält man auf Grund der Periodizität der Approximationsfunktionen eine geschlossene Kurve, die keine Stützstellen S_i interpoliert. Soll eine Stützstelle interpoliert werden, so muss sie (k−1)-fach vorhanden sein (Bild 7).

Für beide Typen der B-Spline-Approximation gilt, dass die Kurve bei k kollinearen Stützstellen ein Geradenstück mit dem Polygon gemeinsam hat. Liegen (k−1) kollineare Stützstellen vor, so ist die entsprechende Polygonseite Tangente der Kurve.

Wird k im Hinblick auf geringen Rechenaufwand auf den Bereich $2 \leq k \leq 4$ beschränkt, so können nur drei verschiedene Vektoren U_k mit Approximationspolynomen vorkommen:

$k = 2 : U_2 = (1 - u,\ u)$

$k = 3 : U_3 = \frac{1}{2}\left((1-u)^2,\ (-u^2 + u + \frac{1}{2}),\ \frac{u^2}{2}\right)$ (13)

$k = 4 : U_4 = \frac{1}{6}\left((1-u)^3,\ (3u^3 - 6u^2 + 4),\ (-3u^3 + 3u^2 + 3u + 1),\ u^3\right)$

Bild 8 zeigt die hiermit gegebenen Möglichkeiten.

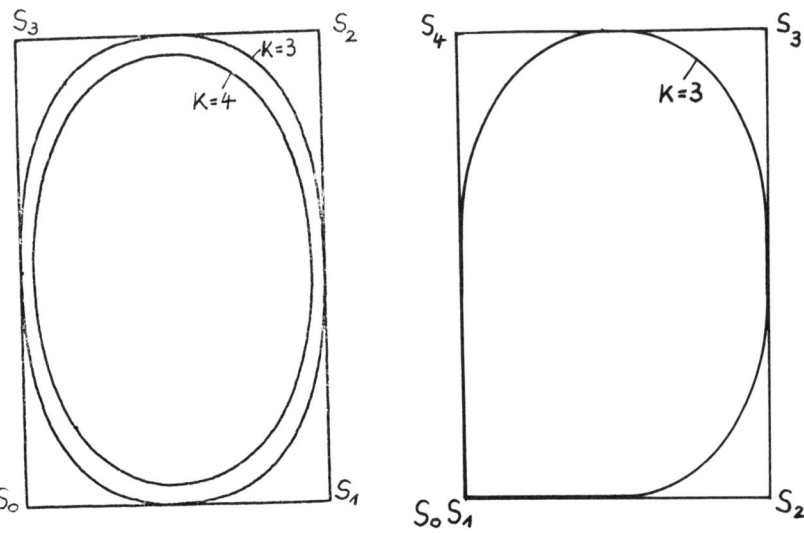

Bild 7: Approximation mit periodischen B-Splines

Die Flächenapproximation mit periodischen B-Splines wird entsprechend Gl. (10) und Gl. (12) berechnet. Sie bietet dem Benutzer zusätzliche Freiheitsgrade. Neben den Stützstellen kann er den Grad der Polynome in u- und v-Richtung vorgeben, in u- und/oder v-Richtung geschlossene und/oder offene Parameterlinien wählen und durch Angabe von Mehrfachstützstellen Unstetigkeiten bzw. Interpolation erzwingen. Dabei kann man sich auf die in Gl. (13) angegebenen Polynome beschränken. Das kantenfreie Zusammenfügen von B-Spline-Pflastern stellt kein Problem dar. An den Rändern der beiden zusammenzufügenden Pflaster müssen nur die Stützstellen des Randpolygons übereinstimmen. Tangentenbedingen sind nicht zu beachten.

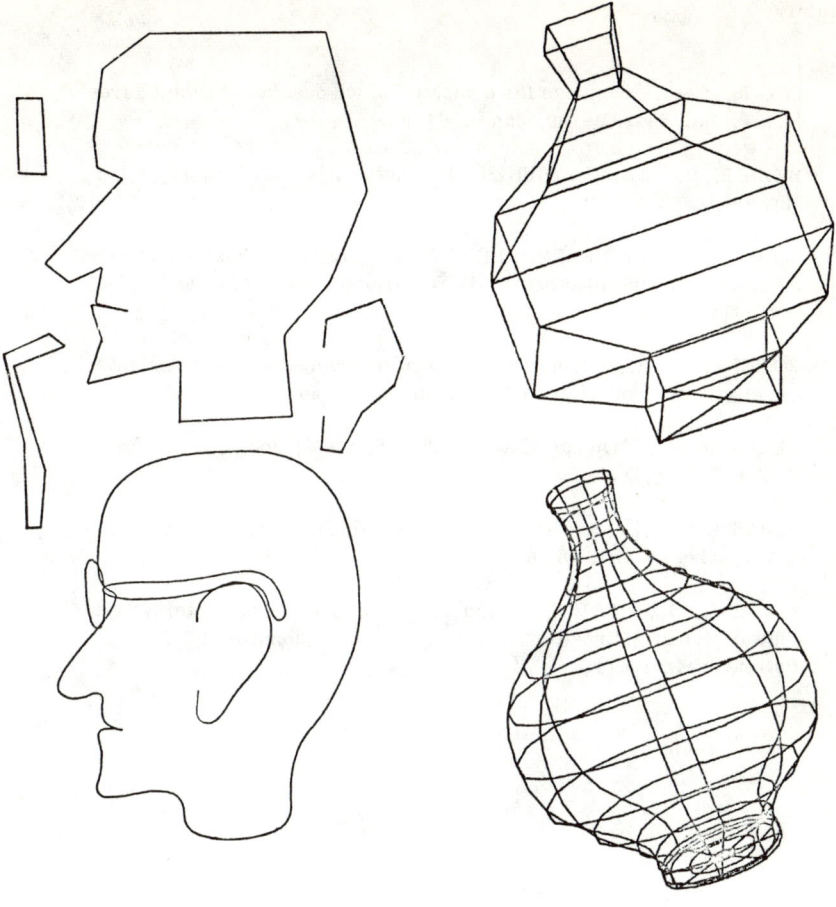

Bild 8: Möglichkeiten der B-Spline-Approximation

Damit steht mit der B-Spline-Approximation ein Verfahren zum Kurven- und Flächenentwurf zur Verfügung, das für den Benutzer einfach zu handhaben ist und durch seinen geringen Rechenaufwand schnelle Antwortzeiten am Display garantiert /7/. Für die Hardwarerealisierung eines Kurven- und Flächengenerators /6/ ist sie bestens geeignet.

Literatur

/1/ COONS, S.A., 'Surfaces for computer-aided design of space figures', M.I.T. ESL 9442-M-139, Jan. 1964

/2/ BEZIER, P., 'Système UNISURF', Automatismes, Vol. 13, No. 5, May 1968

/3/ GORDON, W.J., RIESENFELD, F.R., 'Bernstein-Bézier methods for the computer-aided design of freeform curves and surfaces', GMR-1176, 1972

/4/ FORREST, A.R., 'A new curve form for computer-aided design', University of Cambridge, CAD Document No. 66

/5/ DE BOOR, C., 'On calculating with B-Splines', Journal of Approximation Theory, Vol. 6, No. 1, July 72

/6/ STRASSER, W., 'Schnelle Kurven- und Flächenerzeugung auf grafischen Sichtgeräten', Dissertation, TUB, 1974

/7/ BÖLLING, G., "FABIAN" - Ein Programmsystem zum interaktiven Entwurf von B-Spline-Kurven und -Flächen, Diplomarbeit TUB 73, Betreuer: Strasser.

9. ANWENDUNGEN: GEOGRAPHIE, KONSTRUIEREN

ANWENDUNGEN IN DER GEOGRAPHIE
K.Ch. HASE

R.W. HESSDORFER

RECHNERGESTÜTZTES KONSTRUIEREN
M.J.E. COOLEY

H. FLESSNER, P. GORNY, H.-P. HAAKE, W. HANSMANN

EIN BENUTZERORIENTIERTES INFORMATIONSSYSTEM
FUER LANDESPLANERISCHE APPLIKATIONEN

K.Ch. Hase
Institut für Orts-,
Regional- und Landesplanung
ETH Zürich

1. Einführung

Ausgehend von den in überkommunaler Planung üblichen Engpässen hinsichtlich rationeller Datensammlung und Auswertung wurde am Institut für Orts-, Regional- und Landesplanung der ETH Zürich eine erste, recht pragmatische Aufgabenstellung für ein landesplanerisches Informationssystem entwickelt. Schwerpunkte dieser von Planern konzipierten Aufgabenstellung waren:
- Sammlung von planungsrelevanten Informationen auf Landesebene nach einheitlichen Kriterien.
- Integration der Datenbestände in einer Datenbank mit flexiblen Zugriffsmöglichkeiten.
- Realisierung von Auswertungsalgorithmen in einer eigenen, leicht verständlichen Abfragesprache für den computerunkundigen Planer in Forschung und Praxis.

Die Datenbasis umfasst im wesentlichen drei Datenstrukturen:
- Geographisch lokalisierbare Merkmale über Bodennutzung und Bodenbeschaffenheit dargestellt in einem orthogonalen Hektarraster für die ganze Schweiz (Flächendatei).
- Angaben über die (ca.3000) Schweizer Gemeinden hinsichtlich demographischer, wirtschaftlicher und ausstattungsmässiger Merkmale (Gemeindedatei).
- Verkehrs-, Versorgungs- und Kommunikationsnetze mit geographischer Linienführung und Angabe skalarer Parameter wie Kapazitäten etc. für die Teilstücke (Liniendatei).

Bisher sind Flächendatei und Gemeindedatei realisiert und seit Sommer 73 mit der zugehörigen Abfragesprache im Einsatz. Hierauf beziehen sich alle folgenden Ausführungen.

2. Datenbankstruktur und Benützersprache

2.1 Die Flächendatei

Die Merkmale im Hektarraster sind vorwiegend qualitativer Natur und derart in sog. Merkmalsstufen unterteilt, dass sich je zwei Stufen eines Merkmals, bezogen auf einen Punkt, ausschliessen. So umfasst z.B. das Merkmal Bodennutzung die Stufen 1: Oedland, 2: Fluss, 3: See, 4: Wald, ... 12: Industrieanlagen. Jede Hektare wird in der Flächendatei durch einen Bitstring repräsentiert, der pro Merkmal die dominante Stufe enthält. Die Codierung der Stufen erfolgt in der Bit-Anzahl, die zur binären Darstellung der höchsten Stufe des betreffenden Merkmals notwendig ist. Das Merkmal Bodennutzung mit 12 Stufen benötigt z.B. $\log_2 16 = 4$ Bit zur internen Darstellung. Aber selbst bei dieser komprimierten Codierung belegt die Flächendatei mit ca. 4 Mio Hektaren und bis zu 40 Merkmalen mit durchschnittlich 6-8 Stufen noch ca. 80 Mio Zeichen (à 6 Bit).

Die Zuordnung der Merkmale zu den Teilbereichen des pro Hektare reservierten Bitstrings erfolgt dynamisch in folgendem Sinne: Der durch das Löschen eines nicht mehr in der Datenbank benötigten Merkmals freiwerdende Substring wird in der Merkmalsbeschreibungs-Tabelle als verfügbar markiert und gegebenenfalls mit angrenzenden verfügbaren Substrings konkateniert. Bei der Definition eines neuen Merkmals wird aus den verfügbaren Substrings ein möglichst passender ausgewählt und dem neu einzufügenden Merkmal zugeordnet.

Dadurch wird die Möglichkeit eröffnet, Merkmale, die nicht von allgemeinem Interesse sind, für Spezialauswertungen vorübergehend in die Flächendatei zu integrieren, mit anderen, ständig gespeicherten Merkmalen zu verknüpfen und anschliessend wieder zu löschen. Auf diese Weise wird die Kapazitätsbeschränkung der Flächendatei auf ca. 40 Merkmale (s.o.) in der Praxis 'umgangen'. Es tritt jedoch neu das Problem der schlechten Verwendbarkeit kurzer, nicht zusammenhängender Substrings auf. Eine dadurch bedingte vorzeitige Kapazitätserschöpfung führt dann zu einer Reorganisation der Flächendatei durch Zusammenschieben der belegten Felder im Bitstring.

Aufgrund des Charakters der Flächenmerkmale wurden Fragestellungen mittels Bool'scher Ausdrücke gewählt. Die Syntax wurde im Hinblick auf den Benutzerkreis bewusst einfach gestaltet. Die merkmalsbezogenen Kriterien für eine Auswahl von Gebieten werden z.B. folgendermassen spezifiziert:

```
FRAGE =      merkmalsname = stufe [,stufe] ...
         [UND merkmalsname = stufe [,stufe] ...] ...
  [ODER          "      =   "    [,  "   ] ...
         [UND merkmalsname = stufe [,stufe] ...] ...] ...;
```

wobei das Komma in der Stufenliste ein _implizites_ ODER repräsentiert (mit höherer Priorität als das UND).
(Dabei sind die Ausdrücke in den eckigen Klammern fakultativ und die Punkte '...' danach bedeuten, dass sich die Ausdrücke in den Klammern mehrfach wiederholen dürfen).
Vom Ergebnis kann durch
'GRAPH = zeichenkombination [,zeichenkombination] ...;'
eine kartographische Darstellung (ähnlich SYMAP, aber mit einem 'Grundkarten-Layout', welches durch die Fragestellung induziert wird) oder durch die Anweisung 'TAB'; eine tabellarische Zusammenfassung verlangt werden.

2.2 Die Gemeindedatei

Die Gemeindedatei enthält hauptsächlich quantitative Merkmale, die in floating-point-Codierung (zur Vereinfachung der Arithmetik) je ein Wort belegen. Damit umfasst diese Datei in der Implementierung auf einer CDC 6000 im Maximalausbau mit 600 Merkmalen ca. 20 Mio Zeichen (à 6 Bit). Dieses Speichervolumen wird nicht von Anfang an reserviert, sondern mit wachsendem Datenbestand schrittweise für je 50 Merkmale neu zugewiesen.

Die Abfragen der Gemeindedatei werden mittels in höheren Programmiersprachen üblicher Ausdrücke formuliert, d.h. mit arithmetischen, vergleichenden und logischen Operatoren. Für die resultierende Tabelle werden durch eine OUTPUT-Ausweisung die gewünschten Kolonnen durch arithmetische Ausdrücke spezifiziert.

Aufbauend auf den Gemeinden kann man in der Abfragesprache beliebige höhere Aggregate (z.B. Regionen) definieren, Gemeindemerkmale aufsummieren und auf diesem (höheren) Niveau mit der Abfragesprache der Gemeindedatei weiteroperieren.

Beispiel einer Gemeindeabfrage mit erzeugtem Output:

GEMEINDEFRAGE VOM Ø1/1Ø/74

ANWEISUNGEN:
    :NUM=1-253;
    FRAGE=(AUSL6Ø/EINW6Ø > AUSL7Ø/EINW7Ø) UND (EINW7Ø > 2ØØØ);
    TITEL=ALTERSSTRUKTUR IN 2Ø-JAHRES-KLASSEN;
    TEXT1= EINW. I N   P R O Z E N T;
    TEXT2= 197Ø Ø-19 2Ø-39 4Ø-59 UEB6Ø JAHRE;
    FORMAT=F(7),' *',4F(6,1);
    OUTPUT=EINW7Ø,ALØØ19/EINW7Ø*1ØØ,AL2Ø39/EINW7Ø*1ØØ,
       AL4Ø59/EINW7Ø*1ØØ,AL6Ø9Ø/EINW7Ø*1ØØ;

ALTERSSTRUKTUR IN 2Ø-JAHRES-KLASSEN

NR.	NAME	EINW. 197Ø		Ø-19	2Ø-39	4Ø-59	UEB6Ø	JAHRE
				I N	P R O	Z E N T		
139	RUESCHLIKON	4797.	*	25.7	28.2	26.2	19.8	
152	HERRLIBERG	4Ø83.	*	32.2	29.Ø	24.3	14.5	
154	KUESNACHT (ZH)	12193.	*	26.Ø	26.2	26.4	21.4	
16Ø	ZUMIKON	3Ø13.	*	33.1	3Ø.7	24.8	11.4	
227	SEUZACH	3258.	*	37.3	28.3	23.3	11.1	
244	GEROLDSWIL	2818.	*	36.8	42.4	16.Ø	4.7	
TOTAL FUER 6 GEMEINDEN		3Ø162.	*	29.7	29.1	24.6	16.5	

2.3 Datenfluss zwischen den Dateien

Vornehmlich zur Kartographischen Darstellung von Gemeindedaten wurde folgendes Distributionsmodell entwickelt:

Der Wert eines Gemeindemerkmals wird auf alle zum Gemeindegebiet gehörenden Rasterfelder (d.h. Hektare) verteilt und in frei wählbaren Stufen diskretisiert. Die Verteilung kann gleichmässig erfolgen oder mit frei wählbaren Faktoren gewichtet gemäss den Stufen eines bestehenden Flächenmerkmals.

Beispiel: Einwohnerverteilung nach bestehenden Bodennutzungen. Dieses neu in die Flächendatei integrierte Merkmal ist dann wie alle anderen Flächenmerkmale weiteren Abfragen zugänglich.

Umgekehrt kann man die von den Stufen eines Merkmals belegten Flächen gemeindeweise ermitteln und als neue Merkmale in der Gemeindedatei abspeichern.

Beispiel: Berechnung der Arealstatistik aus dem Flächenmerkmal Bodennutzung.

3. Realisierung eines ersten Testsystems

Um möglichst frühzeitig Erfahrungen mit der Benützersprache hinsichtlich der postulierten Flexibilität für die heterogenen Applikationswünsche zu sammeln, wurde aufbauend auf einem vereinfachten Datenbank-Modell ein erstes Testsystem für die Abfragesprache in Zusammenarbeit mit der IBM Zürich entwickelt für ein Modell IBM/360 (siehe [1]).

Von der Zielsetzung her wurde nicht die Effizienz, sondern eine möglichst rasche Realisierung des Systems in den Vordergrund gestellt. Deshalb wurde PL/I als Komfortable Implementierungsprache gewählt. Auf diese Weise war es z.B. möglich, Anweisungen der Gemeindeabfragen via 'Preprocessor' direkt in den entsprechenden Programm-Modul zu integrieren und via 'Compiler' zu übersetzen. Gesteuert wird das Abfragesystem von einem Assembler-Kontrollprogramm, welches bei Bedarf den PL/I-Compiler und den 'Linkage Editor' dynamisch aufruft.

Diese an sich recht elegante Methode bringt natürlich Effizienzverluste aufgrund des System-'Overheads', sie hat es jedoch ermöglicht, das Abfragesystem in nur 600 Stunden zu programmieren und zu testen. Anzumerken ist noch, dass wegen des vereinfachten DB-Modells auf ein eigenständiges Datenbank-Zugriffssystem zu diesem Zeitpunkt verzichtet wurde und die ('regional' organisierten) Dateien direkt vom Abfragesystem gelesen und modifiziert wurden.

4. Endgültige Implementierung

Die während der Zwischenphase gewonnenen Erkenntnisse und die Forderung nach Flexibilität und Portabilität des Systems führten schliesslich zu der im Folgenden skizzierten Realisierung des Gesamtmodells.

4.1 Konzept und angewandte Methoden

Der Wunsch nach Ausbaufähigkeit legte eine klare Trennung zwischen einem eigenständigen DB-Zugriffssystem und der Abfragesprache nahe. Letztere figuriert somit als Applikationsprogramm unter anderen (Abbildung siehe nächste Seite).

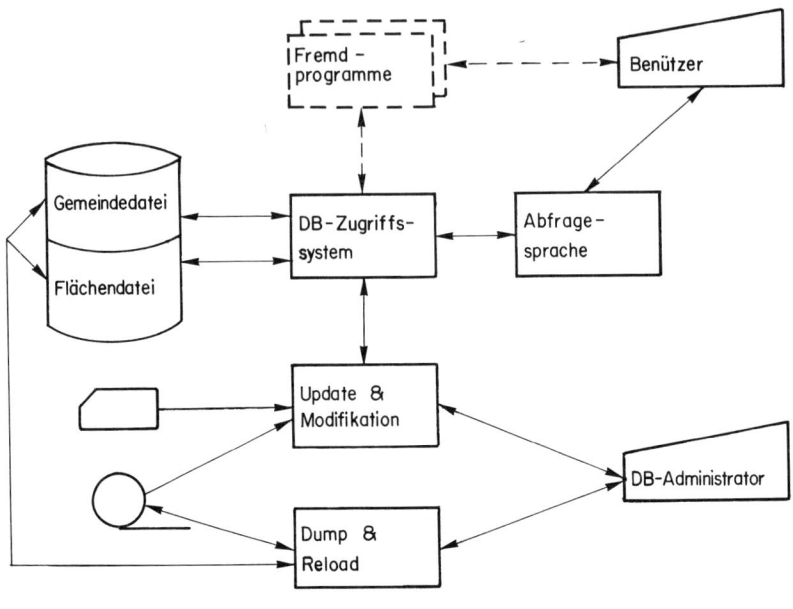

System - Aufbau

Bei der Wahl der Zugriffs-Methode wurde wegen der verlangten Portabilität und der guten Unterstützung durch fast alle Grossrechner-Systeme der indexsequentiellen Fileorganisation (mit Direktzugriff) der Vorzug gegeben.

Für die Abfragesprache wurde zur Vermeidung eines ungerechtfertigten System-'Overheads' (siehe 3.) ein ins DB-System integrierter eigener (Mini-)Compiler entwickelt. In der Syntaxanalyse hat der konsequente Einsatz von (teilweise rekursiven) Erkennungsautomaten viel zur Sicherheit und Fehlerkennung beigetragen. Die der Sprache PASCAL entliehenen Ausdrücke in den Gemeindeabfragen brachten den Vorteil von deterministischen Automaten ('one symbol look ahead') mit sich, ohne die Vielfalt der Ausdrücke einzuschränken.

Bis auf die vollkommen frei wählbaren boole'schen und artithmetischen Ausdrücke liessen sich alle anderen Abfragefunktionen durch parametrisierte Routinen realisieren. Bei den oben genannten Ausdrücken der Gemeindeabfragen entschieden wir uns aus Gründen der Portabilität für die Erzeugung eines Nicht-Maschinen-Codes, der zur Ausführungszeit von einem effizienten Interpretations-Algorithmus ausgewertet wird.

4.2 Implementationssprache

Der auf der CDC 6000 zur Verfügung stehende Fortran-Compiler FTN gestattet mit seinen effizienten Inline-Funktionen für Masking- und Shift-Operationen eine derartige 'Maschinennähe', dass auf die Verwendung einer niedrigeren Sprache verzichtet werden konnte.

Bei der gegenwärtig stattfindenden Implementierung auf einem Modell IBM/370 war dieser Schritt jedoch nötig, da IBM-Fortran indexsequentielle Files und Bitmanipulationen nicht unterstützt. Um Effizienzverluste durch PL/I zu vermeiden, werden für Bitmanipulationen die 'maschinennahe' Sprache PL 360 (siehe [2]) und für die Behandlung der indexsequentiellen Files Assembler-Macros verwendet.

Die Rekursivität der Erkennungsautomaten liess sich auch im Fortran relativ einfach durch eigene 'Stack'-Verwaltung realisieren.

5. Rückblick und Schlussfolgerungen

Nach gut einjährigem Einsatz des Informationssystems lassen sich die ersten Aussagen hinsichtlich Erfüllung der Aufgabenstellung und Angemessenheit der Vorgehensweise machen. Alle drei genannten Aufgaben (siehe 1.) wurden von _einer_ Arbeitsgruppe realisiert, mit einer zwischen 3 und 6 schwankenden Mitarbeiteranzahl.

Die Betreuung der Datensammlung und Erfassung garantierte zwar die Einhaltung der diesbezüglich geforderten einheitlichen Kriterien und schärfte den Blick der System-'Entwickler' für die Charakteristik der zu 'verwaltenden' Information. Diese Aufgabe sollte jedoch von einer Entwicklungsgruppe nur während einer Startphase übernommen werden, da ihr hier nicht in jedem Fall der adäquate Stellenwert zugemessen wird. Die Integration der Bestände in die Datenbank hat sich - wie erwartet - positiv auf den Aufwand für die Informationsbereitstellung ausgewirkt.

Der Einsatz der Abfragesprache, die den für einfache Auswertungen kaum schnell genug (oder gar nicht) verfügbaren Anwendungsprogrammierer ersetzen sollte, erwies sich in der Praxis bisher als recht problematisch. Der (normalerweise) computerunkundige DB-Benützer aus der Planung scheut grossteils die "Mühsal" der syntaktischen Regeln und hat z.T. Verständnisschwierigkeiten hinsichtlich der Semantik. Das führt dann häufig zu dem unerwünschten Resultat, dass der Benützer nach wie vor verbale Problemstellungen anstelle der fertig 'codierten' Abfragen liefert. Ganz abgesehen von dem Mehraufwand für DB-Service-Mitarbeiter (direkter Terminalanschluss ist nur in Ausnahmefällen realisiert), bergen derartige verbale Formulierungen oft genug (und nicht immer rechtzeitig erkannte) Mehrdeutigkeiten in sich.

Bevor man aufwendigere Projekte für den gleichen Benützerkreis an die Hand nimmt, sollte man durch gesteigerte Motivation den Lernprozess zwischen Forschung und Praxis forcieren zur möglichst umfassenden Klärung folgender Fragen:

- Bis zu welchem Grad kann der Normalbenützer komplexe Datenbank-Strukturen inhaltlich beherrschen, und von welcher Stufe an benötigt man den DB-Operator oder den Applikationsprogrammierer als Bindeglied zwischen Benützer und Datenbank?
- Wie kann man auf sprachlicher Ebene dem Benützer ein besseres Verständnis ermöglichen?
- Wie lassen sich mit angemessenem Aufwand 'self contained systems' für Substrukturen komplexer DB-Modelle entwickeln?

Ein m.E. erfolgversprechender Ansatz zur zweiten und dritten Frage wird von E.F. Codd (siehe [3]) geliefert mit dem experimentellen Abfrage-Formulierungs-Subsystem RENDEZVOUS, welches den Benützer im Dialog von der 'umgangs-englischen' zur 'system-englischen' (und damit auch eindeutigen) Formulierung seiner Abfrage führt.

Literaturhinweise:

(1) K.Ch.Hase, C.Hidber, U.Wähli: "Grundzüge eines Informationssystems für die Orts-, Regional- und Landesplanung", IBM-Nachrichten Heft 211, Juli 1972.

(2) N.Wirth: "PL 360, A Programming Language for the 360 Computers", Journal of the ACM, Vol. 15, No. 1, 1968, pp. 37-74.

(3) E.F.Codd: "Seven steps to rendezvous with the casual user", Proc. IFIP TC-2 Working Conference on Data Base Management Systems, Cargese, Corsica, 1.-5.April 1974, North-Holland.

CAMS : Computer Augmented Mapping System

R. W. Hessdorfer
Bundesforschungsanstalt für
Landeskunde und Raumordnung
53 Bonn-Bad Godesberg

An interactive computer-graphics system to increase the ability of geographers to visualize and manipulate geographical and statistical data in the form of thematic maps is currently being developed in the "Bundesforschungsanstalt für Landeskunde und Raumordnung" in Bonn. This system, named CAMS for Computer Augmented Mapping System, is not only based on the need for the map designer to choose representation techniques and to place legends, symbols, and text, but also on the need of the researcher to explore a variety of data combination and grouping techniques to clarify his understanding of the data.

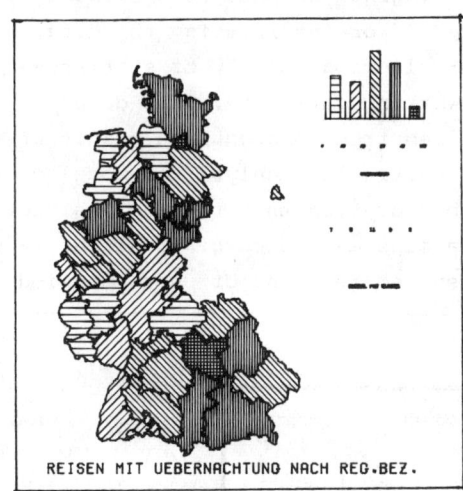

Figure 1: A thematic map indicates both the relative frequencies and spatial distribution of several data groupings by gradations of color, shading, or symbol size. This is an example of the kind of shaded map produced by CAMS on the BfLR Calcomp 738 plotter.

SYSTEM DESCRIPTION:

Because the system will, in the first instance, assist non-programming researchers in the BfLR in the preparation of an Atlas of the Federal Republic of Germany, an important factor in the design of the entire system has been the development of command language and interaction procedures which are as simple, self-explanatory, and user-friendly as possible. User replies are in free-format natural language using key word commands. CAMS allows the advanced user to write lists of complete commands when they are error free; a beginner can request an input explanation at each command point by simply typing a blank line.

Command menus are displayed at strategic points in the dialog so that the user can oversee the options available. In order to allow a maximum of connection to the normal working procedure, the geographical map is used as the basic filter for exploring large "problem-oriented" data sets. The user first displays on the graphics screen the map or map section appropriate to his problem. If the map does not exactly satisfy his needs, the user may change it by either adding areas from the master file, or by eliminating unwanted areas. This geographic map, or list of geographic areas, is then used to search through the "problem-oriented" data sets, combining data set variables for each map area according to a mathematical or logical function. The resulting "working" data set, or data map, is thus a one to one mapping of the data onto the geographical base map.

Output from CAMS lies in one or more of three major information areas. On the simplest level CAMS can produce listings of data sets either entered ("problem-oriented") or produced ("working") during the data mapping process. At the next level CAMS allows a variety of statistical analysis to be performed on these working data sets. This data analysis may be thought of as the work required to produce a resultant data set that reflects the researchers particular analysis or model of the problem situation; or as the data preparation that the map designer must do prior to displaying a map. Data maps may be combined algebraically or logically or transformed by system resident or user supplied

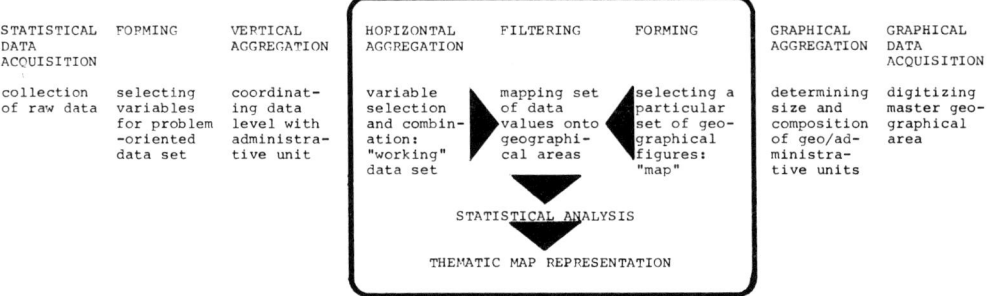

Figure 2: Although CAMS is conceived as both a medium and a method for the synthesis of geographic (areal) and demographic (statistical) data, it is concerned with only a part of the total data analysis problem. Currently, another interactive system, CADS, supplies geographical data sets at any particular level of spatial aggregation, while an information system to supply problem oriented statistical data is still in the design stage.

analysis programs (regression analysis, grouping, factor analysis). Frequency diagrams, mean and standard deviation calculations may be displayed and checked for accuracy of problem characteriation. The resultant data set may then be displayed or plotted as data values in a two-dimensional geographical field. This allows a representation which preserves the integrity of the geographical relationships in the data lost with simple chart output. The highest level of output, thematic maps, is what CAMS is all about. CAMS will produce maps of area boundaries, symbol maps, or shaded maps, both on the display and on the plotter. The user may determine the map size, scale, or section to be drawn; the relationships of the map within the drawn page; the type of shading, color, or symbols to be used to represent the data characteristics; and the placement of labels, legend, special graphical figures, and text on the map page. Once the user has composed his picture on the display screen, the completed map may be directly drawn on the plotter as hard copy, or output to a bulk storage device (dectape, magtape, disk) for later plotting or display.

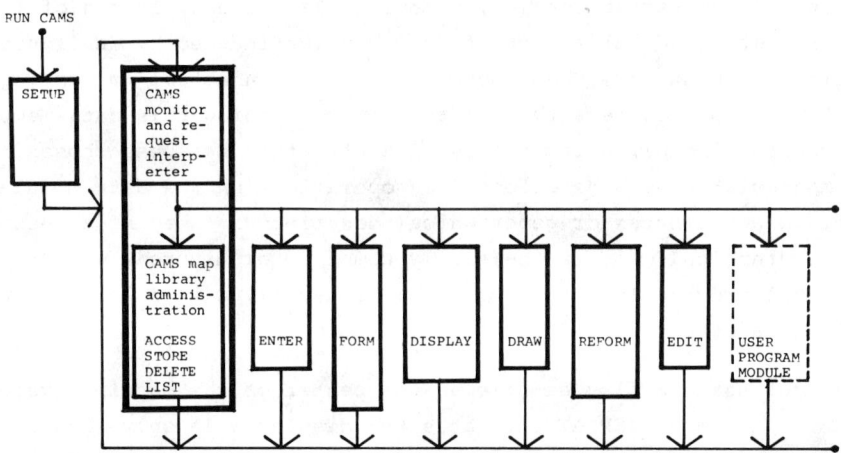

Figure 3: CAMS has been designed as a modular, open-ended system. Each structurally independent module is administered through the CAMS monitor and operates on the CAMS library files. The addition of new modules or programs, either permanent system or temporary user-supplied, is trivial.

In addition to this display and plotting ability, CAMS allows the user to create and administer a permanent system-resident library of up to thirty-five geographic, data, or symbol maps. These maps can then be accessed at any time, edited, deleted, combined, or output to external bulk storage.

General System Mechanisms:

In order to increase the data analysis capabilities of CAMS, a strategy has been adopted that separates geographical coordinate data (x, y values) from the main program data structure. Instead, an intermediate "list" structure serves to incorporate both geographical and statistical data sets into one basic data structure. A geographical map is defined as an ordered list of geographical figures, each having a unique statistical identification number or figure name. A figure is defined as an ordered list of line segments defining the common boundary between any particular figure and its neighbor, or an exterior ground. A line segment thus becomes an ordered list of x, y coordinate values begining with, and ending with, a node by which any particular line segment is connected with the next or previous line segment. Using these definitions, a general CAMS "map" can be considered to consist of two associated parts: (1) A map description record containing structural and identifying attributes (eg. number of list items, length of list, name of list); and (2) a list of data modules indexed by an figure identification number. These modules may contain actual values (eg. a "data" map), or pointers to file records containing this data (eg. a "geographical" map). Because this list structure has been chosen, data manipulation can be effected by operations on the data module lists alone, no coordinates or geographical descriptions need be accessed. Even geographical maps can be easily combined or altered, without the additional programming or space problems usually caused by large coordinate data sets.

Instead of using a display file as the center of the mapping system, the CAMS' command DISPLAY recreates the display file only when it is specifically requested by using the figure list of a map to filter through the line segment file. The resultant display file contains coordinate lists and other display information which make it completely independent of either the original map lists, or the original geographical data files. Only the coordinates which correspond to a particular map list are placed in the display file, and of these, only the coordinates that are visible in the current virtual window - all clipped points are excluded. Simple special figures, such as windows, borders, text labels, and register marks are included in the display file itself, and can become a part of the map list. For more complicated special figures, only the special figure subroutine parameters will be included. Because of the independence from the main coordinate data file, the PLOT command can simply plot on the plotter the

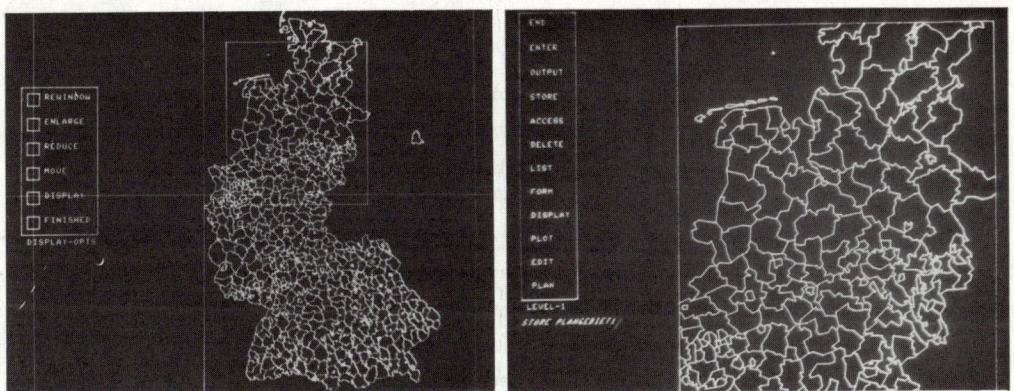

Figure 4: An example of a simple graphical manipulation - "windowing" a displayed map. The system can plot this picture on the Calcomp 738 exactly as it appears on the screen but at any size or scale, or can associate data with only the visible geographic areas. Note also the list of keywords that the user can request when he is uncertain of the command syntax or the options that are available to him.

display file that has been created for the graphical display. The drawing will appear with all the same size relationships (proportional) as on the screen, but can be drawn to any actual size or scale. The screen window of the first map (assumed to be the largest map) is scaled to the requested size and drawn as the page outline (unless specifically suppressed). If the map has been windowed (i.e. only a portion of the map shown) only the lines visible in the original virtual window will be drawn. Since maps can be additively displayed (i.e. added to the existing display file instead of replacing it), more than one map can be drawn within a plotter page, at different scales, in different locations and with different pens. All of these differences, however, must be determined within the DISPLAY command.

Since it is assumed that the user, or a number of users, will be involved with more that one map at a time, any maps either entered or created can be permanently retained in the system library files. Thereafter, these maps can be quickly accessed for the purpose of displaying, plotting or changing the original map. The ACCESS command allows the user to reload any map currently in the map library into the system-working area. Since all map changes (editing figures, data, or specifying display options) are done by changing the map list record, ACCESS creates a duplicate of the orginal map in the working area. This map is placed in the map library with a slightly altered name, and flagged as a temporary map. For convenience, when a data map (data, symbols, names) is accessed, the corresponding geographical ("mother") map is also duplicated and loaded into the working space. Thus any changes in these data maps can result in corresponding changes in the "mother" map. A temporary map may be changed to permanent library entry by using the STORE command and renaming the map. If the name given is the same as an existing map in the library, the old map is deleted, and the new map assumes its place in the library. This access and store strategy allows the user to easily make changes in any map while still retaining the original copy if so desired. If a temporary map is not permanently stored, it will be automatically deleted from the map library when the working session is concluded. Temporary maps appear in the normal library listing and are flagged with a "T". If temporary "mother" map has also been created, it may stored by simply specifying the word "mother" and giving it a unique name within the normal STORE command.

System Implementation:

CAMS is being implemented on a Digital Euqipment Corporation PDP 11/45 mini-computer system with 28 k-words of dynamic storage, and both fixed-head and interchangeable disks. This system is connected to a Tektronix 4002A Graphic Computer Terminal with a joy-stick input device and keyboard, and a Calcomp 738 flatbed plotter. Geographic base data in the form of line segments and coordinates is supplied by a sister system, CADS (Computer Aided Digitizing System), also working online with the PDP 11/45 and a D-mac Digitizer.

Designing an interactive computer graphic system for a mini-computer involves many problems not encountered in programming in a large computer environment. Because of the limited core capacity in any small system, most program data must be kept in exterior disk storage. This means that (1) file structures must be carefully constructed for both flexibility and uniformity; and (2) special programming procedures must be developed to handle frequent file I/O and administration requirements. The word "interactive" in the system description means that a major programming activity will be the translation and checking of user reponses. However, because of core limitations large text blocks or dictionaries in core will be impossible. To compound these difficulties, the CAMS system, because it is rather large and still growing, must be designed as a series of chained program modules, each of which can have a hierarchical structure of program segments in an "overlay" system.

In recognition of these problems CAMS' operating strategy considers that each program module or segment consists of a "Working space" part (passed from program to program and containing a number of file buffers), and a "procedure" part which (operating upon the buffers in the working space and unique for each program segment). In general when an operation on a file buffer has been successfully completed, the buffer is written into the appropriate disk file, and a new (the next) record is read into the working space. This exchanging process, usually involving a number of buffers simultaneously, continues until the procedure has been completed either on the entire list of active records in a file, or a particular sublist. CAMS is supported by three major subsystems which serve to both standardize and facilitate the programming of this system operating strategy.

(1) <u>File handling</u>: For major flexibility all systems files (there are currently six) are direct-access, two-way lists of fixed length records. To save core space the two pointers, indicating the previous record and the next record in the list, are stored on the record itself. This two-way feature, combined with an empty record list, enables records to be added or deleted anywhere within the list (file) without moving any other records, and without necessitating garbage collection on unused records scattered throughout the file. Because the files all have different logical record lengths, different numbers of records, and different external device assignments, each file is separately administrated by a file administration buffer which is permanently stored as the first record of each file. A package of subroutines is available to append, delete, insert, or locate records within any file. For programming efficiency changes in any file may be effected by simply changing the entry in a file table (resident in "working space") corresponding to the desired new attribute. Since all system subroutines use this table to determine file characteristics, no programming changes are necessary.

(2) <u>Text manipulation</u>: To facilitate a flexible, free-format user/

system dialog, all CAMS text I/O passes through a system of subroutines which read and analyze user requests or provide system responses. The read subroutine, which performs the first checks on the input string for special system function keys - escape, line erase, screen erase, etc, functions in combination with several other subroutines which scan for text sub-strings, numbers, and mathematical or logical operators. This package of text handling routines also allows the user to intersperse commands written at the display console with commands read from an external file. This feature combined with the ability to copy user commands made at the console into an external file offers the opportunity to construct standard procedures out of command language requests which can be recalled and executed whenever useful.

Figure 5: A sample system dialog. In this example the user enters a data set called 'auslaender' into the system library. He does this by enumerating the attributes of the data set, including writing eleven text names for the variables. When he is finished, he lists the entire data description, including the data values, to the line printer (lp:). He then, after first forgetting, loads a geographical map to serve as a filter, and forms a working data set consisting of two variables: 'totaus' and 'toterw'. When this 'data map probeeins' has been formed, he stores the map in the CAMS library and proceeds to the next step: making a simple statistical analysis (ranking) of the data values. Since this is an advanced user, who is reasonably familiar with the command requests, the system only interrupts him (capital letters) when he makes an input mistake.

```
enter data auslaender file dk:apop70.dat
ascii       (8a1,f4.0,10f5.0)
yes 71
ERROR: NUMBER OF VARIABLES MAY NOT EXCEED 64
NUMBER OF VARIABLES
(EXCLUDING "STATISTISCHE KENNZIFFER") : 11
descriptive
erwerbsp a16-21j a21-35j, a35-50j    a50-65j
totaus70, totein70
ENTER 4 VARIABLE LABELS (MAX 8 CHARS)
geburta, geburtd,  totwandr  deutwand
DATA SET AUSLAENDER SUCCESSFULLY ENTERED
list pdata auslander to lp:    all
form data probeeins from auslaender
ERROR: NO MAP IS IN THE WORKING SPACE
access bundeskreis
form data probeeins from auslaender   totaus= totaus70,
     toterw = (totaus70 / totein70) + erwerbsp  :
DATA MAP PROBEEINS HAS BEEN FORMED
store probeeins
form rank ausgrouped
```

(3) **Key word display:** The CAMS command language utalizes a combination of hierarchially organized keyword requests at the first level of request sorting, and individually determined program segment requests at the local level. This means that once a particular subprogram or module has been selected by the first level sort, the continuing system requests do not have to be fit within a particular keyword or response pattern. However, at any level where a number of keyword options exist, these options can be displayed on the screen as a menu or list of allowed user responses. The administration and preparation of these text lists, including positioning on the screen, is accomplished by a subsystem called MAKBUT. These text lists reside in files exterior to the CAMS file system, but can be quickly and easily located, displayed, and interrogated by subroutine call. User replies can be either typed or chosen with the cusor directly from the displayed text list.

All the subroutines described in (1), (2), and (3) above reside in a program library, CAMLIB, so that thay are readily available for normal systems programming, or to users who want to create their own special program modules.

Summary

CAMS has been designed to be a flexible instrument for the researcher who wants to explore statistical data while maintaining a close relationship to its spatial context. While CAMS is neither a general information system, nor a general graphic editor, it manages to include both areas sufficiently "to get the job done" by defining its competence rather carefully. This attitude of programming pragmatism has resulted in simple, but workable solutions to many problems which on the general level would have been difficult to solve. Often the theoretical systems designer seeks to enumerate the universe of possible system operations and to make a complete solution which encompasses each and every known problem. However, it is the nature of interactive systems that, because they allow the user to explore problems instead of "just" solving them, they tend to lead to new working procedures and, therefore, to new system requirements which did not exist prior to the implementation of the system. The task of the "pragmatic" systems designer is, then, to construct a system framework which allows for a partial or incomplete solution - he must design a system which provides the user with a number of general procedures with which he can solve or explore a core of the predicted problems, and to which the user can easily attach specific procedures to solve rare, unexpected, or "not-yet-discovered" problems. It is within this kind of "heuristic" systems approach that CAMS has been conceived and is currently being implemented.

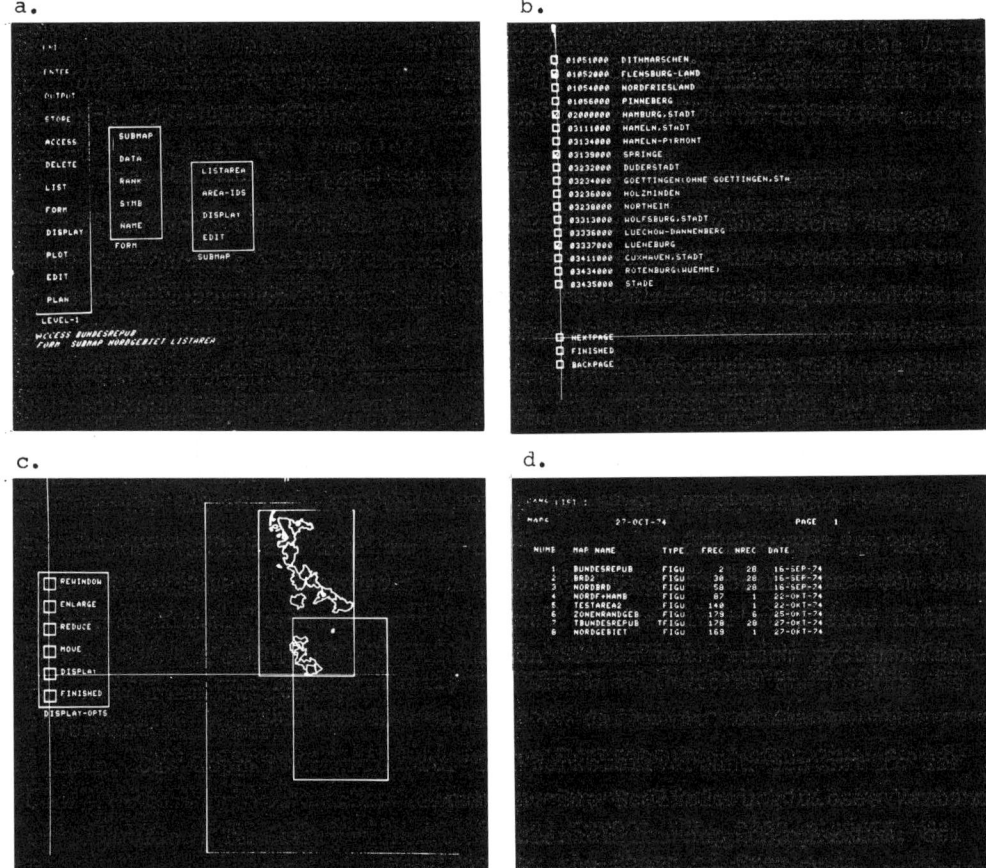

Figure 6: An example of a CAMS procedure. The user will form a submap - a selection of geographical figures from a larger map - in order to study a particular subregion. First he accesses a map called 'bundesrepub' from his existing map library to serve as the base map. Then he issues the "FORM SUBMAP" command, but because he is uncertain about the correct syntax, he requests a list of the possible options at each level in the command hierarchy (Figure 6a). The chosen option "LISTAREA" display to the user a listing of the names and statistical identification numbers of the geographical figures in the base map from which he can select his new map areas with the graphical cursor (Figure 6b). When finished paging through the base map to find the desired figures, the user chooses to display his newly formed submap. Because the map figures are not centered in the 'screen page', he moves the entire assemblage using the "DISPLAY-OPTIONS" (Figure 6c). When the user is satisfied with his new map, both in terms of graphics and geography, he uses the "STORE" command to place map 'nordgebiet' permanently in his library (Figure 6d).

Bibliography:

1. Blum, Helmut,,Das kommunale Planungs-, Informations- und Analyse-System (KOMPAS) der Landeshauptstadt München, <u>Öffentliche Verwaltung und Datenverarbeitung, Heft 11, November 1973, S. 495 - 503</u>

2. Ganser, K., Die Aufgabe der thematischen Karte im Informationssystem Raumentwicklung. <u>Vortrag beim 23. Deutschen Kartographentag 1974 in Bonn-Bad Godesberg</u>

3. Hessdorfer, R.W., System Dokumentation 1: CAMS, Computer Augmented Mapping System. Bundesforschungsanstalt für Landeskunde und Raumordnung, Bonn-Bad Godesberg, <u>Unveröffentlichtes Manuskript, Juli 1974</u>

4. Rase, W.D.,Schäfer, H., Computerunterstützte Herstellung thematischer Karten, <u>Öffentliche Verwaltung und Datenverarbeitung, Heft 5, 1974</u>

5. Rase, W.D., Definition und maschinelle Erfassung flächenhafter Bezugseinheiten, <u>Öffentliche Verwaltung und Datenverarbeitung, Heft 8, 1973</u>

6. Rase, W.D., Bereitstellung der geometrischen Grundlagen für die computerunterstützte Zeichnung thematischer Karten, <u>Unveröffentlichtes Manuskript, Juni 1974</u>

7. Schäfer, H., Grobkonzept für das Informationssystem Raumentwicklung, Bundesforschungsanstalt für Landeskunde und Raumordnung, <u>Informationssystem für Raumordnung und Landesplanung, Heft 6, 1974</u>

COMPUTER AIDED DESIGN - SOME OCCUPATIONAL AND SOCIAL IMPLICATIONS.
M.J.E. COOLEY.   Past President   Amalgamated Union of Engineering Workers.
(Technical and Supervisory Section).

There is a widespread belief that automation, computerisation and the use of robotic devices will automatically liberate men from routine, backbreaking and soul destroying tasks, and leave them free to engage in more creative, worthwhile activities. It is a belief carefully nurtured and developed by the salesmen of high capital equipment. Large Combines and Monopolies look hopefully to the introduction of high capital equipment as a means of negating the "Law of Diminishing Returns". Up to five years ago, the application was in the main in the field of manual work - albeit in some highly skilled jobs involving complex decision making routines. The workers involvevolved, whether it be at Fiat in Italy, British Leyland in Britain, or Ford in the United States would not be prepared to agree that this opened the door to the industrial paradise which the salesmen had suggested. Designers and technologists, in some instances themselves the originators of the equipment, took a neutral, disconnected view about the consequences of the equipment they were designing, or alternatively, held a rather smug view that this kind of equipment would in any case never affect their own "intellectual activity".

The past five years have demonstrated for those who wish to read the signs, that the design office is no industrial sanctuary. Concrete experience tends to demonstrate that the introduction of high capital equipment into the design environment is unlikely to be any more liberating than it has been on the shop floor, yet the idea persists that the drudgery and hackwork of design will be indertaken by computer, and the designer will be free to give full vent to his creativity and in consequence we will automatieally have better designs, quicker and by more satisfied design staffs.

It is the purpose of this paper to challenge this assumption and to demonstrate that there are objective economic laws which in our profit oriented society will inevitably result in the further subordination of the worker (designer) to the machine (computer). Further, an attempt will be madeto demonstrate that the unthinking a application of machinery to a range of productive processes including the production of intellectual output can in fact stifle creativity.

In selling the idea of computers to the design community, it is suggested that the computer will merely deal with the quantitative factors and the designer will deal with value judgements and the creative elements of the design process. It is of course true that the design process is, amongst other things, an interaction of two dialectical opposites, the quantitative and the qualitative. It is not however true, that design methodology is such that these can be separated into two disconnected elements which can then be applied almost as a chemical compound. The process by which these two dialectical opposites are united by the designer to produce a new whole is a complex and as yet ill defined and researched area.

The sequential basis on which the elements interact is of extreme importance. The nature of that sequential interaction, and indeed the ration of the qualitative to the quantitative depends on the commodity under design consideration. Even where an attempt is made to define the proportion of the work that is 'creative' and the proportion that is 'non-creative' what cannot be readily stated is the stage at which the creative element has to be introduced when a certain stage of the non-creative work has been completed. The very subtle process by which the designer reviews the quantitative information he has assembled and then makes the qualitative judgement is extremely complex. Those who seek to introduce computrised equipment into this interaction, attempt to suggest that the quantitative and the qualitative can be arbitrarily divided, and the computer handle the quantitative.

Since C.A.D. dramatically increased the rate at which the quantitative is handled, a serious distortion of this dialectical interaction takes place, frequently to the detriment of the qualitative. There are therefore, good grounds for assuming that the crude introduction of the computer into the design process in keeping with the Western Ethic of 'the faster the better' may well result in a deterioration of the design quality. It is typical of the narrow fragmented and short term view which Capitalism takes of all productive processes, that these important philosohical considerations are ignored. Much design research is limited to considerations of design techniques and associated hardware and software with precious little regard for the objective requirements of the design staff involved. Such research accurately reflects our economic base. Equipment and hence capital first; people last. Indeed it is now clear that many of the schemes to divide the design activity into its 'creative' and 'non- creative' elements are actually an extension of the historical division between manual and intellectual work. Worse still, they are used as a "Trojan Horse" to import the repressiveness of 'Taylorism' into the field of intellectual work.

I do not deny that the introduction of C.A.D. could liberate designers from the routine, soul destroying tasks, and provide them with more time in which to engage in creative work. What I fundamentally question is that this will happen in our profit oriented society. C.A.D. systems are a further manifestation of the great creativity and ingenuity of man in providing implements to meet his primitive need of food, shelter and a safe environment in which to reproduce his own kind. As such, however sophisticated complicated and ingenious they might be, they are merely another 'means of production'. It follows therefore that C.A.D. being a unit of production, will abide by the general laws of technological change, and its implication in my view can only be fully understood when analysed in that historical context.

Viewed historically, the following are important in this context:-

1. The rate of technological change is exponential.
2. The rate of obsolescence of applied knowledge is increasing. (Sir Frederick warner and others have produced mathematical models for

some occupations)
3. There is an ever shorter life of fixed capital. (some equipment is now obsolete in three years).
4. The cost of the <u>Total</u> means of production continues to increase.

Confronted by equipment which is getting obsolete literally by the minute, and has involved enormous capital investment, the employer will seek to recoup that investment by exploiting the equipment for 24 hours a day, and will seek to subordinate the operators more and more to the machine in order to get the maximum performance. He will insist that either the equipment is worked on shifts to attain a 24 hour exploitation, or is used on a continuous overtime basis. This trend had long since been evident on the workshop floor, and is now beginnig to be discernible in a whole series of white collar occupations including design. Thus, far from leading to a shorter working week and longer holidays, the tendency is actually to maintain hours at existing levels, or in fact to increase them.

I would contend therefore, that in our profit oriented society, automation, computerisation and robotic devices will only be introduced in narrow areas of the economy there to be exploited for 24 hours a day. The economic base of our society will prevent the widespread introduction of this kind of equiment and through its general use, the introduction of a shorter working week and longer holidays. Indeed, the effect will be to create a frantic work tempo for some, whilst creating a permanent pool of unemployed persons. What happend in practice is that the introduction of this type of equipment changes the organic composition of capital; by that I mean industry becomes capital intensive rather than labour intensive. Thus we find emphasis on what is called a high wage, high productivity, low cost economy. The consequencies of such an economy have become evident in the United State for dome time. In spite of all the technological change, and the artificial stimulus to the manufacturing industries of the Vietnam war, they have had something like 5 million to 6 million paople permanently unemployed for the last eight years.

Structural unemployment is now growing in many E.E.C. countries, and as in the U.S. will not be confined to unskilled and manual workers. (The Nobel Prizewinner Linus Pauling recently pointed out that 18% of the PhD.s in some fields of technology are unemployed in the U.S.)

In ensuring that the equopment is fully exploited, we see growing pressure for workers to accept shiftwork. We should be quite clear about the consequences of shiftworking. Studies in West Germany inducate that the ulcer rate amongst workers on a rotating shift is eight times as high as those working normal hours. The divorce rate is approximately 80% higher, and the juvenile delinquency rate of their children some 50% greater.

Due to the enormous 'rate of production' of these devices, every effort is made to ensure that the human being who 'feeds them' is capable of responding to the machine at the maximum rate of work. It is now commonplace for systems designers to refer to the operator as the component in the total man-machine system. In order that the response rate of the man be as high as possible to interface with the machine, a number of productivity agreements are now introducing medical checks. In these checks a man is tested like a diode to ensure that his response rate is fast enough. We know that in the steel industry for example, some men whose response rate was not high enough were downgraded, and they were allocated second rate work at £15 per week less. There is a growing tendency also to work out the life expectancy of the operator when working at this frantic tempo. In Standard Triumph in Coventry, it is reckoned that a man is "burned up" in ten years on the main production line. The company actually attempted to get the manual workers to agree that only those under the age of 30 would be recruited for this high tempo work.

In general, this type of equipment means that the operator is further subordinated to the machine with little or no control over the rate at which he works. The process, not the worker sets the tempo. Any initiative displayed by the operator is regarded as disruptive.

It is vitally important that engineers and technologists understand that this is how employers and their sociologists regard human beings. If it is felt that this is a polarised view, let me quote one of them, Robert Boguslaw who recently pointed out:- "Our immediate concern, let us remember, is the exploitation of the operating unit approach to systems design, no matter what materials are used. We must take care to prevent this discussion from degenerating into a single sided analysis of the complex characteristics of one type of system material, namely human beings. What we need is an inventory of the way in which the human behaviour can be controlled and description of some instruments which will help us to achieve control. If this provides us with sufficient 'handles' on human materials so that we can think of them as one thinks of metal parts, electrical power or chemical reactions, then we have succeeded in placing human material on the same footing as any other materials and can proceed with our problems of systems design".

This then is the objective dehumanisation which takes place side by side with this advanced technology. Boguslaw eve goes as far as comparing the human being to other materials:-

"There are however, many disadvantages in the use of human operating units. They are somewhat fragile, they are subject to fatigue, obsolescence, disease and death. They are frequently stupid, unreliable and limited in memory capacity. But beyond all this, they sometimes seek to design their own circuitry. This, in a material is unforgivalbe. Any system utilising them must devise appropriate safeguards".

This then is the real economic and political context in which C.A.D. is being introduced into the design environment. It would be both foolish and elitist to believe that the work in which we as designers are engaged is so complex that the consequences will not be similar to that which has been experience on the shop floor. The concrete experience of my union tends to demonstrate that the conditions I've described on the shop floor are now beginning to apply also in design offices. There is the same desire, when a C.A.D. system has been introduced, to exploit it 24 hours a day. This is not a suggestion that thsi will happen in tha far distant future. Two years ago my union was involved in a very bitter dispute with Rolls Royce. That dispute cost the union a quarter of a million pounds, and it is worthwhile considering some of the conditions which the Comapny sought to impose on the design staffs in a productivity agreement.

"The acceptance of shift work in order to exploit high capital equipment. The acceptance of work measurement techniques. The division of work into basic elements, and the setting of times for these elements, such terms to be compared with actual performance."

This then is the harsh reality which confronts designers when this kind of equipment is introduced into their areas. Those involved at Rolls Royce were some of the finest aerodynamicists in the world.

The problem for older workers, which I mentioned in respect of the shop floor manifests itslef also in a more sophisticated way in design areas. It is now fashionable to talk about intellectual workers as having 'peak performance' ages. The Sunday Times some time ago, gave a list of these for mathematicians, engineers, physicists and others. For some of these the peak performance age was 29 to 32. A number of American studies have recently pointed ou these peak performance ages and it is suggested that they should be followed by a careers plateau for two or three years. Thereafter the employees in question is either moved out of the area or subjected to a "careers de-escalation".

Our practical experience tends to demonstrate that as these new techniques are introduced, and rationalisation takes place, older men are being eliminated in the consequential redundancies. An analysis we have made of the design staffs over 40 indicates that their likelihood of being employed at the same level of salary and the same status is about one third of these at the age of 30. Thus it appears that as C.A.D. is introduced into design areas, the contradictions that we have examined earlier on the shop floor apply also to the design environment. In particular, the worker is further subordinated to the machine. He is compelled to attempt to respond to the machine's speed. <u>In the Man/Machine interface, the man is slow, inconsistent, unreliable.but highly creative, whilst the machine is the dialectical opposite - fast, consistent, reliable but non-creative.</u> As the designer attempts to cope with this interaction the stress upon him is enormous. Some C.A.D. systems seek to eliminate all the so called routine reference work. The department of Labour in the United States has pointed out that creative designers are only engaged on design decisions for about 5% of their time. The rest is on this routine, semi clerical work. When this is handled by the computer it can mean that in certain design proceedures the "Decision Making Rate" is actually increased by 1,900% !

Decision making at such increased rates implies the use of specialists. Such specialisation fits conveniently into the general historical fragmentation of skills and has been evident in the design field since the thirties. During the thirties, the design draughtsman was the centre of the design activity. He would design the commodity, draw it, stress it, specify its lubrication, liaise with the workshops for its manufacture, write the test proceeddures and in many instances commission it. With the increased complexity of technology, each of these functions was divided into a separate discernible task. Thus the draughtsman drew, the designer designed, the metallurgist specified the material, the streesmen carried out the calculations and so on. In consequence, fewer of those in the design field are capable of seeing the design activity in a panoramic way. The computer actually consolidated this highly undesirable historical tendency, hence we repeatedly find references to 'dedicated men' for 'dedicated systems'. The whole educational system is increasingly being subordinated to meeting the requirements of the monopolies for 'dedicated men'. Thus we get narrow, specialised education which trains a man to do a job but does not educate him to think.

This subordination of the operator to the machine is now spreading right through the design spectrum. There were those involved in highly creative fields, such as architecture, who seem to believe that these problems would never expend to their preserves. In fact systems such as the Harness System now exist where the architect is reduced to disposing pre determined architectural elements about a harness. Clearly his creative scope is thereby limited.

On the shop floor, when a productive process has been optimised, it is then almost impossible to change it until the entire environment is changed to introduce a new 'Commodity Model'. The same is beginning to happen in the design environment. Optimisation routines, which imply that the optimum means of dealing with a design problem has been arrived at, frequently leads to the fossilisation of the design in that the employer is not prepared to allow further expenditure to improve on a sub routine which he believes has already reached its optimum. It is an over simplification to suggest that module building techniques where the best elements of a number of soft ware packages can be taken to create a new design will provide a satisfactory solution to this problem.

Seen at a general level, it appears to hold good that the introduction of automatic and computerised equipment into any area of activity will result in the proletarianisation of those involved.

Those such as the aerodynamicists at Rools Royce whom the company sought to subject to stop watch techniques and shiftworking, quickly begin to realise that they need to organise collectively to defend their working conditions. Further, they begin to realise that they have a community of interest with all those others who attempt to ensure that machinery is used to improve the quality of their lives, and not to contribute to its detriment. <u>C.A.D. therefore results in a shift in the cultural, social and political position of design staffs.</u> C.A.D. forces on Design Staffs a growing recognition of the implications of their work for other sections of the community. In the engineering industry, we have seen a number of joint actions of design staffs and those on the shop floor, since frequently design systems where the output is a tape for an N.C. machine tool, can have enormous consequences on the shop floor by eliminating some of the most skilled jobs such as jig boring. But most of all, thoughtful designers are beginning to recognise that they are gradually being ensnared in a proceedure which more and more ties them to the machine, and reduces them to the whims of the system. At the Conference on Robot Technology at Nottingham University in April, a programmable draughting or design system was accapted by definition as being a robot. One of the manufacturers of robotic equipment pointed out:-

"Robots represent industry's logical search for an obedient workforce" That, it seems to me, is a very dangerous philosophy. The great thing about people is that they are sometimes disobedient. Most human development, technical, cultural and political, depended on those who were prepared to 'disobey' the norms of the societies in which they lived. For too long, as designers and technologists, we have been prepared to produce equipment blindly, at the whim of the employers and those whose interests they represent. It seems now time that we stood back and took a deep philosophical view of the work on which we are engaged. C.A.D. has brought the problem to our own doorsteps, we are now in danger of being drawn into an 'intellectual production line' by devices we have originated. We now have a profound and indeed historical responsibility to see that the products of skill and ingenuity are used to provide the economic basis for a more full and dignified existance for the commu ity as a whole, not merely to maximise profits for the few.

The author is engaged in research in the topics covered in this paper. He would welcome an exchange of information (in German or English) from anyone workingi in similar fields.

ADDRESS: M.J.E. Cooley
            75, Talbot Ave,
            Langley,
            New Berks,
            U.K.

ENTWICKLUNG UND EINSATZ

EINES INTERAKTIVEN KONSTRUKTIONSPLATZES (IKP)

H. Flessner +)
P. Gorny
H.-P. Haake
W. Hansmann

1. AUFGABENSTELLUNG

Beim rechnerunterstützten Entwerfen und Konstruieren ist es ein Haupthindernis, daß ein großer Teil der notwendigen Daten in Form von Zeichnungen und Skizzen vorliegt und für den Einsatz von CAD-Programmen erst in alphanumerische Form unter Verwendung von Datenformularen oder Datensprachen gebracht werden müssen. Die Vorlagen können dabei maßstäblich (soweit Papierverzug und Zeichengenauigkeit es zulassen) oder unmaßstäblich mit Maßbeschriftung vorliegen. Je nach Konstruktionsaufgabe müssen unterschiedliche Daten daraus entnommen werden: z.B. aus der Architektenzeichnung eines Gebäudes u.a. die Systemlinien des Tragwerks zur statischen Berechnung, die genauen Körperabmessungen einzelner Tragwerksteile zur Berechnung ihrer Tragfähigkeit und der Materialmengen (Stücklisten, Massenberechnungen), Detailpunkte zur Herstellung von Fertigungszeichnungen von Konstruktionselementen (z.B. Bewehrungspläne), Innenmaße zur Berechnung und Zeichnung von Installationsplänen, Flächen- und Raummaße zur Berechnung von Heizwerten sowie zur Berechnung des Mietwerts und - nicht zu vergessen - einige perspektivische Ansichten für Bauherrn und Behörden.

Nur wenige der Daten für die einzelnen Schritte bei Entwurfs- und Konstruktionsvorgängen - im Bauwesen ebenso wie in anderen Ingenieurbereichen - lassen sich direkt aus den Daten anderer Schritte ermitteln, so daß komplizierte Umsetzvorgänge oft unter Zuhilfenahme anderer schnell alternder Informationsquellen (Gesetze, Normen, Patente, Zulassungsvorschriften für Baustoffe, firmeninterne Standards, Lagerbestände, Lie-

---

+) Adressen:
Prof. Dr.-Ing. Hermann Flessner, Dipl.-Ing. Heinz-Peter Haake,
Dipl.-Ing. Werner Hansmann:
Arbeitsgruppe Angewandte Informatik im Ingenieurwesen,
Ruhr-Universität Bochum, D-4630 Bochum, Postfach 2148
Prof. Dr.-Ing. Peter Gorny:
Angewandte Informatik, Universität Oldenburg,
D-2900 Oldenburg, Postfach 943

fermöglichkeiten, Preislisten etc.) erforderlich werden.
Die bisherigen CAD-Programme behandeln entweder nur Einzelprobleme mit eigener alphanumerischer Eingabe und alphanumerischer und grafischer Ausgabe oder sie integrieren mehrere Schritte auf Kosten der Gestaltungsfreiheit und Wirtschaftlichkeit durch straffe Reglementierung des Katalogs der verwendbaren Konstruktionselemente. Außerdem gibt es eine Reihe von Systemen zum interaktiven Konstruieren am Display mit Hilfe eines Lichtgriffels, bei denen jedoch durchweg von einer leeren Zeichenfläche ausgegangen werden muß.

Im Rahmen eines aus Mitteln des 2. DV-Programms der Bundesregierung geförderten Forschungsvorhabens /1/ werden gegenwärtig Geräte und Methoden untersucht, die mit Hilfe eines "Interaktiven Konstruktionsplatzes" ermöglichen sollen,

- Konstruktionsdaten grafisch bei interaktiver Eingabekontrolle eingeben zu können,
- Änderungen und Ergänzungen an bereits früher automatisch erstellten Konstruktionszeichnungen vornehmen zu können,
- Konstruktionszeichnungen ausgeben zu können und
- unabhängige CAD-Programme teilweise zu Systemen integrieren zu können /2/.

Eine weitere wesentliche Randbedingung des Vorhabens ist die Beachtung der Wirtschaftlichkeit und Praxisorientierung von Konfiguration und Verfahren.

2. HARDWARE

Der von der Bochumer Arbeitsgruppe verwendete "Interaktive Konstruktionsplatz" (IKP) (Bild 1 und 2) umfaßt folgende Geräte:
für die grafische Eingabe
- Digitizer (Koordinatenerfassungsgerät HAROPEN, Fa. Hagen Systems, DIN A 1, 0.1 mm Auflösung, Digitalisierstift).
 Ein anderes mit Lupe ausgestattetes Digitalisiergerät hatte sich für den vorgesehenen Zweck als zu schwerfällig erwiesen.

für die grafische Ausgabe
- passives grafisches Display (Siemens Industriemonitor über Tektronix Video-Scanner). Auf ein Display mit Lightpen wurde bewußt verzichtet, da passive Displays erheblich billiger sind und mit dem Digitalisierstift ähnliche Funktionen ausgeübt werden können.

Bild 1: Der Interaktive Konstruktionsplatz

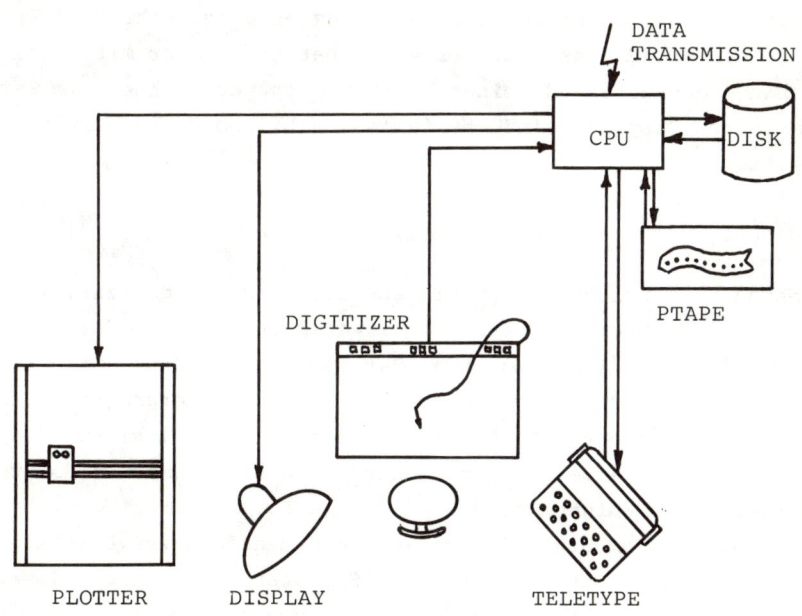

Bild 2: Konfiguration des IKP

- Plotter (Zeichentisch GRAPHOMAT 9004, Fa. Hagen Systems, DIN A 1, 0.05 mm Inkrement)

für die alphanumerische Eingabe
- Konsolschreibmaschine (Siemens Blattschreiber Tsend 100)

Als Steuereinheit für die Geräte dient der Digitalrechner Siemens 404/3, zu dem auch noch Lochstreifen E/A-Geräte gehören. Da sowieso ein Rechner benötigt wurde, konnte mit nur geringen Mehrkosten für zusätzlichen Kernspeicher (insgesamt 64 KB) und einen Plattenspeicher (6 MB) die Möglichkeit geschaffen werden, nicht nur die oben genannten Aufgaben zu erfüllen, sondern auch einen großen Teil der Berechnungen direkt durchzuführen, so daß nur für umfangreiche CAD-Programme eine Verbindung zu einem Großrechner hergestellt werden muß. Tatsächlich konnte bisher die geplante Verbindung zu den Großrechnern TR 440 und Siemens 4004 nur über externe Datenträger (Lochstreifen) simuliert werden.
Eine geplante Erweiterung ist ein akustisches Ausgabegerät (Voice Response Unit) mit digitaler Ansteuerung von auf Tonband gesprochenen Texten.
Zwei Jahre nach Entwurf der beschriebenen Konfiguration könnte man heute aufgrund der technischen Entwicklung entweder mehrere IKPs an einem Rechner der Preisklasse der 404/3 betreiben oder mit wesentlich geringeren Kosten für einen kleinen Computer rechnen. Im Bereich der grafischen Displays sind ebenfalls erhebliche Verbesserungen erzielt worden.

3. MENÜTECHNIK

Eine besondere Erweiterung der Eingabe bietet der Digitizer. Mit Hilfe eines eigenen Menüfeldes, dessen frei wählbare Lage auf der Digitalisierfläche durch Antippen von zwei Passpunkten dem Programm bekanntgemacht wird, kann jeder Programmierer über einen Unterprogrammaufruf /3/ eine beliebige Menge von zusätzlichen Zeichen (Symbolen) für den Benutzer definieren. Außerdem können die Kästchen des Menüfelds Programmsteueranweisungen aufnehmen.
Bild 3 zeigt auf dem Digitalisiertisch ein Menüfeld zur Herstellung von Rohrnetzzeichnungen. Es enthält neben Symbolen von Rohrnetzelementen, die anhand einer danebenliegenden Topologie-Skizze aneinandergereiht werden, auch die Möglichkeit der Zahleneingabe und eine Reihe von Steueranweisungen für den Dateiverkehr, die Ausgabe der fertigen Zeichnung und die Korrektur.
Wegen seiner außerordentlichen Flexibilität kann das Menüfeld softwareseitig wie ein gesondertes Eingabegerät behandelt werden.

Bild 3: *Menüfeld zur Herstellung von Rohrnetzplänen*

4. DIALOG ZWISCHEN KONSTRUKTEUR UND IKP

Nach dem Start eines Programms wird auf die - im Rahmen des gegebenen Menüs - heuristischen Eingaben des Benutzers eine deterministische Reaktion des IKP verlangt. Der so entstehende schnelle Wechsel von Ein- und Ausgabe, der üblicherweise etwas euphemistisch als Dialog bezeichnet wird, läßt sich grob in zwei Themenbereiche unterteilen und ist etwa so strukturiert:

1.) *Steuerung des Konstruktionsvorgangs*
    a) <u>IKP</u>: Anforderung von Steueranweisungen durch Programmsystem
        (über Konsolschreibmaschine (KSM), Display oder Sprach-
        Ausgabegerät (VRU))
    b) <u>Konstrukteur</u>: Steueranweisung zur Auswahl des nächsten Pro-
        gramms/Unterprogramms (über KSM-Tastatur oder Menüfeld)
    c) <u>IKP</u>: Quittung, weiter bei 2a; oder Fehlermeldung, weiter bei
        1a (über KSM, Display, VRU)

2.) *Konstruktionsvorgang*

    a) **IKP**: Anforderung von Daten durch Konstruktionsprogramm (über KSM, Display, VRU)

    b) **Konstrukteur**: Mitteilung über Adresse der Daten auf Hintergrundspeicher oder Eingabe der Daten (über KSM-Tastatur, Digitizer, Menüfeld)

    c) **IKP**: Quittung oder Fehlermeldung. Anfrage, ob Daten geändert oder ergänzt werden sollen (über KSM, Display, VRU)

    d) **Konstrukteur**: Ja, weiter bei 1b oder 2a; oder Nein, weiter bei 2e (über KSM-Tastatur, Menüfeld)

    e) **IKP**: Start des Berechnungsprogramms (auf Kleinrechner oder über DFÜ auf Großrechner)
Ausgabe der Ergebnisse (über KSM, Display, Plotter, Drucker o.a.)
Weiter bei 1a oder 2a.

Jede Konstruktionszeichnung kann aus gerichteten Graphen zusammengesetzt interpretiert werden, bei denen jeder Ast ein Zeichnungselement darstellt. Sie läßt sich deshalb in einem *Wechselschrittverfahren* herstellen:

    1. Schritt: Eingabe des Graphenknotens, an dem fortgesetzt werden soll, und der Richtung des neuen Graphenastes.

    2. Schritt: Ersetzen des abstrakten Graphenastes durch ein reelles Zeichnungselement.

Falls keine Verzweigungen bei einem speziellen Problem möglich sind, wird natürlich der 1. Schritt implizit vom Programm vorgenommen werden (z.B. Reihung von Schriftzeichen, von Maschinenelementen auf einer Welle). Der 2. Schritt kann so erweitert werden, daß nicht nur die geometrische Gestalt des Zeichnungselements auf Sichtgerät oder Plotter ausgegeben wird, sondern auch die physikalischen oder technischen Eigenschaften eines Elements gespeichert werden können, so daß nach Fertigstellung einer größeren Konstruktionseinheit ihre Eigenschaften berechnet werden können.

Mit dem Symbolverwaltungssystem SYMBOS /4/ wurde das Wechselschrittverfahren eingeführt, das den Anschluß vieler Konstruktionsprogramme ermöglicht. SYMBOS geht von einer in Bild 4 dargestellten Struktur einer Zeichnung, dort "Bild" genannt, aus. Die Elemente eines Bildes können in Gruppen zusammengefaßt sein und enthalten programmtechnisch lediglich Verweise auf grafische Muster sowie die Transformations- und Darstellungsparameter (Strichstärke, Flackern, Abdunkeln etc.). Das SYMBOS-Menüfeld (Bild 5) erlaubt die Manipulation des Bildes, der Gruppen und der Elemente. Es gestattet auch das Kreieren, Löschen oder Verschieben von bestimmten herausgehobenen Punkten (Basispunkten) eines Bildes -

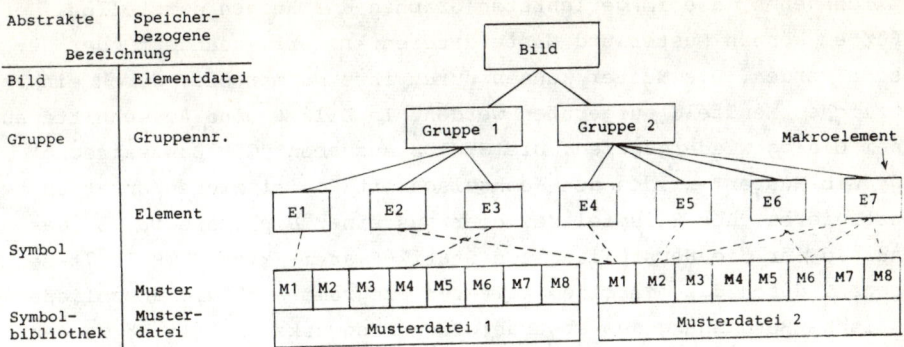

Bild 4: Struktur eines SYMBOS-Bildes

OPERATION	OBJEKT	DARSTELLUNGSART			
KREIEREN	BILD (Elementdatei)		STOP		
EINFÜGEN		BKS	WIEDERHOLE LETZTES SIG-BILD *		
EINFÜGEN MIT VERSCHIEBEN	GRUPPE	PKS	PLOTTER		
LÖSCHEN		SKS	SICHTGERÄT		
LÖSCHEN MIT VERSCHIEBEN	MAKRO- ELEMENT	SKS AUSSCHNITT	DRUCKER		
VERSETZEN		SKS VOLLE GRÖSSE	GERÄTEKANAL- NUMMER		
VERZERREN	ELEMENT	GEHOBENER STIFT	EINGABE ENDE		
SPIEGELN		FLACKERN **			
IDENTIFIZIEREN		FLACKERN AUFHEBEN **	DATEI BEREINIGEN		
KENNZEICHNEN	BASIS- PUNKT	STRICHSTÄRKE 1	CURSOR FIXIEREN		
WANDELN		STRICHSTÄRKE 2	−	E 10	Zahl löschen
AUSGEBEN	MUSTER		7	8	9
DARSTELLUNGSART ÄNDERN			4	5	6
SIG-AUSGABE UNTERDRÜCKEN	MUSTER- DATEI	MUSTER ÜBER NUMMER	1	2	3
UNTERDRÜCKUNG AUFHEBEN		KOORD.-EINGABE ÜBER MENÜFELD	0	,	Zahl- ende

* *Nur für Sichtgeräte mit Storage-CRT oder Refreshing-CRT*
** *Nur für Sichtgeräte mit Bildwiederholspeicher*

Bild 5: Menüfeld für SYMBOS

nämlich jenen, die im gerichteten Graphen die Knoten darstellen. Außerdem können Muster und Musterdateien kreiert, geändert oder gelöscht werden. Die Muster können durch ihre Nummer oder durch ein zusätzliches Menüfeld aufgerufen werden. In Bild 6 sind Ausschnitte aus einem Dialog wiedergegeben. Die SYMBOS-Ausgaben "Gib Basisstrecke" und "Gib Muster" bilden den Wechselschritt Positionieren/Ersetzen beim Konstruieren. Als Beispiel sei hier aus einer Diplomarbeit /5/ das Menüfeld für die Herstellung von Statik-System-Skizzen (Bild 7) herangezogen, durch das mit einem weiteren Programm auch die anschließende statische Berechnung des abstrahierten Tragwerks ermöglicht werden soll. In Bild 8 ist die Entwicklung einer Systemskizze dargestellt.

SYMBOS-AUSGABE über Sichtgerät	BENUTZER-EINGABE über Digitalisierfläche	SYMBOS-BILDPROTOKOLL über Blattschreiber
GIB OPERATION UND OBJEKT	[KENNZEICHNEN] [GRUPPE]	
GIB GRUPPENNUMMER	[5] [ZAHLENDE]	
GIB OPERATION UND OBJEKT	[KENNZEICHNEN] [MUSTERDATEI]	SYMBOLBIBLIOTHEK 'ROHRNETZ'
GIB DATEINUMMER	[3] [ZAHLENDE]	MUSTERDATEI NR 3
GIB PASSWORT	[6] [7] [ZAHLENDE]	
--- FALSCHES PASSWORT		
GIB PASSWORT	[6] [7] [8] [ZAHLENDE]	
GIB OPERATION UND OBJEKT	[DARSTELLUNG ÄNDERN] [PKS]	
GIB NULLPUNKT	(1 Punkt digitalisieren)	
GIB MASSFAKTOR X	[1] [.] [7] [ZAHLENDE]	
GIB MASSFAKTOR Y	[1] [.] [7] [ZAHLENDE]	
GIB DREHWINKEL	[ZAHLENDE]	
⋮		
GIB OPERATION UND OBJEKT	[KREIEREN] [ELEMENT]	
GIB BASISSTRECKE	(2 Punkte digitalisieren)	P118= (28.138, 1.200) P119= (28.139, 1.900)
GIB MUSTER	MUSTER ÜBER NUMMER [2] [9] [ZAHLENDE]	G5/E13 3/29 ROHRSTUECK P118-P119
GIB OPERATION UND OBJEKT	[VERZERREN] [ELEMENT]	
GIB ELEMENTNUMMER	[1] [3] [ZAHLENDE]	
GIB VERZERRFAKTOR	[2] [.] [5] [ZAHLENDE]	G5/E13 3/29 ROHRSTUECK P118-P119 ZERR= 2.500
GIB OPERATION UND OBJEKT		
⋮		

Bild 6: Dialog mit SYMBOS zum Aufbau eines Bildes

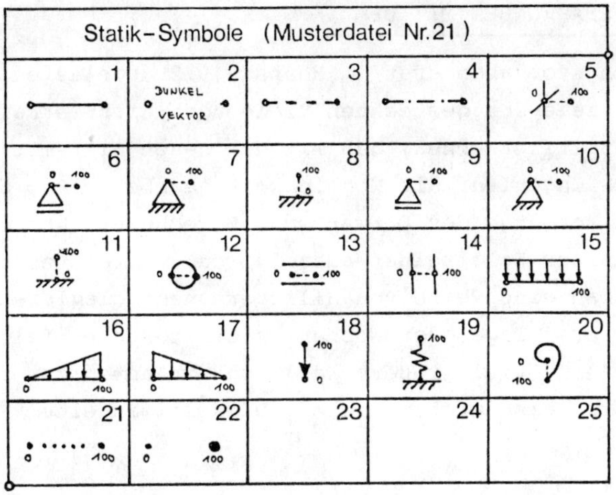

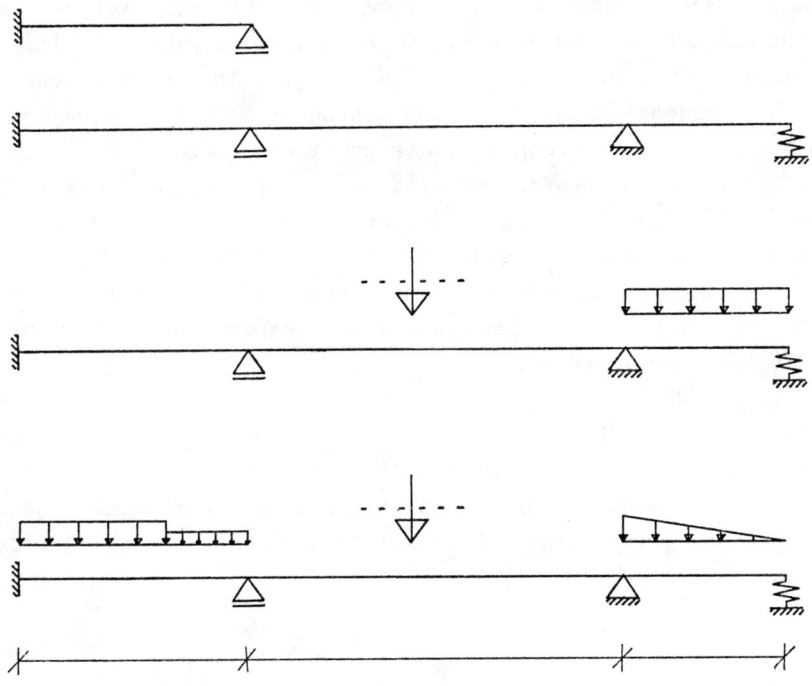

Bild 7: Menüfeld zum Skizzieren von statischen Systemen

Bild 8: Aufbau von statischen Systemen aus Einzelelementen unter SYMBOS

5. BISHERIGE ERFAHRUNGEN MIT DEM IKP

Da das Forschungsvorhaben erst im Herbst 1973 angelaufen ist, sind natürlich heute viele der gesteckten Ziele noch nicht erreicht. Es läßt sich jedoch bereits erkennen, daß mit dem neuen Hilfsmittel IKP dem konstruierenden Ingenieur die Möglichkeit gegeben wird, die iterativ auszuführenden Vorgänge des Entwerfens, Berechnens, Auslegens und Zeichnens in kurzer Zeit selbst auszuführen, während er bisher diese Arbeiten meist an eine Reihe von Hilfspersonen delegieren mußte und die Ergebnisse erst Tage oder Wochen später zurückerhielt. Es wird jetzt möglich, eine viel größere Zahl von Varianten zur Lösung eines Konstruktionsproblems durchzuspielen. Dies sei an einem Beispiel verdeutlicht.

Gegenwärtig wird aus Mitteln des Bundesministeriums für Forschung und Technologie westlich von Sylt in 30 m Wassertiefe eine Forschungsplattform errichtet, für die der Gründungskörper zu gestalten war. Wegen der geplanten Fertigstellung der Insel vor Einbruch der Herbststürme standen jedoch nur wenige Tage für den Entwurf zur Verfügung. Mit dem IKP konnten trotzdem eine Vielzahl von sehr komplizierten Formen des Gründungskörpers auf SChwimmfähigkeit und statisches Verhalten untersucht werden, bis eine Lösung (Stahlbetonhohlkasten von 11 000 t Gewicht) gefunden war, die zu einer Abminderung der Baukosten um 2.4 Millionen DM gegenüber der anfangs vorgesehenen Konstruktion führte. Selbst bei der Anwendung konventioneller bautechnischer Programme hätte diese spektakuläre Einsparung nicht erzielt werden können, da mit der Aufstellung der alphanumerischen Eingabedaten und der Auswertung der alphanumerischen Ergebnisse mehrere Ingenieure monatelang beschäftigt gewesen wären.

Mit der grafischen Eingabe über Digitalisierstift und der grafischen Ausgabe über Display und Plotter wird der dem Ingenieur gewohnte Datenträger Zeichnung in der automatischen Datenverarbeitung anwendbar. Mit dem Interaktiven Konstruktionsplatz wird der Computer dem Ingenieur nähergerückt.

LITERATUR

/1/ Flessner, H.: Rechnerunterstütztes Planen und Konstruieren im Bauwesen über einen Interaktiven Konstruktionsplatz (IKP). Antrag an das BMFT auf Förderung aus dem 2. DV-Programm der Bundesregierung. Ruhr-Universität Bochum, Arbeitsgruppe Angewandte Informatik im Ingenieurwesen. Bochum, 1972.
-: Rechnerunterstütztes Planen und Konstruieren über einen Interaktiven Konstruktionsplatz (IKP) - Einführender Bericht. Ruhr-Universität Bochum, Arbeitsgruppe Angewandte Informatik im Ingenieurwesen, IKP-Bericht 1/74. Bochum 1974.

/2/ Gorny, P.: Interaktive Konstruktionssysteme - Hardware und Software. In: CAD-Mitteilungen 1/73. Ges. f. Kernforschung Karlsruhe, S. 391-404. Karlsruhe 1973.

/3/ Hansmann, W.: Unterprogrammsystem MENUE. Ruhr-Universität Bochum, Arbeitsgruppe Angewandte Informatik im Ingenieurwesen. IKP-Bericht 2/74. Bochum 1974.

/4/ Gorny, P.: Entwurf eines Verwaltungssystems für grafische Symbole zum interaktiven Konstruieren. Ruhr-Universität Bochum, Arbeitsgruppe Angewandte Informatik im Ingenieurwesen, IKP-Bericht 3/74. Bochum 1974.

/5/ Kaufmann, H.: Entwicklung und Programmierung der Strukturen zum automatischen Zeichnen von statischen Systemen im Dialog an einem Interaktiven Konstruktionsplatz (IKP). Ruhr-Universität Bochum, Abteilung für Bauingenieurwesen. Diplomarbeit. Bochum 1974.

10. AUSBILDUNG

DIDAKTISCHE KONZEPTE
W. COY

S. E. BINNS, A. R. WEST

R. LANGEBARTELS, O. HECKER, J. HINRICHS, S. MADALO, K.-H. RÖDIGER

BERUFSBILD DES INFORMATIKERS
H.-Ch. ZEDLITZ

H. FRANCK, Th. SPITTA

STUDIENPLÄNE
Ch. FLOYD

N. ORIS

U. BOSLER, W. BOOKHAGEN, O. HECKER, W. KOCH, O. RABUS

BERICHT VON EINER DREISEMESTRIGEN SEMINAR-REIHE ÜBER EIN THEMA AUS DEM HARDWARE-BEREICH

Wolfgang Coy
Technische Hochschule Darmstadt

Die Diskrepanz zwischen der umfangreichen Wissensaneignung, wie sie durch ein tradiertes Grundstudium den meisten Studenten bis zum Vordiplom zukommen soll und der weitgehenden Unsicherheit bezüglich der wissenschaftlichen Vorgehensweise zur Lösung umfangreicher Probleme (Studien- und Diplomarbeiten), sowie die mangelhafte Kooperationsfähigkeit und die Unsicherheit in der Beurteilung der Grenzen und des Sinns der erlernten methodischen Schritte, sind als Mangel der herkömmlichen Ausbildung bekannt und sind in der hochschul-didaktischen und hochschul-politischen Diskussion der letzten Jahre aufgegriffen worden (z.B. /1/).

Strategien zur Lösung dieses Problems sind von verschiedener Seite und mit unterschiedlichen Intentionen diskutiert worden, so von studentischer Seite und eng damit verbunden (wenn auch mit dem reduzierten Blick auf den zukünftigen "Forscher") von der BAK /1/, aber auch in diversen Regierungsvorlagen /2/ und vom Bundesverband der deutschen Industrie /3/. Als ein vorläufiges, unbefriedigendes Ergebnis dieser Diskussion kann die Studienordnung der Universität Bremen /4/ und ihre verbesserte Version an der Universität Oldenburg /5/ angesehen werden, wo das "Projekt" als grundlegende Einheit der Aneignung wissenschaftlicher (und beruflicher) Fähigkeiten postuliert wurde. Als Widerschein dieser Diskussion mag auch die Reformprüfungs-Ordnung NORIS der TU Berlin (im Fachbereich Kybernetik) /6/ gelten. An den meisten Hochschulen der Bundesrepublik hat sich aber das oben beschriebene Unbehagen nicht oder kaum in den Studien- und Prüfungs-Ordnungen niedergeschlagen, obwohl auch an diesen Hochschulen Begriffe wie "Gruppenarbeit", "Projekt", "kritisches Lernen" und "forschendes Lernen" im Gespräch sind. Es scheint auf lange Dauer gesehen unumgänglich, daß sich (zumindest in einem so extrem an die technologische und ökonomische Entwicklung angekoppeltem Fachgebiet wie der Informatik) alle Hochschulen dieser Diskussion stellen /7/. Zentraler Aspekt muß dabei zweifellos die umfassende hochschul-didaktische und hochschul-politische Diskussion sein (die aus verschiedenen Gründen verzögert und verschleppt wird); diesem untergeordnet, aber wegen der Dringlichkeit der Situation nicht mehr aufschiebbar, ist das Problem der Veränderung der tradierten Studienformen, so daß die Studienformen Raum für veränderte Studien-Inhalte bieten.

In diesem Zusammenhang soll hier über eine drei-semestrige Seminar-Reihe berichtet werden, deren Intention darin lag, einige der Schwierigkeiten des tradierten Grund- und Fachstudiums zu überwinden, ohne daß eine umfassende Neuordnung des Studiums vorgenommen werden konnte.

1. BERICHT

Auf Grund der besonderen Aufbau-Situation des Fachbereichs Informatik an der Technischen Hochschule Darmstadt bot sich vor zwei Jahren die Möglichkeit an, einen Teilversuch zur fach-systematischen Neu-Ordnung der Phase zwischen dem 3. und 6. Semester durchzuführen. Dabei konnte für einen Ausbildungsschwerpunkt (nämlich die theoretische Informatik) eine neue Arbeitsform erprobt werden, ohne daß die bestehenden Prüfungsbestimmungen und die übrigen Ausbildungsbedingungen verändert werden konnten. Die Anregung zur Erprobung dieser neuen Arbeitsform ging auf H.Walter zurück und wurde von diesem zusammen mit dem Verfasser initiiert und durchgeführt.

Es galt ein Thema aus dem Bereich der Kern-Informatik zu finden, in das sich Studenten des 3. Semesters in kurzer Zeit einarbeiten konnten und bei dem als Ziel nicht primär die Erarbeitung eines neuen Wissensgebietes stand, sondern die Erlernung kooperativer Arbeitsweisen und der Fähigkeit zur selbstständigen Arbeit an der "Grenze der Forschung". Dabei war es notwendig, dieses Vorhaben möglichst friktionslos in einen bestehenden, traditionell ausgelegten Studoen- und Prüfungsplan einzubetten.

Auf Grund der gegebenen Rahmenbedingungen wurde als Form der Veranstaltung eine Folge von einem Pro-Seminar und zwei aufbauenden Seminaren gewählt. Zum Thema wurde das Gebiet der "Fehlerdiagnose digitaler Schaltkreise" gewählt, da mit diesem Thema vier wesentliche Lernziele für das Pro-Seminar erreichbar schienen:

- die Vermittlung der mathematischen und technischen Grundlagen zur Behandlung kombinatorischer Schaltkreise

- die beispielhafte Erschließung der ökonomischen Bedeutung der Forschung im Bereich der theoretischen Informatik

- die Einführung in die grundlegenden Arbeiten eines Forschungs-Gebietes bis zum neuesten Stand

- die Vermittlung der formalen Arbeitsweisen der Informatik durch angeleitete und eigenständige Arbeit

Der Vorteil dieser langfristigen Arbeitsform wurde deutlich in der Behandlung der unvermeidbaren Anfänger-Schwierigkeiten. Es gab keine Möglichkeit diese Schwierigkeiten mit Hinweis auf das nahende Semester-Ende zu unterdrücken oder zu überspielen und es zeigte sich in den beiden folgenden Semestern, daß die wesentlichen Schwierigkeiten bei allen Teilnehmern überwunden wurden. Andererseits zeigte sich aber, daß die Möglichkeit relativ selbstständiger Arbeit (im Rahmen dieses einen Arbeitsvorhabens) nur sehr beschränkt genutzt wurde. Dies muß eindeutig dem Widerspruch zwischen einem singulären Arbeitsprojekt mit der Möglichkeit und Forderung selbstständiger Arbeit und der tradierten Ausbildung in den übrigen Unterrichtsfächern (mit der starken Neigung zur Motivation durch Prüfungsdruck) zugeschrieben werden.

Über diese prinzipielle Schwierigkeit hinaus, sei noch auf zwei weitere Probleme hingewiesen:

- Trotz der nun recht breit geführten Diskussion über die Frage der Berufspraxis des Informatikers, ist es immer noch sehr schwierig Material zu finden, das über die konkreten Fragen der Berufspraxis des Informatikers z.B. in der Forschung und Entwicklung berichtet. Für den Rahmen eines Proseminars kann dadurch die Frage der Berufspraxis nur sehr allgemein bestimmt werden und eine Verbindung dieser Frage mit den konkreten Studien-Inhalten ist problematisch

- Die Frage der (mikro-) ökonomischen Faktoren bei der Entwicklung von Rechnern (konkret die Frage nach dem Anteil der Fehlerbehandlung an den gesamten Konstruktionskosten) wird in der Literatur (soweit sie zugänglich ist) nur äußerst vage behandelt, so daß auch hier eine Verbindung von ökonomischer und ingenieurswissenschaftlicher Arbeit kaum darstellbar ist.

Mit diesen Grundlagen und Beschränkungen wurde das Pro-Seminar in zwei aufeinanderfolgenden Seminaren fortgesetzt; dabei wurden im wesentlichen drei Lernziele verfolgt:

- die aktuellen Grenzen, Ziele und Entwicklungsrichtungen der Forschung sollten für das gewählte Thema deutlich werden
- die Kritik-Fähigkeit bei der Interpretation wissenschaftlicher Ergebnisse sollte erarbeitet werden
- die Perspektive eigener wissenschaftlicher Arbeit sollte am fremden Beispiel deutlich werden.

Als Vehikel zur Erreichung dieser Lernziele wurde vor allem die Arbeit mit Dissertationen benutzt, die in gewisser Weise einen besseren Einblick in die Wege, Ziele und Zwänge der wissenschaftlichen Forschung geben als dies Zeitschriften-Beiträge oder gar Lehrbücher können. Durch die Seminar-Folge wurden alle Studenten die Möglichkeit eröffnet, sich mit dem behandelten Gebiet selbstständig (also auch in Form einer Studien- oder Diplomarbeit) auseinanderzusetzen.(Dabei fehlt natürlich der zum Studien-Abschluß notwendige breite Überblick über das Gebiet der Informatik).

2. SCHWIERIGKEITEN UND KRITIK

Während die fach-immanenten Lernziele (wie Einarbeitung in ein wesentliches Gebiet der Kern-Informatik bis hin zur Fähigkeit selbstständiger Arbeit in diesem Gebiet) ohne prinzipielle Schwierigkeiten mit Hilfe des gewählten Themas und der Form der Vermittlung erreichbar scheinen, ergaben sich für die übrigen Lernziele grundlegende Schwierigkeiten. Eine schrittweise Veränderung der Ausbildungsziele vom prüfungsbestimmten Lernen zu einer Ausbildung in der die oben beschriebenen Lernziele erreicht werden sollen, ist im Licht der hier vorgetragenen (partikulären) Erfahrungen schwierig oder gar unmöglich. Grundlage einer Vermittlungsform, die den Begriffen "Projekt", "Berufbezogenheit", "kritischem" oder "forschendem Lernen" gerecht werden soll, muß eine umfassende Diskussion der Studien-Ordnung sein; dabei ist es dringend notwendig auch für die Informatik die folgenden drei Aspekte zukünftiger Informatik-Ausbildung zu erarbeiten:

- Eine klare Richtziel-Bestimmung bezüglich der zu erarbeitenden und zu erlernenden methodischen und fachlichen Fähigkeiten,

- die Klärung des Verhältnisses von Ausbildung und Beruf auf Grund einer umfassenden Berufspraxis-Analyse,

- die Entwicklung neuer Studien- und Lehrformen zur Erreichung der Richtziele in einer kontrollierten und umfassend reflektierten Weise.

/1/ Forschendes Lernen - Wissenschaftliches Prüfen, Schriften der Bundes-Assistenten-Konferenz 5, Bonn, 1970

/2/ Wissenschaftsrat, Empfehlungen zur Struktur und zum Ausbau des Bildungswesens im Hochschulbereich nach 1970, Bonn, 1970

/3/ Zur Lage von Forschung, Lehre und Studium an den Hochschulen der Bundesrepublik Deutschland 1971, Stellungnahme des Präsidialarbeitskreises des Bundesverbandes der Deutschen Industrie e.V., Heft 2 der Veröffentlichungen des Präsidialarbeitskreises, BDI-Drucksache Nr. 93, Köln, 1971

/4/ Elin-Birgit Berndt u.a., Erziehung der Erzieher: das Bremer Reform-Modell, Hamburg, 1972

/5/ Hinrichsen/Knauer/Zessin, Projektstudium in Mathematik - Überlegungen und Vorschläge zur Curriculumplanung, Materialien zur Berufspraxis des Mathematikers Nr. 10, Bielefeld, 1973

/6/ Technische Universität Berlin, Fachbereich 20 - Kybernetik, Studienführer INFORMATIK, Berlin, 1973

/7/ Basisgruppe Mathematik-Informatik der TU Karlsruhe, Beitrag zum Berufsbild des Mathematikers und Informatikers, Bielefelder Materialien zur Berufspraxis des Mathematikers Nr. 8, Bielefeld, 1972

APPENDIX I

Im folgenden soll ein fachsystematischer Literatur-Vorschlag zur Erarbeitung des Themenkreises "Fehlerdiagnose digitaler Schaltkreise" gemacht werden, der sich auf die im obigen Bericht geschilderten Erfahrungen stützt. Es ist deshalb zwischen der Literatur für die Einführungs-Phase (Pro-Seminar) und der weiterführenden Literatur für die Aufbau-Phase (Seminar) getrennt.

a) Einführungs-Phase

D.B. AMSTRONG, On finding a nearly minimal set of fault detction tests in combinational logic nets, IEEE Trans. on Comp., Vol. EC-15, No.1, Feb. 1966, pp 66-73

W.G. BOURICIUS/E.P. HSIEH/G.R. POTZOLU/J.P. ROTH/P.R. SCHNEIDER C.-J.-TAN, Algorithms for detection of faults in logic circuits, IEEE Trans. on Comp.Vol. C-2o, No. 11, Nov. 1971, pp. 1258-1264

H.Y. CHANG/ E.G. MANNING/G. METZE, Fault Diagnosis of Digital Systems, New York, 1970

A.D. FRIEDMANN/P.R. MENON, Fault Detection in Digital Circuits, Englewood Cliffs, 1971

W. GÖRKE, Fehlerdiagnose digitaler Schaltungen, Stuttgart, 1973

W.H. KAUTZ, Fault testing and diagnosis in combinational digital cicuits, IEEE Trans. on Comp., Vol. EC-16, April 1968, pp. 352-366

J.F. POAGE, Derivation of optimum tests to detect faults in combinational digital circuits, in"Mathematical Theory of Automata", Brooklyn, 1962

J.P. ROTH, Diagnosis of automata failures: A calculus and a method, IBM Journal of Res. and Dev., Vol. 1o, Juli 1966 pp. 278-289

J.P. ROTH/W.G. BOURICIUS/P.R. SCHNEIDER, Programmed algorithms to compute tests to detect and distinguish between failures in logic circuits, IEEETrans. on Comp., EC-16, No. 5, Okt. 1967 pp. 567-58o

F.F. SELLERS/ M.Y. HSIAO/ L.W. BEARNSON, Analyzing errors with the boolean difference, IEEE Trans. on Comp., Vol. C-17, No. 7, Juli 1968, pp.676-683

D.R. SCHERTZ/G. METZE, On the indistinguishability of faults in digital systems, Proc. 6th Allerton Conf. on Circuit and Systems Theory pp.752-760

D.R. SCHERTZ/ G. METZE, A new representation for faults in combinational digital circuits, IEEE Trans. on Comp., Vol. C-21, No.8, Aug. 1972, pp. 858-866

P.R. SCHNEIDER, On the necessity to examine D-chains in diagnostic test generation - an example, IBM Journal of Res. & Dev., Jan. 1967, pp. 114

b) Aufbau-Phase

S.B. AKERS, Universal test sets for logic networks, IEEE Trans. on Comp., Vol. C-22, No. 9, Sept. 1973, pp. 835-839

R. BETANCOURT, Derivation of minimum test sets for unate logical circuits, IEEE Trans. on Comp., Vol. C-20 No. 11, Nov. 1971, pp. 1264-1270

D.C. BOSSEN/ D.L. OSTAPKO/ A.M. PATEL, Optimum test patterns for parity networks, ACM FJCC, 1970, pp. 63-68

M.A. BREUER, Generation of fault tests for linear logic networks, IEEE Trans. on Comp., Vol. C-21 No. 1, Jan 1972, pp. 79-83

J.W. GAULT/ J.P. ROBINSON/S.M. REDDY, Multiple fault detection in combinational networks, IEEE Trans. on Comp., Vol. C-21, No. 1 Jan 1972 pp. 31-36

J.P. HAYES, On realization of boolean functions requiring a minimal or near-minimal number of tests, IEEE Trans. on Comp. Vol C-20, Dez. 1971 pp. 1506-1513

J.P. HAYES, A nand model for fault diagnosis in combinational logic networks, IEEE Trans. on Comp., Vol. C-20, No. 12, Dez. 1971 pp.1496-1506

Z. KOHAVI, Fault detection in fanout-free combinational networks, GMD IFAS-Bericht, Nr. 60, St Augustin, Dez. 1972

P.N. MARINOS, Derivation of minimal complete sets of test input sequences using boolean differences, IEEE Trans on Comp., Vol C-20, No. 1, Jan. 1971, pp. 25-32

S.M. REDDY, Complete test sets for logic functions, IEEE Trans on Comp., Vol C-22, No. 11 Nov. 1973, pp. 1016-1020.

AN UNDERGRADUATE GROUP PROJECT IN SOFTWARE ENGINEERING

S. E. Binns
Computing Laboratory
The University
Canterbury
Kent

A. R. West
Dept. of Computer Science
Queen Mary College
London University
Mile End Road
London
(formerly University of Kent at Canterbury)

Software engineering as a discipline arose in response to the 'software crisis' recognised about ten years ago and which gave rise to the two NATO conferences in Garmisch and Rome [1], [2]. These two conferences provided the impetus for the introduction of a course in software engineering as part of the computers and cybernetics degree course at the University of Kent. Software engineering lacks a unified theoretical basis except for certain specialised areas, compiler writing and some aspects of operating system design for example. These areas being the ones which are covered anyway in the traditional computer science degree course. This course therefore emphasises the aspects of software engineering directly concerned with the production of large items of software. One can formalise this as follows:
The aim of the course is to introduce students to some of the problems, with techniques for their solution, which arise in large software projects. It would be ideal at this point to have a list of problem areas with possible solutions and to create a sequence of independant tasks for the students which would illuminate in turn each of the problems and demonstrate how they may be solved. This does not seem possible partly because the problems themselves arise from the interactions which only occur in projects above a certain size. Also the problems are not well enough understood to be isolated in this fashion. The alternative which was adopted was to split the students into groups of four or five with a staff member assigned as project leader to each group. Each group undertakes a substantial project, working on aver-

age, one day per week for three ten week terms (trimesters). The next section of the paper discusses how such projects might be organised and assessed.

Initial problems are choosing projects and fixing the student groups. This is handled very informally, interested staff members put forward projects they are willing to supervise and the students arrange themselves into groups of at least four and choose a project. So far the students have all opted for very practical work as opposed to anything in the nature of research. Typical projects chosen include:-
   (1) Implementing a BCPL like systems programming language
   (2) Producing a package to perform track layout on printed circuit boards.
   (3) Transporting a large Algol program (which uses backing store) from an ICL 1900 to the local computer.
   (4) Implementing an assembler for the NOVA 1210 on a PDP11.

These represent a wide choice of project, some demanding application of standard techniques as (4) above, others require a specialised knowledge of local facilities as (1) and (3), yet again in (2) there is an example of an open ended project. The role of the project leader is rather different in these situations. However, two extremes have to be avoided. These are, exerting too rigid a control, treating the students like coders or on the other hand giving the students their heads. In which case they would certainly make many mistakes but rarely profit greatly from them. The role of the project supervisor is probably best handled by keeping a tight grip on the reins to start with, especially in the design stage, and to give the students more freedom during implementation and testing stages. A danger to avoid here, is that of the project supervisor performing the design stage himself without documenting decisions fully.

One formal meeting a week of the project team is generous once the design phase is finished. A very beneficial side effect of the meetings however is that they can provide feedback from the students on the progress of other courses.

Assessment of group projects might be thought to be particularly difficult. Rather limited experience at Kent however is that it is no more difficult than individual projects. Assessment is based on three items taken in decreasing order of importance: 1) assessment by the project leader based on work done and documentation produced; 2) An individual report each student produces on the course of the project and 3) a short (15 minute) viva. The viva is taken by the project leader and one other member of staff. The project leader acting generally in a neutral role. The extra member of staff in the viva also acts as a second examiner for the individual reports.

In conclusion after one complete year the project seems viable. What is now most important is to develop the course as experience is gained. The individual reports produced by the students will be available to future projects so that experience and knowledge is accumulated. At some further stage, one hopes, it will be possible to apply more structure to the projects or to use them as a test bed for new techniques. A useful particular extension to the projects in future would be to make the groups work to a nominal budget.

The next section of this paper is presented by a Mr.A.West who, as a student took part in one of these projects. He will give a student-eye-view of the course.

Mr. Binns has described some of the considerations that lie behind planning, running and assessing group projects. I would now like to describe briefly the technical nature of the particular group project from which we derived our ideas, and present some of our conclusions.

The four students in the group accepted a proposal from Mr. Binns to design and implement a systems programming language. It was decided that the system would be modelled on the programming language BCPL [3].

The system consists of a one-pass compiler for the language, which we decided to call SYMPL, and an interpreter. The compiler produces an intermediate code, for a virtual stack machine, which is then interpreted.

The compiler consists of about 2000 SYMPL statements and the interpreter consists of about 1500 instructions in assembly language. There are also about 300 pages of systems documentation available.

It was decided that the compiler should itself be written in SYMPL so that we could gain some experience of the language we were trying to implement. The SYMPL statements in the finished compiler would then be mapped automatically into equivalent ALGOL 60 statements using the general-purpose macroprocessor, ML/I [4].

This process would then yield as an ALGOL 60 program, a version of the SYMPL compiler which could be compiled and run. After testing and debugging this ALGOL 60 version of the compiler, it could then be used to compile the SYMPL version of the compiler.

By the time this was accomplished, it was hoped that a working interpreter would be available and debugging of the complete system could then proceed.

Broadly speaking, the tasks involved in implementing the SYMPL system were;
- (i) Write the lexical Analyser and Compiler in SYMPL,
- (ii) Write and test the ML/I mapping macros to map the compiler written in SYMPL into an ALGOL 60 program,
- (iii) Test the compiler,
- (iv) Write and test the interpreter in assembly language
- (v) Test and document the complete system.

One student wrote the lexical Analyser for the compiler and the ML/I mapping macros and two students worked on the rest of the compiler and the documentation. These three students also worked on the testing of the complete compiler. The remaining student wrote and debugged the interpreter. Systems testing was attacked by all members of the group.

The four students in the group worked under the supervision of Mr. Binns, and his guiding role, although necessarily strong at first, became less and less pronounced as time went by.

Once each week the group met with Mr. Binns and discussed any problems which had arisen. At first, discussion centred on defining the scope of the project and planning the implementation, but later, discussion was necessary to clarify the small ambiguities and interfaces that existed between students working on different modules of the project. Decisions were recorded in a minutes book so that they could be referred to later.

The exact nature of the individual report that each student was required to write was not specified by the Board of Examiners. We were unsure whether they required a technical report on what each of us had done or a summary of our views as to the general course and efficiency of the project. In practice the reports tended to discuss both approaches.

By the time the students came to the end of the scheduled time, a working system was available. Full debugging was abandoned in favour of completing the documentation.

The project was very successful both viewed as an industrial product and as an educational aid. This, in my opinion is due to three main factors.

Firstly, the students' motivation to work on the project was high. The field of compiler writing is very interesting and full of challenges. We wanted to do a good job since we knew the system would be used by others and not simply discarded.

Secondly, the project divided neatly into several self-contained modules such as the Lexical Analyser, mapping macros, interpreter. After the interfaces between modules had been defined, work on each module could proceed independently and in parallel with work on other modules. Obstacles in one section would not affect the progress of the others.

Lastly, the attitude of the supervisor, an important factor, was very productive. Mr. Binns succeeded in exciting the curiosity of the students involved without hampering their work. He had a clear idea of what we were trying to achieve and helped us by suggesting the various paths open to our exploration.

The time of 4½ man-months allocated to the project was exceeded by 50% because the students wanted to work on the project and produce something worthwhile.

The project was successful as an educational aid. We learned a great deal about the method of tackling large problems as a group. We all felt that this particular project probably formed the most interesting and useful single part of our undergraduate studies. It was much more fun discovering things than simply being told them.

It was unfortunate that although one of the courses which the students involved in the project had to attend as part of their other studies was a course on compiling techniques, this was scheduled for the final trimester of the project and no direct use could be made of its content. This also had several advantages, however. Since what we learned about compiling techniques was learned by hard work, we are unlikely to forget it. Although we adopted an *ad hoc* approach to writing the compiler, we found that the project helped us to understand the lecture course easily.

The ability to estimate the resources necessary to tackle a large project is important and we gained much experience in assessing our individual capabilities. Many times, the period estimated as being necessary to complete one section of the project was vastly exceeded but towards the end the estimates began to be more and more representative.

We found that the maximum number of people who can work in a group and yet follow completely what the others are doing without formal communication is about three. Notes about the decisions we made proved to be essential. It is very important that the initial design phase is completely understood. Many decisions made at this time are forgotten by the time a month or two has passed.

Bad terminology proved to be a great hindrance to understanding the workings of programs and, although it is a small point, it is worth striving hard to define a set of terms and instructions which really do reflect their function. This is especially true of identifiers in programs and names of files on disc. The naming system should be flexible enough to allow for further extension since, at the time when the terminology is designed and required, no clear idea is available about future needs.

It is very important that if a project is to be carried out in a limited time, considerations of efficiency should be discarded in favour of producing something which works. Once the compiler was working progress accelerated since we had the high-level tools necessary to make alterations. My own feeling about our work is that we should have done less but done it better.

Lastly, we were held up for long periods because we adopted a system of updating and editing files which was not suited to our system. The on-line system which was available facilitates efficient editing but on-line working does not (normally) allow you to keep a record of the changes that are made. At the time when we were working on the project, new discs were being installed and the computer was not functioning as reliably as at other times. Several times we lost files and programs and eventually adopted a batch system where the latest state of the files could be easily regenerated from cards.

References

[1] Software Engineering 1969 Conference report. Editors P. Naur, B. Randell. Scientific Affairs Division, NATO, Brussels 39, Belgium.

[2] Software Engineering Techniques 1970, Conferences report. Editors J. N. Buxton, B. Randell. Scientific Affairs Division, NATO, Brussels 39, Belgium.

[3] 'BCPL - A tool for Compiler Writing and System Programming' M. Richards; AFIPS SJCC 1969 pp 557-566.

[4] ML/I User's Manual. P. J. Brown, University of Kent at Canterbury.

Acknowledgment

Dr. E. B. Spratt at the University of Kent first suggested the course discussed in the paper and has been active in its development.

Mr. P. Rautenbach, Mr. N. Pope and Mr. S. Walton contributed to the project described by Mr. West.

EIN DIALOGPROGRAMMIERSYSTEM FÜR DEN UNTERRICHT IN PROGRAMMIERSPRACHEN

R. Langebartels, O. Hecker, J. Hinrichs, S. Madalo und K.-H. Rödiger

Zusammenfassung: Es wird ein Programmierkurs für Anfänger vorgeschlagen, der sich aus einer Lehrveranstaltung über Algorithmik und einem computerunterstützten Lehrsystem für eine Programmiersprache zusammensetzt. Aus der Sicht des Unterrichts werden Anforderungen an das Dialogprogrammiersystem, den wesentlichen Teil des CUU-Lehrsystems für den Programmiersprachenunterricht, entwickelt. Die Anforderungen beziehen sich auf die Programmiersprache, den Monitor/Editor, die Syntaxanalyse, das Definieren von Subsets, das Debugging und die Implementierung.

1 EINLEITUNG

Die Forschungsgruppe Computergestütztes Lernen im Fachbereich Kybernetik der Technischen Universität Berlin arbeitet seit 1971 an einem Projekt, das die Automatisierung des Unterrichts in der Programmierung von Computern zum Gegenstand hat. Vorrangiges Ziel dieser Arbeiten ist, nicht das Lehrpersonal der Programmierkurse zu substituieren oder die Unterrichtskosten zu vermindern, sondern die Qualität des Programmierunterrichts durch den Einsatz von Computern in diesem Unterricht zu verbessern.

2 PROGRAMMIERUNTERRICHT

Das Lehrziel des Programmierunterrichts für Anfänger sollte darin bestehen, bei den Lernenden die Fähigkeit auszubilden, Probleme mit Hilfe der Werkzeuge Computer und Programmiersprache zu lösen. Entsprechend diesem Lehrziel sind im Programmierunterricht zwei verschiedene, aber in enger Wechselbeziehung stehende Sachgebiete angesprochen:
- die Lösung von Problemen und
- die Formulierung von Problemlösungen in Programmiersprachen.

Der praktisch vorherrschende und populäre Typ von Programmierkursen ist ein Kurs, in dem der Unterricht in der Lösung von Problemen völlig überwuchert ist durch den Unterricht in einer bestimmten Programmiersprache und deren syntaktischen Detailkonstrukten. Als Ergebnis dieser Kurse verfügen die Lernenden oft über genaue Kenntnisse der Einzelheiten einer Programmiersprache, aber nicht über die Fähigkeit, ein Problem mit Hilfe eines Computers zu lösen.

Diese negativen Erfahrungen und die Ergebnisse der Forschung über das Programmieren als Entwurfstätigkeit (1)(2) führen zu dem Vorschlag, den Programmierunterricht in zwei aufeinander bezogene Lehrveranstaltungen zu trennen (vgl. hierzu (3)):

- eine Lehrveranstaltung über Algorithmik und
- eine Lehrveranstaltung über eine Programmiersprache.

In einer Lehrveranstaltung Algorithmik sollen die Lernenden die Fähigkeit entwickeln, zur Lösung eines Problems einen Algorithmus zu konstruieren und diesen in einer Notation zu formulieren, die unabhängig von einer bestimmten Programmiersprache ist. Wird der Algorithmus in Form eines Flußdiagramms dargestellt, so ergibt sich zwar ein anschauliches Bild des Lösungsweges des Problems. Das Flußdiagramm hat aber den Nachteil, durch die Unterschiedlichkeit der Darstellungsweise zum ausführbaren Computerprogramm das Konstruieren sowie Formulieren des Algorithmus strikt und unnötig von dessen Umsetzung in das entsprechende Computerprogramm zu trennen. Sinnvoller erscheint es, den Algorithmus mit Hilfe von strukturierten Anweisungen, den Kontrollstrukturen (1) zu formulieren.

Der Unterricht in einer Programmiersprache hat die Aufgabe, die Fähigkeit des Lernenden zu entwickeln, einen vorgegebenen Algorithmus in ein lauffähiges Computerprogramm abzubilden. Der Lernende muß befähigt werden, die Objekte der Algorithmen in der Programmiersprache zu repräsentieren, die im Algorithmus angegebenen Teilhandlungen durch die in der Programmiersprache vorgesehenen elementaren Algorithmen auszudrücken und die Kontrollstrukturen des Algorithmus in der Programmiersprache zu formulieren.

3 COMPUTERUNTERSTÜTZTER UNTERRICHT IN PROGRAMMIERSPRACHEN

Im Rahmen der Forschungsarbeiten wurde das computerunterstützte Lehrsystem COGEL (4) entworfen und auf einer Rechenanlage PDP 10 implementiert. Der Entwurf berücksichtigt Erfahrungen mit dem TEACH-System, das von Fenichel, Weizenbaum u.a.(5) am MIT entwickelt wurde, und Vorstellungen von Nievergelt u.a.(6) am PLATO IV Computer-Based Education System der University of Illinois. Folgende Eigenschaften kennzeichnen das Lehrsystem COGEL:

- Die Kenntnisse über eine Programmiersprache werden computerunterstützt nach einem Lehralgorithmus vermittelt, der den Lernenden in weitem Maße die Entscheidung überläßt, welche der angebotenen Informationen sie abrufen möchten. Der gesamte Lehrstoff einer Programmiersprache ist nach den verschiedenen Programmiertechniken, die in der Sprache möglich sind, in aufeinander aufbauende Lektionen gegliedert.
- Auf Wunsch wird der Lernende, ohne daß er das Lehrsystem verlassen muß, in ein Dialogprogrammiersystem verzweigt, in dem er einen vorgegebenen oder von ihm konstruierten Algorithmus in ein Computerprogramm umsetzen oder auch zunächst nur die in einer Lektion eingeführten Sprach-

elemente erproben kann.
- An das Dialogprogrammiersystem ist ein computerunterstütztes Auskunftlehrsystem angeschlossen, durch das der Lernende ad hoc, ohne das Dialogprogrammiersystem zu verlassen, für seine Problemsituation erforderliche Informationen erfragen kann.

Die folgende Abbildung zeigt den Aufbau des Lehrsystems COGEL und dessen Integration in den Programmierunterricht für Anfänger:

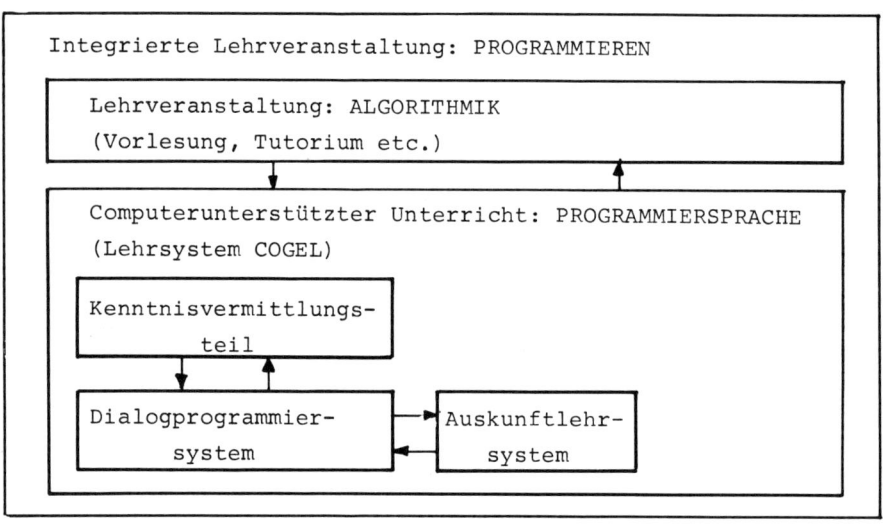

Die Hypothese des Entwurfs, daß sich durch die Verkopplung von computerunterstützter Kenntnisvermittlung, Dialogprogrammiersystem und computerunterstütztem Auskunftlehrsystem die Qualität des Programmiersprachenunterrichts verbessert, wurde in ersten praktischen Erprobungen (7) an einem BASIC-Kurs bestätigt.

Gleichzeitig wurden aber auch die Mängel und Unzulänglichkeiten bestehender Dialogprogrammiersysteme, wie z.B. BASIC, für den Einsatz im Programmierunterricht für Anfänger deutlich: zum strukturierten Programmieren ungeeignete Sprachen, unzulängliche Syntaxanalyse etc. Deshalb wurde aus der Sicht des Unterrichts eine Reihe von Anforderungen an Dialogprogrammiersysteme aufgestellt und begonnen, ein geeignetes System zu realisieren.

4 ANFORDERUNGEN AN EIN DIALOGPROGRAMMIERSYSTEM
Ein Dialogprogrammiersystem enthält als Kern den Prozessor für eine Programmiersprache eingefaßt von einer Dialogumgebung, die Monitor-, Edi-

tor- und Debugfunktionen erfüllt.

4.1 PROGRAMMIERSPRACHE

Eine für Ausbildungszwecke, insbesondere den Anfängerunterricht geeignete Programmiersprache sollte über ein klar formuliertes algorithmisches Konzept verfügen und zum strukturierten Programmieren geeignet sein.

Wirth (8) stellt die Forderung auf:"Die Sprache oder Notation soll... die wesentlichen und typischen Bestandteile von Algorithmen klar, verständlich und auf natürliche Weise widerspiegeln und auf die grundlegenden Eigenschaften und Grenzen von digitalen Rechenanlagen Rücksicht nehmen." und fährt fort:"Darüberhinaus sollen die sprachlichen Aufbauregeln einfach, zweckmäßig und systematisch sein, sodaß deren Erlernen keine besonderen Schwierigkeiten bereitet." Lecarme (9) faßt die Anforderungen an eine Programmiersprache zusammen:"We want a clean language, easy to teach, easy to learn, concise, machine-independent (if such a beast exists in our world), not a too high-level one. In other words we want a language which has its feet on the ground."

Diese Anforderungen stimmen im wesentlichen mit den Anforderungen überein, die Fenichel für die im TEACH-System implementierte Sprache UNCL (10) aufstellte. Allerdings scheint es nicht sinnvoll, allein für den Programmierunterricht eine spezielle Programmiersprache zu entwerfen, da die Sprachen der ALGOL-Familie eine Reihe der oben angeführten Anforderungen erfüllen.

Für das Dialogprogrammiersystem wurde aus der ALGOL-Familie die von Wirth (11) entwickelte Sprache PASCAL ausgewählt. Dabei gaben folgende Gründe den Ausschlag:
- PASCAL verfügt über alle notwendigen und wünschenswerten Kontrollstrukturen des Programmierens:

    1. zusammengesetzte Anweisung

    begin A1; A2;...; AN **end**

    2. bedingte Anweisungen

    if B **then** A1 **else** A2 und

    if B **then** A

    3. repetierte Anweisungen

    while B **do** A und

    repeat A **until** B und

    for I:=IA **to** IE **do** und

    for I:=IA **downto** IE **do**

    4. selektive Anweisung

    case E **of** w1:A1; w2:A2;...; wn:AN **end**

- PASCAL gibt die Möglichkeit der Blockschachtelung von ALGOL 60 zugunsten eines klareren Prozedurkonzeptes auf.
- PASCAL verfügt relativ zu ALGOL 60 über zusätzliche Objekttypen wie char und erlaubt damit ein größeres Anwendungsgebiet.

Für das Dialogprogrammiersystem im Programmiersprachenunterricht wurde ein Subset von PASCAL definiert, der alle Kontrollstrukturen, sowie die Deklaration und den Aufruf von Prozeduren und Funktionen beinhaltet. Die goto-Anweisung und Labels sind nicht vorgesehen. Die Objekttypen sind zunächst auf integer, real, bool, char und array beschränkt. Ein ähnlicher Subset wird in der Vorlesung "Einsatz von Rechenanlagen" an der ETH Zürich verwendet.

4.2 MONITOR/EDITOR

Im Dialogprogrammiersystem stehen dem Lernenden als Editorfunktionen Befehle zum Erstellen, Korrigieren und Speichern von Dateien im on-line Betrieb am Terminal zur Verfügung und als Monitorfunktionen Befehle, die sonst vom Betriebssystem der Rechenanlage ausgeführt werden.

Um den Lernenden nicht zusätzlich zu belasten, muß das Monitor/Editor-System einfach zu handhaben und der Umgang mit ihm leicht zu erlernen sein. Folgende Entscheidungen bestimmen den Entwurf des Systems:
- Beschränkung auf die unerläßlichen Funktionen
    Es ist nicht Ziel, eine Dialogumgebung zu schaffen, die umfangreich und mächtig ist.
- Wahl einprägsamer, mnemonischer Befehle
    Die Befehle sollen nicht vorrangig aus wenigen Zeichen bestehen, sondern einprägsam sein und auch bei späterer Lektüre des Terminalprotokolls leicht zu verstehen sein.
- Beschränkung auf zeilenorientiertes Editieren mit Zeilennummerierung
    Obwohl das zeilenorientierte Editieren schwerfälliger ist, schienen die didaktischen Vorteile gegenüber dem zeichenorientierten Editieren schwerwiegender: Wegfall der Zeigerpositionierbefehle und größere Klarheit und damit geringere Fehlermöglichkeiten bei der Korrektur auf Grund der Zeilennummerierung.

Das Dialogprogrammiersystem verfügt neben Befehlen zur Ein- und Ausgabe und zum Löschen von Zeilen sowie zum Ändern der Zeilennummerierung der aktiven Programmdatei im Arbeitsbereich über Befehle zur Ausgabe, zum Speichern, Umbenennen, Aktivieren und Löschen von Programmdateien auf einem Plattenspeicher. Daneben existieren Befehle zum Compilieren und Executieren des Programms in der aktiven Datei, zum Start des Debug-Systems, zur Wiederholung einer Lektion bzw. zum Start einer neuen Lektion

des Kenntnisvermittlungsteils des Lehrsystems COGEL und zum Aufruf des
Auskunftlehrsystems.

4.3 FEHLERDIAGNOSE UND -KORREKTUR

Erfahrungsgemäß weisen Programme, die im Anfängerunterricht implementiert
werden, viele Fehler auf, die auf die geringe Vertrautheit der Lernenden
im Umgang mit dem Terminal (Tippfehler) und im Umgang mit der Syntax der
Programmiersprache zurückzuführen sind. Als Konsequenz aus solchen Erfahrungen stellen Fenichel u.a.(5) folgende Anforderung auf:"The system must
detect student errors as quickly as possible, whenever possible in a highly localized context. Once an error is detected, it is to be pointed out
to the student in as unambiguous a fashion as possible. Finally, the system must permit the student to correct errors locally, i.e. without forcing him to reconstruct large portions of error-free work."

Um dieses Entwurfskriterium in dem hier dargestellten Dialogprogrammiersystem zu realisieren, werden dem Lernenden für die Erkennung und Korrektur seiner Fehler folgende Hilfsmittel zur Verfügung gestellt:
- zeilenweise Syntaxanalyse
  Nach jeder Zeile wird der in dieser Zeile editierte Teil des Programms
  sofort auf seine syntaktische Korrektheit überprüft.
- Möglichkeit zum dynamischen Debugging
  Zum Erkennen und Korrigieren von Laufzeitfehlern wird dem Lernenden die
  aktuelle Wertebelegung der Variablen seines Programms während der Ausführung zugänglich gemacht.

4.3.1 ZEILENWEISE SYNTAXANALYSE

Mit der Syntaxanalyse während des Editierens ist dem Lernenden die Möglichkeit gegeben, einen Fehler dann zu beseitigen, wenn dessen Wirkung
im Kontext des Programms erkannt wird. Die Wiederholung eines Fehlers
und Folgefehler können damit weitgehend vermieden werden.

Um die Anzahl der Fälle zu vermindern, in denen der Lernende mehr als
eine fehlerfreie Zeile seines Programms nach der Erkennung eines syntaktischen Fehlers nochmals editieren muß, wird dem Lernenden vorgeschrieben,
daß das Zeilenende nur an bestimmten Stellen des Programms auftreten darf.
So wird u.a.gefordert, daß in jeder Zeile des Anweisungsteils von Programmen, Prozeduren und Funktionen mindestens eine PASCAL-Anweisung beginnen muß (Ausnahmen: _end_ darf allein in einer Zeile stehen; Leerzeilen
sind zulässig.). Diese Beschränkung, die für einen PASCAL-Compiler ohne
Bedeutung ist, ergibt sich als Konsequenz aus der Forderung nach zeilenweiser Syntaxanalyse. Andererseits hat diese Bedingung aber den didakti-

schen Vorteil, daß die editierten Programmtexte besser lesbar und übersichtlicher werden.

Um dauernde Recompilationen zu vermeiden, sollte der Lernende, ähnlich wie in dem Dialogprogrammiersystem von Schild (12) vorgeschrieben, sein Programm sequentiell editieren. Da der Lernende das Dialogprogrammiersystem im Rahmen des computerunterstützten Programmiersprachenunterrichts dann benutzt, wenn er ein vollständiges Programm entworfen hat, ist zu erwarten, daß diese Vorschrift den Lernenden nicht merklich behindert. Nachträgliches Einfügen bzw. Ändern von vorangehenden Zeilen erfordert allerdings Recompilation und damit möglicherweise Wartezeiten für den Lernenden.

4.3.2 DYNAMISCHES DEBUGGING
Um die oben angegebenen Anforderungen an Diagnose und Korrektur von syntaktischen Fehlern auch für Laufzeitfehler in einem syntaktisch korrekten Programm zu erfüllen, wurde ein Trace- und Debugging-System mit folgenden Eigenschaften entworfen:
- Trace
  Der Lernende kann beim Start des Programms Variablen benennen und erhält daraufhin während des Programmlaufs die Werte dieser Variablen mit Angabe der Nummer der Zeile ausgedruckt, in der sich die Werte der Variablen verändert haben.
- Dump
  Ein post mortem dump stellt sicher, daß die Symboltabelle auch dann erhalten bleibt, wenn das Programm auf Grund eines Laufzeitfehlers abgebrochen wird. Der Lernende hat in diesem Fall u.a. die Möglichkeit, Wertebelegungen von einzelnen Variablen zum Zeitpunkt des Abbruchs abzufragen.
- symbolisches, dynamisches Debugging
  Beim Start des Programms kann der Lernende Haltepunkte auf einzelne Zeilen des Programms setzen. Er hat damit die Möglichkeit, sein Programm schrittweise ausführen und bei jedem Halt die Werte von Variablen auf Wunsch ausdrucken zu lassen, sowie die Werte dieser Variablen zu verändern. Die Darstellung der Werte der Variablen bei Ein- und Ausgabe richtet sich nach dem jeweils deklarierten Typ.

4.4 DEFINITION VON SUBSETS
Untersuchungen zur Didaktik des Programmiersprachenunterrichts (5)(7) zeigen die Notwendigkeit, die Kenntnisse über die Programmiertechniken einer Programmiersprache aufeinander aufbauend zu vermitteln. Dementsprechend sollte das Dialogprogrammiersystem dem Lernenden erlauben, nur

die Sprachelemte zu benutzen, die er bisdahin im Kenntnisvermittlungsteil des Lehrsystems kennengelernt hat. Diese Anforderung stellen auch
Fenichel u.a.(10) und Nievergelt u.a.(6) auf. Z.B. sollte der Lernende
die Deklaration und den Aufruf von Prozeduren und Funktionen solange
nicht verwenden können, bis er nicht mindestens einmal an mehreren Stellen in einem Programm eine Folge von Anweisungen in genau oder fast genau der gleichen Form formuliert hat und ihm so das Prozedurkonzept auch
praktisch einsichtig werden kann.

Ausgehend von den Lektionen des Kenntnisvermittlungsteils sind somit für
das Dialogprogrammiersystem Subsets der Sprache zu definieren, die nacheinander vorgestellt und zuletzt verbunden die ganze Mächtigkeit der
Sprache wiedergeben. Im Scanner des Dialogprogrammiersystems können auf
Grund des aktuellen Kenntnisstandes des Lernenden Schalter gesetzt werden, die die Benutzung z.B. einer Anweisung solange nicht gestatten, wie
diese noch nicht erklärt worden ist.

Dadurch ist weiter gesichert, daß der Lernende nicht durch Fehlermeldun-
gen, die sich auf im Kurs bisher noch nicht eingeführte Elemente der
Sprache beziehen, verunsichert wird. Diese Eigenschaft erhält ihre besondere Bedeutung in den implementierten Sprachversionen, in denen die
PASCAL-Grundsymbole, die durch englische Wörter dargestellt sind, als
solche ausgeschrieben werden und nicht als Bezeichner für Objekte im
Programm verwendet werden dürfen. Der Tippfehler eines Lernenden, der
statt der Anweisung "form:=form+1" die Anweisung "for_m:=form+1" editiert,
führt dann nicht auf die Fehlermeldung "!unvollständige Schleifenanweisung!", die dem Lernenden unverständlich bleiben muß, solange er die
Lektion über die Schleifenanweisung noch nicht bearbeitet hat.

4.5 COMPUTERUNTERSTÜTZTES AUSKUNFTLEHRSYSTEM

Durch Angabe eines Steuerbefehls kann der Lernende aus dem Dialog mit
dem Programmiersystem ein computerunterstütztes Auskunftlehrsystem (13)
aufrufen. Zum Formulieren seiner Anfragen benutzt der Lernende eine di-
daktisch orientierte Abfragesprache, die grundsätzlich folgenden einfachen syntaktischen Aufbau hat:
<Anfrage>::=<Befehlsliste>:<Vokabelliste>
    <Befehlsliste>::=<Befehl>|<Befehlsliste>,<Befehl>
    <Vokabelliste>::=<Vokabel>|<Vokabelliste>,<Vokabel>
Die Liste der Vokabeln beschreibt den Sachverhalt, zu dem der Lernende
eine Information abrufen möchte. Mit einem Befehl spezifiziert der Lernende die Art der gewünschten Information. Folgende Befehle werden verwendet:

<u>erklärung</u>	- verbale Erklärung
<u>syntax</u>	- syntaktische Definition in BNF
<u>beispiel</u>	- Beispiel
<u>anwendung</u>	- Erklärung der Anwendung
<u>zusammenhang</u>	- Angabe des Zusammenhangs zwischen den Vokabeln bzw. Stellung der Vokabel im Begriffsnetz

Durch die Möglichkeit der Reihung von Befehlen in einer Anfrage kann der Lernende Lehrsequenzen zusammenstellen. Diese Eigenschaft des Auskunftlehrsystems erlaubt es, das Dialogprogrammiersystem auch ohne den Kenntnisvermittlungsteil des Lehrsystems COGEL im Unterricht zu benutzen.

Zwei Beispiele sollen den Wert des Auskunftlehrsystems veranschaulichen:
- Mit der Anfrage <u>syntax</u>:TYP erhält der Lernende die syntaktische Definition in Backus-Naur-Form des non-terminals TYP in PASCAL.
- Die Antwort auf die Anfrage <u>erklärung</u>,<u>beispiel</u>:CASE ist die Abfolge von zwei Lehrtexten, in denen die PASCAL-Kontrollstruktur <u>case</u>...<u>of</u>... verbal erklärt und ein Beispiel angegeben wird.

4.6 IMPLEMENTIERUNG

Der Prozessor für die Programmiersprache wird als Interpreter realisiert, der ein Quellenprogramm, das in dem PASCAL-Subset geschrieben ist, in eine interne Form übersetzt und das Programm in dieser internen Form ausführt. Ein Interpreter ist zwar langsamer in der Ausführung als ein äquivalentes Programm in Maschinensprache, doch ist es wesentlich leichter, gute Möglichkeiten zum Debugging vorzusehen als in einem Compiler. Diese Entscheidung geht von der Erwartung aus, daß die Lernenden die meiste Zeit kürzere Quellenprogramme editieren und debuggen.

Um die Implementierungsarbeiten gering zu halten und das Dialogprogrammiersystem auf weitere Rechenanlagen übertragen zu können, sollen der Monitor/Editor und der PASCAL-Interpreter einschließlich des Debugging-Systems mit Hife einer maschinenunabhängigen Technik implementiert werden. Hierzu bietet sich die von Koster (14) entwickelte Programmiersprache CDL (Compiler Description Language) an, die auf mehreren Rechenanlagen implementiert ist.

Bei der technischen Realisierung des Dialogprogrammiersystems ist weiter darauf zu achten, daß die einzelnen Teile des Systems -Monitor/Editor, Interpreter, Debugging-System und Auskunftlehrsystem- definiert voneinander getrennt sind. Ein Softwaresystem, das im Unterricht eingesetzt, wird, muß besonders flexibel für den Einbau von Änderungen sein, die nach einer durchgeführten Evaluation eventuell notwendig werden können.

5 LITERATUR

(1) Dijkstra, E.W., Notes on Structured Programming, in:Dahl, O.-J.u.a., Structured Programming, London 1972, S.1-82

(2) Wirth, N., Program Development by Stepwise Refinement, CACM 14(1971) No.4, S.221-227

(3) Fisher, P., Hankley, W. and V. Wallentine, Separation of Introductory Programming and Language Instruction, ACM SIGCSE Bulletin 5(1973) No.1, S.9-14

(4) Langebartels, R., COGEL -Ein computerunterstütztes Lehrsystem für den Unterricht in Programmiersprachen, in:Brunnstein, K.u.a.(Hrsg.), Fachtagung Rechner-Gestützter Unterricht, Berlin 1974, S.95-103

(5) Fenichel, R.R., Weizenbaum, J. and J.C. Yochelson, A Program to Teach Programming, CACM 13(1970)No.3, S.141-146

(6) Nievergelt, J., Reingold, E.M. and T.R. Wilcox, The Automation of Introductory Computer Science Courses, in:Günther, A.u.a.(Eds.), Proceedings International Computing Symposium, Amsterdam 1974, S.495-501

(7) Langebartels, R., Konzept und technische Realisierung eines computerunterstützten Unterrichtssystems für die elementare Programmierausbildung, Dissertation TU Berlin, Berlin 1974

(8) Wirth, N., Systematisches Programmieren, Stuttgart 1972, S.7 u.37

(9) Lecarme, O., What Programming Language Should We Use for Teaching Programming, in:Turski, W.M.(ed.), Programming Teaching Techniques, Amsterdam 1973, S.64 und
ders., Structured Programming, Programming Teaching and the Language PASCAL, ACM SIGPLAN Notices 9(1974)No.7, S.15-21

(10) Fenichel, R.R., Design of Languages for Elementary Programming Instruction:Lessons of the TEACH Project, in:Scheepmaker, B. and K.L. Zinn (Eds.), 1. IFIP World Conference on Computer Education, Groningen 1970, S.III/175-177

(11) Wirth, N., The Programming Language PASCAL, Acta Informatica 1(1971), S.35-63

(12) Schild, R., Interactive Structured Programming, in:Günther, A.u.a. (Eds.), Proceedings International Computing Symposium, Amsterdam 1974, S.81-84

(13) Hecker, O., Das computerunterstützte Auskunftlehrsystem CALS für die Programmiersprache BASIC, Diplomarbeit TU Berlin, Berlin 1974

(14) Koster, C.H.A., A Compiler Compiler, Bericht MR 127/71 Mathematisch Centrum, Amsterdam 1971

BERUFSBILD UND PERSPEKTIVEN DES INFORMATIKERS

Dr. Hans-Christian Zedlitz
Diebold Deutschland GmbH
Frankfurt/Main

In einer Untersuchung für den Bundesminister für Forschung und Technologie erhob die Diebold Deutschland GmbH den Bedarf an ADV-Fachkräften in der Bundesrepublik Deutschland bis 1978 je Berufstyp und Ausbildungsgang. Bisher wurden die hochgerechneten Planzahlen der ADV-Anwender und Hersteller veröffentlicht. Die Ergebnisse weiterführender Analysen des Erhebungsmaterials werden im November dem zuständigen Fachausschuß des Ministeriums vorgelegt. Dieser wird dann gültige Bedarfszahlen nennen.

Die aus der Analyse des Materials gewonnenen Erkenntnisse über Bedarf an und Einsatz von Informatikern sollen Ihnen hier vorgestellt werden.

1. Ausbildungsinhalte

   Die Erhebung unterscheidet folgende elf Informatik-orientierte Ausbildungsinhalte:

   1) Diplom-Informatiker systemorientiert

   2) Diplom-Informatiker anwendungsorientiert

   3) Diplom-Ingenieur Fachrichtung Informatik

   4) Ingenieur Fachrichtung Informatik (Grad.)

   5) Informatiker

   6) Informationstechniker

   7) Informationselektroniker

   8) Diplom-Betriebswirt Fachrichtung Informatik

   9) Betriebswirt Fachrichtung Informatik (Grad.)

   1o) Betriebswirt DV

   11) Datenverarbeitungs-Kaufmann

2. Voraussichtliche Bedarfsentwicklung an Informatikern je Ausbildungsabschluß bis 1978

Die hochgerechneten Personalplanzahlen der ADV-Anwender und Hersteller ergeben einen hohen Bedarf an Informatikern. Unter Berücksichtigung absehbarer Laufbahnstrukturen ergibt sich ein zusätzlicher extern zu deckender Bedarf bis 1978 von

9.000   Diplom-Informatikern,
4.500   Diplom-Ingenieuren Fachrichtung Informatik,
3.000   Diplom-Betriebswirten Fachrichtung Informatik,
5.500   Informatikern,
2.700   Informationstechnikern,
9.700   Betriebswirten DV,

d.h., daß 40 % der für die Wahrnehmung von DV-Aufgaben neu eingestellten Hochschulabsolventen einen Informatik-orientierten Ausbildungsabschluß haben sollen. Bei den Fachschulabsolventen wurde ein Anteil von 80 % errechnet.

Die Viabilität dieser Bedarfszahlen muß im strengen Sinne überprüft werden, um bedarfsgerechte Ausbildungskapazitäten sicherzustellen. So führt unser Haus in Zusammenarbeit mit dem Institut für Arbeitsmarktforschung im Auftrag des Bundesministers für Forschung und Technologie weiterführende Analysen des Erhebungsmaterials durch. Dabei stellte sich deutlich heraus,

- daß viele der befragten Entscheidungsträger Ausbildungsinhalte und Einsatzmöglichkeiten der Informatiker nicht oder nur unzureichend kannten,

- zu hohe oder falsche Erwartungen vorliegen,

- der Informatiker z.T. als "Prestige-Fachmann" eingestellt werden soll.

3. **Vorstellungen der DV-Anwender und Hersteller über den Einsatz der Informatiker je Ausbildungsabschluß**

Die im Rahmen unserer Erhebung befragten für die Einstellung von ADV-Fachkräften verantwortlichen Entscheidungsträger trafen überwiegend folgende Zuordnungen von Ausbildungsgang zu ADV-Berufstyp:

AUSBILDUNG	EINSATZ ALS
Diplom-Informatiker systemorientiert	Technisch-wissenschaftlicher Systemanalytiker
Diplom-Informatiker anwendungsorientiert	Anwendungsprogr., Technisch-wissenschaftlicher Systemanalytiker, kaufmännisch/administrativer Systemanalytiker
Diplom-Ingenieur Fachrichtung Informatik	Konsoloperator, Anwendungsprogrammierer, Technisch-wissenschaftlicher Systemanalytiker
Diplom-Betriebswirt Fachrichtung Informatik	Anwendungsprogrammierer, kaufmännisch/administrativer Systemanalytiker
Informatiker	Programmierer, Technisch-wissenschaftlicher Systemanalytiker
Informationstechniker	Operator, Technisch-wissenschaftlicher Systemanalytiker
Betriebswirt DV	Operator, Programmierer, kaufmännisch/administrativer Systemanalytiker, DV-Organisator, DV-Koordinator, Mitarbeiter im technisch-wissenschaftlichen Systembetrieb

Ein hoher Prozentsatz dieser Informatiker soll in der Fachabteilung seine DV-Aufgaben wahrnehmen.

4. Kritik der DV-Anwender und Hersteller am Berufsbild des Informatikers

Die häufig in der Fachwelt zu hörende Kritik am Berufsbild des Informatikers beinhaltet eine Menge von Argumenten, die primär für Psychologen und Soziologen von Interesse sind. Daneben gibt es Argumentenketten, die sehr ernst zu nehmen sind. Sie kommen in der Mehrzahl von Fachleuten, die engagiert an der Definition von Ausbildungsinhalten mitwirkten und einsahen, daß die sich stark wandelnden Anforderungen an die ADV ein Festschreiben differenzierter Ausbildungsmodule nicht zulassen.

Vereinfacht lassen sich die Argumente zu folgender Kritik zusammenfassen:

. Der Informatiker verfügt über ein zu enges Methoden- und Verfahrenwissen, das ihn von den Bedarfsträgern nach DV-Leistungen eher isoliert.

. Der Informatiker erhält im Rahmen seiner Ausbildung ein "abgepacktes DV-Wissen", das als enzyklopädische Kenntnis von veralteten Fakten beschrieben werden kann. Diese Wissenslast beschränkt seine Flexibilität.

. Daraus resultierend verfügt der Informatiker nicht über ein ausreichendes Wissen und Verständnis um die Abläufe in Organisationseinheiten, die durch die ADV unterstützt werden sollen. Er hilft also nicht Probleme zu erkennen und zu lösen sondern er wird zum weiteren Problem - zum Kommunikationsproblem.

5. Erkennbare langfristige Tendenzen der Einsatzmöglichkeiten des Informatikers aus der Sicht der Diebold Deutschland GmbH

Die zitierte Kritik ist nach Meinung unseres Hauses zu undifferenziert, sie reflektiert zu wenig die sich unterschiedlich wandelnden Anforderungen an die DV-orientierten Aufgabenblöcke oder Tätigkeitsfelder bei den Anwendern:

- Erfassung und Transformation von Daten
- Verarbeitung von Daten
- Verwaltung von Daten und Transformation zu Informationen
- Entwicklung und Pflege von DV-Anwendungssystemen
- Sicherheitsmaßnahmen.

Alle diese Tätigkeitsfelder erfordern in unterschiedlicher Verteilung systemorientiertes und anwendungsorientiertes Wissen und Können. Zur Lösung der Aufgaben hat sich die Wissenskombination in Form einer Mitarbeitergruppe (Team) bewährt. Die Aufgabenblöcke bei Herstellern von Hardware und Software erfordern ähnliche Lösungswege, sind aber quantitativ mehr systemorientiert.

Die Nutzung von DV-Leistungen durch die Fachbereiche geschieht heute noch überwiegend über den zwischengeschalteten ADV-Fachmann (Analytiker, Arbeitsvorbereiter etc.). Diebold erwartet, daß in absehbarer Zukunft die tagesbezogene Nutzung der Rechner und ihrer Peripherie durch die Fachabteilung direkt erfolgen wird. Die ADV-Fachleute werden primär die Erhaltung der Stabilität dieser Infrastruktur sicherstellen.

Das legitime Interesse der Hersteller, ihre Wachstumsraten zu erhalten, zwingt diese, die systemorientierten Tätigkeitsfelder zu rationalisieren, um den wachsenden Anteil der Personalkosten in einem ADV-Budget zu stabilisieren. Die Dezentralisierung einiger Tätigkeitsfelder in die Fachabteilungen wiederum erfordert die Wahrnehmung weiterer Aufgabenblöcke wie

- Entwicklung, Pflege und Kontrolle von Standards je Tätigkeitsfeld,
- Wartung und Steuerung des Informationswesens

um die wirtschaftliche Wahrnehmung von Aufgabenblöcken wie z.B. Entwicklung und Pflege von Anwendungssystemen in den Fachabteilungen sicherzustellen. Diese Ausführungen lassen erkennen, daß

- systemorientiertes Wissen und Können langfristig bei Anwendern wie Herstellern notwendig bleibt

- weitere Tätigkeitsfelder an Gewicht zunehmen werden.

- ein fundiertes breites Methoden- und Verfahrenswissen für die sich abzeichnenden Veränderungen benötigt wird

- der quantitative Bedarf an "Nur DV-Fachleuten" je Anwender langfristig erheblich zurückgehen wird.

Lassen Sie mich abschließend die letzten Sätze unseres Gutachtens zitieren. Sie unterstreichen unsere Befürchtung, daß Ausbildungsinhalte, die dem systemorientierten Faktenwissen das Schwergewicht zuordnen, den absehbaren Bedarf nicht genügend berücksichtigen:

"Die sich verändernden Umweltvariablen bei den ADV-Fachkräften, die bei Anwendern beschäftigt sind, stellen Ausbildungsgänge in Frage, die eine erkannte Leistungsartenkombination als beständig erkennen - z.B. Informatiker -. Vielmehr muß eine Verbreitung des Wissens um die Einsatzmöglichkeiten der ADV wie um die Methodik der Problemanalyse und -definition auf allen Ausbildungsebenen gefördert werden. Die sich rasch verändernden organisatorischen Erfordernisse sowie die darauf reagierende Entwicklung der Informationstechnologie verweisen auf absehbare Sicht die Vermittlung von ADV-Fachwissen in den Bereich der Weiterbildung. Neben dem Fachwissen fordert der ADV-Bereich von morgen Mitarbeiter, die komplexe Strukturen erkennen und analysieren können. Die Anforderungen an das Denkvermögen steigen, gleichgültig in welchem Ausbildungsgang es vermittelt wird. Außerdem wird die Bereitschaft verlangt, in kürzer werdenden Abständen das Wissen zu aktualisieren unter Berücksichtigung der Erfordernisse der Institution als ganzes, die den Mitarbeiter beschäfigt. Der Neueinstellung einer ADV-Fachkraft liegt zwar ein Anforderungsprofil zugrunde, das u.a. ein für die Lösung der Aufgaben notwendiges Fachwissen beschreibt. Doch sei abschließend mit aller Deutlichkeit gesagt, daß neben vielen anderen Eigenschaften wie Denkvermögen, Kommunikationsfähigkeit, Belastbarkeit usw. das Fachwissen oft schneller vermittelt werden kann."

Wir sind überzeugt, daß wir viele anwendungs- wie systemorientierte Informatiker benötigen, die gelernt haben, komplexe Probleme zu strukturieren und in Zusammenarbeit mit Fachleuten anderer Disziplinen zu lösen. Wir sind bemüht, den fundierbaren Bedarf zu quantifizieren. Die Erfahrung lehrt uns, daß ein **Festschreiben** von Ausbildungsinhalten nur grob geschehen darf, auf jeden Fall die

Methodik Vorrang erhalten muß. Die absehbare Zukunft schließlich sollte uns auf einen starken latenten Bedarf an Informationswissenschaftlern aufmerksam machen. Diese haben nur wenig gemeinsam mit den "Computer-Scientists".

Konzept und Studienplan für eine Fachrichtung "Wirtschaftsinformatik" im Studiengang "Informatik" der TU Berlin

Holger Franck, Thorsten Spitta
Institut f. Angewandte Informatik: Lehreinheit EDV

1. Berufsbild eines "Wirtschaftsinformatikers"

Der Kern des Berufsbildes "Wirtschaftsinformatik" wird von allen einschlägigen Untersuchungen zu diesem Problemkreis als "Entwicklung von Informationssystemen und deren Implementierung in eine Organisation" angesehen (vgl. ACM p.367; Grochla, S. 82ff; IFIP, pp. 1ff; Wahl, S. 35off). Der Begriff "Information" ist so weit wie möglich zu nehmen; weitreichende Planungsinformationen gehören ebenso dazu wie etwa einfache Fakturierungen. Ausgeklammert werden sollen allerdings die Gebiete der Ingenieur-Informatik, da diese einer ebenfalls umfassenden Behandlung bedürfen.
Die Betonung des ACM-Papiers auf Informationssysteme in Unternehmungen kann nicht einleuchten. Grundsätzlich sind alle Organisationen Tätigkeitsobjekte, für die zur Debatte steht, Informationsbedürfnisse durch DV-gestützte Informationssysteme befriedigen zu lassen.
Der Tätigkeitsbereich innerhalb einer Organisation liegt zwischen dem reinen Nutzer und dem reinen Betreiber des Informationssystems. Dieser Bereich sorgt neben den o.g. (originären) Tätigkeiten auch für die Bewertung und Umsetzung der von den Nutzern laufend geäußerten Informationsbedürfnisse in eine entsprechende Gestaltung des Informationssystems. Eine Herauslösung dieser Tätigkeiten aus den Rechenzentren in eine mit relativer Unabhängigkeit ausgestattete Abteilung scheint sich in letzter Zeit durchzusetzen. Hierbei ergeben sich zwei verschiedene Schwerpunkte:
1. "Design notwendiger Informationsflüsse", der dem Benutzer nähersteht
2. "System Design", der dem Rechner nähersteht.

2. Kenntnisbereiche

Sowohl ACM als auch IFIP gehen von zwei großen Bereichen aus, die das Wissen bereitstellen sollen, um Informationssysteme zu entwickeln: Wissen über menschliche Organisationen und über Computer. Zwar erscheinen mehr Kenntnisbereiche bei ihnen, aber bei genauerem Hinsehen erweist sich:
ACM (p.373) sieht in ihnen die beiden Aspekte der Umwelt von Informationssystemen (die konzeptionell mit Hilfe des Systemansatzes vereinigt werden); IFIP (p. 6ff) fügt zwar noch Techniken des Management Science ein, sieht deren Sinn jedoch wiederum darin, die Relevanz quantitativer Ansätze sowohl für "Management Probleme" (i.e. Organisationsprobleme) als auch für System Design Probleme aufzuzeigen.

Deutsche Vorschläge zum Wirtschaftsinformatiker versuchen immer nur zu einem "ausgewogenen Verhältnis zwischen dem wirtschaftswissenschaftlichen und dem informatorischen und mathematischen Lehrangebot" (Grochla S. 88) zu kommen. Ein Konzept zur inhaltlichen Umgestaltung des Lehrangebots in Hinblick auf den Wirtschaftsinformatiker über das Nebeneinanderstellen von Vorlesungen aus den verschiedenen Bereichen hinaus fehlt. So stehen Vorlesungen über Geldtheorie, Konjunkturtheorie oder Automatentheorie und Formale Sprachen dem Studenten zur Auswahl (Grochla S. 88), ohne daß die Relevanz für das Studienziel ersichtlich wird. IFIP und ACM gehen insofern einen Schritt weiter, indem sie erkennen, daß die Voraussetzung zum Entwurf von Informationssystemen nicht durch Anbieten von Stoff über Teilaspekte eines Betriebes geschaffen wird, sondern nur durch das vorherige Entwickeln einer Gesamtperspektive des Objektsystems, der Organisation. Hieran soll in diesem Curriculum angeschlossen werden. Allerdings soll in diesem Vorschlag der Organisationsbereich in Hinblick auf Informationssysteme eine noch fundamentalere Bedeutung und vertiefte Analyse erhalten. Für den Organisationsbereich gilt:

1. An erster Stelle hat die Analyse der Organisation zu stehen; aus ihr erwachsen erst die Probleme und Lösungsbedürfnisse, die zur Installierung von DV-gestützten Informationssystemen führen. Dieser Gesichtspunkt hat drei Auswirkungen:
   (1) Er fordert auf zum Hinterfragen der bestehenden Organisationsstrukturen und -prozesse, ihren Implikationen für Informationsverhältnisse.
   (2) Er fordert auf zu untersuchen, inwieweit sich Organisationen erst durch Informationssysteme manifestieren.
   (3) Er macht eingehende wissenschaftliche Analysen erforderlich über das Verhältnis zwischen Problemarten und Problemlösungsverfahren im Computerbereich und im Bereich menschlicher Organisationen. Eine simple Annahme - wie im ACM-Papier (p. 375) gemacht -, daß operationale Modelle für beide Bereiche anwendbar sind, ohne das Ausmaß der Anwendbarkeit zu diskutieren, erscheint als zu oberflächlich. Stehen im Bereich des Computers Problemarten im Vordergrund, deren Formulierung und Kriterien für die Lösung relativ klar sind, ist gerade dies im Bereich der menschlichen Organisationen beim gegenwärtigen Stand unseres Wissens die Hauptschwierigkeit. Sind die Problemlösungsverfahren im Bereich des Computers algorithmisch (insbesondere mit den Eigenschaften "finit" und "definitiv"), sprechen Erfahrungen über das Lösen von Problemen im sozialen Bereich eher für nicht finite und unklare Prozeduren.

2. Es muß darauf geachtet werden, den Studenten schon zu Beginn ihres Studiums eine Perspektive der Gesamtorganisation einschließlich ihrer

Umwelt zu vermitteln. Eine zu frühzeitige isolierte Betrachtung von
Teilbereichen (s. in der Betriebswirtschaftslehre: Bilanzen, Steuerlehre,
Kostenrechnung, Absatz usw.) führt zur Verschleierung der Interdependenzen zwischen den Teilbereichen, die gerade für den Entwurf von Informationssystemen von grundlegender Bedeutung sind.
3. Die am Anfang stehende Konzentration auf die Organisation als Ganze
macht den Studenten eher fähig, sich in Problemstellungen schnell einzuarbeiten, die sich aus der besonderen Art von Organisationen ergeben, in
denen Informationssysteme installiert werden sollen.

Die Gestaltung des Computerbereiches kann sich weitgehend an den IFIP-
Vorschlag anschließen.

Es ergeben sich damit folgende Kenntnisfelder:

      1. Computer und Informationssysteme
      2. Quantitative Methoden
      3. Organisationsanalyse
      4. Entwurf von Informationssystemen

Zum Bereich 4 ist zu sagen: Es gibt kein geschlossenes Konzept, das man
als Kenntnisbereich "information system development" ansprechen könnte.
Vielmehr gilt die Feststellung aus IFIP (p. 62):

    "There exist few generally accepted and many more or less
    'incompatible' approaches in this field."

Möglich nach dem derzeitigen Wissensstand ist nur, eine Reihe von Einzelkenntnissen in diesem Bereich zu vermitteln und in Projekten zur Anwendung zu bringen. Notwendige Kenntnisse z.B. sind:

- Kenntnisse systemtheoretischer Ansätze
- Kenntnisse von Beschreibungs- und Dokumentations-Normen und Ansätzen
- Beherrschung der Anwendung quantitativer Analyseverfahren
- Kenntnis automatisierter Entwurfs-Techniken (z.B. CASCADE, SYSTEMATICS)

Es kann als gesichert gelten, daß nur das Anwenden der o.a. und anderer
Einzelkenntnisse in Analyse- und Entwurfsprojekten hinreichende Kenntnisse darüber vermittelt, was Systementwurf umfaßt. Ein isoliertes Aneinanderreihen von Methoden ist in jedem Fall zu vermeiden.

Die vier Kenntnisbereiche lassen sich überblickartig wie folgt grafisch
darstellen:

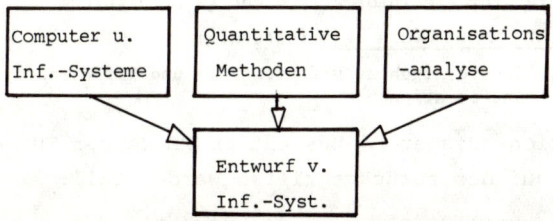

3. Studienplan im Rahmen des Informatik-Studienganges der TU-Berlin

Im Abschnitt 3 wird entlang der vorangegangenen Gliederung in Kenntnisbereiche, untergliedert in Grund- und Hauptstudium, inhaltlich umrissen, welche Lehrgebiete und Lehrveranstaltungen den Studiengang abdecken sollen. Dabei werden bestehende Veranstaltungen nur kurz beschrieben und als solche gekennzeichnet, neu zu schaffende ausführlicher.

3.1. Das Grundstudium

3.1.1. Informatik-Grundlagen

Dieser Bereich entspricht weitgehend den Informatik-Zyklen

- Algorithmen und
- Rechnerorganisation

mit den Veranstaltungen

<u>Algorithmen I</u> (6stündig) Inhalte:
<u>Algorithmen II</u> (4stündig) vgl. Vortrag der NORIS-GRUPPE der
<u>Algorithmen III</u> (4stündig) GI-Tagung

<u>Rechnerorganisation I/W</u> (4stündig) ("W" = Wirtschaftsinformatik)

(v. Neumannsches Modell, Informationsdarstellung, Befehlsvorrat, Adressierung, Maschinenprogrammierung),

<u>Rechnerorganisation II/W</u> (4stündig)

(Betriebsprogramme; Wechselwirkung Hardware-Software im Betriebssystem - weitgehend identisch mit RO III)

RO/W unterscheidet sich also vom bisherigen Zyklus dadurch, daß die Hardware-Bestandteile gestrichen wurden.

3.1.2. Quantitative Methoden

In diesen Bereich fallen:

Mathematik   Operations Research   Statistik

Die Mathematikausbildung wird gegenüber der bisherigen mehr theoretisch ausgerichteten der Informatiker stärker anwendungsorientiert sein müssen, wozu Mathematik II modifiziert wird:

<u>Mathematik für Informatiker I</u>   (6stündig)

(Strukturelle Mathematik; math. Begriffsbildung, math. Methoden zur Behandlung formalisierter und abstrakter Modelle anhand der Mengenlehre, für die Informatik wichtige Strukturen)

<u>Mathematik für Informatiker II/W</u> (6stündig)

(Analysis, lineare Algebra, Differential- und Differenzengleichungen, Transformationen)

Im Gebiet "Operations Research" besteht am FB 2o der TUB ein umfassendes Lehrangebot, auf das zurückgegriffen werden soll:

<u>Einführung in Operations Research</u> (4stündig)

Wahlpflichtfach Operations Research (2stündig)

    entweder   Entscheidungstheorie
    oder   Heuristische Methoden
    oder   Graphentheorie

Im Gebiet "Statistik" wird ebenfalls schon eine entsprechende Lehrveranstaltung angeboten

Statistik für Informatiker (6stündig)

Voraussetzung: Mathematik I und II

    (Indices, Zeitreihen, Regression, statistische Erhebung, statistische Tests, Problematik statistischer Verfahren)

3.1.3. Organisationsanalyse

In diesem Bereich gibt es praktisch kein Lehrangebot, nicht einmal Konzepte. Im folgenden ein Ansatz dazu:

Organisationsanalyse I (6stündig)

(Organisationsanalyse herrschender Organisationslehren, ihre historische Entwicklung, Konzepte und sich daraus ergebende Probleme; Verdeutlichung des Zusammenhangs zwischen Wertsystem, Organisationslehre und Organisationsanalyse)

1. Teilaspekte betonende Organisationslehren und deren ökonomische Kategorien

    (klassische Organisationslehre (Taylor); human relations Ansatz ("neoklassischer"); Bürokratiemodell (Weber); entscheidungsorientierter Ansatz (March, Simon); marxistischer Ansatz)

2. Systemanalytische Organisationslehre

    als mögliche Integrierung der von den bisherigen Lehren betrachteten Teilaspekte

3. Probleme und Möglichkeiten der Demokratisierung in Organisationen

Organisationsanalyse II (4stündig)

(methodische Fragen)

1. Interdependenz von Problemerkennung, Problemlösungsverfahren, Beobachtung und Realität

    (Beobachtungssätze, Hypothesen, Wertfreiheitsproblem am Beispiel der Organisationsanalyse, empirische Adäquanz, Begriffsbildung: Fruchtbarkeit von Begriffssystemen, Konsistenz, Validität)

2. Problemarten und Problemstellungen in sozialen Organisationen einerseits und Informatik andererseits

    (am Beispiel der historischen Entwicklung der Systemwissenschaften (insbes. OR) sollen die Schwierigkeiten und Fehllösungen aufgezeigt werden, die entstehen, wenn versucht wird, für technische Problemstellungen entwickelte Verfahren auf soziale Systeme zu übertragen)

3. Stufenweise Formalisierung von Problembeschreibungen in den Sozialwissenschaften und in der Informatik

    (Prädikaten- und Aussagenlogik, strukturelle wie z.B. graphentheoretische Methoden, Algorithmen, Differential- und Differenzengleichungen)

4. Auswahl von Beobachtungsmaterial, Gestaltung empirischer Überprüfungsprozesse

    (vgl. statistische Methoden)

Organisationsanalyse III (6stündig)

(Bildung operationaler Modelle bei der Analyse von Organisationen)

1. Modellarten mit Beispielen

    (statische-dynamische, deterministische-probabilistische-funktionale, deskriptive-normative, ikonische-analoge Modelle)

2. Funktion von Modellen

3. Anwendung von Operations Research Modellen bei der Organisationsanalyse

    (Behandlung einfacher Beispiele)

4. Beispiele formalisierter Modellierungen von Organisationen

    (G. Hage's "axiomatische Theorie": Beispiel für ein axiomatisches System verbaler Aussagen über Organisationen, aus denen weitere Aussagen deduziert werden können; Holt-Modgliani-Muth-Simon-Optimierungsmodell: Reihenfolgenoptimierung; Forrester's "Industrial Dynamics"-Ansatz; Bonini's "Behavioral Theory"-Ansatz: Informations- und Entscheidungssysteme in einer Unternehmung)

5. Verhältnis von Informationssystem und Organisation

Organisationsanalyse IV (6stündig)

(praktischer Entwurf von Organisations-Teilsystemen)

Praktischer Entwurf und Analyse von Informationsflüssen in einem Betrieb am Beispiel des betrieblichen Rechnungswesens als umfassend gedachtes Kontrollinstrument; Kosten-Nutzen-Analyse möglicher Systementwürfe; Vergleich mit Realisationen in der Praxis.

3.1.4. Übersicht über das Grundstudium

Gebiet / Sem	Inf.-Grundlagen		Quant. Methoden		Org.-Analyse	SWStd
1.	Alg. I (6)		Math. I (6)		I (6)	18
2.	Alg. II (4)	RO I (4)	Math. II (6)		II (4)	18
3.	Alg. III (4)	RO II (4)	Op.Res. (Einführ) (4)		III (6)	18
4.			OpRes (WP) (2)	Statistik (6)	IV (6)	14
Summe	22		24		22	68

Studienplan: Grundstudium

3.2. Das Hauptstudium

Für das Hauptstudium ergibt sich, in Abänderung der bisherigen Informatik-Prüfungsordnung, folgender Fächerkatalog:

    S = Software
    P = Praktische Informatik
    Q = Spezielle Quantitative Methoden
    AG = Organisationsanalyse spezieller Anwendungsgebiete
    E = Entwurf von Informationssystemen

Q, AG und E sind eine notwendige Spezifizierung des bisherigen Faches A (= Anwendungen); P (= Theoretische Informatik) und H (= Hardware) wurden weggelassen.

Der Fächerkatalog müßte folgende Struktur haben:

> Im Mittelpunkt steht die Entwicklung von spezifischen Informationssystemen. Nach der Problembeschreibung für das jeweilige System erfolgt eine projektgebundene Vertiefung in den Grundlagenfächern, mit Hilfe derer dann das Projekt bearbeitet wird.

G r a f i s c h

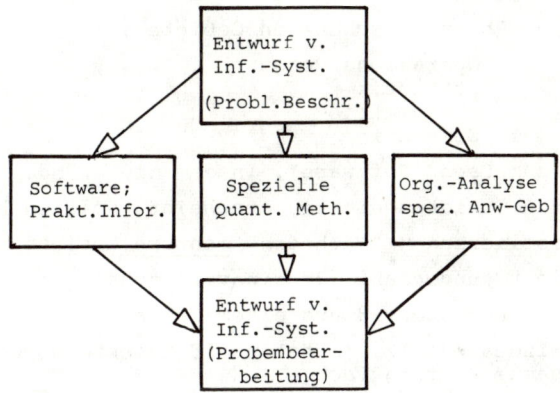

Struktur des Hauptstudiums (Zielvorstellung)

Dieser von der Sache her eigentlich notwendige Aufbau des Hauptstudiums ist jedoch bei der derzeitigen Studienorganisation noch nicht zu verwirklichen. Er verlangt alternative, bis ins Detail durchstrukturierte Projekte, die es gestatten, den Studenten zu Beginn des Hauptstudiums die für das von ihnen gewählte Projekt notwendigen Vertiefungsveranstaltungen zu nennen.

Bis dahin muß konventionell vorgegangen werden, indem man die Vertiefungen vor die Projekte stellt. Damit geht man allerdings den Nachteil ein, daß die Studenten Vertiefungen relativ losgelöst von Projektfragestellungen studieren. Die in den Prüfungsfächern enthaltenen Gebiete werden wieder im einzelnen erläutert.

3.2.1. Software

Im Fach "Software" kann unter drei Prüfungsgebieten ausgewählt werden:

> Betriebssysteme
> Datenbankmanagementsysteme
> Softwaretechnik (Anwendungssoftware)

Die Stundenzahl für dieses Wahlpflichtfach sollte zwischen 8 und 12 liegen.

3.2.2. Praktische Informatik

In dieses Prüfungsfach fallen Gebiete, die eine vielfältige Spezialisierung erlauben, wie

> Computer Graphics
> Prozeßrechnertechnik
> numerische Mathematik

Das Fach sollte nicht in den Pflichtkanon aufgenommen werden, es können jedoch bis zu 8 Wochenstunden gewählt werden (Wahlfach).

3.2.3. Spezielle Quantitative Methoden

In diesem Bereich kann auf ein reichhaltiges Angebot zurückgegriffen werden. Es ist zu wählen zwischen den Gebieten:

> Operations Research
> Statistik
> Ökonometrie
> Simulation

Im Gegensatz zum Fach "Software", in dem die gründliche Durchdringung eines _einzelnen_ Gebietes wichtig erscheint, sollten bei den z.T. gut voneinander zu isolierenden "Methoden" _mehrere_ Gebiete gewählt werden. Daher wird als Pflichtstundenzahl für sinnvoll gehalten:
- mindestens 4, höchstens 8 aus einem Gebiet
- insgesamt mindestens 12, höchstens 18 Semesterwochenstunden (SWStd) für das gesamte Prüfungsfach.

3.2.4. Organisationsanalyse spezieller Anwendungsgebiete

Dieses Prüfungsfach dient dem Kennenlernen der spezifischen Probleme verschiedener Anwendungsbereiche und dem Gewinnen eines gewissen Überblicks über verschiedenartige Problemstellungen.
Während im kommerziellen, insbesondere im industriellen Sektor ein Lehrangebot existiert, besteht im öffentlichen Bereich noch ein erheblicher Bedarf. Durch Koordination mit anderen Fachbereichen und Lehrbeauftragten aus der Praxis lassen sich die Lücken jedoch schließen. Der Umfang dieses Prüfungsfaches sollte zwischen 10 und 12 SWStd liegen.

3.2.5. Entwurf von Informationssystemen

Dieses Kernfach ist noch überaus schwach repräsentiert und erfordert die umfassendste konzeptionelle Arbeit. Folgende Gebiete erscheinen sinnvoll:

Projektmanagement
   Systemerhebung (Ist-Analyse und Sollkonzeption)
   Systementwurf
   Systemimplementierung

Das Gebiet Projektmanagement wäre durch eine vierstündige Vorlesung
mit Übung abzudecken. In den Gebieten Systemerhebung, Systementwurf
und Systemimplementierung müssen zunächst zweisemestrige Projekte stattfinden, nach Möglichkeit in Kooperation mit Industrie und kommunalen Verwaltungen. Die Projekte sollen je 6stündig durchgeführt werden. Erste Erfahrungen in diesem Bereich liegen vor mit der erstmalig im SS 74 abge-
haltenen Veranstaltung "Programmierprojekt kommerzielle EDV" (6stündig),
die jedoch den hier gestellten Ansprüchen nicht genügen kann, da sie für
Informatik-Studenten mit Nebenfach "Wirtschaftswissenschaften" im Grundstudium konzipiert war. Die Teilnahme an einem Projektzyklus könnte dann
einmünden in eine 6monatige Diplomarbeit im Rahmen eines Forschungspro-
jektes. Im Fach "Entwurf von Informationssystemen" sollte die Teilnahme
an zwei Projekten Pflicht sein, also ein Umfang von mindestens 12 SWStd.
Die Höchstzahl in diesem Fach sollte bei 18 Stunden liegen.

3.2.6. Überblick über das Hauptstudium

Der Übersicht wegen seien noch einmal die Prüfungsfächer und die wählbaren Gebiete zusammengetragen:

Pr-Fach	Gebiete	Pflichtstundenzahlen	
		Min	Max
S	Betriebssysteme Softwaretechnik Datenbankmanagementsysteme	8	12
P	Computer Graphics Prozeßrechnertechnik Numerische Mathematik	0	8
Q	Operations Research Statistik Ökonometrie Simulation	12	18
AG	DV-Anwendungen in - Industrie u. Dienstleistungen - öff. Bereich	10	12

E	Projektmanagement
	System-Erhebung
	  " -Entwurf
	  " -Implementierung
		12	18

Summe		42	68

Fächerkatalog: Hauptstudium

Wenn man die hohe Intensität betrachtet, mit der die Projekte in Fach E, aber auch die Veranstaltungen in S und Q ablaufen - dies zeigt die Erfahrung des bisherigen Informatik-Studiums an der TUB -, so wird man 5o SWStd. als die maximale Pflichtstundenzahl im Hauptstudium ansehen müssen.

4. Schlußbemerkung

Dieses Papier hat zwei Funktionen:

(1) Es wurde ein Beitrag geliefert, der über das bloße Kombinieren von Informatik- und Wirtschaftswissenschafts-Fächern hinausgeht und damit eher in der Lage ist als bisher vorliegende deutsche Vorschläge, den Anspruch

> Ausbildung "des methodisch-systematisch geschulten Fachmannes, der ein breit angelegtes Grundlagenwissen mit ad hoc erworbenen Kenntnissen über spezielle Problembereiche kombinieren kann" (Grochla, S. 82)

einzulösen.

(2) Durch Bezugnahme auf einen realen Studiengang wurde ein Beweis für die Realisierbarkeit des Konzepts angetreten. Die Verfasser meinen, daß eine Übertragung auf andere Informatik-Studiengänge der BRD ohne weiteres möglich ist.

Literatur:

ACM: ASHENHURST, R.L. (ed): Curriculum Recommendations for Graduate Professional Programs in Information Systems, CACM 15 (1972), No. 5, pp. 363-398

GROCHLA, E., u.a.: Ein Vorschlag für einen Studiengang "Diplom-Betriebswirt der Fachrichtung Informatik", Angew. Informatik 14 (1972), H. 2, S. 81-9o

IFIP: An International Curriculum for Information System Designers, Zusammenfassung der Ergebnisse der IFIP-Workshops, Fribourg 1969, Ghent 1971, Shrivenham 1971: London 1973

MERTENS, P.: Industrielle Datenverarbeitung, Bd. 1,2; neu bearb. Aufl. Wiesbaden 1972

MERTENS, P.: "Ausbildung in betrieblicher Datenverarbeitung (Betriebsinformatik) an der ... Universität Erlangen-Nürnberg", internes Studienberatungs-Papier 1974

NORIS-GRUPPE: Erfahrungen mit dem Versuch eines integrierten Informatik-Grundstudiums, 4. GI-Tagung, Berlin 1974

WAHL, M.: Gedanken zu einem universitären Wirtschaftsinformatikstudium in: Hansen, H. u. Wahl, M.(Hrsg.) Probleme beim Aufbau betrieblicher Informationssysteme, München 1973

WEDEKIND, H.: Studienplan zum Studiengang Diplom-Wirtschaftsinformatiker, internes Arbeitspapier der TH Darmstadt v. 16.3.1973

WEDEKIND, H.: Systemanalyse (Die Entwicklung von Anwendungssystemen für Datenverarbeitungsanlagen), München 1973

Grundausbildung in Informatik

Ch. Floyd   SOFTLAB, München

Ein mehrsemestriger Grundkurs in Informatik sollte in der Anlage und im pädagogischen Aufbau davon ausgehen, daß die Hochschulausbildung in diesem Gebiet einen stark differenzierten Hörerkreis anspricht:

- angehende Informatiker, denen eine Grundausbildung in ihrem Fach vermittelt werden muß,
- Naturwissenschaftler anderer Disziplinen, welche die Informatik als Nachbar- oder Hilfswissenschaft betreiben wollen,
- Hörer anderer Fakultäten (Wirtschaftswissenschaftler, Juristen, Sprachwissenschaftler, Mediziner), welche im Rahmen eines "studium generale" Grundbegriffe der Informatik kennen lernen wollen, ohne schon eine differenzierte Vorstellung von der späteren Verwendung dieses Wissens in ihren Berufsleben zu haben.

Die letzten beiden Gruppen dürfen im Lehrveranstaltungsangebot der Hochschule keineswegs vernachlässigt werden. Aus ihnen rekrutiert sich nämlich der "qualifizierte Anwenderkreis" der EDV - Wirtschaftler, Politiker und Wissenschaftler, die später sowohl den sinnvollen, sozial nützlichen Einsatz der Datenverarbeitung als auch ihre Weiterentwicklung mindestens ebenso stark mitbestimmen wie die Fachinformatiker selbst.

Für diesen Hörerkreis genügt es nicht, eine Vorlesung über die Einsatzmöglichkeiten des Computers zu besuchen, sondern sie müssen die algorithmische Denkweise selbst kennenlernen, insbesondere sich Programmiererfahrung aneignen. Sie sollten daher die normalen Grundkurse (evtl. mit Verzicht auf eine parallele, vertiefende Ergänzungsvorlesung) so lange besuchen können, bis ihre Anforderungen an Vertiefung ihrer Kenntnisse auf diesem Gebiet erfüllt sind - entsprechend etwa der Grundausbildung in Physik für Nicht-Physiker.

Das Ziel einer solchen gemeinsamen Grundausbildung ist vor allem die Überwindung der Kommunikationsbarriere zwischen Fachinformatikern, Anwendern und Laien, die heute erschreckend hoch ist, und für die der zunehmenden Computerisierung ausgesetzten Öffentlichkeit schädliche Auswirkungen hat. Es ist deswegen notwendig, einen gemeinsamen Bezugsrahmen zu schaffen, der einerseits dem Informatiker eine konkrete Grundlage für die Abstraktionen seiner Wissenschaft liefert, den anderen Interessenten eine für sie verständliche Einführung in die Grundprinzipien der algorithmischen Datenverarbeitung vermitteln.

Dies läßt sich kaum realisieren, wenn nur Einführungsvorlesungen über Datenverarbeitung geboten werden, in denen ein hardwareorientierter Standpunkt betont wird. Dieses Ziel kann jedoch durch eine Folge von Lehrveranstaltungen über die Prinzipien der Softwarekonstruktion erreicht werden, die streng nach einem logischen Top Down-Prinzip angelegt wird und von den anwendungsorientierten zu den technologischen Problemen fortschreitet. Jede Lehrveranstaltung besteht aus einer Kombination von aufeinander abgestimmten Vorlesungen und Übungen. In den Übungen arbeiten die Studenten von der ersten Woche an am Computer; Zusammenarbeit in Gruppen ermöglicht später die Lösung komplexerer Aufgaben und gibt gleichzeitig eine wirklichkeitsnahe Einführung in die Arbeitsweise des praktischen Informatikers. Ein viersemestriger Grundkurs hätte dementsprechend etwa folgenden Aufbau:

1. Semester : Strukturierte Programmierung von Algorithmen für leicht verständliche Anwendungsprobleme (in einer maschinenunabhängigen Programmiersprache wie PASCAL oder ALGOL W) und problembezogene Datenstrukturierung. Dabei wird die Erlernung der algorithmischen Denkweise in den Vordergrund gestellt.

2. Semester : Das Konzept der hierarchischen Strukturierung. Übergänge von höherer auf tiefere Ebene : abstrakte Maschinen, Grundkonzepte der Übersetzung und Interpretation.

3. Semester : Maschineninterne Darstellung von Programmen. Das Betriebssystem als Realisierung der asynchronen Vorgänge (E/A, Multiprogrammierung, Multitasking, Prozeßkommunikation) und der Betriebsmittelverwaltung.

4. Semester : Die reale Maschine (Mikroprogramme, logische Grundstruktur der CPU, Kanäle, Steuerungen, Geräte, Datenübertragung).

Auf diese Weise hat der Nicht-Fachinformatiker die Möglichkeit, in dem ersten Semester bzw. in den ersten beiden Semestern eine "problemnahe" Einführung in die algorithmische Denkweise zu erhalten, ohne – für ihn uninteressante und allenfalls verwirrende – technologische Details der realen Maschine erlernen zu müssen. Für den beginnenden Fachinformatiker andererseits bildet diese, von der Anwendung zur Maschinentechnologie fortschreitende Vorlesungsfolge einen leichteren Zugang zu seinem Gebiet.

Zum Erfolg dieses Grundkurses ist es wesentlich, den Studenten von vornherein die Mehrschichtigkeit des gebotenen Stoffes klarzumachen:

- die Grundprinzipien der Softwarekonstruktion,
- die Problematik der verwendeten Anwendungsbeispiele,
- die Eigentümlichkeiten der verwendeten Sprache bzw. Software,
- die praktische Arbeit im Rechenzentrum.

Der Student erlebt sich so von Anfang an einerseits als Entwickler, andererseits als kritischer Benutzer bereits existierender Systeme. Dadurch wird es auch möglich, sehr schnell Qualitätskriterien für Programmsysteme wie Benutzergerechtheit, funktionale Transparenz, Effektivität, Verständlichkeit usw. und ihre Beziehung zueinander herauszuarbeiten, wie sie in zunehmenden Maße von Theoretikern und Anwendern gefordert werden.

Nicht zuletzt bietet ein solcher Grundkurs einen geeigneten Rahmen für die Betrachtung der Rolle des Computers in der Gesellschaft. Bezüge können schon an Hand der verwendeten Beispiele hergestellt werden. Vor allem aber weist die stark benutzerorientierte Denkweise auf die Verantwortung des Informatikers hin, den Gebrauch des Computers als sinnvolles Werkzeug in der heutigen Welt entscheidend mit zubestimmen.

Erfahrungen mit dem Versuch eines integrierten
Informatik-Grundstudiums
N. Oris

Technische Universität Berlin
Fachbereich Kybernetik

1. Einleitung

Wenn im folgenden von den Überlegungen, die zu dem heutigen Informatik-Studiengang an der TU Berlin führten, von den Erfahrungen, die bisher damit gemacht wurden, und den Modifikationen, denen er möglicherweise unterworfen sein wird, berichtet werden soll, kann das nicht geschehen, ohne Voraussetzungen und Randbedingungen wenigstens kurz zu beleuchten. Es waren im wesentlichen zwei Dinge, welche die Entwicklung entscheidend beeinflußten: das neue Berliner Universitätsgesetz von 1969 und die Förderung der Datenverarbeitung durch die Bundesregierung. Ersteres schuf die hochschulpolitischen Voraussetzungen, letzteres die materielle Grundlage der Studienreform.

Eine konkrete Auswirkung des Universitätsgesetzes war die Bildung von Fachbereichen, die zeitlich mit dem Beginn der Informatik-Förderung zusammenfiel. So war es kein Zufall, daß der Fachbereich Kybernetik entstand, der die Informatik und die wichtigsten ihrer Anwendungsgebiete umfaßt (quantitative Wirtschaftswissenschaften, Automatisierung). In diesem Fachbereich konnte sich die vom Gesetz intendierte Demokratisierung der Universität am ehesten verwirklichen, weil er nicht so stark wie in den meisten anderen Fällen, wo nur Fakultäten in mehrere Fachbereiche aufgeteilt wurden, mit den überkommenen Strukturen belastet war, sondern in vielem neu beginnen mußte. Hinzu kommt eine zweifache Auswirkung der massiven Informatik-Förderung durch die Bundesregierung: Zum einen konnte innerhalb kurzer Zeit eine Reihe von Assistentenstellen mit Hochschulabsolventen besetzt werden, deren Reformvorstellungen und -eifer nicht zuletzt durch die Studentenbewegung in der zweiten Hälfte der 6oer Jahre geprägt worden waren. Zum anderen machte und macht es der schnelle und gleichzeitige Aufbau der Informatik an etwa einem Dutzend Hochschulen schwierig, genügend qualifizierte Hochschullehrer zu finden. Beides führte dazu, daß der Mittelbau den Aufbau des Informatik-Betriebes weitgehend allein zu verantworten hatte. Dieser Vorgang - von manchen das "Berliner bottom-up-Verfahren" genannt - hat andernorts sehr viel Kritik hervorgerufen und zeitweilig sogar zu einer gewissen Isolierung der Berliner Informatik geführt. Hier muß aber hervorgehoben werden, daß gerade diese Art des Aufbaus von unten nach oben der Humus für die Studienreform, für die Ne̲uo̲rdnung des I̲nformatik-S̲tudiums (NORIS) war.

2. Entstehung und Intentionen des neuen Studienplans

Lehrveranstaltungen für einen Studiengang Informatik existieren an der TU Berlin seit dem Frühjahr 1970, wenngleich die zugehörige Prüfungsordnung zu diesem Zeitpunkt vom Senator für Wissenschaft und Kunst noch nicht genehmigt worden war. Studiengang und Prüfungsordnung waren von einer Gemeinsamen Kommission aus Mitgliedern verschiedener Fakultäten vor der Neugliederung der Universität in Fachbereiche erarbeitet worden. Der informatische Kern des Studienplans für das Grundstudium war durch Modifizierung und Erweiterung bereits existierender Lehrveranstaltungen "Programmierung" und "Logischer Entwurf" zustandegekommen. Ferner wurden existierende Lehrveranstaltungen in Mathematik und Elektrotechnik verwendet.

Noch vor der endgültigen Genehmigung der Prüfungsordnung im September 1972 führte eine wachsende Unzufriedenheit mit den Inhalten der Lehrveranstaltungen des Grundstudiums - insbesondere beim Mittelbau - zur Bildung einer Arbeitsgruppe - der NORIS-Gruppe - die einen völlig neuen Studienplan entwarf. Mit diesem Studienplan wurde dann im WS 72/73 der Informatik-Studiengang offiziell eingerichtet. Seit jenem Zeitpunkt existieren zwei Informatik-Prüfungsordnungen (A und B), eine vom Senator stammende (A), die der Rahmenprüfungsordnung Informatik entspricht, und die erwähnte, in der Universität erarbeitete Prüfungsordnung B, deren Einsetzung als Reformversuch auf zunächst zwei Jahre befristet wurde, vgl. [Inf 72]. Seit dem Sommer dieses Jahres kämpft der Fachbereich Kybernetik energisch um eine Verlängerung dieser Reformprüfungsordnung und ihrer Essentials Boolescher Benotung, unbegrenzter Wiederholbarkeit von Prüfungen, Gruppendiplomarbeit. Die Studenten ziehen bis auf vereinzelte Ausnahmen die Prüfungsordnung B vor. Alle folgenden Ausführungen in diesem Bericht beziehen sich auf die Prüfungsordnung B.

Grundlage für die Mitarbeit in der NORIS-Gruppe war für alle Beteiligten zunächst nur die diffuse Unzufriedenheit mit den Inhalten der existierenden Lehrveranstaltungen und der Wunsch, diese Inhalte "informatischer" zu gestalten. Was schließlich als Resultat zahlloser Diskussionen sowie wiederholter Revision von Arbeitspapieren entstand, war ein völlig neu gegliedertes Grundstudium mit ausschließlich neu konzipierten Lehrveranstaltungen, auch in den Bereichen Mathematik und Elektrotechnik. Die Intentionen dieses neuen Grundstudiums können zwar im nachhinein zusammenfassend dargestellt werden - was im folgenden geschehen soll -, dies heißt jedoch nicht, daß sie in voller Klarheit am Anfang der Arbeit der NORIS-Gruppe gestanden hätten; sie wurden vielmehr erst durch den Diskussionsprozeß herauspräpariert.

Zentrales Anliegen des Studienplans für das Grundstudium ist die Vermittlung von Grundlagenwissen der Informatik derart, daß

- begrifflich unabhängige Stoffe nicht unzulässig vermengt, d.h. in einunddieselbe Lehrveranstaltung gepackt werden,
- die Querbeziehungen zwischen den in getrennten Lehrveranstaltungen behandelten Gebieten deutlich gemacht und

- die Bezugspunkte zu Anwendungen, historischer Entwicklung und gesellschaftlichen Implikationen herausgearbeitet werden.

Die Entscheidung für die Beibehaltung eines Grundlagenstudiums bedeutet keine Ablehnung des Projektstudiums, sondern resultiert aus den Zwängen einer bezüglich der Studiengänge konventionell organisierten Hochschule. Wir glauben, daß mit unserem Modell einigen Mißständen des herkömmlichen Grundstudiums erfolgreich begegnet werden kann.

In vielen Bereichen der Kerninformatik greifen rechnerunabhängige und rechnerabhängige Fragen eng ineinander und sind oft nur schwer zu trennen. Dennoch können die zentralen Gebiete Algorithmik und Rechnerorganisation durchaus getrennt voneinander dargestellt werden - und dies ist dem Verständnis sogar förderlich. Elegante Lösungen komplexer Probleme sind ohne eine derartige Trennung undenkbar (Beispiele: Übersetzerbau: Syntaxanalyse - Codegenerierung; Betriebssysteme: Synchronisation - Prozessor-Multiplexing[+]; Ein-/Ausgabe: logische Geräte - physikalische Geräte). Die Trennung von "Informatik-Grundlagen" in Algorithmik und Rechnerorganisation dürfte einen ähnlichen Stellenwert haben wie die der "Mathematik-Grundlagen" (z.B. unter der Bezeichnung "Höhere Mathematik") in Lineare Algebra und Analysis.

Für den eigentlichen Informatik-Kern des Grundstudiums wurden daher zwei Zyklen eingerichtet, "Algorithmen" (4-semestrig), im folgenden "A" abgekürzt, und "Rechnerorganisation" (3-semestrig), abgekürzt "RO". Der Algorithmen-Zyklus ist mit dem "Programming Systems" in der anglo-amerikanischen Computer Science verwandt, wenngleich er mehr auf algorithmisches Denken und strukturierte Programmierung zielt als auf Programmiertechnik im konventionellen Sinn. Die "RO" entspricht in etwa dem "Computer Systems" und umfaßt gleichermaßen Rechnerstrukturen, maschinennahe Programmierung und Elemente der Systemprogrammierung - im Interesse einer integrierten Sicht von Rechnerarchitektur und deren Verfügbarmachung für den Benutzer (zu Programming Systems und Computer Systems vgl. [Den 72]).

Als dritter und letzter Zyklus des Grundstudium-Kerns wurde eine eigene "Mathematik für Informatiker" (4-semestrig), Abkürzung "M", geschaffen. Ein frei wählbares Ergänzungsfach, welches sich im allgemeinen über zwei Semester erstreckt, rundet das Grundstudium ab.

Die Daten des zweiten DV-Programms [DVP 71] machen klar, daß vor allem anwendungsorientierte Informatiker benötigt werden, und ferner, daß die große Mehrheit der Informatiker, ob bei Herstellern oder Anwendern beschäftigt, in keiner Weise mit elektrotechnischen Problemen konfrontiert sein wird. Um dem Rechnung zu tragen, wurde

- ein Alternativstudienplan mit einem umfangreicheren Ergänzungsfach vorgesehen (durch Abwählen von "M IV" und "A IV"),
- eine zweisemestrige "Elektrotechnik und Elektronik für Informatiker" nicht als Pflichtfach, sondern als Ergänzungsfach eingerichtet.

[+] Saltzer spricht in diesem Zusammenhang von "intrinsic" vs. "technological" problems [Sal 66]

Mit den so entstandenen Studienplänen (s. Abschnitt 3) konnte eines der didaktisch-organisatorischen Ziele fast verwirklicht werden:

- den Studenten nicht mehr als drei Lehrveranstaltungen je Semester zuzumuten; lediglich in einem der vier Grundstudiensemester ist eine vierte Lehrveranstaltung notwendig.

Weitere didaktisch-organisatorische Charakteristika des Grundstudiums sind:

- 2 Stunden Tutorium in kleinen Gruppen (1o-2o Teilnehmer) sind Bestandteil jeder Lehrveranstaltung der drei Kernzyklen. Die Arbeit im Tutorium dient nicht so sehr der Behandlung der Übungsaufgaben als vielmehr der gemeinsamen Erarbeitung und Vertiefung von Teilen des Stoffs.
- In "A" und "RO" werden bei allen Lehrveranstaltungen (außer "RO I") praktische Übungen am Rechner durchgeführt.

3. Inhalte der Lehrveranstaltungen

3.1 Algorithmen

Der Algorithmen-Zyklus ist die rechnerunabhängige Komponente des Informatik-Grundstudiums, deren Ziel es ist, das systematische Konstruieren und Formulieren von Algorithmen zu lehren. Unabhängig von der konkreten Stoffauswahl für die einzelnen Semester sind eine Reihe von Prinzipien und Überlegungen für den gesamten Zyklus von großer Bedeutung:

1) Er ist der Methode des strukturierten Programmierens (Dijkstra, Hoare, Wirth) verpflichtet. Das heißt - um diesen beinahe zum Modewort gewordenen Begriff wenigstens schlagwortartig zu umreißen - daß Algorithmen nach der Methode der zunehmenden Verfeinerung (top-down) entwickelt werden. Dabei sind für die verwendeten Prozeduren und Variablen ausdrucksstarke, die intendierte Verwendung charakterisierende Namen zu verwenden (Verbalisierung). Trickreiches Programmieren ist ebenso zu vermeiden wie die Verwendung von Rückwärts-goto's und der undisziplinierte Gebrauch globaler Variablen.

2) Ausgehend von der Einsicht, daß ein erfolgreicher Test nicht die Abwesenheit von Programm-Fehlern sichert, gelangen Korrektheitsbetrachtungen immer stärker in den Vordergrund. Sie sollen daher so weitgehend wie möglich in den A-Zyklus miteinbezogen werden. Dabei wird die Verifikationsmethode (Floyd, Hoare) Anwendung finden und auch - wegen der heute noch weitaus größeren praktischen Bedeutung - das systematische strukturierte Programmieren als Grundlage der Entwicklung von korrekten Programmen aus korrekten Programmen.

3) Von entscheidender Bedeutung ist die Wahl der im A-Zyklus verwendeten Porgrammiersprache(n); denn - so Wirth - "Programmierer operieren oft zeitlebens mit jener Sprache, die sie als erste erlernt haben...Mit der ersten Sprache erlernt man nicht nur ein Vokabular und eine Grammatik, sondern man erschließt sich eine Gedankenwelt". ([Wi 72], S.8) Ohne hier die Gründe näher darlegen zu können, sei gesagt, daß eigent-

lich jede Sprache aus der ALGOL-Familie (ALGOL 60, ALGOL W, SIMULA 67, PASCAL, ALGOL 68) sich als erste Sprache eignet, daß aber jede Assemblersprache, FORTRAN, COBOL oder PL/I ausgeschlossen werden muß.

Die beiden ersten Semester des A-Zyklus behandeln die Grundlagen sequentieller Algorithmen und legen das Schwergewicht auf die Operationsstruktur bei gleichzeitiger Einfachheit der zu manipulierenden Objekte. Demgegenüber stellt das dritte Semester komplexe Datenstrukturen in den Vordergrund , während sich das vierte nichtsequentiellen Algorithmen zuwendet. Vergleicht man den Zyklus mit dem Curriculum 68 [Curr 68], so kann man sagen, daß "A I" und "A II" eine "Teil-Ober-Menge" des Kurses B1 (Introduction to Computing) ist, daß "A III" dem Kurs I1 (Data Structures) entspricht und "A IV" kein Pendant hat.

Algorithmen I (Sequentielle Algorithmen)

Was ist Informatik? Algorithmische Problemlösung. Formulierung von Algorithmen in natürlicher Sprache. Naive Definition des Algorithmus. Übergang zu präziserer Ausdrucksweise: algorithmische Sprache aus der ALGOL-Familie. Elementare Datentypen, Werte, Variablen, Ausdrücke, Zuweisungs-, bedingte, selektive,Wiederholungsanweisungen. Korrektheit von Algorithmen. Syntax, Semantik. Felder. Prozeduren.

Algorithmen II (Sequentielle Algorithmen)

Parametermechanismen. Rekursive Prozeduren. Verschiedene Techniken: numerische Verfahren Sortieren, Suchen; heuristische Methoden. Effizienzanalyse. Einige Aspekte der Implementierung von Programmiersprachen: Syntaxanalyse, Formelübersetzung, Parameterübergabe; Interpreter vs. Compiler.

Algorithmen III (Datenstrukturen)

Typenkonzept für komplexe Strukturen: Aufzählungs-, Teilabschnittstypen, Strukturen, Vereinigungstypen, Potenzmengen, Felder. Operationen auf diesen Typen, Speicherrepräsentation (s. dazu Hoare: "Notes on Data Structuring" in [DDH 72]). Zeiger zum Aufbau verketteter Strukturen. Lineare Listen, Bäume, mehrfach verkettete und zyklische Strukturen. Freispeicherverwaltung und garbage collection. Datenstrukturen auf Hintergrundspeichern. Dünn besetzte Matrizen. Aspekte von software engineering: geschützte Datenstrukturen, au die nur mittels spezieller Algorithmen zugegriffen werden kann. Beispiel einer Listensprache: LISP.

Algorithmen IV (Nichtsequentielle Algorithmen)

Begriff der Nebenläufigkeit. Kommunikation und Synchronisation von nebenläufigen sequentiellen Prozessen. Determiniertheit, deadlocks. Koroutinen und ihre Beziehung zum class-Konzept (SIMULA) und own-Konzept (ALGOL 6o). Sequentialisierung nichtsequentieller Algorithmen mittels Koroutinen. Datenstrukturen mit synchronisierten Zugriffsalgorithmen. Verwendete Sprache ist SIMULA. Literatur: [Dij 65]; Teil III aus [DDH 72]; Kapitel 3 und 7 aus [BrHa 73].

3.2 Rechnerorganisation

Verständnis für die Funktionsweise von Rechnern zu vermitteln ist die Aufgabe dieses Zyklus. Neben der funktionellen Beschreibung der Hardware werden auch die Probleme von deren Nutzbarmachung berücksichtigt: Techniken der maschinenorientierten Programmierung, Nahtstellen zwischen Hardware und Betriebs-Software. Durch die integrierte Darstellung von Hardware und ihrer Programmierung soll der häufig sichtbaren Barriere zwischen dem Hardware- und dem Software-Spezialisten entgegengewirkt werden.

Ein Vergleich mit dem Curriculum 68 ist nicht leicht. Der gesamte Zyklus enthält in etwa den Stoff der Kurse B2 (Computers and Programming), I3 (Computer Organisation) und Teile von I4 (Systems Programming), allerdings in anderer Anordnung.

Rechnerorganisation I (Rechnerstrukturen)

Struktur des klassischen Universalrechners (Steuerwerk, Rechenwerk, Arbeitsspeicher, E/A-Werk). Zahlensysteme, Codes. Boolesche Algebra (soweit sie im folgenden gebraucht und nicht in "M I" behandelt wird). Schaltnetze als Realisierung Boolescher Funktionen; Minimierung (algebraisch, graphisch, algorithmisch); Schaltnetze in Rechenanlagen (Addierer, Code-Umsetzer u.ä.). Schaltwerke als rückgekoppelte Schaltnetze; Beschreibungsmethoden (Übergangsfunktionen, -diagramme, -matrizen); asynchrone und synchrone Schaltwerke; verschiedene Flipflop-Typen; Aufbau komplexerer Schaltwerke, wie sie in Rechenanlagen verwendet werden (Zähler, Register, Multiplizierer u.ä.).

Rechnerorganisation II (Maschinenorientierte Programmierung)

Rechnerarchitektur: Instruktionen, Register, Arbeitsspeicher, Adressierung. Assembler-Programmierung, Debug-Techniken. Unterprogrammtechnik, Parameterübergabe. Externe Bezugnahmen, Binden als Nachübersetzen. Makroinstruktionen.

Rechnerorganisation III (Mehrbenutzersysteme)

Vertiefung der maschinenorientierten Programmierung: Binden und Laden. reusable code, reentrant code, rekursive Routinen. Rechnersysteme: Funktionsweise von Arbeitsspeicher und Peripheriegeräten. Zusammenwirken von Zentraleinheit und Peripherie. Beispiele für typische Rechnerkonfigurationen. Elemente der Betriebs-Software und der zugehörigen Hardware-Eigenschaften: Betriebsarten (Stapel-, Teilnehmerbetrieb u.a.), Multiprogramming. Speicherschutz und Speicherverwaltung. Privilegierte Instruktionen, Unterbrechungen und Unterbrechungsbehandlungen. Virtueller Speicher. Datei-Systeme. Neuere Rechnerstrukturen und -systeme: stack architecture, array processing. Mehrfach-Systeme und Verbund-Systeme.

3.3 Mathematik für Informatiker

Die Konzeption eines Zyklus Mathematik, der speziell auf Informatiker ausgerichtet ist hat erhebliche Schwierigkeiten bereitet, weil anzustreben war, daß sich in den vier Lehrveranstaltungen nicht unsystematisch Stoff aus mathematischen Theorien ansammelt, sondern ein informatisch motivierter roter Faden stets auffindbar bleiben sollte, andererseits eine Übernahme von "klassischen" Mathematik-Lehrveranstaltungen aber nicht möglich war, wollte man das Ziel einer Mathematik für Informatiker nicht aufgeben.

Es ist naheliegend, den Zyklus mit einer Einführung in die strukturelle Mathematik zu beginnen, die den Studienanfänger über die Kenntnisse der Oberschule hinaus mit den Begriffsbildungen struktureller Mathematik vertraut machen will und die dem Inhalt nach in etwa dem Kurs B3 des Curriculums 68 entspricht, und im zweiten Semester eine weitere Lehrveranstaltung über strukturelle Mathematik folgen zu lassen. Wenn aber gesichert sein soll, daß im 3. Semester Elektronik und Elektrotechnik als Ergänzungsfach gewählt werden kann für eine spätere Hardware-Spezialisierung und daß numerische Mathematik innerhalb des Grundstudiums wählbar bleibt, so sind im ersten oder zweiten Semester Analysis und Differentialgleichungen anzubieten. Eine Analysis-Veranstaltung dient darüberhinaus als Klammer, die dem Zerfallen des Mathematik-Zyklus in Teilchen entgegenwirkt, dadurch daß hier eine mathematische Theorie als ganze vorgeführt wird, wobei dann allerdings ein informatischer roter Faden nicht sichtbar wird.

Da zwei parallele Mathematik-Veranstaltungen (Analysis, strukturelle Mathematik) neben zwei Informatik-Lehrveranstaltungen in einem Grundstudium-Semester für Studenten eine zu hohe Arbeitsbelastung mit schlechten Lernerfolgen bedeuten, blieb nur die willkürlich anmutende Lösung, die strukturelle Mathematik in "M I" und "M IV" zu zerlegen, als "M II" Analysis zu betreiben und Differentialgleichungen in "M III" zu behandeln.

<u>Mathematik für Informatiker I</u> (Strukturelle Mathematik)

Mengenlehre; Relationen und Abbildungen. Elemente der Aussagenlogik, Beweistechniken (insbesondere Induktion). Behandlung der Mengenoperationen und der Wahrheitsfunktionen als Operationen in Booleschen Algebren. Ordnungsrelationen. Verhältnis Zerlegungen und Äquivalenzrelationen. Strukturierte Mengen und ihre Morphismen. Formale Sprachen: Erzeugbarkeit (CFL) und Erkennbarkeit (endl. Automat).

<u>Mathematik für Informatiker II</u> (Analysis)

Differential- und Integralrechnung einer reellen Variablen bis zum Hauptsatz:
  Aufbau der reellen Zahlen, Folgen, Reihen, Konvergenz, Stetigkeit, Differenzierbarkeit, Integrierbarkeit; und falls möglich: Eigenschaften der elementaren Funktionen, Potenzreihen, Reihenentwicklung, relative Extrema, numerische Integration.

<u>Mathematik für Informatiker III</u> (Analysis)

Erweiterung der Analysis-Kenntnisse in drei Richtungen:
- Übertragung der Begriffe der Analysis wie Konvergenz etc. auf die komplexen Zahlen.
- $\mathbb{R}^n$ als Vektorraum (lineare Abbildungen, Matrizen, Determinanten, lineare Gleichungssysteme) und Differentialrechnung im $\mathbb{R}^n$
- gewöhnliche Differentialgleichungen

Mathematik für Informatiker IV (Strukturen und Prozesse)

Organisierendes Prinzip eines Teils dieser Lehrveranstaltung ist die Möglichkeit, "Computations" als Prozesse zu beschreiben (d.h. als Folgen von Zustandsübergängen).

Graphen, Verbände, Kombinatorik, Wahrscheinlichkeitstheorie. Prozesse: gerichtete markierte Graphen; deterministische, nondeterministische, stochastische Automaten; Markoffsche Ketten.

4. Querbeziehungen zwischen den Lehrveranstaltungen

In der Abbildung des Studienplans sind einige Querbeziehungen zwischen den Lehrveranstaltungen kenntlich gemacht. Dabei fällt vor allem zweierlei auf:

- die (intendierte) Beziehungslosigkeit von "Algorithmen" und "RO" im 1. Semester, die im 2. und 3. Semester von einer starken Interdependenz abgelöst wird;
- der (bedauerlich) geringe Zusammenhang der Analysis mit den übrigen Lehrveranstaltungen.

Auf einige uns wichtig erscheinende Querbeziehungen wollen wir im folgenden näher eingehen. Da ist zunächst die Beziehung zwischen Schaltalgebra einerseits und Aussagenlogik u. Boolescher Algebra andererseits. Ihre besondere Bedeutung liegt darin, daß die Studenten hier sehr frühzeitig einen Fall unmittelbarer Anwendbarkeit von Mathematik bzw. (umgekehrt) ein Beispiel für die Formalisierung von sehr praktischen Sachverhalten kennenlernen. Dies vermag die Motivation für den M-Zyklus, um die es ohnehin schlecht bestellt ist, zu fördern. Anzustreben ist hier der folgende Zugang: man wird die Schaltalgebra in "RO I" soweit wie für die Praxis unmittelbar notwendig (aber durchaus mathematisch präzise) einführen, um sie anschließend in "M I" aufzugreifen und weiterzuentwickeln. – Ein entsprechendes Vorgehen ist für den Komlex BNF-Syntax/CF-Sprachen möglich.

Wenn in "M I" besonderer Wert gelegt wird auf das Herausarbeiten der Elemente der Beweistechnik (Was ist ein Beweis? Definition und Beweis durch vollständige Induktion), so findet dieses Bemühen in "A II" Anschauungsmaterial: der Unterschied zwischen Testen (mit Einzelbeispielen) und Beweisen wird verdeutlicht, und es wird problematisiert, daß Algorithmen eines Korrektheitsbeweises bedürfen. Die Verifikationsmethode verwendet Logik und vollständige Induktion (Schleifeninvariante). Für die Entwicklung von a priori korrekten Programmen durch strukturierte Programmierung ist ein Beweis vonnöten, daß bei schrittweiser Verfeinerung die Korrektheit erhalten bleibt.

Im 2. Semester können die Zweige "A" und "RO" erstmalig zusammengeführt werden. Einerseits kann an elementaren Beispielen die Problematik der Sprachübersetzung verdeutlicht werden (Anwendung von Rechnern zur Ausführung von Algorithmen), andererseits erweisen sich algorithmische Sprachen als hilfreich zur Vorformulierung von Maschinenprogrammen, die man von Hand erstellen will (Anwendung der Algorithmik zur Beschreibung von Programmen). Der Begriff der abstrakten Maschine schließt dann die Lücke zwischen Algorithmen

Sem.	Algorithmen	Rechnerorganisation	Mathematik f. Informatiker	Ergänzungsfächer	SWSt
1. (WS)	Sequent.Algorithmen, 6 Std. BNF-Syntax	Rechnerstrukturen, 4 Std. Schaltalgebra	Strukturelle Mathem., 6 Std. Aussagenlogik, Boolesch.Alg. CF-Sprachen Vollst. Induktion Graphen		16
2. (SS)	Sequent.Algorithmen, 4 Std. Korrektheitsbeweise Übersetzung Parameterübergabe Rekursion Sprachen	Maschinenorient.Prog., 6 Std. Maschinencode Anschlußkonventionen Makros	Analysis, 6 Std. Diff.u.Integralrechnung		16
3. (WS)	Datenstrukturen, 4 Std. Verkettete Strukturen Speicherverwaltung: Keller Speicherverwaltung: Halde Dateisysteme	Mehrbenutzersysteme, 4 Std. reentrant code Systemoptimierung Speicherverwaltung(Segm.) Prozesse	Analysis, 6 Std. Differentialgleichungen	E-Technik u. Elektronik, 6 Std. zeitveränderliche elektrische Größen	20
4. (SS)	Nichtsequ.Algorithm., 4 Std. Prozesse		Strukturen u.Prozesse, 6 Std. Prozesse	E-Technik u. Elektronik, 6 Std. zeitveränderliche elektrische Größen	16
				Summe:	68

STUDIENPLAN des Grundstudiums (mit Querbeziehungen) in einer "Kern-Informatik"-Variante. Der stark umrandete Block ist obligatorisch (46 Std.). Ferner müssen Lehrveranstaltungen in Ergänzungsfächern freier Wahl belegt werden (22 Std.).

und Rechnerorganisation. - Wichtige Anknüpfungspunkte zwischen den Lehrveranstaltungen sind im einzelnen:

- Übersetzung von einfachen Sprachelementen: Formeln, indizierte Variable, bedingte Anweisung, Laufanweisung.
- Kontrollstrukturen bei höheren und niedrigen Sprachen (z.B. ALGOL - FORTRAN - Assembler).
- Bedeutung der Makrotechnik.
- Implementierung der Parameterübergabe in den Fällen call by reference und call by value.

Um die Bezüge zu vertiefen, sollte eine größere Programmieraufgabe von den beiden beteiligten Dozenten gemeinsam entworfen und für beide Lehrveranstaltungen angerechnet werden (Beispiel: Entwurf von Makros zur Realisierung einiger FORTRAN-Statements).

Die Probleme der Implementierung höherer Sprachen werden auch zu Beginn von "RO III" berührt. Nach der Behandlung von dynamischer Speicherverwaltung (Keller) und reentrant code sollte darüber, was sich zur Laufzeit eines ALGOL- bzw. FORTRAN-Programms abspielt, weitgehend Klarheit bestehen. Als Abrundung bietet sich die Behandlung des Bindens von Moduln mit verschiedenen Quellensprachen an (Beispiel: Codeprozeduren). - Der Kontakt zwischen "A" und "RO" wird im 3. Semester weiter gepflegt bei den folgenden Themen:

- Gestreute Speicherverwaltung, sowohl durch das auf der Halde operierende Laufzeitsystem als auch durch das Betriebssystem bei der Verwaltung von Segmenten im Arbeitsspeicher und auf Hintergrundspeichern;
- Datenstrukturen auf Hintergrundspeichern (Dateisysteme, Datenbanksysteme).

In "RO III" taucht zum ersten Mal der Prozeßbegriff auf, der dann im 4. Semester in "A" und "M" ausführlicher behandelt wird. Die Querbeziehungen (über den Prozeßbegriff) zwischen "A IV" und "M IV" sind von zweifacher Art:

- intuitiver Begriff des "sequentiellen Prozesses" und elementare Formalisierungen dieses Begriffs.
- die Halbordnung als elementarste Formalisierung des Begriffs "nichtsequentieller Prozeß" (Bezug zu Verbänden und Netzplänen).

Die Analysis bleibt im Grundstudium leider ein Fremdkörper, insbesondere für denjenigen, der nicht "Elektrotechnik und Elektronik" hört. Beziehungen ergeben sich in der Tat erst zu Lehrveranstaltungen des Hauptstudiums, so daß die Mathematik in diesem Teil (Analysis) für die Studenten ein typisches Grundlagenfach bleibt ("Ihr werdet es später brauchen!").

5. Der erste Durchgang

Erwartungsgemäß förderten die ersten vier NORIS-Semester (WS 72/73 bis SS 74) eine Reihe von Problemen zutage, von denen einige als typische Anfangsschwierigkeiten bezeichnet werden müssen, während andere durchaus Anlaß zu Konzeptänderungen geben. Im folgenden sollen - unter Verzicht auf mancherlei, oftmals nur dem Insider verständliche Details - die wichtigsten Problembereiche skizziert werden.

1. Die angestrebte Herausarbeitung der Querbeziehungen zwischen den parallelen Zyklen konnte nicht geleistet werden. Die Querbeziehungen lagen zwar vor, jedoch fand keinerlei Synchronisation zwischen den Lehrveranstaltungen statt, von gemeinsamen Übungsaufgaben gar nicht zu reden. Das lag vor allem daran, daß beim ersten Durchgang die Dozenten mangels ausgearbeiteten Materials das Hauptgewicht jeweils auf die Entwicklung ihrer eigenen Lehrveranstaltung und die Erstellung von Skripten legen mußten.

2. Es zeigte sich die paradoxe Situation, daß im Informatik-Grundstudium der Mathematik-Zyklus die meisten Schwierigkeiten bereitet. Erst jetzt ist seine Durchführung beim Fachbereich Mathematik organisatorisch gesichert, während er bislang von Informatikern durchgeführt wurde, und manches Mal die Frage, ob er überhaupt stattfinden würde, weit vor den inhaltlichen Fragen rangierte. Darin ist natürlich auch ein entscheidendes Hemmnis für die im vorigen Absatz angesprochene Kooperation zu sehen. Vor allem aber ist die Gestaltung einer Mathematik für Informatiker ein nicht nur in Berlin ungelöstes Problem.

3. Der Leser, der im 2. Abschnitt erfahren hat, daß eine wesentliche Triebfeder für die grundlegende Umgestaltung des Grundstudiums Unzufriedenheit mit existierenden Lehrveranstaltungen war, wird sich fragen, wie denn die Durchführung des NORIS-Konzepts ohne oder gar gegen jene Teile des Lehrkörpers möglich war, welche die Opposition auf den Plan gerufen hatten. Es ging in der Tat nicht ohne Reibungsverluste ab. Da war zunächst einmal der "Sprachenstreit", bei dem es um die Frage ging, ob PL/I als erste Programmiersprache geeignet sei. Der NORIS-Kreis hat dazu nicht nur in einer sorgfältig begründeten Stellungnahme gegen PL/I und für eine Sprache der ALGOL-Familie Position bezogen (s. dazu FB 2o INFO, Nr. 11, Okt. 1973), sondern sich schließlich, als deutlich wurde, daß von der Gegenseite kein Einlenken zu erwarten war, gezwungen gesehen, in "A I" und "A II" Alternativveranstaltungen anzubieten. Diese Belastung des Lehrkörpers, der sich ohnehin in einer schwierigen Lage befand, wurde noch verschlimmert, als auch noch wegen der absoluten Kooperationsunwilligkeit eines weiteren Hochschullehrers Alternativveranstaltungen in "RO" erforderlich wurden. Dem Außenstehenden mag die Konsequenz, mit der diese Auseinandersetzungen geführt wurden, unverständlich erscheinen, aber er möge sich klarmachen, daß das NORIS-Konzept zur Makulatur geworden wäre, wenn man seiner Durchlöcherung gerade in der Anfangsphase der Realisierung nicht Widerstand entgegengesetzt hätte.

4. Ein entscheidendes Problem jeder Informatik-Ausbildung, nämlich das der Anwendungsfächer, ist auch während der ersten beiden NORIS-Jahre immer deutlicher hervorgetreten. Nicht nur, daß das dritte Semester, in dem mittels der Ergänzungsfächer der Zugang zu den Anwendungen erschlossen werden soll, so sehr mit Veranstaltungen der Kerninformatik ausgefüllt ist, daß den Studenten für andere Dinge kaum noch Arbeitskapazität zur Verfügung steht, sondern es ist auch deutlich geworden, daß es an einer wohlkonzipierten Palette verschiedenster Anwendungsfächer fehlt. Die Bereitstellung eines einigermaßen brauchbar strkturierten wirtschaftswissenschaftlichen Ergänzungsfachs ist nicht viel mehr als ein bescheidener Anfang.

5. Und schließlich muß konstatiert werden, daß eine ganz wesentliche Zielsetzung des NORIS-Konzepts - die Einbeziehung der gesellschaftlichen Implikationen der Informatik in das Studium - praktisch nicht eingelöst werden konnte. Von wenigen bescheidenen Versuchen abgesehen, derartige Fragestellungen in einer Fachveranstaltung zu reflektieren, muß dieser Anspruch nach wie vor als Wechsel, gezogen auf die Zukunft, angesehen werden. Wir werden auf die Ursachen dafür im Abschnitt 6 noch eingehen.

Die Aufnahme des neuen Studiengangs durch die Studenten war und ist uneinheitlich. Die trotz der insgesamt "nur" 68 Semesterwochenstunden von Anfang an geübte und auch heute noch fortdauernde Kritik wegen der zu großen Stoffülle scheint nur für das 3. Semester berechtigt zu sein (vier Lehrveranstaltungen parallel). Die Einrichtung der Tutorien wird allgemein begrüßt, jedoch ist es nur in wenigen Fällen gelungen, dort einen für die ganze Gruppe produktiven Arbeitsstil zu finden; manche Tutorengruppen sterben gegen Semesterende ganz aus.

Die Programmierübungen am Rechner werden teils als motivierend, teils als lästig empfunden. Letzteres ist zum Teil auf technisch-organisatorische Schwierigkeiten beim Umgang mit dem Rechner zurückzuführen, denen durch geeignete Vorbereitung abgeholfen werden kann. Manchmal waren die Programmieraufgaben auch zu umfangreich.

6. Konsequenzen

Die NORIS-Gruppe ist nach Einrichtung des neuen Studiengangs nicht auseinandergegangen, sondern hat in regelmäßigen Treffen die bei der Realisierung auftretenden inhaltlichen und organisatorischen Probleme beraten. Eine Weiterentwicklung des Grundstudienplans ist beabsichtigt, jedoch sind Einzelheiten noch nicht diskutiert. Einige Tendenzen sollen nun im folgenden dargestellt werden.

Nachdem nun im ersten Durchgang die meisten der Lehrveranstaltungen "stehen", dürfte sich die Zusammenarbeit der Dozenten zur Förderung der Querbezüge unter den LV stärken. Darüberhinaus ist anzustreben, möglichst alle Dozenten mit der Durchführung aller Grundstudium-Veranstaltungen zu betrauen. Es wird dadurch verhindert, daß vonseiten des Hauptstudiums unrealistische Forderungen an die Stoffauswahl des Grundstudiums herangetragen werden. Außerdem wird die von allen erwünschte gemeinsam akzeptierte und entwickelte Konzeption des Informatik-Grundstudiums am sichersten erreicht, wenn jeder Dozent sein Urteil bildet und sich nicht auf die "A-Dozenten", "RO-Dozenten" oder "M-Dozenten" verlassen muß. Ob das in naher Zukunft realisierbar wird, bleibt abzuwarten.

Der Mathematik-Zyklus muß erneut als ganzer zur Diskussion gestellt werden, da es nicht zu einer einheitlichen Konzeption gekommen ist. Dieses Ziel ist kaum zu erreichen, trotzdem könnte man zur Förderung der Querbezüge gewisse Leitmotive in die Mathematik einbauen, z.B. den Gegensatz zwischen (math.) Existenz und Konstruierbarkeit. Ferner ist eine inhaltliche Variante diskutierbar, nämlich Kombinatorik und diskrete Wahrscheinlichkeitsrechnung in das erste Drittel von "M II" zu verlegen und die Analysis so nach hinten zu verschieben, daß die Differentialgleichungen in "M III" gestrichen werden. Damit werden neue Bezüge zu "A II", "A III" und "RO III" möglich (Effizienzbetrachtungen),

aber die Elektrotechnik des Ergänzungsfachs wird schwerer wählbar.
Im Algorithmen-Zyklus ist das 3. Semester stofflich überfüllt und das 4. Semester
bringt mit nichtsequentiellen Algorithmen u.E. Hauptstudium-Stoff, so daß sich anbietet, "A III" auszudünnen und die überzähligen Themen in "A IV" anzusiedeln zusammen mit
Prinzipien des software engineering soweit sie rechnerunabhängig formulierbar sind.
"Nichtsequentielle Algorithmen" würde dann Hauptstudium-Veranstaltung.
Diese Maßnahme erleichtert das 3. Semester, das mit vier Lehrveranstaltungen eine starke Belastung für die Studenten darstellt. Eine Reduktion der vier LV zu nur drei parallelen scheint nicht möglich, so daß den Studenten bis auf weiteres dieser Stress zugemutet werden muß.
In "RO" kommt die Darstellung des funktionellen Aufbaus der Hardware zu kurz, so daß möglicherweise eine "RO IV" konzipiert werden könnte.
Das Problem des unzureichenden Lehrangebots in den Anwendungsfächern kann nicht am grünen Tisch gelöst werden. Eine Lösung ist nur von einer weiteren Entwicklung der anwendungsorientierten Einheiten innerhalb des Fachbereichs zu erwarten.

Abschließend soll anhand einer pragmatischen Einschätzung, was Studienreform sein sollte, der Stellenwert von NORIS etwas genauer bestimmt werden. Eine Reform des herkömmlichen Studiums muß mindestens umfassen:

> (i) Verbindung von "Fach"studium und Studium der gesellschaftlichen Auswirkungen in <u>einem</u> Studium(der Informatik),
>
> (ii) Anpassung des Stoffs an Berufsanforderungen,
>
> (iii) Reform des Prüfungswesens,
>
> (iv) Reform der Lehr- und Lernformen,
>
> (v) Bewältigung der Stoffülle.

Im NORIS-Papier (vgl.[NOR 72]) sind (i), (ii), (iv) und (v) thematisiert und ihre Einlösung als Aufgabe gestellt. Im vorliegenden Papier ist hauptsächlich über (v) berichtet worden, weil dort die meisten Fortschritte erzielt sind. In (ii) sind die wenigen verwertbaren Informationen, die überhaupt über die Berufssituation zu erhalten waren, eingeflossen. Im Abschn. 5.5 ist schon dargelegt, daß (i) nicht erzielt worden ist. Es wird sehr schwer sein, Fortschritte in (i) zu erreichen, weil die totale Ausklammerung der gesellschaftlichen Implikationen aus den math.-naturwiss.-technischen Studiengängen der Hochschulen ein Verständnis von Wissenschaft bei Dozenten und Studenten geprägt hat, welches, wenn überhaupt, nur langsam in Richtung auf (i) zu verändern ist. Die Frage,wie weitgehend und in welchen Zeiträumen diese Trennung aufgehoben werden kann, bedürfte einer eingehenden Analyse, die hier nicht geleistet werden kann.

Der vorliegende Bericht wurde verfaßt von Eberhard Bergmann, FG Programmiersprachen u. Compiler I, außer der Einleitung; Ernst Denert, FG Automatentheorie und Formale Sprachen; Klaus-Peter Löhr, FG Betriebssysteme. Wir betonen jedoch, daß die eigentliche Sustanz dieses Papiers nicht einzelnen Personen, sondern der NORIS-<u>Gruppe</u> zu verdanken ist.

Literatur

[BrHa 73]   Brinch Hansen, O., Operating System Principles, Prentice Hall, 1973

[Curr 68]   Curriculum 68, Recommendations for Academic Programs in Computer Science, CACM Vol. 11, No.3, March 1968, pp. 151-197

[DDH 72]   Dahl, Dijkstra, Hoare, Structured Programming, Academic Press, 1972

[Den 72]   Dennis, P.J., Operating systems principles and undergraduate computer science curricula, SJCC 72, pp. 849-855

[Dij 65]   Dijkstra, E.W., Cooperating Sequential Processes, Report EWD 123 Techn.Univ. Eindhoven 1965

[DVP 71]   Zweites Datenverarbeitungsprogramm der Bundesregierung, Bonn 1971

[Inf 72]   Bergmann, Eggers, Spiller, Weber, Informatik an der TUB, in TUB, Zeitschrift für die TUB, 4 Heft 3 (1972)

[NOR 72]   Neuordnung des Informatik-Studiums (NORIS), in: Info 2o, Informations- und Diskussionsblatt für die Mitglieder des FB 2o der TUB, Nr. 1, 1972

[PTT 72]   Programming Teaching Techniques, W.M. Turski (ed), Proceedings of the IFIP TC-2 Working Conference on Programming Teaching Techniques, Zakopane, Poland, Sept. 1972

[Sal 66]   Saltzer, J.H., Traffic Control in Multiplexed Computer Systems, Sc.D. Thesis, Project MAC, MIT, 1966

[Wi 72]   Wirth, N., Systematisches Programmieren, Teubner Studienbücher Informatik, 1972

Informatik an allgemeinbildenden Schulen

Überlegungen zur Gestaltung von Unterrichtsinhalten
und Erfahrungen bei der Organisation des Unterrichts

U. Bosler, W. Bookhagen, O. Hecker, W. Koch, O. Rabus

Zusammenfassung: Es wird ein Konzept für den Informatik-Unterricht an allgemeinbildenden Schulen dargelegt, das Algorithmik in den Vordergrund stellt und über die Arbeit des "Berliner Arbeitskreises für Informatik in der Schule" berichtet.

1. Die Arbeitsgruppe

Die Einführung der Informatik als Unterrichtsgegenstand in allgemeinbildenden Schulen wird auch in der Bundesrepublik seit geraumer Zeit gefordert. In einigen Ländern laufen Unterrichtsprojekte. Eine allgemein akzeptierte Begründung für Informatik als Schulfach steht noch aus. Wegen der mangelnden Unterrichtserfahrungen sind Curricula oder wenigstens Lernzielkataloge und Unterrichtsmaterialien für die Hand des Lehrers kaum entwickelt.

Der Berliner "Arbeitskreis für Informatik in der Schule" besteht seit Februar 1973. Er sieht seine Aufgabe darin, in enger Zusammenarbeit von Schule und Universität, Informatik-Unterricht in Berliner Schulen zu ermöglichen und auszubauen, um schließlich die eingangs geschilderte Situation verbessern zu helfen. Die Arbeitsgruppe ist eine Interessengemeinschaft, der z.Zt. nicht nur etwa 10 Mitglieder des Fachbereichs Kybernetik der TU Berlin angehören, die teilweise selbst Unterricht in der Schule erteilen, sondern auch ca. 12 Lehrer Berliner Oberschulen.

Die Zielsetzungen der Arbeitsgruppe sind:

1) Äußere Organisation:
   Bereitstellung von Rechnerkapazität (vorerst nur durch die TU Berlin),
   Beratung beim Rechnerzugang und der Organisation der Programmherstellung.
2) Entwicklung und Erprobung eines einheitlichen Konzepts.
3) Entwicklung von Lernziel-Katalogen, Bereitstellung von Unterrichtsmaterial und exemplarische Planung von Unterrichtseinheiten.
4) Organisation bzw. Reorganisation der Lehrerfort- und Weiterbildung in Informatik.
5) Initiierung und Ausbau der Zusammenarbeit mit Institutionen, die die Entwicklung des Informatik-Unterrichts fachlich und organisatorisch unterstützen, wie staatliche Stellen und Forschungsinstitutionen.

2. Informatik als Unterrichtsfach

2.1. Argumente für Informatik in der Schule.

1.Begründung: Vorteile der Algorithmik im Unterricht.

Die zentrale Methodik der Informatik, nämlich die algorithmische Denkweise zusammen mit strukturierter Problemlösung, soll für das Folgende als Algorithmik bezeichnet werden. Algorithmik war schon immer eine Voraussetzung für wissenschaftliches Arbeiten in naturwissenschaftlichen und technischen Disziplinen. Zumindest hier ist daher algorithmisches Denken fundamental. Daß dies für andere Bereiche ohne weiteres ebenfalls gilt, wird hier nicht behauptet. Für Fächer aus den Sozialwissenschaften etwa ist möglicherweise algorithmisches Denken nützlich aber nicht fundamental.

Die Entwicklung von DV-Anlagen als Werkzeug zur automatischen Ausführung von Algorithmen hat eine systematische, direkt vom Problem ableitbare strukturierte Formulierung von Algorithmen gefördert und weitgehend erzwungen. Denn DV-Anlagen erlauben die Lösung von Aufgaben hohen Komplexitätsgrades, der wiederum erhöhte Denkökonomie beim Entwurf zugehöriger Algorithmen erzwingt. Dies betrifft die Verwendung angemessener sogenannter "problemorientierter" Beschreibungsmittel ebenso wie die Technik der sinnvollen Benutzung vorgefertigter Bausteine und die Vorgehensweise beim Entwurf eines Algorithmus, etwa durch die Methode der schrittweisen Verfeinerung bis zu Teilalgorithmen, die im jeweiligen Kontext als primitiv anzusehen sind.

Im Informatik-Unterricht werden geistige Fähigkeiten wie "dynamische" Denkweise, Verbalisierung, Abstraktion, Verallgemeinerung, Erkennen und Übertragen von Strukturen entwickelt und gefördert. Die Klassifizierung von Daten und Methoden wird genau so systematisch geschult und verbessert wie die Qualitäten exakte Planung, Modellbildung, Selbständigkeit und Aktivität.

Die Benutzung des Rechners führt zur Erhöhung der Motivation und zur realen Einschätzung der eigenen Arbeit. Der Unterricht enthält durch diese Erfolgskontrolle und unmittelbare Rückkopplung auf die Herstellung von Algorithmen eine neue Komponente, die andere Schulfächer im allgemeinen in weit geringerem Maße fördern.

Notwendige Bedingungen für erfolgreichen Algorithmik-Unterricht sind die folgenden Werkzeuge:

- ein Rechner hinreichender Größe
- eine nicht nur algorithmisches Denken sondern auch strukturierte Programmierung unterstützende Programmiersprache.

2.Begründung: DV als gesellschaftsbestimmende Erscheinung.

Das Eindringen der Anwendungen der DV in immer neue Bereiche des täglichen Lebens sehen wir ebenfalls als entscheidenden Grund für die Notwendigkeit des Informatik-Unterrichts an. Es geht dabei nicht um Ausbildung von Informatikern oder DV-Praktikern, d.h. um eine Berufsausbildung im engeren Sinn. Vielmehr ist es Aufgabe der allgemeinbildenden Schule, Voraussetzungen zu schaffen nicht nur für das Verständnis des Aufbaues und der Funktionsweise von DV- Anlagen und ihres Einsatzes, sondern auch der gesellschaftlichen Auswirkungen dieses Einsatzes. Daraus folgt, daß neben Algorithmik als dem zentralen Thema des Informatik-Unterrichts andere Teilgebiete der Informatik zu behandeln sind, wie gesellschaftliche Konsequenzen des Computereinsatzes, äußere Organisation, spezielle Programmiersprachen und ihre Verwendung, Aufbau und Wirkungsweise von Computern und die logischen und technischen Grundlagen.

2.2. Informatik als eigenes Unterrichtsfach.

Informatik-Unterricht im eben beschriebenen Umfang sprengt naturgemäß den Rahmen eines Faches, dem Informatik zuzuordnen wäre.

Beschränkt man sich auf Algorithmik als Methode verbunden mit Rechnerbenutzung und Verwendung einer Programmiersprache, so wird gelegentlich davon gesprochen, Algorithmik in denjenigen Fachunterricht einzubauen, in dem algorithmisch lösbare Aufgaben vorkommen und auf die Eigenständigkeit des Algorithmik-Unterrichts zu verzichten. Der zugrundeliegende Gedanke ist zu begrüßen. Guter Algorithmik-Unterricht lebt von der Vielseitigkeit der Aufgaben und ist von vornherein fächerübergreifend. Deshalb ist eine ausschließliche Zuordnung zu nur einem Fach, insbesondere zur Mathematik oder Physik zu vermeiden. Denn einseitige Zuordnung verhindert gerade die Darstellung der Vielseitigkeit der Anwendungen. Aber wegen schulischer Randbedingungen halten wir zum gegenwärtigen Zeitpunkt eine völlige Eingliederung in relevanten Fachunterricht für unrealistisch. Gründe dafür sind:

a) Algorithmik als Methode sollte zunächst im eigenen Fachunterricht entwickelt und danach als Werkzeug für spätere Verwendung in anderen Fächern bereitgestellt werden. Diese Eingliederung wird auch neue Fachdidaktiken erfordern. Es sollte auf jeden Fall darauf geachtet werden, daß nicht eine Verselbständigung des Algorithmik-Unterrichts eintritt, die keine Auswirkungen auf andere Fächer hat.

b) Lehrer sind für den Informatik-Unterricht unzureichend ausgebildet. Die wenigen Lehrer, die Informatik-Kurse betreiben sind z.Zt. ausschließlich Mathematiker oder Physiker.

c) Fachlehrer sind mangelnd informiert über die Methodik und den Rechnereinsatz und haben unzureichende Möglichkeiten der Weiterbildung.

3. Methodik

Im Weiteren wird vom gesamten Spektrum des Informatik-Unterrichts nur die Algorithmik als Methode mit Rechnereinsatz und Benutzung einer Programmiersprache behandelt.

Wir sind der Meinung, daß die Algorithmik entsprechend ihrer zentralen Stellung innerhalb der Informatik am Anfang des Informatik-Unterrichts stehen sollte. Algorithmische Denkweise und damit ein Verständnis für Lösungen einer möglichst großen Problemklasse sollte mit Hilfe einer minimalen Anzahl vernünftiger Kontroll- und Datenstrukturen eingeführt werden, die sich unmittelbar mit Hilfe von Konstruktionen der Muttersprache ausdrücken lassen. Anschließend sind aus den oben angeführten didaktischen Gründen Programmiersprache und Rechner unverzichtbare Werkzeuge. Von den z.Zt. existierenden Programmiersprachen sind wenige für den Schuleinsatz geeignet. Wir haben uns für eine Teilmenge von ALGOL 60 entschieden. Wir halten es für falsch in dieser Phase allzu genau auf die Erklärung der Maschine, selbst ihrer funktionellen Bestandteile und prinzipiellen Organisation einzugehen.

Wir sind für den folgenden Weg: Zunächst die Darstellung der Methodik mit dem Rechner als Werkzeug, später Vermittlung des prinzipiellen Rechneraufbaus; schließlich ist nach Bereitstellung der nötigen Kenntnisse aus Mathematik und Technik der Rechner selbst Gegenstand der Untersuchung und ein vorhandenes Gerät dient der Demonstration einer möglichen Realisierung. Wir sehen für diese Entscheidung folgende Gründe:

1) Unter dem Gesichtspunkt, daß die algorithmische Problemlösung Hauptziel des Unterrichts ist, erscheint der Weg von der anfänglichen Behandlung der Rechnerbestandteile über die Funktionsweise des Rechners zur Problemlösung als zu lang.

2) Einführung in die Informatik mit Klein- und Demonstrationsrechnern führt oft nur zu einer Aneignung spezieller Kenntnisse des Fabrikats. Ihr Einsatz ist in den Phasen des Informatik-Unterrichts gerechtfertigt, in denen der Rechner Unterrichtsgegenstand ist.

3) Die mit Klein- bzw. Tischrechnern erreichbare Stufe einer maschinennahen Programmierung bei systematischer Einführung der Problemlösung über die Maschinensprache erlaubt nur die Lösung von Problemen äußerst geringer Komplexität. Außerdem sind wegen der Rechnerarchitektur fast ausschließlich rein numerische Anwendungen sinnvoll.

4) Gegen die Einführung von Informatik über die Hardware spricht auch, daß Schüler allgemeinbildender Schulen später DV-Anwender im weitesten Sinne sind.

5) Aufgaben aus der Schülerumwelt zur algorithmischen Lösung lassen sich in allen Altersstufen finden. Es ist daher sinnvoll mit Algorithmik in allen Schulstufen zu beginnen und den Rechner als Werkzeug zu benutzen. Demgegenüber ist eine wirklich befriedigende Vorgehensweise vom Rechner zum Problem erst auf einer höheren Altersstufe möglich, weil nicht nur die Aufnahmefähigkeit jüngerer Schüler für

zahlreiche Details noch nicht allzu stark entwickelt ist, sondern notwendige Kenntnisse über die physikalischen und mathematischen Grundlagen der Rechnerkonstruktion und der Codierung fehlen.

6) Der Einstieg über die Algorithmik bedeutet nicht die Ausartung des Unterrichts in einen Programmiersprachenkurs. Demzufolge stellen Eigenschaften und Konstruktionen von Programmiersprachen, die fast ausschließlich maschinenorientiert sind, keinen Unterrichtsgegenstand dar.

4. Lerninhalte

Im Folgenden werden nur die wichtigsten Lerninhalte angegeben. Die Aufzählung entspricht nicht unbedingt der zeitlichen Abfolge im Unterricht.

4.1. Anfangsphase

- Einüben der algorithmischen Denkweise durch Analyse und Aufstellung von Algorithmen des täglichen Lebens, Problematik der Reihenfolge von Teilschritten.

- Verbalisierung sämtlicher Teilschritte unter Verwendung von intuitiven Konstruktionen der deutschen Sprache. Dies schließt die Benennung von Unteralgorithmen ein. Einführung einer Darstellung von Algorithmen.

- Einführung der Kontrollstrukturen Auswahl und Wiederholung bereits in der Anfangsphase. Konstruktionen wie "solange ... gilt, wiederhole ..." und "wiederhole ... bis...". ist der Vorzug zu geben. Zählschleifen können als Sonderfall eingeführt werden. Die Verwendung von Ablaufdiagrammen ist problematisch, besonders für Zählschleifen.

4.2. Abstraktionsstufe

- Intuitive Aufstellung der Eigenschaften von Algorithmen. Besonderer Wert ist zu legen auf Eingangs- und Ausgangsparameter, Termination und Prüfung der Korrektheit, ohne diese Begriffe explizit einzuführen.

- Übergang zum Begriff der Variablen durch sorgfältig gewählte Beispiele und später durch Verwendung eines Speichermodells. Anfangs ist darauf zu achten, die Schüler nicht durch Einführung des Begriffs der Adresse zu verwirren, da die Adressierung eine auf dieser Stufe unnötige Vorstellung von der Linearität des Speichers vermittelt und die saubere Unterscheidung zwischen Begriffen wie Name, Adresse, Inhalt behindert.

- Abstraktion relevanter Eigenschaften. Übergang von allgemeinen Objekten des Algorithmus zu Daten im Computer.

- Einführung der Grundoperation Zuweisung.

4.3. Arbeit mit der Programmiersprache

- Einführung der Kontrollstrukturen Wiederholung, Auswahl, Reihung; eines arithmetischen Datentyps, wenn möglich des Datentyps "Text" oder "Zeichen" der jeweiligen Programmiersprache. Variable, Konstante und ihre Bereitstellung für den Algorithmus. Anwendung auf Aufgaben aus 4.2.

- Grundoperationen der Ein- und Ausgabe der Programmiersprache, Standardfunktionen und weitere primitive Bausteine soweit sie benötigt werden.

- Schachtelung der Kontrollstrukturen durch komplexere Beispiele.

- Operatoren, Formeln und Priorität, Klammerung. Man sollte möglichst die Verwendung von Anweisungsklammern durch Einführung von Prozeduranweisungen verhindern. Bei Sprachen, die Anweisungsklammern verlangen, sollte auf die Analogie zu Ausdrucksklammern verwiesen werden.

- Unteralgorithmen und ihre Formulierung, zunächst ohne Parameter, später mit Parametern.

- Der Begriff des formalen Parameters läßt sich einfach einführen, wenn eine saubere Unterscheidung zwischen Name und Inhalt einer Variablen gemacht worden ist. Man sollte zunächst Variable als aktuelle Parameter verwenden, später Konstante und schließlich Ausdrücke. Eigenheiten der Sprache beim Parametermechanismus sind soweit als möglich zurückzudrängen. Saubere Einführung von Begriffen wie Wert und Effekt eines Algorithmus. Vermeidung von Nebeneffekten und sprachabhängigen Programmiertricks.

4.4. Erweiterung der Datenstrukturen.

- Verbale Beispiele von komplexen Datenstrukturen.

- Felder (allerhöchstens der Dimension 2) und die Abbildung von Datenstrukturen auf Felder.

- Iteration und Rekursion. Bei Rekursion sollte mehr Wert gelegt werden auf natürliche und übersichtliche Formulierungsmöglichkeiten als auf Effizienzfragen.

5. Realisierungsmöglichkeiten

Die Lehrer der Berliner Arbeitsgruppe versuchen z.T. schon über ein Jahr nach Überwindung beträchtlicher äußerer Schwierigkeiten, Informatik-Kenntnisse im Unterricht zu vermitteln. Unterricht wird sowohl in der 9. und 10. Jahrgangsstufe als auch in der Sekundarstufe 2 (11. - 13. Jahrgang) erteilt. Bei durchschnittlicher Schüler-Gruppenfrequenz von 15 laufen derzeit 11 Kurse. Weitere befinden sich in der Planung.

Es muß klar gesagt werden, daß Konzept und Realisierung noch erheblich auseinanderklaffen. Wir halten dies für eine normale Situation nach einer relativ kurzen Arbeitsphase.

Um die Berliner Situation zu verdeutlichen, einige Worte zur "Neugestaltung der gymnasialen Oberstufe". Im Kursunterricht der Sekundarstufe 2 gibt es die Möglichkeit Informatik-Kurse abzuhalten. Informatik als eigenes Fach ist im sogenannten Wahlbereich unterzubringen. Benötigt wird ein vom Fachlehrer zu stellender Antrag an den Senator für Schulwesen, der auch vom Schulleiter entsprechend unterstützt werden muß. Nach Genehmigung kann ein bis zu 2-semestriger Zug durchgeführt werden.

Die Besonderheit ist dabei, daß es in Berlin ein ausgearbeitetes "Grundprogramm für das Fach Informatik" gibt. Dieses Grundprogramm ist für 2 Semester konzipiert, basiert auf der Arbeit mit Tischcomputern und kommt damit der Realität in einigen Berliner Schulen entgegen. Wir sehen unsere Aufgabe darin, diesem curricularen Grundprogramm ein zweites gegenüberzustellen. Die absehbare Fehlentwicklung, Informatik als Rechnerkunde zu betreiben, deren Konsequenz in der Ausstattung der Schulen mit Tischrechnern besteht, soll vermieden werden. Ein angestrebtes alternatives Grundprogramm im Sinne des oben dargelegten Konzepts läßt sich im Berliner Rahmen wegen der großen "Rechnerdichte" zu Ausbildungszwecken auch von den äußeren Gegebenheiten her in die Tat umsetzen.

Genehmigungen zur Durchführung von Informatik-Grundkursen werden vom Senator für Schulwesen immer dann ausgesprochen, wenn sie nach seinem vorliegenden "Tischrechner-Programm" konzipiert sind. Die Genehmigung kann auch ausgesprochen werden, wenn ein alternatives Curriculum vorgelegt wird. Dieses bereitet naturgemäß einem einzelnen Lehrer erhebliche Schwierigkeiten. Deshalb wurde ein solches Curriculum über die Gruppe erstellt. Die Genehmigung ist erteilt, sodaß demnächst ein 4-semestriger Kurs beginnen kann.

In der Anfangsphase mußte sehr pragmatisch vorgegangen werden. Es lagen weder Unterrichtsmaterialien noch Erfahrungen noch ein Konzept vor, von der fehlenden Qualifikation der Lehrer und der fehlenden Möglichkeit der Fortbildung ganz zu schweigen. Deswegen wurden Anfänge des Informatik-Unterrichts in der Sekundarstufe 2 in Mathematik-Grundkursen und Arbeitsgemeinschaften angesiedelt. Wegen fehlender Lehrerstunden und starker Schülerfluktuation sind Arbeitsgemeinschaften selten.

Relativ günstig ist die Situation im Sekundarbereich 1. Hier laufen im Wahlpflichtbereich einige Kurse überwiegend an Berliner Gesamtschulen über jeweils 2 Jahre mit 4 Wochenstunden. Die Anfangsergebnisse sind hier zufriedenstellend. Trotz dieser Einschränkungen ist es der Arbeitsgruppe gelungen, einige Arbeitsmaterialien zu sammeln und zu entwickeln, ein Konzept für den Sekundarstufenbereich zu erarbeiten sowie über die Lehrerfortbildung erste Voraussetzungen für den Informatik-Unterricht zu schaffen.

6. Lehrerfort- und -weiterbildung

Die oben genannten Vorstellungen über Inhalt und Form des Informatik-Unterrichts lassen sich nur dann verwirklichen, wenn eine ausreichende Anzahl von Lehrern kurzfristig die notwendige Qualifikation erhalten kann.

Eine umfassende Lehrerfortbildung wurde deshalb aus folgenden Gründen von der Arbeitsgruppe begonnen und unterstützt:

- Es gibt noch keine Fachausbildung der Informatik für Lehrer an den Berliner Hochschulen.
- Keiner der wenigen vorliegenden Curriculum-Vorschläge enthält genügend Hinweise auf vorhandene oder von Lehrern selbst zu erstellende Unterrichtsmaterialien.
- Das Interesse der Lehrer an der Informatik und dem Einsatz von Computern in verschiedenen Unterrichtsfächern wächst.
- Eine gewisse Fehlentwicklung des Informatik-Unterrichts durch Überbetonung der Hardware oder der Betrachtung bestimmter Rechnerkonfigurationen soll durch eine einheitliche fundierte Ausbildung vermieden werden.

Im Rahmen der Lehrerfort- und weiterbildung des Senators für Schulwesen wurde daher von der Arbeitsgruppe ein geschlossenes Kurssystem entworfen (siehe Bild), das für den berufsbildenden Zweig weiterentwickelt werden muß. Dabei wurde von den folgenden Zielgruppen ausgegangen:

1. Lehrer an allgemeinbildenden Oberschulen, die Informatik unterrichten wollen (Wahlpflichtfächer, Grund- und Leistungskurse).
2. Lehrer mit Unterrichtsfächern, in denen Methoden der Informatik oder der Rechner als Hilfsmittel eingesetzt werden können. Beispiele sind mathematisch-naturwissenschaftliche Fächer, sprachwissenschaftliche oder gesellschaftswissenschaftliche Fächer.
3. Lehrer an berufsbildenden Schulen, die vor allem an Aufbau und Einsatz von DV-Anlagen, sowie der Darstellung betrieblicher Abläufe unter dem Gesichtspunkt des DV-Einsatzes interessiert sind.
4. Lehrer mit Informatik-Vorkenntnissen, die Interesse an speziellem DV-Einsatz haben, wie z.B. Stundenplanerstellung, Bedienung und Einsatz von Kleinrechnern.
5. Lehrer, die einen grundsätzlichen Überblick über den Aufbau (Rechnerkonfiguration) und den Einsatz (z.B. Informatik-Unterricht, Computerunterstützter Unterricht, Schulverwaltung, Stundenplanerstellung) von DV-Anlagen erhalten wollen.

Im dargestellten Kurssystem werden die Kurse A, B, C, G, bereits durchgeführt.

Zugrundeliegende Literatur:

1. Automatisierte Daten-Verarbeitung im Unterricht.
   Arbeitsgruppe "Schulcomputer" beim Kultusminister des Landes Nordrhein-Westfalen, 1973.

2. Frobel et. al.: Tätigkeitsbericht der CUU-Gruppe Gelsenkirchen, 1969-1973.

3. Einführung der Datenverarbeitung in Bildungswesen, Schriften des Bayerischen Staatsministeriums für Unterricht und Kultus, Reihe B, Heft 4, 1974.

4. Entwurf eines curricularen Grundprogramms für das Fach Informatik, Fachbeirat für Informatik, Berlin.

5. Bosler, Koch (Ed.): Informatik in der Schule.
   Übersetzung des holländischen Schulbuches "Computerkunde". Bericht Nr. 73-19 des FB 20 der TU Berlin, 1973.

6. Vorschlag zur Förderung des Informatikunterrichtes in Berliner Schulen.
   Berliner Arbeitskreis für Informatik in der Schule, 1973.

7. Entwurf eines Grundprogramms für das Fach Informatik Grundkurs Sekundarstufe II (neugestaltete Oberstufe).
   Berliner Arbeitskreis für Informatik in der Schule, 1974.

8. Zielsetzungen und Lerninhalte des Informatikunterrichtes.
   Unterausschuß "Informatik an Gymnasien und Berufsschulen" des Ausschusses "Ausbildung" der GI, Mai 1974.

9. Bauer, Weinhart: Informatik, Bayerischer Schulbuch-Verlag, 1974

10. Lehnert: Die Förderung der Entwicklung geistiger Fähigkeiten durch den Einsatz von Rechnern im Unterricht, ZeF 7 (1973).

11. Computer Sciences in Secondary Education.
    Centre for Educational Research and Innovation (CERI), 1971.

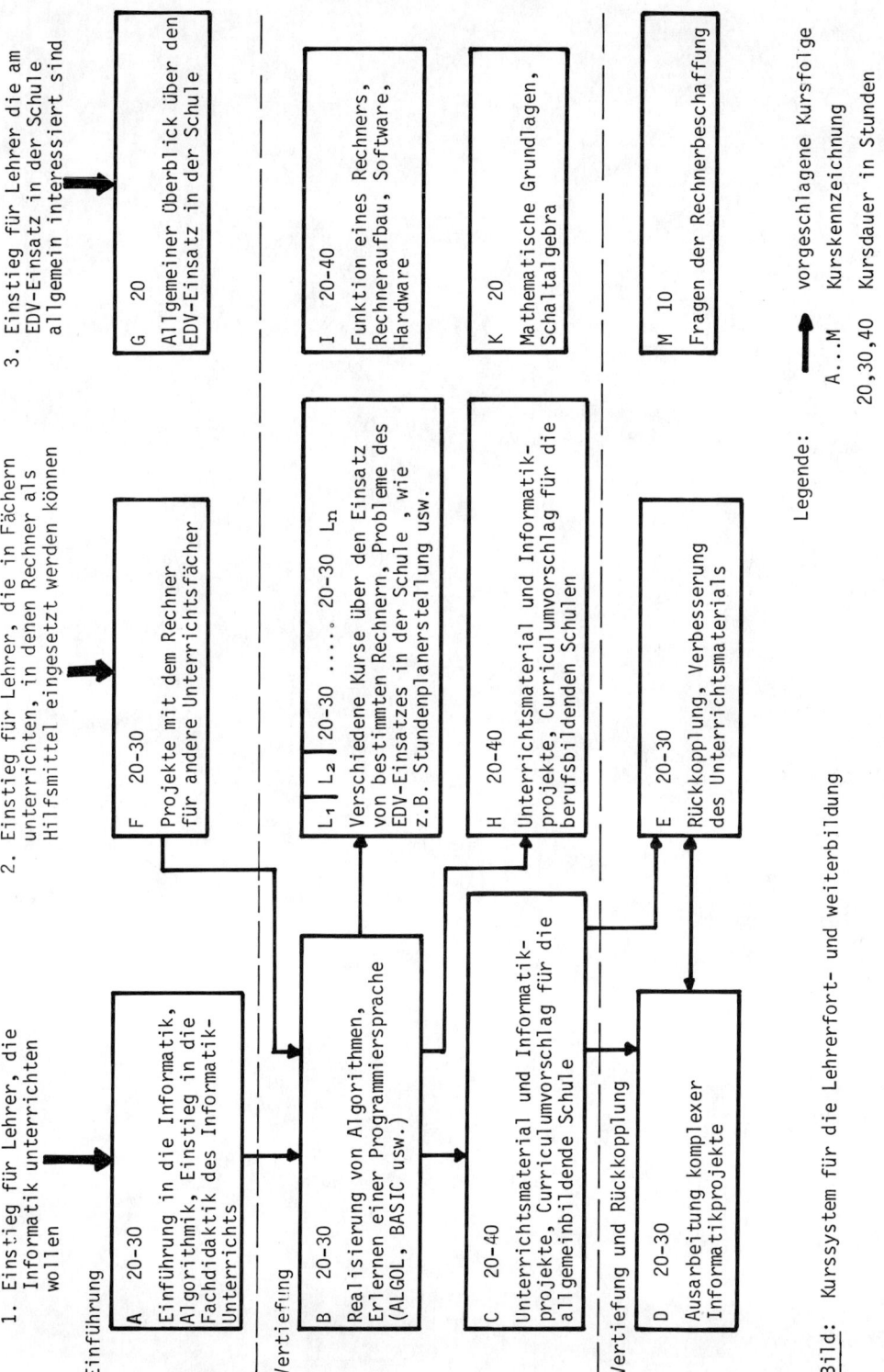

Bild: Kurssystem für die Lehrerfort- und weiterbildung

AUTORENVERZEICHNIS

M. Amirchahy (siehe D. Neel)

P. Ancilotti
Istituto di Elaborazione dell'Informazione, C.N.R.
Via S. Maria, 46
56100 PISA, Italia

A. P. Armit (siehe H.U. Lemke)

H. M. Aus
Max-Planck-Institut für Biophysikalische Chemie
Karl-Friedrich-Bonhoeffer-Institut
3400 Göttingen
Postfach 968

D. Baum
HMI für Kernforschung Berlin GmbH
Bereich DV und Elektronic
1 Berlin 39
Glienicker Str. 100

E. Becker
FG 15 (Spezielle Anwendung) des überregionalen
Forschungsprogramms Informatik an der RWTH Aachen
51 Aachen
Seffenter Weg 23 (RZ)

H. J. Becker
Inst. f. Angewandte Math. und Informatik
Abt. f. Informatik I der Universität Bonn
53 Bonn
Colmantstr. 37

A. Bertoni
Gruppo di Elettronica e Cibernetica
Facoltà di Scienze Fisiche
Università di Milano
Via Viotti, 5
20133 Milano, Italia

W. Bibel
Math. Inst., TU München
8000 München 2
Postfach 20 24 20

S. E. Binns
Computing Laboratory
The University Canterbury,
Kent

W. Bookhagen (siehe U. Bosler)

U. Bosler, Fachbereich Kybernetik, Technische Universität Berlin

F. Brakhagen
Inst. f. Grafische DV und Strukturerkennung
der Ges. f. Math. und DV mbH
5205 St. Augustin
Schloß Birlinghoven
Postfach 1240

J. C. Browne   (siehe S.W. Sherman)

S. Buder   (siehe S. Schindler)

J. Conradi
DATEV e.G.
85 Nürnberg 1
Postfach 824

M. J. E. Cooley
AUEW GH-Doughty,
75, Talbot Ave. Langley Bucks
New Berkshire, England

W. Coy
TH Darmstadt, Fachbereich Informatik
61 Darmstadt
Magdalenenstr. 11

G. Dathe
Betriebsforschungsinstitut GmbH
4 Düsseldorf
Sohnstr. 65

E. Denert, Fachbereich Kybernetik, Technische Universität Berlin

W. M. Denny
Burroughs Corporation
Santa Barbara Plant,
6300 Holliter Ave.,
Goleta, Ca 93017, USA

A. Dörrscheidt, Fachbereich Kybernetik, Technische Universität Berlin

K.-H. Dreckmann   (siehe G. Dathe)

H. Feuerhahn, Fachbereich Kybernetik, Technische Universität Berlin

H. Fiedler
Ges. f. Math. und DV
Abt. f. Behördliche DV-Systeme (A2)
5205 St. Augustin 1
Schloß Birlinghoven
Postfach 1240

H. Flessner
Arbeitsgruppe Angewandte Informatik im
Ingenieurwesen, Ruhr-Universität Bochum
4630 Bochum
Postfach 2148

Ch. Floyd
Softwarelabor f. Systementwicklung
und EDV-Anwendung
8 München 2
Mozartstr. 17   (siehe auch J. Martin)

H. Franck, Fachbereich Kybernetik, Technische Universität Berlin

R. Franck   (siehe E. Denert)

M. Fusani   (siehe P. Ancilotti)

H. Fuss
Institut f. Informationssystemforschung in
der Ges. f. Math. und DV (GMD)
5205 St. Augustin 1
Schloß Birlinghoven
Postfach 1240

P. Gorny
Angewandte Informatik
Universität Oldenburg
2900 Oldenburg
Postfach 943

H.-J. Gottschalk, Fachbereich Kybernetik, Technische Universität Berlin

H. P. Haake   (siehe H. Flessner)

P. Haberäcker
RZ Oberpfaffenhofen d.Dtsch. Forschungs- und
Versuchsanstalt f. Luft- und Raumfahrt e.V.
8031 Oberpfaffenhofen
Post Weßling

W. Händler
Inst. f. Math. Maschinen und DV (III)
der Universität Erlangen-Nürnberg
852 Erlangen
Martensstr. 1

W. Hansmann   (siehe H. Flessner)

J. Harms
CICE, Université de Genève
Promenade des Bastions
1211 Genève 4

J. Hartmanis
Dept. of Computer Science
Cornell University
Ithaca, New York 14853, USA

K.Ch. Hase
Inst. f. Orts-, Regional- und Landesplanung
ETH Zürich
8006 Zürich
Weinbergstr. 35

O. Hecker   (siehe U. Bosler)
                                   (siehe R. Langebartels)

S. Heilbrunner
Hochschule der Bundeswehr München
Fachbereich Informatik
8 München 40
Schwere-Reiter-Str. 35
Postfach 400 030

M. Heinz
Telefunken GmbH
7751 Dettingen 1
Ringstr. 123 B

R. W. Hessdorfer
Bundesforschungsanstalt f. Landeskunde
und Raumordnung
53 Bonn-Bad Godesberg 1
Postfach 130

J. Hinrichs   (siehe R. Langebartels)

S. Hoener
Informatik FG 3
RWTH Aachen
51 Aachen
Schinkelstr. 2

M. Höpner
Inst. f. Informatik
Universität Hamburg
2 Hamburg
Schlüterstr. 70

H.-J. Hoffmann   (siehe H.H. Kron)

J. H. Howard, Jr.
University of Texas at Austin (siehe S.W. Sherman)

J. Jürgens
RZ d. TU München, Arbeitsgruppe
für Betriebssysteme
8000 München 2
Arcisstr. 21

M. Käckell   (siehe H.M. Aus)

J. Klonk
Fakultät f. Informatik (II)
Universität Karlsruhe
75 Karlsruhe 1
Zirkel 2, Postfach 6380

W. Koch, Fachbereich Kybernetik, Technische Universität Berlin

K. Koschel   (siehe H.M. Aus)

C.H.A. Koster, Fachbereich Kybernetik, Technische Universität Berlin

F. Kröger
Math. Inst. d. Universität München
8000 München 2
Postfach 20 24 20

H. H. Kron
TH Darmstadt, Fachbereich Informatik
61 Darmstadt
Magdalenenstr. 11

M. Kudlek
Inst. f. Informatik,
Universität Hamburg
2 Hamburg 13
Schlüterstr. 70

P. Kühn
Inst. f. Nachrichtenvermittlung und DV
Universität Stuttgart
7 Stuttgart 1
Seidenstr. 36

R. Langebartels, Fachbereich Kybernetik, Technische Universität Berlin

M. Langenbach-Betz   (siehe P. Kühn)

M. Lehner   (siehe P. Haberäcker)

H. U. Lemke
415 Krefeld-Oppum
Buschdonk 90

N. Lijtmaer   (siehe P. Ancilotti)

K.-P. Löhr, Fachbereich Kybernetik, Technische Universität Berlin

S. Madalo, Fachbereich Kybernetik, Technische Universität Berlin

J. Martin
HALORG, Saarbrücken

M. Mazaud   (siehe D. Neel)

J.J. Martin
Dept. of Computer Science
Virginia Polytechnic Inst. and
State University
Blacksburg, Va. 24061, USA

S. G. van der Meulen
Math. Inst. (ACCU) der RU
Boedapestlaan
Utrecht/Uithof, Holland

V. ter Meulen   (siehe H.M. Aus)

R. Nagel   (siehe J. Martin)

P. Naur
DIKU, Datalogisk Institut,
Københavns Universitet
Sigurdsgåde 41
DK 2200 København
Danmark

D. Neel
IRIA
Domaine de Voluceau
Rocquencourt
78150 Le Chesnay, France

P. G. Neumann
Computer Science Group
Stanford Research Institute
Menlo Park,
California 94025, USA

N. ORIS, Fachbereich Kybernetik, Technische Universität Berlin

I. M. Osman
Computing Dept.
Durham University
Durham DH 1 3 LE, U.K.

A. Pirotte
MBLE Research Laboratory
2 av. Van Becelaere,
1170 Brussels, Belgium

O. Rabus   (siehe U. Bosler)

P. Raulefs
Inst. f. Informatik I
Universität Karlsruhe
7500 Karlsruhe 1
Postfach 6380

F. Reutter
51 Aachen
Seffenter Weg 23 (RZ)

K.-H. Rödiger   (siehe R. Langebartels)

R. Rossi
Università degli Studi di Bologna
Istituto di Automatica, Facoltà di
Ingegneria
Viale Risorgimento 2
40136 Bologna, Italia

H. Roth
Lehrstuhl f. math. Verfahrensforschung
und DV der Universität Göttingen
34 Göttingen
Nikolausbergerweg 9b

S. W. Sherman
NASA Langley Research Center
Inst. for Computer Applications in
Science and Engineering
Hampton, Va. 23365, USA

J. Simon   (siehe J. Hartmanis)

M. Spadoni   (siehe R. Rossi)

Th. Spitta   (siehe H. Franck)

S. Schindler, Fachbereich Kybernetik, Technische Universität Berlin

J. Schlörer
Abt. f. Med. Statistik, Dokumentation
und DV der Universität Ulm
79 Ulm-Wiblingen
Schloßbau 38

H. A. Schmid   (siehe J. Klonk)

H. J. Schneider
Friedrich-Alexander-Universität
Erlangen-Nürnberg
Inst. f. Math. Maschinen und DV II
852 Erlangen
Egerlandstr. 13

P. Schnupp   (siehe J. Martin)

W. Scholz   (siehe H.M. Aus)

D.-H. Schrödter   (siehe D. Baum)

R. Schroff
Math. Inst. der TU München
8000 München 2
Postfach 20 24 20

F. Schwenkel
Inst. f. Informatik
Universität Hamburg
2 Hamburg 13
Schlüterstr. 66 - 72

W. Straßer, Fachbereich Kybernetik, Technische Universität Berlin

W. Streng   (siehe E. Denert)

S.-A. Tärnlund
University of Stockholm
Schweden

C. Thanos   (siehe P. Ancilotti)

P. Toth   (siehe R. Rossi)

U. Trambacz, Fachbereich Kybernetik, Technische Universität Berlin

H. Vogel   (siehe H.J. Becker)

H. Weber, Fachbereich Kybernetik, Technische Universität Berlin

A.R. West
Dept. of Computer Science,
Queen Mary College, London
University
Mile End Road, London
England

R. Wilhelm
TU München, Abt. Math.
8000 München 2
Arcisstr. 21

G. Winkler   (siehe H.H. Kron)

O. Wörz   (siehe J. Martin)

H.-Ch. Zedlitz
Diebold-Deutschland GmbH
Geschäftsleitung
6000 Frankfurt/M.
Feuerbachstr. 8

QA
76
G44a
4th, 1974

JAN 1 4 1976